AUTOCOURSE™

THE WORLD'S LEADING GRAND PRIX ANNUAL

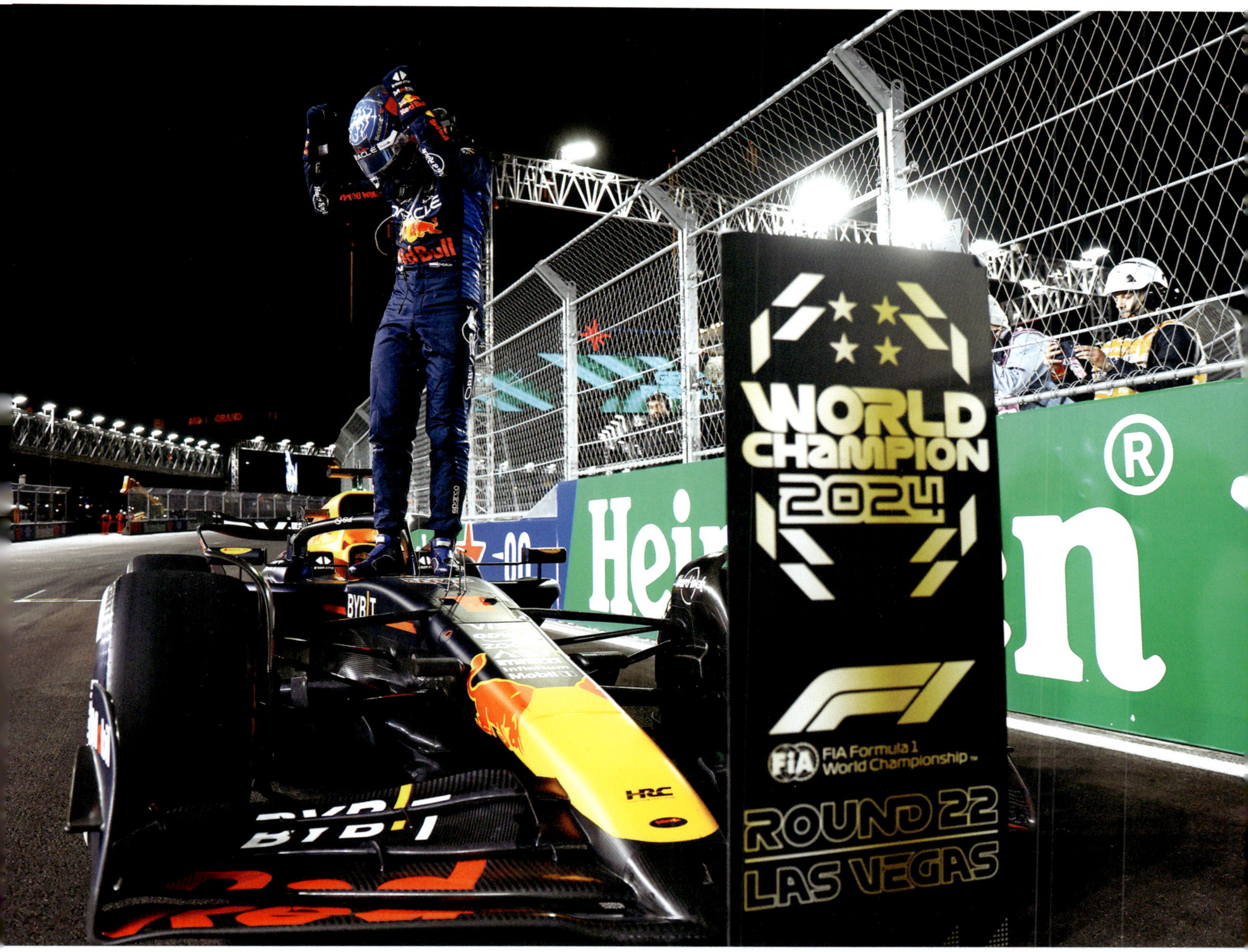

icon
PUBLISHING LIMITED

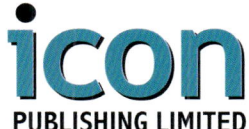

SERGIO PEREZ

CONTENTS

MAX VERSTAPPEN Four-times world champion	6
EDITOR'S INTRODUCTION	8
THE TOP TEN DRIVERS OF 2024 Ranked by the Editor	12
THE HARDEST YARDS... Tony Dodgins reviews the 2024 season	24
STELLAR BY NATURE With more than 20 years of F1 experience, Andrea Stella has led McLaren back to the top after a quarter-century wait. Tony Dodgins profiles him.	34
BRAINS TRUST Four highly intelligent women are passionate about F1 strategy, their roles and STEM opportunities for youngsters. Maurice Hamilton found out how they got to the F1 paddock.	40
DRIVING FORWARD Aston Martin owner Lawrence Stroll has raised the stakes in his quest for the world championship. Tony Dodgins looks at the dramatic reshape of the team.	46
APPRECIATIONS by Maurice Hamilton	52
FORMULA ONE TEAM-BY-TEAM REVIEW by Mark Hughes and Adrian Dean	54
FORMULA ONE CHASSIS LOGBOOK compiled by David Hayhoe	96
2024 GRANDS PRIX by Tony Dodgins and Maurice Hamilton	103
2024 FORMULA ONE STATISTICS compiled by David Hayhoe	344
FORMULA 2 REVIEW by Craig Llewellyn	346
FORMULA 3 REVIEW by Craig Llewellyn	356
FORMULA E REVIEW by Sam Smith	362
SPORTS & GT REVIEW by Gary Watkins	372
TOURING CAR REVIEW by Matt Salisbury	382
US RACING REVIEW by Gordon Kirby	392
MAJOR RESULTS WORLDWIDE compiled by David Hayhoe and João Paulo Cunha	413

AUTOCOURSE 2024–2025

Is published by:
Icon Publishing Limited
2 Redesdale House,
85 The Park,
Cheltenham,
Gloucestershire,
GL50 2RP
United Kingdom

Tel: +44 (0)1242 245329

Editorial office:
Park Farm Barn,
New Street,
Deddington,
OX15 0SS
United Kingdom

Tel: +44 (0)7836 271998

Email: info@autocourse.com
Website: www.autocourse.com

Printed in the United Kingdom by
Gomer Press Ltd
Llandysul Enterprise Park,
Llandysul,
Ceredigion,
SA44 4JL
Tel: 01559 362371
email: sales@gomer.co.uk

© Icon Publishing Limited 2024.
No part of this publication may be reproduced, stored in a retrieval system or transmitted, in any form or by any means, electronic, mechanical, photocopying, recording or otherwise, without prior permission in writing from Icon Publishing Limited.

ISBN: 978-1910584-58-3

DISTRIBUTORS

Gardners Books
1 Whittle Drive, Eastbourne,
East Sussex, BN23 6QH
Tel: +44 (0)1323 521555
email: sales@gardners.com

Chaters Wholesale Ltd
25/26 Murrell Green Business Park,
Hook, Hampshire, RG27 9GR
Tel: +44 (0)1256 765443
Fax: +44 (0)1256 769900
email: books@chaters.co.uk

NORTH AMERICA
NATIONAL BOOK NETWORK
NBN
4501 Forbes Boulevard,
Suite 200,
Lanham, MD 20706
Tel: (301) 459-3366
Fax: (301) 429-5746

www.autocourse.com

publisher
STEVE SMALL
steve.small@iconpublishinglimited.com

commercial director
BRYN WILLIAMS
bryn.williams@iconpublishinglimited.com

editor
TONY DODGINS

grand prix correspondents
TONY DODGINS
MAURICE HAMILTON

f1 technical editor
MARK HUGHES

text editor
IAN PENBERTHY

results and statistics
DAVID HAYHOE

lap chart compiler
PETER McLAREN

f1 car and circuit illustrations
ADRIAN DEAN
f1artwork@blueyonder.co.uk

Acknowledgements

France: ACO, Fédération Française du Sport Automobile, FIA (Mohammed Ben Sulayem, Tom Wood, Roman De Lauw); **Germany:** Mercedes-Benz (Toto Wolff, James Allison, Bradley Lord, Adam McDaid, Rosa Herrero Venegas, Charlotte Davies); **Great Britain:** Formula One Group (Stefano Domenicali, Liam Parker), Maurice Hamilton, Mark Hughes, McLaren (Zak Brown, Andrea Stella, Steve Atkins, Sophie Ogg, Harry Bull, Charlie Russell, Sophie Almeida, Maria Galea), Red Bull Racing (Christian Horner, Helmut Marko, Pierre Waché, Paul Monaghan, Paul Smith, Alice Hedworth, Madeliene Coe, Anna Webster), Alpine F1 (Oliver Oakes, David Sanchez, Sam Mallinson), Aston Martin (Mike Krack, Dan Fallows, Tom McCullough, Andy Stevenson, Adrian Atkinson, Will Hings, Eve Merrell, Michael Clayton), Williams F1 (James Vowles, Dave Robson, Rebecca Banks, Dominique Heyer-Wright); **Italy:** Commissione Sportiva Automobilistica Italiana, Scuderia Ferrari (Frédéric Vasseur, Silvia Hoffer, Roberta Colleluori, Mia Djacic), RB-Honda (Laurent Mekies, Jody Egginton, Jonathan Eddolls, Fabiana Valenti, Andrea Saveri), Pirelli (Mario Isola, Luca Colajanni, Anthony Peacock); **Switzerland:** Stake F1 Team Kick Sauber (Alessandro Alunni Bravi, James Key, Will Ponissi); **USA:** Haas (Andrea de Zordo, Stuart Morrison, Jessica Borrell), IndyCar/Penske Entertainment Corp., Indianapolis Motor Speedway.

Photographs published in AUTOCOURSE 2024–2025 have been contributed by:

Aston Martin Aramco F1 Team; BMW Alpine F1 Team; Mercedes-AMG Petronas F1 Team; McLaren F1 Team; MoneyGram Haas F1 Team; Red Bull Content Pool/Getty Images; Scuderia Ferrari; Stake F1 Team Kick Sauber; Williams Racing; Pirelli; DTM; FTW; Japanese Super Formula; F1.com Formula E/LAT; WEC; BTCC/Jacob Ebrey; TCR; LAT Photographic/Motorsport Images; IndyCar/Penske Entertainment Corp.; Grand Prix Photo/Peter Nygaard; Lukas Gorys; Atsuo Sakurai; Bryn Williams; XPB Images.

Dust jacket: The 2024 FIA World Drivers' Champion, Max Verstappen.
Photo: Bryn Williams

Title page: Verstappen celebrates his fourth consecutive drivers' championship in Las Vegas.
Photo: Red Bull Content Pool/Getty Images

STILL LEADING THE FIELD

www.autocourse.com

MAX VERSTAPPEN
FOUR TIMES CHAMPION

FOUR TIMES world champion. That sounds very good! You grow up racing and seeing the stats of legendary drivers. You're thinking. yes, that sounds very impressive and you hope that one day you can just be on the podium. Or win a race. Maybe even a championship.

It's already hard enough to win one. You need also a bit of luck to be in the right team situation, and we had that. But that was more the first three championships. In 2024, we hit the ground running, but then had a lot of tough races. And that's something I'm very proud of – where we definitely didn't have the fastest car, but kept it together as a team.

After 2023, you don't expect another year like that. But the car was really difficult to drive and it was about working with the team because these moments can be very demotivating. But actually they are really important moments to keep it together and work harder to understand. If you give up, you are giving up the championship as well.

We remained calm most of the time and barely made any mistakes. Maybe we even over-performed sometimes. And in some places our opposition definitely didn't grab the points that they should have. All those things matter at the end.

I'm very loyal to the team and appreciate what they have done for me, picking me up out of F3 and giving me an F1 seat. You are going through all these emotions over the years with these key people. When there are tough times, it's very easy to say goodbye or forget about that. But I think it's actually way more important to go through it together, deal with it and just move on. Next year, I think, is going to be a big battle.

Every year there are always things going through your head. Like how long do I still want to do this? Where do I want to do this? How do I want to do this? There are things in your private life that happen as well, but that's fine. I'm generally quite relaxed. I'm not someone who makes very drastic decisions and, at the same time, I'm just very happy where I'm at right at the moment.

EDITOR'S INTRODUCTION
THE HARDEST YARDS

Above: Max Verstappen and Red Bull celebrated a fourth successive drivers' championship in Las Vegas.
Photo: Red Bull Content Pool/Getty Images

Top right: Lando Norris produced a superb drive in Abu Dhabi to ensure that McLaren secured the constructors' honours.
Photo: McLaren F1 Team

Above right: Ferrari's season was up and down, but they still garnered five wins between Leclerc and Sainz.
Photo: Scuderia Ferrari

Right: The Abu Dhabi result was the culmination of years of hard work for Zak Brown in re-establishing McLaren as a championship force.
Photo: McLaren F1 Team

BOTH Christian Horner and Max Verstappen think that the Dutchman's fourth world championship win was his best. Not the most dominant or dramatic, but one that was full of resilience and mental strength with barely an error across a season when he didn't have the best car 70 per cent of the time.

The championship 'fight', such as it was, never truly ignited due to Verstappen's seven wins in the first ten races of 2024. You can't give a generational talent such as his more than 50 points head start and then expect to catch him. But, as Horner said at the end of the year, the 2025 season, the final one under the current regulations, could be absolutely epic.

He's right. After F1's longest ever 24-race season, you'd imagine that the F1 circus would be preoccupied with a well-deserved break, looking ahead only as far as the turkey, wine, mince pies and Christmas pudding. And yet, as the paddock emptied in Abu Dhabi, the talk was all about Melbourne '25.

At the time of writing, the internet is alive with news that Liam Lawson has beaten Yuki Tsunoda to the second Red Bull seat alongside Verstappen in 2025. I can't help feeling that's a bit like fighting to be first on to the executioner's chopping block… I felt similar vibes when I heard that Michael Andretti was planning on coming to F1 from Indy car racing, that he was going to commute back and forth across the Atlantic and take on Ayrton Senna at McLaren. He'd have needed good luck with that! Michael doesn't seem to have a lot of luck when it comes to F1, but perhaps you make your own.

Making it worse for Andretti was that F1 had been at the height of its gizmo age before such as active suspension was banned. Martin Whitmarsh once told me a great story about McLaren's Steve Hallam producing a lovely leather-bound manual, which explained the intricacies of the steering-wheel controls to help out the drivers before the year's first test. Hallam was a bit put out when, at the end of the briefing, Senna shook his head and said no, he was a professional racing driver and didn't need it, leaving the manual on the desk as he walked out.

So Andretti also stood up and said, "No thank you, I'm a professional racing driver, too," and he walked out, leaving his manual on the table. Whereupon Ayrton, who was waiting around the corner until Michael had gone, nipped back in and put the manual in his briefcase, with a wink. Lawson is unlikely to get any of that from the straight-shooting Verstappen, just pure, raw, unadulterated, mind-rattling pace. But if he's anywhere near in his first full season of F1, it will be the making of him.

Intriguingly, at the time of writing, the bookmakers do not see Verstappen as favourite for a fifth consecutive world title, a feat achieved only once, by Michael Schumacher in the dominant Ferrari team of the early 2000s. They have Lando Norris at 21/10, marginally ahead of Max, 9/4, then Charles Leclerc, 7/2, Oscar Piastri, 8/1 and Lewis Hamilton, 9/1! Poor old George Russell is good value at 20/1. Or, there's a wild punt on Kimi Antonelli, 80/1, as the next Messiah.

The bookies don't often get it wrong, but I can see some potential banana skins. When you read Mark Hughes' AUTOCOURSE team technical reviews, it becomes clear that the big brains believe that quantum steps taken by McLaren and Mercedes in 2024, allowing them to win ten races between them, were substantially due to progress with aero-elasticity, or 'bendy wings' if you like. It is a grey area that, outside of its static load tests, the FIA finds very difficult to police.

If that is low-hanging fruit, why didn't Red Bull, renowned for exploiting it for years, and Ferrari, not put more emphasis on it? Well, firstly, the fruit is not so low hanging. It's a difficult thing to do and it needs resource. Christian Horner said that Red Bull were hemmed in by the cost cap and that they had less aero testing capability through being constructors' champions. On top of that

there was a further ten per cent reduction in aero testing for 12 months starting in October, 2022, due to breaching the cost cap in '21. By the end of '23, that would have impacted development of the '24 car.

Formula 1 is no longer like it was when budgets were unrestricted and you could go in any development direction you fancied, as long as you had the money and the people. When Nigel Mansell joined Ferrari back in the day, apparently he had a mind-boggling array of brake pedals from which to choose! Now, though, you allocate development budget judiciously. At Ferrari, Frédéric Vasseur was loathe to commit money to technology he believed to be illegal and that might be curbed by the FIA. Thus Maranello was late to the party.

Heading into 2025, you might logically conclude that there is scope for significant gains at both Red Bull and Ferrari. Remember, too, that Ferrari temporarily engineered itself into a mid-season hole in 2024. Across the season, the team averaged just over 27 points per race, but in the five races from Canada to Hungary, an 'upgrade' brought back the dreaded bouncing and that average dropped to just over 14 points. The team had but one podium, assisted by Norris and Verstappen colliding in Austria, before another upgrade addressed its issues.

When you weigh it all up and realise that if Ferrari gets it right, it's going to have a man with more than 100 wins and pole positions in one of its cockpits, those odds of 9/1 start to look enticing! That desire for an eighth title is still there. Lewis's biggest challenges will be overcoming his dislike of the heavy, understeering current-generation F1 car and the man on the other side of the garage.

But what if Red Bull makes strides, too? How do you beat Verstappen? Well, there's a theory that racing drivers slow down a bit when they have children. And Kelly Piquet, Max's partner, is pregnant. Straw-clutching, I know, but with Max, you've got to take all you can get. Hang on to your hats – F1 2025 is going to be great!

Above: In a very close and competitive WEC season, Toyota took the manufacturers' title at the final round in Bahrain.
Photo: WEC

Top right: Josef Newgarden kisses the trophy after his second consecutive Indianapolis 500 win.
Photo: IndyCar/Penske Entertainment Corp.

Top centre right: Joey Logano ensured that Penske was still the team to beat in NASCAR.
Photo: Nigel Kinrade/NKP/LAT Images

Top far right: A third Vanderbilt trophy in just four years for Alex Palou.
Photo: IndyCar

Above right: Porsche's Pascal Wehrlein took the Formula E drivers' title.
Photo: Porsche

Above far right: Heading for the very top? Gabriel Bortoleto conquered F2 and now heads to Sauber/Audi.
Photo: XPB Images

Right: Ferrari triumphed once more at Le Mans.
Photo: Scuderia Ferrari

Below right: Hyundai's Norbert Michelisz heads team-mates Azcona and Girolami in Macau.
Photo: TCR

In the FIA WEC championship, Kévin Estre, André Lotterer and Laurens Vanthoor claimed the drivers' championship with Penske Porsche Motorsport after victories in Qatar and Fuji. But in a 'tweak' to the Porsche roster, involving the reduction of the full-time line-up from three drivers to two in the WEC, veteran Lotterer stands down for 2025.

For the second successive year, Ferrari won at Le Mans, bringing its wins total in the Sarthe classic to 11, behind only Porsche and Audi. Antonio Fuoco, Miguel Molina and Nicklas Nielsen were the winning drivers for AF Corse. They also finished second in the championship, two points clear of Toyota Gazoo Racing pairing Kamui Kobayashi and Nyck de Vries, who won the Imola round with Mike Conway. Conway missed out on Le Mans with a broken collarbone and ribs following a cycling accident. At Spa, British drivers Callum Ilott and Will Stevens claimed the first customer victory of the Hypercar era with a well-timed stop that allowed them to beat the Ferraris.

At the final round in Bahrain, Toyota claimed a sixth consecutive manufacturers' title with Sébastian Buemi, Brendon Hartley and Ryo Hirakawa, winning the Sakhir race to add to their victory at Interlagos.

In F2, the FIA's premier F1 feeder category, Brazilian Gabriel Bortoleto, a Fernando Alonso protégé, joined Charles Leclerc, George Russell and Oscar Piastri in securing back-to-back rookie titles in F3 and F2. Bortoleto will partner Nico Hülkenberg at Sauber in 2025, after taking feature-race wins at Red Bull Ring and Monza.

The championship battle went down to the Abu Dhabi season finale with Red Bull junior driver Isack Hadjar, who could boast feature-race wins in Melbourne, Imola, Silverstone and Spa. With Bortoleto starting second and Hadjar third, the French-Algerian called it the worst moment of his life when he stalled on the grid. He was still hopeful of a promotion to the sport's top tier pending the F1 driver machinations at Red Bull.

Estonian Paul Aron also impressed on his way to third in the championship, winning in Lusail and earning a reserve driver role with Alpine for 2025. Barbadian Zane Maloney scored a rare feature/sprint-race double in the Bahrain season-opener and had second places in both Silverstone races.

Two more F2 men who were already announced as F1 graduates, with the season barely under way, were Prema drivers Kimi Antonelli – replacing Lewis Hamilton at Mercedes no less! – and Ollie Bearman, who finished a fine seventh in the Saudi Arabian GP for Ferrari when Carlos Sainz was sidelined with appendicitis. Bearman will be in a Haas in 2025. Antonelli won the Silverstone sprint race and the Hungaroring feature event, but he and Bearman could only manage sixth and 12th in the championship as Prema struggled unexpectedly with F2's new chassis and engine issues.

American Jak Crawford won the Barcelona feature race, and Franco Colapinto the Imola sprint prior to being called up by Williams to replace Logan Sargeant. Joshua Dürksen claimed the Baku sprint and Yas Marina feature, while Dennis Hauger won the Jeddah sprint, but changes direction to Indy NXT with Andretti Global in 2025.

The FIA F3 series was won by Italian Leonardo Fornaroli at Trident, who moves up to F2 with Invicta. While he didn't actually win a round, consistency delivered second in Melbourne and at the Monza final round, with further podiums in Imola, Barcelona, Budapest and Spa. Second place in the series went to countryman Gabriele Minì, who won in Monaco and finished ahead of British driver Luke Browning, who was first past the chequered flag in the Bahrain season-opening feature race and won at Red Bull Ring as well. Arvid Lindblad finished fourth, with wins in the Bahrain sprint and Barcelona feature, and a sprint/feature double at Silverstone.

In the tenth Formula E season, Pascal Wehrlein clinched his first title at the final round in London, driving for TAG Heuer Porsche, as the Kiwi pairing of Mitch Evans and Nick Cassidy took Jaguar TCS Racing to its first World

Teams' Championship. Wehrlein won in Mexico City, Misano and London, Evans in Monaco, and Cassidy in Diriyah and Berlin. António Félix da Costa was fifth after wins in Berlin and Shanghai, and a double in Portland. Oliver Rowland also took two wins en route to fourth in the series, while other race winners were Jake Dennis, Max Günther and Sam Bird.

The TCR World Tour regained FIA status, Norbert Michelisz beating Swede Thed Björk to the crown with wins in Vallelunga and Interlagos in a BRC Hyundai Elantra. Björk won in Mid-Ohio, Uruguay and Macau for Lynk & Co, for whom Yann Ehrlacher also won three times.

The IndyCar series in the US brought a third title and second in succession for Alex Palou with Chip Ganassi Racing, taking wins on the Indy road course and at Laguna Seca. Colton Herta was his nearest challenger for Andretti Global, victorious in Toronto and at the Nashville Superspeedway. Kiwi Scott McLaughlin was third, with victories in Alabama, Iowa and Milwaukee for Penske.

Will Power also won at Road America, Iowa and Portland for 'the Captain', but had to be content with fourth place in the series. Pato O'Ward was Arrow McLaren's highest-placed driver, fifth, with victories at Mid-Ohio and on the Milwaukee Mile. Penske also claimed a 20th Indy 500 win when Josef Newgarden pulled off a great last-lap pass of O'Ward to become the first back-to-back Indy 500 winner since Hélio Castroneves in 2002. Evergreen six-times champion Scott Dixon was sixth in the championship, with wins in Long Beach and Detroit.

Whether it was an aeroscreen or roof didn't seem to matter to Penske. After becoming the 16th team to win back-to-back NASCAR titles with Joey Logano and Ryan Blaney in 2022 and '23, Penske went one better with a treble, Logano coming out on top in a 1-2 finish as the pair duelled it out again.

Tony Dodgins
December, 2024

FIA F1 WORLD CHAMPIONSHIP 2024
TOP TEN DRIVERS
THE EDITOR'S CHOICE

MAX VERSTAPPEN

1

FROM the point the Miami upgrade went on Lando Norris's McLaren for round six, Max Verstappen no longer had the fastest car. Yet he won a 24-race championship by 63 points.

Verstappen knew the writing was on the wall, but the Red Bull was not suddenly miles off. He started from the front row in four of the next five races, taking important wins in Imola, Montreal and Barcelona. They were important in the context of what was to follow.

Such a margin allowed Max to get his elbows out, which he was not averse to doing. He and Norris might have been buddies, but out on the track, you'd never have known. In Austria, Max got physical at Turn Three, contact between them consigning Lando to retirement while the penalised Max recovered to fifth and pushed his lead out to 81 points.

At McLaren, Andrea Stella was unimpressed. He harked back to the 2021 title battle with Hamilton when, in Stella's opinion, driving tactics adopted by Max were not punished, which he felt was coming back to bite.

You didn't need to be Einstein to work out that for Norris to close the gap, he needed bigger point swings that came only with winning races. In Austin, Max drove Lando wide at Turn One and didn't care that Leclerc got through – it suited him actually. He knew that the stewards allowed more leeway in the chaos of an opening lap. Later on, there was Turn 12. Then, in Mexico, Turns Four and Eight, the latter well over the top. There were penalties for both, but that was okay; Ferrari was up the road again.

"He's so good," Stella had shrugged, "Why does he need to do it?" In Brazil a week later, Max drove a sublime race from the back to one of his best ever wins. Different class. It's called ruthless competitiveness. It was there with Senna and it was there with Schumacher.

CHARLES LECLERC

SOMETIMES, Leclerc is pigeonholed as a great qualifier, but less strong in races and prone to the odd error. The make-up of the 2023 Ferrari furthered that perception, as he took five poles, but invariably went backwards with degrading rear tyres. But that was the car, not him.

Conceptually, the 2024 car had opposing characteristics. Sometimes, Leclerc would struggle to generate enough soft-tyre temperature for the first sector of a Q3 lap, notably Singapore, but the payback was better tyre usage on Sunday, allowing him a fine season, spoiled only by a mid-year blip when the team's Spain 'upgrade' brought back the dreaded bouncing and Ferrari was off the pace for half a dozen races.

On a street circuit, he has always been peerless and, helped by the slow-corner strengths of the Ferrari, poles in Monte Carlo and Baku could be taken for granted. Finally, he took an emotional win on his home streets. But he will kick himself over Baku. With the race seemingly in the bag, Ferrari left him out for a lap longer than they should have done before changing tyres, allowing Piastri to close and then mug him into Turn One.

There were further wins in front of the ecstatic *tifosi* at Monza, where he managed a one-stopper to beat the two-stopping McLarens, and in Austin. He finished in the top four 18 times from 24 starts and, Monza apart, delivered other strong tyre-saving drives at Suzuka and Zandvoort.

You winced when he made a crucial track-limits error in Q2 in Abu Dhabi as Ferrari fought for the constructors' title, but then he produced one of the greatest opening laps ever seen. He is a phenomenal talent who likes a strong front end as much as Verstappen and Hamilton, and the current cars don't suit him – his qualifying delta over team-mate Sainz averaged just 0.049s over the year. Next year, Charles and Lewis can complain about that together!

LANDO NORRIS

IT was a toss-up between Leclerc and Lando for No.2 spot. As soon as Norris got his hands on a car with podium-scoring and race-winning potential, he delivered. Highly regarded for so long now, it seems bizarre to recall Miami as his first win. The number of drivers who gave him a post-race pat on the back spoke volumes.

Norris has it all: great qualifying speed, the ability to resist pressure when leading, strong tyre management, a strong racing brain and a pragmatic approach. He is totally honest as well, almost too self-critical, more self-deprecating even than Leclerc.

Miami apart, he won by a huge margin in Verstappen's backyard at Zandvoort, dominated Singapore and then sealed McLaren's constructors' title with the coolest of performances in Abu Dhabi. It wasn't as easy as it looked, as Sainz and Ferrari showed greater pace than McLaren had anticipated.

Norris's qualifying laps were often sublime. Piastri is no slouch, yet Lando outqualified him 20–4 over the course of the season, with an average 0.174s delta between them – impressive by any standards.

Mistakes were few and far between, mostly involving opening laps – either sub-optimal starts or car placement, such as putting himself in a vulnerable position on the outside of Hamilton as Lewis got the jump on him off the line in the Shanghai sprint. Or, on pole in Austin, allowing Verstappen down the inside, from where Max drove him off the road. Then there was the costly missing of the yellow in Qatar, where a 30s stop-go penalty amid a safety-car period was unduly harsh.

You could accuse him of being a little passive in his wheel-to-wheel tussles with Verstappen and say he needs to toughen up. But again, that's harsh. With a huge points deficit, he couldn't afford to, and intimidation is not his way. He has the belief though, and when he said that 2025 is going to be *his* year, he meant it.

GEORGE RUSSELL

WHO is better, Norris or Russell? If your life depended on answering that correctly, you wouldn't know what to say. Both are top drawer, and George proved it with a year when he got the better of his seven-times world champion team-mate.

With nothing to choose between Russell and Hamilton for qualifying speed over the previous two seasons, George was suddenly an average 0.173s quicker for single-lap pace, and he outqualified Lewis 19–5 over the season (24–6 if you include the sprints).

Why? Running these heavy understeer-in/oversteer-out ground-effect chassis as low as a track will allow – with flat aero platforms and no pitch – in search of greater downforce, makes handling peaky and can sap confidence. George, it seems, was more adaptable.

Russell was first past the chequer on three occasions. He picked up the pieces in Austria when Verstappen and Norris tangled. But there was nothing fortunate about Spa, quite the opposite, as he eked out a one-stop strategy brilliantly – the call was his – and used his battery deployment intelligently to fend off a closing Hamilton, on faster rubber. Only to be disqualified for being 1.5kg underweight due to a combination of tyre tread loss from the one-stopper, plank wear from the compression at Eau Rouge and George himself being a fraction lighter than usual.

Put the Mercedes on a smooth track with low temperature – Las Vegas had both – and suddenly it was in a different league. Russell put it on pole and won as he pleased. But most grands prix are held in sunny conditions with blistering track temperatures. Russell making the final step and challenging for championships in 2025 will depend upon Mercedes giving him the car to do it. And now he must lead the development team, as rookie Kimi Antonelli joins Mercedes for 2025.

4

Photo: Mercedes AMG Petronas F1 Team

CARLOS SAINZ

5

POOR Carlos was a victim of circumstance in 2024. When Ferrari found themselves with an unexpected opportunity to sign Lewis Hamilton, it was obvious they would not pass it up. And while Sainz is very good, he's not quite Leclerc, and Charles was already on a long-term contract. After four years with Ferrari, Carlos was facing the exit door.

This was all known pre-season, and the kind of year Sainz subsequently delivered was a measure of his great character, commitment and professionalism.

He started strongly with a podium in Bahrain, before being taken ill with appendicitis in Jeddah, where Ollie Bearman was called in for qualifying and the race. Sainz's return, in Melbourne, was stunning. He qualified on the front row and, benefiting from pole-man Verstappen's early retirement, dominated the race.

The performance in Mexico was even better, winning from pole in front of visiting family and friends to take one more victory in red. His dedication to the Ferrari cause was evident right to the last lap of the last race in Abu Dhabi, where he chased Norris for all he was worth as their two teams fought for the constructors' championship.

He was outqualified 14–9 (17–12 including sprints) by Leclerc, but with an average of less than five-hundredths between them. Acknowledging Charles's single-lap speed, that is far from shabby.

The low points were a spin and contact with Alex Albon in Montreal, a tangle with Sergio Pérez that took out both of them on the penultimate lap in Azerbaijan, and two crashes in the wet, usually his forte, in Brazil.

With Red Bull's lack of a strong back-up for Verstappen exposed by the team dropping behind McLaren and Ferrari, surely Carlos was the answer. So why didn't the team sign him? You can only conclude that Christian Horner had a gun to his head. But you can imagine Sainz going down very well with James Vowles at Williams.

OSCAR PIASTRI

AFTER an impressive start to his F1 career in 2023, Piastri jumped to the next level. He scored his first GP win in Budapest, although the shine was taken off by the circumstances.

Outqualified by team-mate Norris as McLaren locked out the front row, Oscar got the better start and led confidently. He only lost his lead when Norris was needlessly prioritised at the pit stops, but Lando had strong pace in the final stint and it needed a team order to ensure that he let Oscar back past.

That revealed two things: first, there was nothing in Piastri's contract that disadvantaged him vis à vis Lando; second, Norris was honourable enough to respect the team's wishes. It did not turn into Vettel/Webber Malaysia, 2013. 'Gifted' wins never feel quite the same, though, even if the bonus dollars still hit the bank account!

But there was nothing gifted about Azerbaijan. It was Leclerc's fourth Baku pole in succession, but he'd never won there – failings of his car, rather than his own. This time, with decent race pace to boot, he appeared unstoppable. Piastri had other ideas, though. After the pit stops, with one chance as Leclerc brought his tyres in, he pulled off a sensational pass – possibly the move of the year, at Turn One. Without it, Ferrari, not McLaren, would have won the championship.

He qualified on the front row and kept Leclerc honest in Monaco en route to second, and was the only driver to complete every racing lap. Post-Baku, though, his season petered out somewhat, and he was outqualified and outraced by Norris everywhere. He did hand his team-mate the Interlagos sprint race while Norris was still in the championship mathematically, and was repaid in Qatar.

If McLaren is competitive from the off in 2025, does he have the ultimate pace to challenge his team-mate over a season? The 20–4 qualifying deficit with a 0.174s average delta will be a concern.

LEWIS HAMILTON

IT was not a vintage season by the standards of a seven-times world champion, and Hamilton's travails were rooted in an inability to get the best out of the Mercedes in qualifying.

There was an interesting little cameo, slightly tense, in the Budapest cool-down room after McLaren had finished 1-2 ahead of Lewis, and Lando Norris was still narked at having to concede the win to Piastri.

"Phew, you guys are fast," Lewis observed innocently.

"You had a fast car seven years ago," Lando replied, a little tersely. "You made the most of it, and now it's us."

He had a point. People, who look at Hamilton's 104 pole positions and think of him as the GOAT, wonder how he can be the better part of two-tenths slower than a man in the same car across a season, with a 19–5 (24–6) qualifying deficit.

Not to denigrate Lewis's mighty achievements, they fail to factor in the unprecedented amount of time he spent in a superior car (2014–20). In his 246 starts with Mercedes across 12 seasons, he had 78 poles (31.7 per cent). Not as overwhelming as you might think, his stats having taken a hit since the current regs in 2022. What would those numbers have looked like for a Senna or Schumacher? Who knows?

Retired drivers like Rosberg and Button say that as you age, it's the one-lap pace that goes first. But with Lewis, 40 in January, 2025, you suspect that it's more about the current generation of ground-effect cars being so badly suited to his aggressive style. And second, Russell is just bloody quick.

As for any lack of desire, forget it. Lewis's emotional ninth Silverstone win, breaking a victory drought back to 2021, was fabulous. He was excellent at Spa, and just look at those recovery drives in Vegas and Abu Dhabi. Leclerc, trying to win a first title at Ferrari, needs Hamilton like a hole in the head. Good luck with that one, Fred…

FERNANDO ALONSO

BY the standards of his multiple-podium 2023 season, Alonso had a disastrous 2024 season, but he was still 'best of the rest' outside the top four teams. You wouldn't have expected anything less, but he still scored nearly 30 points more than anyone else.

Developing the current cars, which effectively is the same as heaping more downforce upon them, is not straightforward. McLaren was the only team for whom every upgrade correlated on track with what had been seen in the wind tunnel and simulation. Even Red Bull, Ferrari and Mercedes experienced backward steps. At Aston Martin, though, practically everything that went on to the car was a retrograde step.

If the future didn't look so bright in terms of investment and opportunity through Lawrence Stroll's largesse, you could imagine Alonso, at 43, forcibly ejecting toys from the pram.

Who knows what he said behind closed doors – even in public, it was obvious that frustration was building. "It's time to work hard, deliver more and talk less," he espoused after qualifying 11th and finishing 12th in front of his home supporters in Barcelona.

On track, though, Fernando doesn't give up. When the car worked with him, he got the most out of it, qualifying fourth in Jeddah – where commitment is rewarded – and a fine third in Shanghai. There was a three-race period when he seemed to have lost the will to live: out-qualified by Stroll in Miami, Imola and Monaco, which corresponded with a big upgrade not delivering, but he was back in the top six in Montreal.

A season where fifth place in Jeddah was his best result is not good enough for Fernando, a man who still wants a third world championship. His big hope is Stroll's substantial investment and the clean sheet of paper for 2026. He'll just have to trust that by then, his teammate is not Verstappen.

NICO HÜLKENBERG

9

NICO HÜLKENBERG finished just one point behind tenth place in the drivers' championship, driving for a Haas team that had been a solid last in 2023.

It was a strong reflection on both driver and team. With Ayao Komatsu brought in to replace Guenther Steiner as team principal, some good work over the winter was able to solve Haas's Achilles heel from the previous season – disastrous race tyre degradation.

The team engineered the car in a direction that gave it much better tyre usage, but not without robbing it of single-lap speed. That much was apparent from some remarkable qualifying efforts from Hülkenberg. He was a fine sixth on the grid at Silverstone – ahead of both bouncing Ferraris! – and an absolutely remarkable fourth in Abu Dhabi, which put the wind up Alpine as the two teams battled for the extra lucre that came with finishing sixth in the championship.

The highlights of Hülkenberg's season were a brace of sixth places in Austria and Silverstone, but he also scored points in Jeddah, Melbourne, Shanghai, Singapore, Austin, Mexico, Las Vegas and Abu Dhabi. On top of that, he finished one place shy of the points on no fewer than seven occasions, underlining a consistency that was the foundation of an unexpectedly strong and rewarding season for Haas. They will be sorry to see Nico go as Esteban Ocon and Ollie Bearman come in for 2025.

It's been an awful long time, 14 years, since Hülkenberg claimed that wet-weather pole position for Williams at Interlagos. Now with 227 GP starts behind him, he's the sort of driver you suspect would do a good job for Red Bull, but 37 is not the age of driver they are ever going to sign. It looks like a top car is going to elude him, but a multi-year deal with Audi is no more than he deserves.

PIERRE GASLY

PIERRE GASLY has bounced back well from the confidence-sapping experience of spending a dozen races as Max Verstappen's team-mate at Red Bull in 2019, before being demoted back to its junior team.

Outside of the top four teams and Fernando Alonso, Nico Hülkenberg and Gasly were the 2024 standouts, with Nico just getting the nod due to his consistency. Okay, Pierre beat him to tenth in the championship by a point, but much of that was down to a fine third place in Brazil, where, like Verstappen, both Alpine drivers gained from staying out on-track and benefiting from a timely red flag for a free tyre change.

If Hülkenberg amazed with his fourth place on the grid in Abu Dhabi, Gasly went one better in Las Vegas, where, helped by a chassis that brought its soft tyres up to temperature quickly in the cold, he managed to split the Ferraris on the grid and qualify third!

There were points in Monaco, Canada, Austria and Zandvoort, before Gasly's season really took an upward trajectory with a strong Alpine upgrade in Austin. A power-unit issue put him out in Vegas after that mighty qualifying, but Pierre kept the momentum going with a strong fifth place in Qatar and seventh at the season-closer in Abu Dhabi.

In 2023, the qualifying delta between Gasly and team-mate Esteban Ocon had been the smallest on the grid, just a couple of hundredths. It was the same again in 2024, Gasly quicker this time, by an average of just 0.046s! Ocon shaded the head-to-head 12–11, but was 14–15 down if you included the sprints. It was that tight. Esteban, moving on to Haas, would argue that he didn't get the strong Austin upgrade. They survived one more year of intense rivalry, with Ocon making contact after lunging Gasly at Monaco's Portier, the stress point!

MISSION ACCOMPLISHED

After 14 years of Red Bull and Mercedes domination, McLaren won its first F1 Constructors' Championship in 26 years. It was a hard-fought battle that went down to the wire in Abu Dhabi, as TONY DODGINS relates...

Above: Max Verstappen's dominant start to the season proved decisive, as he claimed a fourth successive world title.
Photo: Pirelli

Above right: A tough year for Christian Horner, but he ended it at Buckingham Palace to receive a CBE.

Right: Sergio Pérez's loss of form led to him agreeing to a mutual split from the team after four seasons.
Photos: Red Bull Content Pool/Getty Images

Opening spread: A jubilant tableau for McLaren's pit-lane celebrations in Abu Dhabi.
Photo: McLaren F1 Team

WHEN Red Bull began the defence of its drivers' and constructors' titles with a dominant 1-2 in the Bahrain season-opener, neutrals feared another year of crushing dominance à la 2023, when the team had won every race bar Singapore.

Speaking post-race, team principal Christian Horner said, "It's just one circuit, with very cool temperatures [the race had an 18.00 local start time]. Next week in Jeddah, we have a street track with much higher temperatures. We're going to need three, four, even five races before we see a true pattern. From testing, the field has converged. We're going to face some big challenges – Ferrari, Mercedes and Aston Martin all looked very competitive."

Note: Horner neglected to mention McLaren, for whom Lando Norris and Oscar Piastri had qualified seventh and eighth, and finished sixth and eighth respectively at Sakhir. That evening, what odds would you have been offered on a final championship top three of: 1, McLaren, 666 points; 2, Ferrari, 652; 3, Red Bull, 589?

After Max Verstappen won seven of the first ten races, plus sprint races in Shanghai and Miami, who could have imagined that a championship fight with Norris would be the story line that ran as far as Las Vegas in the second half of the season?

Certainly, it was a difficult season for Horner, who had to contend with superstar designer Adrian Newey's announcement in May that he was leaving; the influence of his recently-departed chief designer, Rob Marshall, at McLaren; the loss of long-term stalwarts Jonathan Wheatley (sporting director) and Will Courtenay (chief strategist) to Sauber/Audi and McLaren respectively; and a dramatic drop-off in form from Sergio Pérez that ultimately cost Red Bull the title.

By the time the curtain came down on F1's 24-race, longest ever season, Horner's Bahrain prediction had been spot on. When George Russell won in Las Vegas, he made it seven drivers with multiple wins in the same season, which had not happened since 1981. And not since 1977 had four different constructors won at least three races in one year.

Horner rates 2024 as Verstappen's best season and Max agrees: "Last year, I had a dominant car, but I always felt that not everybody appreciated what we achieved as a team, winning ten races in a row. The car was not as dominant as people thought, but this year, I'd say that 70 per cent of the time we didn't have the fastest car."

When McLaren arrived at round six in Miami, its heavily upgraded car became the class of the field. "But, actually, we still extended our lead, so that's something I'm very proud of," Verstappen pointed out. Pre-Miami, he had led Norris by 52 points, while at season's end, the margin was 63 points.

"You always have to believe, but in the middle of the season, we had a lot of issues where we didn't really understand what was going on with the car," Max admitted, "But I'm proud of how the team reacted and turned it around from Austin, and put us in the fight a bit more, so all credit to them for that."

Doubtless, many drivers on the F1 grid could have won the championship in Verstappen's 2023 car. But how many could have won it in his '24 car? The chasm between Verstappen and team-mate Pérez underlined that it was Max who made the difference. The average qualifying delta between them across the season was 0.486s, the largest on the grid. To put that in context, Valtteri Bottas was quicker than Zhou Guanyu by a similar margin at Sauber, but, other than that, no team-mate delta was greater than a quarter of a second.

While Verstappen won nine times, Pérez was the only driver in the top four teams without a victory. After four podiums in the first five races, he went on a 19-race streak without one and finished a distant eighth in the championship, 70-odd points behind seventh-placed Lewis Hamilton. Such had been Red Bull's dominance in 2023 that Pérez had finished the championship second to Verstappen. But, as the field converged, every driver in the rival top three teams got between them. The constant pressure and questions over his future only exacerbated the situation, and although Sergio had a Red Bull contract for 2025, he'd lost confidence by year's end. A mutual parting of the ways was agreed, and Liam Lawson has the unenviable task of sitting alongside Verstappen in 2025.

Above: "Where did you come from?" Charles Leclerc and Oscar Piastri after a clinical move had clinched a second and significant race win for the young Aussie.
Photo: XPB Images

Top right: Piastri crosses the line in Hungary to score his maiden win.
Photo: McLaren F1 Team

Above right: Having followed team orders, Lando Norris congratulates Piastri on his Hungaroring success.
Photo: Atsuo Sakurai

Right: Flawless under pressure, Norris sealed the deal for McLaren by delivering a fourth win in Abu Dhabi.
Photo: McLaren F1 Team

After McLaren's great turnaround in 2023, CEO Zak Brown was targeting championships, and his team's first constructors' championship since 1998 was the feel-good story of the season.

Both Lando Norris and Oscar Piastri scored their first grand prix wins – Lando in Miami and Oscar in Hungary – as the team's MCL38 became the car to beat. There were further emphatic wins for Norris in Zandvoort and Singapore, and a superb drive to win in Abu Dhabi and clinch the constructors' championship under strong early pressure from Carlos Sainz and Ferrari.

Piastri also stood on the podium's top step in Baku after mugging Charles Leclerc in a race that it seemed the Monégasque couldn't lose. You can never say that a championship is down to one race, but if Piastri hadn't made that superb opportunist pass into Turn One from way back, which Oscar himself described as 50/50, only just keeping the McLaren out of the wall on exit, the team would not have won the constructors' championship. It created a 14-point swing between Piastri and Leclerc at that race, which was the amount by which McLaren beat Ferrari at season's end. Had Leclerc won Baku and not Piastri, the teams would have finished the season level on points, with Ferrari taking the title on a win countback by six races to five. Not that we wish to give Charles sleepless nights…

How had McLaren closed the gap to Red Bull and overhauled them? Zak Brown has always given enormous credit to the leadership of Andrea Stella (*see feature, page 34*), who had taken over as team principal in December, 2022. And, as mentioned, the team had also poached Red Bull chief designer Rob Marshall after 18 years at Milton Keynes. Marshall, whose CV includes a spell at Rolls-Royce, is renowned for his strong knowledge of aero-elasticity, which, via flexi-wings, was a key component in addressing one of the great challenges of the current generation of ground-effect cars – a tendency towards low-speed understeer and high-speed oversteer. A rear wing that backs off its power at high speed allows the front wing to be sufficiently aggressive to combat low-speed understeer.

Just how influential has Marshall been at McLaren? Stella, reflecting on the season, admitted that his impact had been even greater than expected.

"We had not focused enough on aero-elasticity before," Stella said. "It can deliver performance, but only if you do specific studies. We were able to do these because we had expanded the team and added resources, gained quite a lot of efficiency, stimulated by the cost-cap requirement. This allowed us to take on more projects."

Flexi-wings have been part of F1 for aeons, of course, but only a few weeks after rival teams had been jumping up and down about McLaren's front wing, the team introduced a new family of rear wings 'upgraded around some more modern concepts' at Spa.

It wasn't long before this was being referred to as McLaren's 'mini DRS' rear wing – very useful at places with a lot of high-speed running, such as Spa, Azerbaijan and Monza.

And so, back to Azerbaijan. Leclerc, as usual, had been in a class of his own around Baku in qualifying and had taken a fourth consecutive pole by more than three-tenths. He had the race fully under control during the opening stint on the medium tyre. But Ferrari kept him out a lap longer than they should have done before pitting for hards, allowing Piastri to move too close. Then Oscar caught out Charles with that great late lunge. Leclerc, concentrating on bringing his hard tyres in gently, had checked his mirrors, concluded that the McLaren was too far back and hadn't covered off the inside.

Still, Leclerc wasn't unduly concerned, thinking that he would easily repass the McLaren later with DRS down the long straight. But he could not. The top element of McLaren's rear wing was twisting slightly at its outer bottom edges, opening a slight gap between the two wing elements and giving a mini-DRS effect when Piastri did not have DRS.

It reduced drag and provided Oscar with a straight-line speed boost, albeit small. Data from qualifying showed that, of the leading cars, McLaren had the slowest top speed when DRS was active, but the highest top speed when it was inactive. Even from just over half a second behind entering the DRS zone, Leclerc could not get a move done, whereas Piastri had passed the Ferrari from 0.7s back.

Rival teams lobbied the FIA to take action, estimating that the wing had been worth a couple of tenths. A week later in Singapore, Zak Brown revealed that he had told the FIA that McLaren would not use it again. The personification of magnanimity? Or the action of a man who knew that it would only be needed again in Las Vegas, where, coincidentally, McLaren had its weakest race... All part of the F1 game!

Why didn't everyone go down the flexi-wing route to the same extent as McLaren? Mercedes did, and made significant gains to the point where the team could win four races, more than in any other season since ground effect had returned in 2022. Red Bull probably underestimated the extent to which its advantage would be eroded, particularly after Verstappen's start to the season, and was also hemmed in by the cost cap. And at Ferrari, Frédéric Vasseur was wary of committing resource to an area that the FIA might potentially have stamped on.

After a 2023 season in which Ferrari often had demonstrated strong qualifying pace, but high tyre degradation in races, the 2024 car was conceptually

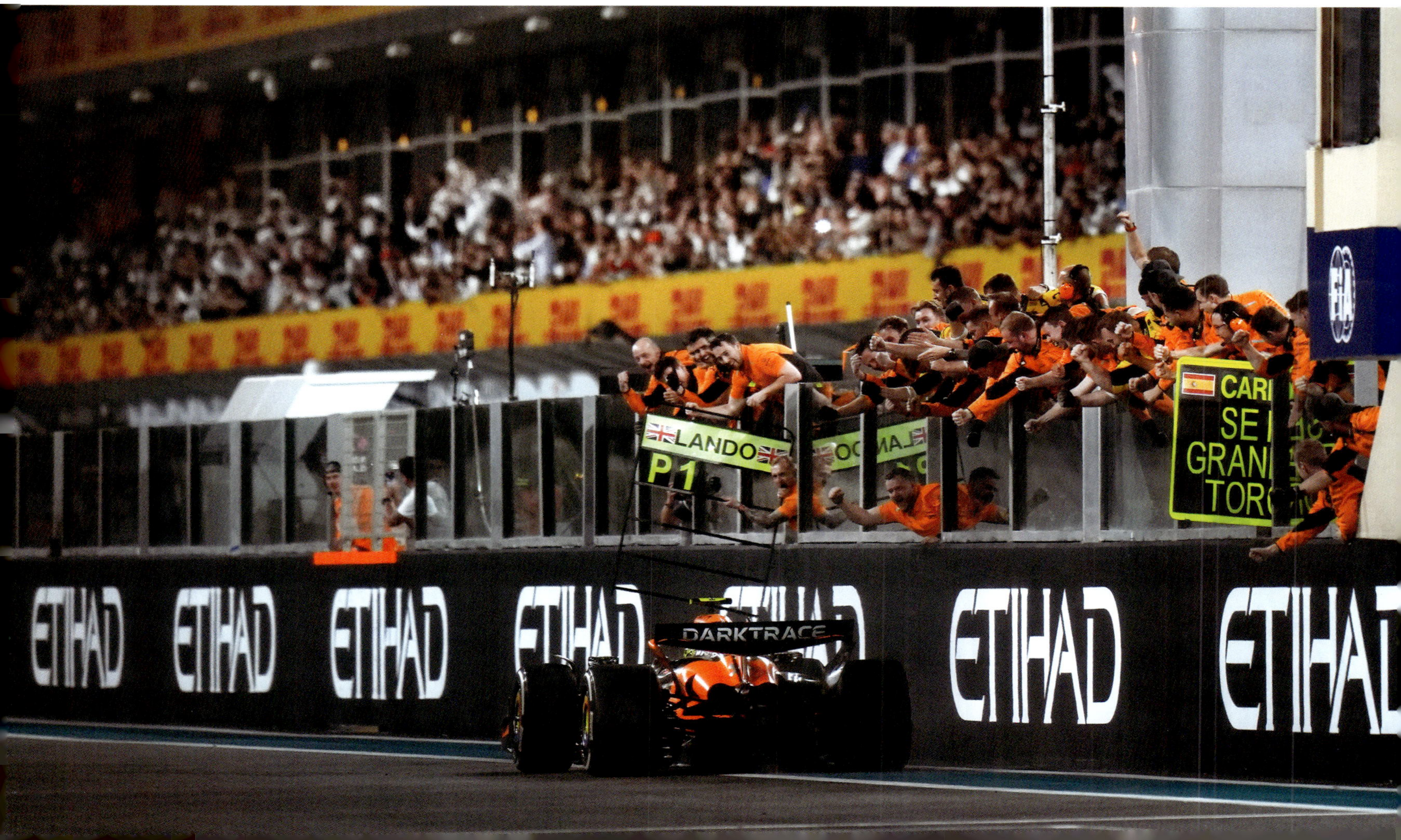

Above: A dream came true for Charles Leclerc, who finally won his home grand prix in Monte Carlo.

Top right: Leclerc took three wins, including a dominant drive at the United States GP in Austin.

Above right: Done the gigs, got the T-shirt! Carlos Sainz proudly sports his successes with Ferrari.

Photos: Scuderia Ferrari

Right: Mercedes hit the sweet spot as George Russell was utterly dominant in Las Vegas.

Photo: Mercedes-AMG Petronas F1 Team

different and had opposing characteristics. Sometimes, it struggled to generate front tyre temperature in qualifying, but benefited from relatively benign tyre usage in races. Leclerc used this to great effect at Suzuka, Zandvoort and especially Monza, where he managed to beat the McLarens by one-stopping to take an emotional second win in front of the *tifosi*.

Monte Carlo might have been one of the most tedious GPs in living memory, with the first ten on the grid finishing in the same order for the first time in F1 history, but it was a tense couple of hours for Leclerc followers. Brought up in Monaco, Charles has always had super-high-level performance around his home streets – any streets for that matter – but zero luck. As usual, he was on pole, and this time he finally shook the monkey off his back. A third strong win came in Austin, where he took full advantage of Verstappen driving Norris into the next state at Turn One, and was never seen again.

Carlos Sainz had the best of his four seasons at Ferrari, with a great win in Melbourne just a couple of weeks after missing Jeddah through appendicitis. It was surpassed, though, by his drive in Mexico, where he took pole and dominated.

Sainz has a strong racing brain and intelligence, and sometimes could adapt and generate tyre temperature in qualifying where Leclerc could not. His approach, levels of effort and professionalism speak volumes for a man who loved being a Ferrari driver, but knew that he was being replaced by Lewis Hamilton at the end of the season. In Abu Dhabi, he was still giving his all.

When Leclerc won Monaco and a Ferrari upgrade was just around the corner, a championship challenge appeared to be on the cards. Unfortunately, the new configuration introduced for round ten in Barcelona reinstated the dreaded bouncing and was a backward step. For a key batch of four or five mid-season races, Ferrari spent time back-to-backing different set-ups in an attempt to solve its issues, which it did finally with another significant upgrade at Monza. By then, it was too late, although the team did take McLaren to the wire.

At Mercedes, George Russell and Hamilton finished the year sixth and seventh in the championship respectively – the first time that Lewis had been outside the top six in his F1 career following a topsy-turvy year. After a tricky start, during which neither drivers nor team could fathom the car, finding it tricky to balance, an aero-elastic front wing introduced at Monaco gave the car more speed. Having regularly been qualifying on the third or fourth row, suddenly Russell took pole in Canada.

"Montreal was a reward for all the hard work and dedication from the team because sometimes you're thinking, 'When are we going to get a reward?'" George said. "This is the first time we really feel the momentum shift and had a clear idea of what we needed."

Two races later, he won in Austria, albeit fortuitously after Verstappen and Norris had collided, and then took pole at Silverstone as Mercedes locked out the front row. Retirement with a water leak was a blow, but a fine drive by Hamilton broke a winless spell for the seven-times champion that dated back to 2021. Then he produced

another fine performance at Spa, but was narrowly beaten by George eking out his tyres to make a one-stop work. Frustratingly for Russell, though, the car was marginally underweight and he was disqualified, Lewis taking the win.

From early in the season, if the surface was flat, allowing the car to be run low, and track temperature was low, the Mercedes was right there. But when the temperature came up, it was a different story. In Melbourne, for example, Hamilton was top of the time sheets in FP1 and FP2 on a cold day, but then didn't even make Q3.

Las Vegas, though, was right up the W15's street. With temperatures dictating parkas and bobble hats, Russell put the car on pole and controlled the race, while Hamilton was super-strong, driving through the field to second from tenth after a qualifying mistake.

This was by no means the first qualifying issue for Lewis who, puzzlingly, struggled much more relative to his team-mate. Remember Russell at Williams, one of the quickest one-lap drivers on the grid with his 'Mr Saturday' nickname? When he was given his Mercedes promotion, many predicted that he might get the better of Hamilton in qualifying, if not the race. It was always super-tight, and for two seasons they were separated by mere hundredths. In 2024, Russell outqualified Hamilton 19–5 (24–6 if you include the sprints) by an average of 0.173s.

It was one of the big question marks of the season, but clearly no surprise to Lewis. As early as Monaco, he said, "I don't anticipate being ahead of George in qualifying this year. I already know that I'm going to lose two-tenths going into qualifying."

Above: Lewis Hamilton signed off his Mercedes career in style.
Photo: Atsuo Sakurai

Top right: Who the f**k needs Steiner? Ayao Komatsu took over the reins at Haas to great effect with a limited budget.
Photo: MoneyGram Haas F1 Team

Above right: Lawrence Stroll's ambition is as strong as ever, but his team went backwards in 2024.
Photo: Aston Martin Aramco F1 Team

Top far right: Pierre Gasly enhanced his reputation with some sparkling late-season performances for Alpine.
Photo: BWT Alpine F1 Team

Right: Despite occasional spats throughout the season, George Russell and Lando Norris remained on good terms with the champion.
Photo: Red Bull Content Pool/Getty Images

As the year progressed, he regressed to "I suck in qualifying" and even, after qualifying in Vegas, "I'm not fast any more." The latter, of course, was seized upon and spun into stories about how worrying such a declaration must be for Messrs Elkann and Vasseur at Maranello.

But of course, Lewis Hamilton doesn't forget how to drive fast. It's just that in the sound-bite confines of a TV interview, he doesn't have the time or inclination to go into specifics.

Hamilton is a driver who likes a car 'on the nose' with a sharp turn-in. He likes to brake late, carry a lot of speed into the corner and then sort out the rear end. But the current generation of F1 cars are bigger and heavier than ever, with the low-speed understeer and snap oversteer already mentioned. Those characteristics are worsened by the rakeless flat platform needed for consistent downforce, which removes any pitch to load up the front.

"Lewis has particularly struggled on single laps," Mercedes trackside engineering director Andrew Shovlin said in Hungary. "His long-run pace is always there. It's more about the way that he wants to attack a corner. When you do that, then the car snaps to oversteer. You start to build tyre temperature. So, most of our work has been trying to give him a car that you can drive in his very attacking style and extract the lap time, without it breaking away on the way in and catching him by surprise."

Leclerc drives in a similar manner and hates understeer. Interestingly, at Ferrari, the qualifying delta versus Sainz was much closer in 2024, less than five-hundredths across the season. It will be fascinating to see how Charles and Lewis compare.

Outside the top four, Aston Martin finished fifth once more, but had a disappointing season. Lawrence Stroll is investing a fortune (see *feature, page 46*), but that is very much about the future. In the present, the car's development lost ground to the opposition, and Fernando Alonso's multi-podiums of 2023 were way out of reach. A fifth place in round two at Jeddah was the highlight of the Spaniard's year. Technical director Dan Fallows, who had joined from Red Bull in 2022, paid the price and moved elsewhere in the organisation as Stroll attracted heavy hitters like Adrian Newey and Andy Cowell.

Alpine had a season of upheaval, with Hitech GP boss Oliver Oakes coming in as team principal and Flavio Briatore brought back as executive advisor by Renault Group CEO Luca de Meo. After a difficult start to the year, things improved, and a late-season Austin upgrade helped the team retain its top-six position in the teams' pecking order, along with some top-quality performances from Pierre Gasly, which saw off the challenge from Haas. The latter did a strong job, Ayao Komatsu having taken over from Guenther Steiner as team principal, and Nico Hülkenberg in particular doing a fine job to finish in the championship top ten.

In the final analysis, nobody was ever going to give Verstappen a 50-point start in the championship and catch him, without the aid of unreliability from Red Bull, which, after Max retired in Melbourne, didn't occur again. When it began to get a bit close, Max became more physical and there were some flash points, in Austria and Austin specifically.

A slow Red Bull pit stop at Red Bull Ring had allowed Norris to close in and, with seven laps to go, he tried to pass Verstappen into Turn Three. The resulting collision gave both punctures. The stewards gave Verstappen a 10s penalty for being "predominantly at fault", but while Lando retired, Max went on to finish fifth, his penalty having no effect.

"I looked forward to a strong fair battle, but I wouldn't say that's what it was in the end," Norris lamented. "A tough one to take. It was a mistake-free race from my side, but I got taken out."

Norris felt that Verstappen had ignored the rule that precluded moving in the braking zone. "You're not allowed to react to the other driver, and that's what he did, three times out of three," he claimed. "Twice I managed to avoid

it and not run into him, and the third time he ran into me. There's rules, and if they aren't followed, there's nothing I can do."

So long as Verstappen avoided any big points swings to Norris, he was safe. Ferrari's late-season performance jump was actually a boon for Max. In Austin, where Norris and Verstappen were on the front row, Max went down the inside, ushered Lando wide on exit and allowed Leclerc through into a lead that Charles never surrendered as Ferrari finished 1-2.

Later in the race, Lando attempted to go around the outside of Verstappen into Turn 12 with the aid of DRS. But, thanks to regulations that give the corner to the driver ahead at the apex, all Max had to do was go deep on the brakes and run Lando wide. Norris passed off-track, did not give the place back and earned a penalty.

What McLaren was hoping was that with Verstappen off the track on exit himself, either he would receive a penalty for forcing another driver off, or the overtake would be allowed to stand. That didn't happen, though. Should it have? Probably, yes, because if that was legitimate defence, how is anyone ever going to make a successful overtake? It led to much debate and the feeling that a rule tweak was necessary.

Then, a week later in Mexico, they were at it again, Norris trying to go around the outside of the Red Bull in Turn Four and Verstappen forcing him off. This time, Max was given a 10s penalty, then another when he forced Norris off at Turn Eight in a much more dubious manner. Was 10s enough for that?

As at Turn One in Austin, Leclerc was the beneficiary. This was Verstappen operating in the grey areas. He knew that on that particular day, he didn't have the necessary pace in the Red Bull to fight Norris, but that the Sainz/Leclerc Ferraris did, so he was hoping that Norris would lose ground and potentially points to the Ferraris.

Quite what you think of such tactics depends on your perspective. Verstappen knew the rule book, and so long as he didn't do anything outrageous enough to earn a race ban, well, so be it, that's racing. Accusations of ruthless tactics had been levelled at other greats, such as Senna and Schumacher before him.

Niggles and inconsistencies that developed in the latter part of the season – how on earth was Russell penalised for an inside pass of Valtteri Bottas in Austin? – led to a feeling that the FIA should be concentrating on bigger issues, such as driving standards and racing guidelines, gravel traps or future regulations, rather than giving Verstappen community service for swearing, or fining Charles Leclerc for the same offence. It led to the Grand Prix Drivers Association (GPDA) issuing a letter asking to be treated like adults.

Okay, F1 drivers are role models, but F1 bleeps out most of the swearing in radio transmissions anyway and fans like to see emotions coming out. Imagine if footballers were miked up while a game was going on! Swearing in a press conference is slightly different, but, even then, it was hardly a big deal, and kids hear far worse in a school playground on a daily basis.

Neils Wittich leaving his role as race director came out of the blue with three races still to go. He was replaced by F2/F3 race director Rui Marques, the BBC reporting that Wittich had left as a result of his relationship with FIA president Mohammed Ben Sulayem.

With just a year left before swingeing changes for 2026, the last year of the existing regulations could produce a truly epic 2025 season if the closeness of the current grid is any barometer. One difference, will be the absence of the fastest-lap bonus point, introduced in 2019.

Opinion is polarised, but most drivers agree that it did not serve the purpose of rewarding the quickest driver. Instead, it came down to whomever had a pit-stop gap behind them through race circumstances and could take on a set of fresh tyres. And, in some cases, it was open to abuse by second or affiliated teams. In Singapore, for instance, VCARB, the Red Bull junior team, pitted Daniel Ricciardo for softs in his last GP, which prevented McLaren from picking up an extra point. And in Abu Dhabi, Haas, which uses Ferrari engines, did likewise with Kevin Magnussen, which again stopped McLaren, who had the quickest car, from going for an additional point, which might have been crucial. How about an extra point for pole position? Altogether more deserved and sensible?

STELLAR BY NATURE

When Zak Brown first offered Andrea Stella the team principal's role at McLaren, he declined. Three years later, he took it on. TONY DODGINS considers the background to that decision and the Italian's thoughts on putting McLaren back on top after a quarter-century wait...

Above: Andrea Stella's calm, measured approach is appreciated at McLaren.

Right: Abu Dhabi, 14th October, 2010 – the day that the championship slipped from Fernando Alonso's grasp at the final round.

Above right: Brazil, 2014. The younger Stella chats with Alonso.

Photos: XPB Images

FERRARI, McLaren and Williams used to be F1's goliaths, in the same way that Red Bull and Mercedes dominated the sport for 14 consecutive years from 2010 to 2023. When Ayrton Senna beat Alain Prost to win the 1993 season-closer in Adelaide, it marked the end of an era. Senna was leaving McLaren after six years and three world titles; Prost had just driven his last GP after four championships and a then-record 51 victories. The Australian win was a milestone for Ron Dennis's McLaren – for the first time, it moved one race ahead of Ferrari as the F1 team with the most wins, and from a history that was 16 years shorter.

Since then, Ferrari has redressed the balance. After Abu Dhabi, 2024, the numbers look like this: Ferrari, 248 wins; McLaren, 189; Mercedes, 129; Red Bull, 122. Much of that is down to five years of Maranello's total dominance in the early 2000s – the Michael Schumacher era. Woking's last constructors' championship, before 2024's fabulous turnaround, was in 1998.

That phenomenal Schumacher-era Ferrari team was where Andrea Stella, the man today's McLaren CEO Zak Brown credits with returning the team to the top of the pile, cut his racing teeth.

Stella, 53, hails from Orvieto in Umbria, Italy, midway between Florence and Rome, where he graduated in aerospace engineering from the Sapienza University. He also has a PhD in mechanical engineering and had mentioned his interest in F1 to his thesis tutor at the same time as Ferrari had approached universities in their search for suitable candidates. He joined the Scuderia in his late twenties as a performance engineer specialising in data analysis.

At first, Stella worked with the test team before moving on to the race team with Schumacher. One driver who encountered him was Brazilian Luciano Burti, whose own F1 career had ended after a huge shunt at Spa, following a collision with Eddie Irvine. However, he was taken on by Ferrari as a test driver. Burti mentioned two of Stella's qualities: an uncanny grasp of data and what to do with it, as if he'd been in the car with the driver, and nurturing. These human qualities made him feel part of the team.

Ferrari's super-team had been structured by Jean Todt, whose work ethic was famed throughout the paddock. Stella found himself working around high-quality, senior people. Men like Ross Brawn, Rory Byrne, James Allison, Nicolas Tombazis, all led by the charismatic Luca Montezemolo, whom Stella described as a team builder.

Talking to F1's *Beyond The Grid* podcast, Stella said that many of the individuals there could have accepted lucrative offers elsewhere, but they remained in their Ferrari roles because there was a sense of wanting to be part of the team and to work with their mates.

"Michael's desire to win was so great that you almost needed a team to manage it," he said. "He was the emotional engine. He was very connected at a personal level, very sensitive. I was exposed to excellent people and the level of motivation needed, which is beyond what most people are comfortable with. You needed to be comfortable with feeling uncomfortable."

After a spell working on engine braking and differential control, Stella became Kimi Räikkönen's Ferrari race engineer in 2009 and then spent five years working with Fernando Alonso, with whom he formed a strong relationship. They narrowly missed out on winning the championship in both 2010 and 2012.

That 2010 Abu Dhabi season finale in particular was a shattering blow for both. Going in, Alonso was leading the championship with 246 points to Mark Webber's 238, Sebastian Vettel's 231 and Lewis Hamilton's 222. Hamilton could only take the title if he won the race and the other three failed to score significant points, so effectively it was Alonso and Ferrari versus Red Bull. Alonso had that eight-point cushion over Webber, and if Vettel won, Fernando needed to be fourth.

When Vettel took pole, the pressure was increased, but with Alonso third on the grid, things were under control. Even when Jenson Button beat the Ferrari off the line, Fernando ran fourth. With Webber fifth, directly behind him, Ferrari saw the Australian as the only threat to that all-important fourth place. But they were wrong. A first-lap collision between Michael Schumacher's Mercedes and Tonio Liuzzi, brought out the safety car, and both Nico Rosberg's Mercedes and Vitaly Petrov's Renault were among those that pitted for the prime (hard tyre), which then would go to the end.

When Red Bull pitted Webber early – too early to have a pit window to Rosberg and Petrov – a dubious strategy, Ferrari covered him with Alonso. It was a mistake, which dropped Fernando behind Rosberg, Petrov and Robert Kubica in the sister Renault, who had started on the prime tyre after qualifying outside the top ten.

This was a year before DRS arrived and a year before Pirelli control tyres. A driver could run around Yas Marina on Bridgestone primes all day long without any significant degradation. Further, Renault was running very little rear wing and also had a highly efficient F-duct (remember them?). Although slow through the twisty final sector, where they couldn't be passed anyway, the Renaults were ballistic down the straight. And at the first running of the Abu Dhabi GP the previous year, there had been just four successful overtakes.

"Use your talent," Stella, who had not been responsible for the strategy call, encouraged Alonso on the radio. But with all those contributory factors, the Good Lord himself wouldn't have passed a Renault around Abu Dhabi that evening. The frustrated Spaniard was trapped behind Petrov for the rest of race and finished seventh, while Vettel won and took his first championship. The Italian media? Well, you can imagine. It was as though someone had shot the Pope…

Inevitably, on Saturday night in Abu Dhabi, 2024, with Stella on the brink of leading McLaren to its first constructors' title in 26 years, the disappointment reared its head.

"Going back to this track 14 years ago, it was potentially the most painful day in my F1 career," Andrea reflected. "But if I look back now, and I've talked about this with Fernando a couple of times, we actually feel proud of what we achieved in 2010. That we were there fighting in Abu Dhabi, in a year where we didn't enjoy any technical advantage. It was thanks to great execution and great driving by Fernando that we were fighting for the championship at that last race.

"Ultimately, over time, while you are proud of your victories, sometimes when you don't win, it's what counts the most in making you what you are today. I hope that in some of the learning and even the emotional toughness that you gain, I have been able to add something to my career. And, also, to my contribution to McLaren."

That contribution, according to Zak Brown, has been huge. As he said when AUTOCOURSE interviewed him a year ago, "Our turnaround is 100 per cent people related. Andrea has been awesome, and we've had a total change of leadership: new team principal, new technical director and new head of aero. The other 997 people are the same. The difference between how the team is led now and before is night and day."

In 2015, when Alonso left Ferrari for McLaren after five years, he recommended Stella as a man who could make a difference. This was before Brown had taken over the reins, when the team was at a low point in its history, struggling financially and about to embark on a difficult season, with Honda entering F1's turbo hybrid formula a year earlier than it would have liked at Ron Dennis's behest. Stella joined as head of race operations. With a wife, Michela, and two sons, Edoardo and Federico, committing to a move to England was a big decision.

Once Brown had his feet properly under the table and the time to take stock, he was impressed by Stella, who was promoted to performance director in 2018. The following season, Zak sounded him out about becoming team principal, but feeling that he wasn't ready, Stella turned it down. McLaren appointed Andreas Seidl from Porsche instead, with Stella becoming executive director, racing. Finally, he accepted the TP role in December, 2022, when Seidl departed for a new role at Sauber/Audi.

Reflecting as the champagne flowed post-race in Abu

35

Above: The McLaren MCL38, which finally returned the constructors' title to Woking after 26 years.

Top right: Oscar Piastri is hugged by Stella after his victory in Hungary.

Above right: Lando and Zak Brown celebrate their victory in Abu Dhabi.

Right: Gil de Ferran is not forgotten at McLaren. Lando and the team convene for a tribute in Miami.
Photos: McLaren F1 Team

Dhabi, Stella said, "From the time I joined McLaren to celebrating a championship means, if you want, that we have come almost through a circle. I often mention to the team that in the first race in 2015 in Australia, between our best lap in Q1 [Button's McLaren-Honda] to the pole position [Lewis Hamilton's Mercedes], there were five seconds. And we have gone all the way thanks to great resilience and great belief.

"I would like to thank in particular Zak, Paul Walsh [McLaren Group executive chairman] and all our shareholders for their faith in the changes that gradually have been implemented and put McLaren in a very solid position. When you are trusted, when you start to be able to deliver the investments necessary, you can compete at the top.

"The final bit of the circle came through unlocking the people. But I'm not sure that you can actually appreciate what that means if you're not actually part of seeing the rapid progress of 1,000 people. But that's what has happened. Hopefully, this is not a high point, but a starting point.

"You cannot do anything if you are a one-man show, even if you are team principal. You need the support of your chairman, CEO, shareholders, and we need to be aligned, otherwise you don't create a culture. Zak walks the factory with me very often and we have several conversations. Ultimately, it is the accumulation of these numerous, numerous conversations that change the culture and trust in an organisation. They see that as a TP or CEO, you are one of them. And thanks to conversations, we build the way we want to be as a group. And then we will guarantee that the way we want to build will be implemented. That's where you really make a difference as a TP or CEO. Not because you bring new staff, but because what we agree altogether will be guaranteed.

"This is the process we went through and the reason why I wear this pin," Stella said poignantly as he pointed to a helmet badge in the colours of Gil de Ferran affixed to his shirt.

The late Brazilian, twice Champ Car champion and Indy 500 winner, was McLaren's sporting director from 2018 to 2020, and then acted as an adviser from May, 2023, until his death from a heart attack in December of that year while karting with his son.

"Gil was the first person I talked to when the proposal to be team principal came across," Stella related. "Because of his friendship, wisdom, and incredible qualities at a human level and his intelligence. And he was always a great racer. It was very clear that whatever I was going to build, I was going to build it with Gil. He was my advisor, my personal consultant, and if we implemented the culture and created the belief, if we were able to increase the standards to the level required, this is also because Gil was part of the process.

"So, it was easy for us and straightforward to dedicate our first victory in Miami to Gil. I wear this pin all the time when I am at the factory, and for the final race, I needed to give a clear message to myself and to everyone that Gil was with us throughout the season."

This unlocking or empowering of people within an organisation, constantly developing and concentrating on the human side, seems to come naturally to Stella. While there's an abundance of courses and books espousing such things, the importance of open-minded personal relationships was demonstrated to him first-hand at Ferrari.

When asked about the cultural differences between the two teams, he said, "Before we talk about differences, I would say that there are fundamentals that are very, very similar. The commitment of the people, the passion.

Sometimes I hear about the passion in the Italian team and more of a cold approach [in the British one], which I can definitely say is not true. The motivation, the passion that we have at McLaren is definitely comparable with what I was used to at Ferrari.

"Moving from one team to the other, I didn't have to think in a different way. What I've found very powerful at McLaren is that when we have agreement, when we identify common solutions, when we put in place, let's call it, rules or behaviours, or principles that can form the culture, then the team members are consistent in sticking with what was agreed. It's made progress easy."

In a major 1,000-plus-people organisation like an F1 team, full of highly competent, competitive individuals, the need to put senior people in the right places, empower them and have them all pull in the same direction, leaving egos at the door, is easy to say, but not easy to do. When it worked in the way Stella witnessed at Ferrari, the results were spectacular. As they were when Toto Wolff achieved it at Mercedes, and Christian Horner at Red Bull – excellent communicators both.

But there are always ripples in the road. Stella had to cope with one at the start of the 2024 season. In February, 2023, the decision was taken to part company with technical director James Key and to establish a new three-pronged technical leadership in the key areas of aerodynamics, performance development and engineering. Three technical directors would report directly to Stella. The highly-respected Peter Prodromou would head up the aero side; Neil Houldey, a McLaren design engineer since 2006, after five years at Lola, would take care of engineering; and David Sanchez, who had resigned from Ferrari, would join in charge of car concept and performance on 1st January, 2024, after a period of gardening leave.

But then, in May, 2023, McLaren had the opportunity to poach the highly-regarded Rob Marshall from Red

Above: Team players. Piastri and Norris give the team a strong and youthful driver pairing going forward.

Top right: Job done. Stella points to the screen as Norris takes the crucial win in Abu Dhabi.

Above right: Norris launched his championship bid by securing a win at Zandvoort.

Right: Victory in Singapore kept up the momentum, before Lando's challenge just fell short.
Photos: McLaren F1 Team

Bull, at 56 still a live wire steeped in F1. A race engineer at Benetton in 1994, he had joined Red Bull as chief designer in 2006 and was promoted to chief engineering officer in 2016. His early career included a spell at Rolls-Royce, and he is renowned for a keen understanding of aero-elasticity, a key area of F1 performance, especially in the ground-effect era.

When Sanchez arrived, there was a problem. Houldey had 'taken one for the team' and, despite his promotion, had accepted a deputy role on the engineering side to allow McLaren to accommodate Marshall. However, Sanchez was not prepared to play ball.

"The role we envisioned and had agreed to was not aligned with the reality of the position I found," Sanchez said. McLaren admitted that the Frenchman was "more senior" than the role the squad could offer him. After just three months, he was off to Alpine and Marshall was made chief designer.

There is no doubt that Marshall is a highly significant and perhaps even decisive addition to McLaren's strength (*see Season Review, page 24*). "Rob came with a reputation," Stella said, "and myself, the other technical directors and the team have all been impressed even more than we expected.

"His knowledge of how you design a car, especially from a layout point of view – and this will be very important in 2025 for the 2026 regulations – is very strong. Sitting next to him and seeing him working on the screen, I'm thinking it was really a good idea to get Rob. Because he's doing all the work in terms of layout for '25 and '26. We did miss this kind of role at McLaren before.

"In addition, he brings fantastic human qualities. He's a very positive person that everyone enjoys working with. He's full of energy. You can see him in the garage, often laying under the car. Everyone appreciates his incredible knowledge and experience, but at the same time, his hands – and sometimes even his head! – are dirty."

You can have the personnel, but without the infrastructure and tools, an F1 team is not going to win. One of the things that impressed Marshall was the correlation between wind tunnel/CFD and the track. Every upgrade that McLaren brought worked, which could not be said of Red Bull, Ferrari or Mercedes. After years of using Toyota's wind tunnel in Cologne, McLaren now has its own recommissioned tunnel, a big project, fully on stream.

"The new wind tunnel is definitely a big step forward," Stella said, "but that step is above all from a logistical point of view. I always stress that last year's car, both for the upgrades in Austria and for Singapore, was designed in the Toyota wind tunnel. But to develop things in the Toyota tunnel, you have the part ready and then it's tested two days after just because of the shipment. Now, we have the part ready and it's tested two hours later. You just gain so much efficiency.

"But in reality, chasing efficiency is not only thanks to the wind tunnel, but is in the whole approach to aerodynamic development. We have seen and experienced ourselves that even if you have more and more restrictions from a development point of view [as McLaren will have in terms of reduced wind tunnel/CFD time as a result of being champions], the way you generate the knowledge, the efficiency, is by far the most important thing. It's not like if you have three times the wind tunnel time, you will develop the car three times faster – that's not the case. And we have seen this in 2024 very well, because there were developments taken trackside by some teams that didn't necessarily represent progress. We are very much investing in quality."

McLaren's reliability throughout 2024 was also hugely

impressive. Lando Norris failed to finish just twice, on both occasions through contact, while Oscar Piastri was the only driver to complete every racing lap of the season.

"From an operational and reliability point of view, the team has achieved standards that make me think of the early 2000 years at Ferrari, where reliability was a religion," Stella said. "This is a result of investing in this area, and changing the organisation and culture. But with reliability in F1, you're as good as yesterday, there is no accumulated credit!"

One of the reasons why Stella was perhaps diffident in accepting the team principal role when it was first offered is that inevitably there is a public-facing role, and the man is a doer rather than a talker. But the pure common sense, immediacy, intelligence and eloquence that he offers to a camera or microphone, in other than his mother tongue, has been revelatory. And he doesn't pull his punches.

In Austria, after Norris's contact with Verstappen, for which Max was given a 10s penalty, but finished fifth while Lando retired, Stella opined, "The problem behind it is that if you don't address these things honestly, they come back. And they have come back today because they were not addressed properly in the past when there were some fights [involving Verstappen] with Lewis that needed to be punished in a harsher way. The fact is that we have so much respect for Red Bull, so much respect for Max that they don't need to do this. To almost compromise your reputation. Why would you do that?"

Then, clearly irked after Norris was given a five-second penalty, which cost him a podium, for overtaking Verstappen off-track in Austin, when Max had pushed him there and also left the track, Stella said, "The way the stewards interfered with a beautiful piece of motorsport was inappropriate because both cars went off-track and therefore gained an advantage. It costs us a podium in a race where we stayed patient after getting pushed off at the first corner [also by Verstappen] and accepted it."

Predictably, Stella didn't think much of Verstappen's first-corner collision with Piastri in Abu Dhabi either: "When you have teams fighting for the championship, it is the pinnacle and time to harvest the efforts of a season. That felt a little unnecessary. But sometimes adversities give you the opportunity to show your strengths, and I think that's what happened. First of all because Oscar never gave up and came back to score a point that could have been very important, if not the two points that would have been decisive in case of a swap between Carlos and Lando.

"And Lando showed his strengths delivering a perfect race when all the pressure was on him. He stayed very calm. He was calm on the radio as he considered some difficult options that we gave him, like when we said, 'Would you pit in the case of a safety car for a new set of tyres?' We saw him at his best, and his best is just incredibly competitive. I cannot wait to see Lando and Oscar in the future with a competitive car right from race one.

"And for me, the opportunity to show the team strengths was in Lando's pit stop. The whole season was on that last stop. A problem there, and we could have lost the position to Carlos and the championship. And the guys delivered what I think was the best stop of the season. It confirmed the trajectory, which was not only car performance, but the overall maturity, mentality and emotional resilience of the entire team. All this was given the opportunity to be shown thanks to the accident in corner one."

One thing that McLaren's rivals can bank on is that under Stella, nobody at the team will be resting on any laurels. "It would be naïve and arrogant to think that we have achieved something, that now we are perfect and can relax," he affirmed. "The best philosophy now is that you start as if you had lost. And that's what we are going to do." You don't doubt him.

THE BRAINS TRUST

That cliché about women and multi-tasking? There could be something in it. An F1 strategist's role is the ultimate manifestation of multi-tasking. Until recently, 40 per cent of F1's chief strategists were women. The ratio has only dipped because two have swapped the pit wall for the broadcast booth. All four are passionate about encouraging young women towards STEM subjects and motorsport. MAURICE HAMILTON spoke to them...

Above: A focused Hannah Schmitz at the Red Bull coalface.
Photo: Red Bull Content Pool/Getty Images

Inset, above right: Elf's Valerie Jorquera was one of F1's pioneering women in the seventies.
Photo: Elf

Far right: Ruth Buscombe has moved on from Sauber to work with F1TV.
Photo: F1TV

FIFTY years ago, Valerie Jorquera worked as a petro-chemist for Elf in the French company's role as supplier of Formula 1 fuel and lubricants. The French woman was treated as a novelty; a female in the paddock doing something other than being the partner of a driver or team boss. The wives and girlfriends might have applied impressive mental dexterity when using stop watches in the essential function of time-keeping, but this was patronisingly dismissed as merely giving the women something to do.

Jorquera was viewed as a curiosity, particularly when it became known that previously she had worked as a mechanic in her father's garage. An interest in motor racing had led Valerie to a minor administrative role within Elf, before she learned about chemistry and took exams as a means of actually getting a job in the paddock. In the seventies, this was a highly unusual career path. Now, such an option is enthusiastically embraced by young women, to such an extent that their influence in the successful running of any race team is widespread and much admired, both within the paddock and beyond.

The increase in female participation has been gradual, but inexorable over the decades. By the nineties, engineering had become a common means of entry.

Diane Holl was a senior member of John Barnard's design team in England, working for Ferrari. In Maranello itself, Morena Ferrari (no relation to the company founder) had been appointed as a fluid dynamics engineer. Dina Clark worked in the rapidly expanding electronics department at Benetton in Oxfordshire, while at Goodyear, Janet Melia, a chemical engineering graduate from Pittsburgh, Pennsylvania, had joined the racing division straight from college. In 1993, Sauber set a precedent by arriving in F1 with Carmen Ziegler as a team manager who was more than capable of holding her own.

Despite this obvious change in attitude, a feature in the colour supplement of a British Sunday newspaper in the early nineties chose not to recognise the significant shift. Under the heading 'Life's The Pits', the embellished piece focused on drivers' partners and concluded, "Women are thus reduced to the legion of worshippers or to the primal role of sex object in a macho world." The writer (a woman) would have difficulty in finding an excuse to employ such phraseology today. To coin an appropriate phrase, it would be a foolhardy strategy.

Female strategists along the pit wall have grown in number. This is not a tactful move on the part of politically-correct teams, keen to be seen to be 'doing the right thing'. The strategist's role is crucial and not one to be held hostage to social divergence. It is, in a stationary sort of way, as vital to a team's success as the driver exercising his skill in the cockpit. Both players need to react instantly to the many and varied curve balls that come their way – and remain totally calm while doing so. For an hour-and-a-half on a race-day afternoon, the effort and expectation of more than 900 people rest on the strategist and driver getting it right on their behalf. One wrong decision made in the blink of an eye can send weeks of preparation down the pan. It is not a responsibility that can be borne lightly. And yet, in this so-called macho world, at least four women are not only capable of doing it, but also of earning the hard-won respect of their predominantly male colleagues.

The strategist has to take a multitude of factors on board: track position; tyre degradation; tyre choice remaining; computer predictions; long-run performances during free practice; approaching weather; second guessing the strategy of rivals; race history on the track in question; information flowing from mission control back at team HQ; brief, but urgent conversations between drivers and their race engineers; the likelihood of a safety car; known intelligence about the driver in front and the challenger behind; the mind-set of the team's drivers on that particular weekend, and their history when under pressure or dealing with traffic; not to forget coping with the rising need to visit the bathroom in a race elongated by incidents and safety cars. All of the foregoing tension is being generated in the midst of a relentless cacophony of noise and vibration while the sun beats on their back and exacerbates an ambient pit-wall temperature of 30°C and more. There's no respite whatsoever.

Then, suddenly: "Safety car! Do we pit? We need to know NOW! Both cars? Which one first? Who's nearest pit entry? What's everyone else doing? Quick! Make up your mind!" It takes multi-tasking to a whole different level. Who on earth could cope with that? Why would anyone want to cope with that? Is this a singular female trait?

"I don't think so," says Ruth Buscombe. "One of the traits that makes a good strategist – male or female – is being very competitive. A bit like drivers; deep down, they all think they're the best. Strategists, in the same selfish way, think they're the best. Saying that, we have to keep our egos in check because it's easy to get it wrong. To be a good strategist, you have to enjoy and live for the pressure of a race. There's lots of other great jobs you can do in F1 if strategy isn't for you."

Above: Bernie Collins spent many years working for Force India and its subsequent guise as Aston Martin.
Photo: Aston Martin Aramco F1 Team

Above right: After a support strategist role at Ferrari, Ruth Buscombe moved trackside for Alfa Romeo Sauber.
Photo: Sauber

Above far right: An open mind and free thinking helped Rosie Wait find her perfect role at Mercedes.
Photo: Mercedes-AMG Petronas F1 Team

Right: Hannah Schmitz's skills have contributed to many of Red Bull's victories.
Photo: Red Bull Content Pool/Getty Images

Bernie Collins, a former strategist at Force India/Aston Martin, has also experienced the pressure of being the focal point on the pit wall.

"I'm good at thinking things through; that's one of my strengths," says Bernie. "Is it a female trait? I really don't know. Conversely, you could say a weakness of mine is a female peculiarity. If, say, there was an issue on the pit wall, I sometimes found difficulty moving on to the next problem. I was in danger of overthinking what's just happened and wondering if I could have done anything differently. Or if one of the engineers shouted at me, rather than taking it personally, I had to tell myself it was based on the situation, whatever it was, and not on me. Just move on! That is maybe a female thing, although saying that, I've spoken to guys who've said they'd react in the same way in a similar situation. So, who's to say? The one certainty is it's part of the strategist's job."

Another certainty is that such a scenario would have been far from future strategists' minds when studying at university. Most of them had never heard of the role, never mind imagined that eventually they would play such a focal part in the success or otherwise of a team operating on an annual budget of squillions of dollars. Hannah Schmitz (Red Bull), Rosie Wait (Mercedes) and Ruth Buscombe (ex-Ferrari/Sauber) are all Cambridge graduates. Bernie Collins studied for her engineering degree at Queens University, Belfast.

"I believe engineering has the power to solve a lot of the world's problems," says Collins. "I think it's really important. Something that's changing positively is the way people view it. They used to assume that you're in overalls, building a car, like a mechanic. Very few considered an engineer in the really high-tech aspect that it should be thought of. I think we're gradually changing the assumption that it's a dirty career. That's why a lot of females were put off becoming an engineer. But that attitude is changing, partly, I believe, from the success and profile emerging with the girls working as engineers and strategists in F1."

Rosie Wait recognises the importance of engineering, but appreciates the value of maintaining an open mind. In a Q+A on the Mercedes-AMG Petronas F1 web site, she said, "At school, I was very focused on studying the subjects I enjoyed, primarily maths and physics. This led me to an engineering degree at university, after which I moved into F1 in the vehicle dynamics department at McLaren. My advice to the younger generation would be not to get too hung up on the exact job you want, too early. Instead, focus on learning what you enjoy doing, what you are good at and what is important to you. Once you have a clear idea of these three things, then you can find a job that matches you, rather than trying to fit yourself into the job you think you want."

Hannah Schmitz's road to head of strategy at Red Bull began with an interest in cars and physics. "Early on," she says, "my parents noticed that I was playing with cars and Lego, not dolls. I was more interested in how things worked and putting them together. No one in my household watched motor racing, but I got interested and Dad was into watching any sport. I loved maths and physics at school, and had a really inspirational teacher. He taught us the application of physics in the real world and that's what got me interested in cars. I knew I wanted to do engineering in something automotive, and the pinnacle is obviously F1. It was at university that I started to see a route into it as a career. The year I graduated, I'd been sponsored in London by a building services company, which is where I was supposed to go, but then came the big economic crash and no one was hiring. Red Bull does a student placement scheme in Milton Keynes, and my supervisor from my final-year project, which was doing the suspension for a solar-powered car, thought it was something I'd be really interested in. I applied before I'd graduated and, fortunately, within three months of doing that placement, someone resigned and there was a full-time job. I knew as soon as I started that it was where I wanted to be."

Motorsport was furthest from Collins's mind when she began her studies at university. A turning point came when she joined Formula Student, part of a degree-level project that involved designing, building and racing a little single-seater race-car.

"Formula Student was a really useful and revealing mix of engineering experience and running a mini company," she says. "You needed to work together to make sure the chassis and components were ready in time; everything needed to come together while working to a very low budget. It allowed me to see a potential career. I could do the academic stuff and I could do the design work. I could figure out the best way to make something work.

"I hadn't really thought about automotive as a career. Formula Student made me realise that motorsport combines academic and practical aspects, both of which I really like. Even so, Formula 1 seemed a world away from whatever I might choose as a career. During my final year, McLaren Racing sent an advertisement directly to universities, saying they were looking to take on two newly-qualified mechanical or aerodynamic engineers for their graduate scheme. I gave it some thought, but didn't do anything. It was only through my lecturer actively encouraging me that I applied – almost as an afterthought. I got the job."

In common with other strategists, Bernie's journey to the pit wall included experience in various departments, from gearbox design to being a race engineer (with Jenson Button), before jumping in at the deep end with a

44 THE BRAINS TRUST

move to Force India as strategist. The structure and final result of her path is typical of what Ruth Buscombe refers to as, "Showing women that engineering and strategy is a job that's bankable; it's *available*. Previously, women didn't realise that."

Collins and Buscombe were the first to move away from the pit wall and lend their unique experience to media work, Bernie taking on a role with Sky F1, Ruth with F1TV. Their input has been a revelation, mainly because a strategist has never been free in the past to reveal in fascinating detail what is actually going on at the pit wall during a race weekend. Formula 1 being the secretive, suspicious business that it is, strategists were never allowed to breathe a word to anyone outside the team. A positive side effect of this exposure is having such intricate detail explained by women who clearly know what they're talking about – far in advance, usually, of their male co-presenters. To drive the point home, Collins has written a best-selling book, *How To Win A Grand Prix*, on the subject.

"I've had quite a surprise at the book signings," says Collins. "I'd say it was 50/50 male and female. And, of the women, I'd estimate up to 40 per cent of them are under the age of 20. They're not necessarily asking about engineering; some want to talk about, say, journalism or broadcasting. Their interest has been aroused by [Netflix series] *Drive to Survive*, or maybe seeing me on Sky F1. I've been impressed by the number of girls from many different backgrounds that are doing STEM [science, technology, engineering, mathematics] or want to get into engineering. It's so encouraging to see that."

Wait says, "I totally agree that we are seeing a transformation in motorsport and how many females are getting involved in all areas, which is great to be part of. We are seeing a lot more women joining the team in all departments, which is encouraging compared to ten years ago. But there is still a way to go, particularly in the more senior roles. I think this is important to give the more junior women the confidence that F1 can be a viable long-term career for them. I think the sport has done well to bring in more female commentators and analysts, and has challenged and removed some of the less appropriate historic elements, which projected the wrong image."

"I think the point is, yes, we do want the best people for the job, and that's not always a man," adds Schmitz. "So you need to open up the opportunities to meet those people that will be the best for the job. Don't be deterred just because there aren't many women. That's changing all the time and, to be honest, it doesn't really matter. People are proud to show what they do and to help encourage women, young girls to stay in STEM. There's so many exciting careers for them, and there are so many incredible women across motorsport. I'm really happy to help represent that."

Buscombe agrees: "It's particularly encouraging when you get a message – or perhaps a young girl comes up to you at a race-track – and they say, 'I'm in engineering because of you.' Or 'I'd never really thought of F1 as something I could be involved with, but hearing what you say has made that seem possible.' If I can inspire just one woman to be an engineer, that's good enough for me. It's brilliant to have such a wonderful opportunity to do that."

Such a wonderful proposition would never have crossed – indeed, never have been allowed to cross – Valerie Jorquera's mind in what we can recognise now as another age entirely.

Above: This can be stressful! Hannah tries to assimilate meteo maps, track data and a busy pit lane – all at the same time.
Photo: Red Bull Content Pool/Getty Images

Top left: Bernie Collins has transitioned successfully into her role with Sky TV.

Above left: Bernie, with Anthony Davidson, analysing race action.
Photos: FTW

Left: Rosie Wait makes a point. Messrs Wolff and Lord take it on board.
Photo: Mercedes-AMG Petronas F1 Team

DRIVING FORWARD

Lawrence Stroll is passionate, enthusiastic, persuasive – and a multi-billionaire. A dangerous combination. His goal is the F1 World Championship. Given the extraordinary off-track developments at Aston Martin in 2024, with Adrian Newey and Andy Cowell on board, TONY DODGINS wonders whether it would be a bigger shock if he failed, rather than succeeded…

Above: The perspective of a multi-billionaire allows Lawrence Stroll to consider his new managing technical partner, Adrian Newey, a bargain!

Right: Title sponsor Aramco is already hard at work on fuels and combustion, key parts of F1's new power-unit regulations for 2026.

Photos: Aston Martin Aramco F1 Team

HOW do you achieve a net worth of $4bn? Lawrence Sheldon Strulovic was born in Montreal in 1959 to a fashion importer father, who purchased the Canadian licences for Polo and Ralph Lauren clothing. By the age of 17, Lawrence was handling Pierre Cardin and soon began expanding Ralph Lauren in Europe with friend and Hong Kong textile manufacturer Silas Chou. Chou also made clothes for Tommy Hilfiger, and the partners went on to buy a majority share in the brand through a newly-formed company, Sportswear Holdings. Together, they boosted sales volumes tenfold to almost $2bn by the millennium.

Sportswear Holdings invested in the Michael Kors brand in 2003, paying $100m for 85 per cent of the business according to the *Financial Times*. When it was floated on the New York Stock Exchange in 2011, Michael Kors was valued at $3.6bn. At that point, Stroll sold some of his holding, followed by the remaining 5.7 per cent in 2014, when the value had risen to $20bn, netting another $1bn plus.

Always a huge car and racing enthusiast, Stroll owns a private car collection worth $150m plus, including some of the most collectable Ferraris, having owned a Quebec Ferrari dealership as well as the Mont-Tremblant racing circuit. He was not shy of using his fortune to further son Lance's racing ambitions. He bought a stake in the crack Italian Prema Powerteam to ensure top equipment in the junior formulae, Lance going on to win the Italian F4 championship and the European F3 title with the squad in 2016. That facilitated an F1 Superlicence, and Stroll Sr put a reputed $80m into the Williams team to buy Lance a seat on the F1 grid in 2017, alongside Felipe Massa.

Some have suggested that Stroll's move into team ownership could have been Williams, even accusing Claire Williams of mismanaging an opportunity. Williams has since admitted that "it drives her nuts" – she wanted to stay in the F1 business – but in fact, it was simply bad timing. In 2017, Williams finished fifth in the constructors' championship, and it was not until the end of 2019, when title sponsor ROKiT allegedly reneged on sponsorship commitments, that she was forced to sell.

By then, Stroll had purchased Force India after Vijay Mallya's team had gone into administration in mid-2018. In doing his due diligence, Stroll had been impressed that Force India had managed to finish fourth in the constructors' championship in 2016 and 2017 (with double the points of any team below them) while operating on a budget that was roughly a quarter of that spent by any of F1's top three teams, and with a staffing level that was less than half. But still he was cautious, having numerous conversations with Liberty's F1 boss, Chase Carey, specifically concerning the imposition of F1's projected cost cap, before making the commitment and paying £90m for the team.

An old cliché says that the only way to make a small fortune out of motor racing is to start with a big one – unless your name happens to be Bernie Ecclestone! And yet Stroll, in the habit of increasing the value of his fashion investments at least tenfold, has done it again in motor racing. In November, 2023, he sold a minority

shareholding in his team to Arctos Partners, a Dallas-based private equity firm dedicated to the sports industry, valuing the rebranded Aston Martin F1 team at £1bn. And currently, there is talk of a further 20–25 per cent sell-off, which could value the team north of £1.5bn.

But that's not because he is cashing in his chips. On the contrary, Stroll has a vision and dream for his bespoke F1 super-facility just across the road from Silverstone, on which he has already spent £200m and counting. The climb in value of the team is down to three things.

First, F1 has never been more popular, thanks in large part to the reach of Netflix's *Drive to Survive* series. Revenues, which the teams share in, are climbing. Second, the renaming and association of the team with niche brand Aston Martin. Not only did Stroll buy Force India, but also, in January, 2020, he led a consortium that invested $235m for 16.7 per cent of the Aston Martin car company, of which he is executive chairman. And third, the state-of-the-art HQ, and recruitment of names like Newey and Cowell.

"When Force India went into bankruptcy, there was no plan," Stroll said. "But after getting the asset, yes, I had a very clear vision that this is an automotive company. And I had a dream that, being based at Silverstone for almost three decades, it had to be a British brand. And for me, there was only one British brand that justifies being on the pedestal of F1. And that was Aston Martin."

Although McLaren has just won the constructors' championship as a private rather than a works team for the first time since Brawn in 2009, conventional wisdom said that to launch a championship bid, especially with new engine regulations on the slate for 2026, a major manufacturer tie-up was crucial. For Stroll, Honda's timeline worked out swimmingly.

After an initially difficult time with McLaren in the 1.6-litre V6 turbo hybrid era, Honda got its act together, and by 2021, with Red Bull, it was a match for Mercedes. Even though Toto Wolff's squad won the teams' championship, Max Verstappen won the drivers' title, and once again Honda was behind the world champion's shoulders.

Honda withdrawing again from F1 at this stage came as a surprise. And it was the catalyst behind Red Bull taking the decision to become an engine manufacturer. The late Dietrich Mateschitz made a huge investment in Red Bull Power Trains, while Red Bull inked a tie-up with Ford.

At this point, Honda performed a U-turn. But they no longer had a team. Enter Stroll. Rather than continue as a Mercedes customer heading into another regulation and power-unit change scheduled for 2026, he actively courted Honda. Helping him, in a new role as CEO of performance technologies, was Martin Whitmarsh, who had a strong relationship with the Japanese manufacturer dating back to the McLaren-Honda days of the late eighties and early nineties.

An Aston Martin/Honda works alliance was announced at Monaco in 2023. Aston had made a quantum performance leap and was on a strong upward trajectory across all departments as it moved into Building One of its new technology campus. Fernando Alonso, who had signed in 2022, finished on the podium in six of the first eight 2023 grands prix.

Having formerly been working out of the old Jordan factory with the addition of a few Portakabins, now the team can house all of its manufacturing and racing resources within a single 400,000sq.ft, three-building complex on a 40-acre site. The very latest in facilities and machinery includes a new wind tunnel and simulator, planned to be fully operational by the end of 2024, in time for the new 2026 regulations. It is complete with gym, restaurant and wellness centre, as well as esports facilities and on-site walking/cycling trails.

And, as 2024 progressed, Stroll was able to announce his keynote signings, further signalling his seriousness of intent, just in case anyone was in any doubt. In July, it was announced that Andy Cowell would take over from Whitmarsh as Group CEO, starting on 1st October, while Enrico Cardile joins as chief technical officer in 2025, having left Ferrari. Then, in September, the great coup – Adrian Newey signed as managing technical partner, with a shareholding and due to start on 1st March, 2025.

Cowell, 55, is steeped in motor racing, having watched sprints and hillclimbs with his father from the age of five. He might just as easily have gone the chassis route, rather than into engine design, accepting a Reynard scholarship

Above: Former Mercedes HPP boss Andy Cowell was tempted back to the F1 front line by Aston Martin's ambitious plans.

Top right: Former CEO Martin Whitmarsh helped put the building blocks into place with Honda.

Above right: Team principal Mike Krack with performance director Tom McCullough.

Right: Fernando Alonso was unable to make much of an impression on the front-runners with the AMR24.

Photos: Aston Martin Aramco F1 Team

in a year out from university before graduating. Then he went into a graduate placement scheme with Cosworth.

"Cosworth was an established engineering organisation," Cowell told F1's *Beyond The Grid* podcast. "I thought I'd go there for three or four years and then maybe go into race-cars. When I went there, I'd class myself as knowing nothing about engines."

That rapidly changed. Cowell worked as an integration engineer on the McLaren project, when McLaren and Ayrton Senna lost Honda at the end of 1992 and were running a Cosworth V8 that was supposed to be a spec behind the works units used by Michael Schumacher and Benetton. When McLaren switched catastrophically to Peugeot for 1994, Cowell did the detail design on the cylinder head for that year's Cosworth HB engine.

Then he took his know-how to BMW, where he was involved in the development of the super-powerful P81 V10 engines of the early 2000s, before returning to Cosworth as principal engineer for F1 design and development in 2001. He made the move to Mercedes-Ilmor in 2004 and became engineering director for Mercedes HPP from July, 2008, to January, 2013, responsible for technical and programme leadership of all engine and powertrain projects. He became managing director in 2013.

It was in this role that he oversaw development of the innovative V6 hybrid with its 'hidden' turbo. Comfortably the best powertrain in the first year of the new F1 turbo-hybrid era, it powered Mercedes to an unprecedented spell of F1 domination, during which the team won eight successive constructors' titles.

Stories that Brixworth had a head start with the requisite high-performance requirements are not strictly true. The first port of call for detailed know-how was actually the Mercedes truck division! Those who have worked with Cowell hold him in high regard as a leader, whose great strengths include lateral-thinking and problem-solving.

When Cowell left at the end of 2020 to pursue other projects, he admits that his family and close friends thought he was as mad as a box of frogs. Now sated after his break and ready to begin again, he is a great signing for Stroll. Lawrence's cheque book might have helped, but for Cowell, the engineering challenge is likely to be just as important.

"It's my first time in the paddock since Abu Dhabi, 2019, when I hung up my cans next to Niki Lauda's slot," Cowell smiled when he arrived in Austin for the first time wearing green. "I'm glad to be back, to be honest. When Lawrence got in touch around Easter time, I'd spoken to several F1 teams, mostly on the power-unit side, but I guess I didn't want to do the same. I probably became more of an F1 'bobble hat'. I watched it intently. I wouldn't say I'd missed it to point where I needed to come back, but Lawrence's enthusiasm for what's being built – Aston, Honda, Aramco, the key personnel. You think, crikey, that's all a bit exciting!"

Cowell was only 18 days into the job, but already had spent a couple of weeks in the new factory, and had been to Saudi to meet the Aramco people (combustion is going to be key to the 2026 engine regulations) and to Honda in Sakura, Japan.

"Aramco is exceptional in terms of ambition, facilities and global reach, and they are working well with Honda, which is a key," Cowell explained. "In Japan, we had a steering committee meeting for a couple of hours, and the rest of the time was talking to their engineers, which was a blast down memory lane, but they are hugely competent. I was looking in awe at their test facilities and blown away by their determination and pride. I want to help, but not hinder."

Cowell was also impressed by the enthusiasm at Silverstone, despite 2024 being a tough season for the team, which was fifth in the constructors' championship again, and a distant fifth after the promise of 2023.

"We're disappointed at where we are, everyone is," he admitted. "I've not met anyone living in a bubble of happiness. It's everywhere that we need to get better. Not a single area of the business is saying to me that we're perfect and ready to win championships.

"It was all a bit of a data overload in terms of technology and people. Everyone knows my name and I know nobody's! We're quite a young organisation in terms of a team targeting being at the front, even though Jordan goes back 20 years and more. There's a lot to be done, including setting up our own wind tunnel and establishing class-leading simulation tools. And at the same time as 2025, we've got to make a gearbox to go on the back of the Honda power unit for 2026. If senior leaders take on some of those tasks, we'll get to the front quicker.

"For me, it's about getting to know the way people at Silverstone work, how we create aero upgrades, who does what. And with Adrian coming and Enrico, making the organisational changes that I think will help everyone going forward, so that it's not just a desk waiting for people, but a structure that has their name in it, so their first day is a working day. That's how I see my role as CEO.

"When I was at Mercedes HPP, the thing I hated was wasting time. If something is not efficient, that made me grumpy. Overlap of responsibility makes me grumpy, as do gaps. You're wanting people to work as one brain. Meetings and reports I don't really like. I don't want two-page job descriptions, it's bullet points. A relentless drive forward with the mission as the beacon. I've spoken to Lawrence and thanked him for the opportunity and for what he's put together. He's the mastermind and we are trying to deliver on his vision."

Above: Aston Martin's new 400,000sq.ft campus, complete with interconnecting walkways, will house everything, including a state-of-the-art wind tunnel.

Top right: Dan Fallows paid the price for the failings of the 2024 car, finding himself redeployed.

Top far right: Lance Stroll continues his difficult quest in the hunt for championship glory.

Above right: Key figures in the Aston Martin F1 story. *Left to right:* Martin Whitmarsh, Dan Fallows, Andy Cowell, Fernando Alonso, Adrian Newey, Lawrence and Lance Stroll, Tom McCullough, Luca Furbatto, Andy Stevenson.

Right: Can Fernando Alonso win a third world championship in an Adrian Newey car at 45?

Photos: Aston Martin Aramco F1 Team

Stroll and Newey revealed that they had had several chance meetings at the gym, usually over race weekends in the Middle East, where Newey was impressed by the Canadian's passion, commitment and enthusiasm. Ultimately, they were the factors that convinced him a move to Aston Martin was the right one.

"He's very persuasive," Newey said. "The reality is, if you go back 20 years, then what we now call team principals were actually the owners of the teams: Frank Williams, Ron Dennis, Eddie Jordan, etc. In this modern era, Lawrence is actually unique in being the only properly active team owner, and I think that does bring a different feeling. It's back to the old-school model, and for me to have the chance to be a shareholder and partner is something that hasn't been offered to me before. It became a very natural choice."

When, in May, the shock news came that Newey was leaving Red Bull after 20 years, Ferrari was widely tipped as his next destination. Almost 40 years ago, in 1987, Carl Haas paid Newey $400,000 to race engineer Mario Andretti's Indy car in the US, a colossal sum of money then. By way of comparison, previously Newey had been on $60,000 with the Kraco team, engineering Mario's son, Michael. Haas hadn't taken leave of his senses, though. As the US importer for Lola, he wanted Newey's input into Lola's Indy car and to keep him away from rival March, which had won the previous two Indy 500s with Adrian's input.

In Formula 1, Newey's earnings started to become seriously stratospheric when Ron Dennis was forced to almost double his McLaren salary, to an estimated $5m, to prevent him from defecting to Jaguar in 2001 to join old friend Bobby Rahal, who was running the team at the time. Then, when he joined Red Bull in 2005, owner Dietrich Mateschitz was said to have almost swallowed his can of Red Bull upon learning of Newey's salary requirements, before phoning his mate, Gerhard Berger, to ask about the wisdom of it. In reply, Berger asked him what it was worth to make his car go a second a lap quicker. So Mateschitz paid.

That was 20 years ago, and it was widely thought that Ferrari would be the team with the desire and wherewithal to persuade the now 65-year-old Newey to abandon his sabbatical, although moving to Italy might have been a stumbling block. But when Newey had left Williams for McLaren in 1997, it was said that the offer of shares in the team and greater influence in the decision making might have persuaded him to stay. At McLaren, likewise, no stake was offered, with only an intention, not a timeline, from Ron Dennis regarding more control. He was never going to have a shareholding at Ferrari.

The other thing that Newey points out is that he joined Williams at a time when the team was going through a lean spell, and ditto McLaren. And Red Bull, although taking over the Jaguar team was effectively a start-up when it came to the need for cutting-edge simulation tools, facilities and mind-set. Newey prefers to take on a project that he can influence rather than join an already successful team.

A man with 13 drivers' titles and 12 constructors' has nothing to prove and wants to enjoy any new working environment. He was impressed by a private tour of Aston's amazing new facility and by Stroll's enthusiasm. And doubtless the reported offer of £20m per annum,

rising to £30m with bonuses and a 2.5 per cent (£37.5m) stake in a team valued at £1.5bn would have been a nice sweetener, too!

If an Aston Martin-Honda sets the pace in 2026 or is close to it, who will win them a world championship? As much as Lawrence Stroll wants to win a championship, Fernando Alonso also wants to win a third. Could he really do it 20 years after winning his second?

It's 50 years since legendary broadcaster the late Harry Carpenter uttered, "Oh my God, he's won back the title at 32!" when Muhammad Ali floored George Foreman in the eighth round of their Rumble in the Jungle in Zaire. The boxing ring, above all, is the place where any physical decline or lack of sharpness is cruelly exposed, but such is the progress in sports science, conditioning and nutrition, that 30-odd years later, Bernard Hopkins was taking Joe Calzaghe close at 43.

So, yes, Fernando could do it. He wouldn't even be F1's oldest world champion – that was Fangio in 1957, at 46 years and 41 days. But you can bet that the final piece of Lawrence Stroll's jigsaw is Max Verstappen. Ostensibly, the Dutchman is under contract to Red Bull until 2028, but in F1, who knows?

Could Aston Martin win a constructors' title with Lance in one of its cars? If Newey, Cowell, Honda and Co came up with something as dominant as Mercedes did in 2014, yes, it could. But what if Verstappen wanted to join for 2026 and Lawrence wants Alonso, who is contracted for that season, to have the chance of a last hurrah? Well, perhaps he might persuade Lance to drive the Valkyrie WEC car for a season instead. Whatever happens will be fascinating to watch.

51

APPRECIATIONS 2024
By MAURICE HAMILTON

ALAN REES

THE contribution by ALAN REES to front-line motorsport went far beyond a distant ninth place in a Cooper-Maserati at the 1967 British Grand Prix, the Welshman's only GP entry in a pukka Formula 1 car.

He raced twice in the Formula 2 category of the German Grand Prix, retiring in 1966 and finishing seventh the following year. On both occasions, Rees drove a Brabham entered by Roy Winkelmann Racing, for whom he raced for several seasons, often with success and, on two occasions, beating F2 pace-setters Jochen Rindt and Jackie Stewart.

Rees had started racing with a Lotus 11 before switching to single-seaters and becoming British Formula Junior champion in 1961. Away from the cockpit, he called on his business and management skills (he had a degree in economics) in 1969 when he became a founding member of the ambitious March Engineering concern, along with Max Mosley, Robin Herd and Graham Coaker.

In 1973, he was recruited by Don Nichols to help establish Shadow as a Formula 1 team. He left the American operation in 1978 to co-found the newly formed Arrows outfit, acting as team principal and remaining with the F1 team when it became Footwork following a Japanese buy-out. Subsequently, Rees regained ownership of the team (with Jackie Oliver) in 1991. His involvement with F1 ended when Tom Walkinshaw took a controlling interest in 1996.

Following a long illness, Alan Rees passed away at the age of 86 on 6th September, 2024.

DAVE WALKER

DAVE WALKER came to prominence in 1970 when he joined the works Lotus Formula 3 team and won the Lombank championship, claiming two more titles the following year. He won 25 of 32 race starts in F3. However, a logical step up to Formula 1 with Lotus for 1971 proved less successful.

Walker's debut with the Lotus 56B at Zandvoort set the tone when he crashed in the rain on a day when the four-wheel-drive Pratt & Whitney turbine car had had a performance advantage that was good enough to move the Australian from 22nd to tenth in the first five laps. Ten GPs with the Lotus 72 were riddled with mechanical failures in 1972, the year his problems were exacerbated by Emerson Fittipaldi winning the championship in the other JPS Lotus 72. His best result was fifth in the non-championship Brazilian GP.

After sporadic outings in F2, F5000 and sports cars, Walker's competition career was not helped by injuries sustained in two road accidents. He retired in 1975 and eventually returned to Australia, where he ran a boat charter business before passing away at the age of 82 on 24th May, 2024.

JOHN WEBB

JOHN WEBB was a marketing genius who will be forever associated with the growth of Brands Hatch into a successful grand prix venue.

When Webb formed a press and promotions company in 1953, one of his first clients was the Kent circuit, which at the time was no more than a kidney-shaped club racing venue. The introduction of a loop to Druids, followed by the extension to Westfield, opened the opportunity for Brands Hatch to stage a world championship grand prix in 1964. When Grovewood Securities took ownership, the investment company made Webb full-time executive director.

With support from his wife, Angela, Webb became a powerhouse of innovation, introducing the non-championship Race of Champions, air displays at the grands prix, as well as offbeat trackside entrainment. He was also responsible for dreaming up myriad racing concepts, from Formula Ford and Thundersports to Sports 2000 and Formula 5000.

Webb retired to Spain in 1989, where he passed away on 12th January, 2024, at the age of 92.

ALBERTO COLOMBO

ALBERTO COLOMBO, who died aged 77 on 7th January, 2024, failed to qualify for three grands prix in his attempt to break into Formula 1. Born in Varedo, not far from Monza, he won the 1974 Italian Formula 3 Championship.

A move to Formula 2 with a variety of teams across four seasons brought a few worthwhile results and encouraged the dream of reaching Formula 1. An opportunity to make his debut (then aged 32) arose in 1978, when Jean-Pierre Jarier left ATS after three races.

Unfamiliar with the car, Colombo failed to make the grid for the Belgian Grand Prix at Zolder. When he suffered another DNQ at Jarama, he was replaced by Keke Rosberg.

Colombo was given a final grand prix opportunity with a second Merzario in the Italian Grand Prix at Monza, but that also brought non-qualification and a return to Formula 2 with his own team, Sanremo Racing, for 1979 and 1980.

When Colombo retired from the cockpit, he continued to run the team in F2 and then Formula 3000 throughout the 1980s.

TED TOLEMAN

THE owner of a successful car transportation business, TED TOLEMAN went from being a club racer to the entrant of the grand prix team that gave Ayrton Senna his Formula 1 debut.

As well as racing a Sports 2000 Lola in the 1970s, Toleman gradually increased his involvement through sponsorship, specifically of Rad Dougall, the South African driver who dominated FF2000 in 1977.

Toleman Racing took a major step forward by hiring Rory Byrne and entering a March-BMW in the 1978 F2 championship. Ultimately, this led to Byrne designing a Toleman F2 car powered by a Hart engine, which was entered in the 1980 European Championship.

When Brian Henton and Derek Warwick dominated the series, Toleman took the plunge into F1 for 1981. From a hesitant start with Hart's turbo-powered four-cylinder, Toleman became a genuine force, Senna almost winning the Monaco Grand Prix in his debut season in 1984.

Toleman Racing was sold to Benetton when Toleman withdrew from motorsport in 1986. He died, aged 86, on 10th April, 2024.

WILSON FITTIPALDI

ALTHOUGH perpetually living in the shadow of his younger brother, Emerson, WILSON FITTIPALDI was a Formula 1 points scorer and constructor in his own right. After racing saloons, sports cars and Formula Fords in Brazil, he moved to Europe in 1970 and raced Formula 3, before joining his brother in F2 the following year.

A step up to F1 for 1972 might have brought sixth place on his debut in the non-championship Brazilian Grand Prix, but the season turned out to be a struggle in what effectively was the third works Brabham. With Graham Hill moving on in 1973, Fittipaldi fared much better as Carlos Reutemann's team-mate, the highlight being a strong drive into what would have been third place at Monaco but for a fuel system failure on the BT42. He scored points twice, his best result being fifth in the German GP on the Nürburgring Nordschleife.

With his heart set on establishing a Brazilian F1 team, Wilson struggled to make the Copersucar-Fittipaldi competitive in its debut season in 1975. When Emerson moved from McLaren in 1976, Wilson took on a management role, the highlight being second place in their home race in 1978. He returned to the cockpit in 1982 to compete in stock car and GT racing while managing the career of his son, Christian. Wilson Fittipaldi passed away at the age of 80 on 23rd February, 2024.

RUPERT KEEGAN

HAILED as the next James Hunt, RUPERT KEEGAN matched the 1976 World Champion out of the car, but failed to progress on track. The Englishman took part in 25 grands prix with a variety of lower-order teams over four seasons. He was supported by his father, Mike, whose aviation business provided backing through the ranks of Formula Ford and Formula 3, Rupert winning the British F3 Championship in 1976.

Propelled straight to Formula 1, he did well to qualify for all 12 races entered with an uncompetitive Hesketh 308E and finish seventh in the Austrian GP. It didn't get any better when he switched to Surtees for 1978, when he started just six races and finished once.

A step down to the Aurora F1 series brought five wins and the championship with an Arrows A1, but a return to grand prix racing with a RAM Williams FW07B in 1980, followed by a final shot with a March 821 the following year, brought ninth at Watkins Glen as the best result from seven starts.

He switched to endurance racing, making three appearances at Le Mans between 1982 and 1984. The following year, he tried his hand at single-seaters again, scoring four points in his three Indycar outings in a March 85C-Cosworth.

Rupert Keegan succumbed to cancer at the age of 69 on 23rd September, 2024.

GIL DE FERRAN

THE loss of GIL DE FERRAN, at the age of 56, reverberated around the racing world. Born in Paris, but raised in Brazil (his father was a director of Ford of Brazil), de Ferran began karting at an early age and went on to win the 1987 Brazilian Formula Ford title.

Arriving in the UK, he raced in Formula Ford 1600, Opel/Vauxhall Lotus and Formula 3, winning the British F3 title in 1992 with Paul Stewart Racing. A progression to Formula 3000 with PSR brought three wins and a run to the championship wire in 1994, but not the final step to Formula 1, despite test drives with Arrows and Williams.

A move to the USA brought great success in Indy car racing – he won the Champ Car series in 2001 and 2002, and the Indianapolis 500 race the following year. He was recognised as an outstanding talent, helped in no small part by his diligent approach and keen interest in engineering.

After switching to racing management, de Ferran joined BAR-Honda as sporting director between 2005 and 2007, then returned to the cockpit, establishing his own team in the American LeMans Series and, later, IndyCar. F1 became part of his life once more with two spells at McLaren, the first as sporting director, from July, 2018 to early 2021. He returned as a consultant at the behest of Zak Brown in 2023.

De Ferran suffered a heart attack while at a private event not far from his home in Fort Lauderdale, Florida, on 29th December, 2023.

TEAM-BY-TEAM
FORMULA 1 REVIEW

Team Reviews: MARK HUGHES

Car Illustrations: ADRIAN DEAN

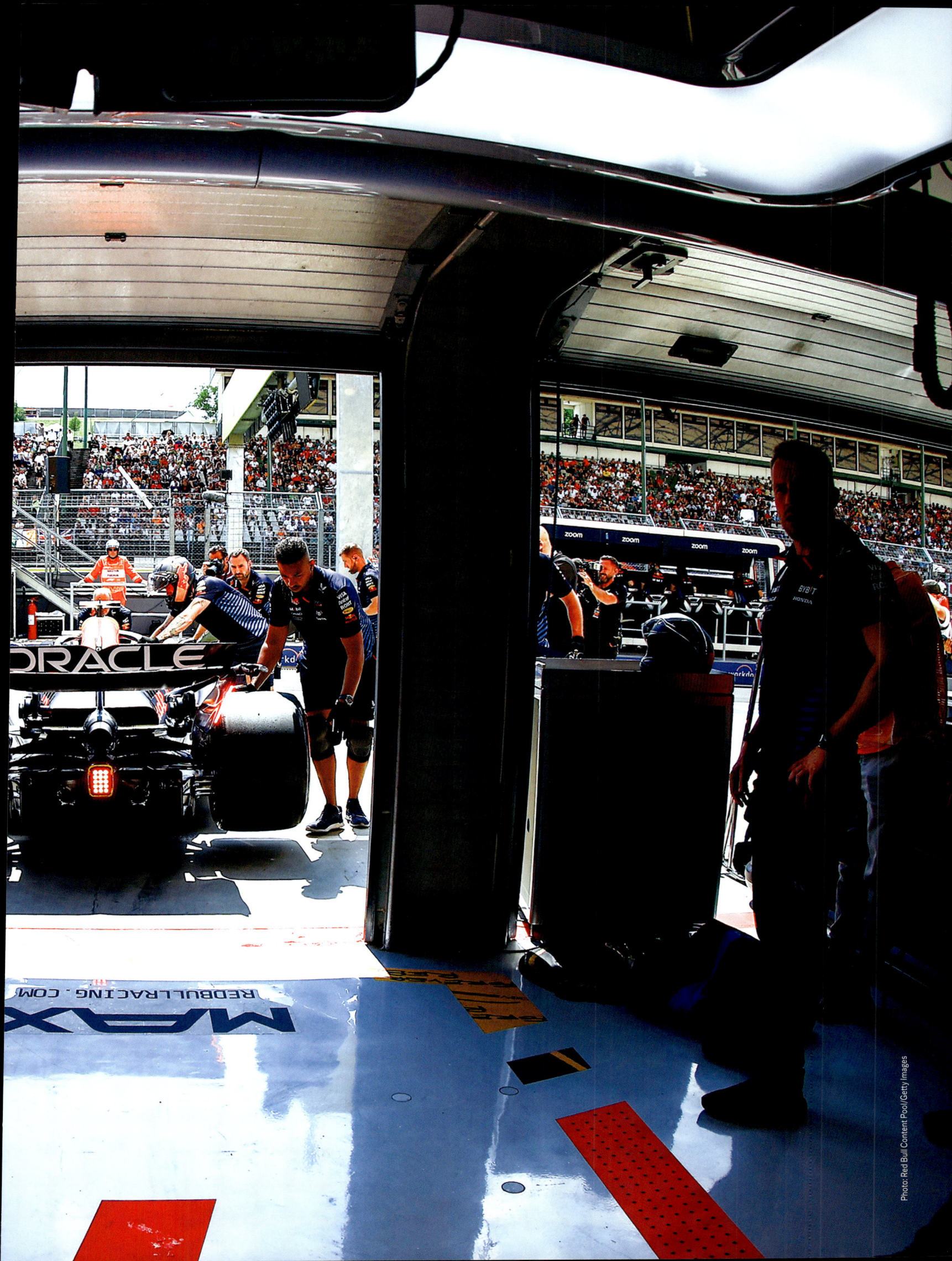

McLAREN F1 TEAM

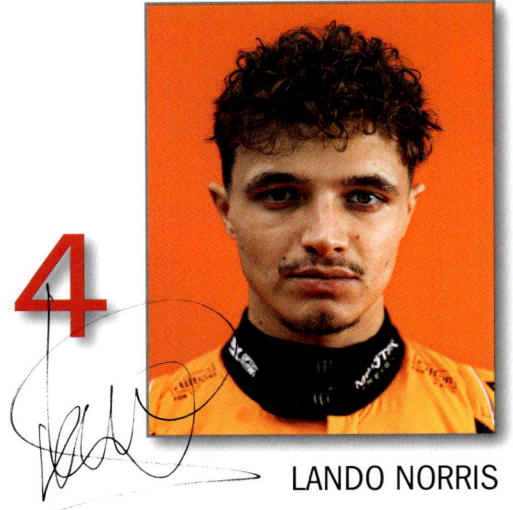

LANDO NORRIS

OSCAR PIASTRI

McLaren's spectacular rise continued in 2024 as it transitioned from occasional lead chaser of Red Bull in 2023 to being able to go head to head with the previously all-conquering squad. It culminated in the team's first constructors' world championship since 1998, while Lando Norris was runner-up to Max Verstappen in the drivers' championship. In all, McLaren took six victories and eight pole positions in 2024. It was very much back, after such a long absence from the regular victories that used to be so routine. It was a further step in a remarkable progression from the doldrums of 2018, when occasionally it had fielded the slowest car of all, and it reflects enormously well on the steering of the team by Andrea Stella in his second year as principal.

The MCL38 was a continuation of the previous season's car, visually distinguished from it only by a more tightly-shaped sidepod and new radiator inlet arrangement. This was made possible by some of the radiators being resited higher and further back. The cockpit position was slightly further forward. Again, Mercedes supplied the power unit only, McLaren making its own gearbox. The suspension remained pull-rod front/push-rod rear.

Although there was no particular vice with the car at the beginning of the season, generally it was only the fourth fastest, and it was clear that Red Bull, Ferrari and Mercedes had all made bigger gains during the off-season. This reflected a development cycle that stretched back to mid-2023, as recalled by Stella: "Last year [2023], we cashed in some accelerated understanding in-season, and that was reflected in the Austria and Singapore upgrades. We spent a lot of the knowledge in-season, which meant when we went to the '24 car, we found Ferrari and Red Bull had made a bigger step during the winter than we did. Early season, the Red Bull was winning everything, and this is where Verstappen got most of the advantage in the drivers' championship. This was sort of expected, as they had not delivered many upgrades last year and so cashed in the accumulated knowledge with their '24 car. Also, there was good work by Ferrari in making a good step.

"Our big step came with our upgrade in Miami. When we cashed in with a big improvement there, it put us among the best cars. In some specific medium/high-speed corners, the actual best car. Ferrari was the best in low-speed, Red Bull in high."

That Miami update coincided with Lando Norris's first grand prix victory, and thereafter the MCL38 was a contender for victory everywhere, with a more rounded set of strengths than any of its rivals, but with a big points deficit, courtesy of Red Bull's early domination. With Oscar Piastri also taking his first grand prix victories in the car, the team was scoring more heavily in the constructors' championship than Red Bull, overcoming the deficit.

McLAREN MCL38

FORMULA 1 PARTNERS	Mastercard · OKX · Google · Chrome · BAT · Cisco · DP World · Dell Technologies · Darktrace · Monster Energy · Arrow · Jack Daniel's · Salesforce · Alteryx Hilton · Estrella Galicia 0,0 · Dropbox · Unilever · DeWalt · Goldman Sachs · Workday · Cadence · Webex · Coca-Cola · Ecolab · Airwallex · Webex Abercrombie & Fitch · Get Your Guide · Logitech · Google Cloud · Deloitte · eBay · Splunk · Optimum Nutrition · T Mobile · VMware · CNBC · Richard Mille Udemy · TUMI · FX Pro · Smartsheet · Medallia · Castore · Halo ITSM · New Era · K-Swiss · Immersive Labs · Reiss · FAI Aviation Group · Levis · Sanofi Stanley Black & Decker · T-Mobile · Sikkens · Alpinestars · Ashurst · Pirelli · Lego · Stratasys · Kaust · SunGod
POWER UNIT	Type Mercedes-AMG M14 E Performance No. of cylinders (vee angle): V6 (90°) No. of valves: 24 Max rpm (ICE): 15,000 Electronics: McLaren Applied, including chassis control, power-unit control, data acquisition, sensors, data analysis and telemetry Fuel: Petronas E10 Lubricants: Petronas
TRANSMISSION	Gearbox: Eight forward speeds and one reverse, seamless-shift, carbon-composite casing Clutch: Electro-hydraulically operated carbon multi-plate
CHASSIS	Monocoque: Carbon-fibre composite, incorporating driver controls and fuel cell Front suspension: Carbon-fibre/titanium suspension legs, pull-rod-actuated inboard torsion-bar spring and damper system Rear suspension: Carbon-fibre/titanium suspension legs, push-rod-actuated inboard torsion-bar spring and damper system Brakes: AP Racing calipers and master cylinders, Carbone Industrie carbon discs and pads, McLaren/AP Racing brake-by-wire rear brake control system Steering: McLaren power-assisted rack-and-pinion Instruments: McLaren Applied dashboard display Wheels: BBS, 18in diameter Tyres: Pirelli P Zero
DIMENSIONS	Not disclosed Formula weight: 798kg, including driver and camera

LANDO NORRIS

ZAK BROWN

McLAREN F1 TEAM: PERSONNEL

Chief Executive Officer: Zak Brown

Team Principal: Andrea Stella

Chief People and Sustainability Officer: Daniel Gallo

Executive Director, Chief of Staff: Chloe Todd

Chief Financial Officer: Laura Bowden

Chief Communications Officer: Steve Atkins

Chief Marketing Officer: Louise McEwen

Co-Chief Commercial Officer: Matt Dennington

Co-Chief Commercial Officer: Nick Martin

Executive Director, Chief Designer: Rob Marshall

Executive Director, Technical Director, Aerodynamics: Peter Prodromou

Executive Director, Technical Director, Engineering: Neil Houldey

Chief Operating Officer: Piers Thynne

Executive Director, Technical Director, Performance: Mark Temple

Director, Race Engineering, Race Engineer (Norris): Will Joseph

Director, Human Performance, Race Engineer (Piastri): Tom Stallard

Director, Tyres and Brakes: Hiroshi Imai

Director, F1 Communications: Sophie Ogg

Above: The team celebrates winning the constructors' championship in Abu Dhabi.

Right: Oscar Piastri turned in a fine drive to beat Charles Leclerc's Ferrari in Baku.

Centre right: Team principal Andrea Stella was the lynchpin in the team's rise to the top.

Far right: McLaren mechanics complete a rapid pit stop as Lando Norris heads for his first ever grand prix win at Miami.

Photos: McLaren F1 Team

PETER PRODROMOU

ROB MARSHALL

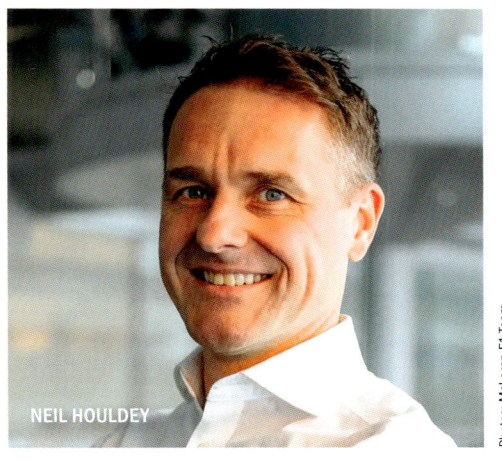
NEIL HOULDEY

PIERS THYNNE

MARK TEMPLE

The Miami upgrade was extensive and included an all-new floor, further resited radiators, and new sidepods and radiator inlet bodywork. The whole package energised the underfloor performance substantially. It represented the team's latest understanding in what Stella described as a "voyage of discovery".

"It takes a lot of work over many years to build this kind of accumulated knowledge. There's no click change. It's a build. Across a group. It's not even elite knowledge. There are more than 100 people in the aero groups, and you need to get concepts and criteria understood and contributed to. That has been the key."

The specification of the car remained very stable after the Miami upgrade. The next new floor didn't appear until Mexico, for example. But there was a much better correlation between upgrades and on-track performance than with any of the rival cars. A two-part upgrade spread over the Zandvoort and Monza weekends resulted in a change in the floor edges and sidepod shape.

Rob Marshall joined the team from Red Bull at the beginning of the year, and he played an important role in accelerating progress in aero-elasticity. The low-downforce rear wing used in Spa, Monza and Baku achieved a 'mini DRS' effect through flexure at the outboard ends beyond a certain speed, and although the FIA admitted that it broke no regulation, the team was asked to ensure that it did not flex so much in future.

"We had not focused enough on aero elasticity before," said Stella. "It can deliver performance, but only if you do some specific studies. We were able to do these because we had expanded the team and added resources, gained quite a lot of efficiency, stimulated by the cost-cap requirement. This has given us capacity, and we have invested human resources which allowed us to take on more projects, including aero elasticity."

This was crucial in addressing one of the key difficulties of this generation of car: that of low-speed understeer and high-speed oversteer. A rear wing that backed off its power at high speed allowed the front wing to be aggressive enough to combat low-speed understeer.

Rear wing development was a feature of the latter half of the team's season, with new versions of both the high-downforce (at Zandvoort) and medium-downforce (at Brazil) wings appearing. They eradicated the former deficit to Red Bull in the amount of speed that was boosted when in DRS mode.

It all added to the car's strength as a great all-rounder, one that might go down in F1 history as the car that returned the team to its former glory.

CHARLES LECLERC

OLLIE BEARMAN

CARLOS SAINZ

SCUDERIA FERRARI

Ferrari's decision to change the aerodynamic philosophy of its car – from the previous fat outwash sidepods to a more conventional undercut arrangement – proved fruitful. The team was in contention for the constructors' world championship right until the final round, falling short by just 14 points to McLaren.

The SF-24 won five races (three for Charles Leclerc, two for Carlos Sainz), set three poles and qualified an average of 0.181s slower than the Red Bull, 0.151s adrift of the McLaren.

Like its predecessors, it had quite distinctive performance characteristics, with the absolute best slow-corner performance and low-speed acceleration, but it experienced some difficulty in faster, long-duration corners. It was much better with the tyres than its predecessor and generally proved much more responsive to development.

The technical department that created the car was headed by Enrico Cardile, but he left before mid-season after accepting an offer from Aston Martin. He was replaced by Loïc Serra, recruited from Mercedes.

Although the aerodynamic surfaces of the SF-24 were very different from those of the 2023 car, the mechanical layout (push-rod front suspension/pull-rod rear) remained as something of an outlier from the fashion. Similarly, its power unit remained the only one not to utilise a split turbo-compressor. Its long inlet tracts and relatively small turbo

FERRARI SF-24

SPONSORS	AWS · Bitdefender · CEVA Logistics · Chivas Regal · DXC Technology · Genesys · Harman · HCL Software · OIIR Automotive · Palantir · Peroni 0.0 · Philip Morris International · Ray-Ban · Richard Mille · Shell · Santander · VGW Play · ZCG
OFFICIAL SUPPLIERS	B&O · Bell · Brembo · Celcius · Ecopol · Garrett · Giorgio Armani · Iveco · Mahle · Manpower Group · NGK · Öhlins · Pirelli · Puma · Riedel · Riva · Sabelt · SKF · Techno Gym · Vista Jet
POWER UNIT	Type: Ferrari 066/10 1.6-litre turbo hybrid No. of cylinders (vee angle): V6 (90°) No. of valves: 24 Maximum rpm: 15,000 Electronics: Magneti Marelli Fuel: Shell Oil: Shell
TRANSMISSION	Gearbox: Ferrari eight-speed-plus-reverse, longitudinally-mounted, electronically-controlled, sequential semi-automatic with quick-shift mechanism
CHASSIS	Monocoque: Moulded carbon-fibre and honeycomb composite structure Front suspension: Double wishbones with push-rod-actuated inboard springs Rear suspension: Double wishbones with pull-rod-actuated inboard springs Brakes: Brembo ventilated carbon-fibre discs front and rear, brake-by-wire control for rear brakes Wheels: OZ Racing, 18in diameter Tyres: Pirelli P Zero
DIMENSIONS	Not disclosed Formula weight: 798kg, including driver and camera

CHARLES LECLERC

FRÉDÉRIC VASSEUR

Photo: Scuderia Ferrari

SCUDERIA FERRARI: PERSONNEL

Chairman: John Elkann	Head of Quality & Project Management Office: Francesco Marino
Chief Executive Officer: Benedetto Vigna	Head of Finance: Luigi Centenari
Team Principal & General Manager: Frédéric Vasseur	Race Engineer (Leclerc): Bryan Bozzi
Technical Director Power Unit: Enrico Gualtieri	Race Engineer (Sainz): Riccardo Adami
Technical Director Chassis: Loïc Serra	No.1 Mechanic (Leclerc): Alessandro Fusaro
Sporting Director: Diego Ioverno	No.1 Mechanc (Sainz): Filippo Milani
Deputy Team Principal: Jérôme d'Ambrosio	Head of Communications: Silvia Frangipane Hoffer
Head of Track Engineering: Matteo Togninalli	
Head of Race Strategy Operations: Ravin Jain	
Head of PU Operations: Luigi Fraboni	
Head of Supply Chain & Manufacturing: Enrico Racca	

Above: Carlos Sainz scored two wins in a distinguished season for the Scuderia.
Photo: Bryn Williams

Right: Charles Leclerc secured his third victory of the year at the US GP in Austin.

Above right: Ollie Bearman stood in for Sainz in Saudi Arabia and performed admirably.

Above far right: Sainz tucked in and ready to go.

Below right: A win at last on home soil for Leclerc.

Below far right: Monaco post-race, and a celebratory dive into the Med for Leclerc and Vasseur.
Photos: Scuderia Ferrari

ENRICO GUALTIERI

DIEGO IOVERNO

LOÏC SERRA

MATTEO TOGNINALLI

RAVIN JAIN

continued to mark it out too, but in performance, it was at least on a par with the rival PUs of Honda and Mercedes.

The chassis was lengthened by 5cm compared to the previous car, to facilitate a shorter gearbox casing that would create more volume around the diffuser for the aerodynamicists to exploit. The anti-dive angle of the front suspension was increased to better control the aerodynamic platform. It was a fairly cautious revamp beneath new clothes, with Cardile explaining at the launch, "We have taken on board what the drivers have told us, and turned those ideas into engineering reality with the aim of giving them a car which is easier to drive and therefore easier to get the most out of and push to its limits. We did not set ourselves any design constraints other than delivering a strong and honest racing car, which can reproduce on the race-track what we see in the wind tunnel."

In those aims, it succeeded. The aero gains made over the 2023 car were considerable and, given the initial difficulties of McLaren and Mercedes, they made Ferrari the closest rival to the early dominance of Red Bull.

At Imola, the team made its first major upgrade. A slim vertical opening adjacent to the front of the chassis had been used previously as the inlet for an S-duct, which exited through the top bodywork near the front of the cockpit. This feature had been dropped and instead the inlet was conjoined with the horizontal one above to feed the radiators, giving quite a Red Bull-like arrangement. A lip above the horizontal inlet, rather than below it, allowed a concave curvature as the shroud merged with the sidepod, creating a low-pressure region to accelerate the airflow.

The redesign had allowed the sidepod undercut to be enhanced. The 'coke bottle' in-sweep of the lower bodywork at the rear was also improved, the aero team more fully exploiting the room created there by the 2024 gearbox.

It was with the car in this specification that Leclerc won in Monaco. But Imola was just the first of a two-part upgrade, the remainder being introduced in Barcelona and comprising even further enhanced undercut, lowered roof of the front of the floor and a fully-reshaped 'canoe' section (the flat part of the underfloor between the tunnels). In theory, this gave a very significant downforce boost. But it proved to be a misstep, as it took the car into the dreaded 'bouncing' territory.

Without all the old parts – some of which had been cannibalised to make new ones – it was not possible to revert immediately to the previous specification, although this had happened by Hungary. Meanwhile, a more fully considered version of the update – with another new floor, floor edges and revised expansion ramp to the diffuser – was introduced at Monza. These changes together with a cut-out around the 'coke bottle' section kept the car away from the bouncing threshold while delivering the aero gains that had been hoped for at Barcelona.

Team principal Frédéric Vasseur talked about that whole sequence, saying, "In the third year of these regulations, you cannot expect to find 15 points [of downforce] from one upgrade. This will not happen. It means that each time that we are bringing something, it's marginal, but still crucially important when you are fighting for hundredths of a second. So if each time you can bring two or three points, it can make a huge difference. The issue is that when you expect to bring a couple of points on the car, if you have a downside, either on bouncing or set-up, the impact of the downside can be bigger than the couple of points that you bring. And this is what happened.

"The response of the team to this was very, very positive. They went back to the wind tunnel in the evening at Barcelona to try to understand what we did wrong, but there were absolutely no internal fights. We messed up by introducing the bouncing; it was not expected, but the reaction of the team allowed us to correct it. But it meant we struggled for three or four races in succession."

The recovery was slowed somewhat by the refurbishing and re-equipping of the wind tunnel taking longer than the allocated summer break. But with that corrective update, the car went on a very productive spree, winning in Monza, only narrowly losing out at Baku, and taking consecutive comfortable victories at Austin and Mexico. But the fast, long corners of Qatar presented a more difficult challenge. The aero map of the car, which gave it that great short-corner performance, worked against it in longer turns. "Yes, it's in the aero map," confirmed Vasseur. "It's about the sensitivity to the roll or to the steer. We did a good step forward compared to last year on this. Last year, we are struggling a lot with the wind, much less this season, and we have to continue to push on the weaknesses of the car, but it's a clear characteristic of the car."

Playing its part in this conflict of balance between corner types was the fact that Ferrari did not follow the lead of McLaren and Mercedes in developing aero-elastic front wings. "This was frustrating," admitted Vasseur, who believes that such developments did not meet the regulations and who queried the governing body on how it would react to them. "Because it's clear performance, and we waited for the decision to know if it's legal or not. You have always to keep in mind the cost cap, which means that you have to be efficient with the budget. So if you start to do a development, and at the end, it's ruled not legal, you burn 600,000 euros. Which is out of a development budget of three of four million. If you burn half a million of that for nothing, you cannot spend it somewhere else. We said, 'Okay, let's wait the decision,' and we pushed too late."

The expectation for 2025 and the arrival of Lewis Hamilton is immense.

ORACLE RED BULL RACING

MAX VERSTAPPEN — 1

SERGIO PÉREZ — 11

The Red Bull RB20 was good enough to take Max Verstappen to a fourth consecutive world title, but not good enough to maintain the team's general dominance of the previous two seasons. Verstappen won more races – nine - than anyone else, but the low-scoring of the second car driven by Sergio Pérez left the team only third in the constructors' championship.

As Verstappen won four of the first five races, initially it looked like a continuation of the team's 2023 dominance. But from the moment McLaren introduced its updated car for round six in Miami, the RB20 was essentially fighting a rearguard action. As Red Bull development stalled – extra downforce was coming at the expense of poor balance – so Ferrari and Mercedes were also able to compete and, on occasion, beat the team. This was the season in which the others finally caught up with the big lead Red Bull had established in the ground-effect era of 2022.

That lead had been created by a superior integration of suspension and underfloor design in Adrian Newey's RB18. Less extreme contours than others around the diffuser choke point, amid a very intricate floor geometry, had allowed the Red Bulls of 2022 and '23 to give a better spread of downforce through the speed range. A crucial part in making this work was a suspension that, though super-stiff by the standards of pre-2022, was soft enough to tune the car's front-rear handling balance as required. When McLaren introduced an aero-elastic front wing as part of its Miami upgrade, and Mercedes followed suit a couple of races later, Red Bull's manner of achieving balance essentially became obsolete. With aero-elastic front wings, the balance conflict between low-speed understeer and high-speed oversteer could be resolved without resorting to softer suspension and sacrificing peak downforce.

Red Bull was limited in its ability to respond, partly because of the F1 cost cap. "The cost cap is one aspect," said Pierre Waché, the man in technical charge since the mid-season departure of Newey. "It's the whole global aspect of resource. We did some development on this, but you have to also develop the two cars for '25 and '26. It's a resource limitation – of money and people."

Visually, the RB20 represented a considerable aerodynamic evolution over what had gone before. As the other teams had all produced visual clones of the previous Red Bulls, the RB20 appeared at its launch to have moved the game on.

A completely reconfigured underfloor had been made possible by a massive undercut around the front sidepods, which, in turn, had been facilitated by a radically reworked cooling system. A revolutionary approach had been taken with multiple cooling routes for specific components, forming a network rather than the usual bigger all-encompassing routes. In this way, the cooling levels could

ORACLE RED BULL RACING RB20

TITLE PARTNERS	Red Bull · Oracle
TEAM PARTNERS	Bybit · TAG Heuer · Built for Athletes · Castore · Sui · Athletic Propulsion Labs · Blenders · Rauch · Hard Rock International · Telcel · Claro · VISA · Inter.mx Heineken · Rokt · PATRÓN Tequila · Armor All · Gold Standard · Pepe Jeans · EA Sports · Sparco
TECHNICAL PARTNERS	Honda · CDW · Mobil 1 · Esso · Zoom · Siemens · Hewlett Packard Enterprise · Arctic Wolf · AT&T · DMG Mori · Hexagon · Ansys · PWR · HP Poly · Pirelli
POWER UNIT	Red Bull Honda RBPT001 1.6-litre turbo No. of cylinders (vee angle): V6 (90°) No. of valves: 24 Max. rpm (ICE): 15,000 Electronics: MESL standard electronic control unit Fuel: Esso Synergy Oil: Mobil 1
TRANSMISSION	Red Bull Racing eight-speed gearbox, longitudinally mounted with hydraulic power-shift and clutch operation
CHASSIS	Monocoque: Carbon-fibre composite with engine as fully stressed member Front suspension: Aluminium uprights, carbon-fibre double wishbones with pull-rod-actuated springs, dampers and anti-roll bar Rear suspension: Aluminium uprights, carbon-fibre double wishbones with push-rod-actuated springs, dampers and anti-roll bar Brakes: Carbone Industrie pads and discs, Brembo calipers Wheels: BBS Racing, 18in diameter Tyres: Pirelli P Zero
DIMENSIONS	Not disclosed Formula weight: 798kg, including driver and camera

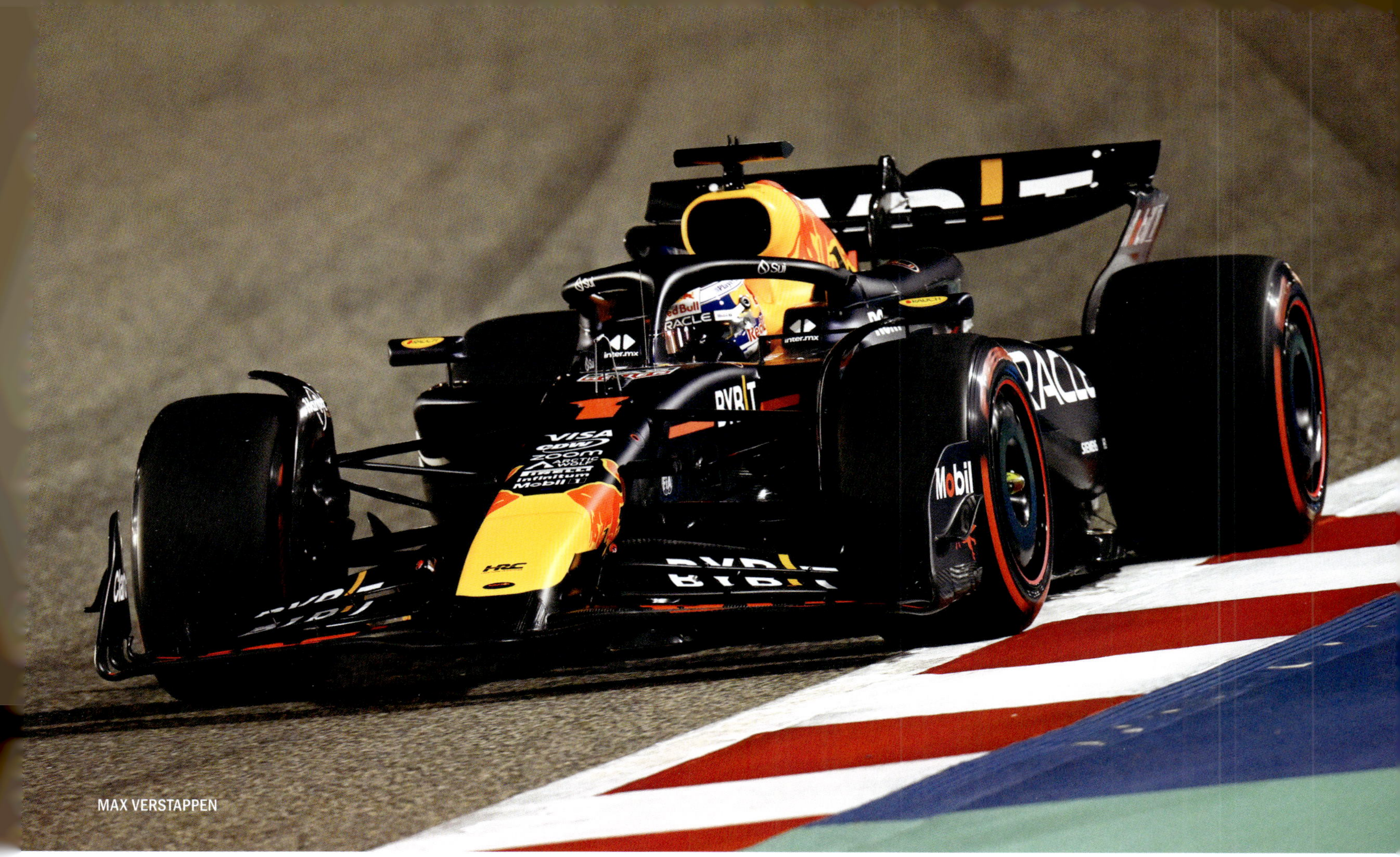

MAX VERSTAPPEN

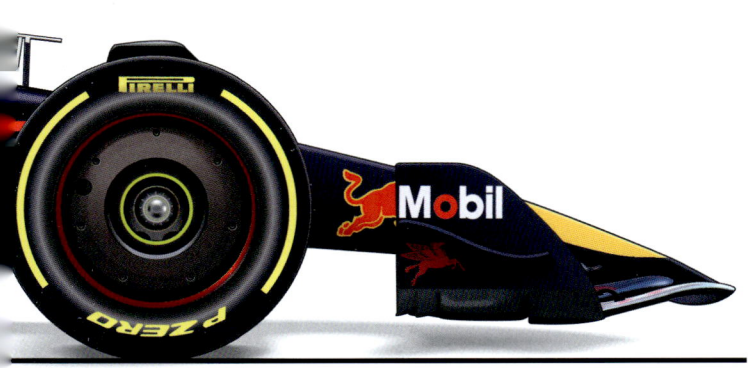

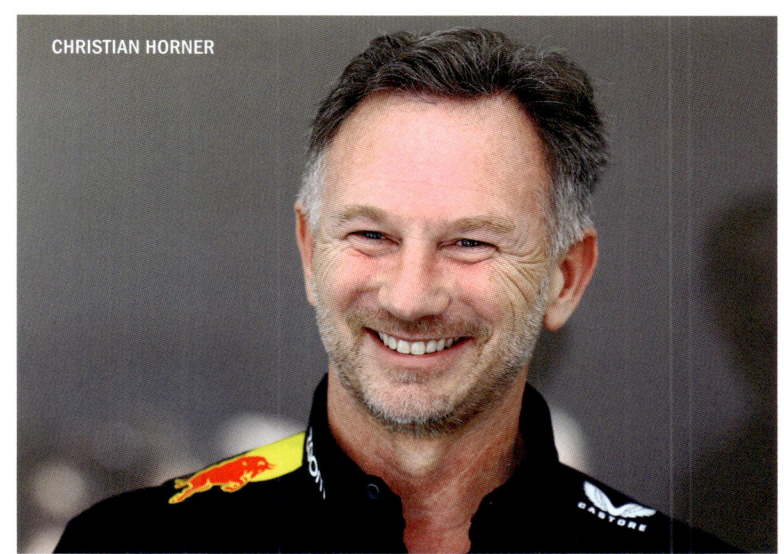

CHRISTIAN HORNER

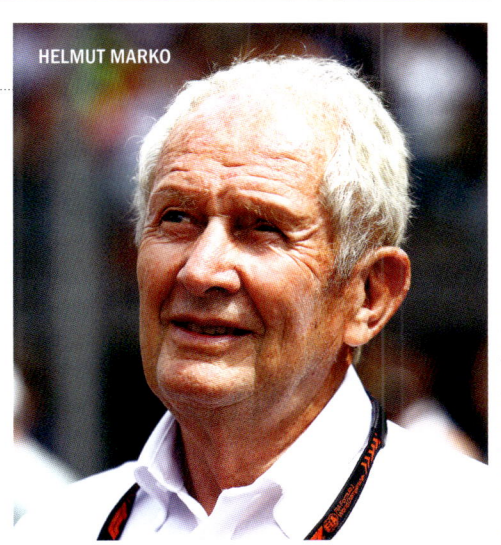

ORACLE RED BULL RACING: PERSONNEL

CEO and Team Principal: Christian Horner CBE

Technical Director: Pierre Waché

Technical Director, Red Bull Powertrains: Ben Hodgkinson

Chief Designer: Craig Skinner

Head of Performance Engineering: Ben Waterhouse

Head of Aerodynamics: Enrico Balbo

Sporting Director: Jonathan Wheatley

Chief Engineer, Car Engineering: Paul Monaghan

Head of Simulation: Simon Rennie

Chief Engineer, Aerodynamics: Sean Whitehead

Race Engineer (Verstappen): Gianpiero Lambiase

Race Engineer (Pérez): Hugh Bird

Chief Mechanic: Chris Gent

No.1 Race Mechanic (Verstappen): Matt Caller

No.1 Race Mechanic (Pérez): Jonathan Caller

Chief Marketing Officer: Oliver Hughes

Director of Brand & Communications: Kelly Brittain

Director of Communications & Social Media: Paul Smith

HELMUT MARKO

Photos: Red Bull Content Pool/Getty Images

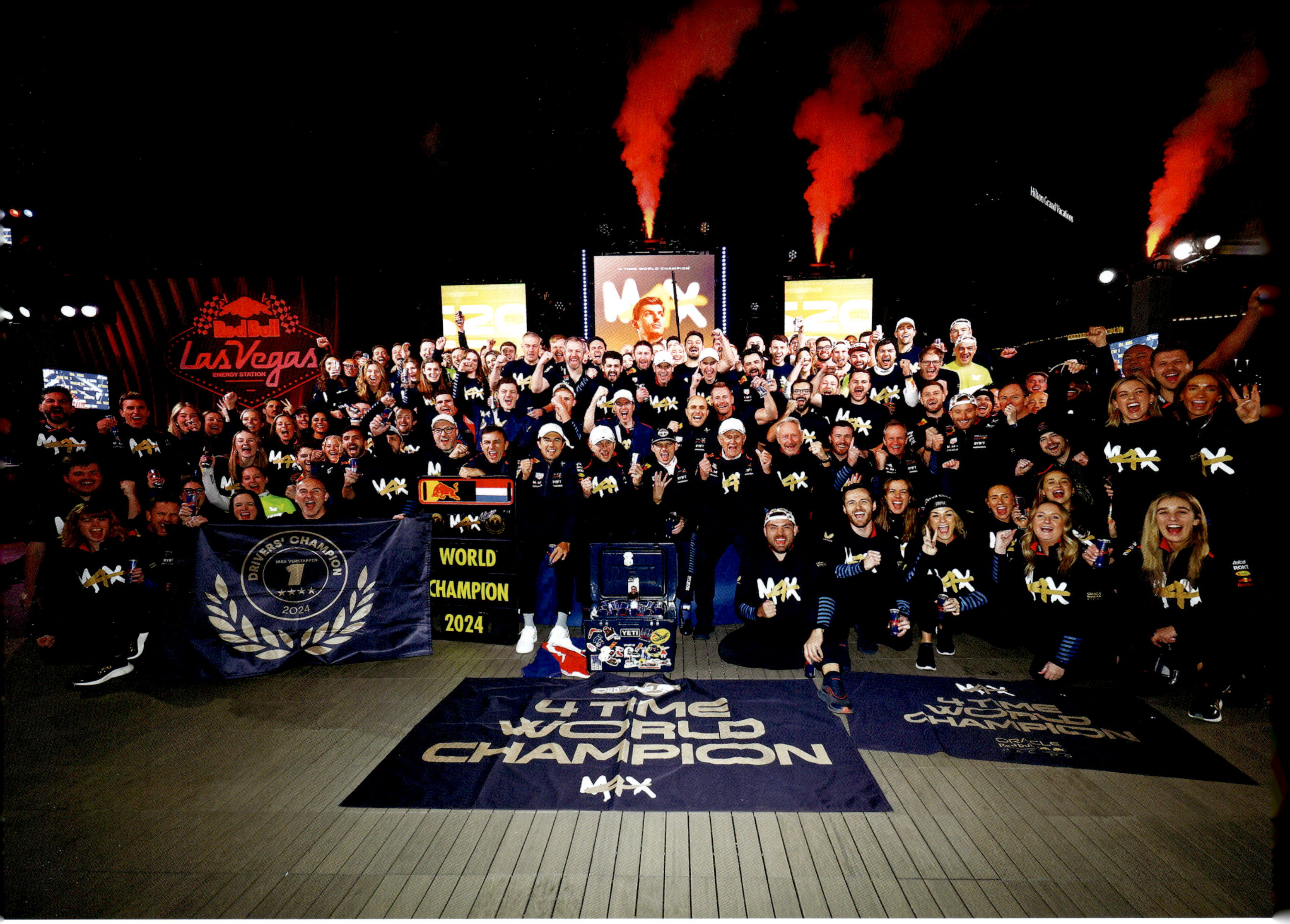
Red Bull
Las Vegas
4 TIME
WORLD
CHAMPION
WORLD
CHAMPION
2024

Above: The Red Bull team celebrates a fourth consecutive world drivers' championship at Las Vegas.

Far right: In a season dominated by his team-mate, Sergio Pérez was on the podium in Bahrain *(right)*, followed by races in Saudi Arabia and Japan, but he struggled thereafter.
Photos: Red Bull Content Pool/Getty Images

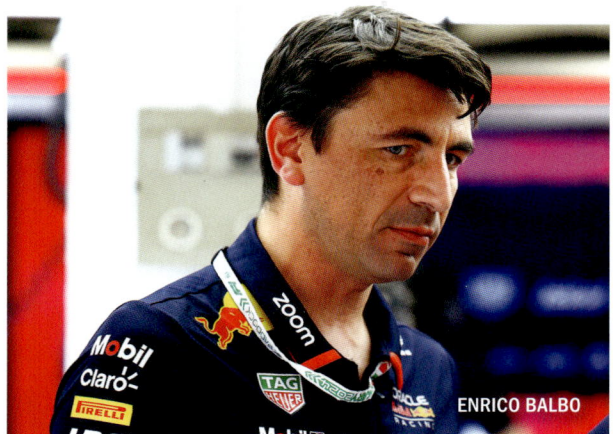

ENRICO BALBO

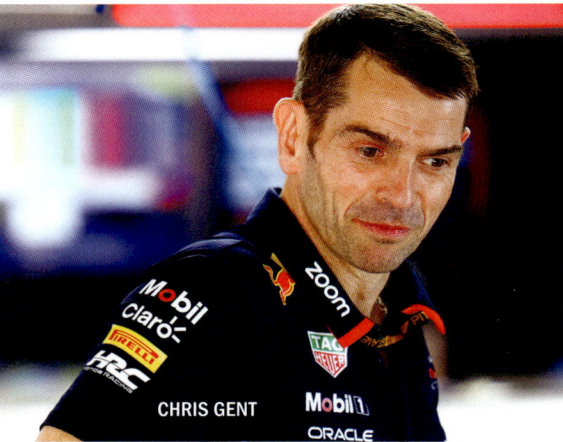

CHRIS GENT

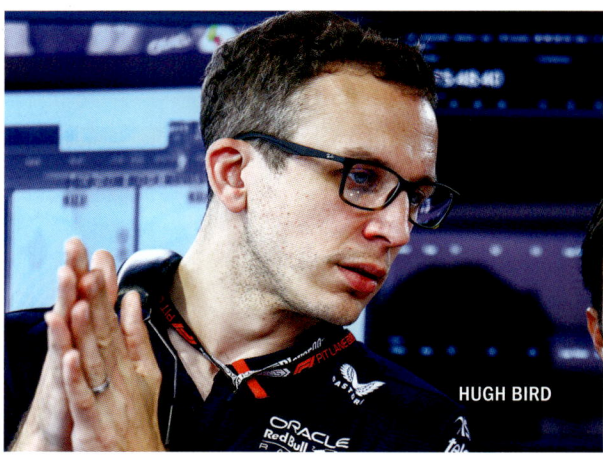

HUGH BIRD

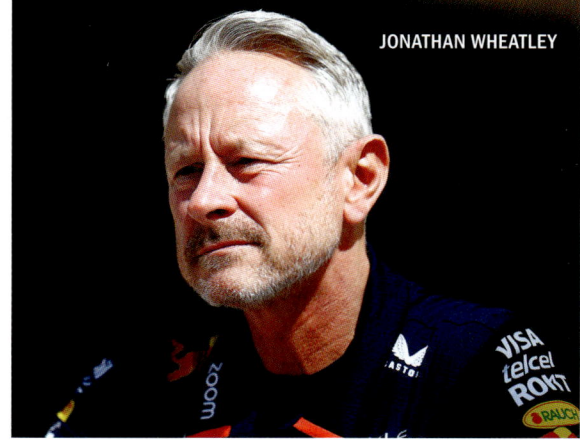

JONATHAN WHEATLEY

PIERRE WACHÉ

GIANPIERO LAMBIASE

PAUL MONAGHAN

be varied much more intricately according to the demands of any given circuit.

With so many separate channels, the chosen level of cooling could be more specific to individual radiators and less 'global'. At some tracks where the electrical demand is high and the amount of straight-line running low, the battery and electrical cooling would need to be accentuated. But the oil and water cooling might be less critical. At other tracks, that demand is balanced quite differently. With more individual cooling available, the radiators can be reduced in size.

It all contributed to a car with a notably small radiator area, allowing its mass to be more centralised, and with a lower centre of gravity. The inlet for the sidepod radiators was an inverted L-shape, with a slim vertical channel on the cockpit side and a slim horizontal one beneath an extended bodywork lip at the top of the sidepods. Compared to the conventional oval-type inlet shape, it made for a hugely-enhanced undercut to the sidepod.

In the way the layout maximised the aerodynamic surfaces, it was a much more sophisticated car than any on the grid. But the performance benefit of this startling approach ended up being overwhelmed by the aero-elastic front wings, which Red Bull did not master to the same extent.

"In trying to continue/develop our aero concept even further, we saw an area of the bodywork which could offer us a good performance gain," said Waché of the car's concept. "We tried to maximise that, and clearly the undercut is very important. That affected cooling and how we could extract the most from it to be able to cool the car and to maximise this aspect, too. It was quite a risk, to be able to cool the car with this concept, and I think we achieved this with reasonable success."

Regular tweaks were made to the front wing, sidepod and floor details as part of the general development. For Hungary, a specific high-downforce bodywork was introduced without the high sidepod shoulders of the original car. Subsequently, the two bodywork types were mixed and matched according to the circuit traits. Regardless of bodywork, though, it was evident that the car was becoming steadily more difficult to balance as development attempted to increase downforce. "The lower you go [on ride height] and still have control of the bouncing, the better – which was way lower than in '22, for example – then the characteristics around this area of balance become more fundamental," said Waché.

"We had missed some characteristic of the car which we… I wouldn't say we didn't spot it, but it was not highlighting a massive loss of performance previously. It had been there already from mid-'23. But more and more when you extract performance, you start to expose these characteristics. These are highlighted at very low downforce, high ride heights, and suddenly the driver cannot drive the car. The problem was really highlighted at Monza."

Based upon this new understanding, a mini recovery was staged in the latter part of the season, with a series of upgrades at Baku and Austin, which made the conflict between low- and high-speed balance less extreme. With the car like this, Verstappen won in the wet of Brazil and through the high-speed bends of Qatar. But it remained a difficult car to set up and more usually was outperformed by the McLaren.

Development in the third year of this formula was generally in the region of diminishing returns for Red Bull, exacerbated by the limitations of its very old wind tunnel in Bedford. "We had some correlation issues," Waché admitted. "The main problem is accuracy and repeatability. When you develop a new concept, this tunnel could work very well. It's more when you are fighting the flattening development curve, it's difficult to work with it because we are very dependent on the temperature in the UK, big swings between cold and hot. It's very difficult for us. We've tried to improve it inside and have developed it a lot over the years, but some physical aspects you cannot change. For sure, it affected our rate of development compared to other teams." An all-new tunnel at the team's Milton Keynes site is being built, but it won't be ready until at least 2026.

While the car was considerably faster than its dominant predecessor, F1 performance is always relative to the competition. Furthermore, Waché accepted that the RB20 had some quite stubborn limitations. "The ride is not nice," he said.

This was clear at Monaco, where the relatively soft vertical stiffness and very high roll stiffness made it a bouncing handful, unable to deal with bumps and kerbs. "It's natural with this type of very stiff and heavy car," said Waché. "In terms of damping, you cannot really get what you need because the regulation removed the inertia damper, which was very efficient at very low movement compared to what you have with a viscous damper. So the natural ride of this regulation is not nice, but I think our car is particularly not good. We have to try to improve it for next year. In '23, we had the same issue, but we had enough of a performance delta over the others that it wasn't obvious."

Which neatly encapsulates the challenge Red Bull faced in 2024.

44

LEWIS HAMILTON

63

GEORGE RUSSELL

MERCEDES-AMG PETRONAS F1 TEAM

Four grand prix victories was the best seasonal haul for Mercedes since the advent of the ground-effect regulations in 2022, and at Silverstone, Spa and Vegas, its car really did appear to be the class of the field. But 2024 was yet another perplexing season of varying competitiveness for the squad, which was in its final year with Lewis Hamilton.

Technically, the W15 represented a new approach. The forward-cockpit, mid-wing concept had been abandoned, in its place a car with a much more conventional layout and a switch to the more commonplace push-rod rear suspension from the previous pull-rod arrangement. A novel feature was its front wing with a 'legality strip' of carbon fibre connecting the top flap to the nose (as required by the regulations), but otherwise minus around a third of the flap's span. This was used to boost airflow to the rear. It was an ingenious exploitation of a regulation loophole, but was made obsolete by probably the most important upgrade the car received: the aero-elastic front wing introduced at Monaco.

To accommodate the more rearwards cockpit, the gearbox casing had been shortened by around 10cm. This still left the cockpit slightly further forwards than that of the Red Bull, but brought it into line with the McLaren and Ferrari. Much of the 2023 car's tricky behaviour at low speeds had been attributed to a mechanical limitation at the rear, something the team sought to address with this car, as highlighted by technical director James Allison at its launch.

"A big focus has been on improving the previous car's unpredictable rear axle," he said. "We have worked hard to ensure that both axles, but particularly the rear axle, retain better control of the tyre than on the W14. There's also been some housekeeping on areas in which we had room for improvement, including the DRS effect and pit-stop performance."

Of the switch from the rear pull-rod arrangement to push-rod, trackside engineering chief Andrew Shovlin outlined the thinking: "The pull-rod packaging means it's very difficult to do changes, and heave spring changes in particular, damper changes, etc. And on balance, we decided the push-rod was the way to go. In terms of being able to rapidly change set-up, this conventional layout is far easier to work with."

But it didn't hit the ground in a happy place, the drivers finding that they could have it with either speed-sapping understeer at slow speeds or edgy oversteer at high. For much of the first part of the season, it was regularly only the fifth-fastest car in qualifying, behind even the identically-powered Aston Martin.

As the team delved into why it was proving such a difficult car to balance, there was what James Allison described as an, 'Oh, my God. How could

MERCEDES-AMG F1 W15 EQ Power+

TITLE PARTNER	Petronas **PRINCIPAL PARTNER** Ineos
TEAM PARTNERS	UBS · Team Viewer · CrowdStrike · Snapdragon · G42 · Akkodis · Hewlett Packard Enterprise · IWC Schaffhausen · The Ritz-Carlton · AMD · SAP Pure Storage · Einhell · Solera · Tommy Hilfiger · Nuvei · WhatsApp · Fastly · Sherwin Williams
TEAM SUPPLIERS	Puma · Police · BetterUp · Endless · Pirelli
POWER UNIT	Type: Mercedes-AMG F1 M15 E Performance No. of cylinders (vee angle): V6 (90°) No. of valves: 24 Max. rpm (ICE): 15,000 Electronics: FIA standard ECU and FIA homologated electronic & electrical system Instrumentation: McLaren Electronic Systems (MES) Fuel: Petronas Primax Lubricants: Petronas Syntium
TRANSMISSION	Gearbox: Eight forward gears plus one reverse, carbon-fibre main case, sequential, semi-automatic, hydraulic activation Clutch: Carbon plate
CHASSIS	Monocoque: Moulded carbon-fibre and honeycomb composite structure Front suspension: Carbon-fibre wishbone and push-rod-actuated torsion springs and rockers Rear suspension: Carbon-fibre wishbone and push-rod-actuated inboard springs and dampers Brakes: Carbone Industrie carbon/carbon discs and pads, Brembo calipers, rear brake-by-wire Steering: Power-assisted rack-and-pinion Wheels: BBS, 18in diameter Tyres: Pirelli P Zero
DIMENSIONS	Length: Over 5000mm · Width: 2000mm · Height: 970mm · Formula weight: 798kg, including driver and camera

LEWIS HAMILTON

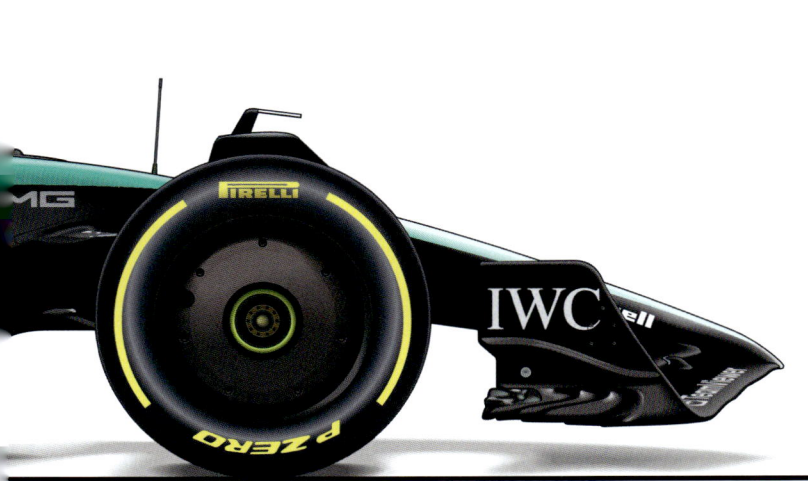

TOTO WOLFF

MERCEDES-AMG PETRONAS F1 TEAM: PERSONNEL

Team Principal & CEO: Toto Wolff	Sporting Director: Ron Meadows
Technical Director: James Allison	Head of Race Strategy: Rosie Wait
Managing Director, High Performance Powertrains: Hywel Thomas	Senior Race Engineer (Hamilton): Peter Bonnington
Chief Operating Officer: Rob Thomas	Senior Race Engineer (Russell): Marcus Dudley
Trackside Engineering Director: Andrew Shovlin	Performance Engineer (Hamilton): Michael Sansoni
Director Of Car Design: John Owen	Performance Engineer (Russell): Hugues Bretonnier
Engineering Director: Giacomo Tortora	Chief Mechanic: Matt Deane
Aerodynamic Director: Jarrod Murphy	Reserve Driver: Andrea Kimi Antonelli
Chief Engineer, Car Design: Ashley Way	Chief Engineer Trackside: Simon Cole
Head Of Vehicle Dynamics Group: Emiliano Gianguilio	Chief Communications Officer: Bradley Lord

Photos: Mercedes-AMG Petronas F1 Team

Above: The team celebrates Lewis Hamilton's record-breaking ninth win in the British Grand Prix.
Photo: Mercedes-AMG Petronas F1 Team

Above right: Russell on the limit at Silverstone in his quest for pole position.
Photo: Bryn Williams

Right: Russell's car is kept cool on the grid as the countown to the start in Singapore nears.

Centre right: Fist pump for Russell after his stunning win in Las Vegas.

Far right: Joy and relief for Lewis after his brilliant drive to win at Silverstone.
Photos: Mercedes-AMG Petronas F1 Team

PETER BONNINGTON

JAMES ALLISON

ANDREA KIMI ANTONELLI

we have been so dumb?' moment. This was a reference to how much more powerful the front wing had become now that they were able to run the car much lower than before.

"The front wings on these cars are very big, and they probably like being near the ground most of all. That tends to make a car get more nervous as it goes faster, because proportionately more is moving to the front axle than you might wish. And so you're fighting that with these rules. And the more you find downforce near the ground, the worse that gets.

"There is always a tendency for low-speed understeer and high-speed oversteer. But the more extreme you make it, the more tricky the car feels to the driver. You can do things with the mechanical balance [to counteract that], but if you take away the aerodynamic unhappiness that that mechanical balance is fighting, then you can have a less extreme mechanical balance migration, and a car that feels more consistent and predictable to the driver."

The solution to this was the new front wing, introduced on Russell's car in Monaco and Hamilton's in Montreal. It featured the sort of aero-elasticity already seen on the front wing McLaren had introduced two races before, but had been in development from much earlier in the season. While passing all the required load tests, the flaps would begin to flex downwards beyond a certain speed in response to the load and in doing so would become less powerful relative to the rear wing at higher speeds. This allowed the set-up window to be much wider, using a more aggressive front flap angle to counteract the low-speed understeer without the concomitant worsening of the high-speed stability.

Like McLaren's similar wing, it had an immediate effect, with Russell setting pole and leading for much of the way in Montreal. His victory two races later in Austria was fortunate (owing to the Verstappen/Norris clash well ahead of him), but Hamilton's ninth British Grand Prix victory the following week was won from the front after engaging the McLarens in battle. After taking a 1-2 on the road at Spa (but with on-the-road winner Russell disqualified for being underweight), that made it three victories in four races for the team.

But such form wasn't maintained. Although the car showed well on fast corners and on a cool track, it still struggled on slow corners and/or a hot track. It also responded badly to bumps – as Russell explained after dominating around the cold, smooth track of Las Vegas: "It still has a narrow window, and when we can set the car up in a way that we exploit that window, we have a race-winning car. But when you go to different circuits and you have to change where you position the set-up, we totally fall outside of our working window… When the track is bumpy, we have to lift the car and go softer on the suspension. Certain circuits require us to be in a [ride-height] window the car doesn't like. But on smooth circuits like this, where we can run it low and stiff, we fly."

A steady development programme kept the car in the mix – new floors at Spa and Austin, together with revised sidepods and an enhanced-outwash front wing at the latter venue – but only within those environmental parameters outlined by Shovlin.

Where the lessons from 2024 might take the team in the final year of this regulation set in 2025 is an intriguing speculation.

ASTON MARTIN ARAMCO F1 TEAM

14 FERNANDO ALONSO

18 LANCE STROLL

A fifth place in the constructors' championship, many points clear of sixth, might not sound disastrous, but the pattern of Aston Martin's season was troubling. It became ever less competitive, having begun the season neck and neck with Mercedes and ended it qualifying behind Sauber as the slowest car in both Brazil and Vegas. In between, several of the development upgrades only seemed to make the car less competitive. Attempts to add aerodynamic load to the car invariably led to it becoming more difficult to drive – and the attempts at reducing its deficit in high-speed corners only seemed to lose it its previous good low/medium-speed form.

The story of its season was that of a car unable to resolve the conflict of requirements at different corner speeds and circuit characteristics.

Dan Fallows – who stepped down from his position as technical director after the Mexican Grand Prix – believes that it was not about the basic architecture of the car, but rather "the interactions of the aero with the suspension and the tyres, which makes the job doubly, triply complicated."

Aerodynamically, the AMR24 was not radically different from the previous year's car. The radiator inlets had been reshaped, the front wing mounted on the bottom flap rather than the mainplane below, the sidepods made mildly different in profile. Still taking its power unit and rear end from Mercedes meant a switch to push-rod suspension from pull-rod at the rear (the front remained push-rod), in line with the works team. The gearbox casing was shorter, which moved the cockpit position slightly further back.

As far as Aston was concerned, the Mercedes mechanical changes were all considered to be positive for its car. "Going to a push-rod rear suspension made life a lot easier in terms of adjustment on race weekends," said Fallows, "because a lot more of the suspension components are above the gearbox, instead of buried internally in it. Aerodynamically, that layout lends itself a bit better to managing airflow around the rear corner in a way that we would like to do, particularly with the layout of the lower wishbone and how that interacts with the devices outboard on the brake ducts. So we were kind of hoping [Mercedes] would go down that route."

As for the cockpit repositioning, "It was about making the exposed area of the chassis underneath the radiator inlet narrower. So it gives you more area to control flow around the sidepods and around the floor edge. Because a lot of the trick with these regulations, particularly with the sidepods, is about managing airflow to the floor itself and to the rear. And the more air you can suck in to start off with, the easier your job is to manage it as it goes rearward."

The drivers reported that it retained the 2023 car's decent low-speed behaviour, but it definite-

ASTON MARTIN AMR24

TITLE PARTNER	ARAMCO
GLOBAL PARTNERS	Ma'aden · Cognizant · BOSS · Valvoline · Glenfiddich · NexGen · Velocity Black · Citi Banco Master · SentinelOne · Juniper Networks · Banco Master · JCB NetApp · Circle8 · Avatrade Service Now · Regent Cruises · Girard Perregaux · Epos · Bombardier · Globe Trotter · Wolfgang Puck · Pirelli · Financial Times · TikTok
OFFICIAL SUPPLIERS	Oakley · Ogio · OMP · Stilo
POWER UNIT	Type: Mercedes-AMG F1 M15E EQ Power+ No. of cylinders (vee angle): V6 (90°) No. of valves: 24 Max rpm (ICE): 15,000 Electronics: FIA single ECU with in-house-designed electrical harness Fuel: E10s Fuel: E10
TRANSMISSION	Gearbox: Mercedes AMG F1 eight-speed, semi-automatic, seamless-shift Clutch: AP Racing
CHASSIS	Monocoque: Carbon-fibre composite with Zylon anti-intrusion panels
	Front suspension: Carbon-fibre wishbone and push-rod suspension elements operating inboard heave unit, anti-roll bar and damper system
	Rear suspension: Carbon-fibre wishbone and push-rod suspension elements operating inboard torsion-bar and damper system
	Brakes: Carbon-fibre discs and pads, Brembo calipers, in-house-designed brake-by-wire system
	Wheels: BBS, 18in diameter Tyres: Pirelli P Zero
DIMENSIONS	Length: 5600mm Width: 2000mm Wheelbase 3600mm Formula weight: 798kg, including driver and camera

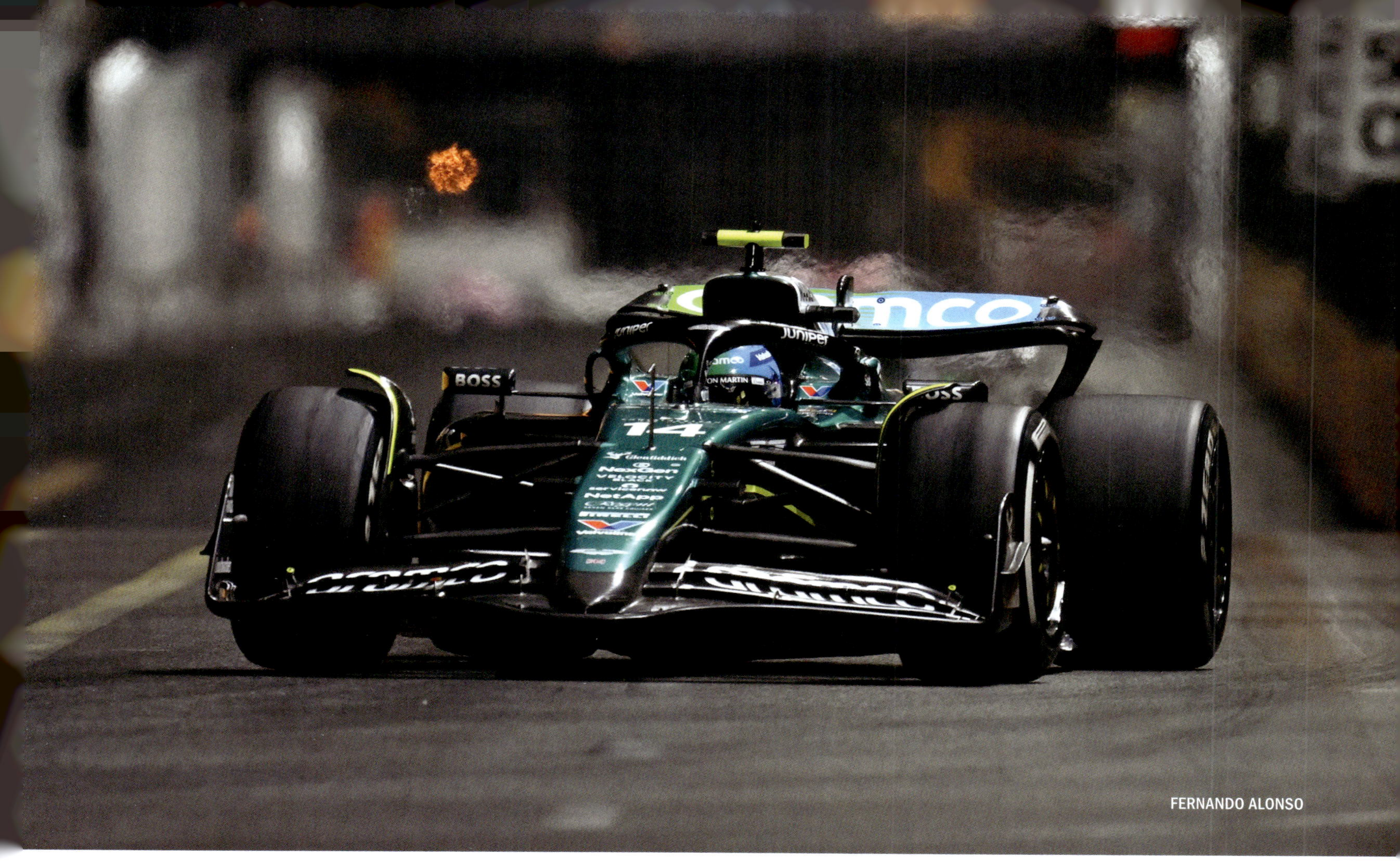

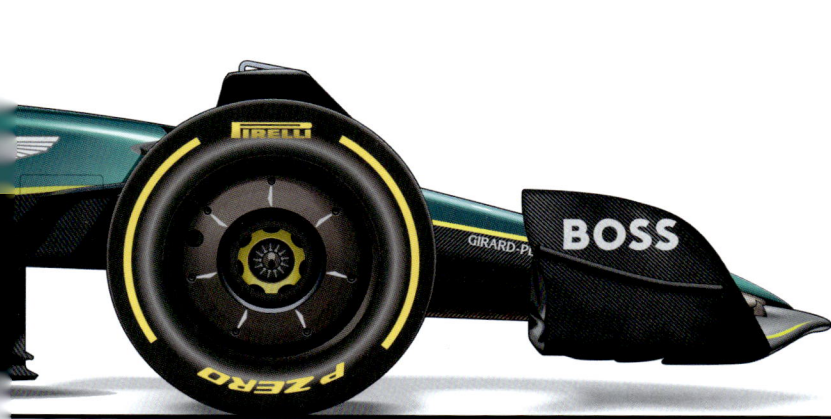

FERNANDO ALONSO

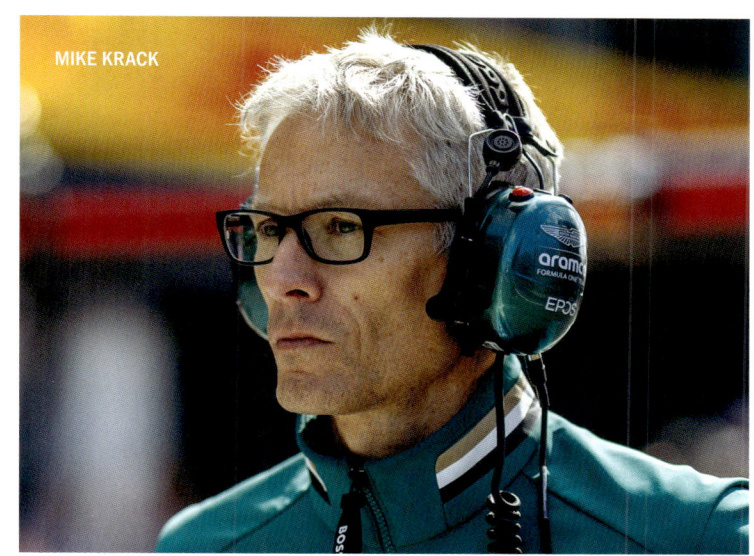

MIKE KRACK

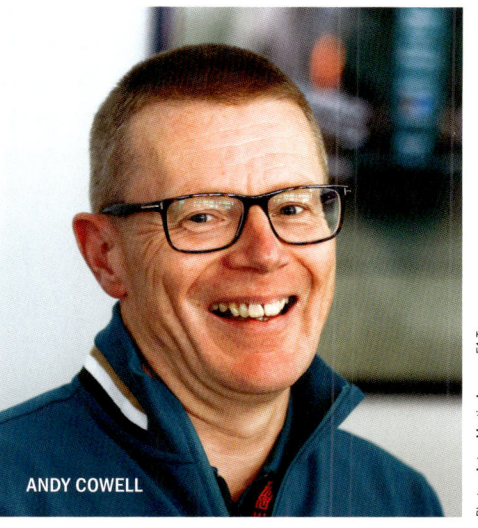

ASTON MARTIN ARAMCO F1 TEAM: PERSONNEL

- Executive Chairman: Lawrence Stroll
- Group CEO: Andy Cowell
- Team Principal: Mike Krack
- Chief Technical Officer: Enrico Cardile (joining In 2025)
- Executive Director, Technical: Bob Bell
- Deputy Technical Director: Eric Blandin
- Performance Director: Tom McCullough
- Sporting Director: Andy Stevenson
- Engineering Director: Luca Furbatto
- Chief Designer: Akio Haga
- Head of Trackside Systems Integration: Joe Robinson
- Race Engineer (Alonso): Chris Cronin
- Race Engineer (Stroll): Andrew Vizard
- Chief Mechanic: Curtis Stones
- No.1 Mechanic (Alonso): Michael Brown
- No.1 Mechanic (Stroll): Harry Rush
- Reserve Drivers: Felipe Drugovich & Zak Crawford
- Managing Director, Commercial: Jefferson Slack
- Director of Communications: Adrian Atkinson
- Head of Media & Communications: Will Hings

ANDY COWELL

Photos: Aston Martin Aramco F1 Team

Above: Last-minute adjustments are carried out on Lance Stroll's Aston on the grid in Miami.

Right: Off we go. Fernando Alonso heads out into the pit lane.

Far right: An impromptu team photo at Silverstone.
Photos: Aston Martin F1 Team

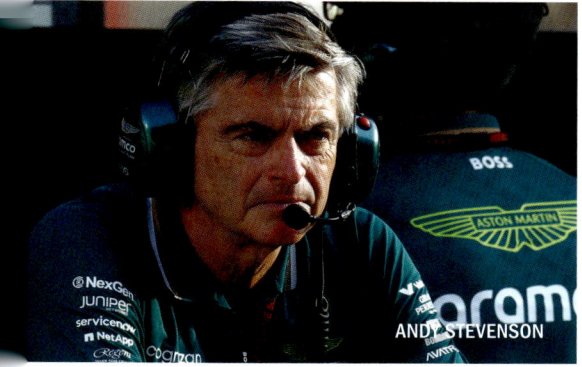
ANDY STEVENSON

TOM McCULLOUGH

ERIC BLANDIN

LAWRENCE STROLL

ZAK CRAWFORD

FELIPE DRUGOVICH

ly lacked the performance of the top cars in the high-speed sections. At Suzuka, the first planned upgrade – comprising an all-new floor and diffuser – generally retained the car's initial gap to the front of around 0.5 per cent in qualifying, much the same as Mercedes at that time. Fernando Alonso insisted that this spec, while not a huge improvement on the original, was the car at its best.

For Imola, just three races later, there was another update, with a front wing that had a different load distribution across its width to rework the airflow being supplied to the floor. There were accompanying changes to the floor edges and diffuser. These were more specifically configured to give a better balance window through the full range of corner speeds. This coincided with a step-change reduction (from 0.5 to 1.6 per cent) in competitiveness. Thereafter, each time an update was applied to the car, there would be a few races of recovering some of the deficit, before another update increased it again. This happened with both the Hungary and Austin packages.

After neither driver reported favourably on the Austin upgrade, the team reverted to mixing and matching floors, which it had been doing for a few races before. It was as if the team had despaired of trying to make a single floor work over a variety of corner speeds, so ended up developing two in tandem and choosing according to track characteristics. The Austin upgrade was an attempt at introducing a floor that would work at all tracks. In Brazil, Alonso was back to the round-four (Japan) floor, as he had been pushing to do since Baku six weeks earlier.

"We have had to decide on a race-by-race basis where we think the most lap time is going to be gained," said Fallows, "and where we can afford to maybe compromise a car a little bit. Obviously, that's not a situation we want to be in.

"It's been speed range, but it's also things like the track characteristics, bumps and certain combinations of corners. That has been quite a challenge, particularly with these regulations, with the big floors running so close to the ground. So when you have subtle changes in ride heights, roll angles, yaw conditions with wind, etc, it can upset the aerodynamics of the floor in particular. So we've been trying to make sure that as you add performance to the car, it doesn't then destroy some of the good characteristics that you get in some conditions."

After providing a good boost in performance at the beginning of 2023, the Fallows-led technical team at Aston simply had not kept pace with the tricky demands of developing this generation of car. For a team of such soaring ambition and heavy investment, this wasn't deemed acceptable. The spectacular recruitment of Andy Cowell and Adrian Newey (as well as Ferrari's former technical director, Enrico Cardile, who starts as chief technical officer in 2025) will place an even larger spotlight on the team.

BWT ALPINE FORMULA 1 TEAM

10 PIERRE GASLY

31 ESTEBAN OCON

61 JACK DOOHAN

Alpine took some bold steps in the conception of its all-new A524 – and it bit them. A very difficult gestation led to the team being weeks behind in its development of the car pre-season, putting it firmly at the back in the early races and leading to the resignations of Matt Harman as technical director and aero chief Dirk de Beer after the first race.

Although the car moved up the grid as the team caught up with development, the big improvement came late in the season from an impressive upgrade made under the supervision of new technical director David Sanchez. It helped the team to secure sixth place in the constructors' championship, but there had been many high-level casualties along the way.

In May, Renault automotive CEO Luca de Meo recruited the team's former boss, Flavio Briatore, as executive advisor for the Formula 1 division. In effect, he returned as the boss, and shortly afterwards Bruno Famin stepped down from that role.

De Meo had clearly given Briatore scope to do whatever he considered necessary, and he quickly created waves by confirming that he was considering severing the links with Renault's power unit supply for the future. The Renault PU was reckoned to be costing around 0.3s per lap, and Briatore's plan was confirmed with the November announcement of a Mercedes customer supply from 2026, thus leaving the historic Renault Sport Viry

ALPINE A524

TITLE PARTNER	BWT
PREMIUM PARTNERS	Castrol · BP Ultimate · H. Moser & Cie · Renault E-Tech
OFFICIAL PARTNERS	ApeCoin · Businessolver · Binance · Mobilize · Microsoft · Boeing · XBOX · MNTN · Amazon Music · Qatar Airways · Infinox · Banco BRB · Kappa · Delphi Canel's · Eurodatacar · Sprinklr · The Venetian Resort Las Vegas · Shamir · Yahoo!
OFFICIAL SUPPLIERS	3D Systems · Alpinestars · Alpine Eyewear · GCaps · Hexis · KWay · Johnson Health Tech (Matrix) · Pirelli · Roland · Trak Racer · JAAQ
POWER UNIT	Type: Type: Renault E-Tech 2024 Hybrid No. of cylinders (vee angle): V6 (90°) No. of valves: 24 Max rpm (ICE): 15,000 Electronics: MES-Microsoft standard electronic control unit Fuel: BP Oil: Castrol
TRANSMISSION	Gearbox: Eight-speed-plus-reverse, semi-automatic, quick-shift system Clutch: AP Racing
CHASSIS	Monocoque: Moulded carbon-fibre and aluminium-honeycomb composite Front suspension: Upper and lower carbon-fibre wishbones, push-rod-actuated torsion-bar springs, dampers and anti-roll bar Rear suspension: Upper and lower carbon-fibre wishbones, pull-rod actuated torsion-bar springs and transverse-mounted damper units, aluminium uprights Brakes: Brembo calipers, carbon discs and pads Master cylinders: AP Racing Wheels: BBS, 18in diameter Tyres: Pirelli P Zero
DIMENSIONS	Length: 5620mm Width: 2000mm Front track: 2000mm Rear track: 2000mm Height: 1100mm Formula weight: 798kg, including driver and camera

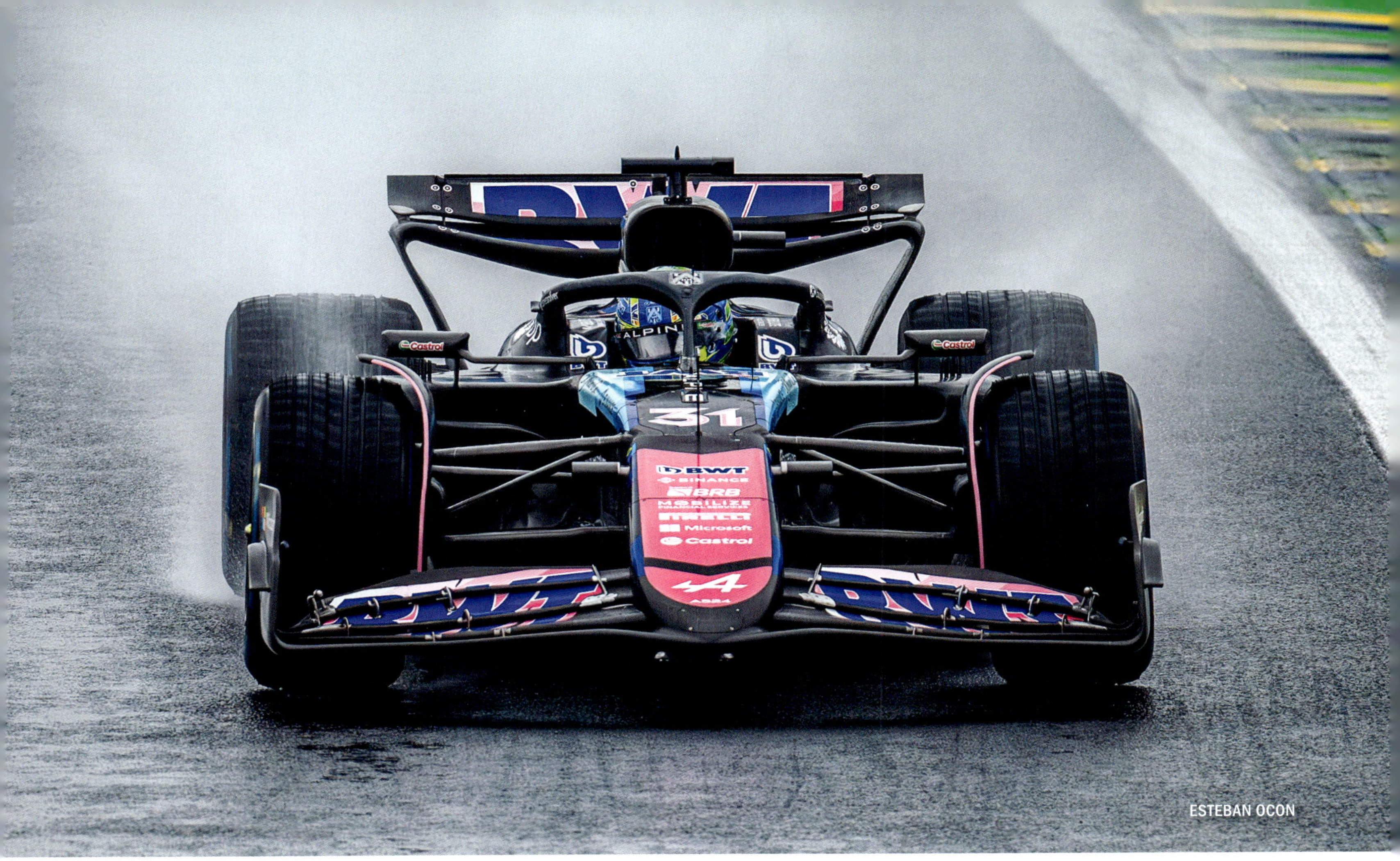

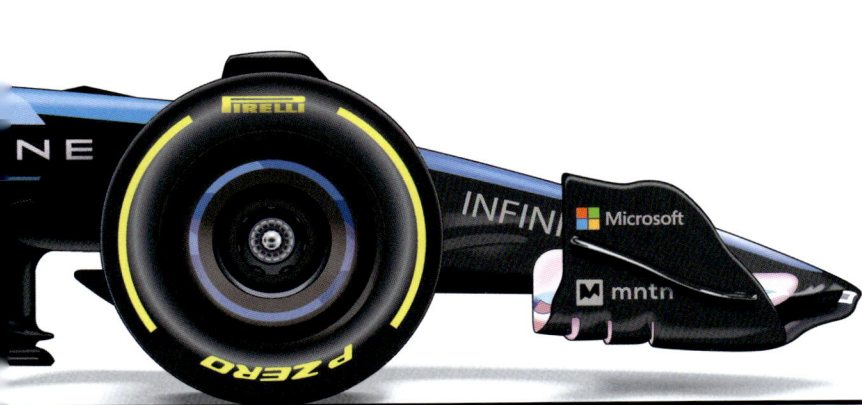

ESTEBAN OCON

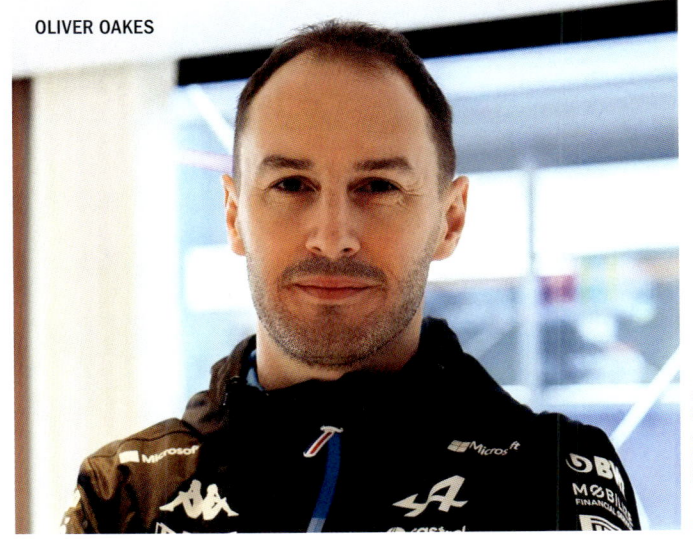

OLIVER OAKES

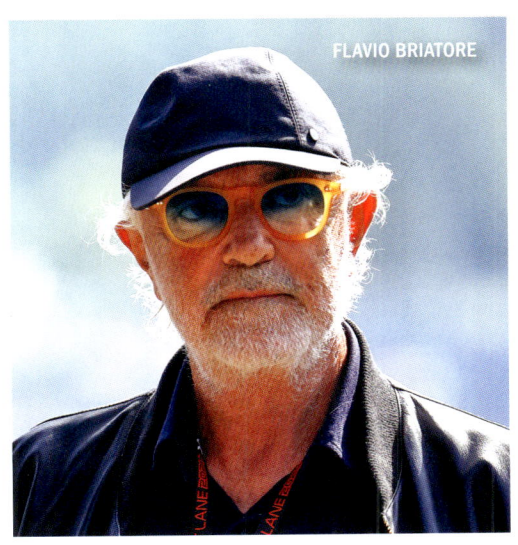

Photos: BWT Alpine F1 Team

BWT ALPINE FORMULA 1 TEAM: PERSONNEL

CEO Alpine: Philippe Krief

Team Principal: Oliver Oakes

Executive Advisor: Flavio Briatore

Executive Technical Director: David Sanchez

Technical Director Viry-Châtillon: Eric Meignan

Sporting Director: Julian Rouse

Race Team Manager: Rob Cherry

Deputy Head of Trackside Engineering: Karel Loos

Technical Director, Engineering: Joe Burnell

Chief Aerodynamicist: Michael Broadhurst

Technical Director, Performance: Ciaron Pilbeam

Chief Mechanic: Jason Milligan

Head of Vehicle Performance: Vin Dhanani

Race Engineer (Gasly): John Howard

Race Engineer (Ocon/Doohan): Josh Peckett

Senior Strategy Engineer: Oriol Isern

FLAVIO BRIATORE

Photo: XPB Images

Above: A double podium brought unexpected joy for Gasly, Ocon and the Alpine team in São Paulo.

Right: With Ocon's departure, Pierre Gasly has assumed the role of undisputed team leader.

Above right: Rooster-tails from the Alpine as Gasly heads for third place in Brazil.
Photos: BWT Alpine F1 Team

DAVID SANCHEZ

ERIC MEIGNAN

JULIAN ROUSE

ROB CHERRY

CIARON PILBEAM

JOE BURNELL

factory with no F1 role from that time. In the meantime, Briatore had recruited Oliver Oakes – owner of the Hitech F2/F3 team – as the new team principal. Previously, Hitech had had its application to join the F1 grid turned down.

This was a radically different group of senior people to the one the team had started with just a few months earlier. In the meantime, the technical departments had pressed on with trying to make up for the time lost to the A524's difficult birth. The all-new chassis was supposed to facilitate greater stiffness for the same weight. The rear suspension, while still push-rod, was completely new to address the previous car's poor ride and associated aero problems. The bodywork featured a much bigger undercut to the sidepod and a new floor.

The difficulties began with the decision to make the chassis as a single piece, which is quite routine for the leading teams. But manufacturing difficulties – exacerbated by having to make late-notice alterations when it was realised that driver Esteban Ocon would not fit – resulted in the chassis failing its crash test. Thus the car was in a very under-developed state – and significantly overweight – in the first few races. It took until round six in Miami, with Pierre Gasly's modest tenth place, for the team to score its first point.

Shortly after Sanchez's arrival as technical director, he ordered a halt to the development direction the team was pursuing. He realigned it according to his own understanding of the nuances of ground-effect aerodynamics. "When I joined, obviously the big question mark was why the car was so far back. Was it a lack of ideas, a lack of directions or a lack of skills? On the nice side, I found very competent people and pretty good facilities. But the bad performance at the start of the season was from a car which was very heavy, and the direction which had been taken to develop it was a little arguable.

"The limitations of the car were very obvious, and the way to try and drag it out of this corner was also quite obvious. So that's why, first few weeks, we made a bit of a status update of what we had in the pipeline: What do we keep? What do we stop? What do we refocus? Especially in aero, and we made a plan to try and deliver a complete upgrade package – and we introduced this at Austin."

That package comprised a new floor, new details along the floor edge and a reshaped 'coke bottle'/ rear engine cover to further aid the underbody flow. Sanchez explained the philosophy behind the changes: "There's an easy trap to fall into with these ground-effect cars. You want downforce, and if you just develop the car at low ride heights, you find a lot of big downforce in the tunnel. But then with all the issues about porpoising, ride and so on, you have a very high peak of downforce, but you can't go there, you can't run it. And because you have developed the aero around this low ride height, as soon as you deviate from this small window, as you lift the car up to stop the bouncing, the car is just slow."

The Austin upgrade represented a more sympathetic generation of downforce through all the ride heights, speed ranges, and angles of roll and pitch the car will experience.

"So as well as the clarity of direction and the sort of characteristics we were looking for, we also sought to optimise all the tools available and not simply focus on the wind tunnel in a very specific area of the map. These days, CFD is very good and it gives a lot more information; it's where we design the car. So instead of saying, well, the wind tunnel is the tool for aero, well no, it's one of them; there are a few others. There's data from the race-car, there is CFD data and showing what the flow is like, how to manipulate it, and then the wind tunnel is another layer. Trying to blend all these three environments, you try and build a lot of confidence on where you're trying to get to. But also if the wind tunnel is happy, but the CFD says 'Don't go there,' you shouldn't go there."

In addition to the weight loss, another area of improvement came with the team's eager pursuit of aero-elasticity once McLaren and Mercedes had shown what was possible and permitted. "It was a direction we had to catch up with," said Sanchez. "The regulations allow a certain amount, and wherever you think you can gain a bit of performance, you have to go and grab it. We made good progress with this through the season."

The combination of this technology made the Austin upgrade quite spectacular. Gasly qualified comfortably in Q3, and two races later, in the rain of Brazil, the team scored a spectacular 2-3 result. Although aided by the conditions and smart strategy, the car had qualified on the second row, a feat it repeated in Las Vegas.

So a dramatic season and one of considerable upheaval, but the direction and speed of competitive travel was impressive.

MONEYGRAM HAAS F1 TEAM

20 KEVIN MAGNUSSEN

OLLIE BEARMAN

27 NICO HÜLKENBERG

50

The 2024 season was very positive for the reshuffled Haas team. New team principal Ayao Komatsu took over the reins from the departing Guenther Steiner and refashioned the team according to his own observations in his previous role of performance director.

Former technical director Simone Resta left with Steiner, as did former head of aero Aaron Melville. In their place, Komatsu promoted former chief designer Andrea de Zordo to TD and former aerodynamicist David Paganelli to head of aero. Replacing de Zordo as chief designer was Tom Coupland. In addition, Komatsu created a new role of performance director to better link the aero department with trackside engineering. This was filled by Damien Brayshaw.

Komatsu had no great expectation of being able to lift Haas from its 2023 position of a solid last in the constructors' championship, but instead focused on eradicating what he saw as previous bottlenecks and problems within the team's processes. Chief among these was improving communication between departments, and between the design centre within Ferrari's Maranello campus and the race team in Banbury, UK. Despite the new way of working being applied to a car that had been largely created by the previous group, the team was pleasantly surprised at the outcome: the VF-24 had none of the tyre degradation problems of 2023 and had a very rounded performance over

HAAS VF-24

TITLE SPONSOR	MoneyGram
SPONSORS	Haas Automation · Play'n GO · Chipotle · TravisMathew · Palm Angels · Taittinger · Tricorp · OAKBERRY · Mphasis · Orion180 · UChicago Medicine · MGM · Mercari
SUPPLIERS	Alpinstars · Pirelli · Schuberth
POWER UNIT	Type: Ferrari 066/10 Hybrid 1.6-litre turbo No. of cylinders (vee angle): V6 (90°) No. of valves: 24 Max. rpm (ICE): 15,000 Electronics: FIA standard ECU and FIA homologated electronics and electrical system Fuel & lubricants: Shell
TRANSMISSION	Gearbox: Ferrari eight-speed-plus-reverse, longitudinally-mounted, electronically-controlled, sequential semi-automatic with quick-shift mechanism Clutch: AP Racing
CHASSIS	Monocoque: Carbon-fibre and honeycomb composite structure Front suspension: Double wishbones, push-rod-actuated torsion-bar springs, anti-roll bar Rear suspension: Double wishbones, pull-rod actuated torsion-bar springs, anti-roll bar Dampers: ZF Sachs/Öhlins Brakes: Six-piston calipers, carbon discs and pads Wheels: BBS, 18in diameter Tyres: Pirelli P Zero
DIMENSIONS	Not disclosed Formula weight: 798kg, including driver and camera

NICO HÜLKENBERG

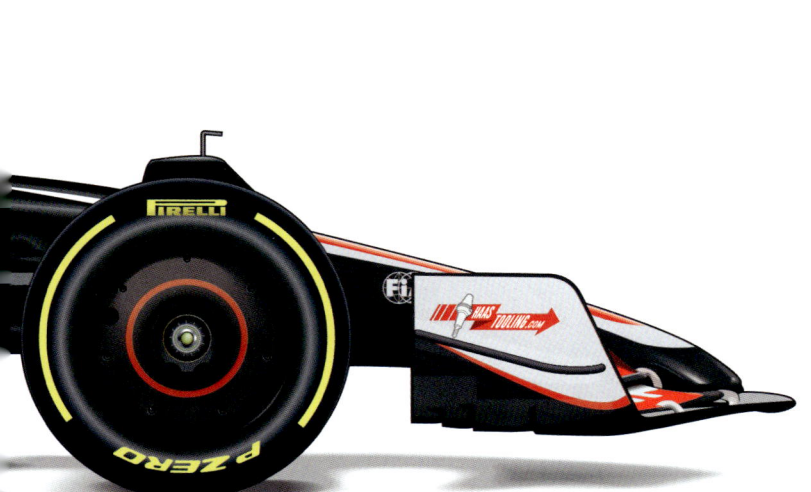

AYAO KOMATSU

MONEYGRAM HAAS F1 TEAM: PERSONNEL

Founder & Chairman: Gene Haas	Race Engineer (Hülkenberg): Gary Gannon
Chief Operating Officer: Joe Custer	Race Engineer (Magnussen/Bearman): Mark Slade
Team Principal: Ayao Komatsu	Chief Mechanic: Toby Brown
Team Manager: Peter Crolla	Race Mechanic (Hülkenberg): Matt Thompson
Race Team Co-ordinator: Neil Hanley	Race Mechanic (Magnussen/Bearman): Elliot Parkes
Technical Director: Andrea de Zordo	Head of Communications: Stuart Morrison
Chief Designer: Tom Coupland	Senior Communications Manager: Jessica Borrell
Performance Director: Damien Brayshaw	Director of Marketing: Mark Morrell
Head of Performance Engineering: Dom Haines	Reserve Drivers: Pietro Fittipaldi & Oliver Bearman
Chief Aerodynamicist: Rhodri Moseley	

GENE HAAS

Photos: MoneyGram Haas F1 Team

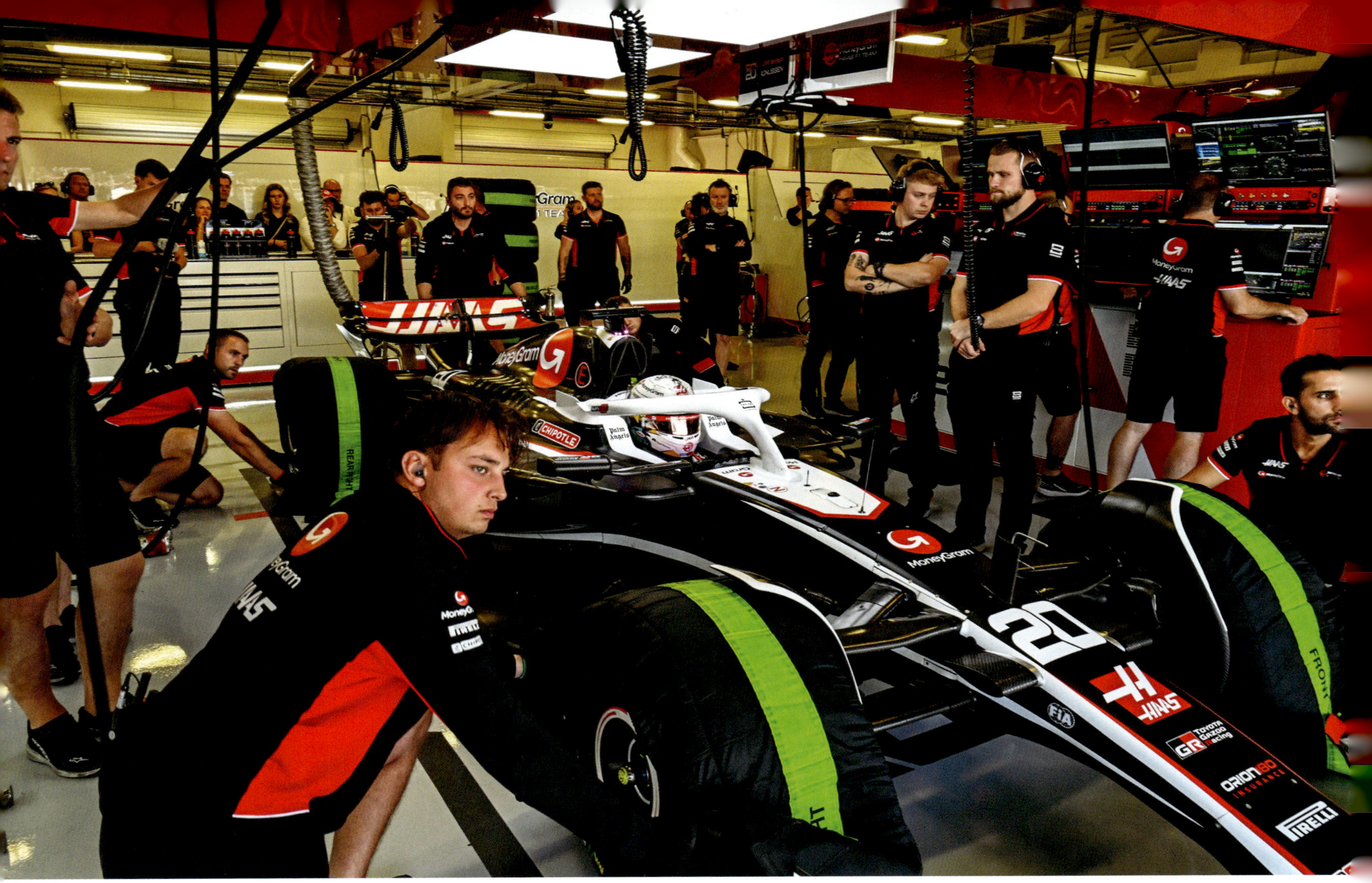

Above: The tyre warmers are about to come off as Kevin Magnussen prepares for action.

Right: Plenty to digest in the Haas team's mission control.

Above right: Nico Hülkenberg posted some tremendous performances in qualifying, such as his sixth place at Silverstone for the British GP.

Top far right: Ollie Bearman stood in for Magnussen in Baku, where he brought his car home tenth to score a valuable point for the team.

Photos: MoneyGram Haas F1 Team

ANDREA DE ZORDO

PIETRO FITTIPALDI

all types of track, which allowed the team to vie for sixth place in the constructors' championship. In outright pace, it was 0.3s closer to the front than the previous car, averaging just 0.9s off in qualifying (and only 0.65s off the identically-powered Ferrari). Highlights were Nico Hülkenberg's brace of sixth places in Austria and Silverstone, but the car was almost always vying for points.

In appearance, the VF-24 was quite similar to the 2023 Austin upgraded car, with similar undercut sidepods. Ferrari – which continued to supply the power unit, gearbox and running gear – provided a gearbox that was 5cm shorter than the previous version, creating more volume around the diffuser. Better packaging allowed more development potential for the aero group.

Improving the previous car's disastrous tyre degradation traits was a top priority, and quite aside from having produced a car with more downforce that slid its rear tyres less, pre-season testing at Bahrain was almost entirely devoted to fully understanding how it responded to different setups to gain a much fuller understanding than before of tyre usage.

"We started the season quite scared about the race pace," admitted de Zordo. "So we focused on that during pre-season testing. We also tested a few things – like a hypothesis, something not proven. From that, we started to develop the car around what we found in this test. For the following development, it was quite important. In general, it was more robust than the previous year, and so we understood the car better right from the start."

De Zordo also highlighted the big improvements made in the way the team worked: "The main difference was that trackside, development and design were more aligned, like bridges together. Before, they were sometimes separate entities, sometimes even in competition with each other! Now we really worked together. We discuss things a lot more. Every time there's been an upgrade, we discuss more openly about what worked and didn't work.

"Another change which paid off well was we tried to give people more freedom in their work. The head of aero [Paganelli] has done good work, giving the people more freedom to work and get better recognition of their work. Previously, it was more they were forced to work in a certain way. Now they are freer to express themselves, and are happier and deliver better things. We then put it all together. We are freer and it has freed more resource.

"Ayao Komatsu put in a lot of effort in getting Banbury and Maranello to work better together, and helped the people in Italy to work well. When all the change happened, the people here in Italy were a bit scared because they didn't know what was going to happen. Was it all going to the UK? But he made clear the design office would remain in Italy and really made a lot of effort to make the people happy. He tried to send more people trackside and organised visits from Italy to UK to see the other factory. The mood here improved a lot."

Informed by what they had discovered in pre-season testing, the first upgrade was on the car early, in China for round five. "We changed something in the floor to help make it more stable," explained de Zordo, "and from then, we could push the aero more."

The new floor came with a new engine cover plus a few accompanying details. The engine cover was narrowed significantly, giving more airflow capacity to the rear wing. The geometry of the floor was altered in such a way that, in combination with the greater performance being squeezed from that rear wing, it gave a better spread of downforce, making the car more driveable.

"At the start of the season, we understood we were relatively weak in high-speed," explained de Zordo, "so we started working on that. Fixing this problem was relatively easy. You develop the car, put more effort in a certain speed range. For the medium-speed. it's a bit different – I don't think we made it worse. We just improved the high-speed, the medium not as much."

As with the other two major upgrades brought to the car – at Silverstone and Austin – the China upgrade correlated with a significant jump in competitiveness. For Silverstone, a totally new floor geometry was at the centre of changes that included all-new radiator-inlet bodywork, diffuser and engine cover. In Austin, there was a significantly deeper sidepod undercut, making possible a more aggressive floor expansion area, which, in turn allowed the diffuser to be reprofiled further. Floor fences and floor edges were reprofiled accordingly.

There was also a new front wing, at Zandvoort, with reduced camber inboard and increased camber mid-section. This concentrated the load towards the middle of the wing, giving a cleaner flow over the nose, which overlapped with the first element of the wing. This was designed to give a more efficient central flow to feed the floor.

The rate of development was much better than it had been in 2023, but it did begin to suffer as the top teams began to delve more deeply into aero elasticity of wings. "For a team of this size, it's very difficult to explore that area," admitted de Zordo. "It really requires a lot of resources – in terms of design, simulation, calculation, testing. For us, that's a very difficult area. If we want to compete at this level in coming years, we must be stronger in those areas."

The team's new tie-up with Toyota (which began at the US Grand Prix) should provide the sort of technical resource to compete in the more intense level of research needed for such technology. Things are definitely looking far brighter at Haas than 12 months ago.

VISA CASH APP RB F1 TEAM

Under its new Racing Bull (or RB) identity, the former AlphaTauri team battled with Alpine and Haas for sixth place in the constructors' championship, ultimately finishing eighth. It did so with a car named the VCARB 01, which was a close evolution of the 2023 AlphaTauri AT04. At an average of 0.9s adrift of the identically-powered Red Bull in qualifying, it was a couple of tenths closer to the front than its predecessor.

The main differences between the late 2023-spec car and the launch version of the new car were mechanical. In place of the previous push-rod front suspension was the pull-rod system of the 2023 Red Bull RB19. Until the Las Vegas GP, the rear suspension remained Red Bull '23-spec push-rod, as introduced by the junior team at Singapore that year. For the last three races, the car ran with the full 2024-spec Red Bull rear end. Honda continued to supply the power unit and Red Bull Technologies the gearbox.

Aside from a different radiator inlet bodywork, the aero surfaces were largely unchanged. This included the floor, which essentially was that which had been introduced at the final race of 2023, in Abu Dhabi. This strong carry-over of a car that had shown good form at the end of the previous season was probably responsible for a similarly strong start to 2024. In the early part of the season, the VCARB was usually clear of the Haas/Alpine/Williams group, with Yuki Tsunoda a Q3 regular. But

22 YUKI TSUNODA

3 DANIEL RICCIARDO

30 LIAM LAWSON

VCARB 01

PARTNERS	Red Bull · Orlen · Honda · Epicor · XMTrading · Randstad Italia · P448 · Pirelli · Ravenol · NEFT Vodka · Piquadro · Tudor · Hugo Eyewear · Riedel · Siemens
POWER UNIT	Type: Honda Red Bull RBPTH001 No. of cylinders (vee angle): V6 (90°) No. of valves: 24 Max rpm (ICE): 15,000 Electronics: MESL standard electronic control unit Fuel and lubricants: E10
TRANSMISSION	Gearbox: Red Bull eight-speed, carbon-composite main case, longitudinally mounted with hydraulic power-shift Clutch: Carbon multi-plate
CHASSIS	Monocoque: Red Bull moulded carbon-fibre and honeycomb composite structure
Front suspension: Carbon-composite wishbones and uprights, pull-rod-actuated inboard torsion bars and dampers
Rear suspension: Red Bull Technology carbon-composite wishbones, pull-rod-actuated inboard torsion bars and dampers
Brakes: VCARB/Red Bull Technology Steering: VCARB power-assisted
Wheels: F1 standard supply component, 18in diameter Tyres: Pirelli P Zero
DIMENSIONS	Not disclosed Formula weight: 798kg, including driver and camera

YUKI TSUNODA

LAURENT MEKIES

Photos: Red Bull Content Pool/Getty Images

VISA CASH APP RB F1 TEAM: PERSONNEL

Team Owner: Red Bull GmbH	Head of Vehicle Performance: Guillaume Dezoteux
Team Principal: Laurent Mekies	Chief Race Engineer: Jonathan Eddolls
CEO: Peter Bayer	Senior Race Engineer: Mattia Spini
Chief Technical Officer: Tim Goss	Race Engineer (Tsunoda): Ernesto Desiderio
Technical Director: Jody Egginton	Race Engineer (Ricciardo/Lawson): Pierre Hamelin
Deputy Technical Director: Guillaume Cattelani	Chief Mechanic: Domiziano Gacchinetti
Head of Aerodynamics: Johl Guru	Director of Marketing & Communications: Fabian Wrabetz
Racing Director: Alan Permane	Head of Communications & Digital: Fabiana Valenti
Sporting Director: Marco Perrone	

PETER BAYER

GUILLAUME DEZOTEUX

JONATHAN EDDOLLS

the competitiveness took a dive from the Spanish Grand Prix (round ten) onwards. This coincided with a substantial upgrade, which did not deliver what simulation had suggested it would.

The team's technical director, Jody Eggington explained: "The '23 car was developed fairly late and the rear end we started the year with was the same we'd ended up with at the end of '23. So we knew our launch car was quite well understood, and that served us quite well and also we'd seen a good improvement in the tunnel during the winter. We were well prepared for the start of the season." Certainly, they were much further along in understanding their car than Alpine, Haas and Williams, so could hit the ground running.

The Barcelona upgrade majored on an all-new underfloor geometry, with a higher forward part, and accompanying changes to the alignment and geometry of the inlet fences. Also, it encompassed a new engine cover/upper sidepod profile to improve airflow to the rear wing, and a reshaped radiator-inlet leading edge. Somewhere among those changes, however, the car lost its previous driveable balance.

"The update didn't work as we hoped," said Eggington, "and that cost us a bit of momentum. It delivered in load terms; we improved the downforce across the speed range. But the car was a bit more disconnected and harder to balance through corners, so we couldn't really convert the aero points to lap time. It was a bit more difficult on corner entry, a bit more imbalanced mid-corner and a little bit on exit. Put all that together and you're not able to make use of all the load. If the driver is unhappy on corner entry, it's over before it's started. So we undid a couple of bits of that update in the next few races to understand which bit was disconnecting the balance, and which bit was providing a load benefit without extra sensitivities. It took us a bit of time to unwind that.

"But we had to do that because there was goodness in the floor, which we've carried forward, but we had to separate what was good from what wasn't. It's been a while since we had to do that. We took the decision quickly. It was important to get the aero department clear on what we needed to do and not be left wondering. We reverted and did it all in CFD and aero. We didn't do track tests, we didn't 'cut and shut' the floor. We took it back, said to the aero guys, take another look at this in CFD, recorrelate, put it back in the simulator, let's understand what's not delivering. Some parts of it came back in the Monza upgrade."

Tsunoda and Daniel Ricciardo mixed and matched the floor specs for a few races as the puzzle was worked out, but in the meantime, Haas, Alpine and Williams all made good progress. So even when the problem was understood and the car improved by a new floor, introduced at Monza, generally it didn't achieve the level of competitiveness seen in the early season (with the exception of wet qualifying in Brazil, where Tsunoda qualified P3).

The team shares time in Red Bull's Bedford wind tunnel. The senior team said that the limitations arising from the tunnel's vintage played a part in their difficulties in 2024. Eggington acknowledged these limitations, but didn't consider them to be first-order contributors to the VCARB's difficulties. "It's the same tool and we've faced the same challenges. Temperature control is tricky. It's a harder tool to work with on a very cool day or a very hot day. You have to keep your wits about you to ensure you've not inadvertently lost control of the baseline. That's a bigger topic than it would be with a new tunnel. But we're aware of it. I wouldn't lay a lot of the reason for our performance on that.

"The bigger the operating window you can give, the bigger the envelope for the engineers and the drivers. In former times, we gave the drivers a nice platform to work with. The '22 car had that, and we've lost some of that in pursuit of performance. We're always trying to put load on the car, but you have to have the balance window to work with regardless of new driver or a veteran."

Like Haas, half the team is based in Italy and half in the UK. However, the move from Bicester to within Red Bull's main campus in Milton Keynes is due to be completed in the 2024–25 off-season, ready for what will be the team's final season with Honda power.

Left: Daniel Ricciardo's F1 return with RB failed to convince the Red Bull hierarchy and he was replaced by Liam Lawson after the Singapore Grand Prix.

Far left: Lawson scored a point in Austin and earned the dubious privilege of being Max Verstappen's team-mate at Red Bull in 2025.

Bottom: The team assembles for the end-of-season photo in Abu Dhabi.

Photos: Red Bull Content Pool/Getty Images

JODY EGGINTON

ALAN PERMANE

PIERRE HAMELIN

2
LOGAN SARGEANT

FRANCO COLAPINTO

23
ALEX ALBON

43

WILLIAMS RACING

A scant 17 points, ninth place in the constructors' and a huge repair bill from multiple crashes by all three of its drivers made for an extremely challenging season for Williams. But behind that apparent chaos, actually some real progress was made in updating the team's knowledge and processes.

The FW46 had been created incorporating far more contemporary standards of construction than Williams cars of the past few years, with an aerodynamic profile that relied far less than previously upon simply being a 'low-drag special' and the hope of scoring points at the few tracks where that would confer an advantage. Team boss James Vowles had requested much more of an all-rounder from the technical team. "I told them that they should dare to do something different [from what we had]," he said. "If we failed, then I would take the blame. But if we didn't take a new path, then we would stay where this team has been for the last ten years. We can't be satisfied with seventh or eighth place in the medium term. That's why we've taken full risks everywhere."

There were downsides to that decision, as it turned out. But they were of an operational nature, rather than performance. There were several occasions when the car showed itself to be at least a match for the 'mid-pack' lower Q3 contenders, and with a more straightforward season probably it would have averaged around the same perfor-

WILLIAMS FW46

PARTNERS	Komatsu · Stephens · Kraken · Gulf · Duracell · My Protein · Globant · Mercado Libre · Vast · Keeper · Dorilton Ventures · FanCapital · Michelob Ultra · ZOOX · Jumeirah · Ingenuity Commerce · Puma · PureStream · Pirelli · Crew Clothing · Life Fitness · Spinal Injuries Association
POWER UNIT	Type: Mercedes-AMG F1 M15 E Power+ No. of cylinders (vee angle): V6 (90°) No. of valves: 24 Max. rpm (ICE): 15,000 Fuel injection: High-pressure direct injection (max. 500 bar, one injector/cylinder) Max. fuel flow rate: 100kg/hr (above 10,500rpm) Pressure charging: Single-stage compressor and exhaust turbine on common shaft Exhaust turbine max. rpm: 125,000 Electronics: FIA standard SECU control unit ERS: Mercedes-AMG HPP Fuel: Gulf
TRANSMISSION	Gearbox: Mercedes-AMG, eight forward speeds plus reverse, seamless, sequential, semi-automatic shift, electro-hydraulic actuation Clutch: Carbon multi-plate
CHASSIS	Monocoque: Moulded carbon-fibre and honeycomb composite structure Front suspension: Double wishbone, push-rod-actuated springs and anti-roll bar Rear suspension: Double wishbone, pull-rod-actuated springs and anti-roll bar Brakes: Brembo six-piston front and rear calipers, carbon discs and pads Steering: Williams power-assisted rack-and-pinion Wheels: F1 standard supply component, 18in diameter Tyres: Pirelli P Zero
DIMENSIONS	Length: Not disclosed Width: 2000mm Height: 970mm Wheelbase: Not disclosed Formula weight: 798kg, including driver and camera

ALEX ALBON

JAMES VOWLES

WILLIAMS RACING: PERSONNEL

Co-founders: Sir Frank Williams & Sir Patrick Head	Engineering Director: Dave Worner
Williams Board: Matthew Savage, James Matthews	Deputy Chief Designer & Head of Design: Jonathan Carter
Team Principal: James Vowles	Chief Engineer: Dave Robson
Board Adviser: Peter Kenyon	Head of Aerodynamics: Adam Kenyon
Chief Operating Officer: Frederic Brousseau	Chief Race Engineer: Paul Williams
Sporting Director: Sven Smeets	Head of Strategy: Richard Lockwood
General Counsel: Mark Biddle	Performance Engineer: Luke Dardis
Chief Human Resources Officer: Ann Perrins	Senior Race Engineer (Albon): James Urwin
Chief Financal Officer: Steve Cripps	Senior Race Engineer (Sargeant/Colapinto): Gaeten Jago
Operations Director: Scott Williams	Team Manager: Dave Redding
Marketing Director: Marcus Prosser	Head of Communications: Craig Woodhouse
Commercial Director: James Bower	F1 Communications Lead: Rebecca Banks
Chief Technical Officer: Pat Fry	Communications Manager: Dominique Heyer-Wright

Above: Celebration time for the team after both Colapinto and Albon scored points in Baku.

Above right: Alex Albon carried the weight of the team on his shoulders until the arrival of Colapinto, but a sterner test lies ahead when Sainz joins for 2025.

Above far right: Williams gave Logan Sargeant a second season to prove his worth, but sadly the American failed to convince and he was dropped after Zandvoort.

Right: An eight-mechanic team is needed to get Colapinto on to the Monza grid.

Photos: Williams Racing

 DAVE ROBSON
 SVEN SMEETS
 JAMES MATTHEWS
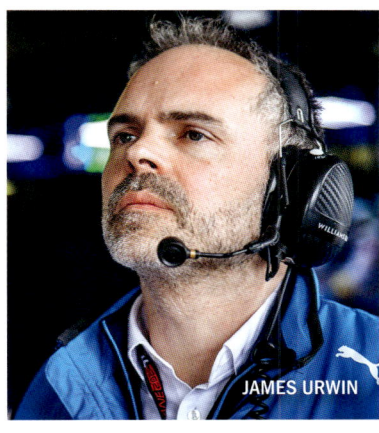 JAMES URWIN

mance as the Haas and RB, rather than a quarter-second behind. Relative to the gap to the front, it qualified an average of 1.0s off the fastest, compared to 1.2s for its predecessor.

Ironically, it was in choosing to completely update the way in which the chassis was made – to make it both lighter and simpler to manufacture – that led to the car being completed late and beginning the season overweight! The late completion of the car meant that there was no time to put all the components through the usual stress analysis, and some were even fashioned in metal rather than carbon fibre for speed of production. Initially, this more than offset the 14kg reduction in the base chassis weight compared to the 2023 car.

Aerodynamically, the car was all new, with a much wider nose to aid the outwash of the airflow and a more svelte-looking sidepod arrangement. To maximise time spent on the design of the car, Williams opted to retain the 2023 Mercedes rear end rather than wait until the 2024 spec had been confirmed. This meant the retention of pull-rod rear suspension rather than the Merc '24 push-rod layout. It also meant the longer '23 gearbox casing.

Dave Robson, head of vehicle performance, explained the background to creating the FW46 with new technologies when the team was in the midst of replacing outdated tools: "Apart from the technical changes, we were also putting in a different structure of people, many of them new. It takes a little bit of time to knit together and make that operate slickly.

"But technically, we made some fairly big changes in modernising how we go about designing and making the chassis. That did yield a big weight reduction in the chassis, and the simpler manufacturing process will reap rewards. But it was a longer process than we expected it to be when we set out. Once you're behind on the chassis work, then everything starts to get behind; the designers took longer to do the chassis than we'd originally planned, and in terms of manufacturing everything gets knocked back. So ideally, we would have started everything earlier and not gone through that."

With production of parts running so late, the last thing the team needed was an early sequence of crashes. But that's what it got. Alex Albon's crash in Melbourne led to Logan Sargeant giving up his car for him at that race, as there was no spare. The factory worked flat out in getting two raceworthy cars ready for the next round, in Suzuka, where Sargeant crashed heavily in practice and Albon collided with Daniel Ricciardo in the first lap of the race. There were further crashes in the second half of the season from Sargeant, Albon and Sargeant's replacement, Franco Colapinto.

This all put the team on the back foot for its aero development programme, as there simply wasn't the production capacity to keep up with the wind tunnel, because it was busy remaking parts. As a result, there was only one major upgrade for the car, at Zandvoort after the summer break, followed by a smaller tweak in Singapore.

It all impacted heavily upon the car's competitiveness. Before it was out-developed by the others, it was overweight by as much as 10kg (around 0.3s-worth at most tracks). "Easy to say, but had we not been overweight at the start of the season, we'd have been in pretty good competitive shape in those early races," said Robson. Indeed, subtract that nominal 0.3s and it would have regularly been the fifth-fastest car.

The front locking problem, which had beset Williams cars ever since the advent of these regulations in 2022, was finally banished. "Because we'd improved the aero characteristics, it opened up some different set-up windows," explained Robson, "which allows us to ultimately make the front of the car more responsive and less prone to the front locking turn in, and then the whole corner gets better from there.

"In involves getting the load from the front wing and forward part of the floor to stay with you as you slow the car down and begin to turn it in. It also involves changing the characteristics of the rear end, allowing you to change the mechanical set-up so you can get a bit more consistency and grip, because of the way the front of the car works mechanically and the way you present the tyre. So it's a bit of everything, but what it really all stemmed from was saying very early in the concept phase, 'This is what we're going to do, this is how we're going to do it and therefore this is what we need the wind tunnel to work on.' That's probably where we've worked a bit differently to how we have in the past. There was a different emphasis right from the concept phase because those things are so embedded into the aero and they're very difficult to unwind."

As work continues on modernising and expanding the facility, Williams hopes that the pain endured in 2024 will begin paying back in '2025.

STAKE F1 TEAM KICK SAUBER

24

ZHOU GUANYU

77

VALTTERI BOTTAS

Temporarily resurrecting the Sauber team name as preparation gets under way for Audi's F1 debut in 2026, the Hinwil team had a difficult season. It was lodged firmly at the bottom of the constructors' championship on just two points. This came amid tempestuous changes at board level of the parent Audi company, which increased its previous minority shareholding in the team to 100 per cent ownership at the beginning of the year.

In July, Audi dismissed team CEO Andreas Seidl after only 19 months in the role, together with his boss, Oliver Hoffman (the ex-Audi automotive engineering chief who was only made chairman of the Sauber group in March). New Audi boss Gernot Döllner appointed former Ferrari team principal Mattia Binotto as a replacement for them both.

But as these big corporate moves played out, the Sauber team itself remained one of the smallest. Technical director James Key – who had taken the role only towards the end of 2023 – assessed the team's resource as, "lacking the manpower to get into great detail on, for example, aero-elasticity. But there is no lack of brainpower here."

Key inherited the C44, largely created under the control of his predecessor. It was the slowest car on the grid, on average, at 1.5s off the front, a couple of tenths further adrift than the year before, while its nearest rivals closed the gap to the front. Like all Saubers of recent years, it used a Ferrari power unit and gearbox internals, but Sauber's own casing and running gear. Aerodynamically, it was a mild evolution of the 2023 car, but the move to pull-rod front suspension from push-rod was made for aerodynamic reasons, especially the easier adoption of anti-dive geometry to keep the aero platform more stable. It was a plan already in place when Key arrived, and which he described as being ambitious.

"I know how tricky that is, and that's really why not everyone's done it. For the size of team, it was a brave move, and the team pulled it off pretty well because there's a lot of pitfalls there… Basically, a pull-rod is a much less mechanically efficient solution. You can often find yourself adding weight or losing mechanical advantage on the springs and dampers, which means you have to have stiffer elements that move less, which is always prone to more friction and hysteresis. A ground-effect car is very ride-height sensitive, and with a pull-rod your authority of the vertical stiffness is less because of the geometry. Then you've got an element in tension, which is far more difficult to cope with structurally than if it's in compression. So all of those things are really bad, but you do it for aerodynamic gain. So to do it and not make any of those challenges a deficit is pretty brave. And by and large, the team achieved that, which I thought was a great effort."

Key cited the team's scale as being responsible

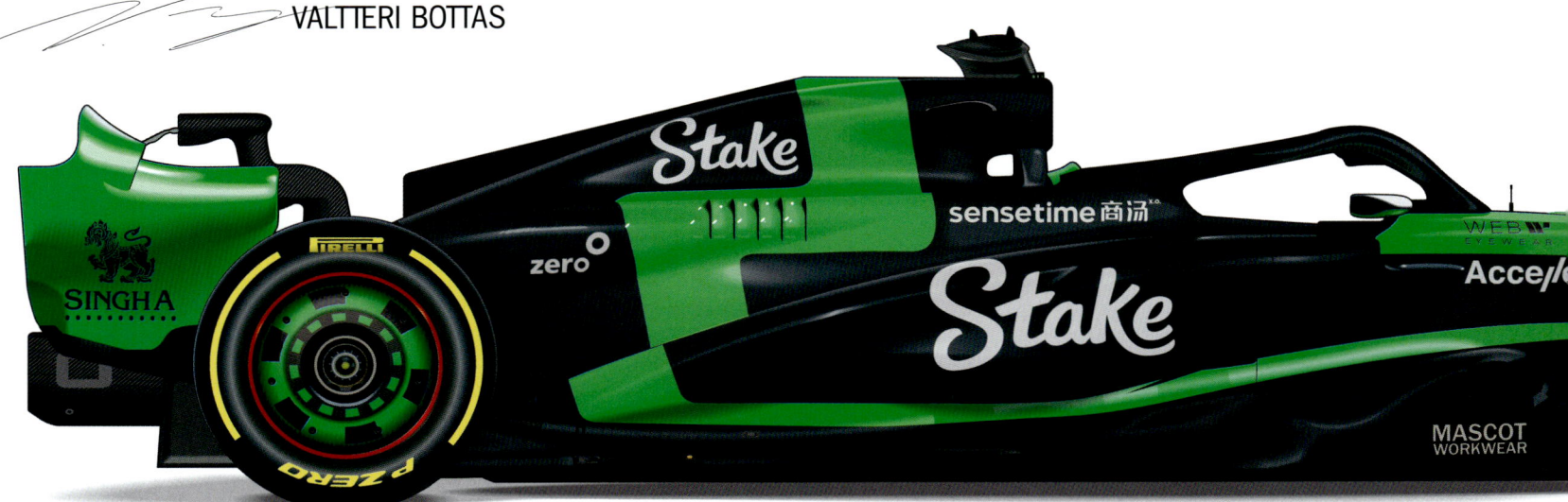

SAUBER C44

TITLE PARTNER	Stake **CHASSIS NAMING RIGHTS PARTNER:** KICK
OFFICIAL PARTNERS	Accelleron · Agilis · Ambrosial · Camozzi · Cielo · Ciesse Piumini · CODE-ZERO · Edelweiss · Everdome · Extreme Networks · Ferrari Trento · FIX Network GeorgFischer · GlobeAir · Hewlett Packard Enterprise · Hyland · JigSpace · Marelli · MASCOT Workwear · MindMaze · Mitsubishi Electric · Pirelli · PUMA · Sabelt Save The Children · Scania · SenseTime · Singha Corporation · Sunoco · Tucano · Vibratech · Walter Meier · WEB Eyewear · WhistlePig · Zero Petroleum
POWER UNIT	Type: Ferrari Hybrid 1.6-litre turbo No. of cylinders (vee angle): V6 (90°) No. of valves: 24 Max. rpm: 15,000 Electronics: MESL standard electronic control unit
TRANSMISSION	Stake F1 Team KICK Sauber carbon-fibre maincase with Ferrari cassette containing eight forward speeds plus reverse, sequential, semi-automatic, longitudinally mounted Clutch: Carbon composite
CHASSIS	Monocoque: Carbon-fibre and honeycomb composite structure Front suspension: Double wishbones, inboard spring-and-damper elements actuated by pull-rods Rear suspension: Multi-link, inboard spring-and-damper elements actuated by push-rods Dampers: Öhlins Brakes: Brembo carbon-composite calipers, pads and discs; brake-by-wire Steering: power-assisted rack-and-pinion Wheels: BBS, 18in diameter Tyres: Pirelli P Zero
DIMENSIONS	Length: 5500mm Width: 2000mm Front track: 1650mm Rear track: 1550mm Height: 970mm Wheelbase: 3600mm Formula weight: 798kg, including driver and camera

VALTTERI BOTTAS

MATTIA BINOTTO

STAKE F1 TEAM KICK SAUBER: PERSONNEL

COO & CTO: Mattia Binotto	Head of Race Engineering: Giampaolo Dall'Ara
Team Representative: Alessandro Alunni Bravi	Senior Strategy Engineer: Rithvik Dhananjay Reddy
Operations Director: Axel Kruse	Race Engineer (Bottas): Steven Petrik
Technical Director: James Key	Race Engineer (Zhou): Carlo Pasetti
Chief Designer: Eric Gandelin	Chief Mechanic: Lee Stevenson
Head of Vehicle Dynamics: Antoine Brissat	Chief Communications Officer: Florian Buengener
Head of Aero Operations & Technology: Alessandro Cinelli	Senior Communications Manager: Will Ponissi
Sporting Director: Beat Zehnder	
Racing Director: Xevi Pujolar	

ALESSANDRO ALUNNI BRAVI

Photo: Stake F1 Team Kick Sauber

Above: Preparing Zhou's car in the garage at Imola.

Above right: Zhou is briefed on the grid in Qatar, where he scored four face-saving points for the team.

Right: Valtteri Bottas was left high and dry at season's end. The Finn felt badly let down by events after former team boss Fred Vasseur left for Ferrari.

Far right: A new sponsor and garish livery at the team photo in Bahrain.
Photos: Stake F1 Team Kick Sauber

for the difficult season it endured. "It's basically where the team was in '23, but with the difference that our main competitor [Haas] had a very particular problem with their car which they seemed to fix for this year.

"At the beginning of this year, we were a small, independent, private team, and if we look at the teams we're fighting with, Alpine is a works team already, they're at the cost cap, they've got their workforce, etc. We've got two teams [Haas and RB] which have bigger brothers, so they source a lot of their parts from them, share a wind tunnel, etc, so reducing the workload. And then there's Williams, which is probably most similar to us, but has got significantly more people. So actually, we're small, but we do almost all the design apart from the gearbox internals and engine; the whole of the rest of the car is a Hinwil car. So actually, our workload is higher, but we're probably the smallest properly independent team."

The Audi ramp-up is beginning, and there are around 100 more people at Hinwil than a year ago, but that still leaves it below 700.

The biggest single problem that the team faced all year only became apparent at the season's first pit stop, which took a disastrously long time, as initially the front wheels could not be detached from the stub axles. This was repeated for the next few races and, unfortunately, it coincided with the car being at its most competitive, when it could have scored points. "The one time in those early races we didn't have the problem was at China," said Key, "and that was our most competitive race all season, and we could have been on for good points. But then we had a power-unit issue…"

As for the cause of the wheel problem, Key said, "We can only assume it was to do with the different heat expansion of the different materials, but we don't have the facilities here to prove that in a controlled way. You can heat stuff up, but it isn't the same as the track. We didn't have a pit-stop car, so we had to make a rig to try and replicate a car for the pit crew to change tyres on and get roughly the right kind of movements and dynamics around each corner. Every other pit stop we did pre-season, all the R&D tests we've done were all cold, but even in pre-season testing, it wasn't apparent. The materials we were using were very standard materials – titanium axle, aluminium wheelnuts.

"But aluminium is always risky, and even before the problem came up, I said let's get a steel axle/titanium wheelnut solution on the way. Which we introduced in Imola, and it's been fine ever since."

The basic limitation of the car was high-speed oversteer. In slow- and mid-corner performance, the C44 was competitive with the cars around it on the grid. All the deficit was at high speed.

"It was clear at the end of last year that we'd lost quite a lot to where the other cars were," said Key. "In September [2023], I asked our chief aero to draw me up the most aggressive development plan feasible for the first seven races, and we went with that. In that earlier period, the team absolutely knocked it out of the park in delivering those updates; Japan [race four] was our third floor spec, which for the size of team we are was absolutely outstanding, and the Japan step was pretty damn good, actually. Had we not had the pit-stop thing where we got passed by everyone in the pit lane, I think that would have been another point-scoring opportunity early on.

"Previously, the development lead times here were really uncompetitive. But in the key aerodynamic areas, particularly the floor, we halved the amount of time it took to make them – and that's without any expenditure, just mind-set, and organising and really strong teamwork between production design, aero, etc."

Had that development rate continued, Sauber might have been able to get into the fight with Williams, etc, in the latter part of the season. But a big planned update stubbornly refused to work, even in the tunnel, so it was never produced. "We wanted to get a bigger step on the aero side with a potential change of philosophy to address some of the limiting characteristics," said Key. "We put a lot of resource and time into it, but it didn't pay off. It can happen sometimes. So we didn't have a big mid-season step in contrast to Williams, who did."

As Sauber transitions into Audi, the uncomfortable spotlight will shine more intensely. Hopefully, 2024 represented just growing pains.

CHASSIS LOGBOOK 2024

COMPILED BY DAVID HAYHOE

McLAREN MCL38

ROUND 1 BAHRAIN GP

RED BULL-HONDA RBPT
| 1 | Max Verstappen | RB20/02 |
| 11 | Sergio Pérez | RB20/03 |

MERCEDES
| 44 | Lewis Hamilton | F1 W15/03 |
| 63 | George Russell | F1 W15/02 |

FERRARI
| 16 | Charles Leclerc | SF-24/ |
| 55 | Carlos Sainz | SF-24/ |

McLAREN-MERCEDES
| 4 | Lando Norris | MCL38/ |
| 81 | Oscar Piastri | MCL38/ |

ASTON MARTIN-MERCEDES
| 14 | Fernando Alonso | AMR24/02 |
| 18 | Lance Stroll | AMR24/01 |

ALPINE-RENAULT
| 10 | Pierre Gasly | A524/02 |
| 31 | Esteban Ocon | A524/03 |

WILLIAMS-MERCEDES
| 2 | Logan Sargeant | FW46/02 |
| 23 | Alexander Albon | FW46/01 |

RB-HONDA RBPT
| 3 | Daniel Ricciardo | VCARB 01/ |
| 22 | Yuki Tsunoda | VCARB 01/ |

SAUBER-FERRARI
| 24 | Zhou Guanyu | C44/03 |
| 77 | Valtteri Bottas | C44/02 |

HAAS-FERRARI
| 20 | Kevin Magnussen | VF-24/02 |
| 27 | Nico Hülkenberg | VF-24/03 |

ROUND 2 SAUDI ARABIAN GP

RED BULL-HONDA RBPT
| 1 | Max Verstappen | RB20/02 |
| 11 | Sergio Pérez | RB20/03 |

MERCEDES
| 44 | Lewis Hamilton | F1 W15/03 |
| 63 | George Russell | F1 W15/02 |

FERRARI
16	Charles Leclerc	SF-24/
55	Carlos Sainz	SF-24/(Thu)
38	Oliver Bearman	SF-24/(Fri+Sat)

McLAREN-MERCEDES
| 4 | Lando Norris | MCL38/ |
| 81 | Oscar Piastri | MCL38/ |

ASTON MARTIN-MERCEDES
| 14 | Fernando Alonso | AMR24/02 |
| 18 | Lance Stroll | AMR24/01 |

ALPINE-RENAULT
| 10 | Pierre Gasly | A524/02 |
| 31 | Esteban Ocon | A524/03 |

WILLIAMS-MERCEDES
| 2 | Logan Sargeant | FW46/02 |
| 23 | Alexander Albon | FW46/01 |

RB-HONDA RBPT
| 3 | Daniel Ricciardo | VCARB 01/ |
| 22 | Yuki Tsunoda | VCARB 01/ |

SAUBER-FERRARI
| 24 | Zhou Guanyu | C44/03 |
| 77 | Valtteri Bottas | C44/02 |

HAAS-FERRARI
| 20 | Kevin Magnussen | VF-24/02 |
| 27 | Nico Hülkenberg | VF-24/03 |

ROUND 3 AUSTRALIAN GP

RED BULL-HONDA RBPT
| 1 | Max Verstappen | RB20/02 |
| 11 | Sergio Pérez | RB20/03 |

MERCEDES
| 44 | Lewis Hamilton | F1 W15/03 |
| 63 | George Russell | F1 W15/02 |

FERRARI
| 16 | Charles Leclerc | SF-24/ |
| 55 | Carlos Sainz | SF-24/ |

McLAREN-MERCEDES
| 4 | Lando Norris | MCL38/ |
| 81 | Oscar Piastri | MCL38/ |

ASTON MARTIN-MERCEDES
| 14 | Fernando Alonso | AMR24/02 |
| 18 | Lance Stroll | AMR24/03 |

ALPINE-RENAULT
| 10 | Pierre Gasly | A524/02 |
| 31 | Esteban Ocon | A524/03 |

WILLIAMS-MERCEDES
| 2 | Logan Sargeant | FW46/02 (until Sat P3) |
| 23 | Alexander Albon | FW46/02 (01-Fri P1) |

RB-HONDA RBPT
| 3 | Daniel Ricciardo | VCARB 01/ |
| 22 | Yuki Tsunoda | VCARB 01/ |

SAUBER-FERRARI
| 24 | Zhou Guanyu | C44/03 |
| 77 | Valtteri Bottas | C44/02 |

HAAS-FERRARI
| 20 | Kevin Magnussen | VF-24/02 |
| 27 | Nico Hülkenberg | VF-24/03 |

ROUND 4 JAPANESE GP

RED BULL-HONDA RBPT
| 1 | Max Verstappen | RB20/04 |
| 11 | Sergio Pérez | RB20/03 |

MERCEDES
| 44 | Lewis Hamilton | F1 W15/03 |
| 63 | George Russell | F1 W15/02 |

FERRARI
| 16 | Charles Leclerc | SF-24/ |
| 55 | Carlos Sainz | SF-24/ |

McLAREN-MERCEDES
| 4 | Lando Norris | MCL38/ |
| 81 | Oscar Piastri | MCL38/ |

ASTON MARTIN-MERCEDES
| 14 | Fernando Alonso | AMR24/02 |
| 18 | Lance Stroll | AMR24/01 |

ALPINE-RENAULT
| 10 | Pierre Gasly | A524/02 |
| 31 | Esteban Ocon | A524/03 |

WILLIAMS-MERCEDES
| 2 | Logan Sargeant | FW46/01 |
| 23 | Alexander Albon | FW46/02 |

RB-HONDA RBPT
3	Daniel Ricciardo	VCARB 01/
40	Ayumu Iwasa	VCARB 01/(Fri P1)
22	Yuki Tsunoda	VCARB 01/

SAUBER-FERRARI
| 24 | Zhou Guanyu | C44/01 (03-Fri+Sat) |
| 77 | Valtteri Bottas | C44/02 |

HAAS-FERRARI
| 20 | Kevin Magnussen | VF-24/02 |
| 27 | Nico Hülkenberg | VF-24/03 |

ROUND 5 CHINESE GP

RED BULL-HONDA RBPT
| 1 | Max Verstappen | RB20/04 |
| 11 | Sergio Pérez | RB20/03 |

MERCEDES
| 44 | Lewis Hamilton | F1 W15/03 |
| 63 | George Russell | F1 W15/02 |

FERRARI
| 16 | Charles Leclerc | SF-24/ |
| 55 | Carlos Sainz | SF-24/ |

McLAREN-MERCEDES
| 4 | Lando Norris | MCL38/ |
| 81 | Oscar Piastri | MCL38/ |

ASTON MARTIN-MERCEDES
| 14 | Fernando Alonso | AMR24/02 |
| 18 | Lance Stroll | AMR24/03 |

ALPINE-RENAULT
| 10 | Pierre Gasly | A524/02 |
| 31 | Esteban Ocon | A524/04 |

WILLIAMS-MERCEDES
| 2 | Logan Sargeant | FW46/01 |
| 23 | Alexander Albon | FW46/02 |

RB-HONDA RBPT
| 3 | Daniel Ricciardo | VCARB 01/ |
| 22 | Yuki Tsunoda | VCARB 01/ |

SAUBER-FERRARI
| 24 | Zhou Guanyu | C44/01 |
| 77 | Valtteri Bottas | C44/03 |

HAAS-FERRARI
| 20 | Kevin Magnussen | VF-24/02 |
| 27 | Nico Hülkenberg | VF-24/03 |

ROUND 6 MIAMI GP

RED BULL-HONDA RBPT
| 1 | Max Verstappen | RB20/04 |
| 11 | Sergio Pérez | RB20/03 |

MERCEDES
| 44 | Lewis Hamilton | F1 W15/03 |
| 63 | George Russell | F1 W15/02 |

FERRARI
| 16 | Charles Leclerc | SF-24/ |
| 55 | Carlos Sainz | SF-24/ |

McLAREN-MERCEDES
| 4 | Lando Norris | MCL38/ |
| 81 | Oscar Piastri | MCL38/ |

ASTON MARTIN-MERCEDES
| 14 | Fernando Alonso | AMR24/02 |
| 18 | Lance Stroll | AMR24/03 |

ALPINE-RENAULT
| 10 | Pierre Gasly | A524/04 |
| 31 | Esteban Ocon | A524/03 |

WILLIAMS-MERCEDES
| 2 | Logan Sargeant | FW46/01 |
| 23 | Alexander Albon | FW46/02 |

RB-HONDA RBPT
| 3 | Daniel Ricciardo | VCARB 01/ |
| 22 | Yuki Tsunoda | VCARB 01/ |

SAUBER-FERRARI
| 24 | Zhou Guanyu | C44/01 |
| 77 | Valtteri Bottas | C44/02 |

HAAS-FERRARI
| 20 | Kevin Magnussen | VF-24/02 |
| 27 | Nico Hülkenberg | VF-24/03 |

ROUND 7 EMILIA ROMAGNA GP

RED BULL-HONDA RBPT
| 1 | Max Verstappen | RB20/04 |
| 11 | Sergio Pérez | RB20/03 |

MERCEDES
| 44 | Lewis Hamilton | F1 W15/03 |
| 63 | George Russell | F1 W15/02 |

FERRARI
| 16 | Charles Leclerc | SF-24/ |
| 55 | Carlos Sainz | SF-24/ |

McLAREN-MERCEDES
| 4 | Lando Norris | MCL38/ |
| 81 | Oscar Piastri | MCL38/ |

ASTON MARTIN-MERCEDES
| 14 | Fernando Alonso | AMR24/02 |
| 18 | Lance Stroll | AMR24/03 |

ALPINE-RENAULT
| 10 | Pierre Gasly | A524/04 |
| 31 | Esteban Ocon | A524/03 |

WILLIAMS-MERCEDES
| 2 | Logan Sargeant | FW46/03 |
| 23 | Alexander Albon | FW46/02 |

RB-HONDA RBPT
| 3 | Daniel Ricciardo | VCARB 01/ |
| 22 | Yuki Tsunoda | VCARB 01/ |

SAUBER-FERRARI
| 24 | Zhou Guanyu | C44/04 |
| 77 | Valtteri Bottas | C44/03 |

HAAS-FERRARI
20	Kevin Magnussen	VF-24/02
50	Oliver Bearman	VF-24/02 (Fri P1)
27	Nico Hülkenberg	VF-24/03

ROUND 8 MONACO GP

RED BULL-HONDA RBPT
| 1 | Max Verstappen | RB20/04 |
| 11 | Sergio Pérez | RB20/03 |

MERCEDES
| 44 | Lewis Hamilton | F1 W15/03 |
| 63 | George Russell | F1 W15/02 |

FERRARI
| 16 | Charles Leclerc | SF-24/ |
| 55 | Carlos Sainz | SF-24/ |

McLAREN-MERCEDES
| 4 | Lando Norris | MCL38/ |
| 81 | Oscar Piastri | MCL38/ |

ASTON MARTIN-MERCEDES
| 14 | Fernando Alonso | AMR24/02 |
| 18 | Lance Stroll | AMR24/03 |

ALPINE-RENAULT
| 10 | Pierre Gasly | A524/04 |
| 31 | Esteban Ocon | A524/03 |

WILLIAMS-MERCEDES
| 2 | Logan Sargeant | FW46/03 |
| 23 | Alexander Albon | FW46/02 |

RB-HONDA RBPT
| 3 | Daniel Ricciardo | VCARB 01/ |
| 22 | Yuki Tsunoda | VCARB 01/ |

SAUBER-FERRARI
| 24 | Zhou Guanyu | C44/04 |
| 77 | Valtteri Bottas | C44/03 |

HAAS-FERRARI
| 20 | Kevin Magnussen | VF-24/02 |
| 27 | Nico Hülkenberg | VF-24/03 |

FERRARI SF-24

Scuderia Ferrari

RED BULL RB20

ROUND 9 CANADIAN GP
	RED BULL-HONDA RBPT	
1	Max Verstappen	RB20/04
11	Sergio Pérez	RB20/02
	MERCEDES	
44	Lewis Hamilton	F1 W15/03
63	George Russell	F1 W15/02
	FERRARI	
16	Charles Leclerc	SF-24/
55	Carlos Sainz	SF-24/
	McLAREN-MERCEDES	
4	Lando Norris	MCL38/
81	Oscar Piastri	MCL38/
	ASTON MARTIN-MERCEDES	
14	Fernando Alonso	AMR24/02
18	Lance Stroll	AMR24/03
	ALPINE-RENAULT	
10	Pierre Gasly	A524/04
31	Esteban Ocon	A524/03
61	Jack Doohan	A524/03 (Fri P1)
	WILLIAMS-MERCEDES	
2	Logan Sargeant	FW46/03
23	Alexander Albon	FW46/02
	RB-HONDA RBPT	
3	Daniel Ricciardo	VCARB 01/
22	Yuki Tsunoda	VCARB 01/
	SAUBER-FERRARI	
24	Zhou Guanyu	C44/04
77	Valtteri Bottas	C44/03
	HAAS-FERRARI	
20	Kevin Magnussen	VF-24/02
27	Nico Hülkenberg	VF-24/03

ROUND 10 SPANISH GP
	RED BULL-HONDA RBPT	
1	Max Verstappen	RB20/05
11	Sergio Pérez	RB20/03
	MERCEDES	
44	Lewis Hamilton	F1 W15/03
63	George Russell	F1 W15/02
	FERRARI	
16	Charles Leclerc	SF-24/
55	Carlos Sainz	SF-24/
	McLAREN-MERCEDES	
4	Lando Norris	MCL38/
81	Oscar Piastri	MCL38/
	ASTON MARTIN-MERCEDES	
14	Fernando Alonso	AMR24/03
18	Lance Stroll	AMR24/04
	ALPINE-RENAULT	
10	Pierre Gasly	A524/03
31	Esteban Ocon	A524/04
	WILLIAMS-MERCEDES	
2	Logan Sargeant	FW46/03
23	Alexander Albon	FW46/02
	RB-HONDA RBPT	
3	Daniel Ricciardo	VCARB 01/
22	Yuki Tsunoda	VCARB 01/
	SAUBER-FERRARI	
24	Zhou Guanyu	C44/02
77	Valtteri Bottas	C44/03
	HAAS-FERRARI	
20	Kevin Magnussen	VF-24/02
27	Nico Hülkenberg	VF-24/03
50	Oliver Bearman	VF-24/03 (Fri P1)

ROUND 11 AUSTRIAN GP
	RED BULL-HONDA RBPT	
1	Max Verstappen	RB20/05
11	Sergio Pérez	RB20/03
	MERCEDES	
44	Lewis Hamilton	F1 W15/03
63	George Russell	F1 W15/02
	FERRARI	
16	Charles Leclerc	SF-24/
55	Carlos Sainz	SF-24/
	McLAREN-MERCEDES	
4	Lando Norris	MCL38/
81	Oscar Piastri	MCL38/
	ASTON MARTIN-MERCEDES	
14	Fernando Alonso	AMR24/03
18	Lance Stroll	AMR24/04
	ALPINE-RENAULT	
10	Pierre Gasly	A524/03
31	Esteban Ocon	A524/04
	WILLIAMS-MERCEDES	
2	Logan Sargeant	FW46/03
23	Alexander Albon	FW46/02
	RB-HONDA RBPT	
3	Daniel Ricciardo	VCARB 01/
22	Yuki Tsunoda	VCARB 01/
	SAUBER-FERRARI	
24	Zhou Guanyu	C44/02
77	Valtteri Bottas	C44/03
	HAAS-FERRARI	
20	Kevin Magnussen	VF-24/02
27	Nico Hülkenberg	VF-24/03

ROUND 12 BRITISH GP
	RED BULL-HONDA RBPT	
1	Max Verstappen	RB20/05
11	Sergio Pérez	RB20/03
37	Isack Hadjar	RB20/03 (Fri P1)
	MERCEDES	
44	Lewis Hamilton	F1 W15/03
63	George Russell	F1 W15/02
	FERRARI	
16	Charles Leclerc	SF-24/
55	Carlos Sainz	SF-24/
	McLAREN-MERCEDES	
4	Lando Norris	MCL38/
81	Oscar Piastri	MCL38/
	ASTON MARTIN-MERCEDES	
14	Fernando Alonso	AMR24/03
18	Lance Stroll	AMR24/04
	ALPINE-RENAULT	
10	Pierre Gasly	A524/03
61	Jack Doohan	A524/03 (Fri P1)
31	Esteban Ocon	A524/04
	WILLIAMS-MERCEDES	
2	Logan Sargeant	FW46/03
45	Franco Colapinto	FW46/03 (Fri P1)
23	Alexander Albon	FW46/02
	RB-HONDA RBPT	
3	Daniel Ricciardo	VCARB 01/
22	Yuki Tsunoda	VCARB 01/
	SAUBER-FERRARI	
24	Zhou Guanyu	C44/02
77	Valtteri Bottas	C44/03
	HAAS-FERRARI	
20	Kevin Magnussen	VF-24/02
50	Oliver Bearman	VF-24/02 (Fri P1)
27	Nico Hülkenberg	VF-24/03

ALPINE A524

ALPINE A524

HAAS VF-24

ROUND 13 HUNGARIAN GP

	RED BULL-HONDA RBPT	
1	Max Verstappen	RB20/05
11	Sergio Pérez	RB20/03
	MERCEDES	
44	Lewis Hamilton	F1 W15/01
63	George Russell	F1 W15/02
	FERRARI	
16	Charles Leclerc	SF-24/
55	Carlos Sainz	SF-24/
	McLAREN-MERCEDES	
4	Lando Norris	MCL38/
81	Oscar Piastri	MCL38/
	ASTON MARTIN-MERCEDES	
14	Fernando Alonso	AMR24/03
18	Lance Stroll	AMR24/04
	ALPINE-RENAULT	
10	Pierre Gasly	A524/03
31	Esteban Ocon	A524/04
	WILLIAMS-MERCEDES	
2	Logan Sargeant	FW46/03
23	Alexander Albon	FW46/02
	RB-HONDA RBPT	
3	Daniel Ricciardo	VCARB 01/
22	Yuki Tsunoda	VCARB 01/
	SAUBER-FERRARI	
24	Zhou Guanyu	C44/02
77	Valtteri Bottas	C44/04
	HAAS-FERRARI	
20	Kevin Magnussen	VF-24/02
27	Nico Hülkenberg	VF-24/03
50	Oliver Bearman	VF-24/03 (Fri P1)

ROUND 14 BELGIAN GP

	RED BULL-HONDA RBPT	
1	Max Verstappen	RB20/05
11	Sergio Pérez	RB20/03
	MERCEDES	
44	Lewis Hamilton	F1 W15/01
63	George Russell	F1 W15/02
	FERRARI	
16	Charles Leclerc	SF-24/
55	Carlos Sainz	SF-24/
	McLAREN-MERCEDES	
4	Lando Norris	MCL38/
81	Oscar Piastri	MCL38/
	ASTON MARTIN-MERCEDES	
14	Fernando Alonso	AMR24/03
18	Lance Stroll	AMR24/04
	ALPINE-RENAULT	
10	Pierre Gasly	A524/03
31	Esteban Ocon	A524/04
	WILLIAMS-MERCEDES	
2	Logan Sargeant	FW46/03
23	Alexander Albon	FW46/02
	RB-HONDA RBPT	
3	Daniel Ricciardo	VCARB 01/
22	Yuki Tsunoda	VCARB 01/
	SAUBER-FERRARI	
24	Zhou Guanyu	C44/02
77	Valtteri Bottas	C44/04
	HAAS-FERRARI	
20	Kevin Magnussen	VF-24/02
27	Nico Hülkenberg	VF-24/03

MERCEDES F1 W15

ROUND 15 DUTCH GP

RED BULL-HONDA RBPT
1	Max Verstappen	RB20/05
11	Sergio Pérez	RB20/02

MERCEDES
44	Lewis Hamilton	F1 W15/01
63	George Russell	F1 W15/03

FERRARI
16	Charles Leclerc	SF-24/
55	Carlos Sainz	SF-24/

McLAREN-MERCEDES
4	Lando Norris	MCL38/
81	Oscar Piastri	MCL38/

ASTON MARTIN-MERCEDES
14	Fernando Alonso	AMR24/03
18	Lance Stroll	AMR24/04

ALPINE-RENAULT
10	Pierre Gasly	A524/04
31	Esteban Ocon	A524/02

WILLIAMS-MERCEDES
2	Logan Sargeant	FW46/03
23	Alexander Albon	FW46/01

RB-HONDA RBPT
3	Daniel Ricciardo	VCARB 01/
22	Yuki Tsunoda	VCARB 01/

SAUBER-FERRARI
24	Zhou Guanyu	C44/03
77	Valtteri Bottas	C44/04
97	Robert Shwartzman	C44/04(Fri P1)

HAAS-FERRARI
20	Kevin Magnussen	VF-24/02
27	Nico Hülkenberg	VF-24/03

ROUND 16 ITALIAN GP

1	Max Verstappen	RB20/05
11	Sergio Pérez	RB20/02

MERCEDES
44	Lewis Hamilton	F1 W15/01
63	George Russell	F1 W15/03
12	A. Kimi Antonelli	F1 W15/03(Fri P1)

FERRARI
16	Charles Leclerc	SF-24/
55	Carlos Sainz	SF-24/

McLAREN-MERCEDES
4	Lando Norris	MCL38/
81	Oscar Piastri	MCL38/

ASTON MARTIN-MERCEDES
14	Fernando Alonso	AMR24/03
18	Lance Stroll	AMR24/04

ALPINE-RENAULT
10	Pierre Gasly	A524/04
31	Esteban Ocon	A524/02

WILLIAMS-MERCEDES
23	Alexander Albon	FW46/01
43	Franco Colapinto	FW46/03

RB-HONDA RBPT
3	Daniel Ricciardo	VCARB 01/
22	Yuki Tsunoda	VCARB 01/

SAUBER-FERRARI
24	Zhou Guanyu	C44/03
77	Valtteri Bottas	C44/04

HAAS-FERRARI
20	Kevin Magnussen	VF-24/02
27	Nico Hülkenberg	VF-24/03

ROUND 17 AZERBAIJAN GP

RED BULL-HONDA RBPT
1	Max Verstappen	RB20/05
11	Sergio Pérez	RB20/03

MERCEDES
44	Lewis Hamilton	F1 W15/02
63	George Russell	F1 W15/03

FERRARI
16	Charles Leclerc	SF-24/
55	Carlos Sainz	SF-24/

McLAREN-MERCEDES
4	Lando Norris	MCL38/
81	Oscar Piastri	MCL38/

ASTON MARTIN-MERCEDES
14	Fernando Alonso	AMR24/03
18	Lance Stroll	AMR24/04

ALPINE-RENAULT
10	Pierre Gasly	A524/04
31	Esteban Ocon	A524/02

WILLIAMS-MERCEDES
23	Alexander Albon	FW46/01
43	Franco Colapinto	FW46/03

RB-HONDA RBPT
3	Daniel Ricciardo	VCARB 01/
22	Yuki Tsunoda	VCARB 01/

SAUBER-FERRARI
24	Zhou Guanyu	C44/04
77	Valtteri Bottas	C44/02

HAAS-FERRARI
50	Oliver Bearman	VF-24/02
27	Nico Hülkenberg	VF-24/03

ROUND 18 SINGAPORE GP

RED BULL-HONDA RBPT
1	Max Verstappen	RB20/05
11	Sergio Pérez	RB20/04

MERCEDES
44	Lewis Hamilton	F1 W15/02
63	George Russell	F1 W15/03

FERRARI
16	Charles Leclerc	SF-24/
55	Carlos Sainz	SF-24/

McLAREN-MERCEDES
4	Lando Norris	MCL38/
81	Oscar Piastri	MCL38/

ASTON MARTIN-MERCEDES
14	Fernando Alonso	AMR24/03
18	Lance Stroll	AMR24/04

ALPINE-RENAULT
10	Pierre Gasly	A524/04
31	Esteban Ocon	A524/02

WILLIAMS-MERCEDES
23	Alexander Albon	FW46/01
43	Franco Colapinto	FW46/03

RB-HONDA RBPT
3	Daniel Ricciardo	VCARB 01/
22	Yuki Tsunoda	VCARB 01/

SAUBER-FERRARI
24	Zhou Guanyu	C44/04
77	Valtteri Bottas	C44/02

HAAS-FERRARI
20	Kevin Magnussen	VF-24/02
27	Nico Hülkenberg	VF-24/03

WILLIAMS FW46

SAUBER C44

RB VCARB 01

ROUND 19 UNITED STATES GP

RED BULL-HONDA RBPT		
1	Max Verstappen	RB20/05
11	Sergio Pérez	RB20/04
MERCEDES		
44	Lewis Hamilton	F1 W15/03
63	George Russell	F1 W15/02
FERRARI		
16	Charles Leclerc	SF-24/
55	Carlos Sainz	SF-24/
McLAREN-MERCEDES		
4	Lando Norris	MCL38/
81	Oscar Piastri	MCL38/
ASTON MARTIN-MERCEDES		
14	Fernando Alonso	AMR24/03
18	Lance Stroll	AMR24/04
ALPINE-RENAULT		
10	Pierre Gasly	A524/04
31	Esteban Ocon	A524/03
WILLIAMS-MERCEDES		
23	Alexander Albon	FW46/02
43	Franco Colapinto	FW46/03
RB-HONDA RBPT		
22	Yuki Tsunoda	VCARB 01/
30	Liam Lawson	VCARB 01/
SAUBER-FERRARI		
24	Zhou Guanyu	C44/04
77	Valtteri Bottas	C44/02
HAAS-FERRARI		
20	Kevin Magnussen	VF-24/02
27	Nico Hülkenberg	VF-24/03

ROUND 20 MEXICO CITY GP

RED BULL-HONDA RBPT		
1	Max Verstappen	RB20/05
11	Sergio Pérez	RB20/04
MERCEDES		
44	Lewis Hamilton	F1 W15/03
12	A. Kimi Antonelli	F1 W15/03 (Fri P1)
63	George Russell	F1 W15/04 (02-Fri)
FERRARI		
16	Charles Leclerc	SF-24/
38	Oliver Bearman	SF-24/(Fri P1)
55	Carlos Sainz	SF-24/
McLAREN-MERCEDES		
4	Lando Norris	MCL38/
29	Patricio O'Ward	MCL38/(Fri P1)
81	Oscar Piastri	MCL38/
ASTON MARTIN-MERCEDES		
14	Fernando Alonso	AMR24/03
34	Felipe Drugovich	AMR24/03(Fri P1)
18	Lance Stroll	AMR24/04
ALPINE-RENAULT		
10	Pierre Gasly	A524/04
31	Esteban Ocon	A524/02
WILLIAMS-MERCEDES		
23	Alexander Albon	FW46/02
43	Franco Colapinto	FW46/03
RB-HONDA RBPT		
22	Yuki Tsunoda	VCARB 01/
30	Liam Lawson	VCARB 01/
SAUBER-FERRARI		
24	Zhou Guanyu	C44/04
97	Robert Shwartzman	C44/04(Fri P1)
77	Valtteri Bottas	C44/02
HAAS-FERRARI		
20	Kevin Magnussen	VF-24/02
27	Nico Hülkenberg	VF-24/03

ROUND 21 SÃO PAULO GP

RED BULL-HONDA RBPT
| 1 | Max Verstappen | RB20/05 |
| 11 | Sergio Pérez | RB20/03 |

MERCEDES
| 44 | Lewis Hamilton | F1 W15/03 |
| 63 | George Russell | F1 W15/04 |

FERRARI
| 16 | Charles Leclerc | SF-24/ |
| 55 | Carlos Sainz | SF-24/ |

McLAREN-MERCEDES
| 4 | Lando Norris | MCL38/ |
| 81 | Oscar Piastri | MCL38/ |

ASTON MARTIN-MERCEDES
| 14 | Fernando Alonso | AMR24/03 |
| 18 | Lance Stroll | AMR24/04 |

ALPINE-RENAULT
| 10 | Pierre Gasly | A524/04 |
| 31 | Esteban Ocon | A524/03 |

WILLIAMS-MERCEDES
| 23 | Alexander Albon | FW46/01 |
| 43 | Franco Colapinto | FW46/03 |

RB-HONDA RBPT
| 22 | Yuki Tsunoda | VCARB 01/ |
| 30 | Liam Lawson | VCARB 01/ |

SAUBER-FERRARI
| 24 | Zhou Guanyu | C44/04 |
| 77 | Valtteri Bottas | C44/02 |

HAAS-FERRARI
| 27 | Nico Hülkenberg | VF-24/03 |
| 50 | Oliver Bearman | VF-24/02 |

ROUND 22 LAS VEGAS GP

RED BULL-HONDA RBPT
| 1 | Max Verstappen | RB20/05 |
| 11 | Sergio Pérez | RB20/03 |

MERCEDES
| 44 | Lewis Hamilton | F1 W15/02 |
| 63 | George Russell | F1 W15/03 |

FERRARI
| 16 | Charles Leclerc | SF-24/ |
| 55 | Carlos Sainz | SF-24/ |

McLAREN-MERCEDES
| 4 | Lando Norris | MCL38/ |
| 81 | Oscar Piastri | MCL38/ |

ASTON MARTIN-MERCEDES
| 14 | Fernando Alonso | AMR24/02 |
| 18 | Lance Stroll | AMR24/04 |

ALPINE-RENAULT
| 10 | Pierre Gasly | A524/04 |
| 31 | Esteban Ocon | A524/03 |

WILLIAMS-MERCEDES
| 23 | Alexander Albon | FW46/02 |
| 43 | Franco Colapinto | FW46/03 |

RB-HONDA RBPT
| 22 | Yuki Tsunoda | VCARB 01/ |
| 30 | Liam Lawson | VCARB 01/ |

SAUBER-FERRARI
| 24 | Zhou Guanyu | C44/04 |
| 77 | Valtteri Bottas | C44/02 |

HAAS-FERRARI
| 20 | Kevin Magnussen | VF-24/02 |
| 27 | Nico Hülkenberg | VF-24/03 |

ROUND 23 QATAR GP

RED BULL-HONDA RBPT
| 1 | Max Verstappen | RB20/05 |
| 11 | Sergio Pérez | RB20/03 |

MERCEDES
| 44 | Lewis Hamilton | F1 W15/02 |
| 63 | George Russell | F1 W15/03 |

FERRARI
| 16 | Charles Leclerc | SF-24/ |
| 55 | Carlos Sainz | SF-24/ |

McLAREN-MERCEDES
| 4 | Lando Norris | MCL38/ |
| 81 | Oscar Piastri | MCL38/ |

ASTON MARTIN-MERCEDES
| 14 | Fernando Alonso | AMR24/02 |
| 18 | Lance Stroll | AMR24/04 |

ALPINE-RENAULT
| 10 | Pierre Gasly | A524/04 |
| 31 | Esteban Ocon | A524/03 |

WILLIAMS-MERCEDES
| 23 | Alexander Albon | FW46/02 |
| 43 | Franco Colapinto | FW46/01 |

RB-HONDA RBPT
| 22 | Yuki Tsunoda | VCARB 01/ |
| 30 | Liam Lawson | VCARB 01/ |

SAUBER-FERRARI
| 24 | Zhou Guanyu | C44/04 |
| 77 | Valtteri Bottas | C44/02 |

HAAS-FERRARI
| 20 | Kevin Magnussen | VF-24/02 |
| 27 | Nico Hülkenberg | VF-24/03 |

ROUND 24 ABU DHABI GP

RED BULL-HONDA RBPT
1	Max Verstappen	RB20/05
37	Isack Hadjar	RB20/05 (Fri P1)
11	Sergio Pérez	RB20/03

MERCEDES
| 44 | Lewis Hamilton | F1 W15/02 |
| 63 | George Russell | F1 W15/03 |

FERRARI
16	Charles Leclerc	SF-24/
55	Carlos Sainz	SF-24/
39	Arthur Leclerc	SF-24/(Fri P1)

McLAREN-MERCEDES
4	Lando Norris	MCL38/
81	Oscar Piastri	MCL38/
28	Ryō Hirakawa	MCL38/(Fri P1)

ASTON MARTIN-MERCEDES
14	Fernando Alonso	AMR24/02
18	Lance Stroll	AMR24/04
34	Felipe Drugovich	AMR24/04 (Fri P1)

ALPINE-RENAULT
| 10 | Pierre Gasly | A524/04 |
| 61 | Jack Doohan | A524/02 |

WILLIAMS-MERCEDES
23	Alexander Albon	FW46/02
46	Luke Browning	FW46/02(Fri P1)
43	Franco Colapinto	FW46/01

RB-HONDA RBPT
22	Yuki Tsunoda	VCARB 01/
40	Ayumu Iwasa	VCARB 01/(Fri P1)
30	Liam Lawson	VCARB 01/

SAUBER-FERRARI
| 24 | Zhou Guanyu | C44/04 |
| 77 | Valtteri Bottas | C44/02 |

HAAS-FERRARI
| 20 | Kevin Magnussen | VF-24/02 |
| 27 | Nico Hülkenberg | VF-24/03 |

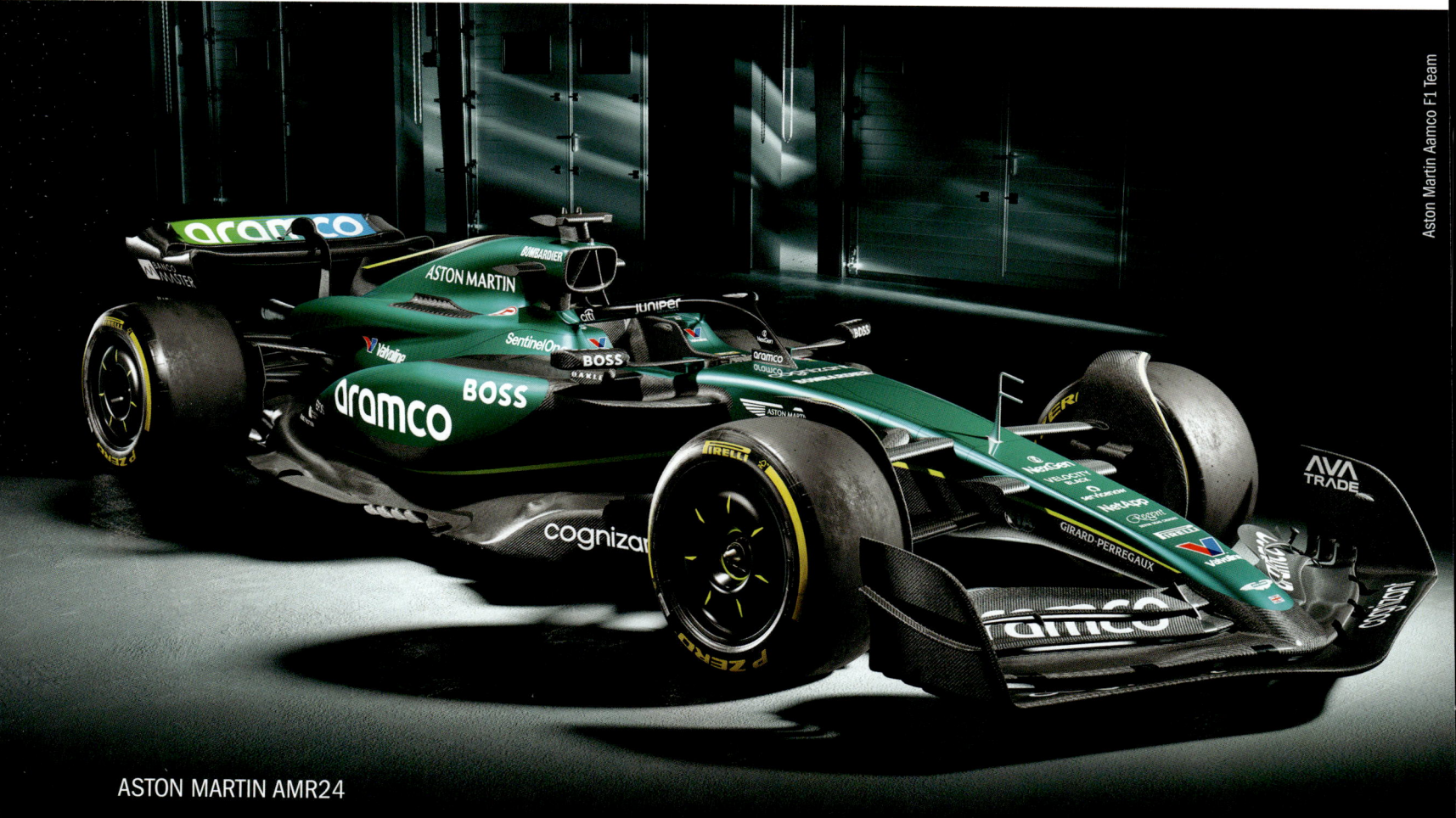

ASTON MARTIN AMR24

FIA FORMULA 1 WORLD CHAMPIONSHIP

GRANDS PRIX 2024

BY TONY DODGINS and MAURICE HAMILTON

SAKHIR QUALIFYING

A RELATIVELY quiet off-season, for the first time in championship history without even one team line-up change, suddenly burst into life. After ten years with Haas, team principal Guenther Steiner was sacked. Clearly, becoming a star of Netflix's *Drive to Survive* was not enough. After five seasons when the team finished ninth, ninth, last, eighth and last in the constructors' championship, Gene Haas said, "It's clear that we need to improve our on-track performance."

He went about it by promoting 47-year-old Ayao Komatsu, previously the team's engineering director, adding, "Fundamentally, we now have engineering at the heart of our management."

That news was dwarfed, however, by the announcement that Lewis Hamilton would join Charles Leclerc at Ferrari for 2025! Hamilton's two-year Mercedes contract extension, signed in August, 2023, evidently included a two-way option clause for the second year. After some deep thought, he decided to exercise it and put pen to Maranello paper at the expense of Carlos Sainz.

The word was that Lewis had been seeking a much longer deal from the three-pointed star, including a lucrative ambassadorial role when it came time to hang up his crash helmet, but that the Stuttgart board was not playing ball. Toto Wolff also alluded to missing out on Max Verstappen ten years before because he'd been tied to Lewis and Nico Rosberg long term and didn't have a cockpit to offer the Dutchman. Now, his eyes were on rising star Kimi Antonelli, who was being fast-tracked through F2. Toto wanted to keep his options open.

Then, in early February, a female employee accused Red Bull boss Christian Horner of controlling and coercive behaviour, prompting an investigation by the parent company. It dismissed the charges against him while revealing no details, but as the paddock assembled in Bahrain for round one, text leaks to the F1 media, as well as to FOM and the FIA, had the likes of Wolff and McLaren boss Zak Brown calling for greater transparency for the good of the sport. And, of course, with Horner's wife being former Spice Girl Geri Halliwell, the gossip columnists were having a field day.

Three days of pre-season testing at Sakhir had indicated that Red Bull's RB20, described as "an aggressive evolution", was still the class of the field, but with Ferrari, the new-concept Mercedes W15 and McLaren narrowing the gap. And that is how things looked when the new season got under way on Thursday in Bahrain. Thursday because the following race, a week later in Saudi Arabia, was scheduled for Saturday, as Ramadan was due to begin the following day. The logistics meant that Sakhir would also begin a day early, with the season-opener held on Saturday.

By the end of the 2023 season, Ferrari had been showing impressive single-lap pace, with Leclerc taking pole in three of the last five grands prix and starting them all from the front row. The Scuderia's problem was rear tyre degradation in the race, leaving them well shy of Red Bull's Sunday pace. Much work had gone into improving that, but Thursday afternoon showed that Red Bull still had highly impressive and superior long-run pace, especially on the soft-compound Pirellis.

And when the chips were down, Max Verstappen even managed to begin his quest for a fourth consecutive world title from pole position, although Leclerc's Q2 time was actually the fastest lap of Bahrain qualifying. It was Verstappen's 33rd F1 pole, equalling Jim Clark and Alain Prost, and moving him one clear of Nigel Mansell.

Leclerc's failure to take pole was rooted in the need – which he disputed – for two sets of softs to clear Q1. His first run was three-tenths shy of team-mate Sainz, who topped the session. Ferrari, mindful of the track gripping up and the tightness of the field, sent him out for a second run while Ferrari No.55 remained in the garage. In fact, Leclerc didn't need to do another hot lap to get through, but the mileage on that second set meant that he had scrubbed rubber for his first Q3 run, while Red Bull had two new sets.

"I lost the rhythm with the used softs and had to re-adapt to the new tyres with the track changing in Q3," he admitted. "The track is evolving and you go out with new tyres. How much front wing do you put on for the last run? I'm not happy... I thought we had enough margin in Q1, but the team didn't want to risk it."

Although his Q2 time was 0.2s quicker than Verstappen's, in Q3, Leclerc couldn't quite get it together and lapped almost a quarter of a second slower, although still fast enough for the front row.

"I'm happy to be on pole of course," Max acknowledged, "but it's a little unexpected. The track had a lot of grip, but the wind made it hard to get the lap together."

Mercedes had finally scrapped its zero-pod concept with the new W15, and both Hamilton and George Russell had been happier with their new steed in testing. But while Russell managed a lap that was just 0.08s behind Leclerc and a couple of hundredths quicker than Sainz in the second Ferrari, Hamilton could manage only ninth quickest, behind Sergio Pérez with the second Red Bull, Fernando Alonso's Aston Martin and both McLarens.

Lewis lapped almost a quarter of a second slower than his team-mate, putting it down to a different set-up. "George showing the car's potential is great for the team," he said, looking for the positives. "Yesterday, George and I were on the same set-ups, but today he went left and I went right, and right wasn't good for single-lap pace."

Alonso was delighted to be sixth, just four-hundredths behind Sainz and a hundredth shy of Pérez. "I didn't expect to be that competitive," he said candidly. "Being on the same tenth as Ferrari is unexpected for us."

Lando Norris, 0.43s behind pole, was seventh, but had mixed feelings. "I made mistakes on my second Q3 run in Turn One and Turn Four, and my first sector time was 0.3s off what it should have been," he grimaced. "I think P2 was possible, but on the positive side, as it cools down, the balance comes together and the car comes alive, and at a track we were not expecting to be strong for us, so not all bad."

By contrast, team-mate Oscar Piastri, just 0.07s and one place back, was less comfortable than he had been on practice day, but, like Norris, was grateful to see that those ahead weren't on a different planet.

Behind Hamilton, Nico Hülkenberg delivered one of his trademark sterling qualifying efforts to put a Haas into the top ten. Team-mate Kevin Magnussen made Q2, behind the Visa Cash App RB (formerly AlphaTauri) cars of Yuki Tsunoda (11th) and Daniel Ricciardo (14th), the Faenza cars sandwiching Lance Stroll's Aston Martin and Alex Albon's Williams. Falling at the first hurdle were the Saubers of Valtteri Bottas and Zhou Guanyu, Logan Sargeant's Williams, and the two Alpines of Esteban Ocon and Pierre Gasly.

As the grid formed up for the start of what would be Formula 1's longest ever season, at 24 races, the F1 world was anxious to see whether the winter's development had closed Red Bull's margin of superiority. Single-lap pace was one thing, but the proof of the pudding would come over a race distance.

Tyre degradation pointed towards a two-stop race, and that was confirmed by every car lining up for the 20th anniversary of the first Bahrain GP on Pirelli's red-walled soft tyre.

As the red lights extinguished, it became clear that Max Verstappen's sharpness had not been dulled by the winter break. Immediately, he jinked right to repel a slightly better getaway by Charles Leclerc, then blocked off a look around the outside of Turn One by the Ferrari. George Russell ran third, with a fast-starting Sergio Pérez harrying the Mercedes. Then came Carlos Sainz in the second Ferrari, from Fernando Alonso's Aston Martin, the McLarens of Lando Norris and Oscar Piastri, Lewis Hamilton's Mercedes and Yuki Tsunoda's newly (and awkwardly) renamed Visa Cash App RB completing the top ten. Further back, Nico Hülkenberg's qualifying effort for Haas came to nought when he rear-ended Lance Stroll's Aston Martin after being too late on the brakes down the inside into Turn One. Stroll spun to the back while 'The Hulk' headed to the pits and took on a set of hard tyres, rejoining half a minute off the back of the pack.

By lap three, it was evident that Leclerc was in for an afternoon with his Ferrari. As Russell's Mercedes relieved it of second place, Charles suffered a lock-up into Turn Ten. In the second Maranello machine, however, Sainz was going well, reporting to Ferrari that he had more pace than the guys in front. "Good to know," they replied. He wasn't referring to Verstappen, however, the triple-champion 5.5s to the good after just six laps…

Pérez now began to attack the struggling Leclerc, who had wildly different front brake temperatures and suffered another lock-up into T10, the Red Bull going by down the inside into Turn 11.

With Russell running second for Mercedes, at last there was something to cheer for the Hamilton fans when Lewis got a DRS run on Alonso's Aston Martin, moving up to eighth place into Turn One, just a couple of seconds behind the McLaren twins.

Sainz, in the better-handling Ferrari, now wanted to be past his team-mate so that he could get after Russell and Pérez, but Leclerc didn't give it up easily as Carlos came down the inside of Turn One with the benefit of DRS. They very nearly made contact as the former hung on to the inside line into Turn Two before being forced to lift. A diplomatic incident was narrowly averted.

The pit stops began in earnest on lap 12, with Russell and Leclerc in to switch to the hard-compound tyre, rejoining 12th and 14th respectively, separated by Valtteri Bottas's Sauber. A lap later, Pérez, Piastri and Hamilton were all in to cover off the earlier stoppers. The Red Bull rejoined still behind Russell, but managed to maintain position versus Leclerc. McLaren was forced to pit Norris on the next lap to cover off his team-mate and Hamilton.

Pérez was now all over the back of Russell's Mercedes, forcing him to defend the inside into Turn Four, then getting a better exit to promote himself to what would become second place once all the stops had played out. Sainz made his stop on lap 15 and, no doubt to his frustration, rejoined just behind Leclerc once more. Potentially, this was only a temporary state of affairs, as Leclerc told Ferrari, "I just cannot get out of front locking, everywhere!"

It didn't take long for Sainz to begin attacking him once more, the evidence indicating that Ferrari had better

Above: The sun sets over the Sakhir circuit as Norris and Piastri's McLarens lead Hamilton's Mercedes and Hülkenberg's Haas.
Photo: Pirelli

Left: Alpine's Esteban Ocon was facing a tough season ahead.
Photo: BWT Alpine F1 Team

Below left: Lewis Hamilton's announcement of his move to Ferrari for 2025 still reverberated through the paddock.
Photo: XPB Images

Below far left: Ayao Komatsu took over the reins at Haas, replacing Guenther Steiner.
Photo: Haas F1 Team

Opening spread: Max Verstappen takes control at the start. The Red Bull driver led every lap of the season's opening race.
Photo: Red Bull Content Pool/Getty Images

Above: The Ferraris of Leclerc and Sainz fought out the final podium place behind the Red Bulls.
Photo: Atsuo Sakurai

Top right: Valtteri Bottas (with front wing endplate still awry) and Pierre Gasly race away from their pit stop on lap 12.
Photo: Stake F1 Team Kick Sauber

Above right: A shower of sparks from George Russell's Mercedes during his opening-stint pursuit of Max Verstappen.
Photo: Atsuo Sakurai

Right: Fireworks signal the end of the race for Daniel Ricciardo, whose strategy was frustrated by team-mate Tsunoda.
Photo: Red Bull Content Pool/Getty Images

pace than Russell's Mercedes on the harder tyre. Despite Leclerc having DRS from the Mercedes as well, Carlos managed a late lunge down the inside of the other Ferrari to go by for the second time as the Monégasque suffered yet another lock-up.

At this point, Verstappen was half a minute in front, an 18-lap stint on his starting softs depressing his rivals by providing another example of just how well the Red Bulls looked after their tyres. He rejoined still comfortably in front of team-mate Pérez after a leisurely – by Red Bull standards – 2.9s stop.

Meanwhile, a frustrated Leclerc was busy informing Ferrari that his car was pulling fully to the right under braking – post-race, the team revealed that there was as much as a 100-degree difference between the right and left front brake temperatures. Ferrari had experienced brake material and consistency problems in practice; in Leclerc's case, it was clear that they hadn't got on top of it.

Meanwhile, Sainz was setting fastest lap as he attacked Russell, going around the outside of the Mercedes at Turn Four. Verstappen now led team-mate Pérez by 5s on his much fresher tyres, with Sainz just 2.5s behind the second Red Bull as the race approached the 20th of its 57 laps. Behind Russell and Leclerc, Norris's McLaren was a further 5s in arrears, 1.8s clear of Piastri's sister car. Hamilton was running a relatively lonely eighth, 4s behind the young Australian and 5s in front of Alonso's Aston, which had Zhou Guanyu's Sauber in close attendance.

Any fleeting hopes that this might be a closer contest than first thought disappeared rapidly when Verstappen left his pursuers gasping during his first hard-tyre stint, disappearing up the road by almost a second per lap over the next ten laps!

As the second pit-stop window opened, Russell, as at the opening stops, was first in for another set of the hard-compound rubber on lap 32, and back out without undue drama. The same could not be said of Valtteri Bottas, however, the Sauber stationary for no less than 52s as the team encountered a cross-threaded left-front wheel-nut issue that would become a recurring theme. It was rooted in new lightweight parts from an external supplier, but had not been experienced during pre-season testing or practice, only becoming apparent with the heat build-up during race conditions. Unfortunately, the option of reverting to the 2023-specification hubs and nuts did not exist, thanks to heavily redesigned front suspension.

Both Norris and Hamilton stopped on lap 34, with Leclerc and Piastri in next time around in a bid to cover. Leclerc managed to clear Norris, but Piastri was unable to hold off Hamilton for eighth on his cold tyres. Sainz stopped on the next lap and came back out 3.5s up on team-mate Leclerc, with second-placed Pérez responding next time around, reappearing on new softs rather than a second set of hards. He covered off Sainz by around 1.7s, but would have to make his tyres last for the final 16 laps of the race. Verstappen mirrored the move on the next lap.

Entering the final ten laps, Verstappen had a comfortable 17s cushion to team-mate Pérez, while Sainz, just over 3s behind the Mexican, was waiting in vain for his hard-compound tyres to be quicker than Sergio's softs.

Meanwhile, Leclerc was beginning to get to grips with his brake issues and had managed to close in on Russell. This time, it was actually George who ran wide at Turn Ten, allowing the Ferrari down the inside of Turn 11, their roles reversed from earlier in the afternoon.

The points-paying positions were now occupied by the Red Bulls, Ferraris, Mercedes, McLarens and Aston

Above: Sergio Pérez ensured a Red Bull 1-2, after holding off the challenge of Ferrari's Carlos Sainz.
Photo: Red Bull Content Pool/Getty Images

Top right: A year is a long time in F1; a podium had become a pipe-dream for Fernando Alonso.
Photo: Aston Martin Aramco F1 Team

Above right: Sainz claimed the final podium place for Ferrari.
Photo: Scuderia Ferrari

Right: A clenched fist and a satisfied smile from Verstappen after his dominant win.
Photo: Red Bull Content Pool/Getty Images

Martins. With six laps to go, the honour of 'best of the rest' was held by Zhou Guanyu's Sauber. Just over 2s behind him was Kevin Magnussen, the Haas promisingly showing much improved levels of tyre degradation over the race distance at what was a high-deg track. Dogging the Dane's wheel-tracks, though, without being able to find a way by, was Yuki Tsunoda, who had been caught by RB team-mate Daniel Ricciardo.

Ricciardo, like the Red Bull drivers, was on softs for the final stint.

"Yuki, driver swap, driver swap," went out the instruction from the pit wall.

"Are you kidding me? Now?" Tsunoda responded.

Into Turn One, it didn't happen. "I don't need to say anything," Ricciardo radioed, making his feelings clear. Finally, it did happen, by which time, Daniel had missed the sweet spot of his fresh softs to attack Magnussen. Sarcastically, Tsunoda radioed, "Thanks guys, I appreciate it." On the slowdown lap, he would practically side-swipe his team-mate, prompting a "What the ****!" from Daniel.

As the chequer greeted a 55th GP win for Verstappen, the sobering reality for the opposition was a 22s margin over Sergio Pérez, and a Red Bull 1-2. A positive for Ferrari, though, was driver-of-the-day Sainz staying within 2.5s of the second Red Bull and a 3-4 for Maranello, despite tricky circumstances for Leclerc.

Russell's fifth place was a disappointing start for new-direction Mercedes, with Norris's McLaren, sandwiching the two Silver Arrows. Piastri was eighth in the second McLaren, 5s adrift of Hamilton, while Aston Martin also had suffered a disappointing start, with nothing like the euphoria of a year earlier when Alonso had stood on the podium. This time, he was ninth, almost 20s behind Piastri, with team-mate Stroll completing a solid recovery after his opening-lap punt from Hülkenberg.

"I had a lot of fun," Verstappen smiled. "It's always very special to have this kind of day. Because they don't happen that often when it all goes perfect." Who was he trying to kid?

"I think we got the race spot on," Christian Horner said, "but let's wait for five or six races before we get a pattern. I've still got a feeling that the pack is going to be much closer this year." Worried-looking rivals up and down the paddock did not appear so convinced!

One man who had been convincing, however, was Sainz, who now, of course, was looking for alternative employment. He revealed that he also had been contending with brake issues.

"In the first stint and the beginning of the second, whenever we were in traffic, we were having a lot of brake vibrations, and the pedal at one point started to go long," he explained. "It was always a balancing act between going for it, and trying to get rid of the dirty air and overtake people, or saving my brakes because they were going to fail. I started saving by moving a bit on the straight to cool the side that was getting hotter and the vibration started to get better. And then I could start to make moves forward.

"It was good to be close to Checo, but I wasn't getting too excited.

"We'd been testing here three days and saw that Red Bull's degradation on the soft was exactly the same as ours on the hard. But we're at one of their strongest tracks with very high tyre deg at the rear. Hopefully, when we go to a more front-limited track, our car will come alive and we will be able to challenge."

So, some cause for optimism there. Meanwhile, Russell explained that Mercedes' afternoon had been far from perfect, too: "For whatever reason, we both had massive engine overheating and the battery wasn't working properly. I had a good start, got up to second and suddenly big red alarms on the steering wheel. We had no battery left, had to turn the power down and I was losing about four-tenths a lap just in power, so it was difficult, and I don't think we got to show the potential of the car."

Yes, Red Bull had dominated once more, but nobody else had the same perfect afternoon as the defending multiple champions.

FIA FORMULA 1 WORLD CHAMPIONSHIP

VIEWPOINT
AS YOU WERE

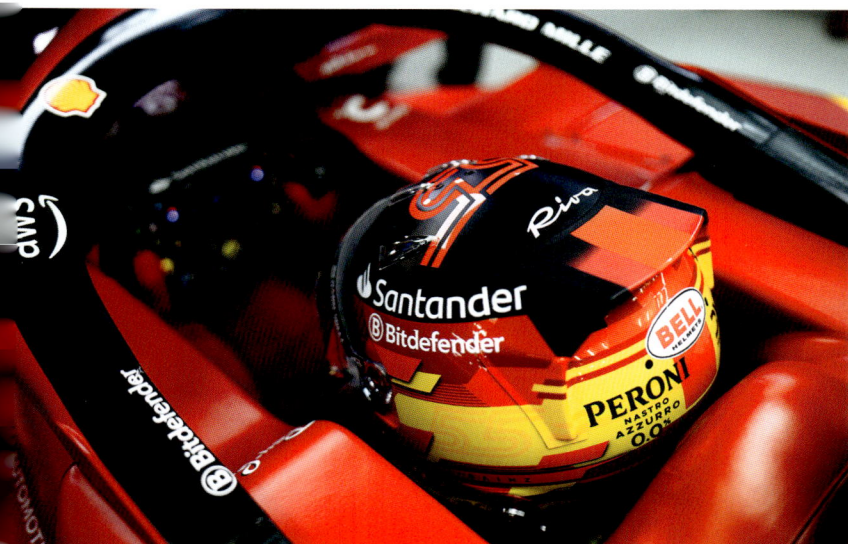

THERE had been the usual pre-season hype; anything to give the sense that Red Bull might not have it easy in 2024. A front-page headline in the 15th-February edition of *Autosport* shouted, 'RED BULL IS BEATABLE'. Reading the small print, it became evident that this was the wishful thinking of Aston Martin at the launch of their new car. No harm in saying it. The proof would be evident in lap times a couple of weeks later.

Classifications from the three free practice sessions, plus Q1 and Q2, had four different names at the top. And not one of them was Max Verstappen. But wait... At the end of Q3, there was the world champion, a couple of tenths ahead of Charles Leclerc.

Race-day? Car No.1 leads all the way and sets the fastest lap to win by 22 seconds. There was a feeling that it could have been 32 seconds. Or any number you like. The sense of *déjà-vu* was compounded by Sergio Pérez giving Red Bull a clean sweep. The fact that Checo was 'only' 2.65 seconds ahead of Leclerc was an irrelevance.

Writing in the next edition of *Autosport*, Kevin Turner began his editorial with a resigned, "Well, for the neutral, that was pretty much the worst-case scenario."

Inside the magazine, GP editor Alex Kalinauckas did his best to suggest that things could be, might be, maybe with a following wind, different to this familiar scenario. But that could not detract from a sense of foreboding exacerbated by the thought of 23 similar races by December.

There had been some tinkering around the edges, the use of DRS now being allowed from the end of lap one instead of lap two. Which was about as much use as nicking Adrian Newey's pencil. With Verstappen completing the first lap 0.978s ahead of Leclerc, the tiny chance of an overtake was already hobbled by the beginning of brake trouble on the Ferrari. With Max 1.5s to the good at the end of lap two, it was game over. The first Aston Martin was already six seconds behind. So much for Red Bull being unbeatable. Christian Horner was adamant that his team would face on-track challenges in 2024. He was right. But just not yet."

Maurice Hamilton

FORMULA 1 GULF AIR BAHRAIN GRAND PRIX 2024

SAKHIR 29 FEBRUARY–02 MARCH

RACE DISTANCE: 57 laps, 191.530 miles/308.238km
RACE WEATHER: Dry/dark (track 22–24°C, air 19°C)

BAHRAIN INTERNATIONAL CIRCUIT, SAKHIR
Circuit: 3.363 miles/5.412km, 57 laps
● Sector ▬ DRS Zone

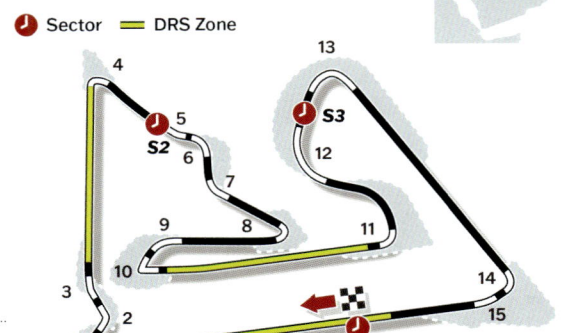

RACE – OFFICIAL CLASSIFICATION

Pos.	Driver	Nat.	No.	Entrant	Car/Engine	Laps	Time/Retirement	Speed (mph/km/h)	Gap to winner	Fastest race lap
1	Max Verstappen	NL	1	Oracle Red Bull Racing	Red Bull RB20-Honda RBPT H002 V6	57	1h 31m 44.742s	125.257/201.581		1m 32.608s 39
2	Sergio Pérez	MEX	11	Oracle Red Bull Racing	Red Bull RB20-Honda RBPT H002 V6	57	1h 32m 07.199s	124.748/200.762	22.457s	1m 34.364s 40
3	Carlos Sainz	E	55	Scuderia Ferrari	Ferrari SF-24-066/12 V6	57	1h 32m 09.852s	124.688/200.666	25.110s	1m 34.507s 44
4	Charles Leclerc	MC	16	Scuderia Ferrari	Ferrari SF-24-066/12 V6	57	1h 32m 24.411s	124.361/200.139	39.669s	1m 34.090s 36
5	George Russell	GB	63	Mercedes-AMG Petronas F1 Team	Mercedes-AMG F1 W15-M15 E Perf. V6	57	1h 32m 31.530s	124.202/199.883	46.788s	1m 35.065s 40
6	Lando Norris	GB	4	McLaren Formula 1 Team	McLaren MCL38-Mercedes F1 M15 E Perf. V6	57	1h 32m 33.200s	124.164/199.822	48.458s	1m 34.476s 35
7	Lewis Hamilton	GB	44	Mercedes-AMG Petronas F1 Team	Mercedes-AMG F1 W15-M15 E Perf. V6	57	1h 32m 35.066s	124.122/199.755	50.324s	1m 34.722s 39
8	Oscar Piastri	AUS	81	McLaren Formula 1 Team	McLaren MCL38-Mercedes F1 M15 E Perf. V6	57	1h 32m 40.824s	123.993/199.548	56.082s	1m 34.983s 39
9	Fernando Alonso	E	14	Aston Martin Aramco F1 Team	Aston Martin AMR24-Mercedes F1 M15 E Perf. V6	57	1h 32m 59.629s	123.576/198.876	1m 14.887s	1m 34.199s 48
10	Lance Stroll	CDN	18	Aston Martin Aramco F1 Team	Aston Martin AMR24-Mercedes F1 M15 E Perf. V6	57	1h 33m 17.958s	123.171/198.225	1m 33.216s	1m 35.632s 30
11	Zhou Guanyu	CHN	24	Stake F1 Team Kick Sauber	Sauber C44-Ferrari 066/12 V6	56			1 lap	1m 35.458s 30
12	Kevin Magnussen	DK	20	MoneyGram Haas F1 Team	Haas VF-24-Ferrari 066/10 V6	56			1 lap	1m 35.570s 34
13	Daniel Ricciardo	AUS	3	Visa Cash App RB Formula One Team	RB VCARB 01-Honda RBPT H002 V6	56			1 lap	1m 35.163s 37
14	Yuki Tsunoda	J	22	Visa Cash App RB Formula One Team	RB VCARB 01-Honda RBPT H002 V6	56			1 lap	1m 35.833s 37
15	Alexander Albon	T	23	Williams Racing	Williams FW46-Mercedes F1 M15 E Perf. V6	56			1 lap	1m 35.723s 40
16	Nico Hülkenberg	D	27	MoneyGram Haas F1 Team	Haas VF-24-Ferrari 066/10 V6	56			1 lap	1m 34.834s 46
17	Esteban Ocon	F	31	BWT Alpine F1 Team	Alpine A524-Renault E-Tech RE24 V6	56			1 lap	1m 36.226s 34
18	Pierre Gasly	F	10	BWT Alpine F1 Team	Alpine A524-Renault E-Tech RE24 V6	56			1 lap	1m 34.805s 45
19	Valtteri Bottas	FIN	77	Stake F1 Team Kick Sauber	Sauber C44-Ferrari 066/12 V6	56			1 lap	1m 36.202s 33
20	Logan Sargeant	USA	2	Williams Racing	Williams FW46-Mercedes F1 M15 E Perf. V6	55			2 laps	1m 34.735s 42

DHL Fastest race lap (scores 1 point): Max Verstappen on lap 39, 1m 32.608s, 130.726mph/210.383km/h.
Lap record: Michael Schumacher (Ferrari F2004 V10), 1m 30.252s, 134.263mph/216.074km/h (2004, 3.366-mile/5.417km circuit).
Lap record (current configuration): Pedro de la Rosa (McLaren MP4-20-Mercedes V10), 1m 31.447s, 132.386mph/213.054km/h (2005).

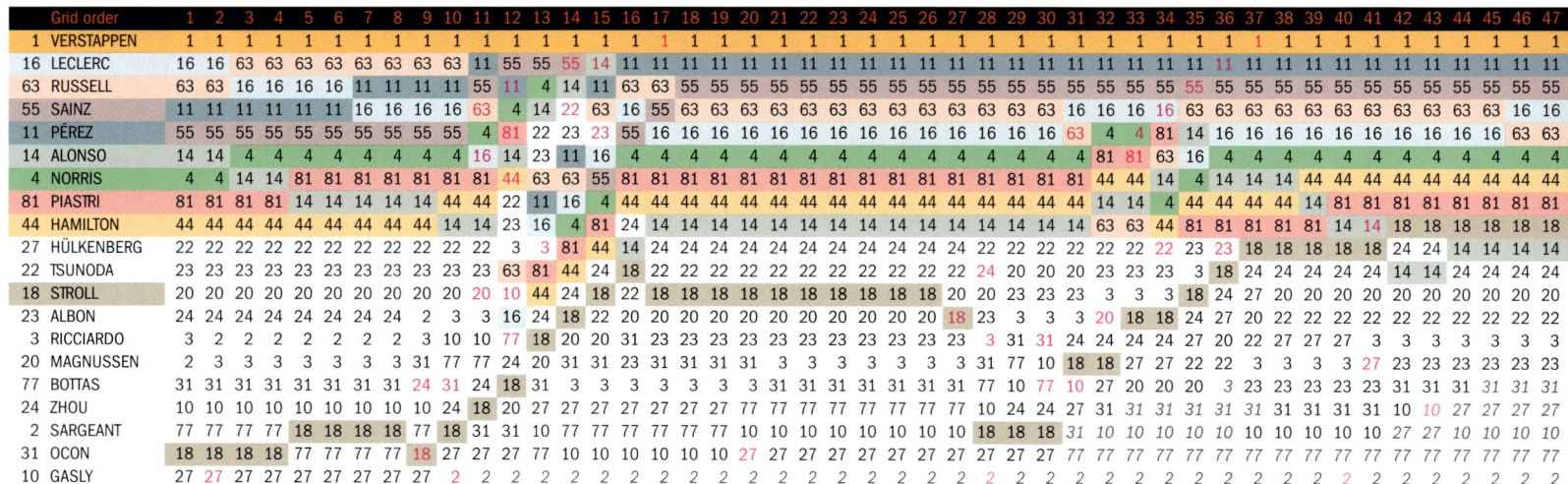

TIME SHEETS

PRACTICE 1 (THURSDAY)
Weather: Dry/sunny
Temperatures: track 32-35°C, air 19-20°C

Pos.	Driver	Laps	Time
1	Daniel Ricciardo	23	1m 32.869s
2	Lando Norris	25	1m 32.901s
3	Oscar Piastri	25	1m 33.113s
4	Yuki Tsunoda	24	1m 33.183s
5	Fernando Alonso	20	1m 33.193s
6	Max Verstappen	21	1m 33.238s
7	George Russell	25	1m 33.251s
8	Charles Leclerc	24	1m 33.268s
9	Lewis Hamilton	22	1m 33.302s
10	Valtteri Bottas	21	1m 33.354s
11	Carlos Sainz	26	1m 33.385s
12	Sergio Pérez	24	1m 33.413s
13	Alexander Albon	17	1m 33.583s
14	Lance Stroll	20	1m 33.868s
15	Zhou Guanyu	16	1m 33.923s
16	Logan Sargeant	19	1m 34.213s
17	Esteban Ocon	21	1m 34.807s
18	Pierre Gasly	24	1m 35.144s
19	Kevin Magnussen	25	1m 37.477s
20	Nico Hülkenberg	27	1m 37.938s

PRACTICE 2 (THURSDAY)
Weather: Dry/dark
Temperatures: track 21-22°C, air 17°C

Pos.	Driver	Laps	Time
1	Lewis Hamilton	25	1m 30.374s
2	George Russell	23	1m 30.580s
3	Fernando Alonso	22	1m 30.660s
4	Carlos Sainz	25	1m 30.769s
5	Oscar Piastri	27	1m 30.784s
6	Max Verstappen	25	1m 30.851s
7	Nico Hülkenberg	23	1m 30.884s
8	Lance Stroll	26	1m 30.891s
9	Charles Leclerc	26	1m 31.113s
10	Sergio Pérez	26	1m 31.115s
11	Alexander Albon	26	1m 31.333s
12	Daniel Ricciardo	26	1m 31.516s
13	Logan Sargeant	27	1m 31.715s
14	Kevin Magnussen	27	1m 31.764s
15	Yuki Tsunoda	29	1m 31.881s
16	Pierre Gasly	25	1m 31.951s
17	Valtteri Bottas	24	1m 32.001s
18	Esteban Ocon	25	1m 32.027s
19	Zhou Guanyu	28	1m 32.048s
20	Lando Norris	25	1m 32.608s

PRACTICE 3 (FRIDAY)
Weather: Dry/sunny
Temperatures: track 29-34°C, air 20-21°C

Pos.	Driver	Laps	Time
1	Carlos Sainz	18	1m 30.824s
2	Fernando Alonso	18	1m 30.965s
3	Max Verstappen	16	1m 31.062s
4	Charles Leclerc	17	1m 31.094s
5	Lando Norris	12	1m 31.118s
6	George Russell	12	1m 31.190s
7	Oscar Piastri	13	1m 31.210s
8	Sergio Pérez	17	1m 31.248s
9	Nico Hülkenberg	13	1m 31.278s
10	Lance Stroll	17	1m 31.396s
11	Daniel Ricciardo	13	1m 31.449s
12	Lewis Hamilton	20	1m 31.452s
13	Yuki Tsunoda	14	1m 31.631s
14	Kevin Magnussen	20	1m 31.671s
15	Alexander Albon	17	1m 31.965s
16	Zhou Guanyu	17	1m 32.000s
17	Valtteri Bottas	16	1m 32.096s
18	Esteban Ocon	11	1m 32.124s
19	Logan Sargeant	16	1m 32.125s
20	Pierre Gasly	14	1m 32.382s

QUALIFYING (FRIDAY)
Weather: Dry/dark Temperatures: track 21-22°C, air 18°C

Pos.	Driver	First	Second	Third	Qualifying Tyre
1	Max Verstappen	1m 30.031s	1m 29.374s	**1m 29.179s**	Soft (n)
2	Charles Leclerc	1m 30.243s	**1m 29.165s**	1m 29.407s	Soft (n)
3	George Russell	1m 30.350s	1m 29.922s	1m 29.485s	Soft (n)
4	Carlos Sainz	**1m 29.909s**	1m 29.573s	1m 29.507s	Soft (n)
5	Sergio Pérez	1m 30.221s	1m 29.932s	1m 29.537s	Soft (n)
6	Fernando Alonso	1m 30.179s	1m 29.801s	1m 29.542s	Soft (n)
7	Lando Norris	1m 30.143s	1m 29.941s	1m 29.614s	Soft (n)
8	Oscar Piastri	1m 30.531s	1m 30.122s	1m 29.683s	Soft (n)
9	Lewis Hamilton	1m 30.451s	1m 29.718s	1m 29.710s	Soft (n)
10	Nico Hülkenberg	1m 30.566s	1m 29.851s	1m 30.502s	Soft (u)
11	Yuki Tsunoda	1m 30.481s	1m 30.129s		
12	Lance Stroll	1m 29.965s	1m 30.200s		
13	Alexander Albon	1m 30.397s	1m 30.221s		
14	Daniel Ricciardo	1m 30.562s	1m 30.278s		
15	Kevin Magnussen	1m 30.646s	1m 30.529s		
16	Valtteri Bottas	1m 30.756s			
17	Zhou Guanyu	1m 30.757s			
18	Logan Sargeant	1m 30.770s			
19	Esteban Ocon	1m 30.793s			
20	Pierre Gasly	1m 30.948s			

QUALIFYING: head to head

Verstappen	1	0	Pérez
Hamilton	0	1	Russell
Norris	1	0	Piastri
Leclerc	1	0	Sainz
Gasly	0	1	Ocon
Alonso	1	0	Stroll
Albon	1	0	Sargeant
Bottas	1	0	Zhou
Tsunoda	1	0	Ricciardo
Magnussen	0	1	Hülkenberg

FOR THE RECORD

30th GP 1-2 FINISH: Red Bull

DID YOU KNOW?

This was the 20th Bahrain Grand Prix.

POINTS

DRIVERS

1	Max Verstappen	26
2	Sergio Pérez	18
3	Carlos Sainz	15
4	Charles Leclerc	12
5	George Russell	10
6	Lando Norris	8
7	Lewis Hamilton	6
8	Oscar Piastri	4
9	Fernando Alonso	2
10	Lance Stroll	1

CONSTRUCTORS

1	Red Bull	44
2	Ferrari	27
3	Mercedes	16
4	McLaren	12
5	Aston Martin	3

9 · HAMILTON · Mercedes   7 · NORRIS · McLaren   5 · PÉREZ · Red Bull   3 · RUSSELL · Mercedes   1 · VERSTAPPEN · Red Bull

10 · HÜLKENBERG · Haas   8 · PIASTRI · McLaren   6 · ALONSO · Aston Martin   4 · SAINZ · Ferrari   2 · LECLERC · Ferrari

RACE TYRE STRATEGIES

	Driver	Race Stint 1	Race Stint 2	Race Stint 3	Race Stint 4
1	Verstappen	Soft (u): 1-17	Hard (n): 18-37	Soft (n): 38-57	
2	Pérez	Soft (u): 1-12	Hard (n): 13-36	Soft (n): 37-57	
3	Sainz	Soft (u): 1-14	Hard (n): 15-35	Hard (n): 36-57	
4	Leclerc	Soft (u): 1-11	Hard (n): 12-34	Hard (n): 35-57	
5	Russell	Soft (u): 1-11	Hard (n): 12-31	Hard (n): 32-57	
6	Norris	Soft (u): 1-13	Hard (n): 14-33	Hard (n): 34-57	
7	Hamilton	Soft (u): 1-12	Hard (n): 13-33	Hard (n): 34-57	
8	Piastri	Soft (u): 1-12	Hard (n): 13-34	Hard (n): 35-57	
9	Alonso	Soft (u): 1-15	Hard (n): 16-41	Hard (n): 42-57	
10	Stroll	Soft (n): 1-9	Hard (n): 10-27	Hard (n): 28-57	
11	Zhou	Soft (n): 1-9	Hard (n): 10-28	Hard (n): 29-56	
12	Magnussen	Soft (n): 1-11	Hard (n): 12-32	Hard (n): 33-56	
13	Ricciardo	Soft (u): 1-13	Hard (n): 14-35	Soft (n): 36-56	
14	Tsunoda	Soft (n): 1-14	Hard (n): 15-34	Hard (n): 35-56	
15	Albon	Soft (u): 1-15	Hard (n): 16-34	Hard (n): 35-56	
16	Hülkenberg	Soft (n): 1	Hard (n): 2-20	Hard (n): 21-41	Soft (u): 42-56
17	Ocon	Soft (n): 1-10	Hard (n): 11-30	Hard (n): 31-56	
18	Gasly	Soft (n): 1-12	Hard (n): 13-31	Hard (n): 32-43	Soft (n): 44-56
19	Bottas	Soft (u): 1-12	Hard (n): 13-30	Hard (n): 31-56	
20	Sargeant	**Soft (n): 1-10**	Hard (n): 11-28	Hard (n): 29-40	Soft (n): 41-55

The tyre regulations stipulate that at least two of three dry tyre specifications must be used during a dry race.
Selected compounds for Sakhir: Red = Soft (C3); Yellow = Medium (C2); White = Hard (C1). (n) new (u) used

Lap chart (laps 48-57)

48	49	50	51	52	53	54	55	56	57	
1	1	1	1	1	1	1	1	1	1	1
11	11	11	11	11	11	11	11	11	11	2
55	55	55	55	55	55	55	55	55	55	3
16	16	16	16	16	16	16	16	16	16	4
63	63	63	63	63	63	63	63	63	63	5
4	4	4	4	4	4	4	4	4	4	6
44	44	44	44	44	44	44	44	44	44	7
81	81	81	81	81	81	81	81	81	81	8
14	14	14	14	14	14	14	14	14	14	9
18	18	18	18	18	18	18	18	18	18	10
24	24	24	24	24	24	24	24			
20	20	20	20	20	20	20	20			
22	22	22	22	3	3	3	3			
3	3	3	3	22	22	22	22			
23	23	23	23	23	23	23	23			
31	31	31	31	31	31	31	31			
10	10	10	10	10	10	10	10			
77	77	77	77	77	77	77	77			
2	2	2	2	2	2	2	2			

27 = Pit stop   *2* = One lap or more behind

JEDDAH QUALIFYING

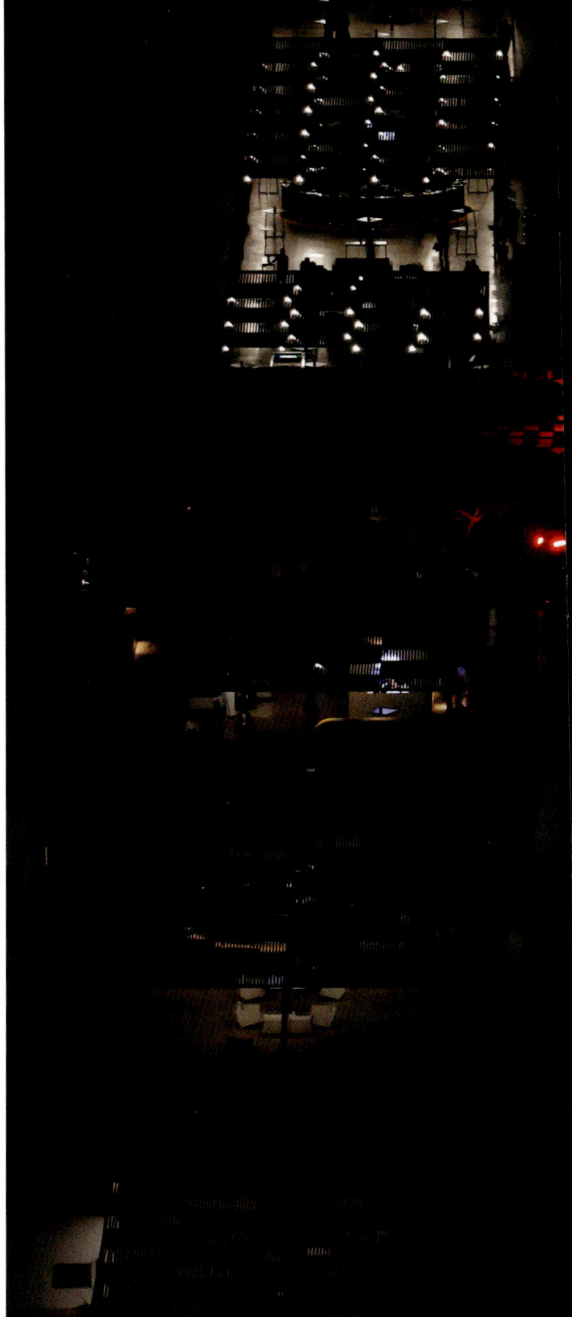

A WEEK is a long time in motor racing. As Saudi Arabian qualifying began, opening-round driver-of-the-day Carlos Sainz was absent. After completing the opening practice day around the formidable high-speed Jeddah Corniche circuit with what he thought was a stomach bug, he was diagnosed with appendicitis and taken to hospital for surgery. Cue a surprise opportunity for 18-year-old Ferrari Academy driver and upcoming British talent Oliver Bearman, who had just put his Prema F2 car on pole. He received the call from Ferrari's Fred Vasseur at around 2pm on Friday (the first two practice sessions being run on Thursday, as in Bahrain), less than two hours before FP3, his only chance to acclimatise to the 2024 Ferrari ahead of qualifying. A formidable task. As Vasseur said, "We're talking Jeddah, not Barcelona…" Bearman wasn't totally green, having tested the previous year's Ferrari and completed a couple of 2023 FP1 sessions with Haas.

Sainz apart, another fine Bahrain performer, Zhou Guanyu, who had been the first Sakhir finisher outside the acknowledged top five teams, missed qualifying due to a crash in FP3, giving Sauber too much to do in the time available.

The hope among Red Bull's rivals, so comprehensively vanquished in Bahrain, was that the very different Jeddah circuit – with its kerbs, high-speed blind corners and 27-turn, 3.8-mile second-longest lap on the calendar – would allow them to be closer. But, it was not to be…

With Sergio Pérez having been the pole-man on the previous two visits to Saudi, Max Verstappen was chasing his first pole at the venue. His first Q3 run proved that he had every intention of claiming it. He was 0.33s quicker than his team-mate and fastest in all three sectors.

The man expected to offer the sternest challenge to the RB20s was Charles Leclerc, shooting for a seventh consecutive front-row start. On his first run, though, it wasn't happening for the Monégasque. He tried two tyre-preparation laps, but could only manage fourth fastest, fully 0.8s shy of Verstappen's pace and two-tenths behind his own Q2 lap.

The suspicion was that he'd overheated the rubber, and Ferrari went back to just the one prep lap for the all-important final runs. Leclerc improved enough to split the Red Bulls, beating Pérez by a couple of hundredths to claim that front-row slot. The sobering reality, however, was that he was still more than three-tenths behind Verstappen after a lap where he'd left nothing on the table.

"I'm very happy with that," Verstappen smiled. "We made some improvements to the car after Thursday and I felt much more comfortable today, which is important around here."

After an underwhelming race in Bahrain, the single-lap pace of Fernando Alonso's Aston Martin looked very strong in Jeddah, and there was no doubting the 42-year-old's commitment as he qualified on the second row, just 0.04s behind the second Red Bull. Team-mate Lance Stroll backed him up by also putting the second car into the top ten.

The McLarens were a further quarter of a second away for one-lap pace, Oscar Piastri the quicker of the two drivers this time as the papaya cars locked out the third row.

"There may have been a tiny bit more to be had, but not enough to move me further up," was his assessment. "It's a relief actually, because I hit the wall pretty hard in Q1 and I thought that was my day done, but they make 'em strong in Woking!"

Just 0.05s behind was team-mate Lando Norris, who was happy with his lap, but not overly optimistic about the team's race prospects, given that this was a much lower tyre-degradation circuit, hence a reduced delta between car performance making overtaking tougher. Not helped by a McLaren straight-line speed deficit.

George Russell was the lead Mercedes driver again, outqualifying Lewis Hamilton for the fourth consecutive race, but he was disappointed with his seventh place, 0.15s ahead of his team-mate. "My first Q3 run on used tyres was a good one and I was P4, but on my new-tyre run, I made a mistake at Turn Nine. It could have been better," he admitted.

Hamilton elaborated on that, saying that the bouncing that had been a serious issue with the previous Mercedes cars was still a problem with the W15, particularly through Turns Six to Eight in sector one, a high-speed section with lateral load and yaw on the car. Verstappen, he pointed out, had a much more stable platform and was flat through there, whereas the Mercedes drivers were constantly having to make corrections.

Yuki Tsunoda did another strong job to put his RB ninth, five slots ahead of his struggling team-mate, Daniel Ricciardo.

And so, what of Ollie Bearman? Well, despite his lack of cockpit time and the daunting nature of the track, he only failed to bump Hamilton out of Q3 by 0.036s! His Q2 time was half a second shy of Leclerc, who was just a tenth down on Verstappen, but still he wasn't happy. "It was a messy Q2 from me," he revealed, "so not that happy overall with my performance, but it's a great opportunity!"

Vasseur was much happier, though: "I told him to build up to it, and I'm impressed."

So, too, was Verstappen: "I was watching him in FP3 to see how quickly he was pushing, and he did a really good job. Then, six-tenths away in qually with no FP1 or FP2 – you can't ask for more than that."

Also eliminated in Q2 were Alex Albon's Williams, Ricciardo and the two Haas cars, Nico Hülkenberg red-flagging the session when he pulled off at Turn Eight with a fuel-system issue. Valtteri Bottas went out in Q1 by just seven-hundredths, while Alpine's awful start to the year continued as the team was left to contemplate 17th and 18th for Esteban Ocon and Pierre Gasly, with only Logan Sargeant's Williams slower.

There had been more personnel upheaval at Enstone in the wake of technical director Matt Harman and head of aerodynamics Dirk de Beer tendering their resignations. Technical advisor Bob Bell had also left to take up a position with Aston Martin.

News of the resignations had broken during Alpine's desultory Bahrain weekend, and a restructure followed with what the team called "a new three-pillared approach" – meaning a trio of technical directors appointed to work on the chassis side. Joe Burnell was now technical director (engineering), with David Wheater technical director (aerodynamics) and former Mark Webber race engineer Ciaron Pilbeam technical director (performance). Power unit tech director Eric Meignan, based at Viry-Chatillon, remained, all four reporting to team principal Bruno Famin.

WITH the season-opener in Bahrain a two-stop race on account of the higher tyre degradation, Jeddah, with much more benign tyre usage, was expected to be a medium-hard one-stopper. Thus it was no surprise, when the tyre covers came off, that all but two cars were on the medium-compound Pirelli. The exceptions were Oliver Bearman's Ferrari and Valtteri Bottas's Sauber.

While computer simulations might have shown the medium-hard route to be quicker, a shorter opening stint on the soft and longer second stint on the hard was feasible for the 50 laps, and Ferrari chose that route for 18-year-old Bearman – the youngest starter in the history of the Scuderia's F1 team and the first driver since Arturo Merzario in 1972 to make his F1 debut in red ('Little Art' scored a point for sixth in the British GP at Silverstone, aged 29). Ferrari thought that Bearman would benefit from the additional grip for his first mid-pack race start. Only Max Verstappen and Lance Stroll had started a GP at a younger age.

Compounding Alpine's early-season woes, Pierre Gasly reported a gearbox problem on the formation lap and was pulled into the pits to retire at the end of the opening lap.

When the starting lights went out, Max Verstappen made no mistake and converted his pole position. Team-mate Sergio Pérez looked like making it a Red Bull 1-2 as he got around the outside of Charles Leclerc's Ferrari at the first turn. Leclerc, though, hung on through Turn Two and had the inside for Turn Four, keeping the Ferrari in second place. Further back, new team-mate Bearman made a decent first F1 start and retained his 11th qualifying position despite being edged wide at Turn Four by Kevin Magnussen's Haas. He even had the audacity to have a brief look down the inside of Yuki Tsunoda's RB into Turn Six before thinking better of it.

Over the line at the end of the opening lap they flashed, in the order Verstappen, Leclerc, Pérez, Fernando Alonso, Oscar Piastri, Lando Norris, George Russell, Lewis Hamilton, Lance Stroll, Tsunoda, Bearman, Magnussen, Alex Albon, Nico Hülkenberg, Daniel Ricciardo, Esteban Ocon, Bottas, Logan Sargeant and Zhou Guanyu.

With DRS now available on the second lap, Piastri wasted no time in pulling a fine move around the outside of Alonso's Aston in Turn One to go fourth. A couple of laps later, Pérez managed to displace Leclerc, this time going down the inside of the Ferrari at the first turn.

On lap seven, Lance Stroll, running ninth in the second Aston, suffered a heavy accident at Turn 23, bringing out the safety car. The Canadian, as he'd done in practice, had clipped the wall in Turn 22 with the left front, which fired him across the track and into the barrier.

His engineer, clearly looking at data rather than a TV screen, asked, "Can you bring it back, Lance?"

"No, I'm in the ****ing wall!" retorted his frustrated driver.

Immediately, Ferrari was on the radio, telling Bearman to pit to get rid of his starting softs. Pretty much the entire field followed suit to make a cheap stop on to the hard-compound Pirelli and then manage a long stint to the end of the race. With their cars running close together, McLaren and Mercedes opted not to lose time by double-stacking. They prioritised their first cars,

Above: Mechanics make last-minute checks before the start of the race.
Photo: XPB Images

Left: The implacable Williams team principal, James Vowles, on the grid.
Photo: Williams Racing

Opening spread: Max Verstappen makes an early pit stop on lap eight, switching to hard-compound Pirellis for the rest of the race.
Photo: Red Bull Content Pool/Getty Images

Piastri pitting at McLaren and Russell at Mercedes, while Norris and Hamilton continued circulating. Further down, Hülkenberg's Haas and Zhou's Sauber continued for similar reasons.

When the safety car came in after nine laps of the race's 50, the order was Norris, Verstappen, Hamilton, Pérez, Leclerc, Piastri, Alonso, Hülkenberg, Russell, Zhou, Tsunoda, Bearman, Magnussen, Albon, Ocon, Bottas, Sargeant and Ricciardo.

At the restart, Bearman, clearly not remotely intimidated in his first GP, managed to put a move on Tsunoda to go 11th, dummying outside and then switching back to the inside of Turn One. That effectively was a net ninth, given that Hülkenberg and Zhou, now ahead of him, had not stopped.

By lap 13, Verstappen on his new hards was pushing Norris on his used mediums, and he retook the race lead down the inside into Turn One. At the same time, team-mate Pérez mirrored the DRS move to relieve Hamilton's Mercedes of third.

Further back, a tangle between Magnussen and Albon left the Haas with floor damage and the Williams with a left-front vibration. The Anglo-Thai driver complained that the Dane had left him nowhere to go, something of a familiar refrain.

The race stewards were also looking into a potential jump-start by Norris and Red Bull's release of Pérez in front of Alonso during the pit stops. Norris would get away with it, as he had stopped the car shortly after it moved and gained no advantage. Pérez, who was not expected to pit again, would have 5s added to his race time. Magnussen was given a 10s penalty for his cack-handedness with Albon.

Next time around, Bearman's progress continued when he relegated Zhou's Sauber with a DRS pass into Turn One, putting himself into the top ten. Leclerc, now with Piastri close behind, was anxious to be past Hamilton on his old mediums and got a move done into Turn One to take fourth, just 2s behind the penalised Pérez, who re-established Red Bull's 1-2 when he went by Norris into Turn One on lap 19.

Bearman, after his opening-lap jockeying with Magnussen, now had the other Haas on his radar, Hülkenberg still circulating on his starting mediums some 20 laps in. "Mate, he's so slow," Bearman offered. Not wanting to wear hards that would have to do a long stint in the dirty air behind the Haas, he got a simple DRS pass done into Turn One on lap 21.

Just to further sour Magnussen's afternoon, before half-distance came news of another 10s penalty for leaving the track and gaining an advantage. He had passed Tsunoda's RB into Turn One and then run ever so slightly wide on exit, so it seemed somewhat harsh. An instruction to give the place back might have been more appropriate.

The medium-tyre runners who had not stopped were trying to extend as much as possible in the hope of another safety car, but now they were losing performance. In the event of another intervention, of course, everyone would probably stop again, meaning that their elevated out-of-synch positions would become true race positions, so they fought on for each place, although Norris reported that doing so was becoming "tricky".

Leclerc went by Lando into Turn One on lap 27, by which time he was almost 8s behind Pérez's second Red Bull, which had already overcome its 5s penalty.

Further back, an almighty scrap for 12th place was being fought by Magnussen's Haas, Tsunoda's RB, Ocon's Alpine and the Williams pair of Albon and Sargeant. Magnussen's defence was as stubborn as ever, and as he was now 19s behind tenth-placed team-mate Hülkenberg,

Above: **Ferrari's Charles Leclerc under pressure from Lewis Hamilton and Oscar Piastri.**
Photo: Scuderia Ferrari

Top left: **A single point for Nico Hülkenberg and Haas, aided in no small part by team-mate Magnussen.**
Photo: Haas F1 Team

Above left: **Oscar Piastri consolidated his strong start to the season with fourth place.**
Photo: McLaren F1 Team

Left: **To help Ollie Bearman off the line in his first GP, Ferrari started him on the soft-compound Pirellis.**
Photo: Scuderia Ferrari

Above: Kevin Magnussen's obdurate tactics kept Tsunoda, Ocon, Albon and Sargeant from reaching team-mate Hülkenberg.
Photo: Haas F1 Team

Top right: Sergio Pérez took a comfortable second place behind Verstappen.
Photo: Lukas Gorys

Above right: A more convincing display by Fernando Alonso, who claimed a tenacious fifth place.
Photo: Aramco Aston Martin F1 Team

Right: 'Driver of the day'. Ollie Bearman shone on his unexpected debut with Ferrari.
Photo: Scuderia Ferrari

who had yet to stop, the Haas tactic seemed to be about making a gap for 'The Hulk' to get in and out while remaining on course for a vital point.

With 18 laps to go, Will Joseph was on the radio to fourth-placed Norris: "Lando, I've got to ask you a question. At some point, we've just got to go for Plan A [a normal stop] and then drive back through those cars. Do you think it's going to be possible?"

"Yes," replied Norris, "but I think box as late as we can." Presumably to allow the soft tyre to be bolted on for his final stint.

Hülkenberg made his all-important stop on lap 34 and, indeed, managed to exit on his new hards in front of the rest of the field, now lined up behind his team-mate. And, confirming what the game had been about, Magnussen's race engineer, the vastly experienced Mark Slade, complimented his driver on a job well done.

Pete Bonnington was also on the radio to his man Hamilton, who was finally preparing to stop with 13 laps remaining in the absence of the desired safety car: "We are thinking softs to the end?" Lewis agreed.

McLaren brought in Norris next time around to cover Hamilton. He rejoined just in front of the Mercedes, also on the red-walled tyre, after a slightly delayed 4.1s stop.

With ten laps remaining, Verstappen was stroking it around 9s in front of his team-mate, who was 12s clear of Leclerc's Ferrari. Charles had a similar margin over Piastri's McLaren, which had Alonso 4s behind it. Russell was almost within DRS range of the Aston, with the impressive Bearman just 5.7s behind. The debutant could not relax, though, the soft-tyred and closing Norris/Hamilton duo just 5.5s behind.

On lap 42, Bearman asked, "At this pace, will Norris catch us or not?"

"Yeah, we believe so," Ferrari told him, whereupon he upped his pace slightly. At this point, he was just 23s behind team-mate Leclerc, having started 11th, as opposed to Charles's front-row grid position, which was a fine effort.

"How far away is Hamilton?" Oliver wanted to know a lap later.

"We might have a chance to stay ahead of them both, so just focus to the end," the team told him.

After 43 laps on his starting mediums, Zhou Guanyu was finally called in from tenth by Sauber. In the absence of a safety car, he was always likely to drop to the back of the pack, but a wheel-nut issue, of the type suffered by Bottas in Bahrain, ensured it.

The final few laps were all about drivers fighting rear-guard actions. Alonso was keeping Russell at bay for fifth, a much more convincing display by Aston Martin than in Bahrain. And with three to go, Bearman was still 2.5s to the good over the closing Norris, who had Hamilton breathing down his neck.

On the last lap, Leclerc, with a DRS tow, pinched the point for the race's fastest lap from the soft-tyred Hamilton. Bearman also set his own personal best, just three-tenths slower than Leclerc's as he closed to within 3s of Russell's sixth at the flag, actually extending his advantage over Norris.

"The tyres were a little bit cold at the end," Verstappen told his team to explain why he'd allowed Leclerc and Ferrari to claim an extra point. For the second time in his career, he had won nine consecutive grands prix.

Fittingly, Bearman was voted 'driver of the day'. "It's been a bit of a whirlwind to be honest," he admitted. "I knew I might have a bit of a delta on the softs at the start, but once you've overdone it a bit, it punishes you. I was a bit cramped in the car, being quite tall, so I'm feeling it a bit in the back and neck, but the bulk of the second stint on the hard, flat out, was insane. I'll take the pain for the result!"

It had been a fine effort. So, too, was a point for the Haas team from Hülkenberg, facilitated by team-mate Magnussen, who had fought as though his life depended on it, despite his penalties, creating the opportunity for his team-mate. With such a tight midfield pack, points opportunities had threatened to be rare, to the extent that conversations were already being held about rejigging the points allocation to reward more than just the first ten positions.

Tony Dodgins

VIEWPOINT
BRILLIANT BEARMAN

TALK about a best-case/worst-case scenario. You are the reserve driver at Ferrari, hoping on the off chance to get a race if something befalls either Charles Leclerc or Carlos Sainz. That moment not only arrives when you least expect it, but also comes halfway through a race weekend at Jeddah. Being pitched into one of the most high-profile race seats in the world at, say, Silverstone or Barcelona is one thing. Being told to be ready for FP3 in a couple of hours at a concrete-encased, blind-corner track with a 155mph average is something else entirely.

That was the situation that caught Oliver Bearman unawares as he made his way to the track in the belief that his mission of the day would be making the most of a pole-position start in an F2 race. His world changed dramatically with the news that Sainz had been sidelined with appendicitis and the sudden need for the 18-year-old British driver to swap his Prema Racing overalls for a red driving suit with the Prancing Horse emblem.

There would be scarcely time for Bearman to seek advice from Leclerc when familiarising himself with Ferrari's plan for the final free practice session. And all of this on a track where the smallest error would make FP3 a pointless exercise if the car were damaged. Not only that, but Bearman would then be launched straight into qualifying with scant knowledge of how the SF-24 was performing at its maximum on this unique track. He completed 22 trouble-free laps and carried that momentum through to qualifying, where he failed by just 0.036s to make it into Q3.

Twenty-four hours later, Ollie Bearman became Britain and Ferrari's youngest F1 racer as he mastered the complex start process and completed the first lap in 11th place. But what about the remaining 49 laps on an anti-clockwise track with punishing G-forces?

No problem. At the end of an impressive drive, Bearman set his fastest race lap as he dealt with potential attacks by Lando Norris and Lewis Hamilton on fresher tyres. This had been the Brit's big chance – and he had grabbed it with both hands.

Maurice Hamilton

FORMULA 1 STC SAUDI ARABIAN GRAND PRIX 2024

2

JEDDAH 07–09 MARCH
RACE DISTANCE: 50 laps, 191.662 miles/308.450km
RACE WEATHER: Dry/dark (track 27-29°C, air 25°C)

JEDDAH CORNICHE CIRCUIT
Circuit: 3.836 miles/6.174km, 50 laps

RACE – OFFICIAL CLASSIFICATION

Pos.	Driver	Nat.	No.	Entrant	Car/Engine	Laps	Time/Retirement	Speed (mph/km/h)	Gap to winner	Fastest race lap	
1	Max Verstappen	NL	1	Oracle Red Bull Racing	Red Bull RB20-Honda RBPT H002 V6	50	1h 20m 43.273s	142.462/229.270		1m 31.773s	50
2	Sergio Pérez	MEX	11	Oracle Red Bull Racing	Red Bull RB20-Honda RBPT H002 V6	50	1h 20m 56.916s *	142.062/228.626	13.643s	1m 32.273s	37
3	Charles Leclerc	MC	16	Scuderia Ferrari	Ferrari SF-24-066/12 V6	50	1h 21m 01.912s	141.916/228.391	18.639s	1m 31.632s	50
4	Oscar Piastri	AUS	81	McLaren Formula 1 Team	McLaren MCL38-Mercedes F1 M15 E Perf. V6	50	1h 21m 15.280s	141.527/227.765	32.007s	1m 32.310s	45
5	Fernando Alonso	E	14	Aston Martin Aramco F1 Team	Aston Martin AMR24-Mercedes F1 M15 E Perf. V6	50	1h 21m 19.032s	141.418/227.590	35.759s	1m 32.387s	43
6	George Russell	GB	63	Mercedes-AMG Petronas F1 Team	Mercedes-AMG F1 W15-M15 E Perf. V6	50	1h 21m 23.209s	141.297/227.395	39.936s	1m 32.254s	42
7	Oliver Bearman	GB	38	Scuderia Ferrari	Ferrari SF-24-066/12 V6	50	1h 21m 25.952s	141.217/227.267	42.679s	1m 32.186s	50
8	Lando Norris	GB	4	McLaren Formula 1 Team	McLaren MCL38-Mercedes F1 M15 E Perf. V6	50	1h 21m 28.981s	141.130/227.127	45.708s	1m 31.944s	40
9	Lewis Hamilton	GB	44	Mercedes-AMG Petronas F1 Team	Mercedes-AMG F1 W15-M15 E Perf. V6	50	1h 21m 30.664s	141.081/227.048	47.391s	1m 31.746s	38
10	Nico Hülkenberg	D	27	MoneyGram Haas F1 Team	Haas VF-24-Ferrari 066/10 V6	50	1h 22m 00.269s	140.232/225.682	1m 16.996s	1m 32.366s	49
11	Alexander Albon	T	23	Williams Racing	Williams FW46-Mercedes F1 M15 E Perf. V6	50	1h 22m 11.627s	139.910/225.163	1m 28.354s	1m 32.307s	50
12	Kevin Magnussen	DK	20	MoneyGram Haas F1 Team	Haas VF-24-Ferrari 066/10 V6	50	1h 22m 29.010s *	139.418/224.372	1m 45.737s	1m 32.338s	47
13	Esteban Ocon	F	31	BWT Alpine F1 Team	Alpine A524-Renault E-Tech RE24 V6	49			1 lap	1m 33.481s	48
14	Logan Sargeant	USA	2	Williams Racing	Williams FW46-Mercedes F1 M15 E Perf. V6	49			1 lap	1m 33.026s	49
15	Yuki Tsunoda	J	22	Visa Cash App RB Formula One Team	RB VCARB 01-Honda RBPT H002 V6	49	*		1 lap	1m 33.523s	44
16	Daniel Ricciardo	AUS	3	Visa Cash App RB Formula One Team	RB VCARB 01-Honda RBPT H002 V6	49			1 lap	1m 33.323s	47
17	Valtteri Bottas	FIN	77	Stake F1 Team Kick Sauber	Sauber C44-Ferrari 066/12 V6	49			1 lap	1m 32.706s	49
18	Zhou Guanyu	CHN	24	Stake F1 Team Kick Sauber	Sauber C44-Ferrari 066/12 V6	49			1 lap	1m 32.208s	49
	Lance Stroll	CDN	18	Aston Martin Aramco F1 Team	Aston Martin AMR24-Mercedes F1 M15 E Perf. V6	5	accident			1m 35.560s	5
	Pierre Gasly	F	10	BWT Alpine F1 Team	Alpine A524-Renault E-Tech RE24 V6	1	gearbox			no time	
EW	Carlos Sainz	E	55	Scuderia Ferrari	Ferrari SF-24-066/12 V6		appendicitis; withdrew after FP2				

* Magnussen: 10s time penalty for causing a collision with Albon; 10s time penalty for leaving the track and gaining an advantage (originally finished 11th).
* Pérez: 5s time penalty for unsafe release. * Tsunoda: 5s time penalty for unsafe release (originally finished 14th).

DHL Fastest race lap (scores 1 point): Charles Leclerc on lap 50, 1m 31.632s, 150.721mph/242.561km/h.
Lap record: Lewis Hamilton (Mercedes F1 W12 V6), 1m 30.734s, 152.212 mph/244.962km/h (2021).

20 · ZHOU · Sauber   18 · GASLY · Alpine   16 · BOTTAS · Sauber   14 · RICCIARDO · RB   12 · ALBON · Williams

19 · SARGEANT · Williams   17 · OCON · Alpine   15 · HÜLKENBERG · Haas   13 · MAGNUSSEN · Haas   11 · BEARMAN · Ferrari

Grid order		1	2	3	4	5	6	7	8	9	10	11	12	13	14	15	16	17	18	19	20	21	22	23	24	25	26	27	28	29	30	31	32	33	34	35	36	37	38
1	VERSTAPPEN	1	1	1	1	1	1	1	4	4	4	4	4	1	1	1	1	1	1	1	1	1	1	1	1	1	1	1	1	1	1	1	1	1	1	1	1	1	1
16	LECLERC	16	16	16	11	11	11	11	1	1	1	1	1	4	4	4	4	11	11	11	11	11	11	11	11	11	11	11	11	11	11	11	11	11	11	11	11	11	11
11	PÉREZ	11	11	11	16	16	16	16	44	44	44	44	44	11	11	11	11	4	4	4	4	4	4	4	4	16	16	16	16	16	16	16	16	16	16	16	16	16	16
14	ALONSO	14	81	81	81	81	81	81	11	11	11	11	11	44	44	16	16	16	16	16	16	16	16	16	16	4	4	4	4	4	4	4	4	4	4	4	4	4	81
81	PIASTRI	81	14	14	14	14	14	14	16	16	16	16	16	16	16	44	44	44	44	44	44	44	44	44	44	44	44	44	44	44	44	44	44	44	44	44	81	81	14
4	NORRIS	4	4	4	4	4	4	4	81	81	81	81	81	81	81	81	81	81	81	81	81	81	81	81	81	81	81	81	81	81	81	81	81	81	81	44	14	63
63	RUSSELL	63	63	63	63	63	63	63	14	14	14	14	14	14	14	14	14	14	14	14	14	14	14	14	14	14	14	14	14	14	14	14	14	14	14	14	63	38
44	HAMILTON	44	44	44	44	44	44	44	27	27	27	27	27	27	63	63	63	63	63	63	63	63	63	63	63	63	63	63	63	63	63	63	63	63	63	38	4
22	TSUNODA	18	18	18	18	18	22	22	63	63	63	63	63	63	27	38	38	38	27	38	27	38	38	38	38	38	38	38	38	38	38	38	38	38	38	44	44
18	STROLL	22	22	22	22	22	38	38	22	24	24	24	24	24	38	38	38	27	38	27	38	27	27	27	27	27	27	27	27	27	27	27	27	27	27	24	24	24	24
38	BEARMAN	38	38	38	38	38	20	20	22	38	38	38	38	38	24	24	24	24	24	24	24	24	24	24	24	24	24	24	24	24	24	24	24	27	27	27	27
23	ALBON	20	20	20	20	20	23	23	38	38	22	22	22	22	22	22	22	22	22	22	22	22	22	22	22	22	22	20	20	20	20	20	20	20	20	20	20	20	20
20	MAGNUSSEN	23	23	23	23	23	27	27	20	20	20	20	20	20	20	20	20	20	20	20	20	20	20	20	20	20	20	22	22	22	31	31	31	31	31	31	31
3	RICCIARDO	27	27	27	27	27	3	3	23	23	23	23	23	23	23	23	23	23	23	23	23	23	23	23	23	23	23	23	23	23	22	22	22	22	22	22	22
27	HÜLKENBERG	3	3	3	3	3	31	31	31	31	31	31	31	31	31	31	31	31	31	31	31	31	31	31	31	31	31	31	31	31	2	2	2	2	2	2	2
77	BOTTAS	31	31	31	31	31	77	77	77	77	77	77	77	77	2	2	2	2	2	2	2	2	2	2	2	2	2	2	2	2	3	3	3	3	3	3	3
31	OCON	77	77	77	77	77	2	2	2	2	2	2	2	2	77	77	77	77	77	77	77	77	77	77	77	77	77	77	77	77	77	77	77	77	77	77	77
10	GASLY	2	2	2	2	2	24	24	3	3	3	3	3	3	3	3	3	3	3	3	3	3	3																
2	SARGEANT	24	24	24	24	24																																	
24	ZHOU	10																																					

SC Safety Car deployed on laps 7-9

TIME SHEETS

PRACTICE 1 (THURSDAY)
Weather: Dry/sunny
Temperatures: track 34-41°C, air 26-29°C

Pos.	Driver	Laps	Time
1	Max Verstappen	24	1m 29.659s
2	Fernando Alonso	24	1m 29.845s
3	Sergio Pérez	23	1m 29.868s
4	George Russell	23	1m 29.939s
5	Charles Leclerc	24	1m 30.030s
6	Carlos Sainz	24	1m 30.164s
7	Lando Norris	26	1m 30.231s
8	Lewis Hamilton	21	1m 30.236s
9	Lance Stroll	18	1m 30.580s
10	Alexander Albon	26	1m 30.747s
11	Valtteri Bottas	26	1m 30.783s
12	Daniel Ricciardo	25	1m 30.917s
13	Esteban Ocon	27	1m 30.945s
14	Logan Sargeant	27	1m 30.966s
15	Oscar Piastri	22	1m 30.977s
16	Yuki Tsunoda	25	1m 31.036s
17	Pierre Gasly	25	1m 31.046s
18	Zhou Guanyu	24	1m 31.131s
19	Nico Hülkenberg	19	1m 31.411s
20	Kevin Magnussen	18	1m 31.577s

PRACTICE 2 (THURSDAY)
Weather: Dry/dark
Temperatures: track 27-28°C, air 25°C

Pos.	Driver	Laps	Time
1	Fernando Alonso	28	1m 28.827s
2	George Russell	24	1m 29.057s
3	Max Verstappen	27	1m 29.158s
4	Charles Leclerc	25	1m 29.180s
5	Sergio Pérez	27	1m 29.300s
6	Lance Stroll	27	1m 29.336s
7	Carlos Sainz	26	1m 29.455s
8	Lewis Hamilton	22	1m 29.504s
9	Pierre Gasly	29	1m 29.528s
10	Oscar Piastri	27	1m 29.594s
11	Yuki Tsunoda	28	1m 29.666s
12	Lando Norris	23	1m 29.758s
13	Zhou Guanyu	27	1m 29.777s
14	Alexander Albon	28	1m 29.789s
15	Esteban Ocon	27	1m 29.901s
16	Logan Sargeant	27	1m 29.934s
17	Kevin Magnussen	24	1m 29.985s
18	Nico Hülkenberg	26	1m 30.077s
19	Daniel Ricciardo	29	1m 30.088s
20	Valtteri Bottas	27	1m 30.153s

PRACTICE 3 (FRIDAY)
Weather: Dry/sunny
Temperatures: track 34-40°C, air 25-28°C

Pos.	Driver	Laps	Time
1	Max Verstappen	13	1m 28.412s
2	Charles Leclerc	16	1m 28.608s
3	Sergio Pérez	13	1m 28.906s
4	George Russell	17	1m 28.964s
5	Lando Norris	11	1m 28.971s
6	Fernando Alonso	14	1m 29.038s
7	Lance Stroll	14	1m 29.127s
8	Oscar Piastri	11	1m 29.213s
9	Lewis Hamilton	19	1m 29.268s
10	Oliver Bearman	22	1m 29.306s
11	Kevin Magnussen	12	1m 29.485s
12	Pierre Gasly	13	1m 29.546s
13	Yuki Tsunoda	18	1m 29.572s
14	Esteban Ocon	13	1m 29.575s
15	Nico Hülkenberg	11	1m 29.675s
16	Daniel Ricciardo	15	1m 29.740s
17	Alexander Albon	13	1m 29.808s
18	Valtteri Bottas	21	1m 30.083s
19	Zhou Guanyu	12	1m 30.739s
20	Logan Sargeant	2	no time

QUALIFYING (FRIDAY)
Weather: Dry/dark   Temperatures: track 28-31°C, air 25°C

Pos.	Driver	First	Second	Third	Qualifying Tyre
1	Max Verstappen	1m 28.171s	1m 28.033s	1m 27.472s	Soft (n)
2	Charles Leclerc	1m 28.318s	1m 28.112s	1m 27.791s	Soft (n)
3	Sergio Pérez	1m 28.638s	1m 28.467s	1m 27.807s	Soft (n)
4	Fernando Alonso	1m 28.706s	1m 28.122s	1m 27.846s	Soft (n)
5	Oscar Piastri	1m 28.755s	1m 28.343s	1m 28.089s	Soft (n)
6	Lando Norris	1m 28.805s	1m 28.479s	1m 28.132s	Soft (n)
7	George Russell	1m 28.749s	1m 28.448s	1m 28.316s	Soft (u)
8	Lewis Hamilton	1m 28.994s	1m 28.606s	1m 28.460s	Soft (n)
9	Yuki Tsunoda	1m 28.988s	1m 28.564s	1m 28.547s	Soft (n)
10	Lance Stroll	1m 28.250s	1m 28.578s	1m 28.572s	Soft (n)
11	Oliver Bearman	1m 28.984s	1m 28.642s		
12	Alexander Albon	1m 29.107s	1m 28.980s		
13	Kevin Magnussen	1m 29.069s	1m 29.020s		
14	Daniel Ricciardo	1m 29.065s	1m 29.025s		
15	Nico Hülkenberg	1m 29.055s	no time		
16	Valtteri Bottas	1m 29.179s			
17	Esteban Ocon	1m 29.475s			
18	Pierre Gasly	1m 29.479s			
19	Logan Sargeant	1m 29.526s			
20	Zhou Guanyu	no time			

QUALIFYING: head to head

Verstappen	2	0	Pérez
Hamilton	0	2	Russell
Norris	1	1	Piastri
Leclerc	1	0	Sainz
Leclerc	1	0	Bearman
Gasly	0	2	Ocon
Alonso	2	0	Stroll
Albon	2	0	Sargeant
Bottas	2	0	Zhou
Tsunoda	2	0	Ricciardo
Magnussen	1	1	Hülkenberg

FOR THE RECORD

100th PODIUM & 60th FRONT ROW: Max Verstappen
1st GP START & 1st POINTS: Oliver Bearman
10,000th GP LAP RACED: Max Verstappen

DID YOU KNOW?
Oliver Bearman at 18 years and 306 days becomes the third-youngest driver to start in the F1 World Championship, behind Verstappen and Stroll.

POINTS

DRIVERS
1	Max Verstappen	51
2	Sergio Pérez	36
3	Charles Leclerc	28
4	George Russell	18
5	Oscar Piastri	16
6	Carlos Sainz	15
7	Fernando Alonso	12
8	Lando Norris	12
9	Lewis Hamilton	8
10	Oliver Bearman	6
11	Nico Hülkenberg	1
12	Lance Stroll	1

CONSTRUCTORS
1	Red Bull	87
2	Ferrari	49
3	McLaren	28
4	Mercedes	26
5	Aston Martin	13
6	Haas	1

10 · STROLL · Aston Martin

8 · HAMILTON · Mercedes

6 · NORRIS · McLaren

4 · ALONSO · Aston Martin

2 · LECLERC · Ferrari

9 · TSUNODA · RB

7 · RUSSELL · Mercedes

5 · PIASTRI · McLaren

3 · PÉREZ · Red Bull

1 · VERSTAPPEN · Red Bull

Lap chart

39	40	41	42	43	44	45	46	47	48	49	50	·	
1	1	1	1	1	1	1	1	1	1	1	1		1
11	11	11	11	11	11	11	11	11	11	11	11		2
16	16	16	16	16	16	16	16	16	16	16	16		3
81	81	81	81	81	81	81	81	81	81	81	81		4
14	14	14	14	14	14	14	14	14	14	14	14		5
63	63	63	63	63	63	63	63	63	63	63	63		6
38	38	38	38	38	38	38	38	38	38	38	38		7
4	4	4	4	4	4	4	4	4	4	4	4		8
44	44	44	44	44	44	44	44	44	44	44	44		9
24	24	24	27	27	27	27	27	27	27	27	27		10
27	27	27	20	20	20	20	20	20	20	20	20		
20	20	20	23	23	23	23	23	23	23	23	23		
31	31	31	23	31	31	31	31	31	31				
23	23	23	22	22	22	22	22	22	22	22	22		
22	22	22	2	2	2	2	2	2	2	2	2		
2	2	2	3	3	3	3	3	3	3	3	3		
3	3	3	77	77	77	77	77	77	77	77	77		
77	77	77	24	24	24	24	24	24	24	24	24		

81 = Pit stop   **77** = One lap or more behind

RACE TYRE STRATEGIES (PIRELLI)

	Driver	Race Stint 1	Race Stint 2	Race Stint 3
1	Verstappen	Medium (n): 1-7	Hard (n): 8-50	
2	Pérez	Medium (n): 1-7	Hard (n): 8-50	
3	Leclerc	Medium (n): 1-7	Hard (n): 8-50	
4	Piastri	Medium (n): 1-7	Hard (n): 8-50	
5	Alonso	Medium (u): 1-7	Hard (n): 8-50	
6	Russell	Medium (n): 1-7	Hard (n): 8-50	
7	Bearman	Soft (n): 1-7	Hard (n): 8-50	
8	Norris	Medium (n): 1-37	Soft (u): 38-50	
9	Hamilton	Medium (n): 1-36	Soft (u): 37-50	
10	Hülkenberg	Medium (n): 1-33	Hard (n): 34-50	
11	Albon	Medium (n): 1-7	Hard (n): 8-50	
12	Magnussen	Medium (n): 1-7	Hard (n): 8-50	
13	Ocon	Medium (n): 1-7	Hard (n): 8-49	
14	Sargeant	Medium (n): 1-7	Hard (n): 8-49	
15	Tsunoda	Medium (n): 1-7	Hard (n): 8-49	
16	Ricciardo	Hard (n): 1-7		
17	Bottas	Soft (n): 1-7	Hard (n): 8-35	Soft (n): 36-49
18	Zhou	Medium (n): 1-41	Soft (n): 42-49	
	Stroll	Medium (u): 1-5 (dnf)		
	Gasly	Medium (n): 1 (dnf)		

The tyre regulations stipulate that at least two of three dry tyre specifications must be used during a dry race.
Selected compounds for Jeddah: Red = Soft (C4); Yellow = Medium (C3); White = Hard (C2).   (n) new   (u) used

FIA FORMULA 1 WORLD CHAMPIONSHIP · ROUND 3

AUSTRALIAN GRAND PRIX

MELBOURNE CIRCUIT

MELBOURNE QUALIFYING

AFTER Red Bull's dominant start to the year in the Middle East, on to the feel-good factor of Melbourne and, finally, their rivals' hopes of a different narrative. At the end of the opening day, Charles Leclerc had a margin of almost four-tenths over Max Verstappen for single-lap pace and, perhaps more importantly, his Ferrari was also demonstrating an unusual longer-run advantage.

But there was a caveat. Verstappen had run wide over the kerb at Turn Ten in FP1, damaging his Red Bull's floor, which cost him the first 20 minutes of FP2 while repairs were completed. Neither his soft-tyred push-lap nor his race simulation was truly representative.

The other Friday story was Alex Albon losing his Williams on the exit of Turn Six – as he had in 2023's race – and cannoning into the walls on both the right- and left-hand sides of the track, to the terminal detriment of his Williams chassis. The team's outdated manufacturing process, which had to cope with wholesale changes to the 2024 FW46, left the build programme well behind, and Williams lacked a spare tub for at least the first three flyaway races.

Aware that Albon was the team's stronger driver, team principal James Vowles commandeered team-mate Logan Sargeant's car for the rest of the weekend, rendering the Floridian a spectator.

Sargeant called it the toughest moment of his career, while Vowles admitted that the lack of a spare tub was, "Unacceptable in modern-day F1" and an illustration of why the team needed to go through significant change. "While Logan shouldn't have to suffer for a mistake he didn't make," Vowles said, "every race counts when the midfield is tighter than ever. The decision was not made lightly. We cannot thank Logan enough; he's a true team player."

On Saturday, the picture changed. In FP3, the medium-compound C4 Pirelli proved quicker than the soft C5. It was the first time that Pirelli had brought the C5 in 2024, and it proved a tricky tyre to get the best from in cooler temperatures. Verstappen summed it up: "I don't know why in the high speed I can't go faster on the soft tyre compared to the medium. The tyre is moving around too much." Carlos Sainz, still recovering from the appendicitis operation that had kept him out of Jeddah, actually topped FP3 on the medium!

Mercedes endured a troubled practice, especially on Lewis Hamilton's side of the garage, where widespread set-up changes between the two Friday sessions had backfired badly. Suddenly, though, the Mercs were in the picture in FP3, albeit briefly.

In the three-and-a-half hours between FP3 and qualifying, the temperatures rose just enough (ambient, 18 degrees; track temperature, 34 degrees) to allow the softs to work better. With Verstappen now fully up to speed and Ferrari not getting the best out of the car in qualifying, it added up to Max puncturing expectations of that narrative change with a lap in 1m 15.915s to give him yet another pole, by a relatively comfortable 0.27s.

"A bit unexpected today," he admitted, "but very happy with Q3. Both laps felt nice. We got there in the end."

Closest to him was Sainz, not Leclerc. Charles's obvious confidence in the car that had allowed him to dominate Friday was not there on Saturday morning. Suddenly, he was getting understeer through Turns One and Two. To counter it, he dialled in a bit more front wing, but by the time he got to the high-speed left/right of Turns Nine and Ten, the car was not as balanced and planted as the previous day, the rear snappy.

The problem was bringing in the soft-compound fronts sufficiently for sector one. Attempting to solve this with more front wing put extra demand on the rears, overheating them by Turns Nine and Ten. Sainz had the same issue. His best Q3 lap was on a par with Verstappen's as far as Turns Nine and Ten, where he also experienced a snap. Pole had been a genuine possibility, but, still, he was happy: "If you'd told me five days ago that I'd be on the front row, I wouldn't have believed it," Carlos smiled. "I'm not in my best state, but I can get it done. It's discomfort rather than pain. I can adapt."

In Q2, the Ferraris had been quickest, Sainz a tenth up on Leclerc, with Verstappen a further tenth back. In Q3, however, Leclerc went too aggressive with the front wing and aborted his second run after a mistake at Turn 12, allowing both Sergio Pérez's Red Bull and Lando Norris's McLaren to qualify ahead of him, as well as his team-mate and Verstappen. Rather than an eighth straight front-row start, he was left contemplating fifth, although that became fourth when Pérez was handed a three-place grid penalty for impeding Nico Hülkenberg in Q1, Red Bull having failed to give him sufficient warning of the German's impending arrival.

Home hero Oscar Piastri looked impressive all through practice, the stronger of the two McLaren drivers, but when the chips were down, it was Norris who unexpectedly outqualified a Ferrari.

"A good turnaround on a weekend when I've not felt that comfortable," Lando said. "It felt like I managed to unlock a bit of potential, which I've not had in a while," he added, typically self-deprecating. Piastri, by contrast, had mixed feelings, believing he'd left something on the table in qualifying sixth, but failing to nail Turn One on either of his Q3 runs.

Some eight-tenths down on Verstappen's pole, George Russell was the lone Mercedes to make Q3, with Hamilton, eight-times Melbourne pole-man (a single-event record beaten only by his nine in Budapest), missing the Q2 cut by five-hundredths. It was the fifth successive time that Russell had outqualified Hamilton. Clearly, Mercedes was still struggling, and for the first time since 2011, there was no Silver Arrow in an F1 grid's top six.

"We have a car with which you can be narrowly in and out of the window," said Toto Wolff, after the W15 had looked a particular handful through Turns One and Two. "It's more complex than just rear instability. It's the whole interaction of aerodynamics, the mechanical side and the tyres."

A fine effort from Yuki Tsunoda put a Visa Cash App RB eighth, with Lance Stroll managing a rare outqualification of team-mate Fernando Alonso as the Aston Martins completed the top ten.

Alex Albon thanked Sargeant for his largesse by qualifying the lone Williams 12th. Valtteri Bottas, Kevin Magnussen and Esteban Ocon were the other Q2 casualties. Those falling at the first Q1 hurdle were Daniel Ricciardo (whose 12th-quickest lap was deleted for exceeding track limits at Turn Four, dropping him to 18th), Nico Hülkenberg, Pierre Gasly and Zhou Guanyu.

PRACTICE and qualifying had evolved through Ferrari setting the pace to Red Bull hitting back and Max Verstappen claiming another pole position. However, a real race was still anticipated in Melbourne.

Why so? Well, the combination of the smooth, resurfaced (in 2022) Albert Park track and a step softer tyre compounds from Pirelli had thrown up considerable graining on both the soft and medium tyres, while nobody had so much as run the hard tyre, expected to be the prime race compound, prior to the start.

Whereas thermal degradation was the area where Red Bull had previously demonstrated regular superiority, Melbourne would be all about graining and wear. And Friday's evidence suggested that Ferrari was perhaps in better shape than Red Bull. Such had also been the case at the penultimate 2023 race in Las Vegas, where only an inopportune safety car had scuppered Charles Leclerc.

"I think we have a fight on our hands with Ferrari because the degradation is going to be high," Sergio Pérez confirmed post-qualifying. And whereas traditionally Australia had been a one-stop race, almost certainly this one would involve two stops.

Of course, graining is exacerbated by running in dirty air, so the start was even more significant. The first nine all took to the grid on the medium-compound tyre, while Fernando Alonso's tenth-placed Aston Martin lined up on the hard. Behind him, Lewis Hamilton's Mercedes was sporting a set of red-walled softs, no doubt in the hope of a good launch and then perhaps an early safety car that would allow him to run two stints on the hard compound. Further back, Nico Hülkenberg's Haas started on the hard, with both Daniel Ricciardo and Zhou Guanyu (from the pit lane after *parc fermé* modifications) opting for softs. Everyone else took the medium compound.

Verstappen made no mistake when the lights went out and converted his pole, the field streaming through Turns One and Two behind him in well-behaved fashion. The first five were all in grid order, but George Russell managed to pinch a place from Pérez, going around the outside of the second Red Bull in Turn Three. Further back, Alex Albon was down two slots in the Williams as he went in search of that championship point to justify the appropriation of his team-mate's car!

Carlos Sainz managed to keep his Ferrari within a second of Verstappen around the opening lap (DRS being enabled on lap two in 2024 remember), and the first indication that all was not well with the RB20 came with a puff of smoke from the right rear of Max's car as he ran a little deep into Turn Three on the second lap, losing time. That allowed the Ferrari to stay close enough to sweep by the three-times champion with the help of DRS on the long run down to Turn Nine. From hospital bed to Australian GP race lead in two weeks!

"I just lost the car, really weird," Verstappen informed his team, explaining the *faux pas* at Turn Three. Then, shortly after, "The car is loose." He had an issue. The right rear brake was binding on, which had caused the Turn Three problem, and now heat build-up was causing ever increasing smoke from the back of the Red Bull. As his rivals started to stream by, Verstappen toured into the pits, flames licking from the back of his car. Winning ten successive grands prix for the second time in his career was not going to happen. His 43-race finishing streak, dating back to Melbourne, 2022, was over.

Predictably, Hamilton, without his hoped-for early safety car, was first into the pits on lap eight of the 58 to get rid of his starting softs, the Mercedes rejoining 14th on the hard tyre. A lap later, team-mate George Russell

Above: Smoke pours from the brakes of Verstappen's Red Bull as Carlos Sainz takes over the lead on the second lap.

Above left: Logan Sargeant was left on the sidelines.
Photos: XPB Images

Left: Alex Albon wrecked his Williams in Friday's second practice.
Photo: FTW

Below left: "It was this close." Daniel Ricciardo explains his Turn Four lap-time deletion in qualifying.
Photo: Red Bull Content Pool/Getty Images

Opening spread: Carlos Sainz returned from his recent appendix operation to take a popular triumph in Melbourne.
Photos: Scuderia Ferrari and Pirelli

Above: An early-race tussle between the Haas cars of Magnussen and Hülkenberg, the Alpines of Ocon and Gasly, and the RB of Ricciardo.
Photo: BWT Alpine F1 Team

Top right: Lance Stroll took a strong sixth place for Aston Martin.
Photo: Aramco Aston Martin F1 Team

Above right: Yuki Tsunoda was placed seventh, well ahead of team-mate Ricciardo.
Photo: Red Bull Content Pool/Getty Images

Right: Team orders helped Lando Norris claim third place for McLaren.
Photo: McLaren F1 Team

and Aston's Lance Stroll were both in as well, swapping their starting mediums for hards.

After the first ten laps, Sainz had a 2.8s lead over Lando Norris, with Charles Leclerc's Ferrari still within DRS range of the McLaren. Behind him, Oscar Piastri was similarly within DRS range of the second Ferrari. Russell's pit stop had put undercut pressure on those ahead and also released Pérez, who was now 4s behind Piastri. Yuki Tsunoda ran 2.5s behind the Mexican and was being harried by Fernando Alonso.

Sainz, orchestrating things from his cockpit, told Ferrari, "Let's open the gap now to go long. The car feels very good." Meanwhile, team-mate Leclerc pitted after ten laps in response to Russell, rejoining behind Nico Hülkenberg and Pierre Gasly, both yet to pit, but comfortably clear of the Mercedes.

As good as his word, Sainz had stretched his lead over second-placed Norris to almost 7s by lap 13. Pérez, now third on the road and still to make his first stop, was a similar distance behind the McLaren and telling his team, "I think we overdid it on this tyre; the grip from the rear is quite low."

Both Norris and Pérez pitted on lap 15, Lando rejoining behind the earlier-stopping Leclerc and Piastri, but with a handy tyre offset, while Sergio just managed to pit out and keep the early-stopping Hamilton at bay. Once the Red Bull's tyres were up to temperature, though, it dropped the Mercedes rapidly. "Jeez, that car's fast," Hamilton confirmed. Ultimately, it didn't matter, the seven-times champion ending his race with engine failure after 17 laps.

Sainz was controlling the race. His pace on his starting mediums was still on a par with those who had stopped for hards. Carlos went as far as lap 16, six laps further than his team-mate and Piastri, before pitting for hards. His stop put Alonso, on hard tyres, narrowly into the lead, and a virtual safety car (VSC) for Hamilton's parked Mercedes facilitated a cheap stop, saving around seven seconds. Fernando emerged fifth, behind the two Ferraris, two McLarens and around 5s ahead of Russell's Mercedes. Further back, Hülkenberg and Gasly also took advantage of the VSC to make stops.

Pérez was soon making headway on his new set of hard-compound boots. Having taken seventh place from Lance Stroll's Aston Martin, he rapidly closed down Russell's Mercedes and swept into the top six around the outside of the Mercedes into Turn Nine. Echoing Hamilton's earlier sentiment, George was on the radio, telling the Mercedes pit, "That car is a rocket ship!" As if they didn't know…

With just over a third of the race complete, Sainz led by 1.6s from team-mate Leclerc, with a 2s gap to Piastri, aiming to be the first Australian driver ever to stand on the podium in his home event. Norris was 2.5s back, with a 7s advantage over Alonso, who had Pérez just 5s behind and closing. Behind Russell and Stroll, Yuki Tsunoda was just 1.5s back with the first of the RBs, while Albon's Williams completed the top ten. Within striking distance, though, were the two Haas cars, Kevin Magnussen on the hard-compound tyre and team-mate Hülkenberg on the medium. The team would soon order a swap so that Nico could make best use of his mediums while Kevin ran deeper before a second stop.

Thirteenth place, a further 4s back, was not what the doctor ordered for Daniel Ricciardo in his home race. He had not been helped by his track-limits penalty in qualifying of course, but if he was serious about a return to the main Red Bull team in 2025, he needed to be beating Tsunoda…

As the race approached half-distance, Sainz had his lead over Leclerc out to 4.5s. If anything, Charles was being reeled in by Piastri's McLaren, now just 2s back, with Norris lapping even quicker in the second papaya car and only 1.2s behind the home hero. Leclerc was not thrilled with his car's balance on his first set of hard Pirellis. If they were not to fall victim to a McLaren undercut, Ferrari needed to pit Leclerc again soon.

Alonso could not match the Ferrari/McLaren pace and had dropped 11.5s back from the second McLaren, with his mirrors full of Pérez's Red Bull. There was nothing he could do to stop the Mexican from flying by with DRS before Turn Nine to take fifth place. Surprisingly, though, Sergio did not disappear up the road to threaten the leading four, but began to lose pace, not helped by a visor tear-off compromising the floor's aero performance and costing a tenth or two per lap according to Christian Horner. Alonso, on his mediums, was actually able to use DRS to good effect and stay close, helping him to drop Russell's Mercedes.

McLaren did not want to compromise Norris's pace on his fresher tyres and, at half-distance, ordered Piastri to move over. It was the right call, but not a popular one in Melbourne! Oscar did as he was bid, however.

"My tyre is gone, front left," Leclerc told Ferrari on lap 34 of the 58. "I think we cannot wait too much." They

Above: Oscar Piastri's second successive fourth place put him neck and neck with team-mate Lando Norris in the driver standings.
Photo: Atsuo Sakurai

Top right: Distracted by Alonso's Aston, George Russell crashes his Mercedes on lap 56.

Above right: Russell's car upturned on the track.
Photos: FTW

Right: A great day for the Scuderia as Sainz and Leclerc celebrate their 1-2 finish with a selfie in *parc fermé*.
Photo: Scuderia Ferrari

responded by calling him in, sending him on his way again after an efficient 2.1s stop. It was in the nick of time, as he rejoined only just in front of Pérez and Alonso. He fended them off through Turns One and Two, which was just as well in view of Norris setting a personal-best lap just as the Ferrari pitted. If Charles had lost any more time, an overcut would have been on for Lando. Pérez pitted a couple of laps later for his new hards.

At two-thirds-distance, Sainz had a 10s margin over Norris's McLaren, with Piastri some 8s behind his team-mate after losing some time with a grassy moment out of Turn 13. All three still had to make their second stops. Leclerc, happier on his second set of hards, was 26s behind his race-leading team-mate.

McLaren brought in Norris for his final stop with 17 laps remaining, Lando accelerating back into the fray just under 4s behind Leclerc, but with a decent tyre offset. As the Monégasque set the race's fastest lap, Sainz was on the radio, requesting that Ferrari did not make his pit stop too tight versus his team-mate!

With Verstappen out, a win for Leclerc would have put him at the top of the championship table, and there had been times at Ferrari when such a tactic – or even the order of a straight swap – would have been enacted. But not with Fred Vasseur at the helm, on a weekend when the recovering Sainz had been superb. The Spaniard was called in with 16 to go, pitting out still 6s clear of Leclerc.

Further back, there was a tasty battle between Haas and Williams for the last point. Hülkenberg was in possession of it, while Albon was a couple of seconds back, under severe pressure from Magnussen who, at one stage, unbelievably contemplated a lunge down the inside of Turn Nine. Mercifully, he thought better of it! A couple of laps later, he went the more conventional route and swept around Albon's outside in Turn Nine with DRS.

With 15 laps to go, Russell, who had yet to make a second stop, told Mercedes, "The tyres are feeling good," raising the possibility that, with 5.5s in hand over Pérez, he might try to make it with just the one stop, despite already having 34 laps on his hard Pirellis. But the team went the conventional route, and George would have an entirely different difficult ending to the race…

At the front, the status quo remained, and a delighted Sainz took the flag ahead of Leclerc – under a VSC for an accident involving Russell – to give Ferrari a first 1-2 since Bahrain, 2022.

"Life is a roller coaster, eh?" Carlos chuckled over the radio. A lost drive before the season started, a strong drive in Bahrain, illness in Jeddah, and now this.

Leclerc was quick to congratulate him: "Carlos has done a better job all weekend, or at least from qualifying to the race, so he definitely deserves that victory."

McLaren was delighted to have the pace to keep Leclerc honest, even if Sainz had been out of range. Meanwhile, Pérez's lacklustre fifth made you wonder whether Ferrari might even have got the job done had Verstappen been in the race.

Alonso and Russell had been battling for fifth for the last five laps when, on the penultimate lap, George found himself much closer to the Aston Martin in Turn Six while making a steering-wheel change, ran wide through the gravel on exit and suffered a big shunt, bouncing back into the middle of the track, the car on its side. It was in a highly vulnerable position as George frantically radioed for a red flag. It didn't come, but thankfully, the VSC and radio communications were enough for anyone coming through to navigate the stricken car.

"I was half a second behind Fernando, 100m from the corner, and then suddenly he came towards me extremely quick, I was right in his gearbox," Russell said.

No doubt, Alonso had been trying to slow Russell's exit from the corner to prevent him from going by with DRS into Turn Nine, but had gone a bit too far. A stewards' examination of the Aston's data revealed that the Spaniard had braked briefly on the previous straight, downshifted, then accelerated again and upshifted through the corner. Maybe not a brake-test in the extreme sense, but close…

Tony Dodgins

VIEWPOINT
SICKBAY TO SERIOUSLY GOOD

IF you'd scripted this in a movie, critics would have panned the storyline as fanciful, ridiculous even. The initial premise of having your handsome leading man race for Ferrari would be obligatory. As would a narrative in which Ferrari plans to ditch him for a superstar in 12 months' time and makes the surprise announcement just before the season starts. Further pathos would be added when our hero is struck down with appendicitis after manfully struggling through the opening practice sessions for the second race. Where on earth could this story go after such significant early setbacks?

Simple! He returns to the cockpit two weeks later – and wins a world championship grand prix! Yeah, right.

Not even Netflix would attempt to pass this off as the credible plot for a thriller. But that is exactly what happened on 25th March, 2024, as Carlos Sainz, in the manner of a true leading man, rewrote the anticipated plot and brought consecutive Red Bull victory runs to an end for the second time.

There might have been outside assistance when Max Verstappen retired from the lead with brake trouble, but Sainz, not known for excessive optimism, already felt that he would be able to challenge the Red Bull. That seemed a reasonable assumption when he went on to prove better than Charles Leclerc in making the soft Pirellis work.

Sainz taking care of tyres was one thing, but how about looking after himself, particularly when regularly experiencing 5g? That is a big enough demand on a fit driver, never mind one who has gone through surgery in the previous 14 days.

"When I was about to catch my flight to Australia, I was still in bed and could barely use my abdominal muscles," said Sainz. He had spent two hours each day in a hyperbaric chamber designed to boost oxygen intake and aid healing. But would that be enough?

He said that he felt much better when he reached Australia, an impression that would improve with each relatively pain-free lap in the SF-24. After 58 laps on Sunday, a driver who was due to be unemployed in 2025 had shown true quality and incredible determination. Talk about a story with a happy ending…

Maurice Hamilton

3

FORMULA 1 ROLEX AUSTRALIAN GRAND PRIX 2024

MELBOURNE 22-24 MARCH
RACE DISTANCE: 58 laps, 190.217 miles/306.124km
RACE WEATHER: Dry/sunny (track 40°C, air 21-23°C)

ALBERT PARK GRAND PRIX CIRCUIT, MELBOURNE
Circuit: 3.280 miles/5.278km, 58 laps

RACE – OFFICIAL CLASSIFICATION

Pos.	Driver	Nat.	No.	Entrant	Car/Engine	Laps	Time/Retirement	Speed (mph/km/h)	Gap to leader	Fastest race lap
1	Carlos Sainz	E	55	Scuderia Ferrari	Ferrari SF-24-066/12 V6	58	1h 20m 26.843s	141.869/228.316		1m 20.031s 48
2	Charles Leclerc	MC	16	Scuderia Ferrari	Ferrari SF-24-066/12 V6	58	1h 20m 29.209s	141.799/228.204	2.366s	1m 19.813s 56
3	Lando Norris	GB	4	McLaren Formula 1 Team	McLaren MCL38-Mercedes F1 M15 E Perf. V6	58	1h 20m 32.747s	141.696/228.037	5.904s	1m 19.915s 49
4	Oscar Piastri	AUS	81	McLaren Formula 1 Team	McLaren MCL38-Mercedes F1 M15 E Perf. V6	58	1h 21m 02.613s	140.825/226.636	35.770s	1m 20.199s 54
5	Sergio Pérez	MEX	11	Oracle Red Bull Racing	Red Bull RB20-Honda RBPT H002 V6	58	1h 21m 23.152s	140.233/225.683	56.309s	1m 20.388s 47
6	Lance Stroll	CDN	18	Aston Martin Aramco F1 Team	Aston Martin AMR24-Mercedes F1 M15 E Perf. V6	58	1h 22m 00.065s	139.181/223.990	1m 33.222s	1m 20.930s 49
7	Yuki Tsunoda	J	22	Visa Cash App RB Formula One Team	RB VCARB 01-Honda RBPT H002 V6	58	1h 22m 02.444s	139.113/223.881	1m 35.601s	1m 21.134s 46
8	Fernando Alonso	E	14	Aston Martin Aramco F1 Team	Aston Martin AMR24-Mercedes F1 M15 E Perf. V6	58	1h 22m 07.835s *	138.962/223.637	1m 40.992s	1m 20.493s 52
9	Nico Hülkenberg	D	27	MoneyGram Haas F1 Team	Haas VF-24-Ferrari 066/10 V6	58	1h 22m 11.396s	138.861/223.475	1m 44.553s	1m 21.145s 46
10	Kevin Magnussen	DK	20	MoneyGram Haas F1 Team	Haas VF-24-Ferrari 066/10 V6	57			1 lap	1m 21.082s 44
11	Alexander Albon	T	23	Williams Racing	Williams FW46-Mercedes F1 M15 E Perf. V6	57			1 lap	1m 21.618s 46
12	Daniel Ricciardo	AUS	3	Visa Cash App RB Formula One Team	RB VCARB 01-Honda RBPT H002 V6	57			1 lap	1m 21.239s 46
13	Pierre Gasly	F	10	BWT Alpine F1 Team	Alpine A524-Renault E-Tech RE24 V6	57	*		1 lap	1m 21.090s 51
14	Valtteri Bottas	FIN	77	Kick Sauber F1 Team	Sauber C44-Ferrari 066/12 V6	57			1 lap	1m 21.422s 48
15	Zhou Guanyu	CHN	24	Kick Sauber F1 Team	Sauber C44-Ferrari 066/12 V6	57			1 lap	1m 21.327s 49
16	Esteban Ocon	F	31	BWT Alpine F1 Team	Alpine A524-Renault E-Tech RE24 V6	57			1 lap	1m 21.354s 45
17	George Russell	GB	63	Mercedes-AMG Petronas F1 Team	Mercedes-AMG F1 W15-M15 E Perf. V6	56	accident		2 laps	1m 20.284s 53
	Lewis Hamilton	GB	44	Mercedes-AMG Petronas F1 Team	Mercedes-AMG F1 W15-M15 E Perf. V6	15	power unit			1m 22.444s 11
	Max Verstappen	NL	1	Oracle Red Bull Racing	Red Bull RB20-Honda RBPT H002 V6	3	rear brakes/fire			1m 23.115s 3
EW	Logan Sargeant	USA	2	Williams Racing	Williams FW46-Mercedes F1 M15 E Perf. V6		car taken over by Albon			

* Alonso: Drive-through converted to 20s time penalty for potentially dangerous driving (originally finished 6th).   * Gasly: 5s time penalty for crossing the yellow line at the pit exit.

DHL Fastest race lap (scores 1 point): Charles Leclerc on lap 56, 1m 19.813s, 147.928mph/238.066km/h (new record).
Previous lap record: Sergio Pérez (Red Bull RB19-Honda RBPT V6), 1m 20.235s, 147.150mph/236.814km/h (2023).

19 · ZHOU · Sauber
Car modified in parc fermé; required to start from the pit lane

17 · GASLY · Alpine

15 · OCON · Alpine

13 · BOTTAS · Sauber

11 · HAMILTON · Mercedes

18 · RICCIARDO · RB

16 · HÜLKENBERG · Haas

14 · MAGNUSSEN · Haas

12 · ALBON · Williams

Grid order	1	2	3	4	5	6	7	8	9	10	11	12	13	14	15	16	17	18	19	20	21	22	23	24	25	26	27	28	29	30	31	32	33	34	35	36	37	38	39	40	41	42	43	44	45	46
1 VERSTAPPEN	1																																													
55 SAINZ	55	55	55	55	55	55	55	55	55	55	55	55	55	55	55	55	55	55	55	55	55	55	55	55	55	55	55	55	55	55	55	55	55	55	55	55	55	55	55	55	55	55	55	55	55	55
4 NORRIS	4	1	1	4	4	4	4	4	4	4	4	4	14	14	14	16	16	16	16	16	16	16	16	16	16	16	16	16	16	16	16	16	16	16	4	4	4	4	4	4	4	16	16	16	16	16
16 LECLERC	16	4	4	16	16	16	16	16	11	11	11	11	4	16	16	81	81	81	81	81	81	81	81	81	4	4	4	4	4	4	4	4	4	4	81	81	81	81	16	4	4	4	4	4	4	4
81 PIASTRI	81	16	16	81	81	81	81	81	81	81	81	81	81	4	4	4	4	14	14	14	14	14	14	14	14	14	14	14	14	14	14	14	14	14	11	11	11	11	11	81	81	81	81	81	81	81
11 PÉREZ	11	81	81	63	63	63	63	11	16	27	16	16	16	81	81	14	14	4	4	4	4	4	4	4	81	81	81	81	81	81	81	81	81	81	14	14	14	14	81	63	63	63	63	63	63	63
63 RUSSELL	63	63	63	11	11	11	11	22	81	10	27	81	81	11	11	27	27	63	63	63	63	63	63	63	11	11	11	11	11	11	11	11	11	11	14	14	14	14	14	11	11	11	11	11	63	14
22 TSUNODA	11	11	11	18	18	18	18	14	27	16	81	27	27	27	10	63	18	11	11	11	63	63	63	63	63	63	63	63	63	63	63	63	63	63	11	18	11	11	11	14	14	14	14	14	14	63
18 STROLL	18	18	18	22	22	22	22	31	10	81	10	10	10	10	63	10	11	18	18	18	18	18	18	18	18	18	18	18	18	18	18	18	18	18	18	11	18	18	18	18	18	18	18	18	18	18
14 ALONSO	22	22	22	44	44	44	14	27	22	63	63	63	63	63	18	18	22	22	22	22	22	22	22	22	22	22	22	22	22	22	22	22	22	22	22	10	10	10	22	22	22	22	22	22	22	22
44 HAMILTON	44	44	44	14	14	14	77	10	63	18	18	18	18	18	22	22	23	23	23	23	23	23	23	23	23	23	23	23	27	27	27	27	27	27	10	22	22	22	10	27	27	27	27	27	27	27
23 ALBON	14	14	14	77	77	77	31	63	18	44	44	44	44	44	23	23	20	20	20	20	20	20	20	20	27	27	27	27	23	23	23	23	23	23	27	27	27	27	27	23	23	23	20	20	20	20
77 BOTTAS	77	77	77	20	20	20	27	18	44	22	22	22	22	22	20	27	27	27	27	27	27	27	27	27	20	20	20	20	3	3	24	24	24	24	23	23	23	23	23	20	20	20	23	23	23	23
20 MAGNUSSEN	20	20	20	23	23	23	3	44	31	3	3	3	3	3	27	20	3	3	3	3	3	3	3	3	3	3	24	24	10	10	10	10	10	10	20	23	20	20	20	3	3	3	3	3	3	3
31 OCON	23	23	23	31	31	31	44	23	23	31	31	31	31	31	31	3	10	24	24	24	24	24	24	24	24	10	10	10	24	24	10	10	10	10	3	3	3	3	31	77	31	3	3	31	10	10
27 HÜLKENBERG	31	31	31	27	27	10	20	20	20	20	20	20	20	20	3	31	24	10	10	10	10	10	10	10	10	23	3	3	20	20	3	3	3	3	31	77	77	77	3	31	77	77	77	77	31	31
10 GASLY	27	27	27	10	10	23	23	3	3	23	23	23	23	23	77	77	77	77	77	77	77	77	77	77	77	77	77	77	77	77	77	77	77	77	77	31	31	31	77	77	77	77	31	24	24	24
3 RICCIARDO	10	10	10	3	24	3	24	24	24	24	24	77	77	77	31	31	31	31	31	31	31	31	31	31	31	31	31	31	31	31	31	31	31	31	24	24	24	24	24	24	24	24	24	24	24	24
24 ZHOU	3	3	3	24	3	24	77	77	77	77	77	77																																		
	24	24	24																																											

VSC Virtual Safety Car deployed on laps 17-18 and 57-58.

TIME SHEETS

PRACTICE 1 (FRIDAY)
Weather: Dry/sunny
Temperatures: track 37-39°C, air 20-21°C

Pos.	Driver	Laps	Time
1	Lando Norris	23	1m 18.564s
2	Max Verstappen	19	1m 18.582s
3	George Russell	21	1m 18.597s
4	Charles Leclerc	22	1m 18.599s
5	Yuki Tsunoda	26	1m 18.621s
6	Sergio Pérez	23	1m 18.642s
7	Lance Stroll	26	1m 18.667s
8	Carlos Sainz	23	1m 18.686s
9	Lewis Hamilton	20	1m 18.771s
10	Oscar Piastri	25	1m 18.918s
11	Daniel Ricciardo	25	1m 19.274s
12	Alexander Albon	11	1m 19.443s
13	Kevin Magnussen	21	1m 19.489s
14	Logan Sargeant	22	1m 19.519s
15	Esteban Ocon	25	1m 19.561s
16	Nico Hülkenberg	21	1m 19.604s
17	Pierre Gasly	25	1m 19.622s
18	Fernando Alonso	16	1m 19.716s
19	Zhou Guanyu	23	1m 19.989s
20	Valtteri Bottas	21	1m 20.014s

PRACTICE 2 (FRIDAY)
Weather: Dry/sunny
Temperatures: track 36-39°C, air 21°C

Pos.	Driver	Laps	Time
1	Charles Leclerc	26	1m 17.277s
2	Max Verstappen	21	1m 17.658s
3	Carlos Sainz	25	1m 17.707s
4	Lance Stroll	29	1m 17.822s
5	Fernando Alonso	31	1m 17.912s
6	George Russell	24	1m 17.951s
7	Oscar Piastri	29	1m 18.077s
8	Sergio Pérez	33	1m 18.090s
9	Lando Norris	23	1m 18.155s
10	Yuki Tsunoda	27	1m 18.188s
11	Zhou Guanyu	32	1m 18.421s
12	Daniel Ricciardo	30	1m 18.534s
13	Logan Sargeant	23	1m 18.578s
14	Valtteri Bottas	32	1m 18.585s
15	Pierre Gasly	33	1m 18.691s
16	Nico Hülkenberg	28	1m 18.702s
17	Esteban Ocon	32	1m 18.705s
18	Lewis Hamilton	23	1m 18.834s
19	Kevin Magnussen	31	1m 19.275s
-	Alexander Albon	-	-

PRACTICE 3 (SATURDAY)
Weather: Dry/overcast
Temperatures: track 28-31°C, air 18-19°C

Pos.	Driver	Laps	Time
1	Charles Leclerc	22	1m 16.714s
2	Max Verstappen	28	1m 16.734s
3	Carlos Sainz	20	1m 16.791s
4	Lewis Hamilton	20	1m 16.806s
5	George Russell	23	1m 16.886s
6	Fernando Alonso	20	1m 16.997s
7	Sergio Pérez	28	1m 17.014s
8	Oscar Piastri	19	1m 17.087s
9	Lance Stroll	22	1m 17.341s
10	Lando Norris	22	1m 17.490s
11	Yuki Tsunoda	19	1m 17.673s
12	Valtteri Bottas	20	1m 17.752s
13	Alexander Albon	23	1m 17.759s
14	Zhou Guanyu	19	1m 17.876s
15	Esteban Ocon	20	1m 17.920s
16	Nico Hülkenberg	17	1m 17.941s
17	Kevin Magnussen	18	1m 17.961s
18	Daniel Ricciardo	20	1m 17.963s
19	Pierre Gasly	19	1m 18.390s
-	Logan Sargeant	-	-

FOR THE RECORD

20th GP PODIUM & 1,000th POINT: Carlos Sainz

DID YOU KNOW?

There have only been two previous occasions where Ferrari finished 1st and 2nd, and McLaren finished 3rd and 4th (the 1974 Dutch GP and the 2007 Belgian GP.)

POINTS

DRIVERS

1	Max Verstappen	51
2	Charles Leclerc	47
3	Sergio Pérez	46
4	Carlos Sainz	40
5	Oscar Piastri	28
6	Lando Norris	27
7	George Russell	18
8	Fernando Alonso	16
9	Lance Stroll	9
10	Lewis Hamilton	8
11	Yuki Tsunoda	6
12	Oliver Bearman	6
13	Nico Hülkenberg	3
14	Kevin Magnussen	1

CONSTRUCTORS

1	Red Bull	97
2	Ferrari	93
3	McLaren	55
4	Mercedes	26
5	Aston Martin	25
6	RB	6
7	Haas	4

QUALIFYING (SATURDAY)
Weather: Dry/overcast Temperatures: track 34-36°C, air 19-20°C

Pos.	Driver	First	Second	Third	Qualifying Tyre
1	Max Verstappen	1m 16.819s	1m 16.387s	1m 15.915s	Soft (n)
2	Carlos Sainz	1m 16.731s	1m 16.189s	1m 16.185s	Soft (n)
3	Sergio Pérez	1m 16.805s	1m 16.631s	1m 16.274s	Soft (n)
4	Lando Norris	1m 17.430s	1m 16.750s	1m 16.315s	Soft (n)
5	Charles Leclerc	1m 16.984s	1m 16.304s	1m 16.435s	Soft (n)
6	Oscar Piastri	1m 17.369s	1m 16.601s	1m 16.572s	Soft (n)
7	George Russell	1m 17.062s	1m 16.901s	1m 16.724s	Soft (n)
8	Yuki Tsunoda	1m 17.356s	1m 16.791s	1m 16.788s	Soft (n)
9	Lance Stroll	1m 17.376s	1m 16.780s	1m 17.072s	Soft (n)
10	Fernando Alonso	1m 16.991s	1m 16.710s	1m 17.552s	Soft (n)
11	Lewis Hamilton	1m 17.499s	1m 16.960s		
12	Alexander Albon	1m 17.130s	1m 17.167s		
13	Valtteri Bottas	1m 17.543s	1m 17.340s		
14	Kevin Magnussen	1m 17.709s	1m 17.427s		
15	Esteban Ocon	1m 17.617s	1m 17.697s		
16	Nico Hülkenberg	1m 17.976s			
17	Pierre Gasly	1m 17.982s			
18	Daniel Ricciardo	1m 18.085s			
19	Zhou Guanyu	1m 18.188s			
-	Logan Sargeant	-			

QUALIFYING: head to head

Verstappen	3		0	Pérez
Hamilton	0		3	Russell
Norris	2		1	Piastri
Leclerc	1		1	Sainz
Leclerc	1		0	Bearman
Gasly	0		3	Ocon
Alonso	2		1	Stroll
Albon	3		0	Sargeant
Bottas	3		0	Zhou
Tsunoda	3		0	Ricciardo
Magnussen	2		1	Hülkenberg

 9 · STROLL · Aston Martin
 7 · RUSSELL · Mercedes
 5 · PIASTRI · McLaren
 3 · NORRIS · McLaren
 1 · VERSTAPPEN · Red Bull

10 · ALONSO · Aston Martin
8 · TSUNODA · RB
6 · PÉREZ · Red Bull
3-place grid penalty for impeding Hülkenberg during qualifying
4 · LECLERC · Ferrari
2 · SAINZ · Ferrari

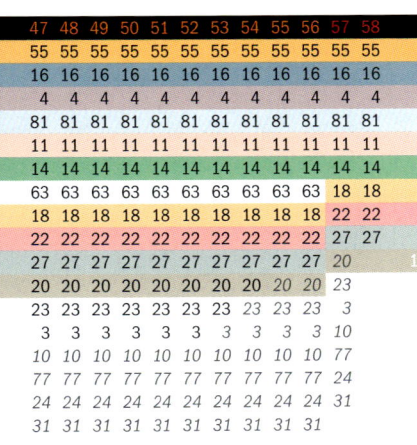

3 = Pit stop   24 = One lap or more behind

VSC VSC

RACE TYRE STRATEGIES

	Driver	Race Stint 1	Race Stint 2	Race Stint 3	Race Stint 4
1	Sainz	Medium (n): 1-16	Hard (n): 17-41	Hard (n): 42-58	
2	Leclerc	Medium (n): 1-9	Hard (n): 10-34	Hard (n): 35-58	
3	Norris	Medium (n): 1-14	Hard (u): 15-40	Hard (u): 41-58	
4	Piastri	Medium (n): 1-9	Hard (n): 10-39	Hard (u): 40-58	
5	Pérez	Medium (n): 1-14	Hard (n): 15-35	Hard (n): 36-58	
6	Stroll	Medium (u): 1-8	Hard (n): 9-37	Hard (n): 38-58	
7	Tsunoda	Medium (n): 1-9	Hard (n): 10-36	Hard (n): 37-58	
8	Alonso	Hard (u): 1-17	Medium (u): 18-41	Hard (n): 42-58	
9	Hülkenberg	Hard (n): 1-17	Medium (n): 18-35	Hard (n): 36-58	
10	Magnussen	Medium (n): 1-7	Hard (n): 8-33	Hard (n): 34-57	
11	Albon	Medium (n): 1-6	Hard (n): 7-27	Hard (n): 28-57	
12	Ricciardo	Soft (n): 1-5	Hard (n): 6-29	Hard (n): 30-57	
13	Gasly	Medium (n): 1-17	Hard (n): 18-41	Hard (n): 42-58	
14	Bottas	Medium (u): 1-8	Hard (n): 9-36	Hard (n): 37-57	
15	Zhou	Soft (n): 1-6	Hard (n): 7-35	Hard (n): 36-57	
16	Ocon	Medium (n): 1-9	Hard (n): 10-16	Hard (n): 17-42	Hard (u): 43-57
17	Russell	Medium (n): 1-8	Hard (n): 9-45	Hard (n): 46-56 (dnf)	
	Hamilton	Soft (n): 1-7	Hard (n): 8-15 (dnf)		
	Verstappen	Medium (n): 1-3 (dnf)			

The tyre regulations stipulate that at least two of three dry tyre specifications must be used during a dry race.
Selected compounds for Melbourne: Red = Soft (C5); Yellow = Medium (C4); White = Hard (C3). (n) new (u) used

SUZUKA QUALIFYING

FERRARI might have won in Melbourne, but the F1 circus arrived at Suzuka fully expecting Red Bull to be firmly back on top, at a circuit where the high-speed Esses of sector one in particular would reward the inherently superior downforce of the RB20.

But there were variables to add to the mix. First, this was a Japanese GP run in April, not late in the year as in the past, and the track/ambient temperatures on the opening day were 11 degrees lower – a different challenge in terms of achieving optimum tyre temperatures and a workable balance.

The opportunity for data gathering was also limited when the second session of free practice on Friday fell victim to the weather – not wet enough to use Pirelli intermediates, not dry enough for slicks.

Standout features of Friday's dry FP1 were improved pace and balance from the two Mercedes. The Red Bulls were indeed quickest, ahead of Melbourne winner Carlos Sainz's Ferrari, but George Russell and Lewis Hamilton managed to split the Maranello cars, Charles Leclerc having a difficult day. Hamilton said that it was the best the car had felt all year. Russell advised caution, though. We had seen pace from the W15 chassis before in cold conditions…

Sure enough, in Saturday's qualifying hour, the McLarens, whose Friday FP1 times had been set on used softs and thus were unrepresentative, were closest to Red Bull, just as they had been the previous September. And this time, it was Red Bulls plural, Sergio Pérez having done a fine job to qualify just 0.06s behind his three-times champion team-mate.

Verstappen, as normal whenever his team-mate gets anywhere near him, was relatively downbeat about his own efforts: "Yeah," he shrugged after his 36th F1 pole, "Not bad… It could have been a better lap, but it doesn't matter."

Whereas Max had lapped almost seven-tenths faster than at Suzuka six months before, Pérez had found almost double that! "I didn't open the lap in the best way, so maybe pole was possible," he mused.

Such was the relentless pace of development that every one of Red Bull's main rivals – McLaren, Ferrari, Aston Martin and Mercedes – also had at least one driver lapping a second or more quicker than six months previously!

For McLaren, that man was Lando Norris, who was just 0.29s behind Verstappen. The MCL36's strength was high-speed corners, and Norris, admirably, was nip and tuck with Verstappen through the Esses, losing his time on traction out of slow-speed corners and on straight-line speed. "A purple sector one is a good feeling!" Lando smiled, no doubt thrilled to have put one over on Verstappen.

For Ferrari, it was Carlos Sainz to the fore once again to qualify fourth, a couple of tenths down on his former team-mate. "I did some good laps in qualifying, where we'd made a step from FP3, and physically I'm feeling much better," he said.

If Carlos was happy with his performance, team-mate Charles Leclerc was not. Although he was only a tenth slower, such was the competitiveness of the fight behind Red Bull that he was four places further back, eighth. And that on a circuit where overtaking is tough.

The root of Leclerc's problem was a poor Q1 first run that required the use of a second set of softs, which translated into just the one Q3 run.

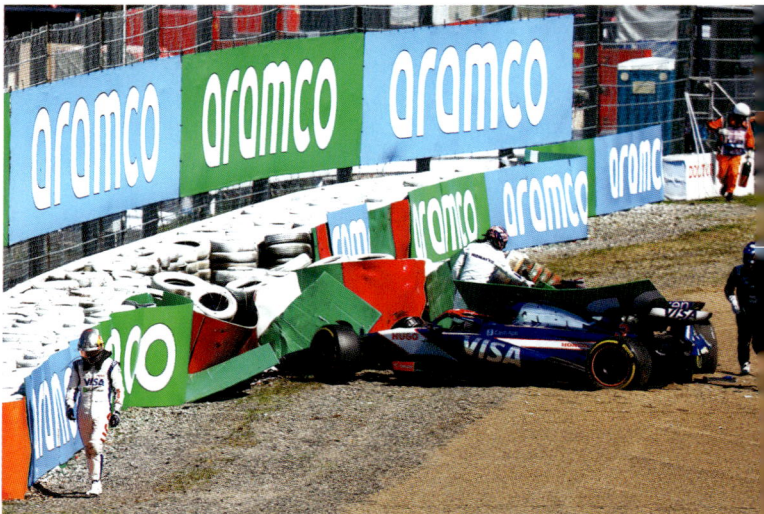

"It was one of those sessions you maybe get once a season," he explained. "Everything feels okay, the balance is not way off, but you look at the time sheet and you're a second off. When that happens, normally you look at the tyres and the way you've brought them up to temperature. I tried many different things today, none of which worked, and for now I don't have an answer. The positive is that our race pace looks a bit stronger."

Separating the Ferraris on the grid were Fernando Alonso's Aston Martin, Oscar Piastri's McLaren and Lewis Hamilton's Mercedes. Alonso was a mighty 1.9s quicker than six months previously, and he missed Sainz's second-row time by just a hundredth, while Piastri, Hamilton and Leclerc were blanketed by just two-hundredths.

"Both Q3 laps were risky and rewarding!" Alonso smiled. A grimacing Piastri admitted that it hadn't been his best of days, however, as he contemplated a time that was a quarter of a second behind his team-mate at a track where he had qualified on the front row the previous September. He identified sector two as his Achilles heel. Hamilton, much happier on Friday, was left to ask, "Where is that missing half-second?" (The gap to Verstappen.) But it was a step forward from the full second that had separated them in 2023.

Russell was outqualified by Hamilton for the first time in six races, 0.23s down, while Yuki Tsunoda qualified his VCARB in the top ten for the third consecutive race, to the delight of the home fans. But he was not thrilled with the balance and, like Leclerc, had just one set of softs after Q2, in which he pipped team-mate Daniel Ricciardo by 0.06s.

Nico Hülkenberg did his usual strong qualifying job to line up 12th, two-hundredths behind the Australian, with Valtteri Bottas putting the first Sauber 13th, ahead of Alex Albon's Williams and Esteban Ocon, who was delighted to haul his Alpine out of Q1.

The Q1 casualties were a bemused Lance Stroll (his significantly upgraded Aston Martin three-quarters of a second down on Alonso's sister car), Pierre Gasly's Alpine, Kevin Magnussen's Haas, Logan Sargeant's Williams and Zhou Guanyu with the second of the Saubers.

AS the grid formed up at Suzuka, it was Red Bull's 27th front-row lockout, although only its third in six years – after Abu Dhabi, 2022 and Bahrain, 2023. Which not only spoke volumes for Max Verstappen, but also raised questions about Sergio Pérez, depending on your point of view. The Red Bulls were clear favourites, but higher-than-predicted race-day track temperature – 40 degrees, the same as in 2023 – and potentially differing tyre strategies pointed to an absorbing race behind Verstappen…

Conventional wisdom said two stops due to the track's high thermal tyre degradation, as opposed to graining, which had been the concern in Melbourne. Red Bull and Ferrari had only one new set of the hard-compound Pirellis available for the race, while Mercedes and McLaren had two. Fernando Alonso, fifth on the grid for Aston Martin, had just one new set each of mediums and hards, and therefore would have to use the soft tyre at some stage. Logic suggested that this would be during the opening stint, not only to ensure a better launch, but also because of the highest likelihood of a safety car. Sure enough, when the tyre blankets came off, the Spaniard was on the red-walled tyre.

Thus second-row starters Lando Norris and Carlos Sainz were desperate to fend off the Aston Martin on the opening lap so as not to lose time behind it as Alonso's tyre condition dropped off. Fernando apart, the first 11 started on Pirelli's medium tyre, with 12th through 17th on the soft.

As the lights blinked out, Verstappen moved right to cover team-mate Pérez into the first corner, and Norris and Sainz managed to resist Alonso's challenge. The top ten all headed through the Esses in grid order, but further back, Yuki Tsunoda did not get the greatest of getaways on his mediums, causing a bottleneck out of Turn Two. Team-mate Daniel Ricciardo was baulked, and Lance Stroll, racy on his Pirelli softs from P16, tried to go around the RB's outside.

Ricciardo, looking in his left-hand mirror, jinked right to avoid the Aston just as Alex Albon shaped to go by on the other side. The RB and the Williams departed stage right and hard into the tyre barrier, bringing out the red flag. Thankfully, both drivers were okay and out of their cars.

After a half-hour delay, the grid reformed with the remaining 18 cars. Because the field had gone through a timing sector, the new starting order allowed Nico Hülkenberg and Valtteri Bottas to keep the elevated tenth and eleventh places they had gained on their original softs after passing the slow-starting Tsunoda. Perhaps more significantly, both seventh-placed Lewis Hamilton and ninth-placed George Russell had switched to the hard-compound Pirelli. The red flag had dispensed with the need to use different compounds, and now Mercedes could potentially execute a one-stopper using their two sets of hards.

The only medium-tyred leading runner behind Hamilton was Charles Leclerc, who did not want to become stuck behind a potentially slower car through his first stint and managed to squeeze inside his future Ferrari team-mate through the Esses. Tsunoda, on the soft tyre this time, also relegated Russell in the second Mercedes.

Verstappen led from Pérez, then Norris, Sainz, Alonso, Oscar Piastri, Leclerc, Hamilton, Tsunoda, Russell, Esteban Ocon, Bottas, Stroll, Pierre Gasly (who had Turn One contact with team-mate Ocon), Kevin Magnussen, Zhou Guanyu, Hülkenberg (who bogged down off the line when the anti-stall kicked in) and Logan Sargeant.

With DRS available down the front straight on lap two, Russell demoted Tsunoda, and Bottas passed Ocon. The order remained stable until the first of the leading runners pitted. This was not Alonso on his softs, as might

Above: The Red Bulls take charge from the start. Max Verstappen and team-mate Sergio Pérez cover off Oscar Piastri, while Carlos Sainz's Ferrari attacks from the other side.
Photo: Red Bull Content Pool/Getty Images

Top left: Zhou Guanyu had plenty of enthusiastic local support.
Photo: Atsuo Sakurai

Above left: Out of sight and out of mind? Formula 2 winner Ayumu Iwasa, now back in Super Formula, was given an FP1 outing with RB.
Photo: Red Bull Content Pool/Getty Images

Left: The crash between Ricciardo and Albon caused a red flag on the opening lap.
Photo: XPB Images

Below left: Imaginary F1 driver Brad Pitt joined the fan mayhem.

Opening spread: Giant banners bearing the images of the drivers flutter in the breeze behind an expectant Suzuka crowd.
Photos: Atsuo Sakurai

Above: Sign here. Carlos Sainz and Charles Leclerc get to grips with Japanese calligraphy at a Ferrari media event.
Photo: Scuderia Ferrari

Top right: Once again, Fernando Alonso split the 'big four' with his sixth place for Aston Martin.
Photo: Aramco Aston Martin F1 Team

Above right: Logan Sargeant's troubled season continued at Suzuka, the Williams driver being the last classified finisher.
Photo: Williams Racing

Right: A third second place in four races for Sergio Pérez.
Photo: Red Bull Content Pool/Getty Images

have been expected, but Lando Norris, who was in just 12 laps into the 53. He rejoined tenth on hards, 5s behind Stroll's Aston.

Piastri was in next time around, McLaren stopping early to cover off potential Ferrari undercuts by Sainz and Leclerc. A couple of seconds behind the second Ferrari, Hamilton would have been expecting his hard-compound Pirellis to start paying dividends as the race progressed, but, in fact, he was struggling with understeer that he figured had been caused by slight damage sustained in a contact with Leclerc on the opening lap. Lewis duly radioed in to ask whether he should let team-mate Russell by, the two Mercs swapping places a lap later.

Alonso now brought his Aston in to go from the softs to mediums and cover off Piastri. At the time of the McLaren stops, Verstappen had a 4.5s margin over team-mate Pérez, with Sainz a similar distance behind the second Red Bull. The Ferrari, now in clean air, actually started to reduce the Mexican's margin, prompting a call from Red Bull to pit before Carlos entered undercut range, both men coming in on lap 16. The two cars rejoined on mediums, with Pérez around 4s behind the early-stopping Norris, but with a softer tyre and a five-lap delta that Red Bull figured would make overtaking straightforward.

The race leader was in a lap later and rejoined still third, just half a second down on Russell's hard-tyred, long-running Mercedes. Leclerc now led by 4s, doing a decent job of eking out a longer stint on his starting mediums, his lowly eighth starting position more or less forcing the strategy upon Ferrari.

Soon it became evident that the extra grip from the fresh Pirellis meant that Norris and Pérez would not be delayed much in traffic. The former ran around the outside of Hamilton into Turn One, and the latter made his move on the Mercedes down the inside of 130R! And, for good measure, repeated the manoeuvre on Russell a lap later.

After just 19 laps, Hamilton was on the radio to Mercedes, reporting of his hard-compound Pirellis that "the tyres are dropping, the front right is dead." He had Sainz right behind him, the Ferrari demoting the Mercedes into Spoon Curve.

On lap 21, Verstappen retook the lead from Leclerc, who nevertheless was doing a sterling job on his starting mediums, still obtaining good pace from them, despite having opened a 13s advantage over seventh-placed Hamilton since passing him early on.

"Change this strategy!" the seven-times champion radioed as Alonso's medium-shod Aston Martin started to reel him in.

"Copy, Lewis, yeah," replied Pete Bonnington. "We are just waiting for the window to clear."

By then, Sainz had caught the lead Mercedes and repeated his Spoon move on Russell to go fifth, some 7s behind Pérez's Red Bull. Meanwhile, Hamilton also had to give best to Alonso's Aston on a fesh set of mediums.

At the front, Verstappen was continuing his serene progress and extending his advantage over Leclerc, who had yet to stop and was just 3s ahead of Pérez in the second Red Bull, the Mexican passing third-placed Norris into the chicane on lap 22.

Next time around, Russell was in for a fresh set of hards. Further back in the midfield, Tsunoda, Magnussen, Stroll, Bottas and Sargeant all piled in at the same time.

A good stop by the VCARB boys was appreciated by the home crowd and set up Tsunoda for some points at home.

On lap 24, Hamilton finally had a window and came in for a new set of boots, rejoining almost 7s behind his team-mate.

"How did I lose so much time?" Lewis wanted to know. "Just traffic and degradation," Bonnington explained.

At half-distance, Leclerc ran wide at the first Degner, letting Pérez through to make it a comfortable Red Bull 1-2 and signalling that his starting mediums had just about had enough. Norris was right on the back of the Ferrari and, despite being just 14 laps into his hard-tyre stint, received the instruction to "Box this lap.'

"Why so early?" he asked, but you didn't need to be Einstein to see that the plan was to undercut the long-running Leclerc. There was also concern about Russell's reshod Mercedes, which was on the cusp of Lando's pit window and had just set a new race fastest lap. Predictably, Ferrari responded by bringing in Leclerc on the same lap as Norris. Ferrari managed a 2.4s stop for Charles, with Mercedes a couple of tenths slower for George. As they blasted back into the fray, Leclerc cleared Russell's Mercedes by the skin of his teeth, while Norris was forced to drop in behind the Mercedes.

He wasn't there for long, despite Russell's hards being just four laps older, the McLaren sweeping around the outside of the Mercedes into Turns One and Two, then setting off after Leclerc. McLaren had not expected to be behind the latter, who had started eighth, at this juncture.

In the other McLaren, Piastri made a more conventionally-timed stop with 20 laps remaining, rejoining 12s adrift of Hamilton on significantly fresher

Above: After his third successive win at Suzuka, Max Verstappen's domination of the race appeared to be an ominous portent for the remainder of the season.

Top right: Three 1-2 finishes in four races for the Red Bull duo.

Above right: Tsunoda celebrates his tenth place to record the first point scored by a Japanese driver at his home race since 2012.

Photos: Red Bull Content Pool/Getty Images

Right: A tough race for Mercedes, Lewis Hamilton being unable to resist the challenge of Piastri in their battle for eighth place.

Photo: Mercedes-AMG Petronas F1 Team

rubber. Behind them, Tsunoda and Stroll, battling for what was likely to be the final point, had caught Hülkenberg on old hards. This might have afforded the Aston an opportunity had Tsunoda not pulled off a great outside pass in the final part of the Esses, to the delight of the crowd.

Pérez made his second stop on lap 34, as did Alonso, the Aston coming out in eighth, still ahead of Piastri's McLaren. Versappen was in next time around for his final stop, which put Sainz, who had yet to stop, into the lead. Max rejoined still ahead of Leclerc, who had Norris 2s behind, Lando now with Pérez breathing down his neck.

Sainz, his medium-compound tyres now 20 laps old, was on the radio to Ferrari: "Let's box soon, I think I'm going to lose time here." The team told him that a bigger offset would be better in the closing laps, so, for the moment, he kept going.

Pérez, with tyres that were seven laps older, made short work of Leclerc's Ferrari, pulling a DRS pass into Turns One and Two to take third, just 8s behind his dominant team-mate, re-establishing a Red Bull 1-2 when Sainz pitted on lap 37. The Ferrari rejoined seventh on its new hards, just over 10s behind team-mate Leclerc, who occupied the last podium position, but Sainz had Hamilton, Russell and Norris to get through first. He made short work of Hamilton, easing down the inside of the Mercedes into Turn One with DRS, while Russell vacated fifth when he abandoned the one-stop plan and pitted for fresh mediums on lap 38, with 15 to go.

Hamilton went a similar route on lap 40 and rejoined 9s behind his team-mate on tyres that were just three laps newer. Lewis might have been the quicker Mercedes in qualifying this time, but George was driving the quicker race on a disappointing afternoon for Mercedes.

"What's the gap ahead?" Lewis wanted to know. "We've lost even more time."

"Yeah, it looks like we lost a bit of time on the in-lap," he was told.

With ten laps to go, Verstappen led Pérez by 10s and Red Bull was set fair for another 1-2, but the final podium place was up for grabs. Leclerc had a tenuous hold on it, some 7.5s behind Pérez, but Norris was just 2s behind him and had Sainz, with his healthy tyre offset, bearing down on him. When Norris suffered a lock-up into Turn 11, the second Ferrari was quickly upon him Carlos making the simplest of DRS passes down the inside into Turn One.

Vasseur-era Ferrari does not do gratuitous team orders, and rather than a "Hold station", the message that went out from the pit wall was to Leclerc and was, "We are racing Norris." In other words, don't take Carlos off and look after your tyres as much as possible.

Charles made his team-mate work for it, but on a higher-degradation surface, with fresher tyres and DRS, there was no resisting Sainz, who maintained his record of finishing on the podium at every race so far in 2024.

Leclerc appeared to have Norris's McLaren under control for fourth place, but 13s further back down the road, Alonso's Aston Martin was under pressure from Piastri's McLaren for sixth, with Russell just half a second behind and closing on his fresh mediums. Knowing all about George's pace, however, Alonso was cannily allowing the young Aussie to stay within DRS range to offer a bit of help in keeping Russell at bay.

With three to go, Russell made a late lunge down the inside of Piastri's McLaren into the hairpin, but Oscar braved it out and kept the position. But he had lost his DRS assistance from Alonso by a tenth, and on the last lap, there was nothing he could do to stop the Mercedes from going by down the inside into Turn One.

After the blip in Melbourne, Red Bull was back, Verstappen taking a 57th GP victory and third straight Japanese win ahead of team-mate Pérez.

The Ferraris were third and fourth across the line, Leclerc beating Norris to the chequer by 3s. Lando was not convinced that the early stop had been the correct call, team principal Andrea Stella admitting that the strategy had put him at a significant disadvantage in terms of total race time on a day when tyre degradation had meant that track position was not all.

Behind Russell and Piastri, Hamilton could do no better than ninth. Some 48s further back, Tsunoda was happy to be the first Japanese driver to score points in a home race since Kamui Kobayashi in 2012.

Tony Dodgins

VIEWPOINT
NO-POINTED STAR

THIS was Mercedes' worst result at Suzuka in over a decade. Lewis Hamilton (a four-times winner at the track) finished ninth, two places behind George Russell. Another statistic Hamilton didn't need reminding of was having failed, for the first time in 17 seasons, to finish higher than sixth in the opening four races. The dire results for both drivers were stark proof of a car that was not working – for the third year running.

The fundamental problem of not truly understanding the implication of the so-called ground-effect formula had stayed with Mercedes from the radical zero-pod W13 of 2022, right through to the latest iteration, W15. There would be flashes of promise, created by an extremely narrow sweet spot, but exacerbated by a knife-edge car that was not working on the track in the same way it had done in the wind tunnel.

Continual tweaks and upgrades could not cure the underlying problem of balance. Signs of desperation had been evident, for instance, in a higher-downforce rear wing that suddenly appeared during FP3 in Jeddah.

"We've had something of a front-limited car all year, especially in the lower-speed corners," said Mercedes technical director James Allison. "Once you've got front tyres that don't want to go around the corner, that means the drivers have to wait an eon to get on the power on the exit of the corner, and you haemorrhage lap time there. In extremis, actually to make the car go around the corner, they have to boot it around the corner with the throttle to loosen up the rear end somewhat, and that kills the rear tyres. So we end up overheating on the rear as a result of being front limited."

At Suzuka, the best Mercedes was 45s away from a win – excusable in part thanks to Red Bull's dominance, but less acceptable because of the 25s deficit to the best non-Red Bull. Mercedes had been expecting to lead the charge, not struggle along in the second division's wake with a car that was consistent only as far as the regular periods of disappointment it was heaping upon this increasingly beleaguered team from one race to the next.

Maurice Hamilton

4

FORMULA 1 MSC CRUISES JAPANESE GRAND PRIX 2024

SUZUKA 05-07 APRIL

RACE DISTANCE: 53 laps, 191.054 miles/307.471km

RACE WEATHER: Dry/sunny-overcast (track 32-39°C, air 22-30°C)

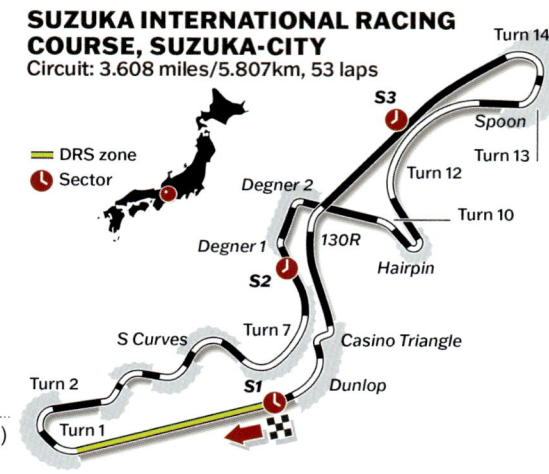

SUZUKA INTERNATIONAL RACING COURSE, SUZUKA-CITY
Circuit: 3.608 miles/5.807km, 53 laps

RACE – OFFICIAL CLASSIFICATION

Pos.	Driver	Nat.	No.	Entrant	Car/Engine	Laps	Time/Retirement	Speed (mph/km/h)	Gap to leader	Fastest race lap	
1	**Max Verstappen**	NL	1	Oracle Red Bull Racing	Red Bull RB20-Honda RBPT H002 V6	53	1h 54m 23.566s	100.209/161.271		1m 33.706s	50
2	**Sergio Pérez**	MEX	11	Oracle Red Bull Racing	Red Bull RB20-Honda RBPT H002 V6	53	1h 54m 36.101s	100.026/160.977	12.535s	1m 33.945s	35
3	**Carlos Sainz**	E	55	Scuderia Ferrari	Ferrari SF-24-066/12 V6	53	1h 54m 44.432s	99.905/160.782	20.866s	1m 33.841s	46
4	**Charles Leclerc**	MC	16	Scuderia Ferrari	Ferrari SF-24-066/12 V6	53	1h 54m 50.088s	99.823/160.650	26.522s	1m 35.044s	53
5	**Lando Norris**	GB	4	McLaren Formula 1 Team	McLaren MCL38-Mercedes F1 M15 E Perf. V6	53	1h 54m 53.266s	99.777/160.576	29.700s	1m 35.186s	51
6	**Fernando Alonso**	E	14	Aston Martin Aramco F1 Team	Aston Martin AMR24-Mercedes F1 M15 E Perf. V6	53	1h 55m 07.838s	99.567/160.237	44.272s	1m 34.726s	53
7	**George Russell**	GB	63	Mercedes-AMG Petronas F1 Team	Mercedes-AMG F1 W15-M15 E Perf. V6	53	1h 55m 09.517s	99.542/160.198	45.951s	1m 34.404s	39
8	**Oscar Piastri**	AUS	81	McLaren Formula 1 Team	McLaren MCL38-Mercedes F1 M15 E Perf. V6	53	1h 55m 11.091s	99.520/160.162	47.525s	1m 34.802s	35
9	**Lewis Hamilton**	GB	44	Mercedes-AMG Petronas F1 Team	Mercedes-AMG F1 W15-M15 E Perf. V6	53	1h 55m 12.192s	99.504/160.136	48.626s	1m 33.952s	41
10	Yuki Tsunoda	J	22	Visa Cash App RB Formula One Team	RB VCARB 01-Honda RBPT H002 V6	52			1 lap	1m 36.342s	51
11	Nico Hülkenberg	D	27	MoneyGram Haas F1 Team	Haas VF-24-Ferrari 066/10 V6	52			1 lap	1m 35.325s	52
12	Lance Stroll	CDN	18	Aston Martin Aramco F1 Team	Aston Martin AMR24-Mercedes F1 M15 E Perf. V6	52			1 lap	1m 35.798s	41
13	Kevin Magnussen	DK	20	MoneyGram Haas F1 Team	Haas VF-24-Ferrari 066/10 V6	52			1 lap	1m 36.654s	24
14	Valtteri Bottas	FIN	77	Stake F1 Team Kick Sauber	Sauber C44-Ferrari 066/12 V6	52			1 lap	1m 36.608s	25
15	Esteban Ocon	F	31	BWT Alpine F1 Team	Alpine A524-Renault E-Tech RE24 V6	52			1 lap	1m 36.232s	52
16	Pierre Gasly	F	10	BWT Alpine F1 Team	Alpine A524-Renault E-Tech RE24 V6	52			1 lap	1m 36.642s	48
17	Logan Sargeant	USA	2	Williams Racing	Williams FW46-Mercedes F1 M15 E Perf. V6	52			1 lap	1m 34.900s	43
	Zhou Guanyu	CHN	24	Stake F1 Team Kick Sauber	Sauber C44-Ferrari 066/12 V6	12	gearbox			1m 37.160s	9
	Daniel Ricciardo	AUS	3	Visa Cash App RB Formula One Team	RB VCARB 01-Honda RBPT H002 V6	0	accident			no time	
	Alexander Albon	T	23	Williams Racing	Williams FW46-Mercedes F1 M15 E Perf. V6	0	accident			no time	

The race was red-flagged on lap 1, following the crash of Albon and Ricciardo. After around 25 minutes, the race resumed from a standing start, for the remaining laps.

DHL Fastest race lap (scores 1 point): Max Verstappen on lap 50, 1m 33.706s, 138.624mph/223.093km/h.

Lap record: Lewis Hamilton (Mercedes F1 W10 V6), 1m 30.983s, 142.773mph/229.770 km/h (2019).

19 · SARGEANT · Williams   17 · GASLY · Alpine   15 · OCON · Alpine   13 · BOTTAS · Sauber   11 · RICCIARDO · RB

20 · ZHOU · Sauber   18 · MAGNUSSEN · Haas   16 · STROLL · Aston Martin   14 · ALBON · Williams   12 · HÜLKENBERG · Haas

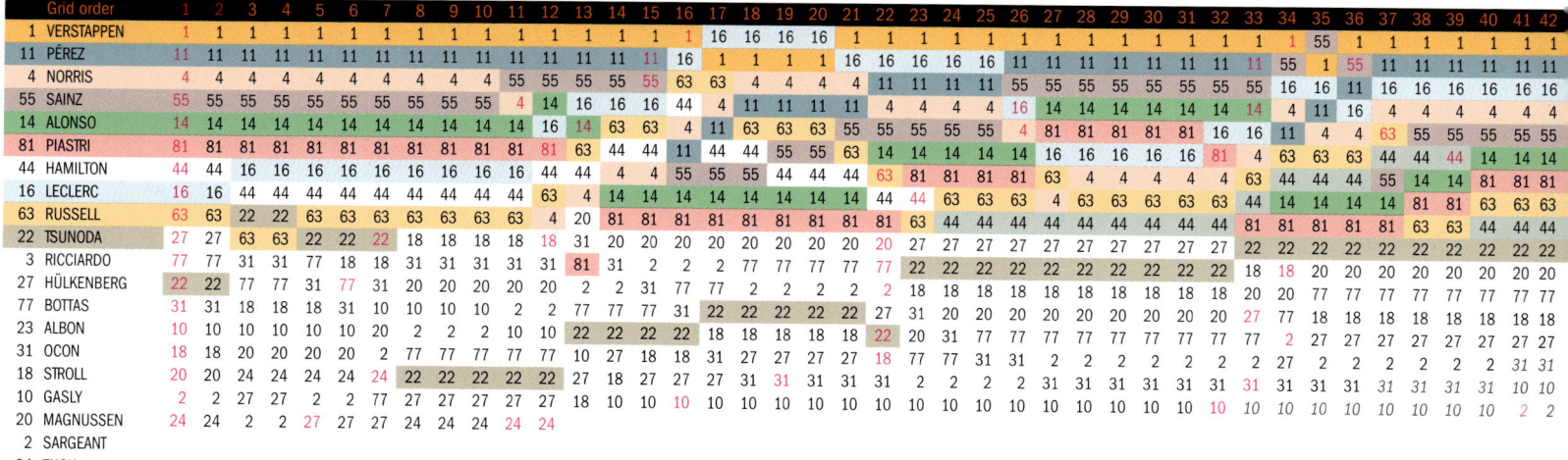

Race red-flagged on lap 1   SC Safety Car deployed on laps 1-2

TIME SHEETS

PRACTICE 1 (FRIDAY)
Weather: Dry/overcast
Temperatures: track 23-25°C, air 17-19°C

Pos.	Driver	Laps	Time
1	Max Verstappen	18	1m 30.056s
2	Sergio Pérez	18	1m 30.237s
3	Carlos Sainz	20	1m 30.269s
4	George Russell	18	1m 30.530s
5	Lewis Hamilton	23	1m 30.543s
6	Charles Leclerc	18	1m 30.558s
7	Fernando Alonso	20	1m 30.599s
8	Oscar Piastri	23	1m 31.165s
9	Yuki Tsunoda	20	1m 31.230s
10	Lando Norris	22	1m 31.240s
11	Esteban Ocon	19	1m 31.935s
12	Alexander Albon	18	1m 31.943s
13	Nico Hülkenberg	19	1m 31.958s
14	Valtteri Bottas	17	1m 32.054s
15	Lance Stroll	17	1m 32.055s
16	Ayumu Iwasa	22	1m 32.103s
17	Pierre Gasly	23	1m 32.277s
18	Zhou Guanyu	18	1m 32.638s
19	Kevin Magnussen	21	1m 32.803s
20	Logan Sargeant	10	1m 33.204s

PRACTICE 2 (FRIDAY)
Weather: Rain/overcast
Temperatures: track 16-17°C, air 12°C

Pos.	Driver	Laps	Time
1	Oscar Piastri	7	1m 34.725s
2	Lewis Hamilton	6	1m 35.226s
3	Charles Leclerc	4	1m 38.760s
4	Yuki Tsunoda	8	1m 40.946s
5	Daniel Ricciardo	9	1m 41.913s
6	Zhou Guanyu	7	no time
7	Valtteri Bottas	7	no time
8	Alexander Albon	5	no time
9	Kevin Magnussen	4	no time
10	Nico Hülkenberg	5	no time
11	Carlos Sainz	3	no time
12	Lando Norris	3	no time
13	Esteban Ocon	3	no time
-	Fernando Alonso	-	-
-	Pierre Gasly	-	-
-	Sergio Pérez	-	-
-	George Russell	-	-
-	Logan Sargeant	-	-
-	Lance Stroll	-	-
-	Max Verstappen	-	-

PRACTICE 3 (SATURDAY)
Weather: Dry/sunny
Temperatures: track 25-29°C, air 20-23°C

Pos.	Driver	Laps	Time
1	Max Verstappen	23	1m 29.563s
2	Sergio Pérez	25	1m 29.832s
3	George Russell	24	1m 29.918s
4	Lewis Hamilton	21	1m 30.037s
5	Fernando Alonso	24	1m 30.082s
6	Lando Norris	14	1m 30.137s
7	Carlos Sainz	27	1m 30.171s
8	Oscar Piastri	19	1m 30.226s
9	Yuki Tsunoda	21	1m 30.341s
10	Charles Leclerc	25	1m 30.383s
11	Alexander Albon	23	1m 30.533s
12	Valtteri Bottas	26	1m 30.546s
13	Daniel Ricciardo	24	1m 30.682s
14	Esteban Ocon	18	1m 31.022s
15	Zhou Guanyu	16	1m 31.067s
16	Nico Hülkenberg	21	1m 31.139s
17	Pierre Gasly	19	1m 31.141s
18	Lance Stroll	23	1m 31.342s
19	Logan Sargeant	20	1m 31.452s
20	Kevin Magnussen	22	1m 31.462s

QUALIFYING (SATURDAY)
Weather: Dry/overcast   Temperatures: track 24-27°C, air 18-20°C

Pos.	Driver	First	Second	Third	Qualifying Tyre
1	Max Verstappen	1m 28.866s	1m 28.740s	1m 28.197s	Soft (n)
2	Sergio Pérez	1m 29.303s	1m 28.752s	1m 28.263s	Soft (n)
3	Lando Norris	1m 29.536s	1m 28.940s	1m 28.489s	Soft (n)
4	Carlos Sainz	1m 29.513s	1m 29.099s	1m 28.682s	Soft (n)
5	Fernando Alonso	1m 29.254s	1m 29.082s	1m 28.686s	Soft (n)
6	Oscar Piastri	1m 29.425s	1m 29.148s	1m 28.760s	Soft (n)
7	Lewis Hamilton	1m 29.661s	1m 28.887s	1m 28.766s	Soft (n)
8	Charles Leclerc	1m 29.338s	1m 29.196s	1m 28.786s	Soft (n)
9	George Russell	1m 29.799s	1m 29.140s	1m 29.008s	Soft (n)
10	Yuki Tsunoda	1m 29.775s	1m 29.417s	1m 29.413s	Soft (n)
11	Daniel Ricciardo	1m 29.727s	1m 29.472s		
12	Nico Hülkenberg	1m 29.821s	1m 29.494s		
13	Valtteri Bottas	1m 29.602s	1m 29.593s		
14	Alexander Albon	1m 29.963s	1m 29.714s		
15	Esteban Ocon	1m 29.811s	1m 29.816s		
16	Lance Stroll	1m 30.024s			
17	Pierre Gasly	1m 30.119s			
18	Kevin Magnussen	1m 30.131s			
19	Logan Sargeant	1m 30.139s			
20	Zhou Guanyu	1m 30.143s			

QUALIFYING: head to head

Verstappen	4	0	Pérez
Hamilton	1	3	Russell
Norris	3	1	Piastri
Leclerc	1	2	Sainz
Leclerc	1	0	Bearman
Gasly	0	4	Ocon
Alonso	3	1	Stroll
Albon	4	0	Sargeant
Bottas	4	0	Zhou
Tsunoda	4	0	Ricciardo
Magnussen	2	2	Hülkenberg

FOR THE RECORD

3,000th GP LAP LED: Max Verstappen

DID YOU KNOW?

This was the 40th World Championship GP in Japan (including the two Pacific GPs).

Verstappen has now won 30 GPs from pole. He stands 4th in the all-time list of wins from pole behind Lewis Hamilton, Michael Schumacher and Sebastian Vettel.

POINTS

DRIVERS

1	Max Verstappen	77
2	Sergio Pérez	64
3	Charles Leclerc	59
4	Carlos Sainz	55
5	Lando Norris	37
6	Oscar Piastri	32
7	George Russell	24
8	Fernando Alonso	24
9	Lewis Hamilton	10
10	Lance Stroll	9
11	Yuki Tsunoda	7
12	Oliver Bearman	6
13	Nico Hülkenberg	3
14	Kevin Magnussen	1

CONSTRUCTORS

1	Red Bull	141
2	Ferrari	120
3	McLaren	69
4	Mercedes	34
5	Aston Martin	33
6	RB	7
7	Haas	4

 9 · RUSSELL · Mercedes
 7 · HAMILTON · Mercedes
 5 · ALONSO · Aston Martin
 3 · NORRIS · McLaren
 1 · VERSTAPPEN · Red Bull

10 · TSUNODA · RB   8 · LECLERC · Ferrari   6 · PIASTRI · McLaren   4 · SAINZ · Ferrari   2 · PÉREZ · Red Bull

RACE TYRE STRATEGIES

	Driver	Race Stint 1	Race Stint 2	Race Stint 3	Race Stint 4	Race Stint 5
1	Verstappen	Medium (n): 1-16	Medium (n): 17-34	Hard (n): 35-53		
2	Pérez	Medium (n): 1-15	Hard (n): 16-33	Hard (n): 34-53		
3	Sainz	Medium (n): 1	Medium (n): 2-15	Medium (u): 16-36	Hard (n): 37-53	
4	Leclerc	Medium (n): 1	Medium (n): 2-26	Hard (n): 27-53		
5	Norris	Medium (n): 1-11	Hard (n): 12-26	Hard (n): 27-53		
6	Alonso	Soft (n): 1-13	Medium (n): 14-33	Hard (n): 34-53		
7	Russell	Medium (n): 1	Hard (n): 2-22	Hard (n): 23-37	Medium (u): 38-53	
8	Piastri	Medium (n): 1-12	Hard (n): 13-32	Hard (n): 33-53		
9	Hamilton	Medium (n): 1	Hard (n): 2-23	Hard (n): 24-39	Medium (u): 40-53	
10	Tsunoda	Hard (n): 1	Soft (u): 2-7	Hard (n): 8-22	Medium (n): 23-52	
11	Hülkenberg	Soft (n): 1-5	Hard (n): 6-33	Hard (n): 34-52		
12	Stroll	Soft (n): 1	Soft (n): 2-12	Medium (n): 13-22	Hard (n): 23-34	Soft (n): 35-52
13	Magnussen	Medium (n): 1	Medium (n): 2-22	Hard (n): 23-52		
14	Bottas	Soft (n): 1-6	Hard (n): 7-22	Hard (n): 23-52		
15	Ocon	Soft (n): 1	Hard (n): 2-19	Hard (n): 20-33	Medium (n): 34-52	
16	Gasly	Soft (n): 1	Hard (n): 2-16	Medium (n): 17-32	Hard (n): 33-52	
17	Sargeant	Soft (n): 1	Hard (n): 2-22	Hard (n): 23-34	Medium (n): 35-41	Soft (n): 42-52
	Zhou	Medium (n): 1	Soft (n): 2-7	Hard (n): 8-12 (dnf)		
	Ricciardo	Medium (n): 0 (dnf)				
	Albon	Soft (n): 0 (dnf)				

The tyre regulations stipulate that at least two of three dry tyre specifications must be used during a dry race.
Selected compounds for Suzuka: Red = Soft (C3); Yellow = Medium (C2); White = Hard (C1). (n) new (u) used

1 = Pit stop   10 = One lap or more behind

FIA FORMULA 1 WORLD CHAMPIONSHIP · ROUND 5
CHINESE GRAND PRIX
SHANGHAI INTERNATIONAL CIRCUIT

SHANGHAI QUALIFYING/SPRINT QUALIFYING & RACE

FORMULA 1's return to the Shanghai International Circuit for the first time since 2019 coincided with the first of six 2024 sprint events, which were run to a revised format. The previous arrangement, introduced in 2021, had Saturday as a stand-alone sprint day, with qualifying for the main GP on Friday afternoon, after just one free practice session in the morning. What many teams and drivers regarded as a largely redundant practice session followed on Saturday morning, while the afternoon's sprint set the grid for Sunday's main event.

Drivers were often reluctant to take risks in the sprint because any mishap threatened to hinder their chances disproportionately in the main race. Thus for 2024, Friday afternoon qualifying would set the grid for the 100km sprint race rather than the main event, the sprint taking place on Saturday morning, but no longer setting the grid for the main race, which would have its own qualifying session on Saturday afternoon. With the number of sprints increased from three to six, the remainder would follow on in Miami, Austin, Austin, Brazil and Qatar.

On an overcast Friday morning, we were treated to the unusual sight of small fires bordering the track at Turns Five and Seven as the skid plates of the low-running cars threw up sparks and set fire to the grass!

In SQ (sprint qualifying) 1, both Alpines, both Williams and Yuki Tsunoda's VCARB were eliminated. The rain forecast for SQ2 duly arrived at the end of the medium-shod second session, when we lost George Russell's Mercedes by 0.03s, the Haas cars of Kevin Magnussen and Nico Hülkenberg, Daniel Ricciardo's VCARB and Lance Stroll's Aston Martin. To the great delight of a packed main grandstand, Zhou Guanyu made it through to SQ3, along with Sauber team-mate Valtteri Bottas!

The intermediate Pirellis were required for SQ3, with rain and a gripless surface producing a spinning Charles Leclerc – he got away with it – and an ever-changing lottery of an order. The McLarens appeared to be quick, but when Lando Norris ran wide out of the final corner and exceeded track limits, his pace-setting time was deleted, Lewis Hamilton's Mercedes topping the times in the dying seconds. However, Norris went back to the top before that lap, too, was initially deleted.

The rules state that if a driver exceeds track limits out of the final corner, he loses that lap and the following one, ostensibly because he has a flying start to the next lap. On this occasion, however, it could be proved that Norris's excursion had actually cost him time, so common sense was applied and his session-heading final lap was reinstated. Nobody seemed to have any real gripe. The order behind Hamilton was Fernando Alonso, Max Verstappen, Carlos Sainz, Sergio Pérez, Leclerc, Oscar Piastri, and then Sauber drivers Bottas and Zhou.

On a track with a dry racing line and the field on slicks, Hamilton made the best getaway and thrust his Mercedes down the inside of the pole-position McLaren into Shanghai's corkscrew sequence of early corners. Norris unwisely tried to brave it out around the outside to have the inside line for Turn Three. Predictably, Hamilton ushered him wide, and all of Lando's qualifying work was undone as he dropped to eighth.

Initially, it was a return to yesteryear as Hamilton battled Alonso, before Verstappen got into his stride and relieved the Aston Martin of second place seven laps into the race's 19. Two laps later, he was past the lead Mercedes down the inside of the Turn 14 hairpin, and that was that.

With three laps to go, there was a great scrap as Alonso tried to hang on to third under pressure from Sainz, Pérez and Leclerc. The fighting Spaniards allowed Pérez to pull an opportunistic move on both. Alonso also lost out to Sainz and, in an attempt to take the place back with a lunge down the inside of Turn Nine, suffered a puncture, forcing him to pit.

Leclerc was now snapping at his team-mate and was unimpressed when Sainz drove him wide at the exit of Turn 14, but ultimately he was able to battle his way past to claim fourth. McLaren had to be content with sixth and seventh for Norris and Piastri respectively, with Russell bagging the final point for eighth. Home hero Zhou just missed out, a further 6s back.

It felt a little odd returning to qualifying mode after the morning sprint on Saturday, but that's what the new format decreed, and it was a dry track that greeted drivers.

The shock of Q1 was Lewis Hamilton's elimination after his seven-point haul from the sprint race. Joining him on the sidelines after the opening salvo were Zhou (who missed out by just 0.04s), Kevin Magnussen, a dejected Tsunoda and Logan Sargeant after a spin.

Sainz provided the drama in Q2 when he dropped his Ferrari out of the final turn and spun lightly into the tyres on the opposite side of the track, bringing out the red flag. He kept the engine alive, though, got it back to the pits and, in a reflection of the confidence with which he was driving, finished the session third quickest, ahead of team-mate Leclerc. Bottas did a great job to put a Sauber into Q3, pipping Stroll by 0.06s. The other eliminees were Ricciardo, Ocon, Albon and Gasly.

Verstappen always had a fifth successive 2024 pole within his grasp, the first time a driver had achieved that at the start of a season since Mika Häkkinen in 1999. It was also a milestone 100th pole for Red Bull. Behind him, the other front-row slot had been hard-fought. Ultimately, Pérez made it with the second RB20, 0.32s behind his team leader.

Alonso qualified a fine third for Aston Martin, ahead of the Norris/Piastri McLarens. The Australian pipped Leclerc to fifth by a hundredth, with Charles beating team-mate Sainz by the same margin. Russell put the lead Mercedes eighth, from Hülkenberg's Haas and Bottas's Sauber.

Right: Norris runs wide at the start, blowing his pole position.
Photo: XPB Images

Left: The world champion's Red Bull usurped early leader Hamilton at half-distance in the sprint.

Below far right: Hamilton led after his lap-one opportunism, but had no answer to Verstappen's pace.
Photos: Red Bull Content Pool/Getty Images

Below right: A delighted Fernando Alonso after qualifying third for the sprint race.
Photo: Aramco Aston Martin F1 Team

Bottom: Nico Hülkenberg and Alonso jockey for position in the pit-lane scramble for sprint qualifying.
Photo: XPB Images

Opening spread: Max Verstappen takes the lead from Lando Norris on lap 19 on his way to a fifth grand prix win of the year.
Photo: Red Bull Content Pool/Getty Images

Above: Alonso leads Pérez, Norris, Piastri, Russell, Leclerc and the rest across the line at the end of the opening lap.
Photo: Atsuo Sakurai

Top right: With the field under the safety car, Ricciardo's RB is rear-ended by Lance Stroll's Aston.
Photo: XPB Images

Above right: Lewis Hamilton fans were prominent in Shanghai.
Photo: Atsuo Sakurai

Right: Under grey skies, McLaren mechanics prepare their cars for Lando Norris and Oscar Piastri.
Photo: McLaren F1 Team

MAX VERSTAPPEN seldom fails to convert a pole position, and he did so again in China. Fernando Alonso seldom fails to position his car in exactly the right place with controlled aggression on the opening lap, and he demonstrated that once more in Shanghai by making a proper job of what Norris had tried to do to Hamilton in the sprint, successfully demoting Sergio Pérez and grabbing second place.

Norris emerged fourth from the corkscrew sort-out, ahead of McLaren team-mate Oscar Piastri, then George Russell's Mercedes and Nico Hülkenberg's Haas. 'The Hulk' was in his 208th grand prix, equalling the late Andrea de Cesaris's record for the most races contested without a win.

The Ferraris of Charles Leclerc and Carlos Sainz ran eighth and ninth after Leclerc had evened the score with his team-mate for Turn 14 in the sprint, running him wide at the first corner when Carlos somewhat optimistically had a look at the outside. Dead last, apart from Logan Sargeant's Williams, which had started from the pits, was none other than Lewis Hamilton…

It was a mixed opening lap for the two VCARBs. Daniel Ricciardo, having outqualified Yuki Tsunoda for the first time in 2024, fell three places to 15th. Meanwhile, the Japanese driver, who, like Stroll, Hamilton and Sargeant, had opted for the soft-compound Pirelli with the rest of the field on mediums, picked up three slots to run right behind him.

The Ferraris wasted little time in demoting Hülkenberg; two places further back, Alex Albon was less than happy with Esteban Ocon's defence of 12th place: "This guy is moving like a **** everywhere on the brakes…"

Hamilton, unimpressed by the soft tyre in terms of facilitating a chance to make early progress, finally got a move done to relegate Zhou's 18th-placed Sauber, but it looked like being a long afternoon for the seven-times champion. Stroll, on his softs, had managed to pass Hülkenberg for ninth, but had been noted for forcing the Haas off-track.

Verstappen drove serenely away at a second per lap over the opening five laps, while his team-mate tried to find a way back past Alonso. With his natural racer's instinct, the Spaniard resisted for as long as possible, prompting McLaren to tell fourth-placed Norris, "Fernando is pushing his tyres much harder than us. This is good." Alonso finally realised the futility of his defence and allowed Pérez down the inside of Turn Six, making it a Red Bull 1-2.

A couple of laps later, Norris also got by Alonso to put his McLaren into the top three. In sixth, Russell had come under heavy pressure from Leclerc's Ferrari, which demoted the Mercedes around the outside into Turn One on lap 9.

Three laps later, Leclerc had caught Piastri's McLaren and went down the inside of the McLaren into Turn 14 to claim fifth. "I'm happy to go longer if we need to, but the pace is this," Charles told Ferrari.

Race leader Verstappen was into the pits after 14 laps, swapping his starting mediums for a set of hard-compound Pirellis, with Pérez also pitting. Max rejoined fourth, behind Norris, Leclerc and Piastri, but just ahead of Sainz's fifth-placed Ferrari.

In the pits, meanwhile, Alpine had a problematic stop for Pierre Gasly, the right rear wheel not properly affixed as he moved off. The wheel-changer on that corner was sent tumbling, thankfully without serious injury, while Pierre, realising the situation, applied the brakes.

McLaren pulled in Piastri for a second set of mediums on lap 17, Oscar dropping to ninth, while Ferrari was on the radio to Leclerc asking, "What do you think about Plan D for Delta?"

"If you are happy with this pace, yes," Leclerc

FIA FORMULA 1 WORLD CHAMPIONSHIP

responded, suggesting that, after his fine opening stint on mediums the previous time out in Japan, Ferrari was contemplating another one-stopper.

Meanwhile, team-mate Sainz was under heavy pressure from Pérez for fourth, the Red Bull going by the Ferrari at Turn 14. The Spaniard pitted from seventh for a new set of hards on lap 19, the Ferrari rejoining just ahead of Bottas's Sauber and quickly reclaiming a place from Hülkenberg's Haas.

The two-stopping Verstappen was back into the race lead by one-third-distance as he overhauled Norris, who looked as though a one-stop race was the plan.

Further back, the VCARBs were still together, with Ricciardo finally battling his way past Tsunoda on a track where, for once, he appeared to have the upper hand.

On lap 21, Bottas ground to a halt at Turn 11 with a power unit failure. With Race Control initiating a VSC period, Leclerc got a well-timed pit stop on to the hard compound, the Ferrari rejoining fifth on its fresh rubber, just behind Alonso's Aston. Hamilton also took the opportunity to stop for a new set of boots, while Norris, for the moment, continued on, which was a little unfathomable. But, with the Sauber still stranded, the VSC period lasted long enough for Lando to get in next time around.

By lap 23, the VSC had been upgraded to a full safety car. By the time it ended, a lap prior to half-distance, the order behind Bernd Maylander was Verstappen, Norris, Leclerc, Pérez, Sainz, Alonso, Russell, Piastri, Hülkenberg, Ricciardo, Ocon, Hamilton, Tsunoda, Magnussen, Albon, Sargeant, Zhou and Gasly, with Stroll's Aston in the pits. Pulling off in the second sector with a flat right rear tyre was Tsunoda.

Behind the safety car, Stroll had heavily rammed the back of Ricciardo's VCARB as the field bunched up into the hairpin.

"This idiot just slammed on the brake, check for wing

Above: Sergio Pérez holds off the McLarens of Norris and Piastri.
Photo: Red Bull Content Pool/Getty Images

Top right: A nice moment for Zhou Guanyu, who was allowed to take the post-race plaudits at the finish.
Photo: Stake F1 Team Kick Sauber

Right: Alex Albon sported a panda-inspired helmet for the race.
Photo: Williams Racing

Below right: Tyre issues kept Charles Leclerc from challenging for a place on the podium.
Photo: Scuderia Ferrari

Far right: Lando Norris was surprised, but delighted, with his unexpected second place.
Photo: XPB Images

damage," Stroll radioed. But Ricciardo had braked to avoid Piastri in front of him, and Stroll would soon receive a 10s penalty. Daniel hadn't quite managed to avoid his countryman, however, and consequently Oscar had reduced rear downforce for the rest of the afternoon.

Meanwhile, Tsunoda had been involved in an entirely separate incident when he was the victim of a late lunge by Kevin Magnussen at Turn Six, for which the Dane would also receive a 10s penalty. The safety car was deployed again while Tsunoda's car was removed, finally pulling off again on lap 31, with 25 laps remaining.

While most of the front-runners had taken on hard-compound Pirellis at their free pit stop, Alonso had a new set of softs available and was going to be interesting to watch. He hassled Pérez for fourth place for a while, but the edge soon went off the red-walled tyres.

As a result of his assault by Stroll, Ricciardo had lost so much rear downforce that soon he was going backwards, ceding places to Hamilton, Ocon and Albon. "I've got no rear on exits," he confirmed to RB, which prompted the decision to retire the car – a black afternoon for the team.

Ricciardo, always level headed, nonetheless was frustrated with Stroll. "It wasn't a little misjudgement, it was miles off," he said later. "I've watched his onboard, and he's not even looking at me, he's looking in his mirror or at the apex of the corner. It's a restart, you know, you have to be vigilant…"

Sargeant, after his pit-lane start, was enjoying one of his stronger races, but it was scuppered by a 10s penalty when he was adjudged to have passed Hülkenberg under safety car conditions. Nico had been emerging from the pits and had narrowly beaten the Floridian to the safety car line. Sargeant didn't realise that and was somewhat bemused as to why neither Race Control nor his team had told him to drop back behind the Haas, feeling that the time addition and two licence penalty points were somewhat harsh.

On lap 39, Pérez thrust his Red Bull down the inside of Leclerc's Ferrari at Turn Six to move back up to third place, setting his sights on Norris's second-placed McLaren, some 5s further up the road.

Lando had been struggling a little with understeer, the team suggesting that he increase the amount of engine braking. Doing that is a little like putting in a bit of handbrake as the car is turned in, helping it to rotate. The trade-off is an increase in rear tyre temperature and wear, so he declined their invitation.

Alonso had had enough of his soft tyres by lap 44 and was in from seventh place to swap them for mediums, rejoining out of the points in 12th place, but on rubber that was at least 20 laps newer than all of those ahead of him. He was soon lapping at least 2s quicker, and made short work of Albon, Ocon and Hülkenberg. Hamilton's eighth-placed Mercedes was just 2.5s ahead and only 1.5s behind Piastri.

With seven laps remaining, Alonso suffered an almighty tank-slapper out of the final corner as he came within DRS range of Hamilton, but somehow he gathered it together – nothing at all wrong with his 42-year-old reactions! He demoted Hamilton down the inside of Turn Six, and Piastri had to give best at the hairpin as the Aston returned to the seventh place it had been in when Alonso had jettisoned his softs. Now, however, it had the benefit of an additional point for fastest lap.

Five races, and four wins for Verstappen as he cruised across the finish line 10s clear of Norris, who took his 15th F1 podium.

Depressingly for Red Bull's rivals, the world champion reported that the RP20 had "felt amazing, basically on rails. I could do whatever I wanted with it."

If that wasn't entirely surprising, second place for Norris came as something of a shock for McLaren. "We came here thinking that it was damage limitation so, clearly, we have to fine-tune something in our understanding!" smiled team principal Andrea Stella. His driver admitted that he'd taken a wager with engineer Will Joseph that Ferrari would be half a minute quicker for race pace given the performance in Saturday's sprint. It was a bonus that the team was more than happy to take.

Leclerc, too, had been surprised at McLaren's race pace, as the Ferraris could do no better than fourth and fifth. "I thought that we would be able to put Lando under pressure," he said, "and on the medium tyre, we were okay, but as soon as we put the hard tyres on, they were half a second quicker, which is difficult to understand. There's nothing too positive to take away from a weekend like this, but we hope the game-changer will be the upgrades." But they would not arrive until the Imola race, a month away.

Tony Dodgins

VIEWPOINT
ORANGE OPTIMISM

BEFORE the grand prix, Lando Norris genuinely did not expect to have the pace of the Ferraris across 56 laps. He based his prediction on the McLaren's performance during the sprint race on the previous day. Even allowing for him being pessimistic (in his usual self-deprecating way), after having blown the sprint start from pole, this seemed a reasonable prophecy based on a race where he had finished sixth, and had struggled to match Sainz and Leclerc.

Things were different on Sunday. The ambient temperature and the wind had dropped. Unlike in the sprint, Norris found that he was able to move ahead of Fernando Alonso's Aston Martin and easily control his pace for the rest of the race. So much so that he was only 14 seconds off Max Verstappen's winning Red Bull, albeit after a safety car, and capable of preventing Sergio Pérez from making it a Red Bull clean sweep.

Despite all that Norris had said going into the race, keeping Red Bull honest was not such a surprise in the overall scheme of things. From the early days of testing, Lando had spoken about being able to fight against Red Bull and possibly taking a win at some point in 2024. Given his penchant for keeping expectations in check, this was clearly not a familiar F1 public relations sound bite.

"I still feel the same," Norris reiterated after the race in Shanghai. "Okay, it's not going to come easy and it's not going to come for a while. But, the right day, right time and good conditions which suit our car a little bit more, then 100 per cent I have faith in the team and my ability to be able to pull it off. But it does need to be right place, right time. I don't think we're close enough for the time being, but I want to believe. It's not often that I have faith in something, whether it's myself or whatever it is I'm trying to change, but that's how I feel right now."

It was encouraging news, not just for Norris and McLaren fans, but also for anyone hoping for a change in script – which included just about everyone bar Red Bull. And it turned out to be prophetic…

Maurice Hamilton

5

FORMULA 1 LENOVO CHINESE GRAND PRIX 2024

SHANGHAI 19–21 APRIL

RACE DISTANCE: 56 laps, 189.559 miles/305.066km
RACE WEATHER: Dry/cloudy (track 26–30° C, air 20–22° C)

SHANGHAI INTERNATIONAL CIRCUIT
Circuit: 3.387 miles/5.451km, 56 laps

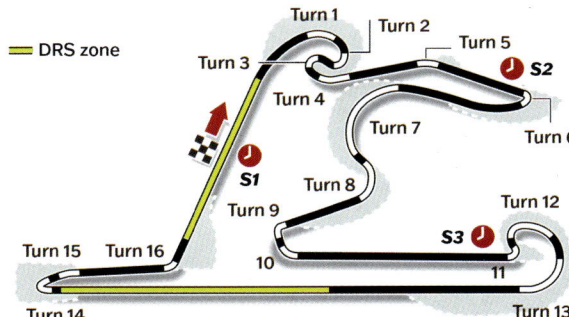

RACE – OFFICIAL CLASSIFICATION

Pos.	Driver	Nat.	No.	Entrant	Car/Engine	Laps	Time/Retirement	Speed (mph/km/h)	Gap to leader	Fastest race lap
1	Max Verstappen	NL	1	Oracle Red Bull Racing	Red Bull RB20-Honda RBPT H002 V6	56	1h 40m 52.554s	112.748/181.450		1m 38.406s 33
2	Lando Norris	GB	4	McLaren Formula 1 Team	McLaren MCL38-Mercedes F1 M15 E Perf. V6	56	1h 41m 06.327s	112.492/181.038	13.773s	1m 38.751s 33
3	Sergio Pérez	MEX	11	Oracle Red Bull Racing	Red Bull RB20-Honda RBPT H002 V6	56	1h 41m 11.714s	112.392/180.877	19.160s	1m 39.388s 33
4	Charles Leclerc	MC	16	Scuderia Ferrari	Ferrari SF-24-066/12 V6	56	1h 41m 16.177s	112.309/180.744	23.623s	1m 39.384s 33
5	Carlos Sainz	E	55	Scuderia Ferrari	Ferrari SF-24-066/12 V6	56	1h 41m 26.537s	112.118/180.437	33.983s	1m 39.764s 19
6	George Russell	GB	63	Mercedes-AMG Petronas F1 Team	Mercedes-AMG F1 W15-M15 E Perf. V6	56	1h 41m 31.278s	112.031/180.296	38.724s	1m 40.112s 39
7	Fernando Alonso	E	14	Aston Martin Aramco F1 Team	Aston Martin AMR24-Mercedes F1 M15 E Perf. V6	56	1h 41m 35.968s	111.945/180.158	43.414s	1m 37.810s 45
8	Oscar Piastri	AUS	81	McLaren Formula 1 Team	McLaren MCL38-Mercedes F1 M15 E Perf. V6	56	1h 41m 48.752s	111.711/179.781	56.198s	1m 39.739s 18
9	Lewis Hamilton	GB	44	Mercedes-AMG Petronas F1 Team	Mercedes-AMG F1 W15-M15 E Perf. V6	56	1h 41m 50.540s	111.678/179.728	57.986s	1m 40.835s 34
10	Nico Hülkenberg	D	27	MoneyGram Haas F1 Team	Haas VF-24-Ferrari 066/10 V6	56	1h 41m 53.030s	111.632/179.655	1m 00.476s	1m 40.815s 32
11	Esteban Ocon	F	31	BWT Alpine F1 Team	Alpine A524-Renault E-Tech RE24 V6	56	1h 41m 55.366s	111.590/179.586	1m 02.812s	1m 40.937s 33
12	Alexander Albon	T	23	Williams Racing	Williams FW46-Mercedes F1 M15 E Perf. V6	56	1h 41m 58.060s	111.540/179.507	1m 05.506s	1m 40.790s 34
13	Pierre Gasly	F	10	BWT Alpine F1 Team	Alpine A524-Renault E-Tech RE24 V6	56	1h 42m 01.777s	111.473/179.398	1m 09.223s	1m 39.198s 40
14	Zhou Guanyu	CHN	24	Stake F1 Team Kick Sauber	Sauber C44-Ferrari 066/12 V6	56	1h 42m 04.243s	111.428/179.326	1m 11.689s	1m 38.633s 42
15	Lance Stroll	CDN	18	Aston Martin Aramco F1 Team	Aston Martin AMR24-Mercedes F1 M15 E Perf. V6	56	1h 42m 15.340s *	111.226/179.001	1m 22.786s	1m 39.444s 37
16	Kevin Magnussen	DK	20	MoneyGram Haas F1 Team	Haas VF-24-Ferrari 066/10 V6	56	1h 42m 20.087s *	111.140/178.863	1m 27.533s	1m 41.077s 45
17	Logan Sargeant	USA	2	Williams Racing	Williams FW46-Mercedes F1 M15 E Perf. V6	56	1h 42m 27.664s *	111.004/178.643	1m 35.110s	1m 41.000s 14
	Daniel Ricciardo	AUS	3	Visa Cash App RB Formula One Team	RB VCARB 01-Honda RBPT H002 V6	33	accident damage			1m 40.994s 16
	Yuki Tsunoda	J	22	Visa Cash App RB Formula One Team	RB VCARB 01-Honda RBPT H002 V6	26	accident			1m 41.593s 11
	Valtteri Bottas	FIN	77	Stake F1 Team Kick Sauber	Sauber C44-Ferrari 066/12 V6	19	engine			1m 41.276s 11

* Magnussen: 10s time penalty for causing a collision with Tsunoda (originally finished 15th),   * Sargeant: 10s time penalty for overtaking under Safety Car conditions.
* Stroll: 10s time penalty for causing a collision with Ricciardo (served at pit stop).

DHL Fastest race lap (scores 1 point): Fernando Alonso on lap 45, 1m 37.810s, 124.666mph/200.629km/h.

Lap record: Michael Schumacher (Ferrari F2004 V10), 1m 32.238s, 132.196mph/212.749km/h (2004).

19 · TSUNODA · RB   17 · MAGNUSSEN · Haas   15 · GASLY · Alpine   13 · OCON · Alpine   11 · STROLL · Aston Martin

20 · SARGEANT · Williams   18 · HAMILTON · Mercedes   16 · ZHOU · Sauber   14 · ALBON · Williams   12 · RICCIARDO · RB
Car modified in parc fermé; required to start from the pit lane

Grid order	1	2	3	4	5	6	7	8	9	10	11	12	13	14	15	16	17	18	19	20	21	22	23	24	25	26	27	28	29	30	31	32	33	34	35	36	37	38	39	40	41	42	43	44	45	46	47
1 VERSTAPPEN	1	1	1	1	1	1	1	1	1	1	1	1	1	4	4	4	4	4	1	1	1	1	1	1	1	1	1	1	1	1	1	1	1	1	1	1	1	1	1	1	1	1	1	1	1	1	1
11 PÉREZ	14	14	14	14	11	11	11	11	11	11	11	11	4	16	16	1	1	1	4	4	4	4	4	11	4	4	4	4	4	4	4	4	4	4	4	4	4	4	4	4	4	4	4	4	4	4	4
14 ALONSO	11	11	11	11	14	14	4	4	4	4	4	4	11	1	1	16	16	16	16	16	16	16	16	4	16	16	16	16	16	16	16	16	16	16	16	16	11	11	11	11	11	11	11	11	11	11	11
4 NORRIS	4	4	4	4	4	4	14	14	14	14	16	16	16	81	81	55	11	11	11	11	11	16	14	16	11	11	11	11	11	11	11	11	11	11	11	16	16	16	16	16	16	16	16	16	16	16	16
81 PIASTRI	81	81	81	81	81	81	81	81	81	81	81	81	55	55	11	55	14	14	14	14	14	14	16	14	81	55	55	14	14	14	14	14	14	14	14	14	14	14	14	14	14	14	55	55	55	55	55
16 LECLERC	63	63	63	63	63	63	63	63	63	16	16	55	55	11	11	81	14	63	63	63	63	63	81	55	14	14	55	55	55	55	55	55	55	55	55	55	55	55	55	55	55	55	63	63	63	63	63
55 SAINZ	16	16	16	16	16	16	16	16	63	63	14	3	3	14	14	14	63	81	81	81	81	81	63	14	63	63	63	63	63	63	63	63	63	63	63	63	63	63	63	63	63	63	14	81	81	81	81
63 RUSSELL	27	55	55	55	55	55	55	55	55	55	63	20	14	63	63	63	18	18	18	18	18	55	55	63	55	81	81	81	81	81	81	81	81	81	81	81	81	81	81	81	81	81	81	44	44	44	44
27 HÜLKENBERG	55	18	18	18	18	18	18	18	18	18	18	18	10	3	14	63	3	55	55	55	55	18	27	81	27	27	3	3	3	3	27	44	44	44	44	44	44	44	44	44	44	44	44	27	27	31	27
77 BOTTAS	18	27	27	27	27	27	77	77	10	3	20	63	20	20	20	27	27	31	27	27	27	31	3	18	18	3	27	27	27	27	44	44	27	27	27	27	27	44	44	44	44	44	27	31	31	14	31
18 STROLL	77	77	77	77	77	77	27	31	77	20	10	18	18	27	27	77	77	77	31	31	31	3	31	27	31	44	44	44	44	44	31	31	31	31	31	31	31	31	31	31	31	31	31	23	14	23	14
3 RICCIARDO	31	31	31	31	31	31	31	23	3	2	2	27	27	77	77	31	31	44	3	22	18	2	44	31	3	31	31	31	31	31	3	23	23	23	23	23	23	23	23	23	23	23	23	14	23	23	23
31 OCON	23	23	23	23	23	23	10	31	18	18	27	77	77	31	31	44	44	44	3	2	22	31	44	20	23	23	23	23	23	23	23	2	2	2	2	2	2	10	24	2	2	2	20	20	20	20	20
23 ALBON	10	10	10	10	10	10	10	3	23	27	77	77	31	44	44	20	22	3	22	44	3	22	20	22	22	22	2	10	10	10	10	10	10	10	10	2	2	2	2	20	20	20	2	2	2	2	2
10 GASLY	3	3	3	3	3	3	3	27	20	77	22	22	22	22	22	3	22	22	23	3	44	44	24	3	24	2	10	2	2	2	2	2	2	2	2	10	10	24	10	10	10	10	10	10	10	24	24
24 ZHOU	22	22	22	22	22	22	44	2	31	31	44	22	23	23	23	22	2	24	2	10	10	10	10	23	10	10	10	24	24	24	24	24	24	24	10	24	24	10	10	24	24	24	24	24	24	24	10
20 MAGNUSSEN	24	20	20	44	44	44	44	20	44	22	23	44	23	3	22	2	44	44	2	24	20	20	22	24	20	20	20	20	20	18	20	18	18	18	18	18	18	18	18	18	18	18	18	18	18	18	18
44 HAMILTON	20	24	44	20	20	20	2	27	23	44	44	23	44	24	2	24	10	10	10	20	2	24	23	10	24	24	24	18	18	18	18	18	3														
22 TSUNODA	44	44	24	24	24	24	22	22	44	23	24	2	2	10	10	10	20	20	20	20	20	10	10	10	18																						
2 SARGEANT	2	2	2	2	2	2	24	24	24	24	10	10	10	10	10	10	10	20	20																												

VSC Virtual Safety Car deployed on laps 22–23   SC Safety Car deployed on laps 24–31   1 = Pit stop   10 = One lap or more behind

TIME SHEETS

PRACTICE 1 (FRIDAY)
Weather: Dry/cloudy
Temperatures: track 40-41°C, air 25-27°C

Pos.	Driver	Laps	Time
1	Lance Stroll	21	1m 36.302s
2	Oscar Piastri	24	1m 36.629s
3	Max Verstappen	25	1m 36.660s
4	Sergio Pérez	24	1m 36.690s
5	Nico Hülkenberg	23	1m 37.101s
6	Kevin Magnussen	23	1m 37.118s
7	Esteban Ocon	23	1m 37.213s
8	Alexander Albon	19	1m 37.229s
9	Daniel Ricciardo	25	1m 37.238s
10	Valtteri Bottas	24	1m 37.530s
11	Zhou Guanyu	24	1m 37.626s
12	Yuki Tsunoda	27	1m 38.006s
13	Charles Leclerc	20	1m 38.090s
14	Carlos Sainz	19	1m 38.284s
15	Logan Sargeant	23	1m 38.286s
16	Lando Norris	21	1m 38.630s
17	George Russell	21	1m 38.806s
18	Lewis Hamilton	24	1m 38.839s
19	Fernando Alonso	22	1m 38.936s
20	Pierre Gasly	21	1m 39.276s

SPRINT QUALIFYING (FRIDAY)
Weather: Dry-wet/cloudy
Temperatures: track 24-29°C, air 18-22°C

Pos.	Driver	First	Second	Third	Qualifying Tyre
1	Lando Norris	1m 36.384s	1m 36.047s	1m 57.940s	Soft (n)
2	Lewis Hamilton	1m 37.181s	1m 36.287s	1m 59.201s	Soft (n)
3	Fernando Alonso	1m 36.883s	1m 36.119s	1m 59.915s	Soft (n)
4	Max Verstappen	1m 36.456s	1m 35.606s	2m 00.028s	Soft (n)
5	Carlos Sainz	1m 36.719s	1m 36.052s	2m 00.214s	Soft (n)
6	Sergio Pérez	1m 36.110s	1m 35.781s	2m 00.375s	Soft (n)
7	Charles Leclerc	1m 36.537s	1m 35.711s	2m 00.566s	Soft (n)
8	Oscar Piastri	1m 36.542s	1m 35.853s	2m 00.990s	Soft (n)
9	Valtteri Bottas	1m 37.112s	1m 36.056s	2m 01.044s	Soft (n)
10	Zhou Guanyu	1m 37.544s	1m 36.307s	2m 03.537s	Soft (n)
11	George Russell	1m 37.310s	1m 36.345s		
12	Kevin Magnussen	1m 37.033s	1m 36.473s		
13	Nico Hülkenberg	1m 36.924s	1m 36.478s		
14	Daniel Ricciardo	1m 37.321s	1m 36.553s		
15	Lance Stroll	1m 36.961s	1m 36.677s		
16	Pierre Gasly	1m 37.632s			
17	Esteban Ocon	1m 37.720s			
18	Alexander Albon	1m 37.812s			
19	Yuki Tsunoda	1m 37.892s			
20	Logan Sargeant	1m 37.923s			

FOR THE RECORD

10,000th GP LAP RACED: Carlos Sainz

100th GP POLE POSITION: Red Bull

QUALIFYING: head to head

Verstappen	5	0	Pérez
Hamilton	1	4	Russell
Norris	4	1	Piastri
Leclerc	2	2	Sainz
Leclerc	1	0	Bearman
Gasly	0	5	Ocon
Alonso	4	1	Stroll
Albon	5	0	Sargeant
Bottas	5	0	Zhou
Tsunoda	4	1	Ricciardo
Magnussen	2	3	Hülkenberg

QUALIFYING (SATURDAY)
Weather: Dry/sunny
Temperatures: track 31-34°C, air 23-24°C

Pos.	Driver	First	Second	Third	Qualifying Tyre
1	Max Verstappen	1m 34.742s	1m 33.794s	1m 33.660s	Soft (n)
2	Sergio Pérez	1m 35.457s	1m 34.026s	1m 33.982s	Soft (n)
3	Fernando Alonso	1m 35.116s	1m 34.652s	1m 34.148s	Soft (n)
4	Lando Norris	1m 34.842s	1m 34.460s	1m 34.165s	Soft (n)
5	Oscar Piastri	1m 35.014s	1m 34.659s	1m 34.273s	Soft (n)
6	Charles Leclerc	1m 34.797s	1m 34.399s	1m 34.289s	Soft (n)
7	Carlos Sainz	1m 34.970s	1m 34.368s	1m 34.297s	Soft (n)
8	George Russell	1m 35.084s	1m 34.609s	1m 34.433s	Soft (n)
9	Nico Hülkenberg	1m 35.068s	1m 34.667s	1m 34.604s	Soft (n)
10	Valtteri Bottas	1m 35.169s	1m 34.769s	1m 34.665s	Soft (n)
11	Lance Stroll	1m 35.334s	1m 34.838s		
12	Daniel Ricciardo	1m 35.443s	1m 34.934s		
13	Esteban Ocon	1m 35.356s	1m 35.223s		
14	Alexander Albon	1m 35.384s	1m 35.241s		
15	Pierre Gasly	1m 35.287s	1m 35.463s		
16	Zhou Guanyu	1m 35.505s			
17	Kevin Magnussen	1m 35.516s			
18	Lewis Hamilton	1m 35.573s			
19	Yuki Tsunoda	1m 35.746s			
20	Logan Sargeant	1m 36.358s			

SPRINT (SATURDAY)
RACE DISTANCE: 19 laps, 64.237 miles/103.379km
RACE WEATHER: Dry/cloudy Temperatures: track 26-28°C, air 20-21°C

Pos.	Driver	Laps	Time/Retirement	Speed (mph/km/h)	Gap to leader	Fastest race lap		Grid
1	**Max Verstappen**	19	32m 04.660s	120.152/193.366		1m 40.331s	3	4
2	**Lewis Hamilton**	19	32m 17.703s	119.343/192.064	13.043s	1m 40.420s	3	2
3	**Sergio Pérez**	19	32m 19.918s	119.207/191.845	15.258s	1m 41.065s	4	6
4	**Charles Leclerc**	19	32m 22.146s	119.070/191.625	17.486s	1m 41.003s	4	7
5	**Carlos Sainz**	19	32m 25.356s	118.874/191.309	20.696s	1m 40.962s	4	5
6	**Lando Norris**	19	32m 26.748s	118.789/191.172	22.088s	1m 40.951s	4	1
7	**Oscar Piastri**	19	32m 29.373s	118.628/190.914	24.713s	1m 41.107s	3	8
8	**George Russell**	19	32m 30.356s	118.569/190.818	25.696s	1m 41.505s	5	11
9	Zhou Guanyu	19	32m 36.611s	118.190/190.208	31.951s	1m 41.502s	5	10
10	Kevin Magnussen	19	32m 42.058s	117.862/189.680	37.398s	1m 42.092s	5	12
11	Daniel Ricciardo	19	32m 42.500s	117.835/189.637	37.840s	1m 42.234s	6	14
12	Valtteri Bottas	19	32m 42.955s	117.808/189.593	38.295s	1m 42.140s	6	9
13	Esteban Ocon	19	32m 44.501s	117.715/189.444	39.841s	1m 42.191s	4	17
14	Lance Stroll	19	32m 44.959s	117.688/189.400	40.299s	1m 42.258s	5	15
15	Pierre Gasly	19	32m 45.498s	117.655/189.348	40.838s	1m 42.017s	4	16
16	Yuki Tsunoda	19	32m 46.530s	117.594/189.249	41.870s	1m 42.056s	4	19
17	Alexander Albon	19	32m 47.658s	117.526/189.140	42.998s	1m 42.389s	8	18
18	Logan Sargeant	19	32m 51.012s	117.326/188.818	46.352s	1m 42.516s	7	20
19	Nico Hülkenberg	19	32m 54.290s	117.132/188.505	49.630s	1m 42.315s	5	13
20	Fernando Alonso	17	accident damage *		2 laps	1m 40.537s	3	3

* 10s time penalty for causing a collision with Sainz

Fastest race lap: Max Verstappen on lap 3, 1m 40.331s, 121.533mph/195.588km/h.

9 · HÜLKENBERG · Haas

7 · SAINZ · Ferrari

5 · PIASTRI · McLaren

3 · ALONSO · Aston Martin

1 · VERSTAPPEN · Red Bull

10 · BOTTAS · Sauber   8 · RUSSELL · Mercedes   6 · LECLERC · Ferrari   4 · NORRIS · McLaren   2 · PÉREZ · Red Bull

Lap chart (laps 48-56)

48	49	50	51	52	53	54	55	56	
1	1	1	1	1	1	1	1	1	1
4	4	4	4	4	4	4	4	4	2
11	11	11	11	11	11	11	11	11	3
16	16	16	16	16	16	16	16	16	4
55	55	55	55	55	55	55	55	55	5
63	63	63	63	63	63	63	63	63	6
81	14	14	14	14	14	14	14	14	7
44	81	81	81	81	81	81	81	81	8
14	44	44	44	44	44	44	44	44	9
27	27	27	27	27	27	27	27	27	10
31	31	31	31	31	31	31	31	31	
23	23	23	23	23	23	23	23	23	
20	20	20	20	20	10	10	10	10	
10	10	10	10	24	24	24	24	24	
2	24	24	24	20	20	20	20	20	
24	2	2	2	2	2	2	18	18	
18	18	18	18	18	18	18	2	2	

RACE TYRE STRATEGIES

	Driver	Race Stint 1	Race Stint 2	Race Stint 3	Race Stint 4	Race Stint 5
1	**Verstappen**	Medium (n): 1-13	Hard (n): 14-23	Hard (n): 24-56		
2	Norris	Medium (n): 1-22	Hard (n): 23-56			
3	Pérez	Medium (n): 1-13	Hard (n): 14-23	Hard (n): 24-56		
4	Leclerc	Medium (n): 1-21	Hard (n): 22-56			
5	Sainz	Medium (n): 1-17	Hard (n): 18-56			
6	Russell	Medium (n): 1-11	Medium (n): 12-23	Hard (n): 24-56		
7	Alonso	Medium (n): 1-11	Medium (n): 12-23	Soft (n): 24-43	Medium (n): 44-56	
8	Piastri	Medium (n): 1-16	Medium (u): 17-24	Hard (n): 25-56		
9	Hamilton	Soft (n): 1-9	Medium (n): 10-21	Hard (n): 22-56		
10	Hülkenberg	Medium (n): 1-8	Hard (n): 9-23	Hard (n): 24-56		
11	Ocon	Medium (n): 1-9	Hard (n): 10-23	Hard (n): 24-56		
12	Albon	Medium (n): 1-9	Medium (n): 10-23	Hard (n): 24-56		
13	Gasly	Medium (n): 1-11	Medium (n): 12-23	Hard (n): 24-38	Medium (n): 39-56	
14	Zhou	Medium (n): 1-8	Hard (n): 9-23	Hard (n): 24-40	Soft (n): 41-56	
15	Stroll	Soft (n): 1-9	Medium (n): 10-21	Hard (n): 22-26	Medium (n): 27-35	Hard (u): 36-56
16	Magnussen	Hard (n): 1-17	Medium (n): 18-27	Medium (n): 28-56		
17	Sargeant	Soft (n): 1-12	Medium (n): 13-24	Hard (n): 25-56		
	Ricciardo	Medium (n): 1-14	Medium (n): 15-33 (dnf)			
	Tsunoda	Soft (n): 1-8	Medium (n): 9-23	Hard (n): 24-26 (dnf)		
	Bottas	Medium (n): 1-9	Hard (n): 10-19 (dnf)			

The tyre regulations stipulate that at least two of three dry tyre specifications must be used during a dry race.
Selected compounds for Shanghai: Red = Soft (C2); Yellow = Medium (C3); White = Hard (C2). (n) new (u) used

POINTS

DRIVERS
1	Max Verstappen	110
2	Sergio Pérez	85
3	Charles Leclerc	76
4	Carlos Sainz	69
5	Lando Norris	58
6	Oscar Piastri	38
7	George Russell	33
8	Fernando Alonso	31
9	Lewis Hamilton	19
10	Lance Stroll	9
11	Yuki Tsunoda	7
12	Oliver Bearman	6
13	Nico Hülkenberg	4
14	Kevin Magnussen	1

CONSTRUCTORS
1	Red Bull	195
2	Ferrari	151
3	McLaren	96
4	Mercedes	52
5	Aston Martin	40
6	RB	7
7	Haas	5

FIA FORMULA 1 WORLD CHAMPIONSHIP · ROUND 6
MIAMI GRAND PRIX
MIAMI CIRCUIT

MIAMI QUALIFYING/SPRINT QUALIFYING & RACE

MIAMI free practice and sprint qualifying on Friday pointed to strong progress from a substantially upgraded McLaren, but ended with Max Verstappen's Red Bull on pole again. The McLaren threat waned when the team was unable to get the best out of the soft-compound (C4) Pirellis that were mandatory for SQ3, but with Sunday's main race likely to be a medium/hard-compound one-stopper, the evidence pointed to McLaren being a genuine threat in the main event.

Lando Norris was fastest in both SQ1 and SQ2, but dropped to ninth in SQ3 on the soft compound. And Verstappen's pole time was half a tenth slower than Norris had managed in SQ2 on mediums!

"I just pushed too hard, simple as that," said the disappointed Norris. "Just silly. A couple of mistakes at Turn One, and it just spiralled from there."

The first half of Norris's SQ3 lap was messy, but he was quickest in the final sector, and his self-deprecation didn't tell the full story. Team principal Zak Brown admitted, "We didn't get the softs to work on either car, and we'll have to look at how we brought them in."

The soft was so easy to overheat – as Verstappen found in FP1, when he had to do four consecutive cool-down laps to bring the temperatures back under control after overworking them on his out-lap. Norris's SQ3 lap was actually the first time he'd tried the soft tyre, having spent all of FP1 on the hard compound back-to-backing the upgraded McLaren with Oscar Piastri's less developed version ("Upgrade light" as Brown described it, the young Australian due to receive the full package at Imola). Not ideal, and it demonstrated the challenges of introducing an upgrade package on a sprint weekend.

Bringing in the soft was a challenge for everyone, not just McLaren, illustrated by Verstappen's surprise that his SQ3 lap, which included a sideways moment in T13/14, was good enough for pole. "Where was everyone?" he asked. "I'll take it, but my lap wasn't great…"

One man who was grateful that qualifying conditions were so different on the soft was Charles Leclerc, who lost all of free practice when he clobbered the inside kerb at Turn 16, spun his Ferrari, couldn't select reverse and caused the session to be red-flagged. He made a good recovery to qualify alongside Verstappen on the sprint front row.

Team-mate Carlos Sainz's hot SQ3 lap was on a par with Leclerc as far as a mistake at Turn 17, and he lined up fifth, behind Sergio Pérez in the second Red Bull and a delighted Daniel Ricciardo, who was finally a stand-out, using an upgraded floor allied to his new China chassis to put his RB Cash App a fine fourth. The top ten for the sprint was completed by Piastri, the Aston Martins of Lance Stroll and Fernando Alonso (in that order), Norris and Nico Hülkenberg's Haas.

When the lights went out for the 19-lap sprint, Leclerc got a slightly better launch than Verstappen, but the Red Bull chopped across to claim the inside for Turn One. Pérez ran a little wide on exit and Ricciardo snatched third. Further back, Hamilton arrived down the inside "like a bull", in the words of Alonso. The Spaniard jinked left to miss him, which in turn sent teammate Stroll, on his outside, into Norris. Lance and Lando were both out on the opening lap. Russell also lost out in the mêlée, dropping three positions from his 11th starting slot. A safety car deployment while the mess was sorted out would have consequences for Hamilton.

As soon as DRS was enabled, Pérez put a move on Ricciardo to reclaim third place, with Sainz and Piastri also right with the RB, but unable to get past. By lap ten, there was a gap of a couple of seconds behind the McLaren to Hülkenberg's Haas and the sister car of Kevin Magnussen, which occupied the final points-paying position, eighth.

And here lay the main story of the race. As Hamilton bore down on Magnussen, Kevin fought as though his life depended on it, attracting no fewer than three 10s penalties (five penalty points would accrue by the end of the weekend!) for straight-lining the chicane. That was strategic, an attempt to keep Hamilton out of DRS on the following straight.

Magnussen was totally frank: "The penalties were all deserved. On one lap, Nico [Hülkenberg] straight-lined the chicane and broke my DRS. It would have been better if he hadn't so we could have better defended Hamilton. After that, it was all about protecting him, like I did in Jeddah, to get points for the team. It's not how I like to go racing, but…"

At one point, the Dane's defence was so extreme that Hamilton, no doubt to his fury, was passed by Tsunoda. Lewis retook Yuki on the last lap to claim that final point. Or so he thought, until a penalty for speeding in the pit lane as the safety car had led the pack through it added 20s to his race time.

Reverting to main-race qualifying mode after racing was still a bit counter-intuitive, but Friday's quick men were still the quick men over a lap on Saturday, with Verstappen claiming a sixth straight pole. Leclerc, his main rival once more, was 0.141s adrift this time and just eight-hundredths quicker than Ferrari team-mate Sainz, who pipped Pérez to the second row by 0.005s. The McLarens locked out row three, the top six drivers covered by just over four-tenths.

The gap to Mercedes was almost double that as Russell outqualified Hamilton once more by the slimmest of margins as the Silver Arrows took row four. Hülkenberg made it through to Q3 for the third time in six races for Haas, with Tsunoda completing the top ten. Stroll missed out on the top-ten shootout by a tenth, but outqualified Alonso (15th), while both Alpines made Q2, Pierre Gasly outqualifying Esteban Ocon for the first time in the season. Alex Albon was a disappointed 14th, claiming that he could make Pirelli's softs last for only six corners.

The big questions were just how close McLaren's upgrade would put the team to Red Bull in a race situation and whether Woking could leapfrog Maranello as main challengers. Asked if the upgrade was as big as the previous year's upgrade in Austria, team principal Andrea Stella said, "Not quite, but it's very significant."

Above: A fine fourth place for Daniel Ricciardo in the sprint race.
Photo: Red Bull Content Pool/Getty Images

Top left: As well as introducing a new sponsor, Ferrari ran with pale blue trims on their cars as a nod to their 1964 championship-winning season.
Photo: Scuderia Ferrari

Above left: Mario Andretti and Fernando Alonso – F1 legends both.
Photo: Aramco Aston Martin F1 Team

Left: Verstappen took pole for the sixth straight race, with Leclerc and Sainz just behind the Red Bull driver.

Far left: Verstappen leads Leclerc in the sprint race.
Photos: Red Bull Content Pool/Getty Images

Below far left: 'The Hulk' garnered more sprint points for Haas.
Photo: Haas F1 Team

Opening spread: Victory at last for a joyous Lando Norris.
Photo: McLaren F1 Team

Above: Sergio Pérez nearly takes out his team-mate as he overshoots the corner ahead of the Ferraris.
Photo: Atsuo Sakurai

Right: Esteban Ocon finally scored his first point of the year for Alpine.
Photo: BWT Alpine F1 Team

Below right: Seventh place for the RB of Yuki Tsunoda ahead of George Russell's Mercedes.
Photo: Red Bull Content Pool/Getty Images

To mark the 70th anniversary of Ferrari's presence in North America, the cars were decked out in a special one-off Miami colour scheme, which featured two historic shades of blue – *Azzurro La Plata* and *Azzurro Dino* – the drivers and team personnel also in light blue, along with the wings, wheel fairings and halos on the SF24s. A new title sponsor for the first time since 2021 had arrived in the shape of Hewlett-Packard, but off-track, the paddock gossip surrounded Adrian Newey's recently-announced decision to leave Red Bull Racing after nigh on 20 years (*see* Viewpoint).

Once again, Max Verstappen got the power down to lead into Turn One, and Charles Leclerc got lucky after a slow getaway. Initially, he had been swallowed up by team-mate Carlos Sainz off the line, but suddenly a torpedo appeared down Leclerc's inside in the shape of Sergio Pérez. Sainz also had to take avoiding action as he turned in, allowing Leclerc to switch back inside both of them as Pérez went in too deep. In fact, the Mexican almost took out Verstappen!

Oscar Piastri did well out of it, too, up to third with the first of the McLarens. Behind him, as they streamed across the line at the end of the opening lap, were Sainz, Pérez, Lando Norris, Lewis Hamilton, Nico Hülkenberg, Yuki Tsunoda, George Russell (down three places), Lance Stroll, Fernando Alonso (up three places), Pierre Gasly, Esteban Ocon (the Alpine pair doing almost the entire first lap side by side!), Alex Albon, Logan Sargeant, Kevin Magnussen, Zhou Guanyu, Valtteri Bottas and Daniel Ricciardo.

A one-stop race was widely anticipated and practically everyone had started on the medium-compound Pirelli, save for Hamilton, Alonso, Magnussen and Ricciardo, who had gone for the hards, while Bottas's Sauber had a set of softs.

At the front, Verstappen edged just far enough away to keep himself out of DRS range, but Leclerc's second-place Ferrari was under heavy pressure from Piastri's McLaren, which snatched second place down the inside of Turn 17 on lap five.

Approaching one-third-distance, Verstappen led Piastri by 3s, with Leclerc just half a second behind the McLaren as he set a new race fastest lap, and Sainz 2s behind his team-mate. Carlos had dropped Pérez by 4.5s, and Sergio was under heavy pressure from Norris for his fifth place. Mercedes' race pace was no better than its single-lap performance, and Hamilton had dropped 10s behind Norris in 19 laps on his harder tyres, with team-mate Russell a further 2s back and only a couple of seconds clear of Tsunoda. Ocon was a similar distance further back, tenth, while Alonso was having a rare uninspiring afternoon back in 11th with the first Aston.

Pérez was the first to pit, swapping his starting mediums for hards, Red Bull turning him around sub-2s.

As soon as Pérez came in, McLaren was on the radio to Norris: "Sainz is the car ahead. We should go after him rather than protect against Pérez," they told him.

"Yeah, agreed, I'll go get him!" replied a confident-sounding Lando. Remembering his blistering Friday pace on the mediums, once Pérez was out of the way, the team was clearly confident enough that they could forget about him and open up a pit window to the Mercs. Right on cue, Norris set the fastest lap of the race.

With 20 laps down, Leclerc's Ferrari was in for hards and back out again after another ballistic 1.9s pit stop, rejoining between the two Mercedes. He didn't want to waste any time behind Hamilton and pulled off a fine pass of the Mercedes around the outside of Turn 11. Laying down a marker for 2025?

Suddenly, there was a cone lying on the circuit. "I hit a bollard in Turn 15, check the front wing," Verstappen advised Red Bull. He had run wide over the kerb on the way in, clobbering the cone, which now lay in the middle of the track.

With Russell reporting that it had blown on to the racing line, race control designated a VSC. Ocon, Alonso and Magnussen all took advantage to make a pit stop, while Verstappen headed to the pits on lap 23, handing the race lead to Piastri who, along with Sainz, ran to lap 27 before stopping. That handed the race lead to Norris.

Clearly, Verstappen was not in the kind of sweet spot he'd enjoyed in Shanghai. "It's really low grip," he told his team. "I locked up again." He was 11.5s behind the yet-to-stop Norris, who was about to enjoy a huge stroke of good fortune. Magnussen had attempted to go around the outside of Sargeant into Turn One, but when Logan defended deep, he switched back and attempted to get a better exit and make the move through Turns Two and Three. It all seemed a bit cack-handed, and the Williams

exited backwards and hard into the Tecpro, prompting a full safety car.

In came Norris on lap 30 for fresh hards, emerging still in the lead. Meanwhile, the safety car had erroneously picked up Verstappen as the race leader, requiring Bernd Maylander to release everyone to catch Norris and then wait for the McLaren to lead the pack around.

The race went green again on lap 32, with 25 laps separating Norris from his first GP win, but with Verstappen right on his rear wing. With a clear track in front of him, could Lando demonstrate Friday's searing race pace once again on the hard tyre?

The new race order was Norris, Verstappen, Leclerc, Piastri, Sainz, Pérez, Tsunoda, Hamilton, Russell, Ocon, Alonso, Gasly, Albon, Zhou, Ricciardo, Hülkenberg, Stroll, Bottas and Magnussen. All of the front-runners were now on hards, save for Pérez, Hamilton and Alonso on the yellow-walled medium.

All the early evidence suggested that Norris and McLaren had the necessary pace, Lando managing to get Verstappen out of DRS range straight away.

Meanwhile, Sainz had a go at Piastri's McLaren around the outside of Turn 11, as Leclerc had done to Hamilton. Oscar was having none of that, however, and closed the door on him.

"He pushed me off," Sainz claimed, but it had looked more like hard racing, despite a light brush between the McLaren's right rear and the Ferrari's left front. Sainz didn't think so, though, telling his team, "Just tell him to give me the position back and he doesn't get a penalty. Tell McLaren to be telling him because they need to be telling him."

Eventually, McLaren did get on the radio to Piastri, telling him, "Oscar, a couple of laps ago in Turn 11, when Sainz went off-track, it looked like you were ahead at the apex of the corner. Ferrari think you should give the position up, but we do not." The stewards concurred with McLaren and deemed no further action.

"Stay focused, 20 laps to go," Riccardo Adami radioed to Sainz.

"Yeah, leave me alone, Ricky, leave me alone," Carlos responded, clearly rattled by the lack of action.

Meanwhile, Hamilton had made use of his softer rubber to take seventh from Tsunoda.

Verstappen was unable to do much about Norris, who had opened up a 2.6s lead. "I can't get the car to turn, it's a disaster," Max told Red Bull.

Sainz was determined to be past Piastri and went deep into Turn 17 down the inside, the Ferrari getting a little sideways on the brakes, its right rear wheel clipping Piastri's left front wing endplate. Sainz emerged ahead, but was slower out of the final turn, allowing Piastri to go back around his outside into Turn One. But he also ran too deep into the corner, allowing Sainz to retake fourth.

On lap 40 of the 57, it was Pérez's turn to mug Piastri at Turn 11, with an opportunistic Hamilton following him through, relegating the second McLaren to seventh.

"Oscar, we see front wing damage, so we think we should box and replace it," was a message that Piastri did not want to hear, bringing him into the pits for a second time on lap 41 and ruining what would have been a well-deserved helping of points. Had the safety car come out just a couple of laps earlier, he could have won the race. Fine margins…

Piastri tumbled right down the order to 17th and had to start battling back through, now on a set of medium-compound tyres. He soon caught the VCARB of Ricciardo, his countryman and the man whose McLaren seat he had taken in 2023. Daniel was not about to yield without a fight, and it was then that McLaren came on the radio to tell Oscar, "Just a reminder, Lando is leading the race. We do not want to cause a safety car here." A penny for his thoughts, but the call made sense.

Above: Lando Norris heads to his maiden grand prix win against an Ayrton Senna backdrop.
Photo: Atsuo Sakurai

Top right: Norris stuck with McLaren when they were in the doldrums, so his victory was all the sweeter.
Photo: McLaren F1 Team

Above right: Leclerc and Sainz were classified third and fourth after Pérez's time penalty.
Photo: Scuderia Ferrari

Right: Adrian Newey addresses the Red Bull crew after announcing his decision to move on.
Photo: Red Bull Content Pool/Getty Images

More likely to occupy Bernd Maylander, though, was Alonso battling with old Alpine team-mate Esteban Ocon, with more than one bout of previous. The McLaren pit-wall crew must have breathed a collective sigh of relief when Fernando got by unscathed for ninth.

There was more anxiety for them as Alex Albon, trying to defend 15th in his Williams, locked up and went straight on at Turn 11, allowing Ricciardo, Bottas and Magnussen to go through while he dropped to the tail of the pack.

But, finally, after 15 podiums, Norris got it done and was able to stand on the top step. True, he'd had a stroke of good fortune with the optimal safety car timing, but the important thing was that thereafter, in his upgraded McLaren, he had been able to drive away from Verstappen. He crossed the line with 7.5s in hand to give McLaren, the second most successful team in terms of F1 victories, just its second win in 12 years.

"I knew on Friday we had the pace," Lando said. "There were a couple of mistakes over the weekend, but I managed to put it together. I'm just really proud. A lot of people, I guess, doubted me along the way. This one is also for the team. I stuck with McLaren because I believe in them, and today proved why."

Behind Norris and Verstappen, Leclerc and Sainz were third and fourth for Ferrari, ahead of Pérez, who admitted that he'd been fortunate to get away with the first corner and wouldn't have gone up the inside had he appreciated quite how little grip there was.

Hamilton, sixth, had his most enjoyable race of 2024 thus far, which is not saying much, and Tsunoda equalled his best seventh-place 2024 result from Melbourne. Russell brought the second Mercedes home eighth, ahead of Alonso's Aston, with Ocon claiming his first point of the year for Alpine.

The genuine delight for Norris from his peers was warming to witness, the likes of Hamilton and Alonso offering hugs and hearty congratulations as well as generational peers such as Verstappen, Leclerc, Sainz and Russell.

As regards the rest of the season, though, it was clear that McLaren had taken a step forward, both Verstappen and Leclerc referring to the SQ2 time Norris had set on mediums on the Friday. Another big question was whether McLaren had made a giant stride or Red Bull had underperformed.

"I didn't really see Lando in the beginning because I was more focused on Oscar behind and the Ferraris," Verstappen explained. "But then I boxed and I heard the pace he was doing on the used mediums. I was like, 'I mean, that's quite insane.' I would have never been able to do that.

"So I knew even if there wouldn't have been a safety car that when he would come out on fresh tyres, I would have had to push on quite a lot to be able to keep him behind. Then the safety car: sometimes it works for you, sometimes against you. We clearly weren't quick enough after it. And once I realised that, I just settled for second.

"I never really felt comfortable the whole weekend. I think on the medium tyre, it was still okay-ish, but on the hard, it was quite a disaster: just low grip, very tricky balance in the low-speed. I couldn't really lean on the rear, and in the high-speed, I was understeering a lot. When you have these two issues, you cannot balance it out."

Obviously, the picture would change from circuit to circuit, and certainly nobody left Miami thinking that Red Bull was a spent force. But the team now had its challenges, on-track and off (see Viewpoint).

Tony Dodgins

VIEWPOINT
MOVING ON

MIAMI'S paddock scuttlebutt was dominated by the news that Red Bull technical genius Adrian Newey would leave the team at the end of the year, after 20 years at Milton Keynes. A seismic shock.

Newey appreciates stability in his working environment. A quarter of a century ago, Bobby Rahal, a former Indycar driver whom Newey engineered, and a close friend now heading up the Jaguar F1 team, almost succeeded in poaching Adrian from McLaren. A decisive factor in Newey eventually staying put was McLaren boss Ron Dennis pointing out that Rahal was embroiled in a political battle with Niki Lauda at Jaguar. Newey had signed a pre-agreement, but changed his mind.

This time, the controversy surrounding Christian Horner had unsettled him, but he admitted in Miami that the decision had not come out of the blue. Asked if he'd been considering an exit for some time, he said, "If I'm honest, kind of. I'm in a very lucky position where I don't need to work to live. I work because I enjoy it. I just felt that now is a good time to step back and take a bit of a break and take stock of life.

"I think Mandy, my wife, and the dogs, we'll probably go travelling. We'll probably get a motorhome or something, go down through France and just enjoy life. And then maybe at some point, I don't know when, I'll be standing in the shower and say, 'Right, this is going to be the next adventure.' But right now, there is no plan."

Of course, there was much speculation over where 'the next adventure' would take him. Ferrari was favourite, and Lewis Hamilton said, "If I was to do a list of people that I'd love to work with, he would absolutely be at the top of that."

Lawrence Stroll had supposedly offered £450k a week for Newey to join Aston, and even new Williams team principal James Vowles was actively courting him: "Williams is where Adrian really cut his teeth. It could fit perfectly now for someone wanting to potentially dig into a challenge. We're not driven by an OEM. We're driven by a group of individuals that want to be there. It's all about racing. And hopefully that plays to his strengths."

A team cannot lose someone of Newey's calibre without feeling it, but you only have to look around the Milton Keynes site and the new Red Bull Power Trains facility to appreciate the fine job Horner has done in establishing the team as an F1 powerhouse, facilitated by Dietrich Mateschitz's largesse. The technical department has strength in depth. There would be challenges ahead, forgetting immediate ones from McLaren and Ferrari, but modern F1 is no one-man show. Anyone predicting a Red Bull demise would be misguided.

Tony Dodgins

6

FORMULA 1 CRYPTO.COM MIAMI GRAND PRIX 2024

MIAMI 03-05 MAY

RACE DISTANCE: 57 laps, 191.585 miles/308.326km

RACE WEATHER: Dry/sunny (track 45-47°C, air 29-30°C)

MIAMI INTERNATIONAL AUTODROME, FLORIDA
Circuit: 3.363 miles/5.412km, 57 laps

RACE – OFFICIAL CLASSIFICATION

Pos.	Driver	Nat.	No.	Entrant	Car/Engine	Laps	Time/Retirement	Speed (mph/km/h)	Gap to leader	Fastest race lap
1	Lando Norris	GB	4	McLaren Formula 1 Team	McLaren MCL38-Mercedes F1 M15 E Perf. V6	57	1h 30m 49.876s	126.573/203.699		1m 30.980s 55
2	Max Verstappen	NL	1	Oracle Red Bull Racing	Red Bull RB20-Honda RBPT H002 V6	57	1h 30m 57.488s	126.378/203.385	7.612s	1m 31.261s 48
3	Charles Leclerc	MC	16	Scuderia Ferrari	Ferrari SF-24-066/12 V6	57	1h 30m 59.796s	126.324/203.299	9.920s	1m 31.084s 56
4	Sergio Pérez	MEX	11	Oracle Red Bull Racing	Red Bull RB20-Honda RBPT H002 V6	57	1h 31m 04.526s	126.215/203.123	14.650s	1m 30.855s 55
5	Carlos Sainz	E	55	Scuderia Ferrari	Ferrari SF-24-066/12 V6	57	1h 31m 06.283s *	126.174/203.058	16.407s	1m 30.928s 55
6	Lewis Hamilton	GB	44	Mercedes-AMG Petronas F1 Team	Mercedes-AMG F1 W15-M15 E Perf. V6	57	1h 31m 06.461s	126.170/203.051	16.585s	1m 31.233s 54
7	Yuki Tsunoda	J	22	Visa Cash App RB Formula One Team	RB VCARB 01-Honda RBPT H002 V6	57	1h 31m 16.061s	125.949/202.695	26.185s	1m 31.682s 55
8	George Russell	GB	63	Mercedes-AMG Petronas F1 Team	Mercedes-AMG F1 W15-M15 E Perf. V6	57	1h 31m 24.665s	125.751/202.377	34.789s	1m 31.921s 43
9	Fernando Alonso	E	14	Aston Martin Aramco F1 Team	Aston Martin AMR24-Mercedes F1 M15 E Perf. V6	57	1h 31m 26.983s	125.698/202.292	37.107s	1m 31.727s 55
10	Esteban Ocon	F	31	BWT Alpine F1 Team	Alpine A524-Renault E-Tech RE24 V6	57	1h 31m 29.622s	125.638/202.194	39.746s	1m 32.037s 51
11	Nico Hülkenberg	D	27	MoneyGram Haas F1 Team	Haas VF-24-Ferrari 066/10 V6	57	1h 31m 30.665s	125.614/202.156	40.789s	1m 31.941s 56
12	Pierre Gasly	F	10	BWT Alpine F1 Team	Alpine A524-Renault E-Tech RE24 V6	57	1h 31m 34.834s	125.519/202.003	44.958s	1m 32.055s 56
13	Oscar Piastri	AUS	81	McLaren Formula 1 Team	McLaren MCL38-Mercedes F1 M15 E Perf. V6	57	1h 31m 39.632s	125.409/201.826	49.756s	1m 30.634s 43
14	Zhou Guanyu	CHN	24	Stake F1 Team Kick Sauber	Sauber C44-Ferrari 066/12 V6	57	1h 31m 39.855s	125.404/201.818	49.979s	1m 31.991s 56
15	Daniel Ricciardo	AUS	3	Visa Cash App RB Formula One Team	RB VCARB 01-Honda RBPT H002 V6	57	1h 31m 40.832s	125.382/201.782	50.956s	1m 32.122s 57
16	Valtteri Bottas	FIN	77	Stake F1 Team Kick Sauber	Sauber C44-Ferrari 066/12 V6	57	1h 31m 42.232s	125.350/201.731	52.356s	1m 32.098s 55
17	Lance Stroll	CDN	18	Aston Martin Aramco F1 Team	Aston Martin AMR24-Mercedes F1 M15 E Perf. V6	57	1h 31m 45.049s *	125.286/201.628	55.173s	1m 31.588s 57
18	Alexander Albon	T	23	Williams Racing	Williams FW46-Mercedes F1 M15 E Perf. V6	57	1h 32m 05.967s	124.812/200.865	1m 16.091s	1m 30.849s 55
19	Kevin Magnussen	DK	20	MoneyGram Haas F1 Team	Haas VF-24-Ferrari 066/10 V6	57	1h 32m 14.559s *	124.618/200.553	1m 24.683s	1m 31.774s 33
	Logan Sargeant	USA	2	Williams Racing	Williams FW46-Mercedes F1 M15 E Perf. V6	27	accident			1m 33.452s 15

* Magnussen: 10s time penalty for causing a collision with Sargeant; drive-through for entering the pits during a Safety Car period and not changing tyres, converted to 20s time penalty (originally finished 18th).
* Sainz: 5s time penalty for causing a collision with Piastri (originally finished 4th). * Stroll: 10s time penalty for leaving the track and gaining an advantage (originally finished 13th).

DHL Fastest race lap: Oscar Piastri on lap 43, 1m 30.634s, 133.573mph/214.965km/h.

Lap record: Max Verstappen (Red Bull RB19-Honda RBPT V6), 1m 29.708s, 134.952mph/217.184km/h (2023).

19 · ZHOU · Sauber 17 · SARGEANT · Williams 15 · ALONSO · Aston Martin 13 · OCON · Alpine 11 · STROLL · Aston Martin

20 · RICCIARDO · RB 18 · MAGNUSSEN · Haas 16 · BOTTAS · Sauber 14 · ALBON · Williams 12 · GASLY · Alpine

3-place grid penalty for overtaking under Safety Car conditions at the Chinese GP

Grid order	1	2	3	4	5	6	7	8	9	10	11	12	13	14	15	16	17	18	19	20	21	22	23	24	25	26	27	28	29	30	31	32	33	34	35	36	37	38	39	40	41	42	43	44	45	46
1 VERSTAPPEN	1	1	1	1	1	1	1	1	1	1	1	1	1	1	1	1	1	1	1	1	1	1	81	81	81	81	4	4	4	4	4	4	4	4	4	4	4	4	4	4	4	4	4	4	4	4
16 LECLERC	16	16	16	81	81	81	81	81	81	81	81	81	81	81	81	81	81	81	81	81	81	81	1	55	55	55	81		1	1	1	1	1	1	1	1	1	1	1	1	1	1	1	1	1	1
55 SAINZ	81	81	81	16	16	16	16	16	16	16	16	16	16	16	16	16	16	55	55	55	55	55	4	4	4	55	16	16	16	16	16	16	16	16	16	16	16	16	16	16	16	16	16	16	16	16
11 PÉREZ	55	55	55	55	55	55	55	55	55	55	55	55	55	55	55	55	55	16	4	4	4	4	1	1	1	1	81	81	81	81	81	81	81	81	81	81	55	55	55	55	55	55	55	55	55	55
4 NORRIS	11	11	11	11	11	11	11	11	11	11	11	11	11	11	4	4	4	4	44	16	16	16	16	16	16	16	55	55	55	55	55	55	55	55	55	55	81	11	11	11	11	11	11	11	11	11
81 PIASTRI	4	4	4	4	4	4	4	4	4	4	4	4	4	4	11	44	44	44	16	44	44	44	44	11	11	11	11	11	11	11	11	11	11	11	11	11	44	44	44	44	44	44	44	44	44	44
63 RUSSELL	44	27	27	27	27	27	27	27	44	44	44	44	44	44	44	63	63	63	63	63	63	63	11	44	22	22	22	22	22	22	22	44	44	44	44	44	22	22	22	22	22	22	22	22	22	22
44 HAMILTON	27	44	44	44	44	44	44	44	27	63	63	63	63	63	63	22	22	22	22	22	22	22	22	22	44	44	44	44	44	44	44	22	22	22	22	22	63	63	63	63	63	63	63	63	63	63
27 HÜLKENBERG	22	22	22	63	63	63	63	63	63	22	22	22	22	22	22	11	11	11	11	11	11	11	63	14	3	4	63	63	63	63	63	63	63	63	63	63	31	14	14	14	14	14	14	14	31	31
22 TSUNODA	63	63	63	22	22	22	22	22	22	31	31	31	31	31	31	31	31	31	31	31	31	31	14	24	3	63	24	31	31	31	31	31	31	31	31	31	14	31	31	31	31	14	14	14	14	14
18 STROLL	18	18	18	18	18	18	18	18	14	14	14	14	14	14	14	14	14	14	14	14	14	24	3	31	63	3	31	14	14	14	14	14	14	14	14	14	81	10	10	10	10	10	10	10	10	27
10 GASLY	14	10	10	10	10	10	10	10	10	10	10	10	10	10	10	10	10	14	27	24	24	24	24	14	27	31	63	31	14	3	14	14	3	10	10	10	10	10	10	10	10	10	27	27	27	10
31 OCON	10	14	14	14	14	14	14	14	31	24	24	24	24	24	24	24	24	10	3	3	3	3	31	27	14	14	3	23	23	23	23	23	23	23	23	23	23	23	23	23	23	23	23	23	23	23
23 ALBON	31	23	23	23	23	23	23	23	3	3	3	3	3	3	3	3	20	18	10	10	10	10	10	10	23	23	14	27	27	27	27	24	24	24	24	24	24	27	24	24	24	24	24	24	24	24
14 ALONSO	23	31	31	31	31	31	31	31	2	18	18	18	18	18	18	18	18	3	18	18	18	18	18	18	10	10	10	24	24	24	24	3	3	3	3	3	3	24	3	3	3	3	3	3	3	18
77 BOTTAS	2	2	2	2	2	2	24	2	77	77	77	77	77	77	77	77	77	77	77	77	77	77	18	18	18	18	18	10	10	10	10	10	10	27	27	27	27	3	18	18	18	18	18	18	3	3
2 SARGEANT	20	24	24	24	24	24	24	24	18	2	2	2	2	2	2	2	2	20	20	20	20	20	20	23	18	18	18	18	18	18	18	18	18	18	18	18	18	18	18	18	18	77	77	77	77	77
20 MAGNUSSEN	24	77	77	77	77	77	77	23	23	23	23	23	23	23	23	23	23	23	23	23	23	23	2	2	2	2	2	77	77	77	77	77	77	77	77	77	77	77	77	77	77	20	20	20	20	81
24 ZHOU	77	20	20	20	20	20	20	77	2	2	2	2	2	2	2	20	20	20	20	20	20	20	20	20	20	20	20	20	20	20	20	20	20	20	20	20	20	81	81	81	81	81	81	81	81	20
3 RICCIARDO	3	3	3	3	3	3	3	23	77	77	77	77	77	77	77	77	77	77	77	77	77	77	77	77	77	77																				

VSC Virtual Safety Car deployed on lap 23   SC Safety Car deployed on laps 29-32

TIME SHEETS

SPRINT QUALIFYING (FRIDAY)

Weather: Dry/sunny

Temperatures: track 46-48°C, air 30°C

Pos.	Driver	First	Second	Third	Qualifying Tyre
1	Max Verstappen	1m 28.194s	1m 28.001s	1m 27.641s	Soft (n)
2	Charles Leclerc	1m 28.537s	1m 27.977s	1m 27.749s	Soft (n)
3	Sergio Pérez	1m 28.681s	1m 27.865s	1m 27.876s	Soft (n)
4	Daniel Ricciardo	1m 28.700s	1m 28.122s	1m 28.044s	Soft (n)
5	Carlos Sainz	1m 28.435s	1m 28.262s	1m 28.103s	Soft (n)
6	Oscar Piastri	1m 28.056s	1m 28.163s	1m 28.161s	Soft (n)
7	Lance Stroll	1m 28.807s	1m 28.323s	1m 28.375s	Soft (u)
8	Fernando Alonso	1m 28.192s	1m 28.189s	1m 28.419s	Soft (n)
9	Lando Norris	1m 27.939s	1m 27.597s	1m 28.472s	Soft (n)
10	Nico Hülkenberg	1m 29.040s	1m 28.330s	1m 28.476s	Soft (u)
11	George Russell	1m 28.387s	1m 28.343s		
12	Lewis Hamilton	1m 28.736s	1m 28.371s		
13	Esteban Ocon	1m 28.873s	1m 28.379s		
14	Kevin Magnussen	1m 28.377s	1m 28.614s		
15	Yuki Tsunoda	1m 28.687s	no time		
16	Pierre Gasly	1m 29.185s			
17	Zhou Guanyu	1m 29.267s			
18	Valtteri Bottas	1m 29.360s			
19	Logan Sargeant	1m 29.551s			
20	Alexander Albon	1m 29.858s			

QUALIFYING (SATURDAY)

Weather: Dry/sunny Temperatures: track 48-51°C, air 29-31°C

Pos.	Driver	First	Second	Third	Qualifying Tyre
1	Max Verstappen	1m 27.689s	1m 27.566s	1m 27.241s	Soft (n)
2	Charles Leclerc	1m 28.081s	1m 27.533s	1m 27.382s	Soft (n)
3	Carlos Sainz	1m 27.937s	1m 27.941s	1m 27.455s	Soft (n)
4	Sergio Pérez	1m 27.772s	1m 27.839s	1m 27.460s	Soft (n)
5	Lando Norris	1m 27.913s	1m 27.871s	1m 27.594s	Soft (n)
6	Oscar Piastri	1m 28.032s	1m 27.721s	1m 27.675s	Soft (n)
7	George Russell	1m 28.159s	1m 28.095s	1m 28.067s	Medium (n)
8	Lewis Hamilton	1m 28.167s	1m 27.697s	1m 28.107s	Medium (n)
9	Nico Hülkenberg	1m 28.383s	1m 28.200s	1m 28.146s	Soft (n)
10	Yuki Tsunoda	1m 28.324s	1m 28.167s	1m 28.192s	Soft (n)
11	Lance Stroll	1m 28.177s	1m 28.222s		
12	Pierre Gasly	1m 27.976s	1m 28.324s		
13	Esteban Ocon	1m 28.209s	1m 28.371s		
14	Alexander Albon	1m 28.343s	1m 28.413s		
15	Fernando Alonso	1m 28.453s	1m 28.427s		
16	Valtteri Bottas	1m 28.463s			
17	Logan Sargeant	1m 28.487s			
18	Daniel Ricciardo	1m 28.617s			
19	Kevin Magnussen	1m 28.619s			
20	Zhou Guanyu	1m 28.824s			

PRACTICE 1 (FRIDAY)

Weather: Dry/sunny

Temperatures: track 51-54°C, air 30-31°C

Pos.	Driver	Laps	Time
1	Verstappen	25	1m 28.595s
2	Piastri	24	1m 28.700s
3	Carlos Sainz	24	1m 28.711s
4	George Russell	26	1m 28.784s
5	Lance Stroll	25	1m 28.817s
6	Sergio Pérez	23	1m 28.868s
7	Lewis Hamilton	24	1m 29.012s
8	Yuki Tsunoda	25	1m 29.056s
9	Esteban Ocon	23	1m 29.163s
10	Pierre Gasly	27	1m 29.175s
11	Daniel Ricciardo	27	1m 29.178s
12	Kevin Magnussen	26	1m 29.189s
13	Nico Hülkenberg	25	1m 29.314s
14	Alexander Albon	24	1m 29.393s
15	Zhou Guanyu	24	1m 29.445s
16	Lando Norris	21	1m 29.495s
17	Valtteri Bottas	23	1m 29.636s
18	Logan Sargeant	23	1m 29.891s
19	Fernando Alonso	22	1m 30.023s
20	Charles Leclerc	3	1m 32.099s

SPRINT (SATURDAY)

RACE DISTANCE: 19 laps, 63.796 miles/102.670km

RACE WEATHER: Dry/sunny Temperatures: track 46-47°C, air 29-31°C

Pos.	Driver	Laps	Time/Retirement	Speed (mph/km/h)	Gap to leader	Fastest race lap		Grid
1	**Max Verstappen**	19	31m 31.383s	121.427/195.418		1m 30.415s	4	1
2	**Charles Leclerc**	19	31m 34.754s	121.211/195.071	3.371s	1m 30.807s	4	2
3	**Sergio Pérez**	19	31m 36.478s	121.101/194.893	5.095s	1m 30.921s	19	3
4	**Daniel Ricciardo**	19	31m 46.354s	120.474/193.884	14.971s	1m 31.505s	4	4
5	**Carlos Sainz**	19	31m 46.605s	120.458/193.858	15.222s	1m 31.568s	17	5
6	**Oscar Piastri**	19	31m 47.133s	120.425/193.805	15.750s	1m 31.393s	19	6
7	**Nico Hülkenberg**	19	31m 53.437s	120.028/193.166	22.054s	1m 31.963s	8	10
8	**Yuki Tsunoda**	19	32m 01.199s	119.543/192.386	29.816s	1m 31.844s	16	15
9	Pierre Gasly	19	32m 03.263s	119.414/192.179	31.880s	1m 32.148s	6	16
10	Logan Sargeant	19	32m 05.738s	119.261/191.932	34.355s	1m 32.192s	6	18
11	Zhou Guanyu	19	32m 06.461s	119.216/191.860	35.078s	1m 32.131s	7	17
12	George Russell	19	32m 07.138s	119.175/191.793	35.755s	1m 32.173s	8	11
13	Alexander Albon	19	32m 07.469s *	119.154/191.760	36.086s	1m 32.223s	6	20
14	Valtteri Bottas	19	32m 08.275s *	119.104/191.680	36.892s	1m 32.462s	7	19
15	Esteban Ocon	19	32m 09.123s *	119.052/191.595	37.740s	1m 32.218s	19	13
16	Lewis Hamilton	19	32m 20.730s *	118.340/190.449	49.347s	1m 31.830s	16	12
17	Fernando Alonso	19	32m 30.792s	117.729/189.467	59.409s	1m 32.355s	7	8
18	Kevin Magnussen	19	32m 37.686s *	117.315/188.800	1m 06.303s	1m 32.113s	5	14
	Lance Stroll	1	*accident damage*			no time		7
	Lando Norris	0	*accident*			no time		9

* Albon: Car modified in parc fermé; required to start from the pit lane.

* Bottas: 3-place grid penalty for driving unnecessarily slowly and impeding Piastri during qualfying.

* Hamilton: Drive-through converted to 20s time penalty for speeding in the pit lane (originally finished 8th).

* Magnussen: 10+10+10s time penalty for leaving the track and gaining an advantage; 5s time penalty for leaving the track without a justifiable reason multiple times (originally finished 10th)

* Ocon: 10s time penalty for unsafe release and collision with Leclerc (served at pit stop).

Fastest race lap: Max Verstappen on lap 4, 1m 30.415s, 133.897mph/215.486km/h.

FOR THE RECORD

1st GP WIN: Lando Norris

40,000th GP LAP RACED: Red Bull

DID YOU KNOW?

Lando Norris had more podiums (15) before his first victory than any other driver in the history of the championship

QUALIFYING: head to head

Verstappen	6	0	Pérez
Hamilton	1	5	Russell
Norris	5	1	Piastri
Leclerc	3	2	Sainz
Leclerc	1	0	Bearman
Gasly	1	5	Ocon
Alonso	4	2	Stroll
Albon	6	0	Sargeant
Bottas	6	0	Zhou
Tsunoda	5	1	Ricciardo
Magnussen	2	4	Hülkenberg

9 · HÜLKENBERG · Haas

7 · RUSSELL · Mercedes

5 · NORRIS · McLaren

3 · SAINZ · Ferrari

1 · VERSTAPPEN · Red Bull

10 · TSUNODA · RB

8 · HAMILTON · Mercedes

6 · PIASTRI · McLaren

4 · PÉREZ · Red Bull

2 · LECLERC · Ferrari

47	48	49	50	51	52	53	54	55	56	57	•
4	4	4	4	4	4	4	4	4	4	4	1
1	1	1	1	1	1	1	1	1	1	1	2
16	16	16	16	16	16	16	16	16	16	16	3
55	55	55	55	55	55	55	55	55	55	55	
11	11	11	11	11	11	11	11	11	11	11	5
44	44	44	44	44	44	44	44	44	44	44	6
22	22	22	22	22	22	22	22	22	22	22	7
63	63	63	63	63	63	63	63	63	63	63	8
31	14	14	14	14	14	14	14	14	14	14	9
14	31	31	31	31	31	31	31	31	31	31	10
27	27	27	27	27	27	27	27	27	27	27	
10	10	10	10	10	10	10	10	10	10	10	
23	23	23	23	23	18	18	18	18	18	18	
24	18	18	18	18	24	24	24	24	24	81	
18	24	24	24	24	23	3	81	81	81	24	
3	3	3	3	3	3	81	3	3	3	3	
77	81	81	81	81	81	77	77	77	77	77	
81	77	77	77	77	77	20	20	20	20	20	
20	20	20	20	20	20	23	23	23	23	23	

23 = Pit stop

RACE TYRE STRATEGIES

PIRELLI

	Driver	Race Stint 1	Race Stint 2	Race Stint 3
1	Norris	Medium (n): 1-29	Hard (n): 30-57	
2	Verstappen	Medium (n): 1-23	Hard (n): 24-57	
3	Leclerc	Medium (n): 1-19	Hard (n): 20-57	
4	Pérez	Medium (n): 1-17	Hard (n): 18-28	Medium (u): 29-57
5	Sainz	Medium (n): 1-27	Hard (n): 28-57	
6	Hamilton	Hard (n): 1-26	Medium (u): 27-57	
7	Tsunoda	Medium (n): 1-28	Hard (n): 29-57	
8	Russell	Medium (u): 1-24	Hard (n): 25-57	
9	Alonso	Hard (u): 1-22	Medium (u): 23-57	
10	Ocon	Medium (n): 1-22	Hard (n): 23-57	
11	Hülkenberg	Hard (n): 1-12	Hard (n): 13-28	Medium (n): 29-57
12	Gasly	Medium (n): 1-12	Hard (n): 13-57	
13	Piastri	Medium (n): 1-27	Hard (n): 28-40	Medium (u): 41-57
14	Zhou	Medium (n): 1-28	Soft (n): 29-57	
15	Ricciardo	Hard (n): 1-28	Medium (u): 29-57	
16	Bottas	Soft (n): 1-11	Hard (n): 12-29	Medium (n): 30-57
17	Stroll	Medium (u): 1-11	Hard (u): 12-28	Medium (u): 29-57
18	Albon	Medium (n): 1-10	Hard (n): 11-53	Soft (n): 54-57
19	Magnussen	Hard (n): 1-22	Medium (n): 23-28	Medium (n): 29-57
	Sargeant	Medium (n): 1-11	Hard (n): 12-27 (dnf)	

The tyre regulations stipulate that at least two of three dry tyre specifications must be used during a dry race.
Selected compounds for Miami: Red = Soft (C4); Yellow = Medium (C3); White = Hard (C2). (n) new (u) used

POINTS

DRIVERS

1	Max Verstappen	136
2	Sergio Pérez	103
3	Charles Leclerc	98
4	Lando Norris	83
5	Carlos Sainz	83
6	Oscar Piastri	41
7	George Russell	37
8	Fernando Alonso	33
9	Lewis Hamilton	27
10	Yuki Tsunoda	14
11	Lance Stroll	9
12	Oliver Bearman	6
13	Nico Hülkenberg	6
14	Daniel Ricciardo	5
15	Esteban Ocon	1
16	Kevin Magnussen	1

CONSTRUCTORS

1	Red Bull	239
2	Ferrari	187
3	McLaren	124
4	Mercedes	64
5	Aston Martin	42
6	RB	19
7	Haas	7
8	Alpine	1

IMOLA QUALIFYING

THE record books will show that Max Verstappen took an eighth consecutive F1 pole position for the 2024 Emilia Romagna GP, fittingly enough equalling a record by the late, great Ayrton Senna, who was killed at Imola in perhaps F1's blackest weekend 30 years ago (see Viewpoint).

But that tells nothing like the full story. This was not a routine dominant Red Bull/Verstappen practice and qualifying. On the opening day, the world champion was struggling. In FP1, he was on the radio explaining that T11 (Acque Minerale) was a disaster: "There's no grip there and I can't brake late because the car is bottoming really badly. Then on apex entry, I just have no front end."

With a revised aero set-up for FP2, he was happier on the medium compound (Pirelli brought the softest tyres in its range to Imola, the C3/4/5, a step softer than on the previous visit in 2022), but as soon as he took on the softs for a qualifying simulation, he was in strife again: "My God, it's so difficult. This time, suddenly the front grips up so much I almost spun!"

The Red Bull's balance just wasn't there. On Friday's long runs, McLaren had appeared highly impressive once again, both Miami winner Lando Norris and Oscar Piastri had the full raft of upgrades after the Australian had raced in the US in 'upgrade-lite' spec as team principal Zak Brown had put it. Second quickest for single-lap pace, 0.1s behind Charles Leclerc's heavily upgraded Ferrari (revised sidepod inlet, floor and rear wing), Piastri was fastest of all on the long runs.

But almost inevitably, Red Bull dug themselves out of the mire, not least due to an all-nighter in the operations centre back at Milton Keynes, following a ten-hour stint in the simulator by Sébastian Buemi. The RB20 was at its weakest at front-limited circuits, as we'd seen in Melbourne, where Ferrari had had more pace, but on Saturday, Verstappen found he had a better front end and balance, and at the end of Q1, there he was at the top of the time sheet again.

There were some surprises to behold: Nico Hülkenberg topped the session with a second soft-tyre run until Verstappen and Charles Leclerc beat him, while Yuki Tsunoda was fourth quickest at the home race just a few kilometres from his team's Faenza base.

Fernando Alonso was in trouble after an off in FP3, which heavily damaged his Aston Martin and gave his crew a busy lunchtime. He ran with heavy fuel in Q1 to do the consecutive laps he had missed in FP3, but on his qualifying lap proper, he was forced to pit with an "unknown technical problem." Which turned out to be a lack of fuel... Sunday, at a track where overtaking is difficult, would likely be a taxing day, so Fernando elected to change the car and start from the pit lane.

Joining Alonso as Q2 spectators were the two Sauber drivers, Valtteri Bottas and Zhou Guanyu, then a frustrated Kevin Magnussen who had had his hot lap blocked by Oscar Piastri. This would have consequences later for the young Aussie, and the under-pressure Logan Sargeant, who was within a couple of tenths of Williams team-mate Alex Albon, but had his laps deleted for track-limits infringements.

Meanwhile, a Q2 casualty was none other than Sergio Pérez. The Mexican, on used softs for his first run, was surprised by the grip afforded by new rubber and lost time at Tosa. He ended up more than half a second behind Verstappen and, more importantly, 0.16s adrift of tenth-placed Daniel Ricciardo.

With that, the average qualifying deficit between Verstappen and Pérez (0.339s) became the largest delta across the entire grid, greater even than the 0.313s between Albon and Sargeant, with Verstappen now owning the only team-mate whitewash across both main and sprint qualifying formats. At the other end of the spectrum, the two closest team-mate deltas were those between the rival McLaren and Ferrari drivers, ramping up pressure on Sergio to retain his seat.

The Q2 eliminees with Pérez were the improving Alpine drivers Esteban Ocon and Pierre Gasly, Williams' Alex Albon and Lance Stroll, who capped a disappointing day for the Aston team. The Canadian was underwhelmed by a substantial upgrade package that the team had brought to Imola. "It feels the same as it's felt all year," he grimaced.

At the front, the pack was closer than ever. Before Verstappen made his second Q2 run, the first five – Leclerc, Yuki Tsunoda, Norris, Max and Piastri – were all blanketed by a mind-boggling 0.079s!

While Verstappen might have taken the pole, it was not without the aid of a handy tow from Hülkenberg's Haas, which allowed Max to pip Piastri's McLaren by just seven-hundredths.

"I'm more than happy with that one!" Verstappen beamed. "It's been a difficult weekend, even this morning, and I touched the gravel out of the second Rivazza on my best lap."

Piastri beat team-mate Norris to the front row by 0.02s, but was left contemplating what might have been after a three-place grid drop for the Magnussen incident: "It was a bit of a scruffy last corner, but we're on the pace and confidence is high," he reported.

Leclerc and Carlos Sainz could only manage fourth and fifth for Ferrari. "You never know what the fuel loads are on Friday, and the others were obviously a bit heavier than we thought, which was a surprise," Leclerc admitted. "We know where we are losing, which is the first few turns, so we'll have to look at that." Which implied that Ferrari hadn't got its tyre preparation right.

George Russell put the first Mercedes sixth on the grid, two slots and a quarter of a second ahead of team-mate Lewis Hamilton. The silver cars were split by the excellent Tsunoda, who achieved his best starting slot of the season so far. Daniel Ricciardo was a couple of tenths and two positions in arrears with the second VCARB, his first time in Q3 in 2024, with Hülkenberg's Haas making it into the top ten for the fourth time in seven 2024 races.

THERE is always a special flavour about a grand prix in Italy, even more so at Imola, with F1 enjoying its surge in popularity, and Ferrari hoping that its upgrades would close the gap to dominant Red Bull and emerging McLaren. Lando Norris might have pipped Charles Leclerc to the front row, but Oscar Piastri's three-place grid penalty for impeding Kevin Magnussen meant that the red cars filled row two and were in the fight. The packed grandstands seethed with swaying red.

A medium/hard one-stopper was the predicted strategy on a track with a long 27–28s pit-stop loss, 15 of the 20 starters and all of the top ten going to the grid on Pirelli's medium compound. Sergio Pérez had opted for the hard from his lowly 11th starting position, while further back, Pierre Gasly and the pit-lane-starting Alonso went for softs, hoping for some strong early laps and then a safety car.

With overtaking notoriously difficult around Imola, some opening-lap fireworks were anticipated, but in fact it was all highly orderly as the field filed through the first chicane and around the opening lap. Across the line, it was starting order for the first six as Max Verstappen led Norris, Leclerc, Sainz, Piastri and George Russell. Lewis Hamilton was up a place to seventh and Nico Hülkenberg ran eighth for Haas, both VCARBs dropping a couple of positions, Yuki Tsunoda and Daniel Ricciardo being ninth and 11th respectively, split by Sergio Pérez, who had picked up a position despite his harder-compound tyres. Esteban Ocon was running 12th, ahead of Lance Stroll, Alex Albon, Pierre Gasly, Kevin Magnussen (who had managed to jump both Saubers – Valtteri Bottas ahead of Zhou Guanyu), with Logan Sargeant and Alonso bringing up the rear.

Verstappen broke DRS range to Norris's McLaren early, but was not running away, while everyone focused on staying in touch without taking too much out of the rubber on heavy fuel.

Alonso soon became tired of tooling around at the back and, despite no early safety car, was into the pits on lap eight to swap his starting softs for hards, his front brakes on fire as he resumed! Albon, Gasly and Bottas all stopped a lap later. While Gasly had also thrown the dice and gone to the grid on the softs, the Williams and Sauber were on mediums, so the stop looked like an attempt to force a reaction from those just outside the top ten in the hope of an undercut. Nobody responded though, and it all went awry for Albon, the new right front not being attached properly, forcing him to stop again and take a 10s penalty for an unsafe release.

With a dozen laps down, Verstappen led Norris by 3s, with Leclerc's Ferrari another couple of seconds behind the lead McLaren. Sainz was a similar distance behind his team-mate, but under heavy pressure from Piastri, who was clearly quicker, but unable to find a way by. Mercedes didn't quite seem to have the race pace, with Russell falling away 3s behind Piastri and Hamilton still in touch. Hülkenberg, a further 8s down, still ran ninth, but had Tsunoda, Pérez and Ricciardo in close attendance. Daniel was next in for a switch to hards to apply some potential undercut pressure to the three ahead. Tsunoda covered him a lap later with a stop that leapfrogged Hülkenberg when the Haas pitted next time around.

At the front, meanwhile, the strategy games could not quite begin yet, the leading trio needing to be mindful that Pérez, now eighth, was running the reverse strategy on his hard-compound tyres and that they might struggle to put a DRS pass on him even with fresh rubber. Leclerc had closed in on Norris's second place and looked well placed to try an undercut, but he didn't have the necessary gap to the midfield, Ferrari telling him, "We are going plan B." But just then, Pérez helped the situation somewhat by locking up and running across the gravel into the first Rivazza, costing himself around 5s.

Verstappen, now with more than 6s in hand over Norris at the front, was on the radio, telling Red Bull, "My front left tyre is not good."

The first of the top six to pit, however, was Russell's Mercedes, George getting away in 2.4s with his shiny new

Above: Leclerc and Sainz were on duty to keep the *tifosi* happy.
Photo: Scuderia Ferrari

Top left: Once again, Tsunoda shone in qualifying, seventh quickest.
Photo: Pirelli

Above left: Under pressure. Logan Sargeant's best times were deleted after he exceeded track limits.
Photo: Williams Racing

Left: Pérez goes airborne in his Red Bull while attempting to make Q3.
Photo: Atsuo Sakurai

Below left: Damon Hill chats with Ollie Bearman, Britain's bright new F1 hopeful.
Photo: Haas F1 Team

Opening spread: An orderly getaway as Lando Norris and Max Verstappen lead the field towards the first chicane.
Photo: Red Bull Content Pool/Getty Images

Above: Lando Norris just failed to catch Verstappen, but managed to take second place, after resisting the late-race charge of Charles Leclerc.
Photo: XPB Images

Above right: A three-place grid penalty for impeding Kevin Magnussen in qualifying cost Oscar Piastri a front-row slot. The young Australian had to be content with fourth after a tough race.
Photo: McLaren F1 Team

Top far right: Lance Stroll was the race's last unlapped runner, coming home in ninth place.
Photo: Aramco Aston Martin F1 Team

Above far right: Ferrari couldn't quite get it done for the home fans. That would have to wait until Monza.
Photo: Scuderia Ferrari

Right: McLaren celebrates after second and fourth-place finishes.
Photo: McLaren F1 Team

hards. He came out behind Ocon's Alpine, but was able to go by comfortably down the main straight with DRS.

Norris received the call to box on lap 23 and, frustratingly, came back out still just behind Pérez. Again, though, a DRS pass was accomplished with greater ease than McLaren might have feared, Lando losing minimal time as Ferrari extended Leclerc's stint, no doubt hoping to repeat the approach that had allowed him to beat Norris at Suzuka.

Next time around, Piastri was in, having spent the whole stint trapped behind Sainz. Verstappen stopped on lap 25, which meant that, temporarily, Ferrari was running 1-2. Leclerc, however, was in three laps after Norris and rejoined also just behind Pérez, having covered off Piastri. Could the Ferrari go by the Red Bull as comfortably as the McLaren? The answer was yes, Leclerc getting by Pérez before Piastri became too much of a nuisance.

Sainz was in on lap 27 as Hamilton, after a brief excursion at Acque Minerale, followed him in. But the late stop, three laps after Piastri, had cost the Spaniard, the McLaren driver now 6s up the road by the time Sainz also made his way past Pérez on 30-lap-old hards.

As Piastri pushed to stay within DRS range of Leclerc, who was now 3s behind Norris's lead McLaren, his team was telling him, "Degradation on all cars looks higher than expected, but we think this is Plan B, not Plan C."

Leclerc, meanwhile, was starting to eat into the deficit to Norris, who wasn't slow to notice and asked, "Where am I so much slower than the guys behind?"

The reassurance from the pit wall was, "Lando, they're using their tyres a lot more than we are."

"Yeah," Lando replied, "but I have no pace…"

After a brief battle keeping Hamilton at bay for a couple of laps, Pérez finally pitted to swap his starting hards for mediums with 25 laps remaining. He rejoined just out of the points behind Tsunoda, Hülkenberg and Ricciardo.

Leclerc was now starting to look like a threat to Norris's second place, putting a couple of seconds between himself and Piastri, and closing almost to within DRS range of the lead McLaren.

"Last couple of laps Leclerc is trying to push on a bit," McLaren told Norris. "The lap before, he did a 21.0 and his last lap was a 20.5, so he's trying."

"Yep, me too, I'm trying," responded Lando, "and he's a lot quicker…"

With his fresh mediums, Pérez was soon back past Ricciardo, Hülkenberg and Tsunoda, but with Hamilton 30s ahead, that was as far as the Mexican would go on a lacklustre weekend. After 46 laps, his team-mate was leading the race comfortably, almost a minute up the road…

Leclerc might have got to within DRS range of Norris, but he would go no further and had used a lot of tyre getting there: witness a straight-on moment at Variante Alta that signalled the end of his challenge as the gap started to open again.

It looked like there might have been some kidology in those "I'm trying" messages from Norris as, not only did he start putting some distance on the Ferrari, but also he started to close the gap to Verstappen. It was down to under 5s with a dozen laps remaining.

"The main losses to Lando are Turn Two and Turn Six," Red Bull told Max.

"Yeah, my tyres don't work, mate," Verstappen replied, the Red Bull clearly not as happy on the hard Pirelli as on the medium.

"Just information, Max, that's all," 'GP' Lambiase told his man.

"Yeah, same for me," Max replied, each seemingly as keen not to upset the other!

At McLaren, Will Joseph was also encouraging his man to get his clog down. "Max is struggling with tyres," Lando was told.

"Yep, yep, I'm pushing…" Norris confirmed.

Top: Before and after the race…
Photos: Atsuo Sakurai

Above: Ferrari's Charles Leclerc received enthusiastic home support.
Photo: Scuderia Ferrari

Above right: Max Verstappen was made to work hard for his victory.
Photo: Red Bull Content Pool/Getty Images

Above far right: Thirty years on, Ayrton Senna was remembered with a variety of tribute stickers placed on the cars.
Photo: Haas F1 Team

Right: Past and present merge as Verstappen speeds his Red Bull through a sea of Brazilian flags.
Photo: Red Bull Content Pool/Getty Images

With ten laps to go, it was a surprise to see Russell called into the pits for tyres. He was running sixth, some 7.8s behind Sainz's Ferrari and with team-mate Hamilton just 3.5s adrift. Behind Lewis, there was a tight pit window to Pérez, on his mediums. In ten laps, there was no chance of George re-catching Lewis, so he stood to lose two points in the drivers' championship to earn the team an extra fastest-lap point in the constructors' championship. With George ahead, you wondered why Mercedes didn't chase the extra point with Lewis instead, but that would have dropped him behind Pérez.

With Norris still closing, 'GP' was now interested in covering all the bases: "With the gap now under 5s, we really can't afford any track limits," Max was told, having been warned earlier in the race. In effect, "Get on with it, but make sure you stay on the black stuff." Not easy on worn hards…

Norris had the gap down to a second-and-a-half with six laps to go and excitement was growing on the McLaren pit wall. "Lando, happy to push Turn Nine a little bit more," Norris was told.

With a hint of exasperation, he responded, "I'm pushing as hard as I can, mate, thank you."

Verstappen upped his pace a fraction, and it looked like he had it under control, but Norris gathered himself for one last push and had the gap down to 1.2s with two to go, almost within DRS range.

"The battery is almost empty," Verstappen informed his pit crew.

"If we want to top up the battery, it will be mode seven, Max, but you will clip more in mode seven."

As they flew towards the start of the final lap, Norris failed to get DRS by just 0.04s at the detection point and Verstappen was safe barring any last-lap error. There wasn't one. Max and Red Bull had answered the questions Norris had posed with his Miami win, but clearly, there was finally healthy competition at the front in F1 again. Ferrari was not far behind either, Leclerc easing back and taking the flag some 7s adrift of the lead pair.

"I had to work for that," Verstappen said with a laugh over the radio, "but great race considering how the weekend started."

"That's two wins in a day for you!" Christian Horner pointed out, referencing a 24-hour SIM race Verstappen had been competing in, including a four-hour stint post-qualifying!

It had been so finely balanced that Norris was left to contemplate what might have been if Verstappen had not enjoyed that tow from Hülkenberg in qualifying. Piastri had backed up McLaren's strength.

At Ferrari, Leclerc enjoyed his first Imola podium, but he had wanted more, while team-mate Sainz, fifth, was not happy with the overall pace and some battery deployment issues.

Mercedes still had work to do and, publicly at any rate, Russell had no problem with sacrificing his sixth place.

"At the end of the day, as a team we scored one extra point," he said with a resigned expression. "I lost my position to Lewis, but I'm not going to sulk over losing a P6, to be honest… We're a little bit in no-man's land behind Ferrari and McLaren, and ahead of the midfield."

Eighth place, his worst result of the season, was not what Red Bull was looking for from Sergio Pérez, but Lance Stroll brought some cheer to Aston Martin after a difficult weekend with ninth place. Yuki Tsunoda rewarded the VCARB factory staff, at Imola in strength, with the final point. Hülkenberg, after a strong weekend, was the most unfortunate of those who left empty handed, 11th.

Tony Dodgins

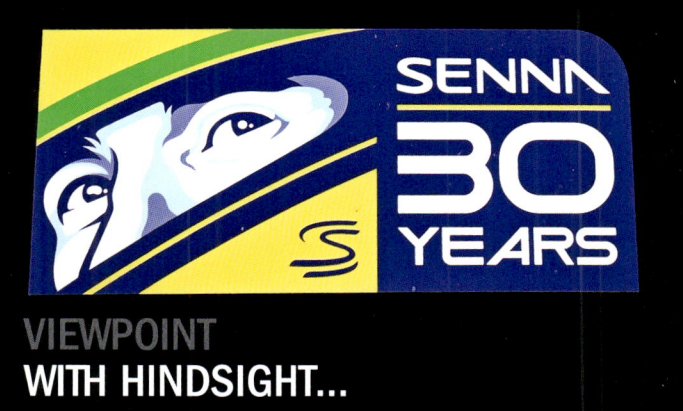

VIEWPOINT
WITH HINDSIGHT...

HAD Ayrton Senna been around, he would have relished the challenge faced by Max Verstappen and Red Bull as the weekend unfolded at Imola. A car that usually had been a dream to drive had become an unbalanced handful.

There were no simulators in the early 1990s, but had there been, Senna might have given serious thought to flying back to base and spending several hours in the sim, much as Sébastien Buemi had done throughout Friday night on behalf of Verstappen at the Red Bull campus in Milton Keynes.

As it was, Senna would have sat through the best part of the evening with his engineer in the team truck as they analysed each corner, from entry to exit and every centimetre in between. The discussion would largely have been between the two of them, with occasional input from the tyre engineer and the engine supplier's technical representative.

In today's situation, with an army of technicians examining every conceivable permutation on their computers in factory-based mission-control centres, Senna would have taken a deep dive into the mountain of information waiting for him on arrival at the track on Saturday morning. Given the unexpected struggle experienced by Williams-Renault with their FW16 during the first two races of 1994, there is every chance that Ayrton would not have slept much had today's detailed scrutiny and evaluations been available.

It's also reasonable to suggest that Adrian Newey and Williams would have been on top of FW16's shortcomings much sooner. But making such an assumption is as frustrating as envisaging an altogether different outcome had the opening laps of the 1994 San Marino Grand Prix been run under strict safety procedures since fashioned by painful experience.

Much had happened for the better during the previous 30 years. It was three decades since that terrible weekend at Imola and yet, with Senna's exhilarating memories still fresh in the minds of those fortunate to have witnessed his thrilling presence, it seemed like no time at all.

Maurice Hamilton

7

FORMULA 1 MSC CRUISES GRAN PREMIO DEL MADE IN ITALY E DELL'EMILIA-ROMAGNA 2024

AUTODROMO ENZO E DINO FERRARI, IMOLA
Circuit: 3.050 miles/4.909km, 63 laps

IMOLA 17-19 MAY

RACE DISTANCE: 63 laps, 192.034 miles/309.049km
RACE WEATHER: Dry/partly cloudy (track 47-50°C, air 32-33°C)

RACE – OFFICIAL CLASSIFICATION

Pos.	Driver	Nat.	No.	Entrant	Car/Engine	Laps	Time/Retirement	Speed (mph/km/h)	Gap to leader	Fastest race lap
1	Max Verstappen	NL	1	Oracle Red Bull Racing	Red Bull RB20-Honda RBPT H002 V6	63	1h 25m 25.252s	134.885/217.077		1m 20.366s 38
2	Lando Norris	GB	4	McLaren Formula 1 Team	McLaren MCL38-Mercedes F1 M15 E Perf. V6	63	1h 25m 25.977s	134.866/217.046	0.725s	1m 19.994s 54
3	Charles Leclerc	MC	16	Scuderia Ferrari	Ferrari SF-24-066/12 V6	63	1h 25m 33.168s	134.677/216.742	7.916s	1m 19.935s 27
4	Oscar Piastri	AUS	81	McLaren Formula 1 Team	McLaren MCL38-Mercedes F1 M15 E Perf. V6	63	1h 25m 39.384s	134.514/216.480	14.132s	1m 19.907s 25
5	Carlos Sainz	E	55	Scuderia Ferrari	Ferrari SF-24-066/12 V6	63	1h 25m 47.577s	134.300/216.135	22.325s	1m 20.220s 63
6	Lewis Hamilton	GB	44	Mercedes-AMG Petronas F1 Team	Mercedes-AMG F1 W15-M15 E Perf. V6	63	1h 26m 00.356s	133.968/215.600	35.104s	1m 20.331s 43
7	George Russell	GB	63	Mercedes-AMG Petronas F1 Team	Mercedes-AMG F1 W15-M15 E Perf. V6	63	1h 26m 12.406s	133.656/215.098	47.154s	1m 18.589s 54
8	Sergio Pérez	MEX	11	Oracle Red Bull Racing	Red Bull RB20-Honda RBPT H002 V6	63	1h 26m 20.028s	133.459/214.781	54.776s	1m 19.686s 52
9	Lance Stroll	CDN	18	Aston Martin Aramco F1 Team	Aston Martin AMR24-Mercedes F1 M15 E Perf. V6	63	1h 26m 44.808s	132.824/213.759	1m 19.556s	1m 20.570s 58
10	Yuki Tsunoda	J	22	Visa Cash App RB Formula One Team	RB VCARB 01-Honda RBPT H002 V6	62			1 lap	1m 20.936s 14
11	Nico Hülkenberg	D	27	MoneyGram Haas F1 Team	Haas VF-24-Ferrari 066/10 V6	62			1 lap	1m 21.700s 3
12	Kevin Magnussen	DK	20	MoneyGram Haas F1 Team	Haas VF-24-Ferrari 066/10 V6	62			1 lap	1m 21.009s 58
13	Daniel Ricciardo	AUS	3	Visa Cash App RB Formula One Team	RB VCARB 01-Honda RBPT H002 V6	62			1 lap	1m 21.569s 13
14	Esteban Ocon	F	31	BWT Alpine F1 Team	Alpine A524-Renault E-Tech RE24 V6	62			1 lap	1m 21.304s 37
15	Zhou Guanyu	CHN	24	Stake F1 Team Kick Sauber	Sauber C44-Ferrari 066/12 V6	62			1 lap	1m 21.016s 37
16	Pierre Gasly	F	10	BWT Alpine F1 Team	Alpine A524-Renault E-Tech RE24 V6	62			1 lap	1m 21.371s 10
17	Logan Sargeant	USA	2	Williams Racing	Williams FW46-Mercedes F1 M15 E Perf. V6	62			1 lap	1m 21.229s 55
18	Valtteri Bottas	FIN	77	Stake F1 Team Kick Sauber	Sauber C44-Ferrari 066/12 V6	62			1 lap	1m 21.455s 11
19	Fernando Alonso	E	14	Aston Martin Aramco F1 Team	Aston Martin AMR24-Mercedes F1 M15 E Perf. V6	62			1 lap	1m 19.004s 62
	Alexander Albon	T	23	Williams Racing	Williams FW46-Mercedes F1 M15 E Perf. V 6	51	withdrew *			1m 21.274s 48

* Albon: 10s stop-and-go penalty for car released in an unsafe condition.

DHL Fastest race lap (scores 1 point): George Russell on lap 54, 1m 18.589s, 139.728mph/224.871km/h.
Lap record: Lewis Hamilton (Mercedes F1 W11 V6), 1m 15.484s, 145.476mph/234.121km/h (2020).

 19 · SARGEANT · Williams
 17 · ZHOU · Sauber
 15 · GASLY · Alpine
 13 · STROLL · Aston Martin
 11 · PÉREZ · Red Bull

 20 · ALONSO · Aston Martin
Car modified in parc fermé; required to start from the pit lane
 18 · MAGNUSSEN · Haas
 16 · BOTTAS · Sauber
 14 · ALBON · Williams
 12 · OCON · Alpine

Grid order	1	2	3	4	5	6	7	8	9	10	11	12	13	14	15	16	17	18	19	20	21	22	23	24	25	26	27	28	29	30	31	32	33	34	35	36	37	38	39	40	41	42	43	44	45	46	47	48	49	50
1 VERSTAPPEN	1	1	1	1	1	1	1	1	1	1	1	1	1	1	1	1	1	1	1	1	1	1	1	1	1	55	55	55	1	1	1	1	1	1	1	1	1	1	1	1	1	1	1	1	1	1	1	1	1	1
4 NORRIS	4	4	4	4	4	4	4	4	4	4	4	4	4	4	4	4	4	4	4	4	4	4	16	16	16	16	44	1	4	4	4	4	4	4	4	4	4	4	4	4	4	4	4	4	4	4	4	4	4	4
16 LECLERC	16	16	16	16	16	16	16	16	16	16	16	16	16	16	16	16	16	16	16	16	16	16	4	55	55	44	1	4	16	16	16	16	16	16	16	16	16	16	16	16	16	16	16	16	16	16	16	16	16	16
55 SAINZ	55	55	55	55	55	55	55	55	55	55	55	55	55	55	55	55	55	55	55	55	55	55	55	81	44	1	4	81	81	81	81	81	81	81	81	81	81	81	81	81	81	81	81	81	81	81	81	81	81	81
81 PIASTRI	81	81	81	81	81	81	81	81	81	81	81	81	81	81	81	81	81	81	81	81	81	81	81	44	4	11	16	11	55	55	55	55	55	55	55	55	55	55	55	55	55	55	55	55	55	55	55	55	55	55
63 RUSSELL	63	63	63	63	63	63	63	63	63	63	63	63	63	63	63	63	63	63	63	63	44	44	11	11	11	16	81	55	55	11	63	63	63	63	63	63	63	63	63	63	63	63	63	63	63	63	63	63	63	63
22 TSUNODA	44	44	44	44	44	44	44	44	44	44	44	44	44	44	44	44	44	44	44	44	63	11	4	18	81	81	11	63	63	63	11	11	11	11	11	11	44	44	44	44	44	44	44	44	44	44	44	44	44	44
44 HAMILTON	27	27	27	27	27	27	27	27	27	27	27	27	27	27	27	27	27	27	27	27	11	11	11	11	11	11	18	18	18	18	18	18	18	44	44	44	44	11	22	22	22	22	22	11	11	11	11	11	11	11
3 RICCIARDO	22	22	22	22	22	22	22	22	22	11	27	18	18	18	18	18	18	18	18	18	18	18	63	63	63	63	63	18	44	44	44	18	18	18	18	18	11	22	11	11	11	11	11	22	22	22	22	22	22	22
27 HÜLKENBERG	11	11	11	11	11	11	11	11	11	18	18	31	31	31	31	31	31	31	31	63	31	31	20	20	20	20	20	20	20	20	20	20	20	20	20	20	22	3	11	27	27	27	27	27	27	27	27	27	27	18
11 PÉREZ	3	3	3	3	3	3	3	3	3	3	18	22	31	20	20	20	20	20	20	20	20	20	31	24	24	24	24	24	24	22	22	22	22	22	22	27	11	3	3	3	18	18	18	27	27	27	27	27	27	27
31 OCON	31	31	31	31	31	31	31	31	31	31	18	31	20	24	24	24	24	24	24	24	24	24	22	22	22	22	22	22	22	27	27	27	27	27	27	20	77	77	18	18	3	3	3	3	3	3	3	3	3	3
18 STROLL	18	18	18	18	18	18	18	18	18	31	3	20	24	2	2	2	2	2	2	2	2	2	27	27	27	27	27	27	27	3	3	3	3	3	3	18	18	18	77	77	77	77	77	77	77	77	77	77	77	77
23 ALBON	23	23	23	23	23	23	23	23	23	24	24	24	2	22	22	22	22	22	22	22	22	22	3	3	3	3	3	3	3	24	77	77	77	77	77	77	31	31	31	31	31	31	31	31	31	31	31	31	31	20
10 GASLY	10	10	10	10	10	10	10	10	10	23	24	2	22	27	27	27	27	27	27	27	27	27	2	2	2	2	2	2	2	77	24	24	24	24	24	31	14	14	14	14	14	14	14	14	14	14	14	14	14	14
77 BOTTAS	20	20	20	20	20	20	20	20	24	2	2	3	3	3	3	3	3	3	3	3	3	3	10	10	10	10	10	10	10	2	14	31	31	14	14	14	20	20	20	20	20	20	20	20	20	20	20	20	24	24
24 ZHOU	77	77	77	77	77	77	77	77	2	10	10	10	10	10	10	10	10	10	10	10	10	10	77	77	77	77	77	77	77	10	14	31	31	24	24	24	24	20	20	20	20	20	20	20	20	10	10	10	10	10
20 MAGNUSSEN	24	24	24	24	24	24	10	77	77	77	77	77	77	77	77	77	77	77	77	77	77	77	14	31	31	14	14	31	31	14	24	14	14	31	31	10	10	10	10	10	10	10	10	10	10	2	2	2	2	2
2 SARGEANT	2	2	2	2	2	2	77	14	14	14	14	14	14	14	14	14	14	14	14	14	14	14	31	31	31	31	10	2	2	2	2	2	2	2	2	2	14	14	14	14	14	14	14	14	14	14	14	14	14	14
14 ALONSO	14	14	14	14	14	14	14	23	23	23	23	23	23	23	23	23	23	23	23	23	23	23	23	23	23	23	23	23	23	23	23	23	23	23	23	23	23	23	23	23	23	23	23	23	23	23	23	23	23	23

TIME SHEETS

PRACTICE 1 (FRIDAY)
Weather: Dry/sunny
Temperatures: track 49-50°C, air 27-28°C

Pos.	Driver	Laps	Time
1	Charles Leclerc	30	1m 16.990s
2	George Russell	28	1m 17.094s
3	Carlos Sainz	25	1m 17.120s
4	Sergio Pérez	23	1m 17.233s
5	Max Verstappen	21	1m 17.240s
6	Yuki Tsunoda	29	1m 17.388s
7	Lewis Hamilton	27	1m 17.408s
8	Lando Norris	17	1m 17.602s
9	Oscar Piastri	25	1m 17.807s
10	Fernando Alonso	18	1m 17.867s
11	Pierre Gasly	21	1m 17.905s
12	Lance Stroll	22	1m 18.072s
13	Daniel Ricciardo	26	1m 18.142s
14	Esteban Ocon	29	1m 18.612s
15	Oliver Bearman	31	1m 18.667s
16	Valtteri Bottas	23	1m 18.827s
17	Zhou Guanyu	18	1m 19.129s
18	Logan Sargeant	22	1m 19.901s
19	Alexander Albon	8	1m 20.050s
20	Nico Hülkenberg	20	1m 21.059s

PRACTICE 2 (FRIDAY)
Weather: Dry/sunny
Temperatures: track 36-42°C, air 26-28°C

Pos.	Driver	Laps	Time
1	Charles Leclerc	29	1m 15.906s
2	Oscar Piastri	30	1m 16.098s
3	Yuki Tsunoda	32	1m 16.286s
4	Lewis Hamilton	29	1m 16.297s
5	George Russell	32	1m 16.311s
6	Carlos Sainz	30	1m 16.423s
7	Max Verstappen	23	1m 16.447s
8	Sergio Pérez	25	1m 16.552s
9	Nico Hülkenberg	28	1m 16.826s
10	Fernando Alonso	29	1m 16.838s
11	Daniel Ricciardo	32	1m 16.967s
12	Lando Norris	30	1m 16.980s
13	Lance Stroll	26	1m 16.991s
14	Esteban Ocon	31	1m 17.008s
15	Pierre Gasly	32	1m 17.064s
16	Valtteri Bottas	28	1m 17.088s
17	Kevin Magnussen	32	1m 17.129s
18	Alexander Albon	23	1m 17.135s
19	Zhou Guanyu	28	1m 17.606s
20	Logan Sargeant	22	1m 17.848s

PRACTICE 3 (SATURDAY)
Weather: Dry/sunny
Temperatures: track 51-53°C, air 28-29°C

Pos.	Driver	Laps	Time
1	Oscar Piastri	15	1m 15.529s
2	Lando Norris	15	1m 15.829s
3	Carlos Sainz	22	1m 16.067s
4	Charles Leclerc	20	1m 16.087s
5	George Russell	16	1m 16.095s
6	Max Verstappen	21	1m 16.366s
7	Alexander Albon	14	1m 16.470s
8	Esteban Ocon	19	1m 16.481s
9	Lance Stroll	24	1m 16.543s
10	Nico Hülkenberg	15	1m 16.547s
11	Daniel Ricciardo	15	1m 16.560s
12	Sergio Pérez	18	1m 16.631s
13	Yuki Tsunoda	14	1m 16.668s
14	Valtteri Bottas	15	1m 16.695s
15	Logan Sargeant	16	1m 16.794s
16	Kevin Magnussen	12	1m 16.923s
17	Lewis Hamilton	16	1m 16.960s
18	Fernando Alonso	10	1m 17.339s
19	Pierre Gasly	17	1m 17.361s
20	Zhou Guanyu	15	1m 17.891s

QUALIFYING (SATURDAY)
Weather: Dry/overcast Temperatures: track 44-47°C, air 29-30°C

Pos.	Driver	First	Second	Third	Qualifying Tyre
1	Max Verstappen	1m 15.762s	1m 15.176s	1m 14.746s	Soft (n)
2	Oscar Piastri	1m 15.940s	1m 15.407s	1m 14.820s	Soft (n)
3	Lando Norris	1m 15.915s	1m 15.371s	1m 14.837s	Soft (n)
4	Charles Leclerc	1m 15.823s	1m 15.328s	1m 14.970s	Soft (n)
5	Carlos Sainz	1m 16.015s	1m 15.512s	1m 15.233s	Soft (n)
6	George Russell	1m 16.107s	1m 15.671s	1m 15.234s	Soft (n)
7	Yuki Tsunoda	1m 15.894s	1m 15.358s	1m 15.465s	Soft (n)
8	Lewis Hamilton	1m 16.604s	1m 15.677s	1m 15.504s	Soft (n)
9	Daniel Ricciardo	1m 16.060s	1m 15.691s	1m 15.674s	Soft (n)
10	Nico Hülkenberg	1m 15.841s	1m 15.569s	1m 15.980s	Soft (n)
11	Sergio Pérez	1m 16.404s	1m 15.706s		
12	Esteban Ocon	1m 16.361s	1m 15.906s		
13	Lance Stroll	1m 16.458s	1m 15.992s		
14	Alexander Albon	1m 16.524s	1m 16.200s		
15	Pierre Gasly	1m 16.015s	1m 16.381s		
16	Valtteri Bottas	1m 16.626s			
17	Zhou Guanyu	1m 16.834s			
18	Kevin Magnussen	1m 16.854s			
19	Fernando Alonso	1m 16.917s			
20	Logan Sargeant	no time			

QUALIFYING: head to head

Verstappen	7	0	Pérez
Hamilton	1	6	Russell
Norris	5	2	Piastri
Leclerc	4	2	Sainz
Leclerc	1	0	Bearman
Gasly	1	6	Ocon
Alonso	4	3	Stroll
Albon	7	0	Sargeant
Bottas	7	0	Zhou
Tsunoda	6	1	Ricciardo
Magnussen	2	5	Hülkenberg

FOR THE RECORD

150th GRAND PRIX START: Lance Stroll

2,000th GP LAP LED: Spanish drivers

1,000,000th GP Km RACED: Ferrari engines

DID YOU KNOW?

Verstappen is now level with Senna on consecutive GP pole positions (8).

This was the 300th world championship GP started by Mercedes.

POINTS

DRIVERS

1	Max Verstappen	161
2	Charles Leclerc	113
3	Sergio Pérez	107
4	Lando Norris	101
5	Carlos Sainz	93
6	Oscar Piastri	53
7	George Russell	44
8	Lewis Hamilton	35
9	Fernando Alonso	33
10	Yuki Tsunoda	15
11	Lance Stroll	11
12	Oliver Bearman	6
13	Nico Hülkenberg	6
14	Daniel Ricciardo	5
15	Esteban Ocon	1
16	Kevin Magnussen	1

CONSTRUCTORS

1	Red Bull	268
2	Ferrari	212
3	McLaren	154
4	Mercedes	79
5	Aston Martin	44
6	RB	20
7	Haas	7
8	Alpine	1

9 · RICCIARDO · RB   7 · TSUNODA · RB   5 · PIASTRI · McLaren
3-place penalty for impeding Magnussen during qualifying
3 · LECLERC · Ferrari   1 · VERSTAPPEN · Red Bull

10 · HÜLKENBERG · Haas   8 · HAMILTON · Mercedes   6 · RUSSELL · Mercedes   4 · SAINZ · Ferrari   2 · NORRIS · McLaren

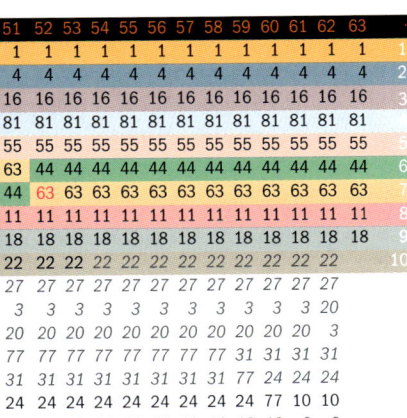

14 = Pit stop   23 = One lap or more behind

RACE TYRE STRATEGIES

	Driver	Race Stint 1	Race Stint 2	Race Stint 3	Race Stint 4
1	Verstappen	Medium (n): 1-24	Hard (n): 25-63		
2	Norris	Medium (n): 1-22	Hard (u): 23-63		
3	Leclerc	Medium (n): 1-25	Hard (n): 26-63		
4	Piastri	Medium (n): 1-23	Hard (u): 24-63		
5	Sainz	Medium (n): 1-27	Hard (n): 28-63		
6	Hamilton	Medium (n): 1-27	Hard (n): 28-63		
7	Russell	Medium (n): 1-21	Hard (n): 22-52	Medium (u): 53-63	
8	Pérez	Hard (n): 1-37	Medium (n): 38-63		
9	Stroll	Medium u): 1-37	Hard (u): 38-63		
10	Tsunoda	Medium (n): 1-12	Hard (n): 13-62		
11	Hülkenberg	Medium (n): 1-13	Hard (n): 14-62		
12	Magnussen	Medium (n): 1-37	Hard (n): 38-62		
13	Ricciardo	Medium (n): 1-11	Hard (n): 12-62		
14	Ocon	Medium (n): 1-25	Hard (n): 26-62		
15	Zhou	Hard (n): 1-33	Medium (n): 34-62		
16	Gasly	Soft (n): 1-8	Hard (n): 9-30	Medium (n): 31-62	
17	Sargeant	Hard (n): 1-31	Medium (n): 32-62		
18	Bottas	Medium (n): 1-8	Hard (n): 9-62		
19	Alonso	Soft (n): 1-7	Hard (u): 8-40	Medium (u): 41-58	Soft (n): 59-62
	Albon	Medium (n): 1-8	Hard (n): 9	Medium (u): 10-28	Medium (u): 29-51 (dnf)

The tyre regulations stipulate that at least two of three dry tyre specifications must be used during a dry race.
Selected compounds for Imola: Red = Soft (C5); Yellow = Medium (C4); White = Hard (C3). (n) new (u) used

FIA FORMULA 1 WORLD CHAMPIONSHIP · ROUND 8
MONACO GRAND PRIX
MONTE CARLO CIRCUIT

MONTE CARLO QUALIFYING

CHARLES LECLERC dominated Friday practice in Monaco for a race that everyone acknowledges is won on Saturday, in qualifying. He headed into his home race with the most F1 pole positions (23) of any driver without a world championship to his name, almost 40 per cent of them at street circuits – Monaco, Baku, Miami, Singapore and Las Vegas. The home hero's Ferrari looked the class of the field on Friday with a strong front end, compliant ride and a slow-speed corner advantage. It dominated both Friday practice sessions by a margin and only failed to top the FP1 times because Ferrari elected not to do a soft-tyre run.

At the end of FP2, Lewis Hamilton, who described Monaco Friday as the best day of Mercedes' season so far, managed to get within two-tenths of his future Ferrari team-mate, but, along with Fernando Alonso's third-place time, these laps were set later on after strong track evolution.

Red Bull looked like they were facing another Imola as they tried to turn around an opening day on which Max Verstappen was only fourth quickest, more than half a second behind Leclerc's pace, with Sergio Pérez 11th. With Monte Carlo's crowns, cambers and kerbs, this one looked like it might be a trickier fix than San Marino.

"It's jumping like a kangaroo. I'm getting headaches, it's crazy!" Verstappen complained. The problems continued into qualifying, the world champion clearing Q1 only seventh as he fought to beat Ayrton Senna's record of eight consecutive poles. That didn't look too likely!

Meanwhile, Sergio Pérez was slower than all bar the Saubers of Valtteri Bottas and Zhou Guanyu, but the margins were miniscule. Monaco is a short lap. George Russell's Q1 session-topping lap was 1m 11.492s. Fernando Alonso's Aston Martin was the first Q1 casualty, 16th, but his time was only 0.527s shy of Russell. Pérez, 18th, was just 0.568s away, the first time in 2024 that a Red Bull had gone out in Q1. Anyone remember 1988, when Senna's pole had beaten the second-place car, his team-mate Alain Prost's McLaren, by 1.42s?

If Q1 was tight, in Q2, the top four were covered by just nine-hundredths! The McLarens, resplendent in a lovely green and yellow tribute livery to the great Senna, a man who had won six times in Monte Carlo and who had died this month some 30 years ago, started to show their hands. Lando Norris went quickest, a hundredth faster than an improving Verstappen, and two-hundredths quicker than team-mate Oscar Piastri. Leclerc, picking up the pace after a conservative Q1, was 0.09s behind the ultimate pace. Further back, Esteban Ocon's Alpine, Nico Hülkenberg's Haas, Daniel Ricciardo's VCARB, Lance Stroll's Aston Martin and Kevin Magnussen's Haas missed the Q2 cut.

On the opening Q3 runs, Leclerc went quickest for the first time, his 1m 10.418s lap just 0.03s clear of Piastri. Meanwhile, Carlos Sainz was a quarter of a second away in third place with the second Ferrari. Verstappen's first run put him within a tenth-and-a-half, third, ahead of Sainz.

There's a special thrill about Monte Carlo's Q3 second runs. Verstappen's pole challenge was over with a radio message that he had hit the wall. Often quickest in sector one, the world champion had gone into Sainte Devote a little hot and clipped the barrier.

"Ah man ... this car is slippery as ****," was his frustrated take.

Lewis Hamilton, 6–1 down in the qualifying head-to-head with team-mate Russell, went fifth, and the tiny Principality held its collective breath as Leclerc emerged for his final run. Without being quickest in any sector, nonetheless he improved his pole time to 1m 10.270s.

Oscar Piastri did his damnedest to respond, but was 0.15s behind the Ferrari as he claimed a spot on the front row. Sainz improved to third, quick enough to bump Norris to fourth, while Russell had to be content with fifth, quicker than Hamilton once again, but with an upgraded front wing on his W15 that his team-mate was yet to receive. Verstappen would start sixth, between the two Mercedes, with Yuki Tsunoda's VCARB, Alex Albon's Williams and Pierre Gasly's Alpine completing the top ten.

"I'm not so disappointed with the position as with our performance," Verstappen said. "It's not something that came as a surprise though, because I knew our limitations coming into the weekend. It's been bad. I can't take any kerbs, and in the middle sector, I'm driving around them. It feels like I'm driving a go-kart with no suspension or damping."

This was Leclerc's third Monaco GP pole, Piero Ferrari on hand to witness the Scuderia's milestone 250th F1 pole.

"I'm really happy with the lap," Leclerc smiled. "The excitement here [he meant pressure!] is so high, but as I know from the past, qualifying is not everything. Now we need to put everything together."

Meanwhile, Piastri thought he might have done even better: "If you took the second half of my first lap in Q3 and the first half of the second one, it would have been enough, but there were a couple of mistakes at the end. But credit to Charles, he'd been incredibly quick all weekend. I don't think anyone thought we were going to get close to him, so nice to be starting on the front row and good momentum built."

Sainz, too, was happy: "Today is an improvement. I've been struggling all weekend with confidence and feel, so P3 was a step forward. The long runs looked better though, so hopefully we are in a good place. The priority tomorrow will be to win with Charles."

Would this be the race for Leclerc to shake off the proverbial Monaco monkey on his back? Throughout his career, he had produced some electrifying performances on his home streets, but lady luck had never smiled on him. The fact that he had not converted his previous 12 poles, a statistic that he was constantly reminded of, was more down to the race shortcomings of a car that he'd often overqualified. But it had to be in the back of his mind, nonetheless.

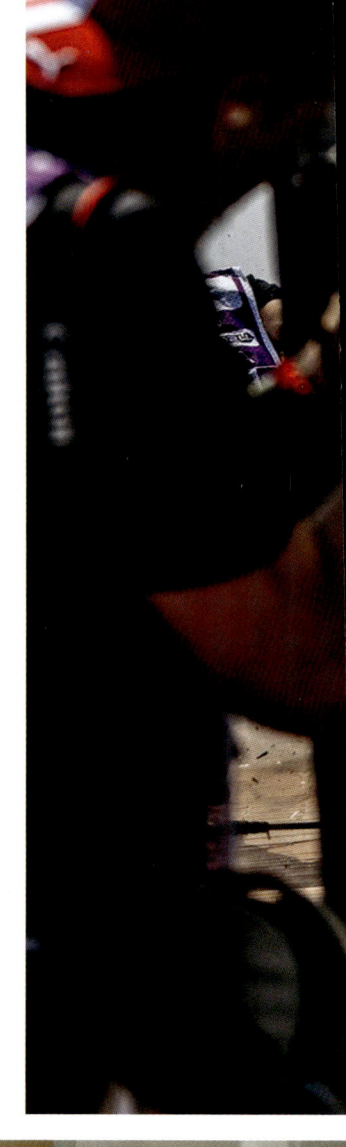

Right: Motor racing is dangerous. Sergio Pérez's Red Bull smashes into the barriers, with a brave photographer still at close quarters!
Photo: FTW

Below: Pérez's mangled car is winched away.
Photo: Red Bull Content Pool/Getty Images

Bottom: A frustrated Hülkenberg was a victim of the collision.
Photo: Haas F1 Team

Bottom right: Pérez was left to survey the damage.
Photo: Red Bull Content Pool/Getty Images

Opening spread: Follow my leader. The opening-lap crash and red flag left little room for race strategies. Here, leader Leclerc heads Piastri, Sainz and Norris through the Rascasse hairpin.
Photo: Pirelli

WHAT banana skin was Charles Leclerc going to slip on this time? A personal error? A strategy error? Freak weather? The last did not look like being an issue as sunshine greeted the grid. And, with the first four all lining up on the medium-compound Pirelli, there was no great potential for strategic variation among the pace-setters. George Russell's fifth-placed Mercedes was the first car on a different tyre – the hard compound – a selection also made by Max Verstappen and Lewis Hamilton behind him.

Meanwhile, right at the back were the two Haas cars. An internal communications breakdown meant that the team's upgraded rear wing was actually outside the rules, so Nico Hülkenberg and Kevin Magnussen, who qualified 12th and 15th respectively, were disqualified.

Leclerc cleared the first hurdle when he got away well as the lights extinguished and negotiated the short 200m dash into Sainte Devote with his nose in front. Momentarily, it looked as though Carlos Sainz was going to demote Oscar Piastri down the inside and make it a Ferrari 1-2, but the Australian kept his boot in and Sainz had to cede position. There was light contact, though, and Sainz was sparking at Massenet before running straight on in Casino Square, his left front tyre punctured.

But Carlos received a huge stroke of good fortune in the form of a red flag for a bigger coming-together near the back of the field. As the cars bunched up into the first corner, Magnussen got a good run down the inside of one of the Saubers and his own team-mate, Hülkenberg. Up the hill, he kept his foot hard down and tried to draw alongside Pérez's Red Bull. Sergio squeezed him, though, and the contact spun the Red Bull hard into the barrier, from where it rebounded and collected Hülkenberg in the second Haas. Not a race to remember for Gene Haas's men! Conventional wisdom seemed to be that Magnussen should have lifted and was fortunate not to receive licence penalty points that would have seen him facing a race ban.

There had also been aggravation between the Alpine drivers further around the lap before the red flag was flown, with Esteban Ocon trying to nip inside his team-mate at Portiers, his left rear becoming airborne over Pierre Gasly's right front and bouncing Ocon straight out of the race.

"What did he do? Why did he try to attack me? The whole car is damaged now!" stormed an irate Gasly. Ocon would receive a five-place grid drop for the next race in Canada and two penalty points. The good news for Sainz was that with the red coming on the opening lap, the restart would be taken from the lap before, hence grid order.

The interesting aspect was tyres. With the need to run both compounds now negated, would everyone bolt on hards and try to run the whole race on them? Once again, the strategy of the first four mirrored each other as they did just that. And, once again, Russell, Verstappen and Hamilton did something different, this time all going for the mediums.

Above: Charles Leclerc led every lap of the restarted race, the top ten finishers running in the same order throughout.
Photo: Scuderia Ferrari

Top right: Yuki Tsunoda finished one lap down, but garnered more valuable points for RB.
Photo: Red Bull Content Pool/Getty Images

Above right: Captured mid-pack, Alex Albon scored his first points of the season for Williams.
Photo: Atsuo Sakurai

Right: Pierre Gasly's Alpine speeds up the hill towards Casino Square.
Photo: BWT Alpine F1 Team

Yuki Tsunoda and Alex Albon restarted on hards, Gasly took mediums, as did Lance Stroll and Fernando Alonso in the Aston Martins. Daniel Ricciardo opted for hards, Valtteri Bottas for mediums, while Logan Sargeant and Zhou Guanyu completed the remaining 16 on hards.

Leclerc converted his pole again at the second time of asking, and this time the field was orderly as it filed through Sainte Devote and snaked away up the hill.

As the mediums came in quicker, Russell hassled Norris without any realistic chance of going by the McLaren. "George, no need to stick this close, just manage the tyres at this stage," Russell was told.

"This is the only opportunity," he responded, somewhat optimistically

Russell did as he was bid for a few laps and, as a 3s gap opened up, came back on to the team and asked, "Do you want me to manage everywhere, or just in three, four and five [Massenet, Casino and Mirabeau]? Because if I continue at this pace, we are going to open up a pit stop for them."

Everyone, it seemed, was managing, which did not make for spectacular viewing. Max Verstappen's race engineer, 'GP' Lambiase, was telling his man that he didn't understand why Russell was going quite so slowly. Third-place man Sainz was getting a little jumpy, too, as he followed closely behind his race-leading team-mate and Piastri.

"Charles is managing, I guess?" Sainz asked the Ferrari pit wall by way of confirmation. "Because that was close with Piastri. One lap, he might just send it…"

To give an idea of the degree of tyre management going on, Bottas, whom Sauber had pitted to go from the hard to medium Pirellis, was suddenly in free air and lapping in the 1m 16s, while Leclerc, leading, was doing 1m 20s, some 10s off his pole-position pace.

As the race approached the 30-lap point, Norris was on the radio, telling McLaren, "A little bit of abrasion on the left front."

The comforting reply was, "We see it, Lando, it's about the same as Ferrari had ten laps ago." Further explanation of the managing going on, especially if, like Mercedes, the aim was to get through on a set of mediums. But did it mean that Piastri and Norris were going to be in better shape than Leclerc and Sainz in the closing stages, especially with the further message that Sainz had evidence of front left graining?

The gap from Norris to Russell was 13.4s with 34 of the 78 laps completed, with around 19s needed for a pit stop. Sainz was starting to realise that if the gap grew enough to allow Norris to stop, the McLaren would be potentially threatening on a new set of softs.

So, Ferrari got on the radio to Leclerc: "If you can, we need to slow down a bit."

"Yeah, I mean, what's the scope of that?" the race leader wanted to know.

"We are preventing McLaren having a pit-stop window," he was told.

"That makes me push in the slow speed, which I don't like," Leclerc replied.

Meanwhile, Piastri had spotted Leclerc's predicament: "He really doesn't seem to be slowing down. They must be worried about something, otherwise I feel like he'd just be slowing down."

With 45 of the 78 laps down, Norris wanted a tyre

Above: The racing in Monte Carlo can often be processional, but the draw for spectators remains irresistible.
Photo: Stake F1 Team Kick Sauber

Top right: Lewis Hamilton flashes between the walls of advertising hoardings.
Photo: Atsuo Saurai

Above right: Second-placed Oscar Piastri hussles his McLaren through the tunnel.
Photo: McLaren F1 Team

Right: The happiest man on earth. Leclerc's home victory brought unbridled joy to his team.
Photo: Scuderia Ferrari

report. "How is my front left looking compared to them?" he asked.

"Of the four of you, you are the best," he was told. Which was good to know.

Further back, the Aston Martins had been running line astern just outside the points, with Stroll ahead of Alonso. Which led to the rather bizarre situation of Alonso going slowly enough to drop back and create a pit-stop window for Stroll, so that Lance could take on a new set of tyres in the hope of attacking Gasly and challenging for points. All very well until Lance suffered a puncture after clipping the barrier at the entry to the harbour-front chicane. Thus he had to pit again with 28 laps remaining, taking softs and rejoining dead last.

With 26 laps remaining, Hamilton pitted for a new set of hards. The medium-compound starters, with Russell at the front, had dropped 16s behind Norris's fourth place. Verstappen and Hamilton were behind him when Lewis pulled the trigger and made the stop.

Verstappen covered him on the next lap and rejoined still sixth, the pair now the best part of 20s behind Russell, who was all on his own.

"Why didn't you tell me the out-lap was critical?" Hamilton complained to Mercedes as Verstappen pitted out still ahead of him. How long had the Englishman been doing this?

Verstappen and Hamilton took no time to re-close the gap to Russell, but when they arrived, Lewis claiming the race's fastest lap, the fresher tyre advantage was still nothing like enough to facilitate an overtaking move. If tyre management wasn't your thing, this was turning into a soporific affair (see Viewpoint).

As it entered its closing stages, Leclerc started to cut loose and with six laps to go, had a comfortable 8s margin over Piastri. Nobody was going to deny him his destiny and, finally, he claimed the race around the streets where he had been born and brought up. Louis Chiron had been the first Monégasque to win the Monaco GP, in 1931, but Leclerc was the first to win an F1 world championship Monaco.

The emotion was palpable. He had to take a moment to compose himself before describing what it meant.

"It's such a difficult race," he explained. "The fact that twice I'd started on pole position and we didn't quite make it, makes it even better in a way. It means such a lot. It is the race that made me dream of becoming an F1 driver one day. Fifteen laps from the end, you are just hoping that nothing happens and already the emotions were coming. I was thinking about my dad [who had passed in 2017] a lot more than I thought while driving. He gave everything for me to be here and it was a dream of ours for me to race here, and to win, so unbelievable."

The victory, his first since Austria, 2022, some 39 races before, moved Leclerc to within 31 points of Verstappen in the championship, and suddenly people were talking about a potential championship challenge. Given Leclerc's street-circuit prowess, however, that might all have been a bit premature.

Verstappen, sixth, was less than enthused by his afternoon: "From lap one of the restart, it was drive four seconds off the pace and … yeah, chill. It was no workout whatsoever – just really, really boring."

He had a point. For the first time in F1 history, the first ten on the grid (Leclerc, Piastri, Sainz, Norris, Russell, Verstappen, Hamilton, Tsunoda, Albon and Gasly) finished in the same top ten positions. Few deny that Monaco is an iconic event and should be on the F1 calendar. But has it reached the stage where some Monaco-specific rules are needed for a Sunday?

Russell – who said he'd never driven a race so slowly as forced to when making mediums last the entire race distance – suggested that Monaco should be run exclusively on the soft tyre, which, he figured, would require everyone to make two pit stops. Or, alternatively, require everyone to use all three compounds of tyre.

Leclerc didn't care about that. He had dominated the weekend from the first moments of opening practice and, finally, that Monte Carlo monkey was off his back.

Tony Dodgins

VIEWPOINT
NO KNEE-JERK NEEDED

FROM the moment the red flag appeared, this GP was doomed. With tyre changes permitted, strategy would no longer be the sole potential creator of interest during the remaining 77 laps. Equally, given the cast-iron reliability of contemporary cars, there would be no chance of a technical problem bringing a change as the top ten set off and, nearly two hours later, finished in exactly the same order. Even by Monaco standards, this was dire.

Should the race be banished because of it? Absolutely not. It would be a different story if others on the 24-race calendar were like this. But Monaco is the outlier. And magnificently so.

Containing an F1 car within these confines remains as unique a challenge as it always was. Fifty years ago, naysayers were complaining that Monaco had no place in 'modern' GP racing. And that was when F1 cars were svelte streamliners compared to today's hefty trucks!

It used to be that teams adapted their cars to suit Monaco. Nose cones would be opened to allow more air to reach the front-mounted radiator; side panels removed to improve driver cooling; hefty Ford GT40 driveshafts fitted to save transmissions.

Now the call is for the track to be adapted to suit the cars. That may be inevitable given that the proposed F1 car profile for 2026 is even more complex and hardly a slimmer's charter. But surely a less invasive cure could be found for Monaco?

Tyres limited to the softest compound, with two mandatory stops? That would at least maintain the element of a 'race', unlike a suggested time trial with the field setting off in reverse qualifying order for a five-lap blast. That's the equivalent of the football World Cup final being purely penalty kicks for fear of having 90 minutes of play end in a nil-nil draw.

This new low on Monaco's boredom chart should not prompt massive change just for the sake of it. Given the intensity of concentration necessary on a constantly changing track surface, the satisfaction of winning at Monaco remains greater than doing so in Bahrain, Barcelona and Abu Dhabi put together. Even during a dull race, as Charles Leclerc's shining face showed all too clearly.

Maurice Hamilton

8 — FORMULA 1 GRAND PRIX DE MONACO 2024

CIRCUIT DE MONACO, MONTE-CARLO
Circuit: 2.074 miles/3.337km, 78 laps

MONTE CARLO 24-26 MAY

RACE DISTANCE: 78 laps, 161.734 miles/260.286km
RACE WEATHER: Dry/sunny (track 40-45°C, air 25-26°C)

RACE – OFFICIAL CLASSIFICATION

Pos.	Driver	Nat.	No.	Entrant	Car/Engine	Laps	Time/Retirement	Speed (mph/km/h)	Gap to leader	Fastest race lap
1	Charles Leclerc	MC	16	Scuderia Ferrari	Ferrari SF-24-066/12 V6	78	2h 23m 15.554s	67.738/109.013		1m 15.162s 71
2	Oscar Piastri	AUS	81	McLaren Formula 1 Team	McLaren MCL38-Mercedes F1 M15 E Perf. V6	78	2h 23m 22.706s	67.681/108.922	7.152s	1m 16.281s 73
3	Carlos Sainz	E	55	Scuderia Ferrari	Ferrari SF-24-066/12 V6	78	2h 23m 23.139s	67.678/108.917	7.585s	1m 14.726s 62
4	Lando Norris	GB	4	McLaren Formula 1 Team	McLaren MCL38-Mercedes F1 M15 E Perf. V6	78	2h 23m 24.204s	67.669/108.903	8.650s	1m 15.742s 64
5	George Russell	GB	63	Mercedes-AMG Petronas F1 Team	Mercedes-AMG F1 W15-M15 E Perf. V6	78	2h 23m 28.863s	67.633/108.844	13.309s	1m 15.228s 73
6	Max Verstappen	NL	1	Oracle Red Bull Racing	Red Bull RB20-Honda RBPT H002 V6	78	2h 23m 29.407s	67.628/108.837	13.853s	1m 14.569s 58
7	Lewis Hamilton	GB	44	Mercedes-AMG Petronas F1 Team	Mercedes-AMG F1 W15-M15 E Perf. V6	78	2h 23m 30.462s	67.620/108.824	14.908s	1m 14.165s 63
8	Yuki Tsunoda	J	22	Visa Cash App RB Formula One Team	RB VCARB 01-Honda RBPT H002 V6	77			1 lap	1m 14.720s 77
9	Alexander Albon	T	23	Williams Racing	Williams FW46-Mercedes F1 M15 E Perf. V6	77			1 lap	1m 17.060s 77
10	Pierre Gasly	F	10	BWT Alpine F1 Team	Alpine A524-Renault E-Tech RE24 V6	77			1 lap	1m 15.625s 77
11	Fernando Alonso	E	14	Aston Martin Aramco F1 Team	Aston Martin AMR24-Mercedes F1 M15 E Perf. V6	76			2 laps	1m 17.939s 68
12	Daniel Ricciardo	AUS	3	Visa Cash App RB Formula One Team	RB VCARB 01-Honda RBPT H002 V6	76			2 laps	1m 17.172s 46
13	Valtteri Bottas	FIN	77	Stake F1 Team Kick Sauber	Sauber C44-Ferrari 066/12 V6	76			2 laps	1m 16.561s 17
14	Lance Stroll	CDN	18	Aston Martin Aramco F1 Team	Aston Martin AMR24-Mercedes F1 M15 E Perf. V6	76			2 laps	1m 16.710s 59
15	Logan Sargeant	USA	2	Williams Racing	Williams FW46-Mercedes F1 M15 E Perf. V6	76			2 laps	1m 15.525s 62
16	Zhou Guanyu	CHN	24	Stake F1 Team Kick Sauber	Sauber C44-Ferrari 066/12 V6	76			2 laps	1m 14.718s 75
	Esteban Ocon	F	31	BWT Alpine F1 Team	Alpine A524-Renault E-Tech RE24 V6	0	accident damage			no time
	Sergio Pérez	MEX	11	Oracle Red Bull Racing	Red Bull RB20-Honda RBPT H002 V6	0	accident			no time
	Nico Hülkenberg	D	27	MoneyGram Haas F1 Team	Haas VF-24-Ferrari 066/10 V6	0	accident			no time
	Kevin Magnussen	DK	20	MoneyGram Haas F1 Team	Haas VF-24-Ferrari 066/10 V6	0	accident			no time

The race was red-flagged on lap 1, following the multi-car collision. After around 40 minutes, the race resumed from a standing start, for the remaining laps.

DHL Fastest race lap (scores 1 point): Lewis Hamilton on lap 63, 1m 14.165s, 100.649mph/161.979km/h.
Lap record: Lewis Hamilton (Mercedes F1 W12 V6), 1m 12.909s, 102.383mph/164.769km (2021).

 20 · MAGNUSSEN · Haas
 18 · ZHOU · Sauber
 16 · PÉREZ · Red Bull
 14 · ALONSO · Aston Martin
 12 · RICCIARDO · RB
 19 · HÜLKENBERG · Haas
 17 · BOTTAS · Sauber
 15 · SARGEANT · Williams
 13 · STROLL · Aston Martin
 11 · OCON · Alpine

Lap chart

Grid order	Laps 1–54
16 LECLERC	16 throughout
81 PIASTRI	81 throughout
55 SAINZ	55 throughout
4 NORRIS	4 throughout
63 RUSSELL	63 throughout
1 VERSTAPPEN	1 throughout
44 HAMILTON	44 throughout
22 TSUNODA	22 throughout
23 ALBON	23 throughout
10 GASLY	10 throughout
31 OCON	18 18 18 ... 18 14 14 14 14 14 14
3 RICCIARDO	3 14 14 14 ... 14 3 3 3 3 3 3
18 STROLL	14 14 3 3 3 ... 3 2 2 77 77 77 77
14 ALONSO	2 2 77 77 ... 77 2 2 24 14 77 2 2 2 2
2 SARGEANT	77 77 2 2 2 ... 2 24 24 24 24
11 PÉREZ	24 24 24 24 24 24 24 77 77 ... 77 18 18 18 18 18
77 BOTTAS	
24 ZHOU	
27 HÜLKENBERG	
20 MAGNUSSEN	

Race red-flagged on lap 1   SC Safety Car deployed on laps 1-2

TIME SHEETS

PRACTICE 1 (FRIDAY)
Weather: Dry/sunny-overcast
Temperatures: track 35-36°C, air 24-25°C

Pos.	Driver	Laps	Time
1	Lewis Hamilton	35	1m 12.169s
2	Oscar Piastri	31	1m 12.198s
3	George Russell	35	1m 12.295s
4	Lando Norris	33	1m 12.396s
5	Charles Leclerc	33	1m 12.397s
6	Fernando Alonso	26	1m 12.775s
7	Lance Stroll	26	1m 12.789s
8	Yuki Tsunoda	34	1m 12.875s
9	Daniel Ricciardo	36	1m 12.901s
10	Carlos Sainz	35	1m 12.954s
11	Max Verstappen	29	1m 12.984s
12	Sergio Pérez	29	1m 13.229s
13	Valtteri Bottas	28	1m 13.248s
14	Kevin Magnussen	33	1m 13.390s
15	Alexander Albon	34	1m 13.425s
16	Nico Hülkenberg	34	1m 13.576s
17	Logan Sargeant	36	1m 14.150s
18	Esteban Ocon	33	1m 14.159s
19	Zhou Guanyu	30	1m 14.570s
20	Pierre Gasly	10	1m 15.574s

PRACTICE 2 (FRIDAY)
Weather: Dry/overcast
Temperatures: track 29-31°C, air 21-23°C

Pos.	Driver	Laps	Time
1	Charles Leclerc	37	1m 11.278s
2	Lewis Hamilton	32	1m 11.466s
3	Fernando Alonso	37	1m 11.753s
4	Max Verstappen	37	1m 11.813s
5	Lando Norris	35	1m 11.953s
6	Carlos Sainz	36	1m 11.962s
7	Lance Stroll	22	1m 12.062s
8	Sergio Pérez	31	1m 12.099s
9	Alexander Albon	38	1m 12.257s
10	George Russell	30	1m 12.260s
11	Yuki Tsunoda	36	1m 12.349s
12	Oscar Piastri	35	1m 12.366s
13	Kevin Magnussen	31	1m 12.473s
14	Esteban Ocon	34	1m 12.554s
15	Nico Hülkenberg	34	1m 12.569s
16	Daniel Ricciardo	37	1m 12.577s
17	Pierre Gasly	35	1m 12.750s
18	Logan Sargeant	36	1m 12.790s
19	Valtteri Bottas	31	1m 13.057s
20	Zhou Guanyu	32	1m 13.773s

PRACTICE 3 (SATURDAY)
Weather: Dry/sunny
Temperatures: track 42-46°C, air 26-30°C

Pos.	Driver	Laps	Time
1	Charles Leclerc	26	1m 11.369s
2	Max Verstappen	27	1m 11.566s
3	Lewis Hamilton	25	1m 11.710s
4	Oscar Piastri	25	1m 11.901s
5	Sergio Pérez	24	1m 11.923s
6	George Russell	33	1m 11.968s
7	Carlos Sainz	26	1m 11.979s
8	Lando Norris	24	1m 11.988s
9	Yuki Tsunoda	27	1m 11.991s
10	Fernando Alonso	25	1m 12.087s
11	Pierre Gasly	26	1m 12.144s
12	Alexander Albon	24	1m 12.180s
13	Nico Hülkenberg	24	1m 12.192s
14	Kevin Magnussen	31	1m 12.216s
15	Lance Stroll	25	1m 12.331s
16	Esteban Ocon	25	1m 12.472s
17	Logan Sargeant	21	1m 12.703s
18	Daniel Ricciardo	28	1m 12.829s
19	Zhou Guanyu	28	1m 13.830s
20	Valtteri Bottas	2	no time

QUALIFYING (SATURDAY)
Weather: Dry/sunny Temperatures: track 35-40°C, air 22-27°C

Pos.	Driver	First	Second	Third	Qualifying Tyre
1	Charles Leclerc	1m 11.584s	1m 10.825s	1m 10.270s	Soft (n)
2	Oscar Piastri	1m 11.500s	1m 10.756s	1m 10.424s	Soft (n)
3	Carlos Sainz	1m 11.543s	1m 11.075s	1m 10.518s	Soft (n)
4	Lando Norris	1m 11.760s	1m 10.732s	1m 10.542s	Soft (n)
5	George Russell	1m 11.492s	1m 10.929s	1m 10.543s	Soft (n)
6	Max Verstappen	1m 11.711s	1m 10.745s	1m 10.567s	Soft (n)
7	Lewis Hamilton	1m 11.528s	1m 11.056s	1m 10.621s	Soft (n)
8	Yuki Tsunoda	1m 11.852s	1m 11.106s	1m 10.858s	Soft (n)
9	Alexander Albon	1m 11.623s	1m 11.216s	1m 10.948s	Soft (n)
10	Pierre Gasly	1m 11.714s	1m 10.896s	1m 11.311s	Soft (u)
11	Esteban Ocon	1m 11.887s	1m 11.285s		
*	Nico Hülkenberg	1m 11.876s	1m 11.440s		
12	Daniel Ricciardo	1m 11.785s	1m 11.482s		
13	Lance Stroll	1m 11.728s	1m 11.563s		
*	Kevin Magnussen	1m 11.832s	1m 11.725s		
14	Fernando Alonso	1m 12.019s			
15	Logan Sargeant	1m 12.020s			
16	Sergio Pérez	1m 12.060s			
17	Valtteri Bottas	1m 12.512s			
18	Zhou Guanyu	1m 13.028s			

* Disqualified from the qualifying classification for non-compliant upper rear wing element.

QUALIFYING: head to head

Verstappen	8		0	Pérez
Hamilton	1		7	Russell
Norris	5		3	Piastri
Leclerc	5		2	Sainz
Leclerc	1		0	Bearman
Gasly	2		6	Ocon
Alonso	4		4	Stroll
Albon	8		0	Sargeant
Bottas	8		0	Zhou
Tsunoda	7		1	Ricciardo
Magnussen	2		6	Hülkenberg

McLaren F1 Team

FOR THE RECORD

250th GP POLE POSITION: Ferrari

DID YOU KNOW?

Charles Leclerc became the first Monégasque to win the Monaco Grand Prix in the modern era.

This was the 70th world championship Grand Prix staged in Monaco.

The first GP where the top 10 on the grid finished in the same positions (the previous record was 6).

The first McLaren car on the Monaco front row since Jenson Button in 2011.

POINTS

DRIVERS
1	Max Verstappen	169
2	Charles Leclerc	138
3	Lando Norris	113
4	Carlos Sainz	108
5	Sergio Pérez	107
6	Oscar Piastri	71
7	George Russell	54
8	Lewis Hamilton	42
9	Fernando Alonso	33
10	Yuki Tsunoda	19
11	Lance Stroll	11
12	Oliver Bearman	6
13	Nico Hülkenberg	6
14	Daniel Ricciardo	5
15	Alexander Albon	2
16	Esteban Ocon	1
17	Kevin Magnussen	1
18	Pierre Gasly	1

CONSTRUCTORS
1	Red Bull	276
2	Ferrari	252
3	McLaren	184
4	Mercedes	96
5	Aston Martin	44
6	RB	24
7	Haas	7
8	Williams	2
9	Alpine	2

10 · GASLY · Alpine

8 · TSUNODA · RB

6 · VERSTAPPEN · Red Bull

4 · NORRIS · McLaren

2 · PIASTRI · McLaren

9 · ALBON · Williams

7 · HAMILTON · Mercedes

5 · RUSSELL · Mercedes

3 · SAINZ · Ferrari

1 · LECLERC · Ferrari

RACE TYRE STRATEGIES

	Driver	Race Stint 1	Race Stint 2	Race Stint 3
1	Leclerc	Medium (n): 1	Hard (n): 2-78	
2	Piastri	Medium (u): 1	Hard (u): 2-78	
3	Sainz	Medium (n): 1	Hard (n): 2-78	
4	Norris	Medium (u): 1	Hard (u): 2-78	
5	Russell	Hard (n): 1	Medium (n): 2-78	
6	Verstappen	Hard (n): 1	Medium (n): 2-52	Hard (u): 53-78
7	Hamilton	Hard (n): 1	Medium (n): 2-51	Hard (u): 52-78
8	Tsunoda	Medium (n): 1	Hard (n): 2-77	
9	Albon	Medium (n): 1	Hard (n): 2-77	
10	Gasly	Hard (n): 1	Medium (n): 2-77	
11	Alonso	Medium (u): 1	Hard (u): 2-76	
12	Ricciardo	Medium (n): 1	Hard (n): 2-76	
13	Bottas	Hard (n): 1	Medium (n): 2-15	Hard (u): 16-76
14	Stroll	Hard (u): 1	Medium (u): 2-42	Soft (n): 43-76
15	Sargeant	Hard (n): 1-57	Medium (n): 58-76	
16	Zhou	Medium (n): 1	Hard (n): 2-70	Soft (n): 71-76
	Ocon	Hard (n): 0 (dnf)		
	Pérez	Hard (n): 0 (dnf)		
	Hülkenberg	Medium (n): 0 (dnf)		
	Magnussen	Hard (u): 0 (dnf)		

The tyre regulations stipulate that at least two of three dry tyre specifications must be used during a dry race.
Selected compounds for Monte Carlo: Red = Soft (C5); Yellow = Medium (C4); White = Hard (C3). (n) new (u) used

11 = Pit stop **23** = One lap or more behind

MONTREAL QUALIFYING

PREDICTABLY, Charles Leclerc's win in Monte Carlo, closing Red Bull's gap in the respective drivers' and constructors' championships to just 31 points and 24 points with a third of the season run, prompted excited speculation about a genuine championship fight. Heading to Montreal, Ferrari appeared to be a threat and McLaren was confident of being in the mix at every track.

Christian Horner was happy to admit that kerb-riding was the Achilles heel of Red Bull's RB20. "It was with the previous car as well," he said, "but now the field has converged…"

Circuit Gilles Villeneuve has always rewarded benign kerb-riding characteristics through the first sequence of corners and the chicanes, particularly the exit of the final one out on to the front straight flirting with 'Champion's Wall'. The feeling was that Red Bull might have its hands full for a second consecutive race.

Friday revealed little about the competitive order. The opening session of free practice was washed out and the FP2 times were not representative because not everyone ran similar tyres at similar times. The quick men got a set of softs fully up to temperature and kept running. They didn't include Max Verstappen, with just the single push-lap before returning to the pits with an ERS fault on a new power unit.

Mercedes looked strong, with George Russell in particular, and when Lewis Hamilton topped Saturday morning's dry FP3 and said that he was delighted with the balance of his car, it looked as though the team was about to join the party at well!

They had shown glimpses of competitiveness in previous sessions throughout 2024, but it had all ebbed away when things turned serious and track temperatures rose. This time, though, the session-topping pace translated in qualifying as well, with both Mercs now fitted with the new front wing that had appeared on Russell's W15 in Monaco, technical chief James Allison confirming that the team's original new-concept wing had been consigned to history.

Previously, the W15 had had strong rear grip at high speed with understeer at low speed or reduced understeer at a cost of a more skittish rear end as it ran lower to achieve greater downforce and the power of the front wing increased. Hitherto, balancing the car had been an insurmountable task. But the new wing broadened the set-up window, and suddenly the Mercedes was the fastest car in Montreal.

Both Russell and Hamilton dipped into the 1m 11s in Q2, the only drivers to do so. The Q3 times were slower because the wind had changed direction, giving a strong headwind down the long straight into the final chicane, but a delighted Russell gave Mercedes its first Canada pole since 2017 with a 1m 12.000s dead. He had achieved it on used softs on his first run, with the aid of a handy tow from his buddy, Alex Albon.

The time was matched to the thousandth by Verstappen's Red Bull as the front-row men recorded identical times for the first time since Jerez, 1997.

"The car has felt awesome all weekend," Russell confirmed. "I think we're homing in on the sweet spot finally." But sounding a note of caution, he was aware that the corner speed range in Canada is not that great and conceded that the upcoming Barcelona race was likely to be a better barometer of whether Mercedes was now truly in the game.

Verstappen was happy enough with his front-row slot, saying, "Going into qualifying, I would definitely have taken P2. We're still struggling with the same thing we did at Monaco, but around here there's more aero involved, so it didn't affect us as badly. On pure pace, we're second. I couldn't have done the times Merc did in Q2."

All the excitement over the identical times tended to distract attention from McLaren being so close as well. Lando Norris was just two-hundredths adrift, with team-mate Oscar Piastri's deficit a whole tenth as the papaya cars locked out row two, the McLarens quicker than anyone through sector two.

So, what of Montreal specialist Hamilton, a man who had won his first GP in Canada, boasted six poles and had never started out of the top five? To his dismay, seventh was the best he could manage, some 0.28s from his team-mate's pole, and behind an inspired Daniel Ricciardo's VCARB and Fernando Alonso's Aston Martin. "The car feels great and I was right there in FP3, but in qualifying the grip just vanished," Lewis shrugged.

Yuki Tsunoda made it two VCARBs in the top eight, while Lance Stroll put the second Aston ninth and a fabulous effort from Alex Albon put Williams into the top ten, somewhat unbelievably at the expense of Ferrari!

It was a reflection of F1's current rude health that there were five different chassis in the top six grid slots, all covered by less than two-tenths! It was the closest top-six spread since the 1961 British GP at Aintree. Ironically, at a time when paddock gossip was all about the draft new rules for 2026 that almost inevitably would spread the pack.

So, what had gone wrong at Ferrari? The SF-24 was the polar opposite of the previous year's car, which had achieved tyre warm-up quickly, but ate its rubber in the race. In the wet, cold conditions of Friday, Ferrari didn't look quick, Carlos Sainz referring back to the wet China sprint, when the team had also struggled with tyre warm-up.

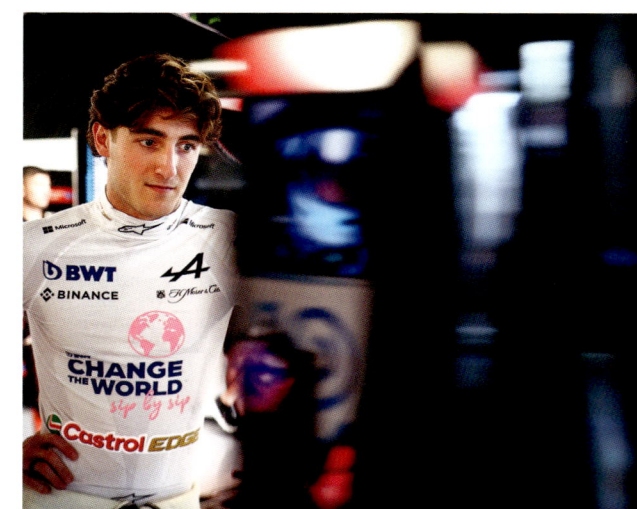

They had the same issue again, the softs not properly up to temperature for sector one of a hot lap, Fred Vasseur confirming that they were bleeding away half of their lap deficit in the first two corners. The situation wasn't helped when, fearing rain later in Q2, the team used new softs for its first run and was on used rubber when the track gripped up at the end of the session. Leclerc in particular was distinctly unimpressed, but it was something McLaren had done as well, and still made it through.

If Leclerc and Sainz were high-profile casualties of Q2, their plight was not as bad as that of Sergio Pérez who, armed with a new two-year Red Bull contract extension, found himself out in Q1 for the second successive race, along with both Sauber drivers – Valtteri Bottas and Zhou Guanyu, Alpine's Esteban Ocon and Haas's Nico Hülkenberg.

With Williams team principal James Vowles openly courting Carlos Sainz, Logan Sargeant's Williams days seemed numbered, but the Floridian made Q2 for the first time in 2024 and put the second Williams 13th on the grid, ahead of Kevin Magnussen and Pierre Gasly.

GEORGE RUSSELL had done a fabulous job of putting Mercedes on pole, with Bahrain the only other time that either of the Silver Arrows had qualified on the front two rows in 2024. In fact, Lewis Hamilton was yet to start a race higher than seventh! But Sunday in Montreal was wet, adding a complication to the mix. The entire field bar the two Haas cars would start on Pirelli's intermediate tyres, with Kevin Magnussen (14th) and Nico Hülkenberg (19th) opting for full wets.

When the lights went out in the murk, Russell moved right to fend off any advances from Max Verstappen as the field skittered through Turns One and Two and off into the first chicane scrabbling for grip. The first four were in grid order, with Verstappen and the McLarens of Lando Norris and Oscar Piastri giving chase to Russell, while Fernando Alonso and Lewis Hamilton gained places at the expense of a slithering Daniel Ricciardo. The man to watch, though, was Magnussen, taking full advantage of his full wets to scythe through the pack up to eighth place, ahead of Stroll by the end of the opening lap.

Charles Leclerc, starting 11th after Ferrari's difficult qualifying, had a good opening to the lap, but the second half was a bit lairy as he ran deep into the Turn Ten hairpin and then went straight on at the final chicane. He was running tenth at the end of the first lap, ahead of Yuki Tsunoda, Alex Albon, Hülkenberg, Carlos Sainz, Logan Sargeant, Esteban Ocon, Sergio Pérez, Pierre Gasly, and Sauber drivers Valtteri Bottas and Zhou Guanyu.

The track still looked very wet as Magnussen continued his inexorable progress, passing Ricciardo and then Hamilton to move into the top six. Hülkenberg had joined in the fun, too, up into the top ten. Magnussen was just 8.5s off the lead after the first two laps, but a radio message from Mercedes, telling Russell that the current level of rain was the worst that they expected, hinted that ultimately the Haas gamble might not pay off.

On lap three, Magnussen took fifth from Alonso, but the gap to Russell actually grew, which suggested that the track was moving towards intermediates rather than full wets.

Leclerc's miserable Montreal continued when he asked the team, "Is everything okay on the engine? We have wheel spins on exits."

"No, it's not," came the response. "We have issues, but keep pushing."

When Verstappen lapped in 1m 33.8s on lap five versus Magnussen's 1m 34.4s, the Dane still behind Norris's third-placed McLaren, it looked as though the honeymoon was over for Haas. Sure enough, the team called in Magnussen on lap eight, when a slow 8.6s pit stop undid much of Kevin's hard work. He rejoined 14th, back where he had started… Meanwhile, Hülkenberg was repassed for seventh by Ricciardo. Bad news for the Australian, though, was a 5s penalty for a false start.

At the front, Russell was not getting away from Verstappen, who had opened up a 7s gap to Norris's McLaren by lap 14, one-fifth-distance. The race leader was told, "We're expecting another rain shower 20 minutes from now."

"Tell me what you'd like me to do then," Russell replied. "These tyres are going to wear very quickly."

"Just be careful not to tear the inter," was the advice from the pit wall.

But suddenly, as a drying line began to emerge, Norris was taking chunks out of the leading pair and the deficit to Verstappen was down to less than 4s. Max, in turn,

Above: **Max Verstappen assumes the lead after the first safety-car period, erstwhile leaders Russell and Norris being consigned to second and third.**
Photo: Red Bull Content Pool/Getty Images

Top left: **Toto Wolff leads the team applause after Russell took pole.**

Above left: **A clenched fist and a contented smile from George.**
Photos: Mercedes-AMG Petronas F1 Team

Centre left: **Charles Leclerc steers his Ferrari well clear of the Wall of Champions.**
Photo: Scuderia Ferrari

Left: **Jack Doohan's projected FP1 run for Alpine was washed out by the rain.**
Photo: BWT Alpine F1 Team

Opening spread: **A dry line emerges for Max Verstappen to negotiate in the tricky conditions before the safety-car intervention.**
Photo: Red Bull Content Pool/Getty Images

Above: Lando Norris lost control of the race bottled up behind the safety car, before stopping for a second set of Inters.
Photo: McLaren F1 Team

Top right: Despite a penalty for a false start, Daniel Ricciardo brought his RB home in eighth place.
Photo: Red Bull Content Pool/Getty Images

Above right: An ill-timed switch to hard slicks was disastrous for Charles Leclerc. Subsequently, he retired with engine issues.
Photo: XPB Images

Right: Despite a five-place grid penalty for his Monaco collision with team-mate Gasly, Esteban Ocon finished tenth to claim the final point.
Photo: BWT Alpine F1 Team

started to get edgy, looking for a way past the leading Mercedes. But, because of the wet conditions, DRS was not yet in operation. Trying a little too hard, the Dutchman ran deep into Turn One and on to the slippery stuff, which gave Russell breathing space and allowed Norris to close to within a second.

When the track dried sufficiently for DRS to be activated, Norris wasted no time in diving around the outside of Verstappen to claim second place into the final chicane with 20 of the race's 70 laps completed. A lap later, he repeated the move on race leader Russell who, in his attempt to defend, ran straight on and also lost position to Verstappen, dropping from first to third in the blink of an eye.

Once into the lead, Norris started to romp away, leaving his pursuers by around 2s a lap over the next five laps. Meanwhile, Verstappen lost further time when Logan Sargeant, who had spun earlier on, lost his Williams at the exit of Turn Four, but that meant a safety car and the end of Norris's advantage.

Worse than that, Lando had gone by the pit-lane entry when the safety car was deployed, while those behind him all managed to get in for fresh intermediates. Norris caught Bernd Maylander on the next lap and so was speed restricted, meaning that by the time he got in and out of the pits, his lead had gone and he was down to third behind Verstappen and Russell, only marginally clearing team-mate Piastri.

With Ferrari not featuring at all, Leclerc decided it was worth a gamble on a set of hard-compound slicks, which was a tad optimistic. His pit stop was also dreadfully slow. The good news for the Monégasque was that Ferrari thought it had fixed his engine issue.

The new restart order was Verstappen, Russell, Norris, Piastri, Hamilton, Alonso, Tsunoda (yet to pit), Stroll, Ocon (yet to pit), Ricciardo, Albon, Bottas, Sainz, Magnussen, Gasly, Pérez, Hülkenberg, Zhou and Leclerc.

"We've got more rain," a frustrated Leclerc told Ferrari as he skated around on his slicks.

"Copy," they replied. "Two laps of rain and then it dries. Just keep it on track and then we will go fast." In the crowd, though, the hoods and umbrellas were going up. In a heartbeat, Leclerc was more than 20s off the back of the pack.

Then came the move of the race as Albon towed past Ricciardo on the outside down the straight into the final chicane, which brought him on to the rear wing of Ocon's Alpine. Taking advantage of the Frenchman's used inters, Albon was able to jink inside and dispense with a second car in what looked like one seamless move. Great confidence. Ocon isn't the easiest man to pass!

Approaching half-distance and with rain still falling, Leclerc abandoned his slick-tyre gamble and pitted once more for more intermediates. It was a day to forget for the Scuderia; Sainz in the other car was battling Bottas's Sauber for 12th and losing his front wing endplate in the process…

Ferrari had got it wrong with Leclerc by about eight laps. By lap 42, the sun was out, the sky was blue and Pierre Gasly brought his Alpine in for a set of slicks. His sector times immediately became the focus of strategists up and down the pit lane. For the moment, though, the leaders all continued to circulate on intermediates, with Verstappen 4s in front of Russell, who had Norris, Piastri and Hamilton all in close attendance, with Alonso 12s further back. Behind the Aston Martin, Tsunoda, Stroll, Albon and Ocon occupied the remaining points positions. It looked as though Gasly's call had been a bit too much of a gamble when his sector-two time proved still to be 5s off the intermediate pace.

Leclerc's Canadian GP came to an end after 43 laps when he received the instruction to retire the car.

By lap 44, Gasly was within 3s of the race-leading pace and Hamilton was the first of the front-runners to dive in for a set of mediums. Further back, Ricciardo, Sainz and Pérez all followed him in.

Russell and Norris, second and third, might have been expected to respond to Hamilton, but instead they continued on another lap. Piastri, though, was into the pits from fourth place.

At the end of lap 45, Verstappen pitted and was followed in by Russell, but Norris continued around for another lap. Just as Lando set the race's fastest lap as he put the hammer down on his one lap in free air, Hamilton set the race's fastest middle-sector time, indicating that the cross-over point had indeed been reached. Norris was in at the end of the lap and pitted out to join the track at Turn Two just as Verstappen was coming by. But on tyres that would take a while to get up to temperature, Norris couldn't quite get the power on the road, and it was Verstappen leading by 1.5s with 22 laps remaining, a gap that was out to 4s as Norris brought his tyres in and crossed the line at the end of the lap with Russell and Piastri right with him.

Verstappen, though, was not entirely comfortable with the Red Bull. "The ride is very bad, it's like a locked suspension again," he told his team.

Next time around, Norris locked up at the Turn Ten hairpin and could not prevent Russell from stealing second place down the straight on the run to the final chicane. Almost immediately, though, George made a mess of the entry to Turn Eight and Norris was back ahead. Some expletives from Russell brought a "Focus, George, focus," from Toto Wolff.

With 16 laps to go, there was a flurry of activity as Pérez damaged his rear wing with an off when he got off the dry line and had to pit, while Sainz spun his Ferrari and

RACE 09 CANADA

Above: A 60th grand prix win for Max Verstappen, who used all his skills to defeat both the opposition and the weather conditions.
Photo: Red Bull Content Pool/Getty Images

Top right: The unlucky Lando Norris had to settle for second place.
Photo: McLaren F1 Team

Above right: Pierre Gasly was an early stopper for hard slicks and eventually was rewarded with ninth.
Photo: BWT Alpine F1 Team

Right: Split strategy by Mercedes as Russell, on mediums, just holds off the challenge from team-mate Hamilton on the hard tyres.
Photo: Mercedes-AMG Petronas F1 Team

collected the hapless Albon. Carlos regained the track after slithering around on the grass, but Albon was in the wall facing the wrong way. Cue a second safety car.

With 15 laps remaining, both Mercedes took the opportunity to pit for fresh slicks, Russell taking mediums, while Hamilton went for hards. It was an interesting move, Russell giving up third place to Piastri to do it. By the time the safety car pulled off, there were 12 racing laps remaining, with the top-ten order: Verstappen, Norris, Piastri, Russell, Hamilton, Alonso, Stroll, Tsunoda, Ocon and Ricciardo.

Verstappen timed the restart perfectly and opened out a lead of almost 2s before they crossed the line again. Russell on his new rubber was hassling Piastri, but the young Australian was resolute in his defence going into the final chicane.

Then McLaren put out a radio message: "Oscar, request to hold position. Do you think you can challenge Verstappen? He was 1:17.4 last lap."

"I need to focus on keeping Russell behind," Piastri replied. "Just leave me to it."

As Verstappen set the race's fastest lap on lap 64, Piastri and Russell went into the final chicane side by side, with George forced to straight-line it, which allowed Hamilton through into fourth.

Next time around, and it was Hamilton pressuring Piastri before going by with DRS where Russell had been unable to do so. George followed him through on the next lap at the same place, however, relegating Piastri to fifth. Russell had seemed the quicker Mercedes all afternoon, and now he set about repassing his seven-times champion team-mate.

"We are racing. Just remember, it goes without saying, keep it clean please," was the message to Russell. He just about managed it, getting bravely down the inside of Hamilton into the final chicane, only just staying on the dry line.

Meanwhile, Tsunoda threw away points with two laps remaining when he ran deep on to the grass at Turn Eight and spun his VCARB.

Verstappen might have started the weekend on the back foot, but when the opportunity came, he grasped it with both hands and took the flag to claim a 60th GP win by just under 4s from Norris, with Russell claiming the final podium spot.

"I loved that one, a lot of fun!" Verstappen beamed. "You need those kind of races once in a while!"

Meanwhile, Norris was happy enough, and philosophical: "I had a lot of pace, but the safety car wasn't great. Just as it helped me in Miami, it's now had me back over."

Russell admitted to a couple of mistakes, and while he regarded the race as a missed opportunity, at least he could enjoy giving Mercedes its first 2024 podium. Competition at the front was hotting up. As well as Red Bull, McLaren and now Mercedes looked like potential winners, even if Ferrari, surprisingly, was further from its winning Monaco form than could possibly have been anticipated. Roll on Barcelona..

Tony Dodgins

VIEWPOINT
HURRY UP AND WAIT

WHEN George Russell finished third in Montreal, it seemed hard to believe that this was the first time a Mercedes driver had finished on the podium in the nine races since the start of the season. The past few years had been a very hard slog ever since the revised formula had highlighted a failure by Mercedes to get their technical heads around ground effect in its latest form. The start of each new season brought fresh hope, and 2024 had been no exception. There were moments of optimism, but none so encouraging as the raft of updates brought to Miami, Imola and Monaco.

The biggest gain appeared to come with a revised front wing, which, coupled with marginally less dependence on ground effect, had given Lewis Hamilton and George Russell a wider and more useful window between the two previous extremes of either high-speed oversteer or low-speed understeer, with nothing in between. At long last, they had a car that was well balanced and easy to drive. Well, easier. At times.

Fickleness continued to raise its head around the Circuit Gilles Villeneuve. Hamilton had been fastest by nearly four-tenths in FP3 and yet, when it came to qualifying, he was close to three-tenths away from Russell on pole. Despite disappointment with this and a race in which Hamilton admitted to making too many mistakes, there was more hope than had been evident for longer than Mercedes cared to remember, Lewis describing the W15 as "becoming a car we can fight with".

Russell led for 20 laps. Then it became a struggle to hold off Lando Norris and McLaren, a drop in tyre performance contributing to a visit to the run-off and a fall to that final place on the podium. But there had been evidence of race pace not seen before.

Given what Mercedes had experienced in recent years, this might have been a breakthrough. But technical director James Allison cautioned against too much expectation. "The characteristics of Montreal made it [W15] look a little quicker than we have a natural right to command at the coming races," he said. The hope was that he was understandably, but unduly circumspect after so long in the doldrums.

Maurice Hamilton

9

FORMULA 1 AWS GRAND PRIX DU CANADA 2024

MONTRÉAL 07-09 JUNE

RACE DISTANCE: 70 laps, 189.686 miles/305.270km

RACE WEATHER: Wet track, rain briefly later/cloudy (track 21-27°C, air 16-20°C)

CIRCUIT GILLES VILLENEUVE, MONTRÉAL

Circuit: 2.709 miles/4.361km, 70 laps

RACE – OFFICIAL CLASSIFICATION

Pos.	Driver	Nat.	No.	Entrant	Car/Engine	Laps	Time/Retirement	Speed (mph/km/h)	Gap to leader	Fastest race lap
1	Max Verstappen	NL	1	Oracle Red Bull Racing	Red Bull RB20-Honda RBPT H002 V6	70	1h 45m 47.927s	107.573/173.122		1m 15.569s 70
2	Lando Norris	GB	4	McLaren Formula 1 Team	McLaren MCL38-Mercedes F1 M15 E Perf. V6	70	1h 45m 51.806s	107.508/173.017	3.879s	1m 15.558s 67
3	George Russell	GB	63	Mercedes-AMG Petronas F1 Team	Mercedes-AMG F1 W15-M15 E Perf. V6	70	1h 45m 52.244s	107.500/173.005	4.317s	1m 14.895s 70
4	Lewis Hamilton	GB	44	Mercedes-AMG Petronas F1 Team	Mercedes-AMG F1 W15-M15 E Perf. V6	70	1h 45m 52.842s	107.490/172.989	4.915s	1m 14.856s 70
5	Oscar Piastri	AUS	81	McLaren Formula 1 Team	McLaren MCL38-Mercedes F1 M15 E Perf. V6	70	1h 45m 58.126s	107.401/172.845	10.199s	1m 16.247s 65
6	Fernando Alonso	E	14	Aston Martin Aramco F1 Team	Aston Martin AMR24-Mercedes F1 M15 E Perf. V6	70	1h 46m 05.437s	107.277/172.646	17.510s	1m 16.303s 70
7	Lance Stroll	CDN	18	Aston Martin Aramco F1 Team	Aston Martin AMR24-Mercedes F1 M15 E Perf. V6	70	1h 46m 11.552s	107.175/172.481	23.625s	1m 16.762s 70
8	Daniel Ricciardo	AUS	3	Visa Cash App RB Formula One Team	RB VCARB 01-Honda RBPT H002 V6	70	1h 46m 16.599s *	107.090/172.344	28.672s	1m 17.076s 68
9	Pierre Gasly	F	10	BWT Alpine F1 Team	Alpine A524-Renault E-Tech RE24 V6	70	1h 46m 17.948s	107.067/172.308	30.021s	1m 17.013s 70
10	Esteban Ocon	F	31	BWT Alpine F1 Team	Alpine A524-Renault E-Tech RE24 V6	70	1h 46m 18.240s	107.062/172.300	30.313s	1m 17.012s 70
11	Nico Hülkenberg	D	27	MoneyGram Haas F1 Team	Haas VF-24-Ferrari 066/10 V6	70	1h 46m 18.751s	107.054/172.286	30.824s	1m 16.683s 67
12	Kevin Magnussen	DK	20	MoneyGram Haas F1 Team	Haas VF-24-Ferrari 066/10 V6	70	1h 46m 19.180s	107.046/172.274	31.253s	1m 16.499s 68
13	Valtteri Bottas	FIN	77	Stake F1 Team Kick Sauber	Sauber C44-Ferrari 066/12 V6	70	1h 46m 28.414s	106.891/172.025	40.487s	1m 17.250s 65
14	Yuki Tsunoda	J	22	Visa Cash App RB Formula One Team	RB VCARB 01-Honda RBPT H002 V6	70	1h 46m 40.621s	106.688/171.697	52.694s	1m 17.309s 70
15	Zhou Guanyu	CHN	24	Stake F1 Team Kick Sauber	Sauber C44-Ferrari 066/12 V6	69	1h 46m 41.455s		1 lap	1m 17.325s 68
	Carlos Sainz	E	55	Scuderia Ferrari	Ferrari SF-24-066/12 V6	52	accident damage			1m 18.957s 51
	Alexander Albon	T	23	Williams Racing	Williams FW46-Mercedes F1 M15 E Perf. V6	52	accident			1m 19.359s 51
	Sergio Pérez	MEX	11	Oracle Red Bull Racing	Red Bull RB20-Honda RBPT H002 V6	51	accident damage			1m 18.819s 51
	Charles Leclerc	MC	16	Scuderia Ferrari	Ferrari SF-24-066/12 V6	40	engine (mileage)			1m 26.012s 39
	Logan Sargeant	USA	2	Williams Racing	Williams FW46-Mercedes F1 M15 E Perf. V6	23	accident			1m 26.484s 19

* Ricciardo: 5s time penalty for false start - moved before the start signal was given (served at pit stop).

DHL Fastest race lap (scores 1 point): Lewis Hamilton on lap 70, 1m 14.856s, 130.321mph/209.730km/h.

Lap record: Valtteri Bottas (Mercedes F1 W10 V6), 1m 13.078s, 133.491mph/214.833km/h (2019).

 19 · BOTTAS · Sauber
Car modified in parc fermé; required to start from the pit lane

 17 · HÜLKENBERG · Haas

 15 · GASLY · Alpine

 13 · SARGEANT · Williams

 11 · LECLERC · Ferrari

 20 · ZHOU · Sauber
Car modified in parc fermé; required to start from the pit lane

 18 · OCON · Alpine
5-place grid penalty for causing a collision with Gasly at the Monaco GP

 16 · PÉREZ · Red Bull

 14 · MAGNUSSEN · Haas

12 · SAINZ · Ferrari

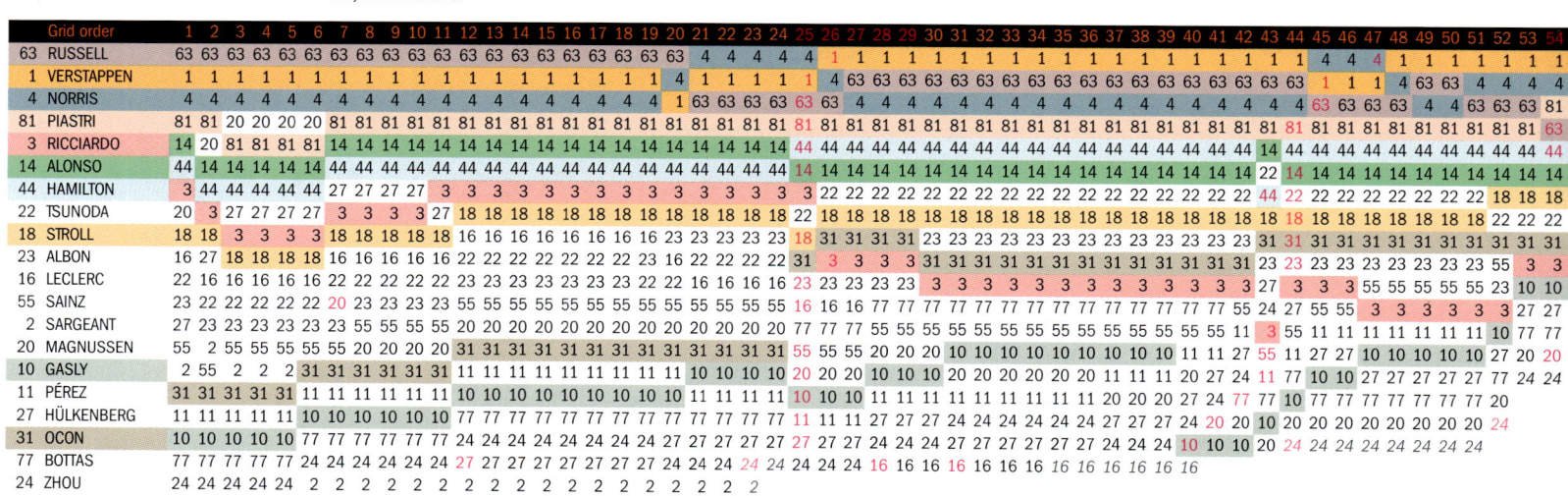

SC Safety Car deployed on laps 25-29 and 54-58

TIME SHEETS

PRACTICE 1 (FRIDAY)
Weather: Dry-wet/cloudy
Temperatures: track 27-30°C, air 20-22°C

Pos.	Driver	Laps	Time
1	Lando Norris	8	1m 24.435s
2	Carlos Sainz	11	1m 24.763s
3	Charles Leclerc	11	1m 25.306s
4	Lewis Hamilton	11	1m 25.970s
5	Max Verstappen	10	1m 26.502s
6	Oscar Piastri	7	1m 26.754s
7	Pierre Gasly	8	1m 27.584s
8	Valtteri Bottas	11	1m 27.670s
9	Sergio Pérez	10	1m 28.058s
10	George Russell	9	1m 28.541s
11	Daniel Ricciardo	9	1m 28.582s
12	Yuki Tsunoda	9	1m 28.723s
13	Kevin Magnussen	8	1m 29.052s
14	Nico Hülkenberg	5	1m 32.826s
15	Fernando Alonso	4	1m 33.411s
16	Logan Sargeant	5	1m 36.586s
17	Lance Stroll	4	1m 40.530s
18	Zhou Guanyu	4	no time
19	Jack Doohan	3	no time
20	Alexander Albon	4	no time

PRACTICE 2 (FRIDAY)
Weather: Dry-wet/cloudy
Temperatures: track 29-31°C, air 22-27°C

Pos.	Driver	Laps	Time
1	Fernando Alonso	25	1m 15.810s
2	George Russell	24	1m 16.273s
3	Lance Stroll	27	1m 16.464s
4	Charles Leclerc	24	1m 16.556s
5	Daniel Ricciardo	23	1m 16.731s
6	Kevin Magnussen	15	1m 16.773s
7	Lewis Hamilton	27	1m 16.908s
8	Yuki Tsunoda	22	1m 16.951s
9	Alexander Albon	22	1m 16.977s
10	Sergio Pérez	19	1m 17.041s
11	Esteban Ocon	31	1m 17.417s
12	Logan Sargeant	22	1m 17.496s
13	Carlos Sainz	27	1m 17.722s
14	Valtteri Bottas	21	1m 17.817s
15	Nico Hülkenberg	20	1m 17.903s
16	Oscar Piastri	20	1m 19.008s
17	Zhou Guanyu	17	1m 19.087s
18	Max Verstappen	4	1m 19.311s
19	Pierre Gasly	26	1m 20.789s
20	Lando Norris	21	1m 20.843s

PRACTICE 3 (SATURDAY)
Weather: Dry/cloudy
Temperatures: track 34-36°C, air 23-25°C

Pos.	Driver	Laps	Time
1	Lewis Hamilton	31	1m 12.549s
2	Max Verstappen	32	1m 12.923s
3	George Russell	33	1m 12.957s
4	Lance Stroll	27	1m 13.026s
5	Oscar Piastri	32	1m 13.266s
6	Daniel Ricciardo	34	1m 13.279s
7	Lando Norris	32	1m 13.293s
8	Fernando Alonso	30	1m 13.340s
9	Sergio Pérez	29	1m 13.342s
10	Charles Leclerc	28	1m 13.349s
11	Kevin Magnussen	30	1m 13.439s
12	Carlos Sainz	33	1m 13.570s
13	Valtteri Bottas	32	1m 13.642s
14	Logan Sargeant	31	1m 13.663s
15	Yuki Tsunoda	31	1m 13.716s
16	Pierre Gasly	29	1m 13.737s
17	Nico Hülkenberg	27	1m 13.777s
18	Alexander Albon	22	1m 13.880s
19	Esteban Ocon	31	1m 14.075s
20	Zhou Guanyu	4	1m 18.656s

FOR THE RECORD

60th GP WIN: Max Verstappen
10th GP FRONT ROW: George Russell

QUALIFYING (SATURDAY)
Weather: Dry/cloudy Temperatures: track 29-31°C, air 21-22°C

Pos.	Driver	First	Second	Third	Qualifying Tyre
1	George Russell	1m 13.013s	1m 11.742s	1m 12.000s	Soft (u)
2	Max Verstappen	1m 12.360s	1m 12.549s	1m 12.000s	Soft (n)
3	Lando Norris	1m 12.959s	1m 12.201s	1m 12.021s	Soft (n)
4	Oscar Piastri	1m 12.907s	1m 12.462s	1m 12.103s	Soft (n)
5	Daniel Ricciardo	1m 13.240s	1m 12.572s	1m 12.178s	Soft (n)
6	Fernando Alonso	1m 13.117s	1m 12.635s	1m 12.228s	Soft (n)
7	Lewis Hamilton	1m 12.851s	1m 11.979s	1m 12.280s	Soft (u)
8	Yuki Tsunoda	1m 12.748s	1m 12.303s	1m 12.414s	Soft (n)
9	Lance Stroll	1m 13.088s	1m 12.659s	1m 12.701s	Soft (n)
10	Alexander Albon	1m 12.896s	1m 12.485s	1m 12.796s	Soft (n)
11	Charles Leclerc	1m 13.107s	1m 12.691s		
12	Carlos Sainz	1m 13.038s	1m 12.728s		
13	Logan Sargeant	1m 13.063s	1m 12.736s		
14	Kevin Magnussen	1m 13.217s	1m 12.916s		
15	Pierre Gasly	1m 13.289s	1m 12.940s		
16	Sergio Pérez	1m 13.326s			
17	Valtteri Bottas	1m 13.366s			
18	Esteban Ocon	1m 13.435s			
19	Nico Hülkenberg	1m 13.978s			
20	Zhou Guanyu	1m 14.292s			

QUALIFYING: head to head

Verstappen	9	0	Pérez
Hamilton	1	8	Russell
Norris	6	3	Piastri
Leclerc	6	2	Sainz
Leclerc	1	0	Bearman
Gasly	3	6	Ocon
Alonso	5	4	Stroll
Albon	9	0	Sargeant
Bottas	9	0	Zhou
Tsunoda	6	3	Ricciardo
Magnussen	3	6	Hülkenberg

POINTS

DRIVERS

1	Max Verstappen	194
2	Charles Leclerc	138
3	Lando Norris	131
4	Carlos Sainz	108
5	Sergio Pérez	107
6	Oscar Piastri	81
7	George Russell	69
8	Lewis Hamilton	55
9	Fernando Alonso	41
10	Yuki Tsunoda	19
11	Lance Stroll	17
12	Daniel Ricciardo	9
13	Oliver Bearman	6
14	Nico Hülkenberg	6
15	Pierre Gasly	3
16	Alexander Albon	2
17	Esteban Ocon	2
18	Kevin Magnussen	1

CONSTRUCTORS

1	Red Bull	301
2	Ferrari	252
3	McLaren	212
4	Mercedes	124
5	Aston Martin	58
6	RB	28
7	Haas	7
8	Alpine	5
9	Williams	2

9 · STROLL · Aston Martin

7 · HAMILTON · Mercedes

5 · RICCIARDO · RB

3 · NORRIS · McLaren

1 · RUSSELL · Mercedes

10 · ALBON · Williams

8 · TSUNODA · RB

6 · ALONSO · Aston Martin

4 · PIASTRI · McLaren

2 · VERSTAPPEN · Red Bull

RACE TYRE STRATEGIES

	Driver	Race Stint 1	Race Stint 2	Race Stint 3	Race Stint 4	Race Stint 5
1	Verstappen	Inter (n): 1-25	Inter (n): 26-45	Medium (n): 46-70		
2	Norris	Inter (n): 1-26	Inter (n): 27-47	Medium (n): 48-70		
3	Russell	Inter (n): 1-25	Inter (n): 26-45	Hard (n): 46-54	Medium (n): 55-70	
4	Hamilton	Inter (n): 1-25	Inter (n): 26-43	Medium (n): 44-54	Hard (n): 55-70	
5	Piastri	Inter (n): 1-25	Inter (n): 26-44	Medium (n): 45-70		
6	Alonso	Inter (n): 1-25	Inter (n): 26-44	Hard (n): 45-70		
7	Stroll	Inter (n): 1-25	Inter (n): 26-44	Hard (u): 45-70		
8	Ricciardo	Inter (n): 1-26	Inter (n): 27-43	Medium (u): 44-70		
9	Gasly	Inter (n): 1-25	Inter (n): 26-40	Hard (n): 41-70		
10	Ocon	Inter (n): 1-44	Medium (n): 45-70			
11	Hülkenberg	Wet (n): 1-12	Inter (n): 13-25	Inter (n): 26-44	Medium (n): 45-70	
12	Magnussen	Wet (n): 1-7	Inter (n): 8-25	Inter (n): 26-41	Medium (n): 42-54	Medium (n): 55-70
13	Bottas	Inter (n): 1-42	Medium (n): 43-70			
14	Tsunoda	Inter (n): 1-44	Medium (n): 45-70			
15	Zhou	Inter (n): 1-24	Inter (n): 25-44	Medium (n): 45-52	Medium (n): 53-69	
	Sainz	Inter (n): 1-25	Inter (n): 26-43	Medium (n): 44-52 (dnf)		
	Albon	Inter (n): 1-25	Inter (n): 26-44	Medium (n): 44-51 (dnf)		
	Pérez	Inter (n): 1-25	Inter (n): 26-43	Medium (n): 44-51 (dnf)		
	Leclerc	Inter (n): 1-25	Inter (n): 26-28	Hard (n): 29-31	Inter (n): 32-40 (dnf)	
	Sargeant	Inter (n): 1-23 (dnf)				

The tyre regulations stipulate that at least two of three dry tyre specifications must be used during a dry race.
Selected compounds for Montréal: Red = Soft (C5); Yellow = Medium (C4); White = Hard (C3). (n) new (u) used

24 = Pit stop   2 = One lap or more behind

FIA FORMULA 1 WORLD CHAMPIONSHIP · ROUND 10

SPANISH GRAND PRIX

BARCELONA-CATALUNYA CIRCUIT

CATALUNYA QUALIFYING

THE big question heading into Barcelona was whether the Mercedes pace that had taken George Russell to the Montreal pole would translate in Spain, or whether Max Verstappen and Red Bull, on a more 'normal' track, would resume their early-season domination.

McLaren team boss Zak Brown was predicting a genuine four-way battle, featuring his own team, Ferrari, Mercedes and Red Bull, but the doubts over Mercedes repeating its Canadian performance surrounded the relatively low speed range of the corners in Canada and the polar opposite at Barcelona. The signs were encouraging, however, when Lewis Hamilton topped FP2 on 1m 13.264s. Carlos Sainz's Ferrari was just 0.02s behind, while Lando Norris's McLaren was only a tad slower.

Verstappen, for the third successive race, was not entirely happy with his RB20, initially reporting turn-in understeer and then, in FP2, a loose feeling that prompted him to change. The car's compromised kerb-riding ability had also clearly been taken seriously, Max conducting a midweek Imola test in a two-year-old RB18 chassis.

The limiting factors in Barcelona are balance and keeping the Pirellis (principally the left front) alive long enough to be quick in both the first and last sectors of the lap, but that was aided by qualifying conditions being significantly cooler than the scorching temperatures of Friday. What was a constant, though, was F1's current hyper competitiveness, as less than three-quarters of a second covered the 15 cars that escaped Q1! They did not include Kevin Magnussen's Haas, the VCARBs of Yuki Tsunoda and Daniel Ricciardo, and the Williams pair, Alex Albon and Logan Sargeant. Albon would start from the pit lane with engine components beyond the standard allocation.

After the first Q2 runs, Lewis Hamilton was down in 12th place, unimpressed with that particular set of soft-compound Pirellis, but he got it together on his second attempt and was bested only by Verstappen. Russell was third quickest, ahead of Norris and Sainz. Sergio Pérez, to his relief, made it through to the top-ten shootout ahead of the improved Alpines of the closely-matched Pierre Gasly and Esteban Ocon. Despite his best efforts, home hero Fernando Alonso missed out by two-hundredths and was joined in the Q3 spectator ranks by Valtteri Bottas, Nico Hülkenberg, Aston team-mate Lance Stroll and Zhou Guanyu.

Alonso refused to be downcast: "To be honest, we were closer than we thought, we were not even sure about Q1," he admitted candidly. Perhaps not the sort of thing Lawrence Stroll wanted to hear!

Verstappen, who had started the season with seven straight poles, was attempting to take his first in three races and pipped Norris's McLaren by just over a tenth in the first Q3 runs. Maintaining the Mercedes upturn, Hamilton and Russell were just hundredths away, while the Ferraris of Sainz and Charles Leclerc were around a quarter of a second behind the ultimate pace. Meanwhile, Oscar Piastri still had work to do after having his first run scratched for abuse of track limits on the exit of Turn Ten. His second attempt was no better, this time running wide on the exit of T11 and off into the gravel, meaning P10 on the grid.

In the meantime, at Mercedes, there seemed to be a bit of a niggle, with Russell feeling that he had been impeded by his team-mate. "What the **** was Lewis doing prepping that lap?" he wanted to know.

"He just… it's fine. We'll talk about it afterwards. Head in the game," was the somewhat enigmatic response. Apparently, both of them had been wanting to pick up a tow, and Russell was less than impressed at how it had worked out.

The second runs looked like being mighty close. Sainz flashed across the line and only failed to beat Verstappen's provisional pole by 0.06s, before Leclerc pipped him by just six-thousands to go second quickest.

Then Max shifted the goalposts, moving the pole target to 1m 11.403s. Norris picked up the gauntlet and was on course with a new quickest second sector, ultimately breaking the timing beam 0.02s ahead of the Red Bull to claim his second F1 pole.

The two Mercedes could not match that, but were quick enough to knock the two Ferraris off the second row, Hamilton beating Russell by a hundredth to outqualify him for only the second time in ten races and start in the top six for the first time in 2024.

"It was pretty much a perfect lap," enthused the delighted Norris. "We've been close all weekend, but this was all about putting together that perfect lap, which I managed to do. We've been very strong since Miami, but I think Max and Red Bull have looked a little stronger than us so far this weekend, so very happy. We made some changes for the final run; there were a couple of places where I needed to improve and did exactly that, so now we can fight for the win tomorrow."

Verstappen, despite a tow from team-mate Pérez down into Turn One, had lost out to McLaren around a track often regarded as a solid barometer of car performance, but was confident that it was all still to play for on Sunday.

"McLaren are on fire!" was one observation from a rival team and, unfortunately, it was not just on the track. The team had to contend with a serious paddock hospitality fire that took the best part of two hours to extinguish and resulted in hospital treatment for one member of the team, thankfully later released without serious harm. Meanwhile, team principal Zak Brown had been conducting business from the FIA offices, while rival teams had been feeding his staff. Nothing like F1 paddock camaraderie.

If the McLaren threat to Red Bull had been reaffirmed, there was a tinge of disappointment from Toto Wolff about the three-tenths gap between Mercedes and Red Bull. This wasn't quite a Montreal repeat.

"We're not quite back in the game," he conceded. "The gap is still quite a lot for this track, and maybe we were thinking that we could have been a bit faster based on Friday, but third and fourth is solid. You have to be a bit humble, though, based on where we were three or four races ago, when we wouldn't have been having an objective to qualify on the front row."

THE Circuit de Catalunya has never been the easiest track on which to overtake, and although DRS has made it possible, a good start is always important. Both front-row men knew that, and it was Max Verstappen who got away slightly better from P2 than pole-man Lando Norris. The latter did his best to squeeze the Red Bull as Verstappen aimed for the inside of Turn One, costing the Dutchman a little bit of momentum as he briefly went rally-crossing on the grass.

The whole grid (bar Albon, who started from the pit lane on mediums) was on the soft-compound tyre, so there was no variance in tyre grip off the line. But making a brilliant start from the second row, George Russell towed Verstappen and then jinked left, forcing Charles Leclerc's fast-starting Ferrari to go further left, and then, with momentum, swept around the outside of both front-row men through Turn One to put Mercedes into the lead. If ever a man was driving with confidence, that was it!

With Norris's fine Saturday work undone in the first few hundred yards, the rest of the field negotiated the first three turns without incident, with a lap-long scrap between Lance Stroll and Valtteri Bottas providing most of the entertainment.

Russell led the field over the line at the end of the opening lap from Verstappen, Norris, Lewis Hamilton, Charles Leclerc, Carlos Sainz, Pierre Gasly, Oscar Piastri, Esteban Ocon, Nico Hülkenberg (up three places), Sergio Pérez, Fernando Alonso, Stroll, Bottas, Yuki Tsunoda, Kevin Magnussen, Zhou Guanyu, Logan Sargeant, Daniel Ricciardo and Alex Albon.

With Verstappen tracking Russell, race engineer 'GP'

Lambiase was on the radio, telling his man, "It might be our best opportunity now, Max. Think wisely." Doubtless, he regarded Norris as the long-term threat and was encouraging his man to put Russell's Mercedes between them as soon as DRS was available.

Verstappen did precisely that, towing up to Russell down the long straight and then, mirroring the move George himself had made on lap one, sweeping majestically around the outside of the Mercedes in Turns One and Two.

Sainz had passed Leclerc into Turn One and things were becoming a little tetchy as Charles tried to take back the place.

"Ah, he closed me down," Leclerc declared on the radio.

"He touched me, we collided and he pushed me off. He touched my rear right, so I was clearly ahead," was Sainz's take on the situation.

With ten laps on the board, Verstappen had not broken away and was still just 2s clear of Russell, with Norris within DRS range of the Mercedes. In turn, Norris, Hamilton, Sainz and Leclerc were still within DRS range of each other, before a 3s gap to Gasly, running a strong seventh in the first Alpine, Piastri separating him from team-mate Ocon.

To the surprise of certain sections of the paddock, Alpine had re-employed Flavio Briatore, now 74, in an 'executive advisor' role. Briatore, of course, had been at the Renault helm in the nineties when Michael Schumacher had won back-to-back championships in 1994 and '95, then returned to oversee Renault's 2005–6 championships with Fernando Alonso before being given

Above: The action begins as George Russell takes advantage around the outside of a squabbling Lando Norris and Max Verstappen.
Photo: Red Bull Content Pool/Getty Images

Top left: Williams' Alex Albon and Logan Sargeant get ready for action.
Photo: Williams Racing

Above left: Audi big chief Oliver Hoffmann was in the Sauber pit.
Photo: Lukas Gorys

Centre left: Some small progress for Alpine, Pierre Gasly qualifying a fine seventh and finishing ninth.
Photo: Atsuo Sakurai

Left: Changes were afoot at Alpine with the arrival of Flavio Briatore in the role of 'executive advisor'. He is seen here with the Renault CEO Luca de Meo.
Photo: XPB Images

Opening spread: Red Bull's Max Verstappen emerged victorious in Barcelona, taking his seventh win of the season.
Photos: Red Bull Content Pool/Getty Images

Above: The win that got away? A bad start compromised Lando Norris, who had to settle for second place.
Photo: McLaren F1 Team

Top right: There was massive support for local hero Carlos Sainz.
Photo: Scuderia Ferrari

Above right: Charles Leclerc upheld Maranello's honour with a fifth place.
Photo: Scuderia Ferrari

Right: Max Verstappen needed only two laps to take the lead from George Russell's Mercedes.
Photo: Lukas Gorys

a lifetime ban for the 'crashgate' scandal in Singapore, 2008, when Nelson Piquet Jr had been asked to crash deliberately to bring out a safety car at an opportune moment for team-mate Alonso.

Briatore's lifetime ban was later overturned by a French court, and in Spain, Alpine team principal Bruno Famin said that it was irrelevant: "I don't really mind about the past, I'm always looking to the future. Flavio has high-level knowledge of F1 and knows a lot of people."

The rumour mill was suggesting that Briatore was backing a move for Renault to ditch its own 2026 engine project and potentially continue in F1 with a customer engine. Which, no doubt, was worrying for the staff at Viry-Chatillon…

As the first pit-stop window approached, Verstappen tried to open up a bigger lead and had a bit of a moment in Turn Seven. Some 16 laps in, with the 66-lap race on the cusp between two and three stops, Russell pitted from second place and was followed in by Sainz. A problem with the right rear at Mercedes meant a 5.3s stop, and George only just managed to prevent Sainz, with a 2.2s Ferrari stop, from going by in the pit lane.

Hamilton responded on the next lap, but despite Russell's slow stop, remained behind him and Sainz on the road, while Norris was asked, "Lando, we could cover Russell on this lap, what do you think?"

"No," Norris replied. "I think we should go and get Max."

Red Bull called in Verstappen for a new set of Pirelli mediums after 18 laps, which put Norris into the lead, some 4s clear of Leclerc and then Piastri, all three of them yet to stop.

Hamilton was anxious to be past Sainz, who was troubled by slower-corner understeer early in his medium-tyre stint. He was strong out of the last corner, though, and it took a bold move by Hamilton down the inside of Turn One to displace the Ferrari after a light touch.

Sainz thought he'd done so unfairly. "He touched and ran me off," he told the Ferrari team. "Check the onboard. He needs to let me by." Race Control noted the incident.

Norris, leading, was told, "The situation is we've lost position to Max, Russell, Hamilton and Sainz, but we're picking up a good tyre delta, six laps on some of them already, keep going." McLaren finally called him in after 23 laps to replace his starting softs with a set of mediums.

Leclerc took over in front until Ferrari pitted him a lap later, and he rejoined seventh, between the Alpines of Gasly and Ocon.

Meanwhile, Sainz was still seeking further feedback on Hamilton's robust pass. The news from the Ferrari pit wall was not what he wanted to hear: "They reported no further investigation. I know it's harsh, but let's concentrate on our race."

"I don't understand why there's a rule book and we don't follow it," replied the frustrated Carlos as he headed towards a tenth consecutive points finish in his home GP since outqualifying and outracing Versappen at Toro Rosso in Barcelona back in 2015.

As Norris caught Sainz, McLaren's strategy was about to be put to the test. Could Lando get the on-track moves done or would he be sat behind, losing time? It was the former, as he walked by with DRS and no undue drama down the inside into Turn One.

At Ferrari, Leclerc did not seem happy with his longer stint. "Why are we on plan A?" he wanted to know.

"We are in line with everyone else. That was the choice," he was told, which, clearly, did not appear to be the case. Nevertheless, he went past Gasly with ease and now ran sixth, some 9s behind his team-mate.

Above: Lewis Hamilton took on a set of soft tyres for his final stint, which helped him seize third place ahead of team-mate Russell.

Above right: Hamilton claimed his first podium of 2024.
Photos: Mercedes-AMG Petronas F1 Team

Right: Ferrari's upgrades appeared not to work in Barcelona, despite Carlos Sainz having shown great pace in practice.
Photo: Scuderia Ferrari

Some 11 laps into his medium-tyre stint, Verstappen, with a 6.6s lead over Russell, told his team, "The tyres are very inconsistent."

After resistance from Hamilton at Turn One when Norris arrived behind him, the McLaren was much closer out of the final turn on the next lap and went by without problem into Turn One as the race approached half-distance.

There was some great racing when Norris homed back in on Russell's second place. When George defended the inside into Turn One, Lando went imperiously around his outside in Turn Three, before Russell returned the compliment around the outside of Turn Four to grab the inside for Turn Five. Norris was back inside at Turn Seven, the scrap allowing Hamilton back with the pair of them.

Russell immediately bailed out into the pit lane for a second time, this time taking on a set of hard-compound Pirellis after a much cleaner stop. Again, Sainz followed him in, did likewise, and they left in the same order. Just six laps into his third stint, though, George was telling the team, "This tyre does not feel good, it's sliding already."

With 23 laps remaining, Norris had almost halved the near-10s gap that Verstappen had managed to eke out and had left Hamilton's third-placed Mercedes some 5s in his wake. Was this shaping up to be a repeat of Imola, when Norris had hassled Verstappen all the way to the chequered flag?

Mercedes had heeded Russell's feedback on the hard-compound tyre, and when Hamilton arrived in the pits with 22 laps remaining, they bolted on a set of the red-walled softs, which, Lewis said, had always been the plan.

Red Bull called in Verstappen on the next lap and also went for the soft-compound tyres. McLaren told Norris, "This is our chance now."

As Hamilton made short work of Sainz's Ferrari to take sixth, McLaren informed Norris, "If we wanted to cover Hamilton, we'd have to do it soon. Do you think if we went for the tyre delta, you'd be able to pass him again?"

"Yeah, I'll pass him," Lando declared confidently, but then thought about it a bit and said, "I'm unsure. It depends if we're here to finish first or third." Over to you on the pit wall…

They brought him in on lap 47, with 19 to go. He pitted out just ahead of Russell and Hamilton in the Mercs, but, provided he could get the tyres in quickly, he wouldn't need to take the edge off his new rubber passing cars.

With 15 laps to go, Verstappen led Norris by just over 6s, both on softs. Russell was 3s adrift on hards, with Hamilton in his wheel tracks on softs. Sainz, on hards, was 4.5s behind the second Mercedes and being closed down by Leclerc, on fresher softs.

Hamilton, on the grippier rubber, wasted no time in relegating Russell from third place, and it was the same scenario at Ferrari as Sainz opened the door to allow Leclerc by with 11 laps to go so that he could get after Russell's fourth-placed Mercedes.

Norris had more pace than Verstappen and claimed the race's fastest lap, but not by a sufficient margin to threaten a second straight win for Max, the Red Bull taking the flag 2.2s ahead. Hamilton claimed his first podium of 2024, the second in succession for his team. Russell just hung on to fourth, crossing the line 0.4s clear of Leclerc's closing Ferrari. Sainz had to be content with sixth in his home GP, some 2.7s clear of Piastri's McLaren.

Pérez was some 25s adrift in the second Red Bull, with the Alpines of Gasly and Ocon taking the final points.

Some eight years on from his first GP victory here in 2016, Verstappen had his 61st. He put it down to taking the lead early on, and then being able to defend against McLaren and Norris's impressive pace.

Asked whether he could have won, Norris was brutally honest, as always: "Not could have, should have," he said. "I got a bad start, simple as that. The car was incredible today and I think we were the quickest, for sure. So, a lot of positives and one negative that ruined everything. I need to tidy up a few little bits and then we'll be on top."

It was a message that, no doubt, was getting through at Red Bull.

Tony Dodgins

VIEWPOINT
FERRARI BOUNCING BACKWARDS

FERRARI was finally on a roll. There was talk of a championship challenge. That seemed to be the genuine Prancing Horse promise in the wake of Charles Leclerc's emotional and powerful win in Monaco, Carlos Sainz's impressive victory in Australia, followed by a successful upgrade at Imola. Things looked likely to improve even further as Ferrari brought another development to Spain.

The trouble with updates is they need to work – immediately. The Ferrari revision not only failed to provide additional performance, but also took the red cars backwards. Or to be more exact, it took them up and down as the dreaded phenomenon of bouncing returned to make the drivers' eyes water. Rather than striding forward on the highway to victory, Ferrari were losing their way and about to enter a development cul-de-sac.

Zero points in Canada had been partially excused by Circuit Gilles Villeneuve being an outlier with its particular demands, coupled with Leclerc having an engine issue and a desperate gamble with hard tyres on a still-damp track. Sainz then added to the deflection away from impending car trouble by spinning off.

Ferrari's upgrade failure would be exacerbated by McLaren and Mercedes making theirs work, thus doubling the agony in subsequent races as the team began to think about returning to the Imola spec, particularly in the light of the Spanish result, Leclerc and Sainz finishing fifth and sixth, half a minute behind.

The situation appeared even more difficult going forward. At forthcoming press conferences, questions for Lewis Hamilton would begin to surface about the wisdom of his move to Ferrari for 2025. And then it was revealed that Ferrari's technical director, Enrique Cardile, would be off to Aston Martin – which prompted snarky social media comments from Ferrari fans about Cardile's suitability for the post in the first place.

Of course, they would say that as Ferrari slipped from number two in the constructors' championship to drop behind McLaren, while Mercedes was coming up strongly on the rails. A championship challenge from Ferrari suddenly seemed fanciful.

Maurice Hamilton

10 FORMULA 1 ARAMCO GRAN PREMIO DE ESPAÑA 2024

BARCELONA 21-23 JUNE

RACE DISTANCE: 66 laps, 190.908 miles/307.236km
RACE WEATHER: Dry/sunny-overcast (track 39-44°C, air 24-25°C)

CIRCUIT DE BARCELONA-CATALUNYA, BARCELONA
Circuit: 2.894 miles/4.657km, 66 laps

RACE – OFFICIAL CLASSIFICATION

Pos.	Driver	Nat.	No.	Entrant	Car/Engine	Laps	Time/Retirement	Speed (mph/km/h)	Gap to leader	Fastest race lap
1	Max Verstappen	NL	1	Oracle Red Bull Racing	Red Bull RB20-Honda RBPT H002 V6	66	1h 28m 20.227s	129.667/208.679		1m 17.776s 54
2	Lando Norris	GB	4	McLaren Formula 1 Team	McLaren MCL38-Mercedes F1 M15 E Perf. V6	66	1h 28m 22.446s	129.613/208.592	2.219s	1m 17.115s 51
3	Lewis Hamilton	GB	44	Mercedes-AMG Petronas F1 Team	Mercedes-AMG F1 W15-M15 E Perf. V6	66	1h 28m 38.017s	129.233/207.981	17.790s	1m 17.809s 46
4	George Russell	GB	63	Mercedes-AMG Petronas F1 Team	Mercedes-AMG F1 W15-M15 E Perf. V6	66	1h 28m 42.547s	129.123/207.804	22.320s	1m 18.290s 50
5	Charles Leclerc	MC	16	Scuderia Ferrari	Ferrari SF-24-066/12 V6	66	1h 28m 42.936s	129.114/207.789	22.709s	1m 17.897s 52
6	Carlos Sainz	E	55	Scuderia Ferrari	Ferrari SF-24-066/12 V6	66	1h 28m 51.255s	128.913/207.465	31.028s	1m 18.539s 39
7	Oscar Piastri	AUS	81	McLaren Formula 1 Team	McLaren MCL38-Mercedes F1 M15 E Perf. V6	66	1h 28m 53.987s	128.846/207.358	33.760s	1m 17.874s 56
8	Sergio Pérez	MEX	11	Oracle Red Bull Racing	Red Bull RB20-Honda RBPT H002 V6	66	1h 29m 19.751s	128.227/206.362	59.524s	1m 17.785s 51
9	Pierre Gasly	F	10	BWT Alpine F1 Team	Alpine A524-Renault E-Tech RE24 V6	66	1h 29m 22.252s	128.167/206.265	1m 02.025s	1m 19.045s 51
10	Esteban Ocon	F	31	BWT Alpine F1 Team	Alpine A524-Renault E-Tech RE24 V6	66	1h 29m 32.116s	127.932/205.887	1m 11.889s	1m 18.982s 54
11	Nico Hülkenberg	D	27	MoneyGram Haas F1 Team	Haas VF-24-Ferrari 066/10 V6	66	1h 29m 39.442s *	127.758/205.606	1m 19.215s	1m 18.609s 49
12	Fernando Alonso	E	14	Aston Martin Aramco F1 Team	Aston Martin AMR24-Mercedes F1 M15 E Perf. V6	65			1 lap	1m 18.334s 50
13	Zhou Guanyu	CHN	24	Kick Sauber F1 Team	Sauber C44-Ferrari 066/12 V6	65			1 lap	1m 18.771s 50
14	Lance Stroll	CDN	18	Aston Martin Aramco F1 Team	Aston Martin AMR24-Mercedes F1 M15 E Perf. V6	65			1 lap	1m 19.318s 50
15	Daniel Ricciardo	AUS	3	Visa Cash App RB Formula One Team	RB VCARB 01-Honda RBPT H002 V6	65			1 lap	1m 19.450s 61
16	Valtteri Bottas	FIN	77	Kick Sauber F1 Team	Sauber C44-Ferrari 066/12 V6	65			1 lap	1m 19.608s 13
17	Kevin Magnussen	DK	20	MoneyGram Haas F1 Team	Haas VF-24-Ferrari 066/10 V6	65	*		1 lap	1m 19.805s 33
18	Alexander Albon	T	23	Williams Racing	Williams FW46-Mercedes F1 M15 E Perf. V6	65			1 lap	1m 19.132s 45
19	Yuki Tsunoda	J	22	Visa Cash App RB Formula One Team	RB VCARB 01-Honda RBPT H002 V6	65	*		1 lap	1m 19.447s 56
20	Logan Sargeant	USA	2	Williams Racing	Williams FW46-Mercedes F1 M15 E Perf. V6	64			2 laps	1m 20.172s 38

* Hülkenberg and Tsunoda: 5s time penalty for speeding in the pit lane.   * Magnussen: 5s time penalty for false start - moved before the start signal was given (served at pit stop).

DHL Fastest race lap (scores 1 point): Lando Norris on lap 51, 1m 17.115s, 135.089mph/217.405km/h.
Lap record: Giancarlo Fisichella (Renault R25 V10), 1m 15.641s, 136.835mph/220.213km/h (2005, 2.875-mile/4.627km circuit).
Lap record (current configuration): Max Verstappen (Red Bull RB19-Honda RBPT V6), 1m 16.330s, 136.479mph/219.641km/h (2023).

 19 · SARGEANT · Williams
3-place grid penalty for impeding Stroll during qualifying

 17 · TSUNODA · RB

 15 · ZHOU · Sauber

 13 · HÜLKENBERG · Haas

 11 · PÉREZ · Red Bull
3-place grid penalty for car being in an unsafe condition at the Canadian GP.

 20 · ALBON · Williams
Car modified in parc fermé; required to start from the pit lane

 18 · RICCIARDO · RB

 16 · MAGNUSSEN · Haas

 14 · STROLL · Aston Martin

 12 · BOTTAS · Sauber

TIME SHEETS

PRACTICE 1 (FRIDAY)
Weather: Dry/sunny
Temperatures: track 46-47°C, air 29°C

Pos.	Driver	Laps	Time
1	Lando Norris	27	1m 14.228s
2	Max Verstappen	27	1m 14.252s
3	Carlos Sainz	31	1m 14.572s
4	George Russell	31	1m 14.614s
5	Sergio Pérez	28	1m 14.692s
6	Oscar Piastri	29	1m 14.867s
7	Lewis Hamilton	28	1m 14.911s
8	Esteban Ocon	30	1m 15.086s
9	Fernando Alonso	26	1m 15.222s
10	Alexander Albon	25	1m 15.417s
11	Charles Leclerc	26	1m 15.434s
12	Valtteri Bottas	24	1m 15.472s
13	Pierre Gasly	21	1m 15.484s
14	Lance Stroll	28	1m 15.512s
15	Daniel Ricciardo	30	1m 15.580s
16	Zhou Guanyu	24	1m 15.616s
17	Kevin Magnussen	30	1m 15.644s
18	Logan Sargeant	25	1m 15.752s
19	Oliver Bearman	29	1m 15.865s
20	Yuki Tsunoda	21	1m 15.916s

PRACTICE 2 (FRIDAY)
Weather: Dry/sunny
Temperatures: track 43-46°C, air 25-26°C

Pos.	Driver	Laps	Time
1	Lewis Hamilton	28	1m 13.264s
2	Carlos Sainz	30	1m 13.286s
3	Lando Norris	31	1m 13.319s
4	Pierre Gasly	27	1m 13.443s
5	Max Verstappen	29	1m 13.504s
6	Charles Leclerc	22	1m 13.597s
7	Oscar Piastri	28	1m 13.622s
8	George Russell	28	1m 13.722s
9	Esteban Ocon	30	1m 13.766s
10	Valtteri Bottas	30	1m 13.924s
11	Kevin Magnussen	32	1m 14.021s
12	Nico Hülkenberg	29	1m 14.053s
13	Sergio Pérez	23	1m 14.081s
14	Fernando Alonso	28	1m 14.091s
15	Yuki Tsunoda	31	1m 14.211s
16	Daniel Ricciardo	29	1m 14.257s
17	Zhou Guanyu	21	1m 14.345s
18	Lance Stroll	28	1m 14.402s
19	Alexander Albon	34	1m 14.807s
20	Logan Sargeant	33	1m 15.070s

PRACTICE 3 (SATURDAY)
Weather: Dry/sunny
Temperatures: track 42-46°C, air 27-28°C

Pos.	Driver	Laps	Time
1	Carlos Sainz	19	1m 13.013s
2	Lando Norris	14	1m 13.043s
3	Charles Leclerc	18	1m 13.050s
4	Max Verstappen	24	1m 13.087s
5	George Russell	20	1m 13.164s
6	Lewis Hamilton	26	1m 13.359s
7	Sergio Pérez	19	1m 13.723s
8	Alexander Albon	14	1m 13.753s
9	Fernando Alonso	21	1m 13.786s
10	Oscar Piastri	14	1m 13.907s
11	Esteban Ocon	18	1m 13.950s
12	Pierre Gasly	14	1m 13.964s
13	Nico Hülkenberg	20	1m 13.975s
14	Valtteri Bottas	19	1m 14.024s
15	Kevin Magnussen	27	1m 14.074s
16	Daniel Ricciardo	17	1m 14.161s
17	Lance Stroll	16	1m 14.254s
18	Yuki Tsunoda	22	1m 14.420s
19	Zhou Guanyu	17	1m 14.572s
20	Logan Sargeant	12	1m 14.729s

QUALIFYING (SATURDAY)
Weather: Dry/sunny Temperatures: track 34-36°C, air 24-25°C

Pos.	Driver	First	Second	Third	Qualifying Tyre
1	Lando Norris	1m 12.386s	1m 11.872s	1m 11.383s	Soft (n)
2	Max Verstappen	1m 12.306s	1m 11.653s	1m 11.403s	Soft (n)
3	Lewis Hamilton	1m 12.143s	1m 11.792s	1m 11.701s	Soft (n)
4	George Russell	1m 12.456s	1m 11.812s	1m 11.703s	Soft (n)
5	Charles Leclerc	1m 12.257s	1m 12.038s	1m 11.731s	Soft (n)
6	Carlos Sainz	1m 12.403s	1m 11.874s	1m 11.736s	Soft (n)
7	Pierre Gasly	1m 12.651s	1m 12.079s	1m 11.857s	Soft (n)
8	Sergio Pérez	1m 12.477s	1m 12.054s	1m 12.061s	Soft (n)
9	Esteban Ocon	1m 12.691s	1m 12.109s	1m 12.125s	Soft (n)
10	Oscar Piastri	1m 12.460s	1m 12.011s	no time	
11	Fernando Alonso	1m 12.505s	1m 12.128s		
12	Valtteri Bottas	1m 12.758s	1m 12.227s		
13	Nico Hülkenberg	1m 12.708s	1m 12.310s		
14	Lance Stroll	1m 12.881s	1m 12.372s		
15	Zhou Guanyu	1m 12.880s	1m 12.738s		
16	Kevin Magnussen	1m 12.937s			
17	Yuki Tsunoda	1m 12.985s			
18	Daniel Ricciardo	1m 13.075s			
19	Alexander Albon	1m 13.153s			
20	Logan Sargeant	1m 13.509s			

QUALIFYING: head to head

Verstappen	10	0	Pérez
Hamilton	2	8	Russell
Norris	7	3	Piastri
Leclerc	7	2	Sainz
Leclerc	1	0	Bearman
Gasly	4	6	Ocon
Alonso	6	4	Stroll
Albon	10	0	Sargeant
Bottas	10	0	Zhou
Tsunoda	7	3	Ricciardo
Magnussen	3	7	Hülkenberg

DID YOU KNOW?

This was the second consecutive Spanish GP with no retirements, Verstappen finishing first and Sargeant last in both.

POINTS

DRIVERS

1	Max Verstappen	219
2	Lando Norris	150
3	Charles Leclerc	148
4	Carlos Sainz	116
5	Sergio Pérez	111
6	Oscar Piastri	87
7	George Russell	81
8	Lewis Hamilton	70
9	Fernando Alonso	41
10	Yuki Tsunoda	19
11	Lance Stroll	17
12	Daniel Ricciardo	9
13	Oliver Bearman	6
14	Nico Hülkenberg	6
15	Pierre Gasly	5
16	Esteban Ocon	3
17	Alexander Albon	2
18	Kevin Magnussen	1

CONSTRUCTORS

1	Red Bull	330
2	Ferrari	270
3	McLaren	237
4	Mercedes	151
5	Aston Martin	58
6	RB	28
7	Alpine	8
8	Haas	7
9	Williams	2

 9 · PIASTRI · McLaren
 7 · GASLY · Alpine
 5 · LECLERC · Ferrari
 3 · HAMILTON · Mercedes
 1 · NORRIS · McLaren
 10 · ALONSO · Aston Martin
 8 · OCON · Alpine
 6 · SAINZ · Ferrari
 4 · RUSSELL · Mercedes
 2 · VERSTAPPEN · Red Bull

53	54	55	56	57	58	59	60	61	62	63	64	65	66	
1	1	1	1	1	1	1	1	1	1	1	1	1	1	1
4	4	4	4	4	4	4	4	4	4	4	4	4	4	2
44	44	44	44	44	44	44	44	44	44	44	44	44	44	3
63	63	63	63	63	63	63	63	63	63	63	63	63	63	
55	55	16	16	16	16	16	16	16	16	16	16	16	16	
16	16	55	55	55	55	55	55	55	55	55	55	55	55	6
81	81	81	81	81	81	81	81	81	81	81	81	81	81	7
10	10	10	10	10	10	10	10	10	10	10	10	10	11	8
11	11	11	11	11	11	11	11	11	11	11	11	11	10	9
31	31	31	31	31	31	31	31	31	31	31	31	31	31	10
27	27	27	27	27	27	27	27	27	27	27	27	27	27	
14	14	14	14	14	14	14	14	14	14	14	14	14	14	
24	24	24	24	24	24	24	24	24	24	24	24	24	24	
18	18	18	18	18	18	18	18	18	18	18	18	18	18	
77	77	77	77	77	77	77	77	77	77	77	77	77	77	
20	20	20	20	20	3	3	3	77	77	77	77	77	77	
3	3	3	3	20	20	20	20	20	20	20	20	20	20	
23	23	23	23	23	23	23	23	23	23	23	23	23	23	
2	2	2	2	2	2	2	2	2	2	2	2	2	22	
22	22	2	2	2	2	2	2	2	2	2	2	2	2	

24 = Pit stop **2** = One lap or more behind

RACE TYRE STRATEGIES

	Driver	Race Stint 1	Race Stint 2	Race Stint 3	Race Stint 4
1	Verstappen	Soft (u): 1-17	Medium (n): 18-44	Soft (n): 45-66	
2	Norris	Soft (n): 1-23	Medium (n): 24-47	Soft (u): 48-66	
3	Hamilton	Soft (n): 1-16	Medium (n): 17-43	Soft (u): 44-66	
4	Russell	Soft (n): 1-15	Medium (n): 16-36	Hard (n): 37-66	
5	Leclerc	Soft (n): 1-24	Medium (n): 25-47	Soft (u): 48-66	
6	Sainz	Soft (n): 1-15	Medium (n): 16-36	Hard (n): 37-66	
7	Piastri	Soft (n): 1-21	Medium (n): 22-46	Soft (u): 47-66	
8	Pérez	Soft (n): 1-13	Soft (u): 14-31	Medium (n): 32-49	Soft (u): 50-66
9	Gasly	Soft (n): 1-14	Medium (n): 15-38	Hard (n): 39-66	
10	Ocon	Soft (n): 1-13	Medium (n): 14-37	Hard (n): 38-66	
11	Hülkenberg	Soft (n): 1-12	Medium (n): 13-38	Hard (n): 39-66	
12	Alonso	Soft (n): 1-19	Medium (u): 20-45	Hard (u): 46-65	
13	Zhou	Soft (n): 1-9	Medium (n): 10-41	Hard (n): 42-65	
14	Stroll	Soft (n): 1-17	Medium (n): 18-37	Hard (n): 38-65	
15	Ricciardo	Soft (n): 1-16	Medium (n): 17-42	Hard (n): 43-65	
16	Bottas	Soft (n): 1-11	Soft (u): 12-28	Hard (n): 29-65	
17	Magnussen	Soft (n): 1-10	Medium (n): 11-29	Hard (n): 30-65	
18	Albon	Medium (n): 1-18	Soft (n): 19-43	Soft (n): 44-65	
19	Tsunoda	Soft (n): 1-9	Medium (n): 10-27	Hard (n): 28-44	Soft (n): 45-65
20	Sargeant	Soft (n): 1-14	Medium (n): 15-34	Hard (n): 35-64	

The tyre regulations stipulate that at least two of three dry tyre specifications must be used during a dry race.
Selected compounds for Barcelona: Red = Soft (C3); Yellow = Medium (C2); White = Hard (C1). (n) new (u) used

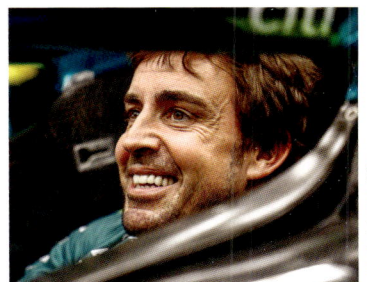

FIA FORMULA 1 WORLD CHAMPIONSHIP · ROUND 11

AUSTRIAN GRAND PRIX

RED BULL RING

FORMULA 1
QATAR AIRWAYS
AUSTRIAN
GRAND PRIX
2024

SPIELBERG QUALIFYING/SPRINT QUALIFYING & RACE

AFTER a brief sensor issue that caused a red flag in practice, Max Verstappen sealed his first pole position in four races ahead of the Red Bull Ring sprint, the third of 2024's six such events.

The world champion was happier with the initial balance of the RB20 than he had been in Monaco, Canada and Spain, even though he ended up less than a tenth clear of Lando Norris on the soft-compound Pirelli used for SQ3. A year on from the start of McLaren's great advance, the team of the moment had a revised front wing and reprofiled front suspension aimed at more downforce and grip in low- and medium-speed corners, with Oscar Piastri qualifying the second car third.

The DRS effect is high in Austria, and the RB20's DRS efficiency gave it a speed advantage at the end of the straights, while it lost out fractionally to McLaren in sector two. But as in Spain, Verstappen made the difference again, his speed and commitment through the sixth-gear Turn Seven a sight to behold. Sergio Pérez was not on the same planet and could only qualify seventh for the sprint.

The Mercedes pace, impressive in the lone practice session on the hard tyre, was further away than George Russell in particular had expected. "I was surprised at the gap to P1," he said, after qualifying fourth, "but I likely pushed too hard on the out-lap and potentially took a little of the peak grip away from the tyre."

Lewis Hamilton – who did not run the soft tyre in practice – lost time in SQ3, having damaged his floor with a trip over the Turn One kerb in SQ1 (in which he squeaked through 13th!), costing him aero performance. Sixth was the best he could manage.

Ferrari had just Carlos Sainz in the top five, as Charles Leclerc had the anti-stall kick in as he waited in the pit lane for SQ3. By the time he got the car fired up and out, he missed the chequered flag by 2s and would start tenth. Team principal Fred Vasseur reported that, as in Barcelona, Ferrari was experiencing high-speed bouncing.

Alpine got both cars through to the top ten again, despite Gasly having "a messy lap", while Kevin Magnussen did a strong job to put his Haas 11th, ahead of both Aston Martins, Lance Stroll marginally quicker than Fernando Alonso. Further back, there seemed to be something about sprints for Logan Sargeant: he had never managed to outqualify Alex Albon for a main race, but, as in Miami, he bested his team-mate for the second time in sprint qualifying.

With the entire field on the medium-compound Pirelli, the first sprint start on Saturday morning was aborted due to photographers being in a dangerous position at Turn One, the extra formation lap reducing the race to 23 laps. Verstappen made another fine getaway and converted his pole. Further back, the frustrated Leclerc was clearly intent on making quick progress, leapfrogging both Alpines and Pérez's Red Bull to run seventh at the end of the opening lap. Team-mate Sainz was on the move, too, going nicely around the outside of Russell's Mercedes in Turn Four to take fourth place.

Verstappen did not run away, however, the McLarens pushing him hard over the opening laps until, on lap five, Norris made a late lunge down the inside of Turn Three to take the lead. But Verstappen got the better exit and when Norris left a gap down the inside of Turn Four, the Red Bull filled it. That forced Lando wide on exit, and Piastri needed no second invitation, pulling off a fine outside pass at Turn Six.

Norris beat himself up about it: "Just a bit silly from my side," he said. "I left the door open for Max like an amateur, did half a job, but didn't finish it off."

After that, it was pretty much stalemate, Piastri not quite having the pace to challenge Verstappen and finishing just over 4s down.

"It's quite hard to get out of the DRS," Verstappen admitted, "but once I did, I could do my own race. They pushed me in the beginning and I think it helped that Lando dropped behind Oscar, because it seemed that Lando was fast."

Norris reported that once the tyres became hot, it wasn't possible to re-pass his team-mate. Behind, Russell retook his fourth place from Sainz after the Spaniard had to 'lift and coast' to cool his brakes and lost the DRS from Piastri. Hamilton finished sixth in the second Mercedes, unhappy with the balance, while Leclerc, too, suffered overheating brakes and had to drop off the back of the queue to cool them, unable to improve on his fine start. A lacklustre Pérez claimed the final point, some 17s behind the sister Red Bull after just 23 laps…

It was back into qualifying mind-set on Saturday afternoon ahead of the main race, with changes permitted to the cars after the sprint in 2024, of course. Alex Albon, Lance Stroll, Sargeant and the Saubers of Valtteri Bottas and Zhou Guanyu all fell at the first hurdle. So close was the competition around the shortest timed lap of the season that had 16th-placed Albon found a quarter of a second, he'd have been fifth!

In Q2, we lost Daniel Ricciardo, Pierre Gasly (whose best lap was deleted for exceeding track limits at T6), Kevin Magnussen, Yuki Tsunoda and Fernando Alonso.

The story of Q3 was post-sprint improvements to the Red Bull that suddenly allowed Verstappen to take a 40th F1 pole, and a fifth at Spielberg, with a 1m 04.314s lap to Norris's 1m 04.718s.

"The car was in a better window," Max explained. "I could push more, and rely on the grip and balance."

There was heartbreak for Piastri, who qualified just 0.07s behind his team-mate, but had his lap scratched for the most marginal of track-limit excesses at Turn Six, meaning P7 on the grid.

"It's embarrassing," the frustrated young Aussie said. "You do all this work for track limits, put in gravel, spend hundreds of thousands if not millions… I mean, I didn't even go off the track! It was probably my best ever Turn Six and it gets deleted." McLaren lodged a protest, but it was deemed inadmissible.

Behind Russell, Hamilton and Sainz, Leclerc was also frustrated. With just the one set of new softs for Q3, after a 1m 05s flat on used rubber, he found three-tenths in the first sector and would have been threatening Norris's front-row time until he went too deep into T4 and locked up, throwing away half his gain. Pushing too hard to recoup it, he dropped a tyre into the T6 gravel and then had a lap-ending tank-slapper in T9. "Totally my fault," he confessed.

Pérez, with no new softs at all for Q3, could manage only eighth, with Hülkenberg's Haas and Ocon's Alpine completing the top ten.

Above: Max Verstappen maintained his dominance by winning the sprint.

Top: A bit of banter between Toto and Christian.

Left: Helmut Marko's influence was still being felt at Red Bull.
Photos: Red Bull Content Pool/Getty Images

Above left: Lando Norris blamed himself for blowing his chances of a win in the sprint race.
Photo: McLaren F1 Team

Far left: Charles Leclerc endured a troubled weekend.
Photo: Scuderia Ferrari

Left: Weighing in after just under half an hour's work, but no points for Sargeant, Tsunoda, Gasly and Albon.

Facing page: Verstappen leads the McLarens of Norris and Piastri at the start of the sprint.
Photos: Red Bull Content Pool/Getty Images

Opening spread: Winner George Russell was in dreamland, having taken full advantage of the collision between Verstappen and Norris.
Photo: Mercedes-AMG Petronas F1 Team

Above: Alpine team-mates Gasly and Ocon clash once more.
Photo: XPB Images

Top right: Still chasing his first win, Oscar Piastri had to settle for another second place.
Photo: McLaren F1 Team

Above right: Eighth place for Kevin Magnussen completed a good weekend for Haas.
Photo: Haas F1 Team

Right: Running three abreast: Ocon, Hülkenberg and Ricciardo head into Turn One at the start.
Photo: XPB Images

THE law of averages says that Max Verstappen must, some day, make a mess of a pole-position start. But it wasn't this day at Spielberg. As in the sprint, the Red Bull was away like a jack rabbit and through Turn One comfortably clear of Lando Norris's McLaren. That sort of thing is important: you control the pace, control the tyre management and break out of DRS. Those in your wake run in dirty air, overheating tyres, brakes and engines, sometimes having to 'lift and coast'.

Behind front-row starter Norris, George Russell was through Turn One in third-place grid order, ahead of Carlos Sainz and team-mate Lewis Hamilton, who went around the Spaniard's Ferrari off-track on the outside of Turn One. It looked as though Hamilton hadn't had much choice, but he was looked at for leaving the track and gaining an advantage.

Behind them, Charles Leclerc's start was nowhere near as decisive as it had been the day before. The Monégasque found himself in the middle of the road on the run into Turn One. A tad circumspect on the brakes perhaps, he was pincered by Sergio Pérez's Red Bull down the inside and Oscar Piastri's McLaren coming around his outside. The meat in the sandwich, Leclerc had to make room for Pérez and suffered damage to his left front wing in light contact with Piastri. Oscar emerged unscathed, but the Ferrari was into the pits at the end of the opening lap for a new nose and a switch from medium to hard Pirellis.

Verstappen was already out of DRS range by the end of the opening lap as Norris, Russell, Hamilton, Sainz, Pérez and Piastri all followed him across the line. Esteban Ocon's Alpine was running eighth, with the Haas cars of Nico Hülkenberg and Kevin Magnussen both in the top ten – timely with Gene Haas himself in the paddock!

Pierre Gasly was 11th with the second Alpine, from Daniel Ricciardo, Fernando Alonso, Yuki Tsunoda, Alex Albon, Valtteri Bottas, Lance Stroll, Zhou Guanyu, Logan Sargeant and Leclerc, stationary in the pits for almost 13s. If ever Charles needed a safety car…

As early as lap three, there was a spirited scrap going on at Mercedes, Hamilton passing Russell with the aid of DRS into Turn Three, only to have his team-mate repass him around the outside into T4. Then Lewis was instructed by the team to give up a place to Sainz for fear of a penalty for his Turn One pass of the Ferrari. Meanwhile, Piastri pulled off a fine outside pass of Pérez's Red Bull in Turn Six to move up to sixth.

With Pirelli's medium the starting tyre of choice, most were anticipating a two-stop strategy, with the first pit stops not expected until 20 laps into the race's 71. It settled into a management phase, with everyone looking after tyres and keeping temperatures under control.

By the time the first pit window opened, Verstappen had stretched out a comfortable 6s cushion to Norris, with Russell a further 4s behind his compatriot and buddy. Sainz had the lone challenging Ferrari just a couple of seconds further back. There was a similar gap to Hamilton, who had a closing Piastri just 1.5s behind aboard the second McLaren. Pérez had dropped 4s behind the young Aussie. He had lost a second per lap to his race-leading team-mate over the opening 20 laps…

Hamilton and Pérez were in on lap 22, Lewis trying the undercut on Sainz, but not without drama.

"I think Hamilton crossed the white line on [pit] entry," Piastri snitched, and indeed he had, the Mercedes leaving a tell-tale black rear tyre mark outside the white line as he gathered up the car after an oversteer moment. Soon would come notification of a 5s penalty.

Russell – who opted for a second set of mediums – and Sainz (on hards) responded to Hamilton a lap later and rejoined still ahead of him, Lewis just 4s clear of the Haas

pair, who had gained time via earlier stops to go on to hards, and now ran seventh and eighth.

Magnussen was attacking Hülkenberg until told that it was important to manage tyres at this point.

"Is that for Nico as well?" he asked, a bit miffed, before responding to a further call for caution with "**** that!"

Then both Verstappen and Norris received the call to pit and were away again after similarly efficient stops, separated by 5.5s. They retook the race's top two slots when Piastri pitted for new boots a lap later.

McLaren, unable to run with Verstappen in the opening medium-tyred stint, was hoping that Norris might be relatively more competitive on the hard compound, but initially it didn't look that way, Verstappen opening out his margin to around 8s as the race approached half-distance. Russell, on the quicker medium, had got the gap to Norris down to below 4s, while Sainz was a similar distance behind and holding his own against Hamilton. It looked like a stalemate as Piastri ran sixth, 4s adrift of the second Mercedes, while Pérez dropped 7s further away.

Magnussen had fallen back to a more respectful 4s behind Hülkenberg, with Ricciardo's VCARB closing down both. Alonso, now on mediums, was in touch, ahead of the Alpines, but received a 10s penalty for rudely punting Zhou's Sauber at Turn Three.

The Alpines, quicker than Alonso, were anxious to be past the Aston, and given the respective histories between Ocon and Fernando, and between Esteban and Gasly, you figured that this could all become a bit feisty. At the start of lap 36, both Alpines got DRS on Alonso, with Ocon making a routine pass down the inside of Turn One.

However, that gave Alonso DRS on the run to Turn Three. He looked at going straight back inside his former team-mate, but received a rude chop as Ocon covered off the inside.

"Wow!" was Alonso's simple reaction over the radio.

Gasly saw the opportunity to go around the outside of both in Turn Three, but was ushered wide on exit by his team-mate. Five laps later, Gasly finally made it past Ocon with a brave move around the outside of Turn Four, which gave him the inside for T6.

On lap 47, Russell made his final stop for a set of hards after a 24-lap stint on mediums, while Sainz's Ferrari pitted next time around for a new set of mediums. Meanwhile, Piastri put a DRS move on Hamilton down the inside of Turn Three to take third.

With 20 laps remaining, Verstappen, with a 7s advantage over Norris, told Red Bull that his tyres were shot. He was called into the pits and followed in by the McLaren. It was an unusually slow 6.5s Red Bull stop due to a sticking left rear.

"Aargh, my God!" was Verstappen's comment as he rejoined, his lead down to just 2.8s. Then he lost more time locking the right front into Turn Four. Max's mediums were a used set, while Norris's were brand new. By lap 54, the McLaren was within DRS range, and on lap 55, he had a brief look down the inside on the run into Turn Three, but Verstappen moved to block.

"He reacted to my move. You're not allowed to do that," Norris complained over the radio. "He saw me move and then he moved."

"Okay, we're on it," McLaren told him.

Verstappen was not his usual composed self. "It feels like there's something wrong with the car, man, just no grip," he said.

Norris needed to be careful, though, receiving a very untimely black-and-white flag for a track-limits infringement. Undeterred, he made a lunge down the inside at Turn Three on lap 59, but ran off-track on exit and was obliged to cede the position back to the Red Bull.

No doubt fearing a 5s penalty for another limits violation, Norris was quick to get his mitigation across: "He can't keep moving after I've moved, it's just

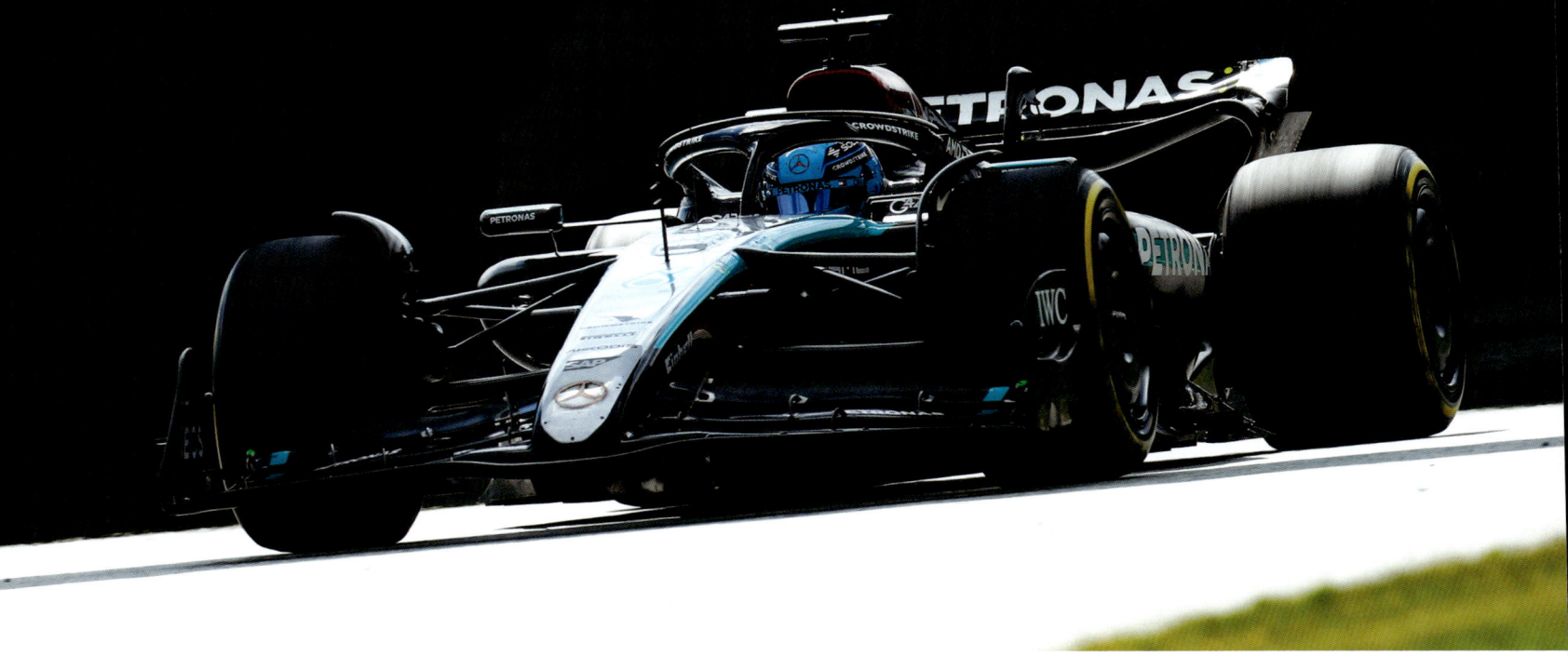

Above: Back on top. George Russell scored a morale-boosting win for Mercedes.
Photo: Mercedes-AMG Petronas F1 Team

Top right: Verstappen and Norris limp away after their collision.
Photo: FTW

Above right: Great work by Red Bull mechanics allowed Verstappen to re-enter the race and claim valuable championship points.
Photo: Red Bull Content Pool/Getty Images

Right: The McLaren driver heads for the pits with a shredded tyre and terminal sidepod damage.
Photo: Atsuo Sakurai

dangerous. We're gonna have a big shunt. He forced me to go wide and lock up."

"Okay, mate, he forced you off," engineer Will Joseph confirmed. "It was the right thing to give the position back, let's get it again."

It was not long before Race Control affirmed that the track-limits violation had been noted and so, to be safe, Norris needed to pass Verstappen and open up a 5s buffer over the remaining ten laps.

On lap 63, Lando again went down the inside of T3, kept it all together and made the turn, while it was Verstappen who ran wide this time, in defence.

"He has to give the position back, I was ahead," Norris complained.

"He forced me off again. He just dive-bombed me. It's not how you overtake," Verstappen claimed.

"It's not clever, is it?" Lambiase concurred, for the benefit of the race stewards no doubt.

Next time around, seven from the end, they finally made contact at T3. Norris went for the outside, Verstappen moved over on him and the resultant collision punctured Max's left rear tyre. But Norris also had a puncture, not to mention a confirmed 5s penalty…

Verstappen made it around to the pits and took on some used softs. Suddenly, a 15s deficit to Norris had morphed into the race lead for George Russell. Not far behind, though, Piastri pulled off a superb outside pass of Carlos Sainz's Ferrari to move up to second, less than 3s behind Russell's race-leading Mercedes. There were six laps remaining.

Verstappen was now fifth and soon came notification of a 10s penalty for the incident with Norris. With just three laps remaining, though, it wouldn't make a difference, with the Red Bull 12s behind Hamilton's fourth-placed Mercedes and 17s clear of Hülkenberg's Haas, which, amazingly, was still ahead of Pérez's Red Bull!

Russell held off Piastri to give Mercedes a victory that, he admitted, they could only have dreamed about after the opening round in Bahrain: "We were only 12–13s behind and have made such good strides. Realistically, we could have won Canada, and this makes up for one or two mistakes there."

Behind Piastri and third-placed Sainz, Hamilton was fourth and generally unhappy. "It was pretty shocking," he said. "I'm really happy for the team of course. On my side, it wasn't for the lack of trying, but we've been just generally slow."

Verstappen finished fifth, picked up ten points and actually extended his championship lead, as both Norris and Leclerc failed to score.

Predictably, the recriminations soon began.

"I looked forward to a strong fair battle, but I wouldn't say that's what it was in the end," Norris grimaced. "A tough one to take. It was a mistake-free race from my side and I felt I did a good job, but got taken out. It's a rule that you're not allowed to react to the other driver. And that's what he did, three times out of three. Three times I managed to avoid it and not run into him, and the third time, he ran into me. He ruined his own race just as much as he ruined mine. There's rules, and if the rules aren't followed, there's nothing I can do about that."

Verstappen countered with, "I felt like he dive-bombs, sometimes he's so late on the brakes. One time, he went straight and I had to go around the sausage kerb, otherwise we'd have touched. It is what it is, but it's never nice to come together. We'll talk about it."

Adding to the world champion's frustration was his feeling that Red Bull's problems had been self-inflicted because of questionable strategy and a poor pit stop.

McLaren team principal Andrea Stella, a man who talks a lot of sense, had a different view: "The problem behind it is that if you don't address these things honestly, they come back. And they have come back today because they were not addressed properly in the past when there were some fights [from Verstappen] with Lewis that needed to be punished in a harsher way. The fact is that we have so much respect for Red Bull, so much respect for Max, that they don't need to do this. To almost compromise your reputation. Why would you do that?"

Tony Dodgins

FIA FORMULA 1 WORLD CHAMPIONSHIP

VIEWPOINT
BANG TO RIGHTS

MAX VERSTAPPEN and Lando Norris collide. It's the denouement of a couple of previous attempts by Norris to take the lead. Both drivers have punctures, their chances of victory up in the air, along with flailing rubber. In each driver's head, blame has already been apportioned. Cue social media going into meltdown, the target of indignation driven by fan affiliation. Exactly as you would expect.

At the height of this partisan dogma, it was enlightening to check out Anthony Davidson's analysis on Sky F1's *SkyPad*. Knowing precisely where each driver would hit the brakes, the former F1 racer (and Mercedes sim driver) was able to add substance to the onboard images during the previous overtaking attempts at the same corner.

In the first, it was clear that Verstappen had moved in the braking area. "That's not allowed," said Davidson, before adding, "They wrote that rule because of Max!"

He was more equivocal about Norris's move up the inside, which had forced Verstappen over the kerb on the exit. Max had called 'foul'. Davidson pulled up a rerun of the 2019 Austrian GP when Verstappen, diving down the inside, had done exactly the same thing to Charles Leclerc – and nothing had been said by the stewards. You might not have approved of the tactic, but at least, as Davidson pointed out, there was consistency in the judgement.

On lap 64, Norris reverted to coming down the outside in the genuine hope of a slingshot as Verstappen dealt with being out of position. This gambit depended on Max leaving a car's width on the outside – as he was formally obliged to do. Lando's onboard showed the space rapidly diminishing to the point where contact was inevitable. "I rest my case," said Davidson.

During the subsequent increasingly angry debate, it was worth remembering Davidson's cheery words as he introduced his piece to camera. "I prefer it this way round – any time – rather than a boring race with one driver disappearing off into the distance. I'm happy in many ways to be able to analyse this."

Amen to that.

Maurice Hamilton

FORMULA 1 QATAR AIRWAYS AUSTRIAN GRAND PRIX 2024

SPIELBERG 28-30 JUNE

RACE DISTANCE: 71 laps, 190.420 miles/306.452km
RACE WEATHER: Dry/cloudy 45-48°C, air 29-30°C)

RED BULL RING, SPIELBERG
Circuit: 2.683 miles/4.318km, 71 laps

RACE – OFFICIAL CLASSIFICATION

Pos.	Driver	Nat.	No.	Entrant	Car/Engine	Laps	Time/Retirement	Speed (mph/km/h)	Gap to leader	Fastest race lap
1	George Russell	GB	63	Mercedes-AMG Petronas F1 Team	Mercedes-AMG F1 W15-M15 E Perf. V6	71	1h 24m 22.798s	135.402/217.908		1m 09.164s 48
2	Oscar Piastri	AUS	81	McLaren Formula 1 Team	McLaren MCL38-Mercedes F1 M15 E Perf. V6	71	1h 24m 24.704s	135.351/217.826	1.906s	1m 08.697s 56
3	Carlos Sainz	E	55	Scuderia Ferrari	Ferrari SF-24-066/12 V6	71	1h 24m 27.331s	135.281/217.713	4.533s	1m 09.282s 56
4	Lewis Hamilton	GB	44	Mercedes-AMG Petronas F1 Team	Mercedes-AMG F1 W15-M15 E Perf. V6	71	1h 24m 45.940s *	134.786/216.917	23.142s	1m 09.562s 61
5	Max Verstappen	NL	1	Oracle Red Bull Racing	Red Bull RB20-Honda RBPT H002 V6	71	1h 25m 00.051s *	134.413/216.316	37.253s	1m 07.719s 68
6	Nico Hülkenberg	D	27	MoneyGram Haas F1 Team	Haas VF-24-Ferrari 066/10 V6	71	1h 25m 16.886s	133.971/215.605	54.088s	1m 10.215s 51
7	Sergio Pérez	MEX	11	Oracle Red Bull Racing	Red Bull RB20-Honda RBPT H002 V6	71	1h 25m 17.470s *	133.955/215.580	54.672s	1m 09.694s 56
8	Kevin Magnussen	DK	20	MoneyGram Haas F1 Team	Haas VF-24-Ferrari 066/10 V6	71	1h 25m 23.153s	133.807/215.341	1m 00.355s	1m 10.125s 45
9	Daniel Ricciardo	AUS	3	Visa Cash App RB Formula One Team	RB VCARB 01-Honda RBPT H002 V6	71	1h 25m 23.967s	133.786/215.307	1m 01.169s	1m 10.426s 49
10	Pierre Gasly	F	10	BWT Alpine F1 Team	Alpine A524-Renault E-Tech RE24 V6	71	1h 25m 24.564s	133.770/215.282	1m 01.766s	1m 09.609s 45
11	Charles Leclerc	MC	16	Scuderia Ferrari	Ferrari SF-24-066/12 V6	71	1h 25m 29.854s	133.632/215.060	1m 07.056s	1m 09.584s 55
12	Esteban Ocon	F	31	BWT Alpine F1 Team	Alpine A524-Renault E-Tech RE24 V6	71	1h 25m 31.123s	133.599/215.006	1m 08.325s	1m 09.649s 45
13	Lance Stroll	CDN	18	Aston Martin Aramco F1 Team	Aston Martin AMR24-Mercedes F1 M15 E Perf. V6	70			1 lap	1m 10.143s 54
14	Yuki Tsunoda	J	22	Visa Cash App RB Formula One Team	RB VCARB 01-Honda RBPT H002 V6	70			1 lap	1m 10.318s 54
15	Alexander Albon	T	23	Williams Racing	Williams FW46-Mercedes F1 M15 E Perf. V6	70	*		1 lap	1m 10.364s 41
16	Valtteri Bottas	FIN	77	Stake F1 Team Kick Sauber	Sauber C44-Ferrari 066/12 V6	70			1 lap	1m 10.449s 48
17	Zhou Guanyu	CHN	24	Stake F1 Team Kick Sauber	Sauber C44-Ferrari 066/12 V6	70			1 lap	1m 10.470s 54
18	Fernando Alonso	E	14	Aston Martin Aramco F1 Team	Aston Martin AMR24-Mercedes F1 M15 E Perf. V6	70	*		1 lap	1m 07.694s 70
19	Logan Sargeant	USA	2	Williams Racing	Williams FW46-Mercedes F1 M15 E Perf. V6	69			2 laps	1m 10.406s 60
20	Lando Norris	GB	4	McLaren Formula 1 Team	McLaren MCL38-Mercedes F1 M15 E Perf. V6	64	accident damage *		7 laps	1m 08.016s 53

* Albon: 5s time penalty for crossing the white line at the pit entry (originally finished 14th).   * Alonso: 10s time penalty for causing a collision with Zhou (served at pit stop).
* Hamilton: 5s time penalty for crossing the white line at the pit entry (served at pit stop).   * Norris: 5s time penalty for leaving the track without a justifiable reason multiple times (retired).
* Pérez: 5s time penalty for speeding in the pit lane (served at pit stop).   * Verstappen: 10s time penalty for causing a collision with Norris.

DHL Fastest race lap: Fernando Alonso on lap 70, 1m 07.694s, 142.688mph/229.633km/h.

Lap record: Nigel Mansell (Williams FW11B-Honda V6 turbo), 1m 28.318s, 150.500mph/242.207km/h (1987, 3.692-mile/5.942km circuit).

Lap record (current configuration): Carlos Sainz (McLaren MCL35-Renault V6), 1m 05.619s, 147.200mph/236.894km/h (2020).

19 · SARGEANT · Williams   17 · STROLL · Aston Martin   15 · ALONSO · Aston Martin   13 · GASLY · Alpine   11 · RICCIARDO · RB

20 · ZHOU · Sauber   18 · BOTTAS · Sauber   16 · ALBON · Williams   14 · TSUNODA · RB   12 · MAGNUSSEN · Haas

Car modified in parc fermé; required to start from the pit lane

Grid order	1	2	3	4	5	6	7	8	9	10	11	12	13	14	15	16	17	18	19	20	21	22	23	24	25	26	27	28	29	30	31	32	33	34	35	36	37	38	39	40	41	42	43	44	45	46	47	48	49	50	51	52	53	54	55
1 VERSTAPPEN	1	1	1	1	1	1	1	1	1	1	1	1	1	1	1	1	1	1	1	1	1	1	1	1	81	1	1	1	1	1	1	1	1	1	1	1	1	1	1	1	1	1	1	1	1	1	1	1	1	1	1	1	1	1	1
4 NORRIS	4	4	4	4	4	4	4	4	4	4	4	4	4	4	4	4	4	4	4	4	4	4	4	4	1	81	4	4	4	4	4	4	4	4	4	4	4	4	4	4	4	4	4	4	4	4	4	4	4	4	4	4	4	4	4
63 RUSSELL	63	63	63	63	63	63	63	63	63	63	63	63	63	63	63	63	63	63	63	63	63	63	63	63	63	4	4	63	63	63	63	63	63	63	63	63	63	63	63	63	63	63	63	63	55	44	81	81	81	44	44	63	63	63	63
55 SAINZ	44	44	44	44	44	55	55	55	55	55	55	55	55	55	55	55	55	55	55	55	55	55	55	55	55	63	63	55	55	55	55	55	55	55	55	55	55	55	55	55	55	55	55	55	63	81	44	44	44	81	63	44	55	55	55
44 HAMILTON	55	55	55	55	55	44	44	44	44	44	44	44	44	44	44	44	44	44	44	44	44	44	44	44	44	55	55	44	44	44	44	44	44	44	44	44	44	44	44	44	44	44	44	44	44	55	63	63	63	63	81	81	44	44	44
16 LECLERC	11	11	11	11	11	11	81	81	81	81	81	81	81	81	81	81	81	81	81	81	81	81	44	44	44	44	44	81	81	81	81	81	81	81	81	81	81	81	81	81	81	81	81	44	44	63	55	55	55	55	55	55	81	44	44
81 PIASTRI	81	81	81	81	81	81	11	11	11	11	11	11	11	11	11	11	11	11	11	11	11	11	27	27	27	27	27	11	11	11	11	11	11	11	11	11	11	11	11	11	11	11	11	11	11	11	11	11	11	11	11	11	27	27	27
11 PÉREZ	31	27	27	27	27	27	27	27	27	27	27	27	31	31	31	31	31	31	31	10	22	20	20	11	11	11	11	27	27	27	27	27	27	27	27	27	27	27	27	27	10	31	22	22	27	27	27	27	27	27	20	20	20	20	20
27 HÜLKENBERG	27	31	31	31	31	31	31	31	31	31	31	31	10	10	10	10	10	10	10	31	22	11	11	20	20	20	20	20	20	20	20	20	20	20	20	20	20	20	31	31	31	22	31	27	20	20	20	20	20	20	3	11	11	11	11
31 OCON	20	20	20	20	20	20	20	20	20	20	22	22	22	22	22	22	22	22	22	20	27	22	22	22	22	22	22	22	18	3	14	14	14	14	14	14	14	14	14	14	14	14	14	14	31	31	3	3	3	3	11	3	3	3	3
3 RICCIARDO	10	10	10	10	10	10	10	10	10	10	10	10	27	22	22	22	18	18	18	18	18	18	18	18	18	18	18	3	14	14	14	14	14	14	14	14	14	14	14	14	14	3	3	31	3	3	16	16	16	16	16	10	10	10	10
20 MAGNUSSEN	3	3	3	3	3	3	3	3	20	23	77	77	77	77	77	77	77	77	77	77	77	77	14	14	23	14	14	14	31	31	31	31	31	31	31	31	31	31	10	10	3	22	18	77	22	16	10	10	10	10	10	16	31	31	31
10 GASLY	14	22	22	22	22	22	22	22	14	18	14	14	14	14	14	14	14	14	14	14	31	31	10	10	10	10	10	10	10	10	10	10	10	10	10	10	10	10	23	23	23	23	27	27	10	10	31	31	31	31	31	31	16	23	18
22 TSUNODA	22	14	14	14	14	14	14	14	3	14	24	27	27	27	27	27	20	20	20	20	14	31	31	31	31	31	31	31	3	22	18	77	77	77	77	77	27	20	16	20	20	10	10	10	16	16	23	23	23	23	23	23	18	18	23
14 ALONSO	23	23	23	23	23	23	23	23	18	77	20	20	20	20	24	24	24	24	24	24	10	10	23	23	3	3	23	23	23	23	23	23	23	23	23	23	23	23	23	77	77	77	77	77	77	77	77	77	77	77	77	77	77	77	77
23 ALBON	77	18	18	18	18	18	18	18	27	3	3	3	3	3	3	3	3	3	3	3	3	10	23	3	16	16	16	16	16	16	16	16	16	16	16	16	16	16	16	16	16	16	16	16	16	16	16	16	16	16	16	16	23	16	16
18 STROLL	18	77	77	77	77	77	77	77	77	20	18	18	18	18	18	18	18	18	18	18	23	23	3	16	14	23	3	24	24	24	24	24	24	24	24	77	77	77	77	16	16	16	23	14	14	14	14	14	14	14	77	77	77	77	77
77 BOTTAS	16	24	24	24	24	24	24	24	24	16	23	23	23	23	23	23	23	23	23	23	16	16	16	16	24	16	16	16	16	24	14	14	14	14	14	14	14	14	14	14	14	14	14	14	77	77	77	77	77	77	77	77	16	14	14
2 SARGEANT	24	16	16	16	16	16	16	16	16	16	16	16	16	16	16	16	16	16	16	16	24	24	24	24	2	24	24	2	24	2	24	2	24	2	24	2	24	2	24	2	24	24	24	2	2	2	2	2	2	2	24	24	24	24	24
24 ZHOU	2	2	2	2	2	2	2	2	2	2	2	2	2	2	2	2	2	2	2	2	2	2	2	2		2	2		2		2		2		2		2		2		2	2	2								2	2	2	2	2

VSC Virtual Safety Car deployed on lap 66

TIME SHEETS

PRACTICE (FRIDAY)

Weather: Dry/cloudy

Temperatures: track 30-42°C, air 22-25°C

Pos.	Driver	Laps	Time
1	Max Verstappen	28	1m 05.685s
2	Oscar Piastri	32	1m 05.961s
3	Charles Leclerc	31	1m 06.055s
4	Carlos Sainz	31	1m 06.128s
5	Lewis Hamilton	39	1m 06.254s
6	Esteban Ocon	30	1m 06.297s
7	Lance Stroll	27	1m 06.384s
8	George Russell	32	1m 06.386s
9	Yuki Tsunoda	30	1m 06.579s
10	Fernando Alonso	30	1m 06.603s
11	Pierre Gasly	28	1m 06.734s
12	Sergio Pérez	24	1m 06.783s
13	Lando Norris	30	1m 06.880s
14	Zhou Guanyu	28	1m 06.919s
15	Valtteri Bottas	29	1m 06.925s
16	Daniel Ricciardo	31	1m 06.962s
17	Nico Hülkenberg	31	1m 06.966s
18	Alexander Albon	28	1m 06.995s
19	Kevin Magnussen	31	1m 07.145s
20	Logan Sargeant	29	1m 07.259s

SPRINT QUALIFYING (FRIDAY)

Weather: Dry/sunny

Temperatures: track 41-42°C, air 29-30°C

Pos.	Driver	First	Second	Third	Qualifying Tyre
1	Max Verstappen	1m 05.690s	1m 05.186s	1m 04.686s	Soft (n)
2	Lando Norris	1m 05.786s	1m 05.561s	1m 04.779s	Soft (n)
3	Oscar Piastri	1m 06.081s	1m 05.379s	1m 04.987s	Soft (n)
4	George Russell	1m 05.764s	1m 05.325s	1m 05.054s	Soft (n)
5	Carlos Sainz	1m 05.781s	1m 05.435s	1m 05.126s	Soft (n)
6	Lewis Hamilton	1m 06.504s	1m 05.539s	1m 05.270s	Soft (n)
7	Sergio Pérez	1m 06.256s	1m 05.612s	1m 06.008s	Soft (n)
8	Esteban Ocon	1m 06.343s	1m 05.686s	1m 06.101s	Soft (u)
9	Pierre Gasly	1m 06.465s	1m 05.757s	1m 06.624s	Soft (u)
10	Charles Leclerc	1m 06.149s	1m 05.526s	no time	
11	Kevin Magnussen	1m 06.387s	1m 05.806s		
12	Lance Stroll	1m 06.037s	1m 05.847s		
13	Fernando Alonso	1m 06.487s	1m 05.878s		
14	Yuki Tsunoda	1m 06.557s	1m 05.960s		
15	Logan Sargeant	1m 06.518s	no time		
16	Daniel Ricciardo	1m 06.581s			
17	Nico Hülkenberg	1m 06.583s			
18	Valtteri Bottas	1m 06.725s			
19	Alexander Albon	1m 06.754s			
20	Zhou Guanyu	1m 07.197s			

FOR THE RECORD

Red Bull Content Pool

250th GRAND PRIX START: Daniel Ricciardo

40th GP POLE POSITION: Max Verstappen

30th FASTEST LAP: Spanish drivers (Alonso, 26; Sainz, 3; de la Rosa, 1)

QUALIFYING: head to head

Verstappen	11	0	Pérez
Hamilton	2	9	Russell
Norris	8	3	Piastri
Leclerc	7	3	Sainz
Leclerc	1	0	Bearman
Gasly	4	7	Ocon
Alonso	6	5	Stroll
Albon	10	1	Sargeant
Bottas	11	0	Zhou
Tsunoda	8	3	Ricciardo
Magnussen	4	7	Hülkenberg

QUALIFYING (SATURDAY)

Weather: Dry/sunny

Temperatures: track 46-50°C, air 32-34°C

Pos.	Driver	First	Second	Third	Qualifying Tyre
1	Max Verstappen	1m 05.336s	1m 04.469s	1m 04.314s	Soft (n)
2	Lando Norris	1m 05.450s	1m 05.103s	1m 04.718s	Soft (n)
3	George Russell	1m 05.585s	1m 05.016s	1m 04.840s	Soft (n)
4	Carlos Sainz	1m 05.263s	1m 05.016s	1m 04.851s	Soft (n)
5	Lewis Hamilton	1m 05.541s	1m 05.053s	1m 04.903s	Soft (n)
6	Charles Leclerc	1m 05.509s	1m 05.104s	1m 05.044s	Soft (u)
7	Oscar Piastri	1m 05.311s	1m 05.070s	1m 05.048s	Soft (n)
8	Sergio Pérez	1m 05.587s	1m 05.144s	1m 05.202s	Soft (u)
9	Nico Hülkenberg	1m 05.596s	1m 05.262s	1m 05.385s	Soft (n)
10	Esteban Ocon	1m 05.574s	1m 05.274s	1m 05.883s	Soft (u)
11	Daniel Ricciardo	1m 05.569s	1m 05.289s		
12	Kevin Magnussen	1m 05.508s	1m 05.347s		
13	Pierre Gasly	1m 05.598s	1m 05.359s		
14	Yuki Tsunoda	1m 05.563s	1m 05.412s		
15	Fernando Alonso	1m 05.656s	1m 05.639s		
16	Alexander Albon	1m 05.736s			
17	Lance Stroll	1m 05.819s			
18	Valtteri Bottas	1m 05.847s			
19	Logan Sargeant	1m 05.856s			
20	Zhou Guanyu	1m 06.061s			

SPRINT (SATURDAY)

RACE DISTANCE: 23 laps, 61.633 miles/99.188km

RACE WEATHER: Dry/cloudy Temperatures: track 44-49°C, air 30-32°C

Pos.	Driver	Laps	Time/Retirement	Speed (mph/km/h)	Gap to leader	Fastest race lap		Grid
1	**Max Verstappen**	23	26m 41.389s	138.553/222.979		1m 09.013s	8	1
2	**Oscar Piastri**	23	26m 46.005s	138.154/222.338	4.616s	1m 08.980s	2	3
3	**Lando Norris**	23	26m 46.737s	138.092/222.237	5.348s	1m 08.935s	2	2
4	**George Russell**	23	26m 49.743s	137.834/221.822	8.354s	1m 09.194s	4	4
5	**Carlos Sainz**	23	26m 51.378s	137.694/221.597	9.989s	1m 09.121s	4	5
6	**Lewis Hamilton**	23	26m 52.596s	137.590/221.429	11.207s	1m 09.265s	5	6
7	**Charles Leclerc**	23	26m 54.813s	137.401/221.125	13.424s	1m 09.352s	5	10
8	**Sergio Pérez**	23	26m 58.798s	137.063/220.581	17.409s	1m 09.420s	4	7
9	Kevin Magnussen	23	27m 05.456s	136.501/219.677	24.067s	1m 09.942s	13	11
10	Lance Stroll	23	27m 11.564s	135.990/218.855	30.175s	1m 10.260s	11	12
11	Esteban Ocon	23	27m 12.228s	135.935/218.766	30.839s	1m 10.254s	9	8
12	Pierre Gasly	23	27m 12.697s	135.896/218.703	31.308s	1m 10.168s	10	9
13	Yuki Tsunoda	23	27m 16.841s	135.552/218.149	35.452s	1m 10.363s	5	14
14	Daniel Ricciardo	23	27m 20.786s	135.226/217.625	39.397s	1m 10.480s	5	16
15	Fernando Alonso	23	27m 24.544s	134.917/217.128	43.155s	1m 10.393s	5	13
16	Logan Sargeant	23	27m 25.465s	134.841/217.006	44.076s	1m 10.488s	6	15
17	Alexander Albon	23	27m 26.062s *	134.792/216.927	44.673s	1m 10.562s	8	20
18	Valtteri Bottas	23	27m 27.900s	134.642/216.685	46.511s	1m 10.590s	8	18
19	Nico Hülkenberg	23	27m 29.812s *	134.486/216.434	48.423s	1m 10.512s	8	17
20	Zhou Guanyu	23	27m 34.532s	134.102/215.817	53.143s	1m 10.613s	6	19

* Albon: Car modified in parc fermé; required to start from the pit lane

* Hülkenberg: 10s time penalty for forcing Alonso off the track (originally finished 14th).

Fastest race lap: Lando Norris on lap 2, 1m 08.935s, 140.119mph/225.499km/h.

9 · HÜLKENBERG · Haas

7 · PIASTRI · McLaren

5 · HAMILTON · Mercedes

3 · RUSSELL · Mercedes

1 · VERSTAPPEN · Red Bull

10 · OCON · Alpine

8 · PÉREZ · Red Bull

6 · LECLERC · Ferrari

4 · SAINZ · Ferrari

2 · NORRIS · McLaren

56	57	58	59	60	61	62	63	64	65	66	67	68	69	70	71	
1	1	1	1	1	1	1	1	63	63	63	63	63	63	63	63	1
4	4	4	4	4	4	4	4	55	81	81	81	81	81	81	81	2
63	63	63	63	63	63	63	63	81	55	55	55	55	55	55	55	3
55	55	55	55	55	55	55	55	1	44	44	44	44	44	44	44	
81	81	81	81	81	81	81	81	44	1	1	1	1	1	1	1	5
44	44	44	44	44	44	44	44	4	27	27	27	27	27	27	27	6
27	27	27	27	27	27	27	27	27	11	11	11	11	11	11	11	7
11	11	11	11	11	11	11	11	11	20	20	20	20	20	20	20	8
20	20	20	20	20	20	20	20	20	3	3	3	3	3	3	3	9
3	3	3	3	3	3	3	3	3	10	10	10	10	10	10	10	10
10	10	10	10	10	10	10	10	10	31	31	31	31	31	16	16	
31	31	31	31	31	*31*	*31*	31	31	16	16	16	16	16	31	31	
18	*18*	*18*	*18*	*18*	*18*	*16*	16	16	18	*18*	*18*	*18*	*18*	*18*		
23	23	23	23	23	23	23	23	23	*22*	*22*	*22*	*22*	*22*	*22*		
22	*16*	*16*	*16*	*22*	*22*	*22*	*22*	*22*	*77*	*77*	*77*	*77*	*77*	*77*		
16	*22*	*22*	*22*	*77*	*77*	*77*	*77*	*77*	*14*	*14*	*14*	*14*	*24*	*24*		
77	*77*	*77*	*77*	*14*	*14*	*14*	*14*	*14*	*24*	*24*	*24*	*24*	*14*	*14*		
14	*14*	*14*	*14*	*24*	*24*	*24*	*24*	*24*	*2*	*2*	*2*	*2*	*2*			
24	*24*	*24*	*24*	*2*	*2*	*2*	*2*	*2*								
2	*2*	*2*	*2*													

16= Pit stop *2 = One lap or more behind*

VSC

RACE TYRE STRATEGIES

PIRELLI

	Driver	Race Stint 1	Race Stint 2	Race Stint 3	Race Stint 4	Race Stint 5
1	Russell	Medium (n): 1-22	Medium (n): 23-46	Hard (n): 47-71		
2	Piastri	Medium (n): 1-25	Hard (n): 26-51	Medium (n): 52-71		
3	Sainz	Medium (n): 1-22	Hard (n): 23-47	Medium (n): 48-71		
4	Hamilton	Medium (n): 1-21	Hard (n): 22-53	Medium (n): 54-71		
5	Verstappen	Medium (n): 1-23	Hard (n): 24-51	Medium (u): 52-64	Soft (u): 65-71	
6	Hülkenberg	Medium (n): 1-11	Hard (n): 12-39	Hard (n): 40-71		
7	Pérez	Medium (n): 1-21	Hard (n): 22-51	Medium (u): 52-71		
8	Magnussen	Medium (n): 1-10	Hard (n): 11-38	Hard (n): 39-71		
9	Ricciardo	Medium (n): 1-10	Hard (u): 11-37	Hard (u): 38-71		
10	Gasly	Medium (n): 1-20	Hard (u): 21-42	Medium (n): 43-71		
11	Leclerc	Medium (n): 1	Hard (n): 2-16	Medium (n): 17-33	Medium (u): 34-51	Medium (u): 52-71
12	Ocon	Medium (n): 1-19	Hard (n): 20-43	Medium (n): 44-71		
13	Stroll	Medium (u): 1-20	Hard (u): 21-43	Hard (u): 44-70		
14	Tsunoda	Medium (u): 1-21	Hard (u): 22-44	Hard (u): 45-70		
15	Albon	Hard (n): 1-12	Hard (n): 13-39	Hard (n): 40-70		
16	Bottas	Hard (n): 1-19	Hard (n): 20-42	Hard (n): 43-70		
17	Zhou	Hard (n): 1-28	Medium (n): 29-51	Hard (n): 52-70		
18	Alonso	Medium (u): 1-11	Medium (u): 12-35	Hard (u): 36-68	Soft (n) 69-70	
19	Sargeant	Medium (n): 1	Medium (u): 2-20	Hard (n): 21-49	Medium (u): 50-69	
20	Norris	Medium (n): 1-23	Hard (u): 24-51	Hard (n): 52-64 (dnf)		

The tyre regulations stipulate that at least two of three dry tyre specifications must be used during a dry race.
Selected compounds for Spielberg: Red = Soft (C5); Yellow = Medium (C4); White = Hard (C3). (n) new (u) used

POINTS

DRIVERS

1	Max Verstappen	237
2	Lando Norris	156
3	Charles Leclerc	150
4	Carlos Sainz	135
5	Sergio Pérez	118
6	Oscar Piastri	112
7	George Russell	111
8	Lewis Hamilton	85
9	Fernando Alonso	41
10	Yuki Tsunoda	19
11	Lance Stroll	17
12	Nico Hülkenberg	14
13	Daniel Ricciardo	11
14	Oliver Bearman	6
15	Pierre Gasly	6
16	Kevin Magnussen	5
17	Esteban Ocon	3
18	Alexander Albon	2

CONSTRUCTORS

1	Red Bull	355
2	Ferrari	291
3	McLaren	268
4	Mercedes	196
5	Aston Martin	58
6	RB	30
7	Haas	19
8	Alpine	9
9	Williams	2

SILVERSTONE QUALIFYING

FRIDAY practice at Silverstone pointed to a continuation of the Red Bull vs McLaren battle that had ended controversially in Austria, but there was a surprise in store. While Lando Norris set the fastest FP2 time and McLaren appeared to have an advantage, Max Verstappen had a moment at Becketts and abandoned his new-tyre push-lap, so his sixth-place time was unrepresentative.

Ferrari seemed to be almost half a second shy for long-run pace, but the emphasis at Maranello was on back-to-backing a car with the recent updates (Charles Leclerc) against one of the previous spec (Carlos Sainz) as the team tried to get a handle on the increased bouncing that had been apparent since Barcelona. Sainz believed that it was costing more time than widely appreciated by eroding driver confidence. Proving the point, Leclerc had a couple of high-speed snaps through Maggotts/Becketts.

Mercedes' Red Bull Ring winner George Russell was realistic ahead of his home GP: "I'd say that the competitive picture looks similar to the past few races – McLaren and Max look a step ahead, and it's close between us and Ferrari."

Silverstone. July. The British summer. Slicks or intermediates? It was anybody's guess. Predictably, the weather forecast was mixed, and when qualifying got under way on Saturday after a wet FP3, it was on a damp, but drying track with intermediate Pirellis the way to go. Initially at least.

There was a red flag halfway through Q1 when Sergio Pérez's recent sub-par run continued after he had changed to slicks, skated off and became beached in the gravel trap at Copse – out in Q1 for the third time in the season.

"I was trying to get some heat into the tyres, but it was quite wet at Turn Nine, and when I downshifted, I locked the rears," he explained.

As ominous clouds gathered, McLaren told Norris that rain was expected in five minutes, so it was possible that the first couple of laps following the restart could be decisive.

Red Bull had an even bigger scare when Verstappen, who was not among the first to get out as the session resumed, almost mirrored his team-mate's error when he was caught out by rain at Copse, but he managed to get the car through the gravel and keep going. With the track improving towards the end of the 15 minutes as the rain stopped again, the Mercedes of Lewis Hamilton and Russell topped the session, and it was Valtteri Bottas, Kevin Magnussen, Pérez, and Alpine's Esteban Ocon and Pierre Gasly (who had a plethora of engine penalties anyway) who took no further part.

The Q2 session was run on slicks and the shock elimination this time was Leclerc's Ferrari, the Monaco winner missing out by a tenth-and-a-half, along with Logan Sargeant, Yuki Tsunoda, Zhou Guanyu and Daniel Ricciardo.

"We are just struggling overall," said a downcast Leclerc. "We just don't have the pace. Especially when it's damp conditions, for some reason, there is either one axle or the other that is not ready, and today it was mostly the front. We paid the price."

The Q3 shootout was on a dry track and it was a fabulous battle between the three Brits, to the delight of a hugely enthusiastic crowd. And in typical 2024 style, it was very tight. The last of the three to deliver a first-run flyer, Russell was at the top of the time sheet by 0.006s from Norris, with Hamilton just a tenth adrift and only marginally quicker than Oscar Piastri with the second McLaren. Verstappen and Red Bull had more than three-tenths to find, which looked unlikely considering Verstappen's floor damage sustained in the Q1 off at Copse.

On his final run, Max found a tenth, which was enough to move him ahead of Piastri, but not enough to get on terms with the British trio. There was a roar when Lewis Hamilton leapt to the top of the time sheet with a lap that was 0.034s quicker than Russell. It was only temporary, though, George moving the goalposts by another tenth-and-a-half to claim his first Silverstone pole and the third of his career.

In the Mercedes garage, Toto Wolff punched the air as Norris backed out of his final attempt and the Silver Arrows were 1-2! It was the 82nd time they had managed it, but it had been a while. It was a British 1-2-3 for the first time in Silverstone history and the first time since the 1968 South African GP, when the men in question had been Jim Clark, Graham Hill and Jackie Stewart.

"We definitely didn't expect to be front row this weekend," Hamilton admitted. "It's huge for us, and the car felt fantastic. It was about getting the tyre temperatures in the right place and then sealing the deal. Ultimately, there was still some time left on the table, which George was able to find, but I feel confident about the car for tomorrow, and with the conditions we have, we can work together to keep Lando behind."

Russell backed up his eight-times Silverstone-winning team-mate's sentiments: "The car really came alive in qualifying and what a joy to drive. We're riding on a bit of a wave, but tomorrow is going to be tight with Lando, and Max will be fast as always."

Verstappen was happy enough with P4, given his damaged floor, while fifth-placed Oscar Piastri lamented getting too close to Sainz starting his final run. Nico Hülkenberg did an absolutely superb job to put his Haas sixth on the grid – ahead of Sainz! – with Lance Stroll, Alex Albon and Fernando Alonso completing the top ten.

THREE British drivers in the top three grid positions at Silverstone. It wasn't scripted, it was reality. But would there be a new British winner of his home race, or a record ninth victory at a single venue for Lewis Hamilton? Or could Max Verstappen spoil the party?

The one certainty was that George Russell, Hamilton and Lando Norris all wanted it as badly as each other. With the eyes of another capacity crowd trained on the starting lights, it was Russell who made no mistake and converted his third career pole, heading Hamilton through Turn One. Norris, trying to get around the outside of the seven-times champion, succeeded only in opening the door for Verstappen, who swept by into third place around Village as Oscar Piastri ran fifth, ahead of Carlos Sainz.

Nico Hülkenberg, after his marvellous sixth in qualifying, had dropped three places to ninth, while Q2 eliminee Charles Leclerc had gone in the opposite direction, up to eighth in the second Ferrari, behind Lance Stroll's Aston Martin. Fernando Alonso completed the top ten, ahead of Yuki Tsunoda, Williams drivers Alex Albon (who lost ground in a first-lap contact with Alonso) and Logan Sargeant, Daniel Ricciardo, Zhou Guanyu, Esteban Ocon, Kevin Magnussen, Valtteri Bottas and Sergio Pérez. Pierre Gasly had been planning to start from the pit lane, but a gearbox problem on the formation lap meant that the Alpine did not take the start.

The top 14 were all on the medium-compound tyre. Zhou and Ocon had opted for the soft, while the out-of-position Pérez was planning on a long opening stint on the hard.

The threatened rain arrived 14 laps into the 52-lap race. Russell, controlling the pace at the front, 1.6s in front of his team-mate, radioed in: "Just keep me posted if anyone is going off because it's coming down harder now."

The lead pair had opened a couple of seconds' advantage over Verstappen, now being hassled by Norris, who had McLaren team-mate Piastri just 1.5s behind. The Ferraris didn't have the pace to run with the leaders, Sainz almost 5s behind the second McLaren, with team-mate Leclerc a similar distance in arrears, having worked his way past Stroll.

To general cheers all around, Norris got a better exit from Becketts and put a DRS pass on Verstappen down into Stowe to move into third. And it wasn't long before Piastri pulled a similar move to relegate the Red Bull to fifth place.

With the surface becoming increasingly slippery, the McLarens seemed to be more comfortable than the Red Bull. Verstappen's race engineer, 'GP' Lambiase, was telling his man, "The target is to try to survive this pocket of rain if you can. Obviously, your call if conditions worsen too much."

Hamilton saw this as his chance, reducing the gap to his team-mate, slipstreaming him down Hangar Straight

Above: George Russell and Lewis Hamilton's Mercedes lead as the race is started in the dry.
Photo: Atsuo Sakurai

Top left: An apprehensive-looking Alex Albon before the start.
Photo: Williams Racing

Above centre left: Lance Stroll beat team-mate Fernando Alonso to take seventh place.
Photo: Aramco Aston Martin F1 Team

Above left: Formula 2 front-runner Isack Hadjar was given a run in the Red Bull in Friday practice.
Photo: Red Bull Content Pool/Getty Images

Left: Russell took pole as Mercedes closed out the front row.

Opening spread: Hamilton shows the winner's trophy to his adoring fans.
Photos: Mercedes-AMG Petronas F1 Team

217

Above: Lap 28, and Piastri pits. Meanwhile, Norris had already switched to inters a lap earlier.
Photo: McLaren F1 Team

Top right: With the track becoming slippery, brollies go up in the crowd and Verstappen gives way to Piastri.
Photo: Bryn Williams

Above right: Another ninth place and two more points for Alex Albon.
Photo: Pirelli

Right: Once again, Nico Hülkenberg overachieved, taking sixth for Haas.
Photo: Bryn Williams

and going by with the aid of DRS on the inside into Stowe on lap 18. As the rain intensified, though, both Mercedes ran off the track at Abbey, allowing Norris to close in and take second from Russell as Race Control disabled DRS.

On lap 20, with the surface ever wetter, it was Norris who seemed to have vastly superior grip as he made short work of Hamilton into Abbey. Piastri was on the move, too, passing first Russell and then Hamilton into Stowe, to make it a McLaren 1-2.

Meanwhile, Ferrari had called in Leclerc to go on to intermediates, but too soon. At the same time, Mercedes was on the radio to Hamilton: "Lewis, we think it's time to jump to inters. Let us know what you think."

"Nope," Hamilton replied. "It's dry in a lot of places."

Sainz, unsurprisingly given his genes as the son of a double world rally champion, also excels in slippery conditions, and while Verstappen had dropped 7s back from Russell, the Ferrari was just half a second behind the Red Bull for fifth as the race reached half-distance.

Piastri was flying, too, now right with Norris as Verstappen decided to pit for intermediates. Sainz followed the Red Bull in. Norris also received the call to pit from the lead on lap 27, while Piastri continued around. Behind him, both Hamilton and Russell came into the pit lane. With the rain intensifying, you had to wonder why McLaren had not simply double-stacked Piastri. Okay, he would have lost a little time, but nothing like as much as he was about to.

By the time Oscar headed into the pit lane, Norris was all but upon him, meaning he'd lost close to a pit stop's worth of time in a single lap… He rejoined sixth, 6s behind Sainz's Ferrari.

The early pit call on to the intermediates had jumped Verstappen past Russell. "Great call on the inter," 'GP' told Max. "Come on, we're back in the race." Norris now led by just over 3s from Hamilton, whose race engineer, Peter Bonnington, told him, "Okay, Lewis, this is our time."

On lap 34, out of nowhere, pole-man Russell received the instruction to retire the car. For the previous ten laps, he had been getting temperature warnings on the steering wheel as Mercedes experienced a water system issue. While the call to stop was not entirely unexpected, therefore, it was cruel luck and, for the crowd, the hopes of an all-British podium were over.

With 15 laps remaining, Norris led Hamilton by 2s, with Verstappen 6s behind and closing. Sainz was a further 12s behind, with the unfortunate Piastri just outside DRS range and Hülkenberg back up to a fine sixth some 20s further in arrears.

With the rain now stopped and the circuit drying, the message to Piastri was, "Competitor cars do not have mediums. Currently, we think medium is the right tyre."

"Yes, yes, it's the best," the young Aussie responded, still obviously somewhat underwhelmed at the way his race had panned out.

Hamilton was in for tyres on lap 39, as was Verstappen, but Norris continued on for another lap. Softs were bolted on to Hamilton's Mercedes, while Max was sent back into the fray on the hard-compound Pirelli. Piastri, as expected, switched to the medium.

As Norris headed into the pits, he was told, "We can choose the medium to cover people like Verstappen, or we can choose the soft to cover people like Hamilton." They went for the soft, but Norris was a bit long on his pit-stop marks and it was a relatively slow 4.5s stop. As Lando rejoined, Hamilton had already gone through and led by 2.5s with 12 laps left.

"Norris is on the same tyre," Bonnington told Lewis.

Above: Verstappen switched to hard tyres on lap 39, then set off in pursuit of Norris and Hamilton.
Photo: Red Bull Content Pool/Getty Images

Top right: Hamilton savours his record ninth British Grand Prix win.
Photo: Mercedes-AMG Petronas F1 Team

Above right: Norris rues the team's decision to put him on soft tyres when a victory had been possible.
Photo: McLaren F1 Team

Right: With the sun shining, Hamilton held off Verstappen's late challenge in a thrilling finish.
Photo: Mercedes-AMG Petronas F1 Team

"Just leave me to it, mate," replied the man chasing his ninth Silverstone win. He knew what he had to do.

With five laps to go, Hamilton seemed to have Norris under control, still 2.7s clear. The danger man appeared to be Verstappen on the hard-compound tyre and now just 1.2s behind the McLaren. He closed that down with ease and, with DRS, demoted the defenceless Norris into Stowe. Some 10s behind, Piastri, on the mediums, was setting fastest laps. Hamilton was now 3.3s up the road. Could Max get him?

Verstappen took back fastest lap from Piastri and, as they headed on to the final lap, had the gap down to 2.5s. But he'd run out of time and the roof almost blew off Silverstone as Hamilton crossed the line to win his ninth British Grand Prix and his 104th GP. Behind Verstappen, Norris, Piastri and Sainz, Hülkenberg was a fine sixth, ahead of the Astons of Stroll and Alonso, with Albon and Tsunoda the remaining points-scorers.

"Get in there, Lewis, you're the man!" roared a delighted Bonnington. "Oh, mate, I've been waiting for this, Jeez…"

Hamilton could barely get the words out. "Thanks, guys," he said, his voice broken. "It means such a lot to get this one."

He was still emotional when he reached the podium. "You've got to dig deep, even when you feel like you're at the bottom of the barrel. There have been days since 2021 where I didn't feel like I was good enough or that I was going to get back to where I am today, but everybody has been so supportive, and it's a big thank you. It's been 945 days, something like that…"

Later, reflecting on the race, he added, "In the first stint, I had a bit of understeer and was just managing because we didn't know how long we had to go on those tyres. I was planning to go longer than George, but when the rain came, I knew that was the moment to pounce.

"But I couldn't understand how McLaren could generate so much heat in the tyres. Then, the last stop, we timed it right and the team did a great job in the pits. George's win last week wasn't on pure pace, and I think this weekend we did do it on pace.

"I think if Lando had made the final stop before us, it would have been very difficult to get by. When he stayed out, I knew that was the moment to undercut him. Then, when Max started to close in, I had to give everything, full attack and the tyre just started to drop off. Another five laps and I don't know if we'd been able to hang on.

"This one really feels different. I had my Mum and Dad there when I first won the championship, but it was difficult to absorb it all at that age. Time with family is always a challenge, but they've been here this weekend, my niece and nephew, and to be able to see them there and share this experience, the last British GP with this team that has been so incredible to me. I have never cried coming from a win, but it just came out of me. I think this win could be the most special to me."

Verstappen had now gone two races without a win for the first time in 2024, but was sanguine: "The beginning was not good. I ran out of tyres and everything was running hot. Lando and Oscar got by, and then the rain came, I had no grip and didn't want to take too much risk. At one point, even Carlos rocked up, and I thought, 'Jesus, this is a bad afternoon.'

"Then, on to slicks, and the hard tyre was the right call. Ultimately, I finished second when it was looking like P5, so I'll take that. We just didn't have the pace, which is something we need to look into."

McLaren did have the pace and probably should have won the race. The decision not to double-stack Piastri, to do the additional lap with Norris before the switch to slicks, and to put Lando on softs rather than mediums at the end all cost a shot at the podium's top step.

"So many things were going well," Norris said ruefully, "and, yes, we threw it away. I think the decision to go on to the softs was wrong, and two calls cost us everything today."

Russell had picked up the pieces when the opportunity presented itself in Austria. And for Mercedes' second successive victory, unthinkable back in Bahrain four short months earlier, Hamilton had done rather more than that. Superb entertainment and a great moment in the sport's history.

Tony Dodgins

VIEWPOINT
MASSIVE RESPECT

AND still the records kept coming. Lewis Hamilton might have been absent from the top step of the podium for two-and-a-half years and reached the ripe old age of 39, but Silverstone would provide a truly significant shout for the seven-times world champion.

On Sunday, 7th July, 2024, his 104th F1 win set two further benchmarks: he had become the first driver to win nine times at the same circuit (this being Silverstone adding another layer of emotion) and the first F1 driver to win a race in 16 different seasons.

Just take a moment to think about that last achievement. To be so consistently competitive in such a high-pressure game is a remarkable tribute to his resilience, professionalism, innate speed – and unequivocal love of the sport. It was that passion for competing and winning that had carried him through a desert of 945 days that, he admitted later, brought occasional moments of doubt. And yet he pushed on, waiting for opportunities such as this.

This British GP win had not been presented on a plate. He had had to work for it – as only he knew how. That moment in the damp, tricky conditions when he took the lead from Mercedes team-mate George Russell; the ability to read the long game when the McLarens briefly swept him aside; the coolness and confidence to cope with the potential menace of an attack from Max Verstappen in the closing stages.

"Leave it to me, mate," he had said when Peter Bonnington appraised him of what needed to be done. 'Bono' had worked as Lewis's race engineer for long enough to know exactly what that message meant. His man had the nous and the capacity to get the job done, despite the personal pressure of the moment.

Small wonder that Lewis Hamilton sobbed during and after his slow-down lap. He had produced arguably one of his greatest drives on this very track in the wet in 2008. And here he was, an incredible 16 years later, doing it all again. Respect.

Maurice Hamilton

12

Official Timepiece

FORMULA 1 QATAR AIRWAYS BRITISH GRAND PRIX 2024

SILVERSTONE 05-07 JULY

RACE DISTANCE: 52 laps, 190.263 miles/306.198km

RACE WEATHER: Wet track, rain briefly later/cloudy (track 25-27°C, air 14-18°C)

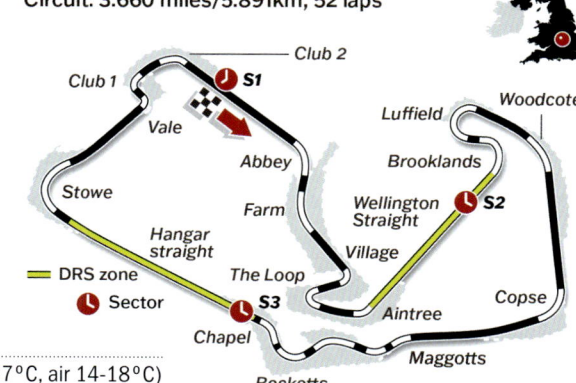

SILVERSTONE CIRCUIT
Circuit: 3.660 miles/5.891km, 52 laps

RACE – OFFICIAL CLASSIFICATION

Pos.	Driver	Nat.	No.	Entrant	Car/Engine	Laps	Time/Retirement	Speed (mph/km/h)	Gap to leader	Fastest race lap
1	Lewis Hamilton	GB	44	Mercedes-AMG Petronas F1 Team	Mercedes-AMG F1 W15-M15 E Perf. V6	52	1h 22m 27.059s	138.455/222.821		1m 29.438s 45
2	Max Verstappen	NL	1	Oracle Red Bull Racing	Red Bull RB20-Honda RBPT H002 V6	52	1h 22m 28.524s	138.414/222.755	1.465s	1m 28.952s 48
3	Lando Norris	GB	4	McLaren Formula 1 Team	McLaren MCL38-Mercedes F1 M15 E Perf. V6	52	1h 22m 34.606s	138.244/222.482	7.547s	1m 29.262s 43
4	Oscar Piastri	AUS	81	McLaren Formula 1 Team	McLaren MCL38-Mercedes F1 M15 E Perf. V6	52	1h 22m 39.488s	138.108/222.263	12.429s	1m 28.748s 51
5	Carlos Sainz	E	55	Scuderia Ferrari	Ferrari SF-24-066/12 V6	52	1h 23m 14.377s	137.143/220.710	47.318s	1m 28.293s 52
6	Nico Hülkenberg	D	27	MoneyGram Haas F1 Team	Haas VF-24-Ferrari 066/10 V6	52	1h 23m 22.781s	136.913/220.340	55.722s	1m 29.836s 43
7	Lance Stroll	CDN	18	Aston Martin Aramco F1 Team	Aston Martin AMR24-Mercedes F1 M15 E Perf. V6	52	1h 23m 23.628s	136.889/220.302	56.569s	1m 29.897s 46
8	Fernando Alonso	E	14	Aston Martin Aramco F1 Team	Aston Martin AMR24-Mercedes F1 M15 E Perf. V6	52	1h 23m 30.636s	136.698/219.994	1m 03.577s	1m 29.710s 47
9	Alexander Albon	T	23	Williams Racing	Williams FW46-Mercedes F1 M15 E Perf. V6	52	1h 23m 35.446s	136.567/219.783	1m 08.387s	1m 29.718s 52
10	Yuki Tsunoda	J	22	Visa Cash App RB Formula One Team	RB VCARB 01-Honda RBPT H002 V6	52	1h 23m 46.362s	136.270/219.306	1m 19.303s	1m 30.229s 43
11	Logan Sargeant	USA	2	Williams Racing	Williams FW46-Mercedes F1 M15 E Perf. V6	52	1h 23m 56.019s	136.009/218.885	1m 28.960s	1m 29.972s 42
12	Kevin Magnussen	DK	20	MoneyGram Haas F1 Team	Haas VF-24-Ferrari 066/10 V6	52	1h 23m 57.212s	135.977/218.833	1m 30.153s	1m 30.093s 42
13	Daniel Ricciardo	AUS	3	Visa Cash App RB Formula One Team	RB VCARB 01-Honda RBPT H002 V6	51			1 lap	1m 30.735s 47
14	Charles Leclerc	MC	16	Scuderia Ferrari	Ferrari SF-24-066/12 V6	51			1 lap	1m 29.748s 43
15	Valtteri Bottas	FIN	77	Stake F1 Team Kick Sauber	Sauber C44-Ferrari 066/12 V6	51			1 lap	1m 31.277s 44
16	Esteban Ocon	F	31	BWT Alpine F1 Team	Alpine A524-Renault E-Tech RE24 V6	50			2 laps	1m 30.875s 46
17	Sergio Pérez	MEX	11	Oracle Red Bull Racing	Red Bull RB20-Honda RBPT H002 V6	50			2 laps	1m 29.707s 50
18	Zhou Guanyu	CHN	24	Stake F1 Team Kick Sauber	Sauber C44-Ferrari 066/12 V6	50			2 laps	1m 31.014s 43
	George Russell	GB	63	Mercedes-AMG Petronas F1 Team	Mercedes-AMG F1 W15-M15 E Perf. V6	33	water system			1m 31.298s 3
NS	Pierre Gasly	F	10	BWT Alpine F1 Team	Alpine A524-Renault E-Tech RE24 V6	–	gearbox failure on formation lap			

DHL Fastest race lap (scores 1 point): Carlos Sainz on lap 52, 1m 28.293s, 149.251mph/240.195km/h..

Lap record: Nigel Mansell (Williams FW11B-Honda V6 turbo), 1m 09.832s, 153.059mph/246.324km/h (1987, 2.969-mile/4.778km circuit).

Lap record (current configuration): Max Verstappen (Red Bull RB16-Honda V6), 1m 27.097s, 151.300mph/243.494km/h (2020).

19 · GASLY · Alpine
NS – gearbox failure on formation lap

17 · MAGNUSSEN · Haas

15 · RICCIARDO · RB

13 · TSUNODA · RB

11 · LECLERC · Ferrari

20 · PÉREZ · Red Bull
Car modified in parc fermé; required to start from the pit lane

18 · OCON · Alpine

16 · BOTTAS · Sauber

14 · ZHOU · Sauber

12 · SARGEANT · Williams

Grid order	1	2	3	4	5	6	7	8	9	10	11	12	13	14	15	16	17	18	19	20	21	22	23	24	25	26	27	28	29	30	31	32	33	34	35	36	37	38	39	40	41
63 RUSSELL	63	63	63	63	63	63	63	63	63	63	63	63	63	63	63	63	63	44	44	4	4	4	4	4	4	4	4	81	4	4	4	4	4	4	4	4	4	4	4	44	44
44 HAMILTON	44	44	44	44	44	44	44	44	44	44	44	44	44	44	44	44	44	63	4	81	81	81	81	81	81	81	81	44	4	44	44	44	44	44	44	44	44	44	55	4	4
4 NORRIS	1	1	1	1	1	1	1	1	1	1	1	1	1	1	1	4	4	4	63	44	44	44	44	44	44	44	44	81	44	1	1	1	1	1	1	1	1	1	44	1	1
1 VERSTAPPEN	4	4	4	4	4	4	4	4	4	4	4	4	4	4	4	1	1	81	81	63	63	63	63	63	63	63	63	1	63	55	55	55	55	55	55	55	55	55	1	81	81
81 PIASTRI	81	81	81	81	81	81	81	81	81	81	81	81	81	81	81	81	81	1	1	1	1	1	1	1	1	1	1	63	55	55	55	55	55	81	81	81	81	81	55	55	55
27 HÜLKENBERG	55	55	55	55	55	55	55	55	55	55	55	55	55	55	55	55	55	55	55	55	55	55	55	55	55	55	55	55	81	81	81	81	81	27	27	27	27	27	27	27	27
55 SAINZ	18	18	18	18	18	18	18	18	18	18	18	18	16	16	16	16	16	16	16	27	27	27	27	27	27	27	14	27	27	27	27	27	27	18	18	18	18	18	18	18	18
18 STROLL	16	16	16	16	16	16	16	16	16	16	16	16	18	18	18	18	18	27	14	14	14	14	14	14	14	14	22	18	18	18	18	18	18	14	14	14	14	14	14	14	14
23 ALBON	27	27	27	27	27	27	27	27	27	27	27	27	27	27	27	27	27	18	18	18	18	18	18	18	18	14	23	14	14	14	14	14	14	22	22	22	22	22	22	22	22
14 ALONSO	14	14	14	14	14	14	14	14	14	14	14	14	14	14	14	14	14	22	22	22	22	22	22	22	22	20	22	22	22	22	22	22	22	23	23	23	23	23	23	23	23
16 LECLERC	22	22	22	22	22	22	22	22	22	22	22	22	22	22	22	22	22	23	23	23	23	23	23	23	23	2	23	23	23	23	23	23	23	20	20	20	20	2	20	20	20
2 SARGEANT	23	23	23	23	23	23	23	23	23	23	23	23	23	23	23	23	23	2	2	20	20	20	20	27	20	20	20	20	20	20	20	2	20	2	2	2	2	20	2	2	2
22 TSUNODA	2	2	2	2	2	2	2	2	2	2	2	2	2	2	2	2	2	20	20	2	2	2	2	18	2	2	2	2	2	2	2	3	3	3	3	3	3	3	3	3	3
24 ZHOU	24	24	24	24	24	3	3	3	3	3	3	20	3	3	3	3	3	3	3	3	3	3	3	3	3	3	3	3	3	3	3	77	77	77	77	77	77	77	77	77	77
3 RICCIARDO	3	3	3	3	3	24	20	20	20	20	20	3	11	11	11	11	11	77	77	77	77	77	77	77	77	77	77	77	77	77	77	16	16	16	16	16	16	16	16	16	16
77 BOTTAS	31	31	31	31	20	11	11	11	11	11	11	11	77	77	77	77	77	16	16	16	16	16	16	16	16	16	16	16	16	16	16	11	11	11	11	11	11	11	31	11	11
20 MAGNUSSEN	20	20	20	20	11	31	31	31	31	31	77	77	20	20	20	20	20	11	11	11	11	11	11	11	11	11	11	11	11	11	11	31	31	31	31	31	31	31	11	31	31
31 OCON	77	77	77	11	31	20	77	77	77	77	31	31	31	31	31	31	31	31	31	31	31	31	31	31	31	31	31	31	31	31	31	24	24	24	24	24	24	24	24	24	24
10 GASLY	11	11	11	77	77	77	24	24	24	24	24	24	24	24	24	24	24	24	24	24	24	24	24	24	24	24	24	24	24	24	24										
11 PÉREZ																																									

TIME SHEETS

PRACTICE 1 (FRIDAY)
Weather: Dry/overcast
Temperatures: track 20-22°C, air 18-19°C

Pos.	Driver	Laps	Time
1	Lando Norris	26	1m 27.420s
2	Lance Stroll	22	1m 27.554s
3	Oscar Piastri	18	1m 27.631s
4	Max Verstappen	25	1m 27.729s
5	George Russell	26	1m 27.738s
6	Fernando Alonso	27	1m 27.794s
7	Lewis Hamilton	26	1m 27.858s
8	Charles Leclerc	26	1m 27.903s
9	Carlos Sainz	27	1m 27.925s
10	Esteban Ocon	24	1m 27.974s
11	Nico Hülkenberg	22	1m 28.082s
12	Valtteri Bottas	26	1m 28.254s
13	Daniel Ricciardo	24	1m 28.477s
14	Oliver Bearman	25	1m 28.536s
15	Zhou Guanyu	24	1m 28.590s
16	Alexander Albon	25	1m 28.649s
17	Jack Doohan	22	1m 28.735s
18	Franco Colapinto	24	1m 29.078s
19	Isack Hadjar	15	1m 29.270s
20	Yuki Tsunoda	5	1m 29.864s

PRACTICE 2 (FRIDAY)
Weather: Dry-heavy rain/overcast
Temperatures: track 19-28°C, air 17-20°C

Pos.	Driver	Laps	Time
1	Lando Norris	26	1m 26.549s
2	Oscar Piastri	24	1m 26.880s
3	Sergio Pérez	25	1m 26.983s
4	Nico Hülkenberg	26	1m 26.990s
5	Charles Leclerc	27	1m 27.150s
6	Lewis Hamilton	26	1m 27.202s
7	Max Verstappen	21	1m 27.233s
8	Carlos Sainz	31	1m 27.249s
9	Lance Stroll	21	1m 27.274s
10	George Russell	26	1m 27.294s
11	Fernando Alonso	25	1m 27.372s
12	Valtteri Bottas	16	1m 27.381s
13	Alexander Albon	26	1m 27.645s
14	Pierre Gasly	24	1m 27.732s
15	Esteban Ocon	19	1m 27.743s
16	Yuki Tsunoda	26	1m 27.745s
17	Logan Sargeant	24	1m 27.809s
18	Zhou Guanyu	19	1m 27.813s
19	Daniel Ricciardo	25	1m 27.916s
20	Kevin Magnussen	20	1m 28.122s

PRACTICE 3 (SATURDAY)
Weather: Rain/overcast
Temperatures: track 13°C, air 11°C

Pos.	Driver	Laps	Time
1	George Russell	23	1m 37.529s
2	Lewis Hamilton	28	1m 37.564s
3	Lando Norris	20	1m 37.714s
4	Carlos Sainz	23	1m 38.139s
5	Max Verstappen	20	1m 38.393s
6	Charles Leclerc	26	1m 38.454s
7	Oscar Piastri	27	1m 38.654s
8	Fernando Alonso	21	1m 38.940s
9	Sergio Pérez	18	1m 39.284s
10	Nico Hülkenberg	16	1m 39.340s
11	Alexander Albon	24	1m 39.603s
12	Lance Stroll	23	1m 39.700s
13	Logan Sargeant	22	1m 39.702s
14	Yuki Tsunoda	26	1m 39.820s
15	Valtteri Bottas	22	1m 40.242s
16	Esteban Ocon	25	1m 40.430s
17	Kevin Magnussen	21	1m 40.539s
18	Daniel Ricciardo	28	1m 40.823s
19	Zhou Guanyu	23	1m 41.785s
20	Pierre Gasly	2	no time

QUALIFYING (SATURDAY)
Weather: Wet-dry/cloudy   Temperatures: track 20-22°C, air 13-14°C

Pos.	Driver	First	Second	Third	Qualifying Tyre
1	George Russell	1m 30.106s	1m 26.723s	1m 25.819s	Soft (n)
2	Lewis Hamilton	1m 29.547s	1m 26.770s	1m 25.990s	Soft (n)
3	Lando Norris	1m 31.596s	1m 26.559s	1m 26.030s	Soft (n)
4	Max Verstappen	1m 31.342s	1m 26.796s	1m 26.203s	Soft (n)
5	Oscar Piastri	1m 30.895s	1m 26.733s	1m 26.237s	Soft (n)
6	Nico Hülkenberg	1m 31.929s	1m 26.847s	1m 26.338s	Soft (n)
7	Carlos Sainz	1m 30.557s	1m 26.843s	1m 26.509s	Soft (n)
8	Lance Stroll	1m 31.410s	1m 26.938s	1m 26.585s	Soft (n)
9	Alexander Albon	1m 31.135s	1m 26.933s	1m 26.640s	Soft (n)
10	Fernando Alonso	1m 31.264s	1m 26.730s	1m 26.917s	Soft (u)
11	Charles Leclerc	1m 30.496s	1m 27.097s		
12	Logan Sargeant	1m 31.608s	1m 27.175s		
13	Yuki Tsunoda	1m 30.994s	1m 27.269s		
14	Zhou Guanyu	1m 31.190s	1m 27.867s		
15	Daniel Ricciardo	1m 31.291s	1m 27.949s		
16	Valtteri Bottas	1m 32.431s			
17	Kevin Magnussen	1m 32.905s			
18	Esteban Ocon	1m 34.557s			
19	Sergio Pérez	1m 38.348s			
20	Pierre Gasly	1m 39.804s			

FOR THE RECORD

20th GP PODIUM: Lando Norris
80th GP 1-2 GRID: Mercedes

DID YOU KNOW?

The only other time of 3 British drivers filling the top 3 grid positions at the British GP was in 1962 (Clark, Surtees and Ireland).

The last occasion of 3 British drivers in the top 3 grid positons was in S. Africa, 1968 (Clark, Hill and Stewart).

POINTS

DRIVERS

1	Max Verstappen	255
2	Lando Norris	171
3	Charles Leclerc	150
4	Carlos Sainz	146
5	Oscar Piastri	124
6	Sergio Pérez	118
7	George Russell	111
8	Lewis Hamilton	110
9	Fernando Alonso	45
10	Lance Stroll	23
11	Nico Hülkenberg	22
12	Yuki Tsunoda	20
13	Daniel Ricciardo	11
14	Oliver Bearman	6
15	Pierre Gasly	6
16	Kevin Magnussen	5
17	Alexander Albon	4
18	Esteban Ocon	3

CONSTRUCTORS

1	Red Bull	373
2	Ferrari	302
3	McLaren	295
4	Mercedes	221
5	Aston Martin	68
6	RB	31
7	Haas	27
8	Alpine	9
9	Williams	4

QUALIFYING: head to head

Verstappen	12	0	Pérez
Hamilton	2	10	Russell
Norris	9	3	Piastri
Leclerc	7	4	Sainz
Leclerc	1	0	Bearman
Gasly	4	8	Ocon
Alonso	6	6	Stroll
Albon	11	1	Sargeant
Bottas	11	1	Zhou
Tsunoda	9	3	Ricciardo
Magnussen	4	8	Hülkenberg

Williams Racing

9 · ALBON · Williams

7 · SAINZ · Ferrari

5 · PIASTRI · McLaren

3 · NORRIS · McLaren

1 · RUSSELL · Mercedes

10 · ALONSO · Aston Martin

8 · STROLL · Aston Martin

6 · HÜLKENBERG · Haas

4 · VERSTAPPEN · Red Bull

2 · HAMILTON · Mercedes

RACE TYRE STRATEGIES

	Driver	Race Stint 1	Race Stint 2	Race Stint 3	Race Stint 4	Race Stint 5
1	Hamilton	Medium (n): 1-27	Inter (n): 28-38	Soft (u): 39-52		
2	Verstappen	Medium (n): 1-26	Inter (n): 27-38	Hard (n): 39-52		
3	Norris	Medium (n): 1-27	Inter (n): 28-39	Soft (u): 40-52		
4	Piastri	Medium (n): 1-28	Inter (n): 29-38	Medium (n): 39-52		
5	Sainz	Medium (n): 1-26	Inter (n): 27-39	Hard (n): 40-50	Soft (u): 51-52	
6	Hülkenberg	Medium (n): 1-26	Inter (n): 27-39	Soft (u): 40-52		
7	Stroll	Medium (n): 1-27	Inter (n): 28-39	Medium (n): 40-52		
8	Alonso	Medium (n): 1-27	Inter (n): 28-38	Medium (n): 39-52		
9	Albon	Medium (n): 1-27	Inter (n): 28-38	Medium (n): 39-52		
10	Tsunoda	Medium (n): 1-27	Inter (n): 28-38	Soft (n): 39-52		
11	Sargeant	Medium (n): 1-27	Inter (n): 28-38	Soft (n): 39-52		
12	Magnussen	Medium (n): 1-27	Inter (n): 28-38	Soft (n): 38-52		
13	Ricciardo	Medium (n): 1-26	Inter (n): 27-37	Soft (n): 38-51		
14	Leclerc	Medium (n): 1-19	Inter (n): 20-27	Inter (n): 28-37	Soft: 38-51	
15	Bottas	Medium (n): 1-26	Hard (n): 27-37	Soft (n): 38-51		
16	Ocon	Soft (n): 1-19	Inter (n): 20-21	Medium (n): 22-26	Inter (n): 27-38	Medium (n): 39-50
17	Pérez	Hard (n): 1-19	Inter (n): 20-28	Inter (n): 29-37	Medium (n): 38-47	Soft (u): 48-50
18	Zhou	Soft (n): 1-12	Medium (n): 13-19	Inter (n): 20-26	Inter (n): 27-37	Soft (u): 38-50
	Russell	Medium (n): 1-27	Inter (n): 28-33 (dnf)			
NS	Gasly	Medium (n): 0				

The tyre regulations stipulate that at least two of three dry tyre specifications must be used during a dry race.
Selected compounds for Silverstone: Red = Soft (C3); Yellow = Medium (C2); White = Hard (C1). (n) new (u) used

7 = Pit stop   88 = One lap or more behind

FIA FORMULA 1 WORLD CHAMPIONSHIP · ROUND 13

HUNGARIAN GRAND PRIX

HUNGARORING CIRCUIT

HUNGARORING QUALIFYING

THE key question at Hungaroring was whether a significantly upgraded Red Bull could restore the competitive advantage that had helped Max Verstappen win seven of 2024's races so far. It had been seriously eroded over the previous six races, during which McLaren had outscored the constructors' champions by 37 points.

The RB20 had a reprofiled nose and front wing with the aim of adding more downforce without producing a negative effect on the airflow downstream. There were also different lower front wishbone shrouds, reprofiled flick-ups around the halo, rear brake duct modifications and a visually different engine cover incorporating cooling gills à la Ferrari and Mercedes.

The revised car seemed to be working well in practice, and amid scorching track temperatures approaching 60 degrees, McLaren made its long run on the hard-compound tyre and appeared to be in good shape as well, at least on Lando Norris's side of the garage.

Was the pressure beginning to get to Verstappen? Conditions were cooler and damper on Saturday, and the track right on the bubble between intermediates and slicks as qualifying began. Max's manner on the radio at the beginning of qualifying betrayed angst, his concern being the rain. As he was being told to calm down by race engineer 'GP' Lambiase, the team suddenly had more to worry about when Sergio Pérez lost the second RB20 at Turn Eight on soft-compound tyres as the drizzle fell. He spun into the tyres and was out.

By the end of Q1, the racing line was almost dry again, and Lewis Hamilton and Verstappen set identical 1m 17.087s times. But when that was suddenly beaten by Daniel Ricciardo with a couple of minutes remaining, it showed that drivers needed to be out right at the end. George Russell had gone too soon, and the previous year's Hungaroring pole-man was caught out, falling at the first hurdle along with the hapless Pérez, Zhou Guanyu, and Alpine drivers Esteban Ocon and Pierre Gasly, who were not on-track at the right time either.

"Why are we not fuelling the car to the end?" Russell wanted to know. "Not having enough fuel is fundamental." It had seemed pretty clear that the last lap was going to be the quickest.

Lewis Hamilton had always been formidable around Hungaroring, a circuit he describes as an overgrown kart track and at which he could boast nine poles. In Q2, though, the seven-times champion was under pressure as Norris set the pace ahead of Verstappen, team-mate Oscar Piastri and the two Ferrari drivers, Charles Leclerc and Carlos Sainz. Next up were the two Aston Martins and VCARBs – only the second time in the season that both Faenza cars had made Q3 – leaving Hamilton a precarious tenth as the midfield all began later final runs. He seemed to be in trouble as Nico Hülkenberg set quicker times in the first two sectors, but Lewis finally squeaked through – by 0.01s!

Toto Wolff was underwhelmed. "It's total underperformance from literally everyone involved here," he stormed. "Losing a car in Q1 is just not on. At the end, we just didn't have the pace, but a very disappointing day. With George, it was 70 per cent the team's fault in not fuelling a lot more."

Valtteri Bottas, 12th, missed out by 0.07s, with the two Williams of Alex Albon and Logan Sargeant 13th and 14th, ahead of Kevin Magnussen's Haas. It was perhaps Sargeant's most impressive qualifying effort to date, the Floridian just over a tenth behind Albon.

With the threat of rain still hanging in the air as Q3 began, it was a little surprising that Alonso and Tsunoda made their first runs on used softs. Norris, however, wasn't hanging around and set provisional pole on his first run with 1m 15.227s, giving him a three-tenths buffer.

Team-mate Oscar Piastri ran him super-close, the Australian just two-hundredths slower. Then it was Verstappen's turn, but the championship leader was unable to displace the McLarens at the head of the pack with 1m 15.273s. Just five-hundredths covered the first three, but, crucially, both McLarens were at the front.

Yuki Tsunoda ensured that it would stay like that when he suffered a big shunt taking too much exit kerb on the way out of Turn Five and deposited his VCARB hard into the barrier. With two minutes remaining, out came the red flag.

"Not an easy qualifying, but I'm happy," smiled Norris after his third F1 pole. "Hopefully, with two cars at the front, we can control it from there. The car's going well, I'm driving well, so it's obvious what the goal is."

Piastri was sanguine: "It's the first qualifying 1-2 for McLaren for a very long time [Brazil 2012], which is great, but missing out by two-hundredths, you think of all the little things you could have done a bit better. But it's amazing. We've got a big task ahead of us trying to win this championship as a team, so we'll be smart."

While Verstappen was a strong favourite for a fourth successive drivers' title, McLaren clearly believed that it was in the hunt for the constructors'. With its drivers so evenly matched and an apparent chasm separating the Red Bull men, perhaps that was justified.

"The whole weekend, we have been a little bit behind," Verstappen summarised. "I would have liked a bit more grip, but it's just not there at the moment. I hope in the race we can follow them. At the moment, I feel that we are chasing."

Meanwhile, McLaren team principal Andrea Stella was playing down its new-found pace-setter status: "We'll try our best, but Max is always the reference, and he will be the favourite tomorrow."

"My Q3 lap was more or less the maximum I could do," said Carlos Sainz, but it was still four-tenths behind the McLaren/Red Bull pace. He did manage to outqualify Charles Leclerc, though, the Ferraris being split on the grid by Hamilton's Mercedes.

The Aston Martins shared row four, Fernando Alonso a couple of tenths quicker than Lance Stroll, with the two VCARBs completing the top ten, Ricciardo 0.03s quicker than the chastened Tsunoda.

As the grid formed up in Budapest, the feeling was that this was very much McLaren's race to lose, notwithstanding that starts had not been the team's strong suit in 2024.

When the lights blinked out, Oscar Piastri made a slightly better getaway than his pole-winning team-mate. Lando Norris moved right to cover him, but the second McLaren was already there and Norris had to switch his attention to Max Verstappen, who was intent on running around the outside of both papaya cars through Turn One. Max was being optimistic, however, and was forced wide and off-track with all four wheels. He rejoined ahead of Norris, forcing him to lift momentarily, which gave Lewis Hamilton the opportunity to run around the outside of the McLaren in Turn Two.

Norris, unimpressed at the prospect of going from pole to fourth, braved it out with Hamilton through Turn Three, getting back in front as he kicked up dust over the kerb on exit.

It took no time for the radio message from the Norris cockpit: "Max has to give back the position. He committed to the outside so that he would run off. Can't do that…"

"We're on it," confirmed McLaren.

The Ferrari drivers had differing fortunes off the line. Carlos Sainz dropped three places from his fourth spot on the grid, while team-mate Charles Leclerc was up a place from sixth to fifth, the pair split by Fernando Alonso's Aston Martin. Lance Stroll ran eighth with the second Aston, ahead of Alex Albon's Williams and Kevin Magnussen's Haas.

Daniel Ricciardo headed VCARB team-mate Yuki Tsunoda, both down a couple of slots from their grid positions, then came Nico Hülkenberg, Esteban Ocon (up four places for Alpine), George Russell, Sergio Pérez, Logan Sargeant (down four places) and Zhou Guanyu.

The information soon arrived that Verstappen had been noted for leaving the track and gaining an advantage, and it really became a question of whether Red Bull would instruct him to give back the position or risk a 5s penalty at his first stop. If he had been leading the race, that might have been a tougher call, but with Piastri setting the pace, there was potential for McLaren to back the Dutchman into the pack and increase the effect of any penalty.

Meanwhile, Verstappen was doing his utmost to influence the stewards. "I got forced off," he claimed. "I was ahead at the apex and he just opened the wheel, so I got forced out."

On the third lap, Sainz pushed his way inside compatriot Alonso at Turn One to move up to sixth. Every one of the top six had started on the medium-compound Pirelli, seventh to tenth were on the softs, with 11th to 14th on mediums. Further back, out-of-position Russell and Pérez were on hards, and obviously planning a long opening stint.

Verstappen's race engineer, 'GP' Lambiase, told him, "Max, the incident is under investigation. Our recommendation is that you let this go. So let Lando past down into Turn One."

"Why can't they say what they think and then we decide?" Verstappen responded, followed by some expletives. Almost immediately, though, he slowed on the run to Turn Two, and McLaren had itself a 1-2, Piastri leading Norris by just under three seconds.

"Okay, so you can just run people off the track, then?" commented a peeved Verstappen.

The pit lane was busy just seven laps into the 70 as Albon, Magnussen and Ocon all stopped to swap their starting softs for hards, with Alonso, Ricciardo and Zhou responding next time around.

Hamilton was the first of the medium-tyre starters to enter the pits, after 17 laps. McLaren responded with a message to Norris: "Hundred per cent pace, please,

Above: Max Verstappen runs wide on the opening lap.

Top left: Yuki Tsunoda made it into Q3, but brought proceedings to an abrupt end when he shunted his RB.
Photos: Red Bull Content Pool/Getty Images

Above left: All okay for Carlos Sainz.
Photo: Scuderia Ferrari

Left: Another weekend was compromised for Sergio Pérez, who crashed out of Q1.
Photo: Lukas Gorys

Opening spread: Oscar Piastri crosses the line to claim his first grand prix victory, while a compliant Lando Norris finishes second.
Photo: Atsuo Sakurai

Above: Lewis Hamilton and Mercedes had no answer to the speed of the McLarens, but he won the race with Ferrari and Red Bull to record his 200th podium.
Photo: Atsuo Sakurai

Top right: Team principal Mike Krack contemplates Aston Martin's return from the Hungarian weekend – a single point from Lance Stroll.

Above right: Finishing last and no sign of progress for Zhou Guanyu.
Photos: Stake F1 Team Kick Sauber

Right: After breaking the winner's trophy in 2023, Lando Norris jokingly sported a porcelain-themed helmet for the weekend.
Photo: McLaren F1 Team

hundred per cent pace," which was followed by the instruction to pit. Lando covered off the Hamilton threat successfully and rejoined fifth.

Out front, Piastri had opened an 8s margin over Verstappen, who seemed even less thrilled with life: "I can't brake, I can't enter corners. Front and rears. It's really bad."

Next time around, McLaren brought in Piastri, who was away again still 2.5s clear of team-mate Norris. Meanwhile, Red Bull waited another two laps before bringing in Verstappen, as Ferrari also serviced Sainz, leaving Leclerc out until lap 23 before going on to hards in what was expected to be a two-stop race.

With 25 laps down, Piastri led Norris by 3.2s, with Hamilton 2.4s behind the second McLaren and Verstappen 5s further back. Then there was a 7s gap to Leclerc, who had a yet-to-pit Tsunoda 4.5s behind him, the VCARB about to be passed by Sainz.

Now Hamilton was paying for the heavy use of his fresh hard tyres to undercut Verstappen into third. Approaching half-distance, Max had closed in on his old foe's Mercedes and was looking for a way by. When Lewis suffered a slight lock-up into Turn One while braking late and defending, Verstappen got a better exit and tried to go around the outside at Turn Two, but went a little too deep. Lewis fended him off.

Cue another frustrated radio transmission from Verstappen: "I'm minus five on brake bias and this thing just doesn't ******* turn. It's unbelievable!"

While his annoyance grew at being trapped behind Hamilton, the McLarens were 7s up the road. Piastri possessed a 1.5s margin over team-mate Norris, while Leclerc's Ferrari, with a handy tyre offset similar to Verstappen's, had set fastest lap and was closing on the battle for third.

On lap 41, Hamilton pitted for his second stop and was followed in by Leclerc, Lewis intent on maintaining track position relative to Verstappen and Charles hoping to undercut him. The Mercedes went on to a set of hards, the Ferrari took mediums.

Verstappen was not impressed and was complaining to his team: "It's quite impressive how we let ourselves get undercut and just completely **** my race!"

Piastri was under more pressure from Norris, who had been told that he was free to race, but he lost a chunk of his lead when he ran wide at Turn 11 while negotiating traffic. Surprisingly, given that McLaren didn't appear to have undue pressure from behind – Norris some 7.2s clear of Verstappen – with 25 laps remaining, the team chose to pit second-placed Norris first, which inevitably would result in him undercutting Piastri into the lead. After an efficient 2.3s pit stop, Lando was on his way on a fresh set of mediums.

As he exited the pits, Piastri was told, "Okay, Oscar, Lando has pitted to make sure he covers Hamilton. We'll manage that situation. Best pace from you now." Surprisingly, he went around again and you began to wonder whether this was McLaren prioritising Norris. When he did make a 2.9s stop on lap 48, he emerged behind his team-mate, both of them now on mediums.

However, the message to Lando was, "Okay, Lando, Oscar has just pitted. He will come out behind you. We would like to re-establish the order at your convenience."

Here was a second dubious call. Had they said, "Swap immediately," it would have left no room for ambiguity and Piastri would still have been in control. Allowed to

operate at his convenience, however, Norris was likely to leave the swap as late as possible. First, in the hope that a late-race safety car might close up the pack and make it a high-risk business, in which case, he no doubt hoped, the team would abandon the idea. And second, if he did it somewhat patronisingly out of the last corner, as Ayrton Senna had done with Gerhard Berger at Suzuka back in 1991, Lando would appear to be the moral victor.

Verstappen was the last of the front-runners to stop, pitting on lap 50 for his final set of mediums and a handy tyre offset. But he was down in fifth, some 5.7s behind Leclerc, who was still harrying Hamilton, and some 15s off the race lead.

Then McLaren issued another message to Piastri: "Okay, Oscar, so once you get to Lando, we will swap position. But we want to avoid Lando having to give up a lot of race time."

Which only added to the ambiguity. Furthermore, Norris was now 3.6s in front with 19 to go. What if Piastri didn't get to him? Would that mean there would be no swap? All a bit confusing and perhaps not what the erstwhile race leader wanted to hear.

Then, just in case Norris might experience 'selective deafness', McLaren radioed, "Lando, radio check please."

"Yes, loud and clear," replied Norris.

"Okay, can you save the tyres at Turn Four and Turn 11 please?" These are the two Hungaroring corners that put heavy loads through the right and left fronts respectively. Effectively a 'slow down' call.

On what was becoming a day of fascinating radio transmissions, the next one came from Lambiase to Verstappen who, with 17 laps to go, had closed on to the back of Hamilton and Leclerc, wiping out the 5s deficit that had existed when he left the pits three laps earlier.

"Well, that's some gentle introduction," said Lambiase, who had obviously instructed his man to bring in his final set of tyres much more gently and hadn't been impressed by an opening lap that was 2s faster than Leclerc, even though it had, for the moment, snared the fastest-lap point, later nicked by a late-stopping Russell.

"No, mate. Don't give me that ****," responded a narked Verstappen. "You guys gave me this **** strategy. Okay? I'm trying to rescue what's left. ****!"

You had to pity the team's strategy chief, Hannah Schmitz, on the pit wall, so often in the past the chief architect of winning Red Bull strategies (see Viewpoint).

Meanwhile, McLaren was starting to take a firmer line with Norris: "We need to save more tyres please, and we do want to let Oscar through."

"Well, you should have boxed him first then, surely, no?" was the reply.

"It doesn't matter," race engineer Will Joseph told him.

"I mean, it does, to me maybe," said Norris, no doubt a reference to his outside chance of the drivers' championship.

Then, a couple of laps later: "Lando, we still think you are using the tyres too much at Turns Four and 11, and the rears at the exit of Turn Six and Turn Nine. Oscar is 3.5s – we know you'll do the right thing."

On lap 57, Verstappen was closer than ever to Leclerc out of the final corner and finally went inside the Ferrari into Turn One to take fourth and set his sights on Hamilton. By lap 63, he was with the Mercedes and took a run around the outside of Turn Two, but was run wide on exit.

"Shouldn't you leave a car's width?" he radioed.

"We think you were behind at the apex, Max," Lambiase told him.

"Whatever, man," replied a grumpy world champion.

Next time around, the Dutchman was closer out of the final corner and went for the inside of Turn One with a late lunge. He locked up, went straight and tagged Hamilton's right front. That flicked the Red Bull around and it briefly departed stage left before resuming between the two Ferraris, Sainz having closed to within a couple of seconds of Leclerc.

"He moved under braking!" Verstappen radioed.

"I'm not even going to get into a radio fight with the other teams, Max," said Lambiase. "We'll let the stewards do their thing. It's childish on the radio. Childish."

With Norris still taking little heed of McLaren's wishes, they tried again: "Okay, Lando, we think both cars are using their tyres too much. Just remember every single Sunday morning meeting we've had."

"Yeah, well tell him to catch up, please."

Piastri could not, however, and that was spelled out by another radio transmission on lap 64: "Lando, he can't catch you up. You've proved your point and it really doesn't matter."

To Norris, though, it did. "He's on quicker tyres," Lando pointed out, "and I would have tried to undercut anyway."

"Mate, we did the stop sequence in this order for the good of the team," Joseph said. "I'm trying to protect you, mate, I promise. There's five laps to go. The way to win a championship is not by yourself, it's with the team. You're going to need Oscar and the team."

With three laps remaining, Piastri legitimately pointed out, "The longer we leave this, the riskier it gets."

"Understood, Oscar, we're managing it," confirmed engineer Tom Stallard.

The final message to Norris from Joseph with three laps to go and no time for a restart if there was a safety car, was firm: "A potential safety car now would make this very awkward. Please do it. Now."

Norris finally obeyed, throttling back from what had become a 6s margin out of the final corner and allowing Piastri past him down the main straight. Oscar had a sprint-race victory to his name from Qatar 2023, but in his 35th race, he could finally celebrate a first full GP win.

He doesn't do histrionics, of course, and it was a muted "Thank you, everyone. Thanks very much. Thanks for the co-ordination. Sorry I made the swap a bit more painful than it needed to be."

Hamilton's fine drive might not have brought him a Silverstone-equalling ninth Budapest win, but it did bring him his 200th F1 podium, the closest to him being Michael Schumacher on 155. Norris, publicly magnanimous with his team-mate and on the podium, looked rattled in the cool-down room, throwing away the second-place cap. And when Lewis pointed out how quick the McLaren was, he retorted, "Well, you had a quick car seven years ago." A bit taken aback, Hamilton said he'd only been complimenting the team…

In the drivers' championship, Norris was still 76 points – more than three victories – behind Verstappen. Piastri, fifth, was 40 points further back. But in the constructors' battle, a McLaren 1-2 and a Red Bull 5-7 indicated a significant shift. McLaren was up to second, just 51 points behind Red Bull and 16 clear of Ferrari.

Behind Leclerc's Ferrari, Verstappen, fifth, believed that Hamilton had turned right in the braking zone when Max was already committed at Turn One and didn't agree with Lewis's 'racing incident' assessment. He was also dismissive of those who thought he'd been a team bully.

"I don't know why you can't be vocal on the radio. This is a sport," he said. "If people don't like it, then stay home."

Behind the drama surrounding the big points, Sainz brought home the second Ferrari in sixth, while Pérez and Russell paid the price for their Q1 exits with seventh and eighth respectively, the final points going to Yuki Tsunoda and Lance Stroll.

In Piastri, F1 had its seventh different winner in 13 races, and perhaps was closer and more compelling than it ever had been.

Tony Dodgins

VIEWPOINT
MAD MAX

GOING into the Hungarian GP, Red Bull revealed that Helmut Marko's contract had been renewed, a move that also seemed to ensure Max Verstappen's continuing presence. Despite having signed a contract extension, it was believed that the world champion had options if his ally, Marko, was no longer on board. Now everything had fallen into place. All would remain sweetness and light.

That was not a summary you would have chosen after the race. Verstappen's petulance on the radio not only hinted at his frustration with the current RB20, but the frequent outbursts also suggested that perhaps he was no longer sure about committing himself to Red Bull Racing in its current state. Either way, there was no excuse for the world champion being ferociously critical of a team that had given such unconditional support for several seasons.

Spats with his race engineer, Gianpiero Lambiase, were one thing ('GP' had proved more than capable of looking after himself during his driver's moments of volatility). But to openly refer to the "sh*t strategy" was a sad and pathetic disregard of Hannah Schmitz, who had played such a significant part in many of Max's victories. The fact that he wasn't getting his own way and being beaten was no excuse for publicly throwing Schmitz under a bus, particularly as the TV camera immediately homed in on the hapless strategist. However, she remained cool (outwardly at least), despite the massive pressure being piled on team members at the pit wall.

Verstappen's frustration was excused by some because "that's who he is and why he is a multiple champion". And there's an element of truth in that. Equally, the experience that comes with such significant success ought to have tempered his exasperation with the thought that he was more or less three clear wins ahead in the championship and all was far from lost.

Timely circumspection might also have prevented the desperate lunge at Lewis Hamilton. Max was lucky to be able to continue and finish fifth. That, too, should have been a mitigating factor on a day when, it was argued, he deserved to score no points all.

Maurice Hamilton

Above: Lap 49, and Lando Norris heads out for his final stint on medium-compound tyres. Having overtaken Oscar Piastri, he seemed well placed for the win before team orders were imposed.

Far left: Piastri greeted his first GP win in his usual sanguine manner.
Photos: McLaren F1 Team

Left: Max Verstappen vented his frustration at the Hungaroring.

Below left: Max's race engineer, Gianpiero Lambiase, is well equipped to handle himself.
Photos: Red Bull Content Pool/Getty Images

13 FORMULA 1 HUNGARIAN GRAND PRIX 2024

HUNGARORING MOGYORÓD, BUDAPEST
Circuit: 2.722 miles/4.381km, 70 laps

BUDAPEST 19-21 JULY
RACE DISTANCE: 70 laps, 190.531 miles/306.630km
RACE WEATHER: Dry/sunny (track 45-49°C, air 33°C)

RACE – OFFICIAL CLASSIFICATION

Pos.	Driver	Nat.	No.	Entrant	Car/Engine	Laps	Time/Retirement	Speed (mph/km/h)	Gap to leader	Fastest race lap	
1	Oscar Piastri	AUS	81	McLaren Formula 1 Team	McLaren MCL38-Mercedes F1 M15 E Perf. V6	70	1h 38m 01.989s	116.612/187.669		1m 21.716s	51
2	Lando Norris	GB	4	McLaren Formula 1 Team	McLaren MCL38-Mercedes F1 M15 E Perf. V6	70	1h 38m 04.130s	116.569/187.600	2.141s	1m 21.712s	50
3	Lewis Hamilton	GB	44	Mercedes-AMG Petronas F1 Team	Mercedes-AMG F1 W15-M15 E Perf. V6	70	1h 38m 16.869s	116.318/187.195	14.880s	1m 22.153s	54
4	Charles Leclerc	MC	16	Scuderia Ferrari	Ferrari SF-24-066/12 V6	70	1h 38m 21.675s	116.223/187.043	19.686s	1m 22.182s	29
5	Max Verstappen	NL	1	Oracle Red Bull Racing	Red Bull RB20-Honda RBPT H002 V6	70	1h 38m 23.338s	116.190/186.990	21.349s	1m 20.908s	51
6	Carlos Sainz	E	55	Scuderia Ferrari	Ferrari SF-24-066/12 V6	70	1h 38m 25.062s	116.156/186.935	23.073s	1m 21.441s	53
7	Sergio Pérez	MEX	11	Oracle Red Bull Racing	Red Bull RB20-Honda RBPT H002 V6	70	1h 38m 41.781s	115.829/186.408	39.792s	1m 21.096s	49
8	George Russell	GB	63	Mercedes-AMG Petronas F1 Team	Mercedes-AMG F1 W15-M15 E Perf. V6	70	1h 38m 44.357s	115.778/186.327	42.368s	1m 20.305s	55
9	Yuki Tsunoda	J	22	Visa Cash App RB Formula One Team	RB VCARB 01-Honda RBPT H002 V6	70	1h 39m 19.248s	115.100/185.236	1m 17.259s	1m 23.533s	57
10	Lance Stroll	CDN	18	Aston Martin Aramco F1 Team	Aston Martin AMR24-Mercedes F1 M15 E Perf. V6	70	1h 39m 19.965s	115.086/185.213	1m 17.976s	1m 22.338s	48
11	Fernando Alonso	E	14	Aston Martin Aramco F1 Team	Aston Martin AMR24-Mercedes F1 M15 E Perf. V6	70	1h 39m 24.449s	115.000/185.074	1m 22.460s	1m 23.063s	52
12	Daniel Ricciardo	AUS	3	Visa Cash App RB Formula One Team	RB VCARB 01-Honda RBPT H002 V6	69			1 lap	1m 22.640s	30
13	Nico Hülkenberg	D	27	MoneyGram Haas F1 Team	Haas VF-24-Ferrari 066/10 V6	69			1 lap	1m 23.461s	54
14	Alexander Albon	T	23	Williams Racing	Williams FW46-Mercedes F1 M15 E Perf. V6	69			1 lap	1m 23.930s	31
15	Kevin Magnussen	DK	20	MoneyGram Haas F1 Team	Haas VF-24-Ferrari 066/10 V6	69			1 lap	1m 23.553s	50
16	Valtteri Bottas	FIN	77	Stake F1 Team Kick Sauber	Sauber C44-Ferrari 066/12 V6	69			1 lap	1m 22.792s	52
17	Logan Sargeant	USA	2	Williams Racing	Williams FW46-Mercedes F1 M15 E Perf. V6	69			1 lap	1m 20.561s	65
18	Esteban Ocon	F	31	BWT Alpine F1 Team	Alpine A524-Renault E-Tech RE24 V6	69			1 lap	1m 21.610s	66
19	Zhou Guanyu	CHN	24	Stake F1 Team Kick Sauber	Sauber C44-Ferrari 066/12 V6	69			1 lap	1m 23.487s	38
	Pierre Gasly	F	10	BWT Alpine F1 Team	Alpine A524-Renault E-Tech RE24 V6	33	hydraulics			1m 23.340s	31

DHL Fastest race lap (scores 1 point): George Russell on lap 55, 1m 20.305s, 122.035mph/196.396km/h.
Lap record: Lewis Hamilton (Mercedes F1 W11 V6), 1m 16.627s, 127.892mph/205.823km/h (2020).

19 · OCON · Alpine   17 · RUSSELL · Mercedes   15 · MAGNUSSEN · Haas   13 · ALBON · Williams   11 · HÜLKENBERG · Haas

20 · GASLY · Alpine   18 · ZHOU · Sauber   16 · PÉREZ · Red Bull   14 · SARGEANT · Williams   12 · BOTTAS · Sauber

Additional power unit elements used and car modified in parc fermé; required to start from the pit lane

Grid order		1	2	3	4	5	6	7	8	9	10	11	12	13	14	15	16	17	18	19	20	21	22	23	24	25	26	27	28	29	30	31	32	33	34	35	36	37	38	39	40	41	42	43	44	45	46	47	48	49	50	51	52	53	54
4	NORRIS	81	81	81	81	81	81	81	81	81	81	81	81	81	81	81	81	81	1	1	1	16	16	81	81	81	81	81	81	81	81	81	81	81	81	81	81	81	81	81	81	81	81	81	81	81	81	81	1	1	4	4	4	4	4
81	PIASTRI	1	1	1	4	4	4	4	4	4	4	4	4	4	4	4	4	4	16	16	16	81	81	4	4	4	4	4	4	4	4	4	4	4	4	4	4	4	4	4	4	4	4	4	4	4	4	4	4	4	81	81	81	81	81
1	VERSTAPPEN	4	4	4	1	1	1	1	1	1	1	1	1	1	1	1	1	1	55	55	55	81	4	44	44	44	44	44	44	44	44	44	44	44	44	44	44	44	44	44	1	1	1	1	55	4	81	81	44	44	16	16	16	16	16
55	SAINZ	44	44	44	44	44	44	44	44	44	44	44	44	44	44	16	16	55	81	81	81	55	44	44	1	1	1	1	1	1	1	1	1	1	1	1	1	1	1	1	44	55	55	55	55	55	4	55	55	55	44	44	44	44	44
44	HAMILTON	16	16	16	16	16	16	16	16	16	16	16	16	16	16	44	55	4	4	4	4	1	1	16	16	16	16	16	16	16	16	16	16	16	16	16	16	16	16	16	16	44	44	44	44	44	16	16	16	16	1	1	1	1	1
16	LECLERC	14	14	55	55	55	55	55	55	55	55	55	55	55	55	55	22	44	44	44	44	22	22	22	55	55	55	55	55	55	55	55	55	55	55	55	55	55	55	55	55	16	16	16	16	16	55	55	55	55	55	55	55	55	55
14	ALONSO	55	55	14	14	14	14	18	18	18	18	18	18	22	22	22	44	22	22	22	22	63	63	63	55	22	22	22	63	63	63	63	14	14	14	11	11	11	11	11	11	11	63	63	63	63	63	63	63	63	11
18	STROLL	18	18	18	18	18	14	22	22	22	22	22	22	18	77	63	63	63	63	11	11	55	63	63	63	22	14	14	14	18	18	14	18	14	18	63	63	63	63	63	11	11	11	11	11	63
3	RICCIARDO	23	23	23	23	3	22	77	77	77	77	77	63	11	11	11	11	11	55	55	11	11	11	11	14	18	18	18	18	18	18	18	18	18	18	22	22	22	22	22	22	22	22	22
22	TSUNODA	20	20	20	20	20	22	3	63	63	63	63	63	11	77	10	10	10	10	10	10	10	10	10	18	22	11	22	63	22	22	22	22	22	22	22	18	14	14	14	14	14	14
27	HÜLKENBERG	3	3	3	3	23	77	11	11	11	11	11	11	10	10	27	27	27	27	27	14	18	27	20	11	11	22	63	63	22	77	77	77	14	14	14	3	3	3	3	3	3
77	BOTTAS	22	22	22	22	22	77	63	2	10	10	10	10	27	14	14	14	14	14	14	27	10	20	11	20	20	77	77	77	77	3	14	14	77	77	3	27	18	18	18	18	18	18
23	ALBON	77	77	77	77	77	20	2	10	27	27	27	27	14	23	18	18	18	18	18	18	27	77	77	77	77	20	3	3	14	3	3	77	23	18	27	27	27	27	27	27
2	SARGEANT	27	27	31	31	31	63	11	27	14	14	14	14	23	23	23	23	23	11	2	2	2	2	27	23	23	3	23	23	23	23	23	18	23	23	23	23	23	23	23	23
20	MAGNUSSEN	31	63	63	63	2	10	14	24	23	23	23	23	20	18	20	20	20	20	18	20	20	23	31	24	10	10	2	27	27	27	27	23	27	23	77	20	20	20	20	20
11	PÉREZ	63	2	2	2	11	24	23	23	20	20	20	20	18	20	3	3	3	3	3	3	3	3	3	3	3	77	31	24	20	24	20	27	24	20	20	20	20	20	20	31	31	31	31	31	31
63	RUSSELL	11	27	11	11	11	24	27	20	3	3	3	3	31	77	77	77	77	77	77	77	77	3	2	10	3	23	20	20	31	31	31	31	31	31	2	2	2	2	2	2
24	ZHOU	2	11	24	24	24	31	23	3	31	31	31	31	77	31	31	31	31	31	31	31	31	31	23	27	27	27	31	31	2	2	2	2	2	2	77	77	77	77	77	77
31	OCON	24	24	10	10	10	10	20	31	2	2	2	2	2	2	2	2	2	2	2	2	2	2	10	27	23	23	2	2	24	24	24	24	24	24	24	24	24	24	24	24	24
10	GASLY	10	10	27	27	27	27	24	24	24	24	24	24	24	24	24	24	24	24	24	24	3	23	31	31	31

TIME SHEETS

PRACTICE 1 (FRIDAY)
Weather: Dry/sunny
Temperatures: track 57-59°C, air 31-32°C

Pos.	Driver	Laps	Time
1	Carlos Sainz	27	1m 18.713s
2	Max Verstappen	20	1m 18.989s
3	Charles Leclerc	29	1m 19.011s
4	George Russell	28	1m 19.137s
5	Zhou Guanyu	24	1m 19.180s
6	Lando Norris	26	1m 19.211s
7	Oscar Piastri	26	1m 19.249s
8	Yuki Tsunoda	26	1m 19.260s
9	Lance Stroll	25	1m 19.265s
10	Lewis Hamilton	29	1m 19.287s
11	Sergio Pérez	22	1m 19.440s
12	Daniel Ricciardo	27	1m 19.578s
13	Fernando Alonso	24	1m 19.686s
14	Alexander Albon	22	1m 19.794s
15	Valtteri Bottas	28	1m 19.804s
16	Logan Sargeant	26	1m 19.885s
17	Pierre Gasly	26	1m 19.976s
18	Esteban Ocon	26	1m 20.023s
19	Kevin Magnussen	27	1m 20.295s
20	Oliver Bearman	27	1m 20.371s

PRACTICE 2 (FRIDAY)
Weather: Dry/sunny
Temperatures: track 42-52°C, air 31-35°C

Pos.	Driver	Laps	Time
1	Lando Norris	24	1m 17.788s
2	Max Verstappen	20	1m 18.031s
3	Carlos Sainz	23	1m 18.185s
4	Sergio Pérez	23	1m 18.255s
5	George Russell	20	1m 18.294s
6	Kevin Magnussen	24	1m 18.315s
7	Lewis Hamilton	20	1m 18.363s
8	Daniel Ricciardo	20	1m 18.371s
9	Alexander Albon	22	1m 18.514s
10	Fernando Alonso	23	1m 18.519s
11	Valtteri Bottas	25	1m 18.586s
12	Logan Sargeant	21	1m 18.611s
13	Oscar Piastri	21	1m 18.618s
14	Esteban Ocon	25	1m 18.754s
15	Nico Hülkenberg	25	1m 18.791s
16	Pierre Gasly	24	1m 18.888s
17	Lance Stroll	25	1m 19.179s
18	Charles Leclerc	8	1m 19.286s
19	Yuki Tsunoda	13	1m 19.606s
20	Zhou Guanyu	25	1m 20.067s

PRACTICE 3 (SATURDAY)
Weather: Dry/overcast
Temperatures: track 37-40°C, air 28-29°C

Pos.	Driver	Laps	Time
1	Lando Norris	17	1m 16.098s
2	Oscar Piastri	17	1m 16.142s
3	Max Verstappen	27	1m 16.379s
4	George Russell	15	1m 16.564s
5	Carlos Sainz	16	1m 16.639s
6	Daniel Ricciardo	15	1m 16.652s
7	Alexander Albon	16	1m 16.661s
8	Nico Hülkenberg	15	1m 16.696s
9	Yuki Tsunoda	16	1m 16.744s
10	Lewis Hamilton	14	1m 16.786s
11	Charles Leclerc	17	1m 16.803s
12	Valtteri Bottas	20	1m 16.804s
13	Sergio Pérez	25	1m 16.954s
14	Fernando Alonso	21	1m 17.001s
15	Lance Stroll	22	1m 17.085s
16	Logan Sargeant	15	1m 17.168s
17	Zhou Guanyu	15	1m 17.291s
18	Pierre Gasly	15	1m 17.499s
19	Kevin Magnussen	17	1m 17.507s
20	Esteban Ocon	16	1m 17.575s

QUALIFYING (SATURDAY)
Weather: Wet-dry/overcast Temperatures: track 29-31°C, air 25°C

Pos.	Driver	First	Second	Third	Qualifying Tyre
1	Lando Norris	1m 17.755s	1m 15.540s	1m 15.227s	Soft (n)
2	Oscar Piastri	1m 17.504s	1m 15.785s	1m 15.249s	Soft (n)
3	Max Verstappen	1m 17.087s	1m 15.770s	1m 15.273s	Soft (n)
4	Carlos Sainz	1m 17.244s	1m 15.885s	1m 15.696s	Soft (n)
5	Lewis Hamilton	1m 17.087s	1m 16.307s	1m 15.854s	Soft (n)
6	Charles Leclerc	1m 17.437s	1m 15.891s	1m 15.905s	Soft (n)
7	Fernando Alonso	1m 17.624s	1m 16.117s	1m 16.043s	Soft (u)
8	Lance Stroll	1m 17.405s	1m 16.075s	1m 16.244	Soft (n)
9	Daniel Ricciardo	1m 17.050s	1m 16.202s	1m 16.447s	Soft (u)
10	Yuki Tsunoda	1m 17.436s	1m 16.121s	1m 16.477s	Soft (u)
11	Nico Hülkenberg	1m 17.362s	1m 16.317s		
12	Valtteri Bottas	1m 17.487s	1m 16.384s		
13	Alexander Albon	1m 17.280s	1m 16.429s		
14	Logan Sargeant	1m 17.770s	1m 16.543s		
15	Kevin Magnussen	1m 17.851s	1m 16.548s		
16	Sergio Pérez	1m 17.886s			
17	George Russell	1m 17.968s			
18	Zhou Guanyu	1m 18.037s			
19	Esteban Ocon	1m 18.049s			
20	Pierre Gasly	1m 18.166s			

QUALIFYING: head to head

Verstappen	13	0	Pérez
Hamilton	3	10	Russell
Norris	10	3	Piastri
Leclerc	7	5	Sainz
Leclerc	1	0	Bearman
Gasly	4	9	Ocon
Alonso	7	6	Stroll
Albon	12	1	Sargeant
Bottas	12	1	Zhou
Tsunoda	9	4	Ricciardo
Magnussen	4	9	Hülkenberg

FOR THE RECORD

1st GP WIN: Oscar Piastri
200th GP PODIUM: Lewis Hamilton

DID YOU KNOW?

This was the first complete front row for McLaren since the 2012 Brazilian GP with Hamilton and Button.

Piastri is the fifth Australian to win a race in the world championship

POINTS

DRIVERS

1	Max Verstappen	265
2	Lando Norris	189
3	Charles Leclerc	162
4	Carlos Sainz	154
5	Oscar Piastri	149
6	Lewis Hamilton	125
7	Sergio Pérez	124
8	George Russell	116
9	Fernando Alonso	45
10	Lance Stroll	24
11	Nico Hülkenberg	22
12	Yuki Tsunoda	22
13	Daniel Ricciardo	11
14	Oliver Bearman	6
15	Pierre Gasly	6
16	Kevin Magnussen	5
17	Alexander Albon	4
18	Esteban Ocon	3

CONSTRUCTORS

1	Red Bull	389
2	McLaren	338
3	Ferrari	322
4	Mercedes	241
5	Aston Martin	69
6	RB	33
7	Haas	27
8	Alpine	9
9	Williams	4

9 · RICCIARDO · RB   7 · ALONSO · Aston Martin   5 · HAMILTON · Mercedes   3 · VERSTAPPEN · Red Bull   1 · NORRIS · McLaren

10 · TSUNODA · RB   8 · STROLL · Aston Martin   6 · LECLERC · Ferrari   4 · SAINZ · Ferrari   2 · PIASTRI · McLaren

27 = Pit stop   31 = One lap or more behind

RACE TYRE STRATEGIES

	Driver	Race Stint 1	Race Stint 2	Race Stint 3	Race Stint 4
1	Piastri	Medium (n): 1-18	Hard (u): 19-47	Medium (u): 48-70	
2	Norris	Medium (n): 1-17	Hard (u): 18-45	Medium (n): 46-70	
3	Hamilton	Medium (n): 1-16	Hard (n): 17-40	Medium (n): 41-70	
4	Leclerc	Medium (n): 1-23	Hard (n): 24-40	Medium (n): 41-70	
5	**Verstappen**	Medium (n): 1-21	Hard (n): 22-49	Medium (n): 50-70	
6	Sainz	Medium (n): 1-21	Hard (n): 22-47	Medium (n): 48-70	
7	Pérez	Hard (n): 1-28	Medium (n): 29-47	Medium (n): 48-70	
8	Russell	Hard (n): 1-33	Medium (n): 34-53	Hard (n): 54-70	
9	Tsunoda	Medium (n): 1-29	Hard (n): 30-70		
10	Stroll	Soft (u): 1-14	Medium (u): 15-45	Hard (u): 46-70	
11	Alonso	Soft (u): 1-7	Medium (u): 8-37	Hard (n): 38-70	
12	Ricciardo	Medium (n): 1-7	Hard (n): 8-28	Hard (n): 29-69	
13	Hülkenberg	Medium (n): 1-2	Hard (n): 3-29	Hard (n): 30-69	
14	Albon	Soft (u): 1-6	Hard (n): 7-29	Hard (n): 30-69	
15	Magnussen	Soft (u): 1-6	Hard (n): 7-34	Hard (n): 35-69	
16	Bottas	Medium (u): 1-16	Medium (n): 17-45	Hard (n): 46-69	
17	Sargeant	Medium (n): 1-8	Hard (n): 9-33	Hard (n): 34-63	Soft (n): 64-69
18	Ocon	Medium (n): 1-6	Hard (n): 7-30	Hard (n): 31-64	Soft (n): 65-69
19	Zhou	Medium (u): 1-7	Hard (n): 8-36	Hard (n): 37-69	
	Gasly	Hard (n): 1-28	Medium (n): 29-33 (dnf)		

The tyre regulations stipulate that at least two of three dry tyre specifications must be used during a dry race.
Selected compounds for Budapest: Red = Soft (C5); Yellow = Medium (C4); White = Hard (C3). (n) new (u) used

SPA-FRANCORCHAMPS QUALIFYING

FOR the teams, Spa is always a trade-off between low drag for sectors one and three, which facilitates attack and defence with 75 per cent of the lap run at full throttle – and the higher downforce needed for the long, high-speed corners of sector two, which degrade tyres in the race.

Max Verstappen had delivered in some astonishing drives at Spa, most notably in 2022, when he started 14th and led after a dozen laps! But that was aboard a Red Bull with huge superiority. Latterly, that advantage had been disappearing fast.

Red Bull's position was complicated by Verstappen's Montreal engine failure. Another power unit had to be added to the pool. It was no surprise that the ten-place grid penalty hit was taken in Belgium, with Spa the calendar's easiest circuit on which to overtake. In theory, anyway.

With a Sunday fight through the field being necessary, Red Bull might have been expected to prioritise straight-line speed, but, in fact, they went in the opposite direction in FP1, running a bigger rear wing and showing ominous pace. The RB20 had a huge sector-two advantage of around eight-tenths, topping the session by almost half a second from Hungary winner Oscar Piastri. In FP2, however, McLaren went a similar route and put Lando Norris and Piastri on top of the times.

The rainy weather forecast for qualifying was another factor that drove car set-up in the direction of high rather than low downforce. A skinny rear wing would make sector two much more challenging.

The forecast was right, and as Q1 began, drivers were faced with a wet track and the prospect of it becoming wetter. They needed to get out early on intermediates and put a lap on the board. But such is the Spa microclimate that teams can never be sure – in fact, the final few minutes, with lighter rain, proved decisive. After a few scares, all the big names made it through. Those to go out in Q1 were the two Haas cars of Nico Hülkenberg and Kevin Magnussen (for the first time since Monaco, 2023), Yuki Tsunoda's VCARB (taking engine penalties anyway), Logan Sargeant's Williams and Zhou Guanyu's Sauber, the Chinese driver also hit with a grid drop for impeding Verstappen.

It was intermediates again for Q2, with light drizzle at the start of the session. But, as in Q1, the track evolved and it was all about going quickest, latest, instinctively finding grip levels on an ever-changing surface. Alex Albon failed to make it through by just three-thousandths of a second for Williams, while the relieved driver on the bubble was a certain Sergio Pérez. Also out were Pierre Gasly's Alpine, Daniel Ricciardo's VCARB, Valtteri Bottas's Sauber and Lance Stroll's Aston Martin. The Canadian was struggling for grip, balance and confidence after a heavy shunt in FP3.

Verstappen enjoyed a healthy superiority in Q3, almost 0.6s quicker than anyone else with a 1m 53.159s lap. Nobody could threaten that. He would start 11th.

Ferrari had not appeared especially quick throughout practice, but once again Charles Leclerc produced a special qualifying lap when it mattered. He beat an improving Pérez to the inherited pole, his 25th in F1, by a hundredth of a second.

"I definitely didn't expect that, not this weekend," Leclerc admitted candidly, "but with the tricky conditions, we could do something above expectations. Without rain, we were probably fighting for P5 with Mercedes."

With the rumour mill once more suggesting that Pérez was a man under pressure and not guaranteed still to be in the second Red Bull after the summer break, a front-row slot on a scrubbed set of inters was a great effort and just what the doctor ordered for the Mexican.

Mercedes had a raft of upgrades in Spa, including front wing, floor and diffuser. They took the new floor off both cars after Friday practice because their configuration for Spa introduced some high-speed bouncing. Lewis Hamilton said that it didn't feel particularly strong on Friday and he struggled more on the soft-compound Pirellis in practice, but on a slippery track in qualifying, he was just fine, only missing Pérez's front-row time by 0.07s.

"I think the Red Bulls and McLarens are much quicker than us here in the dry, and the Ferraris there or thereabouts with us. Holding on to a podium is going to be a hell of a fight, but I'm ready for it," Hamilton insisted. "Obviously, Max will be coming through, but let's see."

With Norris fifth and Oscar Piastri sixth, McLaren was not as quick as many had predicted and just marginally faster than George Russell in the second Mercedes.

"I'll have to overtake some quick cars tomorrow, like Pérez's Red Bull," Lando mused, "but I think that the slightly lower downforce we have, which potentially hurt us a bit today, will pay us back."

"The car is quick," Piastri confirmed, "but there were just a couple of mistakes from my side and the tyre strategy we went for didn't really work. We expected it to rain a bit more than it did, and going for our last new set of tyres early seemed like a sensible call, but, in fact, the track improved. But our dry pace looked strong, so we're still in with a shout."

After a couple of lurid moments, Carlos Sainz was down in eighth, more than seven-tenths behind Leclerc. That was good enough to beat Fernando Alonso's Aston Martin by three-tenths, with Esteban Ocon – newly confirmed at Haas alongside Ollie Bearman for 2025 – completing the top ten.

THIS was an intriguing one. With half of the track resurfaced and rain washing the surface green on Saturday, the thinking was that it would be nigh on impossible to run a hard pace and achieve the usual Spa one-stopper. With varying wing levels, cars at the front that had been quicker in the wet, but now were faced with sun and no prospect of rain, and Max Verstappen starting 11th, predicting a winner was a fool's game.

The first 12 on the grid all opted to start on the Pirelli medium, except Carlos Sainz who, out of position, felt compelled to throw the strategy dice and start on the hard compound.

As the starting lights extinguished, Charles Leclerc converted his pole position and got the Ferrari through La Source with its nose in front, while Sergio Pérez battled hard to fight off a fast-starting Lewis Hamilton. They were wheel to wheel down the hill towards Eau Rouge, the Red Bull ultimately having to give way. Pérez attacked again down the Kemmel Straight, but Hamilton moved early to defend the inside into Les Combes, the Mercedes just hanging on.

Lando Norris ran wide at La Source all on his own, dropping the left rear wheel into a new gravel trap on exit and losing three places. Oscar Piastri took advantage to jump up to fourth, fending off George Russell's Mercedes, while Sainz did a fine job to gain a couple of positions from his eighth grid slot, despite having less grip from his harder tyres. Behind Norris, Fernando Alonso's Aston Martin was eighth, Verstappen slotting in behind as he went around the outside of Alex Albon's Williams into the Bus Stop chicane.

The Alpines of Esteban Ocon and Pierre Gasly flashed across the line 11th and 12th, ahead of Valtteri Bottas's Sauber, Daniel Ricciardo's VCARB, Lance Stroll's Aston, Haas drivers Nico Hülkenberg and Kevin Magnussen, Zhou Guanyu's Sauber, Yuki Tsunoda's VCARB and Logan Sargeant's Williams.

At the front, Leclerc was unable to break the DRS delta to Hamilton's Mercedes, the W15 now going much better in the dry than it had done in Friday practice. With its rear wing open down the front straight, it was on to the back of the Ferrari at La Source and in perfect position to draft the race leader down Kemmel Straight. Without any undue fuss, Hamilton towed past Leclerc to take the lead on lap three.

How was Verstappen doing? It soon became apparent that this was not going to be a repeat of previous years, when he had started low down and simply walked his way to the front. With more wing than Norris and a 75m shorter DRS zone on Kemmel Straight for 2024, the world champion was unable to pass the McLaren.

As everyone began to prioritise tyre management, the race entered a stalemate phase. At quarter-distance, Hamilton had 2s in hand over Leclerc. Pérez, not entirely

Above: The Haas cars of Hülkenberg and Magnussen avoid contact as the field piles into La Source on the opening lap.
Photo: Haas F1 Team

Top left: A reshuffle at Alpine after Bruno Famin announced his decision to stand down as team principal.
Photo: Lukas Gorys

Above left: Laurent Mekies overseeing a much restructured Visa Cash App RB F1 Team.

Left: Max Verstappen elected to take a ten-place grid penalty, leaving pole position to Charles Leclerc.
Photos: Red Bull Content Pool/Getty Images

Opening spread: George Russell used his one-stop strategy to bring his Mercedes home ahead of teammate Lewis Hamilton, before losing the race through disqualification.
Photo: Mercedes-AMG Petronas F1 Team

happy with his Red Bull, was a similar distance behind the Ferrari. There was a 1.5s gap to Piastri, who had Russell and Carlos Sainz behind him. Norris was within DRS range of the Ferrari as Russell, on lap ten, became the first of the front-runners to head for the pits and a potential undercut. Verstappen followed him in. The pair rejoined just behind Tsunoda's 12th-placed VCARB.

Next time around, Hamilton, Pérez and Piastri all responded and pitted, but Leclerc carried on, and with Sainz on his hard tyres still fending off Norris, the Ferraris now ran 1-2. Hamilton rejoined sixth. Pérez came back out eighth, just fending off the undercut from Russell, but Piastri was just behind the second Merc. Although not for long, the McLaren towing back past on Kemmel Straight.

Ferrari called in Leclerc a lap later, Charles responding, "If we are getting undercut, let's go long." Ferrari brought him in anyway and the Monégasque was back out without losing track position, but with Pérez, Piastri, Russell and Verstappen closer behind.

Piastri, benefiting from lower drag, demoted Pérez on the run to Les Combes to move into what would become the top three once Sainz, Norris and Alonso had all made their stops.

McLaren waited until lap 16 to call in Norris, and after a 2.3s stop, he was on his way again. The later stop meant that he had dropped 5.5s behind Verstappen, but he would have a tyre delta later and looked okay in relation to the race-leading Sainz, who was going longer on his hards, but lost 3s when he ran wide through the gravel at Stavelot.

Verstappen, with Russell and his team-mate now in his sights, was clearly favouring attack as the better part of tyre management. "I think we should try to get them mate, what do you think?" he enquired of race engineer Gianpiero Lambiase.

"Have a go," responded 'GP'. Max's immediate problem, however, was that Russell was picking up DRS from Pérez.

Ferrari pitted Sainz from the lead just before half-distance to go on to the medium Pirellis.

Much to Verstappen's relief, with Norris setting fastest lap and halving his deficit to the championship leader for sixth, Russell found a way past Pérez, who then immediately headed for the pits after just ten laps on a second set of mediums, taking on hards.

Hamilton and Leclerc were proving evenly matched at the front, Charles just 2.4s behind as he headed for his second pit stop 26 laps into the race's 44 and a potential undercut. At 3.4s, however, the stop was not one of Ferrari's best.

Mercedes responded with Hamilton on the next lap, at the same time as Russell, 5s behind Piastri's McLaren and 9.5s behind his team-mate, threw in a curve ball with a radio message: "Think about the one-stop…"

Then Verstappen pitted for a set of mediums and rejoined a couple of seconds behind Pérez, who obviously would be moved out of the way. Having covered off Leclerc, Hamilton had 2s in hand over the Ferrari and was running fourth.

Piastri now led by 5.3s from Russell, having just set the fastest lap on 17-lap-old hard tyres. Russell, 5.3s behind, was lapping around half a second slower, with Norris only a couple of seconds behind, all three likely to stop again, leaving Hamilton and Leclerc to fight it out for the race.

McLaren duly pitted Norris on lap 30 for a set of hard-compound Pirellis, and he rejoined within striking distance of Verstappen, but this time with Max on the medium tyre.

Next time around, McLaren brought in Piastri from the lead, ending any conjecture that he might stay out and go to the end. The young Aussie overshot his marks slightly and 4.4s was a slow stop, but he still managed to rejoin

Above: Lewis Hamilton leaves his pit and Oscar Piastri arrives, both making their first stops on lap 11.
Photo: XPB Images

Left: Another podium for Charles Leclerc, but Ferrari was lacking a bit of race pace at Spa.
Photo: Scuderia Ferrari

comfortably clear of Verstappen – who had set a new fastest lap on his mediums – Pérez and Norris.

There was no move from Mercedes to pit Russell, and a radio message with 12 laps remaining confirmed the plan: "George, just confirming that you're happy to stay out?"

"Yes," Russell affirmed.

So there it was, Russell was indeed going for the supposedly unattainable one-stopper! He was leading team-mate Hamilton by 7s, so Lewis needed to take around seven-tenths per lap from him to be able to have a go on the last lap. Leclerc was still in touch with Hamilton, but the Ferrari didn't appear to have the straight-line speed to be a nuisance. And, just over 3s behind, Piastri was flying on his fresh new hards.

"How much quicker do I need to be? Am I on target to beat him, or not?" Hamilton wanted to know.

"It's close, it's close," Peter Bonnington told his man.

On lap 35, Piastri was right with Leclerc and tried to go around the outside of the Ferrari at Les Combes, but Charles defended well.

Verstappen, on mediums remember, was actually losing ground to Piastri and was under pressure from Norris, who had set a new fastest lap on his hards.

'GP' Lambiase was on the radio encouraging his man: "Ten laps to go Max. Let's have ten of your finest mate, come on."

Next time around, lap 36, Piastri narrowly made it past Leclerc into Les Combes and set off after Hamilton, another 5s up the road. The McLaren was now the quickest car on the track.

Pérez, after the promise of that front-row start, had dropped 10s behind Norris and now was passed by Sainz into Les Combes with five laps to go, despite the Spaniard's less-than-optimum race strategy. Not the kind of drive the Mexican had been hoping for.

Up front, with three laps to go, Russell was hanging on, but Hamilton had the gap down to just half a second, while Piastri had closed to within 2.5s of the second Mercedes. Leclerc had dropped 5s behind the McLaren, and his mirrors were full of Verstappen and Norris.

On lap 42, using his battery deployment, Russell fended off his DRS-assisted team-mate at the end of the Kemmel Straight. Hamilton was very close with DRS as they went into La Source on lap 43, but, crucially, went in a little deep and lost time on exit. Which meant that, again, he wasn't close enough to challenge into Les Combes. There would be just one more chance. Meanwhile, Red Bull had decided that the best use of Pérez, who had more than a pit stop's advantage over ninth-placed Alonso behind, was to swap him on to softs to steal the fastest-lap point from Norris.

Into Les Combes for the last time, and Hamilton locked up ever so slightly, and that was enough to get Russell home free. "Oh, yes!" yelled a delighted winner as he crossed the line and punched the air.

"We made a lot of changes from Friday night, and the car and tyres just felt great," Russell explained. "I kept saying that I thought we could do the one-stop, and strategy did a great job. But well done to Lewis, too, because he really controlled that race, and if the circumstances had been slightly different, he'd have the victory."

After another Mercedes 1-2 and the team's third win in four races, Toto Wolff's expression was surprisingly sombre, as if he knew that there would be flack from a certain seven-times world champion who had driven brilliantly all afternoon…

"Congratulations to George. He did a great job going long on the tyres," Lewis acknowledged. "Every stint, I had tyres left, but the team pulled me in, so, yeah, unfortunate, but it's one of those days."

Piastri, too, was less than thrilled, having led Russell when he made a second pit stop, thinking that he couldn't

VIEWPOINT
RACING NOWHERE

MAX VERSTAPPEN was speaking after finishing fifth: "I was stuck in the DRS train and basically just stayed there. It was difficult to pass." This raised two significant questions. Surely, DRS was supposed to make overtaking easier. Was this not the same Verstappen who had started 14th at Spa in 2022 and put himself into the lead within 12 laps?

His summary appeared to show that, in 2024, the powers-that-be had failed to find the middle ground between making DRS ineffective and reducing F1 to a pathetic pass-fest.

Even allowing for the superior qualities of the Red Bull and its driver in 2022, Verstappen had made it look as though he had blue lights flashing on the RB18 as the opposition appeared to back off on the climb from Raidillon to Les Combes. The DRS zone was much too long.

For 2024, they reduced it by 75m. That might have been an excessive cut, but it did produce a couple of hold-your-breath overtakes, Oscar Piastri's move around the outside of Charles Leclerc being particularly impressive. Which, surely, is what motor racing is supposed to be all about, rather than an effortless, no-risk or exhilaration push-to-pass.

Going right back to basics, it questioned the need for DRS in the first place. Even allowing for the closely competitive teams and unbelievable short braking zones, DRS is official jargon for saying these F1 cars with their hugely complex aero packages can't actually run in very close company and therefore can't do what they're supposed to do – which is overtake and go motor racing.

When you have a driver of Verstappen's aggression and sense of opportunism saying that he's stuck in a DRS train and can't do anything, then something must be wrong. It will be 'fixed' next time by adding another 25 metres or so to the DRS zone. But that will be nothing more than papering over a massive crack in the fundamental façade of F1.

Maurice Hamilton

make it through to the end. Russell had proved it could be done.

"I thought I could get the Mercs after the second stop, but it took me a couple of laps to get past Charles and it really overheated the tyres doing that." Oscar said. "Clean air made such a big difference today. Once I got some in the middle stint, I picked up a lot of pace and managed to get a nice tyre delta for the last stop. But I clearly didn't need tyre delta, I just needed to keep going, as George showed. And I lost a bit of time in the pits. That's the second or third time this year I've tried to run over the front jack guy, so I'll try not to do that in future!"

Leclerc had extracted everything he could from a Ferrari that had lacked a bit of pace, having fended off Verstappen and Norris to bring the car home fourth. The Ferrari, Verstappen's Red Bull and Norris's McLaren could have been covered by a blanket as they crossed the line. Leclerc reckoned that the hard tyre was the better race tyre, actually improving as the stint progressed, and Verstappen agreed, figuring that if he'd been on the hard rather than the medium in the final stint, he might have passed Charles. Instead, he rued spending much of the race stuck in a DRS train (see Viewpoint). A despondent Norris regretted his first-corner error. He had not taken advantage of Verstappen's damage limitation.

Behind seventh-placed Sainz and Pérez, Alonso did everything he could with an Aston to finish ninth, while Esteban Ocon scored the final point for Alpine.

Heartbreakingly for Russell, such joy at a fine drive lasted only as long as it took the post-race scrutineers to discover that his W15 was 1.5kg underweight. The combination of plank wear – still legal, but higher than expected – greater rubber loss due to his tyres doing 34 laps and more than the expected 3kg in-race fluid loss from George himself conspired against him. It was a bitter pill for Russell to swallow, his team-mate now inheriting a second win in three races as Daniel Ricciardo picked up an unexpected point for tenth. An absorbing race..

Tony Dodgins

Above: Parc fermé. George Russell already seems to grasp that his brilliant drive will end in disqualification.
Photo: Atsuo Sakurai

Top left: Verstappen and Pérez discuss the Red Bull's lack of pace.
Photo: Red Bull Content Pool/Getty Images

Above left: Alpine ran a special one-off livery, a nod to investor Ryan Reynolds' new movie, *Deadpool and Wolverine*. Esteban Ocon scored points with ninth place.
Photo: BWT Alpine F1 Team

Left: Red Bull ran a bigger rear wing than some, and even with DRS in operation, a 75m-shorter zone made overtaking tougher.
Photo: Red Bull Content Pool/Getty Images

14

Official Timepiece

FORMULA 1 ROLEX BELGIAN GRAND PRIX 2024

SPA-FRANCORCHAMPS 26-28 JULY
RACE DISTANCE: 44 laps, 191.415 miles/308.052km
RACE WEATHER: Dry/sunny (track 40-43°C, air 22-24°C)

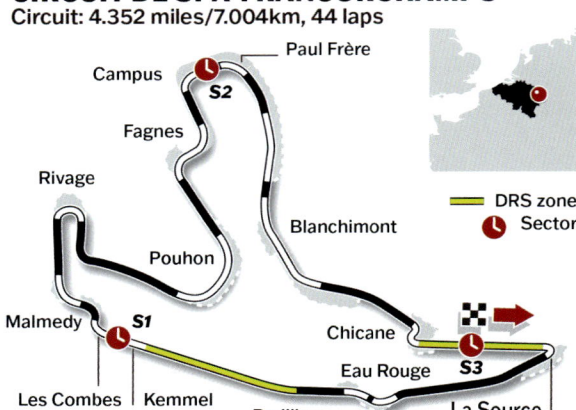

RACE – OFFICIAL CLASSIFICATION

Pos.	Driver	Nat.	No.	Entrant	Car/Engine	Laps	Time/Retirement	Speed (mph/km/h)	Gap to leader	Fastest race lap	
DQ	George Russell	GB	63	Mercedes-AMG Petronas F1 Team	Mercedes-AMG F1 W15-M15 E Perf. V6	44	1h 19m 57.040s *	143.640/231.181		1m 47.113s	44
1	Lewis Hamilton	GB	44	Mercedes-AMG Petronas F1 Team	Mercedes-AMG F1 W15-M15 E Perf. V6	44	1h 19m 57.566s	143.634/231.156		1m 46.653s	33
2	Oscar Piastri	AUS	81	McLaren Formula 1 Team	McLaren MCL38-Mercedes F1 M15 E Perf. V6	44	1h 19m 58.213s	143.614/231.125	0.647s	1m 45.840s	32
3	Charles Leclerc	MC	16	Scuderia Ferrari	Ferrari SF-24-066/12 V6	44	1h 20m 05.589s	143.394/230.770	8.023s	1m 47.013s	33
4	Max Verstappen	NL	1	Oracle Red Bull Racing	Red Bull RB20-Honda RBPT H002 V6	44	1h 20m 06.266s	143.373/230.737	8.700s	1m 46.128s	32
5	Lando Norris	GB	4	McLaren Formula 1 Team	McLaren MCL38-Mercedes F1 M15 E Perf. V6	44	1h 20m 06.890s	143.355/230.707	9.324s	1m 45.563s	31
6	Carlos Sainz	E	55	Scuderia Ferrari	Ferrari SF-24-066/12 V6	44	1h 20m 16.835s	143.059/230.231	19.269s	1m 46.364s	44
7	Sergio Pérez	MEX	11	Oracle Red Bull Racing	Red Bull RB20-Honda RBPT H002 V6	44	1h 20m 40.235s	142.367/229.118	42.669s	1m 44.701s	44
8	Fernando Alonso	E	14	Aston Martin Aramco F1 Team	Aston Martin AMR24-Mercedes F1 M15 E Perf. V6	44	1h 20m 47.003s	142.168/228.798	49.437s	1m 48.051s	42
9	Esteban Ocon	F	31	BWT Alpine F1 Team	Alpine A524-Renault E-Tech RE24 V6	44	1h 20m 49.592s	142.093/228.676	52.026s	1m 46.957s	43
10	Daniel Ricciardo	AUS	3	Visa Cash App RB Formula One Team	RB VCARB 01-Honda RBPT H002 V6	44	1h 20m 51.966s	142.023/228.564	54.400s	1m 47.435s	37
11	Lance Stroll	CDN	18	Aston Martin Aramco F1 Team	Aston Martin AMR24-Mercedes F1 M15 E Perf. V6	44	1h 21m 00.051s	141.787/228.184	1m 02.485s	1m 48.105s	44
12	Alexander Albon	T	23	Williams Racing	Williams FW46-Mercedes F1 M15 E Perf. V6	44	1h 21m 00.691s	141.768/228.154	1m 03.125s	1m 47.996s	44
13	Pierre Gasly	F	10	BWT Alpine F1 Team	Alpine A524-Renault E-Tech RE24 V6	44	1h 21m 01.405s	141.747/228.120	1m 03.839s	1m 47.418s	30
14	Kevin Magnussen	DK	20	MoneyGram Haas F1 Team	Haas VF-24-Ferrari 066/10 V6	44	1h 21m 03.671s	141.681/228.014	1m 06.105s	1m 47.848s	44
15	Valtteri Bottas	FIN	77	Kick Sauber F1 Team	Sauber C44-Ferrari 066/12 V6	44	1h 21m 07.678s	141.565/227.826	1m 10.112s	1m 47.019s	37
16	Yuki Tsunoda	J	22	Visa Cash App RB Formula One Team	RB VCARB 01-Honda RBPT H002 V6	44	1h 21m 13.777s	141.387/227.541	1m 16.211s	1m 47.969s	44
17	Logan Sargeant	USA	2	Williams Racing	Williams FW46-Mercedes F1 M15 E Perf. V6	44	1h 21m 23.097s	141.118/227.107	1m 25.531s	1m 47.490s	43
18	Nico Hülkenberg	D	27	MoneyGram Haas F1 Team	Haas VF-24-Ferrari 066/10 V6	44	1h 21m 25.873s	141.038/226.978	1m 28.307s	1m 48.954s	44
	Zhou Guanyu	CHN	24	Kick Sauber F1 Team	Sauber C44-Ferrari 066/12 V6	5	electrics			1m 52.099s	2

* Russell: Disqualified for car being under the minimum weight limit.

DHL Fastest race lap: (scores 1 point): Sergio Pérez on lap 44, 1m 44.701s, 149.640mph/240.822km/h (new record).
Lap record: Kimi Räikkönen (McLaren MP4-19B-Mercedes V8), 1m 45.108s, 148.465mph/238.931km/h (2004, 4.335-mile/6.976km circuit).
Previous Lap record (current configuration): Valtteri Bottas (Mercedes F1 W09 V6), 1m 46.286s, 147.409mph/237.231km/h (2018).

20 · TSUNODA · RB
Used additional power unit elements; required to start from the back of the grid

18 · SARGEANT · Williams

16 · HÜLKENBERG · Haas

14 · BOTTAS · Sauber

12 · GASLY · Alpine

19 · ZHOU · Sauber
3-place grid penalty for impeding Verstappen during qualifying

17 · MAGNUSSEN · Haas

15 · STROLL · Aston Martin

13 · RICCIARDO · RB

11 · VERSTAPPEN · Red Bull
Used additional power unit element; 10-place grid penalty

Grid order	1	2	3	4	5	6	7	8	9	10	11	12	13	14	15	16	17	18	19	20	21	22	23	24	25	26	27	28	29	30	31	32	33	34	35
16 LECLERC	16	16	44	44	44	44	44	44	44	44	16	16	55	55	55	55	55	55	55	44	44	44	44	44	44	44	81	81	81	81	63	63	63	63	63
11 PEREZ	44	44	16	16	16	16	16	16	16	44	55	4	4	4	44	44	44	44	16	16	16	16	81	81	63	63	63	63	44	44	44	44	44	44	44
44 HAMILTON	11	11	11	11	11	11	11	11	11	55	4	44	44	44	16	16	16	16	55	81	81	81	16	63	1	4	4	4	44	16	16	16	16	16	16
4 NORRIS	81	81	81	81	81	81	81	81	81	4	14	16	16	16	81	81	81	81	63	63	63	63	63	1	4	1	44	16	81	81	81	81	81	81	81
81 PIASTRI	63	63	63	63	63	63	63	63	63	55	11	44	81	81	11	11	11	11	1	1	1	1	4	55	44	16	1	1	1	1	1	1	1	1	1
63 RUSSELL	55	55	55	55	55	55	55	55	55	4	81	11	14	11	11	63	63	63	63	4	4	4	4	4	55	44	16	11	11	4	4	4	4	4	4
55 SAINZ	4	4	4	4	4	4	4	4	63	14	81	11	63	63	1	1	1	1	11	55	55	55	55	16	16	55	1	4	11	11	11	11	11	11	11
14 ALONSO	14	1	1	1	1	1	1	1	31	31	63	1	4	4	4	4	4	4	55	11	11	11	11	11	55	55	55	55	55	55	55	55	55	55	55
31 OCON	1	14	14	14	14	14	14	14	14	18	69	1	20	20	23	23	23	23	31	31	31	31	31	31	31	31	31	31	14	14	14	14	14	14	14
23 ALBON	23	23	23	23	23	23	23	31	31	63	1	20	22	23	3	3	3	3	31	31	14	14	14	14	14	14	14	14	77	77	77	77	77	18	3
1 VERSTAPPEN	31	31	31	31	31	31	10	77	77	77	18	22	3	3	14	14	14	14	23	10	10	10	10	10	10	77	77	77	18	18	18	18	18	3	
10 GASLY	10	10	10	10	10	10	18	18	20	20	23	3	14	14	20	20	31	31	14	14	77	77	77	77	77	18	18	18	3	3	3	3	3	31	
3 RICCIARDO	77	77	77	77	77	77	23	20	20	1	22	18	27	31	31	10	10	10	3	77	18	18	18	18	18	10	3	3	23	31	31	31	31	23	
77 BOTTAS	3	3	3	3	3	3	18	10	22	22	3	23	23	27	31	27	20	27	77	18	20	20	20	20	20	3	3	23	31	23	23	23	23	77	
18 STROLL	18	18	18	18	18	18	20	22	23	27	10	27	10	10	27	31	27	20	18	20	3	3	23	23	23	23	23	20	20	20	20	20	20		
27 HULKENBERG	27	27	27	27	27	27	20	22	23	3	3	27	77	31	22	77	77	18	27	2	2	23	23	23	23	23	20	10	10	10	10	10			
20 MAGNUSSEN	20	20	20	20	20	20	22	3	3	27	27	10	31	77	77	18	18	27	2	2	22	22	22	22	22	10	22	22	22	22	22	22			
2 SARGEANT	24	24	22	22	22	22	2	2	27	10	77	77	2	22	2	22	22	22	22	22	27	27	27	27	27	27	27	27	27	27	27	27			
24 ZHOU	22	22	2	2	2	27	27	27	2	2	2	2	22	2	2	22	22	2	2	2	2	2	2	2	2	2	2	2	2	2	2	2			
22 TSUNODA	2	2	24	24	24																														

TIME SHEETS

PRACTICE 1 (FRIDAY)
Weather: Dry/sunny
Temperatures: track 33-34°C, air 22-23°C

Pos.	Driver	Laps	Time
1	Max Verstappen	23	1m 43.372s
2	Oscar Piastri	24	1m 43.903s
3	Alexander Albon	21	1m 44.099s
4	George Russell	23	1m 44.225s
5	Lewis Hamilton	21	1m 44.279s
6	Charles Leclerc	25	1m 44.306s
7	Sergio Pérez	22	1m 44.329s
8	Lando Norris	24	1m 44.415s
9	Carlos Sainz	24	1m 44.574s
10	Lance Stroll	20	1m 44.699s
11	Pierre Gasly	22	1m 44.833s
12	Fernando Alonso	19	1m 44.921s
13	Daniel Ricciardo	23	1m 44.950s
14	Valtteri Bottas	21	1m 45.155s
15	Logan Sargeant	20	1m 45.311s
16	Yuki Tsunoda	23	1m 45.564s
17	Nico Hülkenberg	19	1m 45.645s
18	Kevin Magnussen	19	1m 45.812s
19	Zhou Guanyu	23	1m 45.995s
20	Esteban Ocon	1	no time

PRACTICE 2 (FRIDAY)
Weather: Dry/sunny
Temperatures: track 30-32°C, air 21-22°C

Pos.	Driver	Laps	Time
1	Lando Norris	19	1m 42.260s
2	Oscar Piastri	23	1m 42.475s
3	Max Verstappen	26	1m 42.477s
4	Charles Leclerc	23	1m 42.837s
5	Carlos Sainz	25	1m 43.098s
6	George Russell	24	1m 43.290s
7	Esteban Ocon	23	1m 43.401s
8	Kevin Magnussen	21	1m 43.485s
9	Sergio Pérez	24	1m 43.504s
10	Lewis Hamilton	25	1m 43.519s
11	Lance Stroll	21	1m 43.532s
12	Fernando Alonso	24	1m 43.538s
13	Valtteri Bottas	24	1m 43.675s
14	Daniel Ricciardo	21	1m 43.823s
15	Pierre Gasly	24	1m 43.829s
16	Nico Hülkenberg	21	1m 43.846s
17	Alexander Albon	23	1m 43.892s
18	Logan Sargeant	24	1m 44.226s
19	Zhou Guanyu	23	1m 44.302s
20	Yuki Tsunoda	24	1m 44.348s

PRACTICE 3 (SATURDAY)
Weather: Wet/overcast
Temperatures: track 22°C, air 18°C

Pos.	Driver	Laps	Time
1	Max Verstappen	4	2m 01.565s
2	Oscar Piastri	4	2m 02.998s
3	Pierre Gasly	5	2m 03.175s
4	Lando Norris	4	2m 03.372s
5	Esteban Ocon	7	2m 05.250s
6	Charles Leclerc	4	2m 06.033s
7	Lance Stroll	4	2m 06.037s
8	Valtteri Bottas	7	2m 06.492s
9	Lewis Hamilton	3	2m 06.751s
10	Sergio Pérez	3	2m 07.103s
11	Alexander Albon	3	2m 07.443s
12	Nico Hülkenberg	5	2m 08.040s
13	Fernando Alonso	4	2m 08.071s
14	Daniel Ricciardo	5	2m 08.410s
15	Yuki Tsunoda	7	2m 09.444s
16	Zhou Guanyu	7	2m 11.109s
17	Logan Sargeant	3	2m 11.220s
18	George Russell	2	no time
19	Carlos Sainz	2	no time
20	Kevin Magnussen	2	no time

QUALIFYING (SATURDAY)
Weather: Wet/overcast Temperatures: track 25-26°C, air 18-19°C

Pos.	Driver	First	Second	Third	Qualifying Tyre
1	Max Verstappen	1m 54.938s	1m 53.837s	1m 53.159s	Inter (n)
2	Charles Leclerc	1m 55.349s	1m 54.193s	1m 53.754s	Inter (n)
3	Sergio Pérez	1m 55.139s	1m 54.470s	1m 53.765s	Inter (u)
4	Lewis Hamilton	1m 55.692s	1m 54.037s	1m 53.835s	Inter (n)
5	Lando Norris	1m 55.582s	1m 54.358s	1m 53.981s	Inter (n)
6	Oscar Piastri	1m 54.835s	1m 54.136s	1m 54.027s	Inter (n)
7	George Russell	1m 55.353s	1m 54.095s	1m 54.184s	Inter (n)
8	Carlos Sainz	1m 55.169s	1m 54.112s	1m 54.477s	Inter (n)
9	Fernando Alonso	1m 55.489s	1m 54.258s	1m 54.765s	Inter (u)
10	Esteban Ocon	1m 55.417s	1m 54.460s	1m 54.810s	Inter (u)
11	Alexander Albon	1m 55.722s	1m 54.473s		
12	Pierre Gasly	1m 54.911s	1m 54.635s		
13	Daniel Ricciardo	1m 55.451s	1m 54.682s		
14	Valtteri Bottas	1m 55.531s	1m 54.764s		
15	Lance Stroll	1m 56.072s	1m 55.716s		
16	Nico Hülkenberg	1m 56.308s			
17	Kevin Magnussen	1m 56.500s			
18	Yuki Tsunoda	1m 56.593s			
19	Logan Sargeant	1m 57.230s			
20	Zhou Guanyu	1m 57.775s			

QUALIFYING: head to head

Verstappen	14	0	Pérez
Hamilton	4	10	Russell
Norris	11	3	Piastri
Leclerc	8	5	Sainz
Leclerc	1	0	Bearman
Gasly	4	10	Ocon
Alonso	8	6	Stroll
Albon	13	1	Sargeant
Bottas	13	1	Zhou
Tsunoda	9	5	Ricciardo
Magnussen	4	10	Hülkenberg

FOR THE RECORD

25th GP POLE POSITION: Charles Leclerc

DID YOU KNOW?

Russell is the first winner to be disqualified since Michael Schumacher at the 1994 Belgian GP for excessive skidblock wear.

This was the third consecutive Belgian GP where Verstappen qualified for pole, but due to a penalty did not line up in pole (at each, a Ferrari inherited pole).

POINTS

DRIVERS

1	Max Verstappen	277
2	Lando Norris	199
3	Charles Leclerc	177
4	Oscar Piastri	167
5	Carlos Sainz	162
6	Lewis Hamilton	150
7	Sergio Pérez	131
8	George Russell	116
9	Fernando Alonso	49
10	Lance Stroll	24
11	Nico Hülkenberg	22
12	Yuki Tsunoda	22
13	Daniel Ricciardo	12
14	Oliver Bearman	6
15	Pierre Gasly	6
16	Kevin Magnussen	5
17	Esteban Ocon	5
18	Alexander Albon	4

CONSTRUCTORS

1	Red Bull	408
2	McLaren	366
3	Ferrari	345
4	Mercedes	266
5	Aston Martin	73
6	RB	34
7	Haas	27
8	Alpine	11
9	Williams	4

10 · ALBON · Williams   8 · ALONSO · Aston Martin   6 · RUSSELL · Mercedes   4 · NORRIS · McLaren   2 · PÉREZ · Red Bull

9 · OCON · Alpine   7 · SAINZ · Ferrari   5 · PIASTRI · McLaren   3 · HAMILTON · Mercedes   1 · LECLERC · Ferrari

Lap chart

	36	37	38	39	40	41	42	43	44	
	63	63	63	63	63	63	63	63	63	DQ
	44	44	44	44	44	44	44	44	44	1
	81	81	81	81	81	81	81	81	81	2
	16	16	16	16	16	16	16	16	16	3
	1	1	1	1	1	1	1	1	1	4
	4	4	4	4	4	4	4	4	4	5
	11	11	11	55	55	55	55	55	55	6
	55	55	55	11	11	11	11	11	11	7
	14	14	14	14	14	14	14	14	14	8
	18	3	3	3	3	31	31	31	31	9
	3	18	31	31	31	3	3	3	3	10
	31	31	18	18	18	18	18	18	18	
	23	23	23	23	23	23	23	23	23	
	20	20	20	20	10	10	10	10	10	
	10	10	10	10	20	20	20	20	20	
	22	22	22	22	22	22	22	22	22	
	77	77	77	77	77	77	77	77	77	
	27	27	27	27	27	27	27	27	27	
	2	2	2	2	2	2	2	2	2	

24 = Pit stop   24 = One lap or more behind

RACE TYRE STRATEGIES

	Driver	Race Stint 1	Race Stint 2	Race Stint 3	Race Stint 4
DQ	Russell	Medium (n): 1-10	Hard (n): 11-44		
1	Hamilton	Medium (n): 1-11	Hard (n): 12-26	Hard (n): 27-44	
2	Piastri	Medium (n): 1-11	Hard (n): 12-30	Hard (n): 31-44	
3	Leclerc	Medium (n): 1-12	Hard (n): 13-25	Hard (n): 26-44	
4	Verstappen	Medium (n): 1-10	Hard (n): 11-28	Medium (n): 29-44	
5	Norris	Medium (n): 1-15	Hard (n): 16-29	Hard (n): 30-44	
6	Sainz	Hard (n): 1-20	Medium (n): 21-28	Hard (n): 29-44	
7	Pérez	Medium (n): 1-11	Medium (n): 12-21	Hard (n): 22-42	Soft (n) 43-44
8	Alonso	Medium (n): 1-13	Hard (n): 14-44		
9	Ocon	Medium (n): 1-12	Hard (n): 13-30	Hard (n): 31-44	
10	Ricciardo	Soft (u): 1-8	Medium (u): 9-21	Hard (n): 22-44	
11	Stroll	Medium (n): 1-12	Hard (n): 13-44		
12	Albon	Medium (n): 1-8	Medium (n): 9-23	Hard (n): 24-44	
13	Gasly	Medium (n): 1-9	Hard (n): 10-28	Hard (n): 29-44	
14	Magnussen	Medium (n): 1-17	Hard (n): 18-44		
15	Bottas	Medium (n): 1-11	Hard (n): 12-35	Medium (n): 36-44	
16	Tsunoda	Medium (n): 1-15	Hard (u): 16-44		
17	Sargeant	Medium (n): 1-6	Medium (n): 7-24	Hard (n): 25-44	
18	Hülkenberg	Medium (n): 1-7	Hard (n): 8-20	Medium (n): 21-44	
	Zhou	Hard (n): 1-5 (dnf)			

The tyre regulations stipulate that at least two of three dry tyre specifications must be used during a dry race.
Selected compounds for Spa-Francorchamps: Red = Soft (C4); Yellow = Medium (C3); White = Hard (C2). (n) new (u) used

ZANDVOORT QUALIFYING

MORE than one driver found that the summer break and a few weeks out of the cockpit had dulled their senses. The banking, flat-out sweeps, gusts and changeable weather of Zandvoort were a rude reawakening!

Max Verstappen, the home hero, had won all three Dutch GPs since the race had returned to the F1 calendar and was aiming to make it four in a row in what would be his 200th F1 start. It was evident that he would face a challenge, however, most notably from McLaren and the resurgent Mercedes team, which had won three of the previous four races. George Russell narrowly pipped Oscar Piastri for single-lap pace on Friday afternoon, while Lando Norris's long-run race pace appeared formidable.

Ferrari was not in the game. After a weather-affected opening practice session, Carlos Sainz lost most of FP2 to a gearbox problem. When FP3 was reduced to a single lap at the end of the session, following a red flag for a heavy crash suffered by Logan Sargeant, it meant that Sainz's first experience of the soft-compound Pirelli was qualifying itself. Meanwhile, Charles Leclerc was three-quarters of a second behind the single-lap pace, and Ferrari's race runs were no stronger.

Sargeant had lost his Williams when he dropped the right front on to wet grass out of Turn Three and kept his boot in, the damage being severe enough to rule the Floridian out of qualifying. Meanwhile, Sainz had been confirmed in the second Williams alongside Alex Albon for 2025 during the break.

With winds gusting off the North Sea – at the back of the Dutch seaside track's main grandstand – the drivers at least had a dry, if quickly evolving track surface for qualifying. The Q1 order changed rapidly. First, Lewis Hamilton was at the top of the time sheet, while team-mate George Russell, who had been quicker in practice, was struggling.

"I don't know what's going on. I'm sliding all over the place!" the perplexed Russell radioed when his first effort was half a second from Hamilton. His team-mate had impeded Sergio Pérez at Turn Nine, however, much to Checo's annoyance, the Mexican needing to burn another set of softs to ensure his progression through to Q2. The four (in addition to the absent Sargeant) who would go no further were Daniel Ricciardo (who missed out by eleven-hundredths), Esteban Ocon, and Sauber drivers Valtteri Bottas and Zhou Guanyu.

The Q2 casualties were altogether more significant and included both Sainz and Hamilton! Carlos missed out by six-hundredths, and Lewis by a tenth. In Sainz's case, it was no great surprise, Ferrari struggling for outright pace in Holland.

Hamilton was more unexpected, however. His best lap was messy, with a snap of oversteer in Turn One, more of the same on the exit of Turn Eight and then time-sapping understeer in Turn Nine. "That was a pretty shocking session," he admitted. "The car didn't feel good at all." If 12th wasn't bad enough, his mood was not improved by a further three-place grid drop imposed by the race stewards for the Pérez block.

After some tough races, stronger performances from both Aston Martins and Pierre Gasly's Alpine had been responsible for the Sainz/Hamilton eliminations. For Alpine, it was a good first appearance on the pit wall for newly confirmed team principal Oliver Oakes. The team also confirmed the signing of reserve driver Jack Doohan for a full race seat in 2025, to replace the departing Ocon.

Also out in Q2 were Yuki Tsunoda's VCARB, and the Haas cars of Nico Hülkenberg and Kevin Magnussen. At the front, Norris pipped McLaren team-mate Piastri by nine-thousandths, and suddenly Russell was within five-hundredths! Verstappen, saving a set of softs, went through eighth – tighter than he might have imagined.

Going into Q3, the two McLaren men and Verstappen were the only drivers with two new sets of softs to call upon. After the first runs, it looked like Verstappen was in with a chance. But on his second run, Norris moved the goal posts. Initially, it seemed that a low 1m 10s lap around the second shortest lap on the calendar would get the job done, until Lando stopped the clock at 1m 09.673s! Nobody else could break 70s, so the McLaren took pole by 0.35s – a whopping margin for 2024 F1!

"It was a really good lap and a smooth qualifying," Lando smiled. "We've got some upgrades for the first time in a while and everything working well." They included revised front suspension to facilitate new brake scoops, as well as reprofiled higher-downforce rear and beam wings.

Verstappen managed to split the McLarens on the grid by lapping a tenth-and a-half quicker than Piastri. "For the whole of qualifying, we lacked a bit of pace and I'm happy to be on the front row," Max said. "The gusts made every lap different."

Russell, fourth and more than half a second from Norris, agreed. "It's a fair result, but it swung so much," he explained. "In Q1, I had no grip, then in Q2 I had the same pace as Lando and Piastri, and thought I had a shot at pole. Then in Q3, it just went away from me a bit. There's a lot of 180-degree corners, tailwinds becoming headwinds and crosswinds. That can make you slide, then you overheat the rears. Also, track temperature dropped a couple of degrees between Q1 and Q2, then again from Q2 to Q3, so you have to drive quicker out-laps to get the tyres into the same window. Same for everyone, but still tricky."

Pérez qualified in the top five for the second consecutive race, having not done so for the previous seven, and Leclerc dragged a lap out of his reluctant Ferrari to end up sixth.

"I cannot do more than this," said Fernando Alonso after putting the first Aston seventh, just 0.06s behind the Ferrari. Not bad for a man who had celebrated another birthday during the summer break, becoming only the second driver (Michael Schumacher was the first) to race beyond his 43rd birthday since Graham Hill in Brazil some 49 years earlier.

Just two-hundredths behind Alonso, Albon was a fine eighth in a significantly upgraded Williams, but, sadly, he was disqualified because the dimensions of the car's new floor marginally infringed the technical regulations. Gasly's Alpine completed the top ten.

AT least race-day at Zandvoort was dry, after the gusty, squawly conditions of practice and qualifying. Kevin Magnussen would start from the pit lane because his car had been fitted with new power unit components, while Alex Albon was at the back after his qualifying disqualification.

Starts had been McLaren's Achilles heel, and although the papaya race pace on Friday had been such that Lando Norris was expected to have the potential to disappear if he could convert his fourth F1 pole, that was no foregone conclusion. And, sure enough, once again, Verstappen got the jump on the McLaren as the lights changed, heading through Tarzan corner comfortably in front. The initial reaction times and getaways of the front-row starters were almost identical, but then the McLaren suffered too much wheelspin in the second phase of the start.

Behind Norris, George Russell got a better start than Oscar Piastri, while Charles Leclerc jumped Sergio Pérez to put his Ferrari fifth. Pierre Gasly ran seventh for Alpine, ahead of Fernando Alonso's Aston Martin, then came Carlos Sainz's Ferrari, Lance Stroll and Nico Hülkenberg with the first Haas.

The first 11 cars started on Pirelli's medium-compound tyre, with a medium/hard one-stopper expected to be the strategy of choice.

Yuki Tsunoda, running 12th, was on the soft, as were Lewis Hamilton's Mercedes and Valtteri Bottas's Sauber behind him. Then came Daniel Ricciardo, Esteban Ocon, Albon, Logan Sargeant and Zhou Guanyu, all on the medium tyre and, from the pit lane, Magnussen all alone on the hard compound.

It took no time at all for Hamilton to demote Tsunoda, and, in the second VCARB, Ricciardo had to get physical to repel the challenge of Ocon. Next on Hamilton's radar was Hülkenberg, but it would take until lap ten before the Mercedes could battle its way past the Haas.

At the front, Verstappen had not been able to shake Norris and was only 1.5s to the good, with Russell's Mercedes 3s further behind. Piastri was almost within DRS range of George, and Leclerc was right with the McLaren, the Ferrari demonstrating better race pace than had been the case in Friday practice. Pérez, too, was still in touch.

Behind, Sainz was all over the back of Gasly's Alpine, forcing a way through on lap 11 after the pair had run the first three corners side by side. This was a good showing by the Frenchman, especially as new team principal Oliver Oakes was present for his first race on the pit wall.

That Norris was feeling super-comfortable in second with the McLaren was confirmed when the team radioed, "Probably Plan A, but Plan B might be a way to beat Max." And Lando responded, "Yeah, the pace is strong."

Meanwhile, Verstappen was beginning to encounter trouble. "The car just doesn't turn at all in Turn Ten," he complained on the radio.

On lap 14, Hamilton worked his way into the points when he took tenth place from Stroll's Aston.

With 17 of the race's scheduled 72 laps down, Norris was beginning to look serious about leading the race, Verstappen having to defend the inside of Tarzan as Lando drew ever closer.

"My tyres are just numb, they don't grip," Verstappen complained again to race engineer Gianpiero Lambiase. And, sure enough, next time around, Norris stayed closer through Zandvoort's final banked turn and walked past the race leader with the benefit of DRS down the front straight to take the inside line into Tarzan and the lead. It would be the last anyone saw of him all afternoon.

By the time the race reached one-third-distance, lap 24, Norris had put 3.5s between himself and Verstappen, who had a cushion of almost 6s to Russell. Piastri was just over a second behind the Red Bull, but under threat from Leclerc's Ferrari, which was within DRS range. Pérez was a respectful 2.5s behind the Monégasque, but being caught by Sainz in the second Ferrari. Gasly was 9s further back and under pressure from Hamilton, going

Above: After Lewis Hamilton's poor qualifying and grid penalty, Mercedes chose to start him on soft-compound tyres.
Photo: Mercedes-AMG Petronas F1 Team

Top left: After a strong showing in qualifying, Alex Albon was disqualified due to a technical infringement.
Photo: Williams Racing

Above left: Ferrari-backed Robert Shwartzman found a berth with Sauber for a run in FP1.
Photo: Stake F1 Team Kick Sauber

Centre left: A front-row place for Max Verstappen alongside Lando Norris.
Photo: Red Bull Content Pool/Getty Images

Below left: Fernando Alonso, 43-years young and still competitive.
Photo: Aston Martin Aramco F1 Team

Opening spread: Max Verstappen made the better start, but there was little the world champion could do when Lando Norris and McLaren got into their stride.
Photo: XPB Images

Above: Another podium place for Charles Leclerc. Ferrari's race pace was strong enough to keep Verstappen honest.
Photo: Scuderia Ferrari

Top right: Ninth for Pierre Gasly brought some cheer at Alpine.
Photo: BWT Alpine F1 Team

Above right: New man at the helm. Oliver Oakes assumed control on the pit wall for Alpine.
Photo: XPB Images

Right: After a hat trick of home wins, Verstappen had to be content with second this time.
Photo: Red Bull Content Pool/Getty Images

well on his softs until pitting to swap them for a set of hard-compound Pirellis.

With Leclerc unable to get around Piastri, Ferrari pitted him on lap 25 to try an undercut, with fastest lap from an earlier-stopping Albon indicating that once again the Pirelli hard had decent warm-up. That dropped Charles into a gap between the Alonso and Stroll Aston Martins, and forced Mercedes to respond on the next lap with third-placed Russell. McLaren could have brought in Piastri at the same time to cover Leclerc, but, with Russell pitting, chose to leave him out in free air.

Russell's stop wasn't the quickest at 3.4s, and with Leclerc wasting no time in passing Alonso, Ferrari's undercut had worked. McLaren, confirming their plan to Piastri, told him, "Okay, Plan A, you've got clear air now, target plus five." But could he go quicker on his used mediums than Leclerc on his fresh hards? No.

Verstappen made his pit stop on lap 28 and McLaren covered him with Norris on the next lap. They waited until lap 33, just three laps shy of half-distance to bring in Piastri for his hards. He'd lost track position to both Leclerc and Russell, but had an eight-lap tyre delta on the Ferrari and seven laps on the Mercedes.

The only real question was whether Norris's pace compared to Verstappen's Red Bull would be as superior on the hard-compound Pirelli as on the medium. That was answered in the affirmative when Lando continued to increase his lead, which was out to 10s by lap 40.

In fact, third-placed Leclerc was now just 5.7s behind, much closer to the Red Bull than Verstappen was to the lead McLaren. Russell was 4s behind the Ferrari and had Piastri, with a new fastest lap, breathing down his neck. Russell could offer no defence and Piastri sailed around his outside in Tarzan at the first time of asking.

With 25 laps remaining, Piastri had caught Leclerc, the pair dropping Russell by just over 5s. Pérez's Red Bull was just 2.5s behind the Mercedes and had Sainz all over it, the second Ferrari also showing strong pace on the hard compound and setting a new fastest lap. Hamilton was running eighth, some 6s further back, having driven a strong race from his lowly 14th on the grid.

After two laps of stern defence by Pérez, never the easiest man to pass, Sainz went around the outside of the Red Bull in Tarzan and set out to catch Russell. But, as things turned out, he wouldn't need to.

Mercedes pitted Hamilton for a second time with 23 laps remaining and bolted on a fresh set of soft tyres, which Lewis had by virtue of not making Q3, taking advantage of a window behind to Hülkenberg. But then they made a similar move with Russell, who had a window back to Hamilton, putting him on scrubbed softs for the remaining 17 laps. They had concluded that George didn't have the pace to resist the closing Sainz and this was a roll of the dice.

It didn't take long for Hamilton to set fastest lap on his fresh softs, but the two-stop plan didn't work out for the other Mercedes. Russell couldn't get closer than 5.5s to Pérez by the time the chequer fell, the Mexican being almost 7s behind Sainz. And Russell, remember, had held track position over both when Mercedes elected to stop him a second time.

Somewhat sobering for Mercedes was that after the

pace shown at Silverstone and Spa, Russell was almost 45s behind when the chequered flag fell on a dominant second GP victory for Norris. And McLaren had the pure pace for Lando to snatch back the fastest-lap point on the 72nd and last lap, on used hard-compound rubber…

"I don't know," Russell mused, "it just felt like I had no grip. I was sliding around like I was on ice, and it was probably something to do with the tyres. The performance does swing circuit to circuit, but this felt a little bit odd."

And the crowd was left to ponder the home hero leading the first 18 laps, but ultimately falling 20s behind Norris by flag fall. Some head scratching to do for Christian Horner and his troops.

"I had a good start and I tried everything I could," Verstappen said, "but throughout the race, I think it was quite clear that we weren't quick enough."

A delighted Norris beamed, "I wouldn't call it a perfect race because of the start again, but afterwards, it was beautiful. The pace was very strong, the car was unbelievable, and I could get comfortable and push. Getting past Max was the tough thing. From quite early on, lap five or six, I was expecting Max to start pushing and get a bit of a gap, but he never did. From that point, I knew we were in with a good chance. He seemed to keep dropping off and my pace was getting better, and once I got into clean air, it was quite a straightforward race."

Leclerc did a fine job to bring a Ferrari, which had looked well out of the ballpark on Friday, home in third place, just 3.7s behind Verstappen and able to repel the threat from Piastri over the last 20 laps. And Sainz proved just how strong Ferrari was for race pace by claiming fifth, just 5.5s behind the Australian after dropping Pérez's Red Bull by more than 7s.

"This year, we have made the car slower in qualifying and faster in the race," Carlos explained. "Last year, was the complete opposite, and we tended to be winners on Saturdays and depressed on Sundays. This year, qualifying is maybe costing a bit much, but in the race, we are definitely stronger."

Within 4s of team-mate Russell by the end, Hamilton had raced as strongly as ever, but eighth place was all he had to show for it. Just over half a minute adrift, Gasly was rewarded with ninth after a feisty drive for Alpine, doing well to take the flag some 5s clear of Alonso's Aston Martin, which claimed the final point.

In the drivers' championship, Verstappen's lead over Norris was still a healthy 70 points, but with nine races remaining, it was not unfeasible that by Abu Dhabi in December, Norris could be a threat. And in the constructors' battle, with Red Bull's advantage down to just 30 points, it could have been said that McLaren, after its dramatic turnaround and strong performances by both drivers, was now actually favourite. Yet another twist in a compelling season.

Tony Dodgins

Above: The extent of Lando Norris's domination presented Red Bull with food for thought.
Photo: Atsuo Sakurai

Right: Norris shares the podium with his race engineer, Will Joseph.
Photo: McLaren F1 Team

Top right: Logan Sargeant pays the price for clipping the grass as his Williams spears across the track.
Photo: XPB Images

Above right: Sargeant prepares for what would be his final grand prix.
Photo: Williams Racing

Far right: One wreck too many for Williams as the track is cleared.
Photo: XPB Images

FIA FORMULA 1 WORLD CHAMPIONSHIP

VIEWPOINT
BREAKING POINT

LOGAN SARGEANT'S F1 career effectively ended 14 minutes into free practice on Saturday morning. The American was unhurt, but the same could not be said for the smoking remains of the Williams he had left behind in the middle of the track. Ultimately, this latest mishap would prompt the realisation that his ambition did not match the talent necessary to cut it at this level. A week later, at Monza, he would be replaced by Franco Colapinto.

Team principal James Vowles was left to tot up a final damage bill covering 17 months that was estimated to have cost Williams north of $4m. Sargeant might have displayed a welcome improvement in form at Silverstone, but this latest episode focused more light on his previous misfortune than future promise.

Logan had been off the road in Suzuka (for the second year in succession), Singapore, Miami (assisted by Magnussen) and Montreal. The final straw was this misjudgement in the Netherlands, which, apart from having a catastrophic result, was clearly down to a schoolboy error.

Accelerating hard out of Turn Three, Sargeant had used the right-hand kerb on exit – and kept his foot in it when the concrete gave way to grass. Assuming he had taken the customary track walk on Thursday – supposedly de rigueur for a driver and his engineers – surely he would have checked the relevant surfaces and noted the potential hazard of both kerb and grass, should they be wet, which unquestionably they were in FP3.

From the moment his right rear Pirelli inter hit the greensward, a fast ride towards the opposite barrier was virtually guaranteed. As was a parting of the ways after a weekend when the hard-pressed Williams crew had worked their socks off to bring a new development package to Zandvoort.

It is true that Sargeant had a raw deal at times (being forced to miss the Australian race because of his team-mate's crash, for example), but it was a sign of the team's reasonable intentions when they chose not to take the more practical option of dismissing one driver and hiring another during the summer break preceding the Dutch GP. Zandvoort had turned out to be one crash too many.

Maurice Hamilton

15

FORMULA 1 HEINEKEN DUTCH GRAND PRIX 2024

ZANDVOORT 23-25 AUGUST

RACE DISTANCE: 72 laps, 190.504 miles/306.587km
RACE WEATHER: Dry/sunny (track 27-31°C, air 19°C)

CIRCUIT ZANDVOORT, NETHERLANDS
Circuit: 2.646 miles/4.259km, 72 laps

RACE – OFFICIAL CLASSIFICATION

Pos.	Driver	Nat.	No.	Entrant	Car/Engine	Laps	Time/Retirement	Speed (mph/km/h)	Gap to leader	Fastest race lap
1	Lando Norris	GB	4	McLaren Formula 1 Team	McLaren MCL38-Mercedes F1 M15 E Perf. V6	72	1h 30m 45.519s	125.941/202.682		1m 13.817s 72
2	Max Verstappen	NL	1	Oracle Red Bull Racing	Red Bull RB20-Honda RBPT H002 V6	72	1h 31m 08.415s	125.414/201.834	22.896s	1m 14.752s 30
3	Charles Leclerc	MC	16	Scuderia Ferrari	Ferrari SF-24-066/12 V6	72	1h 31m 10.958s	125.355/201.740	25.439s	1m 14.585s 62
4	Oscar Piastri	AUS	81	McLaren Formula 1 Team	McLaren MCL38-Mercedes F1 M15 E Perf. V6	72	1h 31m 12.856s	125.312/201.670	27.337s	1m 14.237s 36
5	Carlos Sainz	E	55	Scuderia Ferrari	Ferrari SF-24-066/12 V6	72	1h 31m 17.656s	125.202/201.493	32.137s	1m 14.117s 40
6	Sergio Pérez	MEX	11	Oracle Red Bull Racing	Red Bull RB20-Honda RBPT H002 V6	72	1h 31m 25.061s	125.033/201.221	39.542s	1m 14.587s 69
7	George Russell	GB	63	Mercedes-AMG Petronas F1 Team	Mercedes-AMG F1 W15-M15 E Perf. V6	72	1h 31m 30.136s	124.917/201.035	44.617s	1m 13.927s 57
8	Lewis Hamilton	GB	44	Mercedes-AMG Petronas F1 Team	Mercedes-AMG F1 W15-M15 E Perf. V6	72	1h 31m 35.118s	124.804/200.853	49.599s	1m 13.878s 62
9	Pierre Gasly	F	10	BWT Alpine F1 Team	Alpine A524-Renault E-Tech RE24 V6	71			1 lap	1m 14.855s 54
10	Fernando Alonso	E	14	Aston Martin Aramco F1 Team	Aston Martin AMR24-Mercedes F1 M15 E Perf. V6	71			1 lap	1m 14.758s 34
11	Nico Hülkenberg	D	27	MoneyGram Haas F1 Team	Haas VF-24-Ferrari 066/10 V6	71			1 lap	1m 15.657s 59
12	Daniel Ricciardo	AUS	3	Visa Cash App RB Formula One Team	RB VCARB 01-Honda RBPT H002 V6	71			1 lap	1m 15.222s 52
13	Lance Stroll	CDN	18	Aston Martin Aramco F1 Team	Aston Martin AMR24-Mercedes F1 M15 E Perf. V6	71	*		1 lap	1m 15.255s 51
14	Alexander Albon	T	23	Williams Racing	Williams FW46-Mercedes F1 M15 E Perf. V6	71			1 lap	1m 14.434s 71
15	Esteban Ocon	F	31	BWT Alpine F1 Team	Alpine A524-Renault E-Tech RE24 V6	71			1 lap	1m 15.390s 50
16	Logan Sargeant	USA	2	Williams Racing	Williams FW46-Mercedes F1 M15 E Perf. V6	71			1 lap	1m 15.539s 26
17	Yuki Tsunoda	J	22	Visa Cash App RB Formula One Team	RB VCARB 01-Honda RBPT H002 V6	71			1 lap	1m 15.552s 16
18	Kevin Magnussen	DK	20	MoneyGram Haas F1 Team	Haas VF-24-Ferrari 066/10 V6	71			1 lap	1m 14.954s 42
19	Valtteri Bottas	FIN	77	Stake F1 Team Kick Sauber	Sauber C44-Ferrari 066/12 V6	70			2 laps	1m 15.822s 45
20	Zhou Guanyu	CHN	24	Stake F1 Team Kick Sauber	Sauber C44-Ferrari 066/12 V6	70			2 laps	1m 15.724s 67

* Stroll: 5s time penalty for speeding in the pit lane (originally finished 12th).

DHL Fastest race lap (scores 1 point): Lando Norris on lap 72, 1m 13.817s, 129.064mph/207.708km/h.
Lap record: Lewis Hamilton (Mercedes F1 W12 V6), 1m 11.097s, 134.002mph/215.654km/h (2021).

 19 · ALBON · Williams
 17 · ZHOU · Sauber
 15 · OCON · Alpine
 13 · RICCIARDO · RB
 11 · TSUNODA · RB

 20 · MAGNUSSEN · Haas
Car modified in parc fermé and used additional power unit elements; required to start from the pit lane

 18 · SARGEANT · Williams

 16 · BOTTAS · Sauber

 14 · HAMILTON · Mercedes
3-place grid penalty for impeding Pérez during qualifying

 12 · HÜLKENBERG · Haas

Lap Chart

Grid order	1	2	3	4	5	6	7	8	9	10	11	12	13	14	15	16	17	18	19	20	21	22	23	24	25	26	27	28	29	30	31	32	33	34	35	36	37	38	39	40	41	42	43	44	45	46	47	48	49	50	51	52	53	54
4 NORRIS	1	1	1	1	1	1	1	1	1	1	1	1	1	1	1	1	1	1	4	4	4	4	4	4	4	4	4	4	81	81	81	81	81	4	4	4	4	4	4	4	4	4	4	4	4	4	4	4	4	4	4	4	4	4
1 VERSTAPPEN	4	4	4	4	4	4	4	4	4	4	4	4	4	4	4	4	4	4	1	1	1	1	1	1	1	1	1	1	81	55	4	4	4	81	1	1	1	1	1	1	1	1	1	1	1	1	1	1	1	1	1	1	1	1
81 PIASTRI	63	63	63	63	63	63	63	63	63	63	63	63	63	63	63	63	63	63	63	63	63	63	63	63	81	81	81	11	11	55	1	1	1	16	16	16	16	16	16	16	16	16	16	16	16	16	16	16	16	16	16	16	16	16
63 RUSSELL	81	81	81	81	81	81	81	81	81	81	81	81	81	81	81	81	81	81	81	81	81	81	81	81	63	11	11	55	4	1	16	16	16	63	63	63	63	63	63	63	63	81	81	81	81	81	81	81	81	81	81	81	81	81
11 PÉREZ	16	16	16	16	16	16	16	16	16	16	16	16	16	16	16	16	16	16	16	16	16	16	16	16	11	55	55	1	1	16	63	63	63	11	81	81	81	81	81	81	81	63	63	63	63	63	63	63	63	63	63	63	63	63
16 LECLERC	11	11	11	11	11	11	11	11	11	11	11	11	11	11	11	11	11	11	11	11	11	11	11	11	55	10	10	16	63	10	11	11	11	1	11	11	11	11	11	11	11	55	55	55	55	55	55	55	55	55	55	55	55	63
14 ALONSO	10	10	10	10	10	10	10	10	10	55	55	55	55	55	55	55	55	55	55	55	55	55	55	55	10	16	16	63	10	11	10	55	55	55	55	55	55	55	55	55	55	11	11	11	11	11	11	11	11	11	11	11	11	11
18 STROLL	14	14	14	14	14	14	55	55	10	10	10	10	10	10	10	10	10	10	10	10	10	10	10	10	16	63	63	10	14	55	55	44	44	44	44	44	44	44	44	44	44	44	44	44	44	44	44	44	44	44	44	44	44	44
10 GASLY	55	55	55	55	55	55	14	14	14	14	14	14	14	14	44	44	44	44	44	44	44	44	44	44	14	14	14	14	11	14	44	27	27	27	27	27	27	27	27	27	27	27	27	27	27	27	27	27	27	27	27	27	27	27
55 SAINZ	18	18	18	18	18	18	18	18	18	18	18	18	18	18	18	18	18	18	18	18	18	18	18	18	18	18	18	44	44	44	27	20	20	20	20	20	20	10	10	10	10	10	10	10	10	10	10	10	10	10	10	10	10	10
22 TSUNODA	27	27	27	27	27	27	27	27	44	44	44	44	18	18	18	18	18	18	3	3	3	3	3	20	18	20	20	23	23	23	23	23	23	23	10	23	14	14	14	14	14	14	14	14	14	14	14	14	14	14	14	14	14	14
27 HÜLKENBERG	22	44	44	44	44	44	44	44	27	27	27	27	27	3	3	3	3	3	3	3	3	3	20	20	20	20	44	20	27	23	10	10	10	10	23	14	23	23	23	23	23	18	18	18	18	18	18	18	18	18	18	18	18	18
3 RICCIARDO	44	22	22	22	22	22	22	22	22	22	22	22	22	22	31	31	31	31	31	31	31	20	27	27	27	27	27	22	22	14	14	14	14	14	14	10	10	18	18	18	18	23	3	3	3	3	3	3	3	3	3	3	3	3
44 HAMILTON	77	77	77	77	77	77	77	77	77	77	77	77	77	77	2	2	20	20	20	20	20	31	31	31	31	31	31	31	44	44	3	22	23	18	18	18	18	3	3	3	3	3	23	23	23	23	23	23	23	23	23	23	23	23
31 OCON	3	3	3	3	3	3	3	3	3	3	3	3	3	20	20	20	2	2	2	2	2	27	44	44	44	44	22	18	18	18	18	18	18	3	3	20	77	31	31	31	31	31	31	31	31	31	31	31	31	31	31	31	31	31
77 BOTTAS	31	31	31	31	31	31	31	31	31	31	31	31	77	24	24	24	27	27	27	27	27	22	22	22	22	22	22	31	18	18	3	3	77	77	77	77	77	77	77	77	77	2	2	2	2	2	2	2	2	2	2	2	2	2
24 ZHOU	23	23	23	23	23	23	23	23	23	23	23	23	24	2	27	27	22	22	22	22	22	2	23	23	23	23	23	77	77	77	2	2	2	2	2	2	2	2	2	2	2	22	22	22	22	22	22	22	22	22	22	22	22	22
2 SARGEANT	2	2	2	2	2	2	2	2	2	2	23	20	20	27	22	22	23	23	23	23	23	77	77	77	77	77	77	2	2	2	31	31	31	31	31	31	22	22	77	20	20	20	20	20	20	20	20	20	20	20	20	20	20	20
23 ALBON	24	20	24	24	20	24	20	20	20	24	24	23	23	23	23	23	24	77	77	77	77	24	24	24	24	24	24	24	31	31	22	77	22	22	22	22	31	77	20	77	77	77	77	77	77	77	77	77	77	77	77	77	77	77
20 MAGNUSSEN	20	24	20	20	24	20	24	24	24	20	20	24	2	31	77	77	77	24	24	24	24	23	2	2	2	2	2	24	24	24	24	24	24	24	24	24	24	24	24	24	24	24	24	24	24	24	24	24	24	24	24	24	24	24

TIME SHEETS

PRACTICE 1 (FRIDAY)
Weather: Rain-dry/cloudy-sunny
Temperatures: track 20-24°C, air 19-22°C

Pos.	Driver	Laps	Time
1	Lando Norris	17	1m 12.322s
2	Max Verstappen	13	1m 12.523s
3	Lewis Hamilton	13	1m 13.006s
4	Carlos Sainz	15	1m 13.074s
5	George Russell	17	1m 13.142s
6	Alexander Albon	14	1m 13.159s
7	Oscar Piastri	14	1m 13.230s
8	Nico Hülkenberg	18	1m 13.563s
9	Kevin Magnussen	15	1m 13.597s
10	Zhou Guanyu	15	1m 13.965s
11	Lance Stroll	14	1m 14.151s
12	Sergio Pérez	12	1m 14.279s
13	Charles Leclerc	15	1m 14.306s
14	Yuki Tsunoda	13	1m 14.418s
15	Fernando Alonso	15	1m 14.467s
16	Robert Shwartzman	15	1m 14.658s
17	Logan Sargeant	12	1m 15.605s
18	Esteban Ocon	15	1m 15.796s
19	Daniel Ricciardo	15	1m 16.231s
20	Pierre Gasly	8	1m 22.036s

PRACTICE 2 (FRIDAY)
Weather: Dry/sunny
Temperatures: track 28-30°C, air 23-25°C

Pos.	Driver	Laps	Time
1	George Russell	30	1m 10.702s
2	Oscar Piastri	33	1m 10.763s
3	Lewis Hamilton	30	1m 10.813s
4	Lando Norris	34	1m 10.961s
5	Max Verstappen	33	1m 10.986s
6	Fernando Alonso	30	1m 11.357s
7	Yuki Tsunoda	31	1m 11.374s
8	Kevin Magnussen	33	1m 11.430s
9	Charles Leclerc	31	1m 11.443s
10	Alexander Albon	33	1m 11.550s
11	Lance Stroll	31	1m 11.576s
12	Sergio Pérez	29	1m 11.581s
13	Daniel Ricciardo	31	1m 11.630s
14	Pierre Gasly	33	1m 11.644s
15	Logan Sargeant	32	1m 11.818s
16	Zhou Guanyu	33	1m 11.834s
17	Esteban Ocon	33	1m 12.061s
18	Valtteri Bottas	32	1m 12.206s
19	Carlos Sainz	7	1m 13.108s
20	Nico Hülkenberg	10	1m 13.296s

PRACTICE 3 (SATURDAY)
Weather: Rain/overcast
Temperatures: track 20-23°C, air 17-21°C

Pos.	Driver	Laps	Time
1	Pierre Gasly	5	1m 20.311s
2	Kevin Magnussen	9	1m 20.450s
3	Valtteri Bottas	7	1m 21.155s
4	Lando Norris	6	1m 21.387s
5	Fernando Alonso	6	1m 21.461s
6	Esteban Ocon	4	1m 21.643s
7	Oscar Piastri	10	1m 21.850s
8	Lance Stroll	7	1m 21.941s
9	Nico Hülkenberg	5	1m 22.354s
10	Carlos Sainz	6	1m 22.589s
11	Zhou Guanyu	5	1m 23.240s
12	Logan Sargeant	4	1m 23.287s
13	George Russell	7	1m 23.958s
14	Alexander Albon	5	1m 24.087s
15	Lewis Hamilton	3	1m 24.098s
16	Charles Leclerc	4	1m 24.158s
17	Max Verstappen	3	1m 24.360s
18	Daniel Ricciardo	7	1m 25.433s
19	Yuki Tsunoda	4	no time
20	Sergio Pérez	2	no time

FOR THE RECORD

10th GP FRONT ROW: Lando Norris
15,000th GP LAP RACED: Sergio Pérez
200th GRAND PRIX START: Max Verstappen

POINTS

DRIVERS

1	Max Verstappen	295
2	Lando Norris	225
3	Charles Leclerc	192
4	Oscar Piastri	179
5	Carlos Sainz	172
6	Lewis Hamilton	154
7	Sergio Pérez	139
8	George Russell	122
9	Fernando Alonso	50
10	Lance Stroll	24
11	Nico Hülkenberg	22
12	Yuki Tsunoda	22
13	Daniel Ricciardo	12
14	Pierre Gasly	8
15	Oliver Bearman	6
16	Kevin Magnussen	5
17	Esteban Ocon	5
18	Alexander Albon	4

QUALIFYING (SATURDAY)
Weather: Dry/overcast Temperatures: track 26-28°C, air 24-25°C

Pos.	Driver	First	Second	Third	Qualifying Tyre
1	Lando Norris	1m 11.377s	1m 10.496s	1m 09.673s	Soft (n)
2	Max Verstappen	1m 11.393s	1m 10.811s	1m 10.029s	Soft (n)
3	Oscar Piastri	1m 11.541s	1m 10.505s	1m 10.172s	Soft (n)
4	George Russell	1m 11.049s	1m 10.552s	1m 10.244s	Soft (n)
5	Sergio Pérez	1m 11.006s	1m 10.678s	1m 10.416s	Soft (n)
6	Charles Leclerc	1m 11.370s	1m 10.689s	1m 10.582s	Soft (n)
7	Fernando Alonso	1m 11.493s	1m 10.845s	1m 10.633s	Soft (n)
*	Alexander Albon	1m 11.503s	1m 10.768s	1m 10.653s	Soft (n)
8	Lance Stroll	1m 11.518s	1m 10.661s	1m 10.857s	Soft (n)
9	Pierre Gasly	1m 11.718s	1m 10.815s	1m 10.977s	Soft (n)
10	Carlos Sainz	1m 11.327s	1m 10.914s		
11	Lewis Hamilton	1m 11.375s	1m 10.948s		
12	Yuki Tsunoda	1m 11.603s	1m 10.955s		
13	Nico Hülkenberg	1m 11.832s	1m 11.215s		
14	Kevin Magnussen	1m 11.630s	1m 11.295s		
15	Daniel Ricciardo	1m 11.943s			
16	Esteban Ocon	1m 11.995s			
17	Valtteri Bottas	1m 12.168s			
18	Zhou Guanyu	1m 13.261s			
-	Logan Sargeant	-			

* Disqualified from the qualifying classification due to the floor body lying outside the regulatory volume.

QUALIFYING: head to head

Verstappen	15	0	Pérez
Hamilton	4	11	Russell
Norris	12	3	Piastri
Leclerc	9	5	Sainz
Leclerc	1	0	Bearman
Gasly	5	10	Ocon
Alonso	9	6	Stroll
Albon	14	1	Sargeant
Bottas	14	1	Zhou
Tsunoda	10	5	Ricciardo
Magnussen	4	11	Hülkenberg

CONSTRUCTORS

1	Red Bull	434
2	McLaren	404
3	Ferrari	370
4	Mercedes	276
5	Aston Martin	74
6	RB	34
7	Haas	27
8	Alpine	13
9	Williams	4

9 · GASLY · Alpine

7 · ALONSO · Aston Martin

5 · PÉREZ · Red Bull

3 · PIASTRI · McLaren

1 · NORRIS · McLaren

10 · SAINZ · Ferrari

8 · STROLL · Aston Martin

6 · LECLERC · Ferrari

4 · RUSSELL · Mercedes

2 · VERSTAPPEN · Red Bull

RACE TYRE STRATEGIES

	Driver	Race Stint 1	Race Stint 2	Race Stint 3
1	Norris	Medium (n): 1-28	Hard (n): 29-72	
2	Verstappen	Medium (n): 1-27	Hard (n): 28-72	
3	Leclerc	Medium (n): 1-24	Hard (n): 25-72	
4	Piastri	Medium (n): 1-33	Hard (n): 34-72	
5	Sainz	Medium (n): 1-30	Hard (n): 31-72	
6	Pérez	Medium (n): 1-29	Hard (n): 30-72	
7	Russell	Medium (n): 1-25	Hard (n): 26-54	Soft (u): 55-72
8	Hamilton	Soft (n): 1-23	Hard (n): 24-48	Soft (n): 49-72
9	Gasly	Medium (n): 1-32	Hard (n): 33-71	
10	Alonso	Medium (n): 1-31	Hard (n): 32-71	
11	Hülkenberg	Medium (n): 1-14	Hard (n): 15-71	
12	Ricciardo	Medium (n): 1-29	Hard (n): 30-71	
13	Stroll	Medium (n): 1-30	Hard (n): 31-71	
14	Albon	Medium (n): 1-12	Hard (n): 13-54	Medium (n): 55-71
15	Ocon	Medium (n): 1-30	Hard (n): 31-71	
16	Sargeant	Medium (n): 1-22	Hard (n): 23-71	
17	Tsunoda	Soft (n): 1-14	Medium (n): 15-32	Hard (n): 33-71
18	Magnussen	Hard (n): 1-40	Medium (n): 41-71	
19	Bottas	Soft (n): 1-15	Hard (n): 16-43	Medium (n): 44-70
20	Zhou	Medium (n): 1-18	Hard (n): 19-51	Soft (n): 52-70

The tyre regulations stipulate that at least two of three dry tyre specifications must be used during a dry race.
Selected compounds for Zandvoort: Red = Soft (C3); Yellow = Medium (C2); White = Hard (C1). (n) new (u) used

23 = Pit stop   24 = One lap or more behind

MONZA QUALIFYING

A REVISED Monza, newly resurfaced and with more benign kerbs through the iconic Ascari chicane, produced an incredibly close contest between F1's top four teams of the moment.

For single-lap pace, Lewis Hamilton's Mercedes was fastest in Friday practice by 0.03s from Lando Norris's McLaren, their times set on used tyres, while the Ferrari of third-fastest Carlos Sainz was on a new set. Oscar Piastri had been on course for quickest lap until a snap of oversteer through Ascari cost him. McLaren looked potentially quickest, with the caveat that Max Verstappen's Red Bull had encountered traffic and then a red flag, so didn't set a representative time.

Verstappen was reporting a chassis imbalance in high-speed corners, however, and said that his medium tyres were finished by the end of his 11-lap race stint simulation. His lap averages, though, were on par with McLaren, Mercedes and Ferrari.

Over Friday's long runs, a mere tenth covered six cars from four teams. But, normally a nailed-on one-stopper, suddenly Monza was looking like a two-stop race if tyre degradation did not significantly reduce as the new surface rubbered in.

Mercedes was still trying to validate the new floor, introduced at Spa and discarded at Zandvoort, but the bigger story was the event debut of upcoming Kimi Antonelli who, having turned 18 the previous Monday, drove George Russell's car in FP1. Until he deposited it heavily into the tyres at Parabolica on his second lap, that is!

Surprisingly, this was no gentle easing in. With photographers three rows deep outside the Mercedes garage, the team had given Antonelli two sets of soft tyres and told him to go out and enjoy himself! On his first flying lap, he was quicker than anyone through sector two, but on the next, he carried too much speed into Parabolica (Alboreto these days) and was bitten by an apex oversteer snap.

"Are you okay?" the pit wall team wanted to know.

"Yeah, sorry," a chastened Antonelli replied.

"All good, Kimi, all good," Toto Wolff reassured him.

"What we saw in a lap-and-a-half was astonishing," Wolff said. Antonelli was taken to the medical centre after the 52g impact, while Russell was left hoping that the team could repair the car for FP2, which they did.

Qualifying reflected practice form, with McLaren locking out the front row, Zandvoort winner Norris pipping Piastri to pole by just over a tenth with a 1m 19.327s lap.

"It wasn't a great lap and so pole is a bit of a surprise, but I'll take it," Lando said with a smile.

Incredibly, three-hundredths covered second through fifth as, behind Piastri, Russell stopped the clock in 1m 19.440s, Charles Leclerc's Ferrari recorded 1m 19.460s and team-mate Carlos Sainz, 1m 19.467s. Maranello, as usual, had brought a significant upgrade package to its home event.

Russell was more than happy with third, finding a Q3 lap right at the end after less than optimum runs in Q1 and Q2. Meanwhile, Leclerc had been hoping to challenge for pole, but lined up fourth: "I've had this big issue with too much understeer in the first sector. In FP3, it was gone and everything felt good, but in qualifying, it came back again. In the second and third sector, we were fast, so it's disappointing. I expect it to be a tyre-management race. Whoever does the best job on that should come out on top." Prophetic words.

Sainz actually had the quickest sector-one time and thought he was on for pole, "but then I struggled with understeer in the medium- and high-speed corners at the end of the lap. A mosquito in my eye didn't help!"

After Mercedes had been 1-2 in the final session of free practice on Saturday morning, Hamilton was gutted to qualify sixth, despite being just 0.07s slower than his third-placed team-mate, the Mercs not quite as strong as the ambient and track temperature climbed.

"I'm furious," Lewis grimaced. "I could have been on pole. I lost a tenth-and-a-half at Turn One and then more in the final corner. There's no one to blame but myself. Qualifying has been a weakness for a while and I can't figure it out," he admitted candidly.

Verstappen had even bigger problems and his worst qualifying result since Singapore, 2023. Having appeared competitive with a 1m 19.6s in Q2, he couldn't break 1m 20s in Q3, was half a second slower than Hamilton and would start seventh, just 0.04s ahead of team-mate Sergio Pérez.

"I had understeer on both sets of tyres and had to back out mid-corner," Max explained. "The Q3 balance was completely out."

Alex Albon's Williams and Nico Hülkenberg's Haas completed the top ten, Fernando Alonso's Aston Martin and Daniel Ricciardo's VCARB narrowly missing out. Kevin Magnussen, and the Alpines of Pierre Gasly and Esteban Ocon were the other Q2 casualties.

Meanwhile, out in Q1 had gone Yuki Tsunoda, Lance Stroll, Franco Colapinto

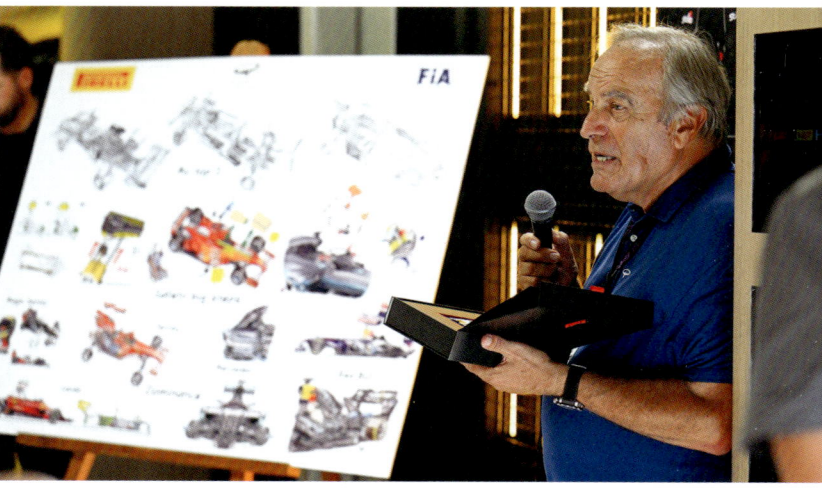

(Logan Sargeant's replacement at Williams), and Sauber drivers Valtteri Bottas and Zhou Guanyu.

Some thought the promotion of 21-year-old Argentine Colapinto into the Williams race team as strange, because with Sainz already signed for 2025, there was no opportunity to parlay it into a full-time seat. If done for performance reasons, it was the first such mid-season move since Renault had replaced Nelson Piquet Jr with Romain Grosjean back in 2009.

Colapinto actually did a fine job to be ninth in FP3, right behind team-mate Albon, and was disappointed to go out in Q1 after running wide at the second Lesmo. His Williams opportunity apparently arose because Mercedes wanted Antonelli to complete his F2/F1 testing programme rather than drive a Williams, and Red Bull was not prepared to lend Liam Lawson. Thus, Colapinto became the 27th Argentine driver to race in F1, the last being Gaston Mazzacane in 2000–01. A certain five-times champion Juan Manuel Fangio is the best known of course, but Carlos Reutemann scored three of his 12 GP wins with Williams in the early eighties.

LANDO NORRIS'S starts from pole and, specifically, his inability to convert them into a first-lap lead, were becoming a bit of a 'thing'. McLaren team principal Zak Brown had been trying to take the pressure off his man. When he was beaten away by Max Verstappen at the previous race in Zandvoort, Brown explained that it had been a traction issue in the second phase of the start. "And that," he said, "was on us, not him."

With the usual fantastic race-day atmosphere in the cauldron that is the Monza Autodromo, all eyes were focused on the starting gantry as the lights extinguished and the papaya front row went away as one. There was no mistake from Norris this time, and he swooped across from the left-hand pole position to cover off team-mate Oscar Piastri and guard the inside line into Turns One and Two.

With a long run into a tight chicane, there is always a lock-up, and this time, the significant example was George Russell, who was forced to take to the escape road as Norris, Piastri and Charles Leclerc's Ferrari headed the pack. As they rushed through Curva Grande and down to the second chicane, Piastri was side by side with Norris and kept coming around the outside as they turned into the left-hander. Lando was forced to back out to avoid a contact.

"I don't know what I could have done differently," he said later. "If I'd braked one metre later, we would probably have crashed, so…"

Norris's compromised exit allowed an opportunistic Leclerc to go inside the McLaren into the first Lesmo. Thus the order across the line at the end of lap one was Piastri, Leclerc, Norris, Carlos Sainz, Lewis Hamilton, Max Verstappen, the delayed Russell (who had suffered right front wing endplate damage), Sergio Pérez, Alex Albon, Fernando Alonso, Daniel Ricciardo, Kevin Magnussen, Pierre Gasly, Yuki Tsunoda, Esteban Ocon, Nico Hülkenberg, Lance Stroll, Franco Colapinto, Valtteri Bottas and Zhou Guanyu.

The general consensus was that a medium/hard one-stopper was a big ask on a track that was at least 50 per cent resurfaced. Alex Albon had articulated it well: "I think it's not actually the temperature that's the problem, it's the tarmac. When it hasn't had time to cure and grip up, it creates this weird graining, very different to normal. It's the whole tyre, and when you get it, you immediately lose seconds. The tyre won't clean up, it's just gone, so a one-stop is going to be very tricky."

As usual, Pirelli's medium compound was the preferred starting tyre, with the top five all on the yellow-walled rubber. The two Red Bulls had gone for the hard to offer a longer opening stint after poor qualifying by their standards, and further down the field, Ocon, Tsunoda, Stroll and Bottas had gone the same route.

Hülkenberg made a good save as he was squeezed on to the grass by Ricciardo and then sustained front wing damage as he tried to go inside Tsunoda at Turn One. He pitted for a new nose and a switch to the hard compound on lap six.

With tyre degradation an unknown, the race pace was measured rather than frenetic. Cautious. Ten laps in, Piastri led Leclerc by 1.7s, and everyone down to eighth-placed Russell sat a respectful 1.5–2s behind the man in front, looking after their rubber.

After a dozen laps, Russell pitted from seventh and had a new nose fitted to his damaged W15 as well as a set of hard-compound Pirellis, costing him 10.5s stationary in the pits.

The McLaren radio waves suddenly became busy, with race-leader Piastri telling the team that he was happy to go with Plan A, and the pit wall telling third-placed Norris

Above: Too fast, too soon? On only his second lap, Kimi Antonelli shunted his Mercedes in FP1.

Above left: No harm done. Toto Wolff confirmed that Antonelli would partner George Russell in 2025.
Photos: Mercedes-AMG Petronas F1 Team

Top: The McLarens of Norris and Piastri take the lead at the start; George Russell is about to take to the escape road in his Mercedes.
Photo: Pirelli

Top left: Carlos Sainz thought that he might have had a shot at pole, but for a pesky mosquito!
Photo: Scuderia Ferrari

Above far left: Franco Colapinto replaced Logan Sargeant at Williams and impressed immediately.
Photo: Bryn Williams

Left: Technical journalist and illustrator Giorgio Piola is presented with an award by F1 for clocking up an amazing 900 grand prix races.
Photo: Pirelli

Opening spread: A sea of red. The *tifosi* fill the track for the victory celebrations.
Photo: Scuderia Ferrari

Above: Carlos Sainz also ran a one-stop strategy for Ferrari, but he could not resist Norris and Piastri's McLarens.
Photo: Scuderia Ferrari

Top right: Outpaced. Lewis Hamilton and Max Verstappen had to be content with fifth and sixth places.
Photo: Mercedes-AMG Petronas F1 Team

Above right: Daniel Ricciardo was given a five-second penalty after colliding with Nico Hülkenberg's Haas.
Photo: Red Bull Content Pool/Getty Images

Right: Lando Norris chases after team-mate Piastri.
Photo: Bryn Williams

on lap 15, "Suggest box to overtake on Leclerc." Lando responded by arriving in the pits wreathed in tyre smoke as he locked up, successfully avoiding a pit-lane speeding transgression. He rejoined sixth.

Leclerc and Hamilton came in on the next lap in an attempt to cover off the McLaren stop. Both were serviced in under 2.5s, but as they blasted back into the fray, Norris was ahead.

Carlos Sainz thought that these stops were all a bit early. "These guys will struggle to go to the end," he told the Ferrari strategists.

McLaren brought in Piastri a couple of laps after Norris, in response to Leclerc and Hamilton. This time, there was no Budapest undercut repeat, car No.81 back out a couple of seconds ahead of Norris, the papaya cars split by Alex Albon's Williams.

Leclerc was not thrilled to make an early stop and be undercut by Norris. "What was that?" he asked. "Why did we pit if we are undercut?" Meanwhile, Sainz was brought in on lap 20 and came back out sixth, just in front of Hamilton.

The two Red Bulls now headed the pack on their hard-compound tyres, Verstappen just a couple of seconds ahead of Pérez, with Piastri 6s behind the Mexican.

"You can pick up the pace, Max" Verstappen was told. But he was in just three laps later, another set of hard-compound tyres confirming that he would be stopping again. A problem with the right rear and 6.2s stationary in the pits was the last thing that he needed. He rejoined eighth, thumping the steering wheel in frustration as he did so, just a couple of seconds in front of Russell.

Pérez would soon pit out of the lead, just as Piastri turned in a new fastest lap on his fresh tyres and Norris was told that he was free to race Oscar under 'papaya rules'. These, Zak Brown had explained earlier, meant that as team-mates they were free to race hard, but it had to be clean, with no touching and due respect. Piastri's opening-lap move had fulfilled the criteria, just, although it had frayed a few nerves on the pit wall and was borderline overly aggressive.

As the race passed 30 of the scheduled 53 laps, however, rather than closing in on Piastri, Norris had dropped to almost 3.5s behind and had Leclerc on him. Ferrari was on the radio to Charles, telling him, "Norris is starting to struggle. This is when Red Bull started to have graining, about 15 laps into the stint." Which told you that Ferrari had been closely monitoring Red Bull's opening stint on the hard compound to work out whether a one-stop was on.

Behind the leading trio, Sainz was around 12s adrift of Leclerc, with Hamilton close to DRS range behind him. The delayed Verstappen was now 7s behind the Mercedes and 4s ahead of team-mate Pérez, who was being hassled by Russell's Mercedes. George tried to go by around the outside of Turn One, but Sergio wasn't having it, and again George missed part of T1/2, being forced to drop back into line on exit. Immediately, he attempted to go around the Red Bull into the second chicane, but Pérez held him off.

A mistake at the Roggia chicane by Norris on lap 31 resulted in Piastri's lead stretching to 5s and put Leclerc right on to the second McLaren's tail, causing Lando to head for his second stop in case Ferrari entertained any hopes of undercutting. He was away again on another set of hards after 3.3s.

Initially, a new fastest first sector by Leclerc suggested that Ferrari was responding to Norris's stop rather than attempting a one-stopper, but the Ferrari kept going.

Meanwhile, on lap 38, about as late as McLaren could leave Piastri before he was potentially undercut by his team-mate, they asked the $64m question: "Oscar, do you think there is any chance that we can one-stop?" Here was Spa all over again.

"I don't think so," he responded. "The front left is pretty dead." The extent to which McLaren had been wearing the front left had been confounding Norris somewhat, too, and brought back to mind Albon's comments.

The feisty battle between Russell and Pérez, who had switched to mediums at his second stop, continued, the Mercedes almost running into the back of the Red Bull at Turn One before Sergio begrudgingly gave George a car's width. The Red Bull took the inside line through Curva Grande, but Russell had strong top speed and guarded the inside into the first chicane.

Piastri was in for a second stop to take on new hards with 14 laps to go, rejoining just in front of Verstappen, who still had a second stop to make.

This was intriguing. Leclerc led on a set of hards that had already done 23 laps. Team-mate Sainz, celebrating his 30th birthday, was 10s behind on fresher hards. Piastri, on his brand-new set, was 8.5s behind the second Ferrari, with Verstappen 1.7s further back and Norris right with his championship rival.

While aware that he had to pit again, Verstappen still took the opportunity to delay Norris's progress, fending him off for a lap until the McLaren got down the inside of the Red Bull into Turn One to begin lap 41. That had increased Piastri's margin over the pole-man to 4s, even forgetting the two Ferraris ahead, as Max did as much damage limitation as possible. Once Norris was through, Verstappen bailed out and pitted for a set of mediums for an 11-lap sprint to the flag, rejoining 12s behind Hamilton's fifth-placed Mercedes.

"The Ferraris are going to try a one-stopper, but it'll be difficult," McLaren told Norris, "so this is qualifying now. Just go for it."

Above: Running for 38 laps on hard Pirellis paid off for Charles Leclerc, who took the chequered flag.

Top right: Frédéric Vasseur accepts the fans' plaudits on the pit wall.

Above right: Leclerc and his ecstatic crew enjoy the moment. Post-race tyre pick-up masks the wear on the Pirellis after his marathon stint.
Photos: Scuderia Ferrari

Right: While Leclerc celebrates his second Monza victory as a Ferrari driver, Piastri and Norris wear expressions suggesting that this was one that got away…
Photo: Bryn Williams

By lap 45, Piastri was on the back of Sainz's Ferrari when Carlos received the message to hold up the young Australian as much as possible.

"My front left has nearly gone, but I guess we try," Sainz acknowledged.

Despite being on tyres that were four laps older than his team-mate's, Leclerc had actually increased his lead over Sainz to 11.5s. It was beginning to look as though this was on for Charles. But would the tyres suddenly fall off the cliff?

Piastri wasted no time in getting by Sainz and up to second, using DRS to clear the Ferrari around the outside on the way into Ascari. Norris would soon demote Carlos, too, and bag the fastest-lap point on his fresh rubber.

With five laps remaining and a 10s advantage over Piastri, Ferrari radioed Leclerc with the instruction, "Brake balance, plus one."

"Leave me alone with this," Charles replied firmly. "If I don't do things you ask, don't ask ten times." A slightly more polite version of Kimi Räikkönen's "Leave me alone, I know what I'm doing!"

Leclerc did. The *tifosi* were starting to understand the game, too, and were going delirious. As he started the 53rd and last lap, Charles still had 4s in hand over Piastri and, all around, the prancing-horse flags were flying. He had made a one-stopper work superbly and, for the second time, won the Italian GP in a Ferrari. For raw emotion, it really doesn't get any better.

"It's just an incredible feeling," Leclerc beamed. "Actually, I thought the first time [in his first year with Ferrari in 2019] would feel like that and the second time, if there was a second time, wouldn't feel as special. But, my God, the emotions in the last few laps were just like in 2019. Monaco and Monza are the two races I want to win every year – and obviously the championship if possible –

but those are the two most important races, and I've won both this year. It's so, so special."

Leclerc's delight was countered by Piastri's disappointment.

"I'm not going to lie, it hurts a lot," Oscar said. "I did a lot of things right today. There were question marks over the strategy going in and from the position we were in with the tyres looking like they did, a one-stop seemed like a very risky call. But, in the end, it was right. I'm very happy with the pace we had, and when you finish second, it hurts."

Behind Sainz, Hamilton brought the first Mercedes home fifth and was left to rue a less than optimum qualifying hour. Verstappen was not thrilled with sixth, but, in the final analysis, lost only eight points to Norris on a day when the differential could easily have been 18.

Russell finished seventh with the second Mercedes, having won his scrap with Pérez. Ninth on the road was Kevin Magnussen, but that position went to Alex Albon after the Dane was penalised 5s for a coming-together with Pierre Gasly.

Just outside the points was Fernando Alonso with the first Aston Martin. Daniel Ricciardo took the flag behind him, but had 15s worth of penalties to add on. The first 5s was for forcing Hülkenberg off in the early laps, with a further 10s added when one of the crew inadvertently touched the car before Ricciardo had served the penalty. That gave 12th to an impressive Colapinto, who had finished his first GP just 14s behind Williams team-mate Albon without any safety-car interventions and having done everything Williams had asked of him.

Now, there was a two-week interlude before the Baku/Singapore double-header, and Red Bull's constructors' championship lead was down to eight points…

Tony Dodgins

VIEWPOINT
UNREASONABLE OR RATIONAL?

THE reception from the *tifosi* in such a theatrical setting might have been a standout moment of the season thus far, but the rapture can only have discomfited the McLaren drivers, despite their presence on the podium. After starting from the front row, one of them should have been on the top step. But which one?

Lando Norris not only left open the door for an opportunist move by Oscar Piastri at the second chicane, but he also allowed Charles Leclerc to nick second place and set in motion a one-stop strategy that worked brilliantly. Cue emotional post-race punditry from Norris supporters, who felt that McLaren should have ordered Piastri to surrender P2 because 'Norris was owed it after Hungary'.

Piastri supporters pointed out that Lando had also presented Oscar with an opportunity to jump ahead on the first lap at the Hungaroring. The subsequent pit-stop place swap had only been brought about because of the team's strategy call. Piastri owed Norris nothing.

Lando's supporters recalled the radio message in Hungary, in which he had been asked to think of the long game and the possible need for future support from his team-mate. The track position situation at Monza, the Norris camp argued, meant that the time for payback was now.

Oscar's fans didn't see it like that. There were eight races to go after this one. That's a long way in terms of potential drama, particularly in a season that was turning out as close as this one. The Piastri faction pointed out that their man had lost significant points through either bad luck or team error on three occasions (Miami, Imola and now Monza due to the missed one-stop option). But then you had Norris advocates arguing that the clash with Verstappen had cost 18 points in Austria.

Mark Webber (Piastri's manager, who knew all about seeing a team-mate win the championship in the same car) noted that Piastri was closer to Norris on the points table than Lando was to Max. And so it went on. The only point beyond any debate at Monza was a classy win in front of the fervent home faithful by tyre whisperer Leclerc.

Maurice Hamilton

16

FORMULA 1 PIRELLI ITALIAN GRAND PRIX 2024

Official Timepiece

MONZA 30 AUGUST-01 SEPTEMBER
RACE DISTANCE: 53 laps, 183.388 miles/295.134km
RACE WEATHER: Dry/sunny-overcast (track 40-52°C, air 33°C)

AUTODROMO NAZIONALE DI MONZA
Circuit: 3.600 miles/5.793km, 53 laps

RACE – OFFICIAL CLASSIFICATION

Pos.	Driver	Nat.	No.	Entrant	Car/Engine	Laps	Time/Retirement	Speed (mph/km/h)	Gap to leader	Fastest race lap	
1	Charles Leclerc	MC	16	Scuderia Ferrari	Ferrari SF-24-066/12 V6	53	1h 14m 40.727s	153.125/246.431		1m 23.226s	33
2	Oscar Piastri	AUS	81	McLaren Formula 1 Team	McLaren MCL38-Mercedes F1 M15 E Perf. V6	53	1h 14m 43.391s	153.034/246.285	2.664s	1m 21.943s	53
3	Lando Norris	GB	4	McLaren Formula 1 Team	McLaren MCL38-Mercedes F1 M15 E Perf. V6	53	1h 14m 46.880s	152.915/246.093	6.153s	1m 21.432s	53
4	Carlos Sainz	E	55	Scuderia Ferrari	Ferrari SF-24-066/12 V6	53	1h 14m 56.348s	152.593/245.575	15.621s	1m 23.219s	53
5	Lewis Hamilton	GB	44	Mercedes-AMG Petronas F1 Team	Mercedes-AMG F1 W15-M15 E Perf. V6	53	1h 15m 03.547s	152.349/245.182	22.820s	1m 21.512s	53
6	Max Verstappen	NL	1	Oracle Red Bull Racing	Red Bull RB20-Honda RBPT H002 V6	53	1h 15m 18.659s	151.840/244.362	37.932s	1m 21.745s	43
7	George Russell	GB	63	Mercedes-AMG Petronas F1 Team	Mercedes-AMG F1 W15-M15 E Perf. V6	53	1h 15m 20.471s	151.780/244.266	39.715s	1m 22.036s	49
8	Sergio Pérez	MEX	11	Oracle Red Bull Racing	Red Bull RB20-Honda RBPT H002 V6	53	1h 15m 34.875s	151.296/243.488	54.148s	1m 22.971s	47
9	Alexander Albon	T	23	Williams Racing	Williams FW46-Mercedes F1 M15 E Perf. V6	53	1h 15m 48.183s	150.854/242.776	1m 07.456s	1m 23.918s	53
10	Kevin Magnussen	DK	20	MoneyGram Haas F1 Team	Haas VF-24-Ferrari 066/10 V6	53	1h 15m 49.029s *	150.826/242.731	1m 08.302s	1m 23.437s	51
11	Fernando Alonso	E	14	Aston Martin Aramco F1 Team	Aston Martin AMR24-Mercedes F1 M15 E Perf. V6	53	1h 15m 49.222s	150.820/242.721	1m 08.495s	1m 22.944s	46
12	Franco Colapinto	RA	43	Williams Racing	Williams FW46-Mercedes F1 M15 E Perf. V6	53	1h 16m 02.035s	150.396/242.039	1m 21.308s	1m 23.728s	53
13	Daniel Ricciardo	AUS	3	Visa Cash App RB Formula One Team	RB VCARB 01-Honda RBPT H002 V6	53	1h 16m 14.179s *	149.997/241.396	1m 33.452s	1m 24.219s	52
14	Esteban Ocon	F	31	BWT Alpine F1 Team	Alpine A524-Renault E-Tech RE24 V6	52			1 lap	1m 24.343s	52
15	Pierre Gasly	F	10	BWT Alpine F1 Team	Alpine A524-Renault E-Tech RE24 V6	52			1 lap	1m 23.755s	51
16	Valtteri Bottas	FIN	77	Stake F1 Team Kick Sauber	Sauber C44-Ferrari 066/12 V6	52			1 lap	1m 23.609s	52
17	Nico Hülkenberg	D	27	MoneyGram Haas F1 Team	Haas VF-24-Ferrari 066/10 V6	52	*		1 lap	1m 23.275s	44
18	Zhou Guanyu	CHN	24	Stake F1 Team Kick Sauber	Sauber C44-Ferrari 066/12 V6	52			1 lap	1m 25.092s	17
19	Lance Stroll	CDN	18	Aston Martin Aramco F1 Team	Aston Martin AMR24-Mercedes F1 M15 E Perf. V6	52			1 lap	1m 22.232s	52
	Yuki Tsunoda	J	22	Visa Cash App RB Formula One Team	RB VCARB 01-Honda RBPT H002 V6	7	accident/floor damage			1m 26.198s	4

* Hülkenberg: 10s time penalty for causing a collision with Tsunoda (served at pit stop). * Magnussen: 10s time penalty for causing a collision with Gasly (originally finished 9th).
* Ricciardo: 5s time penalty for forcing Hülkenberg off the track; 10s time penalty for failure to serve time penalty correctly (originally finished 12th).

DHL Fastest race lap (scores 1 point): Lando Norris on lap 53, 1m 21.432s, 159.134mph/256.100km/h.
Lap record: Rubens Barrichello (Ferrari F2004 V10), 1m 21.046s, 159.892mph/257.320km/h (2004).

All results and data © 2024 Formula One World Championship Limited

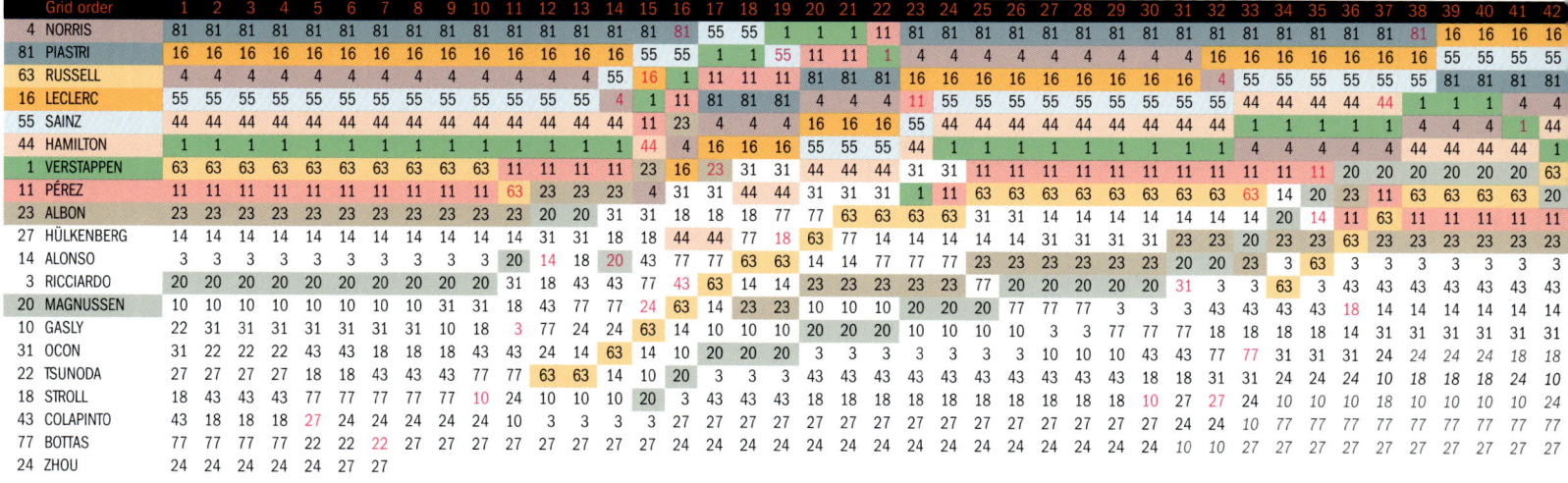

TIME SHEETS

PRACTICE 1 (FRIDAY)
Weather: Dry/sunny
Temperatures: track 50-51°C, air 32-34°C

Pos.	Driver	Laps	Time
1	Max Verstappen	19	1m 21.676s
2	Charles Leclerc	23	1m 21.904s
3	Lando Norris	26	1m 21.917s
4	Carlos Sainz	24	1m 22.126s
5	Valtteri Bottas	21	1m 22.127s
6	Oscar Piastri	23	1m 22.199s
7	Lewis Hamilton	24	1m 22.214s
8	Alexander Albon	24	1m 22.220s
9	Sergio Pérez	21	1m 22.311s
10	Fernando Alonso	18	1m 22.315s
11	Kevin Magnussen	22	1m 22.572s
12	Daniel Ricciardo	21	1m 22.605s
13	Yuki Tsunoda	23	1m 22.714s
14	Pierre Gasly	22	1m 22.763s
15	Zhou Guanyu	22	1m 22.854s
16	Lance Stroll	21	1m 22.864s
17	Franco Colapinto	23	1m 22.880s
18	Esteban Ocon	21	1m 22.880s
19	Nico Hülkenberg	23	1m 23.157s
20	Andrea Kimi Antonelli	5	1m 23.955s

PRACTICE 2 (FRIDAY)
Weather: Dry/sunny
Temperatures: track 40-49°C, air 34°C

Pos.	Driver	Laps	Time
1	Lewis Hamilton	24	1m 20.738s
2	Lando Norris	23	1m 20.741s
3	Carlos Sainz	27	1m 20.841s
4	Oscar Piastri	24	1m 20.858s
5	Charles Leclerc	26	1m 20.892s
6	George Russell	20	1m 21.086s
7	Nico Hülkenberg	25	1m 21.140s
8	Daniel Ricciardo	23	1m 21.300s
9	Fernando Alonso	24	1m 21.316s
10	Lance Stroll	27	1m 21.363s
11	Valtteri Bottas	25	1m 21.461s
12	Kevin Magnussen	11	1m 21.499s
13	Alexander Albon	25	1m 21.592s
14	Max Verstappen	24	1m 21.610s
15	Sergio Pérez	14	1m 21.678s
16	Yuki Tsunoda	20	1m 21.735s
17	Franco Colapinto	20	1m 21.784s
18	Pierre Gasly	23	1m 21.819s
19	Esteban Ocon	22	1m 21.867s
20	Zhou Guanyu	27	1m 22.223s

PRACTICE 3 (SATURDAY)
Weather: Dry/sunny
Temperatures: track 43-46°C, air 31-33°C

Pos.	Driver	Laps	Time
1	Lewis Hamilton	20	1m 20.117s
2	George Russell	24	1m 20.210s
3	Charles Leclerc	22	1m 20.226s
4	Oscar Piastri	15	1m 20.252s
5	Lando Norris	15	1m 20.262s
6	Max Verstappen	24	1m 20.368s
7	Carlos Sainz	20	1m 20.463s
8	Alexander Albon	15	1m 20.596s
9	Franco Colapinto	17	1m 20.905s
10	Nico Hülkenberg	18	1m 20.943s
11	Fernando Alonso	22	1m 20.968s
12	Daniel Ricciardo	18	1m 21.077s
13	Yuki Tsunoda	15	1m 21.141s
14	Pierre Gasly	20	1m 21.155s
15	Lance Stroll	23	1m 21.157s
16	Kevin Magnussen	21	1m 21.208s
17	Esteban Ocon	19	1m 21.258s
18	Sergio Pérez	23	1m 21.287s
19	Valtteri Bottas	20	1m 21.357s
20	Zhou Guanyu	18	1m 22.035s

QUALIFYING (SATURDAY)
Weather: Dry/sunny Temperatures: track 42-49°C, air 33-34°C

Pos.	Driver	First	Second	Third	Qualifying Tyre
1	Lando Norris	1m 19.911s	1m 19.727s	1m 19.327s	Soft (n)
2	Oscar Piastri	1m 20.076s	1m 19.808s	1m 19.436s	Soft (n)
3	George Russell	1m 20.169s	1m 19.877s	1m 19.440s	Soft (n)
4	Charles Leclerc	1m 20.074s	1m 20.007s	1m 19.461s	Soft (n)
5	Carlos Sainz	1m 20.149s	1m 19.799s	1m 19.467s	Soft (n)
6	Lewis Hamilton	1m 20.477s	1m 19.641s	1m 19.513s	Soft (n)
7	Max Verstappen	1m 20.226s	1m 19.662s	1m 20.022s	Soft (n)
8	Sergio Pérez	1m 20.598s	1m 20.216s	1m 20.062s	Soft (u)
9	Alexander Albon	1m 20.542s	1m 20.314s	1m 20.299s	Soft (n)
10	Nico Hülkenberg	1m 20.781s	1m 20.411s	1m 20.339s	Soft (n)
11	Fernando Alonso	1m 20.617s	1m 20.421s		
12	Daniel Ricciardo	1m 20.901s	1m 20.479s		
13	Kevin Magnussen	1m 20.856s	1m 20.698s		
14	Pierre Gasly	1m 20.748s	1m 20.738s		
15	Esteban Ocon	1m 20.764s	1m 20.766s		
16	Yuki Tsunoda	1m 20.945s			
17	Lance Stroll	1m 21.013s			
18	Franco Colapinto	1m 21.061s			
19	Valtteri Bottas	1m 21.101s			
20	Zhou Guanyu	1m 21.445s			

QUALIFYING: head to head

Verstappen	16	0	Pérez
Hamilton	4	12	Russell
Norris	13	3	Piastri
Leclerc	10	5	Sainz
Leclerc	1	0	Bearman
Gasly	6	10	Ocon
Alonso	10	6	Stroll
Albon	14	1	Sargeant
Albon	1	0	Colapinto
Bottas	15	1	Zhou
Tsunoda	10	6	Ricciardo
Magnussen	4	12	Hülkenberg

FOR THE RECORD

1st GRAND PRIX: Franco Colapinto
200,000th GP LAP RACED: Ferrari engine
160th GP POLE POSITION: McLaren

DID YOU KNOW?

Colapinto became the 23rd Argentinian driver to start in the Championship and the first since Gastón Mazzacane at the 2001 San Marino GP.

POINTS

DRIVERS

1	Max Verstappen	303
2	Lando Norris	241
3	Charles Leclerc	217
4	Oscar Piastri	197
5	Carlos Sainz	184
6	Lewis Hamilton	164
7	Sergio Pérez	143
8	George Russell	128
9	Fernando Alonso	50
10	Lance Stroll	24
11	Nico Hülkenberg	22
12	Yuki Tsunoda	22
13	Daniel Ricciardo	12
14	Pierre Gasly	8
15	Oliver Bearman	6
16	Kevin Magnussen	6
17	Alexander Albon	6
18	Esteban Ocon	5

CONSTRUCTORS

1	Red Bull	446
2	McLaren	438
3	Ferrari	407
4	Mercedes	292
5	Aston Martin	74
6	RB	34
7	Haas	28
8	Alpine	13
9	Williams	6

9 · ALBON · Williams

7 · VERSTAPPEN · Red Bull

5 · SAINZ · Ferrari

3 · RUSSELL · Mercedes

1 · NORRIS · McLaren

10 · HÜLKENBERG · Haas

8 · PÉREZ · Red Bull

6 · HAMILTON · Mercedes

4 · LECLERC · Ferrari

2 · PIASTRI · McLaren

43	44	45	46	47	48	49	50	51	52	53	
16	16	16	16	16	16	16	16	16	16	·	
55	55	81	81	81	81	81	81	81	81	81	2
81	81	55	55	55	4	4	4	4	4	4	3
4	4	4	4	4	55	55	55	55	55	55	
44	44	44	44	44	44	44	44	44	44	44	5
1	1	1	1	1	1	1	1	1	1	1	6
63	63	63	63	63	63	63	63	63	63	63	7
20	11	11	11	11	11	11	11	11	11	11	8
11	20	20	20	20	20	20	20	20	20	20	9
23	23	23	23	23	23	23	23	23	23	23	10
3	3	3	14	14	14	14	14	14	14	14	
14	14	14	3	3	3	3	3	3	3	3	
43	43	43	43	43	43	43	43	43	43	43	
31	31	31	31	31	31	31	31				
18	18	18	18	18	18	18	18	18	10	10	
10	10	10	10	10	10	10	10	77	77	77	
24	24	24	24	77	77	77	77	27	27	27	
77	77	77	77	24	24	24	24	24	18	18	
27	27	27	27	27	27	27	27	18			

27 = Pit stop   10 = One lap or more behind

RACE TYRE STRATEGIES

	Driver	Race Stint 1	Race Stint 2	Race Stint 3	Race Stint 4
1	Leclerc	Medium (n): 1-15	Hard (n): 16-53		
2	Piastri	Medium (n): 1-16	Hard (n): 17-38	Hard (n): 39-53	
3	Norris	Medium (n): 1-14	Hard (n): 15-32	Hard (n): 33-53	
4	Sainz	Medium (n): 1-19	Hard (n): 20-53		
5	Hamilton	Medium (n): 1-15	Hard (n): 16-37	Hard (n): 38-53	
6	Verstappen	Hard (n): 1-22	Hard (n): 23-41	Medium (n): 42-53	
7	Russell	Medium (n): 1-11	Hard (n): 12-33	Medium (n): 34-53	
8	Pérez	Hard (n): 1-23	Hard (n): 24-35	Medium (n): 36-53	
9	Albon	Medium (n): 1-17	Hard (n): 18-53		
10	Magnussen	Medium (n): 1-14	Hard (n): 15-53		
11	Alonso	Medium (u): 1-12	Hard (n): 13-35	Hard (u): 36-53	
12	Colapinto	Medium (n): 1-16	Hard (n): 17-53		
13	Ricciardo	Medium (n): 1-11	Hard (n): 12-53		
14	Ocon	Hard (n): 1-31	Medium (n): 32-52		
15	Gasly	Medium (n): 1-10	Hard (n): 11-30	Hard (n): 31-52	
16	Bottas	Hard (n): 1-33	Medium (u): 34-52		
17	Hülkenberg	Medium (n): 1-5	Hard (n): 6-32	Hard (n): 33-52	
18	Zhou	Medium (u): 1-15	Hard (n): 16-52		
19	Stroll	Hard (u): 1-19	Hard (u): 20-36	Medium (u): 37-50	Soft: (n) 51-52
	Tsunoda	Hard (u): 1-7 (dnf)			

The tyre regulations stipulate that at least two of three dry tyre specifications must be used during a dry race.
Selected compounds for Monza: Red = Soft (C5); Yellow = Medium (C4); White = Hard (C3). (n) new (u) used

FIA FORMULA 1 WORLD CHAMPIONSHIP · ROUND 17

AZERBAIJAN GRAND PRIX

BAKU CITY CIRCUIT

BAKU QUALIFYING

CHARLES LECLERC was on a bit of a roll: a podium at Spa after George Russell's disqualification, another at Zandvoort, unexpected after a fine drive, then that tyre-whispering victory at Monza. And Baku, in qualifying at least, was his personal fiefdom with three poles in a row.

Friday practice pointed to another close contest between the top four teams, with Red Bull much more competitive than in Monza. Leclerc's Ferrari, as expected, was quickest, despite a day that was anything but straightforward. He brought out the red flag halfway through FP1 when he carried too much speed into T15 and thumped the tyres. He was unhappy with the repaired Ferrari in FP2, pitting after labelling it "impossible". Then, the undisclosed fault righted, he set quickest FP2 time.

As in Monaco, Baku's short corners played to Ferrari's strengths, and the red cars were also running a skinny rear wing, giving strong straight-line speed. Meanwhile, Red Bull's RB20 looked better balanced and more competitive than it had done for some time, the team without a pole position in nine races! An upgraded floor featured tunnel geometry that had been subtly revised to improve flow downstream, and, like the Ferrari, the car was quick through the circuit's shorter corners.

The first shock of qualifying was a body blow to Lando Norris's championship challenge – he went out in Q1. Track evolution was high and after losing time at T16 on his first run, Norris was caught out by a brief yellow at the same corner and had to back off on his second. The yellow was for Esteban Ocon's slow-moving Alpine, which was limping back to the pits after a hefty contact with the Turn Seven wall. A peeved Norris thought that the white flag would have been more appropriate.

Just how bitter a pill that was to swallow became apparent when McLaren team-mate Oscar Piastri bagged a front-row start. He was the only rival to give Leclerc food for thought, as his second Q3 attempt broke the timing beam 0.07s slower than Charles's first run. Just behind him, though, Leclerc moved the goalposts with a lap in 1m 41.365s, claiming his fourth consecutive Baku pole with more than three-tenths in hand.

Emphasising Ferrari's strength, Carlos Sainz, despite being the better part of half a second slower than his team-mate, still managed to qualify third, beating that other Baku specialist, Sergio Pérez, by a hundredth.

As in 2023, Pérez had the edge on Verstappen in Azerbaijan and, of course, could boast two main-race wins and a sprint-race victory around the 3.7-mile track. It brought to an end Verstappen's 2024 qualifying whitewash. But how much was due to circuit specialism and how much to Red Bull's upgrade?

"I honestly think it's the most significant upgrade we've made, and if we can keep going in that direction, I think we can turn our season around," Pérez said. "If I'd come here with the balance issues I've had for the last few races, I wouldn't have had the confidence, which is what you need here. It's good to be a couple of tenths quicker than Max, but I'd prefer that he was on pole and it wasn't Charles four-tenths away!"

Splitting the Red Bulls, fifth, was George Russell with the first Mercedes, some four-tenths ahead of seventh-placed team-mate Lewis Hamilton. Russell was happy with that after a scrappy practice day when he'd been slower than Lewis. Meanwhile, Hamilton wore a resigned expression when he said, "It's the same old story on a Saturday. The car felt great yesterday, amazing, and I was thinking second row worst case, but then today, the tyres don't work."

On a circuit where driver input is perhaps a bigger percentage of the overall equation, it was no surprise to see Fernando Alonso put his Aston Martin eighth, less than a tenth behind Hamilton.

The Williams pair completed the top ten – a great result for the team and an even better one for Franco Colapinto. The young Argentine had never seen the track before and didn't get off to the greatest of starts when he clobbered the wall at T4 in FP1. But then to have the confidence to flirt so outrageously with the walls in qualifying and actually outqualify Alex Albon was a truly remarkable effort.

Another fine performance came from Oliver Bearman, who had passed the grand old age of 19 after making his Jeddah F1 debut in the absent Carlos Sainz's Ferrari. This time, he was substituting for Kevin Magnussen at Haas, the Dane being the first to suffer a race ban for accumulating 12 penalty points on his F1 super-licence in a 12-month period. The young Briton might have had an Azerbaijan F2 victory on his CV, but it was still a superb effort to just miss out on Q3 by a tenth and to go two-tenths quicker than team-mate Nico Hülkenberg, one of the standout qualifiers of the season, who would start 13th.

Pierre Gasly had actually done a stellar job to qualify an Alpine a couple of hundredths quicker than 'The Hulk', but, alas, he had exceeded the mass fuel flow limit and was disqualified.

Yuki Tsunoda, 12th, was fully half a second quicker than VCARB team-mate Daniel Ricciardo as once more the rumour mill churned with stories of the Australian's impending replacement by Liam Lawson.

Joining the disgruntled Norris outside the top 15 were the hapless Alpine drivers (one with a damaged car, the other disqualified), and Sauber men Valtteri Bottas and Zhou Guanyu. Both Zhou and Ocon elected to take replacement power units, as did Hamilton who, along with Ocon, also made changes to the car and would start from the pit lane.

WITH Oscar Piastri having finished ahead of McLaren team-mate Lando Norris in Monza, much had been made – again – about whether the team should begin prioritising Norris's challenge for the championship.

Heading into the Azerbaijan weekend, team principal Andrea Stella said, "What has changed is that after two-thirds of the season, we are in the quest for the constructors' and the drivers' championships. And we acknowledge, together with Lando and Oscar, that Lando is in the most favourable position. So, if we want to give it a go, we should try to support Lando. We will do this when and if necessary, especially on those 50/50 calls. They will now more naturally end up in Lando's territory while we see if we can make this drivers' championship quest even more realistic. Then we will reassess in a couple of races and see where we are."

Interesting, but with Piastri on the front row and Norris starting 15th (after Lewis Hamilton's pit-lane start), McLaren's new direction was unlikely to be relevant at this particular race!

Charles Leclerc's immediate goal was to convert his third pole position of the year and put Piastri's McLaren outside DRS range as quickly as possible. Traditionally, Baku is a one-stop race, and the first 13 cars on the grid – except Alex Albon – all started on the medium-compound Pirelli. Others seeking to extend the opening stint, thereby growing the window for a cheap tyre stop if there were to be an obliging safety car, were Daniel Ricciardo and the out-of-place Norris, Zhou Guanyu, Alpine drivers Pierre Gasly and Esteban Ocon, and Hamilton.

When the lights went out, Leclerc made no mistake and took the Ferrari cleanly through Turn One in front. Piastri slotted into second and Sergio Pérez got through the first corner side by side with Carlos Sainz. Into Turn Two, Sainz had little option but to cede position. Behind him, Max Verstappen jumped George Russell's Mercedes, with Fernando Alonso, Franco Colapinto, Albon and Oliver Bearman filling the top ten. Behind them came Lance Stroll (soon to report a puncture after contact with Tsunoda), Norris (up a couple of positions), Nico Hülkenberg, Ricciardo, Valtteri Bottas, Gasly, Zhou, and pit-lane starters Hamilton and Esteban Ocon.

Although Leclerc's start and opening lap were good, he was unable to break the DRS to Piastri and was forced to keep a weather eye on the McLaren as they headed down into Turn One to start the third lap. Further back, a 5s gap developed behind Bearman's tenth-placed Haas back to Tsunoda, who was struggling after his opening-lap contact with Stroll, and who had Norris anxious to be past. By forcing Yuki to go defensive into Turn One on lap four, the McLaren got a better exit and was down the inside into Turn Two to claim 11th. Hülkenberg followed him through.

Despite his devastating qualifying speed, Leclerc was not getting away from Piastri, who set quickest lap of the race on lap six to remain within DRS range. Leclerc responded with an even faster lap next time around, however, dropping the McLaren 1.5s behind, with Pérez's Red Bull 2s behind the Australian. Sainz was a similar distance further back, with Verstappen keeping the Spaniard honest, but suffering with brake locking. Nobody was running close enough to risk unnecessary tyre degradation. Hamilton was already reporting that the hard tyre didn't feel great, while Piastri, losing some ground to the leading Ferrari, could feel the rears of his mediums beginning to go away.

Norris whittled down the gap to tenth-placed Bearman, who had fallen 3s behind the Williams duo, with Colapinto still the lead car. Lando got a move done with minimum fuss down the inside of Turn One to move the second McLaren into the points.

By lap nine, Hülkenberg was on the back of his new one-off rookie team-mate, Bearman, the team orchestrating

Above: Charles Leclerc put his Ferrari on pole for the fourth successive time in Baku.
Photo: Scuderia Ferrari

Above left: Lewis Hamilton was somewhat nonplussed at the Mercedes' lack of speed in qualifying.
Photo: Mercedes-AMG Petronas F1 Team

Left: A window on the world captures Sergio Pérez passing in his Red Bull.
Photo: Pirelli

Opening spread: Oscar Piastri managed to grab the lead from Leclerc just before half-distance and held the advantage as the Ferrari wore its tyres in the dirty air.
Photo: XPB Images

Above: George Russell was surprised, but delighted, to finish on the podium for Mercedes.
Photo: Mercedes-AMG Petronas F1 Team

Top right: Franco Colapinto scored points for Williams in only his second grand prix start.

Above right: With Kevin Magnussen serving a one-race ban, Ollie Bearman stepped in for Haas and delivered an impressive tenth place for the team.

Right: Seventh for Alex Albon capped a great haul of points in Baku for Williams.
Photos: Pirelli

a position swap on the following lap, which left the youngster to fend off a closing Ricciardo.

As far as relative tyre performance between the medium and hard was concerned, race engineer Will Joseph told the hard-shod Norris, "The medium is not graining yet. If anything, it's suffering from thermal deg. You are doing a better job than the other car. They are struggling with the rears."

First of the medium runners into the pits, just 11 laps into the race's 51, was Colapinto, suggesting that Williams was thinking about two stops or a very long hard-compound stint. Aston Martin elected to cover him off with Alonso next time around, while Verstappen and Russell were in on lap 13 to switch to hards.

At the front, Leclerc was starting to break away as the pit-stop window for the leaders approached, some 5s clear of Piastri by lap 13. Pérez was still a respectful 2s behind the McLaren, with Sainz following a similar distance back from the Mexican.

On lap 14, Red Bull pitted Pérez in an attempt to undercut Piastri, but, unfortunately, he rejoined just behind Norris, who had been running strongly on his starting hards once in clear air. Surprisingly, though, McLaren did not pit Piastri on the following lap in response as Leclerc set another fastest lap and opened out his lead to 6s.

Realising that they were going to need a bit of help, McLaren got on the radio to Norris and asked him, "Lando, can you do anything to hold Pérez up in the middle sector without hurting yourself?"

"Yes, how long?" Norris wanted to know.

"One or two laps."

In view of Andrea Stella's pre-race, intra-team state-of-play declaration, this was ironic! But it worked a treat, as Oscar stopped on lap 16 and came back out only just ahead of Pérez, who had despatched Norris down the front straight into Turn One.

Ferrari, too, were a bit lackadaisical in pitting the race leader next time around, Leclerc coming back out only just ahead of Albon, who had driven a fine first stint on his hards. Right behind the Williams were Piastri and Pérez, so Charles's hard-earned 6s buffer had been wiped out at a stroke. Ferrari pitted Sainz on the following lap, the second Maranello car only just holding track position over Verstappen.

As Leclerc brought his hard tyres in conservatively, Piastri closed on him all the way around lap 19 to the point where he picked up DRS down the front straight. As they reached the braking area, he was closing, but still appeared to be too far back to dive-bomb the Ferrari down the inside. Leclerc clearly thought so, too, as he didn't bother defending and left the door open.

Piastri, thinking that it might be the only chance he'd get, pulled off a superb overtake that caught Leclerc napping. He only just managed to keep the McLaren out of the tyres on exit, then defended against a counter-pass from the Ferrari.

Leclerc, surprised and no doubt irked, didn't panic. He thought he would have ample opportunity to repay the compliment over the second half of the race, albeit that his Ferrari did not feel as strong on the hard tyre as it had done on the medium.

At half-distance then, Piastri, Leclerc and Pérez were involved in a three-way tussle at the front, with Sainz's Ferrari some 8s further back in fourth place once he had worked his way past Albon. The Williams ran fifth, still on its starting hards, with Norris right behind, but also with a stop to make and under pressure from Verstappen. George Russell was a further 5s back with the first Mercedes, with a 10s margin over Alonso's Aston Martin.

Hamilton was enduring something of a nightmare after his pit-lane start on the hard tyre. "Lewis, anything you can do to bring the surface temperature down?" engineer Pete Bonnington asked him.

"I'm trying," Lewis confirmed as he contemplated life from 14th place, some 25s behind his team-mate with a stop still to make. His only scant consolation was that he was 12s ahead of Ocon's Alpine, which also had started from the pits.

Albon made his pit stop for mediums on lap 32, rejoining just behind team-mate Colapinto. Norris, meanwhile, kept going, still able to fend off a frustrated Verstappen on his fresher tyres. The three-times champion was not happy. "I have no rear grip, the car is just jumping on the rear, losing contact," he complained.

As if to prove the point, he was powerless to resist Russell, who went down the inside of the Red Bull into Turn One to relieve the Dutchman of his sixth place on lap 34.

Meanwhile, Pérez was still very much in the frame at the front. Leclerc had his best look at Piastri's lead into Turn One with 16 laps remaining, but Oscar defended masterfully, in the manner that Charles had failed to do at the beginning of the stint, their brief fight bringing Sergio into DRS range as well.

Meanwhile, Piastri's engineer, Tom Stallard, gave his driver an update on tyres. "Leclerc's tyres look worse than yours at the rear, slightly better on front," he said.

Further back, Hülkenberg moved his Haas into ninth place when he passed Colapinto into Turn One, then set his sights on eighth-placed Alonso, just another 1s ahead.

With 15 laps to go, Leclerc received an unexpected "Box opposite McLaren" instruction from the pits. It didn't seem to make any sense, given that it would mean losing track positions to Pérez, Sainz and possibly Russell, without enough remaining laps to recover them. As Piastri blasted past the pit entry, Leclerc also stayed out, unsurprisingly. If it was supposed to be a bluff, it wasn't a very good one. And McLaren certainly wasn't buying it.

Without a safety car to help Norris's cause, McLaren

269

Above: The crash between Sainz and Pérez promoted Fernando Alonso's Aston Martin into sixth.
Photo: Aston Martin Aramco F1 Team

Top right: Lando Norris drove a brilliant race from 15th to fourth. He had not expected to close the gap to championship rival Verstappen on the grid.
Photo: McLaren F1 Team

Above right: How was it for you? F2 graduates Colapinto and Bearman in *parc fermé* post race.
Photo: XPB Images

Right: McLaren race engineer Tom Stallard and Piastri toast their victory, while Leclerc reflects on a missed opportunity.
Photo: McLaren F1 Team

finally pitted him after 38 laps. He rejoined seventh, some 15s behind Verstappen with 13 laps to go.

On lap 39, Ferrari asked Leclerc, "We are thinking about Plan C, what do you think?"

"It is not stupid," he responded. But given the basic maths involved, if Plan C was a pit stop, it probably was.

Next time around, Leclerc, as close as ever, told his team, "Piastri is starting to struggle."

"Copy, keep it up," they told him. This all felt like Ferrari still trying to bluff McLaren into pitting the race leader again, but that wasn't going to happen.

Meanwhile, Norris was taking chunks out of the gap to Verstappen, nearly 2s in a single lap, but he received a pit message from Will Joseph to temper his enthusiasm. "Imagine Andrea [Stella] on your shoulder saying, 'Zero wheelspin every exit,'" he was told.

On lap 41, Hamilton finally got down the inside of Bearman's Haas to move into 12th place, just 1.5s behind Colapinto, who was 4.5s back from Hülkenberg in the last points position.

As the race entered its closing laps, Leclerc was paying the price for running so close to Piastri for so long and, as McLaren had accurately observed, his rear tyres were in poor shape, and he started to drop out of DRS range to the lead McLaren. He had Pérez back within threatening distance, while Sainz, after a later pit stop, had now caught the Red Bull. Meanwhile, Norris had set the race's fastest lap and was just 2s behind Verstappen for sixth with four laps to go.

"No rear tyres, no rear tyres at all," Leclerc told the Ferrari pit.

Norris had plenty, though, and used them to good effect to demote Verstappen to seventh in a rare move around the outside into Turn One with three to go.

Starting the penultimate lap, Pérez got a DRS run on Leclerc and tried to do to Charles what Lando had done to Max. This time, the Ferrari driver defended the inside, as he should have done with Piastri earlier in the stint, and braved it out side by side with Pérez through T1. Sergio was forced to get out of the throttle briefly, which was all Sainz needed to steal his third place. Unfortunately for Carlos, he ran a little too deep into Turn Two and Pérez got alongside again on exit. Both trying to pick up the slipstream from Leclerc, they made contact and exited needlessly stage left into the wall. Six of one, half a dozen of the other. Pérez was furious, Sainz bemused.

After his best weekend in ages, it was a sad end for the Mexican. It also impacted on his struggling team-mate by elevating Norris to fourth. Not only that, but Verstappen, with a pit-stop window behind him to Alonso, had stopped for a set of softs to pinch Norris's fastest lap and effect a two-point championship swing. But the resulting VSC put paid to that…

With a superb win by Piastri and Norris's fourth place, McLaren had finally knocked Red Bull off the top of the pile and led the constructors' championship for the first time since a brief one-race spell in Melbourne, 2014, at the very beginning of the hybrid era!

"Yesss," Piastri allowed himself quietly over the radio, in the nearest we'd yet seen to unbridled emotion. He quickly checked himself, however, returning immediately to default laid-back mode.

"Well done everybody. That was probably the most stressful afternoon of my life. Thank you. What a day that was," he reflected.

The Ferrari debrief would have been sombre. How had they lost that one? Simple. They had pitted Leclerc a lap too late and put him in jeopardy from Piastri when he hadn't needed to be. And then Charles himself had left the door open. Nobody would have left Azerbaijan more frustrated. But as well as Ferrari losing it, Piastri had truly won it with that superb overtake and then supreme coolness under constant pressure. He was beginning to look genuinely top class.

Russell was very surprised to be on the podium; Norris was delighted with an unexpected fourth – he had not expected to start 15th and finish ahead of Verstappen. The Sainz/Pérez incident promoted Alonso to sixth, and the Williams pair to seventh and eighth, while Colapinto scored his first F1 points in only his second start. Hamilton finished ninth from the pit lane, and the final point went to Bearman, both having passed Hülkenberg, who had suffered front wing damage when he ran over debris from the accident. He thought that the race should have finished under a safety car or even a red flag.

A truly absorbing race. Formula 1's competitiveness had never been closer.

Tony Dodgins

VIEWPOINT
BEYOND ALL DOUBT

THERE might have been a haze of controversy surrounding Oscar Piastri's win in Hungary, but this one was as clear as day. It was down to him – ironically, with a little help from his team-mate. But it was nothing like the awkward team shuffle at the Hungaroring.

Lando Norris was never in contention from the moment a badly timed yellow wrecked his qualifying. Starting back in 15th place, his was a race of damage limitation. It so happened that the strategy had put him in front of Sergio Pérez as the Mexican emerged from his pit stop, looking to undercut Piastri, then in second place. Norris was asked if he could delay the Red Bull within reason and without compromising his own position too much. He did the job perfectly by neutralising Checo. Meanwhile, Piastri had been putting the hammer down, doing enough to get in and out of the pits and be in a position to get on with the job.

Piastri knew exactly what he had to do. So much so that he disregarded a note of caution from Tom Stallard when the engineer warned him not to push too hard, too soon on new tyres when going after Charles Leclerc's leading Ferrari. It was a fair warning, but, in Piastri's mind, outweighed by the advantage of running in clean air. Rather than hold back and damage his tyres in the wake of the Ferrari, Oscar needed to go for it. Now!

It was one of those moves that came from a long way back – as in 'He can't be? Can he? Yes, he has!' That appeared to be Leclerc's unsuspecting view as he left the door open and the McLaren came down the inside with an overtake that, Oscar admitted later, was 50/50 as he j·u·s·t managed to avoid the wall on the exit. Game over.

The admiration for Piastri had to be matched with sympathy for Leclerc. The master of qualifying with a supreme lap that was three-tenths clear for a fourth consecutive Baku pole, he had done absolutely nothing wrong on a day when his team-mate had done everything absolutely right. And some.

Maurice Hamilton

17

FORMULA 1 QATAR AIRWAYS AZERBAIJAN GRAND PRIX 2024

BAKU 13-15 SEPTEMBER
RACE DISTANCE: 51 laps, 190.170 miles/306.049km
RACE WEATHER: Dry/sunny (track 40-45°C, air 27-28°C)

BAKU CITY CIRCUIT
Circuit: 3.730 miles/6.003km, 51 laps

RACE – OFFICIAL CLASSIFICATION

Pos.	Driver	Nat.	No.	Entrant	Car/Engine	Laps	Time/Retirement	Speed (mph/km/h)	Gap to leader	Fastest race lap
1	Oscar Piastri	AUS	81	McLaren Formula 1 Team	McLaren MCL38-Mercedes F1 M15 E Perf. V6	51	1h 32m 58.007s	122.734/197.521		1m 47.060s 47
2	Charles Leclerc	MC	16	Scuderia Ferrari	Ferrari SF-24-066/12 V6	51	1h 33m 08.917s	122.494/197.135	10.910s	1m 47.067s 44
3	George Russell	GB	63	Mercedes-AMG Petronas F1 Team	Mercedes-AMG F1 W15-M15 E Perf. V6	51	1h 33m 29.335s	122.048/196.418	31.328s	1m 46.628s 45
4	Lando Norris	GB	4	McLaren Formula 1 Team	McLaren MCL38-Mercedes F1 M15 E Perf. V6	51	1h 33m 34.150s	121.943/196.249	36.143s	1m 45.255s 42
5	Max Verstappen	NL	1	Oracle Red Bull Racing	Red Bull RB20-Honda RBPT H002 V6	51	1h 34m 15.105s	121.061/194.828	1m 17.098s	1m 46.798s 42
6	Fernando Alonso	E	14	Aston Martin Aramco F1 Team	Aston Martin AMR24-Mercedes F1 M15 E Perf. V6	51	1h 34m 23.475s	120.882/194.540	1m 25.468s	1m 47.057s 48
7	Alexander Albon	T	23	Williams Racing	Williams FW46-Mercedes F1 M15 E Perf. V6	51	1h 34m 25.403s	120.841/194.474	1m 27.396s	1m 46.947s 43
8	Franco Colapinto	RA	43	Williams Racing	Williams FW46-Mercedes F1 M15 E Perf. V6	51	1h 34m 27.548s	120.795/194.400	1m 29.541s	1m 47.274s 44
9	Lewis Hamilton	GB	44	Mercedes-AMG Petronas F1 Team	Mercedes-AMG F1 W15-M15 E Perf. V6	51	1h 34m 30.408s	120.734/194.302	1m 32.401s	1m 47.236s 48
10	Oliver Bearman	GB	50	MoneyGram Haas F1 Team	Haas VF-24-Ferrari 066/10 V6	51	1h 34m 31.134s	120.718/194.277	1m 33.127s	1m 47.048s 47
11	Nico Hülkenberg	D	27	MoneyGram Haas F1 Team	Haas VF-24-Ferrari 066/10 V6	51	1h 34m 31.472s	120.711/194.266	1m 33.465s	1m 47.691s 42
12	Pierre Gasly	F	10	BWT Alpine F1 Team	Alpine A524-Renault E-Tech RE24 V6	51	1h 34m 55.196s	120.209/193.457	1m 57.189s	1m 48.018s 47
13	Daniel Ricciardo	AUS	3	Visa Cash App RB Formula One Team	RB VCARB 01-Honda RBPT H002 V6	51	1h 35m 24.914s	119.584/192.452	2m 26.907s	1m 48.380s 39
14	Zhou Guanyu	CHN	24	Stake F1 Team Kick Sauber	Sauber C44-Ferrari 066/12 V6	51	1h 35m 26.848s	119.544/192.387	2m 28.841s	1m 47.644s 43
15	Esteban Ocon	F	31	BWT Alpine F1 Team	Alpine A524-Renault E-Tech RE24 V6	50			1 lap	1m 48.831s 35
16	Valtteri Bottas	FIN	77	Stake F1 Team Kick Sauber	Sauber C44-Ferrari 066/12 V6	50			1 lap	1m 48.418s 41
17	Sergio Pérez	MEX	11	Oracle Red Bull Racing	Red Bull RB20-Honda RBPT H002 V6	49	accident		2 laps	1m 47.013s 46
18	Carlos Sainz	E	55	Scuderia Ferrari	Ferrari SF-24-066/12 V6	49	accident		2 laps	1m 46.866s 46
19	Lance Stroll	CDN	18	Aston Martin Aramco F1 Team	Aston Martin AMR24-Mercedes F1 M15 E Perf. V6	45	brakes		6 laps	1m 48.148s 31
	Yuki Tsunoda	J	22	Visa Cash App RB Formula One Team	RB VCARB 01-Honda RBPT H002 V6	14	accident damage			1m 50.887s 8

DHL Fastest race lap (scores 1 point): Lando Norris on lap 42, 1m 45.255s, 127.579mph/205.318km/h.
Lap record: Charles Leclerc (Ferrari SF90 V6), 1m 43.009s, 130.361mph/209.795km/h (2019).

20 · OCON · Alpine
Car modified in parc fermé; required to start from the pit lane

18 · GASLY · Alpine

16 · BOTTAS · Sauber

14 · RICCIARDO · RB

12 · HÜLKENBERG · Haas

19 · HAMILTON · Mercedes
Car modified in parc fermé; required to start from the pit lane

17 · ZHOU · Sauber
Used additional power unit elements; required to start from the back of the grid

15 · NORRIS · McLaren

13 · STROLL · Aston Martin

11 · TSUNODA · RB

Grid order	1	2	3	4	5	6	7	8	9	10	11	12	13	14	15	16	17	18	19	20	21	22	23	24	25	26	27	28	29	30	31	32	33	34	35	36	37	38	39	40	41
16 LECLERC	16	16	16	16	16	16	16	16	16	16	16	16	16	16	16	55	16	16	81	81	81	81	81	81	81	81	81	81	81	81	81	81	81	81	81	81	81	81	81	81	81
81 PIASTRI	81	81	81	81	81	81	81	81	81	81	81	81	81	55	55	16	81	81	16	16	16	16	16	16	16	16	16	16	16	16	16	16	16	16	16	16	16	16	16	16	16
55 SAINZ	11	11	11	11	11	11	11	11	11	11	55	55	81	23	81	23	11	11	11	11	11	11	11	11	11	11	11	11	11	11	11	11	11	11	11	11	11	11	11	11	11
11 PÉREZ	55	55	55	55	55	55	55	55	55	55	11	23	23	81	23	11	23	23	23	23	23	55	55	55	55	55	55	55	55	55	55	55	55	55	55	55	55	55	55	55	55
63 RUSSELL	1	1	1	1	1	1	1	1	1	1	23	4	11	11	4	4	55	23	23	23	23	23	4	4	4	4	4	4	4	4	63	63	63	63	63	63	63	63	63	63	63
1 VERSTAPPEN	63	63	63	63	63	63	63	63	63	63	63	11	4	4	55	55	4	4	4	4	4	4	1	1	1	63	63	63	63	4	1	1	1	1	1	1	1	1	1	1	1
14 ALONSO	14	14	14	14	14	14	14	14	14	14	14	23	23	27	27	1	1	1	1	1	1	1	63	63	63	1	1	1	4	4	4	4	4	4	4	4	4	4	4	4	4
43 COLAPINTO	43	43	43	43	43	43	43	43	43	23	14	4	50	1	27	63	63	63	63	63	63	63	63	63	63	23	14	14	14	14	14	14	14	14	14	14	14	14	14	14	14
23 ALBON	23	23	23	23	23	23	23	23	23	4	27	1	10	10	1	14	14	14	14	14	14	14	14	14	14	14	14	14	43	43	43	43	27	27	27	23	23	23	23	23	23
50 BEARMAN	50	50	50	50	50	50	4	4	43	50	4	50	63	63	63	10	10	10	43	43	43	43	43	43	43	43	43	43	27	27	27	27	43	23	23	27	27	27	27	27	27
22 TSUNODA	22	22	4	4	4	4	50	50	4	43	50	27	14	43	43	43	43	43	10	10	10	10	10	10	10	10	27	27	23	23	23	23	23	43	43	43	43	43	43	43	43
27 HÜLKENBERG	4	4	27	27	27	27	27	27	50	3	10	63	50	3	3	3	3	3	27	27	27	27	27	27	27	27	10	10	10	10	50	50	50	50	50	50	50	50	50	50	44
18 STROLL	27	27	3	3	3	3	3	3	3	10	3	14	14	14	14	43	27	27	3	3	3	3	50	50	50	50	50	50	50	50	44	44	44	44	44	44	44	44	44	44	50
3 RICCIARDO	3	3	22	10	10	10	10	10	10	44	44	43	43	24	24	50	50	50	50	50	44	44	44	44	44	44	44	44	44	44	10	10	10	10	10	10	10	10	10	10	10
4 NORRIS	10	10	10	44	44	44	44	44	44	43	43	24	44	44	44	44	44	44	44	44	24	24	24	24	24	24	3	3	3	3	3	3	3	3	3	3	3	3	3	3	3
77 BOTTAS	77	44	44	22	22	22	22	22	22	24	24	31	24	24	31	44	24	24	24	24	31	31	31	31	31	31	24	24	24	24	24	24	24	24	24	31	31	31	31	31	31
24 ZHOU	44	77	77	77	77	77	77	77	24	18	18	44	44	31	31	31	31	31	31	31	31	31	31	31	31	24	18	18	18	18	18	18	18	18	18
10 GASLY	24	24	24	24	24	24	24	24	31	31	31	18	44	44	18	18	18	18	18	77	77	77	77	77	77	18	77	77	77	77	77	77	77	77	77	77	77	77	77	77	77
44 HAMILTON	31	31	31	31	31	31	31	31	77	77	22	77	77	77	77	77	77	77	77	18	18	18	18	18	18	77	24	24	24	24	24	24	24	24	24
31 OCON	18	18	18	18	18	18	18	18	77	77	22	22																													

VSC Virtual Safety Car deployed on lap 51

TIME SHEETS

PRACTICE 1 (FRIDAY)
Weather: Dry/sunny
Temperatures: track 41-45°C, air 32-33°C

Pos.	Driver	Laps	Time
1	Max Verstappen	21	1m 45.546s
2	Lewis Hamilton	19	1m 45.859s
3	Sergio Pérez	17	1m 45.922s
4	Lando Norris	18	1m 46.027s
5	Carlos Sainz	21	1m 46.173s
6	Oscar Piastri	18	1m 46.282s
7	Fernando Alonso	19	1m 46.452s
8	George Russell	18	1m 46.516s
9	Charles Leclerc	11	1m 46.608s
10	Daniel Ricciardo	23	1m 46.687s
11	Oliver Bearman	23	1m 46.973s
12	Nico Hülkenberg	20	1m 47.135s
13	Lance Stroll	15	1m 47.184s
14	Valtteri Bottas	18	1m 47.640s
15	Yuki Tsunoda	21	1m 47.708s
16	Franco Colapinto	12	1m 47.901s
17	Alexander Albon	17	1m 47.955s
18	Pierre Gasly	21	1m 48.712s
19	Zhou Guanyu	19	1m 49.052s
20	Esteban Ocon	3	no time

PRACTICE 2 (FRIDAY)
Weather: Dry/sunny
Temperatures: track 32-33°C, air 28-29°C

Pos.	Driver	Laps	Time
1	Charles Leclerc	20	1m 43.484s
2	Sergio Pérez	23	1m 43.490s
3	Lewis Hamilton	22	1m 43.550s
4	Carlos Sainz	25	1m 43.950s
5	Oscar Piastri	25	1m 43.983s
6	Max Verstappen	24	1m 44.029s
7	Lance Stroll	24	1m 44.093s
8	Nico Hülkenberg	24	1m 44.475s
9	George Russell	16	1m 44.536s
10	Oliver Bearman	24	1m 44.547s
11	Yuki Tsunoda	24	1m 44.645s
12	Fernando Alonso	25	1m 44.683s
13	Alexander Albon	25	1m 44.737s
14	Franco Colapinto	23	1m 44.749s
15	Valtteri Bottas	24	1m 44.785s
16	Daniel Ricciardo	26	1m 45.056s
17	Lando Norris	25	1m 45.156s
18	Pierre Gasly	22	1m 45.391s
19	Esteban Ocon	24	1m 45.810s
20	Zhou Guanyu	25	1m 45.947s

PRACTICE 3 (SATURDAY)
Weather: Dry/cloudy
Temperatures: track 33-37°C, air 28-29°C

Pos.	Driver	Laps	Time
1	George Russell	15	1m 42.514s
2	Charles Leclerc	17	1m 42.527s
3	Lando Norris	15	1m 42.737s
4	Oscar Piastri	14	1m 42.749s
5	Max Verstappen	16	1m 42.862s
6	Carlos Sainz	17	1m 42.968s
7	Sergio Pérez	16	1m 43.024s
8	Alexander Albon	14	1m 43.194s
9	Franco Colapinto	15	1m 43.238s
10	Lewis Hamilton	13	1m 43.301s
11	Fernando Alonso	15	1m 43.474s
12	Yuki Tsunoda	17	1m 43.503s
13	Lance Stroll	19	1m 43.571s
14	Daniel Ricciardo	18	1m 43.870s
15	Pierre Gasly	15	1m 43.876s
16	Nico Hülkenberg	13	1m 44.164s
17	Valtteri Bottas	18	1m 44.187s
18	Zhou Guanyu	20	1m 44.869s
19	Esteban Ocon	1	no time
20	Oliver Bearman	2	no time

QUALIFYING (SATURDAY)
Weather: Dry/sunny   Temperatures: track 34-37°C, air 28-30°C

Pos.	Driver	First	Second	Third	Qualifying Tyre
1	Charles Leclerc	1m 42.775s	1m 42.056s	1m 41.365s	Soft (n)
2	Oscar Piastri	1m 43.033s	1m 42.598s	1m 41.686s	Soft (n)
3	Carlos Sainz	1m 43.357s	1m 42.503s	1m 41.805s	Soft (n)
4	Sergio Pérez	1m 43.213s	1m 42.263s	1m 41.813s	Soft (n)
5	George Russell	1m 43.139s	1m 42.329s	1m 41.874s	Soft (n)
6	Max Verstappen	1m 43.097s	1m 42.042s	1m 42.023s	Soft (n)
7	Lewis Hamilton	1m 43.089s	1m 42.765s	1m 42.289s	Soft (n)
8	Fernando Alonso	1m 43.472s	1m 42.426s	1m 42.369s	Soft (n)
9	Franco Colapinto	1m 43.138s	1m 42.473s	1m 42.530s	Soft (n)
10	Alexander Albon	1m 42.899s	1m 42.840s	1m 42.859s	Soft (u)
11	Oliver Bearman	1m 43.471s	1m 42.968s		
12	Yuki Tsunoda	1m 43.337s	1m 43.035s		
*	Pierre Gasly	1m 43.088s	1m 43.179s		
13	Nico Hülkenberg	1m 43.101s	1m 43.191s		
14	Lance Stroll	1m 43.370s	1m 43.404s		
15	Daniel Ricciardo	1m 43.547s			
16	Lando Norris	1m 43.609s			
17	Valtteri Bottas	1m 43.618s			
18	Zhou Guanyu	1m 44.246s			
19	Esteban Ocon	1m 44.504s			

* DQ from the qualifying classification for a technical infringement (exceeding the instantaneous fuel mass flow limit).

QUALIFYING: head to head

Verstappen	16		1	Pérez
Hamilton	4		13	Russell
Norris	13		4	Piastri
Leclerc	11		5	Sainz
Leclerc	1		0	Bearman
Gasly	7		10	Ocon
Alonso	11		6	Stroll
Albon	14		1	Sargeant
Albon	1		1	Colapinto
Bottas	16		1	Zhou
Tsunoda	11		6	Ricciardo
Magnussen	4		12	Hülkenberg
Bearman	1		0	Hülkenberg

FOR THE RECORD

1st POINTS: Franco Colapinto

500th GP LED: Ferrari

200th GP WITH A PODIUM: Mercedes

100,000th GP KM RACED: Lewis Hamilton

DID YOU KNOW?

Colapinto is the first Argentinian driver to start from the top 10 since Carlos Reutemann at the 1982 Brazilian GP.

Kevin Magnussen's ban from this event, having accrued 12 penalty points, was the first ban since the 2012 Italian GP (Grosjean for dangerous driving in the Belgian GP).

POINTS

DRIVERS

1	Max Verstappen	313
2	Lando Norris	254
3	Charles Leclerc	235
4	Oscar Piastri	222
5	Carlos Sainz	184
6	Lewis Hamilton	166
7	George Russell	143
8	Sergio Pérez	143
9	Fernando Alonso	58
10	Lance Stroll	24
11	Nico Hülkenberg	22
12	Yuki Tsunoda	22
13	Alexander Albon	12
14	Daniel Ricciardo	12
15	Pierre Gasly	8
16	Oliver Bearman	7
17	Kevin Magnussen	6
18	Esteban Ocon	5
19	Franco Colapinto	4

CONSTRUCTORS

1	McLaren	476
2	Red Bull	456
3	Ferrari	425
4	Mercedes	309
5	Aston Martin	82
6	RB	34
7	Haas	29
8	Williams	16
9	Alpine	13

10 · BEARMAN · Haas   8 · COLAPINTO · Williams   6 · VERSTAPPEN · Red Bull   4 · PÉREZ · Red Bull   2 · PIASTRI · McLaren

9 · ALBON · Williams   7 · ALONSO · Aston Martin   5 · RUSSELL · Mercedes   3 · SAINZ · Ferrari   1 · LECLERC · Ferrari

Lap chart (right portion)

42	43	44	45	46	47	48	49	50	51	*
81	81	81	81	81	81	81	81	81	81	1
16	16	16	16	16	16	16	16	16	16	2
11	11	11	11	11	11	11	11	63	63	3
55	55	55	55	55	55	55	55	4	4	4
63	63	63	63	63	63	63	63	1	1	5
1	1	1	1	1	1	1	4	14	14	6
4	4	4	4	4	4	4	1	23	23	7
14	14	14	14	14	14	14	14	43	43	8
23	23	23	23	23	23	23	23	44	44	9
27	27	27	27	27	27	27	27	43	50	10
43	43	43	43	43	43	43	27	27	27	
44	44	44	44	44	44	44	44	10	10	
50	50	50	50	50	50	50	50	3	3	
10	10	10	10	10	10	10	10	24	24	
3	3	3	3	3	3	3	3	3	31	
31	31	31	31	31	31	31	24	24		
18	18	18	77	24	24	24	31	31		
77	77	77	24	77	77	77	77			
24	24	24	18							

18 = Pit stop   *18* = One lap or more behind

VSC

RACE TYRE STRATEGIES

	Driver	Race Stint 1	Race Stint 2	Race Stint 3
1	Piastri	Medium (n): 1-15	Hard (n): 16-51	
2	Leclerc	Medium (n): 1-16	Hard (n): 17-51	
3	Russell	Medium (n): 1-12	Hard (n): 13-51	
4	Norris	Hard (n): 1-37	Medium (n): 38-51	
5	Verstappen	Medium (n): 1-12	Hard (n): 13-49	Soft (u): 50-51
6	Alonso	Medium (u): 1-11	Hard (n): 12-51	
7	Albon	Hard (n): 1-31	Medium (n): 32-51	
8	Colapinto	Medium (n): 1-10	Hard (n): 11-51	
9	Hamilton	Medium (n): 1-12	Hard (n): 13-51	
10	Bearman	Medium (n): 1-14	Hard (n): 15-51	
11	Hülkenberg	Medium (n): 1-15	Hard (n): 16-51	
12	Gasly	Hard (n): 1-50	Soft (n): 51	
13	Ricciardo	Hard (u): 1-49	Soft (n): 50-51	
14	Zhou	Hard (u): 1-34	Medium (n): 35-51	
15	Ocon	Hard (u): 1-49	Soft (n): 50	
16	Bottas	Medium (u): 1-11	Hard (u): 12-50	
17	Pérez	Medium (n): 1-13	Hard (n): 14-49 (dnf)	
18	Sainz	Medium (n): 1-17	Hard (n): 18-49 (dnf)	
19	Stroll	Medium (u): 1	Hard (n): 2-22	Hard (u): 23-45 (dnf)
	Tsunoda	Medium (u): 1-12	Hard (n): 13-14 (dnf)	

The tyre regulations stipulate that at least two of three dry tyre specifications must be used during a dry race.
Selected compounds for Baku: Red = Soft (C5); Yellow = Medium (C4); White = Hard (C3). (n) new (u) used

273

FIA FORMULA 1 WORLD CHAMPIONSHIP · ROUND 18
SINGAPORE GRAND PRIX
MARINA BAY CIRCUIT

MARINA BAY QUALIFYING

BEFORE any on-track action at Marina Bay, there was a minor controversy about swearing and the amount of it broadcast during radio transmissions. FIA president Mohammed Ben Sulayem wanted the show cleaned up. But the way in which he conveyed that didn't sit too comfortably.

"We have to differentiate between our sport – motorsport – and rap music," Ben Sulayem said. "We're not rappers, you know. They say the F-word how many times per minute? We are not on that. That's them and we are [us]."

Lewis Hamilton was unimpressed. "I don't like how he expressed it," he said. "Saying 'rappers' is very stereotypical, as most rappers are black. It really kind of points towards 'We are not like them,' so I think that was the wrong choice of words and there's a racial element there. I agree that things need clearing up a bit, but it's also good to have some emotion. We're not robots."

The general consensus was that when these guys are doing 200mph-plus and someone does something that might put them into the wall, the reaction is unlikely to be the King's English, perfectly enunciated. Besides, fans want emotion and reality. Any kids listening have probably heard worse in the school playground.

But a driver's conduct in the controlled environment of a press conference is different. On Thursday, when Verstappen was asked why, for the first time in 2024, he'd been slower than Sergio Pérez in Baku, he replied, "As soon as I went into qualifying, I knew the car was f**ked."

Some believe that Ben Sulayem had lost the dressing room some time ago, so whether Verstappen's profanity was deliberate was debatable. Whatever, it prompted a stewards' investigation, which found that he was in breach of the FIA's international sporting code. The penalty was a day's work 'in the public interest' – effectively F1 community service.

After qualifying second behind championship rival Lando Norris, in response to a question about Red Bull's turnaround, Verstappen said, "I'd prefer if you asked these questions outside the room." It was his own little protest. Subsequently, he did answer questions outside the conference.

Both pole-man Norris and third-placed Hamilton were sympathetic, Lewis calling it "all a bit of a joke" and adding, "I certainly wouldn't be doing it [the community service] and I hope Max doesn't."

The on-track story was that Norris and McLaren had looked mighty from the time the cars first took to the track on Friday, along with Charles Leclerc and Ferrari again. On the evidence of the first day, both Red Bull and Mercedes were struggling. The RB20 was not renowned for its ability over kerbs and bumps, and Verstappen expected Marina Bay to be the team's biggest challenge, as it had been in 2023. Red Bull had softened the set-up to make the car more benign, but Verstappen still had no feeling and was slow. It was a similar narrative at Mercedes.

But on Saturday morning, after much data study and simulator work, both teams went back stiffer and, further aided by recent circuit resurfacing, suddenly found their respective chassis much more competitive. Ferrari, by contrast, went backwards, Leclerc suddenly the best part of a second off the pace and reporting no grip, the car being highly sensitive to tyre temperature on the C5 Pirelli soft.

Norris was still the pace-setter in qualifying, but Q3 became a one-lap shootout when Carlos Sainz, having moved over on his prep lap to let Oscar Piastri by, suddenly suffered a snap in the final turn as he began his own push-lap. He backed his Ferrari into the barrier, bringing out the red flag and consigned himself to tenth on the grid. Piastri and Nico Hülkenberg were the only drivers with a time on the board, and it would all come down to a single hot lap.

In a further disaster for Ferrari, Leclerc, competitive again in Q2, joined Sainz on the fifth row when he ran all four wheels off at Turn Two and had his lap deleted.

"It was a problem we'd never had throughout the weekend," the Monégasque explained. "The front tyres and blankets not working properly, getting out of the pits with the fronts super-cold and having to push like crazy on the out-lap to recover temperature, which never happened."

Norris's lap (1m 29.525s) wasn't as good as the one he'd been on when Sainz crashed, but nonetheless was good enough to beat Verstappen (1m 29.728s) comfortably to pole, both men more than happy. Max, without a pole in ten races, was relieved at least to be on the front row.

Seldom had a race seen such a topsy-turvy variation in car performance. After their tricky opening day, Hamilton and George Russell suddenly qualified Mercedes on row two!

"Qualifying has been a disaster for me all year, and the car came alive for the first time in a long time," Lewis said. "Suddenly, for the first time, we had a front end."

Asked whether he would have signed for the second row, Russell replied, "At the start of the day, I'd have signed for it; after FP3, I wouldn't have signed for it; and after Q1, I would have begged for it! We didn't change the car from FP3, when I believed that Lando was maybe two-tenths ahead of me and I was four-tenths ahead of the next pack. I was feeling pretty confident that P2 should be the minimum and if I did a great job, maybe I could even fight Lando. Then, suddenly, in Q1, I'm on the verge of getting knocked out! I don't really get it."

If Baku winner Piastri had equalled his Q2 time, he, too, could have been on the front row, but instead he had to be content with fifth. He was ahead of an inspired Nico Hülkenberg, whose sixth place was his best Singapore start, equalling team-mate Kevin Magnussen's performance at the same track in 2023. This time, though, Haas was more hopeful of the race performance bringing a haul of points.

Fernando Alonso's Aston Martin, Yuki Tsunoda's VCARB and the chastened Ferrari pair completed the top ten. Only just missing out was the Williams pair, Alex Albon pipping another fine performance from Franco Colapinto by just 0.007s, despite the Argentine not due to receive the suspension upgrade on Albon's car until Austin. Both were faster than Sergio Pérez – not what Red Bull needed, with McLaren now 20 points ahead in the constructors' championship… Kevin Magnussen's Haas and Esteban Ocon's Alpine were the others to go out in Q2.

Falling at the first hurdle, sadly, was Daniel Ricciardo in what was very possibly his last GP (see Viewpoint). "On every soft tyre that I used, I wasn't competitive at all," he grimaced, "but I'll get a day's community service if I swear, so let's leave it there."

Joining him as Q2 spectators were Lance Stroll, Pierre Gasly, and Sauber drivers Valtteri Bottas and Zhou Guanyu. Bottas was exploring Indycar drives for 2025 as he tried to keep his seat in the team. Alonso protégé Gabriel Bortoleto, the F2 championship leader, and Colapinto were both waiting in the wings.

AS the grid formed up under Marina Bay's evocative lights, Lewis Hamilton, somewhat surprisingly, was on the soft-compound Pirelli, a choice mirrored by Daniel Ricciardo down in 16th place. Everyone else in the top 13 slots was on the medium, while, further back, Kevin Magnussen, Lance Stroll, Bottas and Zhou had gone for the hard tyre.

Lando Norris was intent on converting his pole to lead the opening lap for the first time, while Max Verstappen was chasing a first win in seven races. Most figured that the Dutchman's only real chance was to beat Norris off the line. This time, though, Lando put the power down superbly and completed the short sprint to the tight T1/2 clearly ahead. Hamilton had a brief look at the outside of Verstappen, but then tucked in behind. Further back, Alonso and Leclerc took to the escape road as the pack jostled for position, rejoining in their original positions – seventh and eighth – having gone to the right of the bollard as demanded by the rules.

Across the line at the end of the opening lap, Norris led from Verstappen and Hamilton. Then came George Russell, Oscar Piastri, Nico Hülkenberg, Fernando Alonso, Charles Leclerc, a fast-starting Franco Colapinto (up three places), Sergio Pérez, Yuki Tsunoda, Carlos Sainz (down a further two slots from his tenth place on the grid), Esteban Ocon, Kevin Magnussen, Alex Albon, Daniel Ricciardo, Pierre Gasly, Lance Stroll, Valtteri Bottas and Zhou Guanyu.

Hamilton's soft-tyre gamble was predicated on him being able to use the extra grip to split Norris and Verstappen off the line, but that hadn't happened, and as the front-row men started to drop the Merc, Russell was getting a bit angsty behind: "He needs to increase the pace a bit. The guys at the front are getting away." In other words, hurry up and root those softs, and get out of my way!

With ten laps on the board, Norris had opened up a margin at the front. He was not exerting himself overly, though, as evidenced by his response to a "How's the pace?" enquiry from the pit wall.

"Yeah, I'm pace six or something," he replied, presumably gauging it on a scale of one to ten.

"Okay," Will Joseph responded, "in that case, we'd like to use a bit of that pace to try to get a 5s gap to Max, if possible by the mid-teens."

Norris responded effortlessly, stretching the gap to the requested 5s in just a couple of laps. This was no tyre-management Sunday afternoon stroll, such as we'd seen before at Marina Bay. Hamilton was a further 5s behind Verstappen on his softs, with Russell a couple of seconds adrift, a similar gap to Piastri and another to Hülkenberg, doing a fine job in sixth place for Haas, but being harried by Alonso and Leclerc. Next came the impressive Colapinto, who had picked up his places with an impressive late-on-the-brakes lunge down the inside of Turn One. He was being pushed by Pérez's Red Bull, with Tsunoda and Sainz following closely.

Ricciardo was in on lap 11 to get rid of his starting softs, while Albon was in a lap later – early for mediums – with the undercut reckoned to be worth at least a couple of seconds at Marina Bay. That forced Ferrari to respond with Sainz, who had been bottled up behind Tsunoda, Ocon and Magnussen, the Ferrari only just getting back out ahead of the Williams.

Although a fourth DRS zone had been added to the Marina Bay track layout after Turn 14, the general opinion was that overtaking in Singapore remained difficult to achieve. Pérez, still running tenth and receiving the 'hurry-up' from the Red Bull pit, gave a glowing endorsement of the new Williams recruit when he responded, "He's very good, it's difficult to pass Colapinto." The young Argentine was now the only Williams driver remaining, as team-

Above: Lando Norris converts his pole position ahead of Max Verstappen and Lewis Hamilton's soft-tyred Mercedes.
Photo: McLaren F1 Team

Left: Toto Wolff, happy to see his cars on the second row of the grid.
Photo: Mercedes-AMG Petronas F1 Team

Opening spread: Lord of all he surveys. A dominant Lando Norris led from start to finish.
Photo: Peter Nygaard/GP Photo

Above: The Marina Bay circuit at night provides a spectacular vista.

Top right: Verstappen could not match the pace of Norris, but settled for second and 18 points.
Photos: Red Bull Content Pool/Getty Images

Above right: Nico Hülkenberg moved into tenth place in the chase for the drivers' championship.
Photo: MoneyGram Haas F1 Team

Right: Lap 35, and a feisty battle ensues between Leclerc on mediums and Russell on hard Pirellis. The Ferrari would pit shortly after.
Photo: XPB Images

mate Albon had posted the first retirement with a power-unit problem.

Hamilton, who had fallen 8s behind Verstappen, pitted from third after 18 laps to go on to the hard compound, emerging a couple of seconds behind Magnussen, who had started on the hard and is never the easiest man to negotiate. But Lewis wasted no time in going by with a late lunge into Turn 16, proving that the new DRS zone was of some use after all!

"Did I stop before everyone?" Hamilton asked.

"We are one of the earlier stoppers, but not the earliest," race engineer Peter Bonnington informed him.

"Yeah, we'll be in trouble later – way too short," Lewis responded.

If Baku a fortnight earlier had been grippingly close between three different teams, Singapore was anything but. With just over a third of the race run, Norris's McLaren had a 17s advantage over Verstappen's Red Bull, with Russell's Mercedes a further 12s down. Piastri was just over 1s adrift, with a 10s advantage over Hülkenberg, who'd had Alonso and Leclerc bottled up behind for the whole race.

On lap 26, Leclerc finally found a way past Alonso, who immediately headed into the pits, while Hamilton got around Tsunoda, but not without running too deep into T16 and being repassed. "Something is definitely wrong with the car, mate. The tyres are dropping off," he told the pits. "That's all surface driven," they told him.

Piastri was now hounding Russell for third, and George was in for new boots at the end of lap 27, finally allowing the Baku winner some free air. Another man finally afforded the same luxury was Leclerc who, with a lunge down the inside of Hülkenberg's Haas at Turn 16 on lap 29, could finally get on with it.

With Piastri now lapping much quicker than Verstappen, despite being 10s behind, Red Bull called in Max to go on to the hard-compound tyre just before half-distance. He pitted out behind Leclerc, who was now running at a good pace on his starting mediums as he tried to build a strong tyre offset.

Suddenly, Norris lost 4s to Piastri in a single lap, a result of running too deep into Turn 14 and surviving the lightest of brushes with the wall. The team brought him in for fresh tyres and he re-emerged a couple of seconds ahead of his team-mate, who had yet to stop, of course.

By lap 35, with Piastri still going well on his starting mediums, McLaren was thinking about maximising a tyre offset at the end of the race and asked Oscar, "We're tempted to stay out. That would mean you'd have to overtake Hamilton after the stop. How would that be?"

"Not sure it's a great idea," came the answer.

By lap 36, Russell and Leclerc were involved in a feisty battle, the latter eking out his mediums and the former trying not to lose time behind him on his fresh hards. After defending hard for a couple of laps, Leclerc headed for the pits.

"It will be very tight on exit with Hülkenberg," he was told, the Haas having stopped for fresh hards six laps earlier. A 2.2s Ferrari stop helped the cause and Leclerc pitted out just ahead, setting off after Alonso again. Fernando was now running seventh, 5s further up the road on hards that had done 12 laps.

"It's now starting to get tricky," Piastri told McLaren, who brought him in next time around for fresh hards. He did indeed rejoin behind Hamilton, albeit on tyres 20 laps fresher. Any concern that Oscar had about getting by proved unfounded, as he did so at the first attempt, picking up DRS out of Turn Five and going around the outside of the Mercedes at Turn Seven – another of the clinical moves fast becoming a Piastri staple. He was

Above: Lando Norris was unstoppable in Singapore, but he still trailed Max Verstappen in the championship by more than 50 points.
Photo: Atsuo Sakurai

Top right: The end of what might be the last ever Formula 1 race for an emotional Daniel Ricciardo.

Above right: Waiting in the wings. Liam Lawson, with Laurent Mekies, would take over the Australian's RB seat for the rest of the season.

Right: A late stop for Ricciardo allowed him to set the race's fastest lap, denying Norris an extra point.
Photos: Red Bull Content Pool/Getty Images

now just 2s behind third-placed Russell in the second Mercedes as he set the fastest lap of the race.

Leclerc beat it almost immediately and now was on a charge, too, passing Alonso again and then team-mate Sainz, who was on hard tyres that were 23 laps older and moved over. Hamilton was next on his radar, some 15s further up the road. And Mercedes was also warning Russell about the Ferrari's pace, telling George, "Leclerc still doing high 36s out there. There's a chance of interacting at the very end of the race if he can keep that pace up."

On lap 45, with 17 to go, Piastri repeated his Turn Seven Hamilton move on Russell to take third place, but with Verstappen some 18s ahead of the second McLaren, that was as far as he would go. It's never easy for a driver to watch his team-mate dominate in the same car, especially after the great drive in Baku, but Oscar would maintain his record as the only driver to complete every racing lap so far in 2024.

For superior pace, Norris had been more dominant than anyone in any of the current season's races thus far, but he survived another brush with the right rear against the wall at Turn Ten, which had claimed Russell on the last lap of the 2023 race.

"Maybe I was pushing a bit unnecessarily to do the fastest lap," he admitted later. "It was definitely a bit too close for comfort, but it's also easy to lose concentration and make a mistake if you're taking things easy."

"Okay, Lando, so full concentration now, take a drink," came the instruction from the pit wall.

By lap 50, Leclerc had wiped out his 15s deficit to Hamilton and was on to the back of the Mercedes. Lewis offered no resistance as Charles went down the inside of Turn Seven to move up to fifth and set off after Russell, some 8s ahead. It was almost as though Hamilton was making the point that such an early stop had left him defenceless.

The Mercedes prediction had been correct, and Leclerc did indeed catch Russell in the closing stages, with three laps to go. By then, though, although his tyres were nine laps newer than George's, he'd already taken the best out of them in his determined pursuit.

"They have very good traction again," Leclerc told his crew as he found negotiating the second Mercedes altogether tougher. Fifth was as high as the Monégasque would reach following the frustrating opening stint that was rooted in that deleted Q3 lap. He might not have had quite Norris's race pace, but second should have been on the cards if he'd qualified the Ferrari to its potential.

Norris, having successfully taken back fastest lap from Leclerc, eased off and allowed what had been a half-minute lead to fall way to just over 20s as he took the chequered flag for his third GP victory. He closed Verstappen's championship lead by seven points, rather than eight, because VCARB, Red Bull's junior team, brought in Ricciardo, running last of the 18 cars still circulating, and bolted on a set of softs. Poignantly, Daniel took the fastest-lap point on what was very likely the penultimate lap of his F1 career, after some 257 starts.

"Thank you, Daniel," Verstappen radioed upon being told, as Marina Bay remained the only circuit on the calendar at which Max had never won. His championship lead was down to 52 points with six races to go and three sprints, in Austin, São Paulo and Qatar.

For Ricciardo, soft tyres and low fuel were a good way to finish, if indeed there can be such a thing in F1 (see Viewpoint). Spent physically and clearly emotional, he sat in the cockpit reflecting for a long while before finally climbing out.

Behind sixth-placed Hamilton, Sainz completed the Ferrari damage limitation with seventh, also rueing the qualifying shunt that had dictated a race that had been a far cry from the victory high of a year earlier.

Alonso brought his Aston Martin home eighth, and Hülkenberg delighted Haas with a further two points for ninth, which actually moved him into the championship top ten and his team to within three points of sixth-placed VCARB in the constructors' battle.

Pérez, another to qualify poorly, who had struggled for traction throughout, snatched the last point from the impressive Colapinto, only by pitting a lap earlier and undercutting the Williams. Now there was a second four-week gap before battle recommenced in Austin.

Tony Dodgins

VIEWPOINT
CIAO, DANNY RIC

THERE was a certain poignancy about the way it all ended. Daniel Ricciardo made a third stop, returned to set fastest lap (as a team player, benefiting Max Verstappen and Red Bull by pinching the championship point from Lando Norris) and finish 18th – and last.

It was not the way for an eight-times GP winner to go. The situation was made worse by obfuscation on the part of VCARB and Red Bull because of contractual problems leading into the next race in the United States, where the smiley Aussie remained popular among sponsors and spectators alike.

Ricciardo, normally talkative and direct, had to dance around the subject even though he – and everyone else – knew that his 257th grand prix was likely to have been his last. Indeed, word came shortly after the Singapore weekend that Helmut Marko had wanted rid of him as early as the Spanish GP three months before. Even allowing for the pragmatic Marko's disregard for written agreements, his displeasure was indicative of the pressure Ricciardo had been under from the moment he joined AlphaTauri in 2023. It had been a lifeline following the disastrous two seasons with McLaren. Riccardo's basic mission was to be consistently quicker than Yuki Tsunoda. The points table thus far in 2024 – Tsunoda on 22, Ricciardo 12 – told its own unfortunate story.

Where had it all gone wrong? How could a driver with such natural speed and deft brilliance on the brakes lose a touch that, among other highlights, had brought a sublime victory at Monaco with a down-on-power engine in 2018?

Ricciardo's increasing appearance of weariness suggested that he didn't know the reason any more than the rest of us. There had been plenty of in-depth narrative about cars not suiting his particular driving style. That might have been true, but all of this was underscored by the conundrum that can affect any gifted performer: that deeply frustrating scenario when an innate rhythm is gradually eroded by over-thinking about why it doesn't come easily any more.

The moment had passed for Daniel Ricciardo – and that was desperately sad for his many fans, never mind the man himself.

Maurice Hamilton

18

FORMULA 1 SINGAPORE AIRLINES SINGAPORE GRAND PRIX 2024

SINGAPORE 20-22 SEPTEMBER

RACE DISTANCE: 62 laps, 190.228 miles/306.143km

RACE WEATHER: Dry/dark (track 34-36°C, air 30-31°C)

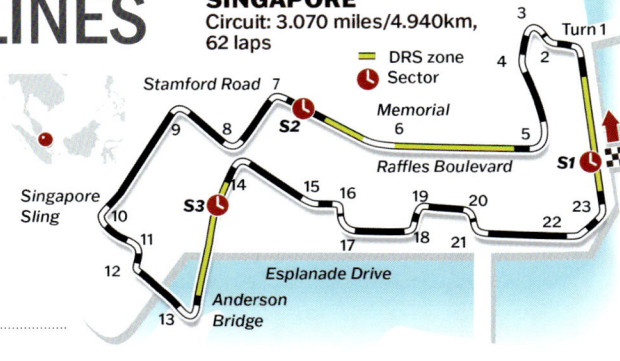

MARINA BAY STREET CIRCUIT, SINGAPORE
Circuit: 3.070 miles/4.940km, 62 laps

RACE – OFFICIAL CLASSIFICATION

Pos.	Driver	Nat.	No.	Entrant	Car/Engine	Laps	Time/Retirement	Speed (mph/km/h)	Gap to leader	Fastest race lap
1	Lando Norris	GB	4	McLaren Formula 1 Team	McLaren MCL38-Mercedes F1 M15 E Perf. V6	62	1h 40m 52.571s	113.145/182.090		1m 34.925s 48
2	Max Verstappen	NL	1	Oracle Red Bull Racing	Red Bull RB20-Honda RBPT H002 V6	62	1h 41m 13.516s	112.755/181.462	20.945s	1m 35.967s 59
3	Oscar Piastri	AUS	81	McLaren Formula 1 Team	McLaren MCL38-Mercedes F1 M15 E Perf. V6	62	1h 41m 34.394s	112.369/180.840	41.823s	1m 35.745s 48
4	George Russell	GB	63	Mercedes-AMG Petronas F1 Team	Mercedes-AMG F1 W15-M15 E Perf. V6	62	1h 41m 53.611s	112.016/180.272	1m 01.040s	1m 37.047s 30
5	Charles Leclerc	MC	16	Scuderia Ferrari	Ferrari SF-24-066/12 V6	62	1h 41m 55.001s	111.990/180.231	1m 02.430s	1m 35.371s 46
6	Lewis Hamilton	GB	44	Mercedes-AMG Petronas F1 Team	Mercedes-AMG F1 W15-M15 E Perf. V6	62	1h 42m 17.819s	111.574/179.561	1m 25.248s	1m 37.393s 43
7	Carlos Sainz	E	55	Scuderia Ferrari	Ferrari SF-24-066/12 V6	62	1h 42m 28.610s	111.378/179.246	1m 36.039s	1m 36.561s 15
8	Fernando Alonso	E	14	Aston Martin Aramco F1 Team	Aston Martin AMR24-Mercedes F1 M15 E Perf. V6	61			1 lap	1m 37.741s 54
9	Nico Hülkenberg	D	27	MoneyGram Haas F1 Team	Haas VF-24-Ferrari 066/10 V6	61			1 lap	1m 37.470s 35
10	Sergio Pérez	MEX	11	Oracle Red Bull Racing	Red Bull RB20-Honda RBPT H002 V6	61			1 lap	1m 37.477s 33
11	Franco Colapinto	RA	43	Williams Racing	Williams FW46-Mercedes F1 M15 E Perf. V6	61			1 lap	1m 37.262s 35
12	Yuki Tsunoda	J	22	Visa Cash App RB Formula One Team	RB VCARB 01-Honda RBPT H002 V6	61			1 lap	1m 36.393s 53
13	Esteban Ocon	F	31	BWT Alpine F1 Team	Alpine A524-Renault E-Tech RE24 V6	61			1 lap	1m 37.964s 48
14	Lance Stroll	CDN	18	Aston Martin Aramco F1 Team	Aston Martin AMR24-Mercedes F1 M15 E Perf. V6	61			1 lap	1m 37.851s 36
15	Zhou Guanyu	CHN	24	Stake F1 Team Kick Sauber	Sauber C44-Ferrari 066/12 V6	61			1 lap	1m 37.461s 47
16	Valtteri Bottas	FIN	77	Stake F1 Team Kick Sauber	Sauber C44-Ferrari 066/12 V6	61			1 lap	1m 37.524s 46
17	Pierre Gasly	F	10	BWT Alpine F1 Team	Alpine A524-Renault E-Tech RE24 V6	61			1 lap	1m 36.927s 46
18	Daniel Ricciardo	AUS	3	Visa Cash App RB Formula One Team	RB VCARB 01-Honda RBPT H002 V6	61			1 lap	1m 34.486s 60
19	Kevin Magnussen	DK	20	MoneyGram Haas F1 Team	Haas VF-24-Ferrari 066/10 V6	57	accident damage		5 laps	1m 37.425s 52
	Alexander Albon	T	23	Williams Racing	Williams FW46-Mercedes F1 M15 E Perf. V6	15	overheating			1m 36.888s 13

DHL Fastest race lap: Daniel Ricciardo on lap 60, 1m 34.486s, 116.953mph/188.218km/h (new record).

Previous lap record: Lewis Hamilton (Mercedes F1 W14 V6), 1m 35.867s, 115.269mph/185.507km/h (2023).

20 · ZHOU · Sauber

18 · GASLY · Alpine

16 · RICCIARDO · RB

14 · MAGNUSSEN · Haas

12 · COLAPINTO · Williams

19 · BOTTAS · Sauber

17 · STROLL · Aston Martin

15 · OCON · Alpine

13 · PÉREZ · Red Bull

11 · ALBON · Williams

Grid order	1	2	3	4	5	6	7	8	9	10	11	12	13	14	15	16	17	18	19	20	21	22	23	24	25	26	27	28	29	30	31	32	33	34	35	36	37	38	39	40	41	42	43	44	45	46	47	48	49	50
4 NORRIS	4	4	4	4	4	4	4	4	4	4	4	4	4	4	4	4	4	4	4	4	4	4	4	4	4	4	4	4	4	4	4	4	4	4	4	4	4	4	4	4	4	4	4	4	4	4	4	4	4	4
1 VERSTAPPEN	1	1	1	1	1	1	1	1	1	1	1	1	1	1	1	1	1	1	1	1	1	1	1	1	1	1	1	1	81	81	81	81	81	81	81	81	81	1	1	1	1	1	1	1	1	1	1	1	1	1
44 HAMILTON	44	44	44	44	44	44	44	44	44	44	44	44	44	44	44	63	63	63	63	63	63	63	63	63	63	81	81	81	1	1	1	1	1	1	1	63	63	63	63	63	81	81	81	81	81	81	81	81	81	81
63 RUSSELL	63	63	63	63	63	63	63	63	63	63	63	63	63	63	63	81	81	81	81	81	81	81	81	81	81	63	16	16	16	16	16	16	16	16	16	44	81	81	81	81	63	63	63	63	63	63	63	63	63	63
81 PIASTRI	81	81	81	81	81	81	81	81	81	81	81	81	81	81	81	44	27	27	27	27	27	27	27	27	27	16	63	63	63	63	63	63	63	63	63	16	44	44	44	44	44	44	44	44	44	44	44	44	44	44
27 HÜLKENBERG	27	27	27	27	27	27	27	27	27	27	27	27	27	27	27	14	14	14	14	14	14	14	14	16	16	43	27	44	44	44	44	44	44	16	55	55	55	55	55	16	16	16	16	16	16	16	16	16	16	44
14 ALONSO	14	14	14	14	14	14	14	14	14	14	14	14	14	14	14	16	16	16	16	16	16	16	16	43	43	63	44	22	22	22	55	55	55	55	14	14	14	16	55	55	55	55	55	55	55	55	55	55	55	55
22 TSUNODA	16	16	16	16	16	16	16	16	16	16	16	16	16	16	16	43	43	43	43	43	43	43	43	11	11	44	43	55	55	55	14	14	14	14	16	16	16	14	14	14	14	14	14	14	14	14	14	14	14	14
16 LECLERC	43	43	43	43	43	43	43	43	43	43	43	43	43	43	43	11	11	11	11	11	11	11	11	14	22	44	22	14	14	14	22	27	27	27	27	27	27	27	27	27	27	27	27	27	27	27	27	27	27	27
55 SAINZ	11	11	11	11	11	11	11	11	11	11	11	11	11	11	11	22	22	22	22	22	22	22	22	44	22	11	55	27	27	27	11	11	11	11	11	11	11	11	11	11	11	11	11	11	11	11	11	11	11	11
23 ALBON	22	22	22	22	22	22	22	22	22	22	22	22	22	22	22	31	31	31	31	44	44	44	44	31	31	14	11	11	11	11	43	43	43	43	43	43	43	43	43	43	43	43	43	43	43	43	43	43	43	43
43 COLAPINTO	55	55	55	55	55	55	55	55	55	55	55	55	55	55	55	31	31	31	31	20	44	44	44	31	31	55	31	10	10	43	43	10	10	3	3	3	22	22	22	22	22	22	22	22	22	22	22	22	22	22
11 PÉREZ	31	31	31	31	31	31	31	31	31	31	20	20	20	20	20	44	20	20	20	20	20	20	20	14	31	43	10	10	10	3	3	10	22	22	22	3	3	3	3	31	31	31	31	31	31	31	31	31	31	31
20 MAGNUSSEN	20	20	20	20	20	20	20	20	20	55	10	10	10	10	10	10	10	10	10	10	10	10	10	55	10	14	14	20	11	24	3	3	22	22	31	31	31	31	31	31	31	31	31	20	20	20	20	18	18	18
31 OCON	23	23	23	23	23	23	23	23	23	10	18	18	18	18	18	18	18	18	18	55	55	55	55	10	14	10	11	24	3	3	22	22	31	31	20	20	20	20	20	20	20	3	18	18	18	24	24	24
3 RICCIARDO	3	3	3	3	3	3	3	3	3	18	24	24	24	24	24	55	55	18	18	18	18	18	18	24	20	3	77	77	3	20	20	20	18	18	18	18	18	18	18	3	24	24	77	77
18 STROLL	10	10	10	10	10	10	10	10	18	23	24	24	77	77	55	55	24	24	24	24	24	24	24	77	77	31	31	3	20	18	18	18	10	24	24	24	24	24	77	77	77	77	10	10
10 GASLY	18	18	18	18	18	18	18	18	24	24	77	77	55	55	55	77	77	77	77	77	77	77	77	3	3	20	20	20	20	77	18	24	24	24	77	77	77	77	77	77	77	10	10	3
77 BOTTAS	77	77	77	77	24	24	24	24	3	77	23	23	23	3	3	3	3	3	3	3	3	3	3	18	18	18	18	18	18	77	77	77	77	10	10	10	10	10	10	10	10	3	3	20	20
24 ZHOU	24	24	24	24	77	77	77	77	77	3	3	3	3	23																																				

TIME SHEETS

PRACTICE 1 (FRIDAY)
Weather: Dry/cloudy
Temperatures: track 37-39°C, air 33-34°C

Pos.	Driver	Laps	Time
1	Charles Leclerc	26	1m 31.763s
2	Lando Norris	25	1m 31.839s
3	Carlos Sainz	27	1m 31.952s
4	Max Verstappen	22	1m 32.097s
5	Yuki Tsunoda	26	1m 32.263s
6	Oscar Piastri	25	1m 32.369s
7	Daniel Ricciardo	21	1m 32.375s
8	Alexander Albon	25	1m 32.451s
9	Fernando Alonso	26	1m 32.610s
10	Esteban Ocon	27	1m 32.615s
11	Franco Colapinto	25	1m 32.618s
12	Lewis Hamilton	24	1m 32.679s
13	Pierre Gasly	27	1m 32.694s
14	Sergio Pérez	22	1m 32.767s
15	Lance Stroll	21	1m 32.778s
16	George Russell	25	1m 33.334s
17	Kevin Magnussen	21	1m 33.377s
18	Valtteri Bottas	25	1m 33.485s
19	Zhou Guanyu	24	1m 33.585s
20	Nico Hülkenberg	24	1m 33.797s

PRACTICE 2 (FRIDAY)
Weather: Dry/dark
Temperatures: track 33-34°C, air 30-31°C

Pos.	Driver	Laps	Time
1	Lando Norris	27	1m 30.727s
2	Charles Leclerc	28	1m 30.785s
3	Carlos Sainz	27	1m 31.356s
4	Yuki Tsunoda	28	1m 31.468s
5	Oscar Piastri	27	1m 31.474s
6	Daniel Ricciardo	26	1m 31.478s
7	George Russell	25	1m 31.488s
8	Sergio Pérez	25	1m 31.598s
9	Alexander Albon	26	1m 31.650s
10	Nico Hülkenberg	26	1m 31.667s
11	Lewis Hamilton	24	1m 31.709s
12	Fernando Alonso	25	1m 31.750s
13	Kevin Magnussen	26	1m 31.793s
14	Lance Stroll	25	1m 31.957s
15	Max Verstappen	24	1m 32.021s
16	Franco Colapinto	26	1m 32.057s
17	Esteban Ocon	27	1m 32.119s
18	Pierre Gasly	27	1m 32.222s
19	Zhou Guanyu	26	1m 32.359s
20	Valtteri Bottas	26	1m 32.786s

PRACTICE 3 (SATURDAY)
Weather: Dry/cloudy
Temperatures: track 34-38°C, air 30-31°C

Pos.	Driver	Laps	Time
1	Lando Norris	16	1m 29.646s
2	George Russell	19	1m 30.125s
3	Oscar Piastri	16	1m 30.431s
4	Max Verstappen	16	1m 30.540s
5	Charles Leclerc	20	1m 30.559s
6	Carlos Sainz	20	1m 30.807s
7	Lewis Hamilton	19	1m 30.864s
8	Alexander Albon	13	1m 30.949s
9	Franco Colapinto	15	1m 30.989s
10	Fernando Alonso	23	1m 31.082s
11	Yuki Tsunoda	16	1m 31.114s
12	Nico Hülkenberg	14	1m 31.187s
13	Kevin Magnussen	14	1m 31.265s
14	Pierre Gasly	22	1m 31.367s
15	Sergio Pérez	15	1m 31.440s
16	Esteban Ocon	20	1m 31.559s
17	Daniel Ricciardo	17	1m 31.561s
18	Lance Stroll	24	1m 31.719s
19	Valtteri Bottas	17	1m 32.098s
20	Zhou Guanyu	19	1m 32.652s

QUALIFYING (SATURDAY)
Weather: Dry/dark Temperatures: track 31-32°C, air 29-30°C

Pos.	Driver	First	Second	Third	Qualifying Tyre
1	Lando Norris	1m 30.002s	1m 30.007s	1m 29.525s	Soft (n)
2	Max Verstappen	1m 30.157s	1m 29.680s	1m 29.728s	Soft (n)
3	Lewis Hamilton	1m 30.393s	1m 29.929s	1m 29.841s	Soft (n)
4	George Russell	1m 30.811s	1m 30.153s	1m 29.867s	Soft (n)
5	Oscar Piastri	1m 30.258s	1m 29.640s	1m 29.953s	Soft (n)
6	Nico Hülkenberg	1m 30.724s	1m 30.150s	1m 30.115s	Soft (n)
7	Fernando Alonso	1m 30.684s	1m 30.450s	1m 30.214s	Soft (n)
8	Yuki Tsunoda	1m 30.716s	1m 30.289s	1m 30.354s	Soft (n)
9	Charles Leclerc	1m 30.786s	1m 29.747s	no time	Soft (n)
10	Carlos Sainz	1m 30.670s	1m 30.108s	no time	Soft (n)
11	Alexander Albon	1m 30.679s	1m 30.474s		
12	Franco Colapinto	1m 30.704s	1m 30.481s		
13	Sergio Pérez	1m 30.624s	1m 30.579s		
14	Kevin Magnussen	1m 30.829s	1m 30.653s		
15	Esteban Ocon	1m 30.958s	1m 30.769s		
16	Daniel Ricciardo	1m 31.085s			
17	Lance Stroll	1m 31.094s			
18	Pierre Gasly	1m 31.312s			
19	Valtteri Bottas	1m 31.572s			
20	Zhou Guanyu	1m 32.054s			

FOR THE RECORD

70th GP FRONT ROW: Max Verstappen

200th GP START: Carlos Sainz

POINTS

DRIVERS

1	Max Verstappen	331
2	Lando Norris	279
3	Charles Leclerc	245
4	Oscar Piastri	237
5	Carlos Sainz	190
6	Lewis Hamilton	174
7	George Russell	155
8	Sergio Pérez	144
9	Fernando Alonso	62
10	Nico Hülkenberg	24
11	Lance Stroll	24
12	Yuki Tsunoda	22
13	Alexander Albon	12
14	Daniel Ricciardo	12
15	Pierre Gasly	8
16	Oliver Bearman	7
17	Kevin Magnussen	6
18	Esteban Ocon	5
19	Franco Colapinto	4

CONSTRUCTORS

1	McLaren	516
2	Red Bull	475
3	Ferrari	441
4	Mercedes	329
5	Aston Martin	86
6	RB	34
7	Haas	31
8	Williams	16
9	Alpine	13

QUALIFYING: head to head

Verstappen	17		1	Pérez
Hamilton	5		13	Russell
Norris	14		4	Piastri
Leclerc	12		5	Sainz
Leclerc	1		0	Bearman
Gasly	7		11	Ocon
Alonso	12		6	Stroll
Albon	14		1	Sargeant
Albon	2		1	Colapinto
Bottas	17		1	Zhou
Tsunoda	12		6	Ricciardo
Magnussen	4		13	Hülkenberg
Bearman	1		0	Hülkenberg

 10 · SAINZ · Ferrari
 8 · TSUNODA · RB
 6 · HÜLKENBERG · Haas
 4 · RUSSELL · Mercedes
 2 · VERSTAPPEN · Red Bull

 9 · LECLERC · Ferrari
 7 · ALONSO · Aston Martin
 5 · PIASTRI · McLaren
 3 · HAMILTON · Mercedes
 1 · NORRIS · McLaren

	51	52	53	54	55	56	57	58	59	60	61	62	
	4	4	4	4	4	4	4	4	4	4	4		1
	1	1	1	1	1	1	1	1	1	1	1	1	2
	81	81	81	81	81	81	81	81	81	81	81	81	3
	63	63	63	63	63	63	63	63	63	63	63	63	4
	16	16	16	16	16	16	16	16	16	16	16	16	5
	44	44	44	44	44	44	44	44	44	44	44	44	6
	55	55	55	55	55	55	55	55	55	55	55	55	7
	14	14	14	14	14	14	14	14	14	14	14	*14*	8
	27	27	27	27	27	27	27	27	27	27	*27*	*27*	9
	11	11	11	11	11	11	11	11	11	11	*11*	*11*	10
	43	43	43	*43*	*43*	*43*	*43*	*43*	*43*	*43*	*43*	*43*	
	22	22	22	22	22	22	22	22	22	22	22		
	31	31	31	31	31	31	31	31	31	31	31		
	18	18	18	18	18	18	18	18	18	18			
	24	24	24	24	24	24	24	24	24	24			
	10	10	10	10	10	10	10	10	10	10			
	3	3	3	3	3	3	*3*	3	3				
	20	20	20	20	20	20	*20*						

3 = Pit stop   *18* = One lap or more behind

RACE TYRE STRATEGIES

	Driver	Race Stint 1	Race Stint 2	Race Stint 3	Race Stint 4
1	Norris	Medium (n): 1-30	Hard (n): 31-62		
2	Verstappen	Medium (n): 1-29	Hard (n): 30-62		
3	Piastri	Medium (n): 1-38	Hard (n): 39-62		
4	Russell	Medium (n): 1-27	Hard (n): 28-62		
5	Leclerc	Medium (n): 1-36	Hard (n): 37-62		
6	Hamilton	Soft (u): 1-17	Medium (n): 18-62		
7	Sainz	Medium (n): 1-13	Hard (n): 14-62		
8	Alonso	Medium (u): 1-25	Hard (u): 26-61		
9	Hülkenberg	Medium (n): 1-29	Hard (n): 30-61		
10	Pérez	Medium (n): 1-28	Hard (n): 29-61		
11	Colapinto	Medium (n): 1-29	Hard (n): 30-61		
12	Tsunoda	Medium (n): 1-33	Soft (u): 34-61		
13	Ocon	Medium (n): 1-29	Hard (n): 30-61		
14	Stroll	Hard (u): 1-26	Medium (n): 27-61		
15	Zhou	Hard (n): 1-34	Medium (n): 35-61		
16	Bottas	Hard (n): 1-33	Medium (n): 34-61		
17	Gasly	Medium (n): 1-37	Soft (n): 38-61		
18	Ricciardo	Soft (n): 1-10	Medium (n): 11-46	Soft (n): 47-58	Soft (u): 59-61
19	Magnussen	Hard (n): 1-28	Medium (n): 29-49	Soft (n): 50-57 (dnf)	
	Albon	Medium (n): 1-11	Hard (n): 12-15 (dnf)		

The tyre regulations stipulate that at least two of three dry tyre specifications must be used during a dry race.
Selected compounds for Singapore: Red = Soft (C5); Yellow = Medium (C4); White = Hard (C3). (n) new (u) used

CIRCUIT OF THE AMERICAS
QUALIFYING/SPRINT QUALIFYING & RACE

THE scuttlebutt going into the Austin weekend was that Red Bull had a cockpit-activated device that could change the height of the floor's leading edge. Such an arrangement was not illegal, and the FIA cleared the team of any wrongdoing. But rivals, especially McLaren, were quick to suggest that if Red Bull were to activate the device in *parc fermé* then, of course, that certainly would have been illegal…

"Yes [the device] exists," responded Red Bull, "although it is inaccessible once the car is fully assembled and ready to run." By the time the action on F1's fourth sprint weekend of the year got under way, it had all become a storm in a teacup.

The big questions were whether Red Bull's latest upgrades, which included a new floor edge and revised engine cover, could stop the rot that had resulted in Verstappen being unable to stay within 20s of the race winner since before the summer break. And how much Ferrari's substantial Monza upgrade would translate on a circuit with more conventional characteristics than the previous two races, in Azerbaijan and Singapore.

Meanwhile, McLaren wanted the recent status quo to remain and turned up at CoTA with the MCL38 sporting Chrome-liveried sidepods in deference to sponsor Google. Alpine confused the issue somewhat with a one-off Indiana Jones/Xbox orange-and-black livery, which made it look as though there were four McLarens out there!

Both real McLarens had substantial upgrades, although Oscar Piastri would have to wait until Mexico for a new front wing. A bigger worry for him, though, occurred when his one push-lap in the first session of sprint qualifying was deleted for exceeding T19 track limits, which eliminated him in SQ1, along with Esteban Ocon, Alex Albon (who spun after taking too much inside kerb at the same corner), and Sauber drivers Valtteri Bottas and Zhou Guanyu.

Sprint qualifying dictates that SQ1 and SQ2 are run on the medium-compound tyre, which suited Ferrari, Charles Leclerc topping the first session and team-mate Carlos Sainz, the second, during which Sergio Pérez, Pierre Gasly, Aston drivers Lance Stroll and Fernando Alonso, and VCARB's Liam Lawson bit the dust.

Bolting on softs for SQ3 shook up the order somewhat, and it was a much happier Verstappen who took pole by 0.012s from a great lap by George Russell, who found seven-tenths on the red-walled Pirellis. That was in stark contrast to bemused team-mate Lewis Hamilton, who had looked competitive on mediums, but actually went slower on softs, languishing in seventh place. Leclerc had to content himself with third, ahead of Lando Norris, Sainz and the impressive Nico Hülkenberg, who was just a tenth shy of the second Ferrari with his Haas! Team-mate Kevin Magnussen, Yuki Tsunoda and the continually high-performing Franco Colapinto completed the top ten.

The 19-lap sprint looked a little ominous for McLaren's championship aspirations, as Verstappen pulled off a lights-to-flag victory from pole to take a valuable eight points.

Behind him, Russell went high into Turn One, allowing Norris bravely through on the inside into Turn Two. And with the Ferraris back on the medium tyre and super-racy, Russell had his hands full. Sainz, in particular, was aggressive as he and Leclerc passed and repassed each other, and Charles's recommendation that they maintain position and concentrate on the others fell on deaf ears.

Sainz, driving beautifully, was the first to get by Russell as George's tyres went away, the Spaniard then chasing down Norris and diving inside the McLaren to take second place on the last lap. Leclerc also demoted Russell and finished right on Norris's tail in fourth, the Ferrari almost being collected as Lando defended the inside of T15.

As Mercedes struggled with overheating rear tyres, Hamilton, who was also contending with a bearing issue, finished sixth, 3s adrift of Russell. Some 7s behind, Magnussen and Hülkenberg delighted Gene Haas with a double helping of home points, seventh and eighth.

As qualifying for the main event began, Verstappen's form continued as he topped Q1 from Leclerc, ahead of a superb third-quickest lap from Lawson, only three-tenths down on the Dutchman and some 0.45s up on VCARB team-mate Tsunoda. The Kiwi was keen to show what he could do, knowing that going further was pointless, given that he had inherited Ricciardo's ten-place grid drop for exceeding engine component supply.

Those to go out at the end of Q1 were the Williams pair (Colapinto just a hundredth shy of Albon), Sauber drivers Bottas and Zhou, and, shockingly, Hamilton. The Mercedes driver described his car as a "nightmare" after changes had been made post-sprint, the W15 offering no grip or balance.

In Q2, Magnussen made it through to the top-ten shootout for the first time in 2024, pipping Tsunoda by three-hundredths. Lawson did not record a time, and the others to fall were Hülkenberg (after a Turn One lock-up cost him four-tenths), Ocon and Stroll.

The title protagonists were left to fight out pole, with Norris fastest after a superb first lap in Q3 that pipped Verstappen by just 0.03s. Max was on course to beat it until Russell suffered a heavy shunt at Turn 19 and red-flagged the session, leaving no time to restart. It was Lando's fourth pole in five races.

The Ferraris were third and fourth, three-tenths down, Sainz outqualifying Leclerc for the first time in six races. Most of Maranello's deficit was through the sweepers in the first sector, and Leclerc was much more confident of the medium-compound race pace. Piastri would line up fifth, but, unusually, was half a second down on Norris, while Russell faced a car rebuild and a pit-lane start. Thus Gasly would start sixth, his and Alpine's best qualifying of the season, ahead of Alonso, Magnussen and the unlucky Pérez, who had been P5 in Q2, but didn't make his hot lap due to the red flag.

Above: Max Verstappen takes control at the start of the sprint race.
Photo: Red Bull Content Pool/Getty Images

Top left: Aston Martin sporting director Andy Stevenson was celebrating his 600th race.
Photo: Aston Martin Aramco F1 Team

Above left: Friendly rivalry between Frédéric Vasseur and Zak Brown.
Photo: XPB Images

Far left: Howdy pardners! F1 pass holders receive a Texan welcome to the paddock.
Photo: Peter Nygaard/GP Photo

Left: Kevin Magnussen took seventh in the sprint for Haas.
Photo: MoneyGram Haas F1 Team

Far left: Musician Sting handed out the trophies for the sprint race.

Opening spread: A bird's-eye view of first-corner action in the main race.
Photos: Pirelli

Above: Esteban Ocon's Alpine is tipped into a spin on the opening lap.
Photo: Peter Nygaard/Grand Prix Photo

Top right: Lando Norris suffered a harsh five-second penalty, which dropped him to fourth behind rival Verstappen at the finish.
Photo: XPB Images

Above right: Carlos Sainz overcame early issues to take second behind team-mate Leclerc.
Photo: Scuderia Ferrari

Right: A special one-off 'Indiana Jones' change of livery for Alpine.
Photo: BWT Alpine F1 Team

Below right: George Russell was forced to start from the back of the grid, but he climbed through the field to finish sixth.
Photo: Mercedes-AMG Petronas F1 Team

AFTER his sizeable qualifying accident, George Russell's Mercedes needed rebuilding and as a result, with component changes, would start the race from the pit lane, while Liam Lawson was the last of those on the grid after inheriting Daniel Ricciardo's ten-place engine penalty.

All eyes were firmly focused on the front, however, where Lando Norris and Max Verstappen occupied the first two spots. The uphill approach to CoTA's wide, multi-line Turn One only heightened the anticipation.

When the lights went out, McLaren enjoyed one of its better starts, and Norris had a car's-length advantage as they blasted up the hill. He moved left to cover off the inside, but not aggressively enough, leaving an open door for Verstappen. Max, predictably, barged through it, running Norris wide on exit. That was an opportunity for the Ferraris, and Charles Leclerc, from grid slot four, was on the inside of the first corner as Carlos Sainz, from third, had to lift momentarily to avoid Norris.

"I knew Max would try something because he had nothing to lose," Leclerc said, "so I placed the car to take advantage, and that's what happened." Verstappen managed to prevent Sainz from making it a Ferrari 1-2, for the moment anyway, and Norris dropped from pole to fourth. Further back, Esteban Ocon was tapped into a spin by Alex Albon's Williams and dropped to the tail of the field.

Scrapping between Verstappen and Sainz, which began in Turn 12 and continued for the balance of the lap, allowed Leclerc to make good his escape, the Monégasque crossing the line 1.6s ahead at the end of the opening lap. Behind Norris, Oscar Piastri ran fifth, ahead of Pierre Gasly, Kevin Magnussen, Yuki Tsunoda, Sergio Pérez, Fernando Alonso, Lewis Hamilton (up five places, despite starting on the hard-compound Pirelli), Lance Stroll, Liam Lawson (also up five on the hard), Zhou Guanyu, Franco Colapinto, Valtteri Bottas, Alex Albon, George Russell and Esteban Ocon.

With a one-stop race the strategy of choice, the first 11 were all on the medium tyre, with Hamilton, Stroll, Lawson, Colapinto and Russell opting for the reverse hard-medium approach further back.

On lap three, in a highly unusual occurrence, Hamilton lost his Mercedes in Turn 19 and ended up beached in the gravel. The incident was almost a carbon copy of his team-mate's downfall in qualifying. It broke F1's long safety-car-free run, the official car neutralising the race so that the W15 could be recovered.

We were under way again on lap six, with Verstappen anticipating Leclerc's restart and remaining close enough out of the final corner to consider a move on the leading Ferrari into Turn One. With no DRS, though, Leclerc had good straight-line speed and covered off the threat, soon becoming clear again before opening a 2.5s advantage over the next three laps.

Sainz was unable to apply the same pressure as before and was on the radio: "No power on the exit of the corners. No power."

"Copy, we do see," came the response. "No option at the moment, we'll keep you posted."

"Yeah, but it's costing me a lot," Carlos complained. "It smells like fuel."

By quarter-distance in the 56-lap race, Leclerc appeared to be comfortable, with a 5.5s gap over Verstappen. Sainz was within 2s of the Red Bull, his issue seemingly under control, while Norris was 3s behind the second Ferrari. Piastri was a further 2.7s back with a 3.5s margin over Gasly's impressive Alpine. Magnussen, Tsunoda, Pérez and Hülkenberg occupied the remaining points-paying positions.

Meanwhile, Russell had progressed from his pit-lane start to 13th, passing Bottas along the way, but in a manner that the stewards didn't like, which earned him a 5s penalty for forcing another driver off the track. It did look exceedingly harsh. Russell, with DRS down the long back straight, had put himself down the inside of Turn 12 and taken the racing line on exit. Bottas had already lost the corner, but chose to keep his foot in and hang on around the outside, going off the track in the process.

When Russell's race engineer, Marcus Dudley, radioed his man about the penalty, George was incredulous: "What?"

On lap 18, seventh-placed Magnussen, running a couple of seconds behind Gasly, dived into the pits to swap his mediums for hards. Gasly was in next time around in an attempt to cover him, but he pitted out significantly behind the Haas.

Four laps later, Ferrari attempted an undercut on Verstappen, pitting Sainz from his third place some 2.5s behind the world champion. A good stop was required to prevent Carlos from pitting out behind Pérez in the second Red Bull and being delayed. The Ferrari crew delivered, and Sainz was on his way again in 2.5s. Figuring that they couldn't prevent the undercut, Red Bull elected to leave Verstappen out for another four laps and have a tyre delta on the Ferrari at the end of the race. The Dutchman came in on lap 26 and pitted out 4.4s behind the Spaniard.

Then Ferrari called in Leclerc, while Norris continued to set competitive lap times on his starting mediums. Piastri, too, was still circulating on his original mediums as Leclerc caught him five laps into his second stint and went by on the inside of Turn 12 without a fight. The McLarens were beginning to lose time to those on fresh hards, so Norris pitted first and then Piastri. Lando would have hards that were six laps fresher than Verstappen's and ten laps newer than Sainz's for the second stint.

Boosting McLaren hopes further was Verstappen's dissatisfaction with the hard compound. "These tyres just aren't good. I can't brake, I can't attack anything," Max told his team. Right on cue, Norris set the race's fastest lap as he began to eat into the gap to the third-placed Red Bull.

Ferrari had appeared to be the car to beat on the medium tyre all weekend, but there was a question mark over its pace on the hard. Everything looked just fine though as Leclerc continued on his serene way with a 7s advantage over team-mate Sainz, who had 5s in hand over Verstappen.

Lawson, having started 19th, remember, went as far as lap 37 on his offset-strategy hards before pitting for a set of mediums. He rejoined just behind Gasly, whose promising afternoon had turned a bit sour with a 5s penalty for running off the track and gaining an advantage. Lawson was also ahead of team-mate Tsunoda, who had been involved in a few midfield battles. "How has this happened?" a miffed Yuki wanted to know.

Magnussen was not happy either. Haas had gone into the race thinking that probably it would be a two-stopper, which, in Magnussen's case, looked more likely after his early lap-18 stop to undercut Gasly. He had gone on to the hard tyre rather than another set of mediums, however, leaving the one-stop option open. By lap 38, Russell, yet to stop, had worked his way up to sixth and had a 16s lead over Colapinto, also yet to stop, and Pérez. Magnussen ran ninth, 4s behind the Mexican, but had team-mate Hülkenberg just 1.5s behind on fresher rubber. Initially, calls to make a second stop were ignored by Magnussen, until he finally pitted on lap 39. The Dane thought that he could have scored points if he'd stayed out. But no doubt the team was keen to avoid an on-track fight between its two drivers… Colapinto was able to cover off Kevin when the Williams pitted, and the two indulged in a feisty scrap when the disgruntled Magnussen rejoined and was unable to displace the spirited rookie.

Russell had run even longer on his starting hards and was up to sixth place when he finally headed for the pits after 41 laps. He resumed eighth, just 4s behind Hülkenberg, with Lawson and Gasly now occupying the final points-scoring positions. Tsunoda had been within DRS range of the Alpine before a clumsy spin at Turn One dropped him behind the battling Colapinto and Magnussen, and Alonso's Aston Martin.

On a bad day for Aston, Fernando was down in 14th,

Above: The Ferrari team, led by Fred Vasseur, celebrates its 1-2 finish.
Photo: Scuderia Ferrari

Top right: Franco Colapinto signs autographs for a large contingent of Argentine fans, who had travelled north to watch him take the final point on offer.
Photo: XPB Images

Above right: Charles Leclerc notched up his third win of the season.
Photo: Scuderia Ferrari

Right: The contentious moment of the race – Verstappen runs Norris wide at T12.
Photo: XPB Images

with Stroll 17th, ahead only of the delayed Albon and Zhou, who had spun to the back earlier.

With ten laps remaining, Leclerc was cruising at the front as Sainz set fastest lap and closed to within 5s. Some 8s behind the Ferraris, Norris had come within DRS range of Verstappen for the first time and things were about to become interesting.

On lap 47, Verstappen locked-up into T1, allowing the McLaren to move closer through the sector-one sweepers, and out of Turn 11 on to the back straight, Norris was right there. Verstappen, was able to cover off the inside of Turn 12, however, and drive a 'wide' car through the third sector.

Max defended superbly for the next five laps, but with another five to go, he made a slightly poorer exit from Turn 11 and moved left early to defend the inside of T12. Norris was forced to go the long way around on the outside line and was not quite a car length ahead, and so was unable able to chop across as they reached the T12 braking zone.

Verstappen, knowing that F1's overtaking guidelines give the car ahead at the apex the right to the corner, came off the brakes to ensure that was the Red Bull, running Norris out wide. Both cars left the track, the McLaren rejoining in front.

"He overtook me outside the track," Verstappen radioed. This was where the rules needed attention, because Norris had no choice but to take avoiding action to prevent contact with a rival who had not remained within track limits (see Viewpoint).

"I think I was ahead at the apex," Norris radioed. "Let me know if you think otherwise."

"We think you were ahead at the apex," was the team's response. Although, in this instance, the law was an ass, Lando was risking a 5s penalty for not giving back the position, despite having a strong case to argue that Max, too, deserved one for forcing him off the track. Certainly, if Russell had been penalised for his fight with Bottas, surely this was a slam-dunk.

"He needs to give it back," Verstappen radioed. Norris, though, showed no sign of doing so, as he had the Red Bull out of DRS range by the time they reached the back straight on lap 53. His best option was to open a 5s advantage on his fresher tyres before the chequered flag.

It was the final lap before a 5s Norris penalty was confirmed for leaving the track and gaining an advantage. Lando began it some 3.3s to the good and by the end of it was 4.1s ahead of the Red Bull – not quite enough.

As an enthralling 2024 season took another twist, Ferrari had confirmed themselves as a force to be reckoned with as a delighted Leclerc led a 1-2 for his third win of the year. Behind Norris and Piastri's McLarens, Russell hunted down Pérez and went by into Turn 12 on the very last lap to pinch sixth after a fine drive from the pits. Hülkenberg brought Haas its fifth points finish in a row, the team moving to sixth in the constructors' battle, nine points clear of VCARB, for whom Lawson was an excellent ninth. The final point went to another fighting performance from Colapinto, who actually had claimed the additional point for fastest lap by means of his second-stint mediums, until Alpine pitted Ocon on to a set of softs to take it away… It was this kind of thing that had been a factor in the FIA deciding to scrap the fastest-lap point from 2025 after a six-year run.

It did not take long for the post-race recriminations to begin, and there was considerable sympathy for the feelings of the rational Andrea Stella.

"The way the stewards interfered with a beautiful bit of motorsport was inappropriate," said the McLaren team principal, "because both cars went off-track, so both cars gained an advantage. It's a shame because it cost us a podium in a race where we stayed patient after we were pushed off at the first corner and accepted it. This kind of decision by the stewards cannot be appealed, so we move on."

On the question of not giving back the place to Verstappen and trying to repass, Stella said simply, "We double-checked that both cars went off-track, and so for us, there was no doubt that the manoeuvre was correct." It was hard to argue against that. Red Bull and Verstappen knew the law, but sometimes the law is an ass. They had got away with one.

Tony Dodgins

VIEWPOINT
PERMISSION TO RUN WIDE

BEFORE the race, Derek Warwick said that a good result would be a quiet afternoon for the stewards with nothing to do. As it turned out, Warwick and his three colleagues were kept quite busy. And some of what they had to say didn't go down well – particularly the crucial verdict when Lando Norris was penalised five seconds for overtaking off the track, even though, in the process, Max Verstappen had also run wide. The stewards were going by the book – a book that needed urgent revision.

It was all about the apex of the corner: in this instance, Turn 12. The rule said that the driver ahead at the apex had the right to the corner. On lap 52, that had been Verstappen. Not by much, but enough. It would have been 'case closed' if then he had remained within track limits. But the fact that the Red Bull also ran wide clouded the issue, Norris having taken the lead by keeping his foot in it while in a different postcode on the run-off.

The rules favoured Verstappen, however – as he knew they would. His crossing of the white line would merely merit a mark against his name on the list of three permitted indiscretions. Norris had used the opportunity to overtake, which was a different matter entirely. A penalty was forthcoming from the moment the McLaren rejoined the track in front of the Red Bull and showed no intention of giving the place back.

In effect, the wording of the relevant regulation had given Verstappen *carte blanche*. He knew that he could come off the brakes early, arrive at the apex first and not worry about the consequences. The corner was his, and Norris would need to sort himself out.

It was argued that Norris should have worked this out for himself. Lando knew his rival well enough to understand that Max had nothing to lose, courtesy of a healthy lead in the championship. If they collided, Norris would have been the biggest loser.

The biggest loser on this day, however, had been F1 itself thanks to the damaging effect of such questionable legislation. Mind you, all of this would have been irrelevant had Turn 12 been fringed by a gravel trap.

Maurice Hamilton

FORMULA 1 PIRELLI UNITED STATES GRAND PRIX 2024

Official Timepiece

AUSTIN 18-20 OCTOBER

RACE DISTANCE: 56 laps, 191.634 miles/308.405km

RACE WEATHER: Dry/sunny (track 43-44°C, air 29-30°C)

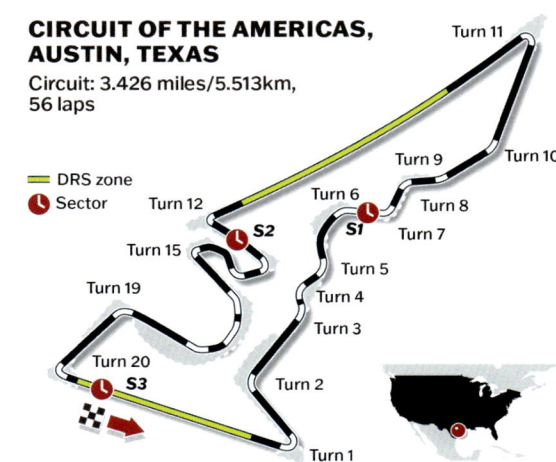

CIRCUIT OF THE AMERICAS, AUSTIN, TEXAS
Circuit: 3.426 miles/5.513km, 56 laps

- DRS zone
- Sector

RACE – OFFICIAL CLASSIFICATION

Pos.	Driver	Nat.	No.	Entrant	Car/Engine	Laps	Time/Retirement	Speed (mph/km/h)	Gap to leader	Fastest race lap
1	Charles Leclerc	MC	16	Scuderia Ferrari	Ferrari SF-24-066/12 V6	56	1h 35m 09.639s	120.827/194.453		1m 37.834s 39
2	Carlos Sainz	E	55	Scuderia Ferrari	Ferrari SF-24-066/12 V6	56	1h 35m 18.201s	120.647/194.162	8.562s	1m 37.763s 42
3	Max Verstappen	NL	1	Oracle Red Bull Racing	Red Bull RB20-Honda RBPT H002 V6	56	1h 35m 29.051s	120.418/193.794	19.412s	1m 38.117s 42
4	Lando Norris	GB	4	McLaren Formula 1 Team	McLaren MCL38-Mercedes F1 M15 E Perf. V6	56	1h 35m 29.993s *	120.398/193.762	20.354s	1m 37.679s 55
5	Oscar Piastri	AUS	81	McLaren Formula 1 Team	McLaren MCL38-Mercedes F1 M15 E Perf. V6	56	1h 35m 31.560s	120.365/193.709	21.921s	1m 37.883s 42
6	George Russell	GB	63	Mercedes-AMG Petronas F1 Team	Mercedes-AMG F1 W15-M15 E Perf. V6	56	1h 36m 05.934s *	119.648/192.554	56.295s	1m 37.656s 42
7	Sergio Pérez	MEX	11	Oracle Red Bull Racing	Red Bull RB20-Honda RBPT H002 V6	56	1h 36m 08.711s	119.590/192.462	59.072s	1m 38.514s 45
8	Nico Hülkenberg	D	27	MoneyGram Haas F1 Team	Haas VF-24-Ferrari 066/10 V6	56	1h 36m 12.596s	119.510/192.332	1m 02.957s	1m 38.404s 51
9	Liam Lawson	NZ	30	Visa Cash App RB Formula One Team	RB VCARB 01-Honda RBPT H002 V6	56	1h 36m 20.202s	119.352/192.079	1m 10.563s	1m 38.091s 54
10	Franco Colapinto	RA	43	Williams Racing	Williams FW46-Mercedes F1 M15 E Perf. V6	56	1h 36m 21.618s	119.323/192.032	1m 11.979s	1m 37.611s 46
11	Kevin Magnussen	DK	20	MoneyGram Haas F1 Team	Haas VF-24-Ferrari 066/10 V6	56	1h 36m 29.421s	119.137/191.773	1m 19.782s	1m 38.210s 56
12	Pierre Gasly	F	10	BWT Alpine F1 Team	Alpine A524-Renault E-Tech RE24 V6	56	1h 36m 40.197s *	118.941/191.417	1m 30.558s	1m 38.311s 55
13	Fernando Alonso	E	14	Aston Martin Aramco F1 Team	Aston Martin AMR24-Mercedes F1 M15 E Perf. V6	55			1 lap	1m 39.261s 52
14	Yuki Tsunoda	J	22	Visa Cash App RB Formula One Team	RB VCARB 01-Honda RBPT H002 V6	55	*		1 lap	1m 39.193s 54
15	Lance Stroll	CDN	18	Aston Martin Aramco F1 Team	Aston Martin AMR24-Mercedes F1 M15 E Perf. V6	55			1 lap	1m 39.214s 54
16	Alexander Albon	T	23	Williams Racing	Williams FW46-Mercedes F1 M15 E Perf. V6	55			1 lap	1m 39.084s 54
17	Valtteri Bottas	FIN	77	Stake F1 Team Kick Sauber	Sauber C44-Ferrari 066/12 V6	55			1 lap	1m 40.575s 53
18	Esteban Ocon	F	31	BWT Alpine F1 Team	Alpine A524-Renault E-Tech RE24 V6	55			1 lap	1m 37.330s 53
19	Zhou Guanyu	CHN	24	Stake F1 Team Kick Sauber	Sauber C44-Ferrari 066/12 V6	55			1 lap	1m 39.272s 53
	Lewis Hamilton	GB	44	Mercedes-AMG Petronas F1 Team	Mercedes-AMG F1 W15-M15 E Perf. V6	1	accident			no time

* Gasly: 5s time penalty for leaving the track and gaining an advantage.   * Norris: 5s time penalty for leaving the track and gaining an advantage (originally finished 3rd).
* Russell: 5s time penalty for forcing Bottas off the track (served at pit stop).   * Tsunoda: 5s time penalty for forcing Albon off the track.

DHL Fastest race lap: Esteban Ocon on lap 53, 1m 37.330s, 126.705mph/203.912km/h.

Lap record: Charles Leclerc (Ferrari SF90 V6), 1m 36.169s, 128.235mph/206.374km/h (2019).

20 · RUSSELL · Mercedes
Car modified in parc fermé; required to start from the pit lane

18 · ZHOU · Sauber
Used additional power unit element; 5-place grid penalty

16 · BOTTAS · Sauber

14 · ALBON · Williams

12 · OCON · Alpine

19 · LAWSON · RB
Used additional power unit elements; required to start from the back of the grid

17 · HAMILTON · Mercedes

15 · COLAPINTO · Williams

13 · STROLL · Aston Martin

11 · HÜLKENBERG · Haas

Grid order	1	2	3	4	5	6	7	8	9	10	11	12	13	14	15	16	17	18	19	20	21	22	23	24	25	26	27	28	29	30	31	32	33	34	35	36	37	38	39	40	41	42	43	44
4 NORRIS	16	16	16	16	16	16	16	16	16	16	16	16	16	16	16	16	16	16	16	16	16	16	16	16	16	16	4	4	4	4	4	16	16	16	16	16	16	16	16	16	16	16	16	16
1 VERSTAPPEN	1	1	1	1	1	1	1	1	1	1	1	1	1	1	1	1	1	1	1	1	1	1	1	1	1	1	4	81	81	81	81	16	81	55	55	55	55	55	55	55	55	55	55	55
55 SAINZ	55	55	55	55	55	55	55	55	55	55	55	55	55	55	55	55	55	55	55	55	55	4	4	4	4	81	16	16	16	16	81	55	1	1	1	1	1	1	1	1	1	1	1	1
16 LECLERC	4	4	4	4	4	4	4	4	4	4	4	4	4	4	4	4	4	4	4	4	4	81	81	81	81	55	55	55	55	55	55	1	4	4	4	4	4	4	4	4	4	4	4	4
81 PIASTRI	81	81	81	81	81	81	81	81	81	81	81	81	81	81	81	81	81	81	81	81	81	55	55	55	55	1	1	1	1	1	1	4	81	81	81	81	81	81	81	81	81	81	81	81
10 GASLY	10	10	10	10	10	10	10	10	10	10	10	10	10	10	10	10	10	11	11	11	11	11	11	11	11	27	63	63	63	63	63	63	63	63	63	63	63	63	63	11	11	11	11
14 ALONSO	20	20	20	20	20	20	20	20	20	20	20	20	20	20	20	20	11	27	27	27	27	27	27	27	27	63	30	30	30	30	30	30	30	30	30	30	11	11	11	11	27	27	27
20 MAGNUSSEN	22	22	22	22	22	22	22	22	22	22	22	22	22	22	11	30	27	30	63	63	63	63	63	63	63	30	43	43	43	43	43	43	43	43	43	43	27	63	63	63	63
11 PÉREZ	11	11	11	11	11	11	11	11	11	11	11	11	11	22	30	30	30	30	30	30	30	30	30	30	30	43	11	11	11	11	11	11	11	11	11	11	20	20	27	30	30	30	30	30
22 TSUNODA	14	14	14	14	14	27	27	27	27	27	27	27	27	30	14	11	31	31	31	31	31	20	20	20	20	20	20	20	20	20	27	27	30	10	10	10	10
27 HÜLKENBERG	27	27	27	27	27	27	14	14	14	14	30	30	30	30	30	63	43	43	43	14	14	14	14	14	11	31	31	31	27	27	27	27	27	10	30	10	22	43	43	43	43
31 OCON	44	18	18	18	18	30	30	30	30	14	14	14	14	14	63	14	31	31	31	31	31	31	20	20	31	27	27	27	31	10	10	10	10	30	10	43	20	20	20
18 STROLL	18	30	30	30	30	24	24	24	24	43	43	43	43	63	63	63	14	18	18	18	20	20	31	18	10	10	10	10	10	22	22	22	22	22	20	20	14	14	14
23 ALBON	30	24	24	24	24	43	43	43	43	77	77	77	77	43	43	43	43	31	31	20	20	18	18	18	18	18	10	22	22	22	22	22	22	23	23	14	14	14	14	22	22	22
43 COLAPINTO	24	43	43	43	43	77	77	77	77	63	63	63	63	77	77	77	77	31	31	23	23	23	23	23	23	23	18	23	23	23	23	23	77	77	77	77	77	77	77	77	77	77	77
77 BOTTAS	43	77	77	77	77	63	63	63	63	31	31	31	31	31	31	23	23	23	23	10	10	10	10	10	10	10	22	77	77	77	77	77	14	14	14	31	31	31	31	31	31	31	31	31
44 HAMILTON	77	63	23	63	63	31	31	31	31	18	18	18	18	18	23	23	18	18	18	22	22	22	22	22	22	22	14	14	14	14	14	14	31	31	31	18	18	18	18	18	18	18	18	18
24 ZHOU	23	23	63	31	31	18	18	18	18	23	23	23	23	23	77	77	77	77	77	77	77	77	77	77	77	14	24	18	18	18	18	18	18	18	18	23	23	23	23	23	23	23	23	23
30 LAWSON	63	31	31	23	23	23	23	23	24	24	24	24	24	24	24	24	24	24	24	24	24	24	24	24	24	24	18	24	24	24	24	24	23	24	24	24	24	24	24	24	24	24	24	24
63 RUSSELL	31																																											

SC Safety Car deployed on laps 3-5

TIME SHEETS

PRACTICE (FRIDAY)

Weather: Dry/sunny-cloudy

Temperatures: track 32-33°C, air 26-27°C

Pos.	Driver	Laps	Time
1	Carlos Sainz	25	1m 33.602s
2	Charles Leclerc	27	1m 33.623s
3	Max Verstappen	23	1m 33.855s
4	Lando Norris	25	1m 33.868s
5	Oscar Piastri	26	1m 33.908s
6	Lewis Hamilton	22	1m 33.963s
7	George Russell	27	1m 34.093s
8	Kevin Magnussen	24	1m 34.096s
9	Fernando Alonso	24	1m 34.112s
10	Yuki Tsunoda	20	1m 34.313s
11	Nico Hülkenberg	24	1m 34.364s
12	Pierre Gasly	24	1m 34.375s
13	Liam Lawson	28	1m 34.443s
14	Alexander Albon	26	1m 34.618s
15	Lance Stroll	24	1m 34.619s
16	Sergio Pérez	24	1m 34.638s
17	Esteban Ocon	24	1m 34.806s
18	Valtteri Bottas	26	1m 35.041s
19	Franco Colapinto	27	1m 35.248s
20	Zhou Guanyu	15	1m 37.219s

SPRINT QUALIFYING (FRIDAY)

Weather: Dry/sunny-cloudy

Temperatures: track 30-32°C, air 28°C

Pos.	Driver	First	Second	Third	Qualifying Tyre
1	Max Verstappen	1m 33.908s	1m 33.290s	1m 32.833s	Soft (n)
2	George Russell	1m 34.125s	1m 33.544s	1m 32.845s	Soft (n)
3	Charles Leclerc	1m 33.647s	1m 33.392s	1m 33.059s	Soft (n)
4	Lando Norris	1m 33.919s	1m 33.566s	1m 33.083s	Soft (n)
5	Carlos Sainz	1m 34.109s	1m 33.274s	1m 33.089s	Soft (n)
6	Nico Hülkenberg	1m 34.825s	1m 33.994s	1m 33.183s	Soft (u)
7	Lewis Hamilton	1m 33.840s	1m 33.370s	1m 33.378s	Soft (n)
8	Kevin Magnussen	1m 34.403s	1m 33.788s	1m 33.398s	Soft (n)
9	Yuki Tsunoda	1m 34.646s	1m 34.052s	1m 33.802s	Soft (n)
10	Franco Colapinto	1m 34.606s	1m 33.952s	1m 34.406s	Soft (u)
11	Sergio Pérez	1m 34.333s	1m 34.244s		
12	Pierre Gasly	1m 34.865s	1m 34.363s		
13	Lance Stroll	1m 34.324s	no time		
14	Fernando Alonso	1m 34.436s	no time		
15	Liam Lawson	1m 34.617s	no time		
16	Oscar Piastri	1m 34.881s			
17	Esteban Ocon	1m 34.917s			
18	Alexander Albon	1m 35.054s			
19	Valtteri Bottas	1m 35.148s			
20	Zhou Guanyu	1m 36.472s			

FOR THE RECORD

100th GP START: Alexander Albon

110th GP PODIUM: Max Verstappen

40th GP PODIUM: Charles Leclerc

300th GP POLE POSITION: British drivers

1st GP FASTEST LAP: Esteban Ocon & Alpine

QUALIFYING: head to head

Verstappen	18	1	Pérez
Hamilton	5	14	Russell
Norris	15	4	Piastri
Leclerc	12	6	Sainz
Leclerc	1	0	Bearman
Gasly	8	11	Ocon
Alonso	13	6	Stroll
Albon	14	1	Sargeant
Albon	3	1	Colapinto
Bottas	18	1	Zhou
Tsunoda	12	6	Ricciardo
Tsunoda	1	0	Lawson
Magnussen	5	13	Hülkenberg
Bearman	1	0	Hülkenberg

QUALIFYING (SATURDAY)

Weather: Dry/sunny

Temperatures: track 32-35°C, air 29-30°C

Pos.	Driver	First	Second	Third	Qualifying Tyre
1	Lando Norris	1m 33.616s	1m 32.851s	1m 32.330s	Soft (n)
2	Max Verstappen	1m 33.046s	1m 32.584s	1m 32.361s	Soft (n)
3	Carlos Sainz	1m 33.556s	1m 32.836s	1m 32.652s	Soft (n)
4	Charles Leclerc	1m 33.241s	1m 32.962s	1m 32.740s	Soft (n)
5	Oscar Piastri	1m 33.864s	1m 33.057s	1m 32.950s	Soft (n)
6	George Russell	1m 33.536s	1m 33.142s	1m 32.974s	Soft (u)
7	Pierre Gasly	1m 33.550s	1m 33.162s	1m 33.018s	Soft (u)
8	Fernando Alonso	1m 33.973s	1m 33.429s	1m 33.309s	Soft (n)
9	Kevin Magnussen	1m 33.564s	1m 33.474s	1m 33.481s	Soft (u)
10	Sergio Pérez	1m 33.611s	1m 33.020s	no time	
11	Yuki Tsunoda	1m 33.795s	1m 33.506s		
12	Nico Hülkenberg	1m 33.601s	1m 33.544s		
13	Esteban Ocon	1m 33.986s	1m 33.597s		
14	Lance Stroll	1m 34.033s	1m 33.759s		
15	Liam Lawson	1m 33.339s	no time		
16	Alexander Albon	1m 34.051s			
17	Franco Colapinto	1m 34.062s			
18	Valtteri Bottas	1m 34.152s			
19	Lewis Hamilton	1m 34.154s			
20	Zhou Guanyu	1m 34.228s			

SPRINT (SATURDAY)

RACE DISTANCE: 19 laps, 64.886 miles/104.424km

RACE WEATHER: Dry/sunny Temperatures: track 37-40°C, air 28-29°C

Pos.	Driver	Laps	Time/Retirement	Speed (mph/km/h)	Gap to leader	Fastest race lap		Grid
1	**Max Verstappen**	19	31m 06.146s	125.172/201.445		1m 37.463s	19	1
2	**Carlos Sainz**	19	31m 10.028s	124.912/201.027	3.882s	1m 37.552s	19	5
3	**Lando Norris**	19	31m 12.386s	124.755/200.773	6.240s	1m 38.045s	17	4
4	**Charles Leclerc**	19	31m 13.102s	124.707/200.697	6.956s	1m 37.748s	11	3
5	**George Russell**	19	31m 21.912s	124.123/199.757	15.766s	1m 38.301s	4	2
6	**Lewis Hamilton**	19	31m 24.870s	123.929/199.444	18.724s	1m 38.372s	17	7
7	**Kevin Magnussen**	19	31m 31.307s	123.507/198.765	25.161s	1m 38.602s	6	8
8	**Nico Hülkenberg**	19	31m 32.734s	123.414/198.615	26.588s	1m 38.746s	16	6
9	Sergio Pérez	19	31m 36.096s	123.195/198.263	29.950s	1m 38.452s	19	11
10	Oscar Piastri	19	31m 43.205s *	122.734/197.522	37.059s	1m 37.567s	19	16
11	Yuki Tsunoda	19	31m 44.509s	122.651/197.387	38.363s	1m 39.136s	19	9
12	Franco Colapinto	19	31m 45.606s	122.580/197.273	39.460s	1m 39.335s	19	10
13	Lance Stroll	19	31m 47.382s	122.466/197.090	41.236s	1m 39.532s	19	13
14	Pierre Gasly	19	31m 48.141s	122.417/197.011	41.995s	1m 39.438s	19	12
15	Esteban Ocon	19	31m 48.950s	122.365/196.928	42.804s	1m 38.835s	7	17
16	Liam Lawson	19	31m 50.154s	122.288/196.804	44.008s	1m 39.237s	7	15
17	Alexander Albon	19	31m 50.710s *	122.252/196.746	44.564s	1m 39.198s	19	18
18	Fernando Alonso	19	31m 52.953s	122.109/196.516	46.807s	1m 39.250s	18	14
19	Zhou Guanyu	19	31m 58.988s	121.725/195.898	52.842s	1m 39.705s	17	20
20	Valtteri Bottas	19	32m 00.622s	121.622/195.731	54.476s	1m 39.642s	16	19

* Albon: Started from the pit lane * Piastri: 5s time penalty for forcing Gasly off the track

Fastest race lap: Max Verstappen on lap 19, 1m 37.463s, 126.532mph/203.634km/h.

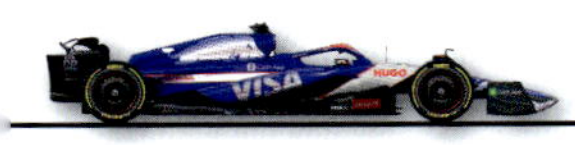

10 · TSUNODA · RB

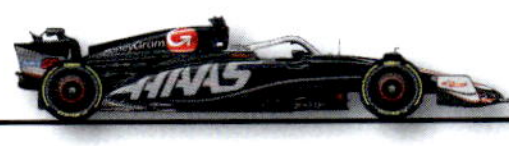

8 · MAGNUSSEN · Haas

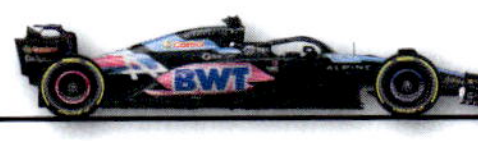

6 · GASLY · Alpine

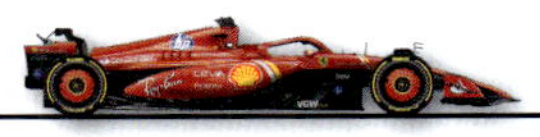

4 · LECLERC · Ferrari

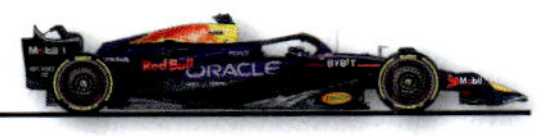

2 · VERSTAPPEN · Red Bull

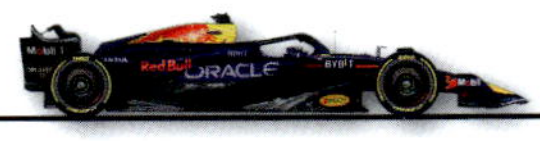

9 · PÉREZ · Red Bull

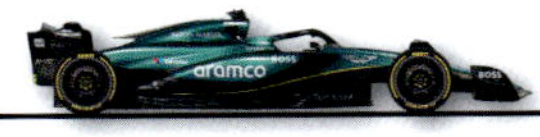

7 · ALONSO · Aston Martin

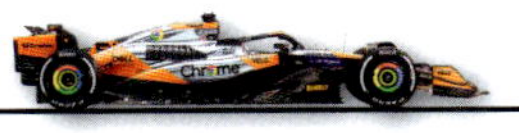

5 · PIASTRI · McLaren

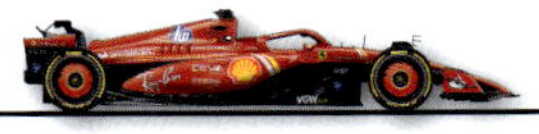

3 · SAINZ · Ferrari

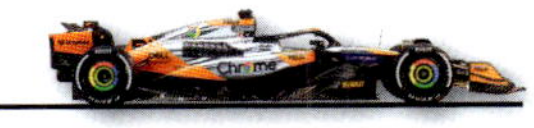

1 · NORRIS · McLaren

45	46	47	48	49	50	51	52	53	54	55	56	
16	16	16	16	16	16	16	16	16	16	16	16	1
55	55	55	55	55	55	55	55	55	55	55	55	2
1	1	1	1	1	1	1	4	4	4	4	4	3
4	4	4	4	4	4	4	1	1	1	1	1	4
81	81	81	81	81	81	81	81	81	81	81	81	5
11	11	11	11	11	11	11	11	11	11	63	63	6
63	63	63	63	63	63	63	63	63	63	11	11	7
27	27	27	27	27	27	27	27	27	27	27	27	8
30	30	30	30	30	30	30	30	30	30	30	30	9
43	43	43	43	43	43	43	43	43	43	43	43	10
10	10	20	20	20	20	20	20	20	20	20	20	
20	20	10	10	10	10	10	10	10	10	10	10	
14	14	14	14	14	14	14	14	14	14	14		
22	22	22	22	22	22	22	22	*22*	*22*	*22*		
31	31	31	*31*	*31*	*31*	*31*	*18*	*18*	*18*	*18*		
18	*18*	*18*	*18*	*18*	*18*	*18*	*23*	*23*	*23*	*23*		
77	*23*	*23*	*23*	*23*	*23*	*23*	*77*	*77*	*77*	*77*		
23	*77*	*77*	*77*	*77*	*77*	*77*	*31*	*31*	*31*	*31*		
24	*24*	*24*	*24*	*24*	*24*	*24*	*24*	*24*	*24*	*24*		

23 = Pit stop *24 = One lap or more behind*

RACE TYRE STRATEGIES

PIRELLI

	Driver	Race Stint 1	Race Stint 2	Race Stint 3
1	Leclerc	Medium (n): 1-26	Hard (n): 27-56	
2	Sainz	Medium (n): 1-21	Hard (n): 22-56	
3	Verstappen	Medium (n): 1-25	Hard (n): 26-56	
4	Norris	Medium (n): 1-31	Hard (n): 32-56	
5	Piastri	Medium (n): 1-32	Hard (n): 33-56	
6	Russell	Hard (n): 1-40	Medium (n): 41-56	
7	Pérez	Medium (n): 1-26	Hard (n): 27-56	
8	Hülkenberg	Medium (n): 1-27	Hard (n): 28-56	
9	Lawson	Hard (n): 1-36	Medium (n): 37-56	
10	Colapinto	Hard (n): 1-39	Medium (n): 40-56	
11	Magnussen	Medium (n): 1-17	Hard (n): 18-38	Medium (n): 39-56
12	Gasly	Medium (n): 1-18	Hard (n): 19-56	
13	Alonso	Medium (n): 1-26	Hard (u): 27-55	
14	Tsunoda	Medium (n): 1-18	Hard (u): 19-55	
15	Stroll	Hard (u): 1-27	Medium (n): 28-55	
16	Albon	Medium (n): 1-3	Medium (n): 4-33	Hard (n): 34-55
17	Bottas	Medium (u): 1-15	Hard (n): 16-55	
18	Ocon	Medium (n): 1-31	Hard (n): 32-51	Soft (u): 52-55
19	Zhou	Medium (u): 1-13	Medium (u): 14-35	Hard (n): 36-55
	Hamilton	Hard (n): 1 (dnf)		

The tyre regulations stipulate that at least two of three dry tyre specifications must be used during a dry race. Selected compounds for Austin: Red = Soft (C4); Yellow = Medium (C3); White = Hard (C2). (n) new (u) used

POINTS

DRIVERS

1	Max Verstappen	354
2	Lando Norris	297
3	Charles Leclerc	275
4	Oscar Piastri	247
5	Carlos Sainz	215
6	Lewis Hamilton	177
7	George Russell	167
8	Sergio Pérez	150
9	Fernando Alonso	62
10	Nico Hülkenberg	29
11	Lance Stroll	24
12	Yuki Tsunoda	22
13	Alexander Albon	12
14	Daniel Ricciardo	12
15	Kevin Magnussen	8
16	Pierre Gasly	8
17	Oliver Bearman	7
18	Franco Colapinto	5
19	Esteban Ocon	5
20	Liam Lawson	2

CONSTRUCTORS

1	McLaren	544
2	Red Bull	504
3	Ferrari	496
4	Mercedes	344
5	Aston Martin	86
6	Haas	38
7	RB	36
8	Williams	17
9	Alpine	13

MEXICO CITY QUALIFYING

FROM Austin to the altitude of lower-grip Mexico City. After CoTA had validated Ferrari's Monza upgrade on a more conventional track, after Baku and Singapore, the big question was whether Maranello could keep the momentum going and become a genuine constructors' championship threat over the balance of the season.

Charles Leclerc had taken a fine win in the USA, but in Mexico, Carlos Sainz was the force to be reckoned with, a pace-setter from the off in Friday practice, the SF24 looking particularly strong on Pirelli's medium compound. Meanwhile, Leclerc was on the back foot. He missed FP1 in favour of Ollie Bearman having a contracted outing for the Scuderia. The other regulars to sit out FP1 were Lewis Hamilton at Mercedes (for Kimi Antonelli), Lando Norris at McLaren (Pato O'Ward), Fernando Alonso – marking his 400th F1 race weekend – at Aston Martin (Felipe Drugovich) and Zhou Guanyu at Sauber (Robert Schwartzman).

Antonelli took a much calmer approach than he had done at the Monza session, where he had crashed on the second lap, learning the circuit through an extended run on the hard-compound Pirelli before taking a set of softs, but, by his own admission, not exploiting the grip fully. He ended up 12th overall, 1.2s adrift of his FP1-topping team-mate, George Russell.

Sainz managed to clear Q1 on a set of mediums; Hamilton, Piastri and Leclerc appeared likely to do the same, but ultimately had to go on to softs. Disastrously for McLaren, however, Oscar had a lap deleted for exceeding track limits at T12, then lost time over a kerb and found himself out in Q1. In 2023, it had been team-mate Norris who had locked up and not managed to put a Q1 time on the board. Piastri would start 17th.

Joining the young Aussie as Q2 spectators were Franco Colapinto and, to groans of disappointment from the huge crowd, home hero Sergio Pérez, Esteban Ocon and Zhou Guanyu.

For Pérez, it was a repeat of Austin, struggling with braking into slow corners and consequently being unable to attack. Once more, the rumours circulated that Liam Lawson had the rest of the season to make a case for himself to partner Max Verstappen in 2025.

The Q2 session was red-flagged with a few seconds remaining after Yuki Tsunoda, who had been third quickest in FP1, put his VCARB into the tyres after a lock-up into Turn 12. That robbed him of an improved lap and made him the first Q2 eliminee, by 0.08s. Ironically, it also robbed team-mate Liam Lawson of the chance to improve, the Kiwi narrowly missing out on Q3, along with Alonso and Lance Stroll's Aston Martins, and Valtteri Bottas's Sauber. Making it worse for VCARB was constructors' rival Haas putting both cars through to Q3 for the first time in 2024.

Initially, it seemed that Ferrari did not gain as much on the soft tyre as had been the case in Austin. It was Norris who topped Q2, a couple of tenths ahead of Verstappen and then the two Ferrari drivers. On the first Q3 run, an attacking lap from the Dutchman (1m 16.368s) was half a second better than Norris's first attempt and pipped Leclerc's Ferrari by five-hundredths. Suddenly, however, Sainz was flying, stopping the clock in 1m 16.055s and putting himself more than three-tenths clear just as Verstappen's time was deleted for exceeding track limits at T2. On his second run, Carlos was even quicker, the only man to dip below 1m 16s with a 1m 15.946s lap to take a sixth career pole and his first of 2024. Either of his laps would have been good enough for pole.

"In Mexico, you often feel like you can't put a lap together for the amount of sliding there is, but my Q3 laps were identical, almost perfect," Sainz beamed. "Since Austin, we've made a step in finding something with the tyre preparation on the out-lap and seem to be going in the right direction. Hopefully, the race pace should be enough to win it," he added confidently.

Verstappen was more than happy with a front-row spot, 0.22s down. Norris was a tenth adrift, third, but mindful that with such a long drag down to Turn One, that was the ideal spot from which to pick up a tow. Team principal Andrea Stella explained that the potential to be closer was there but for overheating the softs too much in Q3.

Leclerc was unimpressed with fourth. "When I got into the car in FP2, I knew I didn't have the feeling," he explained. "In FP3, I was nowhere as well; in qually, I'm nowhere, and the only thing that gives me a bit of optimism is the race pace on Friday. With my driving style, I struggle a bit on low-grip tracks, like Monza and here, especially in qualifying."

After topping that FP1 session, Russell winded himself in a big shunt in FP2. Following his qualifying crash in Austin, the two Mercedes were of different specs, Hamilton's car using the upgraded floor, while Russell's was a later Silverstone specification. He managed to wring fifth place out of it, 0.14s quicker than Lewis, who qualified next up.

Magnussen did a superb job to put the first Haas seventh on the grid, 0.006s quicker than an equally impressive Pierre Gasly for Alpine. Alex Albon qualified his Williams ninth, having recovered well from a crash in FP1, when he had tripped over Bearman, who had been informed of his impending arrival too late, both the Williams and Ferrari suffering damage.

Completing the top ten was Nico Hülkenberg, the one-lap specialist having to give best to his Haas team-mate this time and admitting difficulty in finding a rhythm. Strong top speed, however, meant that 'The Hulk' was confident of racing strongly.

SUCH had been Ferrari's superiority for both one-lap and long-run pace that with a conventional medium/hard one-stop race widely expected for the front-runners, the best chance that either Max Verstappen or Lando Norris had was to make a better start than pole-man Carlos Sainz.

A superior getaway for Verstappen from P2 meant that Sainz was unable to chop across from his outside pole to cover the inside for Turn One, and indeed it was the Red Bull that led into the tight right-left of T1/2. Sainz tried to run wheel to wheel through the turn with Max, but had to back out, take to the run-off and rejoin in front, immediately ceding the place to Verstappen. Norris got through safely in third, ahead of Charles Leclerc. Further back in the pack, contact between Yuki Tsunoda and Alex Albon eliminated both and brought out Bernd Maylander's safety car for the second successive race.

Behind Verstappen, Sainz, Norris and Leclerc, the Mercedes of Lewis Hamilton and George Russell were running fifth and sixth, ahead of Haas pair Kevin Magnussen and Nico Hülkenberg, then Pierre Gasly, Liam Lawson, Lance Stroll, Fernando Alonso, Sergio Pérez, Franco Colapinto, Valtteri Bottas, Zhou Guanyu, Oscar Piastri and Esteban Ocon.

Pérez's excellent launch and five-place gain excited the crowd, but, unfortunately, they had been made from a false position, Sergio having overshot his grid box, which earned him a 5s penalty…

With the debris cleared away, and the stricken VCARB and Williams recovered, the safety car pulled off on lap six, Verstappen gunning it out of Turn 13. With no DRS on the restart lap, of course, all was orderly down through T1/2. Initially, Verstappen was able to keep Sainz's chasing Ferrari just outside DRS range through a fastest lap. Carlos responded, however, setting a fastest lap of his own. On lap nine, noticing flashing red harvesting lights on Verstappen's car, he plunged down the inside of the Red Bull into Turn One. He kept it together through Turn Two and, with a second helping of DRS, was comfortably through Turn Three in front.

The first four were now nose to tail, and it was a tetchy Verstappen on the radio to the pits: "Mate, what can I do with a ******* empty battery? What is this stupid mode?"

It wasn't long before he was more occupied in trying to fend off Norris, who took a look down the outside into Turn Four. Verstappen ran him out wide and Norris short-cut Turn Five across the grass, allowing leader Sainz back ahead before resuming in front of the Red Bull. Verstappen retaliated with an unfeasible move down the inside of Turn Seven that forced them both wide into the run-off. For the second time in seven days, Leclerc gratefully relegated both in one fell swoop to make it a Ferrari 1-2.

"I was ahead the whole way through the corner. This guy is dangerous," radioed a calm, but clearly frustrated Norris. "I just have to avoid a crash. It's the same as last time." Race Control noted both incidents and took little time to notify a 10s penalty for Verstappen for forcing another driver off the track.

Gianpiero Lambiase was quickly on the radio to his man: "So, Max, for info, you've been given a ten-second penalty for forcing Lando off-track at Turn 4."

"That's impressive," Verstappen replied. The Turn Four incident had been debatable if you were worrying about who had been ahead at the apex. If that merited 10s, you did wonder what might be coming for the more unacceptable incident at Turn Seven.

"There was a lot of whingeing," 'GP' pointed out, "a lot." Justifiably, McLaren could claim.

The Mercedes pair had also been involved in a feisty dice ever since Hamilton had beaten Russell off the start. It took George until lap 15 to get a good DRS run on Lewis and go around the outside of his team-mate into Turn One. Doing a commendable job for Haas, Magnussen was

Above: Carlos Sainz was the man to beat throughout the weekend.
Photo: Scuderia Ferrari

Top left: Mexican mayhem. The popular Sergio Pérez was closely guarded by security.
Photo: Red Bull Content Pool/Getty Images

Above left: Yuki Tsunoda's race ended at the first corner, after contact with Alex Albon.
Photo: Atsuo Sakurai

Left: Verstappen, Sainz and Norris ensured a competitive mix at the front of the grid.
Photo: Red Bull Content Pool/Getty Images

Below left: Robert Shwartzman was given a run in the Sauber. The Ferrari driver appeared set to make a career in IndyCar in 2025.
Stake F1 Team Kick Sauber

Opening spread: A farewell win for Carlos Sainz at Ferrari?
Photo: Scuderia Ferrari

Above: Four hundred-up. Well almost, for the seemingly ageless Fernando Alonso.
Photo: Aston Martin Aramco F1 Team

Top right: For once, Ferrari's Charles Leclerc was overshadowed by his team-mate, but he still joined him on the podium.
Photo: Scuderia Ferrari

Above right: Out of the doldrums. Alpine's form picked up in Mexico, where Pierre Gasly grabbed a point. Much, much better was to come a week later…
Photo: BWT Alpine F1 Team

Right: The Haas team's impressive season continued when Kevin Magnussen took seventh. Team-mate Nico Hülkenberg was ninth in a rewarding race for the team.
Photo: MoneyGram Haas F1 Team

still with them, running seventh, team-mate Hülkenberg a couple of seconds further back.

Meanwhile, Alonso's 400th GP weekend (his actual 400th start would come in Qatar) did not work out as he had hoped, his Aston Martin posting a lap-16 early retirement after debris in a brake duct had sent temperatures stratospheric.

Pérez had made it through from his lowly 18th starting position to the fringes of the points and now was with Liam Lawson's tenth-placed VCARB. Both drivers had started on the hard-compound Pirelli to run an offset strategy deeper into the race. All of those ahead were on the medium, and Lawson had done a strong job to be running just over a second behind Gasly's Alpine, which was still in touch with the Haas pair.

Unable, just, to get a move done into T1/2, Pérez, with a second helping of DRS, attempted to go inside Lawson into Turn Four. He ran the VCARB out wide, but the Kiwi came back at him in T5, in turn running the Mexican wide on exit as contact was made, damaging the Red Bull and, according to Christian Horner, robbing it of 65 points of downforce. With all the talk of 2025, this one looked a bit personal, and Pérez was not impressed with the rookie's defence. "What the **** is this idiot doing?" he radioed. Helmut Marko is all for his drivers getting their elbows out – witness a certain three-times world champion – it's just that he'd rather they did it with rival teams than their own!

The race was 20 laps in when the stewards finished their deliberations and hit Verstappen with a second 10s penalty for leaving the track and gaining an advantage, meaning that when Max – still running third, 3s behind Leclerc and ahead of Norris – pitted, it would be 20s before anyone could lay a hand on the Red Bull!

Leclerc, with a new fastest lap, had closed right in on Sainz, prompting a radio message from Carlos: "Charles is taking the piss." Temperatures, of both brakes and engines, are always an issue in Mexico, and the race leader felt that he was being pushed unnecessarily hard at such an early stage.

Pérez's delay in battling Lawson had dropped him into the clutches of Stroll's Aston, which he'd passed earlier, and just 2s behind the Canadian was Colapinto's hard-tyre-shod Williams, under pressure from the second McLaren of the out-of-position Piastri.

On lap 27 of the 71, Red Bull called in Verstappen, who still had a wary Norris bottled up behind him. Ahead of them, Leclerc had heeded warnings, dropped back to around 5s behind his team-mate and was now 'managing'. Verstappen was a similar distance behind the second Ferrari and, with the Red Bull about to serve its penalty, Norris had no need to worry about undercuts or overcuts and was about to be able to demonstrate his true pace. Behind him was a 7s gap to Russell, who had put 4s between himself and Hamilton. Verstappen's stop seemed like an eternity and he re-emerged from the pits in 15th place.

Despite being behind on the road, it was Hamilton who pitted first of the Mercedes drivers, to cover off the delayed Verstappen. McLaren brought in Norris after 31 laps to go on to the hard tyre and see if he could make any impression on the Ferraris.

Ferrari responded by bringing in Leclerc on the next lap, while Mercedes pitted Russell at the same time. Sainz was instructed to come in on the following lap.

"One more lap please, guys, one more lap," responded the race leader, obviously wanting as big a late-race tyre delta as possible over his pursuers. But that was overruled and he was brought in.

Meanwhile, Piastri was still stuck behind Lawson and now had the reshod Hamilton, with a new fastest lap, breathing down his neck. Unlike Sainz, Oscar did want to stop: "Mate, think about pulling me out of this." After fending off Hamilton into T1, Piastri finally got a move done on Lawson down the inside of Turn Four, with Hamilton following him through down the inside of the next corner. Then Lewis successfully negotiated the second McLaren, still on its starting mediums, to claim fifth and be in a position to go after Russell, some 3s further up the road. Piastri was finally brought in after a 40-lap medium-tyre stint.

With 30 laps to go, Sainz led by 7.5s from Leclerc, with Norris 5s behind the second Ferrari and some 16s clear of Russell's Mercedes. Hamilton, starting to take time out of his team-mate, had 8s over Verstappen. Further down, Pérez and Lawson, now on the medium tyre for the final stint, were at it again over 16th place, the VCARB towing past the Red Bull into Turn One, Lawson giving Pérez the middle finger as he went by, still sore about their earlier ding-dong.

For the second consecutive race, Colapinto suddenly set the race's fastest lap, again by dint of going on to the quicker medium tyre for the final stint after running 48 laps on hards with an offset strategy – impressive all the same, even though, as in Austin, it wouldn't last.

At the front, the gaps ebbed and flowed, Leclerc beginning to catch Sainz again, the gap down to less than 5s as, in turn, Norris took time out of Charles. Then, however, Sainz's margin was back out to 7s as Leclerc was slowed by traffic, Norris closing to within 2.5s with a dozen laps to go.

When Leclerc lost more time behind Stroll, Norris set a new fastest lap and put himself within DRS range for the first time. The Ferraris might have had the pace on the medium compound, but on the hard, the McLaren was quicker. Leclerc, on the gas a little too early while trying to keep Norris at bay out of the final corner,

Above: Lewis Hamilton finally got the upper hand over team-mate George Russell after a race-long battle.
Photos: Mercedes-AMG Petronas F1 Team

Top right: Russell seems happy enough with fifth place.

Above right: Another wreck for Williams as Alex Albon rides back to face the music.
Photo: Atsuo Sakurai

Right: Sainz is given a warm embrace by long-time pal Lando Norris.
Photo: XPB Images

Far right: Nowhere man. Out of contention, Red Bull's Sergio Pérez was sent out to try for the fastest lap, but he was beaten to it by Ferrari and Charles Leclerc.
Photo: Red Bull Content Pool/Getty Images

suddenly suffered an almighty tank-slapper. Somehow, he managed to keep the Ferrari out of the wall, but Norris was through. Sainz was another 8s up the road, however, and second was as far as Lando would get. Meanwhile, in the Mercedes war, Russell finally had to give best to Hamilton, who swooped around his outside into Turn One with five laps to go.

Piastri, doing his utmost to limit the damage done by his disastrous Q1 exit, passed Hülkenberg for eighth on lap 57 and was trying to close the gap to Magnussen, a further 5s ahead.

The FIA's decision to do away with the point for fastest race lap from 2025 (see Viewpoint) had polarised opinion, but the teams were making use of it while they could. Colapinto's 1m 20.090s on mediums was lowered to 1m 19.858s by Norris in his hard-tyred pursuit of Leclerc, and then again to 1m 19.691s on lap 68.

However, this coincided with Colapinto trying to win 'the battle of the rookies' by passing Lawson for 12th around the outside into Turn One, which resulted in contact in T2 that damaged Lawson's front wing, and attracted a somewhat harsh 10s time addition and two licence penalty points for the young Argentine. VCARB brought in Lawson for a new nose and a set of softs, and, just as Ricciardo had helped the senior Red Bull team by stealing Norris's fastest-lap point in Singapore, his replacement did likewise with a lap of 1m 19.502s.

But, behind Leclerc, there was a pit-stop gap to Russell, and right at the death, Ferrari called in Charles to go for the extra fastest-lap point – he duly obliged with 1m 18.336s. Red Bull, probably more in hope than expectation, also brought in Pérez for softs, meaning that he would finish what could be his last Mexican GP dead last on the road.

Another absorbing race was won by a delighted Sainz who, unusually, had not just his father, but also his mother and a whole host of friends in tow. He had deeply wanted another win before he left Ferrari, but you couldn't help wondering what he might be feeling at the prospect of the Scuderia starting to look like a championship-challenging outfit just when he wouldn't be able to take advantage.

Norris went home with a ten-point championship swing in his favour, reducing the gap to 47 points with four races and two sprints remaining. In the constructors' championship, first and third for Ferrari allowed them to overhaul Red Bull, moving to within 29 points of McLaren.

Suddenly, the timing of Hamilton's move to Ferrari was beginning to look very good, and he was happy with his fourth place, too: "It was my fault, but we took too much front wing out of the car and I had a load of understeer, which basically knocked out the tyres in that first stint, but after changes at the pit stop, I was much, much better. We also got a lot of information because I could feel exactly where the car was working and where it wasn't, and I could see the difference between George's car and mine."

Despite his penalties, Verstappen was more concerned with Red Bull's race pace, which was still missing after the improvements of Austin. Magnussen, nearing the end of his Haas career, had scored his best result since 2022 in seventh place, having held off Piastri, while Hülkenberg and Gasly took the final points. A sprint weekend in Interlagos beckoned at the end of two brutal season-closing triple-headers. The cauldron was bubbling nicely!

Tony Dodgins

VIEWPOINT
POINTLESS POSTURING

ONCE again tinkering around F1's edges, the FIA announced the elimination of a championship point for fastest lap. They said that the lure of an extra point had not "improved the spectacle".

What, exactly were they expecting? The leaders and their pit crews, having bust a gut to gain a couple of tenths of a second during 90 minutes of racing, to suddenly dive into the pits for fresh tyres, set fastest lap and claim a point – having lost a handful by giving up track position to put on a show? Or perhaps were the officials expecting the leading drivers suddenly to find fast lap pace on tyres that were knackered?

However, the fastest-lap prize did throw a strategy option into the mix. Daniel Ricciardo's last act in the Singapore Grand Prix – and possibly his F1 career – had been to make a late stop, snatch the point away from Lando Norris and debilitate the McLaren driver's championship battle with Max Verstappen, who happened to be driving for RB's senior associate, Red Bull.

Time lost in the pits had made no difference to Ricciardo, since he had been running next to last. The bonus would only be available to a front-runner if there happened to be a large gap – usually in the region of 30 seconds – to the car behind. Ironically, given the timing of the announcement in the days before Mexico, that's exactly what happened to Charles Leclerc. With nothing to lose, he stopped for soft tyres and nicked the point, Norris and McLaren once again being the losers.

Red Bull tried the same thing with Sergio Pérez – which had to be wishful thinking, given that he was up against an infinitely faster driver-car combination and, in any case, his Red Bull had been hobbled by body damage in an earlier incident. It merely exacerbated Checo's misery on a weekend when nothing seemed to go right for the home hero.

The fastest-lap option had brought interest rather than spectacle, given that the extra point could make the difference at the end of the season. The grand gesture of scrapping the point after just six seasons only served to underline F1's pointless posturing.

Maurice Hamilton

20

FORMULA 1 GRAN PREMIO DE LA CIUDAD DE MÉXICO 2024

ROLEX

Official Timepiece

MEXICO CITY 25-27 OCTOBER

RACE DISTANCE: 71 laps, 189.738 miles/305.354km

RACE WEATHER: Dry/overcast (track 28-37°C, air 20-22°C)

AUTÓDROMO HERMANOS RODRÍGUEZ, MEXICO CITY

Circuit: 2.674 miles/4.304 Km, 71 laps

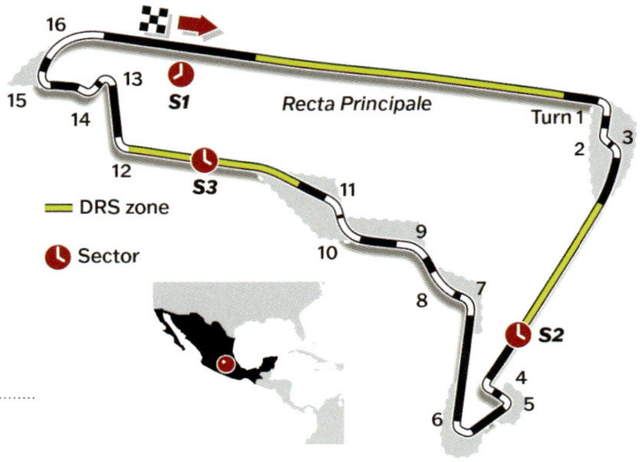

RACE – OFFICIAL CLASSIFICATION

Pos.	Driver	Nat.	No.	Entrant	Car/Engine	Laps	Time/Retirement	Speed (mph/km/h)	Gap to leader	Fastest race lap	
1	**Carlos Sainz**	E	55	Scuderia Ferrari	Ferrari SF-24-066/12 V6	71	1h 40m 55.800s	112.794/181.524		1m 20.137s	62
2	**Lando Norris**	GB	4	McLaren Formula 1 Team	McLaren MCL38-Mercedes F1 M15 E Perf. V6	71	1h 41m 00.505s	112.706/181.383	4.705s	1m 19.691s	68
3	**Charles Leclerc**	MC	16	Scuderia Ferrari	Ferrari SF-24-066/12 V6	71	1h 41m 30.187s	112.157/180.499	34.387s	1m 18.336s	71
4	**Lewis Hamilton**	GB	44	Mercedes-AMG Petronas F1 Team	Mercedes-AMG F1 W15-M15 E Perf. V6	71	1h 41m 40.580s	111.965/180.191	44.780s	1m 20.371s	31
5	**George Russell**	GB	63	Mercedes-AMG Petronas F1 Team	Mercedes-AMG F1 W15-M15 E Perf. V6	71	1h 41m 44.336s	111.897/180.080	48.536s	1m 20.731s	63
6	**Max Verstappen**	NL	1	Oracle Red Bull Racing	Red Bull RB20-Honda RBPT H002 V6	71	1h 41m 55.358s *	111.695/179.756	59.558s	1m 20.872s	53
7	**Kevin Magnussen**	DK	20	MoneyGram Haas F1 Team	Haas VF-24-Ferrari 066/10 V6	71	1h 41m 59.442s	111.621/179.636	1m 03.642s	1m 20.637s	61
8	**Oscar Piastri**	AUS	81	McLaren Formula 1 Team	McLaren MCL38-Mercedes F1 M15 E Perf. V6	71	1h 42m 00.728s	111.597/179.598	1m 04.928s	1m 20.064s	65
9	**Nico Hülkenberg**	D	27	MoneyGram Haas F1 Team	Haas VF-24-Ferrari 066/10 V6	70			1 lap	1m 20.748s	69
10	**Pierre Gasly**	F	10	BWT Alpine F1 Team	Alpine A524-Renault E-Tech RE24 V6	70			1 lap	1m 21.274s	67
11	Lance Stroll	CDN	18	Aston Martin Aramco F1 Team	Aston Martin AMR24-Mercedes F1 M15 E Perf. V6	70			1 lap	1m 21.311s	55
12	Franco Colapinto	RA	43	Williams Racing	Williams FW46-Mercedes F1 M15 E Perf. V6	70	*		1 lap	1m 20.090s	50
13	Esteban Ocon	F	31	BWT Alpine F1 Team	Alpine A524-Renault E-Tech RE24 V6	70			1 lap	1m 20.659s	70
14	Valtteri Bottas	FIN	77	Stake F1 Team Kick Sauber	Sauber C44-Ferrari 066/12 V6	70			1 lap	1m 21.085s	57
15	Zhou Guanyu	CHN	24	Stake F1 Team Kick Sauber	Sauber C44-Ferrari 066/12 V6	70			1 lap	1m 21.553s	56
16	Liam Lawson	NZ	30	Visa Cash App RB Formula One Team	RB VCARB 01-Honda RBPT H002 V6	70			1 lap	1m 19.502s	67
17	Sergio Pérez	MEX	11	Oracle Red Bull Racing	Red Bull RB20-Honda RBPT H002 V6	70	*		1 lap	1m 19.209s	70
	Fernando Alonso	E	14	Aston Martin Aramco F1 Team	Aston Martin AMR24-Mercedes F1 M15 E Perf. V6	15	*brakes*		1 lap	1m 22.722s	7
	Alexander Albon	T	23	Williams Racing	Williams FW46-Mercedes F1 M15 E Perf. V6	0	*accident*			no time	
	Yuki Tsunoda	J	22	Visa Cash App RB Formula One Team	RB VCARB 01-Honda RBPT H002 V6	0	*accident*			no time	

* Colapinto: 10s time penalty for causing a collision with Lawson. * Pérez: 5s time penalty for false start - car's front tyres were ahead of the grid box at the start signal (served at pit stop).

* Verstappen: 10s time penalty for forcing Norris off the track; 10s time penalty for leaving the track and gaining an advantage (both served at pit stop).

DHL Fastest race lap (scores 1 point): Charles Leclerc on lap 71, 1m 18.336s, 122.904mph/197.794km/h.

Lap record: Nigel Mansell (Williams FW14-Renault V10), 1m 16.788s, 128.790mph/207.267km (1991, 2.747-mile/4.421km circuit).

Lap record: (current configuration): Valtteri Bottas (Mercedes F1 W12 V6), 1m 17.774s, 123.792mph/199.223km/h (2021).

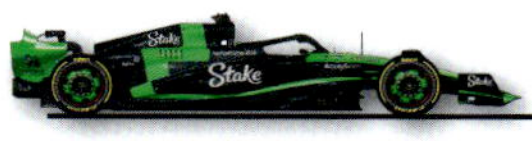

19 · ZHOU · Sauber

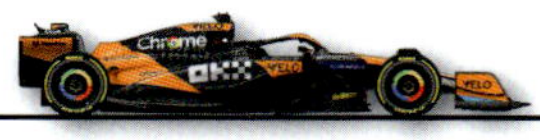

17 · PIASTRI · McLaren

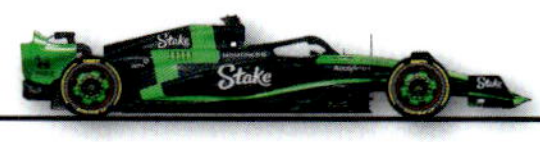

15 · BOTTAS · Sauber

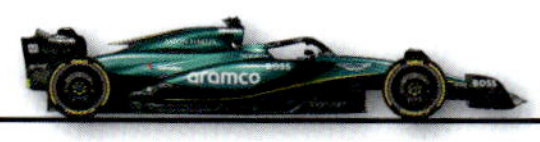

13 · ALONSO · Aston Martin

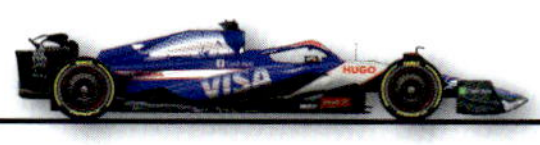

11 · TSUNODA · RB

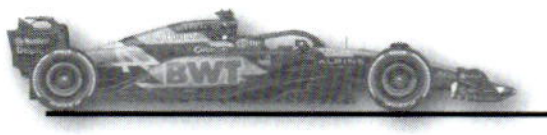

20 · OCON · Alpine
Car modified in parc fermé and used additional power unit elements; required to start from the pit lane

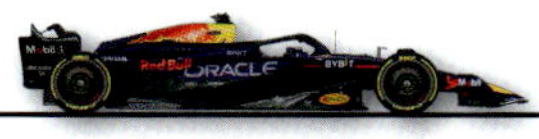

18 · PÉREZ · Red Bull

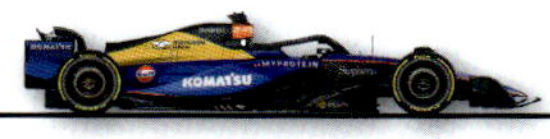

16 · COLAPINTO · Williams

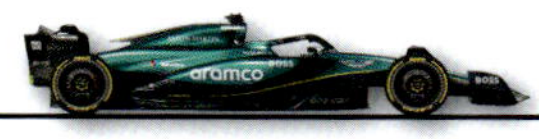

14 · STROLL · Aston Martin

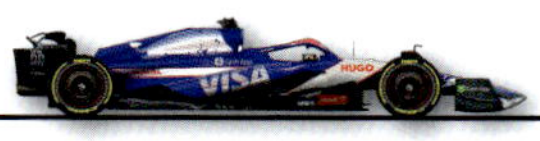

12 · LAWSON · RB

Grid order	1	2	3	4	5	6	7	8	9	10	11	12	13	14	15	16	17	18	19	20	21	22	23	24	25	26	27	28
55 SAINZ	1	1	1	1	1	1	1	1	55	55	55	55	55	55	55	55	55	55	55	55	55	55	55	55	55	55	55	55
1 VERSTAPPEN	55	55	55	55	55	55	55	55	1	16	16	16	16	16	16	16	16	16	16	16	16	16	16	16	16	16	16	16
4 NORRIS	4	4	4	4	4	4	4	4	4	1	1	1	1	1	1	1	1	1	1	1	1	1	1	1	1	4	4	4
16 LECLERC	16	16	16	16	16	16	16	16	16	4	4	4	4	4	4	4	4	4	4	4	4	4	4	4	4	1	63	63
63 RUSSELL	44	44	44	44	44	44	44	44	44	44	44	44	44	44	63	63	63	63	63	63	63	63	63	63	63	63	44	44
44 HAMILTON	63	63	63	63	63	63	63	63	63	63	63	63	63	63	44	44	44	44	44	44	44	44	44	44	44	44	20	20
20 MAGNUSSEN	20	20	20	20	20	20	20	20	20	20	20	20	20	20	20	20	20	20	20	20	20	20	20	20	20	20	27	27
10 GASLY	27	27	27	27	27	27	27	27	27	27	27	27	27	27	27	27	27	27	27	27	27	27	27	27	27	27	10	30
23 ALBON	10	10	10	10	10	10	10	10	10	10	10	10	10	10	10	10	10	10	10	10	10	10	10	10	10	10	30	81
27 HÜLKENBERG	30	30	30	30	30	30	30	30	30	30	30	30	30	30	30	30	30	30	30	30	30	30	30	30	30	30	81	10
22 TSUNODA	18	18	18	18	18	18	18	18	18	18	18	11	11	11	11	11	11	11	11	18	18	18	18	81	81	81	43	43
30 LAWSON	14	14	14	14	14	14	14	14	14	14	11	18	18	18	18	18	18	18	18	43	81	81	81	18	18	43	77	77
14 ALONSO	11	11	11	11	11	11	11	11	11	11	14	14	14	14	43	43	43	43	43	81	43	43	43	43	43	77	24	31
18 STROLL	43	43	43	43	43	43	43	43	43	43	43	43	43	43	81	81	81	81	81	77	77	77	77	77	77	18	31	24
77 BOTTAS	77	77	77	77	77	77	77	77	77	77	77	77	81	81	77	77	77	77	77	11	24	24	24	24	24	24	1	1
43 COLAPINTO	24	24	24	24	24	24	24	24	24	81	81	81	77	77	24	24	24	24	24	24	31	31	31	31	31	31	11	11
81 PIASTRI	81	81	81	81	81	81	81	81	81	24	24	24	24	24	14	31	31	31	31	31	11	11	11	11	11	11	18	18
11 PÉREZ	31	31	31	31	31	31	31	31	31	31	31	31	31	31	31													
24 ZHOU																												
31 OCON																												
	SC	SC	SC	SC	SC	SC																						

Grid order	29	30	31	32	33	34	35	36	37	38	39	40	41	42	43	44	45	46	47	48	49	50	51	52	53	54	55
55 SAINZ	55	55	55	55	55	55	55	55	55	55	55	55	55	55	55	55	55	55	55	55	55	55	55	55	55	55	55
1 VERSTAPPEN	16	16	16	16	16	16	16	16	16	16	16	16	16	16	16	16	16	16	16	16	16	16	16	16	16	16	16
4 NORRIS	4	4	63	4	4	4	4	4	4	4	4	4	4	4	4	4	4	4	4	4	4	4	4	4	4	4	4
16 LECLERC	63	63	4	30	63	63	63	63	63	63	63	63	63	63	63	63	63	63	63	63	63	63	63	63	63	63	63
63 RUSSELL	20	20	30	81	30	81	44	44	44	44	44	44	44	44	44	44	44	44	44	44	44	44	44	44	44	44	44
44 HAMILTON	27	30	81	63	81	44	81	81	81	81	1	1	1	1	1	1	1	1	1	1	1	1	1	1	1	1	1
20 MAGNUSSEN	30	81	44	44	44	30	30	30	30	1	81	20	20	20	20	20	20	20	20	20	20	20	20	20	20	20	20
10 GASLY	81	43	43	43	43	43	43	1	1	30	43	43	43	43	27	27	27	27	27	27	27	27	27	27	27	27	27
23 ALBON	43	44	77	1	1	1	1	43	43	43	20	27	27	27	43	43	43	43	81	81	81	81	81	81	81	81	81
27 HÜLKENBERG	44	77	1	77	77	77	77	20	20	20	30	77	77	77	10	81	81	81	43	10	10	10	10	10	10	10	10
22 TSUNODA	77	1	31	31	20	20	20	77	27	27	27	10	10	10	81	10	10	10	10	77	18	18	18	18	18	18	18
30 LAWSON	31	31	20	20	31	27	27	27	77	77	77	31	81	81	77	77	77	77	77	18	30	30	30	30	30	30	30
14 ALONSO	1	24	27	27	27	31	31	31	10	10	10	81	31	31	31	31	31	31	31	30	77	43	43	43	43	43	43
18 STROLL	24	27	24	24	10	10	10	10	31	31	31	24	24	18	18	18	18	18	18	31	43	77	77	77	77	77	77
77 BOTTAS	10	10	10	10	24	24	24	24	24	24	24	18	18	24	30	30	30	30	30	43	31	31	31	31	31	31	31
43 COLAPINTO	11	11	11	11	11	11	11	11	11	11	11	11	30	30	24	24	24	11	11	11	11	11	11	11	11	11	11
81 PIASTRI	18	18	18	18	18	18	18	18	18	18	18	30	11	11	11	11	11	24	24	24	24	24	24	24	24	24	24
11 PÉREZ																											
24 ZHOU																											
31 OCON																											

SC Safety Car deployed on laps 1-6

TIME SHEETS

PRACTICE 1 (FRIDAY)
Weather: Dry/sunny
Temperatures: track 41-43°C, air 24-25°C

Pos.	Driver	Laps	Time
1	George Russell	24	1m 17.998s
2	Carlos Sainz	25	1m 18.315s
3	Yuki Tsunoda	24	1m 18.699s
4	Max Verstappen	14	1m 18.839s
5	Nico Hülkenberg	18	1m 18.904s
6	Oscar Piastri	24	1m 18.958s
7	Esteban Ocon	22	1m 18.996s
8	Valtteri Bottas	24	1m 19.048s
9	Liam Lawson	26	1m 19.093s
10	Sergio Pérez	23	1m 19.094s
11	Franco Colapinto	21	1m 19.109s
12	Andrea Kimi Antonelli	19	1m 19.200s
13	Patricio O'Ward	21	1m 19.295s
14	Kevin Magnussen	23	1m 19.335s
15	Pierre Gasly	20	1m 19.340s
16	Lance Stroll	18	1m 19.600s
17	Alexander Albon	7	1m 19.812s
18	Felipe Drugovich	17	1m 19.819s
19	Robert Shwartzman	18	1m 19.988s
20	Oliver Bearman	7	1m 21.256s

QUALIFYING (SATURDAY)
Weather: Dry/sunny Temperatures: track 32-41°C, air 23-25°C

Pos.	Driver	First	Second	Third	Qualifying Tyre
1	Carlos Sainz	1m 16.778s	1m 16.515s	**1m 15.946s**	Soft (n)
2	Max Verstappen	1m 16.803s	1m 16.514s	1m 16.171s	Soft (n)
3	Lando Norris	**1m 16.505s**	**1m 16.301s**	1m 16.260s	Soft (n)
4	Charles Leclerc	1m 16.972s	1m 16.641s	1m 16.265s	Soft (n)
5	George Russell	1m 17.194s	1m 16.937s	1m 16.356s	Soft (n)
6	Lewis Hamilton	1m 17.306s	1m 16.973s	1m 16.651s	Soft (u)
7	Kevin Magnussen	1m 17.125s	1m 17.003s	1m 16.886s	Soft (n)
8	Pierre Gasly	1m 17.149s	1m 17.048s	1m 16.892s	Soft (n)
9	Alexander Albon	1m 17.189s	1m 16.988s	1m 17.065s	Soft (n)
10	Nico Hülkenberg	1m 17.186s	1m 16.995s	1m 17.365s	Soft (n)
11	Yuki Tsunoda	1m 17.182s	1m 17.129s		
12	Liam Lawson	1m 17.380s	1m 17.162s		
13	Fernando Alonso	1m 17.307s	1m 17.168s		
14	Lance Stroll	1m 17.407s	1m 17.294s		
15	Valtteri Bottas	1m 17.393s	1m 17.817s		
16	Franco Colapinto	1m 17.558s			
17	Oscar Piastri	1m 17.597s			
18	Sergio Pérez	1m 17.611s			
19	Esteban Ocon	1m 17.617s			
20	Zhou Guanyu	1m 18.072s			

PRACTICE 2 (FRIDAY)
Weather: Dry/sunny
Temperatures: track 29-36°C, air 23-24°C

Pos.	Driver	Laps	Time
1	Carlos Sainz	34	1m 17.699s
2	Oscar Piastri	30	1m 17.877s
3	Yuki Tsunoda	30	1m 17.878s
4	Charles Leclerc	31	1m 17.887s
5	Lando Norris	36	1m 17.948s
6	Kevin Magnussen	34	1m 18.239s
7	Lewis Hamilton	36	1m 18.279s
8	Valtteri Bottas	32	1m 18.351s
9	Sergio Pérez	32	1m 18.392s
10	Liam Lawson	29	1m 18.560s
11	Fernando Alonso	35	1m 18.579s
12	Nico Hülkenberg	34	1m 18.621s
13	Esteban Ocon	30	1m 18.656s
14	Lance Stroll	34	1m 18.890s
15	Franco Colapinto	30	1m 18.908s
16	Pierre Gasly	30	1m 18.942s
17	Zhou Guanyu	37	1m 18.980s
18	George Russell	4	1m 19.041s
19	Max Verstappen	4	no time
-	Alexander Albon	-	-

PRACTICE 3 (SATURDAY)
Weather: Dry/sunny
Temperatures: track 31-38°C, air 20-23°C

Pos.	Driver	Laps	Time
1	Oscar Piastri	18	1m 16.492s
2	Lando Norris	18	1m 16.551s
3	Carlos Sainz	21	1m 16.832s
4	Max Verstappen	26	1m 17.003s
5	Lewis Hamilton	21	1m 17.060s
6	Charles Leclerc	24	1m 17.232s
7	Yuki Tsunoda	20	1m 17.302s
8	George Russell	28	1m 17.341s
9	Kevin Magnussen	19	1m 17.474s
10	Liam Lawson	23	1m 17.494s
11	Alexander Albon	19	1m 17.511s
12	Valtteri Bottas	25	1m 17.639s
13	Franco Colapinto	18	1m 17.712s
14	Sergio Pérez	19	1m 17.787s
15	Fernando Alonso	23	1m 17.798s
16	Nico Hülkenberg	20	1m 17.819s
17	Lance Stroll	26	1m 17.900s
18	Esteban Ocon	19	1m 18.324s
19	Zhou Guanyu	18	1m 18.428s
20	Pierre Gasly	20	1m 18.454s

QUALIFYING: head to head

Verstappen	19	1		Pérez
Hamilton	5	15		Russell
Norris	16	4		Piastri
Leclerc	12	7		Sainz
Leclerc	1	0		Bearman
Gasly	9	11		Ocon
Alonso	14	6		Stroll
Albon	14	1		Sargeant
Albon	4	1		Colapinto
Bottas	19	1		Zhou
Tsunoda	12	6		Ricciardo
Tsunoda	2	0		Lawson
Magnussen	6	13		Hülkenberg
Bearman	1	0		Hülkenberg

FOR THE RECORD

400th GP ENTERED: Fernando Alonso
20,000th GP LAP RACED: Lewis Hamilton
250th GP PODIUM: Lewis Hamilton
10th GP FASTEST LAP: Lando Norris & Carlos Sainz

DID YOU KNOW?

This was the first Ferrari win in Mexico since Prost in 1990. The only other Ferrari win here was Jacky Ickx in 1970.

POINTS

DRIVERS

1	Max Verstappen	362
2	Lando Norris	315
3	Charles Leclerc	291
4	Oscar Piastri	251
5	Carlos Sainz	240
6	Lewis Hamilton	189
7	George Russell	177
8	Sergio Pérez	150
9	Fernando Alonso	62
10	Nico Hülkenberg	31
11	Lance Stroll	24
12	Yuki Tsunoda	22
13	Kevin Magnussen	14
14	Alexander Albon	12
15	Daniel Ricciardo	12
16	Pierre Gasly	9
17	Oliver Bearman	7
18	Franco Colapinto	5
19	Esteban Ocon	5
20	Liam Lawson	2

CONSTRUCTORS

1	McLaren	566
2	Ferrari	537
3	Red Bull	512
4	Mercedes	366
5	Aston Martin	86
6	Haas	46
7	RB	36
8	Williams	17
9	Alpine	14

 9 · ALBON · Williams    7 · MAGNUSSEN · Haas    5 · RUSSELL · Mercedes    3 · NORRIS · McLaren    1 · SAINZ · Ferrari

 10 · HÜLKENBERG · Haas    8 · GASLY · Alpine    6 · HAMILTON · Mercedes    4 · LECLERC · Ferrari   2 · VERSTAPPEN · Red Bull

14 = Pit stop   11 = One lap or more behind

RACE TYRE STRATEGIES

	Driver	Race Stint 1	Race Stint 2	Race Stint 3	Race Stint 4
1	Sainz	Medium (n): 1-32	Hard (n): 33-71		
2	Norris	Medium (n): 1-30	Hard (n): 31-71		
3	Leclerc	Medium (n): 1-31	Hard (n): 32-69	Soft (u): 70-71	
4	Hamilton	Medium (n): 1-28	Hard (n): 29-71		
5	Russell	Medium (n): 1-31	Hard (n): 32-71		
6	Verstappen	Medium (n): 1-26	Hard (n): 27-71		
7	Magnussen	Medium (n): 1-30	Hard (n): 31-71		
8	Piastri	Medium (n): 1-39	Hard (n): 40-71		
9	Hülkenberg	Medium (n): 1-29	Hard (n): 30-70		
10	Gasly	Medium (n): 1-28	Hard (n): 29-70		
11	Stroll	Medium (u): 1-26	Hard (u): 27-70		
12	Colapinto	Hard (n): 1-47	Medium (n): 48-70		
13	Ocon	Hard (n): 1-48	Medium (n): 49-70		
14	Bottas	Hard (u): 1-49	Medium (u): 50-70		
15	Zhou	Hard (n): 1-43	Medium (u): 44-70		
16	Lawson	Hard (n): 1-39	Medium (n): 40-65	Soft (u): 66-70	
17	Pérez	Hard (n): 1-20	Medium (n): 21-43	Medium (n): 44-68	Soft (n): 69-70
	Alonso	Medium (u): 1-15 (dnf)			
	Albon	Medium (n): 0 (dnf)			
	Tsunoda	Medium (n): 0 (dnf)			

The tyre regulations stipulate that at least two of three dry tyre specifications must be used during a dry race.
Selected compounds for Mexico: Red = Soft (C5); Yellow = Medium (C4); White = Hard (C3). (n) new (u) used

INTERLAGOS QUALIFYING/ SPRINT QUALIFYING & RACE

THE news that Max Verstappen would take a sixth engine and incur a five-place grid penalty for the main race at Interlagos was a potential opportunity for Lando Norris to close the championship gap. But with rain forecast for Saturday and Sunday in Brazil, nothing was a given.

The fifth of six sprint events on the 2024 calendar meant that there was another helping of points on offer. At Haas, Kevin Magnussen was ill, so Oliver Bearman was drafted in for another race opportunity ahead of his full-time drive in 2025.

Verstappen might have been no fan of the sprint-race concept, but he could boast a formidable record: 11 out of 16 wins, including the previous six! But from the moment Norris topped the first session of free practice – from George Russell and an inspired Bearman! – McLaren looked like the team to beat. The track had been resurfaced, but most drivers reckoned that it was worse than ever.

"Wow, that was one bumpy ride!" said Russell. Hamilton agreed: "I'm just bouncing across the track everywhere." It seemed to be affecting him more than his team-mate, and that was set to continue.

Oscar Piastri produced a fine lap to pip Norris to a second sprint-race pole, ahead of Charles Leclerc, Verstappen, Carlos Sainz, Russell, Pierre Gasly, Liam Lawson, Alex Albon and Bearman. Hamilton could do no better than 11th, with Sergio Pérez 13th in the second Red Bull, which was a previously used, but different RB20 chassis from the one in which he'd suffered instability and such a disappointing home race in Mexico. Meanwhile, Aston Martin had reverted to a floor that was similar to the one that had last run in Suzuka, but suffered damage on both cars as Alonso and Stroll went out in SQ1. The team elected to raise the ride height, make some other changes and start from the pit lane.

With everyone on the medium-compound Pirellis, McLaren superiority continued in the 24-lap race, Piastri converting his pole and controlling things from the front. It all evolved very much in grid order, save for Hülkenberg, who made a fine start to gain three places up to ninth. With a 40-degree track temperature, however, his tyres suffered from degradation, and he was passed by team-mate Bearman and Pérez before being told to stop the car with a power-unit issue.

Leclerc was another to suffer late degradation, allowing Verstappen to close in. Out of the Senna Esses on lap 18, the Dutchman towed up with DRS and completed a clean outside pass into Turn Four to maximise damage limitation in his points loss to Norris.

Lawson and Pérez continued the spat they had begun in Mexico, when the Kiwi made a late move while trying to defend Turn One with four laps to go. Pérez, though, made it past and grabbed the final point for eighth.

A VSC for Hülkenberg's stricken car prompted McLaren to ask its drivers to swap position, just in case the race finished under yellow. Oscar had been planning to let Lando through on the last lap. That meant there was a three-point, rather than a one-point championship swing when Verstappen narrowly exceeded the VSC delta and earned a 5s penalty, which dropped him to fourth behind Leclerc. Sainz, Russell, Gasly and Pérez claimed the minor points.

As far as dry running was concerned, that was it. As the drivers prepared to revert to qualifying mode for the main race, the elements had other ideas. Dark skies and monsoon conditions on Saturday afternoon dictated that F1 would have the sixth Sunday qualifying session in its history. It would be the earliest in F1 history, too, at 7.30am! Overalls or pyjamas?

Franco Colapinto's arrival on the F1 scene had created huge fervour in Argentina, and although Buenos Aires is more than 1,300 miles from São Paulo by road, the grandstands were full of enthusiastic Argentines waving blue-and-white flags. Sadly, their hero, who had never driven an F1 car in the wet, of course, prompted the first red flag of the day when he lost his Williams out of the Senna Esses and planted it firmly into the tyres.

The biggest shock of Q1 was Lewis Hamilton's elimination, the seven-times champion finding the Mercedes an even bigger handful in conditions in which he so often excels. Super-low ride heights and standing water do not make good bed-fellows. "This damn car, man…" was all Hamilton had to say as he joined Bearman, the chastened Colapinto, Hülkenberg and Zhou as a spectator.

While full wets were needed for the first session, the rain eased sufficiently to allow intermediates in Q2. But the surface was still treacherous, as Sainz demonstrated when he lost the back end of his Ferrari in the most innocuous-looking incident in Turn Two, putting the car into the tyres and causing a second red.

Norris, who had flirted with elimination in Q1, then topped Q2 on intermediates, while the high-profile casualties included both Red Bulls! When the session restarted, the team sent Pérez down to the end of the pit lane. He would have track position, but lose tyre temperature. With Verstappen, they

went the opposite way and, with the team in the first garage, he was at the back of the queue.

That had consequences when Stroll went off at Turn Three and we had a third red flag. There had been a significant delay before the red was thrown, which allowed several to complete their laps, but not Verstappen, who ended up 12th. Pérez, in need of another lap to get his cold tyres back in, was also out.

Verstappen was livid: "I find it unbelievable. I mean, the car goes into the wall, it's broken, clearly destroyed, and they wait 30 to 40 seconds so everyone else can complete their lap, and then those at the back can't. That, of course, ruins qualifying. I just can't get my head around it."

The FIA countered that it had had nothing to do with drivers completing laps. Apparently, they had been able to see on Stroll's on-board that he had been attempting to get the car going, as instructed on the radio, because of the short turnaround time between the delayed qualifying and the race start time, and the need to repair the car. With double-waved yellows in the interim, they had red-flagged the race when it had become obvious that suspension damage was preventing Stroll from moving. Other drivers who did not record times were Gasly and Bottas.

Feeling confident on the intermediates, Norris made the most of his championship rival's woes by planting his car on pole as Q3 produced more chaos. With seven minutes to go, Alonso went off at Turn 11 (Mergulho), causing another red flag and adding to the repair nightmare at Aston Martin.

No sooner had the session resumed than Piastri spun at Turn Three and Tsunoda at Turn Four. Then, under braking for Turn One, Albon lost the rear end of his Williams, suffering a heavy shunt, which prevented him from starting the race. A fifth red flag in a single qualifying session equalled a record established at Imola in 2022.

The conditions had produced a topsy-turvy top ten. Russell qualified on the front row just 0.17s behind Norris, and on row two were Tsunoda and the impressive Ocon. Lawson made it two VCARBS in the top five, ahead of Leclerc, Albon, Piastri and the two crashed Astons.

Above: Oscar Piastri leads Lando Norris in the sprint, before handing his team-mate the win at the finish.
Photo: McLaren F1 Team

Top left: Heavy rain disrupted proceedings, which meant qualifying was held on race-day morning.
Photo: Red Bull Content Pool/Getty Images

Above left: The long, the short and the tall…
Photo: McLaren F1 Team

Left: Alex Albon trashed his Williams in qualifying and didn't make the race as a result.
Photo: Peter Nygaard/Grand Prix Photo

Opening spread: A triumphant Max Verstappen is the Dutch interloper on an otherwise all-French podium as Red Bull's Pierre Waché is joined by delighted Alpine men Esteban Ocon and Pierre Gasly.
Photo: Red Bull Content Pool/Getty Images

Above: Tension mounts as the field arrives on the grid, only for the race to be aborted.
Photo: McLaren F1 Team

Top right: There was no love lost between Liam Lawson and Sergio Pérez. The Kiwi emerged with two points after winning his tussle with the Mexican.
Photo: Red Bull Content Pool/Getty Images

Above right: Nico Hülkenberg spun his Haas harmlessly, but became stranded on the run-off apron. He was disqualified for receiving outside assistance.
Photo: Peter Nygaard/Grand Prix Photo

Right: Pierre Gasly ensured a double podium for Alpine, after just beating George Russell for third place.
Photo: BWT Alpine F1 Team

THERE was much anticipation heading into the São Paulo main race. With Lando Norris on pole and already victorious in the sprint, and Max Verstappen starting 17th, here was a gilt-edged opportunity for the McLaren man to put a significant dent in the triple champion's 44-point series lead. Max, of course, had recovered from 16th to third in Brazil some eight years before, after a mesmerising drive, so how far could he get this time?

With the field on intermediate Pirellis for the early 12.30pm start, drama began on the formation lap when Lance Stroll lost the rear end of his Aston Martin on the brakes for Turn Four, flicking right to make light contact with the wall, slightly damaging the nose of his car. He couldn't get it restarted and climbed out. The start would need to be aborted.

The orange light appeared above the starting gantry and the grid should have remained stationary. But poleman Norris led them off on another formation lap. Some followed, some didn't. When Verstappen radioed that they should have waited for a green light, race engineer Gianpiero Lambiase told him, "All sorts of procedures have been breached here, Max." Meanwhile, Race Control notified a starting procedure infringement by Norris and that the first two rows had been noted. This would have financial, rather than sporting implications.

Around they all went again to form up and be sent off on a third formation lap, the race distance being reduced from 71 to 69 laps. When the red lights went out, George Russell found superior traction from P2 and took his Mercedes inside the pole-position McLaren to lead Norris through the Senna Esses. Yuki Tsunoda, Esteban Ocon and Charles Leclerc tucked in behind, with Liam Lawson sixth as Oscar Piastri and Fernando Alonso disputed seventh. Pierre Gasly's Alpine was ninth, with Verstappen already on tenth-placed Lewis Hamilton's tail as they headed into the tight Turn Eight.

Behind them, Franco Colapinto ran 12th, ahead of Ollie Bearman and Valtteri Bottas, while Sergio Pérez's wretched run continued with a spin that was of his own doing at Turn Ten. That put the second Red Bull dead last, behind Nico Hülkenberg, Zhou Guanyu and Carlos Sainz, who had started from the pit lane with a new power unit after his Q2 crash.

Verstappen was into the points by the start of lap two, after diving decisively down the inside of Hamilton's Mercedes into Turn One. The same move on Gasly's Alpine, on lap five, once again displayed just how much confidence he had on the brakes. It put him up to ninth. DRS, remember, was not in operation due to the wet conditions. A lap later, he was into the top eight, having passed Alonso's Aston Martin.

Meanwhile, Bearman had punted the back of Colapinto's Williams and spun himself around, losing three places and attracting a penalty.

"Ollie, we have a ten-second penalty for the collision," he was informed.

"Why? He didn't even lose any time," came the reply. Bearman had a point. Penalising everything does not encourage racing.

It was interesting that Hamilton, who had produced so many scintillating Interlagos drives himself, was unable to follow Verstappen through the field, especially with his team-mate confidently leading the race. "The ride is really bad, the car is just bouncing so much," he told the Mercedes pit.

Next on Verstappen's radar was Piastri. Could the young Aussie do anything to arrest Max's progress and help his team-mate? We knew the answer soon enough as the Dutchman pulled off another of his signature moves, late on the brakes down the McLaren's inside into Turn One from way back. Next was Lawson, who would not do his 2025 job prospects any good by offering resistance. Considering his aggression against Pérez in Mexico, for which he had been quietly admonished, this was meek and mild, Liam leaving the door open on the inside of Turn Eight. Verstappen was just 11s behind Russell's race lead after 11 laps, with plenty of time in hand.

A measure of Hamilton's struggle was a lock-up and run-off into Junção. Then he suffered the ignominy of Colapinto's Williams diving down his inside into Turn One, to the delight of the Argentine supporting contingent. He lost another slot to Sainz's Ferrari and had Bearman's Haas blow by him down the inside into Turn Four. By this

point, he was ahead only of Pérez's Red Bull, 1s behind, and the two Saubers.

By lap 22, Verstappen had caught Leclerc's fifth-placed Ferrari, which had a bit of a moment into Junção and was slow on exit. Max pulled alongside as they flashed down the front straight, but on the outside this time, Leclerc offering the first bit of strong defence he'd encountered, going deep on the brakes into T1, forcing the Dutchman wide and retaining the position.

"He was squeezing me on to the white line, not leaving a car's width," Verstappen complained on the radio, despite it appearing to be something he would have done himself.

With rain intensifying, Leclerc was first to head for the pits and another set of intermediates on lap 25. He pitted out right behind the Bearman/Hamilton fight, which cost him time. Meanwhile, Norris was becoming impatient behind Russell and asked, "Box to overtake at some point, no?"

"We'll think about it," was the team's response. Lando tried again a lap later, but was told that he would pit out into too much traffic, that the tyres would be okay for a bit longer and that they'd prefer him to stay out.

Piastri tried to go inside Lawson at Turn One, but clipped the VCARB and spun it around, the Kiwi losing positions while Oscar picked up a 10s penalty.

With the weather deteriorating, the smart move was to remain on-track for as long as possible, rather than give up track position, in case there was a stoppage or safety car. McLaren was on the radio, telling Norris, "Lando, Leclerc pitted for a new tyre, he went into traffic and cannot clear it."

On lap 27, Hülkenberg spun on the outside of Turn One and became stranded, bringing out yellows. Race Control threw a VSC, and into the pits from seventh and eighth came Piastri and Alonso. Bearman, Hamilton, Sainz and Pérez followed them in, Checo opting for full wet Pirellis.

Race leaders Russell and Norris stopped next time around, both opting for intermediates, with Tsunoda doing likewise, while new race leader Ocon, Verstappen and Gasly remained out. Hülkenberg had got going again, with outside assistance it transpired, which would have repercussions, but the correspondingly short VSC period meant that Russell and Norris did not benefit from a cheap stop.

The conditions had become treacherous, but the weather radars were forecasting an easing of the rain in a few minutes as the field tiptoed around. Suddenly, Norris, appearing more confident than Russell, took what was now fourth place from his buddy down the inside into Turn Four.

With visibility worsening, Race Control deployed the safety car, but just as it did so, Colapinto lost his Williams up the hill out of Junção, thumped the wall hard and came to rest in the middle of the track. Cue the red flag – a great break and free tyre change for Ocon, Verstappen and Gasly, who hadn't stopped. It was race-changing and brought renewed calls for a rethink of the red-flag rules.

As the race resumed behind the safety car on lap 33, the new order was Ocon, Verstappen, Gasly, Norris, Russell, Tsunoda, Leclerc, Piastri, Alonso, Lawson, Hamilton, Bottas, Sainz, Pérez, Bearman and Zhou. Hülkenberg having been black-flagged, only 16 cars remained.

Sainz was quickly on the radio to race engineer Riccardo Adami with a somewhat unusual enquiry: "Ricky, these are not new inters. Which inter is this? Hello?" According to Pirelli's data, however, they were indeed new.

Proving just how gripless tyres can be without temperature, both Bearman and Zhou suffered grassy moments behind the safety car. As it pulled off and the race was under way once more, Leclerc pinched sixth from Tsunoda in Turn One. Then Norris ran wide at the exit of Turn Four, Russell repassing him to take fourth.

If anyone expected Verstappen to rapidly displace

Above: Esteban Ocon delivered a brilliant performance in the wet to take the runner-up slot.
Photo: BWT Alpine F1 Team

Top right: Wearing his Senna-tribute helmet for the weekend brought little luck for Lewis.
Photo: Mercedes-AMG Petronas F1 Team

Above right: A kiss for Max from partner Kelly.

Right: A champion's drive. Verstappen keeps the Alpines at bay on his way to one of his best ever victories.
Photos: Red Bull Content Pool/Getty Images

Ocon from the lead and disappear up the road, they were mistaken. There had been history between these two in 2018, of course, when Ocon had tried to unlap himself and caused a collision between them in Turn Two, the incident costing Verstappen the race win. Again, Ocon looked as though he would be no pushover as he quickly opened a 2.5s advantage, while team-mate Gasly dropped 3s behind Verstappen. Not having run in the top five all season, Alpine suddenly found itself 1-3!

Meanwhile, Tsunoda dropped another place to Piastri. And Hamilton, finally feeling able to make an aggressive move into Turn One in a car that had been unstable all race, went inside Alonso's Aston to take ninth. Behind Lawson and Pérez, Bearman was harrying Sainz for 13th, but he ran slightly wide into Turn Six, spun and lightly nosed the barrier, before extracting himself and rejoining at the back.

Despite the prospect of a championship swing in Norris's favour an hour or so earlier, it had gone badly pear-shaped, and now he was running fifth, three slots behind Verstappen, as McLaren told him, "If the weather stays as it is, we think it will be these tyres to the end, so it'll be about tyre condition and racing cars on track."

A couple of laps later, Sainz, never comfortable with the Ferrari in the wet – usually a personal strength – also lost the back end, this time into Turn Eight, going in backwards for his second incident of the day. All a bit of a comedown from the highs of Mexico…

With the Ferrari stranded, out came the safety car again with 30 laps remaining – the last thing Ocon needed after confidently opening a 3s advantage over Verstappen. He appeared to be in control, with team-mate Gasly 6s behind the Red Bull and neither Russell nor Norris making significant headway.

But when the race resumed again on lap 42, Verstappen wasted no time in diving down the inside of the lead Alpine into Turn One. Leclerc was aggressive, too, towing past Norris down the main straight in the spray and then diving inside Russell into Turn One. Then Lando did himself no favours by going wide into Turn One and regaining the track seventh, behind team-mate Piastri. Hamilton was repassed by Alonso, relegated further by Lawson and came under attack from Bearman. Then Fernando had his second excursion of the weekend at Mergulho and dropped to the back. It was all happening!

Norris was back up to sixth on lap 46 as McLaren ordered a position swap. Russell had repassed Leclerc, who was struggling with a twitchy-looking Ferrari and had run wide out of Turn Four.

Once again, there was feisty action between Lawson and Pérez. With 14 laps to go, the Mexican went down the inside into Turn One, but the Kiwi kept his boot in. They made light contact through T2, but Lawson hung on. "He drove into the side of me," was his assessment. Meanwhile, Pérez, losing momentum, was passed by Hamilton in T4.

As the rain eased in the closing stages, Verstappen was in another league, setting no fewer than 17 fastest laps as he put 19.5s between himself and Ocon by the chequered flag. But there was delight on the Alpine pit wall as the Enstone team put both drivers on the podium for the first time in 11 years, Gasly beating Russell's Mercedes across the line by 0.7s. A massive haul of 33 points took Alpine to 49 and vaulted them to sixth in the championship, ahead of Haas, VCARB and Williams.

Leclerc fended off Norris to take fifth, with Tsunoda elevated to seventh when Piastri's 10s penalty was applied. Lawson made it two VCARBs in the points with ninth, and the struggling Hamilton was rewarded with the final point as Pérez missed out. "It was like a plank of wood, no suspension, just bouncing on the tyres everywhere, the worst ride we've ever had," said the seven-times champion.

Verstappen rated his fabulous drive more highly than the one in 2016: "This one was more crucial. Back then, I had nothing to lose. I wasn't in a championship fight and was coming back after a strategic mistake we had. This time, there was more at stake and I had to be more controlled. Definitely, this one is the best." A crucial championship blow had been struck. He could now clinch a fourth title in Las Vegas.

Tony Dodgins

VIEWPOINT
ABSOLUTE MAX

RARELY having had to visit Max Verstappen further back than the middle of the grid in 2024, Christian Horner had quite a hike to get to see his man at Interlagos. Interviewed by a TV presenter who had bothered to go down the notorious dip and part the way up the other side to the penultimate row, the Red Bull boss was philosophical.

The irritating events of qualifying earlier in the day were history. The controversial delay in showing the red flag might have accounted for 12th-fastest time – plus a five-place penalty – putting his man 16 places back from championship rival Lando Norris on pole, but, on a day like this, anything could happen. "Any game plan will only evolve with the race," said Horner. How right he was.

Things had already begun to move in Red Bull's favour when Williams withdrew Alexander Albon. Strike one. Another six fell on the first lap. Verstappen made the rest appear pedestrian as he ran around the outside at the exit of Descida do Sol and continued to take chances that were a delicate balance between spontaneous and calculated.

When the Red Bull went no further than P6, a gamble was taken on lap 28 by not following the leaders (George Russell and Norris) into the pits and it began to pay off when the VSC was short lived. More than ever, Red Bull needed a red flag to avoid being stuck on the original tyres at the wrong time.

The timing of Franco Colapinto's shunt might have been very bad news for the beleaguered Williams team, but the subsequent red flag couldn't have been better for Verstappen and others who had stayed out. This element of good luck for the Dutchman cancelled out the bad from quali.

The stage was set as he pulled away at an average of 0.7s per lap from Esteban Ocon. Verstappen had taken the lead from the Alpine with a late braking move (on a treacherous track) that had seemed impossible until it was done. His deft touch made the rest look like amateurs. Good fortune had nothing to do with one of those mesmerising wet-weather performances that earned a place in F1 folklore. And on the same weekend when Ayrton Senna's McLaren MP4/5B had been given an airing by Lewis Hamilton to remind us of two other wet-weather maestros.

Maurice Hamilton

FORMULA 1 LENOVO GRANDE PRÊMIO DE SÃO PAULO 2024

SÃO PAULO 01-03 NOVEMBER

AUTODROMO JOSÉ CARLOS PACE, INTERLAGOS, BRAZIL
Circuit: 2.677 miles/4.309km, 71 laps

RACE DISTANCE: 69 laps, 184.709 miles/297.261km
RACE WEATHER: Rain/overcast (track 26-31°C, air 20-23°C)

RACE – OFFICIAL CLASSIFICATION

Pos.	Driver	Nat.	No.	Entrant	Car/Engine	Laps	Time/Retirement	Speed (mph/km/h)	Gap to leader	Fastest race lap	
1	Max Verstappen	NL	1	Oracle Red Bull Racing	Red Bull RB20-Honda RBPT H002 V6	69	2h 06m 54.430s	87.328/140.540		1m 20.472s	67
2	Esteban Ocon	F	31	BWT Alpine F1 Team	Alpine A524-Renault E-Tech RE24 V6	69	2h 07m 13.907s	87.105/140.182	19.477s	1m 21.771s	64
3	Pierre Gasly	F	10	BWT Alpine F1 Team	Alpine A524-Renault E-Tech RE24 V6	69	2h 07m 16.962s	87.070/140.126	22.532s	1m 21.645s	66
4	George Russell	GB	63	Mercedes-AMG Petronas F1 Team	Mercedes-AMG F1 W15-M15 E Perf. V6	69	2h 07m 17.695s	87.062/140.112	23.265s	1m 21.645s	66
5	Charles Leclerc	MC	16	Scuderia Ferrari	Ferrari SF-24-066/12 V6	69	2h 07m 24.607s	86.983/139.986	30.177s	1m 21.631s	60
6	Lando Norris	GB	4	McLaren Formula 1 Team	McLaren MCL38-Mercedes F1 M15 E Perf. V6	69	2h 07m 25.802s	86.970/139.964	31.372s	1m 21.517s	67
7	Yuki Tsunoda	J	22	Visa Cash App RB Formula One Team	RB VCARB 01-Honda RBPT H002 V6	69	2h 07m 36.486s	86.848/139.769	42.056s	1m 21.828s	69
8	Oscar Piastri	AUS	81	McLaren Formula 1 Team	McLaren MCL38-Mercedes F1 M15 E Perf. V6	69	2h 07m 39.373s *	86.815/139.716	44.943s	1m 21.532s	69
9	Liam Lawson	NZ	30	Visa Cash App RB Formula One Team	RB VCARB 01-Honda RBPT H002 V6	69	2h 07m 44.882s	86.753/139.615	50.452s	1m 22.123s	67
10	Lewis Hamilton	GB	44	Mercedes-AMG Petronas F1 Team	Mercedes-AMG F1 W15-M15 E Perf. V6	69	2h 07m 45.183s	86.750/139.610	50.753s	1m 22.041s	69
11	Sergio Pérez	MEX	11	Oracle Red Bull Racing	Red Bull RB20-Honda RBPT H002 V6	69	2h 07m 45.961s	86.741/139.596	51.531s	1m 22.143s	67
12	Oliver Bearman	GB	50	MoneyGram Haas F1 Team	Haas VF-24-Ferrari 066/10 V6	69	2h 07m 51.515s *	86.678/139.495	57.085s	1m 22.494s	64
13	Valtteri Bottas	FIN	77	Stake F1 Team Kick Sauber	Sauber C44-Ferrari 066/12 V6	69	2h 07m 58.018s	86.605/139.377	1m 03.588s	1m 22.877s	67
14	Fernando Alonso	E	14	Aston Martin Aramco F1 Team	Aston Martin AMR24-Mercedes F1 M15 E Perf. V6	69	2h 08m 12.479s	86.442/139.115	1m 18.049s	1m 22.293s	59
15	Zhou Guanyu	CHN	24	Stake F1 Team Kick Sauber	Sauber C44-Ferrari 066/12 V6	69	2h 08m 14.079s	86.424/139.086	1m 19.649s	1m 23.058s	65
	Carlos Sainz	E	55	Scuderia Ferrari	Ferrari SF-24-066/12 V6	38	accident			1m 24.201s	19
	Franco Colapinto	RA	43	Williams Racing	Williams FW46-Mercedes F1 M15 E Perf. V6	30	accident			1m 24.296s	21
DQ	Nico Hülkenberg	D	27	MoneyGram Haas F1 Team	Haas VF-24-Ferrari 066/10 V6	30	*			1m 23.764s	21
NS	Lance Stroll	CDN	18	Aston Martin Aramco F1 Team	Aston Martin AMR24-Mercedes F1 M15 E Perf. V6		spin on formation lap				
NS	Alexander Albon	T	23	Williams Racing	Williams FW46-Mercedes F1 M15 E Perf. V6		car not ready after accident				

The start was aborted twice, due to Stroll spinning, then cars moving off prematurely at the restart. After around 13 minutes, the race was finally restarted for 69 laps (of the scheduled 71). It was red-flagged on lap 32, following Colapinto's crash, and after around 25 minutes restarted with a rolling start for the remaining laps..

* Bearman: 10s time penalty for causing a collision with Colapinto (served at pit stop).   * Hülkenberg: Disqualified for receiving physical assistance after a spin.

* Piastri: 10s time penalty for causing a collision with Lawson (originally finished 7th).

DHL Fastest race lap (scores 1 point): Max Verstappen on lap 67, 1m 20.472s, 119.780mph/192.767km/h.
Lap record: Lap record: Valtteri Bottas (Mercedes F1 W09 V6), 1m 10.540s, 136.645mph/219.909km/h (2018).

20 · SAINZ · Ferrari
Used additional power unit elements and R-N Components; required to start from the pit lane

18 · HÜLKENBERG · Haas

16 · COLAPINTO · Williams

14 · HAMILTON · Mercedes

12 · PÉREZ · Red Bull

19 · ZHOU · Sauber

17 · VERSTAPPEN · Red Bull
Used additional power unit element; 5-place grid penalty

15 · BEARMAN · Haas

13 · GASLY · Alpine

11 · BOTTAS · Sauber

Lap Chart

Grid order		
4 NORRIS	
63 RUSSELL	
22 TSUNODA	
31 OCON	
30 LAWSON	
16 LECLERC	
23 ALBON	
81 PIASTRI	
14 ALONSO	
18 STROLL	
77 BOTTAS	
11 PÉREZ	
10 GASLY	
44 HAMILTON	
50 BEARMAN	
43 COLAPINTO	
1 VERSTAPPEN	
27 HÜLKENBERG	
31 OCON	
55 SAINZ	

VSC Virtual Safety Car deployed on lap 27
SC   Safety Car deployed on laps 28-33 and 40-42
Race red-flagged on lap 32

TIME SHEETS

PRACTICE (FRIDAY)

Weather: Dry/sunny

Temperatures: track 54-55°C, air 27-29°C

Pos.	Driver	Laps	Time
1	Lando Norris	29	1m 10.610s
2	George Russell	24	1m 10.791s
3	Oliver Bearman	30	1m 10.805s
4	Oscar Piastri	30	1m 10.950s
5	Alexander Albon	28	1m 10.955s
6	Charles Leclerc	31	1m 11.038s
7	Carlos Sainz	30	1m 11.100s
8	Nico Hülkenberg	26	1m 11.124s
9	Fernando Alonso	26	1m 11.215s
10	Pierre Gasly	27	1m 11.216s
11	Liam Lawson	26	1m 11.301s
12	Yuki Tsunoda	25	1m 11.483s
13	Franco Colapinto	31	1m 11.619s
14	Valtteri Bottas	29	1m 11.651s
15	Max Verstappen	30	1m 11.712s
16	Lewis Hamilton	30	1m 11.754s
17	Lance Stroll	26	1m 11.783s
18	Esteban Ocon	26	1m 11.827s
19	Sergio Pérez	28	1m 11.845s
20	Zhou Guanyu	27	1m 12.883s

SPRINT QUALIFYING (FRIDAY)

Weather: Dry/overcast

Temperatures: track 36-40°C, air 20-22°C

Pos.	Driver	First	Second	Third	Qualifying Tyre
1	Oscar Piastri	1m 10.265s	1m 09.239s	1m 08.899s	Soft (u)
2	Lando Norris	1m 09.477s	1m 09.063s	1m 08.928	Soft (n)
3	Charles Leclerc	1m 10.388s	1m 09.248s	1m 09.153s	Soft (n)
4	Max Verstappen	1m 10.409s	1m 09.489s	1m 09.219s	Soft (n)
5	Carlos Sainz	1m 10.503s	1m 09.500s	1m 09.257s	Soft (n)
6	George Russell	1m 10.479s	1m 09.683s	1m 09.443s	Soft (n)
7	Pierre Gasly	1m 10.630s	1m 09.610s	1m 09.622s	Soft (n)
8	Liam Lawson	1m 10.576s	1m 09.827s	1m 09.941s	Soft (n)
9	Alexander Albon	1m 10.366s	1m 09.844s	1m 10.078s	Soft (n)
10	Oliver Bearman	1m 10.442s	1m 09.629s	no time	
11	Lewis Hamilton	1m 10.625s	1m 09.941s		
12	Nico Hülkenberg	1m 10.466s	1m 09.964s		
13	Sergio Pérez	1m 10.392s	1m 10.024s		
14	Franco Colapinto	1m 10.470s	1m 10.275s		
15	Valtteri Bottas	1m 10.861s	1m 10.595s		
16	Fernando Alonso	1m 10.978s			
17	Esteban Ocon	1m 11.052s			
18	Yuki Tsunoda	1m 11.121s			
19	Lance Stroll	1m 11.280s			
20	Zhou Guanyu	1m 12.978s			

QUALIFYING (SUNDAY)

Weather: Rain/overcast Temperatures: track 21-24°C, air 19-21°C

Pos.	Driver	First	Second	Third	Qualifying Tyre
1	Lando Norris	1m 30.944s	1m 24.844s	1m 23.405s	Inter (n)
2	George Russell	1m 29.121s	1m 26.307s	1m 23.578s	Inter (n)
3	Yuki Tsunoda	1m 29.172s	1m 26.464s	1m 24.111s	Inter (n)
4	Esteban Ocon	1m 29.171s	1m 26.206s	1m 24.475s	Inter (n)
5	Liam Lawson	1m 30.758s	1m 25.654s	1m 24.484s	Inter (n)
6	Charles Leclerc	1m 29.839s	1m 26.097s	1m 24.525s	Inter (n)
7	Alexander Albon	1m 29.072s	1m 25.889s	1m 24.657s	Inter (n)
8	Oscar Piastri	1m 30.114s	1m 25.179s	1m 24.686s	Inter (n)
9	Fernando Alonso	1m 30.207s	1m 25.035s	1m 28.998s	Inter (n)
10	Lance Stroll	1m 30.580s	1m 26.334s	no time	
11	Valtteri Bottas	1m 30.633s	1m 26.472s		
12	Max Verstappen	1m 28.522s	1m 27.771s		
13	Sergio Pérez	1m 30.035s	1m 28.158s		
14	Carlos Sainz	1m 30.303s	1m 29.406s		
15	Pierre Gasly	1m 29.420s	1m 29.614s		
16	Lewis Hamilton	1m 31.150s			
17	Oliver Bearman	1m 31.229s			
18	Franco Colapinto	1m 31.270s			
19	Nico Hülkenberg	1m 31.623s			
20	Zhou Guanyu	1m 32.263s			

SPRINT (SATURDAY)

RACE DISTANCE: 24 laps, 64.223 miles/103.356km

RACE WEATHER: Dry/sunny Temperatures: track 50-52°C, air 34-35°C

Pos.	Driver	Laps	Time/Retirement	Speed (mph/km/h)	Gap to leader	Fastest race lap		Grid
1	**Lando Norris**	24	29m 46.045s	129.448/208.327		1m 11.917s	15	2
2	**Oscar Piastri**	24	29m 46.638s	129.405/208.257	0.593s	1m 11.783s	17	1
3	**Charles Leclerc**	24	29m 51.701s	129.040/207.669	5.656s	1m 11.914s	3	3
4	**Max Verstappen**	24	29m 52.542s **	128.979/207.572	6.497s	1m 11.852s	18	4
5	**Carlos Sainz**	24	29m 53.269s	128.926/207.487	7.224s	1m 11.975s	17	5
6	**George Russell**	24	29m 58.551s	128.551/206.882	12.475s	1m 12.142s	12	6
7	**Pierre Gasly**	24	30m 04.206s	128.145/206.230	18.161s	1m 12.400s	19	7
8	**Sergio Pérez**	24	30m 04.762s	128.106/206.166	18.717s	1m 11.678s	24	13
9	Liam Lawson	24	30m 06.818s	127.960/205.931	20.773s	1m 12.596s	18	8
10	Alexander Albon	24	30m 10.651s	127.689/205.496	24.606s	1m 11.692s	24	9
11	Lewis Hamilton	24	30m 15.809s	127.326/204.912	29.764s	1m 12.546s	21	11
12	Franco Colapinto	24	30m 19.278s	127.083/204.521	33.233s	1m 12.701s	15	14
13	Esteban Ocon	24	30m 20.173s	127.021/204.421	34.128s	1m 12.882s	16	16
14	Oliver Bearman	24	30m 21.552s	126.925/204.266	35.507s	1m 12.974s	4	10
15	Yuki Tsunoda	24	30m 27.419s	126.517/203.610	41.374s	1m 12.838s	14	17
16	Valtteri Bottas	24	30m 29.276s	126.389/203.403	43.231s	1m 12.698s	24	15
17	Zhou Guanyu	24	30m 40.184s *	125.640/202.198	54.139s	1m 13.559s	3	20
18	Fernando Alonso	24	30m 42.582s *	125.476/201.934	56.537s	1m 13.111s	16	18
19	Lance Stroll	24	30m 44.028s *	125.378/201.776	57.983s	1m 13.560s	3	19
	Nico Hülkenberg	19	gearbox			1m 12.879s	16	12

* Started from pit lane ** Verstappen: 5-second time penalty for VSC infringement (originally finished 3rd).

Fastest race lap: Sergio Pérez on lap 24, 1m 11.678s, 134.476mph/216.417km/h.

FOR THE RECORD

150th GRAND PRIX START: Pierre Gasly

DID YOU KNOW?

This was the first time since the 1997 Spanish GP (Panis & Alesi) that two French drivers have been on the podium.

Verstappen is the first driver to win from as low as 17th since Räikkönen at the 2005 Japanese GP

QUALIFYING: head to head

Verstappen	20	1	Pérez
Hamilton	5	16	Russell
Norris	17	4	Piastri
Leclerc	13	7	Sainz
Leclerc	1	0	Bearman
Gasly	9	12	Ocon
Alonso	15	6	Stroll
Albon	14	1	Sargeant
Albon	5	1	Colapinto
Bottas	20	1	Zhou
Tsunoda	12	6	Ricciardo
Tsunoda	3	0	Lawson
Magnussen	6	13	Hülkenberg
Bearman	2	0	Hülkenberg

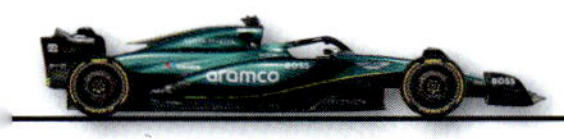
10 · STROLL · Aston Martin
NS - spin on formation lap'

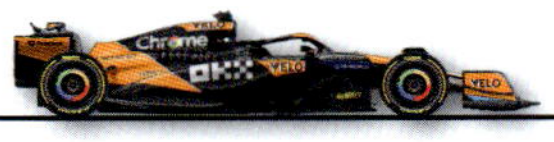
8 · PIASTRI · McLaren

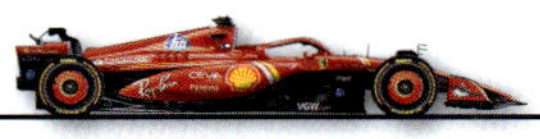
6 · LECLERC · Ferrari

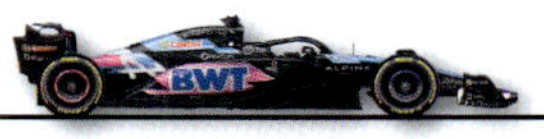
4 · OCON · Alpine

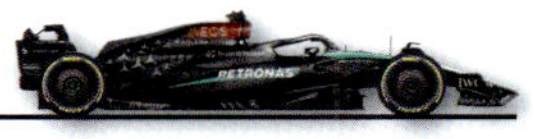
2 · RUSSELL · Mercedes

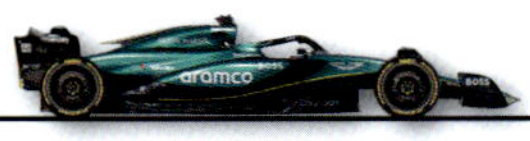
9 · ALONSO · Aston Martin

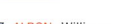

7 · ALBON · Williams
Car not ready after accident - did not start

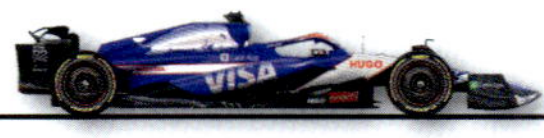
5 · LAWSON · RB

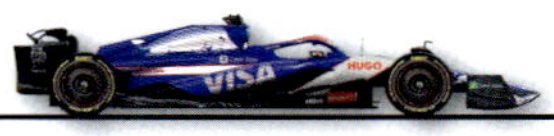
3 · TSUNODA · RB

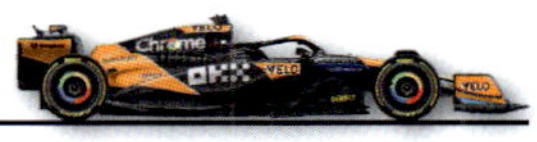
1 · NORRIS · McLaren

56	57	58	59	60	61	62	63	64	65	66	67	68	69	·
1	1	1	1	1	1	1	1	1	1	1	1	1	1	1
31	31	31	31	31	31	31	31	31	31	31	31	31	31	2
10	10	10	10	10	10	10	10	10	10	10	10	10	10	3
63	63	63	63	63	63	63	63	63	63	63	63	63	63	4
16	16	16	16	16	16	16	16	16	16	16	16	16	16	5
4	4	4	4	4	4	4	4	4	4	4	4	4	4	6
81	81	81	81	81	81	81	81	81	81	81	81	81	81	7
22	22	22	22	22	22	22	22	22	22	22	22	22	22	8
30	30	30	30	30	30	30	30	30	30	30	30	30	30	9
44	44	44	44	44	44	44	44	44	44	44	44	44	44	10
11	11	11	11	11	11	11	11	11	11	11	11	11	11	
50	50	50	50	50	50	50	50	50	50	50	50	50	50	
77	77	77	77	77	77	77	77	77	77	77	77	77	77	
24	24	14	14	14	14	14	14	14	14	14	14	14	14	
14	14	24	24	24	24	24	24	24	24	24	24	24	24	

11 = Pit stop *18 = One lap or more behind*

RACE TYRE STRATEGIES

PIRELLI

	Driver	Race Stint 1	Race Stint 2	Race Stint 3	Race Stint 4
1	Verstappen	Inter (n): 1-32	Inter (n): 33-69		
2	Ocon	Inter (u): 1-32	Inter (n): 33-69		
3	Gasly	Inter (n): 1-32	Inter (n): 33-69		
4	Russell	Inter (u): 1-28	Inter (u): 29-32	Inter (u): 33-69	
5	Leclerc	Inter (u): 1-24	Inter (u): 25-32	Inter (u): 33-69	
6	Norris	Inter (u): 1-28	Inter (u): 29-32	Inter (u): 33-69	
7	Tsunoda	Inter (u): 1-28	Wet (n): 29-32	Inter (u): 33-69	
8	Piastri	Inter (u): 1-27	Inter (u): 28-32	Inter (u): 33-69	
9	Lawson	Inter (u): 1-28	Wet (n): 29-32	Inter (u): 33-69	
10	Hamilton	Inter (n): 1-27	Inter (n): 28-32	Inter (n): 33-69	
11	Pérez	Inter (n): 1-27	Wet (u): 28-32	Inter (n): 33-69	
12	Bearman	Inter (n): 1-27	Inter (n): 28-32	Inter (n): 33-69	
13	Bottas	Inter (n): 1-32	Inter (n): 33-69		
14	Alonso	Inter (n): 1-27	Inter (u): 28-32	Inter (n): 33-69	
15	Zhou	Inter (n): 1-27	Inter (u): 28	Wet (n): 29-31	Inter (n): 32-69
	Sainz	Inter (n): 1-27	Inter (n): 28-32	Inter (u): 33-38 (dnf)	
	Colapinto	Inter (n): 1-26	Inter (n): 27-30 (dnf)		
DQ	Hülkenberg	Inter (n): 1-25	Inter (u): 26-27	Wet (n): 28-29	Inter (n): 30 (dnf)
NS	Stroll	Inter (n): 0 (dns)			
NS	Albon				

The tyre regulations stipulate that at least two of three dry tyre specifications must be used during a dry race.
Selected compounds for Brazil: Red = Soft (C5); Yellow = Medium (C4); White = Hard (C3). (n) new (u) used

POINTS

DRIVERS

1	Max Verstappen	393
2	Lando Norris	331
3	Charles Leclerc	307
4	Oscar Piastri	262
5	Carlos Sainz	244
6	George Russell	192
7	Lewis Hamilton	190
8	Sergio Pérez	151
9	Fernando Alonso	62
10	Nico Hülkenberg	31
11	Yuki Tsunoda	28
12	Pierre Gasly	26
13	Lance Stroll	24
14	Esteban Ocon	23
15	Kevin Magnussen	14
16	Alexander Albon	12
17	Daniel Ricciardo	12
18	Oliver Bearman	7
19	Franco Colapinto	5
20	Liam Lawson	4

CONSTRUCTORS

1	McLaren	593
2	Ferrari	557
3	Red Bull	544
4	Mercedes	382
5	Aston Martin	86
6	Alpine	49
7	Haas	46
8	RB	44
9	Williams	17

FIA FORMULA 1 WORLD CHAMPIONSHIP · ROUND 22

LAS VEGAS GRAND PRIX

LAS VEGAS STREET CIRCUIT

LAS VEGAS QUALIFYING

MAX VERSTAPPEN'S superb drive in Brazil, only the fifth time in 1,121 world championship races that a driver had won from 17th on the grid or lower, meant that a fourth consecutive championship would be his in Las Vegas if he could outscore Lando Norris by three points. Vegas had actually been the stage on which the championship had been clinched twice before – by Max's girlfriend Kelly's father, Nelson Piquet, in 1981, and by Keke Rosberg in 1982. But they had been sideshows in a Caesar's Palace car park. Vegas and F1 in the 21st century are rather different!

Off-track, there had been a couple of developments since Interlagos. At Aston Martin, technical director Dan Fallows had paid the price for the underwhelming performance of the 2024 car and was gone from the F1 team. And, in a move unexpected with three races of the season remaining, the FIA had replaced F1 race director Niels Wittich with F2/F3 counterpart Rui Marques.

Meanwhile, the Grand Prix Drivers Association (GPDA) had put out a statement aimed at FIA president Mohammed Ben Sulayem, letting it be known that they did not appreciate being treated like children – a reference to recent sanctions for Verstappen and Charles Leclerc over swearing – and that they felt they were not being listened to. They were very pleasantly surprised, therefore, to arrive on Friday and find that Marques had had the track-limits line redrawn at Turn Four and a more visible pit entry line painted – which they'd drawn attention to in the drivers' briefing.

If there was a lot of hot air in the paddock, none of it was reaching the track, where cold temperatures and a dusty, slippery surface resulted in virtually zero grip as the drivers took to the track for free practice on Thursday (for a Saturday race).

The cold conditions were perfect for Mercedes, as already witnessed in Canada, Silverstone and Spa, the W15's ability to generate tyre temperature a real boon. The Merc was the only front-running chassis that was able to bring the tyres in on its out-lap rather than needing an extra prep lap. It could be fuelled lighter to take advantage of the soft tyre at its best.

Consequently, it enabled Mercedes to top every practice and qualifying session, George Russell claiming a surprise fourth F1 pole for a race where Ferrari had been considered favourite, based on the track layout and the team's 2023 Vegas performance. Russell's time, 1m 32.312s, pipped Carlos Sainz's Ferrari by a tenth.

"This is the lowest-grip track we've been on since Turkey, 2020," Sainz reckoned. "I'm a bit closer to pole than I was expecting. Mercedes is very good at switching on the tyres for sector one, three-tenths up on us, and then we were coming back over the lap." The Ferraris, though, looked best on the long runs, Charles Leclerc in particular. With an eye on its 36-point constructors' championship deficit to McLaren, Ferrari was looking for a win in Sin City, and not expecting to be at its most competitive next time up in Qatar.

The most disappointed man post-qualifying was Lewis Hamilton. At a real low ebb after his dismal race in Brazil, where he had made reference to "our last race together," there was understandable speculation that he might not actually show up in Vegas, allowing Kimi Antonelli to begin his Mercedes race career early. He was present, however, and looked every bit as quick, if not quicker than Russell.

Sadly, after topping Q2, Hamilton's Q3 session was a few minutes to forget. On his first run, he locked the left front into Turn 12 and took to the escape road. On his second, he was over-ambitious on the throttle in Turn Four, lost the rear end, exceeded track limits and had the lap scrubbed. His face said it all. He would start tenth.

Another car able to switch on its tyres was the Alpine. After the team's morale-boosting double podium at Interlagos, igniting the battle for sixth in the constructors' championship with Haas and VCARB, Pierre Gasly took full advantage to qualify a superb third, splitting the Ferraris. Clearly something of a Vegas specialist, the Frenchman had not expected to beat his fourth on the grid in 2023!

Leclerc, who had been on pole for the inaugural Las Vegas GP, was disgruntled with fourth, almost half a second from Russell and with his team-mate on the front row. "Carlos has done a really good job putting the tyres always in the right window," he reckoned. "I couldn't do that. On my last Q3 lap, I have no idea what I did wrong, but I just had no fronts at all." As with Sainz, almost all of the deficit was from sector one.

The two championship contenders had to be content with row three. Verstappen had missed Leclerc's time by a hundredth and was a couple of tenths clear of Lando Norris. Without a super-low-downforce rear wing (Red Bull had not made one due to the cost cap and the fact that it would only be used at Monza and Vegas), the quadruple champion-elect was happy with that and focused purely on getting the job done.

After five poles in the previous seven races from Norris, this was an unfortunate time for McLaren to find itself struggling, relatively speaking. Lando and

team-mate Oscar Piastri could only manage sixth and eighth, split by 0.03s and Yuki Tsunoda's VCARB, which had qualified seventh for the second consecutive race.

"With it very cold and the low grip, the tyres are outside the normal window which you generally optimise them, and we are just struggling and finding it hard to put laps together," team principal Andrea Stella explained. "Hopefully, with continuous laps and more tyre temperature, we can be more competitive in the race."

Nico Hülkenberg did his customary fine job to keep Haas in the frame by qualifying ninth, while team-mate Kevin Magnussen was 12th, behind Esteban Ocon. Zhou Guanyu produced his best qualifying performance of the season so far to put the first Sauber 13th; team-mate Valtteri Bottas would start from the back with extra component penalties.

After its two 40g crashes and incident-strewn Brazil, Williams had worked around the clock to repair two trashed chassis, five floors, five front wings and sundry bodywork sets. To their great credit, they also arrived with a full complement of spares, hoping not to need them. So there were some priceless expressions when Franco Colapinto clipped the inside of Turn 15 and clattered into the wall on the opposite side of the track, prematurely ending Q2. After yet more repair work, he would start from the pit lane with a new gearbox.

Liam Lawson was the other driver to make Q2, but he was more than a second from the stellar Tsunoda, struggling for grip and aborting his second run when he lost the rear at Turn 14.

In the senior Red Bull team, Sergio Pérez's woeful run continued as he went out in Q1, 0.86s adrift of Verstappen and totally gripless. Falling at the first hurdle, too, was Alex Albon, who found himself delayed on both out-laps and unable to generate tyre temperature. Aston Martin's struggles continued, Fernando Alonso out in Q1 for the first time in six months, while Lance Stroll managed only a single lap after the mechanics had been faced with an engine change after a failure in final practice.

WITH a 10pm race start, the low temperatures raised several questions over tyre performance and graining. Tyre management would be key, and the best place to do that was out front. Ferrari's opening-day race runs on the medium compound had looked impressive, and George Russell knew that for his best shot at victory, he needed to convert his pole.

When the red lights blinked out, he did just that, making a great getaway to cover off the inside on the short run to the left-hand Turn One and put the Mercedes through in front of Carlos Sainz. The Spaniard ran a little wide, and team-mate Charles Leclerc, who was already down the inside of Pierre Gasly's Alpine, needed no second invitation to shoot by and move up to second. Behind Gasly, Max Verstappen fended off a first-corner challenge from Lando Norris and emerged still fifth. The rest of the top ten also ran in grid order, Yuki Tsunoda's VCARB heading Oscar Piastri's McLaren, Nico Hülkenberg's Haas and Lewis Hamilton's Mercedes.

Further back, Esteban Ocon led Zhou Guanyu, Liam Lawson, Kevin Magnussen, Fernando Alonso, Sergio Pérez, Alex Albon, Lance Stroll, Valtteri Bottas and, from the pit lane, Franco Colapinto.

There was some hectic side-by-side action through Turns 14–16 as Lawson bravely went around Magnussen, who lost three places on the opening lap, while Pérez sneaked down the inside of Albon.

With DRS enabled, Leclerc immediately put Russell under pressure. On lap four, he was within striking distance of the lead Mercedes, having set fastest lap. Picking up the slipstream, he had a look around the outside into T14, but Russell defended that. Charles then got almost alongside around the flat-out 200mph left-hander on to the short front straight. Brave stuff!

"I couldn't see him. I knew he was there somewhere, but I didn't know where," George said later. Leclerc kept it coming and tried to go around the outside of Turn One, but Russell ushered him wide and hung on to his lead. That was important. So as not to take too much out of his rubber, Leclerc needed to get the move done and hadn't quite managed it.

The first 14 on the grid had all opted for the Pirelli medium in what most anticipated would be a one-stop race. Meanwhile, Alonso had rolled the dice in Vegas and chosen the softs. But they were gone after four laps and, predictably, Fernando was first into the pits. The gamble had been on an early safety car – a fair bet given the lack of grip – but it wasn't forthcoming. Elsewhere, Pérez had done something different after his lowly qualifying and gone for the hard compound, as had Bottas and Colapinto at the back.

With the Ferraris running second and third, and Norris still just sixth, news of a 5s false-start penalty for Oscar Piastri, now ninth behind Hülkenberg, was not the greatest news for Zak Brown's troops in their constructors' championship fight.

Leclerc's early efforts to pass Russell, as fleeting as they had been, had not been good for his mediums, which now were graining and losing him chunks of time. To the extent that he radioed in that Sainz should pass him if he

Above: After qualifying his Alpine in a superb third place, Pierre Gasly faced disappointment on race-day when engine failure forced an early retirement.
Photo: BWT Alpine F1 Team

Top left: Lawrence Stroll cut an unhappy figure as he crossed the pit lane, his cars continuing their slump towards the back of the grid.
Photo: Aston Martin Aramco F1 Team

Above left: Another crash for Colapinto put yet more pressure on his team's resources.
Photo: Williams Racing

Opening spread: Winning from pole position, George Russell dominated proceedings in Las Vegas.
Photos: Mercedes-AMG Petronas F1 Team

Above: Carlos Sainz heads out of his pit on the way to third place.
Photo: Scuderia Ferrari

Top right: Yuki Tsunoda scored valuable points for VCARB in its battle for sixth in the championship.
Photo: Red Bull Content Pool/Getty Images

Above right: A special paint job for Vegas failed to hit the jackpot for Sauber, who left empty-handed for the 22nd time in 2024.
Photo: Stake F1 Team Kick Sauber

Right: Nico Hülkenberg maximised his top-ten qualification to deliver Haas more points with a fine eighth.
Photo: MoneyGram Haas F1 Team

could, which Carlos duly did. Then Leclerc came under threat from Verstappen, the Red Bull going by into Turn 14 on lap eight. Meanwhile, Hamilton had moved up to eighth and was going well, relegating Piastri's McLaren and pressuring Tsunoda's VCARB, which was right with Gasly, who had been passed by Norris as the Alpine began to struggle for pace.

Leclerc wanted rid of his graining mediums, but was told to stay out a while longer as there was a question over the longevity of the hard-compound rubber he would switch to. But he was losing so much time that pitting was the right call, and he was in a lap later.

Ten laps into the race's 50, Hamilton was up to seventh, having gone by Tsunoda, and McLaren also pitted Norris from fifth, as Leclerc wasn't the only one struggling with the mediums. The race was moving in the direction of a two-stopper.

Leclerc and Norris rejoined 14th and 15th respectively. Just as Verstappen took second place from Sainz, with Russell now some 8s in front, Carlos also stopped for tyres, and was followed in by Gasly, Tsunoda and Piastri on lap 11. Frustrated, Oscar had to serve his 5s jump-start penalty before his crew could get to work.

Verstappen came in after a dozen laps and rejoined seventh, behind Bottas, Magnussen, Hülkenberg and the two Mercedes drivers, all of whom had yet to stop. Importantly, though, Max was still ahead of both Ferraris and title rival Norris.

Tsunoda managed to jump Gasly in the pits as they both left practically together. Sadly for the Frenchman, however, his hope of further boosting Alpine's late-season resurgence with more points ended shortly afterwards with a power-unit failure. And the team's situation wasn't helped when Ocon came into the pits, found that the crew wasn't ready and carried on through before arriving back on the next lap.

"We basically gave ourselves a drive-through penalty, and we'll need to review what happened there," Ocon said. Similar confusion at Aston Martin for Lance Stroll was caused by a radio failure, which happened on the opening lap, the Canadian unable to let the team know when he was coming in. Their respective issues dropped both drivers to the back.

Mercedes brought in race leader Russell after a dozen laps, and Hamilton a lap later, Lewis rejoining sixth. By lap 17, one-third-distance, Russell led Verstappen by 10s, with Sainz's Ferrari another 2s behind the Red Bull. Pérez, his starting hard-compound rubber fading, was 1.5s adrift, with Leclerc, Hamilton and Norris all snapping at his heels. Then there was a 9s gap to Tsunoda, who had Magnussen – still yet to stop on his starting mediums and clearly targeting a one-stopper – and Piastri close behind.

By half-distance, Russell had extended his lead over Verstappen slightly to 11s and was totally in control, with Sainz still a couple of seconds behind Max, but under pressure from both Leclerc and Hamilton, who had set fastest lap. Norris had not been able to stay with Charles and Lewis, and had dropped 8s further back. He was under no threat from behind, though, with Tsunoda 12.5s adrift and trying to fend off Hülkenberg's Haas. Zhou was an additional 10s in arears and under threat from Pérez in the final points-scoring slot.

It was not just the medium compound that was graining. Unexpectedly, the hard tyre was as well, and after just 15 laps on them, Sainz, who was now clearly holding up Leclerc, radioed the Ferrari pit: "Let's get off these tyres."

Leclerc looked to go inside at Turn 14 on lap 26, but Sainz shut the door as Hamilton closed on both of them. Meanwhile, Red Bull responded by telling Verstappen to pit to prevent the undercut, but then changed their mind, presumably wondering whether Sainz was bluffing. But the Spaniard's tyre concerns were real enough, and since there was no reaction from his team, midway around lap 27, he tried once more: "Box me, guys." Further back,

Albon had joined Gasly on the casualty list, also with a power-unit failure.

Then Ferrari instructed Sainz to allow Leclerc through, which was a whole lot more difficult than it would have been a lap earlier, given that Lewis was now right on Charles's rear wing. Carlos obliged into Turn 14 and managed to chop across to stay ahead of the Mercedes as both headed for the pits, along with Verstappen ahead. But, at the last minute, Sainz received an instruction to stay out, which he only just managed to do, crossing the solid white line as he veered back on to the track. Hamilton wasted no time in complaining about it.

A penalty was widely anticipated, but because Sainz had not actually entered the pit lane, he wasn't in breach of F1's sporting code and, instead, received only a track-limits lap deletion for effectively cutting the final corner.

Carlos did want to know what had happened, however.

"We were not ready," he was told.

"Wake up, guys. Come on!" was his reply.

Sainz was in for real a lap later and rejoined sixth, just ahead of Tsunoda, but now undercut by Hamilton, who was really flying. Lewis quickly closed down the gap to Verstappen and, given the history, a few nerves were jangled on the Red Bull pit wall.

"Max, just don't lose sight of our aim today here," race engineer Gianpiero Lambiase cautioned him.

"Yeah, yeah, I'm just doing my race," Verstappen confirmed. And, as good as his word, there was no attempt to make things difficult for Lewis, who swept by in the DRS zone on the run down to T14.

At the same time, Leclerc, some 15s ahead, pitted from second place to give Mercedes a 1-2. And here was some more Ferrari controversy. He rejoined just in front of his team-mate and was told that it would be tight with Carlos on exit, but that he had been told not to challenge him.

Above: Four titles in a row for Max Verstappen, who took a measured approach to the race and secured another championship.
Photo: Red Bull Content Pool/Getty Images

Above right: Contrasting emotions on the podium. George Russell celebrates his dominant victory, while Lewis Hamilton reflects on an opportunity to win that had slipped away after his poor qualifying.

Right: From tenth on the opening lap, Hamilton cut his way through the field to finish just eight seconds shy of his team-mate.
Photos: Mercedes-AMG Petronas F1 Team

Thus Leclerc thought he could bring in his second set of hards gently, but was bemused to find Sainz blow straight by him. "Perhaps you should have given him the message in Spanish," he grumbled later.

Once Leclerc had committed to his two-stopper, Mercedes brought in Russell for his second stop. Probably he could have won on a one-stopper, but it was a wise precaution against a late-race safety car. George was now in the happy position of enjoying an 11s lead over Hamilton with a set of tyres that was six laps fresher.

Verstappen was 2s behind the second Mercedes, but being caught by both Ferraris. Hülkenberg was 6s adrift of them with a likely second stop to make and had a 5s margin over Norris, with Piastri's second MCL38 another 10s back. Pérez's second stop dropped him to 15th, behind Lawson, Tsunoda, Alonso and Magnussen, with 17 laps remaining in which to try to salvage a point. He certainly had intent, picking up two places in one go as he went inside both Magnussen and Lawson – battling once again – as the trio entered Turn 14 three abreast!

With Red Bull's outside chance of retaining its constructors' championship in mind, Verstappen wanted to know if he should fight the Ferraris and was told to have a go. With eight laps left, though, Sainz was down his inside into T14 with DRS as the Ferrari drivers tried to maximise their gain in McLaren's least convincing display since its Miami upgrade.

Leclerc now had to overcome the problem caused by his team-mate passing the Red Bull and giving Verstappen DRS, which made getting past into T14 almost impossible. And Carlos didn't seem that keen to hurry along and help his team-mate back on to his tail. All the while, in Leclerc's mind, he should have been in front of the other Ferrari. There would be a very out-of-character foul-mouthed rant to engineer Brian Bozzi post-race.

With five laps to go, Hamilton had Russell's lead down to 5s, but given his favourable tyre delta, you couldn't help but sense that George was just managing the situation.

Hamilton, of course, had nothing to lose and began to push, but started to open up his right front tyre, which put an end to the charge.

There was delight on the Haas pit wall as Hülkenberg passed Tsunoda for eighth, effecting a four-point swing and putting Haas ahead again in the battle with Alpine and RB for sixth in the championship. Just four points separated them, with the Middle Eastern season-closers remaining.

On lap 47, with three to go, Sainz finally put Verstappen out of DRS range, and no sooner had he done so than Leclerc was down the inside of the Red Bull into Turn 14 and up into fourth. That meant an extra two constructors' championship points for Ferrari. Just behind them, Verstappen sealed the championship with a fifth place in Vegas, coincidentally just as Piquet and Rosberg had done over 40 years before.

With that constructors' title still very much in mind now that the drivers' had gone, Norris, with a pit stop's gap to team-mate Piastri, pitted for a set of softs on the penultimate lap to go for the extra fastest-lap point, which he managed comfortably. Now, 24 points separated McLaren and Ferrari, with two races remaining. Pérez claimed the final point for tenth, behind Tsunoda, meaning that Red Bull was now 53 points adrift.

Thus Verstappen left the gambling capital of the world a four-times world champion, matching Alain Prost and Sebastian Vettel, who had also won them consecutively. Christian Horner believed that 2024 was Verstappen's best achievement, and Max agreed.

"For 70 per cent of the season, we didn't have fastest car," Verstappen said. "Mid-season, we had a lot of races where we didn't really understand what was going on. What I'm proud of is that in those tough ones, where we definitely were not fastest, we kept it together, remained calm and barely made any mistakes." Undeniably, man and not machine had made the difference.

Tony Dodgins

VIEWPOINT
BOUNCING BACK

DESPITE saying that he'd thought about packing it in for the rest of the season, following a struggle into tenth place in Brazil – and in the wet, normally his forte – the one thing you could bet on was Lewis Hamilton coming back strong in Las Vegas. He'd done it before. His history, right back to karting, is filled with brilliant demonstrations of the multiple champion being at his most threatening when his back is against the wall.

Added to which, the Mercedes was quick in Vegas. It mattered little that no one could really pinpoint the reason why. A combination of smooth surface, low ride height, cool track and tyres in the working window brought lap times that, unusually for Mercedes, remained competitive right through the weekend. Two crucial mistakes in Q3 put Hamilton P10 and in a different time zone to George Russell in P1. Without the errors, Lewis reckoned that he would have been on pole. We'll never know the truth, but a look back at the 2024 season suggested a touch of over-optimism, Russell having outqualified him 17–5. And three of those were pole positions for car No.63.

Post-race, Hamilton suggested that had he done his job properly during qualifying, the race "would have been a breeze". Later, he softened this *parc fermé* judgement, delivered in the understandable euphoria of a thrusting charge to P2. He paid tribute to George's control of this race from start to finish. There was no question that Russell's drive had demonstrated the calm quality of someone with the speed and confidence to deal with whatever a team-mate, who was 13 years his senior, had to throw at him.

Nonetheless, Hamilton's tingling performance when it really mattered carried the hallmarks of Lewis of old and answered critics who suggested that his best days were history. It set the tone for an intriguing 2025 battle between Hamilton and Charles Leclerc: two drivers prone to occasional errors at critical moments – as Hamilton had shown in Q3.

Maurice Hamilton

22

FORMULA 1 HEINEKEN SILVER LAS VEGAS GRAND PRIX 2024

LAS VEGAS 21-23 NOVEMBER
RACE DISTANCE: 50 laps, 192.599 miles/309.958km
RACE WEATHER: Dry/dark (track 17-18°C, air 17-18°C)

LAS VEGAS STRIP CIRCUIT, NEVADA
Circuit: 3.853 miles/6.201km, 50 laps

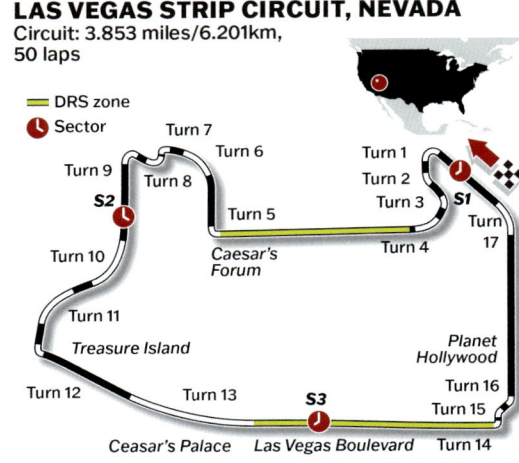

RACE – OFFICIAL CLASSIFICATION

Pos.	Driver	Nat.	No.	Entrant	Car/Engine	Laps	Time/Retirement	Speed (mph/km/h)	Gap to leader	Fastest race lap	
1	George Russell	GB	63	Mercedes-AMG Petronas F1 Team	Mercedes-AMG F1 W15-M15 E Perf. V6	50	1h 22m 05.969s	140.755/226.523		1m 35.717s	46
2	Lewis Hamilton	GB	44	Mercedes-AMG Petronas F1 Team	Mercedes-AMG F1 W15-M15 E Perf. V6	50	1h 22m 13.282s	140.546/226.187	7.313s	1m 35.480s	41
3	Carlos Sainz	E	55	Scuderia Ferrari	Ferrari SF-24-066/12 V6	50	1h 22m 17.875s	140.416/225.977	11.906s	1m 35.875s	44
4	Charles Leclerc	MC	16	Scuderia Ferrari	Ferrari SF-24-066/12 V6	50	1h 22m 20.252s	140.348/225.868	14.283s	1m 35.674s	40
5	Max Verstappen	NL	1	Oracle Red Bull Racing	Red Bull RB20-Honda RBPT H002 V6	50	1h 22m 22.551s	140.283/225.763	16.582s	1m 36.248s	43
6	Lando Norris	GB	4	McLaren Formula 1 Team	McLaren MCL38-Mercedes F1 M15 E Perf. V6	50	1h 22m 49.354s	139.526/224.546	43.385s	1m 34.876s	50
7	Oscar Piastri	AUS	81	McLaren Formula 1 Team	McLaren MCL38-Mercedes F1 M15 E Perf. V6	50	1h 22m 57.334s *	139.303/224.186	51.365s	1m 36.598s	44
8	Nico Hülkenberg	D	27	MoneyGram Haas F1 Team	Haas VF-24-Ferrari 066/10 V6	50	1h 23m 05.777s	139.067/223.806	59.808s	1m 36.585s	48
9	Yuki Tsunoda	J	22	Visa Cash App RB Formula One Team	RB VCARB 01-Honda RBPT H002 V6	50	1h 23m 08.777s	138.983/223.671	1m 02.808s	1m 36.957s	48
10	Sergio Pérez	MEX	11	Oracle Red Bull Racing	Red Bull RB20-Honda RBPT H002 V6	50	1h 23m 09.083s	138.975/223.658	1m 03.114s	1m 36.326s	42
11	Fernando Alonso	E	14	Aston Martin Aramco F1 Team	Aston Martin AMR24-Mercedes F1 M15 E Perf. V6	50	1h 23m 15.164s	138.805/223.385	1m 09.195s	1m 36.553s	39
12	Kevin Magnussen	DK	20	MoneyGram Haas F1 Team	Haas VF-24-Ferrari 066/10 V6	50	1h 23m 15.772s	138.788/223.358	1m 09.803s	1m 36.557s	49
13	Zhou Guanyu	CHN	24	Stake F1 Team Kick Sauber	Sauber C44-Ferrari 066/12 V6	50	1h 23m 20.054s	138.670/223.167	1m 14.085s	1m 36.324s	46
14	Franco Colapinto	RA	43	Williams Racing	Williams FW46-Mercedes F1 M15 E Perf. V6	50	1h 23m 21.141s	138.639/223.118	1m 15.172s	1m 36.867s	37
15	Lance Stroll	CDN	18	Aston Martin Aramco F1 Team	Aston Martin AMR24-Mer.cedes F1 M15 E Perf. V6	50	1h 23m 30.071s	138.392/222.721	1m 24.102s	1m 37.179s	43
16	Liam Lawson	NZ	30	Visa Cash App RB Formula One Team	RB VCARB 01-Honda RBPT H002 V6	50	1h 23m 36.974s	138.823/223.414	1m 31.005s	1m 36.980s	45
17	Esteban Ocon	F	31	BWT Alpine F1 Team	Alpine A524-Renault E-Tech RE24 V6	49			1 lap	1m 36.511s	47
18	Valtteri Bottas	FIN	77	Stake F1 Team Kick Sauber	Sauber C44-Ferrari 066/12 V6	49			1 lap	1m 36.601s	46
	Alexander Albon	T	23	Williams Racing	Williams FW46-Mercedes F1 M15 E Perf. V6	25	power unit			1m 38.008s	21
	Pierre Gasly	F	10	BWT Alpine F1 Team	Alpine A524-Renault E-Tech RE24 V6	15	power unit			1m 38.314s	13

* Piastri: 5s time penalty for incorrect starting position (served at pit stop).

DHL Fastest race lap (scores 1 point): Lando Norris on lap 50, 1m 34.876s, 146.204 mph/235.292 km/h (new record).

Previous lap record: Oscar Piastri (McLaren MCL60-Mercedes V6), 1m 35.490s, 145.264mph/233.779km/h (2023).

20 · COLAPINTO · Williams
Car modified in Parc Fermé and used additional Restricted-Number Components; required to start from the pit lane

18 · STROLL · Aston Martin

16 · ALONSO · Aston Martin

14 · LAWSON · RB

12 · MAGNUSSEN · Haas

19 · BOTTAS · Sauber
Used additional power unit element; 5-place grid penalty

17 · ALBON · Williams

15 · PÉREZ · Red Bull

13 · ZHOU · Sauber

11 · OCON · Alpine

Grid order	1	2	3	4	5	6	7	8	9	10	11	12	13	14	15	16	17	18	19	20	21	22	23	24	25	26	27	28	29	30	31	32	33	34	35	36	37	38	39	40
63 RUSSELL	63	63	63	63	63	63	63	63	63	63	63	44	63	63	63	63	63	63	63	63	63	63	63	63	63	63	63	63	63	63	63	63	63	63	63	63	63	63	63	63
55 SAINZ	16	16	16	16	16	16	55	55	55	1	1	44	63	11	1	1	1	1	1	1	1	1	1	1	16	16	16	16	16	44	44	44	44	44	44	44	44	44	44	44
10 GASLY	55	55	55	55	55	55	16	1	1	55	44	27	11	1	11	55	55	55	55	55	55	55	55	55	1	55	4	1	44	1	1	1	1	1	1	1	1	1	1	1
16 LECLERC	10	10	10	1	1	1	1	16	10	44	27	11	27	55	55	11	16	16	16	16	16	16	16	16	55	1	1	4	1	55	55	55	55	55	55	55	55	55	55	55
1 VERSTAPPEN	1	1	1	10	10	10	10	4	44	27	11	1	1	27	16	16	44	44	44	44	44	44	44	44	44	1	44	44	55	16	16	16	16	16	16	16	16	16	16	16
4 NORRIS	4	4	4	4	4	4	4	10	22	31	31	20	55	16	4	44	4	4	4	4	4	4	4	4	4	44	55	55	27	27	4	4	4	4	4	4	4	4	4	4
22 TSUNODA	22	22	22	22	22	22	22	16	24	20	77	16	4	44	4	11	22	22	22	22	22	22	22	22	22	22	27	27	4	4	27	81	81	81	81	81	81	81	81	81
81 PIASTRI	81	27	27	27	81	81	81	44	81	11	77	55	20	44	20	22	20	22	81	81	81	81	81	81	27	27	22	11	11	11	81	31	22	22	22	22	22	22	22	22
27 HÜLKENBERG	27	81	81	81	27	44	44	81	27	10	24	43	4	20	22	20	23	23	23	27	27	27	27	27	81	11	11	11	24	81	24	27	27	27	27	27	27	27	27	27
44 HAMILTON	44	44	44	44	44	27	27	4	22	43	16	77	77	77	81	14	14	14	14	27	27	27	27	27	24	24	24	24	81	24	31	30	31	14	14	14	14	14	14	14
31 OCON	31	31	31	31	31	31	31	81	55	4	43	43	43	77	23	27	27	27	27	14	14	14	14	14	24	11	30	30	30	30	30	81	31	31	30	27	27	14	31	11	11
20 MAGNUSSEN	24	24	24	24	24	24	20	30	16	22	22	22	22	81	27	27	27	27	27	14	11	31	31	30	30	30	30	30	30	30	22	24	14	30	11	11	31	20		
24 ZHOU	30	30	30	30	30	30	30	11	20	30	10	10	10	14	24	24	30	30	30	30	30	30	30	31	31	81	81	22	22	22	14	14	20	20	20	20	20	20	20	31
30 LAWSON	20	14	14	20	20	20	11	20	77	14	20	14	14	23	43	20	11	11	11	11	31	11	23	81	81	18	14	14	14	20	11	20	43	43	43	43	43	43	43	43
11 PÉREZ	14	20	20	11	11	11	77	20	11	77	23	4	24	10	10	4	77	18	18	18	18	18	18	18	14	43	20	81	43	14	20	11	43	11	43	43	30	24	24	
14 ALONSO	23	11	11	23	23	23	23	77	16	10	81	23	23	24	77	18	18	18	18	18	18	18	18	14	43	20	77	43	18	11	18	11	24	24	24	18	18			
23 ALBON	11	23	23	18	18	18	14	23	4	14	4	24	24	24	18	18	43	43	43	43	43	43	14	20	77	43	43	18	77	77	77	18	18	18	18	30	30			
18 STROLL	18	18	18	77	77	77	18	14	81	24	14	14	30	10	31	10	20	20	20	10	10	10	20	77	43	43	18	18	18	18	18	77	77	77	77	77	77			
77 BOTTAS	77	77	77	14	43	43	43	18	23	23	30	31	31	31	18	77	77	77	77	77	77	77	77	77																
43 COLAPINTO	43	43	43	43	14	14	14	14	18	18	18	18	18	18	18																									

TIME SHEETS

PRACTICE 1 (THURSDAY)
Weather: Dry/dark
Temperatures: track 16-17°C, air 14-15°C

Pos.	Driver	Laps	Time
1	Lewis Hamilton	26	1m 35.001s
2	George Russell	29	1m 35.397s
3	Lando Norris	27	1m 35.954s
4	Charles Leclerc	27	1m 36.007s
5	Max Verstappen	25	1m 36.038s
6	Carlos Sainz	26	1m 36.218s
7	Fernando Alonso	25	1m 36.262s
8	Oscar Piastri	26	1m 36.451s
9	Pierre Gasly	24	1m 36.478s
10	Sergio Pérez	25	1m 36.536s
11	Kevin Magnussen	24	1m 36.811s
12	Lance Stroll	25	1m 36.817s
13	Alexander Albon	26	1m 36.948s
14	Esteban Ocon	25	1m 37.152s
15	Nico Hülkenberg	24	1m 37.200s
16	Valtteri Bottas	25	1m 37.765s
17	Franco Colapinto	28	1m 38.025s
18	Zhou Guanyu	23	1m 38.350s
19	Yuki Tsunoda	23	1m 38.574s
20	Liam Lawson	28	1m 38.730s

PRACTICE 2 (THURSDAY)
Weather: Dry/dark
Temperatures: track 14°C, air 12-13°C

Pos.	Driver	Laps	Time
1	Lewis Hamilton	25	1m 33.825s
2	Lando Norris	25	1m 33.836s
3	George Russell	29	1m 34.015s
4	Carlos Sainz	29	1m 34.105s
5	Charles Leclerc	29	1m 34.313s
6	Pierre Gasly	30	1m 34.651s
7	Kevin Magnussen	20	1m 34.686s
8	Oscar Piastri	26	1m 34.798s
9	Nico Hülkenberg	24	1m 34.818s
10	Yuki Tsunoda	23	1m 34.997s
11	Valtteri Bottas	28	1m 35.020s
12	Esteban Ocon	26	1m 35.221s
13	Lance Stroll	27	1m 35.251s
14	Fernando Alonso	25	1m 35.440s
15	Liam Lawson	24	1m 35.671s
16	Zhou Guanyu	28	1m 35.765s
17	Max Verstappen	25	1m 35.834s
18	Franco Colapinto	30	1m 35.868s
19	Sergio Pérez	25	1m 36.055s
20	Alexander Albon	4	1m 39.629s

PRACTICE 3 (FRIDAY)
Weather: Dry/dark
Temperatures: track 17-18°C, air 15-16°C

Pos.	Driver	Laps	Time
1	George Russell	18	1m 33.570s
2	Oscar Piastri	14	1m 33.785s
3	Carlos Sainz	16	1m 33.918s
4	Lando Norris	14	1m 34.008s
5	Max Verstappen	17	1m 34.137s
6	Lewis Hamilton	17	1m 34.341s
7	Alexander Albon	15	1m 34.407s
8	Franco Colapinto	15	1m 34.723s
9	Kevin Magnussen	13	1m 34.883s
10	Pierre Gasly	15	1m 34.905s
11	Nico Hülkenberg	15	1m 34.908s
12	Charles Leclerc	15	1m 34.941s
13	Sergio Pérez	19	1m 35.061s
14	Esteban Ocon	14	1m 35.460s
15	Fernando Alonso	16	1m 35.938s
16	Yuki Tsunoda	18	1m 36.215s
17	Valtteri Bottas	14	1m 36.412s
18	Liam Lawson	18	1m 36.544s
19	Lance Stroll	13	1m 36.950s
20	Zhou Guanyu	16	1m 36.988s

QUALIFYING (FRIDAY)
Weather: Dry/dark Temperatures: track 14-15°C, air 12-13°C

Pos.	Driver	First	Second	Third	Qualifying Tyre
1	George Russell	1m 33.186s	1m 32.779s	1m 32.312s	Soft (n)
2	Carlos Sainz	1m 33.484s	1m 32.711s	1m 32.410s	Soft (n)
3	Pierre Gasly	1m 33.691s	1m 32.879s	1m 32.664s	Soft (n)
4	Charles Leclerc	1m 33.446s	1m 33.016s	1m 32.783s	Soft (n)
5	Max Verstappen	1m 33.299s	1m 33.085s	1m 32.797s	Soft (n)
6	Lando Norris	1m 33.592s	1m 33.099s	1m 33.008s	Soft (n)
7	Yuki Tsunoda	1m 33.789s	1m 33.089s	1m 33.029s	Soft (n)
8	Oscar Piastri	1m 33.450s	1m 33.024s	1m 33.033s	Soft (n)
9	Nico Hülkenberg	1m 33.920s	1m 33.114s	1m 33.062s	Soft (n)
10	Lewis Hamilton	1m 33.225s	1m 32.567s	1m 48.106s	Soft (n)
11	Esteban Ocon	1m 33.968s	1m 33.221s		
12	Kevin Magnussen	1m 33.991s	1m 33.297s		
13	Zhou Guanyu	1m 34.079s	1m 33.566s		
14	Franco Colapinto	1m 33.746s	1m 33.749s		
15	Liam Lawson	1m 34.087s	1m 34.257s		
16	Sergio Pérez	1m 34.155s			
17	Fernando Alonso	1m 34.258s			
18	Alexander Albon	1m 34.425s			
19	Valtteri Bottas	1m 34.430s			
20	Lance Stroll	1m 34.484s			

QUALIFYING: head to head

Verstappen	21	1	Pérez
Hamilton	5	17	Russell
Norris	18	4	Piastri
Leclerc	13	8	Sainz
Leclerc	1	0	Bearman
Gasly	10	12	Ocon
Alonso	16	6	Stroll
Albon	14	1	Sargeant
Albon	5	2	Colapinto
Bottas	20	2	Zhou
Tsunoda	12	6	Ricciardo
Tsunoda	4	0	Lawson
Magnussen	6	14	Hülkenberg
Bearman	2	0	Hülkenberg

Stake F1 Team Kick Sauber

FOR THE RECORD

4th DRIVERS' WORLD TITLE: Max Verstappen
60th GP 1-2 FINISH: Mercedes

DID YOU KNOW?

Verstappen becomes the 6th driver to win four world titles

POINTS

DRIVERS

1	Max Verstappen	403
2	Lando Norris	340
3	Charles Leclerc	319
4	Oscar Piastri	268
5	Carlos Sainz	259
6	George Russell	217
7	Lewis Hamilton	208
8	Sergio Pérez	152
9	Fernando Alonso	62
10	Nico Hülkenberg	35
11	Yuki Tsunoda	30
12	Pierre Gasly	26
13	Lance Stroll	24
14	Esteban Ocon	23
15	Kevin Magnussen	14
16	Alexander Albon	12
17	Daniel Ricciardo	12
18	Oliver Bearman	7
19	Franco Colapinto	5
20	Liam Lawson	4

CONSTRUCTORS

1	McLaren	608
2	Ferrari	584
3	Red Bull	555
4	Mercedes	425
5	Aston Martin	86
6	Haas	50
7	Alpine	49
8	RB	46
9	Williams	17

10 · HAMILTON · Mercedes

8 · PIASTRI · McLaren

6 · NORRIS · McLaren

4 · LECLERC · Ferrari

2 · SAINZ · Ferrari

9 · HÜLKENBERG · Haas

7 · TSUNODA · RB

5 · VERSTAPPEN · Red Bull

3 · GASLY · Alpine

1 · RUSSELL · Mercedes

41	42	43	44	45	46	47	48	49	50	
63	63	63	63	63	63	63	63	63	63	1
44	44	44	44	44	44	44	44	44	44	2
55	55	55	55	55	55	55	55	55	55	3
1	1	1	1	16	16	16	16	16	16	
16	16	16	16	1	1	1	1	1	1	5
4	4	4	4	4	4	4	4	4	4	6
81	81	81	81	81	81	81	81	81	81	7
22	22	22	27	27	27	27	27	27	27	8
27	27	27	22	22	22	22	22	22	22	9
14	14	14	14	11	11	11	11	11	11	10
11	11	11	11	14	14	14	14	14	14	
20	20	20	20	20	20	20	20	20	20	
43	43	43	43	43	43	43	43	43	24	
31	31	31	24	24	24	24	24	24	43	
24	24	24	31	18	18	18	18	18	18	
18	18	18	18	31	30	30	30	30	30	
30	30	30	30	*31*	*31*	*31*	*31*			
77	77	77	77							

14 = Pit stop **77** = One lap or more behind

RACE TYRE STRATEGIES

	Driver	Race Stint 1	Race Stint 2	Race Stint 3	Race Stint 4
1	Russell	Medium (u): 1-12	Hard (u): 13-32	Hard (u): 33-50	
2	Hamilton	Medium (n): 1-13	Hard (u): 14-27	Hard (u): 28-50	
3	Sainz	Medium (n): 1-10	Hard (n): 11-28	Hard (u): 29-50	
4	Leclerc	Medium (n): 1-9	Hard (n): 10-31	Hard (n): 32-50	
5	Verstappen	Medium (n): 1-11	Hard (n): 12-27	Hard (u): 28-50	
6	Norris	Medium (n): 1-9	Hard (n): 10-30	Hard (n): 31-48	Soft (u) 49-50
7	Piastri	Medium (n): 1-10	Hard (n): 11-25	Hard (n): 26-50	
8	Hülkenberg	Medium (n): 1-14	Hard (n): 15-33	Hard (u): 34-50	
9	Tsunoda	Medium (n): 1-10	Hard (n): 11-29	Hard (n): 30-50	
10	Pérez	Hard (n): 1-17	Medium (n): 18-32	Hard (u): 33-50	
11	Alonso	Soft (n): 1-4	Hard (u): 5-24	Hard (u): 25-50	
12	Magnussen	Medium (n): 1-17	Hard (u): 18-50		
13	Zhou	Medium (u): 1-11	Hard (u): 12-34	Hard (u): 35-50	
14	Colapinto	Hard (u): 1-16	Medium (n): 17-26	Hard (u): 27-50	
15	Stroll	Medium (u): 1-9	Hard (u): 10-28	Hard (u): 29-50	
16	Lawson	Medium (n): 1-11	Hard (u): 12-38	Hard (u): 39-50	
17	Ocon	Medium (n): 1-12	Hard (n): 13-45	Soft (u): 46-49	
18	Bottas	Hard (n): 1-17	Medium (n): 18-35	Hard (n): 36-49	
	Albon	Medium (n): 1-9	Hard (u): 10-25 (dnf)		
	Gasly	Medium (n): 1-10	Hard (n): 11-15 (dnf)		

The tyre regulations stipulate that at least two of three dry tyre specifications must be used during a dry race.
Selected compounds for Las Vegas: Red = Soft (C5); Yellow = Medium (C4); White = Hard (C3). (n) new (u) used

FIA FORMULA 1 WORLD CHAMPIONSHIP · ROUND 23

QATAR GRAND PRIX

LUSAIL CIRCUIT

LUSAIL QUALIFYING/SPRINT QUALIFYING & RACE

JUST a few days after Las Vegas, the vagaries of F1's longest ever calendar dictated a Middle Eastern double-header to finish the year, starting in Qatar, some 8,000 miles away. Max Verstappen might have clinched the drivers' championship in Sin City, but the constructors' title was still up for grabs, with McLaren 24 points clear of Ferrari coming in.

In 2023, the effect of the high-speed track's kerbs on Pirelli's rubber had led the tyre company to mandate an 18-lap maximum on the tyres, so for 2024, the kerbs had been rounded off and gravel strips put in on the outside of Turns 1–5 and 12–15 – to curb enthusiasm, excuse the pun. It all added up to an even faster lap.

"You are really just hanging on in the final sector," Lando Norris admitted. "It's cooler temperatures, but it's still tough physically."

Lusail, in 2023, had been very much a McLaren track, the team leaving with 47 points after a 1-3 in the sprint race and a 2-3 in the main race. Meanwhile, Ferrari had scored just 13 points, and that substantially shaped expectations going in. So, it was a surprise when Charles Leclerc comfortably topped the lone practice session before sprint qualifying, ahead of Lando Norris and Oscar Piastri, with Carlos Sainz next up.

Into sprint qualifying, though, and it was McLaren back on top, with Norris leading every session to take the pole with a lap that was six-hundredths quicker than George Russell. Oscar Piastri was a tenth further back, a similar margin clear of Carlos Sainz, who pipped Leclerc to the honour of being the quicker Ferrari by 0.02s.

"The car looks very competitive on the medium tyre, but we have to acknowledge that the Mercedes in on the same tenth of a second and Ferrari look very close," said a realistic McLaren team principal, Andrea Stella.

The new four-times world champion was seven milliseconds slower than the second Ferrari for Red Bull, not particularly enamoured with the RB20's balance, while Sergio Pérez's dire run in the second car continued when he went out in SQ1, almost seven-tenths slower than Verstappen.

Once again, a dejected-looking Lewis Hamilton was having to rationalise being four-tenths from his front-row-starting team-mate, seventh. "The same as every other qualifying – not that great," he said. "I'm just slow."

The keenly-fought battle for sixth in the constructors' championship was just that once more, with Pierre Gasly eighth for Alpine, Liam Lawson ninth for VCARB and Nico Hülkenberg tenth for Haas as they all chased bonus sprint points, the latter pair swapping positions when Lawson had a lap scratched for exceeding track limits.

Could McLaren go one better than in 2023 and achieve a sprint-race 1-2? The odds looked strong when a great outside pass of Russell in Turn Two by Piastri put the papaya cars first and second. Behind them, Sainz ran a little wide out of the first turn and had to lift, holding up Leclerc behind him, which was all the invitation Hamilton needed to snatch fifth.

With just the one DRS zone around the 3.36-mile lap, the first corner offers the only real overtaking opportunity, and even then it's tricky. Russell had a determined go at getting back past Piastri on lap four, but Oscar is no shrinking violet.

"He just turned into me!" George complained on the radio, to no avail. It would be a frustrating 19 laps for the Las Vegas winner as McLaren asked Norris to moderate his pace to give his team-mate DRS in the battle with the Mercedes. The only time Piastri didn't have the help, lap 14, Russell made another determined bid, but once more the McLaren shut the door. "F**k me, that was late! That's twice now," was George's view.

On the very last lap, out of the final corner, Lando didn't fully pick up the throttle, allowing Piastri to repeat his 2023 sprint win, going by just before the chequer. It was payback for Interlagos, where Oscar had moved over for Lando to maximise his points gain in the ultimately fruitless battle with Verstappen.

Max was still struggling here, substantial oversteer on the first lap causing him to run wide and lose positions to both Hülkenberg and Gasly, which put him ninth and out of the points. It took until lap eight for him to get back past the Alpine.

Having dropped back to conserve his tyres early on, Leclerc began pressuring Hamilton, retaking the place he had lost on the opening lap with some great racing as the pair rounded T1/2 side by side. It was an extra damage-limitation point for Ferrari as McLaren opened its advantage to 30 points. Further back, an excellent drive to seventh by Hülkenberg garnered another two points for Haas in the sixth-place battle as he managed to keep Verstappen's Red Bull at bay.

FIA FORMULA 1 WORLD CHAMPIONSHIP

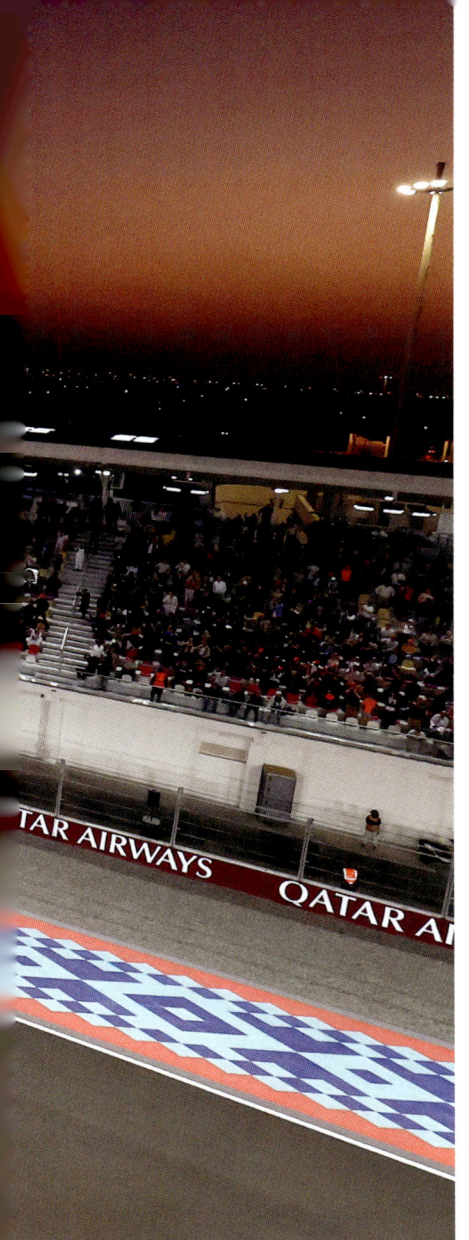

Left: With the circuit groomed to near perfection, Lando Norris and George Russell lead the field away in the sprint race.
Photo: Pirelli

Right: Max's sister, Victoria Jane, and mum, Sophie, on the grid.
Photo: Red Bull Content Pool/Getty Images

Below right: A 1-2 finish and satisfaction at a job well done at McLaren.
Photo: Peter Nygaard/Grand Prix Photo

Below: George and Max were at odds after their qualifying contretemps. The spat would continue to escalate in the coming days.
Photo: Red Bull Content Pool/Getty Images

Bottom: A quiet moment for Valtteri Bottas before the start.
Photo: Kick Sauber F1 Team

Opening spread: A pivotal point in the race. Marshals clear the track as the safety car leads Verstappen, Hamilton and Norris out of the pits.
Photo: XPB Images

With cars no longer in *parc fermé* conditions on Friday night, of course, Red Bull effected a brilliant turnaround, resulting in a significantly better balance – good enough to allow Verstappen to claim his first pole since Austria! Until, that is, he received a one-place grid penalty for impeding Russell, whom he had beaten by 0.055s.

The Dutchman was deeply unimpressed, saying that he'd never seen a driver go to greater lengths to screw someone over than Russell had done in the stewards' room. Many decried the penalty because George had not been on a push-lap when the action had taken place. He had been finishing a second tyre-preparation lap, however, and subsequently did lose time in sector one of his actual push-lap – possibly through lost tyre temperature, so you could see his point. The penalty might have been unusual, but given the five-hundredths separating them, that's not to say it was wrong. A three-place penalty would have dropped Max behind both McLarens and given them a potential buffer to Ferrari.

If unhappy with his penalty, Verstappen was much happier with his car: "I didn't expect that, so well done to the team for giving me a connected car. I didn't expect such a swing in performance – it felt a lot more stable."

The McLarens being a quarter-second off the ultimate pace was a surprise after the opening day, but the important thing was that they still had a margin over Ferrari. With Norris third, Piastri beat Leclerc to the other second-row slot by 0.03s, while Hamilton split the red cars, although he still lapped just over four-tenths slower than his team-mate. However, perhaps reviewing what messrs Elkann and Vasseur might be thinking, he'd changed his "I'm slow" tune to "I've still got it" by Saturday.

Behind Sainz, a happier Fernando Alonso put the first Aston eighth on the grid, ahead of Pérez, who was actually further away from Verstappen (0.9s), despite making the top-ten shootout, than when he had gone out in SQ1! Kevin Magnussen's Haas completed the top ten. Team-mate Hülkenberg, after his sprint heroics, went out in Q1 this time, Haas having failed to get its battery state of charge right.

In his best showing of the season so far, Zhou missed out on Q3 by just 0.06s, while team-mate Bottas, Tsunoda and Stroll went out in Q2. Albon, Lawson, Colapinto and Ocon joined Hülkenberg in failing to clear Q1.

Above: Max Verstappen takes control at the start, edging out pole-sitter George Russell and title rival Lando Norris.
Photo: Red Bull Content Pool/Getty Images

Above right: Esteban Ocon's Alpine career ended on the first lap. The Frenchman, on his way to Haas, was released from his contract before the final race of the season.
Photo: Peter Nygaard/Grand Prix Photo

Right: Pierre Gasly's end-of-year upswing continued with fifth place and ten more points scored.
Photo: BWT Alpine F1 Team

Below right: After sustaining a puncture from Albon's mirror debris, Carlos Sainz fought back to sixth.
Photo: Scuderia Ferrari

MAX VERSTAPPEN had lost his first pole position since Austria – he had been quickest at Spa, but had received an engine penalty – to a one-place grid penalty for impeding George Russell in Q3. If ever a car lined up with 'attitude', it was Max's Red Bull in Qatar and when the lights went out, and he matched Russell's getaway, the intent was obvious. The RB20 was almost alongside, preventing Russell from closing off the inside, and Max went deep into Turn One, making sure that he emerged in front.

For a fleeting moment, Lando Norris looked as though he might get around both, but Verstappen saw the McLaren coming and closed him off, so Russell's pole-position Mercedes dropped from first to third. Behind, Charles Leclerc survived a squirrelly couple of opening corners to run fourth in the first Ferrari, ahead of Oscar Piastri, Carlos Sainz, Sergio Pérez, Fernando Alonso and Lewis Hamilton, who was down three places.

Hamilton had lost those positions because he had edged forwards slightly from his grid box before the red lights had extinguished, then had stopped just as they did so. He was slow getting away again, as well as attracting a 5s penalty.

For those who remembered Norris escaping an almost identical transgression without penalty in the Bahrain season-opener, there were two considerations: first, in Norris's case, although obviously he had moved, he had not triggered a sensor, which, at the time, as per the regulations, had been the sole arbiter of a false start – even though it had been obvious to the naked eye that the car had moved. Hamilton, however, had triggered the sensor. Secondly, after the Norris incident, the wording of the rule had been revised so that the sensor was not the only measure, with visual assessment now valid, so Hamilton would have been penalised anyway, even if he had not triggered the sensor.

The top 17 had all started on the medium-compound tyre, but Nico Hülkenberg, 18th, had gone to the grid on the hard. Nobody had significant data, but, after his strong performance in the sprint, qualifying had been problematic and the German knew that he was out of position, with team-mate Kevin Magnussen having made Q3. Figuring that points would be difficult from his grid spot, even on the medium, he opted for the hard to run a longer opening stint. They offered so little initial grip, however, that he found himself struggling to avoid Albon's Williams into Turn One and hit Esteban Ocon's Alpine, which in turn collected Franco Colapinto's Williams, both going out on the spot and bringing out the safety car.

It was a sad way for Ocon's Alpine career to end. For the previous few races, he'd suspected a chassis issue, but he couldn't pinpoint it, and although the team could see nothing on the data, suddenly he couldn't match team-mate Gasly after the pair had been separated by mere hundredths throughout their time together. In Qatar, Gasly also had an upgraded nose and front wing, and was continuing his impressive recent run of form. So the joint decision was taken to release Ocon a race early, so that he could do the post-Abu Dhabi test for Haas, his new team, while Alpine could give Jack Doohan an early full-race debut.

Compounding the mess and Williams's woe, Lance Stroll also clipped Albon, and although some judged it a racing incident, the Canadian was given a 10s penalty. It mattered little because, having suffered damage in the contact, Stroll was told by Aston to retire the car.

As the field prepared for a lap-four restart, Leclerc found himself slipstreamed by Piastri, who got by into Turn One. At this point, the order was Verstappen, Norris, Russell, Piastri, Leclerc, Sainz, Pérez, Hamilton, Tsunoda, Magnussen, Gasly, Alonso, Zhou, Bottas, Albon, Hülkenberg and Lawson.

Alonso, making his 400th race start in Qatar, rather than his 400th appearance, was suddenly on the radio venting his frustration: "I don't ****** believe it! We have the same ****** problem on the straight for two years!"

He had lost places to Magnussen and Gasly through a battery deployment problem.

"We had some issues," he elaborated later. "It's not the first race that we are lacking top speed after the safety car. I think the car is confused, still thinking that we are behind the safety car. We don't deploy the energy properly out of the last corner when there's a green flag. I think we know what the issue is, just need to find the solution."

Another frustrated man was Yuki Tsunoda. On a super-fast lap full of high-speed corners and with just the single DRS zone, a pass down the inside into Turn One or through the following corners is the only realistic overtaking opportunity in Qatar. But after making up four places on the opening lap, Tsunoda found himself going backwards at a rate of knots, lacking any kind of grip and consequently slow on to the all-important front straight. Magnussen was the first to go bravely around his outside

in T1 on lap nine, with Gasly, Alonso and Zhou following through in short order. Team-mate Liam Lawson was experiencing the same shortcoming, running wide into Bottas's Sauber at the restart and earning a 10s penalty.

At the front, Verstappen was not getting away from Norris, but was controlling things consummately, keeping the McLaren out of DRS range, even though Lando was hardly ever more than 2s back from the lead Red Bull.

By one-third-distance, 19 laps into the race's 57, Russell's Mercedes had dropped 4s away from the second-place McLaren and had Piastri in the second MCL38 just behind. Leclerc had fallen 3s adrift of the Australian, but evidently had been tyre managing, as suddenly he set a couple of fastest laps and closed in again. However, he was concerned about the effect on his tyres. "Can you check the pressures?" he asked, "because the way we're driving, we're likely to get a puncture."

"The pressures are fine, Charles" race engineer Brian Bozzi reassured him. Behind sixth-placed Sainz in the second Ferrari, Pérez was 6s in arrears.

Fearing an undercut attempt by Piastri, Russell was the first of the leading contenders to pit for the switch from medium to hard tyres, coming in after 23 laps. But there was a problem at the right rear, and the Mercedes was stationary for a disastrous 7s, leaving George vulnerable to overcuts by both Ferraris.

It was turning into a difficult day for Mercedes. Hamilton had been reporting understeer and asked the team, "How far are we off the front-runners?"

He was told 1.2s. After a bit of time to digest that, Lewis queried further, "Is something broken or…?"

"No, just unbalanced."

Leclerc, informed about Russell's stop, was now getting on with it, setting his fastest lap, just 0.1s behind Verstappen, who had also just set his.

It didn't take long for Russell to come to dislike the hard-compound tyre. "The car is not turning," he reported, reinforcing his team-mate's understeer experience. He was behind the yet-to-stop Alonso at this point, but couldn't get by and was lapping the better part of a second slower than the Ferraris, still on their starting medium tyres.

McLaren was on course to all but wrap up the constructors' championship, its cars now running second and third, but then a race-changing incident occurred on lap 30. Albon's right-side mirror fell off as he blasted down the straight, possibly a legacy of his opening-lap contact with Stroll. "I was at the back anyway, so had no need of it, so a bit of weight-saving," Alex joked later.

There it sat, off the racing line to the right. Rather than a safety car or a VSC, Race Control displayed double yellow flags a short way down the straight. Subsequently, the FIA explained that it is not usual to deploy a safety car when there is minimal debris off the racing line, and that a VSC was not the answer either, because the field remains spread out and marshals do not have the opportunity to remove the debris safely.

So, what was the right answer? TBA, apparently.

Passing the scene, race leader Verstappen saw the yellows and lifted. Then, as he looked in his mirrors, he saw that Norris was closer to him than previously. "Check that Lando lifted," he told Red Bull.

Shortly afterwards, Bottas received blue flags to warn him that he was about to be lapped by Leclerc's Ferrari. Therefore, he pulled off the racing line down the straight and ran straight over the mirror, instantly transforming it into shards of carbon fire and broken glass.

Not far behind, Sainz and Hamilton drove over the new debris and sustained punctures. Cue another safety car. Just before that, Piastri had pitted, his timing unlucky and his misfortune compounded by the car being stationary for almost 10s as McLaren dealt with a jack issue.

Everyone who had extended their opening medium-

Above: Lewis Hamilton brings his punctured Mercedes into the pits, while Max Verstappen (*hidden behind*) takes full advantage of the safety-car period.
Photo: XPB Images

Top right: Eighth place for Zhou Guanyu broke Sauber's barren season at last.
Photo: Kick Sauber F1 Team

Above right: Park here. Charles Leclerc pulls into the second-place slot as VIPs ready their phones.
Photo: Scuderia Ferrari

Right: Ten seconds seemed like an eternity for Lando as he served his penalty in the pit lane.
Photo: LAT Photographic

tyre stint as far as the safety car now had the benefit of a cheap stop, with Russell taking the opportunity to pit again. He was somewhat dismayed to be sent back out on another set of hards. "Why have we put the hards back on, they're ****!" he complained, clearly annoyed.

It had been a strategic move, rather than an error, the team balancing the choice between new hards and a set of mediums that had done six laps of sprint qualifying.

Meanwhile, at Aston Martin, they had taken a close look at the mediums that had just come off Alonso's car and concluded that they were fine, so Fernando was brought back in again to get rid of his hards in favour of used mediums, the thinking being that it was worth the couple of places it would cost him. They were right, too, as the Spaniard went on to battle back up to seventh and score the team's first points since Singapore.

The in-car snitching continued as Norris reported Hamilton. "Speeding in the pit lane, 100 per cent, and brake-tested me as well," he radioed. In what was proving to be a woeful afternoon, the seven-times champion had indeed failed to activate the limiter. He apologised to the team for his second error, and you got the impression that Abu Dhabi's chequered flag could not come soon enough for him.

The bunched race order behind Bernd Maylander was now Verstappen, Norris, Leclerc, Piastri, Pérez, Gasly, Russell, Sainz, Zhou, Alonso, Magnussen, Tsunoda, Albon, Hülkenberg, Lawson, Hamilton and Bottas.

As the pack dived into Turn One at the restart, Verstappen fended off Norris and Leclerc again, while Piastri brilliantly went wheel to wheel around the first three corners as the Ferrari just held on to third. Meanwhile, Pérez suffered a spin and Hülkenberg went off into the gravel at T3, initiating another safety car, which lasted until lap 42, leaving 15 laps of racing.

As we got under way again, Piastri wanted the front left checked, as he could see sparks and feel a vibration, while checks on his team-mate's conduct under the yellow had been completed and Lando given a 10s stop-go penalty! Not a 10s penalty, a full stop-go, which translated into more like a half minute. With the field all bunched, that was brutal and sent him to the back. Hamilton also received a drive-through for his pit-lane speeding. He wanted to park the car, but was told that if he did, the penalty would carry forward to Abu Dhabi, and that he needed to serve the drive-through and then do one more lap before stopping, which he did.

There was some good comedy as Magnussen and Albon indulged in a feisty scrap over ninth, before the Dane bullied his way by in typically uncompromising fashion, accompanied by the radio message, "F**k off!" To which, the pit-wall response was, "Nice one, Kev." Clearly, with just a single race of his F1 career remaining, he cared little for the FIA's swearing protocol…

Aware that the constructors' battle would go to the wire in Abu Dhabi, Norris was doing his utmost to reach a points-scoring position from the back and managed to relegate Bottas from tenth with three laps to go, also nailing an additional fastest-lap point.

Verstappen's brilliant Brazil win had been in the wet, and on taking the Qatar chequer, win number nine in 2024, he was delighted to prove that Red Bull had turned the car around enough to win on merit in the dry, too.

Once into second, Leclerc had enough pace to keep Piastri behind and score an important result for Ferrari. Russell was disappointed with fourth, the car not having the race pace he'd hoped for, but the excellent Gasly was delighted to be able to keep Sainz's Ferrari behind for fifth and score a vital ten points for his team. That put them five points clear of Haas, for whom the combative Magnussen finished ninth in the team battle for sixth. Ninth because, just ahead of him, a doffing of the cap to Zhou was needed for a fine drive to eighth and Sauber's first points of the season! The failure of VCARB to score meant that it was 13 points behind Alpine and now very much the outsider.

However, the big prize would be sealed at Yas Marina. With a 21-point advantage, a first constructors' championship since 1998 was McLaren's to lose.

Tony Dodgins

VIEWPOINT
MIRROR IMAGE

On lap 30, a mirror flew off Alex Albon's Williams at the end of the main straight. The surprise wasn't so much that it had come adrift, given the almost daily rebuild programme being dealt with by a team out on its feet at the end of a marathon season. The wonder was why the officials – also beleaguered, but as the result of capricious redundancies and job changing – dealt with the hazard in the way they did.

The mirror was off the racing line, but in the overtaking area should a driver be trying to outbrake a rival on the inside. Or, as actually happened in the case of Valtteri Bottas, move out of the way at the behest of a blue flag. Given the approach speed and limited view from the cockpit, drivers could not see the hazard. But trackside cameras made officials aware of precisely what had happened. Their reaction, however, was muddled.

Considering the mirror not to be significantly dangerous – which, technically, it wasn't, until hit by the Sauber and smashed into a hundred pieces – the officials did not call either a VSC or a safety car, preferring instead to show one double-waved yellow to accompany an illuminated yellow panel on the main straight. Lando Norris, chasing Max Verstappen's leading Red Bull, failed to see the yellows and didn't lift off. Given the safety implications of a double yellow, that's a serious offence. But the effect of a heavy-handed punishment – a ten-second stop-go – was exacerbated by a time-consuming pit-lane entry and exit in addition to the field being tightly bunched thanks to a recent safety car. The net result was a back-of-the-field return and a critical points deficiency for McLaren in their tight battle with Ferrari in the constructors' championship. Norris admitted his mistake and recognised the need for a penalty. But this was ruinous collateral damage in a situation that, arguably, would not have happened if officials had called an immediate safety car to allow a marshal to run on to the track, retrieve the mirror and keep everyone's image intact.

Maurice Hamilton

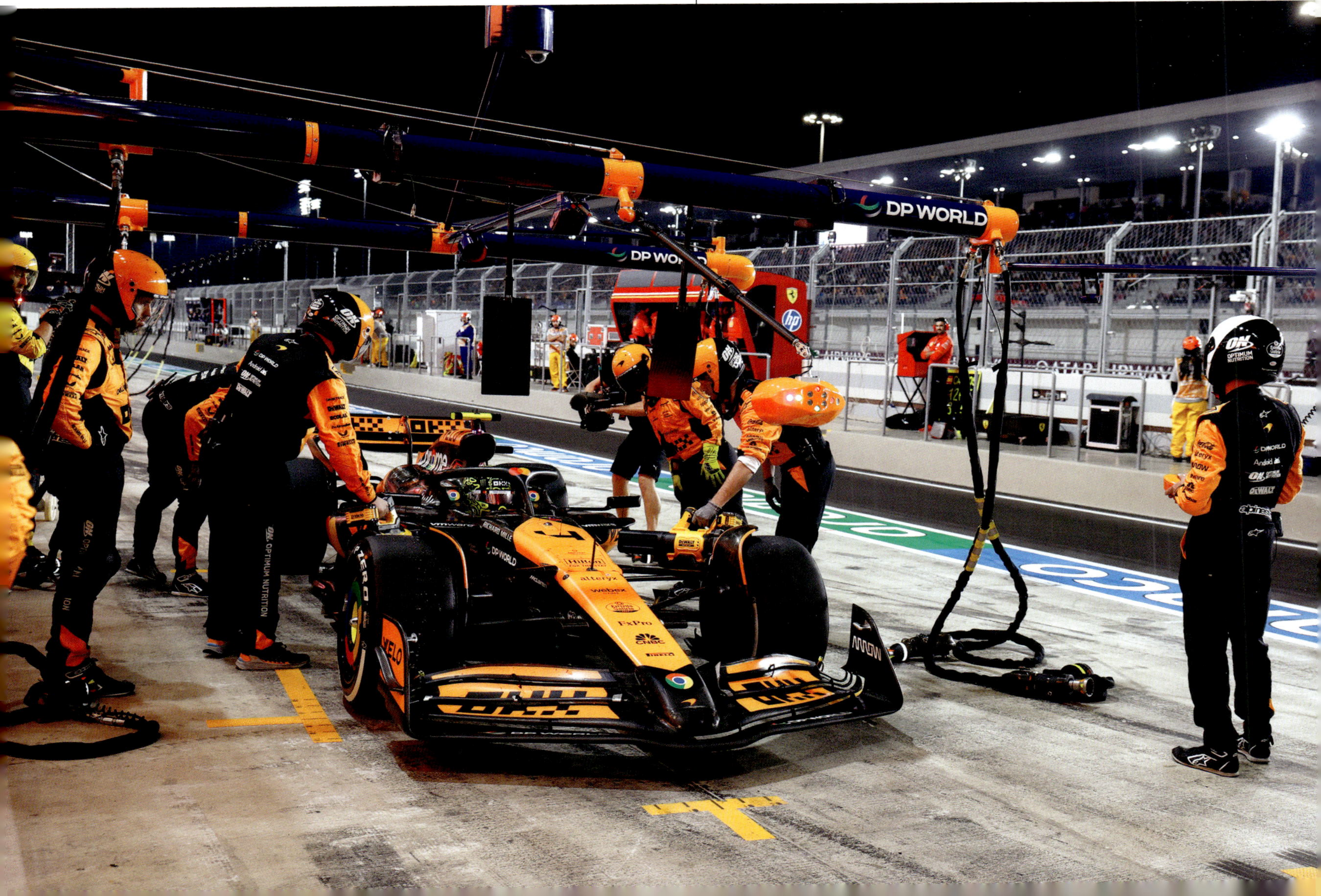

23

FORMULA 1 QATAR AIRWAYS QATAR GRAND PRIX 2024

LUSAIL 29 NOVEMBER–01 DECEMBER
RACE DISTANCE: 57 laps, 191.762 miles/308.611km
RACE WEATHER: Dry/dark (track 21°C, air 18-19°C)

LUSAIL INTERNATIONAL, CIRCUIT, DOHA
Circuit: 3.367 miles/5.419km, 57 laps

RACE – OFFICIAL CLASSIFICATION

Pos.	Driver	Nat.	No.	Entrant	Car/Engine	Laps	Time/Retirement	Speed (mph/km/h)	Gap to leader	Fastest race lap	
1	Max Verstappen	NL	1	Oracle Red Bull Racing	Red Bull RB20-Honda RBPT H002 V6	57	1h 31m 05.323s	126.313/203.281		1m 22.905s	55
2	Charles Leclerc	MC	16	Scuderia Ferrari	Ferrari SF-24-066/12 V6	57	1h 31m 11.354s	126.174/203.057	6.031s	1m 23.242s	53
3	Oscar Piastri	AUS	81	McLaren Formula 1 Team	McLaren MCL38-Mercedes F1 M15 E Perf. V6	57	1h 31m 12.142s	126.156/203.028	6.819s	1m 23.218s	51
4	George Russell	GB	63	Mercedes-AMG Petronas F1 Team	Mercedes-AMG F1 W15-M15 E Perf. V6	57	1h 31m 19.427s *	125.988/202.758	14.104s	1m 23.355s	50
5	Pierre Gasly	F	10	BWT Alpine F1 Team	Alpine A524-Renault E-Tech RE24 V6	57	1h 31m 22.105s	125.926/202.659	16.782s	1m 23.705s	56
6	Carlos Sainz	E	55	Scuderia Ferrari	Ferrari SF-24-066/12 V6	57	1h 31m 22.799s	125.910/202.633	17.476s	1m 23.465s	52
7	Fernando Alonso	E	14	Aston Martin Aramco F1 Team	Aston Martin AMR24-Mercedes F1 M15 E Perf. V6	57	1h 31m 25.190s	125.856/202.545	19.867s	1m 23.667s	57
8	Zhou Guanyu	CHN	24	Kick Sauber F1 Team	Sauber C44-Ferrari 066/12 V6	57	1h 31m 30.683s	125.729/202.342	25.360s	1m 23.889s	57
9	Kevin Magnussen	DK	20	MoneyGram Haas F1 Team	Haas VF-24-Ferrari 066/10 V6	57	1h 31m 37.500s	125.574/202.091	32.177s	1m 24.259s	55
10	Lando Norris	GB	4	McLaren Formula 1 Team	McLaren MCL38-Mercedes F1 M15 E Perf. V6	57	1h 31m 41.085s *	125.492/201.960	35.762s	1m 22.384s	56
11	Valtteri Bottas	FIN	77	Kick Sauber F1 Team	Sauber C44-Ferrari 066/12 V6	57	1h 31m 55.566s	125.162/201.429	50.243s	1m 25.533s	53
12	Lewis Hamilton	GB	44	Mercedes-AMG Petronas F1 Team	Mercedes-AMG F1 W15-M15 E Perf. V6	57	1h 32m 01.445s *	125.029/201.215	56.122s	1m 23.865s	52
13	Yuki Tsunoda	J	22	Visa Cash App RB Formula One Team	RB VCARB 01-Honda RBPT H002 V6	57	1h 32m 06.423s	124.917/201.034	1m 01.100s	1m 26.144s	47
14	Liam Lawson	NZ	30	Visa Cash App RB Formula One Team	RB VCARB 01-Honda RBPT H002 V6	57	1h 32m 07.979s *	124.881/200.977	1m 02.656s	1m 26.076s	46
15	Alexander Albon	T	23	Williams Racing	Williams FW46-Mercedes F1 M15 E Perf. V6	56	*		1 lap	1m 25.559s	47
	Nico Hülkenberg	D	27	MoneyGram Haas F1 Team	Haas VF-24-Ferrari 066/10 V6	39	spin			1m 25.767s	33
	Sergio Pérez	MEX	11	Oracle Red Bull Racing	Red Bull RB20-Honda RBPT H002 V6	38	spin/clutch			1m 25.288s	31
	Lance Stroll	CDN	18	Aston Martin Aramco F1 Team	Aston Martin AMR24-Mercedes F1 M15 E Perf. V6	8	accident damage *			1m 30.935s	6
	Franco Colapinto	RA	43	Williams Racing	Williams FW46-Mercedes F1 M15 E Perf. V6	0	accident			no time	
	Esteban Ocon	F	31	BWT Alpine F1 Team	Alpine A524-Renault E-Tech RE24 V6	0	accident			no time	

* Albon: 10s time penalty for causing a collision with Magnussen (served at pit stop).   * Lawson: 10s time penalty for causing a collision with Bottas (served at pit stop).
* Hamilton: 5s time penalty for false start (served at pit stop); Drive-through penalty for speeding in the pit lane.
* Norris: 10s stop-and-go penalty, for failing to slow for double waved yellow flags.   * Russell: 5s time penalty for falling more than 10 car lengths behind the Safety Car.
* Stroll: 10s time penalty for causing a collision with Albon (served at pit stop).

DHL Fastest race lap (scores 1 point): Lando Norris on lap 56, 1m 22.384s, 147.140mph/236.798km/h (new record).
Previous lap record: Max Verstappen (Red Bull RB16B-Honda V6), 1m 23.196s, 144.655mph/232.799km/h (2021).

 19 · COLAPINTO · Williams
 17 · LAWSON · RB
 15 · STROLL · Aston Martin
 13 · BOTTAS · Sauber
 11 · GASLY · Alpine
 20 · OCON · Alpine
 18 · HÜLKENBERG · Haas
 16 · ALBON · Williams
 14 · TSUNODA · RB
 12 · ZHOU · Sauber

Grid order	1	2	3	4	5	6	7	8	9	10	11	12	13	14	15	16	17	18	19	20	21	22	23	24	25	26	27	28	29	30	31	32	33	34	35	36	37	38	39	40	41	42	43	44	45	46	47
63 RUSSELL	1	1	1	1	1	1	1	1	1	1	1	1	1	1	1	1	1	1	1	1	1	1	1	1	1	1	1	1	1	1	1	1	1	1	1	1	1	1	1	1	1	1	1	1	1	1	1
1 VERSTAPPEN	4	4	4	4	4	4	4	4	4	4	4	4	4	4	4	4	4	4	4	4	4	4	4	4	4	4	4	4	4	4	4	4	4	4	4	4	4	4	4	4	4	4	4	4	4	16	16	16
4 NORRIS	63	63	63	63	63	63	63	63	63	63	63	63	63	63	63	63	63	63	63	63	81	81	81	81	81	81	81	81	81	81	81	81	81	81	16	16	16	16	16	16	16	16	16	16	16	16	16
81 PIASTRI	16	16	16	16	81	81	81	81	81	81	81	81	81	81	81	81	81	81	81	81	16	16	16	16	16	16	16	16	16	16	81	11	81	81	81	81	81	81	81	81	81	81	4	63	63
16 LECLERC	81	81	81	81	16	16	16	16	16	16	16	16	16	16	16	16	16	16	16	16	63	55	55	55	55	55	55	55	55	55	11	81	11	11	11	11	10	63	63	63	63	63	63	10	10
44 HAMILTON	55	55	55	55	55	55	55	55	55	55	55	55	55	55	55	55	55	55	55	55	11	11	11	11	11	11	11	11	11	11	55	10	10	10	10	63	10	10	10	10	10	10	55	55
55 SAINZ	11	11	11	11	11	11	11	11	11	11	11	11	11	11	11	11	11	11	11	11	44	44	44	44	44	44	44	44	44	44	44	10	63	63	63	55	55	55	55	55	55	55	14	14
14 ALONSO	14	14	14	14	44	44	44	44	44	44	44	44	44	44	44	44	44	44	44	44	20	20	10	10	10	10	10	10	10	10	63	14	55	55	55	14	14	14	14	14	14	14	24	24
11 PÉREZ	44	44	44	44	22	22	22	22	20	20	20	20	20	20	20	20	20	20	20	20	10	10	14	14	14	14	14	14	14	14	14	24	14	14	14	24	24	24	24	24	14	14	23	23
20 MAGNUSSEN	22	22	22	22	20	20	20	20	22	22	22	10	10	10	10	10	10	10	10	10	14	14	20	63	63	63	63	63	63	63	24	55	24	14	14	20	20	20	20	23	23	23	20	20
10 GASLY	20	20	20	20	14	10	10	10	10	10	10	22	14	14	14	14	14	14	14	14	63	63	63	24	24	24	24	24	24	24	22	22	20	20	20	22	23	23	23	20	20	20	44	77
24 ZHOU	10	10	10	10	10	14	14	14	14	14	14	14	22	24	24	24	24	24	24	24	24	24	24	22	22	22	22	22	22	22	23	23	22	22	22	23	22	22	22	22	44	44	77	22
77 BOTTAS	77	77	77	77	24	24	24	24	24	24	24	24	24	22	22	22	22	22	22	22	22	22	22	77	77	77	77	77	77	77	77	77	23	23	23	23	27	22	77	77	22	22	44	22	30
22 TSUNODA	30	30	30	30	77	77	77	77	77	77	77	77	77	77	77	77	77	77	77	77	77	77	77	30	30	30	30	30	30	30	20	20	27	30	30	27	77	77	22	44	44	22	30	44
18 STROLL	24	24	24	24	23	23	23	23	23	23	23	23	23	23	23	23	23	27	27	27	30	30	30	27	20	20	44	27	30	30	30	30	44											
23 ALBON	23	23	23	23	27	27	27	27	27	27	27	27	27	27	27	27	27	30	30	30	20	20	20	20	27	27	44	44	44	77														
30 LAWSON	18	18	18	18	30	30	30	30	30	30	30	30	30	30	30	30	30	77	77	77	77	77	77	77	77	77	77																	
27 HÜLKENBERG	27	27	27	27	30	30	18	18																																				
43 COLAPINTO																																												
31 OCON																																												

SC Safety Car deployed on laps 1-4 and 35-42

18 = Pit stop   77 = One lap or more behind

TIME SHEETS

PRACTICE (FRIDAY)
Weather: Dry/twilight
Temperatures: track 23-24ºC, air 20-21ºC

Pos.	Driver	Laps	Time
1	Charles Leclerc	30	1m 21.953s
2	Lando Norris	24	1m 22.378s
3	Oscar Piastri	26	1m 22.425s
4	Carlos Sainz	30	1m 22.535s
5	Yuki Tsunoda	27	1m 23.045s
6	Valtteri Bottas	29	1m 23.064s
7	Lance Stroll	24	1m 23.099s
8	George Russell	27	1m 23.160s
9	Alexander Albon	29	1m 23.161s
10	Lewis Hamilton	26	1m 23.188s
11	Max Verstappen	26	1m 23.213s
12	Fernando Alonso	24	1m 23.227s
13	Nico Hülkenberg	27	1m 23.245s
14	Liam Lawson	29	1m 23.562s
15	Pierre Gasly	28	1m 23.620s
16	Kevin Magnussen	27	1m 23.715s
17	Zhou Guanyu	27	1m 23.880s
18	Sergio Pérez	26	1m 24.039s
19	Franco Colapinto	29	1m 24.200s
20	Esteban Ocon	21	1m 24.280s

SPRINT QUALIFYING (FRIDAY)
Weather: Dry/dark
Temperatures: track 20-21ºC, air 18ºC

Pos.	Driver	First	Second	Third	Qualifying Tyre
1	Lando Norris	1m 21.356s	1m 21.232s	1m 21.012s	Soft (n)
2	George Russell	1m 22.021s	1m 21.488s	1m 21.075s	Soft (n)
3	Oscar Piastri	1m 22.218s	1m 21.548s	1m 21.171s	Soft (n)
4	Carlos Sainz	1m 21.838s	1m 21.809s	1m 21.281s	Soft (n)
5	Charles Leclerc	1m 22.156s	1m 21.818s	1m 21.308s	Soft (n)
6	Max Verstappen	1m 22.033s	1m 21.784s	1m 21.315s	Soft (n)
7	Lewis Hamilton	1m 22.151s	1m 21.734s	1m 21.474s	Soft (n)
8	Pierre Gasly	1m 22.586s	1m 22.352s	1m 21.978s	Soft (u)
9	Nico Hülkenberg	1m 22.569s	1m 22.318s	1m 22.088s	Soft (n)
10	Liam Lawson	1m 22.705s	1m 22.393s	1m 22.577s	Soft (n)
11	Fernando Alonso	1m 22.499s	1m 22.433s		
12	Alexander Albon	1m 22.705s	1m 22.526s		
13	Valtteri Bottas	1m 22.506s	1m 22.538s		
14	Lance Stroll	1m 22.522s	1m 22.599s		
15	Kevin Magnussen	1m 22.560s	1m 22.738s		
16	Sergio Pérez	1m 22.718s			
17	Yuki Tsunoda	1m 22.722s			
18	Esteban Ocon	1m 22.906s			
19	Zhou Guanyu	1m 22.948s			
20	Franco Colapinto	1m 23.423s			

QUALIFYING (SATURDAY)
Weather: Dry/dark Temperatures: track 20-21ºC, air 18-19ºC

Pos.	Driver	First	Second	Third	Qualifying Tyre
1	Max Verstappen	1m 21.579s	1m 20.687s	1m 20.520s	Soft (n)
2	George Russell	1m 21.341s	1m 21.069s	1m 20.575s	Soft (n)
3	Lando Norris	1m 21.578s	1m 20.983s	1m 20.772s	Soft (n)
4	Oscar Piastri	1m 21.821s	1m 21.121s	1m 20.829s	Soft (n)
5	Charles Leclerc	1m 21.278s	1m 21.000s	1m 20.852s	Soft (n)
6	Lewis Hamilton	1m 21.637s	1m 21.095s	1m 21.011s	Soft (n)
7	Carlos Sainz	1m 21.447s	1m 21.199s	1m 21.041s	Soft (n)
8	Fernando Alonso	1m 21.608s	1m 21.208s	1m 21.251s	Soft (n)
9	Sergio Pérez	1m 21.675s	1m 21.425s	1m 21.425s	Soft (n)
10	Kevin Magnussen	1m 21.891s	1m 21.387s	1m 21.500s	Soft (n)
11	Pierre Gasly	1m 21.843s	1m 21.437s		
12	Zhou Guanyu	1m 22.103s	1m 21.501s		
13	Valtteri Bottas	1m 21.927s	1m 21.731s		
14	Yuki Tsunoda	1m 22.364s	1m 21.771s		
15	Lance Stroll	1m 22.011s	1m 21.911s		
16	Alexander Albon	1m 22.390s			
17	Liam Lawson	1m 22.411s			
18	Nico Hülkenberg	1m 22.442s			
19	Franco Colapinto	1m 22.594s			
20	Esteban Ocon	1m 22.714s			

SPRINT (SATURDAY)
RACE DISTANCE: 19 laps, 63.808 miles/102.689km
RACE WEATHER: Dry/dark Temperatures: track 24ºC, air 21ºC

Pos.	Driver	Laps	Time/Retirement	Speed (mph/km/h)	Gap to leader	Fastest race lap		Grid
1	Oscar Piastri	19	27m 03.010s	141.532/227.774		1m 24.494s	17	3
2	Lando Norris	19	27m 03.146s	141.520/227.755	0.136s	1m 24.329s	13	1
3	George Russell	19	27m 03.420s	141.497/227.717	0.410s	1m 24.380s	18	2
4	Carlos Sainz	19	27m 04.336s	141.417/227.588	1.326s	1m 24.405s	16	4
5	Charles Leclerc	19	27m 08.083s	141.091/227.064	5.073s	1m 23.923s	18	5
6	Lewis Hamilton	19	27m 08.660s	141.041/226.984	5.650s	1m 24.337s	18	7
7	Nico Hülkenberg	19	27m 11.518s	140.794/226.586	8.508s	1m 24.284s	18	9
8	Max Verstappen	19	27m 13.378s	140.634/226.328	10.368s	1m 24.577s	18	6
9	Pierre Gasly	19	27m 17.523s	140.278/225.755	14.513s	1m 24.930s	19	8
10	Kevin Magnussen	19	27m 18.495s	140.194/225.621	15.485s	1m 24.568s	18	15
11	Fernando Alonso	19	27m 22.214s	139.877/225.110	19.204s	1m 24.281s	19	11
12	Valtteri Bottas	19	27m 26.361s	139.525/224.543	23.351s	1m 25.447s	12	13
13	Lance Stroll	19	27m 27.431s	139.434/224.398	24.421s	1m 25.369s	18	14
14	Esteban Ocon	19	27m 33.389s	138.932/223.589	30.379s	1m 25.598s	19	17
15	Alexander Albon	19	27m 36.072s	138.707/223.227	33.062s	1m 25.443s	18	12
16	Liam Lawson	19	27m 37.366s	138.598/223.052	34.356s	1m 25.762s	18	10
17	Yuki Tsunoda	19	27m 38.112s	138.536/222.952	35.102s	1m 25.838s	17	16
18	Franco Colapinto	19	27m 38.649s *	138.491/222.880	35.639s	1m 25.599s	18	20
19	Zhou Guanyu	19	28m 14.446s	135.565/218.171	1m 11.436s	1m 25.051s	19	18
20	Sergio Pérez	19	28m 17.381s *	135.331/217.794	1m 14.371s	1m 24.892s	18	19

* Colapinto and Pérez: Car modified in parc fermé; required to start from the pit lane.

Fastest race lap: Charles Leclerc on lap 18, 1m 23.923s, 144.441mph/232.455km/h.

FOR THE RECORD

400th GRAND PRIX START: Fernando Alonso

7,000th GP LAP LED: Red Bull

10th GP PODIUM: Oscar Piastri

3,000th POINT: Max Verstappen

QUALIFYING: head to head

Verstappen	22	1	Pérez
Hamilton	5	18	Russell
Norris	19	4	Piastri
Leclerc	14	8	Sainz
Leclerc	1	0	Bearman
Gasly	11	12	Ocon
Alonso	17	6	Stroll
Albon	14	1	Sargeant
Albon	6	2	Colapinto
Bottas	20	3	Zhou
Tsunoda	12	6	Ricciardo
Tsunoda	5	0	Lawson
Magnussen	7	14	Hülkenberg
Bearman	2	0	Hülkenberg

 9 · PÉREZ · Red Bull

 7 · SAINZ · Ferrari

 5 · LECLERC · Ferrari

 3 · NORRIS · McLaren

 1 · RUSSELL · Mercedes

 10 · MAGNUSSEN · Haas

 8 · ALONSO · Aston Martin

 6 · HAMILTON · Mercedes

 4 · PIASTRI · McLaren

 2 · VERSTAPPEN · Red Bull
1-place grid penalty for driving unnecessarily slowly during qualifying

RACE TYRE STRATEGIES

	Driver	Race Stint 1	Race Stint 2	Race Stint 3
1	Verstappen	Medium (n): 1-35	Hard (n): 36-57	
2	Leclerc	Medium (u): 1-35	Hard (n): 36-57	
3	Piastri	Medium (n): 1-34	Hard (n): 35-57	
4	Russell	Medium (u): 1-23	Hard (n): 24-35	Hard (n): 36-57
5	Gasly	Medium (n): 1-35	Hard (n): 36-57	
6	Sainz	Medium (n): 1-34	Hard (n): 35-57	
7	Alonso	Medium (n): 1-35	Hard (n): 36	Medium (u): 37-57
8	Zhou	Medium (n): 1-35	Hard (n): 36-57	
9	Magnussen	Medium (n): 1-27	Hard (n): 28-57	
10	Norris	Medium (n): 1-35	Hard (n): 36-57	
11	Bottas	Medium (n): 1-27	Hard (n): 28-35	Medium (u): 36-57
12	Hamilton	Inter (n): 1-34	Hard (n): 35-47	
13	Tsunoda	Medium (n): 1-35	Hard (n): 36-40	Soft (n): 41-57
14	Lawson	Medium (n): 1-35	Hard (n): 36-40	Soft (n): 41-57
15	Albon	Medium (n): 1-35	Soft (n): 36-55	Soft (n): 56
	Hülkenberg	Hard (n): 1	Hard (n): 2-31	Medium (n): 32-39 (dnf)
	Pérez	Medium (n): 1-35	Hard (n): 36-38 (dnf)	
	Stroll	Medium (n): 1	Hard (n): 2-7	Hard (n): 8 (dnf)
	Colapinto	Hard (n): 0 (dnf)		
	Ocon	Hard (n): 0 (dnf)		

The tyre regulations stipulate that at least two of three dry tyre specifications must be used during a dry race.
Selected compounds for Lusail: Red = Soft (C3); Yellow = Medium (C2); White = Hard (C3). (n) new (u) used

POINTS

DRIVERS
1	Max Verstappen	429
2	Lando Norris	349
3	Charles Leclerc	341
4	Oscar Piastri	291
5	Carlos Sainz	272
6	George Russell	235
7	Lewis Hamilton	211
8	Sergio Pérez	152
9	Fernando Alonso	68
10	Nico Hülkenberg	37
11	Pierre Gasly	36
12	Yuki Tsunoda	30
13	Lance Stroll	24
14	Esteban Ocon	23
15	Kevin Magnussen	16
16	Alexander Albon	12
17	Daniel Ricciardo	12
18	Oliver Bearman	7
19	Franco Colapinto	5
20	Zhou Guanyu	4
21	Liam Lawson	4

CONSTRUCTORS
1	McLaren	640
2	Ferrari	619
3	Red Bull	581
4	Mercedes	446
5	Aston Martin	92
6	Alpine	59
7	Haas	54
8	RB	46
9	Williams	17
10	Sauber	4

FIA FORMULA 1 WORLD CHAMPIONSHIP · ROUND 24
ABU DHABI GRAND PRIX
YAS MARINA CIRCUIT

YAS MARINA QUALIFYING

AS the curtain came down at Yas Marina, on the longest season in F1 history, it was all about the constructors' championship. Could McLaren, 21 points in front of Ferrari, clinch the championship for the first time since 1998? Could Alpine, five points ahead of Haas, retain sixth place and its attendant healthy cash bonus?

At Ferrari, where Robert Shwartzman was leaving to drive in Indycar in 2025, Charles Leclerc's brother, Arthur, a development driver for the Scuderia, was given the opportunity to drive Carlos Sainz's car in the first session of free practice, and the Leclerc family had flown in to witness a special moment. Charles was suffering from food poisoning, however, and driving was the last thing he felt like doing. But when he failed to emerge from the garage for the first 25 minutes of FP1, it was not because of his health, but rather that of his battery pack. When finally he took to the track, it was with a new energy store and a disastrous ten-place grid penalty. As Sainz put it, "What looked like mission impossible anyway was even worse…"

Carlos, a realist and on his way to Williams for 2025, knew that this was probably the last time for a good while that he would compete near the front. He wanted to make the most of it and gave his all. Ultimately, though, McLaren had more pace, and it was delighted team boss Zak Brown who punched the air as he celebrated an all-papaya front row. Lando Norris claimed his eighth pole of the season with a lap in 1m 22.595s, a couple of tenths up on team-mate Oscar Piastri, who pipped Sainz to the front row by two-hundredths.

"We expected to be a bit better, but it was a good lap," Norris said. "I had a big snap into T9, but otherwise a nice lap. I had a bit to gain because Max was looking quicker than us earlier in qualifying. We're a bit down in straight-line speed to Ferrari and a chunk to Red Bull, but maybe that comes back to us a bit tomorrow." He was referring to the greater downforce the team was running, which could pay back with tyre longevity in the race.

So what of Leclerc? With his ten-place penalty, he needed to qualify as high as possible, and he appeared to be on course when he shot to the top of the times at the end of Q2. But he'd exceeded track limits at Turn One and had the lap scratched.

"No freakin' way," was his reaction when engineer Bryan Bozzi told him the news. But the error was real enough, and you wondered why the lap had needed to be quite so on the edge – a safe passage into Q3 would have sufficed. Instead, Charles would start last.

Quick from first thing Friday and a stunning fourth fastest, Nico Hülkenberg delivered his best qualifying performance of the season, within three-tenths of pole for Haas! That certainly grabbed the attention of the Alpine pit-wall crew, who ordinarily would have been delighted with another top-six qualifying performance from Pierre Gasly, the constructors' combatants being split by none other than Max Verstappen!

Heartbreakingly for Ayao Komatsu's squad, subsequently Hülkenberg was penalised three grid slots for overtaking two cars in the pit lane. He argued, to no avail, that otherwise he wouldn't have got his lap in due to respective garage positions and cars backing up.

Verstappen was P1 after the first Q3 runs, four milliseconds quicker than Norris, and he survived an almighty moment out of the final corner where he had lost the Red Bull's back end, but he kept his boot buried due to the close proximity of the finish line. Somehow, he managed to keep the car out of the wall. Knowing that many of his rivals had been on scrubbed tyres rather than new ones on the first run, he wasn't expecting pole and fell to fifth in the final classification.

"It just highlights our season with this car and how it was very hard to make it work," he said. "If it works, it's good, but today, I was not very happy with the balance, and when you really push to the limit, the car just becomes very peaky. The slide probably looked good, but it's not fast."

Gasly missed Verstappen's time by just 0.04s, while George Russell's Mercedes was seventh quickest. The Qatar pole-man had been quick in practice initially, but then missed a half-second and was slower throughout than team-mate Lewis Hamilton. Part of that might have been due to some experimental set-up work that Russell was doing, with an eye on the future.

There was no fairy-tale ending to Lewis's super-successful 12-year Mercedes career either. He qualified an unfortunate 18th after Kevin Magnussen's Haas had dislodged a track bollard as the Dane, in his farewell GP, tried to get out of the way, also damaging his floor and spoiling his own qualifying in the process. The bollard had lodged itself under the Mercedes for the final four corners, robbing Hamilton of downforce and spelling a tough Sunday afternoon. Toto Wolff apologised, saying it had been "idiotic" that they had put him out so late in the session.

Fernando Alonso qualified the first Aston Martin eighth, after finding it almost undrivable in practice. "We made some changes for FP3. They didn't really work and so we made more for qualifying, suddenly seemed to find the narrow window in which these cars work and it came alive," he smiled.

Even happier was Valtteri Bottas in his last race for Sauber, as the Hinwil team was one of the few to bring upgrades to the season-closer. After suddenly shooting to the top of the times in Q1 and splitting the Ferraris, he ended up qualifying ninth, his best position of the season (he had been tenth in China). "That's as fast as she goes!" he proclaimed.

Completing the top ten was Sergio Pérez, who was adamant that he had not breached track limits when his first Q1 attempt had been deleted. As with Piastri, who suffered the same fate, subsequently the lap was reinstated after closer checks. While the sanguine Aussie was calm, Pérez was anything but. "I told you to check, man!" he stormed at the pit-wall crew. "Why did we waste a new set of tyres?" In the final analysis, it didn't matter and he made it through to Q3, not a given these days.

Out in Q2 went VCARB drivers Yuki Tsunoda and Liam Lawson, Lance Stroll, Magnussen and the frustrated Leclerc, while Alex Albon, Zhou Guanyu, the luckless Hamilton, Franco Colapinto and Jack Doohan (on his Alpine race debut) fell at the first hurdle. Amazingly, just 0.8s covered the entire grid over an 83s lap – a perfect illustration of F1's competitiveness. As McLaren team principal Andrea Stella said, "There are no slow cars any more." Which was not great if you were Leclerc and tasked with starting from the back…

WITH Lando Norris starting on pole, team-mate Oscar Piastri beside him on the front row and Charles Leclerc's Ferrari back in 19th after a ten-place grid penalty for a new energy store and a Q2 lap deletion, McLaren's 21-point constructors' championship lead looked impregnable.

But, on the brink of a great achievement, McLaren team principal Andrea Stella was taking nothing for granted. "It's something that comes with experience," he smiled on Saturday night. Fourteen years earlier, he'd come to the same track with his driver, Fernando Alonso, a strong championship favourite at Ferrari, but with four drivers still in contention mathematically. However, Ferrari had dropped the ball strategically, Alonso couldn't pass Vitaly Petrov and new champion Sebastian Vettel had gone home on top of the championship for the first time all year.

"Actually," Stella smiled when reminded of that race, "I had ten years' experience even before that, but I don't need any of it. I only need look back a week to Qatar. One minute, we were completely on top of everything with Lando, thinking about going for the victory, then next minute, we were at the back. You never know in this sport."

The opening lap of the Abu Dhabi GP proved the wisdom of those words. Ninety seconds after the lights went out, Piastri had been taken out by Max Verstappen at the first corner and was right down at the back. Meanwhile, Leclerc had driven one of the greatest opening laps ever seen in F1, on a par with, if not even better than Ayrton Senna's at Donington in 1993, as he gained 11 places.

Norris had made a solid start, and was away and clear through Turn One, but Verstappen thought he saw a gap up the inside of Piastri's McLaren. He was never sufficiently alongside and clipped Oscar's left rear on exit, spinning the McLaren and delaying his own progress. The Red Bull completed the opening lap in 11th place. Piastri's comment, laced with a healthy dose of sarcasm, was, "Yep, a world-champion move, that one." It was not long before notification came of a 10s penalty for Max.

Norris led the field across the line at the end of the opening lap with Carlos Sainz in hot pursuit, then Pierre Gasly, George Russell, Nico Hülkenberg, Fernando Alonso, fast-starting Kevin Magnussen (up seven places), Leclerc, Lance Stroll, Liam Lawson, Verstappen, Lewis Hamilton, Valtteri Bottas, Zhou Guanyu, Alex Albon, Jack Doohan, Yuki Tsunoda, Franco Colapinto and Piastri. With rumours swirling of Sergio Pérez's imminent replacement at Red Bull by Lawson, what was quite possibly the Mexican's last race for the team ended at Turn Five, where he was clipped by Bottas's Sauber, earning the Finn a 10s penalty in what was his own last race for the Swiss team.

As if not delayed enough, Piastri's chances were further reduced when he clobbered the back of Colapinto's Williams, earning a 10s penalty to be served at his pit stop. At the front, Norris obviously knew all about his team-mate's incident and a glance at a Diamond Vision screen on the second lap alerted him to the fact that somehow Leclerc was eighth, which only added to the nerves. Lando knew that he could not afford to put a foot wrong. Meanwhile, Piastri elected to make an early stop for a front-wing adjust and a switch to hard tyres.

Everyone had started on the medium-compound Pirelli except Hamilton, whose problematic qualifying exit in Q1 had prompted Mercedes to go for the reverse strategy and start him on hards. The opening-lap chaos had helped him up to 12th in his final Mercedes race, and there was a lot more to come.

At the front, Sainz was keeping Norris honest, just over 2.5s behind after half a dozen laps, with the impressive Gasly still third for Alpine, 3.5s further back, having resisted the advances of Russell. Meanwhile, Leclerc had taken seventh from Magnussen on lap six and then demoted Alonso's Aston Martin three laps later. Two laps more, and he was past Hülkenberg's Haas and up to fifth.

Above: Lando Norris escapes as Max Verstappen and Oscar Piastri spin in front of the pack.
Photo: XPB Images

Left: Out of the shadows. Ferrari development driver Arthur Leclerc was handed Sainz's car for first practice.
Photo: Scuderia Ferrari

Below left: Sauber's Beat Zhender called time on his 30-year career with the team.
Photo: Kick Sauber F1 Team

Opening spread: The long wait was over for McLaren, who celebrated clinching the constructors' championship for the first time since 1998.
Photo: Atsuo Sakurai

Above: Having been forced to start from the back of the grid, Charles Leclerc produced a sensational first-lap charge on his drive through the field to third.
Photo: XPB Images

Top right: A long time coming. Jack Doohan finally made his grand prix debut for Alpine, ahead of his full-time ride in 2025.
Photo: BWT Alpine Team

Above right: Never say die. After the unluckiest qualifying session, Lewis Hamilton ended his Mercedes days with a superb reverse-strategy drive to pip George Russell on the very last lap.
Photo: XPB Images

Right: Runner-up Carlos Sainz did all that could be expected of him as he signed off on his Ferrari career.
Photo: Scuderia Ferrari

While most were expected to execute a one-stop strategy, some would go for two, and the early pit visitors after just 11 laps were Magnussen, Zhou, who had a five-second penalty for a jump-start to serve, and Albon. Hülkenberg and Alonso followed suit a lap later, with Gasly in after 14 laps to cover the Haas.

With Verstappen complaining that his front tyres were becoming way too hot and that he couldn't brake properly, McLaren wanted to know how Norris was faring? "I'm struggling a bit more than I was, but I'm maintaining okay now," he reassured them.

Once Leclerc had clear air, he found himself just over 4s behind Russell and closing, but then the gap stabilised, his aggressive stint starting to take a toll on his tyres. Ferrari pitted him on lap 20 to undercut the Mercedes. That meant 38 laps on the hard-compound tyre to make it through on one stop, but that was not excessive. Hamilton, for example, would run a 35-lap opening stint on his hards, with heavier fuel.

Mercedes elected not to cover Leclerc's stop and left Russell out. Charles pitted out into traffic, behind a battling Lawson and Gasly. The Kiwi would need to make two pit visits as his left front was not properly attached at the first. The Ferrari was past the VCARB in short order and Charles, the bit between his teeth, even considered a move on Gasly into Turn 12, before thinking the better of it and going the more conventional route into Turn Six next time around. He lost little time in traffic and was up to third when Russell stopped.

With Norris's lead around 3s, Ferrari pitted Sainz on lap 25, and McLaren responded immediately, bringing in Lando next time around.

"I did a very fast out-lap to try to get within DRS of Lando after his pit stop," Sainz said, "and also, in case they had a slower stop that could put us within reach."

This was the utmost pressure on McLaren. Norris's stop needed to be spot on, and it was, at 2s flat. If Sainz managed to jump them and win, with Leclerc third, Ferrari would score 40 points and McLaren just 18. If Piastri didn't score, which looked unlikely at this stage, Ferrari would win the championship by a single point! Norris could have equalled them by claiming the fastest-lap point, but that option was removed when Haas, which uses Ferrari engines, of course, pitted Magnussen and bolted on a set of softs. Kevin had already been delayed after becoming another victim of Bottas contact, Valtteri having locked up on relatively gripless fresh hards. Being outside the top ten of course, he didn't get the extra point, but neither would McLaren.

In the event that Sainz won, if Piastri got as far as tenth and scored a single point, the two teams would be level on points, but Ferrari would be champions on count-back – with six victories to five. So McLaren needed Norris either to win or finish second, with Piastri at least ninth.

"After Lando came back out still in front of me," Sainz elaborated, "you go through this thought process. 'Do I push like hell now to get within DRS range? Because Lando can also push to keep me out of it, and it means I'm going to destroy my tyres and not have a chance at the end of the race to put him under pressure. Or, do I save my tyres to put him under pressure at the end, like I did in the first stint?' It's a very difficult thing to judge with these tyres, whether to use the first three laps to extract the peak or to save them. But, ultimately, today, I don't think it would have mattered."

That was because, as we'd already seen in 2024, while the McLaren and Ferrari were quite evenly matched on the medium tyre, once the hards went on, the MCL38 was a tenth or two quicker.

"On the medium, I really strongly believed we had a chance, especially with the strength of Charles's comeback," Carlos said, "but little by little with the hard, it was getting tougher and tougher, and it slipped away from us a bit."

FIA FORMULA 1 WORLD CHAMPIONSHIP 24

Norris admitted that the Ferrari's opening-stint pace had grabbed his attention.

"In that first stint, Carlos was probably the quicker driver/car combo," he admitted. "It's just that the dirty air is painful, even when two to three seconds behind. To stay that close for the whole stint was impressive, so I knew that he was very fast. But, the whole season, we've always performed better on harder tyres."

And also going superbly well on his hard tyres was Hamilton. The first-lap mayhem had helped him as well as Leclerc and, on the reverse strategy, he went 35 laps before switching to the quicker medium compound, which brought him back into the reckoning. The team suggesting that he could even make the podium seemed a bit fanciful, but if he'd had the benefit of a timely safety car just before his stop, it might have been possible.

With 22 laps remaining and all the one-stops made, Norris led Sainz by 3s, with Leclerc third, 20s further back. Russell was 3.5s behind the second Ferrari, with a 9.5s margin over Gasly's well-driven Alpine. Hülkenberg was 2s back with a fast-closing Hamilton 6s adrift, 3s clear of Verstappen, who had served his 10s penalty at his pit stop.

The new four-times champion certainly wouldn't have endeared himself to the FIA with his comments while stationary in the pits: "Can we ask them for 20 seconds, stupid idiots…" All in all, it hadn't been his finest afternoon.

With Gasly and Hülkenberg relegated, Hamilton was up to fifth and, with 15 laps to go, wanted to know the gap to Russell.

"It's 14 seconds. You can do that!" race engineer Peter Bonnington encouraged him.

At the same time, McLaren was on the radio to Norris, telling him that Leclerc was struggling with some graining

Above: The end of an era for Lewis Hamilton, who signalled his farewell to Mercedes after a dozen trophy-filled seasons.

Top right: The McLaren crew executed a perfect pit stop to keep Norris on course for victory.

Above right: Oscar Piastri recovers from his lap-one spin before embarking on a hard-fought drive to tenth.
Photos: XPB Images

Right: The victors and the vanquished. Triumphant Lando Norris and Zak Brown flanked by Ferrari's valiant losers, Carlos Sainz and Charles Leclerc.
Photo: Scuderia Ferrari

on his hard tyres, 24 laps into the stint. There had been a couple of slightly slower laps from the Ferrari, but nothing dramatic and Leclerc's gap over Russell was actually extending rather than reducing. Ferrari might have had an eye on the flying Hamilton when Leclerc's engineer, Bryan Bozzi, told him to get back into the rhythm.

"What do you mean the rhythm?" a slightly irked Leclerc replied. "This *is* the rhythm!" After the sort of effort he'd put in, doubtless some admonishment from the pit wall was unwelcome!

"The dirty air is terrible, I'm struggling," Norris told McLaren as the race entered its final ten laps and he began to encounter more back-markers, but at this point his margin over Sainz was out to more than 6s, so at least there was some breathing space.

Taking no chances, McLaren urged Piastri, who was 12th, to target that ninth place before the chequered flag was waved by tennis world No.1 Jannik Sinner. Oscar was involved in a feisty scrap with Tsunoda's VCARB, and Alonso's Aston Martin was another 5s up the road. But beyond the Spaniard, Albon's Williams looked potentially out of reach.

Piastri lost some time with an off-track excursion when he lost downforce in the dirty air behind Tsunoda, but he finally made it by into 11th. That became tenth when Albon was caught and passed in the closing stages by the fresher-tyred Alonso and Piastri after a 45-lap second stint on his hards.

Thus McLaren needed Norris to deliver, and deliver he duly did, sealing the deal for the team with his fourth victory of the year to set off the season-ending fireworks and wild celebrations in the McLaren pit – constructors' champions for the first time since 1998!

And Lando had a message: "Next year is going to be my year, too," he said. "This feels incredible, I'm so proud of everyone. Just huge congrats and a big, big thank you. It's gonna be a big night."

Sainz, popular throughout the paddock and in Maranello, had driven his last race for Ferrari after four years as they came up just 14 points shy of their first constructors' crown since 2008. Such was the weekend's focus, he said, that there hadn't been any time to be emotional. But on the slow-down lap, it came out over the radio to race engineer Riccardo Adami.

Leclerc had really wanted the championship for Ferrari, even believing that it was still possible after his issues on Friday and Saturday, and refusing to give up. While he was happy with his own driver-of-the-day performance, his disappointment at falling just short was greater. But a class act as ever, he had some sincere words for his outgoing team-mate: "Carlos is incredibly talented and has improved me in many areas. He has been an incredible team-mate, and if we have done such a big step, a lot of it is down to him. I will miss the fights, we've had our moments on track, but it's been an absolute pleasure, and I wouldn't be the driver I am today without him as team-mate for the last four years."

So that was the top three. But who would be fourth? That 14s gap between Russell and Hamilton had been whittled away to nothing by the time they began their last lap. "Stating the obvious, keep it super-clean, George," Toto Wolff radioed.

"Of course," Russell replied.

Going down to Turn Six, there was no change as Russell defended the inside. Then he did as he was bid as Lewis, taking advantage of the extra grip from his medium-compound Pirellis, launched it around the outside of Turn Nine to take the position and gain the upper hand as they finished their three years as Mercedes team-mates. "That," Wolff told him, "was the drive of a world champion."

"It's been a pleasure all the way," Bono added on the slow-down lap. "The pleasure has been mine," Lewis replied. "Thanks for all the courage, determination, passion and support." Ferrari beckons.

Verstappen crossed the line sixth, while Gasly secured Alpine's' sixth place in the constructors' championship ahead of Haas. Hülkenberg, Alonso and Piastri completed the points-scorers.

What had promised to be another Red Bull whitewash nine months earlier in Bahrain, had finished wrapped in papaya orange. Full of twists, turns, intrigue and incident, F1's longest season was absorbing to the very end. What might 2025 have to offer?

Tony Dodgins

VIEWPOINT
86 MINUTES OF PRESSURE

On paper, it looked relatively simple. McLaren had a 21-point lead. Both cars were on the front row. Ferrari faced a nightmare as Charles Leclerc started from the back. Lando Norris led every lap. Job done.

Not quite. It had turned out to be an incredibly tense hour and 26 minutes – with trouble barrelling down the inside seconds after the start, as Max Verstappen tagged Oscar Piastri's left rear, making it one McLaren at the front of the field and the other at the back. At the end of the first lap, Carlos Sainz, with nothing to lose in his final race for Ferrari, is pushing Norris. Oh, and Leclerc, after a blinding first lap, has put himself into eighth place! Andrea Stella must have taken a deep breath and tried not to think about the same race in 2010.

That's when he had been overseeing Ferrari and hopefully easing Fernando Alonso into his third championship. Before the start, that particular battle with Red Bull had looked good. Unfortunately, Ferrari chose to focus on Mark Webber and not Sebastian Vettel when setting their strategy. The result was Alonso becoming stuck behind Vitaly Petrov while Vettel raced towards his first championship. What could go wrong this time?

Norris was controlling the race. The single pit stop was perfect in terms of strategy and time taken. But the job was not yet done.

Into the closing stages, and Lando reports that he's struggling with the dirty air created by back-markers. Sainz is still close enough to be a worry. Dirty tyres from a single understeer moment for Norris, as team-mate Piastri had demonstrated behind Tsunoda, and his old mate Carlos would be through and away. Stella didn't need to be told that 25 points for Sainz and 15 for the flying Leclerc (now third) would stack against 18 for Norris and none for Piastri (then 11th), the bottom line being that Ferrari could win this by a single point!

Squeaky bum, sweaty palm, call it what you will, but the McLaren pit-wall crew knew all about it in Yas Marina!

Maurice Hamilton

24

FORMULA 1 ETIHAD AIRWAYS ABU DHABI GRAND PRIX 2024

YAS MARINA 06-08 DECEMBER
RACE DISTANCE: 58 laps, 190.253 miles/306.183km
RACE WEATHER: Dry/twilight-dark (track 26-30°C, air 25-27°C)

YAS MARINA CIRCUIT, YAS ISLAND
Circuit: 3.281 miles/5.281km, 58 laps

RACE – OFFICIAL CLASSIFICATION

Pos.	Driver	Nat.	No.	Entrant	Car/Engine	Laps	Time/Retirement	Speed (mph/km/h)	Gap to leader	Fastest race lap	
1	Lando Norris	GB	4	McLaren Formula 1 Team	McLaren MCL38-Mercedes F1 M15 E Perf. V6	58	1h 26m 33.291s	131.884/212.246		1m 27.438s	52
2	Carlos Sainz	E	55	Scuderia Ferrari	Ferrari SF-24-066/12 V6	58	1h 26m 39.123s	131.736/212.008	5.832s	1m 27.765s	55
3	Charles Leclerc	MC	16	Scuderia Ferrari	Ferrari SF-24-066/12 V6	58	1h 27m 05.219s	131.078/210.949	31.928s	1m 28.018s	51
4	Lewis Hamilton	GB	44	Mercedes-AMG Petronas F1 Team	Mercedes-AMG F1 W15-M15 E Perf. V6	58	1h 27m 09.774s	130.964/210.766	36.483s	1m 27.278s	44
5	George Russell	GB	63	Mercedes-AMG Petronas F1 Team	Mercedes-AMG F1 W15-M15 E Perf. V6	58	1h 27m 10.829s	130.937/210.723	37.538s	1m 28.195s	56
6	Max Verstappen	NL	1	Oracle Red Bull Racing	Red Bull RB20-Honda RBPT H002 V6	58	1h 27m 23.138s *	130.630/210.228	49.847s	1m 27.765s	56
7	Pierre Gasly	F	10	BWT Alpine F1 Team	Alpine A524-Renault E-Tech RE24 V6	58	1h 27m 45.851s	130.067/209.322	1m 12.560s	1m 29.251s	30
8	Nico Hülkenberg	D	27	MoneyGram Haas F1 Team	Haas VF-24-Ferrari 066/10 V6	58	1h 27m 48.845s	129.993/209.203	1m 15.554s	1m 29.152s	17
9	Fernando Alonso	E	14	Aston Martin Aramco F1 Team	Aston Martin AMR24-Mercedes F1 M15 E Perf. V6	58	1h 27m 55.664s	129.824/208.932	1m 22.373s	1m 27.948s	51
10	Oscar Piastri	AUS	81	McLaren Formula 1 Team	McLaren MCL38-Mercedes F1 M15 E Perf. V6	58	1h 27m 57.112s *	129.789/208.875	1m 23.821s	1m 27.690s	51
11	Alexander Albon	T	23	Williams Racing	Williams FW46-Mercedes F1 M15 E Perf. V6	57			1 lap	1m 29.438s	46
12	Yuki Tsunoda	J	22	Visa Cash App RB Formula One Team	RB VCARB 01-Honda RBPT H002 V6	57			1 lap	1m 29.200s	41
13	Zhou Guanyu	CHN	24	Kick Sauber F1 Team	Sauber C44-Ferrari 066/12 V6	57	*		1 lap	1m 27.982s	56
14	Lance Stroll	CDN	18	Aston Martin Aramco F1 Team	Aston Martin AMR24-Mercedes F1 M15 E Perf. V6	57	*		1 lap	1m 28.604s	42
15	Jack Doohan	AUS	61	BWT Alpine F1 Team	Alpine A524-Renault E-Tech RE24 V6	57			1 lap	1m 29.121s	56
16	Kevin Magnussen	DK	20	MoneyGram Haas F1 Team	Haas VF-24-Ferrari 066/10 V6	57			1 lap	1m 25.637s	57
17	Liam Lawson	NZ	30	Visa Cash App RB Formula One Team	RB VCARB 01-Honda RBPT H002 V6	55	engine *		3 laps	1m 28.751s	52
	Valtteri Bottas	FIN	77	Kick Sauber F1 Team	Sauber C44-Ferrari 066/12 V6	30	accident/suspension *			1m 29.482s	14
	Franco Colapinto	RA	43	Williams Racing	Williams FW46-Mercedes F1 M15 E Perf. V6	26	engine			1m 29.411s	5
	Sergio Pérez	MEX	11	Oracle Red Bull Racing	Red Bull RB20-Honda RBPT H002 V6	0	accident			no time	

* Bottas: 10s time penalty for causing a collision with Pérez (served at pit stop).   * Lawson: 10s stop-and-go penalty for release from a pit stop in an unsafe condition.
* Piastri: 10s time penalty for causing a collsion with Colapinto (served at pit stop).   * Stroll: 5s time penalty for leaving the track without justifiable reason multiple times (originally finished 12th).
* Verstappen: 10s time penalty for causing a collision with Piastri (served at pit stop).   * Zhou: 5s time penalty for false start - moved before the start signal was given (served at pit stop).

DHL Fastest race lap: Kevin Magnussen on lap 57, 1m 25.637s, 137.946mph/222.002km/h (new record).
Previous lap record: Max Verstappen (Red Bull RB16B-Honda V6), 1m 26.103s, 137.199mph/220.800km/h (2021).

20 · COLAPINTO · Williams
Used additional Restricted-Number Components; 5-place grid penalty

18 · ALBON · Williams
Used additional Restricted-Number Components; 5-place grid penalty

16 · HAMILTON · Mercedes

14 · MAGNUSSEN · Haas

12 · LAWSON · RB

19 · LECLERC · Ferrari
Used additional power unit element; 10-place grid penalty

17 · DOOHAN · Alpine

15 · ZHOU · Sauber

13 · STROLL · Aston Martin

11 · TSUNODA · RB

Grid order	1	2	3	4	5	6	7	8	9	10	11	12	13	14	15	16	17	18	19	20	21	22	23	24	25	26	27	28	29	30	31	32	33	34	35	36	37	38	39	40	41	42	43	44	45	46
4 NORRIS	4	4	4	4	4	4	4	4	4	4	4	4	4	4	4	4	4	4	4	4	4	4	4	4	4	4	4	4	4	4	4	4	4	4	4	4	4	4	4	4	4	4	4	4	4	4
81 PIASTRI	55	55	55	55	55	55	55	55	55	55	55	55	55	55	55	55	55	55	55	55	55	55	55	55	55	55	55	55	55	55	55	55	55	55	55	55	55	55	55	55	55	55	55	55	55	55
55 SAINZ	10	10	10	10	10	10	10	10	10	10	10	10	10	16	16	16	16	16	16	16	16	16	16	16	1	1	1	44	44	44	44	16	16	16	16	16	16	16	16	16	16	16	16	16	16	16
1 VERSTAPPEN	63	63	63	63	63	63	63	63	63	63	63	63	63	10	16	16	16	16	16	16	1	1	1	1	44	44	44	16	16	16	16	63	63	63	63	63	63	63	63	63	63	63	63	63	63	63
10 GASLY	27	27	27	27	27	27	27	27	27	27	27	16	16	1	1	1	1	1	1	1	44	44	44	44	16	16	16	63	63	63	63	10	10	10	10	10	10	10	10	10	10	44	44	44	44	44
63 RUSSELL	14	14	14	14	14	14	14	14	14	14	16	16	27	1	1	44	44	44	44	44	30	30	10	16	16	16	63	10	10	10	10	27	27	27	27	44	44	10	10	10	10	1	1	1	1	1
27 HÜLKENBERG	20	20	20	20	20	20	16	16	16	14	1	27	44	30	30	30	30	30	10	10	10	16	10	10	10	10	10	27	27	27	27	44	44	44	44	27	27	27	1	1	10	10	10	10	10	10
14 ALONSO	16	16	16	16	16	16	20	20	20	1	14	14	1	27	44	22	10	22	10	22	27	27	27	27	27	27	14	14	14	14	14	1	1	1	1	14	14	14	14	14	27	27	27	27	27	27
77 BOTTAS	18	18	18	18	1	1	1	1	20	20	20	44	22	10	10	22	22	27	27	27	30	14	14	14	14	14	81	81	81	81	81	18	1	1	14	14	23	23	23	23	23	23	23	23	23	23
11 PÉREZ	30	30	1	1	18	18	18	18	18	30	44	22	10	22	22	27	27	27	22	22	14	81	81	81	81	81	18	1	1	23	23	23	23	23	23	23	24	22	22	22	22	14	14	14	14	14
22 TSUNODA	1	1	30	30	30	30	30	30	30	18	30	22	27	27	27	61	61	61	61	61	14	81	18	18	18	18	18	23	23	24	24	24	24	14	22	22	22	22	14	14	14	14	14	14	22	22
30 LAWSON	44	44	44	44	44	44	44	44	44	24	61	14	14	14	14	14	14	14	14	14	81	18	20	20	20	20	20	24	23	23	23	18	22	22	22	22	14	14	81	81	81	81	81	81	81	81
18 STROLL	77	77	77	77	77	24	24	24	24	24	22	18	81	81	81	81	81	81	61	20	23	23	23	23	23	20	24	24	24	61	61	61	61	61	81	18	18	18	18	18	18	18	18	18	18	18
20 MAGNUSSEN	24	24	24	24	24	23	23	23	23	23	23	81	18	18	18	18	18	18	18	18	18	18	22	22	22	22	22	61	61	61	61	81	18	18	18	81	61	61	61	61	61	61	61	61	61	61
24 ZHOU	23	23	23	23	23	22	22	22	22	22	18	20	20	20	20	20	20	20	20	24	22	22	22	22	22	22	61	61	18	18	18	18	81	81	81	61	81	81	81	81	61	61	61	61	61	61
44 HAMILTON	61	61	22	22	22	77	61	61	61	61	24	23	23	23	23	23	23	23	23	23	30	61	61	61	61	61	20	20	20	20	20	20	20	20	20	20	20	20	20	20	20	20	20	20	20	20
61 DOOHAN	22	22	61	61	61	61	81	81	81	81	81	24	24	24	24	24	24	24	24	77	77	77	77	77	77	77	30	30	30	30	30	30	30	30	30	30	30	30	30	30	30	30	30	30	30	30
23 ALBON	43	43	81	81	81	81	77	77	77	77	77	77	77	77	77	77	77	77	77	61	61	30	30	30	30	30	77																			
16 LECLERC	81	81	43	43	43	43	43	43	43	43	43	43	43	43	43	43	43	43	43	43	43	43	43	43	43	43																				
43 COLAPINTO																																														

SC Virtual Safety Car deployed on laps 2-3

TIME SHEETS

PRACTICE (FRIDAY)
Weather: Dry/sunny
Temperatures: track 37-38°C, air 28-29°C

Pos.	Driver	Laps	Time
1	Charles Leclerc	19	1m 24.321s
2	Lando Norris	25	1m 24.542s
3	Lewis Hamilton	27	1m 24.806s
4	George Russell	27	1m 25.165s
5	Pierre Gasly	24	1m 25.333s
6	Nico Hülkenberg	23	1m 25.373s
7	Franco Colapinto	24	1m 25.382s
8	Kevin Magnussen	25	1m 25.444s
9	Felipe Drugovich	22	1m 25.471s
10	Sergio Pérez	26	1m 25.483s
11	Fernando Alonso	23	1m 25.504s
12	Liam Lawson	27	1m 25.563s
13	Valtteri Bottas	23	1m 25.611s
14	Ryō Hirakawa	19	1m 25.874s
15	Isack Hadjar	22	1m 25.877s
16	Zhou Guanyu	23	1m 25.921s
17	Ayumu Iwasa	24	1m 26.121s
18	Arthur Leclerc	22	1m 26.179s
19	Jack Doohan	24	1m 26.304s
20	Luke Browning	22	1m 26.519s

PRACTICE 2 (FRIDAY)
Weather: Dry/twilight-dark
Temperatures: track 27-30°C, air 26-27°C

Pos.	Driver	Laps	Time
1	Lando Norris	25	1m 23.517s
2	Oscar Piastri	28	1m 23.751s
3	Nico Hülkenberg	28	1m 23.979s
4	Carlos Sainz	28	1m 24.099s
5	Lewis Hamilton	28	1m 24.119s
6	Charles Leclerc	28	1m 24.201s
7	Valtteri Bottas	24	1m 24.230s
8	Kevin Magnussen	25	1m 24.235s
9	Alexander Albon	22	1m 24.269s
10	Yuki Tsunoda	28	1m 24.497s
11	Liam Lawson	25	1m 24.503s
12	Pierre Gasly	27	1m 24.517s
13	George Russell	24	1m 24.534s
14	Sergio Pérez	27	1m 24.555s
15	Zhou Guanyu	23	1m 24.557s
16	Fernando Alonso	25	1m 24.574s
17	Max Verstappen	26	1m 24.598s
18	Lance Stroll	29	1m 24.686s
19	Jack Doohan	27	1m 24.961s
20	Franco Colapinto	10	1m 25.265s

PRACTICE 3 (SATURDAY)
Weather: Dry/sunny
Temperatures: track 35-37°C, air 29-30°C

Pos.	Driver	Laps	Time
1	Oscar Piastri	16	1m 23.433s
2	Lando Norris	15	1m 23.626s
3	Lewis Hamilton	18	1m 23.823s
4	Max Verstappen	17	1m 23.844s
5	Carlos Sainz	21	1m 23.871s
6	George Russell	18	1m 24.075s
7	Nico Hülkenberg	14	1m 24.093s
8	Kevin Magnussen	14	1m 24.094s
9	Charles Leclerc	20	1m 24.098s
10	Sergio Pérez	17	1m 24.283s
11	Yuki Tsunoda	18	1m 24.343s
12	Alexander Albon	15	1m 24.378s
13	Pierre Gasly	17	1m 24.408s
14	Jack Doohan	17	1m 24.434s
15	Fernando Alonso	19	1m 24.453s
16	Valtteri Bottas	16	1m 24.479s
17	Liam Lawson	19	1m 24.519s
18	Lance Stroll	20	1m 24.531s
19	Zhou Guanyu	16	1m 24.668s
20	Franco Colapinto	15	1m 24.766s

QUALIFYING (SATURDAY)
Weather: Dry/dark Temperatures: track 26-27°C, air 25-26°C

Pos.	Driver	First	Second	Third	Qualifying Tyre
1	Lando Norris	1m 23.682s	1m 23.098s	1m 22.595s	Soft (n)
2	Oscar Piastri	1m 23.640s	1m 23.199s	1m 22.804s	Soft (n)
3	Carlos Sainz	1m 23.487s	1m 22.985s	1m 22.824s	Soft (n)
4	Nico Hülkenberg	1m 23.722s	1m 23.040s	1m 22.886s	Soft (n)
5	Max Verstappen	1m 23.516s	1m 22.998s	1m 22.945s	Soft (n)
6	Pierre Gasly	1m 23.548s	1m 23.086s	1m 22.984s	Soft (n)
7	George Russell	1m 23.678s	1m 23.283s	1m 23.132s	Soft (n)
8	Fernando Alonso	1m 23.794s	1m 23.268s	1m 23.196s	Soft (n)
9	Valtteri Bottas	1m 23.481s	1m 23.341s	1m 23.204s	Soft (n)
10	Sergio Pérez	1m 23.559s	1m 23.379s	1m 23.264s	Soft (n)
11	Yuki Tsunoda	1m 23.735s	1m 23.419s		
12	Liam Lawson	1m 23.733s	1m 23.472s		
13	Lance Stroll	1m 23.729s	1m 23.784s		
14	Charles Leclerc	1m 23.302s	1m 23.833s		
15	Kevin Magnussen	1m 23.632s	1m 23.877s		
16	Alexander Albon	1m 23.821s			
17	Zhou Guanyu	1m 23.880s			
18	Lewis Hamilton	1m 23.887s			
19	Franco Colapinto	1m 23.912s			
20	Jack Doohan	1m 24.105s			

QUALIFYING: head to head

Verstappen	23	1	Pérez
Hamilton	5	19	Russell
Norris	20	4	Piastri
Leclerc	14	9	Sainz
Leclerc	1	0	Bearman
Gasly	11	12	Ocon
Gasly	1	0	Doohan
Alonso	18	6	Stroll
Albon	14	1	Sargeant
Albon	7	2	Colapinto
Bottas	21	3	Zhou
Tsunoda	13	6	Ricciardo
Tsunoda	5	0	Lawson
Magnussen	7	15	Hülkenberg
Bearman	2	0	Hülkenberg

BWT Alpine F1 Team

FOR THE RECORD

9th CONSTRUCTORS' WORLD TITLE: McLaren
1st GRAND PRIX START: Jack Doohan
1,000th POINT: Lando Norris

DID YOU KNOW?

This was McLaren's first constructors' world title since 1998, a record 26-year interval between titles

This has been the first season where 7 drivers won races multiple times

POINTS

DRIVERS

1	Max Verstappen	437
2	Lando Norris	374
3	Charles Leclerc	356
4	Oscar Piastri	292
5	Carlos Sainz	290
6	George Russell	245
7	Lewis Hamilton	223
8	Sergio Pérez	152
9	Fernando Alonso	70
10	Pierre Gasly	42
11	Nico Hülkenberg	41
12	Yuki Tsunoda	30
13	Lance Stroll	24
14	Esteban Ocon	23
15	Kevin Magnussen	16
16	Alexander Albon	12
17	Daniel Ricciardo	12
18	Oliver Bearman	7
19	Franco Colapinto	5
20	Zhou Guanyu	4
21	Liam Lawson	4

CONSTRUCTORS

1	McLaren	666
2	Ferrari	652
3	Red Bull	589
4	Mercedes	468
5	Aston Martin	94
6	Alpine	65
7	Haas	58
8	RB	46
9	Williams	17
10	Sauber	4

10 · PÉREZ · Red Bull   8 · ALONSO · Aston Martin   6 · RUSSELL · Mercedes   4 · VERSTAPPEN · Red Bull   2 · PIASTRI · McLaren

9 · BOTTAS · Sauber   7 · HÜLKENBERG · Haas
Overtook 2 cars in the tunnel section of the pit exit road; 3-place grid penalty   5 · GASLY · Alpine   3 · SAINZ · Ferrari   1 · NORRIS · McLaren

47	48	49	50	51	52	53	54	55	56	57	58	
4	4	4	4	4	4	4	4	4	4	4	4	1
55	55	55	55	55	55	55	55	55	55	55	55	2
16	16	16	16	16	16	16	16	16	16	16	16	3
63	63	63	63	63	63	63	63	63	63	63	44	4
44	44	44	44	44	44	44	44	44	44	44	63	5
1	1	1	1	1	1	1	1	1	1	1	1	6
10	10	10	10	10	10	10	10	10	10	10	10	7
27	27	27	27	27	27	27	27	27	27	27	27	8
23	23	23	14	14	14	14	14	14	14	14	14	9
14	14	14	23	23	81	81	81	81	81	81	81	10
22	81	81	81	81	23	23	23	23	23	23	23	
81	22	22	22	22	22	22	22	18	18	18	18	
18	18	*18*	*18*	*18*	*18*	*18*	22	22	22	22	22	
61	61	61	61	*61*	61	61	61	61	61	61	61	
24	24	24	*24*	*24*	*24*	*24*	*24*	24	24	24	24	
20	20	20	20	20	20	20	20	20	20	20	20	
30	30	30	30	30	30	30	30					

81 = Pit stop   *43* = One lap or more behind

RACE TYRE STRATEGIES

	Driver	Race Stint 1	Race Stint 2	Race Stint 3	Race Stint 4	Race Stint 5
1	Norris	Medium (n): 1-26	Hard (n): 27-58			
2	Sainz	Medium (n): 1-25	Hard (n): 26-58			
3	Leclerc	Medium (n): 1-20	Medium (n): 21-58			
4	Hamilton	Hard (n): 1-34	Medium (u): 35-58			
5	Russell	Medium (u): 1-26	Hard (n): 27-58			
6	Verstappen	Medium (n): 1-29	Hard (n): 30-58			
7	Gasly	Medium (n): 1-14	Hard (n): 15-58			
8	Hülkenberg	Medium (n): 1-13	Hard (n): 14-58			
9	Alonso	Medium (n): 1-13	Hard (u): 14-37	Hard (u): 38-58		
10	Piastri	Medium (n): 1-4	Hard (n): 5-32	Hard (n): 33-58		
11	Albon	Medium (n): 1-12	Hard (n): 13-57			
12	Tsunoda	Medium (n): 1-22	Hard (n): 23-57			
13	Zhou	Medium (n): 1-12	Hard (n): 13-39	Hard (u): 40-57		
14	Stroll	Medium (u): 1-11	Hard (n): 12-32	Hard (n): 33-57		
15	Doohan	Medium (n): 1-22	Hard (n): 23-57			
16	Magnussen	Medium (n): 1-12	Hard (n): 13-29	Hard (n): 30	Soft (n): 31-55	Soft (u): 56-57
17	Lawson	Medium (n): 1-23	Hard (n): 24-55 (dnf)			
	Bottas	Medium (n): 1-6	Hard (n): 7-30 (dnf)			
	Colapinto	Medium (n): 1-3	Hard (n): 4-26 (dnf)			
	Pérez	Medium (n): 0 (dnf)				

The tyre regulations stipulate that at least two of three dry tyre specifications must be used during a dry race.
Selected compounds for Abu Dhabi: Red = Soft (C5); Yellow = Medium (C4); White = Hard (C3). (n) new (u) used

STATISTICS: Compiled by DAVID HAYHOE

DRIVERS' POINTS TABLE: 2024

Position	Driver	Bahrain	Saudi Arabia	Australia	Japan	China Sprint	China	Miami Sprint	Miami	Imola	Monaco	Canada	Spain	Austria Sprint	Austria	Britain	Hungary	Belgium	Netherlands	Italy	Azerbaijan	Singapore	United States Sprint	United States	Mexico City	São Paulo Sprint	São Paulo	Las Vegas	Qatar Sprint	Qatar	Abu Dhabi	Points
1	Max VERSTAPPEN	1pf	1p	Rp	1pf	1f	1p	1pf	2p	1p	6	1	1	1p	5p	2	5	4	2	6	5	2	1pf	3	6	4	1f	5	8	1	6	**437**
2	Lando NORRIS	6	8	3	5	6p	2	R	1	2	4	2	2pf	3f	20*	3	2p	5	1pf	3pf	4f	1p	3	4p	2	1	6p	6f	2p	10f	1p	**374**
3	Charles LECLERC	4	3f	2f	4	4	4	2	3	3	1p	R	5	7	11	14	4	3p	3	1	2p	5	4	1	3f	3	5	4	5f	2	3	**356**
4	Oscar PIASTRI	8	4	4	8	7	8	6	13f	4	2	5	7	2	2	4	1	2	4	2	1	3	10	5	8	2p	8	7	1	3	10	**292**
5	Carlos SAINZ	3	EW	1	3	5	5	5	5	5	R	6	5	3	5f	6	6	5	4	18*	7	2	2	1p	5	R	3	4	6	2	**290**
6	George RUSSELL	5	6	17*	7	8	6	12	8	7f	5	3p	4	4	1	Rp	8f	DQ	7	7	3	4	5	6	5	R	4	1p	3	4p	5	**245**
7	Lewis HAMILTON	7	9	R	9	2	9	16	6	6	7f	4f	3	6	4	1	3	1	8	5	9	6	6	R	4	11	10	2	6	12	4	**223**
8	Sergio PÉREZ	2	2	5	2	3	3	3	4	8	R	8	8	7	17	7	7f	6	8	17*	10	9	7	17	8f	11	10	20	R	R		**152**
9	Fernando ALONSO	9	5	8	6	20*	7f	17	9	19	11	6	12	15	18f	8	11	8	10	11	6	8	18	13	R	18	14	11	11	7	9	**70**
10	Pierre GASLY	18	R	13	16	15	13	9	12	16	10	9	9	12	10	NS	R	13	9	15	12	17	14	12	10	7	3	R	9	5	7	**42**
11	Nico HÜLKENBERG	16	10	9	11	19	10	7	11	11	R	11	11	19	6	6	13	18	11	17	11	9	8	8	9	R	DQ	8	7	R	8	**41**
12	Yuki TSUNODA	14	15	7	10	16	R	8	7	10	8	14	13	14	10	9	16	17	R	12	11	14	15	7	9	17	13	12				**30**
13	Lance STROLL	10	R	6	12	14	15	R	17	9	14	7	14	10	13	7	10	11	13	19	19*	14	13	15	11	19	NS	15	13	R	14	**24**
14	Esteban OCON	17	13	16	15	13	11	15	10	14	R	10	10	11	12	16	18	9	5	14	15	13	15	18f	13	13	2	17	14	R	-	**23**
15	Kevin MAGNUSSEN	12	12	10	13	10	16	18	19	12	R	12	17	9	8	12	15	14	18	10	-	19*	7	11	7		12	10	9		16f	**16**
16	Alexander ALBON	15	11	11	R	17	12	13	18	R	9	R	18	17	15	9	14	12	14	9	7	R	17	16	R	10	NS	R	15	15	11	**12**
17	Daniel RICCIARDO	13	16	12	R	11	R	4	15	13	12	8	15	14	9	13	12	10	12	13	13	18f	-	-	-	-	-	-	-	-	-	**12**
18	Oliver BEARMAN	-	7	-	-	-	-	-	-	-	-	-	-	-	-	-	-	-	-	-	10	-	-	-	-	14	12	-	-	-	-	**7**
19	Franco COLAPINTO	-	-	-	-	-	-	-	-	-	-	-	-	-	-	-	-	-	-	12	8	11	12	10	12	12	R	14	18	R	R	**5**
20	ZHOU Guanyu	11	18	15	R	9	14	11	14	15	16	15	13	20	17	18	19	R	20	18	14	15	19	19	15	19	15	13	19	8	13	**4**
21	Liam LAWSON	-	-	-	-	-	-	-	-	-	-	-	-	-	-	-	-	-	-	-	-	-	16	9	16	9	9	16	16	14	17*	**4**
22	Valtteri BOTTAS	19	17	14	14	12	R	14	16	18	13	13	16	18	16	15	16	15	19	16	16	16	20	17	14	16	13	18	12	11	R	**-**
23	Logan SARGEANT	20	14	EW	17	18	17	10	R	17	15	R	20	16	19	11	17	17	16	-	-	-	-	-	-	-	-	-	-	-	-	**-**
24	Jack DOOHAN	-	-	-	-	-	-	-	-	-	-	-	-	-	-	-	-	-	-	-	-	-	-	-	-	-	-	-	-	-	15	**-**

	TESTERS																															
	A. Kimi ANTONELLI	-	-	-	-	-	-	-	-	-	-	-	-	-	-	-	-	-	-	-	-	-	AP	-	-	-	AP	-	-	-	-	
	Oliver BEARMAN	-	-	-	-	-	-	-	AP	-	-	AP	-	-	AP	AP	-	-	-	-	-	-	-	AP	-	-	-	-	-	-	-	
	Luke BROWNING	-	-	-	-	-	-	-	-	-	-	-	-	-	-	-	-	-	-	-	-	-	-	-	-	-	-	-	-	-	AP	
	Franco COLAPINTO	-	-	-	-	-	-	-	-	-	-	-	-	-	AP	-	-	-	-	-	-	-	-	-	-	-	-	-	-	-	-	
	Jack DOOHAN	-	-	-	-	-	-	-	AP	-	-	AP	-	-	-	-	-	-	-	-	-	-	-	-	-	-	-	-	-	-	-	
	Felipe DRUGOVICH	-	-	-	-	-	-	-	-	-	-	-	-	-	-	-	-	-	-	-	-	-	-	-	-	-	AP	-	-	-	AP	
	Isack HADJAR	-	-	-	-	-	-	-	-	-	-	-	-	-	AP	-	-	-	-	-	-	-	-	-	-	-	-	-	-	-	AP	
	Ryō HIRAKAWA	-	-	-	-	-	-	-	-	-	-	-	-	-	-	-	-	-	-	-	-	-	-	-	-	-	-	-	-	-	AP	
	Ayumu IWASA	-	-	-	AP	-	-	-	-	-	-	-	-	-	-	-	-	-	-	-	-	-	-	-	-	-	-	-	-	-	AP	
	Arthur LECLERC	-	-	-	-	-	-	-	-	-	-	-	-	-	-	-	-	-	-	-	-	-	-	-	-	-	-	-	-	-	AP	
	Patricio O'WARD	-	-	-	-	-	-	-	-	-	-	-	-	-	-	-	-	-	-	-	-	-	-	-	-	AP	-	-	-	-	-	
	Robert SHWARTZMAN	-	-	-	-	-	-	-	-	-	-	-	-	-	-	-	-	-	-	-	AP	-	-	-	-	AP	-	-	-	-	-	

KEY: AP – Also practiced   DQ – Disqualified   EW – Entry withdrawn   NS – Non-starter   R – Retired   * – Placed, but retired   f – fastest lap   p – pole position

POINTS AND PERCENTAGES

GRAND PRIX GRID POSITIONS: 2024

Pos	Driver	Starts	Best	Worst	Average
1	Lando Norris	24	1	15	3.37
2	Max Verstappen	24	1	17	3.54
3	Charles Leclerc	24	1	19	5.42
4	Oscar Piastri	24	2	17	5.42
5	George Russell	24	1	20	5.63
6	Carlos Sainz	23	1	20	5.70
7	Lewis Hamilton	24	2	19	8.83
8	Sergio Pérez	24	2	20	9.38
9	Fernando Alonso	24	3	20	9.42
10	Yuki Tsunoda	24	3	20	11.08
11	Nico Hülkenberg	24	6	19	11.87
12	Oliver Bearman	3	10	15	12.00
13	Lance Stroll	23	8	18	12.78
14	Pierre Gasly	23	3	20	12.87
15	Daniel Ricciardo	18	5	20	13.11
16	Alexander Albon	23	9	20	13.13
17	Liam Lawson	6	5	19	13.17
18	Esteban Ocon	23	4	20	14.30
19	Kevin Magnussen	22	7	20	14.64
20	Valtteri Bottas	24	9	19	15.04
21	Franco Colapinto	9	8	20	16.00
22	Jack Doohan	1	17	17	17.00
23	Logan Sargeant	14	12	20	17.14
24	Zhou Guanyu	24	12	20	17.58

GRAND PRIX RETIREMENTS: 2024

Number of cars to have retired

Grand Prix	Starters	At 1/4-distance	At 1/2-distance	At 3/4-distance	At full distance	Percentage of finishers
Bahrain	20	-	-	-	-	100.0
Saudi Arabia	20	2	2	2	2	90.0
Australia	19	2	2	2	3	84.2
Japan	20	3	3	3	3	85.0
China	20	-	2	3	3	85.0
Miami	20	-	1	1	1	95.0
Emilia-Romagna	20	-	-	-	1	95.0
Monaco	20	4	4	4	4	80.0
Canada	20	-	1	5	5	75.0
Spain	20	-	-	-	-	100.0
Austria	20	-	-	-	1	95.0
Britain	19	-	-	1	1	94.7
Hungary	20	-	-	1	1	95.0
Belgium	20	1	1	1	1	95.0
Netherlands	20	-	-	-	-	100.0
Italy	20	1	1	1	1	95.0
Azerbaijan	20	-	1	1	4	80.0
Singapore	20	1	1	1	2	90.0
United States	20	1	1	1	1	95.0
Mexico City	20	3	3	3	3	85.0
São Paulo	18	-	2	3	3	83.3
Las Vegas	20	-	2	2	2	90.0
Qatar	20	3	3	5	5	75.0
Abu Dhabi	20	1	2	3	4	80.0

GRAND PRIX LAP LEADERS: 2024

Grand Prix	Verstappen	Norris	Leclerc	Russell	Sainz	Piastri	Hamilton	Ocon	Pérez	Total
Bahrain	57	-	-	-	-	-	-	-	-	57
Saudi Arabia	45	5	-	-	-	-	-	-	-	50
Australia	1	-	-	-	57	-	-	-	-	58
Japan	48	-	4	-	1	-	-	-	-	53
China	51	5	-	-	-	-	-	-	-	56
Miami	22	31	-	-	-	4	-	-	-	57
Emilia-Romagna	60	-	-	-	3	-	-	-	-	63
Monaco	-	-	78	-	-	-	-	-	-	78
Canada	42	8	-	20	-	-	-	-	-	70
Spain	55	9	-	2	-	-	-	-	-	66
Austria	62	-	-	8	-	1	-	-	-	71
Britain	-	19	-	17	-	1	15	-	-	52
Hungary	5	18	2	-	-	45	-	-	-	70
Belgium	-	-	4	14	7	4	15	-	-	44
Netherlands	17	51	-	-	-	4	-	-	-	72
Italy	3	-	15	-	2	32	-	-	1	53
Azerbaijan	-	-	18	-	1	32	-	-	-	51
Singapore	-	62	-	-	-	-	-	-	-	62
United States	-	5	51	-	-	-	-	-	-	56
Mexico City	8	-	-	-	63	-	-	-	-	71
São Paulo	27	-	-	28	-	-	-	14	-	69
Las Vegas	-	-	-	49	-	-	-	1	-	50
Qatar	57	-	-	-	-	-	-	-	-	57
Abu Dhabi	-	58	-	-	-	-	-	-	-	58
Total	**560**	**271**	**172**	**138**	**134**	**123**	**31**	**14**	**1**	**1,444**
(Per cent)	**38.8**	**18.8**	**11.9**	**9.6**	**9.3**	**8.5**	**2.1**	**1.0**	**0.1**	**100.0**

GRAND PRIX CAREER PERFORMANCES: 2024

Driver	Races	Championships	Wins	2nd places	3rd places	4th places	5th places	6th places	7th places	8th places	9th places	10th places	Pole positions	Fastest laps	Sprint points	Total Points
Alexander Albon	104	-	-	-	2	3	6	6	4	5	7	6	-	-	2	240
Fernando Alonso	401	2	32	40	34	28	29	25	29	22	18	14	22	26	8	2337
Oliver Bearman	3	-	-	-	-	-	-	1	-	-	1	-	-	-	-	7
Valtteri Bottas	246	-	10	29	28	13	24	9	5	14	7	6	20	19	9	1797
Franco Colapinto	9	-	-	-	-	-	-	1	-	1	-	-	-	-	-	5
Jack Doohan	1	-	-	-	-	-	-	-	-	-	-	-	-	-	-	-
Pierre Gasly	153	-	1	1	3	4	6	12	11	8	13	11	-	3	10	436
Lewis Hamilton	356	7	105	57	40	32	27	14	13	8	12	4	104	67	42	4862.5
Nico Hülkenberg	227	-	-	-	-	3	9	22	20	22	13	19	1	2	-	571
Liam Lawson	11	-	-	-	-	-	-	-	-	3	-	-	-	-	-	6
Charles Leclerc	147	-	8	15	20	14	13	10	10	4	3	5	26	10	67	1430
Kevin Magnussen	185	-	-	1	-	-	4	3	7	9	11	14	1	3	6	202
Lando Norris	128	-	4	13	9	12	11	14	11	8	9	9	12	57	-	1007
Esteban Ocon	156	-	1	2	1	3	5	12	11	17	18	15	-	1	5	445
Sergio Pérez	281	-	6	17	16	19	17	19	30	22	18	22	3	12	53	1638
Oscar Piastri	46	-	2	5	3	6	3	1	3	7	1	3	-	3	42	389
Daniel Ricciardo	257	-	8	6	18	24	16	16	14	9	13	11	3	17	9	1329
George Russell	128	-	3	2	10	13	13	6	7	6	2	1	5	8	50	714
Carlos Sainz	206	-	4	7	16	9	22	26	14	21	10	10	6	4	69	1272.5
Logan Sargeant	36	-	-	-	-	-	-	-	-	-	1	-	-	-	-	1
Lance Stroll	166	-	-	-	3	4	2	7	7	8	14	15	1	-	6	292
Yuki Tsunoda	87	-	-	-	-	1	-	1	5	4	5	10	-	1	4	91
Max Verstappen	209	4	63	32	17	15	17	10	4	6	5	3	40	33	111	3023.5
Zhou Guanyu	68	-	-	-	-	-	-	-	2	3	2	-	2	-	-	16

Drivers retiring on the formation lap are not counted as having started. At the 2001 Belgian GP, which was abandoned and restarted as a new race, Alonso is regarded as a non-starter, as he only started the initial race.
Points awarded in Sprints: in 2021, 3-2-1 points for the top 3 and since 2022, 8-7-6-5-4-3-2-1 points for the top 8. Grand Prix fastest lap scores 1 point for drivers finishing in the top 10.

GRAND PRIX ALL-TIME RECORDS: 2024

STARTS
Fernando Alonso	401
Lewis Hamilton	356
Kimi Räikkönen	349
Rubens Barrichello	322
Michael Schumacher	307
Jenson Button	306
Sebastian Vettel	299
Sergio Pérez	281
Felipe Massa	269
Daniel Ricciardo	257
Riccardo Patrese	256
Jarno Trulli	252

WINS
Lewis Hamilton	105
Michael Schumacher	91
Max Verstappen	63
Sebastian Vettel	53
Alain Prost	51
Ayrton Senna	41
Fernando Alonso	32
Nigel Mansell	31
Jackie Stewart	27
Jim Clark	25
Niki Lauda	25
Juan Manuel Fangio	24

POLE POSITIONS
Lewis Hamilton	104
Michael Schumacher	68
Ayrton Senna	65
Sebastian Vettel	57
Max Verstappen	40
Jim Clark	33
Alain Prost	33
Nigel Mansell	32
Nico Rosberg	30
Juan Manuel Fangio	29
Mika Häkkinen	26
Charles Leclerc	26

YOUNGEST STARTERS
Max Verstappen	17y 166d
Lance Stroll	18y 148d
Oliver Bearman	18y 306d
Lando Norris	19y 124d
Jaime Alguersuari	19y 125d
Mike Thackwell	19y 182d
Ricardo Rodríguez	19y 208d
Fernando Alonso	19y 218d
Esteban Tuero	19y 320d
Chris Amon	19y 324d
Daniil Kvyat	19y 324d
Esteban Ocon	19y 346d

YOUNGEST WINNERS
Max Verstappen	18y 228d
Sebastian Vettel	21y 73d
Charles Leclerc	21y 320d
Fernando Alonso	22y 26d
Bruce McLaren	22y 104d
Lewis Hamilton	22y 154d
Oscar Piastri	23y 106d
Kimi Räikkönen	23y 157d
Robert Kubica	23y 184d
Jacky Ickx	23y 188d
Michael Schumacher	23y 240d
Emerson Fittipaldi	23y 296d

YOUNGEST ON POLE
Sebastian Vettel	21y 73d
Charles Leclerc	21y 166d
Fernando Alonso	21y 237d
Max Verstappen	21y 308d
Lando Norris	21y 317d
Lance Stroll	22y 17d
Rubens Barrichello	22y 97d
Lewis Hamilton	22y 154d
Andrea De Cesaris	22y 308d
Nico Hülkenberg	23y 80d
Robert Kubica	23y 121d
Jacky Ickx	23y 216d

PODIUMS
Lewis Hamilton	202
Michael Schumacher	155
Sebastian Vettel	122
Max Verstappen	112
Fernando Alonso	106
Alain Prost	106
Kimi Räikkönen	103
Ayrton Senna	80
Rubens Barrichello	68
Valtteri Bottas	67
David Coulthard	62
Nelson Piquet	60

FASTEST LAPS
Michael Schumacher	77
Lewis Hamilton	65
Kimi Räikkönen	46
Alain Prost	41
Sebastian Vettel	38
Nigel Mansell	30
Max Verstappen	30
Jim Clark	28
Mika Häkkinen	25
Fernando Alonso/Niki Lauda	24
Juan Manuel Fangio	23
Nelson Piquet	23

YOUNGEST CHAMPIONS
Sebastian Vettel	23y 134d
Lewis Hamilton	23y 300d
Fernando Alonso	24y 58d
Max Verstappen	24y 73d
Emerson Fittipaldi	25y 273d
Michael Schumacher	25y 314d
Niki Lauda	26y 197d
Jacques Villeneuve	26y 200d
Jim Clark	27y 188d
Kimi Räikkönen	28y 4d
Jochen Rindt	28y 169d
Ayrton Senna	28y 223d

DATES OF BIRTH

Alexander Albon	T	23 Mar 96	Lando Norris	GB	13 Nov 99	Andrea Kimi Antonelli	I	25 Aug 06
Fernando Alonso	E	29 Jul 81	Esteban Ocon	F	17 Sep 96	Luke Browning	GB	31 Jan 02
Oliver Bearman	GB	8 May 05	Sergio Pérez	MEX	26 Jan 90	Felipe Drugovich	BR	23 May 00
Valtteri Bottas	FIN	28 Aug 89	Oscar Piastri	AUS	6 Apr 01	Isack Hadjar	F	28 Sep 04
Franco Colapinto	RA	27 May 03	Daniel Ricciardo	AUS	1 Jul 89	Ryō Hirakawa	J	7 Mar 94
Jack Doohan	AUS	20 Jan 03	George Russell	GB	15 Feb 98	Ayumu Iwasa	J	22 Sep 01
Pierre Gasly	F	7 Feb 96	Carlos Sainz	E	1 Sep 94	Arthur Leclerc	MC	14 Oct 01
Lewis Hamilton	GB	7 Jan 85	Logan Sargeant	USA	31 Dec 00	Patricio O'Ward	MEX	6 May 99
Nico Hülkenberg	D	19 Aug 87	Lance Stroll	CDN	29 Oct 98	Robert Shwartzman	IL	16 Sep 99
Liam Lawson	NZ	11 Feb 02	Yuki Tsunoda	J	11 May 00			
Charles Leclerc	MC	16 Oct 97	Max Verstappen	NL	30 Sep 97			
Kevin Magnussen	DK	5 Oct 92	Zhou Guanyu	CHN	30 May 99			

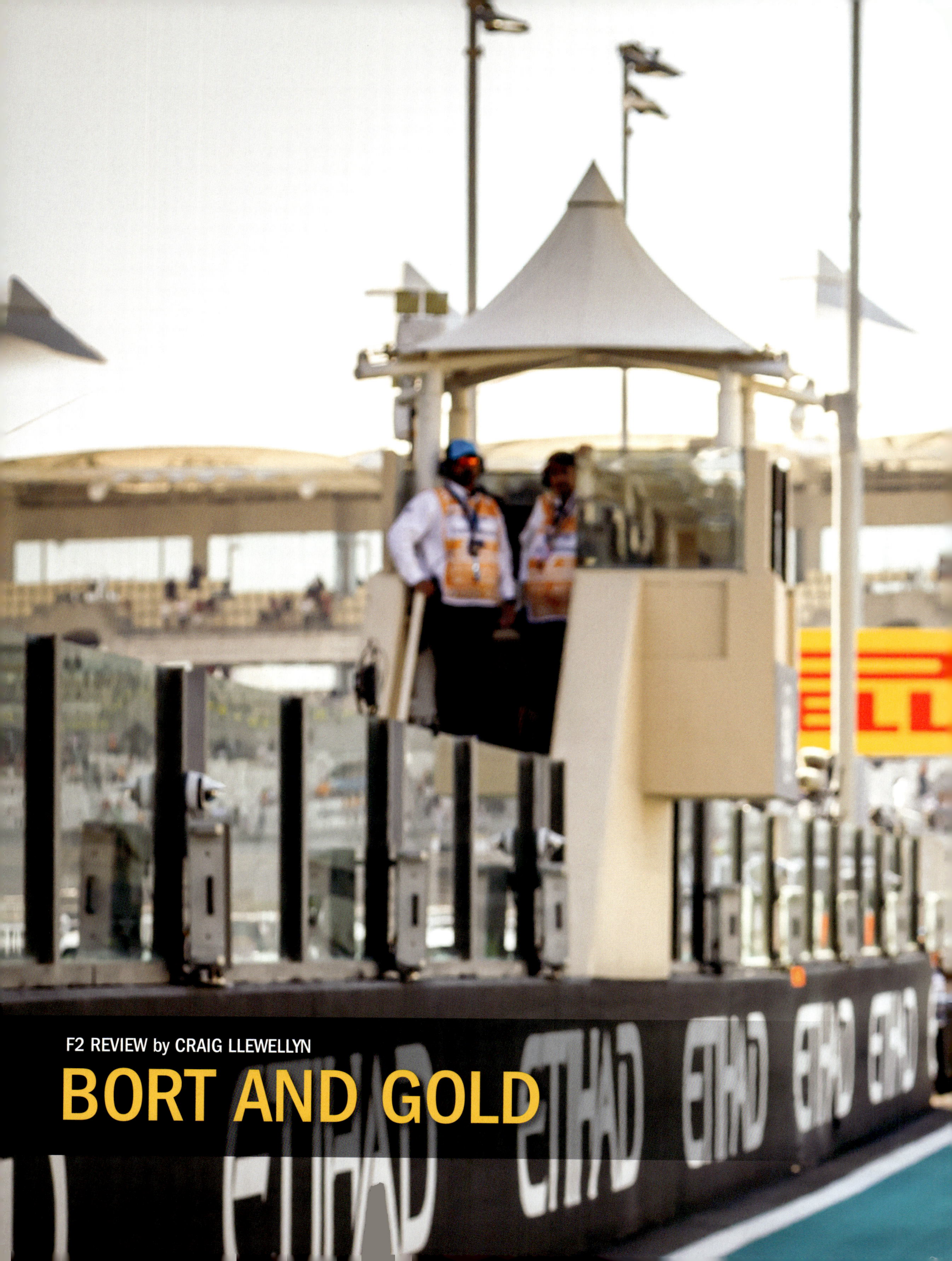

F2 REVIEW by CRAIG LLEWELLYN
BORT AND GOLD

Above: Isack Hadjar began the season strongly, winning the feature race in Melbourne.
Photo: Red Bull Content Pool

Top right: Kush Maini, Enzo Fittipaldi and Dennis Hauger share the feature-race podium in Jeddah, Saudi Arabia.

Above right: Series veteran Victor Martins continued his quest for the title with ART Grand Prix.

Right: Zane Maloney started the season by taking wins in both races in Bahrain.

Opening spread: A rapid rise to the top for new Formula 2 champion Gabriel Bortoleto, who, under the wing of McLaren, was headed to a seat in F1 with Sauber for 2025.

Photos: XPB Images

With two rounds remaining on the 2024 FIA Formula 2 calendar, the title fight looked to have boiled down to a straight head-to-head between a driver already confirmed in an F1 seat for 2025 and another who clearly believed he should be next in line.

Pending an exceptional set of results from Qatar and Abu Dhabi, however, the reality was that no fewer than six drivers (or seven should Franco Colapinto not have already graduated to the top flight) still had championship ambitions heading to Lusail. Reigning FIA F3 champion Gabriel Bortoleto – following a trail already blazed by Oscar Piastri, George Russell and Charles Leclerc – found himself on a collision course with Red Bull protégé Isack Hadjar at the end of a campaign in which they had already come together on numerous occasions.

After the penultimate round, they could hardly have been closer. While the 'exceptional set of results' did not pan out for the majority of their would-be rivals, Bortoleto and Hadjar left Qatar separated by just half a point, and with less than a week to dwell on the situation before they would face off again at Yas Marina.

Bortoleto had arrived in F2 fresh from clinching the 2023 F3 crown, but without opting to step up for a late-season outing at the higher level, while Hadjar was already among a strong cohort of drivers returning for another crack at the title. The French-Algerian was also a participant in a wide-scale game of musical chairs, having left Hitech Pulse-Eight for Campos Racing over the winter, where he teamed up with Red Bull stablemate Pepe Martí as the drinks brand maintained a two-driver presence in the series. Erstwhile Red Bull driver Jak Crawford had joined Hadjar in leaving Hitech, heading instead for DAMS Lucas Oil alongside fellow American Juan Manuel Correa, who had arrived from Van Amersfoort Racing.

In Correa's place, VAR had inked Enzo Fittipaldi, formerly of Rodin Motorsport, and F3 graduate Rafael Villagómez, while its other 2023 pilot, series veteran Richard Verschoor, had joined Trident, where he partnered Roman Staněk, one of the few drivers to remain in situ between seasons. Victor Martins, the highest-placed returnee from 2023, also stayed put with ART Grand Prix, alongside incoming FIA F3 runner-up Zak O'Sullivan, while Oliver Bearman, who had run Martins close for the final top-five spot, remained with a Prema outfit that was eager to reclaim the teams' title after two years of being denied. The Briton, a favourite of the Ferrari Academy, was joined by highly-rated Mercedes protégé Andrea Kimi Antonelli, who had bypassed FIA F3 to join the F2 field as reigning Formula Regional European champion.

Seventh (Fittipaldi), eighth (Dennis Hauger) and ninth (Verschoor) in the 2023 standings also returned to the fray, the Norwegian remaining at MP Motorsport as the benchmark for Colapinto. Zane Maloney, having rounded out the top ten as a member of the Red Bull 'family' the previous season, stayed at Rodin in new Sauber colours, alongside incoming Super Formula champion Ritomo Miyata, the Japanese ace using the F1 feeder series as preparation for his destiny as a Toyota endurance driver.

While the calendar welcomed back Imola after its natural-disaster-induced absence in 2023, and swapped Zandvoort for the Lusail International Circuit in Qatar, there were bigger changes on the technical front, the series introducing a brand-new car and engine package. With the ageing Dallara F2 2018 chassis finally being pensioned off after six years of service, the Italian constructor unveiled the F2 2024, designed to reflect the latest F1 thinking, with overhauled cockpit ergonomics to increase both driver comfort and safety, and all-new bodywork – including a rear wing that looked very different to that seen in the top flight.

The wing, a Dallara design based on FIA investigations into wake generation, had a large top flap that extended upwards through its centre in a bid to increase the DRS efficiency – specifically the speed difference between the flap being open and closed — in a bid to improve racing.

An evolution of the venerable Mecachrome V6 engine, designed to accommodate fully synthetic fuel from the 2025 season, remained the source of power, while a large number of parts were also carried over from the previous model as part of an ongoing move to constrain costs.

Although no one knew the potential significance at the time, the battle between Bortoleto and Hadjar began as soon as the season got under way in Bahrain, the pair colliding in the opening feature race of the campaign before going on to become involved in other incidents that affected their respective results. Bortoleto was the architect of his own affairs, having squandered an inherited pole position with a poor start, before locking up and punting his rival – with whom he had shared the front row – under braking into Turn One, spinning the Campos car and earning a penalty. Hadjar's race became worse when subsequently he was hit by Fittipaldi with enough force that both cars had to retire, the French-Algerian dropping vital early points, while Bortoleto recovered to fifth place, adding ten points to the bonus couple he had received for pole.

Previously, the pair had finished a couple of places apart in a less-eventful sprint, which was won – as was the feature – by Maloney, from eighth and third respectively, the Barbadian having set the pace in pre-season testing at the same Sakhir circuit as he sought to establish his own title credentials after an impressive debut campaign in 2023.

Despite the tighter confines of the Jeddah Corniche street circuit, Hadjar and Bortoleto managed to avoid a repeat of their contretemps in round two, although neither really troubled the scorers, the Campos driver posting a 15th-place finish in the sprint, before retiring once again from the feature race when his car insisted on lapsing into safe mode, a disappointing return after having qualified eighth fastest. Bortoleto was a mechanical DNF in the main event as well, having failed to add to his tally with a mere tenth from a mid-grid qualifying position.

As a result of their relatively poor starts to the season, both drivers were keen to make up the lost ground when the series touched down in Melbourne, but again they found themselves becoming a little too close for comfort. From third on the sprint-race grid, Hadjar inadvertently triggered a shunt that accounted not only for Bortoleto, but also Campos team-mate Martí. Although the No.20 car escaped unscathed from the incident and went on to win comfortably, Hadjar was assessed a 10s penalty, which, in a race twice interrupted by the safety car, was enough to drop him to sixth in the final order, albeit with the fastest-lap bonus.

Despite having qualified eighth and ninth respectively, Hadjar and Bortoleto did not find themselves duelling over track position, the Brazilian dropping back from the start, and then out altogether with a hydraulics issue on his Invicta entry. While Bortoleto's luck appeared to be out for the third consecutive meeting, however, his rival's took a sharp turn for the better after the disappointment of losing sprint-race success. Although his initial progress from row four was slow, Hadjar was perfectly placed – in the pit lane – when the safety car was called to cover the clean-up of early-leader Hauger's accident, and he lost significantly less time than most of the field in making his mandatory tyre change. He still had work to do, but made light of it to claim a first legitimate win of the season, lifting himself into a still-distant fourth in the standings as a result.

Heading into the first mini break of the season, an eight-week interval between leaving Melbourne and rocking up at Imola, Hadjar and Bortoleto barely appeared to be title contenders, let alone the pair that ultimately would dispute the crown. After three rounds, Maloney still held sway in the standings, the Barbadian having added third in the Australian feature and fourth in the sprint in Jeddah to his two opening-round victories. Sitting on 62 points, Maloney enjoyed a 14-point advantage over second-placed Aron, the Estonian having defied his rookie status with a brace of runner-up results to accompany his Bahrain third. Hauger, who should have been kicking himself after the accident that had cost potential victory in Melbourne, was third overall, boosted by a win in the Jeddah sprint, and ensuing podium visits in the Saudi feature and Albert Park sprint. Hadjar, as already mentioned, was up to P4, but seven points adrift of the Norwegian, while Bortoleto was nowhere in comparison, with a meagre 15 points – all from Bahrain – to his credit.

The missing wins at this stage had been claimed by Fittipaldi, who had pulled off a three-wide double pass on Correa and Amaury Cordeel to steal the top step in Jeddah, and Staněk, who had been next up when Hadjar was penalised in Melbourne. Remarkably, neither threatened the podium again thereafter, with Fittipaldi's next best of fourth in Austria the result of multiple penalties ahead of him.

The biggest story outside of the races themselves, however – and one that involved a potential race win that never happened – was Bearman temporarily being promoted to a Ferrari F1 seat, having already claimed pole in Jeddah. The Briton gladly swapped the two-point bonus from his qualifying effort for the opportunity to demonstrate his mettle on the biggest stage, and he would go on to finish seventh on his debut while filling in for an appendicitis-afflicted Carlos Sainz. That would not be Bearman's only F1-induced absence from the 2024 F2 grid, but it meant that one of the pre-season favourites would have to wait for the Melbourne feature before opening his account after a wretched weekend for both Prema cars in Bahrain.

While Bearman and Antonelli toiled, it was a similar story for Martins, the Alpine protégé expected to set the pace from round one. A pair of pointless 11th places book-ended back-to-back retirements through the first two meetings, before the Frenchman finally got on the board with seventh- and eighth-place results 'down under'.

Having seen Bortoleto and then Campos team-mate Martí top the times on the first two days of a much-needed in-season test at Barcelona's Circuit de Catalunya, Hadjar produced the best time of the week on the final morning, but both Imola and Monaco lay between dates in the hills

349

Above: Zak O'Sullivan was fortunate to claim a victory in Monaco, his pit stop being perfectly timed under safety-car conditions.

Top right: Ollie Bearman's F1 opportunities might have hindered his F2 campaign, but he did manage to win races in Austria *(pictured),* Monza and Abu Dhabi.

Above right: Jak Crawford delivered a win for DAMS in the feature race in Barcelona.

Above far right: Franco Colapinto celebrates his victory in Imola. The Brazilian left the series early after being picked by Williams to replace Logan Sargeant in F1.

Centre right: Taylor Barnard celebrates his sprint-race victory in Monte Carlo.
Photos: XPB Images

Right: Kimi Antonelli kisses his trophy after securing a race-one win at Silverstone.
Photo: Mercedes-Benz Group AG

above Barcelona, and it was here that Bortoleto finally put his campaign into some sort of gear – although not before Colapinto had done likewise. The Argentine had squeezed scoring finishes of sixth and fourth in and around an 18th, 11th and a DNF, before being disqualified for a technical infringement from the Melbourne feature, and he was only ninth fastest in qualifying in Emilia-Romagna, but that gave him a front-row start for the sprint, and he wasn't about to waste it. Except he almost did…

A chaotic start to Saturday's event, triggered in part by Colapinto's efforts to regain a lost advantage, led to contact between Staněk and Hadjar, causing a ripple effect that quickly enveloped those around them. While Hadjar spun into the path of Fittipaldi and AIX Racing's Joshua Dürksen with inevitable results, Hauger – who had qualified outside the top ten – hit Staněk's Trident while trying to negotiate the mêlée. Colapinto, who had survived unscathed, was quickly into second at the safety-car restart and harried Aron all the way to the final lap, before pulling off a move around the outside of the Tamburello corner, which had been the scene of the first-lap mayhem, to claim his first win at F2 level.

A repeat on Sunday was unlikely from ninth on the grid without further first-lap shenanigans, and Colapinto only made fifth by the chequered flag. That left him behind Antonelli, who equalled Prema's best result of the year to date, and Dürksen, who claimed his first F2 podium. Ahead of them all, however, was the first proper head-to-head between the drivers who would be on top going into the final round, as Hadjar took advantage of a sloppy getaway from pole-man Bortoleto. The Brazilian, who had scored his first points in six attempts with P6 in the sprint, dropped three places at the start, but benefited from a pit-stop nightmare for Bearman, who had been leading, before jumping fast-starting Dürksen for second. Despite some inadvertent help from the tardy Villagómez, Bortoleto was unable to get close enough to challenge Hadjar for the lead, and the Campos driver duly rattled off a second successive feature-race win to move up another

place in the overall table, closing in on Maloney and Aron as Bortoleto made his first appearance in the top five.

Monaco could, and probably should, have completed a hat trick for Hadjar, only for the Campos driver to be denied two laps from home. He hadn't led for long, having effectively inherited top spot from pole-sitter Verschoor when the Trident driver developed gearbox problems shortly after the pair had pitted in unison, but while Hadjar waited for the assorted pit strategies to unwind, Dürksen stopped on track at Casino after contact with Maloney, prompting a VSC intervention. Normally, drivers would have been prevented from pitting under the caution, but O'Sullivan – who had worked his way forward from 14th while holding out for a late safety car – was already in the pit lane when the AIX machine parked up. That allowed the Briton to rejoin ahead of an infuriated Hadjar, before holding off the Frenchman to claim a first F2 victory.

Maloney having been able to add only tenth in the feature to a sprint-race DNF, the Rodin driver's grip on the top spot in the standings was finally prised loose, as Aron's combination of seventh on Saturday and third in the feature elevated him to first. The Estonian was only two points clear of the surging Hadjar, however, with Bortoleto strengthening his fifth position with a second successive podium as he trailed the other AIX car of Taylor Barnard home in the sprint.

The victory represented Barnard's first appearance in the points, and the Briton would barely scratch the lower scoring positions in the second half of the season, before departing for a plum McLaren seat in Formula E. He had graduated from tenth place in the previous year's F3 standings, having been on a pretty steep trajectory through the junior ranks, but became the sixth different winner in nine races, before O'Sullivan made it seven from ten the following day.

Both Britons had several weeks to reflect on their success as the F2 championship took a brief hiatus while its parent series travelled to Canada, but neither would trouble the scorers, as the list of winners grew further

when the field reconvened in Barcelona. Instead, it was O'Sullivan's ART team-mate, Martins, who was quickest on the draw, claiming a belated first victory of the season in the Saturday event. He came home ahead of Maini and feature-race pole-sitter Aron, while Bortoleto and Hadjar moved line astern to fifth and sixth.

Having been penalised out of third, Correa played the long game in Sunday's feature race, being the last to pit for the soft tyre and then vaulting from sixth as he rejoined to third. His victims? None other than Bortoleto, Hadjar and Aron, Hitech's pole-winner undoing his good work in qualifying by taking to the gravel as he attempted to wrest back the net lead from Crawford. The American had qualified just 0.002s behind Aron, with Colapinto a further 0.004s adrift in third, and victory elevated him to fourth in the standings behind Maloney – whose form had taken something of a dive since back-to-back podiums at Albert Park and Imola – and Aron, who became the first driver to reach 100 points for the year.

The Hitech driver's strong start to the season owed a lot to his natural pace, something he exhibited again with second place in free practice at the Red Bull Ring as the series rolled into the second leg of a tough triple-header linking Spain and Silverstone. Although he qualified a mere fifth, Aron still outscored those around him in the standings in race one, returning to the podium for a seventh time in as many rounds, while Hadjar and Maloney managed only 13th and 17th respectively. For all his speed, however, Aron had yet to reach the top step of the podium through six rounds – an anomaly that also had applied to both Bearman and Bortoleto prior to the series' arrival in Styria.

It seemed somewhat inconceivable that Prema and Invicta would be the ninth and tenth teams to win a race in a season seemingly wide open on race-day. With his stellar F1 debut in Saudi Arabia perhaps putting extra weight on his shoulders through the early rounds, Bearman finally crossed the line first on Saturday at the Red Bull Ring, capitalising on Maini's slow start and cruising to victory ahead of Martí – who also had passed the yellow machine on the opening lap – and Aron, who had spent most of the race with Bortoleto in his mirrors.

Having shown his intent in the shorter of the weekend's two races, the Brazilian followed Bearman's lead and clinched a maiden F2 victory at the 14th time of asking. Despite not having qualified on the front row – that honour went to Hauger and Dürksen – Bortoleto was able to take advantage of a clear run to Turn One after the Norwegian stalled on the formation lap. Although Dürksen held sway early on, it took only four laps for Bortoleto to assume control of the race, something he only lost after the mandatory stops had unwound, as Martí rejoined in front of the No.10 machine. The Spaniard, whose double podium in Bahrain remained by far his best performances for much of the season, subsequently was adjudged to have pitted fractionally after a VSC had been called to cover Maloney's stranded Rodin machine, but Bortoleto was in no mood to wait for the stewards, regaining the net lead shortly after half-distance. Hadjar and Martí led the pursuit until Colapinto – the only driver to have opted for softs over supersofts on the grid – passed both in the closing stages. While Martí's penalty eventually dropped him out of the points entirely, Bortoleto's success was enough to lift him into the top three overall, albeit 30 points off Aron, with Hadjar nine shy of the Estonian.

Hadjar's seemingly inevitable march up the standings finally reached its zenith at Silverstone, where a third feature-race win of the season, secured from pole position, coincided with Aron failing to score and Bortoleto being denied a top-three finish in Saturday's sodden sprint, when he was adjudged to have ended a last-lap scrap – involving team-mate Maini, no less – with a pass made beyond the confines of the circuit. At least the Brazilian was able to add to his tally, with fourth and sixth across the weekend, unlike erstwhile points leader Aron, but he still dropped back to fourth overall as Maloney enjoyed an uptick in performance with a brace of second places.

Above: Paul Aron leads the field at Monza before being punted out of the lead by Pepe Martí.

Top right: Kush Maini secured his only win of the year in Hungary's sprint race.

Above right: Kimi Antonelli took the honours in the Budapest feature race. Two mid-season wins helped the Mercedes-bound youngster to sixth in the championship standings.

Right: Richard Verschoor was overjoyed with his victory in Baku's feature race.

Photos: XPB Images

The Barbadian had recorded six non-scores from eight races since his third place in the Imola sprint, but he mastered the conditions better than most in race one to follow first-time winner Antonelli home at a distance, the pair having started in the same positions on the partially-reversed grid. On Sunday, Maloney crossed the line third, but, like Hadjar, gained a place when Crawford, first across the line, was narrowly unable to erase a five-second penalty earned for an unsafe release that had put him ahead of the Rodin driver.

With the taste of success lingering through the two-week break between the British and Hungarian grands prix, Antonelli wanted more, keen to atone for a season that, until Silverstone, had largely failed to live up to the hype that had accompanied him from FRECA. Prema, with Haas-bound Bearman also struggling, appeared to be lagging behind its rivals in terms of getting to grips with the 2024-spec car, but that did not prevent its Italian star from continually being tipped as Lewis Hamilton's potential replacement at Mercedes for 2025.

Outside the top ten in practice at the Hungaroring, Antonelli qualified seventh for the weekend's feature race and appeared to be on track for another win in the sprint, until his decision to take the soft-compound Pirelli was scuppered by a trip through the gravel and subsequent lock-ups, dropping to 14th at the chequer. In his place, Maini rediscovered the top step for the first time since the 2020 BRDC British F3 Championship, becoming the first Indian driver to win at F2 level, even though he had to wait for the stewards to declare Verschoor's Trident entry illegal at post-race scrutineering.

While Martins took a welcome podium result in second, after making his soft rubber last where Antonelli could not, the hard-shod Hadjar's elevation to third extended his points advantage over Aron to 19, with Bortoleto now 40 adrift after also pitting with tyre woes. The tables would turn in Sunday's feature, however, with Aron the first to lose out when he compounded a slow getaway from pole by sailing long into Turn One. That should have let Fittipaldi, Hadjar or Bortoleto into prime position, but, instead, it was Martins who hit the front, with the two Brazilians in his wake. Bortoleto already knew the opportunity that lay in front of him, as Hadjar – who should have started alongside him on row two – failed to get out of the pit lane before it closed, being relegated to the back. The Brazilian's championship position looked even more positive when Aron, attempting to recover from his lap-one *faux pas*, clattered into the rear of Maloney, ending both their races on the spot.

The ensuing safety car allowed those who had started on the softer rubber – including the top three – to make their mandatory stop, but it also meant that Antonelli, and Saturday pace-setters Verschoor and Maini replaced them at the front. Martins was quickly on the charge and back into second place by lap 18, but another safety car, this time after Cordeel had crashed out, allowed Antonelli to nip in for softs and mount a comeback of his own, scything through from fifth to the lead in just two laps, before racing away from Martins to win by a dozen seconds. The Frenchman held on for another runner-up trophy, with the now soft-shod Verschoor jumping Bortoleto on the final lap for the remaining podium spot.

For Hadjar, classified 18th in the Budapest feature, and Aron, there was just a matter of days to dwell on their misfortune before Spa-Francorchamps took the series into its usual summer break, but the Estonian couldn't shake the hoodoo, as he would carry a ten-place grid penalty to the Ardennes as a result of separate incidents in the Hungarian feature. Ambition undimmed, Aron duly put his car on pole for the third time, but the punishment – assessed on the sprint grid after the partial reversal had been implemented – would hand a definite advantage to

returned to form in time to give Prema victory on home soil in Saturday's sprint, coming through from eighth on the partially-reversed grid was minor in comparison to Bortoleto's rise to that same spot in the finishing order. While Bearman took his first victory – and, indeed, his first podium appearance – since the Red Bull Ring, coming home ahead of Martins and Dürksen, Bortoleto was still denied a full point, as the timing screens showed a dead heat with Hauger, meaning that the pair split the final score right down the middle. With hindsight, it would be a half-point with some significance.

Remarkably, Bortoleto's Sunday was even better and, while there was a major element of luck involved once more, the Invicta driver still had to be in the right place to capitalise. Aron's fortune was still MIA, as despite a lightning start, he was out of the race at the Rettifilio, the victim of a sturdy punt from Martí. Meanwhile, Hadjar had been slower off the line, and he never seemed entirely in tune with his Campos entry, allowing Maloney the opportunity to dream of reigniting his own title ambitions – until Hauger's MP machine became stranded at the chicane just as the majority of those who had started on the supersoft Pirelli emerged from their mandatory stop. Coming from the back, Bortoleto was looking to run longer, but he seized the opportunity to make a leap up the order, rejoining in the net lead ahead of Verschoor and Maloney. Although the Bridgetown native was soon through on to Bortoleto's tail, the pair indulging in a game of cat-and-mouse as they picked their way through the cars ahead of them, the yellow Invicta machine eventually pulled away to the tune of several tenths a lap.

As mesmerising as Bortoleto's race had been, the fate of his two immediate title rivals contributed equally to the shifting balance in the standings. Aron's demise resulted in him dropping back behind Maloney, while Hadjar's slide was eventually arrested in 11th spot, ensuring that the points leader failed to add to his tally for the first time since round two. It also allowed Bortoleto to move to within 11 points of the championship lead with three double-headers remaining.

If Hadjar thought that missing out at Monza was just a hiccup in his campaign, reality bit hard in Baku two weeks later, as again the Campos driver went home empty handed. This time, it was Hadjar's turn to err in qualifying, hitting the barriers deep in the Turn One run-off where, bizarrely, he was joined almost immediately by team-mate Martí. Starting from the penultimate row as a result, Hadjar rose no higher than 12th and 14th in the weekend's two races, opening the door for Bortoleto to not only close the points gap, but also assume control of the championship for the first time. The Brazilian didn't feature on the podium, either, but finishes of fifth (via a hairy moment with the Turn Three barrier) and fourth (with fastest lap) moved him 4.5 points clear at the top of the table, with Aron the other beneficiary, even if he still trailed Maloney overall after netting a pair of sixths.

The usual suspects' absence from the top three allowed some different names to finally take their moment in the spotlight, not least Dürksen, who continued a revelatory campaign with a maiden win in the sprint event. Initially, the Paraguayan had bided his time behind debutants Christian Mansell (in for a frustrated Staněk at Trident) and Gabriele Minì (deputising for Bearman after the Briton had been called upon to replace the suspended Kevin Magnussen in the Haas F1 line-up), before assuming the lead after 13 laps. From there, he built a comfortable advantage twice to win by three seconds and more, while Crawford passed Minì for second, the Italian denying Martins the final podium spot by just 0.020s.

An incident-strewn feature ran four laps shorter than the first race due to a lengthy red-flag period required to clear the grid of a multi-car accident involving Martí and Red Bull stable-mate Oliver Goethe (in for Colapinto at

Bortoleto and Hadjar, who qualified immediately behind the Hitech driver. In the end, however, the weather gods, as so often at Spa, had the final say, not only forcing a delayed start at 18:25 local time, but making just five laps possible, half of which occurred behind the safety car. As a result, only the top five drivers were allocated points, with pole-sitter O'Sullivan again the recipient of the greatest luck, sharing the podium with Hauger and Verschoor as Maloney and Crawford bagged the remaining scores.

While the weather was better for the feature race, the driving was less so, with two safety-car interventions required in the opening laps. Around them, Hadjar assumed a lead that he would only cede through the lengthy pit-stop window, while Bortoleto also got the better of Aron approaching two-thirds-distance. When Lady Luck turned her back on the Estonian during the final lap, Bortoleto was able to vault him in the overall standings. Crawford completed the podium, ahead of O'Sullivan and Verschoor.

With Spa having been given an earlier calendar date, the familiar double-header with Monza was no more, the Italian venue restarting the action after a month of inactivity and delivering a profound shift in the championship dynamic.

Although Maloney continued his recent resurgence with a maiden F2 pole, ahead of fellow contenders Hadjar and Aron, it appeared that the Frenchman's grip on the crown could only tighten, as Bortoleto had ended his session in the gravel at Lesmo 2 with no time on the board. Starting 22nd and last for both races, even at Monza, is usually accompanied by a death knell for any sort of success, not least in a championship where the deficit to P1 was already significant, but the Brazilian remained confident in both his own ability and the propensity for those around him to indulge in chaos.

He was right to believe that, too. Even as Bearman

Above: With Hadjar stuck at the back, Bortoleto heads the field at the Abu Dhabi season finale.

Top right: Pepe Martí finally claimed a win in the Abu Dhabi feature race.

Above right: Rookie Paul Aron's impressive campaign earned him a place as reserve driver with Alpine F1 for 2025.

Above far right: Massive disappointment for championship contender Isack Hadjar, who stalled his car on the grid for the showdown race.

Right: Joshua Dürksen gained attention by claiming race wins in Baku and Abu Dhabi.
Photos: XPB Images

Below right: Japan's new Super Formula champion, Sho Tsuboi.
Photo: Super Formula

MP), who were both unable to avoid Maini's stalled Invicta machine. Verschoor led the late-starting race from pole, but soon ceded to Martins, who then was undone by misfortune at the pit stops, handing the lead back to the Dutchman. Although the ART driver homed in once again in the closing minutes of what became a timed race, his pursuit was ended by the return of the safety car after Minì found the wall at Turn 15, with Antonelli claiming third as the race ended under caution.

Dürksen and Verschoor were the 15th and 16th different winners of an unpredictable season, and that number would swell further over the final two rounds, staged after an interminable 11-week wait, as the powers-that-be had insisted on the culmination of the championship coinciding with an F1 'showdown' long since decided on the drivers' side. Incredibly, neither Hitech nor Aron had featured on the top step of the podium through 12 rounds and 24 races, but again the Estonian put himself in a position to succeed by claiming pole at Lusail, his fourth of the season, the bonus points also drawing him level with Maloney in the title race, while Crawford and Antonelli also retained a mathematical interest.

Aron left Bortoleto trailing to the tune of some three-tenths, with Martins rounding out the top three; Hadjar could manage only ninth. That, of course, meant the Campos driver would line up on the front row for the sprint race, but it was pole-sitter Bearman who prevailed, having opted for the harder tyre, taking a third win of an up-and-down campaign. Intent on battling for every last point, Hadjar's eagerness had got the better of him as his mediums faded, and he spun down to an eventual fourth, as Crawford and Verschoor took advantage of the slip, the Dutchman having jumped back into the MP Motorsport camp following Hauger's decision to prioritise preparation for a 2025 Indy NXT campaign.

Aron and Bortoleto were next across the line, but in keeping with an underlying theme of his season, the former was penalised post-race, dropping to seventh after a clash with fast-starting Martins. Come Sunday, however, the tables were turned, with Bortoleto receiving an in-race penalty for running the wrong side of a marker while aborting a planned tyre stop due to the imposition of a VSC. Unable to pull enough of a gap over Aron and Hadjar, he dropped behind both to set up an intriguing finale where the two leading contenders would start off separated by the half-point that the Brazilian had received at Monza.

For both Bortoleto and Hadjar, the build-up to the final rounds was filled with F1 speculation, but only the Brazilian arrived at Lusail with his future secured, having signed to partner Nico Hülkenberg at Sauber for 2025. For his rival, the coming season remained unclear, although Hadjar insisted that the rumours would not distract him from his immediate goal.

"I would say that chances exist, but, obviously, it does not depend on me," he said of the suggestion that he could step up to fill a seat at one of the Red Bull-owned F1 teams. "Bringing the title home won't decide the future for me, but a lot of things are happening and I am next on the list. It is just a fact."

While, perhaps fittingly, Hadjar and Bortoleto led the way in the final free practice session of the campaign, it was Martins who came out on top in qualifying, by just 0.035s, denying the title protagonists two valuable bonus points. Bortoleto, Aron and Hadjar would be next up, creating a near-perfect grid should the sprint race not put a dent in the showdown scenario, but the Estonian's challenge had ended even before he incurred yet another post-race penalty, scrubbing a ninth podium appearance from his record. Hadjar, too, saw his dream fade a little, a poor start and contact with Maini leaving him with a damaged front wing, while Bortoleto was moving in the opposite direction, vaulting to fifth on the opening lap and quickly making his way to second, albeit unable to do anything about Martí becoming the 18th name in the winners' column after a rapid getaway had propelled him from fourth to first by the opening corner. Hadjar recovered to an eventual fifth place that, despite Bortoleto teasing out an additional five points in the championship battle, ensured that the feature race remained a true winner-takes-all affair.

In the end, however, all the hype and anticipation proved

to be for nothing as Hadjar's car lurched, then stalled as the lights went out on both the starting gantry and his championship dream. "I need an explanation, man," he implored over the radio. "I can't believe all this hard work for that. The worst moment of my life, right now." By the time his car had been recovered, returned to the pit and restarted, Hadjar was two laps down, thereafter pleading to be kept in touch with Bortoleto's position and lap times as he yearned to show what might have been.

For the Brazilian, the task was now much simpler – just keep the car on the road. Bortoleto made the perfect start, capitalising on another slow getaway from pole-man Martins, but his hopes of ending the season on a double high disappeared with two lock-ups while defending from Dürksen immediately after switching to the medium Pirelli. While the Paraguayan went on to claim a second win, and first in a feature, Bortoleto had to overcome Martins before finishing as runner-up – with Verschoor also passing the Frenchman before the chequered flag – but the emotion of achieving his goal was palpable.

"It's one of the best feelings of my life, I think," the new champion admitted. "It's been a very long season, and we have been through a lot of things since the beginning. We struggled a lot in Jeddah and Australia, but the team never gave up, I never gave up and, from that moment on, I think we deserved every single point we achieved. We had luck, but we also created our own luck, with our pace, with our work, the extra hours we did in the sim, the late nights working on new things to bring the car into the right window.

"Going to F1 having won the F2 and F3 titles back to back is a dream, and it's amazing to be included with names like Charles Leclerc, George Russell and Oscar Piastri, and I'm super-proud of it."

Behind the dejected Hadjar, who ultimately trailed the new champion by an unrepresentative 22.5 points in the final standings, Aron was comfortable in third, with Maloney, Crawford, Antonelli, Martins and Verschoor completing the top eight, all recording 100+ points, despite the Italian having withdrawn from both Abu Dhabi races with illness. Colapinto, who had missed the final four rounds after his F1 graduation, was ninth, with the impressive Dürksen rounding out the top ten.

JAPANESE SUPER FORMULA

With no *gaijin* to deflect attention from the homegrown talent, as Liam Lawson had done in 2023, the Super Formula title fight was an all-Japanese affair.

With teams now accustomed to the Dallara SF23, introduced in the previous season, three drivers – Sho Tsuboi (Vantelin Team TOM's), Tadasuke Makino (DoCoMo Team Dandelion Racing) and Tomoki Nojiri (Team Mugen) – headed to the final double-header at Suzuka with a shot at the crown. With the upper hand in the standings, Tsuboi all but eliminated the opposition in the opening leg by finishing second on the road to Kakunoshin Ohta (DoCoMo Team Dandelion Racing), and he repeated the result in the season finale to seal the deal by an eventual margin of 30.5 points.

The title capped a stellar season for Tsuboi, who had been racing in Super Formula since 2019, but had never bettered third in the standings (2020). Moving into outgoing champion Ritomo Miyata's seat at TOM's – and thereby rejoining the open-wheel arm of the team that had taken him to the 2018 Japanese F3 title – proved the catalyst for the 29-year-old who, after finishing third in two of the opening three rounds, added three wins from three at Fuji mid-season to put himself in control of his destiny. Having partnered Miyata to the Super GT title in 2023, Tsuboi also emulated his erstwhile colleague's double by repeating that success in the sportscar series, this time alongside 2019 champion Kenta Yamashita.

F3 REVIEW by CRAIG LLEWELLYN

LEONARDO LEAVES IT LATE

Above: Trident's Leonardo Fornaroli took the F3 title without actually winning a race, but by finishing in the points in all bar two of the season's 20 races.

Above right: Fornaroli celebrates clinching his title at the Monza finale.

Right: Williams Academy driver Luke Browning won the feature race at Silverstone. His third place in the standings earned him a drive in F2 with Hitech Pulse-Eight for 2025.

Photos: XPB Images

LEONARDO FORNAROLI'S run through the chicane had not been ideal, the legacy of his off at the same section earlier in the race, and that left just the back straight and the final corner to achieve his season's goal. It was a long shot, but he knew he had no option. The Italian's cause was not helped by having flat-spotted his tyres when he had locked up into the Rettifilio two laps earlier, but he knew that he might never be in this position again. He could see what he had to do, almost touch the couple of extra points he needed. Heading into the Parabolica, it was now or never, do or…

Fornaroli wasn't the highest-placed returnee from the 2023 season that had propelled the likes of champion Gabriel Bortoleto, Zak O'Sullivan, Paul Aron, Franco Colapinto and Pepe Martí into F2. That 'honour' fell to Dino Beganovic, back at Prema Racing after taking sixth overall in his debut FIA F3 campaign, one place and four points ahead of team-mate Gabriele Minì, who returned to Prema having climbed through the ranks with ART and Hitech. Oliver Goethe, eighth the previous season, was also returning for another crack at the crown, albeit now with Campos Racing, with Fornaroli – a former team-mate of the German's – remaining with the Trident team after just missing a top-ten spot overall in his debut season.

Christian Mansell (ART Grand Prix), Luke Browning (Hitech Pulse-Eight), Sebastián Montoya and Mari Boya (both Campos), and Nikita Bedrin (PHM-AIX Racing) were all back after top-20 efforts in 2023, while the next wave of young talent stepped into plum seats to ensure that there could be no resting on laurels. Reigning GB3 champion Callum Voisin (Rodin), Italian F4 champion Kacper Sztuka (MP Motorsport), Formula Regional Oceania title winner Charlie Wurz (Jenzer Motorsport) and EuroFormula Open king Noel León (Van Amersfoort Racing) all arrived with crowns to display, while Alex Dunne and Joseph Loake (second and third behind Voisin in GB3) had signed with MP and Rodin respectively. Hitech Pulse-Eight signings Martínius Stenshorne (Formula Regional European) and Cian Shields (EuroFormula Open) had been championship runners-up in 2023, while Red Bull protégés Arvid Lindblad (Prema) and Tim Tramnitz (MP) had finished third overall in Italian F4 and FRECA respectively.

The only changes on the team front were PHM-AIX Racing going it alone after letting go of the hand extended by Charouz Racing System in 2023, and the rebranding of the former Carlin team as Rodin Motorsport after a change of ownership. Technically, too, there were barely any differences to the venerable Dallara-Mecachrome F3-2019 as it entered its sixth year of service, save for a further tweaking of Aramco's sustainable fuel and a new specification of Pirelli tyre.

With Browning setting the pace on two of the three days of pre-season testing in Bahrain, it was no surprise to the see the Briton, still a member of the Williams F1 team's talent academy, at the top of the practice-session timesheets. When qualifying came around, however, it was Beganovic on top for Prema, the Swede having pipped Browning to the first points of the year by 0.167s – with Minì off the front row by a scant 0.007s! Meanwhile, Laurens van Hoepen would head an all-ART front row for the opening sprint race, after claiming 12th-fastest time.

Van Hoepen and team-mate Nikola Tsolov spent the first half of the sprint battling over the lead, but that prevented them from pulling away and, with the pack still on their heels, the slightest error proved costly. Lindblad – the youngest driver in the series at just 16 – was the one to capitalise, passing both ART drivers in the space of a couple of laps before going on to take the win. Eventually, van Hoepen got the better of Tsolov to cement second spot, before the Bulgarian was pushed off the podium entirely by Fornaroli.

Having seen his young countryman come away with the spoils in race one, Browning wasted little time in following suit. Taking advantage of an awful start by pole-man Beganovic, the Hitech driver vaulted into a lead that he would not lose over the course of the longer 22-lap event, despite Mansell's best efforts, the Australian eventually crossing the line 1.3s adrift as the race devolved into

a DRS train. Tramnitz passed Meguetounif three laps from home to claim the final podium spot, the delayed Minì only managing sixth, one place ahead of Fornaroli. Beganovic was 13th.

With the F1 schedule opening with back-to-back rounds in Bahrain and Saudi Arabia, three weeks elapsed before the supporting F3 series rejoined the fray in Australia. Undoubtedly, experience of the Albert Park street circuit helped Minì, Fornaroli and Beganovic to lead the way in practice, the top three remaining the same in qualifying, Fornaroli edging Minì for pole by a mere 0.019s, and Beganovic lining up alongside the surprising Bedrin on row two. Championship leader Browning took fifth, ahead of Boya, Tsolov and Lindblad, while van Hoepen secured sprint-race pole once more by rounding out the top dozen.

The Dutchman was in the thick of it again on race-day, too, swapping places with front-row partner Stenshorne several times before the Hitech driver pulled away. Almost inevitably, Lindblad was next on the scene, making short work of second not long before a safety-car interruption put him on Stenshorne's tail – only for the Norwegian to steal a march at the restart and hold on to the win. Behind Lindblad, van Hoepen completed the podium, ahead of Boya, Goethe and Minì, with Fornaroli ninth.

The two Italians had a clearer track ahead of them on Sunday morning, however, although an early safety car prevented either from establishing an advantage. Indeed, it kept the pair vulnerable to attacks from behind and, with no team orders preventing him from challenging Minì, Beganovic moved up to second spot on lap 12. The Swede needed only two more tours to dispose of Fornaroli and, once in front, eased out of DRS range to ensure his first FIA F3 victory. Fornaroli and Minì joined him in the top three, but not before the second Prema driver had repassed Browning, the Briton eventually settling for fourth after a crucial no-score in the sprint.

With nearly eight weeks between rounds two and three, all ten teams convened at Barcelona's Circuit de Catalunya for an in-season test, but while the usual faces were at or near the front of the field, it was Boya and Campos Racing who topped the times on two of the three days. The Spanish team's form carried over to Imola as the competition season resumed in mid-May, with Goethe leading the way in practice and Boya taking third. Despite targeting pole, however, Goethe could manage only eighth as the usual frenetic qualifying shuffle played out. Having led the field ahead of the final runs, the German could only watch as Prema and Trident fought over the top spot, the latter ultimately securing a historic 1-2-3 as Santiago Ramos claimed a maiden pole from team-mates Fornaroli and Meguetounif.

Goethe's weekend got back on track in the sprint race, but not before a spot of chaos and confusion that kept the result in question. León grabbed the lead from pole-sitter Sztuka at the first chicane and resisted repeated challenges from Tramnitz through four safety-car interventions, but was caught unawares by Goethe at the end of a VSC on the final lap, allowing the German to claim victory – or so he thought. Immediately after the race, the Campos driver was relegated by a five-second penalty for a safety-car infringement, only to have the punishment rescinded later. Ironically, León had a penalty stick, dropping to third behind Tramnitz.

It was also a disappointing race for Browning, who retired after contact with Sztuka. With ground to make up, the Briton threw himself back into the fray in Sunday's feature race, dicing with Lindblad, Beganovic and Fornaroli to take an eventual fourth place, one position shy of the Italian, who had had to fight back from a mid-race glitch while leading. Ahead of him, Trident team-mate Meguetounif claimed his first FIA F3 win, but not before having to make up places as DRS proved key.

Above: Gabriele Minì took his only win of the year in the Monaco sprint.

Top right: Alpine Academy driver Minì is set to join Prema for the 2025 F2 season...

Above right: ...while sixth-overall Dino Beganovic moves to DAMS.

Right: Christian Mansell couldn't quite score a win, but he came close, claiming second in the feature race at Monaco.

Photos: XPB Images

Ramos, Fornaroli and Goethe all took turns to lead, but Meguetounif timed his run to perfection, seizing the initiative with five laps to go.

There was little time for the Frenchman to revel in his success before the cars were back on track in Monte Carlo, where Minì was the man to beat, the Monaco specialist claiming his second pole in the Principality by topping the faster qualifying group (for even-numbered cars), which also included Browning and Fornaroli. On the other side of the draw, Prema team-mates Beganovic and Lindblad looked set to battle over the remaining front-row spot before a rash of red flags allowed Mansell to usurp both of them. Minì's success also denied van Hoepen another sprint-race pole, the Dutch driver in the wrong group to deny ART team-mate Tsolov that advantage.

The Bulgarian made good on his opportunity, too, getting enough of a launch off the line to deny Tramnitz into Ste Devote, the German having cleared the second ART car well before the opening corner. Tsolov was required to do it all over again, albeit from a rolling start, after an immediate red flag – caused by Mansell, Lindblad and others coming together at Casino – and he proved up to the task to thwart Tramnitz once more into Turn One. Despite the appearance of the safety car mid-race, the leader made it look easy, eventually winning by four seconds, his pursuers keeping each other occupied. Tramnitz held on to second, echoing his result from Imola, while van Hoepen similarly added his third podium of the season.

Surprisingly, Minì had been unable to make sufficient progress from the outside of row six to add to his points tally, but he knew that he was best placed to claim the maximum in Sunday's 8am feature. With the sun attempting to warm the tarmac, the Sicilian made a perfect start and, with Mansell duly slotting in behind him, had a cushion to his biggest protagonists. Again, the usual Monaco disruptions threatened to slow the leader's progress, but Minì rose above them, even when faced with a last-lap restart with Mansell right on his tail, to claim a second successive feature-race victory on the hallowed streets.

Although the fastest-lap bonus escaped him, the Prema driver accrued sufficient points to move to the top of the standings going into the four-week hiatus while F1 headed to Canada, only to lose out again when racing resumed in Barcelona. The group test there might have suggested that Campos Racing was to the fore, but while Goethe duly went second fastest (and team-mate Montoya was fifth) in practice, it was MP Motorsport and Martínius Stenshorne at the top of the list. Boya rebounded from a late-practice off to threaten the fastest times briefly in qualifying, but the session came down to a last-gasp shootout, in which Mansell claimed his maiden F3 pole – by just 0.036s from Lindblad. Underlining ART's form, Tsolov annexed the inside of row two from Browning, the top four all within a tenth of pole, with Goethe and Fornaroli next up.

Unfortunately for the Campos camp, Montoya's best qualifying time was deleted for a track-limits violation, dropping the Colombian to the last couple of rows, while coincidentally elevating Boya off the front of the reverse grid. With a couple of rapid Trident entries now ahead of him, the Spaniard could have been in for a difficult afternoon, but fate smiled on him, as Ramos and Meguetounif contrived to tangle at the start of lap three, promoting the Campos driver into a lead he would not lose, despite the best efforts of the safety car. Goethe made it a Campos 1-3, sandwiching Dunne, who became the first Irishman on the podium in the series.

With Browning and Minì not scoring on Saturday – the latter following an incident with a fast-rising Montoya – the top of the table had closed up before Sunday's feature race, where another miscue for the Prema driver opened the door further for his rivals. Both Minì and Beganovic had qualified poorly, sharing row eight, but while the Swede moved forward, eventually bagging points for

eighth, his team-mate slipped to 21st, comfortably his lowest finish of the season. All was not lost for Prema, however, as Lindblad bided his time before passing Mansell and then pulled away to ensure that he was far enough ahead to survive the downpour that engulfed the final lap of what was the series' 100th race. Fornaroli and Browning duelled over the final podium spot, determined to make the most of Minì's woes, before the Italian won out, while Browning had slipped behind Goethe by the chequered flag.

While marking the season's mid-point, Barcelona was also the start of a frenetic triple-header with Spielberg and Silverstone, and Fornaroli's tenuous lead in the standings took an immediate blow. Having been disqualified from a practice session in which Austrian rookies Wurz and Joshua Dufek had both tasted top spot, the Italian then lost his fastest time in qualifying to a track-limits violation, meaning that he would have to start from the outside of row 12 for both of the weekend's races.

To make matters worse for Fornaroli, his closest rival, Browning, claimed the bonus points for pole position – his first in the category – despite not benefiting from a tow around the Red Bull Ring's quick layout. The Briton also earned a grid penalty for blocking Beganovic, but to be served in the sprint event rather than the feature, ensuring that he retained pole. Beganovic duly qualified fifth fastest, separated from Browning by team-mates Lindblad and Minì, who sandwiched Tramnitz in P3.

Stenshorne started from the reverse-grid pole, but quickly lost out to front-row partner Mansell, the Australian's ART team-mate, Tsolov, also wanting in on the battle and – after several exchanges of the lead – who found himself at the front when the second safety car of the race was withdrawn with a lap to run. The Bulgarian remained calm under pressure, nailed the restart and was duly rewarded with his second win of the season at the head of an ART 1-3. Neither Fornaroli nor Browning scored, as they finished 12th and 11th respectively, but they remained at the head of the standings, Minì being able to claim only sixth on the road.

Able to start from his earned grid spot in the feature, Browning made no mistake to add his second success of the season. He held the lead off the line and subsequently resisted a triple Prema attack as Minì and Beganovic got the better of Tramnitz to join Lindblad in pursuit. Although subsequently the Red Bull-backed Briton faded following contact with Dunne, his team-mates were relentless, duelling with each other as well as attempting to overcome Browning, while the pack behind benefited from DRS. Mansell briefly threatened the Prema pair as they continued to swap positions, but in the end had to settle for fourth, while Minì eventually bested Beganovic for the second step.

Practice at a rain-affected Silverstone ended with American Max Esterson at the top of an unusual order, ahead of Shields, Tsolov and debutant James Wharton, the Australian deputising for Stenshorne after the Hitech driver had been suspended for having taken part in GB3's round at the same circuit without FIA approval. Esterson had clearly formed an affinity with Silverstone through his time racing in British Formula Ford and GB3, and would also line up on the front row of the grid for the first time in a season that had, to that point, yielded him a single scoring finish, in Bahrain. It was Browning on top again, however, the Briton timing his final lap perfectly to claim back-to-back poles in changing conditions, while Esterson's Jenzer team placed all three of their drivers in the top ten. Meanwhile, Prema were all at sea, with Lindblad their highest qualifier, in 11th, three places ahead of Minì, while Beganovic was back in 19th.

León would start from sprint pole when the weather-delayed race got under way in the early evening, but he lost his advantage almost immediately when Lindblad swept by en route to taking an uncontested third win of the season by nearly six seconds. Esterson's race ended early after he tangled with Goethe, while Browning was also in the wars after contact with Tramnitz had sent him to the pits. Eventually, León would join Lindblad on the podium after coming out on top of a race-long battle with Matías Zagazeta, the Peruvian taking easily his best result of the year just six weeks after missing Monaco with appendicitis.

Despite his nationality, Lindblad has precious little racing experience in the UK, but that presented no obstacle as, aged just 16, he became the series' first ever 'double' winner in a Silverstone feature repeatedly turned on its head by the British weather. The Prema driver was one of several to swap wets for slicks at the end of the formation lap, but then he had to survive a continually wet-dry-wet race until the changeable conditions eventually turned in his favour. Although he crossed the line second on the road, having been as low as 22nd at one point, he knew that countryman Voisin was carrying a ten-second penalty, which would demote him from P1, with Minì also moving in front of the Rodin driver. Meanwhile, both Browning and Fornaroli, who had run 1-2 on wets entering the final ten minutes, were pushed out of the top six.

The Prema 1-2 also ensured that top spot in the drivers' championship changed hands for the fifth consecutive event, with Minì now six points clear of Lindblad who, with a weekend off to catch his breath before heading to Budapest, stood on the verge of series history, having already equalled the record for most wins in the category. Conversely, Fornaroli, in fourth overall, was riding his remarkable consistency to remain in the title race, but neither Lindblad nor the Italian – nor any of the championship hopefuls for that matter – would top a

359

Above: Dino Beganovic had failed to score a single win in 2023, but he soon put that right with a feature-race victory in Melbourne.
Photo: XPB Images

Above right: Red Bull-backed Arvid Lindblad was overjoyed with both of his wins at Silverstone.

Right: Oliver Goethe took a sprint-race win in Imola.
Photos: Red Bull Content Pool

Below right: Nikola Tsolov won three races for ART Grand Prix, but he reached only 11th in the standings.
Photo: XPB Images

session throughout the Hungarian weekend. After Boya and Stenshorne led Browning in practice, the Briton helped shape the grid for Sunday's feature by bringing out the red flag. With the session not restarting, van Hoepen became the surprise pole-sitter after squeezing in an improvement just before the stoppage. Having started the opening reverse-grid races from top spot, this was the young Dutch driver's first feature pole, but he would have a familiar face alongside him, as ART team-mate Tsolov also timed his final run perfectly.

Browning's weekend became worse in the stewards' room after the session, as he was stripped of his fastest lap for causing the red flag and demoted to 15th. With Dufek also being thrown out of the session, the AIX team were left to lament not only losing a place on row three to an underweight car, but also the entire front row for Saturday morning's sprint. Undeterred, however, Bedrin wasted no time in passing pole-sitter Beganovic and resisted any attempt to retake top spot until the Swede dropped to third while trying a move on lap ten. Having kept a watching brief to that point, the second AIX entry of Tasanapol Inthraphuvasak moved up to ensure a 1-2 finish for the German outfit.

With Lindblad and Minì unable to break into the top ten from 13th and 21st on the grid, Fornaroli and Browning took the opportunity to close the points gap in seventh and eighth respectively. Then the Trident driver received another large helping of championship luck in the feature, when all three of his rivals failed to add to their totals, Lindblad contributing to the safety car that resulted in the race finishing under caution to confirm an ART 1-2 and Tsolov's third success of the season. Although he could do nothing about León in his pursuit of yet another top-three finish, Fornaroli collected a handy 12 points to move to within ten of overall leader Minì, before receiving another boost when an underweight van Hoepen was excluded from second spot, promoting the Trident driver to a fifth podium.

After another low-scoring weekend, Browning knew that perhaps he was fortunate still to hold second in the standings heading to Spa, but he showed that he meant business by topping practice with fastest times in both the wet and dry portions of the session. Seventh in a typically frenetic qualifying session later in the day was not the end of the world either, with only Fornaroli of his title rivals lining up ahead of him as Voisin took his maiden F3 pole for the feature.

After a difficult session, Prema pair Minì and Beganovic would share the front row for the sprint, but team-mate Lindblad would have to come from 27th after his best lap was deleted for exceeding track limits. What could have been a routine race for the front-row pair was enlivened by their own battling, and third-placed Tramnitz putting enough pressure on Minì to allow Beganovic to increase a lead that he would not lose. León bettered Tramnitz at the last to complete the podium, but behind them, a slew of track-limits penalties shook up the order, to the detriment of both Fornaroli – who was demoted one place to ninth – and Browning, whose sixth became 12th after two time penalties were applied.

The standings would change again in a damp-but-drying feature, as Minì and Goethe came together on the opening lap, leaving the Prema driver at the back of the field with his points lead suddenly looking vulnerable. Lindblad, too, was having a bad time, eventually being punted into retirement by Mansell, ensuring that he went home empty handed for the second successive weekend. The incident prompted the last of three safety-car interventions, but Voisin remained calm throughout, timing his restarts perfectly to keep both Montoya and Fornaroli at bay as he collected his first win at FIA level. With Minì only recovering to 13th and Browning gaining just one place to finish sixth, Fornaroli's podium was enough to vault him back into a narrow championship lead with one round remaining. Six points covered the top three, with Lindblad, Beganovic and Mansell not entirely

Mansell demoted Minì further at the restart, but just as Fornaroli was handed the opportunity to cruise to the crown, he found himself bouncing through the gravel at Ascari, dropping behind his sole remaining title threat. One lap later, and it had all changed again, with Minì tasting the run-off at Lesmo, allowing Fornaroli to lunge for fourth into Ascari. With Meguetounif out in front at the start of lap ten, both contenders passed Dunne and Mansell within the space of three laps, before the pressure seemed to get to Fornaroli, whose lock-up into Rettifilio allowed Minì to size up an eventual pass. When Mansell followed the Prema through into Roggia on the final lap, it appeared that the Italian team might get to claim both titles – but Fornaroli wasn't done.

His flat-spotted Pirellis notwithstanding, the Italian was all over the rear of Mansell, looking for a way through into Ascari before having to back out. As Minì weaved on the way to Parabolica, Fornaroli seized his opportunity, diving to the inside of the red ART car ahead of him and completing the biggest pass of his career on exit.

"When Gabriele and Mansell passed me, I asked my engineer if I was still champion," Fornaroli revealed. "When he said, 'No,' I knew Ascari was basically the last chance, but I couldn't get it, so, going into the final corner, I told myself, 'Okay, it's all in. I cannot accept to lose the title in the last two laps of the season.'"

In the end, the move proved academic, as Minì was cruelly excluded when his tyre pressures failed to comply with the regulations, promoting Fornaroli to second on the road in a Trident 1-2, and dropping the Sicilian perilously close to losing second overall to Browning. Fornaroli ended the season with the most podiums of any driver – seven – and two poles, but without a win to his name in a year when 12 of his 33 opponents, representing 20 nationalities, had visited the top step.

"He is still a deserving champion," Trident team manager Giacomo Ricci insisted. "For me, especially on the single lap in qualifying, he has been the quickest by far and, at Imola, he was going to win, but was unlucky that the car switched off for a moment. But, even then, he never gave up, and that was the story of his season."

With Mansell and León the only other drivers in the top ten overall not to have won a race of any sort in 2024, the remaining victories were dominated by Lindblad's quartet, although the Briton's title challenge rather fizzled out when he went scoreless over the final three rounds following his Silverstone 'double'. Tsolov demonstrated the value of being at the front of the reverse-grid races by claiming three victories, two of which he collected on Saturdays, while Browning, Beganovic and Meguetounif secured a brace of wins each. Surprisingly, the top three in the points had just three wins between them, with Minì having relied as much on consistency and four podiums as the champion.

Goethe's slim championship bid ended when he took the seat of F1-bound Colapinto in MP Motorsport's F2 line-up, and the German was replaced at Campos by Denmark's Noah Strømsted who, along with Wharton (Hitech), James Hedley (Jenzer) and Tuukka Taponen (ART), was given a one-weekend opportunity to show what he could do at a higher level. None, however, featured among the 28 points scorers, the last of whom, Dufek, got on to the board in the Monza finale.

Fornaroli was one of the first drivers to confirm his elevation to F2 for 2025, the champion joining Invicta Racing shortly after Lindblad had been announced with Campos, but neither was among those to be given an early taste in the 2024 series' final rounds. With Colapinto already in F1, and both Bortoleto and Antonelli set to join him, some plum 2025 seats were available. Browning (ART), Minì (Prema), Beganovic (DAMS), and both Mansell and Esterson (Trident) all jumped at the opportunity of late-season F2 outings.

out of the reckoning, while Prema, who had clinched another teams' title without the need for points in the feature, had all three of their drivers in the hunt for the third time in four years.

Fornaroli's Monza weekend began with the Trident driver being buried deep in the field after suffering from electrical problems in practice, but he made light of the difficulties by topping qualifying by several tenths. The Italian would share the front row with Dunne after the split groups were aggregated, leaving Minì – whose time was closer to the pole-sitter's than the Irishman's – on the inside of row two. Meanwhile, Browning was only seventh in the opening group, putting him 13th on the grid, equidistant between Beganovic and Lindblad, with Mansell ahead of them all.

While the feature grid remained unchanged, the starting line-up for Saturday's sprint was scattered by a rash of positional penalties, including for Fornaroli, Minì and Browning, all of whom would lose four places on the grid for slowing unnecessarily in search of a qualifying tow. Throughout the chaos of multiple safety cars, Tramnitz appeared untroubled as he converted pole position into a first win, but in his wake, positions changed continually before Montoya and Ramos completed the podium. More crucially, Beganovic (fifth), Browning (seventh), Fornaroli (ninth) and Minì (tenth) all scored points to remain in contention heading to the showdown. The luckless Mansell might have fallen by the wayside, but with nothing to lose, he still had a part to play in how the season would be determined.

While Fornaroli quickly squandered the advantage of pole to a determined Dunne, Minì also lost out as Meguetounif took P3 at Rettifilio second time around. With Beganovic and Lindblad already too far back to retain an interest in the title, it appeared that a three-horse race was on the cards – until Browning took himself out of contention by spinning at Ascari, helping to prompt a first safety car.

FORMULA E REVIEW by SAM SMITH

PASCAL PULLS IT OFF

Above: Pascal Wehrlein finally delivered the championship that Porsche had craved so badly.

Above right: Porsche's director of factory motorsport, Florian Modlinger, is a great believer in the German driver's ability.
Photos: Porsche

Right: Former champion António Félix da Costa had an uneven year, but still took four wins, including this one at Portland.
Photo: Formula E

PASCAL WEHRLEIN'S victory in the 2024 ABB FIA Formula E World Championship finally put to bed any doubts about his mentality and ability to execute successful silverware-grabbing seasons.

The once quiet and sometimes diffident Porsche driver has matured significantly since his fitful days in F1 with Sauber and Manor. That showed in 2024, when his pretty much flawless campaign produced three EPrix victories and a brace of runner-up positions with the factory TAG-Heuer Porsche Formula E Team.

That it was done in the second season of the Gen3 rules was all the more impressive, because the notoriously tight field bunched up to such a degree that often grids were separated, top-to-toe, by less than 0.3s.

While Wehrlein rejoiced, overall emotions for Porsche formed a cocktail of elation and relief. After all, this was the German giant's sixth season in the all-electric world championship, which it entered without a title to its name. In any other OEM operation, that would be borderline acceptable, but not at Porsche.

The team entered the season as joint favourites with the Jaguar TCS Racing squad. It knew that the pressure was on, however, as the Porsche board had deliberated on whether to commit to a future in Formula E, which had not completely returned the investment through its TV and media packages, especially in the company's heartland, Germany.

But when eventually it discovered the all-important qualifying range of the Porsche 99X Electric, and Wehrlein hit the ground running at Mexico City – as he had done in 2022, when he had claimed his and Porsche's first victory – the positive air surrounding its present and future endeavours in Formula E began to grow.

The opening race at the Circuit Hermanos Rodriguez in Mexico City suited Wehrlein and Porsche neatly, and he cruised to a dominant win ahead of pole-sitter Sébastien Buemi (Envision Jaguar) and defending champion Jake Dennis (Andretti Porsche).

On the other side of the garage, however, teammate António Félix da Costa was troubled. The 2019/20 champion was in his second season with Porsche after a so-so campaign in 2023, but he was expected to feature strongly in the title fight. In Mexico, he qualified poorly and then made a clumsy opening-lap move on a rival, which forced him to retire with damage. Two weeks later, in Riyadh, he sank completely without trace, subsequently describing his performance as embarrassing.

This was probably the off-track story of the season, as Porsche applied pressure on the always open and frank driver, who is noted for often wearing his heart on his sleeve. Da Costa's form did pick up at the following races in São Paulo and Tokyo, but within the team there was tumult when they elected to test Abt Cupra driver Nico Müller behind closed doors. Naturally, this rankled with da Costa, and at one stage, it seemed as though he might even be replaced mid-season.

But then, as is often the case, he began winning with a combination of inherent strategic brilliance and strategic pack-racing masterclasses. Within hours of him standing on the top step of the podium at Misano in April, however, he was disqualified – for the most bizarre of reasons.

Like many other teams, Porsche had been running an old throttle damper spring since the beginning of the Gen3 era in 2023, after parts supply had been delayed with the new car programme. This came to light in post-Misano technical checks, and da Costa was thrown out of the results. Porsche protested the decision firmly, taking it all the way to the International Appeal Court, but lost its case. This was complicated further by official parts supplier Spark Racing Technologies having not made clear the fact that it had amended the official parts list.

It was a bitter episode between the FIA and Porsche, exemplified by a fierce public argument between senior managers from both sides on the grid at the second Misano race, just hours after the disqualification.

Da Costa, who had conducted himself calmly and professionally throughout, was forced to regroup, and he certainly did so and more. He went on a streak of four race wins – at Berlin and Shanghai, with a double at Portland, to become a distant title challenger as the final races in London came around.

Ultimately, however, it proved too little, too late for the Portuguese driver, but despite the volatility of his season,

he ended it by remaining with Porsche, which was forced to delay its plan to bring in Müller. He was seconded to customer team Andretti for 2025 and will be readied for a potential slot alongside Wehrlein for 2026.

While this played out, Wehrlein was accruing strong points, with a win in the second race at Misano and a second to title challenger Mitch Evans in Shanghai. The Chinese Grand Prix venue was the scene of what might have been a potentially irreversible title-damaging incident when Wehrlein was turfed off the track by over-eager McLaren driver Sam Bird. With a damaged front wing – something of a feature in Gen3 racing – Wehrlein retreated to the pits, resulting in a 25-point deficit to Nick Cassidy, who had gone on one of his customary consistent results gathering sorties, which included wins in Diriyah and Berlin.

At Portland, the penultimate event of the year, Wehrlein was tested again when his front wing was knocked off in the early-race argy-bargy. The early Wehrlein might have crumbled and panicked at this stage, but there was a steelier, more durable edge to him in 2024, even perhaps a calmness that descended when the chips were down. He came fourth on that occasion after an illuminating drive that probably was as central to his success as his three victories.

His laser focus was evident on the team radio, with engineer Fabrice Roussel bringing a soothing element to the communications. It was something that Porsche's director of motorsport, Florian Modlinger, noticed on many occasions, too.

"Look back at some seasons and listen to the radios. We worked on it. Therefore, I enjoy working with Pascal a lot," said Modlinger. "I'm very hard and direct, but all the feedback he gets, he tackles. Listen to season-eight [2022] radios and now; it's a big difference in his approach."

That precision had impressed Porsche when it signed him from Mahindra in 2020, a time when he was still a bit bruised from his fractious parting with Mercedes and faced the realisation that his F1 career was probably over.

"When we took him on board, I was already convinced he was one of the most skilful racing drivers you can get," said Porsche motorsport boss Thomas Laudenbach. "If

Above: At the finale in London, Wehrlein took the spoils. Jaguar's Ian James, Mitch Evans and Nick Cassidy lead the applause for the victor.

Top right: Cassidy claimed two wins for his new team, helping them secure the teams' title.

Above right: Evans triumphed in Monaco, but the New Zealander just fell short in his title bid, trailing Wehrlein by just six points in the final standings.

Right: Evans and Wehrlein go wheel to wheel at the ExCel Arena, London.

Photos: Formula E

you look at his driving style, it's extremely precise, it's extremely clean, and I think that's something that helps him here in Formula E. But maybe he still had to grow, he still had to mature.

"He's another personality today, and I think that's a result of how we work together. We always try to give him the support. He gives it back to us, something that probably throughout the last years really also did grow. To me, he's a more complete racing driver."

Amid the often surreal setting of the Elizabeth Line and Royal Victoria Docks, Wehrlein took the whip-hand with a brilliant Saturday after hunting down the pole-sitter, Jaguar driver Mitch Evans, and teaching the Kiwi some manners with a decisive move.

Meanwhile, Evans's team-mate and fellow title protagonist, Nick Cassidy, suffered an off-day after fluffing his lines in qualifying. Despite a maelstrom of carbon fibre in the midfield pack, he survived and came through to claim a hard-fought seventh. Consequently, heading into the decisive final race, Wehrlein was leading the overall points at 180, with Evans on 177 and Cassidy on 173.

The drama began early for Cassidy in free practice, when an electrical issue confined him to the pits. With just one lap under his belt before the crucial group qualifying session and duel face-offs, the Kiwi had to nail each of them. And he did, in probably the best qualifying display ever seen in the championship, which brought him a brilliant first pole with the Big Cat.

With team-mate Evans in third, behind interloper Maximilian Günther's Maserati, and Wehrlein fourth, the scene was set for a dramatic final act that was far from disappointing.

The Jaguars led 1-2 into the first corner, with Cassidy in charge, and in the early running, they were in complete control, Günther acting as a buffer to Wehrlein. But when the Porsche slipped through to third, Jaguar appeared to panic and things began to fall apart.

Evans and Cassidy had raced hard, but fairly, all season, which undoubtedly helped them to take control of the teams' title, but also left some doubt as to who was in the box seat for the drivers' championship. After Cassidy's Portland disaster, essentially it came down to a fair and winner-takes-all-scrap, but, in full-on 'Nigel Mansell and Nelson Piquet, 1986' fashion, Wehrlein was more than happy to be the 'Prost' element in that scenario and stealthily scoop the big prize.

Cassidy's side of the garage elected for two early attack modes, the second of which allowed Wehrlein to break up the Big Cats. It crumbled from there, with indecision and apparent freestyling of strategy making both Kiwis vulnerable to the lone Porsche.

When Cassidy was sucked into the lower order of the top ten, contact with the front wing of Wehrlein's team-mate, da Costa, deflated his title aspirations as quickly as his left rear Hankook went down. Furious and dejected, he parked his car in the pits and watched as Evans also missed out to a grateful Wehrlein and Porsche, who grasped second behind Oliver Rowland's surging Nissan.

Evans endured a nightmare final few laps as he missed his crucial attack-mode loop transponders twice and fell back. The irony, however, was that his 15 points for third netted Jaguar the teams' and manufacturers' silverware, the first time it had won an international gong since Teo Fabi had sealed the 1991 World Sportscar Championship in the unforgettable XJR14.

The mixed feelings and emotions were palpable in the Jaguar garage after the race, as the celebratory T-shirts, which were rightly worn with pride after a superb season, grated a little with the drivers after Wehrlein had snatched the title from under their noses. Evans and Cassidy's relationship had been stress-tested, but after

a few weeks of silence and reflection, they were working together again as the new season was readied for a December, 2024 start in São Paulo.

"Obviously, after London, it was pretty tense," said Evans. "It was a really tricky moment for Nick and me, in terms of dealing with the emotions of missing out on the championship. You got these kind of conflicting emotions inside you, and obviously the way that it finished in London was tough.

"I think things have changed a bit since then. Obviously, there's been a lot of discussion about how things were dealt with. And, you know, we will see some changes, and hopefully we'll learn from those moments.

"It's one of those moments you just want to kind of move on from, make sure it doesn't happen again, but just move on as quickly as possible. It took me a while to get over that one."

This was all evidenced by the building blocks that Wehrlein put in place in the crucial Saturday race at London's ExCeL Arena, where he secured his third win of the season and avoided being sucked into a needless shunt with an ultra-defensive Mitch Evans.

"He tried to stay out of trouble, he saved energy and he was guided really well by the engineers, but once it came to the point he had to execute, he did it himself," added a delighted Thomas Laudenbach. "You saw that we were running late in taking the attack mode, and we wanted to get him to take the attack mode, and he said 'No, let me get Evans.' So we said, 'Go for it,' and he went for it. If it comes to the point where you have to execute, he's a lot more spot on than I have seen him years ago, and that's great to watch."

The pressure didn't get to Wehrlein any more. It used to, and although that wasn't outwardly visible, he used to become tense, and sometimes self-doubt kicked in. That all changed in 2024.

Above: Shanghai was an important venue for Formula E, which returned to China for the first time since the 2018–19 season.

Top right: Series veteran Jean-Éric Vergne led DS-Penske's challenge, but he could only finish fifth in the final standings.

Above right: Andretti's Jake Dennis celebrates his only win of the season in Diriyah.

Right: Stoffel Vandoorne scored only a single podium during a disappointing campaign.

Below right: Oliver Rowland returned to Nissan and shone brightly at many races, taking two wins. Despite missing the rounds at Portland, he claimed fourth place overall.

Photos: Formula E

"For me, the way he deals with pressure is crucial," Modlinger said. "But this is what I said on the grid before he started in London, too, when I was asked if it was too much pressure for him, and I said, 'No, because Pascal now handles the higher pressure so well.'

"The better we perform, the less pressure, and my job is to keep the team calm. He needs to stay calm in the car, and it was all perfectly executed.

"We actually look for the challenge and therefore we do the sport. It's motorsport, so you have to be like this."

Formula E is so much of a team game, and Wehrlein could not have done what he did without the support of a squad that includes strong and unique characters like Modlinger, team manager James Lindesay, engineer Roussel, chief race engineer Olivier Champenois and team management director Carlo Wiggers.

When it came to becoming champion, however, the buck stopped with Wehrlein. And no one could say that he hadn't earned his title.

"In the end, you're the person in the car; you can also take the decisions you think would be best for you," said Wehrlein. "For example, yesterday [in race one in London], I should have taken the attack mode before I passed Mitch and I said, 'No I'm going to pass him first,' so I denied taking that attack mode and did what I thought was right.

"We're all performing on a really high level. Sometimes, it goes your way, sometimes it doesn't. And I think this weekend has favoured us."

While hierarchies in Formula E are often as brittle as the fragile front wings on the Gen3 cars, it was clear that both Porsche and Jaguar were a cut above in 2024. Evans and Cassidy were consistently far ahead of a lacklustre Sébastien Buemi and Robin Frijns in the customer Envision cars, which apart from topping and tailing the season with podiums for each of them, never featured consistently at the sharp end.

A standout achievement for the Big Cat was undoubtedly at Formula E's jewel-in-the-crown event in Monaco, where the pair dominated, Cassidy electing not to challenge Evans too energetically for victory.

Best of the rest in 2024 was Oliver Rowland, who had by far his best Formula E season since joining the series in 2018. That he did so after returning to the Nissan team with which he had made his debut, after two years away on a fruitless Mahindra odyssey, was no coincidence.

Nissan had recalibrated since forging its own path away from the e.dams organisation in 2022, and it began to pay dividends quickly with a pole and a third place for Rowland in the third round at Riyadh. That performance triggered a remarkable run of results from the British driver, which included another third at São Paulo, a pole and runner-up position on Nissan's home ground, Tokyo, and then an inherited victory in Misano after da Costa's disqualification.

All of a sudden, Rowland went from unlikely front-runner to actually heading the points standings briefly. Had it not been for illness, which made him miss the Portland double-header in June, he'd have been in the title mix.

But while there was fortune in his Misano win, there was also a big dose of bad luck on the day after that. It came on the grid when a team error triggered a series of events where he and the team received erroneous energy-target figures. Leading on the last lap, and seemingly on for double delight, his car ground to a halt, handing Wehrlein the win.

Those missed points and even a conservative haul that he might have mustered at Portland meant that his win in the London finale only hoisted him to fourth place in the

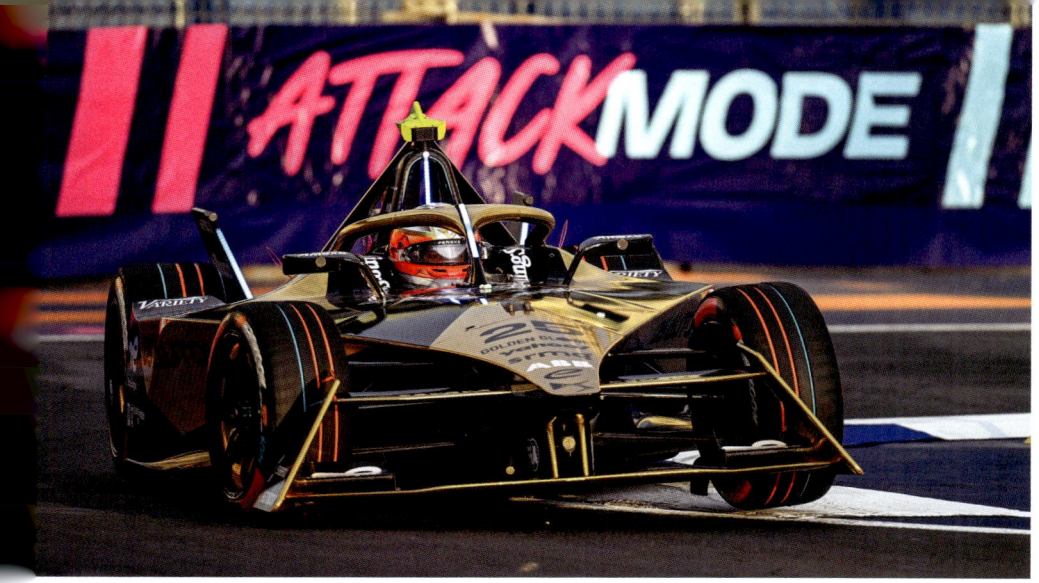

standings, when really he should have been beating down Wehrlein's door for a crack at the title.

But Rowland and Nissan were also realistic in their expectations, firmly focusing on 2025 rather than 2024 as the season in which to challenge for the ultimate prizes.

While Rowland flourished, his team-mate, Sacha Fenestraz, tanked in a season of high frustration and underachievement. This was baffling, because in 2023, the French-Argentine had occasionally dazzled with spiky pace that harnessed a pole in Cape Town and several strong points finishes. But there was little sign of that in his sophomore season, and with a paltry 26 points accrued compared to Rowland's 156, his place in the paddock was under a lot of scrutiny. With Rowland also competing in two fewer races, Nissan had little option but to replace him at season's end, bringing in old boy Norman Nato as Rowland's partner.

Jean-Éric Vergne had a similar campaign to his 2023 effort, although there wasn't the consolation of a victory to add to the Hyderabad success of the previous season. The former Toro Rosso F1 driver celebrated a decade in Formula E in 2024, and clearly he did not have the technical package that was capable of challenging Porsche- and Jaguar-powered cars. The DS Penskes were not that far off the pace, but more often they were not quick in qualifying, while both drivers tended to be shuffled out in the harum-scarum of the pack racing that prevailed once again.

Vergne's highlights included podiums in Berlin and Riyadh during a season in which he was one of the most consistent points scorers. He was quick enough in qualifying, too, beating team-mate Stoffel Vandoorne again and gaining three poles along the way – in Riyadh, Shanghai and Portland.

The biggest off-track news of the season came early in 2024, when it was announced that, in a shock move, former Jaguar technical talisman Phil Charles was leaving the Big Cat to join his former driver Vergne, whom he had engineered in 2012. He didn't mess around and made several changes to the working practices of the team while also formulating plans for the Gen4 era of Jay Penske's entry for 2026 and beyond.

Meanwhile, Vandoorne rather meekly moved across the Stellantis fold to sister brand Maserati MSG for the 2024/25 season, underlining a disappointing two-year stint with the black-and-gold operation. The 2022 champion never quite clicked with the Gen3 car, and despite still being very fast and beating Vergne to third in Monaco, there was simply not enough for him to be given a third season alongside Vergne.

One of the Belgian's self-acknowledged weak spots was taking part in the brutality of the pack-racing fights, which often included tactical or unavoidable contact with other cars. When he tried to engage in these practices, the ultra-smooth racer over-compensated, wiping out himself and others in Berlin.

In the early stages of the championship, outgoing champion Jake Dennis appeared to be on course to defend his title after a win in Riyadh, and podiums in Tokyo and Misano. Yet the Andretti driver faded badly in the second half of the season, he and his side of the garage never really able to get on terms with the factory Porsches with any consistency. His season came to a fractious halt in London, where a true 'school's out' performance sullied his champion's status amid several shunts, penalty points and other sanctions.

Dennis' fourth team-mate in as many years was Norman Nato, who had found himself surplus to requirements at Nissan at the end of the 2023 season. He did a solid, if unspectacular, job at Andretti, gaining a podium in Shanghai, although this was not enough to save him from the revolving door that also let in Nico Müller.

The Swiss driver was one of the true stars of the 2024

Above: Envision's Sébastien Buemi took second place in Mexico.

Above right: A rare bright moment for Mahindra's Edoardo Mortara, who proudly shows off his pole-position trophy in Berlin.

Top: Straddling both WEC and Formula E duties, Nyck de Vries found the going tough with Mahindra.

Above centre right: An unhappy looking Lucas di Grassi marches down the pit lane in Mexico. The Brazilian managed to score just four points with the ABT Cupra Team.

Above far right: A rare bright spot in an injury-hit season for McLaren's Sam Bird came with his win in Brazil.

Right: Max Günther won for Maserati MSG Racing in Japan.

Far right: One to watch. Nico Müller put in some mega-drives for ABT Cupra and could be on the wanted list for some larger teams.

Below right: Flanking race-two winner Félix da Costa in Shanghai, Jake Hughes and Norman Nato enjoyed their only podium visits of the year.

Photos: Formula E

campaign in the ABT Cupra team, which again struggled with a recalcitrant Mahindra powertrain. Müller stepped up to the plate, however, reeling off some astounding performances, such as a miraculous fourth in Misano, which should have brought a podium had it not been for an energy drop-off in the final 50m, which allowed Cassidy's Jaguar to snatch the position.

By this point, he had already tested for Porsche and was in discussions to become a factory driver at Weissach for 2025 and beyond. But he didn't allow that to blindside him at all, instead finishing the season as strongly with four consecutive points finishes. This put experienced team-mate Lucas di Grassi, who scored 48 fewer points, in the shade.

On paper, Maserati MSG had a much less successful season than in 2023, but actually it was quite similar in terms of highlights, with Maximilian Günther claiming a win, as he had done in 2023, at the inaugural Tokyo ePrix in March. In contrast to a woeful start to the 2023 campaign, he came out of the blocks blazing, backing up that win with two further podium places in the first half of the season. But momentum fell away mid-campaign, although largely it was not his fault due to a combination of other accidents and a technical failure at the London round when in line for another crack at the podium.

Maserati's inability to match its 2023 points tally was largely down to the fact that it was essentially a one-car points-scoring operation after Mahindra-bound Edoardo Mortara had been replaced with F2 race winner Jehan Daruvala. The Indian driver did put in some lively performances in Diryah and Berlin, but eight points from 16 races were never going to be good enough to secure his seat and he was replaced by Jake Hughes.

Hughes had shown flashes of his obvious ability with NEOM McLaren alongside Jaguar expat Sam Bird, who had replaced a WEC and DTM compromised René Rast for 2024. While Hughes claimed a brace of pole positions at Misano and Shanghai, the latter being backed up with his first Formula E podium after tailing winner da Costa, Bird's season was much spikier.

On the plus side, Bird claimed McLaren's first ever Formula E win with a typically heroic performance at São Paulo in March, when he executed the ultimate grandstand finish by overtaking a thermally challenged Mitch Evans on the penultimate corner of the race. Just two events later, however, he was sitting in a Monégasque hospital awaiting an X-ray after what initially had looked like a very innocuous accident at Ste Devote during free practice. A fracture in his hand was identified, causing him to miss three races at Monaco and Berlin, which allowed the team's young development driver, Taylor Barnard, into the cockpit.

Barnard did a sterling job in difficult circumstances, scoring points with an eighth and a tenth in Berlin. When Bird returned for Shanghai onward, there were slim pickings, with only an eighth place in London being of any note. Teenager Barnard had done enough, however, to replace the outgoing Hughes. With Nissan said to have made a significant step with its Gen3Evo car for 2025, the F2 race winner could become a significant member of the next generation of Formula E drivers.

The ABT Cupra team had come away from a bruising 2023 with little in the way of prospects with its troublesome Mahindra powertrain, but big in fight and grit. That soon became evident when Nico Müller scored a tenacious seventh at Tokyo, before an even better run at the next event in Misano. There, he had been in line for a remarkable podium when he simply ran out of energy on the run to the finish line, allowing Nick Cassidy to take the final rung of the podium by a ridiculously close 0.050s. Still, a fourth place was a remarkable result considering the deficiencies of the Mahindra package. Müller's stock, already high, went stratospheric.

A trio of excellent sixth places to round out the season underlined the Swiss driver's stellar campaign, and it came as no surprise when he was targeted first by Porsche and then Andretti, where effectively he was placed by the former, for 2025.

By contrast, Lucas di Grassi had perhaps his most difficult and disappointing season in Formula E, with just

two tenth places, in Misano and Berlin, to show for his considerable efforts. Often amid the flying front-wing detritus of the lower midfield, he was comprehensively beaten by his team-mate, and questions began to be asked about his future as he reached the age of 40.

Typically, however, di Grassi came back swinging, committing himself to the new Lola Yamaha Abt outfit, where he will tackle another season alongside F2 front-runner Zane Maloney in 2025.

Mahindra had reshuffled its driver line-up after its *annus horribilis* in 2023, bringing in Edoardo Mortara from Maserati and Nyck de Vries, whose F1 campaign with AlphaTauri in 2023 had been harshly cut short. The UK-based, Indian manufacturer had made several improvements to its overall package ahead of the season, which showed instantly, with Mortara running as high as third in Tokyo before being disqualified for a power over-spike. Better was to come in Berlin, where Mortara took a sensational pole and then the first points of the season with eighth.

More highlights were a fourth each for Mortara in Portland and de Vries in London as a new positive air permeated the Mahindra garage in readiness for the Gen3Evo era in 2025. It will be then that the team is properly judged after several generally poor campaigns.

Holder of the 2024 wooden spoon, and not for the first time, was the Electric Racing Technologies (ERT) squad, which had transitioned from the former NIO and NIO 333 outfits. With two fiery and rapid drivers, Dan Ticktum and Sérgio Sette Câmara, the underfunded team had pulled off some genuine 'David and Goliath' heroics. But as the opposition stretched away through a greater understanding of the Gen3 car, and in particular the pack racing it promoted, ERT was left floundering.

Sette Câmara pulled off some giant-killing qualifying performances in Tokyo and Riyadh, where he took positions on the second row, backing them up with a brilliant sixth behind Ticktum, who secured a barely believable fourth in Misano. These were just crumbs from a very crowded table, however, and by season's end,

Above: The impressive vista of the Autódromo Hermanos Rodríguez stadium in Mexico City offered great viewing for the fans.

Right: London underground. The ExCeL arena provided its own unique atmosphere.

Photos: Formula E

ERT was fighting for survival. The team came through it well, though, thanks to a new American owner, a deal to run year-old Porsche powertrains, and the use of Porsche reserve and development driver David Beckmann.

Notable cameos over the season came from F2 driver Paul Aron and former Dragon driver Joel Eriksson as they filled in for WEC absentee Sébastien Buemi and Robin Frijns in Berlin, Eriksson notching up two points.

In Portland, Indy NXT driver Caio Collet deputised for Rowland, who was on sick leave, while Jordan King and Kelvin van der Linde replaced Nyck de Vries and Nico Müller at Mahindra and ABT respectively, as they were also taking part in the clashing WEC race at Spa during the Berlin double-header weekend.

While Formula E enjoyed one of the most competitive and exciting title fights in its decade-long history, there was plenty of activity, both positive and negative, in the corridors of power at promoter Formula E Holdings and organiser Formula E Operations. There was a sizeable tremor in June, when it was announced that Liberty Global had acquired the majority stake held by Warner Brothers since 2015. This was significant, not only for the stability of a sports business that was still emerging from a very difficult pandemic period, but also because it clearly needs better media exposure and, in particular, better streaming and TV deals.

Within days of the announcement, CEO Jeff Dodds was on a plane to California for talks with broadcasters and streaming services. Expansion for Formula E is badly needed, especially in the USA, the UK and Germany. The latter two received paltry TV engagement through deals with TNT and Servus TV especially, while in the USA, there was some promise early in the season, albeit through the niche Roku TV platform.

It remains to be seen whether the Liberty acquisition will enable Formula E to become what it sometimes likes to call a 'Tier One' sporting business, but there is a growing feeling that it simply has to grow for there to be any significant return on investment for those manufacturers already committed to Gen4 (2026–30) – Jaguar, Nissan, Porsche and Lola.

The fact that Lola, rescued and revitalised by US-based British businessman Till Bechtolsheimer in 2022, is mentioned alongside that trio of OEM behemoths is one of motorsport's best feel-good stories of recent times.

Lola announced its ambition through a technical tie-in with Yamaha in late 2023. Soon after, it registered as a manufacturer for the 2024–25 season in conjunction with ABT, which had endured two difficult seasons with Mahindra power. As of November, 2024, Lola was also the licence holder of the grid slot, with Bechtolsheimer remaining true to his ambition of making Lola a significant player in international motorsport through a two-car operation for 2016/17 Formula E champion Lucas di Grassi and F2 race winner Zane Maloney.

Some apparent stability also came to one of Formula E's most transient teams – ERT – in 2024. Formerly known as Team China Racing, under which name it had taken the first title in 2014/15 with Nelson Piquet Jnr, it became NIO, NIO 333 and then finally ERT. The Chinese owned British-based operation had latterly been a consistent back-marker, and in early 2024, it appeared to be in a fight for survival, with Dan Ticktum and Sérgio Sette Câmara often cutting forlorn figures.

While on-track, points were in short supply, off-track, there was hope. This came through contacts of Liberty, and by October, it was announced that the Forest Road and Ares management companies would work with each

other as the new owners of the squad. Furthermore, there would be a surprise hook-up with Porsche, running the Gen3 homologated powertrain package for Ticktum and Porsche reserve racer David Beckmann.

Beckmann had made his debut in Formula E in 2023 at the Jakarta EPrix, which was missing from the calendar in 2024 due to the national elections. Whereas the Indonesian race will return in 2025, the Hyderabad EPrix was not so lucky, following a late cancellation in January, 2024, when the race was only seven weeks away.

Yet again, the bane of Formula E's image, a stable calendar, had reared its ugly head. That continued for the coming 2024/25 calendar, too, as plans for a first EPrix in Thailand, in the Chiang Mai area, scheduled for March, 2025, were put on ice due to political changes and knock-on effects beyond the series' control. However, many wondered why a replacement race could not have been arranged for the Thai event, which was scratched from the calendar in August, 2024, seven months before it was due to be run.

But while Formula E falls short on its calendar, it can also astonish in a positive sense, such as when it pivoted within 72 hours of the tragic flooding of Valencia and the surrounding area in November, 2024, just ahead of the planned traditional pre-season test at the Circuit Ricardo Tormo. The facility is also Formula E's logistics hub, and at one stage, the disaster appeared to be threatening the coming 2024/25 season, which began in early December in São Paulo, such was the devastation caused around the circuit. A mammoth exercise to transport the test to Jarama was pulled off, however, and the necessary sea freight was shipped to Brazil in time for the opener.

While these dramas were trying, perhaps the biggest challenges are yet to come for Formula E, as it prepares for what is likely to be a crucial step change from the Gen3 cars to the much heralded Gen4 for 2026.

As Formula E's 11th season was about to get under way as AUTOCOURSE went to press, Maserati joined Jaguar, Porsche, Nissan and Lola in committing to the new rules that will herald the fastest ever all-electric motorsport, starting in 2026. That left just DS and Mahindra to make their decisions on Gen4, which are expected early in 2025. If they are also positive, it would mean that all the manufacturers would be retained for the series, which, in the light of a volatile automotive industry and the uncertainty surrounding EV sales, would be a minor miracle.

However, the fact remains that, Lola apart, the last time a major manufacturing brand entered Formula E was in 2019, when Porsche arrived. With Aston Martin, Hyundai (through Genesis), Ford, GM and Alpine all choosing to be involved with other series, it seems that Formula E is still in something of a holding pattern after the disruption of the Covid pandemic.

One aspect the series is keen to promote is fast charging, through energy-boosting pit stops. These were supposed to come into being in 2023, but were delayed while the growing pains of the Gen3 cars were overcome. Testing continued through 2024, but initially complete reliability was difficult to achieve. It was carried on at the 2024/25 pre-season test at Jarama, and will be further tested before a possible introduction partway through the coming season.

The concern remains, however, that with the existing attack-mode power boosting within races – achieved by driving over special transponders off-line – the races will become too complex to understand. This, plus the fact that the energy-top-up pit stops will take at least a minute from start to finish and are devoid of any dynamism, has tested the teams' and manufacturers' patience significantly already.

Much is adaptable in Formula E and usually solutions are found. As with Porsche and Pascal Wehrlein, hard work, dedication and remaining cool under pressure really seem to be rewarded in the world's only all-electric world championship.

SPORTS & GT REVIEW by GARY WATKINS
SHARING THE SPOILS

Above: Once again, Ferrari took victory at Le Mans in a topsy-turvy race that twisted and turned throughout the 24 hours.

Top right: Chasing down the winning Ferrari, the No.7 Toyota of Kamui Kobayashi, Nyck de Vries and José María López took second place.

Above right: The triumphant trio of Miguel Molina, Antonio Fuoco and Nicklas Nielsen celebrate their Le Mans triumph.

Right: Luck was not on the side of the No.8 Toyota of Sébastien Buemi, Brendon Hartley and Ryo Hirakawa, who had to settle for fifth after Hartley's time-consuming spin.

Opening spread: The World Endurance race under way at Fuji, with Porsche, Cadillac, BMW, Toyota and Ferrari all in the mix.
Photos: WEC

FERRARI made it two from two at the Le Mans 24 Hours following the factory's return to the top flight of sportscar racing after an absence of half a century. The Italian manufacturer claimed arguably the biggest prize on offer in the World Endurance Championship, courtesy of Nicklas Nielsen, Antonio Fuoco and Miguel Molina, in the double-points round in June, but it missed the silverware on offer at the end of the season. The WEC drivers' title went to Porsche with Kévin Estre, Laurens Vanthoor and André Lotterer, while Toyota snatched the manufacturers' crown at the death.

So it was kind of honours even for the WEC's big three marques, both historically – they now have a combined total of 35 wins at Le Mans – and in the context of the 2024 campaign: Ferrari, Porsche and Toyota shared the race victories over a calendar that had returned to its traditional eight races after the travails of Covid. But Porsche and Toyota had the consistency throughout the campaign that made them champions at its conclusion.

When it mattered most, however, Ferrari had the pace and the luck to follow up its return triumph at the French enduro in 2023, its 499P Le Mans Hypercar narrowly claiming the victory laurels from Toyota. The difference this time was that it wasn't the only contender. There were an unprecedented number of entries on the lead lap and at least in with a sniff of victory as the time approached four o'clock. Four manufacturers – Porsche, Cadillac, Ferrari and Toyota – provided the nine cars that finished within eight or so miles of the winner. To put that into context, never before had more than two cars been in the hunt at the start of the final lap of the 8.47-mile Circuit de la Sarthe.

The other difference between 2024 and the previous running was the identity of the two Hypercar class entries fighting it out at the front in the final hour. Nielsen, Fuoco and Molina prevailed in the best of the factory AF Corse-run 499Ps by 14s from the Toyota GR010 Hybrid LMH shared by Kamui Kobayashi, Nyck de Vries and late stand-in José María López, who returned to the line-up when Mike Conway was ruled out by injuries sustained in a cycling accident. The second cars from this pair of manufacturers, the two contenders for victory in 2023, ended up third and fifth. James Calado, Alessandro Pier Guidi and Antonio Giovinazzi took the final podium spot for Ferrari; Toyota drivers Sébastien Buemi, Brendon Hartley and Ryo Hirakawa were fifth, with the best of the Porsches, the championship-winning entry, between them. But it could just as easily have been the Toyota – and there is an argument that rightfully it should have been – once again duking it out for the win with Ferrari.

The Ferrari and the Toyota LMH prototypes were evenly matched – there was probably less in it than 12 months previously – over the course of a race that was interrupted by rain on several occasions and six hours' worth of running behind the safety car. The Toyota had the slightest of edges, a reverse of 2023, though the GR010 was undoubtedly the quicker car in wet conditions. That Ferrari ultimately prevailed was due to the fact that, in the final stages of the race, it wasn't the quicker of the Toyotas in the hunt for victory.

A spin for López at the Dunlop Chicane bang on the 23-hour mark as he hunted down Nielsen wasn't the defining moment. That had come exactly an hour before, when Hartley had spun at Mulsanne Corner after a push from

Pier Guidi, a misdemeanour that resulted in the Italian receiving a five-second time penalty at his next stop.

The time loss for Toyota was significant: about 35s on the lap when he had spun and another five on the following lap as he brought his wet-weather Michelins back up to temperature. The deficit of the fifth-placed Toyota to the winning Ferrari at the chequered flag was 62s, but it is important to point out that Hartley dropped back in the pack. That undoubtedly played a part in his ability to mount any kind of useful fight back.

The crew of the Toyota were adamant that the incident had cost them victory. "I guess, without that spin after that little touch, we would have won the race," said Buemi. "We lost something like 40s and we were some way ahead of No.7 [the sister car] at the time." For Hartley, it felt "like the victory just slipped away from us."

Hartley had been just behind the winning Ferrari at the time of the incident and would have assumed the lead when Nielsen had to make an unscheduled pit stop. The driver's door had come open following the car's penultimate stop, and the Dane had no option but to pit because he was being shown the black-and-orange warning flag.

He came in with an hour and 40 left on the clock, or double a normal 50-minute stint on the car's energy allocation. López, chosen to finish the race, despite this being his first time back in a GR010 since the previous November's WEC finale in Bahrain, was 36s behind after making his own second-to-last stop.

His progress towards the Ferrari was halted when he looped the car with an hour to go. The time loss was more or less the 14s by which he lost the race, but it would be wrong to say that Toyota had missed out on the win as a result of an incident that López suspected was caused by some kind of powertrain issue.

Nielsen was backing off at the end; the gap stood at 22s with a couple of laps to go, so López was almost certainly correct when he said that the spin wasn't crucial. The only caveat to that is the fact that Nielsen was in pretty aggressive fuel-save mode as the race approached its

Above: Showdown in Bahrain as Toyota and Porsche go head to head for the manufacturers' title.

Top right: Laurens Vanthoor, André Lotterer and Kévin Estre delivered the drivers' championship for Penske Porsche.

Above right: Toyota's Nyck de Vries, Kamui Kobayashi and Mike Conway celebrate their win at Imola.

Right: The No.6 Penske Porsche took the honours in the season's opener in Qatar.
Photos: WEC

end. His early stop had provided him with no margin for error as he strove to avoid the need for a splash. He knew it would be tight, even with the wet conditions and a brief slow zone, a temporary 80km/h speed limit. Official data showed that he had less than two per cent of his energy allocation for the stint remaining when he took the chequered flag.

"I did quite a bit of fuel-save, but I didn't think about it much," said Nielsen. "If we wanted to go for the win, we only had one option – to save fuel. I just asked the team to give me an energy target per lap, and that's it."

The second-placed Toyota had what might be deemed a messy race. It had to come from the back of the 23-strong Hypercar field after Kobayashi had gone off at Virage Covette at the end of the Porsche Curves as he tried to improve his time in first qualifying. WEC rules demand that a driver loses all his lap times if he or she causes a red flag.

There were multiple issues along the way for this car, though to a greater or lesser extent, their effect was mitigated by the three safety cars that interrupted the race. There were two slow punctures that resulted in unscheduled stops, and the car lost power on Sunday morning when the turbo boost dropped as a result of a sensor issue that took some time to resolve out on track. That explained why the Kobayashi Toyota had to cede position to the sister car, putting Buemi and his teammates in the pound seats as Ferrari's nearest challenger at this point.

Another engine issue, during López's final stint, cost the car time. Somehow, he had ended up with the wrong settings leaving the pits and had to be guided by the team to cycle through the systems to address the problem, all the while trying to make up time on a wet track.

It all went to reinforce Buemi's claim that his car should have won the race. "I think we had the cleanest race of everyone," he said. "This was one that got away."

Porsche might have been in the mix and finished less than 40s down on the winning Ferrari, but when push came to shove, it didn't have the pace to mount a challenge for its 20th Le Mans victory. The 963 LMDh wasn't quite a match for the 499P and GR010, a lack of straight-line speed making it a less raceable machine than its direct competitors. But it was always there or thereabouts through the season.

The factory Porsche squad delivered amazing consistency in 2024. That gave them a first WEC top-class title since the end of the 919 Hybrid LMP1 programme in 2017. Estre, Vanthoor and Lotterer secured a pair of wins – in the new season-opening Qatar fixture on the Losail International Circuit in March, and then at Fuji in September. In the meantime, they were never out of the top six and were on the podium a further three times. So much so that by the time the WEC pitched up in Bahrain for the traditional series curtain-closer, they had one hand on the title and the other poised nearby. And in the end, it mattered not that Estre and his team-mates had their worst race of the season at the finale, scoring only a solitary point.

The German manufacturer and the factory Porsche Penske Motorsport squad had turned a corner at the end of 2023 and continued to improve through the winter. The LMDh hybrid prototype became a more useable race-car and, crucially, a more reliable one. That much

was clear even before the WEC season had started. The US arm of the PPM squad had triumphed over 24 hours at Daytona at the opening round of the IMSA SportsCar Championship in January.

The other factor in PPM's consistency was the Balance of Performance. It always gave the Porsche LMDh a fighting chance, which was not the case for Toyota and Ferrari. There were races when their LMHs weren't quite in the game, most notably at Qatar for both of them, at Interlagos for Ferrari, and Fuji for both again.

There was a new, more reactive system of BoP for 2024. In the previous season, the BoP had been based on simulation and the *potential* of what a car could achieve on-track rather than what it actually did. Also, there was prior notice of when the BoP could change. This time around, it could be altered race by race, based on track performance. And the rule makers – the FIA and the Automobile Club de l'Ouest – didn't always get it right.

Toyota ended up winning more races than any other factory team, taking maximum points at Imola in April, Fuji in July and in November's final round in Bahrain. Those victories were spread across its two entries, two going to the Buemi car and one to Kobayashi's. That meant there was little realistic chance of the WEC drivers' class – which it had won every year since the 2018/19 'superseason' campaign – being retained as the WEC circus headed for its second trip to the Middle East, but it was still very much in with a chance for another manufacturers' title.

That seemed to have disappeared as the eight-hour race entered its final quarter. The Kobayashi/Conway/de Vries entry was out of the race with a high-pressure fuel pump issue and, with 90 minutes to go, Buemi was down in tenth place in the sister car. Then the Swiss driver began an amazing comeback, which took him into the lead, ahead of the second PPM Porsche shared by Matt Campbell, Michael Christensen and Frédéric Makowiecki, and on to a victory margin of more than half a minute. That gave the Japanese marque the all-important manufacturers' prize by just two points.

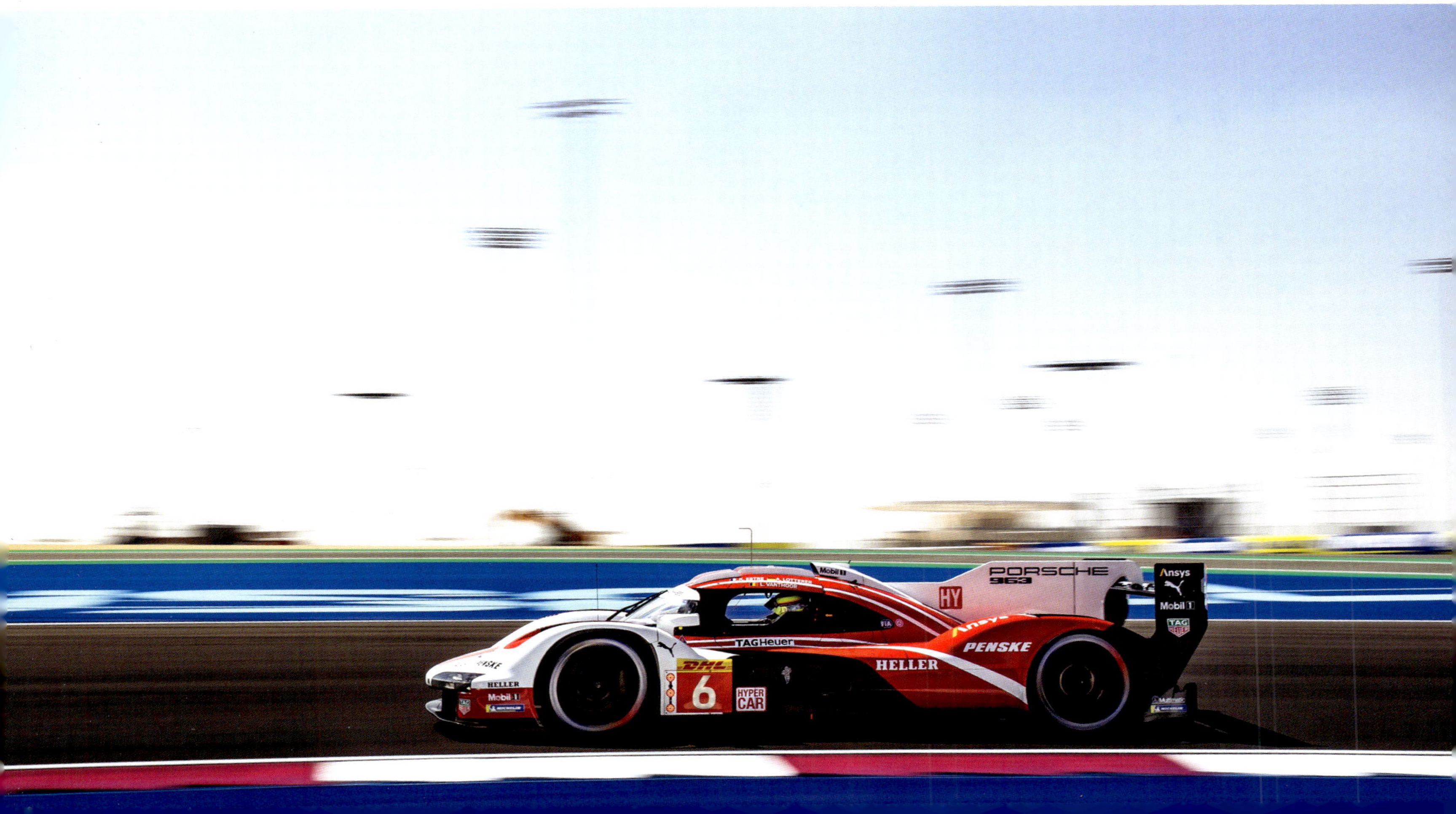

Above: Alpine came to life late in the season, when the No.36 car of Schumacher, Vaxiviere and Lapierre finally clinched a podium in Japan.

Top right: Peugeot ran a heavily revised car in 2024, but found difficulty in breaking the domination of the leading teams.

Top far right: Team Jota's Jenson Button was a big-name driver who committed full-time to the series.

Above right: After a long and painful journey, the popular Robert Kubica became a winner once more.

Above far right: James Calado, Antonio Giovinazzi and Alessandro Pier Guidi took third at Le Mans for Ferrari AF Corse.

Right: Cadillac and BMW fight it out in Fuji.
Photos: WEC

Ferrari ended up second in the drivers' points with Nielsen, Fuoco and Molina, and third in the manufacturers' rankings. It could have been very different for a manufacturer that had stressed ahead of the season that a world championship title was its primary target in 2024. The AF Corse-run factory squad lost two victories in the space of weeks in the spring, missing out in its backyard at Imola and then at Spa. It could have finished 1-2 on both occasions, but it gave away the win in the first of those two races and was plain unlucky in the second.

There was an inexplicable tactical blunder in Italy when the 499Ps were left out on slicks after it had started raining. Three weeks later, in Belgium, the factory Ferraris were again 1-2 when controversially the race was restarted following a red flag after the original scheduled finish time: the 499Ps ended up only third and fourth behind the best of the British Jota team's customer Porsches, driven by Will Stevens and Callum Ilott, and the championship-winning factory car. The eventual top two had pitted just before the red flag and therefore regained much of the time they had lost courtesy of the safety-car restart. Then they jumped to the front when everyone else pitted.

Porsche's victory with one of the three privateer 963s in the field was matched by Ferrari. The so-called customer 499P, run as a satellite operation by AF and driven by Robert Kubica, Yifei Ye and Robert Shwartzman, took the honours at the Circuit of The Americas in Austin in September.

Cadillac was the big disappointment of 2024. It was fourth in the performance pecking order, but ended up nowhere in both championship classifications. There was a series of strong qualifying showings from Lynn, who followed a front-row at Le Mans with pole at Fuji aboard the sole Chip Ganassi Racing-run Caddy V-Series.R LMDh. What he and full-season co-driver Earl Bamber couldn't do was translate those lofty grid positions into anything better than fourth in Austin. (The same result at Qatar was lost to a homologation infringement.)

Yet the GM marque's entry, which Lynn and Bamber drove as a duo in the six-hour races, could have achieved much more. Including at Le Mans, where it was in contention with Ferrari and Toyota with three hours or so to go. After the final safety car, the regular WEC entry, in which Ganassi IndyCar star Alex Palou joined Lynn and Bamber, faded to seventh. In its last year with Cadillac, Ganassi admitted that the car had lost downforce as a result of a gaping hole in the underfloor. It didn't elaborate on the cause.

Elsewhere, Lynn and Bamber might have been on the podium at Spa and Fuji. On both occasions, the latter made mistakes that put the car out of the race, most dramatically in Belgium, where an infinitesimal misjudgement resulted in the biggest of accidents on the Kemel Straight, which triggered the red flag.

Best of the rest, in terms of points scored, was Alpine on its return to the top class of the WEC with its new A424 LMDh. It came out on top of a close battle for fourth in the manufacturers' standings with BMW and Peugeot, each of which – like the Renault brand – scored a solitary podium in the closing stages of the campaign. Over the final three races, Alpine and the Signatech team took a big step forward, the result of that upward development curve and some help from the BoP. There was a pair of fourths that sandwiched a first podium at Fuji for the

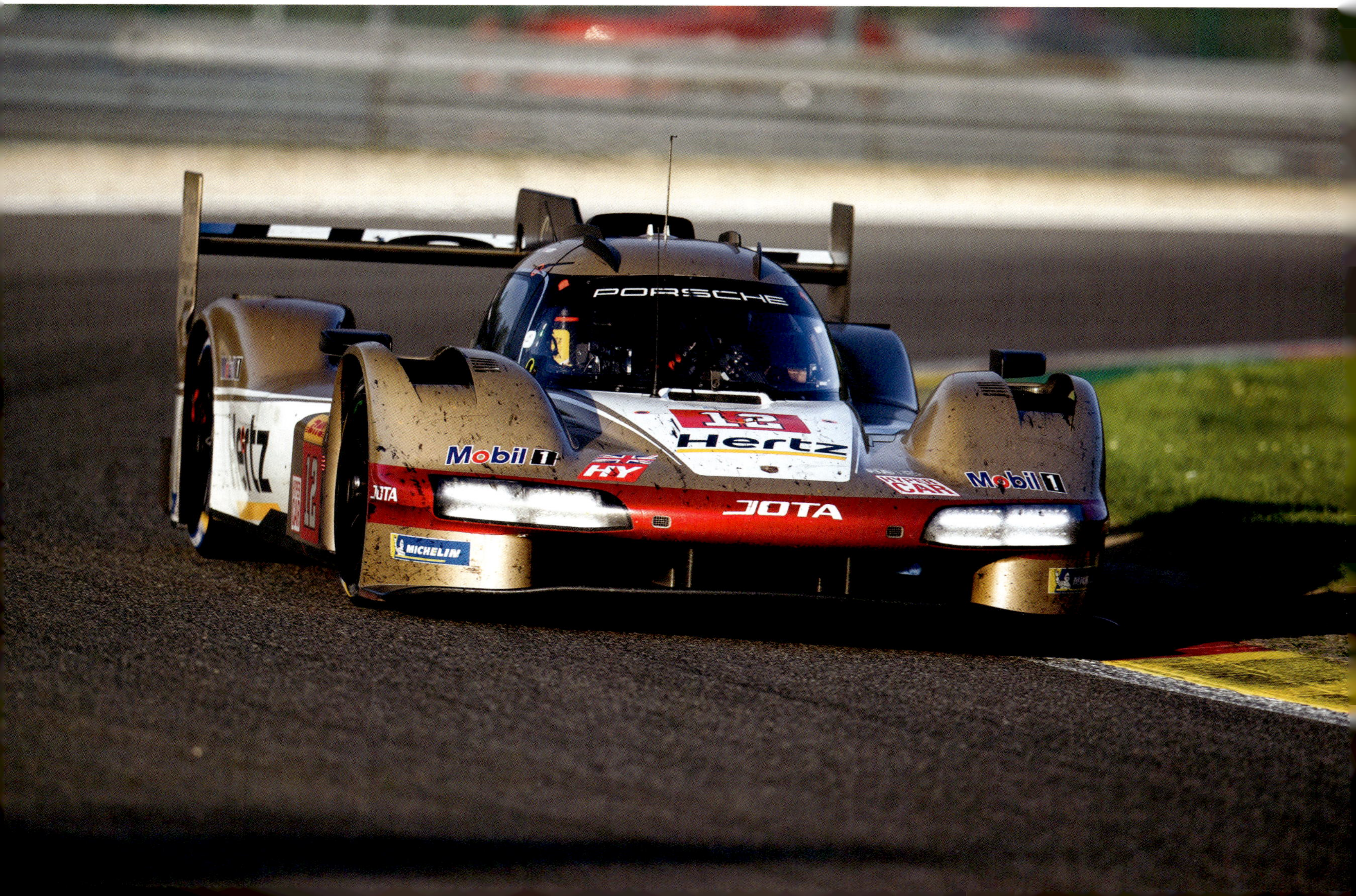

Above: The No.92 Manthey Porsche of Alex Malykhin, Joel Sturm and Klaus Bachler won the opening GT class in Qatar. They went on to secure the FIA Endurance Trophy for LMGT3 drivers.

Above left: The independent Ferrari 499P 3-litre turbo won at CoTA with Robert Kubica, Robert Shwartzman and Yifei Ye at the wheel.
Photos: WEC

Top: United Autosports took class honours at Le Mans with its Oreca-Gibson 07, shared by Oliver Jarvis, Nolan Siegel and Bijoy Garg.
Photo: United Autosports

Left: A surprise win at Spa came the way of Hertz Team Jota, courtesy of the No.12 Porsche driven by Will Stevens and Callum Ilott.
Photo: WEC

entry driven by Mick Schumacher, Nicolas Lapierre and Matthieu Vaxivière.

BMW, new to the WEC's top class after blooding its M Hybrid V8 LMDh in IMSA in 2023, notched up its podium at Fuji, where the best of its WRT-run cars took the fight to Porsche, though the car shared by Dries Vanthoor, Marco Wittmann and Raffaele Marciello wasn't quite quick enough in the final stages to win. Peugeot could take some solace from an otherwise disappointing season after switching at Imola to a heavily-revised car, complete with something approaching a conventional rear wing, that had a late run of decent results. The 9X8 2024 LMH of Mikkel Jensen, Nico Müller and Jean-Éric Vergne crossed the line in fourth at both Fuji and Bahrain. Then it came away with a podium at the finale after the Ferrari of Calado, Pier Guidi and Giovinazzi was penalised for a tyre-allocation infringement.

Porsche also took championship honours, for both drivers and teams, in the new LMGT3 class that took over from GTE Am in 2024. Klaus Bachler, Joel Sturm and Alex Malykhin swept to the title with a round to spare in their Manthey PureRxcing 911 GT3-R, while second went to the sister Manthey EMA entry shared by Richard Lietz, Morris Schuring and Yasser Shahin.

The PureRxcing GT3-R was dominant at the head of a 18-strong field made up of nine manufacturer-chosen customer teams, each entering two cars as per the regulations. Malykhin was the star bronze-rated driver in the field, and quite often he made the difference between the PureRxcing car and its rivals in the pro-am class. The British-based Belarusian and his team-mates won twice, in Qatar and at Interlagos, and were on the podium a further three times. Lietz, Schuring and Shahin also won twice, including at Le Mans where their rivals across the Manthey garage encountered gearbox problems, but also didn't have the same consistency.

The other race winners in LMGT3 were the WRT BMW squad, The Heart of Racing Aston Martin team and Ferrari's AF Corse operation. Motorcycle racing legend Valentino Rossi, a seven-times 500cc/MotoGP champion, contested the WEC with the first of those teams, but ended up with a best result of third at Fuji with team-mates Maxime Martin and Ahmad Al Harthy.

The LMP2 prototype category disappeared from the WEC as scheduled. Not only did the organisers want to make the series easier to understand with a two-class structure, but also they needed to make room for more cars in Hypercar. The secondary prototype category remained, however, an important component of what the ACO liked to call the "pyramid of endurance". It remained the top category in the European Le Mans Series and its Asian counterpart run over the winter months, as well as a component of the IMSA SportsCar Championship in North America. That importance explained why the ACO committed to inviting at least 15 P2s on to the grid at Le Mans, and ended up making room for 16.

United Autosports, for so long a major force in P2 in the WEC and the ELMS, took class honours with its Oreca-Gibson 07 shared by Oliver Jarvis, Nolan Siegel and Bijoy Garg. They triumphed by 18s over 2023 winner Inter Europol Competition with its Oreca driven by Clement Novolak, Vladislav Lomko and Jakub Smiechowski. Top finisher in the pro-am P2 sub-class was the AF-run entry shared by Ben Barnicoat, Nicolás Varrone and François Perrodo in fourth. This Oreca might have beaten the regular entries in class but for a starter-motor issue that lost it vital seconds at every pit stop over the last quarter of the race.

Jarvis was on the driving strength of the United ELMS crew that won more races than any other, the Briton claiming victory in three of the six races with Phil Hanson and Marino Sato. The third of those wins came at the series finale on the Algarve circuit in October, but it wasn't enough to give them the title. That went to the Anglo-Portuguese Algarve Pro Racing line-up of Alex Lynn, James Allen and Kyffin Simpson on the back of an ultra-consistent campaign: they won twice, took a further three podiums and never finished lower than fifth.

It became incorrect in 2024 to talk about the GT World Challenge Europe as representing another code of sportscar racing after the adoption of GT3 rules by the WEC and the ELMS. Yet the series run by the organisation founded by Stéphane Ratel, the architect of GT3 back in 2006, continued to operate in their own orbit with the Spa 24 Hours at the centre.

Just as in the WEC, the GTWCE prizes were divvied out among the manufacturers. Maro Engel and Lucas Auer took the overall title, combining points scored in both the Endurance and Sprint Cup segments of the series in their Winward Racing-run Mercedes-AMG GT3: they were only sixth in the more prestigious Endurance leg, but took the Sprint crown. Meanwhile, AF Ferrari drivers Pier Guidi and Alessio Rovera were triumphant in the Endurance championship.

Together with fellow factory Ferrari driver Davide Rigon, they were on course to take victory in the double-points round at Spa in the summer. Bizarrely, they were deprived of the win when a broken-down car in the pit-lane entry cost Pier Guidi enough time to drop him to second as he made his final stop. The delay allowed Aston Martin to take the chequered flag with the Comtoyou Racing Aston Martin Vantage GT3 shared by Nicki Thiim, Marco Sørensen and Mattia Drudi.

They were driving the new evo version of the second-generation Vantage GT3 racer, which reflected a new commitment to endurance racing at the British manufacturer in a year when it began testing its new Valkyrie LMH WEC and IMSA contender. Aston's previous Spa 24 victory had been in 1948 in the first post-war running of the Belgian classic. The Valkyrie programme was announced with equally lofty ambitions: to win Le Mans for the marque for the first time since 1959.

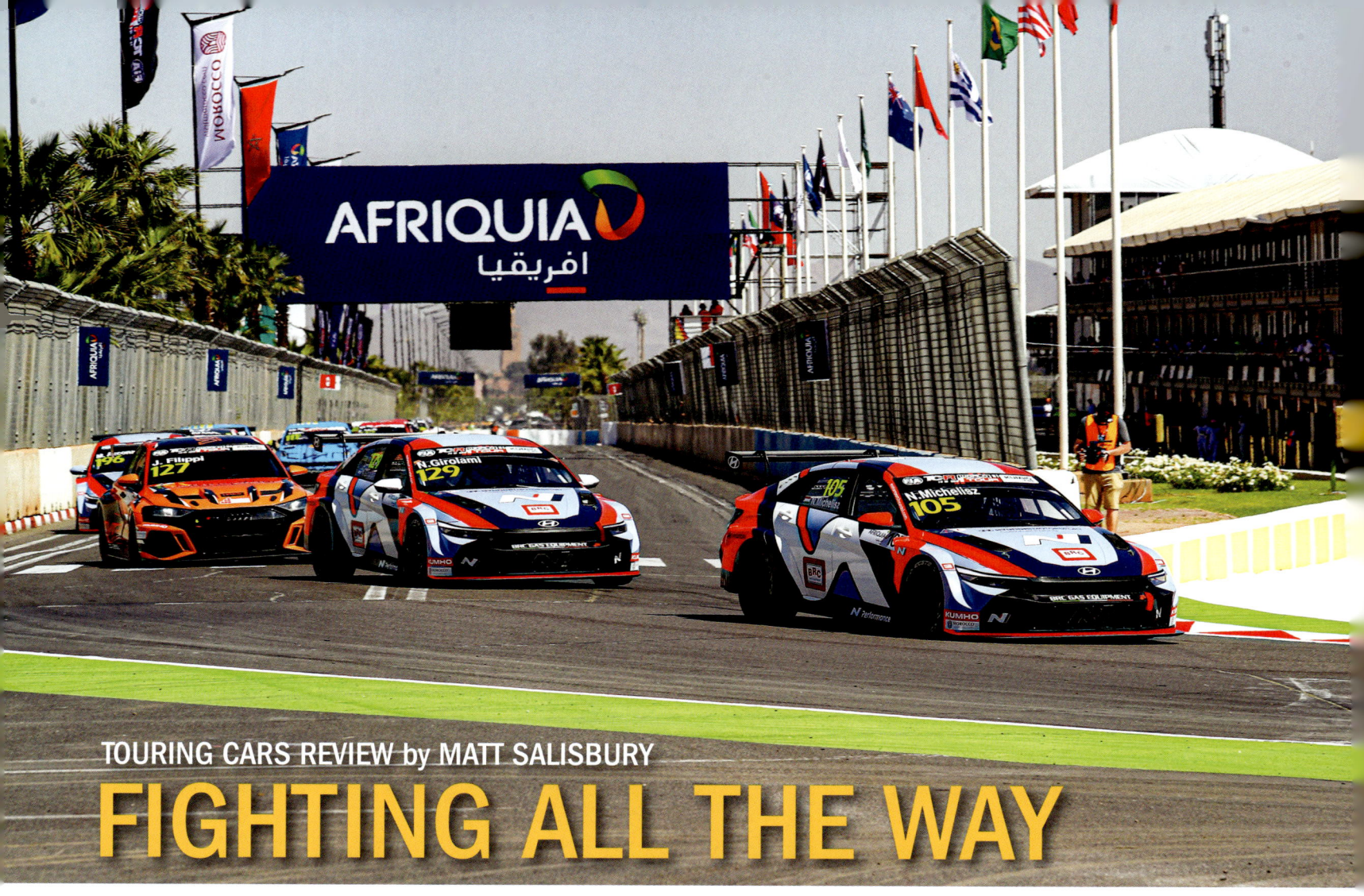

TOURING CARS REVIEW by MATT SALISBURY
FIGHTING ALL THE WAY

Above: Norbert Michelisz leads Hyundai team-mate Nestor Girolami into action at the season's opener in Morocco.

Top right: Yann Ehrlacher took three wins to cement the teams' championship for Cyan Lynk & Co Racing

Top far right: Michelisz scored points in every race to become the series champion for the second season in succession.

Above right: Nestor Girolami took only a single win, in Italy, but his points were crucial in the battle between Lynk & Co and BRC Hyundai.

Above centre right: GOAT Racing's Dušan Borković won for Honda on the streets of Macau.

Above far right: Santiago Urrutia completed Lynk and Co's strong driver line-up.

Right: Mikel Azcona, Yann Ehrlacher and Thed Björk share the podium after race one in El Pinar, Uruguay.
Photos: TCR

AS has become the norm, the world of touring car racing was the place to be for wheel-to-wheel action in 2024 as the fights for the major championship titles all went the distance.

In the case of the TCR World Tour, a familiar name emerged on top after the Macau finale, but in the British Touring Car Championship, the DTM and the Supercars Championship, new names were added to the respective championship trophies as the curtain fell on the season.

TCR WORLD TOUR

The inaugural season for the TCR World Tour in 2023 should have been the precursor for the first TCR World Final, with the top 15 drivers joined by the leading drivers in the TCR World Rankings, which incorporates races across the globe. The event had been scheduled for Portimão in early 2024, but was cancelled in January, while at the same time, eligibility was revised to exclude World Tour drivers.

However, the World Tour had gained FIA status, with a nine-round calendar comprising events on six continents – although subsequently two planned in Australia fell by the wayside.

In total, ten drivers contested the full season, with defending champion Norbert Michelisz spearheading an expanded BRC Hyundai line-up that included Nestor Girolami alongside Mikel Azcona.

Lynk & Co Cyan Racing was unchanged, with the same line-up of Yann Ehrlacher, Thed Björk, Santiago Urrutia and Ma Qing Hua, while Honda was represented by the new GOAT Racing team with Marco Butti and Esteban Guerrieri. Dušan Borković joined them from round two.

Volcano Motorsport rounded out the entry with two Audis for John Filippi and Sami Taoufik, although the latter would depart after two meetings, his car being driven by various names over the remainder of the season.

The campaign kicked off with the only European event at Vallelunga, where Michelisz put his Hyundai on pole before scoring a comfortable victory in the opening race. Ehrlacher followed him home in second, with Guerrieri third as they proved unable to match the pace of the champion. Hyundai doubled up in race two when Girolami ended his first weekend in the Elantra with a straightforward win, despite two safety-car periods, ahead of Uruttia and Butti in a distant third.

Michelisz held the points lead going to Morocco, the event running on a shortened version of the Moulay El Hassan circuit. Ehrlacher led team-mate Urrutia in qualifying for race one, which he headed from start to finish, followed by the Uruguayan, to become the third winner in as many races; Michelisz was third. Then Ma scored his first win of the campaign in race two, the main drama coming at the start when Erhlacher and Michelisz tangled, putting the Frenchman out and leaving the latter outside the top ten.

Despite that, he remained on top of the points as the series headed to the USA for a first visit to Mid-Ohio, where Azcona became the third pole-sitter of the year, having headed Michelisz in the times. Lynk & Co emerged on top in race one, Björk snatching second from Michelisz at the start and then battling his way past Azcona to make it five winners from five. The Swede took third in race two, behind Ehrlacher and Ma, as Lynk & Co locked out the podium, but then he was demoted to sixth for contact on his way through the pack, promoting Guerrieri to third. The Argentine was involved in a bizarre incident post-race when he was hit by Urrutia on the slow-down lap, the latter being excluded from the weekend as a result.

Interlagos marked the halfway stage, and Urrutia made amends somewhat for the incident in the USA by claiming pole ahead of Guerrieri, but the Honda man turned the tables in race one, getting ahead off the line and remaining out front to the finish. Michelisz lined up on pole for the reverse-grid race, and fended off both Ma and Björk to score a vital win, which extended his lead at the top, Ehrlacher having failed to score after early contact.

Just two weeks later, the series headed to El Pinar in

Above: Björk leads the main championship contenders at the start of race one in Macau.
Photo: TCR

Top right: Dan Cammish's Ford Focus was just one of the strong four-car NAPA Racing line-up.

Top far right: Mikey Doble receives the Jack Sears Trophy from series organiser Alan Gow.

Above right: Two-wheeling across Donington's kerbs for Colin Turkington's BMW and Rob Huff's Toyota.

Right: Tom Ingram led the Hyundai challenge for the Bristol Street Motors squad, scoring six wins on his way to second place overall in the championship.
Photos: BTCC/Jakob Ebrey

Uruguay, where Ehrlacher beat the three Hyundai drivers to pole and then led from start to finish in a first race that was impacted by two safety cars. Azcona and Björk rounded out the podium before a chaotic second race, which had to be restarted after confusion at the start caused by an issue with the lighting system. Local driver Pedro Cardoso looked like being the first non-World Tour regular to win until Björk sneaked ahead late on to sit third in the points behind Michelisz and Guerrieri.

Following a two-month break, the action resumed in China, where Urrutia led a Lynk & Co 1-2-3 in qualifying, having topped every session. In the rain-affected opening race, however, no one could match Azcona for pace as he came through from fourth on the grid to take an impressive victory, while Ma secured a popular home win in race two.

Michelisz led the standings going to Macau, with five drivers still in with a realistic chance of emerging on top. In mixed weather conditions, Björk grabbed pole for the opening race of the weekend. Then he took his first win at the challenging street circuit, ahead of Michelisz, to close the gap between them to five points.

Heavy rain delayed race two, which was started under the safety car, with the two title protagonists running on wet tyres. The circuit dried as the race wore on, however, which allowed Borković to lead an impressive 1-2-3 of slick-shod Hondas. Michelisz finished fifth to wrap up the title, being protected by Azcona and Girolami, who kept Björk at bay.

"From the first moment of the season, we didn't put a foot wrong and I scored points in every race," Michelisz said. "I won my first race in the WTCC in Macau and it was an amazing feeling, and I'm a lucky person to have repeated that feeling last year and again this year."

While the calendar for 2025 had yet to be confirmed as AUTOCOURSE closed for press, Australia was scheduled to return with an event at The Bend, and Korea was expected to appear for the first time.

BRITISH TOURING CAR CHAMPIONSHIP

Although the British Touring Car Championship grid was reduced in size for 2024, the quality at the front remained as high as ever.

The top two teams from 2023 – the Alliance Racing-run NAPA Racing UK squad and Bristol Street Motors-backed EXCELR8 – remained unchanged, with Ash Sutton and Tom Ingram leading the respective line-ups.

There were changes elsewhere, however, with West Surrey Racing scaled back to three BMWs for the start of the season, but Speedworks expanded to run four Toyota Corollas with an all-new line-up, including former WTCC title winner Rob Huff, Andrew Watson, and One Motorsport refugees Josh Cook and Aiden Moffat.

The loss of One – the defending Independent champions – and departure of Team HARD left just three non-constructor entries, two of whom were new: Restart Racing and Un-Limited Motorsport.

Restart brought Chris Smiley back to the series after two years away alongside rookie Scott Sumpton, while Un-Limited fielded a single car for teenager Daryl DeLeon for his first full season. Power Maxed Racing rounded out the field with a pair of Vauxhall Astras, one car less than in 2023.

Thus a grid of 20 prepared for the opening round at Donington Park, where the main talking point was expected to be the impact of revisions to the hybrid system, which now gave double the boost it had in 2023.

A new, three-part qualifying system also debuted, with drivers split into two groups based on the results of second practice. Six drivers from each group progressed to Q2, where six more drivers would drop out to leave the 'Quick Six' battling for pole.

Ingram emerged on top in a wet-dry session to score pole, which he converted into victory in an opening race that had been delayed by more than two hours after torrential rain left parts of the circuit under water.

The fast-starting BMW of Jake Hill vaulted to the front when race two kicked off, with Ingram and Sutton giving chase, the battle between the trio offering a taste of what was to come over the season. Ingram fought his way to the front late on to score his second win, while Sutton had overtaken Hill to replicate the race-one result.

Moffat emerged victorious in the reverse-grid finale, the Scot getting ahead of team-mate Huff before holding off the challenges of Colin Turkington, Sutton and Ingram for one of the most impressive wins of his career to date.

Ingram's double win meant that he was leading the standings heading to Brands Hatch for round two, where Turkington and Adam Morgan locked out the front row of the grid for WSR.

Turkington dominated race one, beating Morgan off the line and then racing away from the pack, While his victory was straightforward, the fight for second place was anything but, with Cook battling ahead of Sutton to finish as runner-up after contact had dropped Morgan down the order.

Then Turkington made it two wins from two as Ingram beat Sutton to the runner-up spot in the second race, before the weekend concluded with a new name on the top step of the podium in the shape of Ronan Pearson. The Scot had started from pole, but been beaten off the line by Árón Taylor-Smith, only to power back ahead before the end of lap one. Pearson was followed home by team-mate Tom Chilton and new points leader Sutton, both having passed Taylor-Smith.

Bobby Thompson rejoined the grid in a fourth BMW at Snetterton for what would turn out to be a one-off appearance, but Hill was the star of the weekend, kick-starting his championship challenge in fine style.

Hill powered his Laser Tools-backed car to pole position and became the season's fifth winner with a lights-to-flag win in race one, ahead of Thompson, with Sutton taking third, despite minimal hybrid, as points leader.

The chaotic second race was delayed by heavy rain

Above: Jake Hill, driving the Laser Tools Racing BMW, emerged as a worthy champion in 2024, ahead of Ash Sutton.

Top right: The ever-consistent Josh Cook claimed a couple of victories and seven further podiums in his Toyota Corolla.

Above right: Top Independent Árón Taylor-Smith joins the 'big three' – Ash Sutton, Tom Ingram and Jake Hill – on the podium.

Right: Ingram leads Cook and Hill away from pole position in a wet race one at Silverstone.

Photos: BTCC/Jakob Ebrey

just before the scheduled start, although much of the circuit was dry by the time the action got under way. A number of drivers decided to pit early for slicks, but Hill elected to stay out on wets, his hope of victory seeming to be over when he was hit with a ten-second penalty for an infringement at the start. Having made the right call on tyres when the rain returned, however, he produced the drive of his life to cross the line more than 16 seconds clear of Dan Cammish, overcoming the penalty with ease.

Although Hill looked good for a hat trick in the reverse-grid final race as again he gambled on wet tyres and blasted to the front, this time, the circuit dried, and it turned out to be a dream race for Speedworks, Huff heading Moffat and Cook in a podium lock-out.

Sutton retained the championship lead heading into round four at Thruxton, where Ingram bagged pole ahead of his 100th race with EXCELR8. A poor start by Ingram in race one allowed Hill to blast into the lead from the second row, and he went on to take a third victory ahead of Cammish and Sutton, Ingram battling back to fourth.

Then Ingram stormed to the front of the field to win race two, only to be penalised after the chequered flag for gaining an unfair advantage with a move on Cammish. That dropped him to third, while Hill inherited the win, giving him the championship lead ahead of the reverse-grid finale, where Sutton scored a 40th career victory.

The season hit the halfway stage at Oulton Park, where again Ingram scored pole before taking race-one honours following a wheel-to-wheel battle with Sutton. In race two, Cook took full advantage of his tyre strategy to charge to victory from eighth on the grid, ahead of Ingram and Hill. The latter secured the points lead with victory in race three, passing Mikey Doble on the final lap to prevent him from taking a maiden BTCC win.

The action resumed after the break at Croft, where Turkington scored his 70th career win in the opening race, having qualified on pole. Turkington was removed from the fight for victory in race two following early contact with Sutton, the win going the way of Cook after an impressive battle with Huff at the front.

Hill failed to score after a clash with Chilton, and the Hyundai man went on to win the reverse-grid final race. Team-mate Ingram ended the weekend with two podiums to his name, allowing him to retake the points lead.

Ingram was on the back foot after the opening race at Knockhill, however, when he was forced to retire, while Turkington won again from pole. With Ingram starting down the order in race two, Hill – in his 250th start – took full advantage with a comfortable victory that gave him the points lead once again. Ingram picked up second behind Huff in race three, however, to move back into the top spot, three points clear as they headed to the Donington GP layout.

Cook took pole in qualifying, with Ingram and Hill in fifth and seventh, but it was Turkington who jumped into the lead at the start of race one and picked up his fifth win of the year, with Sutton and Hill giving chase. Ingram dropped outside the top ten after early contact, but had come through to fifth by the finish.

Then Ingram retired from race two after his radiator was holed by a stone, Sutton scoring his second win of the season from Turkington and Hill. That moved Sutton up into second in the standings, behind Hill, but Ingram recovered with a stunning drive in race three as he came from 19th on the grid to second behind Cammish. Hill now held the points lead with two rounds left.

At Silverstone, Ingram claimed a wet pole after Taylor-Smith had been excluded. The two title contenders engaged in a frenetic battle in the opening race, Ingram emerging victorious, but Hill gained the upper hand with the race-two win, while Ingram had slipped to fourth. The soaking-wet finale had to be halted at one stage due to the conditions, but eventually it was run the full distance and was won by Ingram to draw level with Hill at the top.

Effectively, that meant a winner-takes-all finale at Brands Hatch, and it was advantage Ingram after

qualifying when he had taken second behind Turkington, with Hill sixth. Things changed early in race one, however, as Ingram was forced wide at Druids and dropped down the order, while Hill jumped up to second behind Turkington. The team-mates duly swapped positions and Hill took a vital win, Ingram recovering to third.

When Ingram won race two, thanks to early moves on the two BMW drivers, the gap at the top came down to a single point, and he appeared to have the upper hand in the early stages of the finale in his quest for a second title. The mixed weather conditions worked against the Hyundai driver, however, and he had to settle for sixth, while Hill had risen to second, behind race winner Sutton, to secure a popular championship crown.

"This is everything that I have ever wanted, and I can't believe that the dream has finally come true," Hill said. "For so many years, it has been a battle to even be part of the grid, but this makes those battles worthwhile.

"The season has been hard fought from the start, and the fact that there was just one point in it going into race three was pretty fitting. To come out on top is fantastic, and crossing the line knowing I was BTCC champion is an experience that I'll never forget."

Hill's title win helped BMW to secure the manufacturers' crown, although NAPA Racing UK emerged victorious as the leading team. The remaining titles went the way of Power Maxed Racing, with Taylor-Smith and Doble winning the Independents' title and the Jack Sears Trophy.

The big news going into the winter was the departure of the hybrid system after three years, the series revealing that instead it would switch to 100 per cent sustainable fuel and utilise turbo boost to give drivers additional power during races.

Above: Lamborghinis to the fore as Maximilian Paul (71) and Mirko Bortolotti head the pack at Zandvoort.

Top right: Sheldon van der Linde took his Schubert Motorsports BMW to a win at the Nürburgring.

Top far right: Team-mate René Rast was slightly more successful, taking two wins on his way to fifth in the overall standings.

Above right: Winners all. Nicki Thiim at Norisring; Thomas Preining at Lausitz; and Luca Engstler at Oschersleben.

Right: Luca Stolz leads the Mercs of Arjun Maini and Maro Engel at Sachsenring.

Photos: DTM/GroupeC Photography

DEUTSCHE TOURENWAGEN MASTERS

The 2024 DTM season was the fourth to be run under GT3 rules, with the ADAC organising the championship once again, having taken over the previous year following the collapse of ITR.

Thomas Preining returned to defend his title with Manthey Racing and Porsche, joining a reduced grid of 20 cars, several teams having bowed out over the winter.

Manthey was the only one of the three Porsche outfits from 2023 to return, while both Audi and BMW were also represented by single teams after the likes of Team Engstler and Project 1 Racing had departed. Mercedes had lost a team when Team Landgraf withdrew, although there was the addition of a new name, as McLaren joined the grid alongside the Dorr Motorsport squad.

Despite the various team changes, McLaren racer Ben Dorr was the only true rookie, the top six from the previous campaign all returning with the same team and car combinations as in 2023.

Others, such as Luca Engstler and Maro Engel found new homes, which meant that there was no shortage of experience on the grid as the teams prepared for the season to kick off at Oschersleben, where a number of new regulations also came into force. One change meant that any stop carried out during either a full-course caution or a safety-car period would no longer count towards the mandatory pit-stop requirements, which would prove important in the opening rounds.

Ferrari racer Jack Aitken had the honour of topping the first qualifying session of the new season, and the Brit had appeared to be cruising to victory until everything was turned on its head by a safety car to allow the recovery of Dorr's McLaren. Marco Wittmann dived in just before the safety car was deployed to vault into the lead, having started near the back of the grid. However, he slowed with a fuel-pressure issue late on, handing victory to Aitken, ahead of Mirko Bortolotti and Ricardo Feller.

Aitken failed to complete a lap in race two after being caught up in an incident at Turn Two. The win went to Engstler, on his debut weekend with the Grasser Racing squad, after a well-timed pit stop – and issues in the pits for fellow Lamborghini man Bortolotti, who had led the early stages.

Defending champion Preining had endured a tough start to the campaign, but he returned to form to kick-start his championship challenge at the Lausitzring, although he was edged off pole for the opening race by Kelvin van der Linde's Audi, the top three being covered by just 0.025s.

Van der Linde converted pole into victory in the opening race, which was stopped twice because of poor weather conditions, before Preining beat the South African in race two for the first win of his title defence. That wasn't without drama, however, the Schubert squad questioning the move that had allowed the Porsche to get ahead on track.

While van der Linde led the championship standings, his advantage at the top was cut during the opening race at Zandvoort, where Aitken dominated from pole to become the first double winner of the season, ahead of René Rast and Arjun Maini. By contrast, van der Linde was outside the top ten in 13th, a result that would be his lowest finish of the season.

As he had done in the opening round, Wittmann employed a masterful strategy to put himself in contention for victory in race two, but this time he was able to pull it off, scoring his first win of the year from Bortolotti and

Above: The pack jostles for position at Norisring as the Mercedes of Arjun Maini (36) and Lucas Auer (22) squeeze the Audi of Ricardo Feller.

Top right: Consistency paid dividends for Mirko Bortolotti, who won just one race, but took to the podium on five other occasions to clinch the championship.

Above right: Maro Engel emerged as Mercedes' best-placed runner to take third overall in the series.

Above far right: Kelvin van der Linde upheld Audi's honour by scoring three wins and taking second place in the championship.
Photos: DTM/GroupeC Photography

Right: Will Brown beat Triple Eight team-mate Broc Feeney to become Supercar champion in Australia.
Photo: Mark Horsburgh/LAT Images

van der Linde. That was despite a scare shortly after his mandatory stop, when contact with Bortolotti damaged the BMW, although Wittmann eased away in the closing stages for a comfortable win.

The annual trip to the Norisring marked the halfway stage of the season, with challenging weather conditions in the opening race making strategy key. Heavy rain during the latter stages prompted many to dive in for wet rubber, but an inspired call to remain out on slicks made the difference for Rast and Franck Perera as they battled for the lead when the rain stopped. Rast came out on top to win; Engstler, more than half a minute behind the pair, was third.

Race two was dry and ended in victory for Nicki Thiim, making him the first son of a DTM winner also to make it on to the top step of the podium. He had held off Engel and Bortolotti after a late safety-car period, the latter inheriting the championship lead after van der Linde could only manage to finish tenth.

The battle between the pair intensified at the Nürburgring, with van der Linde dominating the opening race to beat his rival by more than 15s, having led all but three laps in tricky wet conditions. That put the Audi man a point clear going into race two, where brother Sheldon scored his first win of 2024 after a race-long battle with Engel, which had ended in his favour when the German suffered a half-spin mid-race following contact with Rast. Engel was still able to take second, with Wittmann third, while van der Linde outscored Bortolotti to extend his championship lead to seven points before the trip to the Sachsenring.

Aitken beat Bortolotti to victory in the opening race as the Italian reclaimed the championship lead, but his time at the top only lasted for 24 hours until van der Linde secured the same result in race two, crossing the line behind Mercedes driver Luca Stolz.

Both drivers had benefited from an unfortunate penalty for Thierry Vermeulen, which resulted in him being called back into the pits while leading. Seventh for Bortolotti meant that the gap at the top remained as it had been going into the weekend. Two top-five finishes for Engel put him third in the standings in what realistically was a three-way title battle across the final rounds – the next five drivers were split by just six points.

The see-saw battle at the top continued apace at the Red Bull Ring, where Bortolotti came from fourth on the grid to win race one on a damp, but drying circuit, despite the best efforts of Engel to get ahead. With van der Linde back in eighth after a difficult qualifying session, the Italian suddenly found himself leading the standings by ten points, following a race that he described as being one of the best of his life.

Although he was unable to convert pole position in race two, which was won by Rast from Preining, Bortolotti again finished ahead of van der Linde to extend his advantage further – 15 points clear of the South African and 20 ahead of Engel going into the season finale.

Bortolotti went into race one knowing that he could lift the title if the result went his way, but instead it was van der Linde who battled his way to a crucial victory, having topped the times in qualifying. The Audi man diced with Lucas Auer's Mercedes throughout before taking maximum points, moving two points ahead of Bortolotti in the standings when he could only take fifth.

Fourth for Engel left him in contention on the final day of the season, when Bortolotti retook the points lead by topping qualifying for three bonus points. Van der Linde had lined up in fifth, but a poor start, and the additional ballast he was obliged to carry, meant that he was unable to match the pace of his rival as Bortolotti followed Engstler home for a second-place finish that wrapped up the title.

"After finishing fourth and second in the past two years, there was a lot of pressure," Bortolotti said. "However, we

did it with our great team. I have been with Lamborghini through thick and thin for ten years, and with this title, I have been able to pay back a little of the trust that they have placed in me."

An unchanged calendar has been confirmed for the 2025 season, when the grid will include at least one new model, HRT Ford Performance bringing the Mustang GT3 to the series. An Evo version of the BMW M4 is also likely to feature, having been revealed midway through the season, but Audi looks set to depart, long-time partner Abt having announced a switch to Lamborghini.

SUPERCARS CHAMPIONSHIP

Down under, the Supercars Championship entered a new era after the departure of triple champion Shane van Gisbergen to NASCAR, his place being taken at Triple Eight by Will Brown, who had left Erebus Motorsport to join the Chevrolet squad.

Erebus had secured the title with Brodie Kostecki in 2023, but when the season got under way in February at Bathurst, he wasn't on the grid, the defending champion sitting out the opening two meetings of the year.

That effectively set up a battle for a new champion, and it was Brown and team-mate Broc Feeney who made the early running by sharing the opening five wins of the year, before Nick Percat sprung a surprise at Albert Park by carrying Matt Stone Racing to victory, ending a personal win drought going back four years.

A first visit to Taupō resulted in a popular win for Kiwi racer Andre Heimgartner, before Brown scored his third win of the campaign to hold a 71-point lead a third of the way into the campaign.

While it would be nearly five months before Brown returned to the top step of the podium, astonishing consistency made him the man to beat in the standings. By the time the series prepared to head for the first endurance event of the campaign, at Sandown, he had only failed to finish on the podium four times in 18 starts.

It meant that Brown was 81 points clear of Chaz Mostert, who had won three times over the summer for Walkinshaw Andretti United to reel in the championship leader, with Feeney having slipped back to third, nearly 200 points behind.

Sandown would be a crucial race in the title hunt, however, with Brown storming to victory alongside Scott Pye, while Feeney took second in a Triple Eight 1-2. With Mostert back in seventh, the gap at the front grew by more than 100 points.

Then Feeney finished second, behind Kostecki at Bathurst – with Brown third – to reclaim second in the standings behind his team-mate. By the end of the weekend at Surfers Paradise, the title fight had come down to two, a tough pair of races for Mostert having knocked him out of contention.

Even then, the title was very much Brown's to lose, and while Feeney was victorious in the opening race of the weekend in Adelaide, Brown followed him home to secure a maiden Supercars crown – adding the title to an impressive resumé that already included success in both Australian F4 and TCR Australia.

The 2025 season will feature a much changed grid and an increased number of races. The first eight rounds will be run as the Sprint Cup, while the Enduro Cup will cover a new endurance event at The Bend as well as Bathurst. At that point, ten drivers – including the winners of the Sprint and Enduro Cups – will battle for the title across the final three events in a system similar to that operated by NASCAR.

Looking further ahead, in 2026, the number of manufacturers involved in the series is set to expand to three for the first time since 2019, Toyota joining the grid with the GR Supra in collaboration with WAU.

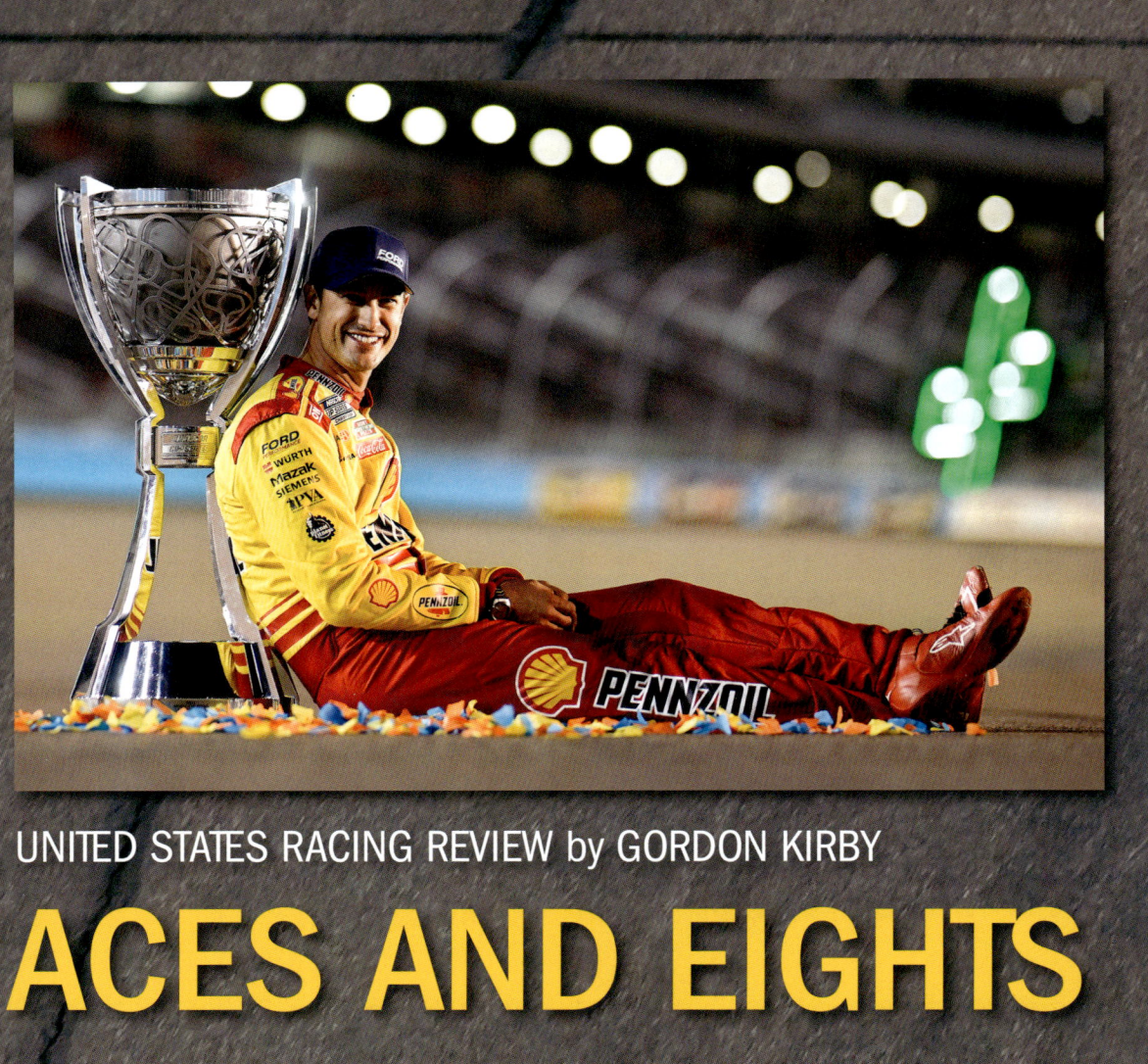

UNITED STATES RACING REVIEW by GORDON KIRBY

ACES AND EIGHTS

Above: Josh Berry, in the No.4 Stewart-Haas Racing Ford Mustang, flips as a precursor to a massive crash that unfolded at Daytona International Speedway in August.

Top right: Kyle Larson won six races, more than anyone else, during the season with Rick Hendrick's Chevrolet Camaro.
Photos: Nigel Kinrade/NKP/LAT Images

Above right: Ryan Blaney, who lost out to Penske team-mate Joey Logano at the end of the 36-race NASCAR season.
Photo: Matthew T. Thacker/NKP/LAT Images

Right: Crash-fests on superspeedways, such as Talladega shown here, became ever more common.
Photo: Nigel Kinrade/NKP/LAT Images

Opening spread: Penske pair Logano (*inset*) and Blaney (12) battled for the title, ending the championship 1-2 and separated by just five points.
Photos: Nigel Kinrade/NKP/LAT Images

AS I've written many times before, NASCAR might not be quite what it was at its height 20 years ago, but it remains the most visible and successful form of American motor racing, enjoying large and very competitive fields of some 40 cars. In an attempt to boost crowds and TV ratings, NASCAR has added road races to the Cup-series calendar in recent years. There are now five such races on the schedule, more than ever.

All 36 races are run with some form of engine air restrictor plates, first introduced at Daytona and Talladega back in 1988. The plates were replaced a few years ago by slightly more high-tech barrels, which were introduced over the past few years at all tracks. The air restrictors cut horsepower substantially, particularly on the big superspeedways – Daytona, Talladega and Atlanta – where NASCAR's big, production-based rocker-arm V8s produce barely 500bhp, half of what they can churn out in unrestricted form.

This makes races on the big tracks particularly close, with the entire field jammed together in a huge multi-car draft lapping some 30mph slower than in the days of yore. The downside to this is that there are often massive multi-car accidents, turning what are supposed to be the series' classic races into crash-fests or 'wreck-um' races. At 2024's fall race at Daytona, there was a 'big one' within a few laps of the chequered flag, which took out no fewer than 27 cars! Most were able to make it back to the pits for repairs and rejoined the race, but these huge accidents only serve to devalue NASCAR's image. They might be attractive to many hardcore NASCAR enthusiasts, but only compel other racing fans to turn up their noses at the series.

Joey Logano claims third NASCAR title, Penske's sixth

Joey Logano won his third NASCAR Cup championship in 2024. He and team-mate Ryan Blaney (defending Cup champion) finished 1-2 in the championship after scoring a sweep of the season finale at Phoenix. It was Penske's fourth NASCAR title in seven years and sixth in total, as well as being Team Penske's 46th national championship across a wide range of motor racing.

All four of Penske's Fords qualified for the 'Play Offs', run over the year's final six of 36 races. Logano, 2018 and '22 champion, won four races; 2023 champion Blaney scored three wins, while Austin Cindric won once. Harrison Burton also won once in the Wood Brothers satellite team.

"To win three championships is really special," Logano said. "What a team! We had a little adversity today and over the season, but the team always persevered. I don't know if I'm the best driver, but I've got the best team. Together, we're very well rounded and able to stand up when it really matters the most. We're a mentally tough team that can make things happen when it matters. I couldn't be more proud of everyone at the shop who build the cars. I don't think anyone works harder than our team and I'm glad we delivered today.

"To be able to race [Blaney] to the end was fun," Logano added. "I knew that he was going to be our toughest competition going into the weekend. I said that to our guys. I said, Blaney is going to have the speed. We've got to beat him on the details. That's where we have the

Above: The blue-riband Daytona 500 season-opener was won by William Byron in a Hendrick Motorsports Axalta Chevrolet Camaro.
Photo: John K. Harrelson/NKP/LAT Images

Top right: 23XI's Tyler Reddick, having led the regular-season standings, made the 'Play Offs'.

Top far right: Vastly experienced racer Denny Hamlin was always a factor with Joe Gibbs Racing's Toyota Camry.
Photos: Nigel Kinrade/NKP/LAT Images

Above right: Christopher Bell scored three wins to make the 'Play Offs', but not the final four.
Photo: Rusty Jarrett/NKP/LAT Images

Above far right: Byron fought with Penske duo Logano and Blaney to the very finish.

Right: The short oval at Bristol under lights exudes 'old school' charm.
Photos: Matthew T. Thacker/NKP/LAT Images

advantage over them. But the speed, he's got turned up pretty high."

The top 16 in points qualify for the 'Play Offs' and the field is whittled down through these closing races to four championship contenders going into the season finale at Phoenix in November. In 2024, the final four were Penske duo Blaney and Logano, plus Tyler Reddick, with 23XI Racing, and William Byron, Hendrick Motorsports.

Reddick was impressive in his second year with 23XI Racing and sixth year in NASCAR's premier Cup series, winning the regular season championship, which covered the year's first 30 races. He won two races during the regular season on the big speedways at Talladega and Michigan, and produced many top-five finishes before racing his way into the final four championship contenders by winning in impressive style at Homestead in October.

All four of Hendrick Motorsports Chevrolets qualified for the 'Play Offs'. Kyle Larson, 2021 champion, was often the man to beat, winning a season-high six races and shaping up as a top title contender, but he failed to make the final four. William Byron took three races and was very competitive in most others, also becoming a top contender. Byron was the only Hendrick driver to make the final four. He ran a strong race in the Phoenix season finale, finishing a close third behind Logano and Blaney. Chase Elliott, 2020 champion, and Alex Bowman in Hendrick's other Chevies also won a race apiece, but neither figured in the fight for the championship.

All four of Joe Gibbs's Toyotas made the 'Play Offs'. Christopher Bell and Denny Hamlin won three races apiece, while 2017 champion Martin Truex and Ty Gibbs made it into the top 16 in points without winning any. After 20 years in NASCAR, Truex announced in mid-summer that he would retire at season's end, although he planned to run the 2025 Daytona 500. Ty Gibbs is the grandson of team owner Joe Gibbs. He won the 2022 Xfinity championship and began racing in the Cup series full time the same year.

Others to win single races in 2024 were 2012 champion Brad Keselowski with one of Roush-Fenway-Keselowski's Fords, Daniel Suarez in a Trackhouse Racing Chevrolet, and Chase Briscoe driving one of Tony Stewart's three Fords. Stewart's team closed its doors at the end of the season, although Stewart himself planned to continue driving himself in NHRA drag racing. Partner Gene Haas aimed to run a one-car NASCAR team in 2025, with Cole Custer driving. Sixteen drivers won races in 2024, and among those who failed to qualify for the 'Play Offs' were two-times champion Kyle Busch, Ross Chastain, Bubba Wallace and Austin Dillon.

NASCAR's second-division Xfinity championship was won by Justin Alllgaier, driving a Chevrolet for Dale Earnhardt Jr's JR Motorsports. Veteran Allgaier had been racing Xfinity cars for 15 years and also won the championship in 2023.

The third-division Truck series championship was won by Ty Majewski, who wrapped up the title with a dominant win in the season finale.

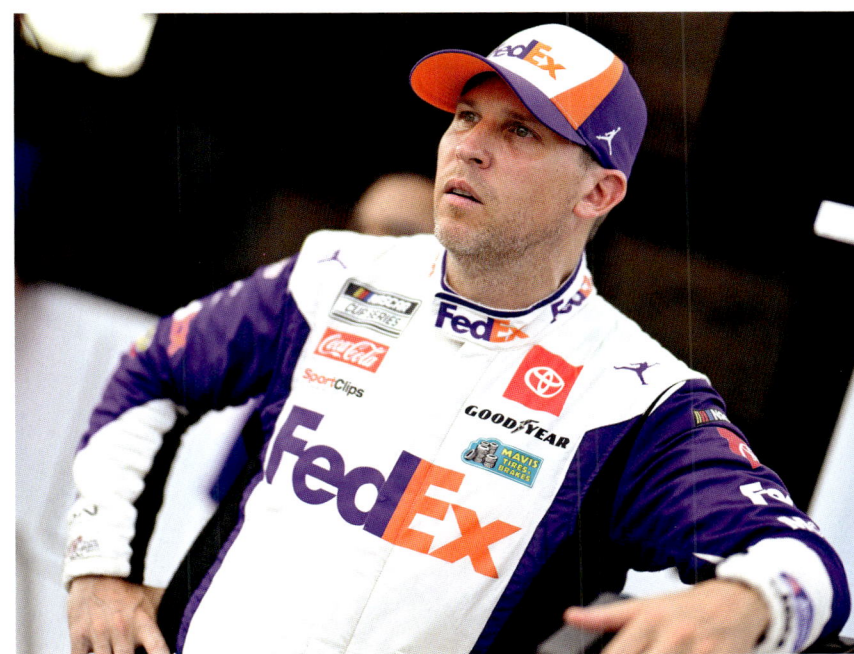

NASCAR sued for monopolist practices

TWO of NASCAR's top teams, 23XI Racing and Front Row Motorsports, have jointly filed an anti-trust suit against NASCAR and its CEO, Jim France, in the Western District of North Carolina. 23XI Racing is owned by retired NBA basketball star Michael Jordan, top NASCAR driver Denny Hamlin and Jordan's long-time business manager and partner, Curtis Polk. Front Row Motorsports is owned by Bob Jenkins, who operates a large chain of fast-food restaurants. Their suit alleges that NASCAR and its leadership have used anti-competitive practices that have prevented fair competition within the sport.

"We share a passion for racing, the thrill of competition, and winning," said a joint statement from 23XI Racing and Front Row Motorsports. "Off the racetrack, we share a belief that change is necessary for the sport we love. Together, we brought this anti-trust case so that racing can thrive and become a more competitive and fair sport in ways that will benefit teams, drivers, sponsors and most importantly, fans."

Added Jordan, "Everyone knows I have always been a fierce competitor, and that will to win is what drives me and the entire 23XI team each and every week out on the track. I love the sport of racing and the passion of our fans, but the way NASCAR is run today is unfair to teams, drivers, sponsors and fans. [Our] action shows we're willing to fight for a competitive market where everyone wins."

Commented Front Row owner Jenkins, "I can tell you, overwhelmingly, even the top-tier teams struggle to break even. If someone in the middle can figure out a way to make it work for them, it's awesome for them. But I don't think you can do that every single year."

The suit is the result of an ongoing dispute between the two teams and NASCAR over the sanctioning body's charter agreement. NASCAR and its

Above: Retired NBA basketball star Michael Jordan, one of the co-owners of 23XI Racing.
Photo: John K. Harrelson/NKP/LAT Images

Main: Nose-to-tail action is typical NASCAR fare for the fans.
Photo: Nigel Kinrade/NKP/LAT Images

teams have been debating the agreement for two years. The teams have argued for the charters to become permanent and for a larger share of NASCAR's revenues. 23XI Racing and Front Row Motorsports were the only two of 15 teams that did not sign the agreement on a deadline of early September.

The lawsuit states that the case "is about the unlawful monopolization of premier stock car racing by the France family in order to enrich themselves at the expense of the premier stock car racing teams that the fans come out to see and that sponsors and broadcasters value."

Jim France is the son of Bill France Jr and grandson of NASCAR founder Bill France Sr. The lawsuit might result in all parties having to turn over their financial records to the court, which would result in the disclosure of France's income. This has never been revealed. It's expected that it will be a year or more before the suit is heard in court.

The anti-competitive practices listed in the lawsuit are: NASCAR buying a majority of premier racetracks that are exclusive to NASCAR races; imposing exclusivity deals on NASCAR-sanctioned tracks; NASCAR acquiring a competitor, the ARCA Menards Series (which prevented it from growing into a more sustainable competitor, becoming instead a NASCAR feeder series); preventing teams from participating in other stock car racing series; NASCAR retaining ownership of Next Gen parts and pieces while forcing teams to buy those parts and pieces from NASCAR-chosen single-source suppliers.

The lawsuit continued, "The France family has used NASCAR to acquire and maintain a monopoly position over premier stock car racing teams through, among other anti-competitive actions, acquisitions of other racing circuits, racetracks, anti-competitive agreements that restrict the availability of racetracks that are suitable for premier stock car racing, monopoly rules regarding the exclusive use of specialized 'Next Gen' cars, and non-compete restrictions that prevent premier stock car teams competing in the Cup Series from also participating in races outside of NASCAR's circuit."

NASCAR's top teams have long depended on sponsorship rather than prize money to fund their operations. Two years ago, four-times champion Jeff Gordon, now vice chairman of Hendrick Motorsports, said that the team had not made a profit for many years. At the same time, NASCAR has benefited from television rights deals that have increased steadily over the past 20 years. A new TV contract begins in 2025 with FOX Sports, NBC Sports, TNT Sports and Amazon. 23XI and Front Row Motorsports' lawsuit claims that NASCAR's broadcast deals have totalled $23.1 billion.

NASCAR first implemented a charter system in 2016. Included in the original agreement was a provision that the teams would not compete in other professional racing series. This provision was expanded in the 2025 charter agreement to prevent any team "from participating in any 'automobile or truck racing' series not sanctioned by NASCAR."

23XI and Front Row are at risk of losing their charters, valued at between $30 million and $50 million. The two teams are seeking an injunction to prevent NASCAR from taking possession of their charters.

Well-known anti-trust attorney Jeffrey Kessler is representing 23XI and Front Row Motorsports. Kessler has worked on a number of landmark anti-trust cases, including the creation of NFL free agency, the implementation of commercial deals in the NCAA and obtaining equal pay for the US women's national soccer team.

The suit concluded with the following declaration: "A competitive market will enable the teams to earn the reasonable profits that are necessary for them to re-invest in their businesses and create an even more exciting product for stock car racing fans, sponsors and broadcasters. The France family and NASCAR are monopolistic bullies. And bullies will continue to impose their will to hurt others until their targets stand up and refuse to be victims. The moment has now arrived."

Above: Alex Palou celebrates his third IndyCar title in four seasons at Nashville.

Top right: Penske's Scott McLaughlin was a factor throughout the year, winning three times, including a race on the oval at Iowa.

Above right: Scott Dixon's mastery of fuel strategy paid dividends, as he secured wins at both Detroit and Long Beach.

Right: Palou claimed the win at Laguna Seca and earlier had won on the Indianapolis road course, but his amazing consistency brought him another title.

Photos: IndyCar/Penske Entertainment Corp.

Palou's third IndyCar title

Alex Palou continued to show outstanding form by winning his third IndyCar championship in four years. The 27-year-old Spaniard won two of 17 championship races and was a little less dominant than in previous years, but he remained the man to beat as he scored Chip Ganassi Racing's 16th CART/IRL/IndyCar championship. Palou is an exceptionally smooth, consistent driver who never seems to get upset or disgruntled and appears destined to become one of IndyCar's most successful drivers ever.

After racing for three years in a variety of European and Japanese small formula cars, Palou broke into IndyCar in 2020 with Dale Coyne's small outfit. He joined Ganassi's top-ranked team in 2021 and went on to win the championship in his first year. He took the title again in 2023 and 2024, and has emerged as IndyCar's best overall driver.

He won the non-championship race at the Thermal Club road course in southern California, and scored two more wins on the Indianapolis road course in May and at Laguna Seca in June. No more wins followed over the summer, however, and Palou hit some bad luck near the end of the season in the second of two races at Milwaukee, where his car suffered an electrical failure at the start. The race was 30 laps old before Palou could rejoin and make it home a distant 19th, salvaging a handful of points from the day. He wrapped up his third title by finishing a lap down in 11th in the season-closer on the 1.3-mile Nashville Speedway, while his primary championship rival, Will Power, lost five laps in the pits fixing an errant seat belt.

"I have to thank everybody on the race team and back at the shop for all the work they did over the season," Alex said. "They pay attention to all the details. It's an amazing team and we've had an amazing year. We only won three races and it was hectic towards the end of the season. We didn't maximise what we had at some races, like Iowa, where I did a mistake and crashed, and Mid-Ohio, where I could have won, but finished second to Pato [O'Ward]. We can improve from here next year."

Team boss Ganassi has great respect for Palou. "Alex never breaks a sweat," he said. "It's amazing, the way he drives. He joined our team three years ago and won his first race with us at Alabama, and it's been smooth sailing ever since."

The only fly in the ointment was the dispute that had raged over Palou's contract in 2023 with Ganassi and McLaren's Zak Brown. Brown had signed Palou to an F1 testing contract in 2022, but an argument over the contract's details erupted in 2023. At the time of writing (late 2024), Palou and Brown had agreed to seek a settlement through arbitration.

Ganassi ran no fewer than five Honda-powered Indy cars in 2024. Six-times champion Scott Dixon finished sixth in points and won two races, at Long Beach and Detroit, both on keen fuel strategy, one of Dixon's many strong suits. Kiwi Marcus Armstrong ran well in many races and finished 14th in points. Swede Linus Lundqvist

came home 16th and won IndyCar's rookie-of-the-year award, earning a podium finish at the Gateway oval in August. Kyffin Simpson drove Ganassi's fifth car and was 21st in points.

Colton Herta beat Penske drivers Scott McLaughlin and Will Power to second in IndyCar's championship by scoring a well-deserved win in the Nashville season finale. Herta had established himself as Andretti Global's lead driver, but he had an uneven year in 2024. He was very competitive in some races, but a midfielder in others, although he was dominant in his two wins of the year at Toronto and Nashville. The latter was Herta's first on an oval in over six years of racing Indy cars.

Kyle Kirkwood was Andretti's second most successful driver in 2024. He didn't win any races, but was a front-runner in many of them and finished seventh in points. He qualified on pole for the Nashville season-closer. Marcus Ericsson, the 2022 Indy 500 winner, moved from Ganassi to Andretti in 2024, but was a midfielder in most races, finishing 15th in points.

Team Penske's three drivers won eight races, more than any other team, with Scott McLaughlin beating Will Power to third in championship points. Both McLaughlin and Power won three races, while Newgarden won twice. Power was able to challenge Palou for the championship, but a spin on a late restart at Milwaukee and a pit stop to fix an unfastened lap belt in the Nashville season-closer knocked the Aussie veteran out of championship contention.

Newgarden won the season-opener at St Petersburg, with McLaughlin and Power finishing third and fourth, but the following month, they were all disqualified and fined after it was discovered that they had illegally used IndyCar's new KERS battery during the St Pete race. The team had tested the KERS system a few weeks earlier, but had left it in place for the race. IndyCar's very basic KERS system wasn't approved for use until Mid-Ohio in July. Penske's team claimed it had been an inadvertent error on their part.

Newgarden was particularly vocal about the matter, which left a bad taste in the mouths of the majority of their competitors and many fans. It was the worst black

mark against his team's name that Roger Penske could ever imagine.

Fifth in championship points was Pato O'Ward, who led McLaren's IndyCar team and won three races, at St Petersburg (following Newgarden's disqualification), Mid-Ohio and Milwaukee. O'Ward was very competitive in many races, but also produced some mediocre runs that prevented him from mounting a championship challenge.

Alexander Rossi had an undistinguished year in one of McLaren's Indy cars, finishing tenth in points, and had not signed a 2024 contract when AUTOCOURSE closed for press. Callum Ilott, Théo Pourchaire and Nolan Siegal shared a third McLaren entry. NASCAR star Kyle Larson made his IndyCar debut in the Indy 500 aboard a fourth McLaren entry and acquitted himself well. After qualifying an impressive fifth, he completed all 200 laps and finished 18th.

Santino Ferrucci had some good races and finished ninth in points, driving for A.J. Foyt's team. Ferrucci re-signed with Foyt to partner David Malukas in 2025. Malukas and Felix Rosenqvist drove for Meyer-Shank Racing in 2024. Both had some competitive races, but achieved little in terms of strong finishes.

Dane Christian Lundgaard was Rahal-Letterman-Lanigan's strongest card in 2024, finishing 11th in points. Graham Rahal and Pietro Fittipaldi drove RLL's other cars, but achieved few results to speak of.

The IndyCar manufacturer's championship was won for the third year in a row by Chevrolet, who beat Honda through the strength of the Penske and McLaren teams.

Newgarden's wins consecutive Indy 500s

The 108th running of the Indianapolis 500 was delayed for almost four hours because of thunderstorms, and the sun was beginning to set when the chequered flag finally flew. But the assembled multitude was treated to an excellent race, Josef Newgarden scoring a very satisfying second consecutive Indy 500 victory by outduelling Pato O'Ward with a superb pass around the outside on the race's last turn to win by a few car lengths. O'Ward finished a deeply disappointed second, just ahead of Scott Dixon and Alexander Rossi.

Newgarden had won the previous year's 500 after a duel with Marcus Ericsson, but there was some controversy surrounding the restart procedure and debate of the legality of the Penske driver going below the track's inner white line on the run to the chequered flag from Turn Four. There was no controversy in 2024, however, and the 33-year old celebrated as he had the previous year by climbing into the grandstands among the fans before going to victory circle.

"There's no better way to win a race than that," Newgarden grinned. "I've got to give it to Pato. He's an incredibly clean driver, and it takes two people to race like that. He could easily have won this race, too. We just had things go our way, and I'm so proud of the whole team and the great work they did all month."

Newgarden qualified on the outside of the front row, beside team-mates Scott McLaughlin and Will Power. Between them, Newgarden and McLaughlin led 90 of the race's 200 laps, with McLaughlin ultimately finishing just two seconds behind his team-mate. Power had an undistinguished race, failing to lead any laps and crashing at three-quarter-distance.

O'Ward qualified on the third row and led some laps in the race's early stages before falling back in traffic. But he recovered well and battled fiercely for the lead in the closing laps. He took the lead at the start of the final lap, eliciting a giant roar from the grandstands, but Newgarden got a good tow from him down the back straight before making the winning pass.

"It's hard to put into words," a devastated O'Ward said. "I'm proud of the work we did today. We recovered, we went back, we went forward, we went back. Some people were driving like maniacs. We had so many near race-enders and we were so close to winning again. I put that car through things I never thought it would be able to do and somehow it came out the other end of the corner."

O'Ward had finished an equally close second to Marcus Ericsson in the 2022 running of the renowned race. "Oh man!" he added. "It's so painful when you put so much into it and then you're two corners short. This place owes me nothing, but it's such a heartbreak when you come so close, especially when it's not the first time and you don't know how many other opportunities like that you will have."

Dixon passed Rossi to take third place with two laps to go, while Ganassi team-mate Alex Palou had an unspectacular 500 to beat McLaughlin to fifth place. Thus he retained his championship points lead, tied with Dixon at that stage of the season.

Above: The white flag is shown and the last-lap drama is about to unfold. McLaren's Pato O'Ward leads Penske's Josef Newgarden over the line.

Top left: Tears of joy for the winner as Newgarden cradles his baby son in Victory Lane.

Above left: Just tears for O'Ward, who again had victory elude him in the Indy 500.

Above far left: Scott McLaughlin took pole at the Speedway for Penske, but had to settle for third place.

Left: O'Ward had the consolation of three wins in a strong season, which included the first race in the Milwaukee double-header.

Photos: IndyCar/Penske Entertainment Corp.

Colton Herta

Marcus Ericsson

Scott Dixon

Kyle Kirkwood

Rinus Veekay

Christian Lundgaard

Linus Lundqvist

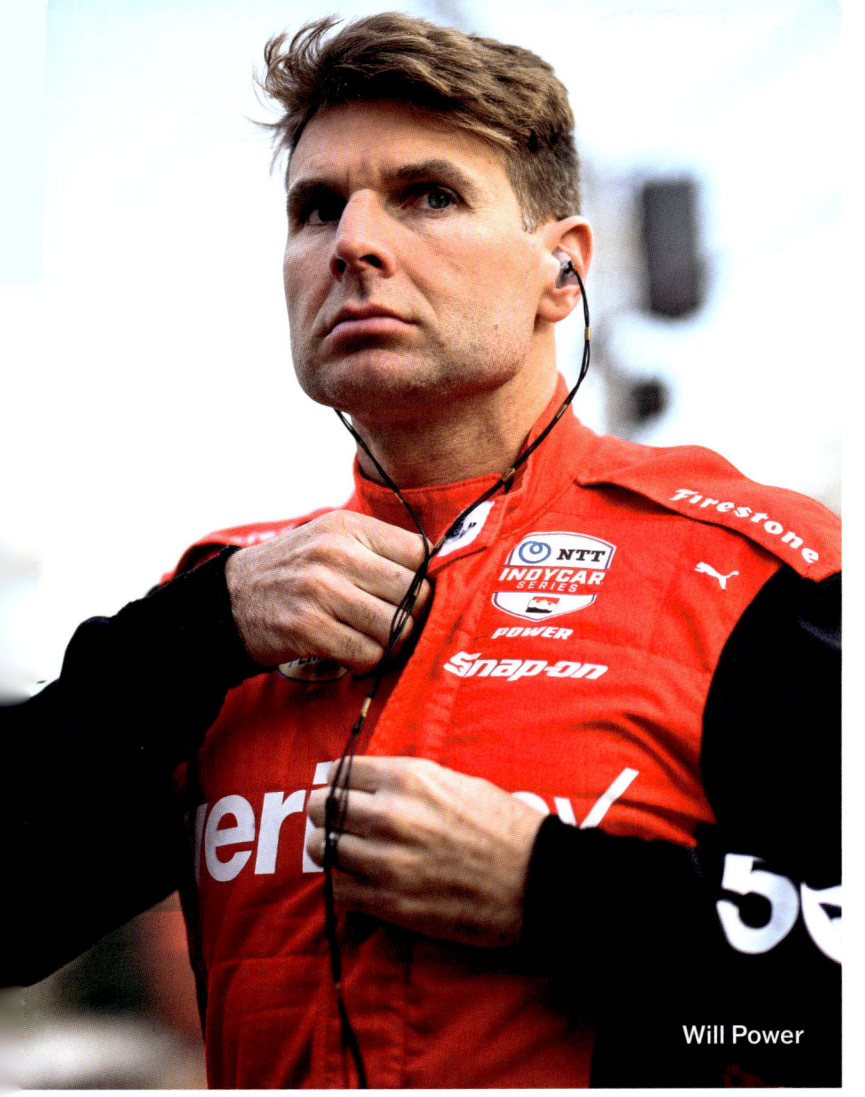

Will Power

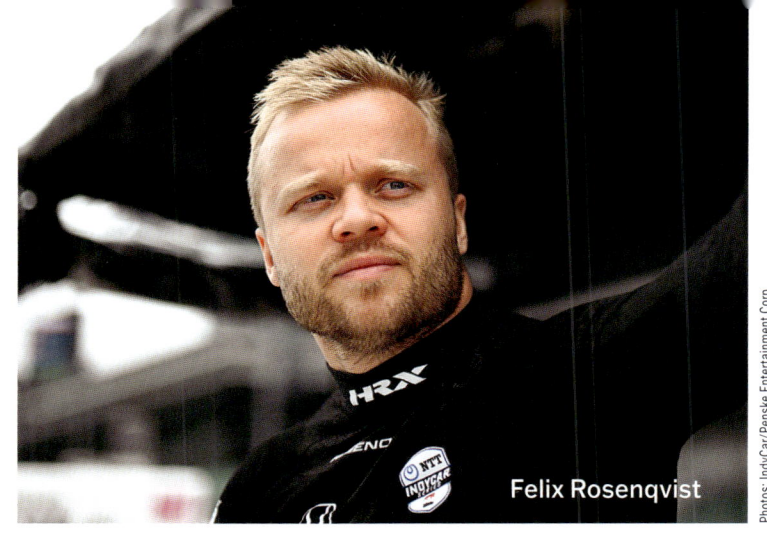

Felix Rosenqvist

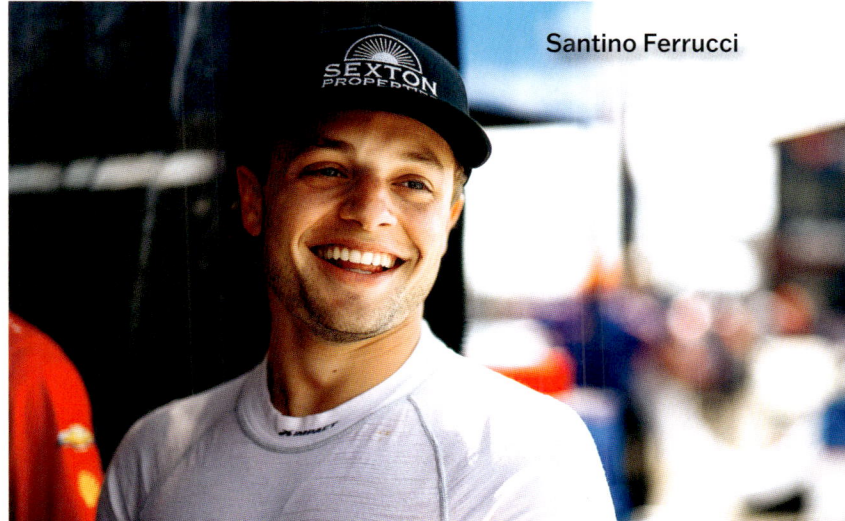

Santino Ferrucci

Photos: IndyCar/Penske Entertainment Corp.

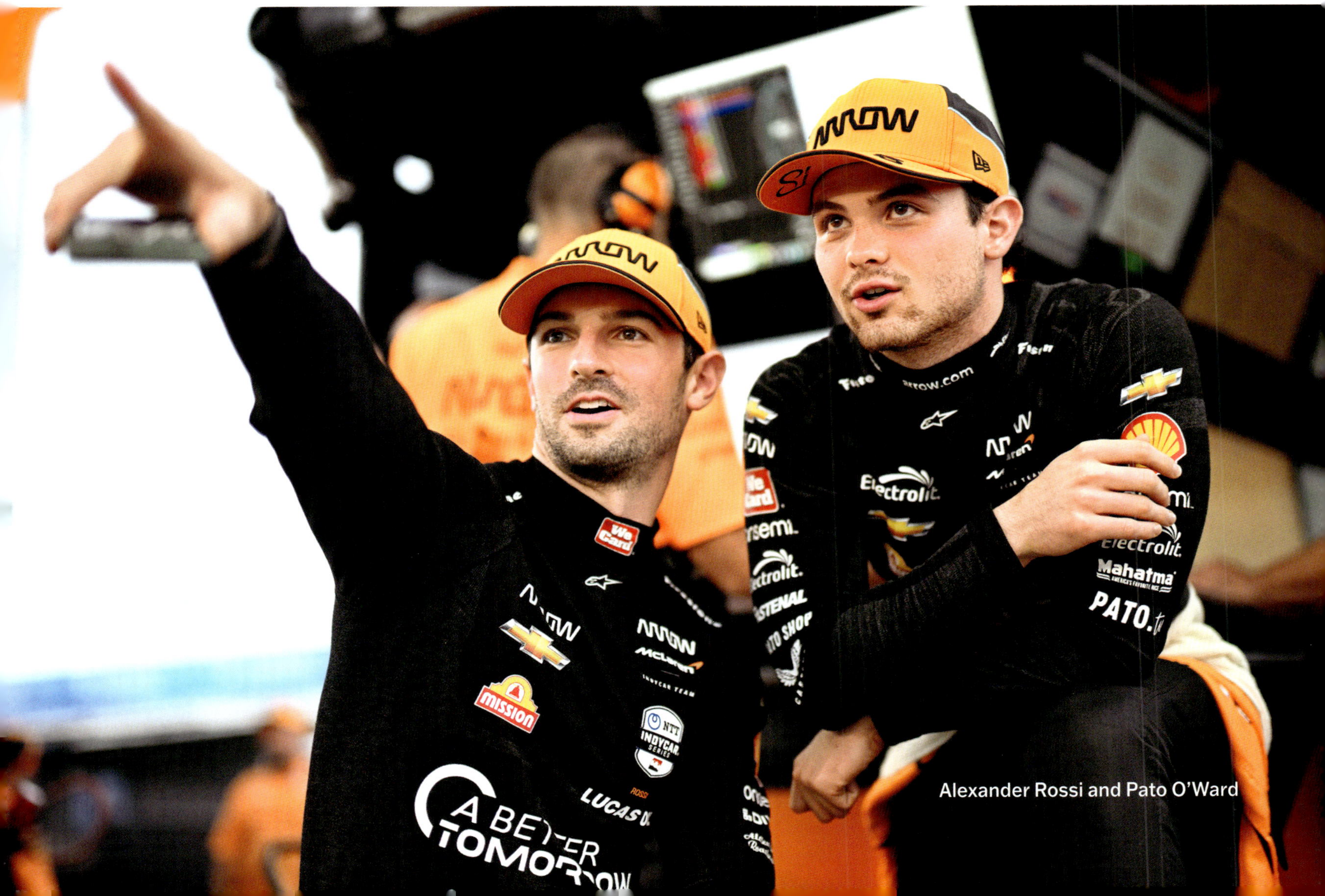

Alexander Rossi and Pato O'Ward

Above: Teams pitched up for an open test at the Milwaukee Mile in the Wisconsin State Fair Park. Even the well-heeled Penske team worked in makeshift conditions. Not very F1.

Top right: Series stalwart Ed Carpenter relies on outside sponsorship for much of his team's budget.

Above right: Serial championship winner Chip Ganassi believes in the charter system for the future health of IndyCar and its teams.

Right: The year marked the end of a dream for Michael Andretti.

Photos: IndyCar/Penske Entertainment Corp.

IndyCar's charter system revealed

Two weeks after the end of the season, IndyCar announced its long-discussed charter system. Starting in 2025, ten teams will be granted charters that will guarantee their cars starting positions in all races save the Indy 500. The charters will also grant the teams participation in IndyCar's Leaders Circle programme, which pays financial rewards to the top 22 finishers in the previous year's points standings. No details of the prize money involved were announced. The charters will also enable the teams to sell investors partnerships in their operations.

Five of the teams will be granted three charters, allowing them to run three cars each; the remaining five will have two charters, allowing them to run two cars each. The three-car teams are Chip Ganassi Racing, Andretti Global, Arrows McLaren, Rahal Letterman Lanigan Racing and Team Penske. The two-car teams are A.J. Foyt Enterprises, Dale Coyne Racing, Juncos Hollinger Racing and Meyer Shank Racing.

It took more than a year of occasionally contentious discussion between IndyCar and its teams to reach agreement on the charter system. Most team owners were effusive in their praise of the charters, but there were some critical words as well.

"When you look back on the modern era of IndyCar racing," said Chip Ganassi, "you will look at a few important moments, the first being the unification of the sport [in 2009], the next being Roger Penske buying the IndyCar series and the IMS, and I truly believe the third will be the charter system."

The day after the announcement, Ed Carpenter announced that his team will partner with and be sponsored by Ted Gelov's Indianapolis-based Heartland Food Products Group. "I don't know that this would be possible without the help of the charter programme," Carpenter said.

McLaren CEO Zak Brown welcomed the charter system, but said that more needs to be done. "We must ensure the financial viability for all the teams," Brown wrote in an open letter to IndyCar. "The charter system is a step in the right direction, but a lot more can be done to lift the sport to new heights. In my view, what's presented doesn't really move the dial.

"We need a structure that aligns the teams with the growth of the series, so perhaps we should look at evolving the charter system into a true franchise model with a defined revenue-sharing stream that ensures long-term viability for the competitors."

Brown went on to list many areas where IndyCar can improve. He began with the calendar, which he believes should be expanded with a race or two in the Northeastern US, and additional races in Canada, Mexico and Brazil. He also suggested standardising the format for race weekends, much like Formula 1, and believes that IndyCar can learn a lot from Liberty Media's takeover of F1. In addition, he considers that the time has come to replace IndyCar's aging Dallara DW12 'spec' chassis, introduced back in 2012. "A new chassis is essential to make the cars nimbler and more drivable," he wrote.

Andretti ousted

The last few years have been exciting, but challenging for Michael Andretti as he attempted to expand into Formula 1, but an unexpected new twist occurred near the end of September when his primary financial investor, Daniel Towriss, took control of what is now known as Andretti Global and pushed Michael to the sidelines.

Towriss is the CEO of Group 1001, an insurance and financial services company based in Zionsville, Indiana. He first became involved in IndyCar in 2018, sponsoring rookie Zach Veach in one of Andretti Autosport's four Indy cars. Zach was unable to forge a career in the class, however, and Towriss switched his support to Colton Herta's car, sponsored by Gainbridge Insurance. Then Towriss became a major investor in Andretti's team, and by 2021, he and Andretti were looking to buy an existing Formula 1 team.

They were spurned by F1's bosses, however, and in 2022, the team was rebranded as Andretti Global. Andretti Acquisitions Corporation was also created with a goal of raising $250 million to invest in a Formula 1 team. Cadillac was intended to be the team's F1 engine partner, but the effort continued to encounter political opposition from most of the F1 teams.

Towriss is said to have invested $250 million of his own money in Andretti Global, and rumours have circulated since the end of 2023 indicating that the relationship between Towriss and Andretti had become strained. With Michael's ousting, it's believed that Towriss will take over as team principal. A statement from Andretti Global suggested that Michael would take on an advisory and ambassadorial role.

"Michael's goal has been to transition to a more strategic role with Andretti Global and focus less on the operational side of the race team," the statement read. "Michael and Dan Towriss have been working closely on developing this new structure, one which Michael is excited to see take shape under Dan's guidance. Michael remains engaged and will continue to serve as a strategic advisor and key ambassador."

Andretti Global runs three cars in the IndyCar series as well as four Indy NXT cars. The team also bought Wayne Taylor's two-car IMSA squad in 2023 and is building a new large headquarters north of Indianapolis to house its fleet of teams and the proposed Formula 1 team. A shake-up in Andretti Global's management and organisation is expected in the wake of Towriss's takeover.

A week after being ousted, Michael Andretti wrote an open letter to his team's fans: "I was born a racer. From an early age, I didn't know anything different than life in the fast lane. Being a 'son of' – be it a proud one – came with a high bar and, once I pressed the gas, I never looked back. I stopped at nothing to find success. I drove for the passion and love of the sport, but I won for the fear of losing. My father's childhood dream became my destiny, and together we built a legacy and a family business.

"When my driving days slowed, I set my sights on creating a space that would inspire future drivers to go faster than I had. I believe that, together with the help of many very qualified and passionate team members, I have been able to do just that. For the past two decades, our team has seen the highest of highs and the lowest of lows. We've grown on a global level that I believe is still untouched in motorsport and we've seen some of the best talent in racing proudly wear the Andretti badge.

"Many of my best memories have come at the wheel of this organization, and I am so proud of what we have built. But decades of running flat out doesn't come without sacrifice and, after much thought and reflection over the past several months, I came to the decision to take a step back. I've had a day-to-day operational role since even before I stepped out of the race car, and it's time now

to pass the baton to my partner and friend, Dan Towriss.

"As I make this decision for myself, my family and this team, I know this is somewhat of a shock to many, especially you, the fans, my extended family. For many of you, you've watched me grow up, or you've grown up right alongside of me, and no matter what moves we've made as a team, you've stuck by our side at every turn. It is not lost on me that the generations of Andretti fans are the best in the business. I'm honored to be considered a fan favorite, a role model and a friend. And I thank you for a lifetime of support and, in some cases, your brutal honesty.

"But I am not going away – I will be serving as an advisor for the team and will be available to help wherever I can. While you might see me less at the racetrack, know that my passion for the sport and my support for our team, and its people, will remain unwavering.

"My hope is that you, as Andretti fans, will keep supporting our team with the same enthusiasm and loyalty that you've so graciously shown myself and my family over the years.

"I'm excited about the opportunity to spend more time with my beautiful family, including my 10-year-old twins, embrace my new Nonno title and explore new things on a personal level and with my other businesses. So, this isn't a goodbye. It is just the turning of the page."

Foster's Indy NXT title

Britain's Louis Foster was the man to beat in the Indy NXT (originally Indy Lights) series. He dominated the season, winning eight races and taking seven poles for Michael Andretti's team. Jacob Abel finished second to Foster, who was expected to graduate to IndyCar in 2025. Max Garcia won the US F2000 championship, while Leonardo Fornareli took the US Formula 3 championship and Nicolas Stati claimed the US Formula 4 title.

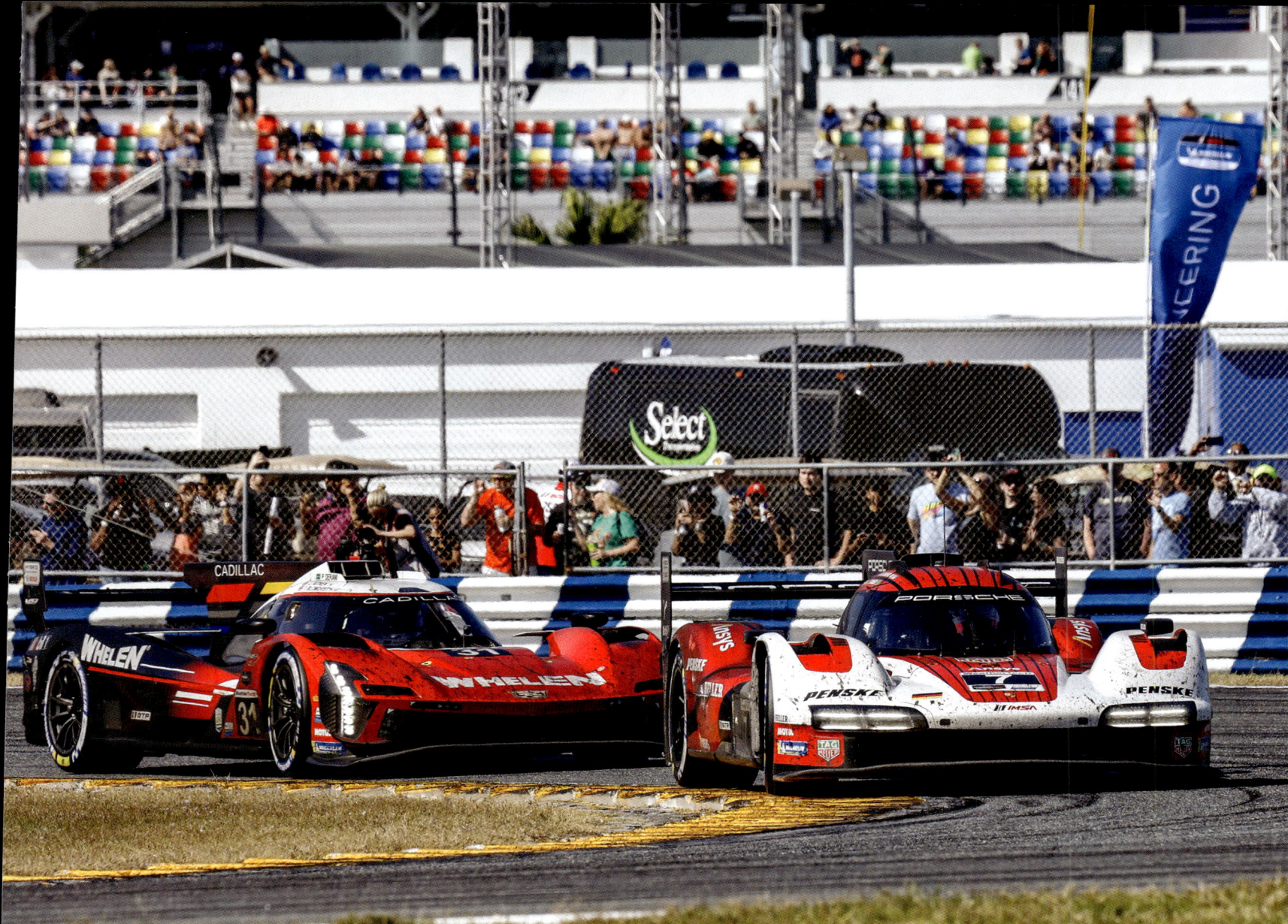

Penske's third outright IMSA championship

Team Penske won IMSA's WeatherTech Sports Car championship with drivers Dane Cameron and Felipe Nasr aboard one of a pair of Porsche 963s. Cameron and Nasr won two of the year's nine races, the Daytona 24 Hours season-opener and Watkins Glen's mid-summer Six Hours.

They were joined at Daytona by Matt Campbell and Josef Newgarden, and wrapped-up the championship by finishing third in the season-closing Petit Le Mans 10 Hours at Road Atlanta. Mathieu Jaminet and Nick Tandy completed a Penske sweep by finishing second in the championship. They also won two races at Laguna Seca and Elkhart Lake.

This was Team Penske's third overall IMSA championship, the team having previously won the DPi title in 2019 and '20. They also had won three consecutive LMP2 championships with Porsche in 2005, '06 and '07. The 2024 IMSA championship was Penske's 45th across all forms of motorsport, including USRRC, Trans Am, Can-Am, Indy cars, NASCAR and IMSA.

Third in 2024 points were Sébastien Bourdais and Renger van der Zande at the wheel of Chip Ganassi's Cadillac V Series R. They were joined in the longer races by IndyCar star Scott Dixon. Bourdais and van der Zande also won two races at Long Beach in the spring and the Petit Le Mans season finale. Van der Zande took the Petit Le Mans win by passing Nick Tandy with just 15 minutes remaining. It was the first time that Ganassi's Cadillac had led the race and was a fitting finish to Ganassi's GTP programme.

Three other teams won races: Louis Delétraz, Colton Herta and Jordan Taylor won the Sebring 12 Hours aboard a Wayne Taylor/Andretti Acura AR-06; Felipe Albuquerque and Ricky Taylor claimed victory in Detroit's street race in another Wayne Taylor/Andretti Acura ARX-06; while Philip Eng and Jeff Krohn earned BMW's first GTP victory on the Indianapolis road course at the wheel of a Rahal-Letterman-Lanigan BMW M Hybrid V8. Lamborghini also ran a single-car GTP effort in 2024. Taylor's two-car team switches from Acura to Cadillac in 2025.

There was a total of 11 IMSA races in 2024, but two of them – at Mosport and Virginia International Raceway – were run without GTP cars, which were deemed too fast for those tracks. Lime Rock was dropped from IMSA's calendar in 2024 and replaced by the Indy road course. The typical IMSA race boasted between 40 and 50 starters, comprising nine GTP hybrids, eight LMP2 cars (all Orecas), 11 GTD Pro cars and 17 GTD entries.

The LMP2 championship was won by Nick Boulle and Tom Dillman driving an Oreca LMP2 07, run by Inter Europol/PR1 Mathiasen Motorsports. The GTD Pro title went to Laurin Heinrich and Martin Christensen's Porsche 911 GT3 R, operated by AO Racing. GTD champions were Russell Ward and Philip Ellis in a Winward Racing Mercedes-AMG GT3.

In many ways, IMSA is the strongest of America's three major circuit racing championships, attracting very good crowds to all of its races and benefiting from a powerful list of 19 manufacturers competing across four categories in the WeatherTech series, plus five additional support series, all of which provides a very complete weekend of racing entertainment for the spectator.

Above: Penske's Dane Cameron and Felipe Nasr claimed IMSA WeatherTech championship honours. Joined by Matt Campbell, they were victorious in the the season's opening race at Daytona.
Photo: Porsche/Gruppe C Photography

Top left: Louis Foster took eight wins in dominant fashion in the Indy NXT feeder series.
Photo: IMS/Chris Jones

Above left: A great moment for Jamie Chadwick, who secured a win over Louis Foster and Jacob Abel at Road America.
Photo: IMS/IndyNXT

Left: Ganassi's Sébastien Bourdais and Renger van der Zande win the prestigious Petit Le Mans, marking Cadillac's farewell to the series, before heading to the WEC in 2025.
Photo: Jake Galstad/LAT Images

APPRECIATIONS
by Gordon Kirby

Parnelli Jones
1933–2024

RUFUS PARNELLI JONES was a tough, crew-cut hombre with chiselled features and a fearsome, cool-eyed stare. He came up through the rough-and-tumble world of jalopy and modified stock car racing in Southern California, and made his mark by winning in stock cars, midget and sprint cars before establishing himself as perhaps the fastest of all the great drivers who tackled the Indianapolis Motor Speedway in the sixties.

"Parnelli Jones was the greatest driver of his era," Mario Andretti said. "He had an aggressiveness and a finesse that no one else possessed, and he won in everything he put his hands on."

Jones dominated three of the seven Indy 500s he started and won the race in 1963, beating Jim Clark. He appeared to be a clear winner again in 1967 with Andy Granatelli's STP turbine car, but a driveshaft bearing broke with only four laps to go. After the race, at the height of his driving prowess, he retired from driving open-cockpit cars. Granatelli wanted him to drive his turbine car again in 1968, but Jones thought that the new Lotus turbine would be quicker and decided against racing the car again.

That was the end of his career in Indy cars, but Parnelli continued to race in Trans Am, Can-Am, and off-road cars and trucks. He won the 1970 Trans Am championship with a Bud Moore Ford Mustang, beating Mark Donohue and Penske Racing by a single point when Trans Am was one of the USA's top racing series, brimming with manufacturer-backed teams. His Trans Am championship year also launched the Boss Mustang, a concept with which he will be forever identified, and which is still being promoted and sold more than half a century later.

Jones also won the Baja 1,000 off-road race in 1970 and '73, setting a record that remains unbroken. His resumé includes four NASCAR stock car victories, the 1964 USAC stock car championship, and the 1961 and '62 USAC Sprint car titles. He also qualified on the first two rows for all seven Indy 500s that he started and led five of those races for a total of 492 laps.

Then there was his career as a team owner, in partnership with Vel Miletich. Vel's Parnelli Jones Racing won the Indy 500 with Al Unser in 1970 and '71, as well as three consecutive USAC championships with Unser and Joe Leonard in 1970, '71 and '72, and a total of 40 USAC Championship races between 1968 and 1977. VPJ also produced the first Cosworth-powered Indy car, developed by John Barnard and driven successfully by Al Unser, and a similar F1 car raced by Mario Andretti from late 1974 through to early '76. VPJ's cars were usually beautiful and often revolutionary.

in addition, VPJ developed a series of Ford and Chevrolet off-road trucks for Parnelli to race while he expanded his business interests with Miletich, becoming a very successful Firestone tyre distributor and property developer in Southern California. His sons, P.J. and Page, pursued racing careers, both winning races in a variety of cars. Parnelli is survived by his wife, Judy, their two sons and six grandchildren.

Bob Riley
1931–2024

BOB RILEY was one of America's most successful racing-car designers. He penned A.J. Foyt's Coyote Indy cars in the mid- to late seventies as well as a long string of Ford-powered IMSA GTP and Trans Am cars. He went on to design the front-engined Ford Mustang GTP car and the Intrepid RM-1 GTP car. In 1990, he formed Riley & Scott with Mark Scott, and the company found considerable success in Trans Am and IMSA with its own Trans Am chassis and Mk III sports car, winning four consecutive championships with Rob Dyson's team and three Daytona 24 Hours triumphs between 1996 and 1999.

During this time, Riley & Scott also built an IRL chassis, followed by a brace of Riley Mk XI sports cars that scored ten Daytona 24 Hours wins between 2005 and 2015 with Pontiac, Lexus, Porsche, BMW and Ford engines. Riley & Scott also developed the Viper GTS-R and GT3-R for ALMS and IMSA competition. Riley's son, Bill, took over the running of the company some ten years ago, and it continues as a vital element of IMSA to this day.

Paul Goldsmith
1925–2024

PAUL GOLDSMITH won races on AMA motorcycles, in NASCAR and USAC stock cars, and also started six Indy 500s, finishing third in the 1960 500. He finished second in the 1954 AMA national championship and won USAC's stock car championship in 1961 and '62, driving for Ray Nichels. Goldsmith finished second in USAC stock car points with Nichels in 1960 and '65. He retired in 1969 to focus on his aviation repair business in Griffith, Indiana. He leaves behind a daughter, Linda Goldsmith-Slifer.

Cale Yarborough
1939–2023

CALE YARBOROUGH was one of the greatest stock car racers of all time. Yarborough won 83 NASCAR Cup races between 1965 and 1988, and took three consecutive championships with Junior Johnson's team in 1976, '77 and '78. He also finished second in points in 1973, '74 and '80, and won the Daytona 500 four times in 1968, '77, '83 and '84.

A football player in his youth, Yarborough was a powerful, bull-necked man, an exciting driver who made up three lost laps to win the 1977 Daytona 500. He stood with Richard Petty, David Pearson and Bobby Allison as one of the superstars of NASCAR's greatest era.

To the wider world, Yarborough is best known for a fist fight with Donnie and Bobby Allison on the infield inside Turn Three on the last lap of the 1979 Daytona 500. While battling for the lead with Donnie, they collided several times before crashing. As Richard Petty went on to win the race, Donnie's brother, Bobby, arrived on the scene, stopped his car, jumped out and indulged in some fisticuffs with Yarborough. The 500 was being televised live by CBS at the time, and a snowstorm across America's northeast resulted in a larger than normal audience – and much increased popularity for NASCAR. "It put NASCAR on the nationwide map," Richard Petty said many years later. "Until then, people thought of NASCAR as a southern sport, but that fight and the snowstorm made for a perfect storm for NASCAR."

Yarborough made his NASCAR debut at Darlington's Southern 500 in 1957, when he was only 18. He scored his first win at the Valdosta, Georgia short track in 1965 and won his last race on the high-banked Atlanta Motor Speedway in 1988. He lived throughout his life in Sardis, South Carolina, where he ran the family farm and owned a Honda dealership. He is survived by his wife, Betty Jo, and three daughters, Julie, Kelley and B.J.

Augie Pabst
1933–2024

AUGIE PABST was the grandson of two Milwaukee beer brewing magnates: Frederick Pabst, founder of the Pabst Brewing Company, and August Uihlein, founder of the Schlitz Brewing Company.

Pabst began racing in 1956 with a Triumph TR3 before switching to an AC Ace-Bristol. He went on to race a Ferrari TR and then a Meister Brauser Scarab, winning the 1959 USAC road racing championship with the latter. He drove a NART Ferrari 250GT at Le Mans in 1960, finishing seventh overall and fourth in class, and won the 1960 SCCA National Sports Car Championship before joining Briggs Cunningham in the 1961 and '62 24-hour races. He finished fourth overall and third in class in the first of them. Pabst also won the Road America 500 twice, in 1961 and '64. He retired from racing in 1966 to become a Pabst Brewing Company executive. He is survived by his wife, Joan, and son, Augie III.

Bill Krause
1933–2024

BILL KRAUSE started racing in midgets and won a local California championship in 1955, but after a couple of accidents, his mother decided that open-wheel racing was too dangerous. Thus his father bought him a D-Type Jaguar, which Bill raced from 1956 to '58. The following year, he raced the Jaguar with a Chevrolet engine, and also a Maserati 450S and a new 'Birdcage' Maserati. Aboard the last of those, he won the *LA Times* GP at Riverside, beating Stirling Moss and Dan Gurney's rear-engined Lotus 19s.

Krause became the first man to race one of Carroll Shelby's Cobras in 1962, before he was hired by Mickey Thompson. He tried to qualify at Indianapolis, but after being sprayed in the face by oil from a blown engine, he went home and raced only sporadically thereafter, retiring in 1966. Krause went on to run a variety of car and motorcycle dealerships, and also worked restoring vintage cars.

Bobby Allison
1937–2024

BOBBY ALLISON was one of NASCAR's greatest drivers, in a career that ran from 1961 to 1988. During that time, he started 718 first-division Cup races, winning 85. He won the 1983 NASCAR championship, driving a Chevrolet for Di Gard Racing, and scored victories in the Daytona 500 three times – in 1978, '82 and '88. He also won the IROC championship in 1980, when that series was at its competitive height, and was voted NASCAR's most popular driver seven times – in 1971–73 and 1980–83.

Bobby was the older brother of Donnie Allison, and in company with Neil Bonnet, they were known as the 'Alabama Gang'. Bobby did a lot of short-track racing over the years, and also raced occasionally in Indy cars, Trans Am and Can-Am. He started two Indy 500s for Team Penske and won four NASCAR races for the team.

"Bobby Allison was a great champion, a NASCAR legend and a real racer," Penske said. "During his four seasons competing with our team, we saw what made Bobby one of our sport's true heroes. He was tough, he was smart and he knew what to do behind the wheel of a race-car. While Bobby earned four wins for us in NASCAR competition, he also raced Indy cars, including two Indianapolis 500s, for Team Penske. Beyond his hall-of-fame career, Bobby was a good man and a good friend, who also had a great connection with race fans of all ages."

Allison achieved a degree of notoriety in 1979 when he pulled over on the last lap of the Daytona 500 to join brother Donnie in some fisticuffs with Cale Yarborough, after the pair had collided while battling for the lead on the last lap. The incident played to a large winter TV audience and helped propel NASCAR's popularity to new heights.

In 1987, Bobby suffered a huge accident at the Talladega superspeedway. Parts of his car flew into the grandstands, injuring spectators, and NASCAR reacted by introducing carburettor restrictor plates at Daytona and Talladega the following year, thus reducing lap speeds by some 30mph. Over the decades that followed, restrictor plates became all-pervasive in NASCAR.

Allison was seriously injured in the summer of 1988 when he crashed at Pocono and was T-boned by another car. He was lucky to survive and spent months in rehab before reluctantly deciding to retire. More tragedy visited the Allison family when his son, Clifford, was fatally injured in an accident during practice at the Michigan Speedway in 1992. The following year, Bobby's other son, Davey, winner of the 1992 Daytona 500, was killed in a crash while landing his helicopter at the Talladega superspeedway. Allison's wife of 55 years, Judy, died in December, 2015, after complications from surgery.

Wally Dallenbach
1936–2024

DURING his 20-year tenure as chief steward of Championship Auto Racing Teams (CART), Wally Dallenbach had a profound effect on the sport. With his deep concerns about driver safety, adherence to a consistent set of rules and calm demeanour in times of crisis, he drew on his own experience as a driver to make Indy car racing a better sport for the drivers, teams and fans alike. He is truly one of the unsung heroes of the period when he served as a key official and decision maker, from 1981 through to his retirement in 2001.

A self-made racer from New Jersey, Dallenbach raced dragsters, stock cars, midgets and sprint cars before making his name as the winner of five Indy car races with Pat Patrick's team in the mid-seventies, including the 1973 California 500. During this time, he moved west to Colorado and started the Colorado 500 motorcycle ride, before retiring in 1980 to become CART's chief steward.

Over the following 20 years, Dallenbach gained a rare reputation as a cool-headed, even-handed steward who became a tremendous proponent of improving all aspects of safety in motor racing. With the assistance of doctors Steve Olvey and Terry Trammell, and safety directors Steve Edwards and Lon Bromley, he developed the sport's most progressive safety and medical team.

And by working closely with the teams and car builders, Dallenbach and his group also influenced many improvements in car and cockpit construction, embracing better ways of absorbing energy on impact. In 1976, he started a rescue team at home in Basalt, Colorado. He began by conscripting 20 friends to take an EMT course, then buying an ambulance. After becoming CART's chief steward, he applied those lessons to the sanctioning body and developed the state-of-the-art safety team, complete with a travelling hospital, doctors and nurses.

Dallenbach could look back with great pride on his work during an era when Indy car racing was at its global height. F1 world champions were in the field, including Mario Andretti, Emerson Fittipaldi and Nigel Mansell, and CART races built a huge worldwide following, challenging Formula 1 for a few years for global supremacy. Over the 115-year history of American championship and Indy car racing, Dallenbach emerged in a class of his own as the most respected chief steward the sport has ever seen.

Wally's wife, Peppy, passed away in 2021. He is survived by two sons, Wally (the 1985 and '86 Trans Am champion, Paul (the 2015 Pike's Peak winner) and daughter Colleen, who is the office manager of Ed Carpenter's IndyCar team.

Rocky Moran
1960–2024

ROCKY MORAN began his racing career driving SCCA races in his native California and first made his mark in the 'new era' Can-Am series. He made his Indy car debut with Dan Gurney's All-American Racers at Watkins Glen in 1981, driving a Chevy-powered Eagle. Moran qualified seventh and led 21 laps before a refuelling gaffe cost him time and dropped him to a sixth-place finish. Gurney hired Moran in 1988 to drive AAR's Toyota IMSA GTO and GTP cars, and he scored Toyota's first Daytona 24 Hours win in 1993, co-driving with PJ Jones and Mark Dismore.

Moran went on to make three Indy 500 starts, in 1988, '89 and '90, the first two with A.J. Foyt's team. He finished 16th in 1988 and 14th in 1989. After retiring from racing, he operated a go-kart track for a few years in partnership with his son, Rocky Jr, who raced successfully in Formula Atlantic, IMSA sports cars and Indy Lights. Moran is survived by his wife, Kayla, a daughter, Kelly, sons Rocky Jr and Cody, and seven grandchildren.

Gil de Ferran
1967–2023

GIL DE FERRAN made a big mark in American racing, winning the 2000 and '01 CART Indy car championships as well as the 2003 Indy 500, driving for Team Penske. Born in France and raised in Brazil, he began racing in karts and won the Brazilian FF1600 championship in 1987. He moved to the UK to race Formula 3 in 1991 and won the 1992 British F3 championship with Paul Stewart Racing, before coming third in the 1994 Formula 3000 championship with Stewart's team.

De Ferran moved to America in 1995 to race for Jim Hall's Indy car team. He scored his first Indy car win at the end of that year at Laguna Seca, and won again at Cleveland in 1996. Hall closed his team at the end of the year and de Ferran joined Derrick Walker's team in 1997. He drove for Walker through 1999, scoring his only win with the team at Portland.

Gil got the big break of his career when he joined Team Penske in 2000, going on to win consecutive CART Indy car championships and the 2003 Indy 500. He also set a world closed-course speed record at 241.428mph in qualifying for the season-closing California 500. He broke his back in a crash on the Phoenix oval early in 2003 and decided to retire at the end of that year. He won the last Indy car race he started that year on the Texas oval. Educated as an engineer, he became an excellent test driver, and because of his seven years racing Indy cars with Honda engines, he was known by Honda's engineers as 'The Human Dynamometer'.

De Ferran returned to racing in 2008 and '09, driving his own Acura LMP2 and P1 cars in the American Le Mans Series, winning five ALMS races in 2009 with co-driver Simon Pagenaud. He retired from driving for good at the end of that year, becoming co-owner of an Indy car team with Roger Penske's youngest son, Jay, in 2010. Raphael Matos drove for the team, but a lack of sponsorship forced its closure at the end of the year.

An amiable, good-humoured man, De Ferran died at 56 after suffering a heart attack at the end of December, 2023. He is survived by his wife, Angela, and two children, Anna and Luke.

MAJOR RESULTS

OTHER CHAMPIONSHIP RACING SERIES WORLDWIDE

Compiled by DAVID HAYHOE and JOÃO PAULO CUNHA – www.forix.com

ABB FIA Formula E World Championship

Officially designated as the 2023–24 season, but all races were held in 2024.

HANKOOK MEXICO CITY E-PRIX, Autódromo Hermanos Rodríguez, Mexico City, D.F., Mexico, 13 January. Round 1. 37 laps of the 1.633-mile/2.628km circuit, 60.420 miles/97.236km.
1 Pascal Wehrlein, D (Porsche 99X Electric Gen3), 50m 15.506s, 72.130mph/116.083km/h; 2 Sébastien Buemi, CH (Jaguar I-Type 6), +1.162s; 3 Nick Cassidy, NZ (Jaguar I-Type 6), +2.079s; 4 Maximilian Günther, D (Maserati Tipo Folgore), +5.780s; 5 Mitch Evans, NZ (Jaguar I-Type 6), +13.064s; 6 Jean-Éric Vergne, F (DS E-TENSE FE23), +13.405s; 7 Jake Hughes, GB (Nissan e-4ORCE 04), +13.916s; 8 Stoffel Vandoorne, B (DS E-TENSE FE23), +14.392s; 9 Jake Dennis, GB (Porsche 99X Electric Gen3), +14.767s; 10 Norman Nato, F (Porsche 99X Electric Gen3), +15.312s; 11 Oliver Rowland, GB (Nissan e-4ORCE 04), +15.485s; 12 Sacha Fenestraz, F (Nissan e-4ORCE 04), +15.718s; 13 Edoardo Mortara, CH (Mahindra M10Electro), +16.214s; 14 Sam Bird, GB (Nissan e-4ORCE 04), +20.600s; 15 Nyck de Vries, NL (Mahindra M10Electro), +23.665s; 16 Jehan Daruvala, IND (Maserati Tipo Folgore), +28.969s; 17 Nico Müller, CH (Mahindra M10Electro), +29.424s; 18 Dan Ticktum, GB (ERT X24), +1m 14.758s; Robin Frijns, NL (Jaguar I-Type 6), -30 laps (DNF-accident); António Félix da Costa, P (Porsche 99X Electric Gen3), -35 (DNF-accident); Lucas di Grassi, BR (Mahindra M10Electro), -35 (DNF-brakes).
Did not start: Sérgio Sette Câmara, BR (ERT X24), technical.
Fastest race lap: Cassidy, 1m 14.746s, 78.648mph/126.572km/h.
Pole position: Wehrlein, 1m 13.298s, 80.202mph/129.073km/h.
Championship points: Drivers: 1 Wehrlein, 28; 2 Buemi, 18; 3 Cassidy, 16; 4 Günther, 12; 5 Evans, 10; 6 Vergne, 8.
Teams: 1 TAG Heuer Porsche Formula E Team, 28; 2 Jaguar TCS Racing, 26; 3 Envision Racing, 18.

DIRIYAH E-PRIX, Diriyah (Riyadh) Street Circuit, Saudi Arabia, 26/27 January. 37 and 36 laps of the 1.550-mile/2.495km circuit.
Round 2 (57.731 miles/92.909km).
1 Jake Dennis, GB (Porsche 99X Electric Gen3), 45m 56.452s, 74.920mph/120.573km/h; 2 Jean-Éric Vergne, F (DS E-TENSE FE23), +13.289s; 3 Nick Cassidy, NZ (Jaguar I-Type 6), +13.824s; 4 Sam Bird, GB (Nissan e-4ORCE 04), +14.620s; 5 Mitch Evans, NZ (Jaguar I-Type 6), +15.174s; 6 Norman Nato, F (Porsche 99X Electric Gen3), +15.661s; 7 Maximilian Günther, D (Maserati Tipo Folgore), +16.267s; 8 Pascal Wehrlein, D (Porsche 99X Electric Gen3), +16.387s; 9 Sérgio Sette Câmara, BR (ERT X24), +26.606s; 10 Robin Frijns, NL (Jaguar I-Type 6), +26.968s; 11 Jake Hughes, GB (Nissan e-4ORCE 04), +27.021s; 12 Sébastien Buemi, CH (Jaguar I-Type 6), +27.472s; 13 Oliver Rowland, GB (Nissan e-4ORCE 04), +27.973s; 14 Stoffel Vandoorne, B (DS E-TENSE FE23), +28.366s; 15 Edoardo Mortara, CH (Mahindra M10Electro), +29.397s; 16 António Félix da Costa, P (Porsche 99X Electric Gen3), +29.885s; 17 Nyck de Vries, NL (Mahindra M10Electro), +30.419s; 18 Nico Müller, CH (Mahindra M10Electro), +30.884s; 19 Lucas di Grassi, BR (Mahindra M10Electro), +31.188s; 20 Jehan Daruvala, IND (Maserati Tipo Folgore), +31.541s; 21 Dan Ticktum, GB (ERT X24), +1m 04.712s; Sacha Fenestraz, F (Nissan e-4ORCE 04), -25 laps (DNF-accident damage).
Fastest race lap: Dennis, 1m 11.399s, 78.168mph/125.800km/h.
Pole position: Vergne, 1m 12.062s, 77.449mph/124.642km/h.

Round 3 (56.181 miles/90.414km).
1 Nick Cassidy, NZ (Jaguar I-Type 6), 43m 51.868s, 76.346mph/122.868km/h; 2 Robin Frijns, NL (Jaguar I-Type 6), +1.192s; 3 Oliver Rowland, GB (Nissan e-4ORCE 04), +1.875s; 4 Jake Hughes, GB (Nissan e-4ORCE 04), +2.931s; 5 Stoffel Vandoorne, B (DS E-TENSE FE23), +3.397s; 6 Sacha Fenestraz, F (Nissan e-4ORCE 04), +4.598s; 7 Pascal Wehrlein, D (Porsche 99X Electric Gen3), +4.816s; 8 Jean-Éric Vergne, F (DS E-TENSE FE23), +5.195s; 9 Maximilian Günther, D (Maserati Tipo Folgore), +5.709s; 10 Mitch Evans, NZ (Jaguar I-Type 6), +6.866s; 11 Edoardo Mortara, CH (Mahindra M10Electro), +10.116s; 12 Jake Dennis, GB (Porsche 99X Electric Gen3), +11.240s*; 13 Nico Müller, CH (Mahindra M10Electro), +14.462s; 14 António Félix da Costa, P (Porsche 99X Electric Gen3), +17.960s; 15 Nyck de Vries, NL (Mahindra M10Electro), +19.295s; 16 Norman Nato, F (Porsche 99X Electric Gen3), +25.235s*; 17 Lucas di Grassi, BR (Mahindra M10Electro), +25.639s; 18 Sérgio Sette Câmara, BR (ERT X24), +26.564s*; Dan Ticktum, GB (ERT X24), -4 laps (DNF-accident damage); Jehan Daruvala, IND (Maserati Tipo Folgore), -11 (DNF-brakes); Sam Bird, GB (Nissan e-4ORCE 04), -14 (DNF-accident damage); Sébastien Buemi, CH (Jaguar I-Type 6), -36 (DNF-accident).
** 5s penalty for overtaking under yellow flag*
Fastest race lap: Dennis, 1m 10.296s, 79.395mph/127.773km/h.
Pole position: Rowland, 1m 10.055s, 79.668mph/128.213km/h.
Championship points: Drivers: 1 Cassidy, 57; 2 Wehrlein, 38; 3 Vergne, 33; 4 Dennis, 28; 5 Evans, 21; 6 Günther, 20.
Teams: 1 Jaguar TCS Racing, 78; 2 DS Penske, 47; 3 TAG Heuer Porsche Formula E Team, 38.

SÃO PAULO E-PRIX, São Paulo Street Circuit, Brazil, 16 March. Round 4. 34 laps of the 1.822-mile/2.933km circuit, 63.606 miles/102.364km.
1 Sam Bird, GB (Nissan e-4ORCE 04), 53m 03.071s, 70.099mph/112.813km/h; 2 Mitch Evans, NZ (Jaguar I-Type 6), +0.564s; 3 Oliver Rowland, GB (Nissan e-4ORCE 04), +3.540s; 4 Pascal Wehrlein, D (Porsche 99X Electric Gen3), +3.629s; 5 Jake Dennis, GB (Porsche 99X Electric Gen3), +3.722s; 6 António Félix da Costa, P (Porsche 99X Electric Gen3), +5.567s; 7 Jean-Éric Vergne, F (DS E-TENSE FE23), +6.006s; 8 Stoffel Vandoorne, B (DS E-TENSE FE23), +6.817s; 9 Maximilian Günther, D (Maserati Tipo Folgore), +8.085s; 10 Sébastien Buemi, CH (Jaguar I-Type 6), +8.610s; 11 Sacha Fenestraz, F (Nissan e-4ORCE 04), +9.277s; 12 Edoardo Mortara, CH (Mahindra M10Electro), +9.762s; 13 Lucas di Grassi, BR (Mahindra M10Electro), +10.819s; 14 Nyck de Vries, NL (Mahindra M10Electro), +13.677s; 15 Jehan Daruvala, IND (Maserati Tipo Folgore), +14.379s; 16 Dan Ticktum, GB (ERT X24), +17.884s; 17 Norman Nato, F (Porsche 99X Electric Gen3), +18.889s*; 18 Robin Frijns, NL (Jaguar I-Type 6), +19.124s; Jake Hughes, GB (Nissan e-4ORCE 04), -3 laps (DNF-technical); Nico Müller, CH (Mahindra M10Electro), -9 (DNF-overheating); Nick Cassidy, NZ (Jaguar I-Type 6), -20 (DNF-accident).
** 5s penalty for causing a collision with di Grassi*
Disqualified: Sérgio Sette Câmara, BR (ERT X24), +17.511s (total energy used was over the maximum of 38.5 kWh).
Fastest race lap: de Vries, 1m 15.502s, 86.897mph/139.847km/h.
Pole position: Wehrlein, 1m 12.789s, 90.136mph/145.060km/h.
Championship points: Drivers: 1 Cassidy, 57; 2 Wehrlein, 53; 3 Evans, 39; 4 Vergne, 39; 5 Dennis, 38; 6 Bird, 37.
Teams: 1 Jaguar TCS Racing, 96; 2 TAG Heuer Porsche Formula E Team, 61; 3 DS Penske, 57.

TOKYO E-PRIX, Tokyo Street Circuit, 30 March. Round 5. 35 laps of the 1.604-mile/2.582km circuit, 56.153 miles/90.370km.
1 Maximilian Günther, D (Maserati Tipo Folgore), 53m 34.665s, 62.884mph/101.202km/h; 2 Oliver Rowland, GB (Nissan e-4ORCE 04), +0.755s; 3 Jake Dennis, GB (Porsche 99X Electric Gen3), +1.405s; 4 António Félix da Costa, P (Porsche 99X Electric Gen3), +1.822s; 5 Pascal Wehrlein, D (Porsche 99X Electric Gen3), +3.897s; 6 Norman Nato, F (Porsche 99X Electric Gen3), +4.573s; 7 Nico Müller, CH (Mahindra M10Electro), +4.983s; 8 Nick Cassidy, NZ (Jaguar I-Type 6), +5.542s; 9 Robin Frijns, NL (Jaguar I-Type 6), +5.929s; 10 Sérgio Sette Câmara, BR (ERT X24), +6.504s; 11 Sacha Fenestraz, F (Nissan e-4ORCE 04), +7.016s; 12 Jean-Éric Vergne, F (DS E-TENSE FE23), +7.583s; 13 Sébastien Buemi, CH (Jaguar I-Type 6), +8.467s; 14 Jake Hughes, GB (Nissan e-4ORCE 04), +8.859s; 15 Mitch Evans, NZ (Jaguar I-Type 6), +9.316s; 16 Stoffel Vandoorne, B (DS E-TENSE FE23), +9.735s; 17 Jehan Daruvala, IND (Maserati Tipo Folgore), +15.096s; 18 Dan Ticktum, GB (ERT X24), +49.418s; 19 Sam Bird, GB (Nissan e-4ORCE 04), -1 lap; Lucas di Grassi, BR (Mahindra M10Electro), -18 (DNF-accident damage); Nyck de Vries, NL (Mahindra M10Electro), -18 (DNF-accident damage).
Disqualified: Edoardo Mortara, CH (Mahindra M10Electro), +4.354s (total energy used was over the maximum of 32kWh).
Fastest race lap: Bird, 1m 19.731s, 72.440mph/116.582km/h.
Pole position: Rowland, 1m 19.023s, 73.089mph/117.626km/h.
Championship points: Drivers: 1 Wehrlein, 63; 2 Cassidy, 61; 3 Rowland, 54; 4 Dennis, 53; 5 Günther, 48; 6 Evans, 39.
Teams: 1 Jaguar TCS Racing, 100; 2 TAG Heuer Porsche Formula E Team, 83; 3 Andretti Formula E, 70.

MISANO E-PRIX, Misano World Circuit Marco Simoncelli, Misano Adriatico, Rimini, Italy, 13/14 April. 28 and 26 laps of the 2.101-mile/3.382km circuit.
Round 6 (58.872 miles/94.745km).
1 Oliver Rowland, GB (Nissan e-4ORCE 04), 40m 05.176s, 88.072mph/141.739km/h; 2 Jake Dennis, GB (Porsche 99X Electric Gen3), +3.003s; 3 Maximilian Günther, D (Maserati Tipo Folgore), +3.788s; 4 Dan Ticktum, GB (ERT X24), +4.554s; 5 Mitch Evans, NZ (Jaguar I-Type 6), +5.673s; 6 Jean-Éric Vergne, F (DS E-TENSE FE23), +7.559s*; 7 Norman Nato, F (Porsche 99X Electric Gen3), +7.588s; 8 Stoffel Vandoorne, B (DS E-TENSE FE23), +7.639s; 9 Sacha Fenestraz, F (Nissan e-4ORCE 04), +7.768s; 10 Lucas di Grassi, BR (Mahindra M10Electro), +7.967s; 11 Nico Müller, CH (Mahindra M10Electro), +8.311s; 12 Sébastien Buemi, CH (Jaguar I-Type 6), +13.447s; 13 Jake Hughes, GB (Nissan e-4ORCE 04), +13.705s; 14 Nyck de Vries, NL (Mahindra M10Electro), +18.051s**; 15 Sérgio Sette Câmara, BR (ERT X24), +57.526s***; 16 Pascal Wehrlein, D (Porsche 99X Electric Gen3), +1m 04.968s; 17 Robin Frijns, NL (Jaguar I-Type 6), +1m 18.360s; Jehan Daruvala, IND (Maserati Tipo Folgore), -1 lap (DNF-accident); Sam Bird, GB (Nissan e-4ORCE 04), -3 (DNF-withdrew); Nick Cassidy, NZ (Jaguar I-Type 6), -5 (DNF-technical); Edoardo Mortara, CH (Mahindra M10Electro), -28 (DNF-technical).
** 5s penalty for causing a collision with Cassidy*
*** 5s penalty for forcing Daruvala off track*
**** Drive-through penalty for overpower usage converted to 50s penalty*
Disqualified: António Félix da Costa, P (Porsche 99X Electric Gen3), originally won in 40m 04.766s.
Fastest race lap: Rowland, 1m 19.730s, 94.886mph/152.705km/h.
Pole position: Evans, 1m 17.068s, 98.164mph/157.979km/h.

Round 7 (54.669 miles/87.981km).
1 Pascal Wehrlein, D (Porsche 99X Electric Gen3), 37m 05.241s, 88.394mph/142.257km/h; 2 Jake Dennis, GB (Porsche 99X Electric Gen3), +1.933s; 3 Nick Cassidy, NZ (Jaguar I-Type 6), +2.221s; 4 Nico Müller, CH (Mahindra M10Electro), +2.271s; 5 Sacha Fenestraz, F (Nissan e-4ORCE 04), +5.230s; 6 Sérgio Sette Câmara, BR (ERT X24), +5.727s; 7 Jean-Éric Vergne, F (DS E-TENSE FE23), +6.794s; 8 Jake Hughes, GB (Nissan e-4ORCE 04), +8.236s*; 9 Jehan Daruvala, IND (Maserati Tipo Folgore), +8.714s; 10 Sam Bird, GB (Nissan e-4ORCE 04), +11.912s; 11 Lucas di Grassi, BR (Mahindra M10Electro), +12.415s**; 12 Maximilian Günther, D (Maserati Tipo Folgore), +13.387s***; 13 Edoardo Mortara, CH (Mahindra M10Electro), +14.171s; 14 Dan Ticktum, GB (ERT X24), +17.875s; 15 Nyck de Vries, NL (Mahindra M10Electro), +21.935s; 16 Norman Nato, F (Porsche 99X Electric Gen3), -1 lap; 17 António Félix da Costa, P (Porsche 99X Electric Gen3), -1; Mitch Evans, NZ (Jaguar I-Type 6), +1m 29.546s; Oliver Rowland, GB (Nissan e-4ORCE 04), -1 (DNF-out of energy); Stoffel Vandoorne, B (DS E-TENSE FE23), -4 (DNF-battery); Sébastien Buemi, CH (Jaguar I-Type 6), -12 (DNF-steering); Robin Frijns, NL (Jaguar I-Type 6), -20 (DNF-accident).
** 5s penalty for not respecting the track limits and overtaking Günther by going off track*
*** 5s penalty for causing a collision with Bird*
**** 5s penalty for causing a collision with Vergne*
Fastest race lap: da Costa, 1m 18.682s, 96.150mph/154.739km/h.
Pole position: Hughes, 1m 16.538s, 98.843mph/159.073km/h.
Championship points: Drivers: 1 Wehrlein, 89; 2 Dennis, 89; 3 Rowland, 80; 4 Cassidy, 76; 5 Günther, 63; 6 Vergne, 53.
Teams: 1 Jaguar TCS Racing, 128; 2 Andretti Formula E, 112; 3 TAG Heuer Porsche Formula E Team, 109.

MONACO E-PRIX, Circuit de Monaco, Monaco, 27 April. Round 8. 31 laps of the 2.074-mile/3.337km circuit, 64.279 miles/103.447km.
1 Mitch Evans, NZ (Jaguar I-Type 6), 58m 15.455s, 66.201mph/106.540km/h; 2 Nick Cassidy, NZ (Jaguar I-Type 6), +0.946s; 3 Stoffel Vandoorne, B (DS E-TENSE FE23), +3.835s; 4 Jean-Éric Vergne, F (DS E-TENSE FE23), +4.799s; 5 Pascal Wehrlein, D (Porsche 99X Electric Gen3), +6.378s; 6 Oliver Rowland, GB (Nissan e-4ORCE 04), +6.792s; 7 António Félix da Costa, P (Porsche 99X Electric Gen3), +7.364s; 8 Sacha Fenestraz, F (Nissan e-4ORCE 04), +7.928s; 9 Maximilian Günther, D (Maserati Tipo Folgore), +8.262s; 10 Norman Nato, F (Porsche 99X Electric Gen3), +9.045s; 11 Lucas di Grassi, BR (Mahindra M10Electro), +9.889s; 12 Nyck de Vries, NL (Mahindra M10Electro), +10.183s; 13 Dan Ticktum, GB (ERT X24), +17.999s; 14 Taylor Barnard, GB (Nissan e-4ORCE 04), +18.128s; 15 Sébastien Buemi, CH (Jaguar I-Type 6), +18.452s; 16 Jake Hughes, GB (Nissan e-4ORCE 04), +18.996s*; 17 Robin Frijns, NL (Jaguar I-Type 6), +19.106s; 18 Sérgio Sette Câmara, BR (ERT X24), +24.573s**; 19 Jake Dennis, GB (Porsche 99X Electric Gen3), +32.032s; 20 Jehan Daruvala, IND (Maserati Tipo Folgore), +1m 12.269s***; Nico Müller, CH (Mahindra M10Electro), -8 laps (DNF-accident); Edoardo Mortara, CH (Mahindra M10Electro), -28 (DNF-accident); Sam Bird, GB (Nissan e-4ORCE 04), -31 (DNF-physical).
** 5s penalty for causing a collision with Müller*
*** 5s penalty for causing a collision with Buemi*
**** 10s stop-and-go penalty for failing to activate attack mode converted to 48s penalty*
Fastest race lap: Daruvala, 1m 31.052s, 81.982mph/131.937km/h.
Pole position: Wehrlein, 1m 29.861s, 83.068mph/133.686km/h.
Championship points: Drivers: 1 Wehrlein, 102; 2 Cassidy, 95; 3 Dennis, 89; 4 Rowland, 88; 5 Evans, 77; 6 Günther, 65.
Teams: 1 Jaguar TCS Racing, 172; 2 TAG Heuer Porsche Formula E Team, 128; 3 Andretti Formula E, 113.

SUN MINIMEAL BERLIN E-PRIX, Tempelhof Airport Street Circuit, Berlin, Germany, 11/12 May. 46 and 41 laps of the 1.456-mile/2.343km circuit.
Round 9 (66.970 miles/107.778km).
1 Nick Cassidy, NZ (Jaguar I-Type 6), 1h 01m 54.939s, 64.898mph/104.443km/h; 2 Jean-Éric Vergne, F (DS E-TENSE FE23), +4.651s; 3 Oliver Rowland, GB (Nissan e-4ORCE 04), +4.915s; 4 Mitch Evans, NZ (Jaguar I-Type 6), +5.340s; 5 Pascal Wehrlein, D (Porsche 99X Electric Gen3), +5.631s; 6 António Félix da Costa, P (Porsche 99X Electric Gen3), +5.760s; 7 Stoffel Vandoorne, B (DS E-TENSE FE23), +6.363s; 8 Edoardo Mortara, CH (Mahindra M10Electro), +7.221s; 9 Sacha Fenestraz, F (Nissan e-4ORCE 04), +9.592s; 10 Taylor Barnard, GB (Nissan e-4ORCE 04), +9.644s; 11 Kelvin van der Linde, ZA (Mahindra M10Electro), +10.133s; 12 Jordan King, GB (Mahindra M10Electro), +10.427s; 13 Paul Aron, EST (Jaguar I-Type 6), +16.598s*; 14 Dan Ticktum, GB (ERT X24), +23.270s**; 15 Jake Hughes, GB (Nissan e-4ORCE 04), +55.538s; 16 Sérgio Sette Câmara, BR (ERT X24), -1 lap***; 17 Jehan Daruvala, IND (Maserati Tipo Folgore), -1; 18 Norman Nato, F (Porsche 99X Electric Gen3), -1; Jake Dennis, GB (Porsche 99X Electric Gen3), -8 (DNF-withdrew); Maximilian Günther, D (Maserati Tipo Folgore), -18 (DNF-accident); Lucas di Grassi, BR (Mahindra M10Electro), -26 (DNF-accident damage); Joel Eriksson, S (Jaguar I-Type 6), -37 (DNF-accident damage).
** 5s penalty for causing a collision with Hughes*
*** 5s penalty for causing a collision with di Grassi*
**** 5s penalty for causing a collsion with Aron*
Fastest race lap: Nato, 1m 02.972s, 83.229mph/133.945km/h.
Pole position: Mortara, 1m 01.741s, 84.889mph/136.615km/h.

Round 10 (59.691 miles/96.063km).
1 António Félix da Costa, P (Porsche 99X Electric Gen3), 47m 55.043s, 74.742mph/120.285km/h; 2 Nick Cassidy, NZ (Jaguar I-Type 6), +0.691s; 3 Oliver Rowland, GB (Nissan e-4ORCE 04), +2.820s; 4 Pascal Wehrlein, D (Porsche 99X Electric Gen3), +4.147s; 5 Jake Dennis, GB (Porsche 99X Electric Gen3), +4.548s; 6 Mitch Evans, NZ (Jaguar I-Type 6), +4.953s; 7 Jehan Daruvala, IND (Maserati Tipo Folgore), +6.032s; 8 Taylor Barnard, GB (Nissan e-4ORCE 04), +6.698s; 9 Joel Eriksson, S (Jaguar I-Type 6), +7.119s; 10 Jean-Éric Vergne, F (DS E-TENSE FE23), +7.357s; 11 Lucas di Grassi, BR (Mahindra M10Electro), +8.204s; 12 Jake Hughes, GB (Nissan e-4ORCE 04), +10.349s; 13 Sérgio Sette Câmara, BR (ERT X24), +10.403s; 14 Paul Aron, EST (Jaguar I-Type 6), +11.124s; 15 Kelvin van der Linde, ZA (Mahindra M10Electro), +11.780s; 16 Edoardo Mortara, CH (Mahindra M10Electro), +12.143s; 17 Dan Ticktum, GB (ERT X24), +12.642s; 18 Jordan King, GB

(Mahindra M10Electro), +16.494s; **19** Norman Nato, F (Porsche 99X Electric Gen3), +20.851s*; **20** Stoffel Vandoorne, B (DS E-TENSE FE23), +36.753s**; Sacha Fenestraz, F (Nissan e-4ORCE 04), -17 laps (DNF-accident); Maximilian Günther, D (Maserati Tipo Folgore), -31 (DNF-accident damage).
** 10s penalty for causing a collision with Fenestraz*
*** 5s penalty for causing a collision with Fenestraz*
Fastest race lap: Nato, 1m 03.553s, 82.468mph/132.720km/h.
Pole position: Dennis, 1m 01.819s, 84.782mph/136.443km/h.
Championship points: Drivers: 1 Cassidy, 140; **2** Wehrlein, 124; **3** Rowland, 118; **4** Dennis, 102; **5** Evans, 97; **6** Vergne, 84.
Teams: 1 Jaguar TCS Racing, 237; **2** TAG Heuer Porsche Formula E Team, 183; **3** Nissan Formula E Team, 144.

SHANGHAI E-PRIX, Shanghai International Circuit, Shanghai, China, 25/26 May. 29 and 28 laps of the 1.896-mile/3.051km circuit.
Round 11 (54.860 miles/88.289km).
1 Mitch Evans, NZ (Jaguar I-Type 6), 38m 03.434s, 86.675mph/139.490km/h; **2** Pascal Wehrlein, D (Porsche 99X Electric Gen3), +0.796s; **3** Nick Cassidy, NZ (Jaguar I-Type 6), +1.498s; **4** Oliver Rowland, GB (Nissan e-4ORCE 04), +1.743s; **5** Jake Dennis, GB (Porsche 99X Electric Gen3), +2.361s; **6** Jean-Éric Vergne, F (DS E-TENSE FE23), +2.599s; **7** Nyck de Vries, NL (Mahindra M10Electro), +2.818s; **8** Sébastien Buemi, CH (Jaguar I-Type 6), +3.610s; **9** Stoffel Vandoorne, B (DS E-TENSE FE23), +4.095s; **10** Lucas di Grassi, BR (Mahindra M10Electro), +4.397s; **11** Sacha Fenestraz, F (Nissan e-4ORCE 04), +4.791s; **12** Robin Frijns, NL (Jaguar I-Type 6), +5.083s; **13** Sérgio Sette Câmara, BR (ERT X24), +5.425s; **14** Norman Nato, F (Porsche 99X Electric Gen3), +5.793s; **15** Nico Müller, CH (Mahindra M10Electro), +6.178s; **16** Jake Hughes, GB (Nissan e-4ORCE 04), +6.566s; **17** Sam Bird, GB (Nissan e-4ORCE 04), +6.944s; **18** António Félix da Costa, P (Porsche 99X Electric Gen3), +7.165s*; **19** Jehan Daruvala, IND (Maserati Tipo Folgore), +7.372s; **20** Dan Ticktum, GB (ERT X24), +7.688s; **21** Maximilian Günther, D (Maserati Tipo Folgore), +13.165s**; Edoardo Mortara, CH (Mahindra M10Electro), -13 laps (DNF-accident damage).
** 5s penalty for forcing Vergne off the track*
*** 10s penalty for causing a collision with Mortara*
Fastest race lap: Dennis, 1m 15.965s, 89.842mph/144.587km/h.
Pole position: Vergne, 1m 13.322s, 93.081mph/149.799km/h.

Round 12 (52.964 miles/85.238km).
1 António Félix da Costa, P (Porsche 99X Electric Gen3), 36m 04.600s, 88.280mph/142.074km/h; **2** Jake Hughes, GB (Nissan e-4ORCE 04), +0.612s; **3** Norman Nato, F (Porsche 99X Electric Gen3), +1.122s; **4** Nick Cassidy, NZ (Jaguar I-Type 6), +2.215s; **5** Mitch Evans, NZ (Jaguar I-Type 6), +3.167s; **6** Stoffel Vandoorne, B (DS E-TENSE FE23), +3.861s; **7** Jean-Éric Vergne, F (DS E-TENSE FE23), +4.374s; **8** Maximilian Günther, D (Maserati Tipo Folgore), +5.077s; **9** Robin Frijns, NL (Jaguar I-Type 6), +7.846s; **10** Oliver Rowland, GB (Nissan e-4ORCE 04), +8.840s; **11** Jake Dennis, GB (Porsche 99X Electric Gen3), +9.634s; **12** Sébastien Buemi, CH (Jaguar I-Type 6), +10.143s; **13** Edoardo Mortara, CH (Mahindra M10Electro), +11.423s; **14** Sacha Fenestraz, F (Nissan e-4ORCE 04), +12.280s; **15** Nico Müller, CH (Mahindra M10Electro), +12.751s; **16** Nyck de Vries, NL (Mahindra M10Electro), +13.102s; **17** Jehan Daruvala, IND (Maserati Tipo Folgore), +15.973s; **18** Sérgio Sette Câmara, BR (ERT X24), +16.419s; **19** Lucas di Grassi, BR (Mahindra M10Electro), +50.057s; **20** Pascal Wehrlein, D (Porsche 99X Electric Gen3), +1m 01.675s; **21** Dan Ticktum, GB (ERT X24), +1m 24.415s; Sam Bird, GB (Nissan e-4ORCE 04), -10 laps (DNF-accident damage).
Fastest race lap: Nato, 1m 15.358s, 90.566mph/145.752km/h.
Pole position: Hughes, 1m 13.921s, 92.326mph/148.585km/h.
Championship points: Drivers: 1 Cassidy, 167; **2** Wehrlein, 142; **3** Evans, 132; **4** Rowland, 131; **5** Dennis, 113; **6** Vergne, 101.
Teams: 1 Jaguar TCS Racing, 299; **2** TAG Heuer Porsche Formula E Team, 226; **3** Nissan Formula E Team, 157.

HANKOOK PORTLAND E-PRIX, Portland International Raceway, Portland, Oregon, USA, 29/30 June. 2 x 27 laps of the 1.982-mile/3.190km circuit.
Round 13 (53.538 miles/86.161km).
1 António Félix da Costa, P (Porsche 99X Electric Gen3), 34m 00.097s, 94.440mph/151.987km/h; **2** Robin Frijns, NL (Jaguar I-Type 6), +0.415s; **3** Jean-Éric Vergne, F (DS E-TENSE FE23), +1.440s; **4** Edoardo Mortara, CH (Mahindra M10Electro), +1.701s; **5** Nico Müller, CH (Mahindra M10Electro), +2.086s; **6** Jake Dennis, GB (Porsche 99X Electric Gen3), +2.634s; **7** Sam Bird, GB (Nissan e-4ORCE 04), +2.858s; **8** Mitch Evans, NZ (Jaguar I-Type 6), +4.507s*; **9** Stoffel Vandoorne, B (DS E-TENSE FE23), +5.183s; **10** Pascal Wehrlein, D (Porsche 99X Electric Gen3), +5.653s; **11** Lucas di Grassi, BR (Mahindra M10Electro), +6.325s; **12** Nyck de Vries, NL (Mahindra M10Electro), +6.477s; **13** Norman Nato, F (Porsche 99X Electric Gen3), +6.487s; **14** Sérgio Sette Câmara, BR (ERT X24), +6.857s; **15** Sacha Fenestraz, F (Nissan e-4ORCE 04), +8.686s; **16** Jehan Daruvala, IND (Maserati Tipo Folgore), +14.031s**; **17** Dan Ticktum, GB (ERT X24), +14.186s***; **18** Caio Collet, BR (Nissan e-4ORCE 04), +15.005s; **19** Nick Cassidy, NZ (Jaguar I-Type 6), +15.445s; **20** Sébastien Buemi, CH (Jaguar I-Type 6), +58.409s; **21** Jake Hughes, GB (Nissan e-4ORCE 04), -1 lap; Maximilian Günther, D (Maserati Tipo Folgore), -5 (DNF-accident damage).
** 5s penalty for causing a collision with Hughes*
*** 5s penalty for causing a collision with Guenther*
**** 5s penalty for not respecting Race Director notes*
Fastest race lap: Hughes, 1m 11.327s, 100.043mph/161.004km/h.
Pole position: Evans, 1m 08.820s, 103.688mph/166.870km/h.

Round 14 (53.538 miles/86.161km).
1 António Félix da Costa, P (Porsche 99X Electric Gen3), 36m 21.519s, 88.318mph/142.134km/h; **2** Robin Frijns, NL (Jaguar I-Type 6), +0.332s; **3** Mitch Evans, NZ (Jaguar I-Type 6), +3.194s; **4** Pascal Wehrlein, D (Porsche 99X Electric Gen3), +3.262s; **5** Jean-Éric Vergne, F (DS E-TENSE FE23), +3.683s; **6** Nico Müller, CH (Mahindra M10Electro), +3.785s; **7** Norman Nato, F (Porsche 99X Electric Gen3), +4.887s; **8** Maximilian Günther, D (Maserati Tipo Folgore), +5.692s; **9** Sébastien Buemi, CH (Jaguar I-Type 6), +6.250s; **10** Jake Dennis, GB (Porsche 99X Electric Gen3), +6.840s; **11** Stoffel Vandoorne, B (DS E-TENSE FE23), +7.490s; **12** Jehan Daruvala, IND (Maserati Tipo Folgore), +7.928s; **13** Nick Cassidy, NZ (Jaguar I-Type 6), +8.078s; **14** Sérgio Sette Câmara, BR (ERT X24), +10.044s; **15** Dan Ticktum, GB (ERT X24), +10.111s; **16** Caio Collet, BR (Nissan e-4ORCE 04), +11.290s; **17** Lucas di Grassi, BR (Mahindra M10Electro), +12.575s*; **18** Sacha Fenestraz, F (Nissan e-4ORCE 04), +20.628s*; Edoardo Mortara, CH (Mahindra M10Electro), -3 laps (DNF-accident damage); Sam Bird, GB (Nissan e-4ORCE 04), -7 (DNF-accident damage); Nyck de Vries, NL (Mahindra M10Electro), -7 (DNF-battery); Jake Hughes, GB (Nissan e-4ORCE 04), -15 (DNF-accident damage).
** 5s penalty for forcing another car off track*
Fastest race lap: Frijns, 1m 10.650s, 101.002mph/162.547km/h.
Pole position: Vergne, 1m 08.779s, 103.750mph/166.969km/h.
Championship points: Drivers: 1 Cassidy, 167; **2** Evans, 155; **3** Wehrlein, 155; **4** da Costa, 134; **5** Rowland, 131; **6** Vergne, 129.
Teams: 1 Jaguar TCS Racing, 322; **2** TAG Heuer Porsche Formula E Team, 289; **3** DS Penske, 184.

HANKOOK LONDON E-PRIX, London ExCel Circuit, Great Britain, 20/21 July. 39 and 37 laps of the 1.292-mile/2.080km circuit.
Round 15 (50.337 miles/81.010km).
1 Pascal Wehrlein, D (Porsche 99X Electric Gen3), 55m 15.663s, 54.727mph/88.075km/h; **2** Mitch Evans, NZ (Jaguar I-Type 6), +0.617s; **3** Sébastien Buemi, CH (Jaguar I-Type 6), +1.457s; **4** Nyck de Vries, NL (Mahindra M10Electro), +2.290s; **5** Edoardo Mortara, CH (Mahindra M10Electro), +13.897s; **6** Nico Müller, CH (Mahindra M10Electro), +14.227s; **7** Nick Cassidy, NZ (Jaguar I-Type 6), +14.725s; **8** Sam Bird, GB (Nissan e-4ORCE 04), +15.209s; **9** Stoffel Vandoorne, B (DS E-TENSE FE23), +15.794s; **10** Norman Nato, F (Porsche 99X Electric Gen3), +16.515s; **11** Lucas di Grassi, BR (Mahindra M10Electro), +16.977s; **12** Sérgio Sette Câmara, BR (ERT X24), +17.419s; **13** Dan Ticktum, GB (ERT X24), +18.249s; **14** Sacha Fenestraz, F (Nissan e-4ORCE 04), +18.712s*; **15** Oliver Rowland, GB (Nissan e-4ORCE 04), +21.036s**; **16** Jake Dennis, GB (Porsche 99X Electric Gen3), +33.186s***; **17** Jean-Éric Vergne, F (DS E-TENSE FE23), +45.199s****; **18** Jehan Daruvala, IND (Maserati Tipo Folgore), -1 lap; Maximilian Günther, D (Maserati Tipo Folgore), -6 (DNF-gearbox); Jake Hughes, GB (Nissan e-4ORCE 04), -29 (DNF-technical); António Félix da Costa, P (Porsche 99X Electric Gen3), -33 (DNF-accident damage); Robin Frijns, NL (Jaguar I-Type 6), -39 (DNF-accident).
** 5s for causing a collision with Nato*
*** 5s penalty for causing a collision with da Costa*
**** 10s penalty for causing a collision with Frijns; 50s penalty for causing a collision with Vergne; 5s penalty for causing a collision with Cassidy*
***** 5s penalty for causing a collision with Daruvala*
Fastest race lap: Evans, 1m 11.701s, 64.892mph/104.433km/h.
Pole position: Evans, 1m 10.622s, 65.883mph/106.029km/h.

Round 16 (47.752 miles/76.850km).
1 Oliver Rowland, GB (Nissan e-4ORCE 04), 54m 30.572s, 52.636mph/84.710km/h; **2** Pascal Wehrlein, D (Porsche 99X Electric Gen3), +1.055s; **3** Mitch Evans, NZ (Jaguar I-Type 6), +3.782s; **4** Sébastien Buemi, CH (Jaguar I-Type 6), +4.004s; **5** Jean-Éric Vergne, F (DS E-TENSE FE23), +4.805s; **6** Nico Müller, CH (Mahindra M10Electro), +5.202s; **7** Robin Frijns, NL (Jaguar I-Type 6), +5.582s; **8** Stoffel Vandoorne, B (DS E-TENSE FE23), +6.104s; **9** Lucas di Grassi, BR (Mahindra M10Electro), +6.667s; **10** Jake Hughes, GB (Nissan e-4ORCE 04), +7.107s; **11** Sérgio Sette Câmara, BR (ERT X24), +7.579s; **12** Norman Nato, F (Porsche 99X Electric Gen3), +8.076s; **13** António Félix da Costa, P (Porsche 99X Electric Gen3), +9.362s*; **14** Dan Ticktum, GB (ERT X24), +9.478s; **15** Sacha Fenestraz, F (Nissan e-4ORCE 04), +19.185s; **16** Nyck de Vries, NL (Mahindra M10Electro), +43.480s; Nick Cassidy, NZ (Jaguar I-Type 6), -4 laps (DNF-accident damage); Maximilian Günther, D (Maserati Tipo Folgore), -9 (DNF-accident damage); Jehan Daruvala, IND (Maserati Tipo Folgore), -29 (DNF-accident); Sam Bird, GB (Nissan e-4ORCE 04), -31 (DNF-accident); Edoardo Mortara, CH (Mahindra M10Electro), -36 (DNF-accident); Jake Dennis, GB (Porsche 99X Electric Gen3), -36 (DNF-accident).
** 5s penalty for causing a collision with Cassidy*
Fastest race lap: Hughes, 1m 11.331s, 65.228mph/104.975km/h.
Pole position: Cassidy, 1m 09.871s, 66.591mph/107.168km/h.

Final championship points
Drivers
1 Pascal Wehrlein, D, 198; **2** Mitch Evans, NZ, 192; **3** Nick Cassidy, NZ, 176; **4** Oliver Rowland, GB, 156; **5** Jean-Éric Vergne, F, 139; **6** António Félix da Costa, P, 134; **7** Jake Dennis, GB, 122; **8** Maximilian Günther, D, 73; **9** Robin Frijns, NL, 66; **10** Stoffel Vandoorne, B, 61; **11** Sébastien Buemi, CH, 53; **12** Nico Müller, CH, 52; **13** Sam Bird, GB, 48; **14** Jake Hughes, GB, 48; **15** Norman Nato, F, 47; **16** Edoardo Mortara, CH, 29; **17** Sacha Fenestraz, F, 26; **18** Nyck de Vries, NL, 18; **19** Dan Ticktum, GB, 12; **20** Sérgio Sette Câmara, BR, 11; **21** Jehan Daruvala, IND, 8; **22** Taylor Barnard, GB, 5; **23** Lucas di Grassi, BR, 4; **24** Joel Eriksson, S, 2.

Teams
1 Jaguar TCS Racing, 368; **2** TAG Heuer Porsche Formula E Team, 332; **3** DS Penske, 200; **4** Nissan Formula E Team, 182; **5** Andretti Formula E, 169; **6** Envision Racing, 121; **7** NEOM McLaren Formula E Team, 101; **8** Maserati MSG Racing, 81; **9** ABT CUPRA Formula E Team, 56; **10** Mahindra Racing, 47; **11** ERT Formula E Team, 23.

FIA Formula 2 Championship

All cars are Dallara F2 2024-Mecachrome F2.

FIA FORMULA 2 CHAMPIONSHIP, Bahrain International Circuit, Sakhir, Bahrain, 1/2 March. Round 1. 23 and 32 laps of the 3.363-mile/5.412km circuit.
Race 1 (77.193 miles/124.230km).
1 Zane Maloney, BB, 42m 13.726s, 109.893mph/176.856km/h; **2** Jak Crawford, USA, +5.490s; **3** Pepe Martí, E, +7.057s; **4** Isack Hadjar, F, +9.783s; **5** Paul Aron, EST, +18.188s; **6** Gabriel Bortoleto, BR, +18.320s; **7** Zak O'Sullivan, GB, +20.135s; **8** Dennis Hauger, N, +21.032s; **9** Ritomo Miyata, J, +21.490s; **10** Richard Verschoor, NL, +21.839s; **11** Victor Martins, F, +23.840s; **12** Juan Manuel Correa, USA, +26.833s; **13** Kush Maini, IND, +27.246s; **14** Andrea Kimi Antonelli, I, +30.260s; **15** Joshua Duerksen, PY, +35.257s; **16** Oliver Bearman, GB, +36.247s; **17** Enzo Fittipaldi, BR, +56.183s; **18** Franco Colapinto, RA, +1m 04.819s; **19** Rafael Villagómez, MEX, +1m 31.558s*; Roman Staněk, CZ, -4 laps (DNF); Taylor Barnard, GB, -7 (DNF); Amaury Cordeel, B, -23 (DNF).
** 10s penalty for causing a collision with Cordeel*
Fastest race lap: Fittipaldi, 1m 45.833s, 114.390mph/184.093km/h.
Pole position: Crawford.

Race 2 (107.459 miles/172.938km).
1 Zane Maloney, BB, 1h 02m 46.435s, 102.854mph/165.528km/h; **2** Pepe Martí, E, +4.621s; **3** Paul Aron, EST, +11.781s*; **4** Zak O'Sullivan, GB, +12.523s; **5** Gabriel Bortoleto, BR, +12.591s; **6** Franco Colapinto, RA, +13.609s; **7** Kush Maini, IND, +14.719s; **8** Dennis Hauger, N, +16.002s; **9** Ritomo Miyata, J, +16.272s; **10** Andrea Kimi Antonelli, I, +20.405s; **11** Joshua Duerksen, PY, +24.035s; **12** Rafael Villagómez, MEX, +29.532s*; **13** Roman Staněk, CZ, +31.193s; **14** Richard Verschoor, NL, +33.702s*; **15** Oliver Bearman, GB, +51.135s; **16** Taylor Barnard, GB, +58.999s; Victor Martins, F, -15 laps (DNF); Jak Crawford, USA, -16 (DNF); Amaury Cordeel, B, -18 (DNF); Juan Manuel Correa, USA, -26 (DNF); Isack Hadjar, F, -32 (DNF); Enzo Fittipaldi, BR, -32 (DNF).
** 5s penalty for speeding in the pit lane*
Fastest race lap: Hauger, 1m 46.743s, 113.415mph/182.524km/h.
Pole position: Bortoleto, 1m 41.915s, 118.788mph/191.171km/h.
Championship points: Drivers: 1 Maloney, 36; **2** Martí, 24; **3** Aron, 19; **4** Bortoleto, 15; **5** O'Sullivan, 14; **6** Crawford, 8.
Teams: 1 Rodin Motorsport, 38; **2** Campos Racing, 29; **3** Invicta Racing, 21.

FIA FORMULA 2 CHAMPIONSHIP, Jeddah Corniche Circuit, Saudi Arabia, 8/9 March. Round 2. 20 and 28 laps of the 3.836-mile/6.174km circuit.
Race 1 (76.572 miles/123.230km).
1 Dennis Hauger, N, 41m 39.473s, 110.507mph/177.845km/h; **2** Paul Aron, EST, +0.782s; **3** Enzo Fittipaldi, BR, +3.984s; **4** Zane Maloney, BB, +6.765s; **5** Jak Crawford, USA, +8.399s; **6** Andrea Kimi Antonelli, I, +11.140s; **7** Pepe Martí, E, +13.663s; **8** Kush Maini, IND, +14.016s; **9** Joshua Duerksen, PY, +17.555s; **10** Gabriel Bortoleto, BR, +18.062s; **11** Franco Colapinto, RA, +18.467s; **12** Ritomo Miyata, J, +25.009s; **13** Taylor Barnard, GB, +25.032s; **14** Rafael Villagómez, MEX, +26.645s; **15** Isack Hadjar, F, -1 lap (DNF); **16** Zak O'Sullivan, GB, -1 (DNF); Juan Manuel Correa, USA, -5 (DNF); Amaury Cordeel, B, -11 (DNF); Victor Martins, F, -20 (DNF).
Withdrawn: Oliver Bearman, GB.
Disqualified: Richard Verschoor, NL, originally won in 41m 38.745s; Roman Staněk, CZ, +17.269s (both for a technical infringement).
Fastest race lap: Aron, 1m 44.607s, 132.026mph/212.475km/h.
Pole position: Aron.

Race 2 (107.262 miles/172.622km).
1 Enzo Fittipaldi, BR, 56m 57.579s, 113.149mph/182.096km/h; **2** Kush Maini, IND, +7.895s; **3** Dennis Hauger, N, +9.348s; **4** Jak Crawford, USA, +9.379s; **5** Amaury Cordeel, B, +9.506s; **6** Andrea Kimi Antonelli, I, +10.044s; **7** Zane Maloney, BB, +10.442s; **8** Richard Verschoor, NL, +11.824s; **9** Rafael Villagómez, MEX, +17.541s; **10** Paul Aron, EST, +25.134s; **11** Victor Martins, F, +25.680s*; **12** Joshua Duerksen, PY, +26.269s**; **13** Taylor Barnard, GB, +30.424s; **14** Juan Manuel Correa, USA, +38.415s; **15** Ritomo Miyata, J, +40.805s; Zak O'Sullivan, GB, -5 laps (DNF); Isack Hadjar, F, -8 (DNF); Franco Colapinto, RA, -14 (DNF); Gabriel Bortoleto, BR, -27 (DNF); Pepe Martí, E, -28 (DNF); Roman Staněk, CZ, -28 (DNF).
** 5s penalty for causing a collision*
*** 10s penalty for leaving the track and gaining an advantage (originally won)*
Withdrawn: Oliver Bearman, GB.
Fastest race lap: Fittipaldi, 1m 44.449s, 132.225mph/212.796km/h.
Pole position: Maini, 1m 42.242s, 135.079mph/217.390km/h.
Championship points: Drivers: 1 Maloney, 47; **2** Fittipaldi, 32; **3** Hauger, 31; **4** Aron, 29; **5** Maini, 27; **6** Martí, 26.
Teams: 1 Rodin Motorsport, 49; **2** Invicta Racing, 42; **3** MP Motorsport, 39.

FIA FORMULA 2 CHAMPIONSHIP, Albert Park Circuit, Melbourne, Victoria, Australia, 23/24 March. Round 3. 23 and 33 laps of the 3.280-mile/5.278km circuit.
Race 1 (75.431 miles/121.394km).
1 Roman Staněk, CZ, 43m 59.337s, 102.885mph/165.578km/h; **2** Dennis Hauger, N, +0.349s; **3** Kush Maini, IND, +1.754s; **4** Franco Colapinto, RA, +2.393s; **5** Ritomo Miyata, J, +2.984s; **6** Isack Hadjar, F, +3.173s*; **7** Victor Martins, F, +3.639s; **8** Zak O'Sullivan, GB, +6.615s; **9** Jak Crawford, USA, +7.297s; **10** Zane Maloney, BB, +7.921s; **11** Juan Manuel Correa, USA, +10.156s; **12** Enzo Fittipaldi, BR, +11.864s; **13** Taylor Barnard, GB, +15.612s; **14** Oliver Bearman, GB, +16.095s**; **15** Rafael Villagómez, MEX, +16.269s; **16** Amaury Cordeel, B, +35.544s; **17** Joshua Duerksen, PY, +44.447s; **18** Paul Aron, EST, +1m 12.351s; Andrea Kimi Antonelli, I, -14 laps (DNF-accident); Richard Verschoor, NL, -14 (DNF-accident); Gabriel Bortoleto, BR, -23 (DNF-accident); Pepe Martí, E, -23 (DNF-accident).
** 10s penalty for causing a collision with Martí*
*** 10s penalty for forcing Durksen off the track*
Fastest race lap: Hadjar, 1m 31.573s, 128.930mph/207.493km/h.
Pole position: Staněk.

Race 2 (108.227 miles/174.174km).
1 Isack Hadjar, F, 56m 42.116s, 114.521mph/184.304km/h; **2** Paul Aron, EST, +4.454s; **3** Zane Maloney, BB, +9.649s; **4** Andrea Kimi Antonelli, I, +12.990s; **5** Ritomo Miyata, J, +13.652s; **6** Richard Verschoor, NL, +18.059s; **7** Rafael Villagómez, MEX, +23.600s; **8** Victor Martins, F, +25.080s; **9** Oliver Bearman, GB, +29.442s; **10** Jak Crawford, USA, +31.199s; **11** Amaury Cordeel, B, +33.841s; **12** Kush Maini, IND, +34.041s; **13** Pepe Martí, E, +34.594s*; **14** Juan Manuel Correa, USA, +41.772s; **15** Roman Staněk, CZ, +58.194s; **16** Taylor Barnard, GB, +59.319s; **17** Enzo Fittipaldi, BR, +1m 09.169s; Dennis Hauger, N, -24 laps (DNF); Joshua Duerksen, PY, -28 (DNF); Zak O'Sullivan, GB, -28 (DNF); Gabriel Bortoleto, BR, -28 (DNF).
** 10s penalty for causing a collision*
Disqualified: Franco Colapinto, RA, +19.741s (technical non-compliance).
Fastest race lap: Crawford, 1m 30.961s, 129.797mph/208.889km/h.
Pole position: Hauger, 1m 28.694s, 133.115mph/214.228km/h.
Championship points: Drivers: 1 Maloney, 62; **2** Aron, 47; **3** Hauger, 41; **4** Hadjar, 34; **5** Maini, 33; **6** Martí, 32.
Teams: 1 Rodin Motorsport, 78; **2** Campos Racing, 60; **3** Hitech Pulse-Eight, 57.

FIA FORMULA 2 CHAMPIONSHIP, Autodromo Enzo e Dino Ferrari, Imola, Italy, 18/19 May. Round 4. 25 and 35 laps of the 3.050-mile/4.909km circuit.
Race 1 (76.122 miles/122.507km).
1 Franco Colapinto, RA, 41m 43.964s, 109.635mph/

176.441km/h; **2** Paul Aron, EST, +1.706s; **3** Zane Maloney, BB, +6.618s; **4** Amaury Cordeel, B, +8.173s; **5** Oliver Bearman, GB, +11.125s; **6** Gabriel Bortoleto, BR, +11.589s; **7** Richard Verschoor, NL, +14.254s; **8** Kush Maini, IND, +16.330s; **9** Zak O'Sullivan, GB, +17.427s; **10** Andrea Kimi Antonelli, I, +18.286s; **11** Rafael Villagómez, MEX, +18.960s; **12** Victor Martins, F, +19.396s; **13** Ritomo Miyata, J, +19.788s; **14** Jak Crawford, USA, +20.089s; **15** Juan Manuel Correa, USA, +20.587s; **16** Pepe Martí, E, +55.602s; Roman Staněk, CZ, -25 laps (DNF); Isack Hadjar, F, -25 (DNF); Joshua Duerksen, PY, -25 (DNF); Enzo Fittipaldi, BR, -25 (DNF); Dennis Hauger, N, -25 (DNF).
Disqualified: Taylor Barnard, GB, finished 7th, +11.920s (failure to engage the start set-up procedure).
Fastest race lap: Colapinto, 1m 30.352s, 121.537mph/195.595km/h.
Pole position: Cordeel.

Race 2 (106.625 miles/171.597km).
1 Isack Hadjar, F, 54m 01.509s, 118.566mph/190.814km/h; **2** Gabriel Bortoleto, BR, +0.569s; **3** Joshua Duerksen, PY, +13.736s; **4** Andrea Kimi Antonelli, I, +18.034s; **5** Franco Colapinto, RA, +18.489s; **6** Paul Aron, EST, +18.815s; **7** Jak Crawford, USA, +20.737s; **8** Juan Manuel Correa, USA, +21.240s; **9** Victor Martins, F, +28.364s; **10** Richard Verschoor, NL, +33.507s; **11** Zane Maloney, BB, +34.107s; **12** Dennis Hauger, N, +34.346s; **13** Zak O'Sullivan, GB, +37.657s; **14** Kush Maini, IND, +37.957s; **15** Ritomo Miyata, J, +38.402s; **16** Rafael Villagómez, MEX, +42.357s; **17** Enzo Fittipaldi, BR, +43.055s; **18** Roman Staněk, CZ, +43.575s; **19** Oliver Bearman, GB, +44.017s; **20** Taylor Barnard, GB, +44.786s; Amaury Cordeel, B, -5 laps (DNF); Pepe Martí, E, -5 (DNF).
Fastest race lap: Martins, 1m 29.580s, 122.584mph/197.280km/h.
Pole position: Bortoleto, 1m 27.056s, 126.138mph/203.000km/h.
Championship points: Drivers: 1 Maloney, 68; **2** Aron, 63; **3** Hadjar, 59; **4** Hauger, 41; **5** Bortoleto, 38; **6** Antonelli, 36.
Teams: 1 Campos Racing, 85; **2** Rodin Motorsport, 84; **3** Hitech Pulse-Eight, 78.

FIA FORMULA 2 CHAMPIONSHIP, Circuit de Monaco, Monaco, 25/26 May. Round 5. 30 and 42 laps of the 2.074-mile/3.337km circuit.
Race 1 (62.205 miles/100.110km).
1 Taylor Barnard, GB, 1h 04m 20.946s, 58.001mph/93.343km/h; **2** Gabriel Bortoleto, BR, +5.246s; **3** Dennis Hauger, N, +5.817s; **4** Andrea Kimi Antonelli, I, +8.213s; **5** Franco Colapinto, RA, +10.857s; **6** Roman Staněk, CZ, +13.594s; **7** Paul Aron, EST, +15.085s; **8** Isack Hadjar, F, +16.495s; **9** Enzo Fittipaldi, BR, +16.890s; **10** Zak O'Sullivan, GB, +17.752s; **11** Oliver Bearman, GB, +18.334s; **12** Juan Manuel Correa, USA, +18.830s; **13** Jak Crawford, USA, +19.225s; **14** Amaury Cordeel, B, +22.049s; **15** Rafael Villagómez, MEX, +24.054s; **16** Richard Verschoor, NL, +24.327s; **17** Ritomo Miyata, J, +25.203s; **18** Joshua Duerksen, PY, +25.915s; Zane Maloney, BB, -8 laps (DNF); Kush Maini, IND, -8 (DNF); Pepe Martí, E, -26 (DNF); Victor Martins, F, -30 (DNF).
Fastest race lap: Antonelli, 1m 22.333s, 90.664mph/145.909km/h.
Pole position: Barnard.

Race 2 (87.088 miles/140.154km).
1 Zak O'Sullivan, GB, 1h 00m 25.696s, 86.470mph/139.160km/h; **2** Isack Hadjar, F, +0.580s; **3** Paul Aron, EST, +8.053s; **4** Oliver Bearman, GB, +9.118s; **5** Juan Manuel Correa, USA, +9.586s; **6** Dennis Hauger, N, +9.945s; **7** Andrea Kimi Antonelli, I, +17.540s; **8** Gabriel Bortoleto, BR, +17.847s; **9** Victor Martins, F, +18.021s; **10** Zane Maloney, BB, +26.555s; **11** Taylor Barnard, GB, +26.983s; **12** Enzo Fittipaldi, BR, +27.418s; **13** Franco Colapinto, RA, +30.213s; **14** Pepe Martí, E, +31.662s; **15** Ritomo Miyata, J, +32.386s; **16** Roman Staněk, CZ, +33.309s; **17** Kush Maini, IND, +33.796s; **18** Joshua Duerksen, PY, -3 laps; Richard Verschoor, NL, -14 (DNF); Rafael Villagómez, MEX, -24 (DNF); Amaury Cordeel, B, -36 (DNF); Jak Crawford, USA, -42 (DNF).
Fastest race lap: Hauger, 1m 22.384s, 90.608mph/145.819km/h.
Pole position: Verschoor, 1m 21.283s, 91.835mph/147.794km/h.
Championship points: Drivers: 1 Aron, 80; **2** Hadjar, 78; **3** Maloney, 69; **4** Hauger, 56; **5** Bortoleto, 50; **6** Antonelli, 48.
Teams: 1 Campos Racing, 104; **2** Hitech Pulse-Eight, 95; **3** MP Motorsport, 94.

FIA FORMULA 2 CHAMPIONSHIP, Circuit de Barcelona-Catalunya, Montmeló, Barcelona, Spain, 22/23 June. Round 6. 26 and 37 laps of the 2.894-mile/4.657km circuit.
Race 1 (75.159 miles/120.956km).
1 Victor Martins, F, 39m 47.280s, 113.455mph/182.588km/h; **2** Kush Maini, IND, +4.411s; **3** Paul Aron, EST, +8.625s; **4** Jak Crawford, USA, +9.096s; **5** Gabriel Bortoleto, BR, +10.742s; **6** Isack Hadjar, F, +11.612s; **7** Ritomo Miyata, J, +12.641s*; **8** Juan Manuel Correa, USA, +12.968s**; **9** Zak O'Sullivan, GB, +25.925s; **10** Joshua Duerksen, PY, +26.814s; **11** Pepe Martí, E, +27.433s; **12** Dennis Hauger, N, +27.834s*; **13** Richard Verschoor, NL, +29.362s; **14** Amaury Cordeel, B, +29.819s; **15** Andrea Kimi Antonelli, I, +29.995s**; **16** Enzo Fittipaldi, BR, +31.765s; **17** Rafael Villagómez, MEX, +33.049s**; **18** Franco Colapinto, RA, +35.554s*; **19** Taylor Barnard, GB, +38.349s; **20** Zane Maloney, BB, +41.445s***; **21** Oliver Bearman, GB, +41.456s; **22** Roman Staněk, CZ, +46.518s*.
** 5+5s penalty for exceeding track limits*
*** 5s penalty for exceeding track limits*
**** 5+5+5s penalty for exceeding track limits*
Fastest race lap: Miyata, 1m 30.617s, 114.960mph/185.011km/h.
Pole position: Maini.

Race 2 (106.990 miles/172.183km).
1 Jak Crawford, USA, 59m 46.800s, 107.461mph/172.941km/h; **2** Franco Colapinto, RA, +1.400s; **3** Juan Manuel Correa, USA, +5.820s; **4** Paul Aron, EST, +11.486s; **5** Isack Hadjar, F, +14.720s; **6** Kush Maini, IND, +19.333s; **7** Zane Maloney, BB, +22.692s; **8** Amaury Cordeel, B, +24.442s; **9** Pepe Martí, E, +24.919s; **10** Gabriel Bortoleto, BR, +25.400s*; **11** Enzo Fittipaldi, BR, +29.155s**; **12** Andrea Kimi Antonelli, I, +35.513s; **13** Ritomo Miyata, J, +35.955s; **14** Oliver Bearman, GB, +37.470s; **15** Zak O'Sullivan, GB, +45.073s***; **16** Rafael Villagómez, MEX, +47.273s; **17** Roman Staněk, CZ, +1m 03.092s; **18** Richard Verschoor, NL, -2 laps (DNF); Joshua Duerksen, PY, -21 (DNF); Taylor Barnard, GB, -26 (DNF); Victor Martins, F, -37 (DNF); Dennis Hauger, N, -37 (DNF).
** 5s penalty for causing a collision with Maini*
*** 5s penalty for exceeding track limits*
**** 5+5s penalty for exceeding track limits*
Fastest race lap: Antonelli, 1m 27.918s, 118.490mph/190.691km/h.
Pole position: Aron, 1m 24.766s, 122.896mph/197.782km/h.
Championship points: Drivers: 1 Aron, 100; **2** Hadjar, 91; **3** Maloney, 75; **4** Crawford, 62; **5** Hauger, 56; **6** Colapinto, 56.
Teams: 1 Campos Racing, 120; **2** Hitech Pulse-Eight, 119; **3** MP Motorsport, 112.

FIA FORMULA 2 CHAMPIONSHIP, Red Bull Ring, Spielberg, Austria, 29/30 June. Round 7. 28 and 40 laps of the 2.683-mile/4.318km circuit.
Race 1 (75.048 miles/120.778km).
1 Oliver Bearman, GB, 37m 22.959s, 120.578mph/194.051km/h; **2** Pepe Martí, E, +1.751s; **3** Paul Aron, EST, +3.003s; **4** Gabriel Bortoleto, BR, +3.655s; **5** Dennis Hauger, N, +11.030s; **6** Jak Crawford, USA, +11.677s; **7** Kush Maini, IND, +13.703s; **8** Joshua Duerksen, PY, +13.887s; **9** Zak O'Sullivan, GB, +15.866s; **10** Victor Martins, F, +19.852s; **11** Franco Colapinto, RA, +21.546s; **12** Taylor Barnard, GB, +22.305s; **13** Isack Hadjar, F, +22.857s; **14** Enzo Fittipaldi, BR, +23.629s; **15** Andrea Kimi Antonelli, I, +23.728s; **16** Juan Manuel Correa, USA, +26.445s; **17** Zane Maloney, BB, +27.184s; **18** Amaury Cordeel, B, +27.597s; **19** Rafael Villagómez, MEX, +28.250s; **20** Richard Verschoor, NL, +29.804s; **21** Roman Staněk, CZ, +29.884s; **22** Ritomo Miyata, J, +46.914s.
Fastest race lap: Miyata, 1m 18.708s, 122.720mph/197.499km/h.
Pole position: Maini.

Race 2 (107.245 miles/172.594km).
1 Gabriel Bortoleto, BR, 53m 59.322s, 119.272mph/191.949km/h; **2** Franco Colapinto, RA, +4.296s; **3** Isack Hadjar, F, +5.553s; **4** Enzo Fittipaldi, BR, +11.399s; **5** Paul Aron, EST, +11.437s*; **6** Joshua Duerksen, PY, +12.562s; **7** Amaury Cordeel, B, +22.557s; **8** Taylor Barnard, GB, +27.634s; **9** Zak O'Sullivan, GB, +32.180s; **10** Jak Crawford, USA, +32.244s; **11** Victor Martins, F, +32.613s; **12** Dennis Hauger, N, +33.470s; **13** Andrea Kimi Antonelli, I, +34.724s; **14** Juan Manuel Correa, USA, +35.143s**; **15** Pepe Martí, E, +36.035s***; **16** Rafael Villagómez, MEX, +49.792s; **17** Kush Maini, IND, +51.433s; **18** Roman Staněk, CZ, +55.494s; Ritomo Miyata, J, -6 laps (DNF); Richard Verschoor, NL, -19 (DNF); Oliver Bearman, GB, -20 (DNF); Zane Maloney, BB, -36 (DNF).
** 5s penalty for more than one change of direction*
*** 5s penalty for crossing the line at pit entry*
**** 10s stop & go penalty converted to 30s penalty for failure to complete mandatory pit stop*
Fastest race lap: Colapinto, 1m 17.868s, 124.044mph/199.630km/h.
Pole position: Hauger, 1m 15.487s, 127.957mph/205.926km/h.
Championship points: Drivers: 1 Aron, 117; **2** Hadjar, 106; **3** Bortoleto, 85; **4** Maloney, 75; **5** Colapinto, 75; **6** Crawford, 66.
Teams: 1 Campos Racing, 143; **2** Hitech Pulse-Eight, 142; **3** MP Motorsport, 137.

FIA FORMULA 2 CHAMPIONSHIP, Silverstone Arena Grand Prix Circuit, Towcester, Northamptonshire, Great Britain, 6/7 July. Round 8. 21 and 29 laps of the 3.660-mile/5.891km circuit.
Race 1 (76.787 miles/123.577km).
1 Andrea Kimi Antonelli, I, 1h 02m 34.856s, 73.699mph/118.607km/h; **2** Zane Maloney, BB, +8.683s; **3** Kush Maini, IND, +11.257s; **4** Gabriel Bortoleto, BR, +15.895s*; **5** Franco Colapinto, RA, +18.064s; **6** Jak Crawford, USA, +18.791s; **7** Dennis Hauger, N, +20.191s; **8** Roman Staněk, CZ, +20.932s; **9** Taylor Barnard, GB, +21.367s; **10** Ritomo Miyata, J, +24.232s; **11** Richard Verschoor, NL, +25.773s; **12** Juan Manuel Correa, USA, +28.071s; **13** Enzo Fittipaldi, BR, +29.749s; **14** Rafael Villagómez, MEX, +32.521s; **15** Amaury Cordeel, B, +33.104s; **16** Joshua Duerksen, PY, +33.960s; Zak O'Sullivan, GB, -5 laps (DNF); Victor Martins, F, -6 (DNF); Oliver Bearman, GB, -7 (DNF); Paul Aron, EST, -14 (DNF); Pepe Martí, E, -14 (DNF); Isack Hadjar, F, -14 (DNF).
** 5s penalty for leaving the track and gaining lasting advantage*
Fastest race lap: Antonelli, 2m 01.267s, 108.667mph/174.883km/h.
Pole position: Antonelli.

Race 2 (106.071 miles/170.705km).
1 Isack Hadjar, F, 54m 48.351s, 116.214mph/187.028km/h; **2** Zane Maloney, BB, +1.657s; **3** Jak Crawford, USA, +1.822s*; **4** Franco Colapinto, RA, +11.991s; **5** Victor Martins, F, +12.228s; **6** Gabriel Bortoleto, BR, +14.510s; **7** Oliver Bearman, GB, +17.478s; **8** Enzo Fittipaldi, BR, +17.990s; **9** Dennis Hauger, N, +23.192s; **10** Pepe Martí, E, +26.778s; **11** Zak O'Sullivan, GB, +32.662s; **12** Paul Aron, EST, +33.270s; **13** Richard Verschoor, NL, +34.951s; **14** Taylor Barnard, GB, +37.294s; **15** Amaury Cordeel, B, +42.346s; **16** Rafael Villagómez, MEX, +45.649s; **17** Ritomo Miyata, J, +46.539s; **18** Roman Staněk, CZ, +50.783s; **19** Kush Maini, IND, +1m 12.301s**; **20** Juan Manuel Correa, USA, +1m 37.471s***; Joshua Duerksen, PY, -27 laps (DNF); Andrea Kimi Antonelli, I, -29 (DNF).
** 5s penalty for exceeding track limits (originally won)*
*** 5+5s penalty for exceeding track limits; 10s penalty for causing a collision with Antonelli*
**** 5s penalty for releasing the clutch early while work was still ongoing to his car during the pit stop*
Fastest race lap: Colapinto, 1m 41.357s, 130.013mph/209.236km/h.
Pole position: Hadjar, 1m 39.368s, 132.616mph/213.424km/h.
Championship points: Drivers: 1 Hadjar, 133; **2** Aron, 117; **3** Maloney, 101; **4** Bortoleto, 98; **5** Colapinto, 92; **6** Crawford, 84.
Teams: 1 Campos Racing, 171; **2** MP Motorsport, 158; **3** Invicta Racing, 156.

FIA FORMULA 2 CHAMPIONSHIP, Hungaroring, Mogyoród, Budapest, Hungary, 20/21 July. Round 9. 28 and 36 laps of the 2.722-mile/4.381km circuit.
Race 1 (76.198 miles/122.628km).
1 Kush Maini, IND, 44m 28.935s, 102.812mph/165.460km/h; **2** Victor Martins, F, +9.564s; **3** Isack Hadjar, F, +15.005s; **4** Dennis Hauger, N, +24.643s; **5** Franco Colapinto, RA, +26.161s; **6** Paul Aron, EST, +32.825s; **7** Taylor Barnard, GB, +37.451s; **8** Juan Manuel Correa, USA, +40.904s; **9** Jak Crawford, USA, +49.354s; **10** Oliver Bearman, GB, +52.613s; **11** Rafael Villagómez, MEX, +54.021s; **12** Ritomo Miyata, J, +54.665s; **13** Zane Maloney, BB, +54.913s; **14** Andrea Kimi Antonelli, I, +55.108s; **15** Roman Staněk, CZ, +55.302s; **16** Gabriel Bortoleto, BR, +56.073s; **17** Pepe Martí, E, +57.437s; **18** Joshua Duerksen, PY, +59.822s; **19** Zak O'Sullivan, GB, +1m 04.702s; **20** Amaury Cordeel, B, +1m 05.863s*; **21** Enzo Fittipaldi, BR, -1 lap.
** 10s penalty for leaving the track and gaining an advantage*
Disqualified: Richard Verschoor, NL, originally won in 44m 27.360s (technical non-conformity).
Fastest race lap: Bortoleto, 1m 32.266s, 106.214mph/170.936km/h.
Pole position: Verschoor.

Race 2 (97.975 miles/157.676km).
1 Andrea Kimi Antonelli, I, 1h 02m 46.691s, 93.663mph/150.736km/h; **2** Victor Martins, F, +12.528s; **3** Richard Verschoor, NL, +13.355s; **4** Gabriel Bortoleto, BR, +14.819s; **5** Enzo Fittipaldi, BR, +18.516s; **6** Dennis Hauger, N, +19.179s; **7** Kush Maini, IND, +20.270s; **8** Ritomo Miyata, J, +20.498s; **9** Taylor Barnard, GB, +21.193s; **10** Rafael Villagómez, MEX, +23.310s; **11** Roman Staněk, CZ, +24.882s; **12** Pepe Martí, E, +26.705s; **13** Franco Colapinto, RA, +28.408s; **14** Zak O'Sullivan, GB, +31.105s; **15** Oliver Bearman, GB, +31.507s; **16** Juan Manuel Correa, USA, +31.883s; **17** Jak Crawford, USA, +32.868s; **18** Isack Hadjar, F, +33.754s; **19** Joshua Duerksen, PY, +44.655s*; Amaury Cordeel, B, -15 laps (DNF); Zane Maloney, BB, -30 (DNF); Paul Aron, EST, -30 (DNF).
** 10s penalty for leaving the track and gaining an advantage*
Fastest race lap: Antonelli, 1m 32.086s, 106.422mph/171.270km/h.
Pole position: Aron, 1m 30.028s, 108.855mph/175.185km/h.
Championship points: Drivers: 1 Hadjar, 140; **2** Aron, 122; **3** Bortoleto, 110; **4** Maloney, 101; **5** Colapinto, 96; **6** Antonelli, 85.
Teams: 1 Invicta Racing, 184; **2** Campos Racing, 178; **3** MP Motorsport, 175.

FIA FORMULA 2 CHAMPIONSHIP, Circuit de Spa-Francorchamps, Stavelot, Belgium, 27/28 July. Round 10. 5 and 25 laps of the 4.352-mile/7.004km circuit.
Race 1 (21.683 miles/34.896km).
1 Zak O'Sullivan, GB, 14m 15.548s, 91.560mph/147.352km/h; **2** Dennis Hauger, N, +0.849s; **3** Richard Verschoor, NL, +1.122s; **4** Zane Maloney, BB, +3.031s; **5** Jak Crawford, USA, +4.051s; **6** Andrea Kimi Antonelli, I, +5.210s; **7** Oliver Bearman, GB, +6.022s; **8** Franco Colapinto, RA, +7.665s; **9** Isack Hadjar, F, +8.907s; **10** Gabriel Bortoleto, BR, +9.907s; **11** Amaury Cordeel, B, +11.187s; **12** Victor Martins, F, +12.642s; **13** Kush Maini, IND, +14.099s; **14** Enzo Fittipaldi, BR, +15.699s; **15** Ritomo Miyata, J, +16.697s; **16** Taylor Barnard, GB, +17.085s; **17** Juan Manuel Correa, USA, +17.851s; **18** Paul Aron, EST, +18.702s; **19** Joshua Duerksen, PY, +19.254s; **20** Roman Staněk, CZ, +20.186s; **21** Rafael Villagómez, MEX, +21.200s; Pepe Martí, E, -4 laps (DNF).
Fastest race lap: O'Sullivan, 2m 19.889s, 111.999mph/180.245km/h.
Pole position: O'Sullivan.

Race 2 (108.725 miles/174.976km).
1 Isack Hadjar, F, 57m 08.495s, 114.243mph/183.857km/h; **2** Gabriel Bortoleto, BR, +2.934s; **3** Jak Crawford, USA, +12.093s; **4** Zak O'Sullivan, GB, +13.741s; **5** Richard Verschoor, NL, +19.392s; **6** Zane Maloney, BB, +21.282s; **7** Ritomo Miyata, J, +21.884s; **8** Amaury Cordeel, B, +25.388s; **9** Andrea Kimi Antonelli, I, +31.800s; **10** Joshua Duerksen, PY, +32.446s; **11** Juan Manuel Correa, USA, +39.528s; **12** Dennis Hauger, N, +42.048s; **13** Taylor Barnard, GB, +43.750s; **14** Roman Staněk, CZ, +53.654s*; **15** Kush Maini, IND, +58.831s*; **16** Paul Aron, EST, -1 lap (DNF); Enzo Fittipaldi, BR, -15 (DNF); Rafael Villagómez, MEX, -22 (DNF); Victor Martins, F, -22 (DNF); Franco Colapinto, RA, -25 (DNF); Oliver Bearman, GB, -25 (DNF); Pepe Martí, E, -25 (DNF).
** 5s penalty for exceeding track limits*
Fastest race lap: Aron, 1m 59.029s, 131.627mph/211.834km/h.
Pole position: Aron, 1m 56.959s, 133.957mph/215.583km/h.
Championship points: Drivers: 1 Hadjar, 165; **2** Bortoleto, 129; **3** Aron, 124; **4** Maloney, 111; **5** Crawford, 100; **6** Colapinto, 96.
Teams: 1 Campos Racing, 203; **2** Invicta Racing, 203; **3** MP Motorsport, 179.

FIA FORMULA 2 CHAMPIONSHIP, Autodromo Nazionale Monza, Monza, Italy, 31 August/1 September. Round 11. 21 and 30 laps of the 3.600-mile/5.793km circuit.
Race 1 (75.400 miles/121.344km).
1 Oliver Bearman, GB, 35m 37.225s, 127.325mph/204.910km/h; **2** Victor Martins, F, +1.694s; **3** Joshua Duerksen, PY, +7.254s; **4** Pepe Martí, E, +12.880s; **5** Zane Maloney, BB, +13.442s; **6** Jak Crawford, USA, +13.486s; **7** Enzo Fittipaldi, BR, +13.587s; **8** Dennis Hauger, N, +14.840s; **8** Gabriel Bortoleto, BR, +14.840s; **10** Isack Hadjar, F, +16.126s; **11** Kush Maini, IND, +17.120s; **12** Amaury Cordeel, B, +19.164s; **13** Ritomo Miyata, J, +22.808s; **14** Richard Verschoor, NL, +23.376s; **15** Roman Staněk, CZ, +24.990s; **16** Rafael Villagómez, MEX, +29.441s; **17** Juan Manuel Correa, USA, +29.713s; **18** Andrea Kimi Antonelli, I, +32.510s; **19** Niels Koolen, NL, +48.820s; **20** Paul Aron, EST, -1 lap*; Oliver Goethe, DK, -21 (DNF); Zak O'Sullivan, GB, -21 (DNF).
** 10s penalty for causing a collision with Maloney*
Fastest race lap: Martins, 1m 33.086s, 139.210mph/224.037km/h.
Pole position: Fittipaldi.

Race 2 (107.796 miles/173.481km).
1 Gabriel Bortoleto, BR, 50m 30.337s, 128.286mph/206.456km/h; **2** Zane Maloney, BB, +9.436s; **3** Richard Verschoor, NL, +11.628s; **4** Andrea Kimi Antonelli, I, +14.173s; **5** Joshua Duerksen, PY, +14.558s; **6** Victor Martins, F, +15.047s; **7** Oliver Bearman, GB, +15.399s; **8** Rafael Villagómez, MEX, +15.753s; **9** Jak Crawford, USA, +17.054s; **10** Enzo Fittipaldi, BR, +17.372s; **11** Isack Hadjar, F, +17.864s; **12** Pepe Martí, E, +18.600s; **13** Zak O'Sullivan, GB, +25.424s; **14** Ritomo Miyata, J, +31.720s*; **15** Kush Maini, IND, +46.981s; **16** Oliver Goethe, DK, +51.605s; **17** Roman Staněk, CZ, +1m 02.455s; **18** Amaury Cordeel, B, +1m 21.694s; **19** Niels Koolen, NL, +1m 26.773s; Juan Manuel Correa, USA, -14 laps (DNF); Dennis Hauger, N, -23 (DNF); Paul Aron, EST, -30 (DNF).
** 10s penalty for causing a collision; 5s penalty for failing to follow Race Director's instructions*
Fastest race lap: Maini, 1m 32.717s, 139.764mph/224.929km/h.
Pole position: Maloney, 1m 32.160s, 140.609mph/226.289km/h.
Championship points: Drivers: 1 Hadjar, 165; **2** Bortoleto, 154.5; **3** Maloney, 135; **4** Aron, 124; **5** Crawford, 105; **6** Antonelli, 99.
Teams: 1 Invicta Racing, 228.5; **2** Campos Racing, 208; **3** MP Motorsport, 179.5.

FIA FORMULA 2 CHAMPIONSHIP, Baku City Circuit, Azerbaijan, 14/15 September. Round 12. 21 and 17 laps of the 3.730-mile/6.003km circuit.
Race 1 (78.267 miles/125.959km).
1 Joshua Duerksen, PY, 44m 00.116s, 106.810mph/171.895km/h; **2** Jak Crawford, USA, +3.444s; **3** Gabriele Minì, I, +4.579s; **4** Victor Martins, F, +4.599s; **5** Gabriel Bortoleto, BR, +7.807s; **6** Paul Aron, EST, +8.793s; **7** Andrea Kimi Antonelli, I, +9.293s; **8** Christian Mansell, AUS, +13.436s; **9** Kush Maini, IND, +15.013s; **10** Zane Maloney, BB, +15.515s; **11**

Luke Browning, GB, +15.740s; **12** Isack Hadjar, F, +16.208s; **13** Enzo Fittipaldi, BR, +17.065s; **14** Dennis Hauger, N, +17.094s; **15** Juan Manuel Correa, USA, +18.039s; **16** Rafael Villagómez, MEX, +20.637s; **17** Richard Verschoor, NL, +22.828s; **18** Amaury Cordeel, B, +47.405s; **19** Pepe Martí, E, +52.191s; **20** Niels Koolen, NL, +56.243s; **21** Oliver Goethe, DK, +1m 42.954s*; Ritomo Miyata, J, -7 laps (DNF-accident).
** 5s penalty for causing a collision with Cordeel*
Fastest race lap: Verschoor, 1m 56.629s, 115.137mph/185.295km/h.
Pole position: Mansell.

Race 2 (63.347 miles/101.947km).
1 Richard Verschoor, NL, 1h 10m 08.415s, 54.243mph/87.296km/h; **2** Victor Martins, F, +0.333s; **3** Andrea Kimi Antonelli, I, +0.567s; **4** Gabriel Bortoleto, BR, +0.819s; **5** Joshua Duerksen, PY, +1.002s; **6** Paul Aron, EST, +1.212s; **7** Luke Browning, GB, +1.351s; **8** Jak Crawford, USA, +1.468s; **9** Dennis Hauger, N, +1.910s; **10** Christian Mansell, AUS, +2.163s; **11** Enzo Fittipaldi, BR, +2.653s; **12** Amaury Cordeel, B, +3.348s; **13** Ritomo Miyata, J, +3.391s; **14** Isack Hadjar, F, +4.127s; **15** Zane Maloney, BB, +42.182s; Gabriele Mini, I, -3 laps (DNF); Juan Manuel Correa, USA, -12 (DNF); Oliver Goethe, DK, -17 (DNF); Rafael Villagómez, MEX, -17 (DNF); Pepe Martí, E, -17 (DNF); Niels Koolen, NL, -17 (DNF).
Disqualified: Kush Maini, IND, -17 (technical non-conformity - failure to engage the start up procedure at the beginning of the race).
Fastest race lap: Bortoleto, 1m 56.417s, 115.346mph/185.632km/h.
Pole position: Verschoor, 1m 54.857s, 116.913mph/188.153km/h.
Championship points: Drivers: 1 Bortoleto, 169.5; **2** Hadjar, 165; **3** Maloney, 135; **4** Aron, 133; **5** Crawford, 116; **6** Antonelli, 113.
Teams: 1 Invicta Racing, 243.5; **2** Campos Racing, 208; **3** MP Motorsport, 181.5.

FIA FORMULA 2 CHAMPIONSHIP, Lusail International Circuit, Doha, Qatar, 30 November/1 December. 23 and 30 laps of the 3.367-mile/5.419km circuit.
Race 1 (77.277 miles/124.365km).
1 Oliver Bearman, GB, 40m 51.281s, 113.736mph/183.040km/h; **2** Jak Crawford, USA, +0.295s; **3** Richard Verschoor, NL, +0.580s; **4** Isack Hadjar, F, +0.910s; **5** Gabriel Bortoleto, BR, +1.227s; **6** Zane Maloney, BB, +1.751s; **7** Paul Aron, EST, +1.059s*; **8** Joshua Duerksen, PY, +1.905s; **9** Victor Martins, F, +2.868s; **10** Dino Beganovic, S, +3.223s; **11** Luke Browning, GB, +3.532s; **12** John Bennett, GB, +4.151s; **13** Ritomo Miyata, J, +1.544s**; **14** Max Esterson, USA, +4.760s; **15** Christian Mansell, AUS, +5.340s; **16** Amaury Cordeel, B, +6.053s; **17** Rafael Villagómez, MEX, +6.517s; **18** Cian Shields, GB, +6.966s; **19** Andrea Kimi Antonelli, I, -3 laps (DNF-accident damage); **20** Kush Maini, IND, -3 (DNF-accident damage); Oliver Goethe, DK, -19 (DNF).
** 2-position penalty for causing a collision with Victor Martins*
*** 4 and 2-position penalties for causing a collision with Beganovic & causing a collision with Antonelli*
Did not start: Pepe Martí, E.
Fastest race lap: Verschoor, 1m 38.630s, 122.903mph/197.793km/h.
Pole position: Bearman.

Race 2 (100.847 miles/162.298km).
1 Paul Aron, EST, 55m 45.433s, 108.701mph/174.937km/h; **2** Isack Hadjar, F, +2.763s; **3** Gabriel Bortoleto, BR, +3.175s*; **4** Oliver Goethe, DK, +3.796s; **5** Dino Beganovic, S, +5.727s; **6** Christian Mansell, AUS, +11.509s; **7** Amaury Cordeel, B, +12.556s; **8** John Bennett, GB, +18.862s; **9** Zane Maloney, BB, +19.818s; **10** Ritomo Miyata, J, +23.297s; **11** Cian Shields, GB, +32.320s; **12** Oliver Bearman, GB, +33.737s; **13** Joshua Duerksen, PY, +46.123s; **14** Kush Maini, IND, +51.909s; **15** Luke Browning, GB, +53.372s; **16** Pepe Martí, E, +1m 05.023s; **17** Richard Verschoor, NL, +1m 09.043s**; **18** Max Esterson, USA, +1m 15.033s; Victor Martins, F, -5 laps; Jak Crawford, USA, -17 (DNF); Rafael Villagómez, MEX, -18 (DNF); Andrea Kimi Antonelli, I, -23 (DNF).
** 5s penalty for failing to follow Race Director's instructions*
*** 10s penalty for unsafe release & 10s stop and go penalty for Safety Car infringement converted to 30s penalty*
Fastest race lap: Bearman, 1m 37.997s, 123.697mph/199.071km/h.
Pole position: Aron, 1m 35.115s, 127.445mph/205.103km/h.
Championship points: Drivers: 1 Bortoleto, 188.5; **2** Hadjar, 188; **3** Aron, 163; **4** Maloney, 140; **5** Crawford, 124; **6** Antonelli, 113.
Teams: 1 Invicta Racing, 262.5; **2** Campos Racing, 231; **3** MP Motorsport, 200.5.

FIA FORMULA 2 CHAMPIONSHIP, Yas Marina Circuit, Abu Dhabi, United Arab Emirates, 7/8 December. 23 and 33 laps of the 3.281-mile/5.281km circuit.
Race 1 (75.402 miles/121.348km).
1 Pepe Martí, E, 38m 36.039s, 117.313mph/188.797km/h; **2** Gabriel Bortoleto, BR, +2.286s; **3** Dino Beganovic, S, +18.828s; **4** Oliver Bearman, GB, +19.547s*; **5** Isack Hadjar, F, +22.980s; **6** Luke Browning, GB, +26.798s; **7** Richard Verschoor, NL, +27.896s; **8** Jak Crawford, USA, +29.768s; **9** Oliver Goethe, DK, +31.618s; **10** Leonardo Fornaroli, I, +33.307s; **11** Ritomo Miyata, J, +33.784s**; **12** Rafael Villagómez, MEX, +34.727s; **13** Amaury Cordeel, B, +36.268s***; **14** Max Esterson, USA, +40.756s; **15** John Bennett, GB, +43.493s****; **16** Christian Mansell, AUS, +45.303s; **17** Kush Maini, IND, +52.570s; **18** Cian Shields, GB, +1m 00.505s; **19** Victor Martins, F, -1 lap; Joshua Duerksen, PY, -5 (DNF).
** 5s penalty for exceeding track limits*
*** 10s penalty for causing a collision with Martins*
**** 10s penalty for causing a collision with Durksen*
***** 5s penalty for exceeding track limits*
Disqualified: Paul Aron, EST, +13.971s (DRS actuator modified).
Withdrawn: Andrea Kimi Antonelli, I.
Fastest race lap: Martins, 1m 39.427s, 118.813mph/191.211km/h.
Pole position: Cordeel.

Race 2 (108.217 miles/174.158km).
1 Joshua Duerksen, PY, **33** laps; **2** Gabriel Bortoleto, BR, 33; **3** Richard Verschoor, NL, 33; **4** Victor Martins, F, 33; **5** Oliver Bearman, GB, 33; **6** Pepe Martí, E, 33; **7** Dino Beganovic, S, 33; **8** Amaury Cordeel, B, 33; **9** Oliver Goethe, DK, 33; **10** Ritomo Miyata, J, 33; **11** Paul Aron, EST, 33; **12** Kush Maini, IND, 33; **13** Leonardo Fornaroli, I, 33; **14** John Bennett, GB, 33; **15** Luke Browning, GB, 33; **16** Christian Mansell, AUS, 33; **17** Max Esterson, USA, 33; **18** Cian Shields, GB, 33; **19** Isack Hadjar, F, -1; Rafael Villagómez, MEX, -28 (DNF); Jak Crawford, USA, -29 (DNF).
Withdrawn: Andrea Kimi Antonelli, I.
Fastest race lap: Verschoor, 1m 38.923s, 119.418mph/192.185km/h.
Pole position: Martins, 1m 35.745s, 123.382mph/198.564km/h.

Final championship points
Drivers
1 Gabriel Bortoleto, BR, 214.5; **2** Isack Hadjar, F, 192; **3** Paul Aron, EST, 163; **4** Zane Maloney, BB, 140; **5** Jak Crawford, USA, 125; **6** Andrea Kimi Antonelli, I, 113; **7** Victor Martins, F, 107; **8** Richard Verschoor, NL, 106; **9** Franco Colapinto, RA, 96; **10** Joshua Duerksen, PY, 87; **11** Dennis Hauger, N, 85.5; **12** Oliver Bearman, GB, 75; **13** Kush Maini, IND, 74; **14** Pepe Martí, E, 62; **15** Enzo Fittipaldi, BR, 61; **16** Zak O'Sullivan, GB, 59; **17** Amaury Cordeel, B, 39; **18** Juan Manuel Correa, USA, 31; **19** Ritomo Miyata, J, 31; **20** Dino Beganovic, S, 22; **21** Taylor Barnard, GB, 18; **22** Roman Staněk, CZ, 14; **23** Oliver Goethe, DK, 14; **24** Rafael Villagómez, MEX, 13; **25** Christian Mansell, AUS, 10; **26** Luke Browning, GB, 7; **27** Gabriele Mini, I, 6; **28** John Bennett, GB, 4.

Teams
1 Invicta Racing, 288.5; **2** Campos Racing, 254; **3** MP Motorsport, 220.5; **4** Hitech Pulse-Eight, 202; **5** Prema Racing, 194; **6** DAMS Lucas Oil, 178; **7** ART Grand Prix, 173; **8** Rodin Motorsport, 171; **9** PHM AIX Racing, 105; **10** Trident, 105; **11** Van Amersfoort Racing, 78.

Japanese Championship Super Formula

All cars are Dallara SF23.

JAPANESE CHAMPIONSHIP SUPER FORMULA, Suzuka International Racing Course, Suzuka-shi, Mie Prefecture, Japan, 10 March. Round 1. 31 laps of the 3.608-mile/5.807km circuit, 111.857 miles/180.017km.
1 Tomoki Nojiri, J (-Honda), 57m 14.911s, 117.233mph/188.669km/h; **2** Kenta Yamashita, J (-Toyota), +1.855s; **3** Naoki Yamamoto, J (-Honda), +3.091s; **4** Kakunoshin Ohta, J (-Honda), +3.845s; **5** Ren Sato, J (-Honda), +13.705s; **6** Nirei Fukuzumi, J (-Honda), +15.716s; **7** Sena Sakaguchi, J (-Toyota), +16.833s; **8** Nobuharu Matsushita, J (-Honda), +17.836s; **9** Ayumu Iwasa, J (-Honda), +18.425s; **10** Tadasuke Makino, J (-Honda), +23.912s.
Fastest race lap: Yamamoto, 1m 39.287s, 130.832mph/210.553km/h.
Pole position: Sakaguchi, 1m 35.789s, 135.609mph/218.242km/h.

JAPANESE CHAMPIONSHIP SUPER FORMULA, Autopolis International Racing Course, Kamitsue-mura, Hita-gun, Oita Prefecture, Japan, 19 May. Round 2. 41 laps of the 2.904-mile/4.674km circuit, 119.076 miles/191.634km.
1 Tadasuke Makino, J (-Honda), 1h 03m 37.202s, 112.300mph/180.730km/h; **2** Ayumu Iwasa, J (-Honda), +5.565s; **3** Sho Tsuboi, J (-Toyota), +8.978s; **4** Naoki Yamamoto, J (-Honda), +25.812s; **5** Kakunoshin Ohta, J (-Honda), +26.311s; **6** Sena Sakaguchi, J (-Toyota), +28.385s; **7** Kenta Yamashita, J (-Toyota), +29.385s; **8** Nirei Fukuzumi, J (-Toyota), +30.041s; **9** Tomoki Nojiri, J (-Honda), +30.286s; **10** Kamui Kobayashi, J (-Toyota), +31.419s.
Fastest race lap: Ben Barnicoat, GB (-Toyota), 1m 30.451s, 115.592mph/186.028km/h.
Pole position: Iwasa, 1m 26.632s, 120.688mph/194.228km/h.

JAPANESE CHAMPIONSHIP SUPER FORMULA, Sportsland-SUGO International Course, Shibata-gun, Miyagi Prefecture, Japan, 23 June. Round 3. 12 laps of the 2.229-mile/3.587km circuit, 26.743 miles/43.038km.
1 Tomoki Nojiri, J (-Honda), 26m 22.982s, 60.818mph/97.877km/h; **2** Ayumu Iwasa, J (-Honda), +0.674s; **3** Sho Tsuboi, J (-Toyota), +1.550s; **4** Tadasuke Makino, J (-Honda), +2.719s; **5** Toshiki Oyu, J (-Toyota), +3.056s; **6** Kenta Yamashita, J (-Toyota), +3.638s; **7** Yuji Kunimoto, J (-Toyota), +5.150s; **8** Kazuto Kotaka, J (-Toyota), +5.247s; **9** Iori Kimura, J (-Honda), +5.789s; **10** Kamui Kobayashi, J (-Toyota), +5.917s.
Fastest race lap: Nojiri, 1m 40.653s, 79.707mph/128.276km/h.
Pole position: Nojiri, 1m 05.244s, 122.966mph/197.894km/h.

JAPANESE CHAMPIONSHIP SUPER FORMULA, Fuji International Speedway, Sunto-gun, Shizuoka Prefecture, Japan, 21 July. Round 4. 41 laps of the 2.835-mile/4.563km circuit, 116.059 miles/186.779km.
1 Sho Tsuboi, J (-Toyota), 59m 40.841s, 116.868mph/188.081km/h; **2** Toshiki Oyu, J (-Toyota), +7.162s; **3** Tomoki Nojiri, J (-Honda), +10.832s; **4** Nirei Fukuzumi, J (-Toyota), +11.642s; **5** Tadasuke Makino, J (-Honda), +13.536s; **6** Yuji Kunimoto, J (-Toyota), +16.180s; **7** Ren Sato, J (-Honda), +17.352s; **8** Kamui Kobayashi, J (-Toyota), +19.949s; **9** Hibiki Taira, J (-Toyota), +20.918s; **10** Naoki Yamamoto, J (-Honda), +22.378s.
Fastest race lap: Nojiri, 1m 24.990s, 120.098mph/193.279km/h.
Pole position: Fukuzumi, 1m 22.543s, 123.658mph/199.009km/h.

JAPANESE CHAMPIONSHIP SUPER FORMULA, Twin Ring Motegi, Motegi-machi, Haga-gun, Tochigi Prefecture, Japan, 25 August. Round 5. 37 laps of the 2.983-mile/4.801km circuit, 110.379 miles/177.637km.
1 Tadasuke Makino, J (-Honda), 1h 00m 10.235s, 110.066mph/177.133km/h; **2** Kenta Yamashita, J (-Toyota), +1.603s; **3** Tomoki Nojiri, J (-Honda), +4.261s; **4** Naoki Yamamoto, J (-Honda), +4.992s; **5** Sho Tsuboi, J (-Toyota), +12.728s; **6** Toshiki Oyu, J (-Toyota), +18.322s; **7** Ayumu Iwasa, J (-Honda), +20.062s; **8** Kazuto Kotaka, J (-Toyota), +23.838s; **9** Nirei Fukuzumi, J (-Toyota), +24.622s; **10** Ren Sato, J (-Honda), +27.471s.
Fastest race lap: Yamamoto, 1m 34.963s, 113.092mph/182.004km/h.
Pole position: Yamashita, 1m 31.995s, 116.740mph/187.875km/h.

JAPANESE CHAMPIONSHIP SUPER FORMULA, Fuji International Speedway, Sunto-gun, Shizuoka Prefecture, Japan, 12/13 October. 2 x 41 laps of the 2.835-mile/4.563km circuit.
Round 6 (116.059 miles/186.779km).
1 Sho Tsuboi, J (-Toyota), 59m 05.287s, 118.040mph/189.967km/h; **2** Ayumu Iwasa, J (-Honda), +4.440s; **3** Kamui Kobayashi, J (-Toyota), +4.853s; **4** Tadasuke Makino, J (-Honda), +5.704s; **5** Nirei Fukuzumi, J (-Toyota), +10.695s; **6** Tomoki Nojiri, J (-Honda), +11.363s; **7** Ren Sato, J (-Honda), +11.898s; **8** Naoki Yamamoto, J (-Honda), +12.799s; **9** Kakunoshin Ohta, J (-Honda), +18.904s; **10** Kenta Yamashita, J (-Toyota), +22.070s.
Fastest race lap: Tsuboi, 1m 24.241s, 121.166mph/194.998km/h.
Pole position: Fukuzumi, 1m 21.726s, 124.895mph/200.998km/h.

Round 7 (116.059 miles/186.779km).
1 Sho Tsuboi, J (-Toyota), 1h 10m 23.732s, 99.080mph/159.453km/h; **2** Nirei Fukuzumi, J (-Toyota), +1.372s; **3** Tadasuke Makino, J (-Honda), +2.857s; **4** Kakunoshin Ohta, J (-Honda), +5.020s; **5** Kamui Kobayashi, J (-Toyota), +5.686s; **6** Ayumu Iwasa, J (-Honda), +6.578s; **7** Tomoki Nojiri, J (-Honda), +8.476s; **8** Kenta Yamashita, J (-Toyota), +8.874s; **9** Iori Kimura, J (-Honda), +10.612s; **10** Toshiki Oyu, J (-Toyota), +11.343s.
Disqualified: Ren Sato, J (-Honda), originally finished 4th, 10s penalty for causing a collision, disqualified for being under minimum weight.
Fastest race lap: Ren Sato, J (-Honda), 1m 24.082s, 121.395mph/195.366km/h.
Pole position: Tsuboi, 1m 21.880s, 124.660mph/200.620km/h.

JAPANESE CHAMPIONSHIP SUPER FORMULA, Suzuka International Racing Course, Suzuka-shi, Mie Prefecture, Japan, 9/10 November. 2 x 31 laps of the 3.608-mile/5.807km circuit.
Round 8 (111.857 miles/180.017km).
1 Kakunoshin Ohta, J (-Honda), 1h 00m 08.862s, 111.583mph/179.575km/h; **2** Sho Tsuboi, J (-Toyota), +4.560s; **3** Tadasuke Makino, J (-Honda), +5.508s; **4** Sena Sakaguchi, J (-Toyota), +7.452s; **5** Tomoki Nojiri, J (-Honda), +8.225s; **6** Nirei Fukuzumi, J (-Toyota), +9.061s; **7** Naoki Yamamoto, J (-Honda), +9.326s; **8** Kenta Yamashita, J (-Toyota), +10.706s; **9** Ayumu Iwasa, J (-Honda), +11.172s; **10** Toshiki Oyu, J (-Toyota), +13.172s.
Fastest race lap: Ohta, 1m 40.588s, 129.140mph/207.830km/h.
Pole position: Ohta, 1m 36.094s, 135.179mph/217.549km/h.

Round 9 (111.857 miles/180.017km).
1 Kakunoshin Ohta, J (-Honda), 53m 45.819s, 124.832mph/200.898km/h; **2** Sho Tsuboi, J (-Toyota), +5.460s; **3** Nirei Fukuzumi, J (-Toyota), +6.691s; **4** Tomoki Nojiri, J (-Honda), +11.787s; **5** Ren Sato, J (-Honda), +13.066s; **6** Naoki Yamamoto, J (-Honda), +21.338s; **7** Ayumu Iwasa, J (-Honda), +22.492s; **8** Tadasuke Makino, J (-Honda), +23.271s; **9** Kenta Yamashita, J (-Toyota), +25.976s; **10** Kamui Kobayashi, J (-Toyota), +26.112s.
Fastest race lap: Iori Kimura, J (-Honda), 1m 40.441s, 129.329mph/208.134km/h.
Pole position: Nojiri, 1m 36.542s, 134.552mph/216.540km/h.

Final championship points
Drivers
1 Sho Tsuboi, J, 117.5; **2** Tomoki Nojiri, J, 87; **3** Tadasuke Makino, J, 86; **4** Kakunoshin Ohta, J, 75; **5** Ayumu Iwasa, J, 63.5; **6** Nirei Fukuzumi, J, 62; **7** Kenta Yamashita, J, 48.5; **8** Naoki Yamamoto, J, 41; **9** Toshiki Oyu, J, 27; **10** Kamui Kobayashi, J, 22.5; **11** Ren Sato, J, 22; **12** Sena Sakaguchi, J, 20; **13** Yuji Kunimoto, J, 7; **14** Kazuto Kotaka, J, 4.5; **15** Iori Kimura, J, 3; **16** Nobuharu Matsushita, J, 3; **17** Hibiki Taira, J, 2.

Teams
1 DoCoMo Team Dandelion Racing, 148; **2** Team Mugen, 131.5; **3** Vantelin Team TOM'S, 112.5; **4** Kids com Team KCMG, 77.5; **5** PONOS Nakajima Racing, 61; **6** Kondo Racing, 50; **7** Vertex Partners Cerumo - INGING, 42; **8** ITOCHU ENEX Team Impul, 9; **9** TGM Grand Prix, 3; **10** San-Ei Gen with B-Max, 3.

FIA Formula 3 Championship

All cars are Dallara F3 2019-Mecachrome V634.

FIA FORMULA 3 CHAMPIONSHIP, Bahrain International Circuit, Sakhir, Bahrain, 1/2 March. Round 1. 19 and 22 laps of the 3.363-mile/5.412km circuit.
Race 1 (63.741 miles/102.582km).
1 Arvid Lindblad, GB, 35m 35.482s, 107.710mph/173.343km/h; **2** Laurens Van Hoepen, NL, +5.478s; **3** Leonardo Fornaroli, I, +5.514s; **4** Nikola Tsolov, BG, +6.717s; **5** Tim Tramnitz, D, +6.927s; **6** Max Esterson, USA, +8.409s; **7** Gabriele Mini, I, +8.413s; **8** Mari Boya, E, +9.183s; **9** Oliver Goethe, DK, +9.938s; **10** Sami Meguetounif, F, +11.245s; **11** Martinius Stenshorne, N, +12.585s; **12** Alex Dunne, IRL, +13.082s; **13** Nikita Bedrin, RUS, +14.987s; **14** Christian Mansell, AUS, +19.282s; **15** Luke Browning, GB, +19.513s*; **16** Tasanapol Inthraphuvasak, T, +19.756s; **17** Callum Voisin, GB, +21.166s; **18** Sebastian Montoya, CO, +22.907s; **19** Charlie Wurz, A, +24.629s; **20** Kacper Sztuka, PL, +26.625s; **21** Santiago Ramos, MEX, +27.349s; **22** Noel León, MEX, +30.135s**; **23** Sophia Flörsch, D, +33.128s**; **24** Josh Dufek, CH, +37.819s; **25** Piotr Wiśnicki, PL, +38.205s; **26** Cian Shields, GB, +40.079s; **27** Joseph Loake, GB, +40.715s; **28** Tom Smith, AUS, +1m 00.473s; **29** Dino Beganovic, S, +1m 30.029s***; Matías Zagazeta, PE, -4 laps (DNF).
** 10s penalty for leaving the track and gaining an advantage*
*** 5s penalty for exceeding track limits*
**** 10s penalty for causing a collision*
Fastest race lap: Hoepen, 1m 50.451s, 109.607mph/176.396km/h.
Pole position: Hoepen.

Race 2 (73.830 miles/118.818km).
1 Luke Browning, GB, 41m 08.012s, 107.914mph/173.670km/h; **2** Christian Mansell, AUS, +1.264s; **3** Tim Tramnitz, D, +2.432s; **4** Sami Meguetounif, F, +5.654s; **5** Santiago Ramos, MEX, +6.930s; **6** Gabriele Mini, I, +8.200s; **7** Leonardo Fornaroli, I, +8.888s; **8** Arvid Lindblad, GB, +9.542s; **9** Alex Dunne, IRL, +16.619s; **10** Oliver Goethe, DK, +17.032s; **11** Nikola Tsolov, BG, +18.076s; **12** Noel León, MEX, +19.451s; **13** Dino Beganovic, S, +20.021s; **14** Martinius Stenshorne, N, +21.734s; **15** Laurens Van Hoepen, NL, +22.676s; **16** Charlie Wurz, A, +23.108s; **17** Sebastian Montoya, CO, +23.679s; **18** Matías Zagazeta, PE, +30.847s; **19** Tasanapol Inthraphuvasak, T, +34.409s; **20** Nikita Bedrin, RUS, +34.902s*; **21** Callum Voisin, GB, +35.839s; **22** Tom Smith, AUS, +37.465s; **23** Joseph Loake, GB, +41.131s; **24** Max Esterson, USA, +42.347s; **25** Piotr Wiśnicki, PL, +52.341s; **26** Cian Shields, GB, +53.921s**; **27** Josh Dufek, CH, +59.979s; **28** Kacper Sztuka, PL, +1m 03.836s; **29** Mari Boya, E, +1m 28.231s***; **30** Sophia Flörsch, D, -1 lap (DNF).
** 5s penalty for exceeding track limits*
*** 10s penalty for causing a collision*
**** 5s penalty for speeding in the pit lane*
Fastest race lap: Beganovic, 1m 50.261s, 109.796mph/176.700km/h.
Pole position: Beganovic, 1m 46.431s, 113.747mph/183.059km/h.
Championship points: Drivers: 1 Browning, 25; **2**

Tramnitz, 21; **3** Mansell, 18; **4** Fornaroli, 15; **5** Lindblad, 14; **6** Meguetounif, 13.
Teams: 1 Trident, 38; **2** ART Grand Prix, 35; **3** Prema Racing, 28.

FIA FORMULA 3 CHAMPIONSHIP, Albert Park Circuit, Melbourne, Victoria, Australia, 23/24 March. Round 2. 20 and 23 laps of the 3.280-mile/5.278km circuit.
Race 1 (65.592 miles/105.560km).
1 Martinius Stenshorne, N, 35m 32.870s, 110.710mph/178.171km/h; **2** Arvid Lindblad, GB, +1.673s; **3** Laurens Van Hoepen, NL, +1.958s; **4** Mari Boya, E, +3.165s; **5** Oliver Goethe, DK, +4.152s; **6** Gabriele Minì, I, +5.158s; **7** Alex Dunne, IRL, +6.485s; **8** Sebastian Montoya, CO, +7.122s; **9** Leonardo Fornaroli, I, +7.311s; **10** Christian Mansell, AUS, +7.747s; **11** Charlie Wurz, A, +8.234s; **12** Tim Tramnitz, D, +8.628s; **13** Dino Beganovic, S, +9.735s*; **14** Joseph Loake, GB, +10.834s; **15** Matías Zagazeta, PE, +11.288s; **16** Kacper Sztuka, PL, +11.967s**; **17** Sami Meguetounif, F, +13.233s**; **18** Callum Voisin, GB, +13.744s; **19** Sophia Flörsch, D, +14.623s; **20** Nikola Tsolov, BG, +15.214s; **21** Nikita Bedrin, RUS, +15.474s***; **22** Josh Dufek, CH, +15.640s; **23** Piotr Wiśnicki, PL, +16.893s; **24** Santiago Ramos, MEX, +17.443s; **25** Cian Shields, GB, +18.250s; **26** Max Esterson, USA, +19.095s**; **27** Tom Smith, AUS, +37.347s****; **28** Luke Browning, GB, -1 lap; Tasanapol Inthraphuvasak, T, -7 (DNF); Noel León, MEX, -8 (DNF).
** 5s penalty for leaving the track and gaining an advantage*
*** 5s penalty for exceeding track limits*
**** 10s penalty for leaving the track and gaining an advantage*
***** 10s penalty for causing a collision with Inthraphuvasak*
Fastest race lap: Browning, 1m 36.186s, 122.747mph/197.542km/h.
Pole position: Hoepen.

Race 2 (75.431 miles/121.394km).
1 Dino Beganovic, S, 41m 23.816s, 109.328mph/175.946km/h; **2** Leonardo Fornaroli, I, +1.682s; **3** Gabriele Minì, I, +3.221s; **4** Luke Browning, GB, +4.050s; **5** Charlie Wurz, A, +16.958s; **6** Sebastian Montoya, CO, +21.230s; **7** Mari Boya, E, +21.492s; **8** Nikita Bedrin, RUS, +25.610s; **9** Oliver Goethe, DK, +26.530s; **10** Christian Mansell, AUS, +26.785s; **11** Arvid Lindblad, GB, +27.009s; **12** Sami Meguetounif, F, +29.437s; **13** Laurens Van Hoepen, NL, +29.512s; **14** Max Esterson, USA, +30.441s; **15** Tim Tramnitz, D, +33.023s; **16** Alex Dunne, IRL, +33.577s; **17** Matías Zagazeta, PE, +34.067s; **18** Kacper Sztuka, PL, +37.812s; **19** Nikola Tsolov, BG, +38.222s; **20** Cian Shields, GB, +42.693s; **21** Callum Voisin, GB, +44.080s; **22** Josh Dufek, CH, +52.748s; **23** Piotr Wiśnicki, PL, +1m 01.595s; **24** Santiago Ramos, MEX, +1m 09.926s*; **25** Noel León, MEX, +1m 10.635s; **26** Martinius Stenshorne, N, +1m 14.235s**; Sophia Flörsch, D, -22 laps (DNF); Tasanapol Inthraphuvasak, T, -23 (DNF); Joseph Loake, GB, -23 (DNF); Tom Smith, AUS, -23 (DNF).
** 5s penalty for leaving the track and rejoining unsafely*
*** 10s penalty for causing a collision with Leon*
Fastest race lap: Beganovic, 1m 35.588s, 123.514mph/198.778km/h.
Pole position: Fornaroli, 1m 33.044s, 126.892mph/204.213km/h.
Championship points: Drivers: 1 Browning, 37; **2** Fornaroli, 37; **3** Minì, 32; **4** Beganovic, 28; **5** Lindblad, 23; **6** Tramnitz, 21.
Teams: 1 Prema Racing, 83; **2** Trident, 60; **3** Hitech Pulse-Eight, 47.

FIA FORMULA 3 CHAMPIONSHIP, Autodromo Enzo e Dino Ferrari, Imola, Italy, 18/19 May. Round 3. 18 and 22 laps of the 3.050-mile/4.909km circuit.
Race 1 (54.770 miles/88.144km).
1 Oliver Goethe, DK, 34m 19.754s, 95.960mph/154.433km/h; **2** Tim Tramnitz, D, +2.157s; **3** Noel León, MEX, +5.340s*; **4** Dino Beganovic, S, +8.266s; **5** Kacper Sztuka, PL, +8.811s; **6** Gabriele Minì, I, +9.404s; **7** Laurens Van Hoepen, NL, +9.795s; **8** Arvid Lindblad, GB, +10.268s; **9** Nikita Bedrin, RUS, +10.829s; **10** Santiago Ramos, MEX, +11.186s; **11** Leonardo Fornaroli, I, +11.675s; **12** Christian Mansell, AUS, +12.352s; **13** Nikola Tsolov, BG, +12.950s; **14** Alex Dunne, IRL, +13.979s; **15** Sophia Flörsch, D, +14.458s; **16** Josh Dufek, CH, +15.500s; **17** Matías Zagazeta, PE, +18.617s; **18** Max Esterson, USA, +18.863s; **19** Cian Shields, GB, +19.224s; **20** Piotr Wiśnicki, PL, +19.541s; **21** Joseph Loake, GB, +20.039s; **22** Martinius Stenshorne, N, +20.680s**; **23** Charlie Wurz, A, +25.023s***; **24** Tom Smith, AUS, +30.860s****; **25** Sebastian Montoya, CO, +33.815s; **26** Luke Browning, GB, -2 laps (DNF-accident); Tasanapol Inthraphuvasak, T, -6 (DNF); Sami Meguetounif, F, -11 (DNF); Callum Voisin, GB, -14 (DNF); Mari Boya, E, -18 (DNF).
** 5s penalty for weaving*
*** 5s penalty for false start*
**** 10s penalty for causing a collision with Voisin*
***** 10s penalty for causing a collision with Boya*
Fastest race lap: Goethe, 1m 33.596s, 117.324mph/188.815km/h.
Pole position: Sztuka.

Race 2 (66.971 miles/107.780km).
1 Sami Meguetounif, F, 35m 12.897s, 114.335mph/184.005km/h; **2** Oliver Goethe, DK, +2.791s; **3** Leonardo Fornaroli, I, +3.368s; **4** Luke Browning, GB, +3.686s; **5** Dino Beganovic, S, +5.724s; **6** Gabriele Minì, I, +6.972s; **7** Arvid Lindblad, GB, +11.575s; **8** Santiago Ramos, MEX, +12.736s; **9** Mari Boya, E, +13.098s; **10** Sebastian Montoya, CO, +14.769s; **11** Tim Tramnitz, D, +18.634s; **12** Sophia Flörsch, D, +21.658s; **13** Laurens Van Hoepen, NL, +22.654s; **14** Martinius Stenshorne, N, +23.516s*; **15** Kacper Sztuka, PL, +23.554s; **16** Alex Dunne, IRL, +24.295s; **17** Matías Zagazeta, PE, +25.720s; **18** Cian Shields, GB, +29.529s; **19** Noel León, MEX, +30.045s*; **20** Christian Mansell, AUS, +31.500s; **21** Max Esterson, USA, +32.271s; **22** Josh Dufek, CH, +35.023s; **23** Piotr Wiśnicki, PL, +37.573s; **24** Charlie Wurz, A, +40.316s; **25** Joseph Loake, GB, +40.585s; **26** Nikola Tsolov, BG, +42.360s; **27** Tom Smith, AUS, +59.188s; **28** Tasanapol Inthraphuvasak, T, +1m 11.428s**; **29** Callum Voisin, GB, +1m 16.623s***; **30** Nikita Bedrin, RUS, -1 lap.
** 10s penalty for forcing another driver off the track*
*** Drive-through penalty for re-joining after receiving mechanical assistance converted to 20s penalty*
**** 10s penalty for causing a collision with Bedrin*
Fastest race lap: Goethe, 1m 33.817s, 117.048mph/188.370km/h.
Pole position: Ramos, 1m 31.767s, 119.663mph/192.579km/h.
Championship points: Drivers: 1 Fornaroli, 52; **2** Browning, 49; **3** Beganovic, 45; **4** Minì, 45; **5** Goethe, 41; **6** Meguetounif, 38.
Teams: 1 Prema Racing, 122; **2** Trident, 107; **3** Campos Racing, 72.

FIA FORMULA 3 CHAMPIONSHIP, Circuit de Monaco, Monaco, 25/26 May. Round 4. 23 and 27 laps of the 2.074-mile/3.337km circuit.
Race 1 (47.691 miles/76.751km).
1 Nikola Tsolov, BG, 59m 09.511s, 48.369mph/77.842km/h; **2** Tim Tramnitz, D, +4.328s; **3** Laurens Van Hoepen, NL, +5.173s; **4** Noel León, MEX, +5.310s; **5** Joseph Loake, GB, +6.489s; **6** Mari Boya, E, +6.891s; **7** Dino Beganovic, S, +7.732s; **8** Luke Browning, GB, +12.658s; **9** Leonardo Fornaroli, I, +12.971s; **10** Oliver Goethe, DK, +14.964s; **11** Gabriele Minì, I, +15.337s; **12** Callum Voisin, GB, +19.472s; **13** Tom Smith, AUS, +20.161s; **14** Max Esterson, USA, +24.341s; **15** Santiago Ramos, MEX, +24.747s; **16** Martinius Stenshorne, N, +25.093s; **17** Tasanapol Inthraphuvasak, T, +27.444s; **18** Sebastian Montoya, CO, +28.335s; **19** Charlie Wurz, A, +29.068s; **20** James Hedley, GB, +43.344s*; **21** Piotr Wiśnicki, PL, +46.393s**; **22** Sami Meguetounif, F, -3 laps (DNF); Nikita Bedrin, RUS, -8 (DNF); Sophia Flörsch, D, -10 (DNF); Kacper Sztuka, PL, -11 (DNF); Arvid Lindblad, GB, -23 (DNF); Christian Mansell, AUS, -23 (DNF); Josh Dufek, CH, -23 (DNF); Alex Dunne, IRL, -23 (DNF); Cian Shields, GB, -23 (DNF).
** 5s penalty for speeding in the pit lane; 5s penalty for Safety Car procedure violation*
*** 10s penalty for leaving the track and gaining an advantage; 10s penalty for causing a collision*
Fastest race lap: Beganovic, 1m 24.919s, 87.903mph/141.466km/h.
Pole position: Tsolov.

Race 2 (55.985 miles/90.099km).
1 Gabriele Minì, I, 44m 15.883s, 75.886mph/122.127km/h; **2** Christian Mansell, AUS, +0.802s; **3** Luke Browning, GB, +1.720s; **4** Arvid Lindblad, GB, +2.197s; **5** Leonardo Fornaroli, I, +2.667s; **6** Dino Beganovic, S, +3.094s; **7** Mari Boya, E, +4.889s; **8** Tim Tramnitz, D, +5.249s; **9** Joseph Loake, GB, +6.602s; **10** Oliver Goethe, DK, +8.007s; **11** Kacper Sztuka, PL, +8.469s; **12** Tom Smith, AUS, +8.959s; **13** Callum Voisin, GB, +9.326s; **14** Santiago Ramos, MEX, +10.963s; **15** Sebastian Montoya, CO, +11.379s; **16** Alex Dunne, IRL, +12.002s; **17** Max Esterson, USA, +12.409s; **18** Tasanapol Inthraphuvasak, T, +13.443s; **19** Sophia Flörsch, D, +13.623s; **20** Josh Dufek, CH, +14.069s; **21** Cian Shields, GB, +15.201s; **22** James Hedley, GB, +15.941s; **23** Noel León, MEX, +17.360s; **24** Nikita Bedrin, RUS, +17.575s; **25** Piotr Wiśnicki, PL, +20.640s*; ***26** Martinius Stenshorne, N, +26.465s**; **27** Nikola Tsolov, BG, +28.566s*; Laurens Van Hoepen, NL, -5 laps (DNF); Sami Meguetounif, F, -8 (DNF); Charlie Wurz, A, -27 (DNF).*
** 10s penalty for causing a collision*
*** 10s penalty for leaving the track and gaining an advantage*
Fastest race lap: Stenshorne, 1m 24.773s, 88.054mph/141.710km/h.
Pole position: Minì, 1m 23.942s, 88.926mph/143.113km/h.
Championship points: Drivers: 1 Minì, 72; **2** Browning, 68; **3** Fornaroli, 64; **4** Beganovic, 58; **5** Lindblad, 44; **6** Goethe, 43.
Teams: 1 Prema Racing, 174; **2** Trident, 119; **3** ART Grand Prix, 85.

FIA FORMULA 3 CHAMPIONSHIP, Circuit de Barcelona-Catalunya, Montmeló, Barcelona, Spain, 22/23 June. Round 5. 21 and 25 laps of the 2.894-mile/4.657km circuit.
Race 1 (60.690 miles/97.671km).
1 Mari Boya, E, 38m 11.211s, 95.479mph/153.658km/h; **2** Alex Dunne, IRL, +0.453s; **3** Oliver Goethe, DK, +0.828s; **4** Martinius Stenshorne, N, +1.068s; **5** Laurens Van Hoepen, NL, +1.263s; **6** Noel León, MEX, +1.735s; **7** Leonardo Fornaroli, I, +1.893s; **8** Dino Beganovic, S, +2.197s; **9** Arvid Lindblad, GB, +2.698s; **10** Tim Tramnitz, D, +2.964s; **11** Christian Mansell, AUS, +3.111s; **12** Luke Browning, GB, +3.375s; **13** Nikola Tsolov, BG, +3.936s; **14** Cian Shields, GB, +4.213s; **15** Joseph Loake, GB, +4.652s; **16** Charlie Wurz, A, +4.982s; **17** Josh Dufek, CH, +5.287s; **18** Tom Smith, AUS, +5.787s; **19** Matías Zagazeta, PE, +6.938s; **20** Sophia Flörsch, D, +7.117s; **21** Santiago Ramos, MEX, +7.370s; **22** Max Esterson, USA, +7.849s; **23** Kacper Sztuka, PL, +8.566s; **24** Piotr Wiśnicki, PL, +8.760s; **25** Tasanapol Inthraphuvasak, T, +16.556s*; Gabriele Minì, I, -4 laps (DNF); Sebastian Montoya, CO, -4 (DNF); Sami Meguetounif, F, -19 (DNF); Callum Voisin, GB, -19 (DNF); Nikita Bedrin, RUS, -19 (DNF).
** 10s penalty for leaving the track and gaining an advantage*
Fastest race lap: Fornaroli, 1m 32.402s, 112.740mph/181.437km/h.
Pole position: Ramos.

Race 2 (72.265 miles/116.299km).
1 Arvid Lindblad, GB, 39m 09.719s, 110.835mph/178.372km/h; **2** Christian Mansell, AUS, +4.447s; **3** Leonardo Fornaroli, I, +5.627s; **4** Oliver Goethe, DK, +6.498s; **5** Luke Browning, GB, +7.388s; **6** Nikola Tsolov, BG, +10.671s; **7** Alex Dunne, IRL, +10.933s; **8** Dino Beganovic, S, +13.419s; **9** Noel León, MEX, +14.159s; **10** Santiago Ramos, MEX, +14.635s; **11** Tim Tramnitz, D, +15.962s; **12** Sebastian Montoya, CO, +20.416s; **13** Charlie Wurz, A, +21.193s; **14** Mari Boya, E, +21.883s*; **15** Sami Meguetounif, F, +22.442s; **16** Callum Voisin, GB, +23.130s; **17** Josh Dufek, CH, +24.231s; **18** Sophia Flörsch, D, +25.842s; **19** Matías Zagazeta, PE, +27.488s; **20** Cian Shields, GB, +33.433s; **21** Gabriele Minì, I, +34.379s; **22** Joseph Loake, GB, +37.395s; **23** Max Esterson, USA, +38.305s; **24** Piotr Wiśnicki, PL, +38.901s; **25** Tom Smith, AUS, +39.534s; **26** Tasanapol Inthraphuvasak, T, +40.613s; **27** Martinius Stenshorne, N, +41.328s; **28** Kacper Sztuka, PL, +47.566s**; **29** Laurens Van Hoepen, NL, -1 lap (DNF); **30** Nikita Bedrin, RUS, -3 (DNF).
** 5+5s penalty for exceeding track limits*
*** 10s penalty for causing a collision with Bedrin*
Fastest race lap: Browning, 1m 31.970s, 113.269mph/182.289km/h.
Pole position: Mansell, 1m 28.463s, 117.760mph/189.516km/h.
Championship points: Drivers: 1 Fornaroli, 84; **2** Browning, 79; **3** Minì, 72; **4** Lindblad, 71; **5** Beganovic, 65; **6** Goethe, 63.
Teams: 1 Prema Racing, 208; **2** Trident, 140; **3** ART Grand Prix, 119.

FIA FORMULA 3 CHAMPIONSHIP, Red Bull Ring, Spielberg, Austria, 29/30 June. Round 6. 21 and 26 laps of the 2.683-mile/4.318km circuit.
Race 1 (56.266 miles/90.552km).
1 Nikola Tsolov, BG, 34m 24.710s, 98.240mph/158.102km/h; **2** Martinius Stenshorne, N, +0.672s; **3** Christian Mansell, AUS, +1.244s; **4** Alex Dunne, IRL, +1.647s; **5** Laurens Van Hoepen, NL, +3.168s; **6** Gabriele Minì, I, +3.496s; **7** Oliver Goethe, DK, +3.750s; **8** Tim Tramnitz, D, +4.053s; **9** Noel León, MEX, +4.498s; **10** Sami Meguetounif, F, +4.886s; **11** Luke Browning, GB, +5.257s; **12** Leonardo Fornaroli, I, +6.118s; **13** Nikita Bedrin, RUS, +7.076s; **14** Callum Voisin, GB, +7.634s; **15** Dino Beganovic, S, +7.690s; **16** Cian Shields, GB, +8.317s; **17** Matías Zagazeta, PE, +8.617s; **18** Max Esterson, USA, +8.726s; **19** Joseph Loake, GB, +9.161s; **20** Charlie Wurz, A, +9.518s; **21** Tom Smith, AUS, +9.811s; **22** Mari Boya, E, +10.759s; **23** Piotr Wiśnicki, PL, +10.976s; **24** Santiago Ramos, MEX, +11.094s; **25** Josh Dufek, CH, +11.350s; **26** Sophia Flörsch, D, +11.766s; **27** Tasanapol Inthraphuvasak, T, +20.645s; Arvid Lindblad, GB, -4 laps (DNF); Sebastian Montoya, CO, -5 (DNF); Kacper Sztuka, PL, -21 (DNF).
Fastest race lap: Tsolov, 1m 23.420s, 115.788mph/186.343km/h.
Pole position: Stenshorne.

Race 2 (69.682 miles/112.142km).
1 Luke Browning, GB, 37m 22.286s, 111.998mph/180.244km/h; **2** Gabriele Minì, I, +1.685s; **3** Dino Beganovic, S, +2.154s; **4** Christian Mansell, AUS, +2.568s; **5** Oliver Goethe, DK, +3.172s; **6** Nikola Tsolov, BG, +7.103s; **7** Arvid Lindblad, GB, +7.803s; **8** Laurens Van Hoepen, NL, +9.912s; **9** Leonardo Fornaroli, I, +10.280s; **10** Alex Dunne, IRL, +13.453s*; **11** Sophia Flörsch, D, +13.877s; **12** Martinius Stenshorne, N, +14.097s**; **13** Santiago Ramos, MEX, +14.568s; **14** Matías Zagazeta, PE, +17.918s; **15** Tim Tramnitz, D, +18.356s*; **16** Kacper Sztuka, PL, +21.323s; **17** Max Esterson, USA, +22.259s; **18** Mari Boya, E, +28.984s***; **19** Piotr Wiśnicki, PL, +30.171s; **20** Sami Meguetounif, F, +33.932s****; **21** Cian Shields, GB, +38.975s****; **22** Tom Smith, AUS, +41.837s**; **23** Noel León, MEX, +47.633s; **24** Joseph Loake, GB, +1m 00.601s; **25** Callum Voisin, GB, +1m 16.678s*; **26** Tasanapol Inthraphuvasak, T, +1m 22.062s; **27** Charlie Wurz, A, -1 lap; Nikita Bedrin, RUS, -16 (DNF); Josh Dufek, CH, -21 (DNF); Sebastian Montoya, CO, -21 (DNF).
** 10s penalty for causing a collision*
*** 5s penalty for exceeding track limits*
**** 5s penalty for exceeding track limits; 10s penalty for causing a collision*
***** 15s penalty for exceeding track limits*
Fastest race lap: Wiśnicki, 1m 23.359s, 115.873mph/186.480km/h.
Pole position: Browning, 1m 20.222s, 120.404mph/193.772km/h.
Championship points: Drivers: 1 Browning, 106; **2** Minì, 95; **3** Fornaroli, 86; **4** Beganovic, 80; **5** Mansell, 78; **6** Lindblad, 77.
Teams: 1 Prema Racing, 252; **2** ART Grand Prix, 169; **3** Trident, 143.

FIA FORMULA 3 CHAMPIONSHIP, Silverstone Arena Grand Prix Circuit, Towcester, Northamptonshire, Great Britain, 6/7 July. Round 7. 18 and 20 laps of the 3.660-mile/5.891km circuit.
Race 1 (65.806 miles/105.904km).
1 Arvid Lindblad, GB, 36m 32.184s, 108.201mph/174.133km/h; **2** Noel León, MEX, +6.560s; **3** Matías Zagazeta, PE, +8.447s; **4** Callum Voisin, GB, +9.409s; **5** Nikola Tsolov, BG, +11.332s; **6** Gabriele Minì, I, +11.453s; **7** Sebastian Montoya, CO, +11.715s; **8** Sami Meguetounif, F, +11.946s; **9** Laurens Van Hoepen, NL, +12.139s; **10** Leonardo Fornaroli, I, +12.646s; **11** Dino Beganovic, S, +17.511s; **12** Christian Mansell, AUS, +20.885s*; **13** Nikita Bedrin, RUS, +21.697s; **14** Piotr Wiśnicki, PL, +22.048s; **15** Joseph Loake, GB, +22.743s; **16** Mari Boya, E, +23.205s; **17** Cian Shields, GB, +23.727s; **18** James Wharton, AUS, +30.851s**; **19** Santiago Ramos, MEX, +35.240s; **20** Tasanapol Inthraphuvasak, T, +36.010s; **21** Tom Smith, AUS, +49.151s***; **22** Alex Dunne, IRL, +1m 14.050s; **23** Josh Dufek, CH, -1 lap; **24** Luke Browning, GB, -1; **25** Tim Tramnitz, D, -1**; Charlie Wurz, A, -7 (DNF); Kacper Sztuka, PL, -12 (DNF); Max Esterson, USA, -15 (DNF); Oliver Goethe, DK, -15 (DNF); Sophia Flörsch, D, -16 (DNF).
** 5+5s penalty for exceeding track limits*
*** 10s penalty for causing a collision*
**** 5s penalty for exceeding track limits; 10s penalty for causing a collision*
Fastest race lap: Lindblad, 1m 47.304s, 122.808mph/197.640km/h.
Pole position: León.

Race 2 (73.127 miles/117.686km).
1 Arvid Lindblad, GB, 47m 12.061s, 93.060mph/149.766km/h; **2** Gabriele Minì, I, +0.874s; **3** Callum Voisin, GB, +9.213s*; **4** Tom Smith, AUS, +19.567s; **5** Piotr Wiśnicki, PL, +42.258s; **6** Oliver Goethe, DK, +46.081s; **7** Leonardo Fornaroli, I, +1m 00.404s; **8** Luke Browning, GB, +1m 03.259s; **9** Nikita Bedrin, RUS, +1m 05.449s; **10** Noel León, MEX, +1m 08.179s; **11** Laurens Van Hoepen, NL, +1m 13.024s; **12** Sami Meguetounif, F, +1m 13.436s; **13** Christian Mansell, AUS, +1m 13.644s; **14** Tim Tramnitz, D, +1m 16.560s; **15** Nikola Tsolov, BG, +1m 16.840s; **16** Santiago Ramos, MEX, +1m 20.201s; **17** Kacper Sztuka, PL, +1m 21.468s; **18** Max Esterson, USA, +1m 23.637s; **19** Dino Beganovic, S, +1m 26.013s**; **20** Tasanapol Inthraphuvasak, T, +1m 26.750s***; **21** James Wharton, AUS, +1m 29.767s; **22** Matías Zagazeta, PE, +1m 33.964s; **23** Mari Boya, E, +1m 36.218s*; **24** Joseph Loake, GB, -1 lap; Charlie Wurz, A, -5 (DNF); Josh Dufek, CH, -12 (DNF); Sebastian Montoya, CO, -13 (DNF); Alex Dunne, IRL, -13 (DNF); Sophia Flörsch, D, -17 (DNF); Cian Shields, GB, -20 (DNF).
** 10s penalty for leaving the track and gaining an advantage (originally won)*
*** 5s penalty for exceeding track limits*
**** 5s penalty for Safety car infringement*
Fastest race lap: Minì, 1m 47.369s, 122.733mph/197.520km/h.
Pole position: Browning, 1m 44.992s, 125.512mph/201.992km/h.
Championship points: Drivers: 1 Minì, 119; **2** Lindblad, 113; **3** Browning, 112; **4** Fornaroli, 93; **5** Goethe, 85; **6** Beganovic, 80.
Teams: 1 Prema Racing, 312; **2** ART Grand Prix, 177; **3** Trident, 153.

FIA FORMULA 3 CHAMPIONSHIP, Hungaroring, Mogyoród, Budapest, Hungary, 20/21 July. Round 8. 18 and 23 laps of the 2.722-mile/4.381km circuit.
Race 1 (48.975 miles/78.818km).
1 Nikita Bedrin, RUS, 29m 41.355s, 99.025mph/159.365km/h; **2** Tasanapol Inthraphuvasak, T, +1.560s; **3** Dino Beganovic, S, +2.189s; **4** Tim Tramnitz, D, +2.629s; **5** Christian Mansell, AUS, +3.483s; **6** Callum Voisin, GB, +3.980s; **7** Leonardo Fornaroli, I, +4.398s; **8** Luke Browning, GB, +4.909s; **9** Laurens Van Hoepen, NL, +5.488s; **10** Sami Meguetounif, F, +5.814s; **11** Oliver Goethe, DK, +6.511s; **12** Noel León, MEX, +7.183s; **13** Martinius Stenshorne, N, +8.174s; **14** Gabriele Minì, I, +8.905s; **15** Arvid Lindblad, GB, +9.367s; **16** Max Esterson, USA, +11.259s; **17** Charlie Wurz, A, +11.890s; **18** Mari Boya, E, +12.434s; **19** Sebastian Montoya, CO, +12.888s; **20** Alex Dunne, IRL, +13.440s; **21** Cian Shields, GB, +13.885s; **22** Josh Dufek, CH, +17.716s; **23** Sophia Flörsch, D, +18.100s; **24** Piotr Wiśnicki, PL, +19.032s; **25** Tom Smith, AUS, +19.562s; **26** Joseph Loake, GB, +32.830s; **27** Kacper Sztuka, PL, +59.688s; **28** Santiago Ramos, MEX, +1m 00.617s; **29** Nikola Tsolov, BG, +1m 10.224s*; Matías Zagazeta, PE, -18 laps (DNF).
** 10s penalty for causing a collision*

Fastest race lap: Loake, 1m 35.669s, 102.436mph/164.855km/h.
Pole position: Beganovic.

Race 2 (62.586 miles/100.723km).
1 Nikola Tsolov, BG, 38m 54.231s, 96.562mph/155.402km/h; **2** Noel León, MEX, +1.114s; **3** Leonardo Fornaroli, I, +1.439s; **4** Christian Mansell, AUS, +1.781s; **5** Santiago Ramos, MEX, +2.091s; **6** Callum Voisin, GB, +2.497s; **7** Nikita Bedrin, RUS, +2.751s; **8** Oliver Goethe, DK, +3.304s; **9** Dino Beganovic, S, +4.008s; **10** Mari Boya, E, +4.443s; **11** Gabriele Minì, I, +5.040s; **12** Luke Browning, GB, +5.139s; **13** Martinius Stenshorne, N, +5.786s; **14** Tasanapol Inthraphuvasak, T, +6.785s; **15** Max Esterson, USA, +7.190s; **16** Alex Dunne, IRL, +7.748s; **17** Cian Shields, GB, +8.206s; **18** Kacper Sztuka, PL, +9.211s; **19** Sebastian Montoya, CO, +9.453s; **20** Tim Tramnitz, D, +9.850s; **21** Piotr Wiśnicki, PL, +10.377s; **22** Josh Dufek, CH, +11.456s; **23** Sophia Flörsch, D, +11.792s; **24** Tom Smith, AUS, +16.104s*; **25** Sami Meguetounif, F, +38.783s; **26** Joseph Loake, GB, -1 lap; **27** Matías Zagazeta, PE, -3; **28** Arvid Lindblad, GB, -3; Charlie Wurz, A, -22 (DNF).
** 5s penalty for exceeding track limits*
Disqualified: Laurens Van Hoepen, NL, +0.605s.
Fastest race lap: Meguetounif, 1m 35.293s, 102.840mph/165.506km/h.
Pole position: Hoepen, 1m 33.935s, 104.327mph/167.899km/h.
Championship points: Drivers: 1 Minì, 119; **2** Browning, 115; **3** Lindblad, 113; **4** Fornaroli, 112; **5** Mansell, 97; **6** Beganovic, 90.
Teams: 1 Prema Racing, 322; **2** ART Grand Prix, 225; **3** Trident, 183.

FIA FORMULA 3 CHAMPIONSHIP, Circuit de Spa-Francorchamps, Stavelot, Belgium, 27/28 July. Round 9. 12 and 15 laps of the 4.352-mile/7.004km circuit.
Race 1 (52.148 miles/83.924km).
1 Dino Beganovic, S, 29m 03.659s, 107.823mph/173.524km/h; **2** Gabriele Minì, I, +1.131s; **3** Noel León, MEX, +2.872s; **4** Tim Tramnitz, D, +5.800s; **5** Sebastian Montoya, CO, +6.815s; **6** Oliver Goethe, DK, +7.237s; **7** Callum Voisin, GB, +7.894s; **8** Santiago Ramos, MEX, +11.049s*; **9** Leonardo Fornaroli, I, +11.937s*; **10** Laurens Van Hoepen, NL, +14.837s; **11** Joseph Loake, GB, +15.976s; **12** Luke Browning, GB, +16.812s**; **13** Nikita Bedrin, RUS, +16.943s; **14** Tuukka Taponen, FIN, +18.384s; **15** Arvid Lindblad, GB, +20.370s**; **16** Christian Mansell, AUS, +22.066s; **17** Matías Zagazeta, PE, +22.454s; **18** Martinius Stenshorne, N, +22.870s*; **19** Sophia Flörsch, D, +24.773s; **20** Kacper Sztuka, PL, +25.416s; **21** Piotr Wiśnicki, PL, +25.974s; **22** Cian Shields, GB, +26.347s; **23** Alex Dunne, IRL, +27.700s**; **24** Josh Dufek, CH, +28.283s; **25** Tom Smith, AUS, +30.721s**; **26** Charlie Wurz, A, +32.293s*; **27** Sami Meguetounif, F, +41.669s***; **28** Mari Boya, E, +49.234s****; **29** Tasanapol Inthraphuvasak, T, 52.996s*****; Max Esterson, USA, -12 laps (DNF-spin).
** 5s penalty for exceeding track limits*
*** 10s penalty for exceeding track limits*
**** 35s penalty for exceeding track limits*
***** 25s penalty for exceeding track limits*
****** 20s penalty for exceeding track limits*
Fastest race lap: León, 2m 08.683s, 121.752mph/195.941km/h.
Pole position: Beganovic.

Race 2 (65.204 miles/104.936km).
1 Callum Voisin, GB, 41m 33.717s, 94.240mph/151.665km/h; **2** Sebastian Montoya, CO, +0.915s; **3** Leonardo Fornaroli, I, +1.662s; **4** Noel León, MEX, +2.191s; **5** Sami Meguetounif, F, +2.871s; **6** Luke Browning, GB, +3.229s; **7** Max Esterson, USA, +3.604s; **8** Santiago Ramos, MEX, +4.088s; **9** Tim Tramnitz, D, +4.852s; **10** Alex Dunne, IRL, +5.345s; **11** Dino Beganovic, S, +6.600s; **12** Laurens Van Hoepen, NL, +7.271s; **13** Gabriele Minì, I, +8.133s; **14** Josh Dufek, CH, +9.522s; **15** Tasanapol Inthraphuvasak, T, +10.686s; **16** Tom Smith, AUS, +11.129s; **17** Matías Zagazeta, PE, +12.148s; **18** Kacper Sztuka, PL, +12.796s; **19** Oliver Goethe, DK, +13.274s; **20** Nikita Bedrin, RUS, +17.763s*; **21** Christian Mansell, AUS, +18.380s**; **22** Cian Shields, GB, +19.997s***; **23** Charlie Wurz, A, +20.236s****; **24** Piotr Wiśnicki, PL, +20.339s*; **25** Joseph Loake, GB, +24.758s*****; Arvid Lindblad, GB, -6 laps (DNF); Mari Boya, E, -6 (DNF); Sophia Flörsch, D, -9 (DNF); Martinius Stenshorne, N, -14 (DNF); Tuukka Taponen, FIN, -14 (DNF).
** 10s penalty for leaving the track and gaining an advantage*
*** 10s penalty for causing a collision with Lindblad*
**** 5s penalty for Safety Car infringement*
***** 5s penalty for speeding in the pit lane*
****** 10s penalty for causing a collision with Floersch*
Fastest race lap: Voisin, 2m 05.770s, 124.572mph/200.480km/h.
Pole position: Voisin, 2m 04.321s, 126.024mph/202.816km/h.
Championship points: Drivers: 1 Fornaroli, 129; **2** Minì, 128; **3** Browning, 123; **4** Lindblad, 113; **5** Beganovic, 100; **6** Mansell, 97.
Teams: 1 Prema Racing, 341; **2** ART Grand Prix, 226; **3** Trident, 217.

FIA FORMULA 3 CHAMPIONSHIP, Autodromo Nazionale Monza, Monza, Italy, 31 August/1 September. Round 10. 17 and 22 laps of the 3.600-mile/5.793km circuit.
Race 1 (61.001 miles/98.172km).
1 Tim Tramnitz, D, 33m 52.339s, 108.391mph/174.439km/h; **2** Santiago Ramos, MEX, +0.911s; **3** Alex Dunne, IRL, +1.375s; **4** Dino Beganovic, S, +1.937s; **5** Sami Meguetounif, F, +4.050s; **6** Luke Browning, GB, +4.126s; **7** Mari Boya, E, +4.360s; **8** Leonardo Fornaroli, I, +4.843s; **9** Gabriele Mini, I, +5.108s; **10** Martinius Stenshorne, N, +5.593s; **11** Sebastian Montoya, CO, +5.779s*; **12** Arvid Lindblad, GB, +5.927s; **13** Laurens Van Hoepen, NL, +6.595s; **14** Matías Zagazeta, PE, +6.773s; **15** Joseph Loake, GB, +6.812s; **16** Sophia Flörsch, D, +6.852s; **17** Noah Strømsted, DK, +6.995s; **18** Kacper Sztuka, PL, +8.668s; **19** Nikola Tsolov, BG, +11.030s; **20** Cian Shields, GB, +12.389s**; **21** Tasanapol Inthraphuvasak, T, +17.500s***; **22** Christian Mansell, AUS, +18.075s****; **23** Tom Smith, AUS, +18.511s*****; **24** Charlie Wurz, A, -1 lap; **25** Callum Voisin, GB, -1; Josh Dufek, CH, -4 (DNF); Max Esterson, USA, -5 (DNF); Piotr Wiśnicki, PL, -5 (DNF); Nikita Bedrin, RUS, -16 (DNF); Noel León, MEX, -16 (DNF).
** 5s penalty for forcing Ramos off the track*
*** 5s penalty for causing a collision with Voisin*
**** 10s penalty for overtaking Loake under Safety Car conditions*
***** 5s penalty for speeding in the pit lane; 5s penalty for forcing Floersch off the track*
****** 10s penalty for causing a collision*
Fastest race lap: Fornaroli, 1m 38.802s, 131.156mph/211.076km/h.
Pole position: Tramnitz.

Race 2 (78.999 miles/127.137km).
1 Sami Meguetounif, F, 39m 58.179s, 118.874mph/191.309km/h; **2** Leonardo Fornaroli, I, +4.587s; **3** Christian Mansell, AUS, +5.522s; **4** Alex Dunne, IRL, +6.862s; **5** Martinius Stenshorne, N, +10.650s; **6** Tim Tramnitz, D, +12.889s; **7** Noel León, MEX, +14.664s; **8** Laurens Van Hoepen, NL, +15.429s; **9** Dino Beganovic, S, +17.071s; **10** Josh Dufek, CH, +18.796s; **11** Tasanapol Inthraphuvasak, T, +21.060s*; **12** Kacper Sztuka, PL, +22.874s; **13** Nikita Bedrin, RUS, +23.472s; **14** Charlie Wurz, A, +23.591s; **15** Tom Smith, AUS, +23.657s; **16** Arvid Lindblad, GB, +25.794s**; **17** Nikola Tsolov, BG, +26.469s; **18** Santiago Ramos, MEX, +26.913s; **19** Joseph Loake, GB, +27.597s; **20** Luke Browning, GB, +31.505s***; **21** Sebastian Montoya, CO, +1m 38.106s****; **22** Callum Voisin, GB, -1 lap; **23** Noah Strømsted, DK, -1*****; Max Esterson, USA, -8 (DNF); Mari Boya, E, -13 (DNF); Piotr Wiśnicki, PL, -19 (DNF); Cian Shields, GB, -20 (DNF); Sophia Flörsch, D, -20 (DNF); Matías Zagazeta, PE, -20 (DNF).
** 10s penalty for failing to follow Race Director's instructions*
*** 10s penalty for causing a collision*
**** 5s penalty for Safety Car infringement; 10s penalty for causing a collision with Loake*
***** 5s penalty for failing to follow Race Director's instructions*
****** 10s penalty for causing a collision with Smith*
Disqualified: Gabriele Minì, I, +3.948s (technical nonconformity – tyre pressures).
Fastest race lap: Stenshorne, 1m 39.435s, 130.322mph/209.732km/h.
Pole position: Fornaroli, 1m 38.287s, 131.844mph/212.182km/h.

Final championship points
Drivers
1 Leonardo Fornaroli, I, 153; **2** Gabriele Mini, I, 130; **3** Luke Browning, GB, 128; **4** Arvid Lindblad, GB, 113; **5** Christian Mansell, AUS, 112; **6** Dino Beganovic, S, 109; **7** Oliver Goethe, DK, 94; **8** Sami Meguetounif, F, 84; **9** Tim Tramnitz, D, 81; **10** Noel León, MEX, 79; **11** Nikola Tsolov, BG, 75; **12** Callum Voisin, GB, 67; **13** Laurens Van Hoepen, NL, 58; **14** Alex Dunne, IRL, 50; **15** Mari Boya, E, 45; **16** Santiago Ramos, MEX, 44; **17** Sebastian Montoya, CO, 40; **18** Martinius Stenshorne, N, 38; **19** Nikita Bedrin, RUS, 25; **20** Tom Smith, AUS, 12; **21** Max Esterson, USA, 11; **22** Charlie Wurz, A, 10; **23** Piotr Wiśnicki, PL, 10; **24** Tasanapol Inthraphuvasak, T, 9; **25** Matías Zagazeta, PE, 8; **26** Joseph Loake, GB, 8; **27** Kacper Sztuka, PL, 6; **28** Josh Dufek, CH, 1.

Teams
1 Prema Racing, 352; **2** Trident, 281; **3** ART Grand Prix, 245; **4** Campos Racing, 179; **5** Hitech Pulse-Eight, 166; **6** MP Motorsport, 137; **7** Van Amersfoort Racing, 91; **8** Rodin Motorsport, 85; **9** PHM AIX Racing, 35; **10** Jenzer Motorsport, 29.

GB3 Championship

All cars are Tatuus MSV-022-Cosworth.

GB3 CHAMPIONSHIP, Oulton Park Circuit, Tarporley, Cheshire, Great Britain, 30 March/1 April. 11, 10 and 12 laps of the 2.692-mile/4.332km circuit.
Round 1 (29.612 miles/47.656km).
1 Louis Sharp, NZ, 20m 24.198s, 87.080mph/140.141km/h; **2** John Bennett, GB, +1.433s; **3** Ugo Ugochukwu, USA, +3.440s; **4** Gerrard Xie, HK, +4.044s; **5** McKenzy Cresswell, GB, +4.920s; **6** Tymoteusz Kucharczyk, PL, +5.663s; **7** Arthur Rogeon, F, +7.789s; **8** Colin Queen, USA, +8.394s; **9** William Macintyre, GB, +8.775s; **10** Jarrod Waberski, ZA, +9.361s.
Fastest race lap: Bennett, 1m 30.514s, 107.068mph/172.310km/h.
Pole position: Sharp, 1m 29.292s, 108.533mph/174.668km/h.

Round 2 (26.920 miles/43.324km).
1 John Bennett, GB, 21m 17.960s, 75.833mph/122.041km/h; **2** Louis Sharp, NZ, +2.898s; **3** McKenzy Cresswell, GB, +7.084s; **4** Ugo Ugochukwu, USA, +8.489s; **5** Gerrard Xie, HK, +12.837s; **6** William Macintyre, GB, +13.440s; **7** Jarrod Waberski, ZA, +20.406s; **8** Hugo Schwarze, D, +21.073s; **9** Patrick Heuzenroeder, AUS, +21.612s; **10** Arthur Rogeon, F, +25.639s.
Fastest race lap: Bennett, 1m 46.490s, 91.005mph/146.459km/h.
Pole position: Sharp, 1m 29.554s, 108.216mph/174.157km/h.

Round 3 (32.304 miles/51.988km).
1 William Macintyre, GB, 25m 55.845s, 74.746mph/120.293km/h; **2** Jarrod Waberski, ZA, +4.082s; **3** Ugo Ugochukwu, USA, +4.899s; **4** Tymoteusz Kucharczyk, PL, +6.516s; **5** Louis Sharp, NZ, +7.059s; **6** Arthur Rogeon, F, +7.504s; **7** Sebastian Murray, UAE, +11.004s; **8** McKenzy Cresswell, GB, +12.980s; **9** Colin Queen, USA, +13.898s; **10** Gerrard Xie, HK, +16.035s.
Fastest race lap: Macintyre, 1m 44.352s, 92.870mph/149.460km/h.
Pole position: Heuzenroeder.

GB3 CHAMPIONSHIP, Silverstone Arena Grand Prix Circuit, Towcester, Northamptonshire, Great Britain, 27/28 April. 10, 10 and 0 laps of the 3.660-mile/5.891km circuit.
Round 4 (36.604 miles/58.908km).
1 Tymoteusz Kucharczyk, PL, 19m 03.166s, 115.271mph/185.511km/h; **2** McKenzy Cresswell, GB, +7.855s; **3** William Macintyre, GB, +9.503s; **4** Louis Sharp, NZ, +12.222s; **5** Gerrard Xie, HK, +12.879s; **6** Ugo Ugochukwu, USA, +14.776s; **7** Jarrod Waberski, ZA, +16.607s; **8** James Hedley, GB, +17.481s; **9** Martinius Stenshorne, N, +18.149s; **10** John Bennett, GB, +20.078s.
Fastest race lap: Kucharczyk, 1m 53.367s, 116.237mph/187.065km/h.
Pole position: Kucharczyk, 2m 05.083s, 105.349mph/169.543km/h.

Round 5 (36.604 miles/58.908km).
1 William Macintyre, GB, 21m 18.191s, 103.094mph/165.914km/h; **2** Ugo Ugochukwu, USA, +0.180s; **3** Tymoteusz Kucharczyk, PL, +0.679s; **4** McKenzy Cresswell, GB, +3.167s; **5** Louis Sharp, NZ, +3.864s; **6** Jarrod Waberski, ZA, +14.942s; **7** James Hedley, GB, +15.788s; **8** John Bennett, GB, +18.049s; **9** Gerrard Xie, HK, +21.330s; **10** Josh Irfan, GB, +24.053s.
Fastest race lap: Kucharczyk, 2m 05.572s, 104.939mph/168.883km/h.
Pole position: Kucharczyk, 2m 05.103s, 105.332mph/169.516km/h.

Round 6
Cancelled due to adverse weather conditions.

GB3 CHAMPIONSHIP, Circuit de Spa-Francorchamps, Stavelot, Belgium, 1/2 June. 8, 7 and 9 laps of the 4.352-mile/7.004km circuit.
Round 7 (34.816 miles/56.031km).
1 Tymoteusz Kucharczyk, PL, 20m 24.588s, 102.351mph/164.718km/h; **2** John Bennett, GB, +1.811s; **3** Louis Sharp, NZ, +3.354s; **4** Ugo Ugochukwu, USA, +5.175s; **5** William Macintyre, GB, +15.057s; **6** Noah Ping, USA, +17.995s; **7** McKenzy Cresswell, GB, +19.391s; **8** Hugo Schwarze, D, +20.709s; **9** Nikita Johnson, USA, +24.230s; **10** Jarrod Waberski, ZA, +26.464s.
Fastest race lap: Macintyre, 2m 31.115s, 103.677mph/166.853km/h.
Pole position: Kucharczyk, 2m 14.596s, 116.402mph/187.331km/h.

Round 8 (30.464 miles/49.027km).
1 Tymoteusz Kucharczyk, PL, 20m 18.681s, 89.991mph/144.827km/h; **2** John Bennett, GB, +0.452s; **3** Louis Sharp, NZ, +0.750s; **4** Ugo Ugochukwu, USA, +0.957s; **5** William Macintyre, GB, +1.370s; **6** Kanato Le, J, +2.097s; **7** Shawn Rashid, USA, +2.410s; **8** Sebastian Murray, UAE, +3.354s; **9** Arthur Rogeon, F, +4.031s; **10** Edward Pearson, GB, +5.148s.
Fastest race lap: Noah Ping, USA, 2m 18.065s, 113.477mph/182.624km/h.
Pole position: Bennett, 2m 14.662s, 116.345mph/187.239km/h.

Round 9 (39.168 miles/63.035km).
1 William Macintyre, GB, 26m 43.414s, 87.940mph/141.526km/h; **2** Gerrard Xie, HK, +0.838s; **3** Noah Ping, USA, +1.405s; **4** Tymoteusz Kucharczyk, PL, +1.705s; **5** Kanato Le, J, +2.370s; **6** McKenzy Cresswell, GB, +2.605s; **7** Hugo Schwarze, D, +3.246s; **8** Arthur Rogeon, F, +3.603s; **9** Colin Queen, USA, +4.123s; **10** Flynn Jackes, PH, +5.940s.
Fastest race lap: Macintyre, 2m 17.160s, 114.226mph/183.829km/h.
Pole position: Schwarze.

GB3 CHAMPIONSHIP, Hungaroring, Mogyoród, Budapest, Hungary, 22/23 June. 11, 11 and 14 laps of the 2.722-mile/4.381km circuit.
Round 10 (29.944 miles/48.191km).
1 Gerrard Xie, HK, 18m 33.309s, 96.828mph/155.830km/h; **2** Tymoteusz Kucharczyk, PL, +0.523s; **3** John Bennett, GB, +3.279s; **4** James Hedley, GB, +4.891s; **5** William Macintyre, GB, +5.843s; **6** McKenzy Cresswell, GB, +6.781s; **7** Louis Sharp, NZ, +7.354s; **8** Patrick Heuzenroeder, AUS, +9.160s; **9** Arthur Rogeon, F, +11.800s; **10** Jarrod Waberski, ZA, +14.868s.
Fastest race lap: Kucharczyk, 1m 40.179s, 97.825mph/157.434km/h.
Pole position: Xie, 1m 39.629s, 98.365mph/158.303km/h.

Round 11 (29.944 miles/48.191km).
1 Louis Sharp, NZ, 18m 25.093s, 97.548mph/156.989km/h; **2** William Macintyre, GB, +4.097s; **3** McKenzy Cresswell, GB, +10.606s; **4** Patrick Heuzenroeder, AUS, +11.808s; **5** Jarrod Waberski, ZA, +15.705s; **6** John Bennett, GB, +16.043s; **7** Noah Ping, USA, +20.089s; **8** James Hedley, GB, +20.928s; **9** Hugo Schwarze, D, +21.697s; **10** Shawn Rashid, USA, +22.565s.
Disqualified: Tymoteusz Kucharczyk, PL, finished 2nd in 18m 27.088s.
Fastest race lap: Sharp, 1m 39.584s, 98.409mph/158.374km/h.
Pole position: Gerrard Xie, HK, 1m 39.720s, 98.275mph/158.158km/h.

Round 12 (38.111 miles/61.334km).
1 Arthur Rogeon, F, 23m 44.027s, 96.346mph/155.054km/h; **2** Josh Irfan, GB, +5.582s; **3** Jarrod Waberski, ZA, +9.875s; **4** Louis Sharp, NZ, +13.278s; **5** Patrick Heuzenroeder, AUS, +13.632s; **6** James Hedley, GB, +14.003s; **7** John Bennett, GB, +14.429s; **8** William Macintyre, GB, +14.818s; **9** McKenzy Cresswell, GB, +17.092s; **10** Hugo Schwarze, D, +18.581s.
Fastest race lap: Tymoteusz Kucharczyk, PL, 1m 40.409s, 97.600mph/157.073km/h.
Pole position: Irfan.

GB3 CHAMPIONSHIP, Circuit Park Zandvoort, Netherlands, 13/14 July. 11, 9 and 16 laps of the 2.646-mile/4.259km circuit.
Round 13 (29.111 miles/46.849km).
1 John Bennett, GB, 20m 44.726s, 84.193mph/135.496km/h; **2** Tymoteusz Kucharczyk, PL, +1.138s; **3** James Hedley, GB, +2.721s; **4** Louis Sharp, NZ, +3.065s; **5** William Macintyre, GB, +3.548s; **6** Hugo Schwarze, D, +4.994s; **7** Colin Queen, USA, +5.371s; **8** Shawn Rashid, USA, +6.122s; **9** Nikita Johnson, USA, +7.013s; **10** Jarrod Waberski, ZA, +8.884s.
Fastest race lap: Bennett, 1m 33.149s, 102.278mph/164.600km/h.
Pole position: Bennett, 1m 40.600s, 94.702mph/152.409km/h.

Round 14 (23.818 miles/38.331km).
1 Tymoteusz Kucharczyk, PL, 17m 05.582s, 83.605mph/134.549km/h; **2** James Hedley, GB, +7.474s; **3** McKenzy Cresswell, GB, +8.222s; **4** Colin Queen, USA, +8.626s; **5** Patrick Heuzenroeder, AUS, +9.623s; **6** Nikita Johnson, USA, +11.704s; **7** Sebastian Murray, UAE, +12.520s; **8** Edward Pearson, GB, +13.169s; **9** Josh Irfan, GB, +15.952s; **10** Aditya Kulkarni, IND, +16.170s.
Fastest race lap: Kucharczyk, 1m 31.584s, 104.025mph/167.413km/h.
Pole position: John Bennett, GB, 1m 40.715s, 94.594mph/152.235km/h.

Round 15 (42.343 miles/68.144km).
1 Nikita Johnson, USA, 26m 19.590s, 96.502mph/155.305km/h; **2** McKenzy Cresswell, GB, +1.644s; **3** Patrick Heuzenroeder, AUS, +2.176s; **4** Hugo Schwarze, D, +2.579s; **5** William Macintyre, GB, +3.052s; **6** Noah Ping, USA, +3.412s; **7** Louis Sharp, NZ, +7.822s; **8** Josh Irfan, GB, +8.276s; **9** Tymoteusz Kucharczyk, PL, +10.171s; **10** John Bennett, GB, +10.604s.
Disqualified: Colin Queen, USA, finished 9th in 26m 29.390s.
Fastest race lap: Johnson, 1m 32.623s, 102.859mph/165.535km/h.
Pole position: Irfan.

GB3 CHAMPIONSHIP, Silverstone Arena Grand Prix Circuit, Towcester, Northamptonshire, Great Britain, 27/28 July. 9, 10 and 12 laps of the 3.660-mile/5.891km circuit.
Round 16 (32.944 miles/53.018km).
1 John Bennett, GB, 21m 03.303s, 93.878mph/151.082km/h; **2** Louis Sharp, NZ, +1.298s; **3** Jarrod Waberski, ZA, +2.317s; **4** Gerrard Xie, HK, +3.293s; **5** Noah Ping, USA, +3.945s; **6** Hugo Schwarze, D, +4.822s; **7** McKenzy Cresswell, GB, +6.013s; **8** Ugo Ugochukwu, USA, +7.228s; **9** Colin Queen, USA, +8.040s; **10** Nikita Johnson, USA, +8.778s.
Fastest race lap: Bennett, 1m 54.229s, 115.359mph/185.653km/h.
Pole position: Cresswell, 1m 52.703s, 116.921mph/188.167km/h.

Round 17 (36.604 miles/58.908km).
1 McKenzy Cresswell, GB, 19m 05.440s, 115.042mph/185.143km/h; **2** Louis Sharp, NZ, +2.234s; **3** John Bennett, GB, +5.790s; **4** Jarrod Waberski, ZA, +6.412s; **5** Tymoteusz Kucharczyk, PL, +6.753s; **6** Ugo Ugochukwu, USA, +12.325s; **7** Shawn Rashid, USA, +13.167s; **8** Noah Ping, USA, +14.672s; **9** Gerrard Xie, HK, +15.249s; **10** Hugo Schwarze, D, +16.316s.
Fastest race lap: Cresswell, 1m 53.840s, 115.754mph/186.288km/h.
Pole position: Cresswell, 1m 52.814s, 116.806mph/187.982km/h.

Round 18 (43.925 miles/70.690km).
1 Arthur Rogeon, F, 24m 26.520s, 107.826mph/173.529km/h; **2** Shawn Rashid, USA, +3.354s; **3** Tymoteusz Kucharczyk, PL, +4.617s; **4** John Bennett, GB, +6.544s; **5** Hugo Schwarze, D, +5.880s*; **6** Gerrard Xie, HK, +7.728s; **7** Louis Sharp, NZ, +8.959s; **8** Patrick Heuzenroeder, AUS, +11.522s; **9** Nikita Johnson, USA, +13.391s; **10** William Macintyre, GB, +13.997s.
** 1-position penalty*
Fastest race lap: Kucharczyk, 1m 54.280s, 115.308mph/185.570km/h.
Pole position: Heuzenroeder.

GB3 CHAMPIONSHIP, Donington Park National Circuit, Castle Donington, Great Britain, 7/8 September. 14, 13 and 17 laps of the 2.487-mile/4.003km circuit.
Round 19 (34.822 miles/56.041km).
1 Louis Sharp, NZ, 20m 03.424s, 104.169mph/167.644km/h; **2** Gerrard Xie, HK, +4.619s; **3** John Bennett, GB, +5.430s; **4** Tymoteusz Kucharczyk, PL, +10.696s; **5** Noah Ping, USA, +12.140s; **6** Freddie Slater, GB, +12.675s; **7** William Macintyre, GB, +15.240s; **8** Hugo Schwarze, D, +16.159s; **9** Jarrod Waberski, ZA, +17.221s; **10** McKenzy Cresswell, GB, +17.815s.
Fastest race lap: Kucharczyk, 1m 24.107s, 106.462mph/171.335km/h.
Pole position: Sharp, 1m 33.263s, 96.011mph/154.514km/h.

Round 20 (32.335 miles/52.038km).
1 Louis Sharp, NZ, 20m 12.587s, 95.997mph/154.493km/h; **2** Tymoteusz Kucharczyk, PL, +2.392s; **3** Noah Ping, USA, +12.648s; **4** Freddie Slater, GB, +8.740s*; **5** Arthur Rogeon, F, +16.066s; **6** Gerrard Xie, HK, +16.259s**; **7** John Bennett, GB, +16.811s; **8** Colin Queen, USA, +18.340s; **9** William Macintyre, GB, +18.744s; **10** McKenzy Cresswell, GB, +19.612s.
** 1-position penalty*
*** 5s penalty for exceeding track limits*
Fastest race lap: Kucharczyk, 1m 31.861s, 97.476mph/156.873km/h.
Pole position: Sharp, 1m 33.436s, 95.833mph/154.228km/h.

Round 21 (42.284 miles/68.050km).
1 Arthur Rogeon, F, 23m 58.296s, 105.835mph/170.325km/h; **2** McKenzy Cresswell, GB, +2.314s; **3** William Macintyre, GB, +3.658s; **4** John Bennett, GB, +4.818s; **5** Freddie Slater, GB, +5.804s; **6** Louis Sharp, NZ, +6.161s; **7** Tymoteusz Kucharczyk, PL, +7.554s; **8** Colin Queen, USA, +7.929s*; **9** Gerrard Xie, HK, +9.163s; **10** Aditya Kulkarni, IND, +13.177s.
** 5s penalty for exceeding track limits*
Fastest race lap: Rogeon, 1m 24.049s, 106.536mph/171.453km/h.
Pole position: Rogeon.

GB3 CHAMPIONSHIP, Brands Hatch Grand Prix Circuit, West Kingsdown, Dartford, Kent, Great Britain, 28/29 September. 15, 14 and 17 laps of the 2.433-mile/3.916km circuit.
Round 22 (36.498 miles/58.738km).
1 McKenzy Cresswell, GB, 20m 01.924s, 109.318mph/175.931km/h; **2** John Bennett, GB, +0.473s; **3** Tymoteusz Kucharczyk, PL, +5.490s; **4** Hugo Schwarze, D, +7.467s; **5** William Macintyre, GB, +8.347s; **6** Nikita Johnson, USA, +15.757s; **7** Louis Sharp, NZ, +16.333s; **8** Arthur Rogeon, F, +17.258s; **9** Callum Voisin, GB, +18.952s; **10** Noah Ping, USA, +19.412s.
Fastest race lap: Bennett, 1m 19.097s, 110.744mph/178.225km/h.
Pole position: Cresswell, 1m 18.479s, 111.616mph/179.628km/h.

Round 23 (34.065 miles/54.822km).
1 Louis Sharp, NZ, 21m 05.917s, 96.873mph/155.902km/h; **2** John Bennett, GB, +0.476s; **3** Tymoteusz Kucharczyk, PL, +1.502s; **4** McKenzy Cresswell, GB, +4.968s; **5** Jarrod Waberski, ZA, +8.090s; **6** Arthur Rogeon, F, +8.832s; **7** Noah Ping, USA, +9.492s; **8** Hugo Schwarze, D, +10.055s; **9** Nikita Johnson, USA, +11.970s; **10** Callum Voisin, GB, +12.476s.
Fastest race lap: Kucharczyk, 1m 19.266s, 110.507mph/177.845km/h.
Pole position: Sharp, 1m 18.622s, 111.413mph/179.301km/h.

Round 24 (41.364 miles/66.570km).
1 Nikita Johnson, USA, 25m 03.711s, 99.029mph/159.372km/h; **2** Callum Voisin, GB, +0.178s; **3** Arthur Rogeon, F, +3.553s; **4** Jarrod Waberski, ZA, +7.841s; **5** William Macintyre, GB, +8.211s; **6** Patrick Heuzenroeder, AUS, +10.051s; **7** Gerrard Xie, HK, +10.554s; **8** Tymoteusz Kucharczyk, PL, +10.826s; **9** John Bennett, GB, +11.421s; **10** Louis Sharp, NZ, +12.008s.
Fastest race lap: Voisin, 1m 19.950s, 109.562mph/176.323km/h.
Pole position: Johnson.

Final championship points
Drivers
1 Louis Sharp, NZ, 478; **2** John Bennett, GB, 456; **3** Tymoteusz Kucharczyk, PL, 443; **4** McKenzy Cresswell, GB, 376; **5** William Macintyre, GB, 372; **6** Jarrod Waberski, ZA, 286; **7** Gerrard Xie, HK, 261; **8** Arthur Rogeon, F, 258; **9** Hugo Schwarze, D, 219; **10** Noah Ping, USA, 211; **11** Nikita Johnson, USA, 193; **12** Patrick Heuzenroeder, AUS, 189; **13** Ugo Ugochukwu, USA, 185; **14** Colin Queen, USA, 178; **15** James Hedley, GB, 151; **16** Josh Irfan, GB, 138; **17** Shawn Rashid, USA, 125; **18** Sebastian Murray, UAE, 111; **19** Aditya Kulkarni, IND, 111; **20** Edward Pearson, GB, 87; **21** Flynn Jackes, PH, 75; **22** Freddie Slater, GB, 51; **23** Kanato Le, J, 46; **24** Callum Voisin, GB, 40; **25** James Wharton, AUS, 30; **26** Max Taylor, USA, 22; **27** Martinius Stenshorne, N, 19; **28** Jacob Douglas, NZ, 18; **29** Tom Mills, GB, 17; **30** Marcus Luzio, GB, 17; **31** Francisco Javier Sagrera, E, 10; **32** Alexandros George Kattoulas, SGP, 6; **33** Rishab Jain, SGP, 4.

Teams
1 Rodin Motorsport, 933; **2** Hitech Pulse-Eight, 908; **3** Elite Motorsport, 729; **4** JHR Developments, 680; **5** VRD by Arden, 528; **6** Fortec Motorsports, 296; **7** Chris Dittmann Racing, 281; **8** Hillspeed, 128; **9** Arden Motorsport, 22.

Super Formula Lights Championship

All cars are Dallara F320-Toyota TGE33.

SUPER FORMULA LIGHTS, Autopolis International Racing Course, Kamit-sue-mura, Hita-gun, Oita Prefecture, Japan, 18/19 May. 21, 14 and 14 laps of the 2.904-mile/4.674km circuit.
Round 1 (60.990 miles/98.154km).
1 Seita Nonaka, J (-Toyota), 36m 46.685s, 99.500mph/160.129km/h; **2** Rikuto Kobayashi, J (-Toyota), +7.272s; **3** Rin Arakawa, J (-Toyota), +9.654s; **4** Kaylen Frederick, USA (-Toyota), +20.090s; **5** Syun Koide, J (-Toyota), +20.549s; **6** Yuga Furutani, J (-Toyota), +21.710s; **7** Souta Arao, J (-Toyota), +22.791s; **8** Nobuhiro Imada, J (-Toyota), +51.330s; **9** Dragon, J (-Toyota), +55.239s; **10** Yasuhiro Shimizu, J (-Toyota), +1m 34.516s.
Fastest race lap: Nonaka, 1m 39.281s, 105.312mph/169.483km/h.
Pole position: Kobayashi, 1m 37.276s, 107.482mph/172.976km/h.

Round 2 (40.660 miles/65.436km).
1 Syun Koide, J (-Toyota), 25m 43.349s, 94.843mph/152.635km/h; **2** Jin Nakamura, J (-Toyota), +0.551s; **3** Seita Nonaka, J (-Toyota), +2.877s; **4** Kaylen Frederick, USA (-Toyota), +4.696s; **5** Yuga Furutani, J (-Toyota), +5.263s; **6** Rin Arakawa, J (-Toyota), +6.027s; **7** Souta Arao, J (-Toyota), +7.344s; **8** Rikuto Kobayashi, J (-Toyota), +8.196s; **9** Nobuhiro Imada, J (-Toyota), +10.940s; **10** Dragon, J (-Toyota), +11.837s.
Fastest race lap: Koide, 1m 38.260s, 106.406mph/171.244km/h.
Pole position: Koide, 1m 37.060s, 107.721mph/173.361km/h.

Round 3 (40.660 miles/65.436km).
1 Seita Nonaka, J (-Toyota), 23m 35.388s, 103.418mph/166.435km/h; **2** Kaylen Frederick, USA (-Toyota), +10.708s; **3** Rikuto Kobayashi, J (-Toyota), +11.244s; **4** Yuga Furutani, J (-Toyota), +12.814s; **5** Rin Arakawa, J (-Toyota), +13.730s; **6** Jin Nakamura, J (-Toyota), +14.260s; **7** Syun Koide, J (-Toyota), +17.935s; **8** Souta Arao, J (-Toyota), +18.997s; **9** Nobuhiro Imada, J (-Toyota), +33.211s; **10** Dragon, J (-Toyota), +34.710s.
Fastest race lap: Nonaka, 1m 40.044s, 104.508mph/168.190km/h.
Pole position: Nonaka.

SUPER FORMULA LIGHTS, Sportsland-SUGO International Course, Shibata-gun, Miyagi Prefecture, Japan, 22/23 June. 26, 18 and 16 laps of the 2.229-mile/3.587km circuit.
Round 4 (57.942 miles/93.249km).
1 Syun Koide, J (-Toyota), 33m 13.506s, 104.636mph/168.395km/h; **2** Jin Nakamura, J (-Toyota), +4.094s; **3** Rin Arakawa, J (-Toyota), +5.931s; **4** Seita Nonaka, J (-Toyota), +6.801s; **5** Yuga Furutani, J (-Toyota), +7.236s; **6** Souta Arao, J (-Toyota), +7.932s; **7** Rikuto Kobayashi, J (-Toyota), +8.272s; **8** Nobuhiro Imada, J (-Toyota), +44.275s; **9** Dragon, J (-Toyota), +57.149s; **10** Makoto Fujiwara, J (-Toyota), +1m 13.846s.
Fastest race lap: Koide, 1m 14.466s, 107.737mph/173.387km/h.:
Pole position: Koide, 1m 13.260s, 109.511mph/176.241km/h.

Round 5 (40.114 miles/64.557km).
1 Jin Nakamura, J (-Toyota), 31m 16.226s, 76.968mph/123.868km/h; **2** Souta Arao, J (-Toyota), +12.107s; **3** Rikuto Kobayashi, J (-Toyota), +13.328s; **4** Rin Arakawa, J (-Toyota), +14.735s; **5** Kaylen Frederick, USA (-Toyota), +17.893s; **6** Yuga Furutani, J (-Toyota), +18.377s; **7** Seita Nonaka, J (-Toyota), +20.254s; **8** Syun Koide, J (-Toyota), +33.195s; **9** Dragon, J (-Toyota), +51.361s; **10** Nobuhiro Imada, J (-Toyota), +1m 00.359s.
Fastest race lap: Nakamura, 1m 32.093s, 87.116mph/140.200km/h.
Pole position: Frederick, 1m 13.025s, 109.863mph/176.808km/h.

Round 6 (35.657 miles/57.384km).
1 Seita Nonaka, J (-Toyota), 30m 27.157s, 70.254mph/113.062km/h; **2** Syun Koide, J (-Toyota), +2.619s; **3** Jin Nakamura, J (-Toyota), +3.939s; **4** Rin Arakawa, J (-Toyota), +5.474s; **5** Rikuto Kobayashi, J (-Toyota), +6.680s; **6** Yuga Furutani, J (-Toyota), +7.456s; **7** Souta Arao, J (-Toyota), +8.024s; **8** Kaylen Frederick, USA (-Toyota), +8.368s; **9** Dragon, J (-Toyota), +17.261s; **10** Nobuhiro Imada, J (-Toyota), +17.936s.
Fastest race lap: Nakamura, 1m 32.454s, 86.776mph/139.652km/h.
Pole position: Koide.

SUPER FORMULA LIGHTS, Fuji International Speedway, Sunto-gun, Shizuoka Prefecture, Japan, 20/21 July. 15, 21 and 15 laps of the 2.835-mile/4.563km circuit.
Round 7 (42.341 miles/68.141km).
1 Syun Koide, J (-Toyota), 23m 42.638s, 107.617mph/173.193km/h; **2** Rin Arakawa, J (-Toyota), +4.871s; **3** Yuga Furutani, J (-Toyota), +5.573s; **4** Souta Arao, J (-Toyota), +6.601s; **5** Jin Nakamura, J (-Toyota), +7.896s; **6** Rikuto Kobayashi, J (-Toyota), +8.150s; **7** Seita Nonaka, J (-Toyota), +9.074s; **8** Kaylen Frederick, USA (-Toyota), +18.016s; **9** Makoto Fujiwara, J (-Toyota), +37.950s; **10** Dragon, J (-Toyota), +44.631s.
Fastest race lap: Koide, 1m 34.114s, 108.455mph/174.542km/h.
Pole position: Nakamura, 1m 33.030s, 109.719mph/176.575km/h.

Round 8 (59.353 miles/95.519km).
1 Rikuto Kobayashi, J (-Toyota), 33m 27.352s, 106.779mph/171.844km/h; **2** Jin Nakamura, J (-Toyota), +5.127s; **3** Souta Arao, J (-Toyota), +11.062s; **4** Seita Nonaka, J (-Toyota), +17.355s; **5** Rin Arakawa, J (-Toyota), +19.600s; **6** Syun Koide, J (-Toyota), +19.929s; **7** Yuga Furutani, J (-Toyota), +22.016s; **8** Kaylen Frederick, USA (-Toyota), +26.366s*; **9** Makoto Fujiwara, J (-Toyota), +50.944s; **10** Dragon, J (-Toyota), +58.758s.
** 5s penalty*
Fastest race lap: Kobayashi, 1m 34.763s, 107.712mph/173.346km/h.
Pole position: Kobayashi, 1m 33.055s, 109.689mph/176.528km/h.

Round 9 (42.341 miles/68.141km).
1 Syun Koide, J (-Toyota), 23m 44.142s, 107.504mph/173.010km/h; **2** Rin Arakawa, J (-Toyota), +7.372s; **3** Seita Nonaka, J (-Toyota), +7.733s; **4** Yuga Furutani, J (-Toyota), +9.544s; **5** Rikuto Kobayashi, J (-Toyota), +12.610s; **6** Souta Arao, J (-Toyota), +16.089s*; **7** Jin Nakamura, J (-Toyota), +17.217s; **8** Dragon, J (-Toyota), +37.556s; **9** Nobuhiro Imada, J (-Toyota), +37.557s; **10** Yasuhiro Shimizu, J (-Toyota), +44.140s.
** 5s penalty*
Fastest race lap: Koide, 1m 34.174s, 108.386mph/174.430km/h.
Pole position: Koide.

SUPER FORMULA LIGHTS, Okayama International Circuit (TI Circuit Aida), Aida Gun, Okayama Prefecture, Japan, 14/15 September. 25, 17 and 18 laps of the 2.301-mile/3.703km circuit.
Round 10 (57.523 miles/92.575km).
1 Syun Koide, J (-Toyota), 37m 35.403s, 91.817mph/147.765km/h; **2** Kaylen Frederick, USA (-Toyota), +5.034s; **3** Rikuto Kobayashi, J (-Toyota), +5.792s; **4** Seita Nonaka, J (-Toyota), +8.669s; **5** Jin Nakamura, J (-Toyota), +9.539s; **6** Souta Arao, J (-Toyota), +10.657s; **7** Yuga Furutani, J (-Toyota), +12.353s; **8** Reimei Ito, J (-Toyota), +14.354s; **9** Dragon, J (-Toyota), +42.645s; **10** Makoto Fujiwara, J (-Toyota), +49.346s*.
** 10s penalty*
Fastest race lap: Koide, 1m 24.035s, 98.571mph/158.634km/h.
Pole position: Koide, 1m 21.671s, 101.424mph/163.226km/h.

Round 11 (39.116 miles/62.951km).
1 Kaylen Frederick, USA (-Toyota), 30m 05.835s, 77.979mph/125.495km/h; **2** Syun Koide, J (-Toyota), +1.190s; **3** Yuga Furutani, J (-Toyota), +5.044s; **4** Jin Nakamura, J (-Toyota), +7.282s; **5** Souta Arao, J (-Toyota), +8.303s; **6** Reimei Ito, J (-Toyota), +10.838s; **7** Rin Arakawa, J (-Toyota), +12.401s; **8** Dragon, J (-Toyota), +46.797s; **9** Makoto Fujiwara, J (-Toyota), +1m 07.410s; Rikuto Kobayashi, J (-Toyota), -13 laps (DNF).
Fastest race lap: Arao, 1m 23.718s, 98.944mph/159.235km/h.
Pole position: Koide, 1m 22.122s, 100.867mph/162.329km/h.

Round 12 (41.417 miles/66.654km).
1 Syun Koide, J (-Toyota), 25m 39.671s, 96.839mph/155.848km/h; **2** Kaylen Frederick, USA (-Toyota), +5.270s; **3** Rikuto Kobayashi, J (-Toyota), +5.963s; **4** Seita Nonaka, J (-Toyota), +7.362s; **5** Souta Arao, J (-Toyota), +7.988s; **6** Jin Nakamura, J (-Toyota), +10.636s; **7** Reimei Ito, J (-Toyota), +11.743s; **8** Rin Arakawa, J (-Toyota), +15.308s; **9** Yuga Furutani, J (-Toyota), +28.684s; **10** Dragon, J (-Toyota), +51.351s.
Fastest race lap: Koide, 1m 24.658s, 97.845mph/157.467km/h.
Pole position: Koide.

SUPER FORMULA LIGHTS, Suzuka International Racing Course, Suzuka-shi, Mie Prefecture, Japan, 9/10 November. 17, 12 and 12 laps of the 3.608-mile/5.807km circuit.
Round 13 (61.341 miles/98.719km).
1 Seita Nonaka, J (-Toyota), 32m 23.702s, 113.612mph/182.841km/h; **2** Souta Arao, J (-Toyota), +0.411s; **3** Rikuto Kobayashi, J (-Toyota), +11.987s; **4** Jin Nakamura, J (-Toyota), +17.011s; **5** Kaylen Frederick, USA (-Toyota), +24.585s; **6** Syun Koide, J (-Toyota), +25.867s; **7** Yuga Furutani, J (-Toyota), +28.145s; **8** Tsubasa Iriyama, J (-Toyota), +50.351s; **9** Yasuhiro Shimizu, J (-Toyota), +1m 08.214s; **10** Dragon, J (-Toyota), +1m 19.457s.
Fastest race lap: Nonaka, 1m 53.103s, 114.850mph/184.833km/h.
Pole position: Nonaka, 1m 51.305s, 116.705mph/187.819km/h.

Round 14 (43.300 miles/69.684km).
1 Rikuto Kobayashi, J (-Toyota), 22m 55.517s, 113.324mph/182.377km/h; **2** Jin Nakamura, J (-Toyota), +1.385s; **3** Yuga Furutani, J (-Toyota), +1.528s; **4** Seita Nonaka, J (-Toyota), +4.621s*; **5** Souta Arao, J (-Toyota), +5.204s; **6** Syun Koide, J (-Toyota), +6.129s; **7** Kaylen Frederick, USA (-Toyota), +11.838s; **8** Nobuhiro Imada, J (-Toyota), +53.047s; **9** Dragon, J (-Toyota), +53.204s; **10** Makoto Fujiwara, J (-Toyota), +54.462s.
** 10s penalty*
Fastest race lap: Nonaka, 1m 53.926s, 114.020mph/183.498km/h.
Pole position: Nakamura, 1m 51.009s, 117.017mph/188.320km/h.

Round 15 (43.300 miles/69.684km).
1 Seita Nonaka, J (-Toyota), 22m 49.810s, 113.796mph/183.137km/h; **2** Souta Arao, J (-Toyota), +3.051s; **3** Jin Nakamura, J (-Toyota), +7.266s; **4** Rikuto Kobayashi, J (-Toyota), +8.802s; **5** Syun Koide, J (-Toyota), +10.445s; **6** Yuga Furutani, J (-Toyota), +12.240s; **7** Kaylen Frederick, USA (-Toyota), +13.306s*; **8** Tsubasa Iriyama, J (-Toyota), +42.921s; **9** Nobuhiro Imada, J (-Toyota), +55.879s; **10** Yasuhiro Shimizu, J (-Toyota), +56.663s.
** 5s penalty*
Fastest race lap: Nonaka, 1m 53.751s, 114.196mph/183.780km/h.
Pole position: Nonaka.

SUPER FORMULA LIGHTS, Twin Ring Motegi, Motegi-machi, Haga-gun, Tochigi Prefecture, Japan, 30 November/1 December. 20, 14 and 14 laps of the 2.983-mile/4.801km circuit.
Round 16 (59.664 miles/96.020km).
1 Syun Koide, J (-Toyota), 35m 11.029s, 101.747mph/163.746km/h; **2** Rikuto Kobayashi, J (-Toyota), +1.146s; **3** Rin Arakawa, J (-Toyota), +10.548s; **4** Souta Arao, J (-Toyota), +10.988s; **5** Jin Nakamura, J (-Toyota), +11.661s; **6** Kaylen Frederick, USA (-Toyota), +19.036s; **7** Yuga Furutani, J (-Toyota), +20.515s; **8** Reimei Ito, J (-Toyota), +26.852s; **9** Togo Suganami, J (-Toyota), +27.535s; **10** Tsubasa Iriyama, J (-Toyota), +35.815s.
Fastest race lap: Kobayashi, 1m 44.762s, 102.514mph/164.980km/h.
Pole position: Koide, 1m 42.779s, 104.491mph/168.163km/h.

Round 17 (41.765 miles/67.214km).
1 Rikuto Kobayashi, J (-Toyota), 24m 35.437s, 101.904mph/163.999km/h; **2** Syun Koide, J (-Toyota), +1.553s; **3** Jin Nakamura, J (-Toyota), +2.850s; **4** Kaylen Frederick, USA (-Toyota), +9.543s; **5** Souta Arao, J (-Toyota), +10.114s; **6** Rin Arakawa, J (-Toyota), +13.247s; **7** Yuga Furutani, J (-Toyota), +14.163s; **8** Seita Nonaka, J (-Toyota), +14.986s; **9** Togo Suganami, J (-Toyota), +17.868s; **10** Reimei Ito, J (-Toyota), +21.580s.
Fastest race lap: Kobayashi, 1m 44.514s, 102.757mph/165.371km/h.
Pole position: Koide, 1m 42.613s, 104.661mph/168.435km/h.

Round 18 (41.765 miles/67.214km).
1 Syun Koide, J (-Toyota), 29m 15.302s, 85.657mph/137.851km/h; **2** Rikuto Kobayashi, J (-Toyota), +2.020s; **3** Yuga Furutani, J (-Toyota), +3.114s; **4** Rin Arakawa, J (-Toyota), +6.530s; **5** Jin Nakamura, J (-Toyota), +7.164s; **6** Seita Nonaka, J (-Toyota), +7.783s; **7** Souta Arao, J (-Toyota), +8.350s; **8** Togo Suganami, J (-Toyota), +10.411s; **9** Reimei Ito, J (-Toyota), +13.280s; **10** Tsubasa Iriyama, J (-Toyota), +15.007s.
Fastest race lap: Koide, 1m 44.996s, 102.285mph/164.612km/h.
Pole position: Koide.

Final championship points.
Drivers
1 Syun Koide, J, 114; **2** Rikuto Kobayashi, J, 86; **3** Seita Nonaka, J, 77; **4** Jin Nakamura, J, 71; **5** Kaylen Frederick, USA, 46; **6** Rin Arakawa, J, 44; **7** Souta Arao, J, 43; **8** Yuga Furutani, J, 34; **9** Reimei Ito, J, 1.

Drivers (Master Class)
1 Dragon, J, 152; **2** Nobuhiro Imada, J, 99; **3** Yasuhiro Shimizu, J, 91; **4** Makoto Fujiwara, J, 68.

Teams
1 TOM'S, 143; **2** B-MAX Racing Team, 124; **3** Toda Racing, 43; **4** Team Dragon, 17; **5** LM Corsa, 1.

Major Non-Championship Formula 3

FIA FR WORLD CUP, Circuito da Guia, Macau, 16/17 November. 10 and 15 laps of the 3.803-mile/ 6.120km circuit.
Race 1 (38.028 miles/61.200km).
1 Ugo Ugochukwu, USA, 47m 40.192s, 47.864mph/ 77.029km/h; **2** Oliver Goethe, DK, +0.221s; **3** Noel León, MEX, +0.445s; **4** Freddie Slater, GB, +0.663s; **5** Enzo Deligny, F, +1.137s; **6** Matteo De Palo, I, +2.196s; **7** James Wharton, AUS, +2.581s; **8** Rashid Al Dhaheri, UAE, +2.792s; **9** Evan Giltaire, F, +3.051s; **10** Dino Beganovic, S, +3.319s.
Fastest race lap: Goethe, 2m 21.520s, 96.735mph/ 155.681km/h.
Pole position: Ugochukwu, 2m 19.107s, 98.413mph/ 158.381km/h.

Race 2 (57.042 miles/91.800km).
1 Ugo Ugochukwu, USA, 1h 06m 58.505s, 51.101mph/ 82.239km/h; **2** Oliver Goethe, DK, +0.412s; **3** Noel León, MEX, +2.426s; **4** Enzo Deligny, F, +2.893s; **5** Cooper Webster, AUS, +6.877s; **6** Alex Dunne, IRL, +7.360s; **7** Mari Boya, E, +8.006s; **8** Dino Beganovic, S, +8.589s; **9** Alexander Abkhazava, GE, +9.660s; **10** Tuukka Taponen, FIN, +9.914s.
Fastest race lap: Goethe, 2m 19.599s, 98.066mph/ 157.823km/h.
Pole position: Ugochukwu.

FIA World Endurance Championship

QATAR 1812 KM, Lusail International Circuit, Doha, Qatar, 2 March. Round 1. 335 laps of the 3.367-mile/5.418km circuit, 1127.638 miles/ 1814.758km.
1 Kévin Estre/André Lotterer/Laurens Vanthoor, F/D/B (Porsche 963), 9h 55m 51.926s, 113.563mph/182.762km/h; **2** Will Stevens/Callum Ilott/Norman Nato, GB/GB/F (Porsche 963), +33.297s; **3** Matt Campbell/Michael Christensen/ Frédéric Makowiecki, AUS/DK/F (Porsche 963), +34.396s; **4** Robert Kubica/Robert Shwartzman/ Yifei Ye, PL/IL/CHN (Ferrari 499P), -1 lap; **5** Mike Conway/Kamui Kobayashi/Nyck de Vries, GB/J/ NL (Toyota GR010 HYBRID), -1; **6** Antonio Fuoco/ Miguel Molina/Nicklas Nielsen, I/E/DK (Ferrari 499P), -2; **7** Paul-Loup Chatin/Ferdinand Habsburg/Charles Milesi, F/A/F (Alpine A424), -2; **8** Sébastien Buemi/Brendon Hartley/Ryo Hirakawa, CH/NZ/J (Toyota GR010 HYBRID), -2; **9** Harry Tincknell/Neel Jani/Julien Andlauer, GB/ CH/F (Porsche 963), -2; **10** Sheldon van der Linde/ Robin Frijns/René Rast, ZA/NL/D (BMW M Hybrid V8), -3.
Fastest race lap: Campbell, 1m 39.748s, 121.503mph/ 195.540km/h.
Pole position: Campbell/Christensen/Makowiecki, 1m 39.347s, 121.993mph/196.330km/h.

6 HOURS OF IMOLA, Autodromo Enzo e Dino Ferrari, Imola, Italy, 21 April. Round 2. 205 laps of the 3.050-mile/4.909km circuit, 625.314 miles/ 1006.345km.
1 Mike Conway/Kamui Kobayashi/Nyck de Vries, GB/J/NL (Toyota GR010 HYBRID), 6h 00m 34.717s, 104.051mph/167.455km/h; **2** Kévin Estre/André Lotterer/Laurens Vanthoor, F/D/B (Porsche 963), +7.081s*; **3** Matt Campbell/Michael Christensen/ Frédéric Makowiecki, AUS/DK/F (Porsche 963), +25.626s; **4** Antonio Fuoco/Miguel Molina/Nicklas Nielsen, I/E/DK (Ferrari 499P), +31.469s; **5** Sébastien Buemi/Brendon Hartley/Ryo Hirakawa, CH/NZ/J (Toyota GR010 HYBRID), +33.777s; **6** Sheldon van der Linde/Robin Frijns/René Rast, ZA/NL/D (BMW M Hybrid V8), -1 lap; **7** Alessandro Pier Guidi/James Calado/Antonio Giovinazzi, I/GB/I (Ferrari 499P), -1; **8** Robert Kubica/Robert Shwartzman/Yifei Ye, PL/ IL/CHN (Ferrari 499P), -1; **9** Mikkel Jensen/Nico Müller/Jean-Éric Vergne, DK/CH/F (Peugeot 9X8 2024), -2; **10** Earl Bamber/Alex Lynn, NZ/GB (Cadillac V-Series.R), -2.
** 5s penalty for overtaking under Safety Car procedures*
Fastest race lap: Fuoco, 1m 31.794s, 119.627mph/ 192.522km/h.
Pole position: Fuoco/Molina/Nielsen, 1m 29.466s, 122.740mph/197.532km/h.

TOTALENERGIES 6 HOURS OF SPA-FRANCORCHAMPS, Circuit de Spa-Francorchamps, Stavelot, Belgium, 11 May. Round 3. 141 laps of the 4.352-mile/7.004km circuit, 613.635 miles/ 987.550km.
1 Will Stevens/Callum Ilott, GB/GB (Porsche 963), 5h 57m 31.542s, 102.980mph/165.730km/h; **2** Kévin Estre/André Lotterer/Laurens Vanthoor, F/D/B (Porsche 963), +12.363s; **3** Antonio Fuoco/Miguel Molina/Nicklas Nielsen, I/E/DK (Ferrari 499P), +1m 14.020s; **4** Alessandro Pier Guidi/James Calado/Antonio Giovinazzi, I/GB/I (Ferrari 499P), +1m 17.710s; **5** Neel Jani/Julien Andlauer, CH/F (Porsche 963), +1m 26.326s; **6** Sébastien Buemi/Brendon Hartley/Ryo Hirakawa, CH/NZ/J (Toyota GR010 HYBRID), +1m 34.955s; **7** Mike Conway/Kamui Kobayashi/Nyck de Vries, GB/J/NL (Toyota GR010 HYBRID), +1m 38.331s*; **8** Robert Kubica/Robert Shwartzman/ Yifei Ye, PL/IL/CHN (Ferrari 499P), +1m 49.162s; **9** Paul-Loup Chatin/Jules Gounon/Charles Milesi, F/F/F (Alpine A424), +2m 07.089s; **10** Mikkel Jensen/ Nico Müller, DK/CH (Peugeot 9X8 2024), -1 lap.
** 5s penalty for causing a collision*
Fastest race lap: Andlauer, 2m 06.459s, 123.892mph/199.385km/h.
Pole position: Matt Campbell/Michael Christensen/ Frédéric Makowiecki, AUS/DK/F (Porsche 963), 2m 03.107s, 127.265mph/204.814km/h.

92ND LE MANS 24 HOURS, Circuit International Du Mans, Les Raineries, Le Mans, France, 16 June. Round 4, 311 laps of the 8.467-mile/13.626km circuit, 2633.176 miles/4237.686km.
1 Antonio Fuoco/Miguel Molina/Nicklas Nielsen, I/E/DK (Ferrari 499P), 24h 01m 55.856s, 109.569mph/176.334km/h; **2** José María López/ Kamui Kobayashi/Nyck de Vries, RA/J/NL (Toyota GR010 HYBRID), +14.221s; **3** Alessandro Pier Guidi/ James Calado/Antonio Giovinazzi, I/GB/I (Ferrari 499P), +36.730s; **4** Kévin Estre/André Lotterer/ Laurens Vanthoor, F/D/B (Porsche 963), +37.897s; **5** Sébastien Buemi/Brendon Hartley/Ryo Hirakawa, CH/NZ/J (Toyota GR010 HYBRID), +1m 02.824s; **6** Matt Campbell/Michael Christensen/ Frédéric Makowiecki, AUS/DK/F (Porsche 963), +1m 45.654s; **7** Earl Bamber/Alex Lynn/Alex Palou, NZ/GB/E (Cadillac V-Series.R), +2m 34.468s; **8** Will Stevens/Norman Nato/Callum Ilott, GB/F/ GB (Porsche 963), +3m 02.691s; **9** Oliver Rasmussen/Phil Hanson/Jenson Button, DK/GB/GB (Porsche 963), +3m 36.756s; **10** Mirko Bortolotti/ Daniil Kvyat/Edoardo Mortara, I/RUS/CH (Lamborghini SC63), -2 laps; **11** Stoffel Vandoorne/Paul Di Resta/Loïc Duval, B/GB/F (Peugeot 9X8 2024), -2; **12** Jean-Éric Vergne/Mikkel Jensen/Nico Müller, F/DK/CH (Peugeot 9X8 2024), -2; **13** Romain Grosjean/Andrea Caldarelli/Matteo Cairoli, F/I/I (Lamborghini SC63), -2; **14** Carl Bennett/Jean-Karl Vernay/Antonio Serravalle, USA/F/CDN (Isotta Fraschini Tipo **6** Competizione LMH), -9; **15** Oliver Jarvis/Bijoy Garg/Nolan Siegel, GB/USA/USA (ORECA 07-Gibson), -14; **16** Jakub Śmiechowski/ Vlad Lomko/Clément Novalak, PL/RUS/F (ORECA 07-Gibson), -14; **17** Paul Lafargue/Job van Uitert/ Reshad De Gerus, F/NL/F (ORECA 07-Gibson), -14; **18** François Perrodo/Ben Barnicoat/Nico Varrone, F/GB/RA (ORECA 07-Gibson), -14; **19** Ryan Cullen/Patrick Pilet/Stéphane Richelmi, IRL/F/ MC (ORECA 07-Gibson), -14; **20** PJ Hyett/Louis Delétraz/Alex Quinn, USA/CH/GB (ORECA 07-Gibson), -16; **21** Alexander Mattschull/Rene Binder/ Laurents Hörr, D/A/D (ORECA 07-Gibson), -16; **22** Matthias Kaiser/Olli Caldwell/Roman De Angelis, FL/GB/CDN (ORECA 07-Gibson), -17; **23** Rodrigo Sales/Mathias Beche/Scott Huffaker, USA/ CH/USA (ORECA 07-Gibson), -18; **24** Naveen Rao/Matthew Bell/Frederik Vesti, USA/GB/DK (ORECA 07-Gibson), -20; **25** Fabio Scherer/David Heinemeier Hansson/Kyffin Simpson, CH/DK/ BB (ORECA 07-Gibson), -20; **26** Lorenzo Fluxá/ Malthe Jakobsen/Ritomo Miyata, E/DK/J (ORECA 07-Gibson), -22; **27** Yasser Shahin/Morris Schuring/Richard Lietz, AUS/NL/A (Porsche 911 GT3 R), -30; **28** Darren Leung/Sean Gelael/Augusto Farfus, GB/RI/BR (BMW M4 GT3), -31; **29** Pipo Derani/Jack Aitken/Felipe Drugovich, BR/GB/BR (Cadillac V-Series.R), -31; **30** Giorgio Roda/Mikkel Overgaard Pedersen/Dennis Olsen, I/DK/N (Ford Mustang GT3), -31; **31** John Hartshorne/Ben Tuck/ Christopher Mies, GB/GB/D (Ford Mustang GT3), -31; **32** Sarah Bovy/Michelle Gatting/Rahel Frey, B/DK/CH (Lamborghini Huracán GT3 Evo2), -32; **33** François Heriau/Simon Mann/Alessio Rovera, F/USA/I (Ferrari 296 GT3), -32; **34** Arnold Robin/ Timur Boguslavskiy/Kelvin van der Linde, F/RUS/ ZA (Lexus RC F GT3), -32; **35** Johnny Laursen/Conrad Laursen/Jordan Taylor, DK/DK/USA (Ferrari 296 GT3), -32; **36** Satoshi Hoshino/Erwan Bastard/ Marco Sørensen, J/F/DK (Aston Martin Vantage AMR GT3), -32; **37** Takeshi Kimura/Esteban Mason/Jack Hawksworth, J/F/GB (Lexus RC F GT3), -32; **38** Hiroshi Koizumi/Sébastien Baud/Daniel Juncadella, J/F/E (Chevrolet Corvette Z06 GT3.R), -33; **39** Mike Wainwright/Daniel Serra/Riccardo Pera, GB/BR/I (Ferrari 296 GT3), -33; **40** Brendan Iribe/Ollie Millroy/Frederik Schandorff, USA/GB/ DK (McLaren 720S GT3 Evo), -36; **41** Alex Malykhin/Joel Sturm/Klaus Bachler, BY/D/A (Porsche 911 GT3 R), -38; **42** Ben Keating/Filipe Albuquerque/ Ben Hanley, USA/P/GB (ORECA 07-Gibson), -39; **43** Tom Van Rompuy/Rui Andrade/Charlie Eastwood, B/P/GB (Chevrolet Corvette Z06 GT3.R), -44; **44** Claudio Schiavoni/Matteo Cressoni/Franck Perera, I/I/F (Lamborghini Huracán GT3 Evo2), -53; **45** Neel Jani/Harry Tincknell/Julien Andlauer, CH/GB/F (Porsche 963), -60; **46** Ryan Hardwick/ Zacharie Robichon/Ben Barker, USA/CDN/GB (Ford Mustang GT3), -84; Robert Kubica/Robert Shwartzman/Yifei Ye, PL/IL/CHN (Ferrari 499P), -63 (DNF); Sébastien Bourdais/Renger van der Zande/Scott Dixon, F/NL/NZ (Cadillac V-Series.R), -88 (DNF); James Cottingham/Nicolas Costa/Grégoire Saucy, GB/BR/CH (McLaren 720S GT3 Evo), -91 (DNF); Hiroshi Hamaguchi/Nico Pino/Marino Sato, J/RCH/J (McLaren 720S GT3 Evo), -99 (DNF); Mathieu Jaminet/Felipe Nasr/Nick Tandy, F/BR/GB (Porsche 963), -100 (DNF); Ian James/Daniel Mancinelli/Alex Riberas, GB/I/E (Aston Martin Vantage AMR GT3), -115 (DNF); George Kurtz/Colin Braun/ Nicky Catsburg, USA/USA/NL (ORECA 07-Gibson), -162 (DNF); John Falb/James Allen/Jean-Baptiste Simmenauer, USA/AUS/F (ORECA 07-Gibson), -199 (DNF); Giacomo Petrobelli/Larry ten Voorde/ Salih Yoluc, I/NL/TR (Ferrari 296 GT3), -199 (DNF); Ahmad Al Harthy/Valentino Rossi/Maxime Martin, OM/I/B (BMW M4 GT3), -202 (DNF); Dries Vanthoor/Raffaele Marciello/Marco Wittmann, B/I/D (BMW M Hybrid V8), -209 (DNF); Sheldon van der Linde/Robin Frijns/René Rast, ZA/NL/D (BMW M Hybrid V8), -215; Nicolas Lapierre/Mick Schumacher/Matthieu Vaxivière, F/D/F (Alpine A424), -223 (DNF); Jonas Ried/Maceo Capietto/Bent Viscaal, D/F/NL (ORECA 07-Gibson), -225 (DNF); Paul-Loup Chatin/Ferdinand Habsburg/Charles Milesi, F/A/F (Alpine A424), -236 (DNF); Thomas Flohr/Francesco Castellacci/Davide Rigon, CH/I/I (Ferrari 296 GT3), -281 (DNF).
Fastest race lap: Kobayashi, 3m 28.756s, 146.010mph/234.981km/h.
Pole position: Estre/Lotterer/Vanthoor, 3m 24.634s, 148.951mph/239.714km/h.

ROLEX 6 HOURS OF SãO PAULO, Autodromo José Carlos Pace, Interlagos, São Paulo, Brazil, 14 July. Round 5. 236 laps of the 2.677-mile/4.309km circuit, 631.887 miles/1016.924km.
1 Sébastien Buemi/Brendon Hartley/Ryo Hirakawa, CH/NZ/J (Toyota GR010 HYBRID), 6h 01m 02.554s, 105.010mph/168.997km/h; **2** Kévin Estre/André Lotterer/Laurens Vanthoor, F/D/B (Porsche 963), +1m 08.811s; **3** Matt Campbell/Michael Christensen/ Frédéric Makowiecki, AUS/DK/F (Porsche 963), +1m 15.993s; **4** Mike Conway/Kamui Kobayashi/Nyck de Vries, GB/J/NL (Toyota GR010 HYBRID), +1m 23.571s; **5** Alessandro Pier Guidi/James Calado/Antonio Giovinazzi, I/GB/I (Ferrari 499P), +1m 27.395s; **6** Antonio Fuoco/Miguel Molina/Nicklas Nielsen, I/E/DK (Ferrari 499P), -1 lap; **7** Jenson Button/Phil Hanson/Oliver Rasmussen, GB/GB/DK (Porsche 963), -1; **8** Mikkel Jensen/Nico Müller/Jean-Éric Vergne, DK/CH/F (Peugeot 9X8 2024), -1; **9** Dries Vanthoor/Raffaele Marciello/Marco Wittmann, B/I/D (BMW M Hybrid V8), -1; **10** Nicolas Lapierre/ Mick Schumacher/Matthieu Vaxivière, F/D/F (Alpine A424), -2.
Fastest race lap: Conway, 1m 24.801s, 113.665mph/ 182.927km/h.
Pole position: Conway/Kobayashi/de Vries, 1m 23.140s, 115.936mph/186.581km/h.

LONE STAR LE MANS, Circuit of the Americas, Austin, Texas, USA, 1 September. Round 6. 183 laps of the 3.426-mile/5.513km circuit, 626.888 miles/ 1008.879km.
1 Robert Kubica/Robert Shwartzman/Yifei Ye, PL/IL/CHN (Ferrari 499P), 6h 00m 23.755s, 104.366mph/167.961km/h; **2** Mike Conway/Kamui Kobayashi/Nyck de Vries, GB/J/NL (Toyota GR010 HYBRID), +1.780s; **3** Antonio Fuoco/Miguel Molina/ Nicklas Nielsen, I/E/DK (Ferrari 499P), +26.282s; **4** Earl Bamber/Alex Lynn, NZ/GB (Cadillac V-Series.R), +46.924s; **5** Paul-Loup Chatin/Ferdinand Habsburg/Charles Milesi, F/A/F (Alpine A424), +1m 10.513s; **6** Kévin Estre/André Lotterer/Laurens Vanthoor, F/D/B (Porsche 963), +1m 36.873s; **7** Matt Campbell/Michael Christensen/Frédéric Makowiecki, AUS/DK/F (Porsche 963), +1m 41.494s; **8** Dries Vanthoor/Raffaele Marciello/Marco Wittmann, B/I/D (BMW M Hybrid V8), -1 lap; **9** Nicolas Lapierre/ Mick Schumacher/Matthieu Vaxivière, F/D/F (Alpine A424), -1; **10** Jenson Button/Phil Hanson/Oliver Rasmussen, GB/GB/DK (Porsche 963), -1.
Fastest race lap: Kobayashi, 1m 52.564s, 109.557mph/176.315km/h.
Pole position: Alessandro Pier Guidi/James Calado/Antonio Giovinazzi, I/GB/I (Ferrari 499P), 1m 50.390s, 111.715mph/179.788km/h.

6 HOURS OF FUJI, Fuji International Speedway, Sunto-gun, Shizuoka Prefecture, Japan, 15 September. Round 7. 213 laps of the 2.835-mile/ 4.563km circuit, 603.922 miles/971.919km.
1 Kévin Estre/André Lotterer/Laurens Vanthoor, F/D/B (Porsche 963), 6h 00m 32.196s, 100.503mph/161.745km/h; **2** Dries Vanthoor/Raffaele Marciello/Marco Wittmann, B/I/D (BMW M Hybrid V8), +16.601s; **3** Nicolas Lapierre/Mick Schumacher/Matthieu Vaxivière, F/D/F (Alpine A424), +42.321s; **4** Mikkel Jensen/Nico Mueller/Jean-Éric Vergne, DK/CH/F (Peugeot 9X8 2024), +45.846s; **5** Will Stevens/Callum Ilott/Norman Nato, GB/GB/F (Porsche 963), +49.689s; **6** Jenson Button/Phil Hanson/Oliver Rasmussen, GB/GB/DK (Porsche 963), +51.916s; **7** Jules Gounon/Ferdinand Habsburg/Charles Milesi, F/A/F (Alpine A424), +54.316s; **8** Paul Di Resta/Loïc Duval/Stoffel Vandoorne, GB/F/B (Peugeot 9X8 2024), +54.324s; **9** Antonio Fuoco/Miguel Molina/Nicklas Nielsen, I/E/DK (Ferrari 499P), +57.874s; **10** Sébastien Buemi/Brendon Hartley/Ryo Hirakawa, CH/NZ/J (Toyota GR010 HYBRID), +58.879s.
Fastest race lap: Milesi, 1m 30.943s, 112.236mph/ 180.627km/h.
Pole position: Earl Bamber/Alex Lynn, NZ/GB (Cadillac V-Series.R), 1m 28.901s, 114.814mph/ 184.776km/h.

BAPCO ENERGIES 8 HOURS OF BAHRAIN, Bahrain International Circuit, Sakhir, Bahrain, 2 November. Round 8. 235 laps of the 3.363-mile/5.412km circuit, 790.272 miles/1271.820km.
1 Sébastien Buemi/Brendon Hartley/Ryo Hirakawa, CH/NZ/J (Toyota GR010 HYBRID), 8h 01m 25.839s, 98.490mph/158.505km/h; **2** Matt Campbell/Michael Christensen/Frédéric Makowiecki, AUS/DK/F (Porsche 963), +29.177s; **3** Mikkel Jensen/Nico Mueller/Jean-Éric Vergne, DK/CH/F (Peugeot 9X8 2024), +36.799s; **4** Paul-Loup Chatin/Ferdinand Habsburg/ Jules Gounon, F/A/F (Alpine A424), +37.404s; **5** Dries Vanthoor/Raffaele Marciello/Marco Wittmann, B/I/D (BMW M Hybrid V8), +47.916s; **6** Earl Bamber/ Alex Lynn/Sébastien Bourdais, NZ/GB/F (Cadillac V-Series.R), +55.841s; **7** Jenson Button/Phil Hanson/Oliver Rasmussen, GB/GB/DK (Porsche 963), +1m 00.834s; **8** Robert Kubica/Robert Shwartzman/ Yifei Ye, PL/IL/CHN (Ferrari 499P), +1m 03.539s; **9** Charles Milesi/Mick Schumacher/Matthieu Vaxivière, F/D/F (Alpine A424), +1m 12.064s*; **10** Kévin Estre/André Lotterer/Laurens Vanthoor, F/D/B (Porsche 963), +1m 19.711s**.
** 5s penalty for an incident with car 50*
*** 2 x 5s penalties*
Fastest race lap: Buemi, 1m 50.492s, 109.567mph/ 176.331km/h.
Pole position: Buemi/Hartley/Hirakawa, 1m 46.714s, 113.446mph/182.573km/h.

Final championship points
Drivers (Hypercar)
1 André Lotterer, D, 152; 1 Kévin Estre, F, 152; 1 Laurens Vanthoor, B, 152; **2** Antonio Fuoco, I, 115; **2** Miguel Molina, E, 115; **2** Nicklas Nielsen, DK, 115; **3** Kamui Kobayashi, J, 113; **3** Nyck de Vries, NL, 113; **4** Brendon Hartley, NZ, 109; **4** Ryo Hirakawa, J, 109; **4** Sébastien Buemi, CH, 109; **5** Frédéric Makowiecki, F, 104; **5** Matt Campbell, AUS, 104; **5** Michael Christensen, DK, 104; **6** Mike Conway, GB, 94; **7** Callum Ilott, GB, 70; **7** Will Stevens, GB, 70; **8** Alessandro Pier Guidi, I, 59; **8** Antonio Giovinazzi, I, 59; **8** James Calado, GB, 59; **9** Robert Kubica, PL, 57; **9** Robert Shwartzman, IL, 57; **9** Yifei Ye, CHN, 57; **10** Norman Nato, F, 45.

Drivers (LMGT3)
1 Alex Malykhin, BY, 139; 1 Joel Sturm, D, 139; 1 Klaus Bachler, A, 139; **2** Morris Schuring, NL, 105; **2** Richard Lietz, A, 105; **2** Yasser Shahin, AUS, 105; **3** Alessio Rovera, I, 97; **3** François Heriau, F, 97; **3** Simon Mann, USA, 97.

Manufacturers (Hypercar)
1 Toyota, 190; **2** Porsche, 188; **3** Ferrari, 137.

Teams (Hypercar)
1 Hertz Team JOTA (car 12), 183; **2** Hertz Team JOTA (38), 153; **3** AF Corse (83), 149.

Teams (LMGT3)
1 Manthey PureRxcing (car 92), 139; **2** Manthey EMA (91), 105; **3** Vista AF Corse (55), 97.

European Le Mans Series

4 HOURS OF BARCELONA, Circuit de Barcelona-Catalunya, Montmeló, Barcelona, Spain, 14 April. Round 1. 139 laps of the 2.894-mile/4.657km circuit, 402.228 miles/647.323km.
1 Lorenzo Fluxá/Malthe Jakobsen/Ritomo Miyata, E/DK/J (ORECA 07-Gibson), 4h 01m 06.862s, 100.092mph/161.082km/h; **2** Matthias Kaiser/Olli Caldwell/Alex Lynn, FL/GB/GB (ORECA 07-Gibson), +16.161s; **3** Filip Ugran/Marino Sato/Ben Hanley, RO/J/GB (ORECA 07-Gibson), +16.905s; **4** Paul Lafargue/Reshad De Gerus/Job van Uitert, F/F/NL (ORECA 07-Gibson), +1m 14.182s; **5** Manuel Maldonado/Charles Milesi/Arthur Leclerc, YV/F/ MC (ORECA 07-Gibson), +1m 20.643s; **6** François Perrodo/Matthieu Vaxivière/Alessio Rovera, F/F/I (ORECA 07-Gibson), -1 lap; **7** Rodrigo Sales/Mathias Beche/Grégoire Saucy, USA/CH/CH (ORECA 07-Gibson), -1; **8** Sebastián Álvarez/Vlad Lomko/ Tom Dillmann, MEX/RUS/F (ORECA 07-Gibson), -1; **9** Jonny Edgar/Louis Delétraz/Robert Kubica, GB/CH/PL (ORECA 07-Gibson), -1; **10** Oliver Gray/ Clément Novalak/Luca Ghiotto, GB/F/I (ORECA 07-Gibson), -1.

Fastest race lap: Rovera, 1m 30.174s, 115.525mph/185.920km/h.
Pole position: Ugran/Sato/Hanley, 1m 28.071s, 118.284mph/190.360km/h.

4 HOURS OF LE CASTELLET, Circuit ASA Paul Ricard, Le Beausset, France, 5 May. Round 2. 125 laps of the 3.586-mile/5.771km circuit, 448.242 miles/721.375km.
1 Sebastián Álvarez/Vlad Lomko/Tom Dillmann, MEX/RUS/F (ORECA 07-Gibson), 4h 00m 47.885s, 111.689mph/179.746km/h; **2** Alejandro García/Paul-Loup Chatin/Frederik Vesti, MEX/F/DK (ORECA 07-Gibson), +14.004s; **3** Jonny Edgar/Louis Delétraz/Robert Kubica, GB/CH/PL (ORECA 07-Gibson), +15.078s; **4** Paul Lafargue/Reshad De Gerus/Job van Uitert, F/F/NL (ORECA 07-Gibson), +20.325s*; **5** Filip Ugran/Marino Sato/Ben Hanley, RO/J/GB (ORECA 07-Gibson), +20.353s; **6** Niels Koolen/Jean-Baptiste Simmenauer/James Allen, NL/F/AUS (ORECA 07-Gibson), +24.186s; **7** Rodrigo Sales/Mathias Beche/Grégoire Saucy, USA/CH/CH (ORECA 07-Gibson), +34.149s; **8** Matthias Kaiser/Olli Caldwell/Alex Lynn, FL/GB/GB (ORECA 07-Gibson), +34.846s; **9** Giorgio Roda/Rene Binder/Bent Viscaal, I/A/NL (ORECA 07-Gibson), +45.906s; **10** Daniel Schneider/Andy Meyrick/Oliver Jarvis, BR/GB/GB (ORECA 07-Gibson), +59.338s.
** 10s penalty due to zig-zagging and blocking another car*
Fastest race lap: Matthieu Vaxivière, F (ORECA 07-Gibson), 1m 42.781s, 125.600mph/202.134km/h.
Pole position: Lafargue/Gerus/Uitert, 1m 40.104s, 128.959mph/207.540km/h.

4 HOURS OF IMOLA, Autodromo Enzo e Dino Ferrari, Imola, Italy, 7 July. Round 3. 133 laps of the 3.050-mile/4.909km circuit, 405.691 miles/652.897km.
1 Manuel Maldonado/Charles Milesi/Arthur Leclerc, YV/F/MC (ORECA 07-Gibson), 4h 01m 32.720s, 100.773mph/162.179km/h; **2** Jonny Edgar/Louis Delétraz/Robert Kubica, GB/CH/PL (ORECA 07-Gibson), +11.357s; **3** Ryan Cullen/Stéphane Richelmi/Felipe Drugovich, IRL/MC/BR (ORECA 07-Gibson), +22.978s; **4** Sebastián Álvarez/Vlad Lomko/Tom Dillmann, MEX/RUS/F (ORECA 07-Gibson), +23.918s; **5** Marcos Siebert/Reshad De Gerus/Job van Uitert, RA/F/NL (ORECA 07-Gibson), +24.092s; **6** Bijoy Garg/Fabio Scherer/Paul Di Resta, USA/CH/GB (ORECA 07-Gibson), +53.601s; **7** Oliver Gray/Clément Novalak/Luca Ghiotto, GB/F/I (ORECA 07-Gibson), +1m 12.605s; **8** Matthias Kaiser/Olli Caldwell/Alex Lynn, FL/GB/GB (ORECA 07-Gibson), -1 lap; **9** Kriton Lendoudis/Richard Bradley/Alex Quinn, GR/GB/GB (ORECA 07-Gibson), -1; **10** François Perrodo/Matthieu Vaxivière/Alessio Rovera, F/F/I (ORECA 07-Gibson), -1.
Fastest race lap: Leclerc, 1m 31.757s, 119.676mph/192.600km/h.
Pole position: Maldonado/Milesi/Leclerc, 1m 30.829s, 120.898mph/194.567km/h.

4 HOURS OF SPA-FRANCORCHAMPS, Circuit de Spa-Francorchamps, Stavelot, Belgium, 25 August. Round 4. 95 laps of the 4.352-mile/7.004km circuit, 413.442 miles/665.370km.
1 Jonny Edgar/Louis Delétraz/Robert Kubica, GB/CH/PL (ORECA 07-Gibson), 4h 01m 28.729s, 102.727mph/165.323km/h; **2** Sebastián Álvarez/Vlad Lomko/Tom Dillmann, MEX/RUS/F (ORECA 07-Gibson), +1.100s; **3** Marcos Siebert/Reshad De Gerus/Job van Uitert, RA/F/NL (ORECA 07-Gibson), +32.436s; **4** Oliver Gray/Clément Novalak/Luca Ghiotto, GB/F/I (ORECA 07-Gibson), +33.731s; **5** Lorenzo Fluxá/Malthe Jakobsen/Ritomo Miyata, E/DK/J (ORECA 07-Gibson), +45.658s; **6** Manuel Maldonado/Charles Milesi/Arthur Leclerc, YV/F/MC (ORECA 07-Gibson), +47.273s; **7** Jonas Ried/Maceo Capietto/Matteo Cairoli, D/F/I (ORECA 07-Gibson), +57.022s; **8** François Perrodo/Matthieu Vaxivière/Alessio Rovera, F/F/I (ORECA 07-Gibson), +1m 01.303s; **9** Giorgio Roda/Rene Binder/Bent Viscaal, I/A/NL (ORECA 07-Gibson), +1m 18.608s; **10** Ryan Cullen/Stéphane Richelmi/Felipe Drugovich, IRL/MC/BR (ORECA 07-Gibson), +1m 25.528s.
Fastest race lap: Milesi, 2m 01.257s, 129.207mph/207.938km/h.
Pole position: Edgar/Delétraz/Kubica, 2m 01.253s, 129.211mph/207.945km/h.

4 HOURS OF MUGELLO, Autodromo Internazionale del Mugello, Scarperia, Firenze (Florence), Italy, 29 September. Round 5. 114 laps of the 3.259-mile/5.245km circuit, 371.536 miles/597.930km.
1 Jonas Ried/Maceo Capietto/Matteo Cairoli, D/F/I (ORECA 07-Gibson), 4h 20m 02.008s, 85.728mph/137.966km/h; **2** Matthias Kaiser/Olli Caldwell/Alex Lynn, FL/GB/GB (ORECA 07-Gibson), +6.580s; **3** Oliver Gray/Clément Novalak/Luca Ghiotto, GB/F/I (ORECA 07-Gibson), +28.308s; **4** Manuel Maldonado/Charles Milesi/Arthur Leclerc, YV/F/MC (ORECA 07-Gibson), +40.703s; **5** Jonny Edgar/Louis Delétraz/Robert Kubica, GB/CH/PL (ORECA 07-Gibson), +43.196s; **6** Bijoy Garg/Fabio Scherer/Paul Di Resta, USA/CH/GB (ORECA 07-Gibson), +47.218s; **7** Sebastián Álvarez/Vlad Lomko/Tom Dillmann, MEX/RUS/F (ORECA 07-Gibson), +50.048s; **8** Rodrigo Sales/Mathias Beche/Grégoire Saucy, USA/CH/CH (ORECA 07-Gibson), +51.579s; **9** Niels Koolen/Jean-Baptiste Simmenauer/James Allen, NL/F/AUS (ORECA 07-Gibson), +1m 01.259s; **10** Kriton Lendoudis/Richard Bradley/Alex Quinn, GR/GB/GB (ORECA 07-Gibson), +1m 02.888s.
Fastest race lap: Cairoli, 1m 34.882s, 123.656mph/199.005km/h.
Pole position: Ried/Capietto/Cairoli, 1m 32.829s, 126.390mph/203.406km/h.

4 HOURS OF PORTIMÃO, Autódromo Internacional do Algarve, Portimão, Portugal, 19 October. Round 6. 127 laps of the 2.891-mile/4.653km circuit, 367.188 miles/590.931km.
1 Lorenzo Fluxá/Malthe Jakobsen/Ritomo Miyata, E/DK/J (ORECA 07-Gibson), 4h 00m 20.026s, 91.669mph/147.527km/h; **2** Jonny Edgar/Louis Delétraz/Robert Kubica, GB/CH/PL (ORECA 07-Gibson), +2.499s; **3** Carl Bennett/Ferdinand Habsburg/Frederik Vesti, USA/A/DK (ORECA 07-Gibson), +3.159s; **4** Sebastián Álvarez/Vlad Lomko/Tom Dillmann, MEX/RUS/F (ORECA 07-Gibson), +4.075s; **5** Oliver Gray/Clément Novalak/Luca Ghiotto, GB/F/I (ORECA 07-Gibson), +9.491s; **6** Bijoy Garg/Fabio Scherer/Paul Di Resta, USA/CH/GB (ORECA 07-Gibson), +12.007s; **7** Niels Koolen/Jean-Baptiste Simmenauer/James Allen, NL/F/AUS (ORECA 07-Gibson), +14.864s; **8** Giorgio Roda/Rene Binder/Bent Viscaal, I/A/NL (ORECA 07-Gibson), +16.120s; **9** Kriton Lendoudis/Richard Bradley/Alex Quinn, GR/GB/GB (ORECA 07-Gibson), +17.115s; **10** Matthias Kaiser/Olli Caldwell/Alex Lynn, FL/GB/GB (ORECA 07-Gibson), +17.585s.
Fastest race lap: Lynn, 1m 32.451s, 112.583mph/181.185km/h.
Pole position: Manuel Maldonado/Charles Milesi/Arthur Leclerc, YV/F/MC (ORECA 07-Gibson), 1m 30.727s, 114.722mph/184.628km/h.

Final championship points
Drivers (LMP2)
1 Louis Delétraz, CH, 93; 1 Jonny Edgar, GB, 93; 1 Robert Kubica, PL, 93; **2** Sebastián Álvarez, MEX, 81; **2** Vlad Lomko, RUS, 81; **2** Tom Dillmann, F, 81; **3** Lorenzo Fluxá, E, 62; **3** Ritomo Miyata, J, 62; **3** Malthe Jakobsen, DK, 62; **4** Arthur Leclerc, MC, 61; **4** Manuel Maldonado, YV, 61; **4** Charles Milesi, F, 61; **5** Matthias Kaiser, FL, 50; **5** Olli Caldwell, GB, 50; **5** Alex Lynn, GB, 50; **6** Reshad De Gerus, F, 50; **6** Job van Uitert, NL, 50; **7** Clément Novalak, F, 47; **7** Luca Ghiotto, I, 47; **7** Oliver Gray, GB, 47; **8** Maceo Capietto, F, 36; **8** Matteo Cairoli, I, 36; **8** Jonas Ried, D, 36; **9** Frederik Vesti, DK, 34; **10** Filip Ugran, RO, 29; **10** Marino Sato, J, 29; **10** Ben Hanley, GB, 29.

Drivers (LMP3)
1 Gael Julien, RI, 99; 1 Michael Jensen, DK, 99; 1 Nick Adcock, GB, 99; **2** Matt Bell, GB, 98; **2** Adam Ali, CDN, 98; **3** Julien Gerbi, F, 90; **3** Gillian Henrion, F, 90; **4** Bernardo Pinheiro, P, 76; **5** Miguel Cristovão, P, 75; **5** Manuel Espirito Santo, P, 75; **6** Alexander Mattschull, D, 53; **6** Wyatt Brichacek, USA, 53; **7** Jean-Baptiste Lahaye, F, 52; **8** Cédric Oltramare, F, 49; **9** Antoine Doquin, F, 44; **9** Jean-Ludovic Foubert, F, 44; **9** Jacques Wolff, F, 44; **10** Oscar Tunjo, CO, 38; **10** Leo Weiss, D, 38; **10** Torsten Kratz, D, 38.

Drivers (LMP2 Pro-Am)
1 Matthieu Vaxivière, F, 98; 1 Alessio Rovera, I, 98; 1 François Perrodo, F, 98; **2** Kriton Lendoudis, GR, 96; **2** Richard Bradley, GB, 96; **2** Alex Quinn, GB, 96; **3** Giorgio Roda, I, 95; **3** Rene Binder, A, 95; **3** Bent Viscaal, NL, 95; **4** Grégoire Saucy, CH, 94; **4** Mathias Beche, CH, 94; **4** Rodrigo Sales, USA, 94; **5** Colin Noble, GB, 70; **5** John Falb, USA, 70; **6** Daniel Schneider, BR, 47; **6** Andy Meyrick, GB, 47.

Drivers (LMGT3)
1 Hiroshi Hamaguchi, J, 76; 1 Andrea Caldarelli, I, 76; 1 Axcil Jefferies, ZW, 76; **2** Takeshi Kimura, J, 74; **2** Daniel Serra, BR, 74; **2** Esteban Masson, F, 74; **3** Valentin Hasse-Clot, F, 66; **3** Derek DeBoer, USA, 66; **3** Casper Stevenson, GB, 66; **4** Sarah Bovy, B, 65; **4** Michelle Gatting, DK, 65; **4** Rahel Frey, CH, 65; **5** Riccardo Pera, I, 64; **5** Mike Wainwright, GB, 64; **5** Davide Rigon, I, 64; **6** Johnny Laursen, DK, 56; **6** Conrad Laursen, DK, 56.

Teams (LMP2)
1 AO by TF (car 14), 93; **2** Inter Europol Competition (43), 81; **3** COOL Racing (37), 62; **4** Panis Racing (65), 61; **5** Algarve Pro Racing (25), 50; **6** Idec Sport (28), 50.

Teams (LMP3)
1 RLR MSport (car 15), 99; **2** EuroInternational (11), 98; **3** Team Virage (8), 90; **4** COOL Racing (17), 75; **5** DKR Engineering (4), 53; **6** Ultimate (35), 52.

Teams (LMP2 Pro-Am)
1 AF Corse (car 83), 98; **2** Algarve Pro Racing (20), 96; **3** Proton Competition (77), 95; **4** Richard Mille by TDS (29), 94; **5** Nielsen Racing (24), 70; **6** United Autosports (21), 47.

Teams (LMGT3)
1 Iron Lynx (car 63), 76; **2** Kessel Racing (57), 74; **3** Racing Spirit of Leman (59), 66; **4** Iron Dames (85), 65; **5** GR Racing (86), 64; **6** Formula Racing (50), 56.

IMSA WeatherTech SportsCar Championship

62ND ROLEX 24 AT DAYTONA, Daytona International Speedway, Daytona Beach, Florida, USA, 28 January. Round 1. 791 laps of the 3.560-mile/5.729km circuit, 2815.960 miles/4531.848km.
1 Dane Cameron/Felipe Nasr/Matt Campbell/Josef Newgarden, USA/BR/AUS/USA (Porsche 963), 23h 58m 24.723s, 117.461mph/189.035km/h; **2** Pipo Derani/Jack Aitken/Tom Blomqvist, BR/GB/GB (Cadillac V-Series.R), +2.112s; **3** Jordan Taylor/Louis Delétraz/Colton Herta/Jenson Button, USA/CH/USA/GB (Acura ARX-06), +14.989s; **4** Nick Tandy/Mathieu Jaminet/Kévin Estre/Laurens Vanthoor, GB/F/F/B (Porsche 963), +15.387s; **5** Gianmaria Bruni/Neel Jani/Alessio Picariello/Romain Dumas, I/CH/B/F (Porsche 963), +44.479s; **6** Tijmen van der Helm/Richard Westbrook/Phil Hanson/Ben Keating, NL/GB/GB/USA (Porsche 963), -2 laps; **7** Connor De Phillippi/Nick Yelloly/Maxime Martin/René Rast, USA/GB/B/D (BMW M Hybrid V8), -13; **8** Jesse Krohn/Philipp Eng/Augusto Farfus/Dries Vanthoor, FIN/A/BR/B (BMW M Hybrid V8), -15; **9** Dwight Merriman/Ryan Dalziel/Connor Zilisch/Christian Rasmussen, USA/GB/USA/DK (ORECA 07-Gibson), -24; **10** George Kurtz/Colin Braun/Toby Sowery/Malthe Jakobsen, USA/USA/GB/DK (ORECA 07-Gibson), -24.
Fastest race lap: Blomqvist, 1m 35.554s, 134.123mph/215.850km/h.
Pole position: Derani/Aitken/Blomqvist, 1m 32.656s, 138.318mph/222.601km/h.

72ND ANNUAL MOBIL 1 TWELVE HOURS OF SEBRING PRESENTED BY CADILLAC, Sebring International Raceway, Florida, USA, 16 March. Round 2. 333 laps of the 3.740-mile/6.019km circuit, 1245.420 miles/2004.309km.
1 Jordan Taylor/Louis Delétraz/Colton Herta, USA/CH/USA (Acura ARX-06), 12h 00m 54.520s, 103.654mph/166.815km/h; **2** Renger van der Zande/Sébastien Bourdais/Scott Dixon, NL/F/NZ (Cadillac V-Series.R), +0.891s; **3** Dane Cameron/Felipe Nasr/Matt Campbell, USA/BR/AUS (Porsche 963), +8.898s; **4** Connor De Phillippi/Nick Yelloly/Maxime Martin, USA/GB/B (BMW M Hybrid V8), +12.056s; **5** Ricky Taylor/Filipe Albuquerque/Brendon Hartley, USA/P/NZ (Acura ARX-06), +13.398s; **6** Jesse Krohn/Philipp Eng/Augusto Farfus, FIN/A/BR (BMW M Hybrid V8), +28.438s; **7** Matteo Cairoli/Andrea Caldarelli/Romain Grosjean, I/I/F (Lamborghini SC63), +28.501s; **8** Gianmaria Bruni/Alessio Picariello/Julien Andlauer, I/B/F (Porsche 963), +44.807s; **9** Nick Tandy/Mathieu Jaminet/Frédéric Makowiecki, GB/F/F (Porsche 963), -2 laps; **10** Dwight Merriman/Ryan Dalziel/Connor Zilisch, USA/GB/USA (ORECA 07-Gibson), -3.
Fastest race lap: Delétraz, 1m 49.497s, 122.962mph/197.889km/h.
Pole position: Pipo Derani/Jack Aitken/Tom Blomqvist, BR/GB/GB (Cadillac V-Series.R), 1m 48.152s, 124.491mph/200.350km/h.

ACURA GRAND PRIX OF LONG BEACH, Long Beach Street Circuit, California, USA, 20 April. Round 3. 68 laps of the 1.968-mile/3.167km circuit, 133.824 miles/215.369km.
1 Renger van der Zande/Sébastien Bourdais, NL/F (Cadillac V-Series.R), 1h 40m 07.318s, 80.197mph/129.064km/h; **2** Pipo Derani/Jack Aitken, BR/GB (Cadillac V-Series.R), +0.564s; **3** Dane Cameron/Felipe Nasr, USA/BR (Porsche 963), +1.675s; **4** Nick Tandy/Mathieu Jaminet, GB/F (Porsche 963), +2.913s; **5** Gianmaria Bruni/Mike Rockenfeller, I/D (Porsche 963), +4.297s; **6** Jesse Krohn/Philipp Eng, FIN/A (BMW M Hybrid V8), +5.047s; **7** Tijmen van der Helm/Richard Westbrook, NL/GB (Porsche 963), +6.892s; **8** Ricky Taylor/Filipe Albuquerque, USA/P (Acura ARX-06), +7.343s; **9** Ben Barnicoat/Parker Thompson, GB/CDN (Lexus RC F GT3), -3 laps; **10** Robby Foley/Patrick Gallagher, USA/USA (BMW M4 GT3), -3.
Fastest race lap: Bourdais, 1m 12.626s, 97.552mph/156.994km/h.
Pole position: Derani/Aitken, 1m 11.388s, 99.244mph/159.717km/h.

MOTUL COURSE DE MONTEREY, WeatherTech Raceway Laguna Seca, Monterey, California, USA, 12 May. Round 4. 119 laps of the 2.238-mile/3.602km circuit, 266.322 miles/428.604km.
1 Nick Tandy/Mathieu Jaminet, GB/F (Porsche 963), 2h 40m 09.438s, 99.773mph/160.569km/h; **2** Pipo Derani/Jack Aitken, BR/GB (Cadillac V-Series.R), +5.764s; **3** Dane Cameron/Felipe Nasr, USA/BR (Porsche 963), +34.673s; **4** Jordan Taylor/Louis Delétraz, USA/CH (Acura ARX-06), +43.445s; **5** Renger van der Zande/Sébastien Bourdais, NL/F (Cadillac V-Series.R), +45.608s; **6** Ricky Taylor/Filipe Albuquerque, USA/P (Acura ARX-06), +46.150s; **7** Connor De Phillippi/Nick Yelloly, USA/GB (BMW M Hybrid V8), +47.615s; **8** Tijmen van der Helm/Richard Westbrook, NL/GB (Porsche 963), +1m 17.343s; **9** Jesse Krohn/Philipp Eng, FIN/A (BMW M Hybrid V8), -1 lap; **10** Gianmaria Bruni/Bent Viscaal, I/NL (Porsche 963), -1.
Fastest race lap: Bourdais, 1m 14.196s, 108.588mph/174.756km/h.
Pole position: van der Zande/Bourdais, 1m 12.445s, 111.213mph/178.979km/h.

CHEVROLET DETROIT SPORTS CAR CLASSIC, Detroit Street Circuit, Michigan, USA, 1 June. Round 5. 75 laps of the 1.645-mile/2.647km circuit, 123.375 miles/198.553km.
1 Ricky Taylor/Filipe Albuquerque, USA/P (Acura ARX-06), 1h 40m 02.133s, 73.999mph/119.089km/h; **2** Nick Tandy/Mathieu Jaminet, GB/F (Porsche 963), +1.132s; **3** Renger van der Zande/Sébastien Bourdais, NL/F (Cadillac V-Series.R), +4.198s; **4** Dane Cameron/Felipe Nasr, USA/BR (Porsche 963), +5.142s; **5** Jordan Taylor/Louis Delétraz, USA/CH (Acura ARX-06), +10.120s; **6** Pipo Derani/Jack Aitken, BR/GB (Cadillac V-Series.R), +10.359s; **7** Jesse Krohn/Philipp Eng, FIN/A (BMW M Hybrid V8), +10.793s; **8** Tijmen van der Helm/Richard Westbrook, NL/GB (Porsche 963), -1 lap; **9** Laurin Heinrich/Seb Priaulx, D/GB (Porsche 911 GT3 R (992)), -1; **10** Jack Hawksworth/Ben Barnicoat, GB/GB (Lexus RC F GT3), -1.
Fastest race lap: Tandy, 1m 05.874s, 89.899mph/144.678km/h.
Pole position: Tandy/Jaminet, 1m 05.390s, 90.564mph/145.749km/h.

SAHLEN'S SIX HOURS OF THE GLEN, Watkins Glen International, New York, USA, 23 June. Round 6. 148 laps of the 3.400-mile/5.472km circuit, 503.200 miles/809.822km.
1 Dane Cameron/Felipe Nasr, USA/BR (Porsche 963), 6h 01m 10.521s, 83.594mph/134.531km/h; **2** Renger van der Zande/Sébastien Bourdais, NL/F (Cadillac V-Series.R), +0.749s; **3** Nick Tandy/Mathieu Jaminet, GB/F (Porsche 963), +2.819s; **4** Jordan Taylor/Louis Delétraz, USA/CH (Acura ARX-06), +22.455s; **5** Jesse Krohn/Philipp Eng, FIN/A (BMW M Hybrid V8), +22.924s; **6** Connor De Phillippi/Nick Yelloly, USA/GB (BMW M Hybrid V8), +23.820s; **7** Gianmaria Bruni/Bent Viscaal, I/NL (Porsche 963), -1 lap; **8** Pipo Derani/Jack Aitken/Tom Blomqvist, BR/GB/GB (Cadillac V-Series.R), -1; **9** Luis Pérez-Companc/Nicklas Nielsen/Lilou Wadoux, RA/DK/F (ORECA 07-Gibson), -1; **10** Gar Robinson/Felipe Fraga/Josh Burdon, USA/BR/AUS (ORECA 07-Gibson), -1.
Fastest race lap: Jaminet, 1m 34.188s, 129.953mph/209.139km/h.
Pole position: Taylor/Delétraz, 1m 32.209s, 132.742mph/213.627km/h.

CHEVROLET GRAND PRIX, Canadian Tire Mosport Park, Bowmanville, Ontario, Canada, 14 July. Round 7. 117 laps of the 2.459-mile/3.957km circuit, 287.703 miles/463.013km.
1 Nick Boulle/Tom Dillmann, USA/F (ORECA 07-Gibson), 2h 40m 34.358s, 107.504mph/173.011km/h; **2** Gar Robinson/Felipe Fraga, USA/BR (ORECA 07-Gibson), +0.658s; **3** Steven Thomas/Scott Huffaker, USA/USA (ORECA 07-Gibson), +4.776s; **4** Ben Keating/Ben Hanley, USA/GB (ORECA 07-Gibson), +5.079s; **5** Daniel Goldburg/Filipe Albuquerque, USA/P (ORECA 07-Gibson), +11.740s; **6** John Farano/Renger van der Zande, CDN/NL (ORECA 07-Gibson), +13.540s; **7** George Kurtz/Colin Braun, USA/USA (ORECA 07-Gibson), +13.641s; **8** PJ Hyett/Louis Delétraz, USA/CH (ORECA 07-Gibson), +13.773s; **9** Luis Pérez-Companc/Pipo Derani, RA/BR (ORECA 07-Gibson), -1 lap; **10** João Barbosa/Lance Willsey, P/USA (Ligier JS P217-Gibson), -2.
Fastest race lap: Dillmann, 1m 08.660s, 128.931mph/207.494km/h.
Pole position: Hyett/Delétraz, 1m 09.582s, 127.223mph/204.745km/h.

IMSA SPORTSCAR WEEKEND, Road America, Elkhart Lake, Wisconsin, USA, 4 August. Round 8. 62 laps of the 4.048-mile/6.515km circuit, 250.976 miles/403.907km.
1 Nick Tandy/Mathieu Jaminet, GB/F (Porsche 963), 2h 40m 44.592s, 93.681mph/150.765km/h; **2** Dane Cameron/Felipe Nasr, USA/BR (Porsche 963), +0.390s; **3** Ricky Taylor/Filipe Albuquerque, USA/P (Acura ARX-06), +1.150s; **4** Pipo Derani/Jack Aitken, BR/GB (Cadillac V-Series.R), +1.449s; **5** Gianmaria Bruni/Bent Viscaal, I/NL (Porsche 963), +10.084s; **6** Tijmen van der Helm/Richard Westbrook, NL/GB (Porsche 963), +10.904s; **7** Jesse Krohn/Philipp Eng, FIN/A (BMW M Hybrid V8), +11.186s; **8** Jordan Taylor/Louis Delétraz, USA/CH (Acura ARX-06), +12.286s; **9** Ben Keating/Ben Hanley, USA/GB (ORECA 07-Gibson), +15.415s; **10** Gerry Kraut/Scott Andrews, USA/AUS (ORECA 07-Gibson), +22.100s.
Fastest race lap: Taylor, 1m 50.385s, 132.018mph/212.462km/h.
Pole position: Taylor/Albuquerque, 1m 48.601s, 134.187mph/215.952km/h.

MICHELIN GT CHALLENGE AT VIR, Virginia International Raceway, Alton, Virginia, USA, 25 August. Round 9. 86 laps of the 3.270-mile/5.263km circuit, 281.220 miles/452.580km.
1 Bryan Sellers/Madison Snow, USA/USA (BMW M4 GT3), 2h 40m 49.112s, 104.921mph/168.854km/h;

2 Harry Tincknell/Mike Rockenfeller, GB/D (Ford Mustang GT3), +3.368s; **3** Ross Gunn/Alex Riberas, GB/E (Aston Martin Vantage GT3 Evo), +4.199s; **4** Joey Hand/Dirk Müller, USA/D (Ford Mustang GT3), +11.688s; **5** Mikaël Grenier/Kenton Koch, CDN/USA (Mercedes AMG GT3), +16.103s; **6** Marvin Kirchhöfer/Oliver Jarvis, D/GB (McLaren 720S GT3 Evo), +16.404s; **7** Jack Hawksworth/Ben Barnicoat, GB/GB (Lexus RC F GT3), +18.620s; **8** Misha Goikhberg/Loris Spinelli, CDN/I (Lamborghini Huracán GT3 Evo2), +19.086s; **9** Laurin Heinrich/Klaus Bachler, D/A (Porsche 911 GT3 R (992)), +19.754s; **10** Russell Ward/Philip Ellis, USA/GB (Mercedes AMG GT3), +20.017s.
Fastest race lap: Spinelli, 1m 44.864s, 112.260mph/180.664km/h.
Pole position: Sellers/Snow, 1m 43.206s, 114.063mph/183.567km/h.

TIRE RACK.COM BATTLE ON THE BRICKS, Indianapolis Motor Speedway, Speedway, Indiana, USA, 22 September. Round 10. 219 laps of the 2.439-mile/3.925km circuit, 534.141 miles/859.617km.
1 Jesse Krohn/Philipp Eng, FIN/A (BMW M Hybrid V8), 6h 00m 54.050s, 88.801mph/142.912km/h; **2** Connor De Phillippi/Nick Yelloly, USA/GB (BMW M Hybrid V8), +1.647s; **3** Tijmen van der Helm/Richard Westbrook/Phil Hanson, NL/GB/GB (Porsche 963), +19.176s; **4** Ricky Taylor/Filipe Albuquerque, USA/P (Acura ARX-06), +52.525s; **5** Gianmaria Bruni/Bent Viscaal/Alessio Picariello, I/NL/B (Porsche 963), -1 lap; **6** Renger van der Zande/Sébastien Bourdais, NL/F (Cadillac V-Series.R), -3; **7** Steven Thomas/Mikkel Jensen/Hunter McElrea, USA/DK/AUS (ORECA 07-Gibson), -4; **8** Nick Boulle/Jakub Śmiechowski/Tom Dillmann, USA/PL/F (ORECA 07-Gibson), -4; **9** Dwight Merriman/Ryan Dalziel/Connor Zilisch, USA/GB/USA (ORECA 07-Gibson), -4; **10** PJ Hyett/Paul-Loup Chatin/Matthew Brabham, USA/F/USA (ORECA 07-Gibson), -4.
Fastest race lap: Bruni, 1m 16.229s, 115.185mph/185.371km/h.
Pole position: van der Zande/Bourdais, 1m 14.592s, 117.712mph/189.440km/h.

MOTUL PETIT LE MANS, Road Atlanta Motorsports Center, Braselton, Georgia, USA, 12 October. Round 11. 443 laps of the 2.540-mile/4.088km circuit, 1125.220 miles/1810.866km.
1 Renger van der Zande/Sébastien Bourdais/Scott Dixon, NL/F/NZ (Cadillac V-Series.R), 10h 00m 36.290s, 112.409mph/180.904km/h; **2** Nick Tandy/Mathieu Jaminet/Kévin Estre, GB/F/F (Porsche 963), +2.948s; **3** Dane Cameron/Felipe Nasr/Matt Campbell, USA/BR/AUS (Porsche 963), +13.832s; **4** Jesse Krohn/Philipp Eng/Augusto Farfus, FIN/A/BR (BMW M Hybrid V8), -1 lap; **5** Pipo Derani/Jack Aitken/Tom Blomqvist, BR/GB/GB (Cadillac V-Series.R), -1; **6** Gianmaria Bruni/Bent Viscaal/Alessio Picariello, I/NL/B (Porsche 963), -2; **7** Jordan Taylor/Louis Delétraz/Colton Herta, USA/CH/USA (Acura ARX-06), -3; **8** Steven Thomas/Mikkel Jensen/Hunter McElrea, USA/DK/AUS (ORECA 07-Gibson), -8; **9** Gar Robinson/Felipe Fraga/Josh Burdon, USA/BR/AUS (ORECA 07-Gibson), -8; **10** Dwight Merriman/Ryan Dalziel/Connor Zilisch, USA/GB/USA (ORECA 07-Gibson), -8.
Fastest race lap: Romain Grosjean, F (Lamborghini SC63), 1m 11.981s, 127.034mph/204.441km/h.
Pole position: Derani/Aitken/Blomqvist, 1m 09.639s, 131.306mph/211.316km/h.

Final championship points.
Drivers (Le Mans Prototype 2)
1 Nick Boulle, USA, 2227; 1 Tom Dillmann, F, 2227; **2** Felipe Fraga, BR, 2166; **2** Gar Robinson, USA, 2166; **3** Ryan Dalziel, GB, 2118; **4** Steven Thomas, USA, 2104; **5** Ben Hanley, GB, 1962; **5** Ben Keating, USA, 1962; **6** PJ Hyett, USA, 1942; **7** Daniel Goldburg, USA, 1884; **8** Luis Pérez-Companc, RA, 1860; **9** John Farano, CDN, 1833; **10** Mikkel Jensen, DK, 1778.

Drivers (Grand Touring Prototype)
1 Dane Cameron, USA, 2982; 1 Felipe Nasr, BR, 2982; **2** Mathieu Jaminet, F, 2869; **2** Nick Tandy, GB, 2869; **3** Renger van der Zande, NL, 2864; **3** Sébastien Bourdais, F, 2864.

Drivers (GT Daytona Pro)
1 Laurin Heinrich, D, 3122; **2** Ross Gunn, GB, 3118; **3** Alexander Sims, GB, 2934; **3** Antonio García, E, 2934.

Drivers (GT Daytona)
1 Philip Ellis, GB, 3266; 1 Russell Ward, USA, 3266; **2** Patrick Gallagher, USA, 3036; **2** Robby Foley, USA, 3036; **3** Mikaël Grenier, CDN, 2661.

Manufacturers (Grand Touring Prototype)
1 Porsche, 3257; **2** Cadillac, 3166; **3** Acura, 3056.

Manufacturers (GT Daytona Pro)
1 Porsche, 3215; **2** Aston Martin, 3158; **3** Chevrolet, 3073.

Manufacturers (GT Daytona)
1 Mercedes, 3532; **2** Lamborghini, 2958; **3** BMW, 2938.

Teams (Le Mans Prototype 2)
1 Inter Europol by PR1 Mathiasen Motorsports (car 52), 2227; **2** Riley (74), 2166; **3** Era Motorsport (18), 2118.

Teams (Grand Touring Prototype)
1 Porsche Penske Motorsport (car 7), 2982; **2** Porsche Penske Motorsport (6), 2869; **3** Cadillac Racing (01), 2864.

Teams (GT Daytona Pro)
1 AO Racing (car 77), 3122; **2** Heart of Racing Team (23), 3118; **3** Corvette Racing by Pratt Miller Motorsports (3), 2934.

Teams (GT Daytona)
1 Winward Racing (car 57), 3266; **2** Turner Motorsport (96), 3036; **3** Korthoff/Preston Motorsports (32), 2661.

Autobacs Super GT Series (Japan)

OKAYAMA GT 300 KM RACE, Okayama International Circuit (TI Circuit Aida), Aida Gun, Okayama Prefecture, Japan, 14 April. Round 1. 82 laps of the 2.301-mile/3.703km circuit, 188.677 miles/303.646km.
1 Sho Tsuboi/Kenta Yamashita, J/J (Toyota GR Supra), 2h 02m 48.219s, 92.184mph/148.356km/h; **2** Yuhi Sekiguchi/Yuichi Nakayama, J/J (Toyota GR Supra), +11.011s; **3** Naoki Yamamoto/Tadasuke Makino, J/J (Honda Civic Type R-GT), +12.262s; **4** Hiroaki Ishiura/Toshiki Oyu, J/J (Toyota GR Supra), +21.100s; **5** Katsumasa Chiyo/Ronnie Quintarelli, J/I (Nissan Fairlady Z), +24.541s; **6** Mitsunori Takaboshi/Atsushi Miyake, J/J (Nissan Fairlady Z), +25.424s; **7** Ukyo Sasahara/Giuliano Alesi, J/F (Toyota GR Supra), +25.776s; **8** Tomoki Nojiri/Nobuharu Matsushita, J/J (Honda Civic Type R-GT), +41.315s; **9** Hiroki Ohtsu/Ren Sato, J/J (Honda Civic Type R-GT), +43.007s; **10** Takuya Izawa/Riki Okusa, J/J (Honda Civic Type R-GT), -1 lap.
Fastest race lap: Tsuboi, 1m 20.674s, 102.677mph/165.242km/h.
Pole position: Tsuboi/Yamashita, 2m 35.561s, 106.496mph/171.390km/h (over **2** laps).

FUJI GT 3 HOURS RACE, Fuji International Speedway, Sunto-gun, Shizuoka Prefecture, Japan, 4 May. Round 2. 117 laps of the 2.835-mile/4.563km circuit, 331.732 miles/533.871km.
1 Mitsunori Takaboshi/Atsushi Miyake, J/J (Nissan Fairlady Z), 3h 01m 16.898s, 109.795mph/176.698km/h; **2** Katsumasa Chiyo/Ronnie Quintarelli, J/I (Nissan Fairlady Z), +13.738s; **3** Koudai Tsukakoshi/Kakunoshin Ohta, J/J (Honda Civic Type R-GT), +36.354s; **4** Sho Tsuboi/Kenta Yamashita, J/J (Toyota GR Supra), +38.002s; **5** Hiroaki Ishiura/Toshiki Oyu, J/J (Toyota GR Supra), +41.637s; **6** Kazuki Hiramine/Bertrand Baguette, J/B (Nissan Fairlady Z), +48.364s; **7** Naoki Yamamoto/Tadasuke Makino, J/J (Honda Civic Type R-GT), +50.361s; **8** Kazuya Oshima/Nirei Fukuzumi, J/J (Toyota GR Supra), +54.666s; **9** Yuhi Sekiguchi/Yuichi Nakayama, J/J (Toyota GR Supra), +1m 14.583s; **10** Yuji Kunimoto/Sena Sakaguchi, J/J (Toyota GR Supra), +1m 26.522s.
Fastest race lap: Takaboshi, 1m 29.559s, 113.971mph/183.418km/h.
Pole position: Tsukakoshi/Ohta, 2m 53.931s, 117.369mph/188.888km/h (over **2** laps).

SUZUKA GT 3 HOURS RACE, Suzuka International Racing Course, Suzuka-shi, Mie Prefecture, Japan, 2 June. Round 3. 92 laps of the 3.608-mile/5.807km circuit, 331.964 miles/534.244km.
1 Ukyo Sasahara/Giuliano Alesi, J/F (Toyota GR Supra), 3h 00m 22.971s, 110.419mph/177.703km/h; **2** Kazuya Oshima/Nirei Fukuzumi, J/J (Toyota GR Supra), +10.968s; **3** Hiroki Ohtsu/Ren Sato, J/J (Honda Civic Type R-GT), +24.573s; **4** Kazuki Hiramine/Bertrand Baguette, J/B (Nissan Fairlady Z), +25.103s; **5** Sho Tsuboi/Kenta Yamashita, J/J (Toyota GR Supra), +32.991s; **6** Koudai Tsukakoshi/Kakunoshin Ohta, J/J (Honda Civic Type R-GT), +46.526s; **7** Naoki Yamamoto/Tadasuke Makino, J/J (Honda Civic Type R-GT), +46.758s; **8** Mitsunori Takaboshi/Atsushi Miyake, J/J (Nissan Fairlady Z), +1m 08.537s; **9** Tsugio Matsuda/Teppei Natori, J/J (Nissan Fairlady Z), +1m 19.706s; **10** Katsumasa Chiyo/Ronnie Quintarelli, J/I (Nissan Fairlady Z), -1 lap.
Fastest race lap: Baguette, 1m 48.752s, 119.445mph/192.228km/h.
Pole position: Sasahara/Alesi, 3m 31.873s, 122.619mph/197.337km/h (over **2** laps).

FUJI GT 350 KM RACE, Fuji International Speedway, Sunto-gun, Shizuoka Prefecture, Japan, 4 August. Round 4. 77 laps of the 2.835-mile/4.563km circuit, 218.319 miles/351.351km.
1 Tomoki Nojiri/Nobuharu Matsushita, J/J (Honda Civic Type R-GT), 2h 00m 43.329s, 108.506mph/174.624km/h; **2** Naoki Yamamoto/Tadasuke Makino, J/J (Honda Civic Type R-GT), +3.277s; **3** Hiroaki Ishiura/Toshiki Oyu, J/J (Toyota GR Supra), +12.233s; **4** Kazuya Oshima/Nirei Fukuzumi, J/J (Toyota GR Supra), +14.725s; **5** Kazuki Hiramine/Bertrand Baguette, J/B (Nissan Fairlady Z), +18.894s; **6** Takuya Izawa/Riki Okusa, J/J (Honda Civic Type R-GT), +24.192s; **7** Sho Tsuboi/Kenta Yamashita, J/J (Toyota GR Supra), +42.439s; **8** Koudai Tsukakoshi/Kakunoshin Ohta, J/J (Honda Civic Type R-GT), +44.929s; **9** Yuji Kunimoto/Sena Sakaguchi, J/J (Toyota GR Supra), +52.143s; **10** Ukyo Sasahara/Giuliano Alesi, J/F (Toyota GR Supra), +55.860s.
Fastest race lap: Sakaguchi, 1m 30.102s, 113.284mph/182.313km/h.
Pole position: Nojiri/Matsushita, 2m 56.359s, 115.754mph/186.288km/h (over **2** laps).

SUZUKA GT 300 KM RACE, Suzuka International Racing Course, Suzuka-shi, Mie Prefecture, Japan, 8 December. Round 5. 51 laps of the 3.608-mile/5.807km circuit, 184.023 miles/296.157km.
This race was scheduled for 1 September but postponed due to Typhoon Shanshan. It retained its original round number.
1 Sho Tsuboi/Kenta Yamashita, J/J (Toyota GR Supra), 1h 44m 15.090s, 105.911mph/170.447km/h; **2** Koudai Tsukakoshi/Kakunoshin Ohta, J/J (Honda Civic Type R-GT), +1.513s; **3** Kazuki Hiramine/Bertrand Baguette, J/B (Nissan Fairlady Z), +9.342s; **4** Naoki Yamamoto/Tadasuke Makino, J/J (Honda Civic Type R-GT), +16.084s; **5** Hiroki Ohtsu/Ren Sato, J/J (Honda Civic Type R-GT), +16.698s; **6** Kazuya Oshima/Nirei Fukuzumi, J/J (Toyota GR Supra), +17.200s; **7** Mitsunori Takaboshi/Atsushi Miyake, J/J (Nissan Fairlady Z), +24.539s; **8** Katsumasa Chiyo/Ronnie Quintarelli, J/I (Nissan Fairlady Z), +31.259s; **9** Hiroaki Ishiura/Toshiki Oyu, J/J (Toyota GR Supra), +33.992s; **10** Yuhi Sekiguchi/Yuichi Nakayama, J/J (Toyota GR Supra), +35.494s.
Fastest race lap: Teppei Natori, J (Nissan Fairlady Z), 1m 47.135s, 121.247mph/195.129km/h.
Pole position: Tsuboi/Yamashita, 3m 27.008s, 125.501mph/201.974km/h (over **2** laps).

SUGO GT 300 KM RACE, Sportsland-SUGO International Course, Shibata-gun, Miyagi Prefecture, Japan, 22 September. Round 6. 84 laps of the 2.228-mile/3.586km circuit, 187.172 miles/301.224km.
1 Ukyo Sasahara/Giuliano Alesi, J/F (Toyota GR Supra), 2h 11m 57.509s, 85.104mph/136.963km/h; **2** Hiroaki Ishiura/Toshiki Oyu, J/J (Toyota GR Supra), +19.957s; **3** Kazuki Hiramine/Bertrand Baguette, J/B (Nissan Fairlady Z), +25.944s; **4** Sho Tsuboi/Kenta Yamashita, J/J (Toyota GR Supra), +41.633s; **5** Naoki Yamamoto/Tadasuke Makino, J/J (Honda Civic Type R-GT), +44.852s; **6** Mitsunori Takaboshi/Atsushi Miyake, J/J (Nissan Fairlady Z), +54.901s; **7** Koudai Tsukakoshi/Kakunoshin Ohta, J/J (Honda Civic Type R-GT), +1m 16.812s; **8** Yuji Kunimoto/Sena Sakaguchi, J/J (Toyota GR Supra), +1m 19.552s; **9** Kazuya Oshima/Nirei Fukuzumi, J/J (Toyota GR Supra), -1 lap; **10** Hiroki Ohtsu/Ren Sato, J/J (Honda Civic Type R-GT), -1.
Fastest race lap: Yuichi Nakayama, J (Toyota GR Supra), 1m 14.907s, 107.088mph/172.341km/h.
Pole position: Hiroaki Ishiura/Toshiki Oyu.

AUTOPOLIS GT 3 HOURS RACE, Autopolis International Racing Course, Kamit-sue-mura, Hita-gun, Oita Prefecture, Japan, 20 October. Round 7. 92 laps of the 2.904-mile/4.674km circuit, 267.195 miles/430.008km.
1 Yuhi Sekiguchi/Yuichi Nakayama, J/J (Toyota GR Supra), 3h 01m 11.604s, 88.478mph/142.391km/h; **2** Katsumasa Chiyo/Ronnie Quintarelli, J/I (Nissan Fairlady Z), +0.885s; **3** Mitsunori Takaboshi/Atsushi Miyake, J/J (Nissan Fairlady Z), +2.966s; **4** Naoki Yamamoto/Tadasuke Makino, J/J (Honda Civic Type R-GT), +3.748s; **5** Kazuki Hiramine/Bertrand Baguette, J/B (Nissan Fairlady Z), +5.353s; **6** Hiroki Ohtsu/Ren Sato, J/J (Honda Civic Type R-GT), +7.647s; **7** Sho Tsuboi/Kenta Yamashita, J/J (Toyota GR Supra), +8.901s; **8** Ukyo Sasahara/Giuliano Alesi, J/F (Toyota GR Supra), +10.242s; **9** Kazuya Oshima/Nirei Fukuzumi, J/J (Toyota GR Supra), +11.981s; **10** Hiroaki Ishiura/Toshiki Oyu, J/J (Toyota GR Supra), +12.152s.
Fastest race lap: Chiyo, 1m 35.832s, 109.101mph/175.582km/h.
Pole position: Tsugio Matsuda/Teppei Natori, J/J (Nissan Fairlady Z), 1m 33.162s, 224.457mph/361.228km/h (over **2** laps).

MOTEGI GT 300 KM RACE, Twin Ring Motegi, Motegi-machi, Haga-gun, Tochigi Prefecture, Japan, 3 November. Round 8. 63 laps of the 2.983-mile/4.801km circuit, 187.942 miles/302.463km.
1 Sho Tsuboi/Kenta Yamashita, J/J (Toyota GR Supra), 1h 53m 50.242s, 99.058mph/159.418km/h; **2** Tomoki Nojiri/Nobuharu Matsushita, J/J (Honda Civic Type R-GT), +20.513s; **3** Hiroaki Ishiura/Toshiki Oyu, J/J (Toyota GR Supra), +27.554s; **4** Hiroki Ohtsu/Ren Sato, J/J (Honda Civic Type R-GT), +27.690s; **5** Yuhi Sekiguchi/Yuichi Nakayama, J/J (Toyota GR Supra), +33.429s; **6** Naoki Yamamoto/Tadasuke Makino, J/J (Honda Civic Type R-GT), +36.618s; **7** Mitsunori Takaboshi/Atsushi Miyake, J/J (Nissan Fairlady Z), +44.710s; **8** Tsugio Matsuda/Teppei Natori, J/J (Nissan Fairlady Z), +45.310s; **9** Katsumasa Chiyo/Ronnie Quintarelli, J/I (Nissan Fairlady Z), +46.199s; **10** Takuya Izawa/Riki Okusa, J/J (Honda Civic Type R-GT), +59.079s.
Fastest race lap: Izawa, 1m 39.702s, 107.716mph/173.352km/h.
Pole position: Izawa/Okusa, 3m 37.911s, 98.568mph/158.629km/h (over **2** laps).

Final championship points
Drivers (GT500)
1 Kenta Yamashita, J, 97; 1 Sho Tsuboi, J, 97; **2** Tadasuke Makino, J, 64; **2** Naoki Yamamoto, J, 64; **3** Mitsunori Takaboshi, J, 54; **3** Atsushi Miyake, J, 54; **4** Hiroaki Ishiura, J, 54; **4** Toshiki Oyu, J, 54; **5** Ukyo Sasahara, J, 51; **5** Giuliano Alesi, F, 51; **6** Kazuki Hiramine, J, 47; **6** Bertrand Baguette, B, 47; **7** Yuichi Nakayama, J, 46; **7** Yuhi Sekiguchi, J, 46; **8** Katsumasa Chiyo, J, 45; **8** Ronnie Quintarelli, I, 45; **9** Tomoki Nojiri, J, 43; **9** Nobuharu Matsushita, J, 43; **10** Kakunoshin Ohta, J, 43; **10** Koudai Tsukakoshi, J, 43.

Drivers (GT300)
1 Yuya Motojima, J, 96; 1 Takashi Kogure, J, 96; **2** Takuro Shinohara, J, 92; **2** Naoya Gamou, J, 92; **3** Yuui Tsutsumi, J, 80; **3** Hibiki Taira, J, 80.

Other Sports Car races

ADAC RAVENOL 24H NÜRBURGRING, Nürburg/Eifel, Germany, 2 June. 50 laps of the 15.769-mile/25.378km circuit, 788.458 miles/1268.900km.
1 Ricardo Feller/Dennis Marschall/Christopher Mies/Frank Stippler, CH/D/D/D (Audi R8 LMS GT3 Evo II), 23h 05m 27.680s, 34.146mph/54.952 km/h; **2** Kévin Estre/Ayhancan Güven/Thomas Preining/Laurens Vanthoor, F/TR/A/B (Porsche 911 GT3 R (992)), +0.603s; **3** Daniel Harper/Max Hesse/Charles Weerts, GB/D/B (BMW M4 GT3), +5.399s; **4** Maximilian Götz/Daniel Juncadella/Luca Stolz, D/E/D (Mercedes-AMG GT3), +5.646s; **5** Marco Mapelli/Jordan Pepper/Kelvin van der Linde, I/ZA/ZA (Lamborghini Huracán GT3 Evo2), +6.168s; **6** Julien Andlauer/Klaus Bachler/Sven Müller/Alessio Picariello, F/A/D/B (Porsche 911 GT3 R (992)), +6.723s; **7** Augusto Farfus/Raffaele Marciello/Maxime Martin/Marco Wittmann, BR/CH/B/D (BMW M4 GT3), +24.601s; **8** Ricardo Feller/Christopher Haase/Frédéric Vervisch/Markus Winkelhock, CH/D/B/D (Audi R8 LMS GT3 Evo II), +25.047s; **9** Antares Au/Indy Dontje/Patrik Kolb/Patric Niederhauser, HK/NL/D/CH (Porsche 911 GT R (992)), +26.078s; **10** Joel Eriksson/Tim Heinemann/Nico Menzel/Martin Ragginger, S/D/D/A (Porsche 911 GT3 R (992), +26.909s.
The race was shortened, due to a 14-hour stoppage because of fog. It only ran for 7h 24m.
Fastest race lap: Felipe Fernandez Laser/Daniel Keilwitz/Luca Ludwig/Nicolás Varrone, D/D/D/RA (Ferrari 296 GT 3), 8m 12.460s, 115.276mph/185.519km/h.
Pole position: Harper/Hesse/Weerts, 8m 10.992s, 115.621mph/186.074km/h.

SPA 24 HOURS, Circuit de Spa-Francorchamps, Stavelot, Belgium, 30 June. 478 laps of the 4.352-mile/7.004km circuit, 2080.296 miles/3347.912km.
1 Mattia Drudi/Nicki Thiim/Marco Sørensen, I/DK/DK (Aston Martin Vantage AMR GT3 Evo), 24h 01m 16.868s, 86.602mph/139.372km/h; **2** Alessandro Pier Guidi/Davide Rigon/Alessio Rovera, I/I/I (Ferrari 296 GT3), +33.604s; **3** Sheldon van der Linde/Dries Vanthoor/Charles Weerts, ZA/B/B (BMW M4 GT3), +38.831s; **4** David Pittard/Henrique Chaves Jr/Ross Gunn, GB/P/GB (Aston Martin Vantage AMR GT3 Evo), +47.815s; **5** Jordan Pepper/Franck Perera/Marco Mapelli, ZA/F/I (Lamborghini Huracán GT3 Evo2), +1m 14.750s; **6** Augusto Farfus/Daniel Harper/Max Hesse, BR/GB/D (BMW M4 GT3), +1m 26.872s; **7** Dominik Baumann/Mikaël Grenier/Philip Ellis/Faisal Al Zubair, A/CDN/GB/OM (Mercedes AMG GT3 Evo), +1m 45.090s; **8** Mathieu Jaminet/Matt Campbell/Frédéric Makowiecki, F/AUS/F (Porsche 911 GT3 R), +1m 45.904s; **9** Patric Niederhauser/Sven Müller/Julien Andlauer, CH/D/F (Porsche 911 GT3 R), -1 lap; **10** Max Hofer/Dylan Pereira/Alexey Nesov/Andrey Mukovoz, A/L/RUS/RUS (Audi R8 LMS GT3 Evo II), -1.
Fastest race lap: Mapelli, 2m 16.105s, 115.113mph/185.257km/h.
Pole position: Pepper/Perera/Mapelli, 2m 13.718s, 117.168mph/188.564km/h.

FIA GT WORLD CUP, Circuito da Guia, Macau, 16/17 November. 12 and 16 laps of the 3.803-mile/6.120km circuit.
Race 1 (45.634 miles/73.440km).
1 Raffaele Marciello, I (BMW M4 GT3), 27m 37.981s, 99.084mph/159.461km/h; **2** Dries Vanthoor, B (BMW M4 GT3), +0.666s; **3** Antonio Fuoco, I (Ferrari 296 GT3), +1.846s; **4** Maro Engel, D (Mercedes AMG GT3 Evo), +4.505s; **5** Augusto Farfus, BR (BMW M4 GT3), +6.388s; **6** Sheldon van der Linde, ZA (BMW M4 GT3), +6.761s; **7** Alessio Picariello, B (Porsche 911 GT3 R (992)), +10.242s; **8** Laurens Vanthoor, B (Porsche 911 GT3 R (992)), +12.107s; **9** Christopher Haase, D (Audi R8 LMS GT3 Evo II), +14.453s; **10** Edoardo Mortara, CH (Lamborghini Huracán GT3 Evo2), +18.258s.

Fastest race lap: van der Linde, 2m 16.710s, 100.139mph/161.158km/h.
Pole position: Marciello, 2m 16.509s, 100.286mph/161.395km/h.

Race 2 (60.845 miles/97.920km).
1 Maro Engel, D (Mercedes AMG GT3 Evo), 45m 44.519s, 79.810mph/128.442km/h*; **2** Augusto Farfus, BR (BMW M4 GT3), +6.641s; **3** Sheldon van der Linde, ZA (BMW M4 GT3), +10.299s; **4** Alessio Picariello, B (Porsche 911 GT3 R (992)), +10.881s; **5** Laurens Vanthoor, B (Porsche 911 GT3 R (992)), +11.205s; **6** Christopher Haase, D (Audi R8 LMS GT3 Evo II), +12.469s; **7** Edoardo Mortara, CH (Lamborghini Huracán GT3 Evo2), +13.025s; **8** Ricardo Feller, CH (Audi R8 LMS GT3 Evo II), +13.821s; **9** Antonio Fuoco, I (Ferrari 296 GT3), +14.853s; **10** Daniel Juncadella, E (Mercedes AMG GT3 Evo), +15.937s.
** 5s penalty for causing a collision*
Fastest race lap: Engel, 2m 32.696s, 89.655mph/144.286km/h.
Pole position: Raffaele Marciello, I (BMW M4 GT3).

Repco Supercars Championship

Cars are: Chevrolet Camaro ZL1 Gen3; Ford Mustang GT Gen3.

THRIFTY BATHURST 500, Mount Panorama, Bathurst, New South Wales, Australia, 24/25 February. 2 x 40 laps of the 3.861-mile/6.213km circuit.
Race 1 (154.423 miles/248.520km).
1 Broc Feeney, AUS (Chevrolet), 1h 36m 15.9437s, 96.248mph/154.896km/h; **2** William Brown, AUS (Chevrolet), +0.3901s; **3** Chaz Mostert, AUS (Ford), +1.1323s; **4** Richie Stanaway, NZ (Ford), +1.5107s; **5** Cameron Hill, AUS (Chevrolet), +2.2634s; **6** Nick Percat, AUS (Chevrolet), +3.0867s; **7** Bryce Fullwood, AUS (Chevrolet), +3.9433s; **8** David Reynolds, AUS (Chevrolet), +4.3837s; **9** Andre Heimgartner, NZ (Chevrolet), +5.1259s; **10** Matthew Payne, NZ (Ford), +5.5967s.
Fastest race lap: Mostert, 2m 08.0797s, 108.511mph/174.631km/h.
Pole position: Brown, 2m 06.3740s, 109.975mph/176.988km/h.

Race 2 (154.423 miles/248.520km).
1 William Brown, AUS (Chevrolet), 1h 27m 19.1560s, 106.109mph/170.766km/h; **2** Chaz Mostert, AUS (Ford), +1.5535s; **3** Broc Feeney, AUS (Chevrolet), +2.7305s; **4** Tom Randle, AUS (Ford), +22.6834s; **5** James Golding, AUS (Chevrolet), +24.0407s; **6** David Reynolds, AUS (Chevrolet), +26.2710s; **7** Matthew Payne, NZ (Ford), +27.3572s; **8** Jack Le Brocq, AUS (Chevrolet), +34.9165s; **9** Nick Percat, AUS (Chevrolet), +35.2489s; **10** Will Davison, AUS (Ford), +42.6161s.
Fastest race lap: Feeney, 2m 07.6228s, 108.899mph/175.257km/h.
Pole position: Feeney, 2m 06.5465s, 109.825mph/176.747km/h.

MELBOURNE SUPERSPRINT, Albert Park Circuit, Melbourne, Victoria, Australia, 21/24 March. 18, 17, 10 and 14 laps of the 3.280-mile/5.278km circuit.
Race 3 (59.033 miles/95.004km).
1 Broc Feeney, AUS (Chevrolet), 33m 13.3790s, 106.611mph/171.575km/h; **2** William Brown, AUS (Chevrolet), +2.3253s; **3** Matthew Payne, NZ (Ford), +4.7124s; **4** Chaz Mostert, AUS (Ford), +5.1586s; **5** Cameron Waters, AUS (Ford), +6.1099s; **6** Nick Percat, AUS (Chevrolet), +8.7801s*; **7** Anton De Pasquale, AUS (Ford), +9.2341s; **8** James Courtney, AUS (Ford), +12.7935s; **9** Todd Hazelwood, AUS (Chevrolet), +14.7979s*; **10** Jack Le Brocq, AUS (Chevrolet), +15.5365s.
** 5s penalty*
Fastest race lap: Feeney, 1m 49.5611s, 107.762mph/173.426km/h.
Pole position: Feeney, 1m 47.7148s, 109.609mph/176.399km/h.

Race 4 (55.753 miles/89.726km).
1 William Brown, AUS (Chevrolet), 31m 40.6618s, 105.600mph/169.947km/h; **2** Mark Winterbottom, AUS (Chevrolet), +0.9693s; **3** Matthew Payne, NZ (Ford), +1.5309s; **4** Broc Feeney, AUS (Chevrolet), +1.8399s; **5** Will Davison, AUS (Ford), +2.4644s; **6** Nick Percat, AUS (Chevrolet), +2.7510s; **7** Cameron Waters, AUS (Ford), +3.3498s; **8** Jack Le Brocq, AUS (Chevrolet), +3.6724s; **9** Todd Hazelwood, AUS (Chevrolet), +8.6315s; **10** Tim Slade, AUS (Chevrolet), +8.7491s.
Fastest race lap: Brown, 1m 49.7203s, 107.605mph/173.174km/h.
Pole position: Waters, 1m 47.4916s, 109.836mph/176.765km/h.

Race 5 (32.796 miles/52.780km).
1 Broc Feeney, AUS (Chevrolet), 26m 32.2808s, 74.148mph/119.330km/h; **2** William Brown, AUS (Chevrolet), +1.7911s; **3** Chaz Mostert, AUS (Ford), +2.7225s; **4** David Reynolds, AUS (Chevrolet), +3.1756s; **5** Jack Le Brocq, AUS (Chevrolet), +3.6926s; **6** Todd Hazelwood, AUS (Chevrolet), +4.6703s; **7** Richie Stanaway, NZ (Ford), +6.5944s; **8** Tim Slade, AUS (Chevrolet), +8.0014s; **9** Nick Percat, AUS (Chevrolet), +8.5072s; **10** Ryan Wood, NZ (Ford), +9.0970s.
Fastest race lap: Mostert, 1m 48.3891s, 108.927mph/175.301km/h.
Pole position: Matthew Payne, NZ (Ford), 1m 46.6541s, 110.699mph/178.153km/h.

Race 6 (45.914 miles/73.892km).
1 Nick Percat, AUS (Chevrolet), 25m 38.3737s, 107.445mph/172.917km/h; **2** William Brown, AUS (Chevrolet), +0.3810s; **3** Broc Feeney, AUS (Chevrolet), +0.9944s; **4** Tom Randle, AUS (Ford), +9.9320s; **5** Chaz Mostert, AUS (Ford), +10.0349s*; **6** Will Davison, AUS (Ford), +14.4397s; **7** Cameron Waters, AUS (Ford), +16.2138s; **8** Richie Stanaway, NZ (Ford), +17.0547s; **9** David Reynolds, AUS (Chevrolet), +17.5480s; **10** Tim Slade, AUS (Chevrolet), +17.9223s.
** 5s penalty*
Fastest race lap: Randle, 1m 48.4542s, 108.862mph/175.196km/h.
Pole position: Mostert, 1m 46.3227s, 111.044mph/178.708km/h.

ITM TAUPŌ SUPER400, Taupo Racetrack, Lake Taupo, New Zealand, 20/21 April. 2 x 60 laps of the 2.064-mile/3.321km circuit.
Race 7 (123.814 miles/199.260km).
1 Andre Heimgartner, NZ (Chevrolet), 1h 44m 15.3390s, 71.256mph/114.675km/h; **2** Will Davison, AUS (Ford), +1.1012s; **3** Anton De Pasquale, AUS (Ford), +2.5641s; **4** Ryan Wood, NZ (Ford), +3.9318s; **5** Jack Le Brocq, AUS (Chevrolet), +21.2535s; **6** Richie Stanaway, NZ (Ford), +23.1340s; **7** James Golding, AUS (Chevrolet), +26.3405s; **8** Cameron Waters, AUS (Ford), +30.5452s; **9** William Brown, AUS (Chevrolet), +30.9350s; **10** Jaxon Evans, NZ (Chevrolet), +35.5458s.
Fastest race lap: David Reynolds, AUS (Chevrolet), 1m 32.7245s, 80.117mph/128.936km/h.
Pole position: Waters, 1m 34.7415s, 78.411mph/126.191km/h.

Race 8 (123.814 miles/199.260km).
1 William Brown, AUS (Chevrolet), 1h 31m 19.5236s, 81.345mph/130.912km/h; **2** Broc Feeney, AUS (Chevrolet), +3.3585s; **3** Anton De Pasquale, AUS (Ford), +14.2612s; **4** Matthew Payne, NZ (Ford), +17.4316s; **5** James Golding, AUS (Chevrolet), +22.6842s; **6** Andre Heimgartner, NZ (Chevrolet), +24.3817s; **7** Chaz Mostert, AUS (Ford), +30.1327s; **8** Jack Le Brocq, AUS (Chevrolet), +30.4356s; **9** Cameron Waters, AUS (Ford), +35.6640s; **10** Ryan Wood, NZ (Ford), +38.0105s.
Fastest race lap: Wood, 1m 27.6151s, 84.789mph/136.455km/h.
Pole position: Payne, 1m 26.8173s, 85.568mph/137.709km/h.

PERTH SUPERSPRINT, Barbagallo Raceway Wanneroo, Perth, Western Australia, Australia, 18/19 May. 2 x 55 laps of the 1.504-mile/2.420km circuit.
Race 9 (82.705 miles/133.100km).
1 Chaz Mostert, AUS (Ford), 52m 11.0965s, 95.090mph/153.032km/h; **2** William Brown, AUS (Chevrolet), +4.9134s; **3** Cameron Waters, AUS (Ford), +13.1297s; **4** Ryan Wood, NZ (Ford), +13.4661s; **5** Broc Feeney, AUS (Chevrolet), +17.8079s; **6** James Courtney, AUS (Ford), +21.7942s; **7** Nick Percat, AUS (Chevrolet), +25.6341s; **8** Matthew Payne, NZ (Ford), +26.0108s; **9** Anton De Pasquale, AUS (Ford), +30.2070s; **10** Tom Randle, AUS (Ford), +31.9240s.
Fastest race lap: Brown, 55.8155s, 96.987mph/156.085km/h.
Pole position: Mostert, 54.5628s, 99.213mph/159.669km/h.

Race 10 (82.705 miles/133.100km).
1 Cameron Waters, AUS (Ford), 52m 11.4767s, 95.078mph/153.014km/h; **2** Chaz Mostert, AUS (Ford), +2.5885s*; **3** William Brown, AUS (Chevrolet), +11.0466s*; **4** Will Davison, AUS (Ford), +12.1004s; **5** Tom Randle, AUS (Ford), +16.8024s; **6** Anton De Pasquale, AUS (Ford), +17.2041s; **7** Broc Feeney, AUS (Chevrolet), +17.4460s; **8** Ryan Wood, NZ (Ford), +19.4364s; **9** Matthew Payne, NZ (Ford), +25.2710s; **10** David Reynolds, AUS (Chevrolet), +25.9148s.
** 5s penalty*
Fastest race lap: Mostert, 55.6345s, 97.302mph/156.593km/h.
Pole position: Waters, 54.5545s, 99.228mph/159.693km/h.

BETR DARWIN TRIPLE CROWN, Hidden Valley Raceway, Darwin, Northern Territory, Australia, 15/16 June. 2 x 48 laps of the 1.783-mile/2.870km circuit.
Race 11 (85.600 miles/137.760km).
1 Broc Feeney, AUS (Chevrolet), 55m 40.4499s, 92.251mph/148.463km/h; **2** Mark Winterbottom, AUS (Chevrolet), +8.6763s; **3** William Brown, AUS (Chevrolet), +10.6426s; **4** James Golding, AUS (Chevrolet), +14.6593s; **5** Chaz Mostert, AUS (Ford), +15.1062s; **6** David Reynolds, AUS (Chevrolet), +17.8120s; **7** Nick Percat, AUS (Chevrolet), +18.6266s; **8** Andre Heimgartner, NZ (Chevrolet), +19.9128s; **9** Anton De Pasquale, AUS (Ford), +20.2235s; **10** Cameron Waters, AUS (Ford), +20.2782s*.
** 5s penalty*
Fastest race lap: Cooper Murray, AUS (Chevrolet), 1m 08.0992s, 94.274mph/151.719km/h.
Pole position: Golding, 1m 06.2302s, 96.934mph/156.001km/h.

Race 12 (85.600 miles/137.760km).
1 Broc Feeney, AUS (Chevrolet), 57m 06.5433s, 89.933mph/144.733km/h; **2** William Brown, AUS (Chevrolet), +1.2255s; **3** Brodie Kostecki, AUS (Chevrolet), +17.4258s; **4** James Golding, AUS (Chevrolet), +27.9601s; **5** Nick Percat, AUS (Chevrolet), +28.6139s; **6** Jack Le Brocq, AUS (Chevrolet), +29.4174s; **7** Will Davison, AUS (Ford), +29.7187s; **8** Anton De Pasquale, AUS (Ford), +30.0323s; **9** Cameron Hill, AUS (Chevrolet), +32.9595s; **10** Richie Stanaway, NZ (Ford), +33.8864s.
Fastest race lap: Brown, 1m 07.6126s, 94.952mph/152.811km/h.
Pole position: Feeney, 1m 05.9205s, 97.390mph/156.734km/h.

NTI TOWNSVILLE 500, Townsville Street Circuit, Queensland, Australia, 6/7 July. 2 x 88 laps of the 1.777-mile/2.860km circuit.
Race 13 (156.387 miles/251.680km).
1 Cameron Waters, AUS (Ford), 1h 54m 21.1327s, 82.055mph/132.055km/h; **2** Chaz Mostert, AUS (Ford), +1.8538s; **3** William Brown, AUS (Chevrolet), +4.6801s; **4** Matthew Payne, NZ (Ford), +6.2778s; **5** Tom Randle, AUS (Ford), +9.1481s; **6** Jack Le Brocq, AUS (Chevrolet), +9.8618s; **7** Broc Feeney, AUS (Chevrolet), +10.1741s; **8** Will Davison, AUS (Ford), +14.6786s; **9** Andre Heimgartner, NZ (Chevrolet), +33.9007s; **10** Cameron Hill, AUS (Chevrolet), +34.5366s.
Fastest race lap: Payne, 1m 15.3079s, 84.953mph/136.718km/h.
Pole position: Waters, 1m 13.7232s, 86.779mph/139.657km/h.

Race 14 (156.387 miles/251.680km).
1 Matthew Payne, NZ (Ford), 1h 54m 21.9164s, 82.045mph/132.040km/h; **2** Cameron Waters, AUS (Ford), +6.0575s; **3** Chaz Mostert, AUS (Ford), +7.6556s; **4** Jack Le Brocq, AUS (Chevrolet), +15.1198s; **5** Tom Randle, AUS (Ford), +16.4005s; **6** Ryan Wood, NZ (Ford), +26.3506s; **7** Broc Feeney, AUS (Chevrolet), +27.0301s; **8** Mark Winterbottom, AUS (Chevrolet), +35.8572s; **9** Cameron Hill, AUS (Chevrolet), +37.4558s; **10** James Golding, AUS (Chevrolet), +37.9764s.
Fastest race lap: Golding, 1m 15.3179s, 84.941mph/136.700km/h.
Pole position: Le Brocq, 1m 14.2467s, 86.167mph/138.672km/h.

PANASONIC AIR CONDITIONING SYDNEY SUPERNIGHT, Sydney Motorsport Park, Eastern Creek, New South Wales, Australia, 20/21 July. 2 x 51 laps of the 2.442-mile/3.930km circuit.
Race 15 (124.541 miles/200.430km).
1 Chaz Mostert, AUS (Ford), 1h 20m 56.8670s, 92.312mph/148.562km/h; **2** Matthew Payne, NZ (Ford), +2.6412s; **3** Tom Randle, AUS (Ford), +4.5639s; **4** Will Davison, AUS (Ford), +18.1193s; **5** Anton De Pasquale, AUS (Ford), +20.3561s; **6** William Brown, AUS (Chevrolet), +27.6433s; **7** Cameron Waters, AUS (Ford), +29.6967s; **8** Nick Percat, AUS (Chevrolet), +33.1724s; **9** Broc Feeney, AUS (Chevrolet), +33.5289s; **10** Brodie Kostecki, AUS (Chevrolet), +36.6762s.
Fastest race lap: Jack Le Brocq, AUS (Chevrolet), 1m 31.1562s, 96.440mph/155.206km/h.
Pole position: Waters, 1m 29.8662s, 97.824mph/157.434km/h.

Race 16 (124.541 miles/200.430km).
1 Chaz Mostert, AUS (Ford), 1h 20m 58.8671s, 92.274mph/148.501km/h; **2** Cameron Waters, AUS (Ford), +7.3643s; **3** William Brown, AUS (Chevrolet), +8.9896s; **4** Matthew Payne, NZ (Ford), +14.8753s; **5** Anton De Pasquale, AUS (Ford), +16.1423s; **6** Will Davison, AUS (Ford), +18.1945s; **7** Brodie Kostecki, AUS (Chevrolet), +26.0143s; **8** Nick Percat, AUS (Chevrolet), +27.1944s; **9** James Golding, AUS (Chevrolet), +27.7813s; **10** Tom Randle, AUS (Ford), +31.2567s.
Fastest race lap: Mostert, 1m 31.3020s, 96.286mph/154.958km/h.
Pole position: Davison, 1m 29.9187s, 97.767mph/157.342km/h.

NED WHISKY TASMANIA SUPERSPRINT, Symmons Plains Raceway, Launceston, Tasmania, Australia, 17/18 August. 2 x 55 laps of the 1.491-mile/2.400km circuit.
Race 17 (82.021 miles/132.000km).
1 Nick Percat, AUS (Chevrolet), 48m 35.2339s, 101.287mph/163.005km/h; **2** Chaz Mostert, AUS (Ford), +0.6142s; **3** Broc Feeney, AUS (Chevrolet), +1.7833s; **4** Cameron Waters, AUS (Ford), +5.1415s; **5** Brodie Kostecki, AUS (Chevrolet), +6.9957s; **6** Cameron Hill, AUS (Chevrolet), +9.8432s; **7** William Brown, AUS (Chevrolet), +12.2851s; **8** Tim Slade, AUS (Chevrolet), +12.8435s; **9** David Reynolds, AUS (Chevrolet), +13.1544s; **10** Bryce Fullwood, AUS (Chevrolet), +24.8849s.
Fastest race lap: Matthew Payne, NZ (Ford), 51.5502s, 104.144mph/167.603km/h.
Pole position: Feeney, 50.9884s, 105.291mph/169.450km/h.

Race 18 (82.021 miles/132.000km).
1 Cameron Waters, AUS (Ford), 55m 52.2101s, 88.083mph/141.757km/h; **2** William Brown, AUS (Chevrolet), +6.3429s; **3** Bryce Fullwood, AUS (Chevrolet), +7.7612s; **4** Chaz Mostert, AUS (Ford), +9.7509s; **5** Jack Le Brocq, AUS (Chevrolet), +10.3532s; **6** Andre Heimgartner, NZ (Chevrolet), +11.4530s; **7** Nick Percat, AUS (Chevrolet), +11.7376s; **8** Ryan Wood, NZ (Ford), +13.3895s; **9** Mark Winterbottom, AUS (Chevrolet), +14.0709s; **10** Tim Slade, AUS (Chevrolet), +15.2727s.
Fastest race lap: Randle, AUS (Ford), 51.6121s, 104.019mph/167.402km/h.
Pole position: Randle, 50.6620s, 105.969mph/170.542km/h.

SANDOWN 500, Sandown International Motor Raceway, Melbourne, Victoria, Australia, 15 September. Round 9. 154 laps of the 1.926-mile/3.100km circuit.
Race 19 (296.643 miles/477.400km).
1 William Brown/Scott Pye, AUS/AUS (Chevrolet), 3h 35m 38.9364s, 82.534mph/132.826km/h; **2** Broc Feeney/Jamie Whincup, AUS/AUS (Chevrolet), +0.4747s; **3** James Golding/David Russell, AUS/AUS (Chevrolet), +2.8804s; **4** Matthew Payne/Garth Tander, NZ/AUS (Ford), +3.2745s; **5** Cooper Murray/Craig Lowndes, AUS/AUS (Chevrolet), +3.6492s; **6** Cameron Waters/James Moffat, AUS/AUS (Ford), +4.1244s; **7** Chaz Mostert/Lee Holdsworth, AUS/AUS (Ford), +4.5343s; **8** David Reynolds/Warren Luff, AUS/AUS (Chevrolet), +5.4678s; **9** Bryce Fullwood/Jaylyn Robotham, AUS/AUS (Chevrolet), +5.8272s; **10** Cameron Hill/Cameron Crick, AUS/AUS (Chevrolet), +6.1012s.
Fastest race lap: Brown/Pye, 1m 08.6615s, 100.995mph/162.536km/h.
Pole position: Brown/Pye, 1m 10.2549s, 98.704mph/158.850km/h.

REPCO BATHURST 1000, Mount Panorama, Bathurst, New South Wales, Australia, 13 October. 161 laps of the 3.861-mile/6.213km circuit.
Race 20 (621.553 miles/1000.293km).
1 Brodie Kostecki/Todd Hazelwood, AUS/AUS (Chevrolet), 5h 58m 03.0649s, 104.156mph/167.622km/h; **2** Broc Feeney/Jamie Whincup, AUS/AUS (Chevrolet), +1.3496s; **3** William Brown/Scott Pye, AUS/AUS (Chevrolet), +13.6404s; **4** Cameron Waters/James Moffat, AUS/AUS (Ford), +15.1169s; **5** Chaz Mostert/Lee Holdsworth, AUS/AUS (Ford), +15.8428s; **6** James Golding/David Russell, AUS/AUS (Chevrolet), +17.5856s; **7** Anton De Pasquale/Tony D'Alberto, AUS/AUS (Ford), +26.7384s; **8** Jack Le Brocq/Jayden Ojeda, AUS/AUS (Chevrolet), +29.7233s; **9** Richie Stanaway/Dale Wood, NZ/AUS (Ford), +32.2044s; **10** Cameron Hill/Cameron Crick, AUS/AUS (Chevrolet), +33.6141s.
Fastest race lap: Feeney/Whincup, 2m 07.8610s, 108.696mph/174.930km/h.
Pole position: Kostecki/Hazelwood, 2m 05.5119s, 110.731mph/178.204km/h.

BOOST MOBILE GOLD COAST 500, Surfer's Paradise Street Circuit, Queensland, Australia, 26/27 October. 2 x 85 laps of the 1.842-mile/2.964km circuit.
Race 21 (156.548 miles/251.940km).
1 Cameron Waters, AUS (Ford), 1h 43m 31.6202s, 90.728mph/146.014km/h; **2** Tom Randle, AUS (Ford), +9.4106s; **3** Broc Feeney, AUS (Chevrolet), +10.1958s; **4** Matthew Payne, NZ (Ford), +19.4413s; **5** Brodie Kostecki, AUS (Chevrolet), +24.7529s; **6** David Reynolds, AUS (Chevrolet), +27.5486s; **7** William Brown, AUS (Chevrolet), +28.8230s; **8** Andre Heimgartner, NZ (Chevrolet), +31.2988s; **9** Richie Stanaway, NZ (Ford), +34.7534s; **10** Chaz Mostert, AUS (Ford), +35.3664s.
Fastest race lap: Feeney, 1m 11.1038s, 93.247mph/150.067km/h.
Pole position: Waters, 1m 11.0581s, 93.307mph/150.164km/h.

Race 22 (156.548 miles/251.940km).
1 Brodie Kostecki, AUS (Chevrolet), 1h 48m 41.8982s, 86.412mph/139.067km/h; **2** William Brown, AUS (Chevrolet), +3.4708s; **3** Broc Feeney, AUS (Chevrolet), +3.9006s; **4** Cameron Waters, AUS (Ford), +4.4819s; **5** Tom Randle, AUS (Ford), +20.8036s; **6** Andre Heimgartner, NZ (Chevrolet), +24.4125s; **7** Richie Stanaway, NZ (Ford), +28.4786s; **8** Jack Le Brocq, AUS (Chevrolet), +28.5669s*; **9** Matthew Payne, NZ (Ford), +29.4943s; **10** David Reynolds, AUS (Chevrolet), +31.2683s.
** 5s penalty*
Fastest race lap: Nick Percat, AUS (Chevrolet), 1m 10.9485s, 93.451mph/150.396km/h.
Pole position: Kostecki, 1m 10.3150s, 94.293mph/151.751km/h.

ADELAIDE 500, Adelaide Street Circuit, South Australia, Australia, 16/17 November. 2 x 78 laps of the 2.001-mile/3.220km circuit.
Race 23 (156.064 miles/251.160km).
1 Broc Feeney, AUS (Chevrolet), 1h 47m 07.6592s, 87.408mph/140.669km/h; **2** William Brown, AUS

(Chevrolet), +12.8028s; **3** Cameron Waters, AUS (Ford), +13.7810s; **4** Matthew Payne, NZ (Ford), +14.0294s; **5** Tom Randle, AUS (Ford), +24.9279s; **6** Brodie Kostecki, AUS (Chevrolet), +34.5023s; **7** Andre Heimgartner, NZ (Chevrolet), +41.0023s; **8** James Courtney, AUS (Ford), +42.0861s; **9** Anton De Pasquale, AUS (Ford), +43.0371s; **10** Ryan Wood, NZ (Ford), +49.0355s.
Fastest race lap: Brown, 1m 20.7939s, 89.151mph/143.476km/h.
Pole position: Waters, 1m 19.9628s, 90.078mph/144.967km/h.

Race 24 (156.064 miles/251.160km).
1 William Brown, AUS (Chevrolet), 1h 50m 34.3754s, 84.684mph/136.286km/h; **2** Chaz Mostert, AUS (Ford), +9.1234s; **3** Tom Randle, AUS (Ford), +9.7295s; **4** Will Davison, AUS (Ford), +9.9663s; **5** Nick Percat, AUS (Chevrolet), +10.2366s; **6** Brodie Kostecki, AUS (Chevrolet), +11.3902s; **7** Broc Feeney, AUS (Chevrolet), +11.5065s; **8** James Golding, AUS (Chevrolet), +12.1660s; **9** Andre Heimgartner, NZ (Chevrolet), +13.3298s; **10** Cameron Waters, AUS (Ford), +23.3590s.
Fastest race lap: Brown, 1m 20.1915s, 89.821mph/144.553km/h.
Pole position: Feeney, 1m 19.9721s, 90.068mph/144.950km/h.

Final championship points
Drivers
1 Brodie Kostecki, AUS, 2888; **2** Shane van Gisbergen, NZ, 2565; **3** Broc Feeney, AUS, 2441; **4** Chaz Mostert, AUS, 2287; **5** William Brown, AUS, 2264; **6** Cameron Waters, AUS, 2099; **7** Andre Heimgartner, NZ, 2016; **8** Anton De Pasquale, AUS, 1818; **9** David Reynolds, AUS, 1806; **10** Will Davison, AUS, 1786; **11** Bryce Fullwood, AUS, 1722; **12** Jack Le Brocq, AUS, 1715; **13** Tom Randle, AUS, 1700; **14** Matthew Payne, NZ, 1673; **15** Mark Winterbottom, AUS, 1579; **16** James Golding, AUS, 1569; **17** James Courtney, AUS, 1568; **18** Scott Pye, AUS, 1524; **19** Tim Slade, AUS, 1497; **20** Nick Percat, AUS, 1230.

Teams
1 Coca-Cola Racing by Erebus, 5152; **2** Red Bull Ampol Racing, 4976; **3** Brad Jones Racing, 3708; **4** Shell V-Power Racing Team, 3694; **5** Tickford Racing, 3667.

FIA TCR World Tour

FIA TCR WORLD TOUR, Autodromo di Vallelunga, Campagnano di Roma, Italy, 20/21 April. 15 and 17 laps of the 2.538-mile/4.085km circuit.
Round 1 (38.075 miles/61.275km).
1 Norbert Michelisz, H (Hyundai Elantra N TCR), 25m 41.522s, 88.917mph/143.098km/h; **2** Yann Ehrlacher, F (Lynk & Co 03 FL TCR), +1.758s; **3** Esteban Guerrieri, RA (Honda Civic Type R FL5 TCR), +2.911s; **4** Mikel Azcona, E (Hyundai Elantra N TCR), +7.809s; **5** Marco Butti, I (Honda Civic Type R FL5 TCR), +11.962s*; **6** Thed Björk, S (Lynk & Co 03 FL TCR), +12.217s; **7** Santiago Urrutia, U (Lynk & Co 03 FL TCR), +13.142s; **8** Ma Qinghua, CHN (Lynk & Co 03 FL TCR), +13.812s; **9** John Filippi, F (Audi RS 3 LMS II TCR), +14.480s; **10** Néstor Girolami, RA (Hyundai Elantra N TCR), +26.940s.
** 5s penalty*
Fastest race lap: Guerrieri, 1m 41.682s, 89.867mph/144.627km/h.
Pole position: Michelisz, 1m 39.249s, 92.070mph/148.172km/h.

Round 2 (43.151 miles/69.445km).
1 Néstor Girolami, RA (Hyundai Elantra N TCR), 35m 17.984s, 73.345mph/118.037km/h; **2** Santiago Urrutia, U (Lynk & Co 03 FL TCR), +3.237s; **3** Marco Butti, I (Honda Civic Type R FL5 TCR), +11.683s; **4** Mikel Azcona, E (Hyundai Elantra N TCR), +12.548s; **5** Thed Björk, S (Lynk & Co 03 FL TCR), +13.668s; **6** Norbert Michelisz, H (Hyundai Elantra N TCR), +14.245s; **7** John Filippi, F (Audi RS 3 LMS II TCR), +16.508s; **8** Esteban Guerrieri, RA (Honda Civic Type R FL5 TCR), +17.034s*; **9** Ma Qinghua, CHN (Lynk & Co 03 FL TCR), +17.086s; **10** Sandro Pelatti, I (Audi RS 3 LMS II TCR), +32.100s.
** 5s penalty*
Fastest race lap: Girolami, 1m 40.174s, 91.220mph/146.804km/h.
Pole position: Girolami.

FIA TCR WORLD TOUR, Circuit International Automobile Moulay El Hassan, Agdal, Marrakesh, Morocco, 4 May. 2 x 36 laps of the 1.057-mile/1.701km circuit.
Round 3 (38.050 miles/61.236km).
1 Yann Ehrlacher, F (Lynk & Co 03 FL TCR), 30m 56.804s, 73.772mph/118.725km/h; **2** Santiago Urrutia, U (Lynk & Co 03 FL TCR), +0.389s; **3** Norbert Michelisz, H (Hyundai Elantra N TCR), +1.086s; **4** Néstor Girolami, RA (Hyundai Elantra N TCR), +2.903s; **5** Mikel Azcona, E (Hyundai Elantra N TCR), +4.812s; **6** John Filippi, F (Audi RS 3 LMS II TCR), +6.141s; **7** Ma Qinghua, CHN (Lynk & Co 03 FL TCR), +10.979s; **8** Thed Björk, S (Lynk & Co 03 FL TCR), +12.814s*; **9** Esteban Guerrieri, RA (Honda Civic Type R FL5 TCR), +13.617s; **10** Sami Taoufik, MA (Audi RS 3 LMS II TCR), +14.583s.
** 5s penalty for causing a collision*
Fastest race lap: Marco Butti, I (Honda Civic Type R FL5 TCR), 50.804s, 74.896mph/120.533km/h.
Pole position: Ehrlacher, 49.641s, 76.650mph/123.357km/h.

Round 4 (38.050 miles/61.236km).
1 Ma Qinghua, CHN (Lynk & Co 03 FL TCR), 31m 00.756s, 73.615mph/118.473km/h; **2** Esteban Guerrieri, RA (Honda Civic Type R FL5 TCR), +2.094s; **3** Dušan Borković, SRB (Honda Civic Type R FL5 TCR), +2.814s; **4** John Filippi, F (Audi RS 3 LMS II TCR), +5.949s; **5** Néstor Girolami, RA (Hyundai Elantra N TCR), +6.400s; **6** Sami Taoufik, MA (Audi RS 3 LMS II TCR), +7.894s; **7** Marco Butti, I (Honda Civic Type R FL5 TCR), +9.583s; **8** Santiago Urrutia, U (Lynk & Co 03 FL TCR), +14.678s; **9** Thed Björk, S (Lynk & Co 03 FL TCR), +15.561s; **10** Mehdi Bennani, MA (Cupra León VZ TCR), +26.077s.
Fastest race lap: Ma, 50.613s, 75.178mph/120.988km/h.
Pole position: Ma.

FIA TCR WORLD TOUR, Mid-Ohio Sports Car Course, Lexington, Ohio, USA, 8 June. 2 x 17 laps of the 2.258-mile/3.634km circuit.
Round 5 (38.386 miles/61.776km).
1 Thed Björk, S (Lynk & Co 03 FL TCR), 25m 39.406s, 89.768mph/144.467km/h; **2** Norbert Michelisz, H (Hyundai Elantra N TCR), +1.339s; **3** Mikel Azcona, E (Hyundai Elantra N TCR), +2.180s; **4** Néstor Girolami, RA (Hyundai Elantra N TCR), +2.953s; **5** Esteban Guerrieri, RA (Honda Civic Type R FL5 TCR), +3.678s; **6** Yann Ehrlacher, F (Lynk & Co 03 FL TCR), +10.990s; **7** Ma Qinghua, CHN (Lynk & Co 03 FL TCR), +23.779s; **8** John Filippi, F (Audi RS 3 LMS II TCR), +33.029s; **9** Dušan Borković, SRB (Honda Civic Type R FL5 TCR), +33.604s; **10** Mark Wilkins, CDN (Hyundai Elantra N TCR), +33.908s.
Disqualified: Santiago Urrutia, U, finished 7th in 26m 02.56s.
Fastest race lap: Azcona, 1m 29.485s, 90.839mph/146.192km/h.
Pole position: Azcona, 1m 27.178s, 93.243mph/150.061km/h.

Round 6 (38.386 miles/61.776km).
1 Yann Ehrlacher, F (Lynk & Co 03 FL TCR), 25m 26.707s, 90.514mph/145.669km/h; **2** Ma Qinghua, CHN (Lynk & Co 03 FL TCR), +0.338s; **3** Esteban Guerrieri, RA (Honda Civic Type R FL5 TCR), +1.503s; **4** Mikel Azcona, E (Hyundai Elantra N TCR), +1.949s; **5** Norbert Michelisz, H (Hyundai Elantra N TCR), +3.688s; **6** Thed Björk, S (Lynk & Co 03 FL TCR), +5.921s*; **7** Dušan Borković, SRB (Honda Civic Type R FL5 TCR), +7.466s; **8** Néstor Girolami, RA (Hyundai Elantra N TCR), +8.653s; **9** John Filippi, F (Audi RS 3 LMS II TCR), +12.816s; **10** Marco Butti, I (Honda Civic Type R FL5 TCR), +16.673s**.
** 5s penalty for pushing Butti and gaining an advantage*
*** 5s penalty for pushing Urrutia and gaining an advantage*
Disqualified: Santiago Urrutia, U, finished 8th in 25m 34.739s (caused a collision with Guerrieri after the chequered flag was given)
Fastest race lap: Michelisz, 1m 28.327s, 92.030mph/148.109km/h.
Pole position: Butti, 1m 29.373s, 90.953mph/146.375km/h.

FIA TCR WORLD TOUR, Autodromo José Carlos Pace, Interlagos, São Paulo, Brazil, 21 July. 14 and 18 laps of the 2.677-mile/4.309km circuit.
Round 7 (37.485 miles/60.326km).
1 Esteban Guerrieri, RA (Honda Civic Type R FL5 TCR), 26m 50.568s, 83.787mph/134.842km/h; **2** Santiago Urrutia, U (Lynk & Co 03 FL TCR), +10.040s; **3** Marco Butti, I (Honda Civic Type R FL5 TCR), +10.860s; **4** Yann Ehrlacher, F (Lynk & Co 03 FL TCR), +11.594s; **5** Thed Björk, S (Lynk & Co 03 FL TCR), +12.605s; **6** Norbert Michelisz, H (Hyundai Elantra N TCR), +13.198s; **7** Ma Qinghua, CHN (Lynk & Co 03 FL TCR), +14.662s; **8** Mikel Azcona, E (Hyundai Elantra N TCR), +14.842s; **9** Dušan Borković, SRB (Honda Civic Type R FL5 TCR), +16.783s; **10** Rafael Suzuki, BR (Peugeot 308 TCR), +21.677s.
Fastest race lap: Guerrieri, 1m 42.950s, 93.627mph/150.678km/h.
Pole position: Urrutia, 1m 41.840s, 94.648mph/152.321km/h.

Round 8 (48.195 miles/77.562km).
1 Norbert Michelisz, H (Hyundai Elantra N TCR), 32m 24.174s, 89.241mph/143.620km/h; **2** Thed Björk, S (Lynk & Co 03 FL TCR), +2.618s; **3** Ma Qinghua, CHN (Lynk & Co 03 FL TCR), +8.698s; **4** Esteban Guerrieri, RA (Honda Civic Type R FL5 TCR), +8.950s; **5** Santiago Urrutia, U (Lynk & Co 03 FL TCR), +10.224s*; **6** Marco Butti, I (Honda Civic Type R FL5 TCR), +14.210s; **7** John Filippi, F (Audi RS 3 LMS II TCR), +15.006s; **8** Rafael Suzuki, BR (Peugeot 308 TCR), +19.601s; **9** Mikel Azcona, E (Hyundai Elantra N TCR), +22.168s; **10** Raphael Reis, BR (Cupra León VZ TCR), +28.569s.
** 5s penalty for overtaking off track limits*
Fastest race lap: Yann Ehrlacher, F (Lynk & Co 03 FL TCR), 1m 43.248s, 93.357mph/150.244km/h.
Pole position: Michelisz.

FIA TCR WORLD TOUR, Autódromo Víctor Borrat Fabini, El Pinar, Uruguay, 4 August. 17 and 22 laps of the 1.942-mile/3.125km circuit.
Round 9 (33.010 miles/53.125km).
1 Yann Ehrlacher, F (Lynk & Co 03 FL TCR), 27m 31.951s, 71.937mph/115.772km/h; **2** Mikel Azcona, E (Hyundai Elantra N TCR), +0.687s; **3** Thed Björk, S (Lynk & Co 03 FL TCR), +2.639s; **4** Norbert Michelisz, H (Hyundai Elantra N TCR), +10.638s; **5** Néstor Girolami, RA (Hyundai Elantra N TCR), +10.734s; **6** Esteban Guerrieri, RA (Honda Civic Type R FL5 TCR), +10.979s; **7** Santiago Urrutia, U (Lynk & Co 03 FL TCR), +11.255s*; **8** Pedro Cardoso, BR (Peugeot 308 TCR), +12.927s; **9** Juan Ángel Rosso, RA (Toyota Corolla GRS TCR), +13.867s; **10** Matías Rossi, RA (Toyota Corolla GRS TCR), +14.599s.
** 5s penalty for causing a collision with Girolami*
Fastest race lap: Ehrlacher, 1m 20.699s, 86.623mph/139.406km/h.
Pole position: Ehrlacher, 1m 20.227s, 87.133mph/140.227km/h.

Round 10 (42.719 miles/68.750km).
1 Thed Björk, S (Lynk & Co 03 FL TCR), 32m 07.780s, 79.775mph/128.386km/h; **2** Pedro Cardoso, BR (Peugeot 308 TCR), +1.281s; **3** Esteban Guerrieri, RA (Honda Civic Type R FL5 TCR), +4.410s; **4** Norbert Michelisz, H (Hyundai Elantra N TCR), +10.790s; **5** Mikel Azcona, E (Hyundai Elantra N TCR), +11.255s; **6** Dušan Borković, SRB (Honda Civic Type R FL5 TCR), +12.488s; **7** Ma Qinghua, CHN (Lynk & Co 03 FL TCR), +12.797s; **8** Néstor Girolami, RA (Hyundai Elantra N TCR), +17.125s; **9** John Filippi, F (Audi RS 3 LMS II TCR), +18.394s; **10** Marco Butti, I (Honda Civic Type R FL5 TCR), +19.256s.
Disqualified: Santiago Urrutia, U, finished 3rd in 32m 09.744s (then 5s penalty added for causing a collision with Guerrieri; disqualified for a technical infringement)
Fastest race lap: Yann Ehrlacher, F (Lynk & Co 03 FL TCR), 1m 21.088s, 86.207mph/138.738km/h.
Pole position: Ma.

FIA TCR WORLD TOUR, Zhuzhou International Circuit, Hunan, China, 19/20 October. 2 x 18 laps of the 2.345-mile/3.774km circuit.
Round 11 (42.211 miles/67.932km).
1 Mikel Azcona, E (Hyundai Elantra N TCR), 40m 34.472s, 62.419mph/100.455km/h; **2** Esteban Guerrieri, RA (Honda Civic Type R FL5 TCR), +7.062s; **3** Thed Björk, S (Lynk & Co 03 FL TCR), +8.441s; **4** Yann Ehrlacher, F (Lynk & Co 03 FL TCR), +9.568s; **5** Santiago Urrutia, U (Lynk & Co 03 FL TCR), +11.629s; **6** Marco Butti, I (Honda Civic Type R FL5 TCR), +13.994s; **7** Norbert Michelisz, H (Hyundai Elantra N TCR), +18.821s; **8** Néstor Girolami, RA (Hyundai Elantra N TCR), +19.825s; **9** Rob Huff, GB (Audi RS 3 LMS II TCR), +22.284s; **10** Jason Zhang, CHN (Lynk & Co 03 FL TCR), +22.464s.
Fastest race lap: Björk, 1m 56.030s, 72.758mph/117.093km/h.
Pole position: Urrutia, 1m 44.684s, 80.644mph/129.784km/h.

Round 12 (42.211 miles/67.932km).
1 Ma Qinghua, CHN (Lynk & Co 03 FL TCR), 35m 40.167s, 71.003mph/114.269km/h; **2** Néstor Girolami, RA (Hyundai Elantra N TCR), +0.378s; **3** Yann Ehrlacher, F (Lynk & Co 03 FL TCR), +4.184s; **4** Santiago Urrutia, U (Lynk & Co 03 FL TCR), +6.987s; **5** Esteban Guerrieri, RA (Honda Civic Type R FL5 TCR), +7.744s; **6** Marco Butti, I (Honda Civic Type R FL5 TCR), +8.026s; **7** Rob Huff, GB (Audi RS 3 LMS II TCR), +8.958s; **8** Norbert Michelisz, H (Hyundai Elantra N TCR), +12.230s; **9** Mikel Azcona, E (Hyundai Elantra N TCR), +12.617s; **10** Thed Björk, S (Lynk & Co 03 FL TCR), +13.085s.
Fastest race lap: Ma, 1m 45.118s, 80.311mph/129.249km/h.
Pole position: Girolami.

FIA TCR WORLD TOUR, Circuito da Guia, Macau, 16/17 November. 11 and 12 laps of the 3.803-mile/6.120km circuit.
Round 13 (41.831 miles/67.320km).
1 Thed Björk, S (Lynk & Co 03 FL TCR), 1h 04m 29.809s, 38.914mph/62.626km/h; **2** Norbert Michelisz, H (Hyundai Elantra N TCR), +1.874s; **3** Mikel Azcona, E (Hyundai Elantra N TCR), +2.529s; **4** Yann Ehrlacher, F (Lynk & Co 03 FL TCR), +3.442s; **5** Néstor Girolami, RA (Hyundai Elantra N TCR), +7.016s; **6** Rob Huff, GB (Audi RS 3 LMS II TCR), +7.807s; **7** Dušan Borković, SRB (Honda Civic Type R FL5 TCR), +29.074s; **8** Martin Cao, CHN (Hyundai Elantra N TCR), +33.002s; **9** Jason Zhang, CHN (Lynk & Co 03 FL TCR), +35.105s; **10** David Zhu, CHN (Lynk & Co 03 TCR), +40.957s.
Fastest race lap: Azcona, 2m 31.590s, 90.309mph/145.339km/h.
Pole position: Björk, 2m 29.816s, 91.379mph/147.060km/h.

Round 14 (45.634 miles/73.440km).
1 Dušan Borković, SRB (Honda Civic Type R FL5 TCR), 39m 14.582s, 69.770mph/112.284km/h; **2** Esteban Guerrieri, RA (Honda Civic Type R FL5 TCR), +3.568s; **3** Marco Butti, I (Honda Civic Type R FL5 TCR), +4.108s; **4** Ma Qinghua, CHN (Lynk & Co 03 FL TCR), +6.546s; **5** Norbert Michelisz, H (Hyundai Elantra N TCR), +11.007s; **6** Mikel Azcona, E (Hyundai Elantra N TCR), +11.314s; **7** Néstor Girolami, RA (Hyundai Elantra N TCR), +11.486s; **8** Thed Björk, S (Lynk & Co 03 FL TCR), +11.975s; **9** Xinzhe Xie, CHN (Honda Civic Type R FL5 TCR), +12.484s; **10** Yann Ehrlacher, F (Lynk & Co 03 FL TCR), +14.372s.
Fastest race lap: Borković, 2m 44.801s, 83.070mph/133.688km/h.
Pole position: Yan.

Final championship points.
Drivers
1 Norbert Michelisz, H, 323; **2** Thed Björk, S, 312; **3** Mikel Azcona, E, 295; **4** Esteban Guerrieri, RA, 291; **5** Yann Ehrlacher, F, 287; **6** Néstor Girolami, RA, 238; **7** Santiago Urrutia, U, 220; **8** Ma Qinghua, CHN, 214; **9** Marco Butti, I, 174; **10** Dušan Borković, SRB, 134; **11** John Filippi, F, 113; **12** Rob Huff, GB, 40; **13** Pedro Cardoso, BR, 38; **14** Martin Cao, CHN, 25; **15** Sami Taoufik, MA, 24; **16** Rafael Suzuki, BR, 24; **17** Juan Ángel Rosso, RA, 20; **18** Jason Zhang, CHN, 18; **19** David Zhu, CHN, 15; **20** Mehdi Bennani, MA, 14.

Teams
1 Lynk & Co Cyan Racing, 735; **2** BRC Hyundai N Squadra Corse, 672; **3** GOAT Racing, 521.

German Touring Car Championship (DTM)

GERMAN TOURING CAR CHAMPIONSHIP (DTM), Motorsport Arena Oschersleben, Germany, 27/28 April. Round 1. 39 and 40 laps of the 2.279-mile/3.667km circuit.
Race 1 (88.864 miles/143.013km).
1 Jack Aitken, GB (Ferrari 296 GT3), 1h 01m 33.741s, 86.609mph/139.384km/h; **2** Mirko Bortolotti, I (Lamborghini Huracán GT3 Evo2), +1.159s; **3** Ricardo Feller, CH (Audi R8 LMS Evo II), +1.595s; **4** Sheldon van der Linde, ZA (BMW M4 GT3), +1.982s; **5** Luca Stolz, D (Mercedes AMG GT3 Evo), +3.744s; **6** Lucas Auer, A (Mercedes AMG GT3 Evo), +4.228s; **7** René Rast, D (BMW M4 GT3), +4.576s; **8** Arjun Maini, IND (Mercedes AMG GT3 Evo), +5.025s; **9** Thierry Vermeulen, NL (Ferrari 296 GT3), +5.177s; **10** Thomas Preining, A (Porsche 911 GT3 R), +5.928s.
Fastest race lap: Feller, 1m 23.099s, 98.712mph/158.861km/h.
Pole position: Aitken, 1m 21.465s, 100.692mph/162.048km/h.

Race 2 (91.143 miles/146.680km).
1 Luca Engstler, D (Lamborghini Huracán GT3 Evo2), 1h 01m 59.094s, 88.224mph/141.983km/h; **2** Maro Engel, D (Mercedes AMG GT3 Evo), +0.300s; **3** Luca Stolz, D (Mercedes AMG GT3 Evo), +18.325s; **4** Arjun Maini, IND (Mercedes AMG GT3 Evo), +20.554s; **5** Kelvin van der Linde, ZA (Audi R8 LMS Evo II), +32.981s; **6** Sheldon van der Linde, ZA (BMW M4 GT3), +35.217s; **7** René Rast, D (BMW M4 GT3), +39.364s; **8** Christian Engelhart, D (Lamborghini Huracán GT3 Evo2), +39.874s; **9** Ricardo Feller, CH (Audi R8 LMS Evo II), +43.730s; **10** Marco Wittmann, D (BMW M4 GT3), +53.667s.
Fastest race lap Engel, 1m 23.245s, 98.539mph/158.582km/h.
Pole position: Mirko Bortolotti, I (Lamborghini Huracán GT3 Evo2), 1m 21.800s, 100.279mph/161.384km/h.

GERMAN TOURING CAR CHAMPIONSHIP (DTM), EuroSpeedway Lausitz, Klettwitz, Dresden, Germany, 25/26 May. Round 2. 38 and 42 laps of the 2.161-mile/3.478km circuit.
Race 1 (82.123 miles/132.164km).
1 Kelvin van der Linde, ZA (Audi R8 LMS Evo II), 1h 34m 55.081s, 51.912mph/83.544km/h; **2** Maro Engel, D (Mercedes AMG GT3 Evo), +2.547s; **3** Thomas Preining, A (Porsche 911 GT3 R), +11.140s; **4** Lucas Auer, A (Mercedes AMG GT3 Evo), +12.344s; **5** Ricardo Feller, CH (Audi R8 LMS Evo II), +14.590s; **6** Sheldon van der Linde, ZA (BMW M4 GT3), +23.396s; **7** Arjun Maini, IND (Mercedes AMG GT3 Evo), +23.849s; **8** Nicki Thiim, DK (Lamborghini Huracán GT3 Evo2), +28.080s; **9** Christian Engelhart, D (Lamborghini Huracán GT3 Evo2), +28.422s; **10** Luca Stolz, D (Mercedes AMG GT3 Evo), +28.462s.
Fastest race lap: van der Linde, 1m 24.399s, 92.182mph/148.352km/h.
Pole position: van der Linde, 1m 20.706s, 96.400mph/155.141km/h.

Race 2 (90.767 miles/146.076km).
1 Thomas Preining, A (Porsche 911 GT3 R), 1h 01m 51.739s, 88.035mph/141.678km/h; **2** Kelvin van der Linde, ZA (Audi R8 LMS Evo II), +1.441s; **3** Ricardo Feller, CH (Audi R8 LMS Evo II), +3.083s; **4** Mirko Bortolotti, I (Lamborghini Huracán GT3 Evo2), +3.721s; **5** Luca Engstler, D (Lamborghini Huracán GT3 Evo2), +7.501s; **6** René Rast, D (BMW M4 GT3), +8.604s; **7** Maro Engel, D (Mercedes AMG GT3 Evo), +10.639s; **8** Sheldon van der Linde, ZA (BMW M4 GT3), +11.504s; **9** Marco Wittmann, D (BMW M4

GT3), +13.496s; **10** Lucas Auer, A (Mercedes AMG GT3 Evo), +14.143s.
Fastest race lap: van der Linde, 1m 21.562s, 95.388mph/153.513km/h.
Pole position: Preining, 1m 20.858s, 96.219mph/154.849km/h.

GERMAN TOURING CAR CHAMPIONSHIP (DTM), Circuit Park Zandvoort, Netherlands, 8/9 June. Round 3. 39 and 38 laps of the 2.646-mile/4.259km circuit.
Race 1 (103.210 miles/166.101km).
1 Jack Aitken, GB (Ferrari 296 GT3), 1h 02m 25.078s, 99.212mph/159.667km/h; **2** René Rast, D (BMW M4 GT3), +2.924s; **3** Arjun Maini, IND (Mercedes AMG GT3 Evo), +5.932s; **4** Clemens Schmid, A (McLaren 720S GT3 Evo), +10.197s; **5** Lucas Auer, A (Mercedes AMG GT3 Evo), +11.492s; **6** Sheldon van der Linde, ZA (BMW M4 GT3), +13.791s; **7** Marco Wittmann, D (BMW M4 GT3), +14.506s; **8** Ricardo Feller, CH (Audi R8 LMS Evo II), +27.237s; **9** Mirko Bortolotti, I (Lamborghini Huracán GT3 Evo2), +27.630s; **10** Luca Stolz, D (Mercedes AMG GT3 Evo), +28.180s.
Fastest race lap: Ben Dörr, D (McLaren 720S GT3 Evo), 1m 33.614s, 101.770mph/163.783km/h.
Pole position: Aitken, 1m 31.762s, 103.824mph/167.089km/h.

Race 2 (100.564 miles/161.842km).
1 Marco Wittmann, D (BMW M4 GT3), 1h 15m 41.704s, 79.712mph/128.285km/h; **2** Mirko Bortolotti, I (Lamborghini Huracán GT3 Evo2), +7.239s; **3** Kelvin van der Linde, ZA (Audi R8 LMS Evo II), +7.373s; **4** Thierry Vermeulen, NL (Ferrari 296 GT3), +7.592s; **5** Luca Stolz, D (Mercedes AMG GT3 Evo), +8.001s; **6** Arjun Maini, IND (Mercedes AMG GT3 Evo), +8.292s; **7** René Rast, D (BMW M4 GT3), +8.601s; **8** Sheldon van der Linde, ZA (BMW M4 GT3), +8.753s; **9** Maximilian Paul, D (Lamborghini Huracán GT3 Evo2), +9.347s; **10** Thomas Preining, A (Porsche 911 GT3 R), +9.977s.
Fastest race lap: Nicki Thiim, DK (Lamborghini Huracán GT3 Evo2), 1m 34.609s, 100.700mph/162.061km/h.
Pole position: Paul, 1m 32.780s, 102.685mph/165.255km/h.

GERMAN TOURING CAR CHAMPIONSHIP (DTM), Norisring, Nürnberg (Nuremberg), Germany, 6/7 July. Round 4. 2 x 69 laps of the 1.343-mile/2.162km circuit.
Race 1 (92.695 miles/149.178km).
1 René Rast, D (BMW M4 GT3), 1h 01m 35.627s, 90.296mph/145.318km/h; **2** Franck Perera, F (Lamborghini Huracán GT3 Evo2), +2.272s; **3** Luca Engstler, D (Lamborghini Huracán GT3 Evo2), +37.075s; **4** Nicki Thiim, DK (Lamborghini Huracán GT3 Evo2), +44.111s; **5** Mirko Bortolotti, I (Lamborghini Huracán GT3 Evo2), +44.479s; **6** Kelvin van der Linde, ZA (Audi R8 LMS Evo II), +44.956s; **7** Sheldon van der Linde, ZA (BMW M4 GT3), +47.506s; **8** Maro Engel, D (Mercedes AMG GT3 Evo), +50.850s; **9** Jack Aitken, GB (Ferrari 296 GT3), +53.488s; **10** Maximilian Paul, D (Lamborghini Huracán GT3 Evo2), +53.749s.
Fastest race lap: Paul, 49.632s, 97.442mph/156.818km/h.
Pole position: Aitken, 48.965s, 98.770mph/158.954km/h.

Race 2 (92.695 miles/149.178km).
1 Nicki Thiim, DK (Lamborghini Huracán GT3 Evo2), 1h 01m 07.550s, 90.988mph/146.430km/h; **2** Maro Engel, D (Mercedes AMG GT3 Evo), +0.777s; **3** Mirko Bortolotti, I (Lamborghini Huracán GT3 Evo2), +1.880s; **4** Arjun Maini, IND (Mercedes AMG GT3 Evo), +3.098s; **5** René Rast, D (BMW M4 GT3), +4.023s; **6** Thomas Preining, A (Porsche 911 GT3 R), +5.211s; **7** Luca Stolz, D (Mercedes AMG GT3 Evo), +5.661s; **8** Ayhancan Guven, TR (Porsche 911 GT3 R), +8.157s; **9** Kelvin van der Linde, ZA (Audi R8 LMS Evo II), +8.489s; **10** Lucas Auer, A (Mercedes AMG GT3 Evo), +9.575s.
Fastest race lap: Thiim, 49.141s, 98.416mph/158.385km/h.
Pole position: Thiim, 48.758s, 99.189mph/159.629km/h.

GERMAN TOURING CAR CHAMPIONSHIP (DTM), Nürburgring, Nürburg/Eifel, Germany, 17/18 August. Round 5. 37 and 41 laps of the 2.255-mile/3.629km circuit.
Race 1 (83.433 miles/134.273km).
1 Kelvin van der Linde, ZA (Audi R8 LMS Evo II), 1h 02m 59.258s, 79.476mph/127.904km/h; **2** Mirko Bortolotti, I (Lamborghini Huracán GT3 Evo2), +15.232s; **3** Maro Engel, D (Mercedes AMG GT3 Evo), +16.377s; **4** Lucas Auer, A (Mercedes AMG GT3 Evo), +28.491s; **5** Jack Aitken, GB (Ferrari 296 GT3), +30.474s; **6** Marco Wittmann, D (BMW M4 GT3), +32.417s; **7** Thomas Preining, A (Porsche 911 GT3 R), +36.799s; **8** Nicki Thiim, DK (Lamborghini Huracán GT3 Evo2), +39.961s; **9** Ricardo Feller, CH (Audi R8 LMS Evo II), +43.820s; **10** Arjun Maini, IND (Mercedes AMG GT3 Evo), +44.262s.
Fastest race lap: van der Linde, 1m 38.011s, 82.826mph/133.295km/h.
Pole position: van der Linde, 1m 25.350s, 95.112mph/153.069km/h.

Race 2 (92.453 miles/148.789km).
1 Sheldon van der Linde, ZA (BMW M4 GT3), 1h 02m 42.337s, 88.464mph/142.369km/h; **2** Maro Engel, D (Mercedes AMG GT3 Evo), +3.256s; **3** Marco Wittmann, D (BMW M4 GT3), +5.813s; **4** Kelvin van der Linde, ZA (Audi R8 LMS Evo II), +12.003s; **5** Ayhancan Guven, TR (Porsche 911 GT3 R), +12.714s; **6** Thierry Vermeulen, NL (Ferrari 296 GT3), +14.742s; **7** Thomas Preining, A (Porsche 911 GT3 R), +14.756s*; **8** Ricardo Feller, CH (Audi R8 LMS Evo II), +17.955s; **9** Mirko Bortolotti, I (Lamborghini Huracán GT3 Evo2), +20.361s; **10** Franck Perera, F (Lamborghini Huracán GT3 Evo2), +21.729s.
** 0.5s penalty to replace change of positions*
Fastest race lap: Guven, 1m 26.696s, 93.636mph/150.692km/h.
Pole position: Engel, 1m 33.750s, 86.590mph/139.354km/h.

GERMAN TOURING CAR CHAMPIONSHIP (DTM), Sachsenring, Oberlungwitz, Germany, 7/8 September. Round 6. 46 and 44 laps of the 2.265-mile/3.645km circuit.
Race 1 (104.185 miles/167.670km).
1 Jack Aitken, GB (Ferrari 296 GT3), 1h 02m 22.683s, 100.213mph/161.278km/h; **2** Mirko Bortolotti, I (Lamborghini Huracán GT3 Evo2), +1.878s; **3** Maro Engel, D (Mercedes AMG GT3 Evo), +3.174s; **4** Luca Stolz, D (Mercedes AMG GT3 Evo), +4.717s; **5** Arjun Maini, IND (Mercedes AMG GT3 Evo), +10.843s; **6** Thomas Preining, A (Porsche 911 GT3 R), +12.217s; **7** René Rast, D (BMW M4 GT3), +14.210s; **8** Kelvin van der Linde, ZA (Audi R8 LMS Evo II), +23.280s; **9** Sheldon van der Linde, ZA (BMW M4 GT3), +23.855s; **10** Jordan Pepper, ZA (Lamborghini Huracán GT3 Evo2), +28.606s.
Fastest race lap: Thierry Vermeulen, NL (Ferrari 296 GT3), 1m 19.500s, 102.561mph/165.057km/h.
Pole position: Aitken, 1m 17.288s, 105.497mph/169.781km/h.

Race 2 (99.656 miles/160.380km).
1 Luca Stolz, D (Mercedes AMG GT3 Evo), 1h 02m 22.057s, 95.872mph/154.292km/h; **2** Kelvin van der Linde, ZA (Audi R8 LMS Evo II), +0.769s; **3** Thierry Vermeulen, NL (Ferrari 296 GT3), +1.315s; **4** Thomas Preining, A (Porsche 911 GT3 R), +2.246s; **5** Maro Engel, D (Mercedes AMG GT3 Evo), +4.422s; **6** Jack Aitken, GB (Ferrari 296 GT3), +8.141s; **7** Mirko Bortolotti, I (Lamborghini Huracán GT3 Evo2), +12.038s; **8** Sheldon van der Linde, ZA (BMW M4 GT3), +13.001s; **9** René Rast, D (BMW M4 GT3), +17.334s; **10** Nicki Thiim, DK (Lamborghini Huracán GT3 Evo2), +18.424s.
Fastest race lap: Vermeulen, 1m 19.082s, 103.104mph/165.929km/h.
Pole position: Vermeulen, 1m 17.311s, 105.465mph/169.730km/h.

GERMAN TOURING CAR CHAMPIONSHIP (DTM), Red Bull Ring, Spielberg, Austria, 28/29 September. Round 7. 38 and 39 laps of the 2.683-mile/4.318km circuit.
Race 1 (101.957 miles/164.084km).
1 Mirko Bortolotti, I (Lamborghini Huracán GT3 Evo2), 1h 01m 36.938s, 99.284mph/159.782km/h; **2** Maro Engel, D (Mercedes AMG GT3 Evo), +1.161s; **3** Arjun Maini, IND (Mercedes AMG GT3 Evo), +8.287s; **4** Luca Stolz, D (Mercedes AMG GT3 Evo), +20.609s; **5** Ayhancan Guven, TR (Porsche 911 GT3 R), +23.641s; **6** Maximilian Paul, D (Lamborghini Huracán GT3 Evo2), +25.181s; **7** Lucas Auer, A (Mercedes AMG GT3 Evo), +27.907s; **8** Kelvin van der Linde, ZA (Audi R8 LMS Evo II), +34.697s; **9** René Rast, D (BMW M4 GT3), +35.446s; **10** Ricardo Feller, CH (Audi R8 LMS Evo II), +36.214s.
Fastest race lap: Engel, 1m 29.929s, 107.408mph/172.856km/h.
Pole position: Maini, 1m 30.128s, 107.171mph/172.475km/h.

Race 2 (104.640 miles/168.402km).
1 René Rast, D (BMW M4 GT3), 1h 01m 30.330s, 102.079mph/164.280km/h; **2** Thomas Preining, A (Porsche 911 GT3 R), +0.668s; **3** Arjun Maini, IND (Mercedes AMG GT3 Evo), +10.367s; **4** Mirko Bortolotti, I (Lamborghini Huracán GT3 Evo2), +14.773s; **5** Kelvin van der Linde, ZA (Audi R8 LMS Evo II), +15.877s; **6** Sheldon van der Linde, ZA (BMW M4 GT3), +17.359s; **7** Ayhancan Guven, TR (Porsche 911 GT3 R), +17.939s; **8** Maro Engel, D (Mercedes AMG GT3 Evo), +24.194s; **9** Franck Perera, F (Lamborghini Huracán GT3 Evo2), +28.612s; **10** Jack Aitken, GB (Ferrari 296 GT3), +29.433s.
Fastest race lap: Preining, 1m 28.665s, 108.939mph/175.321km/h.
Pole position: Bortolotti, 1m 27.921s, 109.861mph/176.804km/h.

GERMAN TOURING CAR CHAMPIONSHIP (DTM), Hockenheimring Grand Prix Circuit, Heidelberg, Germany, 19/20 October. Round 8. 2 x 37 laps of the 2.842-mile/4.574km circuit.
Race 1 (105.160 miles/169.238km).
1 Kelvin van der Linde, ZA (Audi R8 LMS Evo II), 1h 02m 00.072s, 101.765mph/163.776km/h; **2** Lucas Auer, A (Mercedes AMG GT3 Evo), +0.508s; **3** Ayhancan Guven, TR (Porsche 911 GT3 R), +4.194s; **4** Maro Engel, D (Mercedes AMG GT3 Evo), +5.303s; **5** Mirko Bortolotti, I (Lamborghini Huracán GT3 Evo2), +6.010s; **6** Jules Gounon, F (Mercedes AMG GT3 Evo), +6.406s; **7** René Rast, D (BMW M4 GT3), +17.996s; **8** Arjun Maini, IND (Mercedes AMG GT3 Evo), +19.463s; **9** Marco Wittmann, D (BMW M4 GT3), +22.474s; **10** Nicki Thiim, DK (Lamborghini Huracán GT3 Evo2), +24.610s.
Fastest race lap: Gounon, 1m 38.332s, 104.053mph/167.457km/h.
Pole position: van der Linde, 1m 48.797s, 94.044mph/151.350km/h.

Race 2 (105.160 miles/169.238km).
1 Luca Engstler, D (Lamborghini Huracán GT3 Evo2), 1h 01m 52.396s, 101.976mph/164.114km/h; **2** Mirko Bortolotti, I (Lamborghini Huracán GT3 Evo2), +0.455s; **3** René Rast, D (BMW M4 GT3), +1.834s; **4** Thomas Preining, A (Porsche 911 GT3 R), +16.802s; **5** Nicki Thiim, DK (Lamborghini Huracán GT3 Evo2), +18.001s; **6** Ricardo Feller, CH (Audi R8 LMS Evo II), +18.664s; **7** Marco Wittmann, D (BMW M4 GT3), +19.465s; **8** Lucas Auer, A (Mercedes AMG GT3 Evo), +20.558s; **9** Sheldon van der Linde, ZA (BMW M4 GT3), +26.228s; **10** Maro Engel, D (Mercedes AMG GT3 Evo), +29.463s.
Fastest race lap: Engstler, 1m 38.066s, 104.335mph/167.911km/h.
Pole position: Bortolotti, 1m 36.708s, 105.800mph/170.269km/h.

Final championship points
Drivers
1 Mirko Bortolotti, I, 238; **2** Kelvin van der Linde, ZA, 221; **3** Maro Engel, D, 203; **4** René Rast, D, 172; **5** Thomas Preining, A, 158; **6** Sheldon van der Linde, ZA, 142; **7** Arjun Maini, IND, 139; **8** Jack Aitken, GB, 128; **9** Luca Stolz, D, 127; **10** Lucas Auer, A, 116; **11** Ricardo Feller, CH, 115; **12** Marco Wittmann, D, 110; **13** Nicki Thiim, DK, 93; **14** Luca Engstler, D, 92; **15** Thierry Vermeulen, NL, 71; **16** Ayhancan Guven, TR, 69; **17** Franck Perera, F, 39; **18** Maximilian Paul, D, 38; **19** Clemens Schmid, A, 27; **20** Christian Engelhart, D, 15; **21** Jules Gounon, F, 10; **22** Jordan Pepper, ZA, 6; **23** Ben Dörr, D, 4.

Manufacturers
1 Mercedes, 434; **2** Lamborghini, 424; **3** BMW, 382.

Teams
1 Schubert Motorsport, 361; **2** Abt Sportsline, 326; **3** Winward Racing, 316.

British Touring Car Championship

BRITISH TOURING CAR CHAMPIONSHIP, Donington Park National Circuit, Castle Donington, Great Britain, 28 April. 21, 18 and 20 laps of the 1.979-mile/3.185km circuit.
Round 1 (41.521 miles/66.822km).
1 Tom Ingram, GB (Hyundai i30 Fastback N Performance), 32m 23.071s, 76.997mph/123.914km/h; **2** Ash Sutton, GB (Ford Focus ST), +2.485s; **3** Jake Hill, GB (BMW 330e M Sport), +4.239s; **4** Colin Turkington, GB (BMW 330e M Sport), +8.148s; **5** Ronan Pearson, GB (Hyundai i30 Fastback N Performance), +9.153s; **6** Josh Cook, GB (Toyota Corolla GR Sport), +11.511s; **7** Árón Taylor-Smith, IRL (Vauxhall Astra-TOCA), +13.249s; **8** Dan Cammish, GB (Ford Focus ST), +14.382s; **9** Aiden Moffat, GB (Toyota Corolla GR Sport), +19.036s; **10** Andrew Watson, GB (Toyota Corolla GR Sport), +19.488s.
Fastest race lap: Ingram, 1m 15.177s, 94.768mph/152.514km/h.
Pole position: Ingram, 1m 07.845s, 105.009mph/168.997km/h.

Round 2 (35.584 miles/57.267km).
1 Tom Ingram, GB (Hyundai i30 Fastback N Performance), 21m 03.154s, 101.521mph/163.383km/h; **2** Ash Sutton, GB (Ford Focus ST), +0.917s; **3** Jake Hill, GB (BMW 330e M Sport), +1.854s; **4** Josh Cook, GB (Toyota Corolla GR Sport), +5.725s; **5** Colin Turkington, GB (BMW 330e M Sport), +6.775s; **6** Dan Cammish, GB (Ford Focus ST), +8.378s; **7** Adam Morgan, GB (BMW 330e M Sport), +9.004s; **8** Aiden Moffat, GB (Toyota Corolla GR Sport), +11.653s; **9** Rob Huff, GB (Toyota Corolla GR Sport), +12.697s; **10** Dan Rowbottom, GB (Ford Focus ST), +13.294s.
Fastest race lap: Ronan Pearson, GB (Hyundai i30 Fastback N Performance), 1m 09.134s, 103.052mph/165.846km/h.
Pole position: Ingram.

Round 3 (39.542 miles/63.637km).
1 Aiden Moffat, GB (Toyota Corolla GR Sport), 24m 57.046s, 95.178mph/153.174km/h; **2** Colin Turkington, GB (BMW 330e M Sport), +0.520s; **3** Ash Sutton, GB (Ford Focus ST), +1.625s; **4** Tom Ingram, GB (Hyundai i30 Fastback N Performance), +1.981s; **5** Jake Hill, GB (BMW 330e M Sport), +2.284s; **6** Rob Huff, GB (Toyota Corolla GR Sport), +4.041s; **7** Adam Morgan, GB (BMW 330e M Sport), +6.158s; **8** Dan Rowbottom, GB (Ford Focus ST), +6.304s; **9** Josh Cook, GB (Toyota Corolla GR Sport), +9.322s; **10** Dan Cammish, GB (Ford Focus ST), +9.819s.
Fastest race lap: Ingram, 1m 09.257s, 102.869mph/165.551km/h.
Pole position: Huff.

BRITISH TOURING CAR CHAMPIONSHIP, Brands Hatch Indy Circuit, West Kingsdown, Dartford, Kent, Great Britain, 12 May. 24, 27 and 24 laps of the 1.208-mile/1.944km circuit.
Round 4 (28.990 miles/46.654km).
1 Colin Turkington, GB (BMW 330e M Sport), 19m 43.459s, 88.184mph/141.918km/h; **2** Josh Cook, GB (Toyota Corolla GR Sport), +6.826s; **3** Ash Sutton, GB (Ford Focus ST), +8.722s; **4** Jake Hill, GB (BMW 330e M Sport), +14.924s; **5** Dan Rowbottom, GB (Ford Focus ST), +15.386s; **6** Tom Chilton, GB (Hyundai i30 Fastback N Performance), +17.316s; **7** Tom Ingram, GB (Hyundai i30 Fastback N Performance), +19.474s; **8** Andrew Watson, GB (Toyota Corolla GR Sport), +19.763s*; **9** Aiden Moffat, GB (Toyota Corolla GR Sport), +20.669s; **10** Árón Taylor-Smith, IRL (Vauxhall Astra-TOCA), +27.024s.
** 6s penalty for gaining unfair advantage*
Fastest race lap: Turkington, 48.380s, 89.880mph/144.649km/h.
Pole position: Turkington, 47.875s, 90.829mph/146.175km/h.

Round 5 (32.613 miles/52.486km).
1 Colin Turkington, GB (BMW 330e M Sport), 23m 39.873s, 82.689mph/133.075km/h; **2** Tom Ingram, GB (Hyundai i30 Fastback N Performance), +3.397s; **3** Ash Sutton, GB (Ford Focus ST), +3.656s; **4** Adam Morgan, GB (BMW 330e M Sport), +3.681s; **5** Dan Rowbottom, GB (Ford Focus ST), +7.348s; **6** Tom Chilton, GB (Hyundai i30 Fastback N Performance), +7.911s; **7** Dan Cammish, GB (Ford Focus ST), +8.088s; **8** Aiden Moffat, GB (Toyota Corolla GR Sport), +8.585s; **9** Mikey Doble, GB (Vauxhall Astra-TOCA), +10.183s; **10** Árón Taylor-Smith, IRL (Vauxhall Astra-TOCA), +10.388s.
Fastest race lap: Sutton, 48.509s, 89.641mph/144.264km/h.
Pole position: Turkington.

Round 6 (28.990 miles/46.654km).
1 Ronan Pearson, GB (Hyundai i30 Fastback N Performance), 19m 46.603s, 87.950mph/141.542km/h; **2** Tom Chilton, GB (Hyundai i30 Fastback N Performance), +3.655s; **3** Ash Sutton, GB (Ford Focus ST), +4.479s; **4** Árón Taylor-Smith, IRL (Vauxhall Astra-TOCA), +4.679s; **5** Dan Cammish, GB (Ford Focus ST), +5.748s; **6** Dan Rowbottom, GB (Ford Focus ST), +8.077s; **7** Andrew Watson, GB (Toyota Corolla GR Sport), +13.216s; **8** Colin Turkington, GB (BMW 330e M Sport), +13.552s; **9** Rob Huff, GB (Toyota Corolla GR Sport), +14.500s; **10** Adam Morgan, GB (BMW 330e M Sport), +15.344s.
Fastest race lap: Ingram, GB (Hyundai i30 Fastback N Performance), 48.325s, 89.983mph/144.813km/h.
Pole position: Pearson.

BRITISH TOURING CAR CHAMPIONSHIP, Snetterton Circuit, Thetford, Norfolk, Great Britain, 26 May. 3 x 12 laps of the 2.969-mile/4.778km circuit.
Round 7 (35.627 miles/57.336km).
1 Jake Hill, GB (BMW 330e M Sport), 23m 35.164s, 90.630mph/145.855km/h; **2** Bobby Thompson, GB (BMW 330e M Sport), +1.922s; **3** Ash Sutton, GB (Ford Focus ST), +4.009s; **4** Dan Cammish, GB (Ford Focus ST), +5.130s; **5** Andrew Watson, GB (Toyota Corolla GR Sport), +8.021s; **6** Tom Ingram, GB (Hyundai i30 Fastback N Performance), +8.770s; **7** Adam Morgan, GB (BMW 330e M Sport), +12.041s; **8** Colin Turkington, GB (BMW 330e M Sport), +19.824s; **9** Rob Huff, GB (Toyota Corolla GR Sport), +22.219s; **10** Dan Rowbottom, GB (Ford Focus ST), +22.426s.
Fastest race lap: Ingram, 1m 56.404s, 91.818mph/147.767km/h.
Pole position: Hill, 2m 00.876s, 88.421mph/142.300km/h.

Round 8 (35.627 miles/57.336km).
1 Jake Hill, GB (BMW 330e M Sport), 26m 43.848s, 79.967mph/128.695km/h*; **2** Dan Cammish, GB (Ford Focus ST), +6.260s; **3** Josh Cook, GB (Toyota Corolla GR Sport), +9.974s; **4** Mikey Doble, GB (Vauxhall Astra-TOCA), +14.794s; **5** Tom Chilton, GB (Hyundai i30 Fastback N Performance), +15.696s**; **6** Andrew Watson, GB (Toyota Corolla GR Sport), +16.626s; **7** Bobby Thompson, GB (BMW 330e M Sport), +16.643s*; **8** Aiden Moffat, GB (Toyota Corolla GR Sport), +23.431s; **9** Sam Osborne, GB (Ford Focus ST), +26.823s; **10** Daryl DeLeon, PH (Cupra León-TOCA), +29.165s.
** 10s penalty for false start*
*** 5s penalty for gaining unfair advantage*
Fastest race lap: Árón Taylor-Smith, IRL (Vauxhall Astra-TOCA), 2m 0:5.876s, 84.909mph/136.648km/h.
Pole position: Hill.

Round 9 (35.627 miles/57.336km).
1 Rob Huff, GB (Toyota Corolla GR Sport), 25m 37.243s, 83.432mph/134.272km/h; **2** Aiden Moffat, GB (Toyota Corolla GR Sport), +2.338s; **3** Josh Cook, GB (Toyota Corolla GR Sport), +3.297s; **4** Tom Ingram, GB (Hyundai i30 Fastback N Performance), +3.501s; **5** Ash Sutton, GB (Ford Focus ST), +12.830s; **6** Tom Chilton, GB (Hyundai i30 Fastback

N Performance), +14.169s; 7 Colin Turkington, GB (BMW 330e M Sport), +16.470s; 8 Bobby Thompson, GB (BMW 330e M Sport), +19.425s; 9 Jake Hill, GB (BMW 330e M Sport), +20.025s; 10 Mikey Doble, GB (Vauxhall Astra-TOCA), +21.864s.
Fastest race lap: Ingram, 2m 01.251s, 88.148mph/141.860km/h.
Pole position: Osborne.

BRITISH TOURING CAR CHAMPIONSHIP, Thruxton Circuit, Andover, Hampshire, Great Britain, 9 June. 18, 16 and 19 laps of the 2.356-mile/3.792km circuit.
Round 10 (42.408 miles/68.249km).
1 Jake Hill, GB (BMW 330e M Sport), 25m 25.141s, 100.101mph/161.097km/h; 2 Dan Cammish, GB (Ford Focus ST), +1.216s; 3 Ash Sutton, GB (Ford Focus ST), +1.955s; 4 Tom Ingram, GB (Hyundai i30 Fastback N Performance), +2.518s; 5 Josh Cook, GB (Toyota Corolla GR Sport), +13.147s; 6 Tom Chilton, GB (Hyundai i30 Fastback N Performance), +16.739s; 7 Dan Rowbottom, GB (Ford Focus ST), +7.918s*; 8 Adam Morgan, GB (BMW 330e M Sport), +18.765s; 9 Colin Turkington, GB (BMW 330e M Sport), +19.151s; 10 Árón Taylor-Smith, IRL (Vauxhall Astra-TOCA), +19.752s.
** 2-position penalty for overtaking under Safety Car*
Fastest race lap: Hill, 1m 16.246s, 111.239mph/179.023km/h.
Pole position: Ingram, 1m 15.379s, 112.519mph/181.082km/h.

Round 11 (37.696 miles/60.666km).
1 Jake Hill, GB (BMW 330e M Sport), 20m 47.290s, 108.800mph/175.097km/h; 2 Dan Cammish, GB (Ford Focus ST), +1.262s; 3 Tom Ingram, GB (Hyundai i30 Fastback N Performance), -2.628s*; 4 Dan Rowbottom, GB (Ford Focus ST), +2.745s; 5 Ash Sutton, GB (Ford Focus ST), +5.582s; 6 Josh Cook, GB (Toyota Corolla GR Sport), +7.002s; 7 Colin Turkington, GB (BMW 330e M Sport), +7.402s; 8 Adam Morgan, GB (BMW 330e M Sport), +9.809s; 9 Árón Taylor-Smith, IRL (Vauxhall Astra-TOCA), +12.512s; 10 Rob Huff, GB (Toyota Corolla GR Sport), +15.073s.
** 2-position penalty (originally won in 20m 44.662s)*
Fastest race lap: Cammish, 1m 16.467s, 110.918mph/178.505km/h.
Pole position: Hill.

Round 12 (44.764 miles/72.041km).
1 Ash Sutton, GB (Ford Focus ST), 27m 20.097s, 98.256mph/158.128km/h; 2 Dan Cammish, GB (Ford Focus ST), +4.449s; 3 Tom Ingram, GB (Hyundai i30 Fastback N Performance), +7.962s; 4 Adam Morgan, GB (BMW 330e M Sport), +8.039s; 5 Jake Hill, GB (BMW 330e M Sport), +8.198s; 6 Josh Cook, GB (Toyota Corolla GR Sport), +8.376s; 7 Colin Turkington, GB (BMW 330e M Sport), +9.646s; 8 Árón Taylor-Smith, IRL (Vauxhall Astra-TOCA), +10.002s; 9 Rob Huff, GB (Toyota Corolla GR Sport), +10.275s; 10 Ronan Pearson, GB (Hyundai i30 Fastback N Performance), +10.990s.
Fastest race lap: Sutton, 1m 15.753s, 111.963mph/180.188km/h.
Pole position: Morgan.

BRITISH TOURING CAR CHAMPIONSHIP, Oulton Park Circuit, Tarporley, Cheshire, Great Britain, 23 June. 3 x 15 laps of the 2.226-mile/3.582km circuit.
Round 13 (33.390 miles/53.736km).
1 Tom Ingram, GB (Hyundai i30 Fastback N Performance), 21m 39.143s, 92.525mph/148.905km/h; 2 Ash Sutton, GB (Ford Focus ST), +1.913s; 3 Dan Cammish, GB (Ford Focus ST), +4.557s; 4 Adam Morgan, GB (BMW 330e M Sport), +10.230s; 5 Jake Hill, GB (BMW 330e M Sport), +14.700s; 6 Tom Chilton, GB (Hyundai i30 Fastback N Performance), +16.238s; 7 Árón Taylor-Smith, IRL (Vauxhall Astra-TOCA), +26.078s; 8 Josh Cook, GB (Toyota Corolla GR Sport), +26.646s; 9 Aiden Moffat, GB (Toyota Corolla GR Sport), +30.817s; 10 Rob Huff, GB (Toyota Corolla GR Sport), +31.366s.
Fastest race lap: Cammish, 1m 25.358s, 93.882mph/151.088km/h.
Pole position: Ingram, 1m 24.194s, 95.180mph/153.177km/h.

Round 14 (33.390 miles/53.736km).
1 Josh Cook, GB (Toyota Corolla GR Sport), 21m 52.594s, 91.577mph/147.379km/h; 2 Tom Ingram, GB (Hyundai i30 Fastback N Performance), +8.016s; 3 Jake Hill, GB (BMW 330e M Sport), +9.879s; 4 Dan Cammish, GB (Ford Focus ST), +10.430s; 5 Árón Taylor-Smith, IRL (Vauxhall Astra-TOCA), +10.856s; 6 Mikey Doble, GB (Vauxhall Astra-TOCA), +11.452s; 7 Colin Turkington, GB (BMW 330e M Sport), +12.197s; 8 Chris Smiley, GB (Cupra León-TOCA), +13.420s; 9 Dan Rowbottom, GB (Ford Focus ST), +14.705s; 10 Andrew Watson, GB (Toyota Corolla GR Sport), +18.972s.
Fastest race lap: Cook, 1m 26.058s, 93.118mph/149.859km/h.
Pole position: Ingram.

Round 15 (33.390 miles/53.736km).
1 Jake Hill, GB (BMW 330e M Sport), 21m 42.189s, 92.309mph/148.557km/h; 2 Mikey Doble, GB (Vauxhall Astra-TOCA), +0.749s; 3 Árón Taylor-Smith, IRL (Vauxhall Astra-TOCA), +2.410s; 4 Tom Ingram, GB (Hyundai i30 Fastback N Performance), +2.856s; 5 Dan Cammish, GB (Ford Focus ST), +3.714s; 6 Dan Rowbottom, GB (Ford Focus ST), +4.150s; 7 Adam Morgan, GB (BMW 330e M Sport), +6.758s; 8 Josh Cook, GB (Toyota Corolla GR Sport), +7.474s; 9 Chris Smiley, GB (Cupra León-TOCA), +9.744s; 10 Aiden Moffat, GB (Toyota Corolla GR Sport), +12.474s.
Fastest race lap: Ash Sutton, GB (Ford Focus ST), 1m 25.406s, 93.829mph/151.003km/h.
Pole position: Doble.

BRITISH TOURING CAR CHAMPIONSHIP, Croft Racing Circuit, Croft-on-Tees, North Yorkshire, Great Britain, 28 July. 3 x 15 laps of the 2.100-mile/3.380km circuit.
Round 16 (31.502 miles/50.697km).
1 Colin Turkington, GB (BMW 330e M Sport), 20m 50.152s, 90.713mph/145.988km/h; 2 Tom Ingram, GB (Hyundai i30 Fastback N Performance), +1.746s; 3 Dan Cammish, GB (Ford Focus ST), +3.562s; 4 Ash Sutton, GB (Ford Focus ST), +4.114s; 5 Árón Taylor-Smith, IRL (Vauxhall Astra-TOCA), +10.231s; 6 Jake Hill, GB (BMW 330e M Sport), +15.774s; 7 Rob Huff, GB (Toyota Corolla GR Sport), +19.755s; 8 Josh Cook, GB (Toyota Corolla GR Sport), +28.886s; 9 Tom Chilton, GB (Hyundai i30 Fastback N Performance), +31.080s; 10 Dan Rowbottom, GB (Ford Focus ST), +32.165s.
Fastest race lap: Turkington, 1m 22.243s, 91.927mph/147.942km/h.
Pole position: Turkington, 1m 21.072s, 93.254mph/150.079km/h.

Round 17 (31.502 miles/50.697km).
1 Josh Cook, GB (Toyota Corolla GR Sport), 21m 03.148s, 89.779mph/144.486km/h; 2 Rob Huff, GB (Toyota Corolla GR Sport), +0.742s; 3 Dan Rowbottom, GB (Ford Focus ST), +0.954s; 4 Tom Ingram, GB (Hyundai i30 Fastback N Performance), +6.257s; 5 Ash Sutton, GB (Ford Focus ST), +8.115s; 6 Dan Cammish, GB (Ford Focus ST), +8.770s; 7 Árón Taylor-Smith, IRL (Vauxhall Astra-TOCA), +16.772s; 8 Tom Chilton, GB (Hyundai i30 Fastback N Performance), +17.248s; 9 Colin Turkington, GB (BMW 330e M Sport), +17.967s; 10 Aiden Moffat, GB (Toyota Corolla GR Sport), +18.358s.
Fastest race lap: Cook, 1m 22.625s, 91.502mph/147.258km/h.
Pole position: Turkington.

Round 18 (31.502 miles/50.697km).
1 Tom Chilton, GB (Hyundai i30 Fastback N Performance), 20m 56.324s, 90.267mph/145.271km/h; 2 Dan Cammish, GB (Ford Focus ST), +1.504s; 3 Tom Ingram, GB (Hyundai i30 Fastback N Performance), +2.141s; 4 Ash Sutton, GB (Ford Focus ST), +8.219s; 5 Jake Hill, GB (BMW 330e M Sport), +8.760s; 6 Rob Huff, GB (Toyota Corolla GR Sport), +11.151s; 7 Josh Cook, GB (Toyota Corolla GR Sport), +12.550s; 8 Dan Rowbottom, GB (Ford Focus ST), +12.719s; 9 Adam Morgan, GB (BMW 330e M Sport), +17.519s; 10 Ronan Pearson, GB (Hyundai i30 Fastback N Performance), +24.337s.
Fastest race lap: Cammish, 1m 21.989s, 92.211mph/148.400km/h.
Pole position: Chilton.

BRITISH TOURING CAR CHAMPIONSHIP, Knockhill Racing Circuit, Dunfermline, Fife, Scotland, Great Britain, 11 August. 24, 24 and 27 laps of the 1.267-mile/2.039km circuit.
Round 19 (30.406 miles/48.933km).
1 Colin Turkington, GB (BMW 330e M Sport), 20m 53.082s, 87.352mph/140.580km/h; 2 Josh Cook, GB (Toyota Corolla GR Sport), +8.308s; 3 Adam Morgan, GB (BMW 330e M Sport), +9.117s; 4 Árón Taylor-Smith, IRL (Vauxhall Astra-TOCA), +10.073s; 5 Jake Hill, GB (BMW 330e M Sport), +10.503s; 6 Ash Sutton, GB (Ford Focus ST), +12.960s; 7 Dan Rowbottom, GB (Ford Focus ST), +13.765s; 8 Rob Huff, GB (Toyota Corolla GR Sport), +14.076s; 9 Dan Cammish, GB (Ford Focus ST), +15.032s; 10 Mikey Doble, GB (Vauxhall Astra-TOCA), +16.277s.
Fastest race lap: Turkington, 51.300s, 88.905mph/143.079km/h.
Pole position: Turkington, 50.862s, 89.670mph/144.311km/h.

Round 20 (30.406 miles/48.933km).
1 Jake Hill, GB (BMW 330e M Sport), 20m 58.075s, 87.006mph/140.022km/h; 2 Dan Rowbottom, GB (Ford Focus ST), +7.980s*; 3 Colin Turkington, GB (BMW 330e M Sport), +8.717s; 4 Josh Cook, GB (Toyota Corolla GR Sport), +11.800s; 5 Ash Sutton, GB (Ford Focus ST), +12.879s; 6 Adam Morgan, GB (BMW 330e M Sport), +13.248s; 7 Dan Cammish, GB (Ford Focus ST), +14.698s; 8 Aiden Moffat, GB (Toyota Corolla GR Sport), +24.308s; 9 Tom Chilton, GB (Hyundai i30 Fastback N Performance), +24.313s; 10 Tom Ingram, GB (Hyundai i30 Fastback N Performance), +25.841s.
** 5s penalty for being out of position start*
Fastest race lap: Rowbottom, 51.420s, 88.697mph/142.745km/h.
Pole position: Turkington.

Round 21 (34.206 miles/55.050km).
1 Rob Huff, GB (Toyota Corolla GR Sport), 25m 48.020s, 79.548mph/128.020km/h; 2 Tom Ingram, GB (Hyundai i30 Fastback N Performance), +1.395s; 3 Tom Chilton, GB (Hyundai i30 Fastback N Performance), +1.855s; 4 Ash Sutton, GB (Ford Focus ST), +2.614s; 5 Jake Hill, GB (BMW 330e M Sport), +2.972s; 6 Dan Rowbottom, GB (Ford Focus ST), +4.199s; 7 Aiden Moffat, GB (Toyota Corolla GR Sport), +11.142s; 8 Dan Cammish, GB (Ford Focus ST), +12.197s; 9 Colin Turkington, GB (BMW 330e M Sport), +12.307s; 10 Ronan Pearson, GB (Hyundai i30 Fastback N Performance), +15.026s.
Fastest race lap: Ingram, 51.100s, 89.253mph/143.639km/h.
Pole position: Huff.

BRITISH TOURING CAR CHAMPIONSHIP, Donington Park National Circuit, Castle Donington, Great Britain, 25 August. 17, 14 and 17 laps of the 2.487-mile/4.003km circuit.
Round 22 (42.246 miles/67.989km).
1 Colin Turkington, GB (BMW 330e M Sport), 29m 43.663s, 85.342mph/137.344km/h; 2 Ash Sutton, GB (Ford Focus ST), +1.863s; 3 Jake Hill, GB (BMW 330e M Sport), +6.416s; 4 Josh Cook, GB (Toyota Corolla GR Sport), +7.693s; 5 Tom Ingram, GB (Hyundai i30 Fastback N Performance), +10.188s; 6 Adam Morgan, GB (BMW 330e M Sport), +10.817s; 7 Rob Huff, GB (Toyota Corolla GR Sport), +13.884s; 8 Dan Cammish, GB (Ford Focus ST), +14.655s; 9 Árón Taylor-Smith, IRL (Vauxhall Astra-TOCA), +15.259s; 10 Sam Osborne, GB (Ford Focus ST), +16.212s.
Fastest race lap: Turkington, 1m 33.973s, 95.285mph/153.347km/h.
Pole position: Cook, 1m 33.498s, 95.769mph/154.126km/h.

Round 23 (34.784 miles/55.980km).
1 Ash Sutton, GB (Ford Focus ST), 22m 10.948s, 94.187mph/151.579km/h; 2 Colin Turkington, GB (BMW 330e M Sport), +1.712s; 3 Jake Hill, GB (BMW 330e M Sport), +5.121s; 4 Josh Cook, GB (Toyota Corolla GR Sport), +5.540s; 5 Adam Morgan, GB (BMW 330e M Sport), +11.242s; 6 Dan Rowbottom, GB (Ford Focus ST), +13.741s; 7 Rob Huff, GB (Toyota Corolla GR Sport), +15.024s; 8 Árón Taylor-Smith, IRL (Vauxhall Astra-TOCA), +16.376s; 9 Mikey Doble, GB (Vauxhall Astra-TOCA), +18.034s; 10 Sam Osborne, GB (Ford Focus ST), +25.009s.
Fastest race lap: Turkington, 1m 34.026s, 95.231mph/153.260km/h.
Pole position: Turkington.

Round 24 (42.246 miles/67.989km).
1 Dan Cammish, GB (Ford Focus ST), 29m 29.302s, 86.034mph/138.459km/h; 2 Tom Ingram, GB (Hyundai i30 Fastback N Performance), +1.959s; 3 Árón Taylor-Smith, IRL (Vauxhall Astra-TOCA), +2.894s; 4 Josh Cook, GB (Toyota Corolla GR Sport), +3.652s; 5 Jake Hill, GB (BMW 330e M Sport), +4.048s; 6 Mikey Doble, GB (Vauxhall Astra-TOCA), +4.522s; 7 Colin Turkington, GB (BMW 330e M Sport), +5.145s; 8 Adam Morgan, GB (BMW 330e M Sport), +5.712s; 9 Daryl DeLeon, PH (Cupra León-TOCA), +11.337s; 10 Sam Osborne, GB (Ford Focus ST), +12.585s.
Fastest race lap: Ingram, 1m 33.901s, 95.358mph/153.464km/h.
Pole position: Cammish.

BRITISH TOURING CAR CHAMPIONSHIP, Silverstone National Circuit, Towcester, Northamptonshire, Great Britain, 22 September. 22, 22 and 25 laps of the 1.640-mile/2.640km circuit.
Round 25 (36.089 miles/58.079km).
1 Tom Ingram, GB (Hyundai i30 Fastback N Performance), 23m 38.761s, 91.572mph/147.371km/h; 2 Jake Hill, GB (BMW 330e M Sport), +0.641s; 3 Dan Cammish, GB (Ford Focus ST), +0.771s; 4 Ash Sutton, GB (Ford Focus ST), +3.520s; 5 Colin Turkington, GB (BMW 330e M Sport), +8.199s; 6 Josh Cook, GB (Toyota Corolla GR Sport), +15.854s; 7 Tom Chilton, GB (Hyundai i30 Fastback N Performance), +14.666s*; 8 Sam Osborne, GB (Ford Focus ST), +23.412s; 9 Andrew Watson, GB (Toyota Corolla GR Sport), +24.691s; 10 Dan Zelos, GB (Hyundai i30 Fastback N Performance), +24.857s.
** 1-position penalty*
Fastest race lap: Sutton, 1m 03.642s, 92.791mph/149.333km/h.
Pole position: Ingram, 1m 02.380s, 94.668mph/152.354km/h.

Round 26 (36.089 miles/58.079km).
1 Jake Hill, GB (BMW 330e M Sport), 23m 54.086s, 90.594mph/145.797km/h; 2 Colin Turkington, GB (BMW 330e M Sport), +0.822s; 3 Josh Cook, GB (Toyota Corolla GR Sport), +4.562s; 4 Tom Ingram, GB (Hyundai i30 Fastback N Performance), +7.010s; 5 Dan Cammish, GB (Ford Focus ST), +8.439s; 6 Chris Smiley, GB (Cupra León-TOCA), +17.620s; 7 Adam Morgan, GB (BMW 330e M Sport), +17.959s; 8 Dan Zelos, GB (Hyundai i30 Fastback N Performance), +22.649s; 9 Árón Taylor-Smith, IRL (Vauxhall Astra-TOCA), +23.752s; 10 Sam Osborne, GB (Ford Focus ST), +24.541s.
Fastest race lap: Ash Sutton, GB (Ford Focus ST), 1m 03.980s, 92.301mph/148.544km/h.
Pole position: Ingram.

Round 27 (41.010 miles/65.999km).
1 Tom Ingram, GB (Hyundai i30 Fastback N Performance), 58m 51.030s, 41.811mph/67.288km/h; 2 Ash Sutton, GB (Ford Focus ST), +0.293s; 3 Josh Cook, GB (Toyota Corolla GR Sport), +6.234s; 4 Dan Cammish, GB (Ford Focus ST), +13.541s; 5 Jake Hill, GB (BMW 330e M Sport), +12.255s*; 6 Adam Morgan, GB (BMW 330e M Sport), +17.341s; 7 Rob Huff, GB (Toyota Corolla GR Sport), +19.014s; 8 Dan Zelos, GB (Hyundai i30 Fastback N Performance), +13.966s**; 9 Árón Taylor-Smith, IRL (Vauxhall Astra-TOCA), +19.366s; 10 Sam Osborne, GB (Ford Focus ST), +20.986s.
** 1-position penalty*
*** 2-position penalty*
Fastest race lap: Ingram, 1m 03.340s, 93.233mph/150.045km/h.
Pole position: Smiley.

BRITISH TOURING CAR CHAMPIONSHIP, Brands Hatch Grand Prix Circuit, West Kingsdown, Dartford, Kent, Great Britain, 6 October. 18, 15 and 15 laps of the 2.433-mile/3.916km circuit.
Round 28 (43.798 miles/70.485km).
1 Jake Hill, GB (BMW 330e M Sport), 30m 59.950s, 84.771mph/136.427km/h; 2 Colin Turkington, GB (BMW 330e M Sport), +1.105s; 3 Tom Ingram, GB (Hyundai i30 Fastback N Performance), +2.142s; 4 Mikey Doble, GB (Vauxhall Astra-TOCA), +3.375s; 5 Dan Cammish, GB (Ford Focus ST), +9.906s; 6 Árón Taylor-Smith, IRL (Vauxhall Astra-TOCA), +10.861s; 7 Daryl DeLeon, PH (Cupra León-TOCA), +11.891s; 8 Dan Rowbottom, GB (Ford Focus ST), +14.558s; 9 Tom Chilton, GB (Hyundai i30 Fastback N Performance), +15.390s; 10 Andrew Watson, GB (Toyota Corolla GR Sport), +18.942s.
Fastest race lap: Ingram, 1m 30.641s, 96.639mph/155.526km/h.
Pole position: Turkington, 1m 29.333s, 98.054mph/157.803km/h.

Round 29 (36.498 miles/58.738km).
1 Tom Ingram, GB (Hyundai i30 Fastback N Performance), 22m 59.111s, 95.273mph/153.327km/h; 2 Jake Hill, GB (BMW 330e M Sport), +1.421s; 3 Colin Turkington, GB (BMW 330e M Sport), +1.763s; 4 Dan Cammish, GB (Ford Focus ST), +6.016s; 5 Ash Sutton, GB (Ford Focus ST), +7.708s; 6 Árón Taylor-Smith, IRL (Vauxhall Astra-TOCA), +16.292s; 7 Josh Cook, GB (Toyota Corolla GR Sport), +16.646s; 8 Aiden Moffat, GB (Toyota Corolla GR Sport), +16.920s; 9 Tom Chilton, GB (Hyundai i30 Fastback N Performance), +17.763s; 10 Sam Osborne, GB (Ford Focus ST), +19.285s.
Fastest race lap: Ingram, 1m 30.326s, 96.976mph/156.068km/h.
Pole position: Hill.

Round 30 (36.498 miles/58.738km).
1 Ash Sutton, GB (Ford Focus ST), 25m 36.184s, 85.531mph/137.650km/h; 2 Jake Hill, GB (BMW 330e M Sport), +10.269s; 3 Josh Cook, GB (Toyota Corolla GR Sport), +11.730s; 4 Dan Cammish, GB (Ford Focus ST), +17.148s; 5 Colin Turkington, GB (BMW 330e M Sport), +18.339s; 6 Tom Ingram, GB (Hyundai i30 Fastback N Performance), +21.707s; 7 Sam Osborne, GB (Ford Focus ST), +23.001s; 8 Andrew Watson, GB (Toyota Corolla GR Sport), +23.945s; 9 Aiden Moffat, GB (Toyota Corolla GR Sport), +24.360s; 10 Adam Morgan, GB (BMW 330e M Sport), +26.688s.
Fastest race lap: Sutton, 1m 40.667s, 87.014mph/140.036km/h.
Pole position: Cook.

Final championship points
Drivers
1 Jake Hill, GB, 421; 2 Tom Ingram, GB, 413; 3 Ash Sutton, GB, 365; 4 Colin Turkington, GB, 346; 5 Dan Cammish, GB, 346; 6 Josh Cook, GB, 327; 7 Árón Taylor-Smith, IRL, 224; 8 Adam Morgan, GB, 201; 9 Rob Huff, GB, 195; 10 Tom Chilton, GB, 187; 11 Dan Rowbottom, GB, 186; 12 Mikey Doble, GB, 148; 13 Aiden Moffat, GB, 138; 14 Andrew Watson, GB, 120; 15 Sam Osborne, GB, 93; 16 Ronan Pearson, GB, 77; 17 Chris Smiley, GB, 70; 18 Daryl DeLeon, PH, 48; 19 Dan Zelos, GB, 44; 20 Bobby Thompson, GB, 34; 21 Scott Sumpton, GB, 20; 22 Nick Halstead, GB, 7.

Drivers (Independents)
1 Árón Taylor-Smith, IRL, 564; 2 Mikey Doble, GB, 466; 3 Chris Smiley, GB, 396; 4 Daryl DeLeon, PH, 354; 5 Scott Sumpton, GB, 342.

Drivers (Jack Sears Trophy)
1 Mikey Doble, GB, 490; 2 Sam Osborne, GB, 437; 3 Daryl DeLeon, PH, 360; 4 Scott Sumpton, GB, 343; 5 Ronan Pearson, GB, 299; 6 Nick Halstead, GB, 299; 7 Dan Zelos, GB, 147.

Manufacturers
1 BMW, 818; 2 Ford, 795; 3 Hyundai, 694; 4 Toyota, 644.

Teams
1 NAPA Racing UK, 724; 2 Team Bristol Street Motors, 609; 3 Team BMW, 560; 4 LKQ Euro Car Parts with SYNETIQ, 497; 5 Evans Halshaw Power Maxed Racing, 427; 6 Laser Tools Racing with MB Motorsport, 412; 7 Toyota Gazoo Racing UK, 367; 8 Restart

Racing, 181; **9** Duckhams Racing with Bartercard, 85; **10** Zeus Cloud Racing with WSR, 34.

NTT IndyCar Series

All cars are Dallara DW12.

FIRESTONE GRAND PRIX OF ST. PETERSBURG, St. Petersburg Street Circuit, Florida, USA, 10 March. Round 1. 100 laps of the 1.800-mile/2.897km circuit, 180.000 miles/289.682km.
1 Patricio O'Ward, MEX (-Chevrolet), 1h 51m 37.5075s, 96.752mph/155.708km/h; **2** Will Power, AUS (-Chevrolet), +1.1438s; **3** Colton Herta, USA (-Honda), +2.3457s; **4** Alex Palou, E (-Honda), +3.8915s; **5** Felix Rosenqvist, S (-Honda), +6.4923s; **6** Alexander Rossi, USA (-Chevrolet), +7.8732s; **7** Scott Dixon, NZ (-Honda), +8.3843s; **8** Rinus van Kalmthout, NL (-Chevrolet), +10.9225s; **9** Santino Ferrucci, USA (-Chevrolet), +15.1316s; **10** Kyle Kirkwood, USA (-Honda), +16.6755s; **11** Callum Ilott, GB (-Chevrolet), +20.7992s; **12** Kyffin Simpson, BB (-Honda), +21.6541s; **13** Pietro Fittipaldi, BR (-Honda), +24.9054s; **14** Graham Rahal, USA (-Honda), +26.7834s; **15** Tom Blomqvist, GB (-Honda), +32.5605s; **16** Agustín Canapino, RA (-Chevrolet), +34.2126s; **17** Jack Harvey, GB (-Honda), +41.4332s; **18** Christian Lundgaard, DK (-Honda), +50.8226s; **19** Christian Rasmussen, DK (-Chevrolet), -1 lap; **20** Colin Braun, USA (-Honda), -1; **21** Linus Lundqvist, S (-Honda), -3; **22** Romain Grosjean, F (-Chevrolet), -18 (DNF-mechanical); **23** Marcus Ericsson, S (-Honda), -48 (DNF-accident); **24** Sting Ray Robb, USA (-Chevrolet), -67 (DNF); **25** Marcus Armstrong, NZ (-Honda), -75 (DNF-accident).
Most laps led: Newgarden, 92.
Disqualified: Josef Newgarden, USA (-Chevrolet), originally won in 1h 51m 29.5954s; Scott McLaughlin, NZ (-Chevrolet), +0.5456s (both for violation of 'Push to Pass' parameters).
Fastest race lap: Newgarden, 1m 00.6795s, 106.791mph/171.863km/h.
Pole position: Newgarden, 59.5714s, 108.777mph/175.060km/h.
Championship points: Drivers: 1 O'Ward, 50; **2** Herta, 36; **3** Palou, 32; **4** Power, 30; **5** Rosenqvist, 30; **6** Rossi, 28.

ACURA GRAND PRIX OF LONG BEACH, Long Beach Street Circuit, California, USA, 21 April. Round 2. 85 laps of the 1.968-mile/3.167km circuit, 167.280 miles/269.211km.
1 Scott Dixon, NZ (-Honda), 1h 42m 03.1416s, 98.350mph/158.278km/h; **2** Colton Herta, USA (-Honda), +0.9798s; **3** Alex Palou, E (-Honda), +1.7664s; **4** Josef Newgarden, USA (-Chevrolet), +3.9735s; **5** Marcus Ericsson, S (-Honda), +4.3769s; **6** Will Power, AUS (-Chevrolet), +15.7639s; **7** Kyle Kirkwood, USA (-Honda), +16.1788s; **8** Romain Grosjean, F (-Chevrolet), +18.0433s; **9** Felix Rosenqvist, S (-Honda), +18.8155s; **10** Alexander Rossi, USA (-Chevrolet), +32.0915s; **11** Théo Pourchaire, F (-Chevrolet), +33.4409s; **12** Marcus Armstrong, NZ (-Honda), +40.8207s; **13** Linus Lundqvist, S (-Honda), +42.0003s; **14** Rinus van Kalmthout, NL (-Chevrolet), +44.4325s; **15** Agustín Canapino, RA (-Chevrolet), +51.3156s; **16** Patricio O'Ward, MEX (-Chevrolet), +52.9961s; **17** Graham Rahal, USA (-Honda), +1m 02.5190s; **18** Sting Ray Robb, USA (-Chevrolet), +1m 05.5898s; **19** Kyffin Simpson, BB (-Honda), -1 lap; **20** Nolan Siegel, USA (-Honda), -1; **21** Santino Ferrucci, USA (-Chevrolet), -1; **22** Tom Blomqvist, GB (-Honda), -1; **23** Christian Lundgaard, DK (-Honda), -1; **24** Pietro Fittipaldi, BR (-Honda), -1; **25** Jack Harvey, GB (-Honda), -2; **26** Scott McLaughlin, NZ (-Chevrolet), -14; **27** Christian Rasmussen, DK (-Chevrolet), -71 (DNF-accident).
Most laps led: Dixon, 42.
Fastest race lap: Ericsson, 1m 07.7690s, 104.543mph/168.246km/h.
Pole position: Rosenqvist, 1m 06.0172s, 107.317mph/172.711km/h.
Championship points: Drivers: 1 Dixon, 79; **2** Herta, 77; **3** Palou, 67; **4** O'Ward, 64; **5** Power, 59; **6** Rosenqvist, 54.

CHILDREN'S OF ALABAMA INDY GRAND PRIX, Barber Motorsports Park, Birmingham, Alabama, USA, 28 April. Round 3. 90 laps of the 2.300-mile/3.701km circuit, 207.000 miles/333.134km.
1 Scott McLaughlin, NZ (-Chevrolet), 1h 56m 45.7773s, 106.369mph/171.185km/h; **2** Will Power, AUS (-Chevrolet), +1.3194s; **3** Linus Lundqvist, S (-Honda), +2.4421s; **4** Felix Rosenqvist, S (-Honda), +4.5109s; **5** Alex Palou, E (-Honda), +5.3692s; **6** Christian Lundgaard, DK (-Honda), +6.0509s; **7** Santino Ferrucci, USA (-Chevrolet), +6.6055s; **8** Colton Herta, USA (-Honda), +7.5124s; **9** Marcus Armstrong, NZ (-Honda), +8.0375s; **10** Kyle Kirkwood, USA (-Honda), +8.5573s; **11** Graham Rahal, USA (-Honda), +9.0288s; **12** Romain Grosjean, F (-Chevrolet), +9.4495s; **13** Jack Harvey, GB (-Honda), +10.1269s; **14** Kyffin Simpson, BB (-Honda), +10.4415s; **15** Scott Dixon, NZ (-Honda), +11.3628s; **16** Josef Newgarden, USA (-Chevrolet), +12.2355s; **17** Rinus van Kalmthout, NL (-Chevrolet), +13.5092s; **18** Marcus Ericsson, S (-Honda), +13.8437s; **19** Tom Blomqvist, GB (-Honda), +14.5751s; **20** Agustín Canapino, RA (-Chevrolet), +14.6807s; **21** Luca Ghiotto, I (-Honda), +15.6809s; **22** Théo Pourchaire, F (-Chevrolet), -1 lap; **23** Patricio O'Ward, MEX (-Chevrolet), +16.4461s*; **24** Christian Rasmussen, DK (-Chevrolet), -1; **25** Alexander Rossi, USA (-Chevrolet), -30 (DNF-mechanical); **26** Sting Ray Robb, USA (-Chevrolet), -36 (DNF-accident); **27** Pietro Fittipaldi, BR (-Honda), -48 (DNF-accident).
** 1-position penalty for avoidable contact*
Most laps led: McLaughlin, 58.
Fastest race lap: McLaughlin, 1m 07.7544s, 122.206mph/196.672km/h.
Pole position: McLaughlin, 1m 05.9490s, 125.552mph/202.056km/h.
Championship points: Drivers: 1 Herta, 101; **2** Power, 100; **3** Palou, 98; **4** Dixon, 94; **5** Rosenqvist, 87; **6** O'Ward, 71.

SONSIO GRAND PRIX, Indianapolis Motor Speedway, Speedway, Indiana, USA, 11 May. Round 4. 85 laps of the 2.439-mile/3.925km circuit, 207.315 miles/333.641km.
1 Alex Palou, E (-Honda), 1h 45m 27.2320s, 117.956mph/189.832km/h; **2** Will Power, AUS (-Chevrolet), +6.6106s; **3** Christian Lundgaard, DK (-Honda), +8.0900s; **4** Scott Dixon, NZ (-Honda), +13.4262s; **5** Marcus Armstrong, NZ (-Honda), +13.8978s; **6** Scott McLaughlin, NZ (-Chevrolet), +14.2746s; **7** Colton Herta, USA (-Honda), +18.8554s; **8** Alexander Rossi, USA (-Chevrolet), +20.1638s; **9** Graham Rahal, USA (-Honda), +22.1556s; **10** Felix Rosenqvist, S (-Honda), +26.3424s; **11** Kyle Kirkwood, USA (-Honda), +27.4572s; **12** Romain Grosjean, F (-Chevrolet), +29.3108s; **13** Patricio O'Ward, MEX (-Chevrolet), +31.2388s; **14** Pietro Fittipaldi, BR (-Honda), +31.8872s; **15** Kyffin Simpson, BB (-Honda), +32.2895s; **16** Marcus Ericsson, S (-Honda), +34.6582s; **17** Josef Newgarden, USA (-Chevrolet), +36.9649s; **18** Jack Harvey, GB (-Honda), +38.0124s; **19** Théo Pourchaire, F (-Chevrolet), +38.0679s; **20** Christian Rasmussen, DK (-Chevrolet), +39.4219s; **21** Agustín Canapino, RA (-Chevrolet), -1 lap; **22** Sting Ray Robb, USA (-Chevrolet), -1; **23** Tom Blomqvist, GB (-Honda), -1; **24** Linus Lundqvist, S (-Honda), -1; **25** Luca Ghiotto, I (-Honda), -1; **26** Rinus van Kalmthout, NL (-Chevrolet), -1; **27** Santino Ferrucci, USA (-Chevrolet), -30 (DNF-mechanical).
Most laps led: Palou, 39.
Fastest race lap: Palou, 1m 11.1111s, 123.474mph/198.713km/h.
Pole position: Palou, 1m 09.0004s, 127.251mph/204.791km/h.
Championship points: Drivers: 1 Palou, 152; **2** Power, 140; **3** Dixon, 127; **4** Herta, 127; **5** Rosenqvist, 107; **6** McLaughlin, 88.

108TH RUNNING OF THE INDIANAPOLIS 500, Indianapolis Motor Speedway, Speedway, Indiana, USA, 26 May. Round 5. 200 laps of the 2.500-mile/4.023km circuit, 500.000 miles/804.672km.
1 Josef Newgarden, USA (-Chevrolet), 2h 58m 49.4079s, 167.763mph/269.989km/h; **2** Patricio O'Ward, MEX (-Chevrolet), +0.3417s; **3** Scott Dixon, NZ (-Honda), +0.9097s; **4** Alexander Rossi, USA (-Chevrolet), +1.1691s; **5** Alex Palou, E (-Honda), +1.5079s; **6** Scott McLaughlin, NZ (-Chevrolet), +2.0593s; **7** Kyle Kirkwood, USA (-Honda), +2.5379s; **8** Santino Ferrucci, USA (-Chevrolet), +3.6143s; **9** Rinus van Kalmthout, NL (-Chevrolet), +3.9560s; **10** Conor Daly, USA (-Chevrolet), +4.6071s; **11** Callum Ilott, GB (-Chevrolet), +4.9652s; **12** Christian Rasmussen, DK (-Honda), +5.3234s; **13** Christian Lundgaard, DK (-Honda), +6.1824s; **14** Takuma Sato, J (-Honda), +6.6893s; **15** Graham Rahal, USA (-Honda), +7.3608s; **16** Sting Ray Robb, USA (-Chevrolet), +8.5098s; **17** Ed Carpenter, USA (-Chevrolet), +8.9081s; **18** Kyle Larson, USA (-Chevrolet), +9.4846s; **19** Romain Grosjean, F (-Chevrolet), +9.8312s; **20** Hélio Castroneves, BR (-Honda), +10.3602s; **21** Kyffin Simpson, BB (-Honda), +11.0931s; **22** Agustín Canapino, RA (-Chevrolet), -1 lap; **23** Colton Herta, USA (-Honda), -30 (DNF-accident); **24** Will Power, AUS (-Chevrolet), -55 (DNF-accident); **25** Marco Andretti, USA (-Honda), -87 (DNF-accident); **26** Ryan Hunter-Reay, USA (-Chevrolet), -93 (DNF-accident); **27** Felix Rosenqvist, S (-Honda), -145 (DNF-mechanical); **28** Linus Lundqvist, S (-Honda), -173 (DNF-accident); **29** Katherine Legge, GB (-Honda), -178 (DNF-mechanical); **30** Marcus Armstrong, NZ (-Honda), -194 (DNF-mechanical); **31** Tom Blomqvist, GB (-Honda), -200 (DNF-accident); **32** Pietro Fittipaldi, BR (-Honda), -200 (DNF-accident); **33** Marcus Ericsson, S (-Honda), -200 (DNF-accident).
Most laps led: McLaughlin, 66.
Fastest race lap: Lundgaard, 39.7574s, 226.373mph/364.312km/h.
Pole position: McLaughlin, 2m 33.7017s, 234.220mph/376.940km/h (over **4** laps).
Championship points: Drivers: 1 Palou, 183; **2** Dixon, 163; **3** Power, 157; **4** O'Ward, 134; **5** Herta, 134; **6** McLaughlin, 131.

CHEVROLET DETROIT GRAND PRIX PRESENTED BY LEAR, Detroit Street Circuit, Michigan, USA, 2 June. Round 6. 100 laps of the 1.645-mile/2.647km circuit, 164.500 miles/264.737km.
1 Scott Dixon, NZ (-Honda), 2h 06m 07.9684s, 78.251mph/125.933km/h; **2** Marcus Ericsson, S (-Honda), +0.8567s; **3** Marcus Armstrong, NZ (-Honda), +4.9129s; **4** Kyle Kirkwood, USA (-Honda), +6.1249s; **5** Alexander Rossi, USA (-Chevrolet), +8.9532s; **6** Will Power, AUS (-Chevrolet), +10.1045s; **7** Patricio O'Ward, MEX (-Chevrolet), +11.4821s; **8** Felix Rosenqvist, S (-Honda), +15.4998s; **9** Santino Ferrucci, USA (-Chevrolet), +18.2882s; **10** Théo Pourchaire, F (-Chevrolet), +18.8912s; **11** Christian Lundgaard, DK (-Honda), +23.3158s; **12** Agustín Canapino, RA (-Chevrolet), +27.3674s; **13** Pietro Fittipaldi, BR (-Honda), +28.3686s; **14** Rinus van Kalmthout, NL (-Chevrolet), +29.4122s; **15** Graham Rahal, USA (-Honda), +30.1565s; **16** Alex Palou, E (-Honda), +39.0438s; **17** Jack Harvey, GB (-Honda), +46.3377s; **18** Tristan Vautier, F (-Honda), -1 lap; **19** Colton Herta, USA (-Honda), -1; **20** Scott McLaughlin, NZ (-Chevrolet), -1; **21** Sting Ray Robb, USA (-Chevrolet), -1; **22** Linus Lundqvist, S (-Honda), -1; **23** Romain Grosjean, F (-Chevrolet), -3; **24** Kyffin Simpson, BB (-Honda), -4; **25** Hélio Castroneves, BR (-Honda), -5; **26** Josef Newgarden, USA (-Chevrolet), -6; **27** Christian Rasmussen, DK (-Chevrolet), -76 (DNF-mechanical).
Most laps led: Dixon, 35.
Fastest race lap: Herta, 1m 02.7094s, 94.436mph/151.979km/h.
Pole position: Herta, 1m 00.5475s, 97.808mph/157.406km/h.
Championship points: Drivers: 1 Dixon, 216; **2** Palou, 198; **3** Power, 185; **4** O'Ward, 160; **5** Rossi, 150; **6** Kirkwood, 148.

XPEL GRAND PRIX OF ROAD AMERICA PRESENTED BY AMR, Road America, Elkhart Lake, Wisconsin, USA, 9 June. Round 7. 55 laps of the 4.014-mile/6.460km circuit, 220.770 miles/355.295km.
1 Will Power, AUS (-Chevrolet), 1h 45m 00.0267s, 126.154mph/203.025km/h; **2** Josef Newgarden, USA (-Chevrolet), +3.2609s; **3** Scott McLaughlin, NZ (-Chevrolet), +8.0148s; **4** Alex Palou, E (-Honda), +16.7118s; **5** Kyle Kirkwood, USA (-Honda), +24.8662s; **6** Colton Herta, USA (-Honda), +28.3782s; **7** Romain Grosjean, F (-Chevrolet), +29.2710s; **8** Patricio O'Ward, MEX (-Chevrolet), +30.3109s; **9** Marcus Ericsson, S (-Honda), +35.6260s; **10** Graham Rahal, USA (-Honda), +42.8394s; **11** Christian Lundgaard, DK (-Honda), +46.4444s; **12** Linus Lundqvist, S (-Honda), +46.8107s; **13** Théo Pourchaire, F (-Chevrolet), +54.5282s; **14** Felix Rosenqvist, S (-Honda), +59.2412s; **15** Santino Ferrucci, USA (-Chevrolet), +1m 03.7336s; **16** Pietro Fittipaldi, BR (-Honda), +1m 04.7161s; **17** Sting Ray Robb, USA (-Chevrolet), +1m 08.4389s; **18** Alexander Rossi, USA (-Chevrolet), +1m 15.0426s; **19** Hélio Castroneves, BR (-Honda), +1m 15.6918s; **20** Christian Rasmussen, DK (-Chevrolet), +1m 19.0701s; **21** Scott Dixon, NZ (-Honda), +1m 24.4754s; **22** Luca Ghiotto, I (-Honda), +1m 40.1612s; **23** Nolan Siegel, USA (-Chevrolet), -1 lap; **24** Rinus van Kalmthout, NL (-Chevrolet), -2; **25** Jack Harvey, GB (-Honda), -4; **26** Marcus Armstrong, NZ (-Honda), -20 (DNF-mechanical); **27** Kyffin Simpson, BB (-Honda), -50 (DNF-accident).
Most laps led: McLaughlin, 18.
Fastest race lap: Dixon, 1m 43.1076s, 140.149mph/225.548km/h.
Pole position: Lundqvist, 1m 45.1519s, 137.424mph/221.163km/h.
Championship points: Drivers: 1 Power, 236; **2** Palou, 231; **3** Dixon, 225; **4** O'Ward, 184; **5** McLaughlin, 179; **6** Kirkwood, 179.

FIRESTONE GRAND PRIX OF MONTEREY, WeatherTech Raceway Laguna Seca, Monterey, California, USA, 23 June. Round 8. 95 laps of the 2.238-mile/3.602km circuit, 212.610 miles/342.163km.
1 Alex Palou, E (-Honda), 2h 04m 09.8545s, 102.740mph/165.344km/h; **2** Colton Herta, USA (-Honda), +1.9780s; **3** Alexander Rossi, USA (-Chevrolet), +4.5136s; **4** Romain Grosjean, F (-Chevrolet), +4.8243s; **5** Kyle Kirkwood, USA (-Honda), +8.6768s; **6** Scott Dixon, NZ (-Honda), +9.1504s; **7** Will Power, AUS (-Chevrolet), +9.9964s; **8** Patricio O'Ward, MEX (-Chevrolet), +10.6214s; **9** Santino Ferrucci, USA (-Chevrolet), +11.0025s; **10** Marcus Ericsson, S (-Honda), +11.6398s; **11** Felix Rosenqvist, S (-Honda), +12.7088s; **12** Nolan Siegel, USA (-Chevrolet), +13.1305s; **13** Christian Rasmussen, DK (-Chevrolet), +14.3770s; **14** Pietro Fittipaldi, BR (-Honda), +14.7541s; **15** Christian Lundgaard, DK (-Honda), +15.0744s; **16** David Malukas, USA (-Honda), +18.5009s; **17** Linus Lundqvist, S (-Honda), +20.1723s; **18** Agustín Canapino, RA (-Chevrolet), +23.5447s; **19** Josef Newgarden, USA (-Chevrolet), +27.2568s; **20** Sting Ray Robb, USA (-Chevrolet), -1 lap; **21** Scott McLaughlin, NZ (-Chevrolet), -2; **22** Marcus Armstrong, NZ (-Honda), -2; **23** Kyffin Simpson, BB (-Honda), -9 (DNF-accident); **24** Graham Rahal, USA (-Honda), -9 (DNF-accident); **25** Jack Harvey, GB (-Honda), -13 (DNF-mechanical); **26** Rinus van Kalmthout, NL (-Chevrolet), -23 (DNF-mechanical); **27** Luca Ghiotto, I (-Honda), -61 (DNF-accident).
Most laps led: Palou, 48.
Fastest race lap: Ericsson, 1m 08.9728s, 116.811mph/187.990km/h.
Pole position: Palou, 1m 07.1465s, 119.988mph/193.103km/h.
Championship points: Drivers: 1 Palou, 285; **2** Power, 262; **3** Dixon, 253; **4** Herta, 217; **5** Kirkwood, 210; **6** O'Ward, 208.

HONDA INDY 200 AT MID-OHIO PRESENTED BY THE 2025 CIVIC HYBRID, Mid-Ohio Sports Car Course, Lexington, Ohio, USA, 7 July. Round 9. 80 laps of the 2.258-mile/3.634km circuit, 180.640 miles/290.712km.
1 Patricio O'Ward, MEX (-Chevrolet), 1h 33m 22.6191s, 116.071mph/186.799km/h; **2** Alex Palou, E (-Honda), +0.4993s; **3** Scott McLaughlin, NZ (-Chevrolet), +16.1558s; **4** Colton Herta, USA (-Honda), +24.8725s; **5** Marcus Ericsson, S (-Honda), +31.6809s; **6** Alexander Rossi, USA (-Chevrolet), +32.2443s; **7** Christian Lundgaard, DK (-Honda), +32.5714s; **8** Kyle Kirkwood, USA (-Honda), +35.2218s; **9** Christian Rasmussen, DK (-Chevrolet), +40.3182s; **10** Santino Ferrucci, USA (-Chevrolet), +46.9084s; **11** Will Power, AUS (-Chevrolet), +48.6546s; **12** David Malukas, USA (-Honda), +49.3906s; **13** Toby Sowery, GB (-Honda), +49.8866s; **14** Felix Rosenqvist, S (-Honda), +51.8162s; **15** Linus Lundqvist, S (-Honda), +53.4794s; **16** Sting Ray Robb, USA (-Chevrolet), +54.7413s; **17** Marcus Armstrong, NZ (-Honda), +55.8399s; **18** Graham Rahal, USA (-Honda), +58.8681s; **19** Rinus van Kalmthout, NL (-Chevrolet), +1m 00.4550s; **20** Nolan Siegel, USA (-Chevrolet), +1m 05.8591s; **21** Kyffin Simpson, BB (-Honda), +1m 07.0413s; **22** Agustín Canapino, RA (-Chevrolet), -1 lap; **23** Romain Grosjean, F (-Chevrolet), -1; **24** Pietro Fittipaldi, BR (-Honda), -1; **25** Josef Newgarden, USA (-Chevrolet), -1; **26** Jack Harvey, GB (-Honda), -1; **27** Scott Dixon, NZ (-Honda), -40 (DNF-mechanical).
Most laps led: Palou, 53.
Fastest race lap: Newgarden, 1m 06.5386s, 122.167mph/196.608km/h.
Pole position: Palou, 1m 05.3511s, 124.387mph/200.181km/h.
Championship points: Drivers: 1 Palou, 329; **2** Power, 281; **3** O'Ward, 259; **4** Dixon, 258; **5** Herta, 249; **6** Kirkwood, 234.

HY-VEE HOMEFRONT 250 PRESENTED BY INSTACART and HY-VEE ONE STEP 250 PRESENTED BY GATORADE, Iowa Speedway, Newton, Iowa, USA, 13/14 July. 2 x 250 laps of the 0.894-mile/1.439km circuit.
Round 10 (223.500 miles/359.688km).
1 Scott McLaughlin, NZ (-Chevrolet), 1h 44m 41.1172s, 128.098mph/206.154km/h; **2** Patricio O'Ward, MEX (-Chevrolet), +0.4814s; **3** Josef Newgarden, USA (-Chevrolet), +1.5174s; **4** Scott Dixon, NZ (-Honda), +5.0041s; **5** Rinus van Kalmthout, NL (-Chevrolet), +6.5656s; **6** Santino Ferrucci, USA (-Chevrolet), +7.4575s; **7** Kyle Kirkwood, USA (-Honda), +8.4200s; **8** Alexander Rossi, USA (-Chevrolet), +9.3425s; **9** Marcus Ericsson, S (-Honda), +10.3770s; **10** Marcus Armstrong, NZ (-Honda), +11.4006s; **11** Colton Herta, USA (-Honda), +11.8114s; **12** Nolan Siegel, USA (-Chevrolet), +12.1279s; **13** Felix Rosenqvist, S (-Honda), +12.4651s; **14** Kyffin Simpson, BB (-Honda), +13.5048s; **15** Sting Ray Robb, USA (-Chevrolet), +14.0242s; **16** Graham Rahal, USA (-Honda), -1 lap; **17** Katherine Legge, GB (-Honda), -1; **18** Will Power, AUS (-Chevrolet), -9; **19** Pietro Fittipaldi, BR (-Honda), -22 (DNF-accident); **20** Ed Carpenter, USA (-Chevrolet), -22 (DNF-accident); **21** Linus Lundqvist, S (-Honda), -41 (DNF-mechanical); **22** Christian Lundgaard, DK (-Honda), -72 (DNF-accident); **23** Alex Palou, E (-Honda), -75 (DNF-accident); **24** Romain Grosjean, F (-Chevrolet), -202 (DNF-accident); **25** Jack Harvey, GB (-Honda), -222 (DNF-withdrew); **26** David Malukas, USA (-Honda), -250 (DNF-accident); **27** Agustín Canapino, RA (-Chevrolet), -250 (DNF-accident).
Most laps led: McLaughlin, 164.
Fastest race lap: Newgarden, 18.0687s, 178.120mph/286.657km/h.
Pole position: Herta, 17.1506s, 187.655mph/302.002km/h.

Round 11 (223.500 miles/359.688km).
1 Will Power, AUS (-Chevrolet), 1h 26m 38.7472s, 154.768mph/249.075km/h; **2** Alex Palou, E (-Honda), +0.3915s; **3** Scott McLaughlin, NZ (-Chevrolet), +2.3651s; **4** Scott Dixon, NZ (-Honda), +2.5326s; **5** Colton Herta, USA (-Honda), +4.4363s; **6** Patricio O'Ward, MEX (-Chevrolet), +4.6789s; **7** Josef Newgarden, USA (-Chevrolet), +4.8592s; **8** Graham Rahal, USA (-Honda), +18.0556s; **9** Rinus van Kalmthout, NL (-Chevrolet), +18.7648s; **10** Romain Grosjean, F (-Chevrolet), +20.4808s; **11** Santino Ferrucci, USA (-Chevrolet), +20.8311s; **12** Linus Lundqvist, S (-Honda), +25.0235s; **13** David Malukas, USA (-Honda), +26.4773s; **14** Nolan Siegel, USA (-Chevrolet), +28.1296s; **15** Alexander Rossi, USA (-Chevrolet), -1 lap (DNF-accident); **16** Kyle Kirkwood, USA (-Honda), -1 (DNF-accident); **17** Christian Lundgaard, DK (-Honda), -1; **18** Kyffin Simpson, BB (-Honda), -1; **19** Marcus Armstrong, NZ (-Honda), -1; **20** Pietro Fittipaldi, BR (-Honda), -1; **21** Sting Ray Robb, USA (-Chevrolet), -2 (DNF-accident); **22** Ed Carpenter, USA (-Chevrolet), -2 (DNF-accident); **23** Marcus Ericsson, S (-Honda), -2; **24** Katherine Legge, GB (-Honda), -2; **25** Agustín Canapino, RA (-Chevrolet), -29 (DNF-mechanical); **26** Felix Rosenqvist, S (-Honda), -66 (DNF-mechanical); **27** Conor Daly, USA (-Honda), -110 (DNF-mechanical).
Withdrawn: Jack Harvey, GB (-Honda).
Most laps led: Palou, 103.

Fastest race lap: Newgarden, 18.0190s, 178.611mph/287.447km/h.
Pole position: McLaughlin, 17.0966s, 188.248mph/302.956km/h.
Championship points: Drivers: 1 Palou, 379; **2** Power, 344; **3** O'Ward, 327; **4** Dixon, 322; **5** McLaughlin, 314; **6** Herta, 300.

ONTARIO HONDA DEALERS INDY TORONTO, Toronto Street Circuit, Ontario, Canada, 21 July. Round 12. 85 laps of the 1.786-mile/2.874km circuit, 151.810 miles/244.315km.
1 Colton Herta, USA (-Honda), 1h 39m 28.4293s, 91.568mph/147.364km/h; **2** Kyle Kirkwood, USA (-Honda), +0.3469s; **3** Scott Dixon, NZ (-Honda), +0.9680s; **4** Alex Palou, E (-Honda), +1.6911s; **5** Marcus Armstrong, NZ (-Honda), +2.7719s; **6** David Malukas, USA (-Honda), +3.0853s; **7** Christian Lundgaard, DK (-Honda), +3.8925s; **8** Rinus van Kalmthout, NL (-Chevrolet), +4.6346s; **9** Romain Grosjean, F (-Chevrolet), +5.6537s; **10** Graham Rahal, USA (-Honda), +6.1456s; **11** Josef Newgarden, USA (-Chevrolet), +10.4924s; **12** Will Power, AUS (-Chevrolet), +11.5555s; **13** Linus Lundqvist, S (-Honda), -1 lap; **14** Théo Pourchaire, F (-Chevrolet), -1; **15** Toby Sowery, GB (-Honda), -1; **16** Scott McLaughlin, NZ (-Chevrolet), -9 (DNF-accident); **17** Patricio O'Ward, MEX (-Chevrolet), -13 (DNF-accident); **18** Marcus Ericsson, S (-Honda), -13 (DNF-accident); **19** Pietro Fittipaldi, BR (-Honda), -13 (DNF-accident); **20** Santino Ferrucci, USA (-Chevrolet), -13 (DNF-accident); **21** Nolan Siegel, USA (-Chevrolet), -13 (DNF-accident); **22** Kyffin Simpson, BB (-Honda), -19 (DNF-accident); **23** Felix Rosenqvist, S (-Honda), -22 (DNF-mechanical); **24** Hunter McElrea, AUS (-Honda), -28 (DNF-accident); **25** Sting Ray Robb, USA (-Chevrolet), -72 (DNF-mechanical); **26** Agustín Canapino, RA (-Chevrolet), -81 (DNF-accident); **27** Christian Rasmussen, DK (-Chevrolet), -85 (DNF-accident); Alexander Rossi, USA (-Chevrolet), -85 (DNF-accident).
Most laps led: Herta, 81.
Fastest race lap: Dixon, 1m 01.1392s, 105.163mph/169.244km/h.
Pole position: Herta, 59.5431s, 107.982mph/173.781km/h.
Championship points: Drivers: 1 Palou, 411; **2** Power, 362; **3** Dixon, 358; **4** Herta, 354; **5** O'Ward, 340; **6** McLaughlin, 328.

BOMMARITO AUTOMOTIVE GROUP 500, World Wide Technology Raceway, St Louis, Madison, Illinois, USA, 17 August. Round 13. 260 laps of the 1.250-mile/2.012km circuit, 325.000 miles/523.037km.
1 Josef Newgarden, USA (-Chevrolet), 2h 22m 28.2772s, 136.870mph/220.270km/h; **2** Scott McLaughlin, NZ (-Chevrolet), +1.7260s; **3** Linus Lundqvist, S (-Honda), +3.7875s; **4** Alex Palou, E (-Honda), +6.0516s; **5** Colton Herta, USA (-Honda), +6.2646s; **6** Felix Rosenqvist, S (-Honda), -1 lap; **7** Nolan Siegel, USA (-Chevrolet), -1; **8** Marcus Armstrong, NZ (-Honda), -1; **9** Sting Ray Robb, USA (-Chevrolet), -1; **10** Rinus van Kalmthout, NL (-Chevrolet), -1; **11** Scott Dixon, NZ (-Honda), -2; **12** Santino Ferrucci, USA (-Chevrolet), -2; **13** Conor Daly, USA (-Chevrolet), -2; **14** Pietro Fittipaldi, BR (-Honda), -2; **15** Christian Lundgaard, DK (-Honda), -3; **16** Romain Grosjean, F (-Chevrolet), -3; **17** Ed Carpenter, USA (-Chevrolet), -8; **18** Will Power, AUS (-Chevrolet), -10; **19** Alexander Rossi, USA (-Chevrolet), -10 (DNF-accident); **20** Jack Harvey, GB (-Honda), -11 (DNF-accident); **21** David Malukas, USA (-Honda), -22 (DNF-accident); **22** Kyle Kirkwood, USA (-Honda), -53 (DNF-accident); **23** Graham Rahal, USA (-Honda), -99 (DNF-mechanical); **24** Marcus Ericsson, S (-Honda), -109 (DNF-mechanical); **25** Kyffin Simpson, BB (-Honda), -176 (DNF-accident); **26** Patricio O'Ward, MEX (-Chevrolet), -218 (DNF-mechanical); **27** Katherine Legge, GB (-Honda), -253 (DNF-accident).
Most laps led: Power, 117.
Fastest race lap: Newgarden, 25.5721s, 175.973mph/283.201km/h.
Pole position: McLaughlin, 50.0079s, 179.972mph/289.636km/h (over 2 laps).
Championship points: Drivers: 1 Palou, 443; **2** Herta, 384; **3** Dixon, 378; **4** Power, 377; **5** McLaughlin, 370; **6** O'Ward, 345.

BITNILE.COM GRAND PRIX OF PORTLAND, Portland International Raceway, Portland, Oregon, USA, 25 August. Round 14. 110 laps of the 1.964-mile/3.161km circuit, 216.040 miles/347.683km.
1 Will Power, AUS (-Chevrolet), 1h 55m 34.1948s, 112.161mph/180.505km/h; **2** Alex Palou, E (-Honda), +9.8267s; **3** Josef Newgarden, USA (-Chevrolet), +23.2046s; **4** Colton Herta, USA (-Honda), +37.1039s; **5** Marcus Armstrong, NZ (-Honda), +38.0334s; **6** Marcus Ericsson, S (-Honda), +40.7687s; **7** Scott McLaughlin, NZ (-Chevrolet), +42.3498s; **8** Santino Ferrucci, USA (-Chevrolet), +44.8556s; **9** Graham Rahal, USA (-Honda), +49.5811s; **10** Kyle Kirkwood, USA (-Honda), +50.9987s; **11** Rinus van Kalmthout, NL (-Chevrolet), +52.1760s; **12** Alexander Rossi, USA (-Chevrolet), +52.4979s; **13** Christian Lundgaard, DK (-Honda), +55.4967s; **14** Felix Rosenqvist, S (-Honda), +56.7606s; **15** Patricio O'Ward, MEX (-Chevrolet), +58.3930s; **16** Kyffin Simpson, BB (-Honda), +59.4851s; **17** Toby Sowery, GB (-Honda), -1 lap; **18** Sting Ray Robb, USA (-Chevrolet), -1; **19** Jüri Vips, EST (-Honda), -1; **20** David Malukas, USA (-Honda), -1; **21** Nolan Siegel, USA (-Chevrolet), -1; **22** Conor Daly, USA (-Chevrolet), -1; **23** Linus Lundqvist, S (-Honda), -1; **24** Jack Harvey, GB (-Honda), -1; **25** Pietro Fittipaldi, BR (-Honda), -1; **26** Christian Rasmussen, DK (-Chevrolet), -2; **27** Romain Grosjean, F (-Chevrolet), -3; **28** Scott Dixon, NZ (-Honda), -110 (DNF-accident).
Most laps led: Power, 101.
Fastest race lap: Malukas, 59.7452s, 118.343mph/190.454km/h.
Pole position: Ferrucci, 58.2046s, 121.475mph/195.495km/h.
Championship points: Drivers: 1 Palou, 484; **2** Power, 430; **3** Herta, 417; **4** McLaughlin, 396; **5** Dixon, 383; **6** O'Ward, 360.

MILWAUKEE MILE 250, The Milwaukee Mile, Wisconsin State Fair Park, West Allis, Wisconsin, USA, 31 August/1 September. 2 x 250 laps of the 1.015-mile/1.633km circuit.
Round 15 (253.750 miles/408.371km).
1 Patricio O'Ward, MEX (-Chevrolet), 2h 03m 01.3451s, 123.758mph/199.169km/h; **2** Will Power, AUS (-Chevrolet), +1.8215s; **3** Conor Daly, USA (-Chevrolet), +2.4039s; **4** Santino Ferrucci, USA (-Chevrolet), +16.6898s; **5** Alex Palou, E (-Honda), +18.7079s; **6** Linus Lundqvist, S (-Honda), +19.2430s; **7** Alexander Rossi, USA (-Chevrolet), +20.3497s; **8** Scott McLaughlin, NZ (-Chevrolet), +21.0736s; **9** Christian Lundgaard, DK (-Honda), +21.5712s; **10** Scott Dixon, NZ (-Honda), +21.8753s; **11** Christian Rasmussen, DK (-Chevrolet), +22.9117s; **12** Kyle Kirkwood, USA (-Honda), +23.1309s; **13** Felix Rosenqvist, S (-Honda), +26.2308s; **14** Rinus van Kalmthout, NL (-Chevrolet), -1 lap; **15** David Malukas, USA (-Honda), -1; **16** Jack Harvey, GB (-Honda), -1; **17** Nolan Siegel, USA (-Chevrolet), -1; **18** Pietro Fittipaldi, BR (-Honda), -2; **19** Katherine Legge, GB (-Honda), -2; **20** Graham Rahal, USA (-Honda), -2; **21** Marcus Armstrong, NZ (-Honda), -3; **22** Colton Herta, USA (-Honda), -4; **23** Sting Ray Robb, USA (-Chevrolet), -6; **24** Romain Grosjean, F (-Chevrolet), -7; **25** Kyffin Simpson, BB (-Honda), -12; **26** Josef Newgarden, USA (-Chevrolet), -104 (DNF-accident); **27** Marcus Ericsson, S (-Honda), -104 (DNF-accident).
Most laps led: O'Ward, 133.
Fastest race lap: McLaughlin, 23.5855s, 154.926mph/249.329km/h.
Pole position: McLaughlin, 22.5082s, 162.341mph/261.262km/h.

Round 16 (253.750 miles/408.371km).
1 Scott McLaughlin, NZ (-Chevrolet), 2h 06m 31.3981s, 120.334mph/193.658km/h; **2** Scott Dixon, NZ (-Honda), +0.4558s; **3** Colton Herta, USA (-Honda), +5.1263s; **4** Santino Ferrucci, USA (-Chevrolet), +10.9829s; **5** Marcus Ericsson, S (-Honda), +13.7085s; **6** Alexander Rossi, USA (-Chevrolet), +14.3305s; **7** Rinus van Kalmthout, NL (-Chevrolet), +15.2002s; **8** Kyle Kirkwood, USA (-Honda), +15.3219s; **9** Romain Grosjean, F (-Chevrolet), +16.2013s; **10** Will Power, AUS (-Chevrolet), +19.8577s; **11** Felix Rosenqvist, S (-Honda), -1 lap; **12** Christian Lundgaard, DK (-Honda), -2; **13** Kyffin Simpson, BB (-Honda), -2; **14** Jack Harvey, GB (-Honda), -3; **15** Katherine Legge, GB (-Honda), -4; **16** Christian Rasmussen, DK (-Chevrolet), -7; **17** Conor Daly, USA (-Chevrolet), -20 (DNF-withdrew); **18** Sting Ray Robb, USA (-Chevrolet), -29 (DNF-accident); **19** Alex Palou, E (-Honda), -29; **20** Linus Lundqvist, S (-Honda), -35 (DNF-accident); **21** Pietro Fittipaldi, BR (-Honda), -69 (DNF-mechanical); **22** David Malukas, USA (-Honda), -124 (DNF-mechanical); **23** Graham Rahal, USA (-Honda), -127 (DNF-accident); **24** Patricio O'Ward, MEX (-Chevrolet), -163 (DNF-mechanical); **25** Nolan Siegel, USA (-Chevrolet), -226 (DNF-mechanical); **26** Marcus Armstrong, NZ (-Honda), -244 (DNF-accident); **27** Josef Newgarden, USA (-Chevrolet), -245 (DNF-accident).
Most laps led: McLaughlin, 85.
Fastest race lap: Dixon, 23.5149s, 155.391mph/250.077km/h.
Pole position: Newgarden, 22.6980s, 160.983mph/259.078km/h.
Championship points: Drivers: 1 Palou, 525; **2** Power, 492; **3** McLaughlin, 475; **4** Herta, 462; **5** Dixon, 443; **6** O'Ward, 419.

BIG MACHINE MUSIC CITY GRAND PRIX, Nashville Superspeedway, Lebanon, Tennessee, USA, 15 September. Round 17. 206 laps of the 1.330-mile/2.140km circuit, 273.980 miles/440.928km.
1 Colton Herta, USA (-Honda), 1h 43m 15.2534s, 159.207mph/256.219km/h; **2** Patricio O'Ward, MEX (-Chevrolet), +1.8106s; **3** Josef Newgarden, USA (-Chevrolet), +1.9611s; **4** Kyle Kirkwood, USA (-Honda), +4.7175s; **5** Scott McLaughlin, NZ (-Chevrolet), +7.7837s; **6** Santino Ferrucci, USA (-Chevrolet), +9.2336s; **7** Marcus Armstrong, NZ (-Honda), +14.3870s; **8** Linus Lundqvist, S (-Honda), +14.6519s; **9** David Malukas, USA (-Honda), +15.2726s; **10** Conor Daly, USA (-Chevrolet), -1 lap; **11** Alex Palou, E (-Honda), -1; **12** Rinus van Kalmthout, NL (-Chevrolet), -1; **13** Jack Harvey, GB (-Honda), -1; **14** Christian Rasmussen, DK (-Chevrolet), -1; **15** Alexander Rossi, USA (-Chevrolet), -1; **16** Romain Grosjean, F (-Chevrolet), -2; **17** Scott Dixon, NZ (-Honda), -2; **18** Nolan Siegel, USA (-Chevrolet), -2; **19** Christian Lundgaard, DK (-Honda), -2; **20** Sting Ray Robb, USA (-Chevrolet), -2; **21** Pietro Fittipaldi, BR (-Honda), -2; **22** Kyffin Simpson, BB (-Honda), -4; **23** Graham Rahal, USA (-Honda), -4; **24** Will Power, AUS (-Chevrolet), -8; **25** Marcus Ericsson, S (-Honda), -69 (DNF-accident); **26** Katherine Legge, GB (-Honda), -121 (DNF-accident); **27** Felix Rosenqvist, S (-Honda), -151 (DNF-accident).
Most laps led: Kirkwood, 67.
Fastest race lap: O'Ward, 24.2869s, 197.143mph/317.271km/h.
Pole position: Kirkwood, 47.5189s, 201.520mph/324.315km/h (over **2** laps).

Final championship points
Drivers
1 Alex Palou, E, 544; **2** Colton Herta, USA, 513; **3** Scott McLaughlin, NZ, 505; **4** Will Power, AUS, 498; **5** Patricio O'Ward, MEX, 460; **6** Scott Dixon, NZ, 456; **7** Kyle Kirkwood, USA, 420; **8** Josef Newgarden, USA, 401; **9** Santino Ferrucci, USA, 367; **10** Alexander Rossi, USA, 366; **11** Christian Lundgaard, DK, 312; **12** Felix Rosenqvist, S, 306; **13** Rinus van Kalmthout, NL, 300; **14** Marcus Armstrong, NZ, 298; **15** Marcus Ericsson, S, 297; **16** Linus Lundqvist, S, 279; **17** Romain Grosjean, F, 260; **18** Graham Rahal, USA, 251; **19** Pietro Fittipaldi, BR, 186; **20** Sting Ray Robb, USA, 185; **21** Kyffin Simpson, BB, 182; **22** Christian Rasmussen, DK, 163; **23** Nolan Siegel, USA, 154; **24** David Malukas, USA, 148; **25** Jack Harvey, GB, 143; **26** Conor Daly, USA, 119; **27** Agustín Canapino, RA, 109; **28** Théo Pourchaire, F, 91; **29** Katherine Legge, GB, 61; **30** Tom Blomqvist, GB, 46; **31** Ed Carpenter, USA, 45; **32** Toby Sowery, GB, 45; **33** Callum Ilott, GB, 39; **34** Luca Ghiotto, I, 27; **35** Hélio Castroneves, BR, 26; **36** Kyle Larson, USA, 21; **37** Takuma Sato, J, 19; **38** Tristan Vautier, F, 12; **39** Jüri Vips, EST, 11; **40** Colin Braun, USA, 10; **41** Hunter McElrea, AUS, 6; **42** Ryan Hunter-Reay, USA, 6; **43** Marco Andretti, USA, 5.

Rookie of the Year
1 Linus Lundqvist.

Manufacturers
1 Chevrolet, 1475; **2** Honda, 1343.

Other IndyCar races

All cars are Dallara DW12.

$1 MILLION CHALLENGE, The Thermal Club, Palm Springs, California, USA, 24 March. 8, 10 and 20 laps of the 3.067-mile/4.936km circuit.
Heat 1 (24.536 miles/39.487km).
1 Felix Rosenqvist, S (-Honda), 13m 30.9622s, 108.920mph/175.289km/h; **2** Scott McLaughlin, NZ (-Chevrolet), +0.4971s; **3** Josef Newgarden, USA (-Chevrolet), +1.7664s; **4** Christian Lundgaard, DK (-Honda), +6.3835s; **5** Agustín Canapino, RA (-Chevrolet), +8.7479s; **6** Colton Herta, USA (-Honda), +15.8230s; **7** Nolan Siegel, USA (-Honda), +16.4113s; **8** Santino Ferrucci, USA (-Chevrolet), +17.0148s; **9** Will Power, AUS (-Chevrolet), +17.8747s; **10** Kyle Kirkwood, USA (-Honda), +21.4089s; **11** Sting Ray Robb, USA (-Chevrolet), +21.7870s; **12** Scott Dixon, NZ (-Honda), +25.7655s; **13** Rinus van Kalmthout, NL (-Chevrolet), -8 laps (DNF-accident); **14** Romain Grosjean, F (-Chevrolet), -8 (DNF-accident).
Fastest race lap: Dixon, 1m 40.7795s, 109.558mph/176.317km/h.
Pole position: Rosenqvist, 1m 38.5831s, 111.999mph/180.245km/h.

Heat 2 (30.670 miles/49.359km).
1 Alex Palou, E (-Honda), 16m 50.6089s, 109.253mph/175.826km/h; **2** Marcus Armstrong, NZ (-Honda), +5.3375s; **3** Graham Rahal, USA (-Honda), +18.0911s; **4** Linus Lundqvist, S (-Honda), +18.9634s; **5** Pietro Fittipaldi, BR (-Honda), +19.7151s; **6** Alexander Rossi, USA (-Chevrolet), +20.3456s; **7** Patricio O'Ward, MEX (-Chevrolet), +21.0031s; **8** Tom Blomqvist, GB (-Honda), +23.1783s; **9** Callum Ilott, GB (-Chevrolet), +23.3908s; **10** Christian Rasmussen, DK (-Chevrolet), +24.1938s; **11** Kyffin Simpson, BB (-Honda), +25.8233s; **12** Marcus Ericsson, S (-Honda), +26.5815s; **13** Colin Braun, USA (-Honda), +28.8333s.
Fastest race lap: Palou, 1m 39.8051s, 110.628mph/178.038km/h.
Pole position: Palou, 1m 38.5675s, 112.017mph/180.273km/h.

All-Star Race (61.340 miles/98.717km).
1 Alex Palou, E (-Honda), 39m 30.2292s, 93.166mph/149.936km/h; **2** Scott McLaughlin, NZ (-Chevrolet), +5.7929s; **3** Felix Rosenqvist, S (-Honda), +9.7587s; **4** Colton Herta, USA (-Honda), +13.1126s; **5** Marcus Armstrong, NZ (-Honda), +15.0938s; **6** Linus Lundqvist, S (-Honda), +16.1064s; **7** Alexander Rossi, USA (-Chevrolet), +16.5393s; **8** Josef Newgarden, USA (-Chevrolet), +17.6675s; **9** Christian Lundgaard, DK (-Honda), +19.7073s; **10** Agustín Canapino, RA (-Chevrolet), +20.4100s; **11** Graham Rahal, USA (-Honda), -11 laps (DNF-mechanical).
Disqualified: Pietro Fittipaldi, BR (-Honda), failure to follow the directions of IndyCar.
Fastest race lap: Palou, 1m 41.6145s, 108.658mph/174.868km/h.
Pole position: Palou.

NASCAR Cup Series

66TH ANNUAL DAYTONA 500, Daytona International Speedway, Daytona Beach, Florida, USA, 19 February. Round 1. 200 laps of the 2.500-mile/4.023km circuit, 500.000 miles/804.672km.
1 William Byron, USA (Chevrolet Camaro ZL1 '24), 3h 10m 52s, 157.178mph/252.953km/h; **2** Alex Bowman, USA (Chevrolet Camaro ZL1 '24), 200 laps; **3** Christopher Bell, USA (Toyota Camry XSE Next Gen), 200; **4** Corey LaJoie, USA (Chevrolet Camaro ZL1 '24), 200; **5** Darrell Wallace Jr, USA (Toyota Camry XSE Next Gen), 200; **6** A.J. Allmendinger, USA (Chevrolet Camaro ZL1 '24), 200; **7** John Hunter Nemechek, USA (Toyota Camry XSE Next Gen), 200; **8** Erik Jones, USA (Toyota Camry XSE Next Gen), 200; **9** Noah Gragson, USA (Ford Mustang '24), 200; **10** Chase Briscoe, USA (Ford Mustang '24), 200.
Pole position: Joey Logano, USA (Ford Mustang '24), 49.465s, 181.947mph/292.815km/h.
Championship points: Drivers: 1 Byron, 54; **2** Bowman, 50; **3** Bell, 44; **4** Elliott, 42; **5** Wallace Jr, 39; **6** Nemechek, 37.

66TH ANNUAL AMBETTER HEALTH 400, Atlanta Motor Speedway, Hampton, Georgia, USA, 25 February. Round 2. 260 laps of the 1.540-mile/2.478km circuit, 400.400 miles/644.381km.
1 Daniel Suárez, MEX (Chevrolet Camaro ZL1 '24), 3h 28m 11s, 115.398mph/185.716km/h; **2** Ryan Blaney, USA (Ford Mustang '24), +0.003s; **3** Kyle Busch, USA (Chevrolet Camaro ZL1 '24), +0.007s; **4** Austin Cindric, USA (Ford Mustang '24), +0.077s; **5** Darrell Wallace Jr, USA (Toyota Camry XSE Next Gen), +0.112s; **6** Ricky Stenhouse Jr, USA (Chevrolet Camaro ZL1 '24), +0.135s; **7** Ross Chastain, USA (Chevrolet Camaro ZL1 '24), +0.170s; **8** Michael McDowell, USA (Ford Mustang '24), +0.192s; **9** Chris Buescher, USA (Ford Mustang '24), +0.193s; **10** Ty Gibbs, USA (Toyota Camry XSE Next Gen), +0.243s.
Pole position: McDowell, 30.999s, 178.844mph/287.822km/h.
Championship points: Drivers: 1 Busch (Kyle), 77; **2** Byron, 76; **3** Cindric, 76; **4** Wallace Jr, 74; **5** Blaney, 69; **6** Elliott, 65.

27TH ANNUAL PENNZOIL 400 PRESENTED BY JIFFY LUBE, Las Vegas Motor Speedway, Nevada, USA, 3 March. Round 3. 267 laps of the 1.500-mile/2.414km circuit, 400.500 miles/644.542km.
1 Kyle Larson, USA (Chevrolet Camaro ZL1 '24), 3h 00m 25s, 133.192mph/214.351km/h; **2** Tyler Reddick, USA (Toyota Camry XSE Next Gen), +0.441s; **3** Ryan Blaney, USA (Ford Mustang '24), +3.827s; **4** Ross Chastain, USA (Chevrolet Camaro ZL1 '24), +4.356s; **5** Ty Gibbs, USA (Toyota Camry XSE Next Gen), +4.577s; **6** Noah Gragson, USA (Ford Mustang '24), +4.859s; **7** Martin Truex Jr, USA (Toyota Camry XSE Next Gen), +5.418s; **8** Denny Hamlin, USA (Toyota Camry XSE Next Gen), +6.307s; **9** Joey Logano, USA (Ford Mustang '24), +6.794s; **10** William Byron, USA (Chevrolet Camaro ZL1 '24), +7.113s.
Pole position: Logano, 29.291s, 184.357mph/296.694km/h.
Championship points: Drivers: 1 Larson, 118; **2** Blaney, 110; **3** Truex Jr, 104; **4** Byron, 103; **5** Chastain, 98; **6** Busch (Kyle), 95.

20TH ANNUAL SHRINERS CHILDREN'S 500, Phoenix Raceway, Arizona, USA, 10 March. Round 4. 312 laps of the 1.000-mile/1.609km circuit, 312.000 miles/502.115km.
1 Christopher Bell, USA (Toyota Camry XSE Next Gen), 3h 00m 45s, 103.568mph/166.677km/h; **2** Chris Buescher, USA (Ford Mustang '24), +5.465s; **3** Ty Gibbs, USA (Toyota Camry XSE Next Gen), +6.032s; **4** Brad Keselowski, USA (Ford Mustang '24), +9.243s; **5** Ryan Blaney, USA (Ford Mustang '24), +9.448s; **6** Ross Chastain, USA (Chevrolet Camaro ZL1 '24), +9.499s; **7** Martin Truex Jr, USA (Toyota Camry XSE Next Gen), +13.150s; **8** Michael McDowell, USA (Ford Mustang '24), +14.619s; **9** Chase Briscoe, USA (Ford Mustang '24), +14.876s; **10** Tyler Reddick, USA (Toyota Camry XSE Next Gen), +15.348s.
Pole position: Denny Hamlin, USA (Toyota Camry XSE Next Gen), 27.138s, 132.655mph/213.488km/h.
Championship points: Drivers: 1 Blaney, 151; **2** Larson, 141; **3** Truex Jr, 141; **4** Byron, 134; **5** Reddick, 130; **6** Gibbs, 130.

64TH ANNUAL FOOD CITY 500, Bristol Motor Speedway, Tennessee, USA, 17 March. Round 5. 500 laps of the 0.533-mile/0.858km circuit, 266.500 miles/428.890km.
1 Denny Hamlin, USA (Toyota Camry XSE Next Gen), 3h 20m 41s, 79.678mph/128.229km/h; **2** Martin Truex Jr, USA (Toyota Camry XSE Next Gen), +1.083s; **3** Brad Keselowski, USA (Ford Mustang '24), +7.284s; **4** Alex Bowman, USA (Chevrolet Camaro ZL1 '24), +14.342s; **5** Kyle Larson, USA (Chevrolet Camaro ZL1 '24), +15.155s; **6** John Hunter Nemechek, USA (Toyota Camry XSE Next Gen), -1 lap; **7** Chris Buescher, USA (Ford Mustang '24), -1; **8** Chase Elliott,

USA (Chevrolet Camaro ZL1 '24), -1; **9** Ty Gibbs, USA (Toyota Camry XSE Next Gen), -1; **10** Christopher Bell, USA (Toyota Camry XSE Next Gen), -1.
Pole position: Ryan Blaney, USA (Ford Mustang '24), 15.356s, 124.954mph/201.095km/h.
Championship points: Drivers: 1 Blaney, 177; **5** Hamlin, 173; **6** Elliott, 152.

4TH ANNUAL ECHOPARK AUTOMOTIVE GRAND PRIX, Circuit of the Americas, Austin, Texas, USA, 24 March. Round 6. 68 laps of the 3.410-mile/5.488km circuit, 231.880 miles/373.175km.
1 William Byron, USA (Chevrolet Camaro ZL1 '24), 2h 43m 15s, 85.224mph/137.155km/h; **2** Christopher Bell, USA (Toyota Camry XSE Next Gen), +0.692s; **3** Ty Gibbs, USA (Toyota Camry XSE Next Gen), +2.778s; **4** Alex Bowman, USA (Chevrolet Camaro ZL1 '24), +12.675s; **5** Tyler Reddick, USA (Toyota Camry XSE Next Gen), +13.162s; **6** A.J. Allmendinger, USA (Chevrolet Camaro ZL1 '24), +18.979s; **7** Ross Chastain, USA (Chevrolet Camaro ZL1 '24), +20.988s; **8** Chris Buescher, USA (Ford Mustang '24), +24.316s; **9** Kyle Busch, USA (Chevrolet Camaro ZL1 '24), +25.329s; **10** Martin Truex Jr, USA (Toyota Camry XSE Next Gen), +31.628s.
Pole position: Byron, 2m 09.636s, 94.696mph/152.398km/h.
Championship points: Drivers: 1 Truex Jr, 220; **2** Gibbs, 215; **3** Blaney, 211; **4** Hamlin, 206; **5** Larson, 205; **6** Byron, 183.

69TH ANNUAL TOYOTA OWNERS 400, Richmond International Raceway, Virginia, USA, 31 March. Round 7. 407 laps of the 0.750-mile/1.207km circuit, 305.250 miles/491.252km.
1 Denny Hamlin, USA (Toyota Camry XSE Next Gen), 3h 14m 41s, 94.076mph/151.400km/h; **2** Joey Logano, USA (Ford Mustang '24), +0.269s; **3** Kyle Larson, USA (Chevrolet Camaro ZL1 '24), +0.628s; **4** Martin Truex Jr, USA (Toyota Camry XSE Next Gen), +0.640s; **5** Chase Elliott, USA (Chevrolet Camaro ZL1 '24), +0.873s; **6** Christopher Bell, USA (Toyota Camry XSE Next Gen), +1.154s; **7** William Byron, USA (Chevrolet Camaro ZL1 '24), +1.520s; **8** Brad Keselowski, USA (Ford Mustang '24), +1.797s; **9** Chris Buescher, USA (Ford Mustang '24), +2.110s; **10** Tyler Reddick, USA (Toyota Camry XSE Next Gen), +2.114s.
Pole position: Larson, 22.438s, 120.332mph/193.655km/h.
Championship points: Drivers: 1 Truex Jr, 270; **2** Larson, 256; **3** Hamlin, 252; **4** Gibbs, 236; **5** Blaney, 229; **6** Bell, 219.

75TH ANNUAL COOK OUT 400, Martinsville Speedway, Ridgeway, Virginia, USA, 7 April. Round 8. 415 laps of the 0.526-mile/0.847km circuit, 218.290 miles/351.304km.
1 William Byron, USA (Chevrolet Camaro ZL1 '24), 2h 52m 07s, 76.096mph/122.465km/h; **2** Kyle Larson, USA (Chevrolet Camaro ZL1 '24), +0.550s; **3** Chase Elliott, USA (Chevrolet Camaro ZL1 '24), +0.790s; **4** Darrell Wallace Jr, USA (Toyota Camry XSE Next Gen), +0.824s; **5** Ryan Blaney, USA (Ford Mustang '24), +1.023s; **6** Joey Logano, USA (Ford Mustang '24), +1.070s; **7** Tyler Reddick, USA (Toyota Camry XSE Next Gen), +1.320s; **8** Alex Bowman, USA (Chevrolet Camaro ZL1 '24), +1.433s; **9** Ryan Preece, USA (Ford Mustang '24), +1.449s; **10** Chase Briscoe, USA (Ford Mustang '24), +1.566s.
Pole position: Larson, 19.718s, 96.034mph/154.552km/h.
Championship points: Drivers: 1 Larson, 309; **2** Truex Jr, 295; **3** Hamlin, 292; **4** Byron, 261; **5** Blaney, 261; **6** Elliott, 258.

20TH ANNUAL AUTOTRADER ECHOPARK AUTOMOTIVE 400, Texas Motor Speedway, Fort Worth, Texas, USA, 14 April. Round 9. 276 laps of the 1.500-mile/2.414km circuit, 414.000 miles/666.268km.
1 Chase Elliott, USA (Chevrolet Camaro ZL1 '24), 3h 33m 14s, 116.492mph/187.476km/h; **2** Brad Keselowski, USA (Ford Mustang '24), +0.558s; **3** William Byron, USA (Chevrolet Camaro ZL1 '24), +0.678s; **4** Tyler Reddick, USA (Toyota Camry XSE Next Gen), +0.948s; **5** Daniel Suárez, MEX (Chevrolet Camaro ZL1 '24), +1.425s; **6** Chase Briscoe, USA (Ford Mustang '24), +2.079s; **7** Darrell Wallace Jr, USA (Toyota Camry XSE Next Gen), +2.309s; **8** Austin Dillon, USA (Chevrolet Camaro ZL1 '24), +2.310s; **9** Kyle Busch, USA (Chevrolet Camaro ZL1 '24), +3.106s; **10** Carson Hocevar, USA (Chevrolet Camaro ZL1 '24), +3.324s.
Pole position: Kyle Larson, USA (Chevrolet Camaro ZL1 '24), 28.366s, 190.369mph/306.369km/h.
Championship points: Drivers: 1 Larson, 335; **2** Truex Jr, 318; **3** Hamlin, 307; **4** Elliott, 303; **5** Byron, 297; **6** Gibbs, 280.

55TH ANNUAL GEICO 500, Talladega Superspeedway, Lincoln, Alabama, USA, 21 April. Round 10. 188 laps of the 2.660-mile/4.281km circuit, 500.080 miles/804.801km.
1 Tyler Reddick, USA (Toyota Camry XSE Next Gen), 3h 13m 29s, 155.077mph/249.572km/h; **2** Brad Keselowski, USA (Ford Mustang '24), +0.208s; **3** Noah Gragson, USA (Ford Mustang '24), +0.277s; **4** Ricky Stenhouse Jr, USA (Chevrolet Camaro ZL1 '24), +0.487s; **5** Alex Bowman, USA (Chevrolet Camaro ZL1 '24), +0.977s; **6** Anthony Alfredo, USA (Chevrolet Camaro ZL1 '24), +1.262s; **7** William Byron, USA (Chevrolet Camaro ZL1 '24), +1.363s; **8** Todd Gilliland, USA (Ford Mustang '24), +1.575s; **9** Daniel Hemric, USA (Chevrolet Camaro ZL1 '24), +2.002s; **10** Harrison Burton, USA (Ford Mustang '24), +2.297s.
Pole position: Michael McDowell, USA (Ford Mustang '24), 52.609s, 182.022mph/292.936km/h.
Championship points: Drivers: 1 Larson, 359; **2** Truex Jr, 344; **3** Elliott, 337; **4** Byron, 335; **5** Reddick, 316; **6** Hamlin, 308.

55TH ANNUAL WüRTH 400, Dover International Speedway, Delaware, USA, 28 April. Round 11. 400 laps of the 1.000-mile/1.609km circuit, 400.000 miles/643.738km.
1 Denny Hamlin, USA (Toyota Camry XSE Next Gen), 3h 20m 57s, 119.433mph/192.208km/h; **2** Kyle Larson, USA (Chevrolet Camaro ZL1 '24), +0.256s; **3** Martin Truex Jr, USA (Toyota Camry XSE Next Gen), +4.209s; **4** Kyle Busch, USA (Chevrolet Camaro ZL1 '24), +9.646s; **5** Chase Elliott, USA (Chevrolet Camaro ZL1 '24), +9.830s; **6** Noah Gragson, USA (Ford Mustang '24), +10.670s; **7** Ryan Blaney, USA (Ford Mustang '24), +10.827s; **8** Alex Bowman, USA (Chevrolet Camaro ZL1 '24), +11.790s; **9** Daniel Hemric, USA (Chevrolet Camaro ZL1 '24), +12.098s; **10** Ty Gibbs, USA (Toyota Camry XSE Next Gen), +13.594s.
Pole position: Busch, 22.196s, 162.191mph/261.022km/h.
Championship points: Drivers: 1 Larson, 410; **2** Truex Jr, 395; **3** Elliott, 377; **4** Hamlin, 361; **5** Reddick, 354; **6** Byron, 348.

5TH ANNUAL ADVENTHEALTH 400, Kansas Speedway, Kansas City, Kansas, USA, 5 May. Round 12. 268 laps of the 1.500-mile/2.414km circuit, 402.000 miles/646.956km.
1 Kyle Larson, USA (Chevrolet Camaro ZL1 '24), 3h 10m 42s, 126.481mph/203.552km/h; **2** Chris Buescher, USA (Ford Mustang '24), +0.001s; **3** Chase Elliott, USA (Chevrolet Camaro ZL1 '24), +0.060s; **4** Martin Truex Jr, USA (Toyota Camry XSE Next Gen), +0.075s; **5** Denny Hamlin, USA (Toyota Camry XSE Next Gen), +0.609s; **6** Christopher Bell, USA (Toyota Camry XSE Next Gen), +0.693s; **7** Alex Bowman, USA (Chevrolet Camaro ZL1 '24), +0.784s; **8** Kyle Busch, USA (Chevrolet Camaro ZL1 '24), +1.144s; **9** Noah Gragson, USA (Ford Mustang '24), +1.154s; **10** Michael McDowell, USA (Ford Mustang '24), +1.244s.
Pole position: Bell, 29.491s, 183.107mph/294.682km/h.
Championship points: Drivers: 1 Larson, 467; **2** Truex Jr, 438; **3** Elliott, 412; **4** Hamlin, 411; **5** Reddick, 374; **6** Blaney, 367.

5THANNUALGOODYEAR400,DarlingtonRaceway, South Carolina, USA, 12 May. Round 13. 293 laps of the 1.366-mile/2.198km circuit, 400.238 miles/644.121km.
1 Brad Keselowski, USA (Ford Mustang '24), 3h 12m 30s, 124.750mph/200.765km/h; **2** Ty Gibbs, USA (Toyota Camry XSE Next Gen), +1.214s; **3** Josh Berry, USA (Ford Mustang '24), +1.477s; **4** Denny Hamlin, USA (Toyota Camry XSE Next Gen), +3.059s; **5** Chase Briscoe, USA (Ford Mustang '24), +4.245s; **6** William Byron, USA (Chevrolet Camaro ZL1 '24), +6.137s; **7** Darrell Wallace Jr, USA (Toyota Camry XSE Next Gen), +8.554s; **8** Alex Bowman, USA (Chevrolet Camaro ZL1 '24), +9.479s; **9** Justin Haley, USA (Ford Mustang '24), +10.682s; **10** Michael McDowell, USA (Ford Mustang '24), +11.702s.
Pole position: Tyler Reddick, USA (Toyota Camry XSE Next Gen), 28.906s, 170.124mph/273.788km/h.
Championship points: Drivers: 1 Larson, 486; **2** Truex Jr, 456; **3** Hamlin, 447; **4** Elliott, 437; **5** Byron, 400; **6** Reddick, 396.

65TH ANNUAL COCA-COLA 600, Charlotte Motor Speedway, Concord, North Carolina, USA, 26 May. Round 14. 249 laps of the 1.500-mile/2.414km circuit, 373.500 miles/601.090km.
1 Christopher Bell, USA (Toyota Camry XSE Next Gen), 3h 02m 07s, 123.053mph/198.035km/h; **2** Brad Keselowski, USA (Ford Mustang '24), +1.366s; **3** William Byron, USA (Chevrolet Camaro ZL1 '24), +1.923s; **4** Tyler Reddick, USA (Toyota Camry XSE Next Gen), +2.699s; **5** Denny Hamlin, USA (Toyota Camry XSE Next Gen), +3.540s; **6** Ty Gibbs, USA (Toyota Camry XSE Next Gen), +4.163s; **7** Chase Elliott, USA (Chevrolet Camaro ZL1 '24), +4.574s; **8** Ross Chastain, USA (Chevrolet Camaro ZL1 '24), +5.040s; **9** Alex Bowman, USA (Chevrolet Camaro ZL1 '24), +5.711s; **10** Josh Berry, USA (Ford Mustang '24), +6.476s.
Pole position: Gibbs, 29.355s, 183.955mph/296.047km/h.
Championship points: Drivers: 1 Hamlin, 492; **2** Truex Jr, 487; **3** Larson, 486; **4** Elliott, 475; **5** Byron, 461; **6** Reddick, 437.

3RD ANNUAL ENJOY ILLINOIS 300, World Wide Technology Raceway, St Louis, Madison, Illinois, USA, 2 June. Round 15. 240 laps of the 1.250-mile/2.012km circuit, 300.000 miles/482.803km.
1 Austin Cindric, USA (Ford Mustang '24), 2h 48m 03s, 107.111mph/172.378km/h; **2** Denny Hamlin, USA (Toyota Camry XSE Next Gen), +3.844s; **3** Brad Keselowski, USA (Ford Mustang '24), +4.286s; **4** Tyler Reddick, USA (Toyota Camry XSE Next Gen), +6.418s; **5** Joey Logano, USA (Ford Mustang '24), +10.332s; **6** Austin Dillon, USA (Chevrolet Camaro ZL1 '24), +11.021s; **7** Christopher Bell, USA (Toyota Camry XSE Next Gen), +13.034s; **8** Carson Hocevar, USA (Chevrolet Camaro ZL1 '24), +13.392s; **9** Justin Haley, USA (Ford Mustang '24), +13.668s; **10** Kyle Larson, USA (Chevrolet Camaro ZL1 '24), +13.746s.
Pole position: Michael McDowell, USA (Ford Mustang '24), 32.468s, 138.598mph/223.052km/h.
Championship points: Drivers: 1 Hamlin, 534; **2** Larson, 513; **3** Elliott, 507; **4** Truex Jr, 490; **5** Byron, 488; **6** Reddick, 473.

35TH ANNUAL TOYOTA / SAVE MART 350, Sonoma Raceway, California, USA, 9 June. Round 16. 110 laps of the 1.990-mile/3.203km circuit, 218.900 miles/352.285km.
1 Kyle Larson, USA (Chevrolet Camaro ZL1 '24), 2h 56m 14s, 74.526mph/119.938km/h; **2** Michael McDowell, USA (Ford Mustang '24), +4.258s; **3** Chris Buescher, USA (Ford Mustang '24), +6.453s; **4** Chase Elliott, USA (Chevrolet Camaro ZL1 '24), +10.873s; **5** Ross Chastain, USA (Chevrolet Camaro ZL1 '24), +11.089s; **6** A.J. Allmendinger, USA (Chevrolet Camaro ZL1 '24), +13.899s; **7** Ryan Blaney, USA (Ford Mustang '24), +18.855s; **8** Tyler Reddick, USA (Toyota Camry XSE Next Gen), +19.915s; **9** Christopher Bell, USA (Toyota Camry XSE Next Gen), +21.946s; **10** Todd Gilliland, USA (Ford Mustang '24), +24.091s.
Pole position: Joey Logano, USA (Ford Mustang '24), 1m 13.273s, 97.771mph/157.348km/h.
Championship points: Drivers: 1 Larson, 561; **2** Elliott, 547; **3** Hamlin, 535; **4** Reddick, 512; **5** Truex Jr, 508; **6** Byron, 495.

INAUGURAL IOWA CORN 350 POWERED BY ETHANOL, Iowa Speedway, Newton, Iowa, USA, 16 June. Round 17. 350 laps of the 0.875-mile/1.408km circuit, 306.250 miles/492.862km.
1 Ryan Blaney, USA (Ford Mustang '24), 2h 58m 37s, 102.874mph/165.560km/h; **2** William Byron, USA (Chevrolet Camaro ZL1 '24), +0.716s; **3** Chase Elliott, USA (Chevrolet Camaro ZL1 '24), +2.147s; **4** Christopher Bell, USA (Toyota Camry XSE Next Gen), +4.881s; **5** Ricky Stenhouse Jr, USA (Chevrolet Camaro ZL1 '24), +11.586s; **6** Joey Logano, USA (Ford Mustang '24), +12.264s; **7** Josh Berry, USA (Ford Mustang '24), +12.876s; **8** Alex Bowman, USA (Chevrolet Camaro ZL1 '24), +13.121s; **9** Daniel Suárez, MEX (Chevrolet Camaro ZL1 '24), +15.669s; **10** Brad Keselowski, USA (Ford Mustang '24), +15.780s.
Pole position: Kyle Larson, USA (Chevrolet Camaro ZL1 '24), 23.084s, 136.458mph/219.608km/h.
Championship points: Drivers: 1 Elliott, 591; **2** Larson, 583; **3** Hamlin, 553; **4** Byron, 537; **5** Truex Jr, 530; **6** Reddick, 527.

32ND USA TODAY 301, New Hampshire Motor Speedway, Loudon, New Hampshire, USA, 23 June. Round 18. 305 laps of the 1.058-mile/1.703km circuit, 322.690 miles/519.319km.
1 Christopher Bell, USA (Toyota Camry XSE Next Gen), 3h 48m 14s, 84.832mph/136.523km/h; **2** Chase Briscoe, USA (Ford Mustang '24), +1.104s; **3** Josh Berry, USA (Ford Mustang '24), +1.109s; **4** Kyle Larson, USA (Chevrolet Camaro ZL1 '24), +1.371s; **5** Chris Buescher, USA (Ford Mustang '24), +1.751s; **6** Tyler Reddick, USA (Toyota Camry XSE Next Gen), +2.080s; **7** Ricky Stenhouse Jr, USA (Chevrolet Camaro ZL1 '24), +2.420s; **8** John Hunter Nemechek, USA (Toyota Camry XSE Next Gen), +2.523s; **9** Martin Truex Jr, USA (Toyota Camry XSE Next Gen), +2.697s; **10** Ross Chastain, USA (Chevrolet Camaro ZL1 '24), +2.898s.
Pole position: Elliott.
Championship points: Drivers: 1 Larson, 620; **2** Elliott, 620; **3** Hamlin, 580; **4** Truex Jr, 572; **5** Reddick, 560; **6** Bell, 555.

4TH ANNUAL ALLY 400, Nashville Superspeedway, Lebanon, Tennessee, USA, 30 June. Round 19. 331 laps of the 1.330-mile/2.140km circuit, 440.230 miles/708.482km.
1 Joey Logano, USA (Ford Mustang '24), 4h 03m 54s, 108.298mph/174.288km/h; **2** Zane Smith, USA (Chevrolet Camaro ZL1 '24), +0.068s; **3** Tyler Reddick, USA (Toyota Camry XSE Next Gen), +0.071s; **4** Ryan Preece, USA (Ford Mustang '24), +0.251s; **5** Chris Buescher, USA (Ford Mustang '24), +0.275s; **6** Ryan Blaney, USA (Ford Mustang '24), +0.560s; **7** Darrell Wallace Jr, USA (Toyota Camry XSE Next Gen), +0.576s; **8** Kyle Larson, USA (Chevrolet Camaro ZL1 '24), +1.856s; **9** Daniel Hemric, USA (Chevrolet Camaro ZL1 '24), +1.895s; **10** Noah Gragson, USA (Ford Mustang '24), +1.947s.
Pole position: Denny Hamlin, USA (Toyota Camry XSE Next Gen), 29.859s, 160.354mph/258.064km/h.
Championship points: Drivers: 1 Larson, 664; **2** Elliott, 644; **3** Hamlin, 621; **4** Reddick, 611; **5** Truex Jr, 591; **6** Bell, 576.

2ND ANNUAL GRANT PARK 165, Chicago Street Course, Illinois, USA, 7 July. Round 20. 58 laps of the 2.200-mile/3.541km circuit, 127.600 miles/205.352km.
1 Alex Bowman, USA (Chevrolet Camaro ZL1 '24), 2h 19m 24s, 54.921mph/88.387km/h; **2** Tyler Reddick, USA (Toyota Camry XSE Next Gen), +2.863s; **3** Ty Gibbs, USA (Toyota Camry XSE Next Gen), +2.930s; **4** Joey Hand, USA (Ford Mustang '24), +8.513s; **5** Michael McDowell, USA (Ford Mustang '24), +8.584s; **6** Ricky Stenhouse Jr, USA (Chevrolet Camaro ZL1 '24), +12.411s; **7** Todd Gilliland, USA (Ford Mustang '24), +13.212s; **8** William Byron, USA (Chevrolet Camaro ZL1 '24), +13.607s; **9** Kyle Busch, USA (Chevrolet Camaro ZL1 '24), +14.757s; **10** Ryan Blaney, USA (Ford Mustang '24), +16.041s.
Pole position: Kyle Larson, USA (Chevrolet Camaro ZL1 '24), 1m 27.836s, 90.168mph/145.111km/h.
Championship points: Drivers: 1 Larson, 671; **2** Elliott, 660; **3** Reddick, 648; **4** Hamlin, 629; **5** Truex Jr, 601; **6** Byron, 599.

51ST ANNUAL THE GREAT AMERICAN GETAWAY 400 PRESENTED BY VISITPA, Pocono Raceway, Long Pond, Pennsylvania, USA, 14 July. Round 21. 160 laps of the 2.500-mile/4.023km circuit, 400.000 miles/643.738km.
1 Ryan Blaney, USA (Ford Mustang '24), 3h 13m 59s, 123.722mph/199.111km/h; **2** Denny Hamlin, USA (Toyota Camry XSE Next Gen), +1.312s; **3** Alex Bowman, USA (Chevrolet Camaro ZL1 '24), +4.057s; **4** William Byron, USA (Chevrolet Camaro ZL1 '24), +6.160s; **5** Joey Logano, USA (Ford Mustang '24), +6.559s; **6** Tyler Reddick, USA (Toyota Camry XSE Next Gen), +6.865s; **7** Brad Keselowski, USA (Ford Mustang '24), +7.604s; **8** Martin Truex Jr, USA (Toyota Camry XSE Next Gen), +8.512s; **9** Chase Elliott, USA (Chevrolet Camaro ZL1 '24), +9.144s; **10** Darrell Wallace Jr, USA (Toyota Camry XSE Next Gen), +12.089s.
Pole position: Ty Gibbs, USA (Toyota Camry XSE Next Gen), 52.929s, 170.039mph/273.651km/h.
Championship points: Drivers: 1 Elliott, 703; **2** Larson, 700; **3** Reddick, 688; **4** Hamlin, 683; **5** Byron, 646; **6** Truex Jr, 640.

31ST ANNUAL BRICKYARD 400 PRESENTED BY PPG, Indianapolis Motor Speedway, Speedway, Indiana, USA, 21 July. Round 22. 167 laps of the 2.500-mile/4.023km circuit, 417.500 miles/671.901km.
1 Kyle Larson, USA (Chevrolet Camaro ZL1 '24), 3h 29m 09s, 119.770mph/192.752km/h; **2** Tyler Reddick, USA (Toyota Camry XSE Next Gen), +0.282s; **3** Ryan Blaney, USA (Ford Mustang '24), +9.494s; **4** Christopher Bell, USA (Toyota Camry XSE Next Gen), +11.457s; **5** Darrell Wallace Jr, USA (Toyota Camry XSE Next Gen), +11.458s; **6** Todd Gilliland, USA (Ford Mustang '24), +11.458s; **7** Austin Cindric, USA (Ford Mustang '24), +11.459s; **8** Daniel Suárez, MEX (Chevrolet Camaro ZL1 '24), +11.461s; **9** Noah Gragson, USA (Ford Mustang '24), +11.462s; **10** Chase Elliott, USA (Chevrolet Camaro ZL1 '24), +12.888s.
Pole position: Reddick, 49.469s, 181.932mph/292.791km/h.
Championship points: Drivers: 1 Larson, 749; **2** Elliott, 739; **3** Reddick, 734; **4** Hamlin, 706; **5** Blaney, 676; **6** Byron, 654.

67TH ANNUAL COOK OUT 400, Richmond International Raceway, Virginia, USA, 11 August. Round 23. 408 laps of the 0.750-mile/1.207km circuit, 306.000 miles/492.459km.
1 Austin Dillon, USA (Chevrolet Camaro ZL1 '24), 3h 03m 19s, 100.155mph/161.183km/h; **2** Denny Hamlin, USA (Toyota Camry XSE Next Gen), +0.116s; **3** Tyler Reddick, USA (Toyota Camry XSE Next Gen), +0.117s; **4** Darrell Wallace Jr, USA (Toyota Camry XSE Next Gen), +0.278s; **5** Ross Chastain, USA (Chevrolet Camaro ZL1 '24), +0.541s; **6** Christopher Bell, USA (Toyota Camry XSE Next Gen), +0.667s; **7** Kyle Larson, USA (Chevrolet Camaro ZL1 '24), +0.872s; **8** Carson Hocevar, USA (Chevrolet Camaro ZL1 '24), +0.902s; **9** Chase Elliott, USA (Chevrolet Camaro ZL1 '24), +1.273s; **10** Daniel Suárez, MEX (Chevrolet Camaro ZL1 '24), +1.410s.
Pole position: Hamlin, 22.850s, 118.162mph/190.163km/h.
Championship points: Drivers: 1 Larson, 779; **2** Reddick, 774; **3** Elliott, 773; **4** Hamlin, 758; **5** Blaney, 702; **6** Bell, 701.

56TH ANNUAL FIREKEEPERS CASINO 400, Michigan International Speedway, Brooklyn, Michigan, USA, 19 August. Round 24. 206 laps of the 2.000-mile/3.219km circuit, 412.000 miles/663.050km.
1 Tyler Reddick, USA (Toyota Camry XSE Next Gen), 3h 02m 12s, 135.675mph/218.348km/h; **2** William Byron, USA (Chevrolet Camaro ZL1 '24), +0.168s; **3** Ty Gibbs, USA (Toyota Camry XSE Next Gen), +0.590s; **4** Kyle Busch, USA (Chevrolet Camaro ZL1 '24), +1.007s; **5** Brad Keselowski, USA (Ford Mustang '24), +1.546s; **6** Chris Buescher, USA (Ford Mustang '24), +1.789s; **7** Zane Smith, USA (Chevrolet Camaro ZL1 '24), +2.142s; **8** Daniel Suárez, MEX (Chevrolet Camaro ZL1 '24), +2.269s; **9** Denny Hamlin, USA (Toyota Camry XSE Next Gen), +2.306s; **10** Carson Hocevar, USA (Chevrolet Camaro ZL1 '24), +2.567s.
Pole position: Hamlin.
Championship points: Drivers: 1 Reddick, 814; **2** Elliott, 804; **3** Hamlin, 786; **4** Larson, 782; **5** Blaney, 732; **6** Byron, 728.

66TH ANNUAL COKE ZERO SUGAR 400, Daytona International Speedway, Daytona Beach, Florida, USA, 24 August. Round 25. 164 laps of the 2.500-mile/4.023km circuit, 410.000 miles/659.831km.
1 Harrison Burton, USA (Ford Mustang '24), 3h 01m 40s, 135.413mph/217.926km/h; **2** Kyle Busch, USA (Chevrolet Camaro ZL1 '24), +0.047s; **3** Christopher Bell, USA (Toyota Camry XSE Next Gen), +0.139s; **4** Cody Ware, USA (Ford Mustang '24), +0.240s; **5** Ty Gibbs, USA (Toyota Camry XSE Next Gen), +0.282s; **6** Darrell Wallace Jr, USA (Toyota Camry XSE Next Gen), +0.325s; **7** Parker Retzlaff, USA (Chevrolet Camaro ZL1 '24), +0.408s; **8** Brad Keselowski, USA (Ford Mustang '24), +0.409s; **9** Daniel Hemric, USA (Chevrolet Camaro ZL1 '24), +0.429s; **10** Chris Buescher, USA (Ford Mustang '24), +0.446s.
Pole position: Michael McDowell, USA (Ford Mustang '24), 49.136s, 183.165mph/294.776km/h.
Championship points: Drivers: 1 Reddick, 823; **2** Larson, 806; **3** Elliott, 805; **4** Blaney, 755; **5** Byron, 743; **6** Bell, 737.

75TH ANNUAL COOK OUT SOUTHERN 500, Darlington Raceway, South Carolina, USA, 1 September. Round 26. 367 laps of the 1.366-mile/2.198km circuit, 501.322 miles/806.800km.
1 Chase Briscoe, USA (Ford Mustang '24), 3h 55m 14s, 127.870mph/205.787km/h; **2** Kyle Busch, USA (Chevrolet Camaro ZL1 '24), +0.361s; **3** Christopher Bell, USA (Toyota Camry XSE Next Gen), +5.210s; **4** Kyle Larson, USA (Chevrolet Camaro ZL1 '24), +6.092s; **5** Ross Chastain, USA (Chevrolet Camaro ZL1 '24), +6.694s; **6** Chris Buescher, USA (Ford Mustang '24), +7.150s; **7** Denny Hamlin, USA (Toyota Camry XSE Next Gen), +9.665s; **8** Joey Logano, USA (Ford Mustang '24), +9.877s; **9** Corey LaJoie, USA (Chevrolet Camaro ZL1 '24), +9.958s; **10** Tyler Reddick, USA (Toyota Camry XSE Next Gen), +10.461s.
Pole position: Darrell Wallace Jr, USA (Toyota Camry XSE Next Gen), 29.421s, 167.146mph/268.995km/h.
Championship points: Drivers: 1 Larson, 2040; **2** Bell, 2032; **3** Reddick, 2028; **4** Byron, 2022; **5** Blaney, 2018; **6** Hamlin, 2015.

55TH ANNUAL QUAKER STATE 400 AVAILABLE AT WALMART, Atlanta Motor Speedway, Hampton, Georgia, USA, 8 September. Round 27. 266 laps of the 1.540-mile/2.478km circuit, 409.640 miles/659.252km.
1 Joey Logano, USA (Ford Mustang '24), 3h 06m 12s, 132.000mph/212.433km/h; **2** Daniel Suárez, MEX (Chevrolet Camaro ZL1 '24), +0.212s; **3** Ryan Blaney, USA (Ford Mustang '24), +0.213s; **4** Christopher Bell, USA (Toyota Camry XSE Next Gen), +0.368s; **5** Alex Bowman, USA (Chevrolet Camaro ZL1 '24), +0.406s; **6** Tyler Reddick, USA (Toyota Camry XSE Next Gen), +0.446s; **7** Kyle Busch, USA (Chevrolet Camaro ZL1 '24), +0.501s; **8** Chase Elliott, USA (Chevrolet Camaro ZL1 '24), +0.589s; **9** William Byron, USA (Chevrolet Camaro ZL1 '24), +0.665s; **10** Austin Cindric, USA (Ford Mustang '24), +0.826s.
Pole position: Michael McDowell, USA (Ford Mustang '24), 30.926s, 179.267mph/288.502km/h.
Championship points: Drivers: 1 Blaney, 2071; **2** Bell, 2066; **3** Reddick, 2059; **4** Byron, 2059; **5** Logano, 2054; **6** Bowman, 2053.

38TH ANNUAL GO BOWLING AT THE GLEN, Watkins Glen International, New York, USA, 15 September. Round 28. 92 laps of the 2.450-mile/3.943km circuit, 225.400 miles/362.746km.
1 Chris Buescher, USA (Ford Mustang '24), 2h 38m 41s, 85.226mph/137.159km/h; **2** Shane van Gisbergen, NZ (Chevrolet Camaro ZL1 '24), +0.979s; **3** Carson Hocevar, USA (Chevrolet Camaro ZL1 '24), +2.921s; **4** Ross Chastain, USA (Chevrolet Camaro ZL1 '24), +3.311s; **5** Zane Smith, USA (Chevrolet Camaro ZL1 '24), +3.739s; **6** Chase Briscoe, USA (Ford Mustang '24), +3.843s; **7** Michael McDowell, USA (Ford Mustang '24), +3.951s; **8** Corey LaJoie, USA (Chevrolet Camaro ZL1 '24), +4.265s; **9** Ryan Preece, USA (Ford Mustang '24), +4.534s; **10** Austin Cindric, USA (Ford Mustang '24), +4.601s.
Pole position: Chastain, 1m 12.130s, 122.279mph/196.789km/h.
Championship points: Drivers: 1 Bell, 2089; **2** Cindric, 2086; **3** Logano, 2084; **4** Bowman, 2084; **5** Suárez, 2079; **6** Reddick, 2073.

64TH ANNUAL BASS PRO SHOPS NIGHT RACE, Bristol Motor Speedway, Tennessee, USA, 21 September. Round 29. 500 laps of the 0.533-mile/0.858km circuit, 266.500 miles/428.890km.
1 Kyle Larson, USA (Chevrolet Camaro ZL1 '24), 2h 37m 53s, 101.277mph/162.990km/h; **2** Chase Elliott, USA (Chevrolet Camaro ZL1 '24), +7.088s; **3** Darrell Wallace Jr, USA (Toyota Camry XSE Next Gen), +9.729s; **4** Denny Hamlin, USA (Toyota Camry XSE Next Gen), +10.088s; **5** Christopher Bell, USA (Toyota Camry XSE Next Gen), +10.349s; **6** Ryan Blaney, USA (Ford Mustang '24), +11.946s; **7** Ryan Preece, USA (Ford Mustang '24), +13.299s; **8** Chase Briscoe, USA (Ford Mustang '24), +13.791s; **9** Alex Bowman, USA (Chevrolet Camaro ZL1 '24), +14.077s; **10** Ross Chastain, USA (Chevrolet Camaro ZL1 '24), +14.735s.
Pole position: Bowman, 15.142s, 126.720mph/203.937km/h.
Championship points: Drivers: 1 Larson, 3047; **2** Bell, 3032; **3** Reddick, 3028; **4** Byron, 3022; **5** Blaney, 3019; **6** Hamlin, 3015.

24TH ANNUAL HOLLYWOOD CASINO 400 PRESENTED BY ESPN BET, Kansas Speedway, Kansas City, Kansas, USA, 29 September. Round 30. 267 laps of the 1.500-mile/2.414km circuit, 400.500 miles/644.542km.
1 Ross Chastain, USA (Chevrolet Camaro ZL1 '24), 3h 14m 54s, 123.294mph/198.422km/h; **2** William Byron, USA (Chevrolet Camaro ZL1 '24), +0.388s; **3** Martin Truex Jr, USA (Toyota Camry XSE Next Gen), +0.868s; **4** Ryan Blaney, USA (Ford Mustang '24), +2.551s; **5** Ty Gibbs, USA (Toyota Camry XSE Next Gen), +4.437s; **6** Alex Bowman, USA (Chevrolet Camaro ZL1 '24), +5.618s; **7** Christopher Bell, USA (Toyota Camry XSE Next Gen), +6.442s; **8** Denny Hamlin, USA (Toyota Camry XSE Next Gen), +6.833s; **9** Chase Elliott, USA (Chevrolet Camaro ZL1 '24), +9.557s; **10** Zane Smith, USA (Chevrolet Camaro ZL1 '24), +10.131s.
Pole position: Bell, 30.111s, 179.336mph/288.614km/h.
Championship points: Drivers: 1 Byron, 3074; **2** Blaney, 3068; **3** Bell, 3068; **4** Larson, 3058; **5** Hamlin, 3051; **6** Bowman, 3048.

56TH ANNUAL YELLAWOOD 500, Talladega Superspeedway, Lincoln, Alabama, USA, 6 October. Round 31. 195 laps of the 2.660-mile/4.281km circuit, 518.700 miles/834.767km.
1 Ricky Stenhouse Jr, USA (Chevrolet Camaro ZL1 '24), 3h 26m 25s, 150.773mph/242.645km/h; **2** Brad Keselowski, USA (Ford Mustang '24), +0.006s; **3** William Byron, USA (Chevrolet Camaro ZL1 '24), +0.027s; **4** Kyle Larson, USA (Chevrolet Camaro ZL1 '24), +0.080s; **5** Erik Jones, USA (Toyota Camry XSE Next Gen), +0.101s; **6** Christopher Bell, USA (Toyota Camry XSE Next Gen), +0.166s; **7** Justin Haley, USA (Chevrolet Camaro ZL1 '24), +0.178s; **8** Austin Dillon, USA (Chevrolet Camaro ZL1 '24), +0.236s; **9** Darrell Wallace Jr, USA (Toyota Camry XSE Next Gen), +0.259s; **10** Denny Hamlin, USA (Toyota Camry XSE Next Gen), +0.293s.
Pole position: Michael McDowell, USA (Ford Mustang '24), 52.310s, 183.063mph/294.611km/h.
Championship points: Drivers: 1 Byron, 3122; **2** Bell, 3105; **3** Larson, 3100; **4** Hamlin, 3078; **5** Bowman, 3074; **6** Blaney, 3073.

65TH ANNUAL BANK OF AMERICA ROVAL 400, Charlotte Motor Speedway, Concord, North Carolina, USA, 13 October. Round 32. 109 laps of the 2.320-mile/3.734km circuit, 252.880 miles/406.971km.
1 Kyle Larson, USA (Chevrolet Camaro ZL1 '24), 3h 00m 03s, 84.270mph/135.619km/h; **2** Christopher Bell, USA (Toyota Camry XSE Next Gen), +1.511s; **3** William Byron, USA (Chevrolet Camaro ZL1 '24), +8.965s; **4** Austin Cindric, USA (Ford Mustang '24), +9.940s; **5** Chase Elliott, USA (Chevrolet Camaro ZL1 '24), +11.756s; **6** A.J. Allmendinger, USA (Chevrolet Camaro ZL1 '24), +12.919s; **7** Shane van Gisbergen, NZ (Chevrolet Camaro ZL1 '24), +16.970s; **8** Joey Logano, USA (Ford Mustang '24), +17.975s; **9** Darrell Wallace Jr, USA (Toyota Camry XSE Next Gen), +25.570s; **10** Ryan Blaney, USA (Ford Mustang '24), +26.728s.
Pole position: van Gisbergen, 1m 22.704s, 100.987mph/162.522km/h.
Championship points: Drivers: 1 Larson, 4052; **2** Bell, 4032; **3** Reddick, 4029; **4** Byron, 4023; **5** Blaney, 4019; **6** Hamlin, 4015.
Teams: 1 Team Penske (car 22), 5040; **2** Team Penske (12), 5035; **3** Hendrick Motorsports (24), 5034.

7TH ANNUAL SOUTH POINT 400, Las Vegas Motor Speedway, Nevada, USA, 20 October. Round 33. 267 laps of the 1.500-mile/2.414km circuit, 400.500 miles/644.542km.
1 Joey Logano, USA (Ford Mustang '24), 2h 52m 24s, 139.385mph/224.319km/h; **2** Christopher Bell, USA (Toyota Camry XSE Next Gen), +0.662s; **3** Daniel Suárez, MEX (Chevrolet Camaro ZL1 '24), +1.191s; **4** William Byron, USA (Chevrolet Camaro ZL1 '24), +2.648s; **5** Alex Bowman, USA (Chevrolet Camaro ZL1 '24), +5.454s; **6** Martin Truex Jr, USA (Toyota Camry XSE Next Gen), +6.051s; **7** Ross Chastain, USA (Chevrolet Camaro ZL1 '24), +6.735s; **8** Denny Hamlin, USA (Toyota Camry XSE Next Gen), +8.370s; **9** John Hunter Nemechek, USA (Toyota Camry XSE Next Gen), +10.446s; **10** Chris Buescher, USA (Ford Mustang '24), +12.397s.
Pole position: Bell, 29.135s, 185.344mph/298.282km/h.
Championship points: Drivers: 1 Bell, 4086; **2** Larson, 4079; **3** Byron, 4071; **4** Logano, 4061; **5** Hamlin, 4044; **6** Reddick, 4041.

26TH ANNUAL STRAIGHT TALK WIRELESS 400, Homestead-Miami Speedway, Florida, USA, 27 October. Round 34. 267 laps of the 1.500-mile/2.414km circuit, 400.500 miles/644.542km.
1 Tyler Reddick, USA (Toyota Camry XSE Next Gen), 3h 05m 44s, 129.379mph/208.215km/h; **2** Ryan Blaney, USA (Ford Mustang '24), +0.241s; **3** Denny Hamlin, USA (Toyota Camry XSE Next Gen), +0.568s; **4** Christopher Bell, USA (Toyota Camry XSE Next Gen), +1.499s; **5** Chase Elliott, USA (Chevrolet Camaro ZL1 '24), +1.637s; **6** William Byron, USA (Chevrolet Camaro ZL1 '24), +2.346s; **7** Alex Bowman, USA (Chevrolet Camaro ZL1 '24), +2.763s; **8** A.J. Allmendinger, USA (Chevrolet Camaro ZL1 '24), +2.983s; **9** Carson Hocevar, USA (Chevrolet Camaro ZL1 '24), +3.247s; **10** Ryan Preece, USA (Ford Mustang '24), +4.282s.
Pole position: Reddick, 32.248s, 167.452mph/269.488km/h.
Championship points: Drivers: 1 Bell, 4132; **2** Byron, 4110; **3** Larson, 4103; **4** Reddick, 4098; **5** Hamlin, 4092; **6** Blaney, 4072.
Teams: 1 Team Penske (car 22), 5040; **2** Team Penske (12), 5035; **3** Hendrick Motorsports (24), 5034.

76TH ANNUAL XFINITY 500, Martinsville Speedway, Ridgeway, Virginia, USA, 3 November. Round 35. 500 laps of the 0.526-mile/0.847km circuit, 263.000 miles/423.257km.
1 Ryan Blaney, USA (Ford Mustang '24), 3h 28m 31s, 75.677mph/121.791km/h; **2** Chase Elliott, USA (Chevrolet Camaro ZL1 '24), +2.593s; **3** Kyle Larson, USA (Chevrolet Camaro ZL1 '24), +5.172s; **4** Austin Cindric, USA (Ford Mustang '24), +5.263s; **5** Denny Hamlin, USA (Toyota Camry XSE Next Gen), +7.643s; **6** William Byron, USA (Chevrolet Camaro ZL1 '24), +11.887s; **7** Austin Dillon, USA (Chevrolet Camaro ZL1 '24), +11.993s; **8** Ross Chastain, USA (Chevrolet Camaro ZL1 '24), +12.287s; **9** Brad Keselowski, USA (Ford Mustang '24), +12.355s; **10** Joey Logano, USA (Ford Mustang '24), +12.647s.
Pole position: Martin Truex Jr, USA (Toyota Camry XSE Next Gen), 19.686s, 96.190mph/154.803km/h.
Championship points: Drivers: 1 Byron, 5000; **2** Reddick, 5000; **3** Blaney, 5000; **4** Logano, 5000; **5** Bell, 2363; **6** Larson, 2339.
Teams: 1 Team Penske (car 22), 5040; **2** Team Penske (12), 5035; **3** Hendrick Motorsports (24), 5034.

37TH ANNUAL NASCAR CUP SERIES CHAMPIONSHIP RACE, Phoenix Raceway, Arizona, USA, 10 November. Round 36. 312 laps of the 1.000-mile/1.609km circuit, 312.000 miles/502.115km.
1 Joey Logano, USA (Ford Mustang '24), 2h 56m 16s, 106.203mph/170.917km/h; **2** Ryan Blaney, USA (Ford Mustang '24), +0.330s; **3** William Byron, USA (Chevrolet Camaro ZL1 '24), +5.119s; **4** Kyle Larson, USA (Chevrolet Camaro ZL1 '24), +7.169s; **5** Christopher Bell, USA (Toyota Camry XSE Next Gen), +9.752s; **6** Tyler Reddick, USA (Toyota Camry XSE Next Gen), +11.068s; **7** Darrell Wallace Jr, USA (Toyota Camry XSE Next Gen), +11.372s; **8** Chase Elliott, USA (Chevrolet Camaro ZL1 '24), +11.824s; **9** Chris Buescher, USA (Ford Mustang '24), +15.567s; **10** Daniel Suárez, MEX (Chevrolet Camaro ZL1 '24), +21.531s.
Pole position: Martin Truex Jr, USA (Toyota Camry XSE Next Gen), 26.718s, 134.741mph/216.844km/h.
Championship points: Drivers: 1 Logano, 5040; **2** Blaney, 5035; **3** Byron, 5034; **4** Reddick, 5031; **5** Bell, 2412; **6** Larson, 2378.
Teams: 1 Team Penske (car 22), 5040; **2** Team Penske (12), 5035; **3** Hendrick Motorsports (24), 5034.

Final championship points
Drivers
1 Joey Logano, USA, 5040; **2** Ryan Blaney, USA, 5035; **3** William Byron, USA, 5034; **4** Tyler Reddick, USA, 5031; **5** Christopher Bell, USA, 2412; **6** Kyle Larson, USA, 2378; **7** Chase Elliott, USA, 2342; **8** Denny Hamlin, USA, 2328; **9** Alex Bowman, USA, 2318; **10** Martin Truex Jr, USA, 2257; **11** Austin Cindric, USA, 2247; **12** Daniel Suárez, MEX, 2226; **13** Brad Keselowski, USA, 2208; **14** Chase Briscoe, USA, 2184; **15** Ty Gibbs, USA, 2169; **16** Harrison Burton, USA, 2122; **17** Chris Buescher, USA, 930; **18** Darrell Wallace Jr, USA, 878; **19** Ross Chastain, USA, 852; **20** Kyle Busch, USA, 766; **21** Carson Hocevar, USA, 686; **22** Todd Gilliland, USA, 630; **23** Michael McDowell, USA, 624; **24** Noah Gragson, USA, 612; **25** Ricky Stenhouse Jr, USA, 590; **26** Ryan Preece, USA, 584; **27** Josh Berry, USA, 579; **28** Erik Jones, USA, 516; **29** Daniel Hemric, USA, 515; **30** Zane Smith, USA, 505.

Manufacturers
1 Chevrolet, 1309; **2** Ford, 1275; **3** Toyota, 1259.

Teams
1 Team Penske (car 22), 5040; **2** Team Penske (12), 5035; **3** Hendrick Motorsports (24), 5034.

Sunoco Rookie of the Year
Carson Hocevar, USA.

Other NASCAR races

BUSCH LIGHT CLASH AT THE COLISEUM, LA Memorial Coliseum, Los Angeles, California, USA, 3 February. 151 laps of the 0.250-mile/0.402km circuit, 37.750 miles/60.753km.
1 Denny Hamlin, USA (Toyota Camry XSE Next Gen), 1h 08m 46s, 32.937mph/53.008km/h; **2** Kyle Busch, USA (Chevrolet Camaro ZL1 '24), +0.610s; **3** Ryan Blaney, USA (Ford Mustang '24), 151 laps; **4** Joey Logano, USA (Ford Mustang '24), 151; **5** Kyle Larson, USA (Chevrolet Camaro ZL1 '24), 151; **6** Alex Bowman, USA (Chevrolet Camaro ZL1 '24), 151; **7** Chase Briscoe, USA (Ford Mustang '24), 151; **8** Brad Keselowski, USA (Ford Mustang '24), 151; **9** Martin Truex Jr, USA (Toyota Camry XSE Next Gen), 151; **10** William Byron, USA (Chevrolet Camaro ZL1 '24), 151.
Pole position: Hamlin.

BLUEGREEN VACATIONS AT DAYTONA, Daytona International Speedway, Daytona Beach, Florida, USA, 15 February. 2 x 60 laps of the 2.500-mile/4.023km circuit.
Duel 1 (150.000 miles/241.402km).
1 Tyler Reddick, USA (Toyota Camry XSE Next Gen), 53m 35s, 167.963mph/270.310km/h; **2** Chase Elliott, USA (Chevrolet Camaro ZL1 '24), +0.056s; **3** Alex Bowman, USA (Chevrolet Camaro ZL1 '24), 60 laps; **4** Carson Hocevar, USA (Chevrolet Camaro ZL1 '24), 60; **5** Erik Jones, USA (Toyota Camry XSE Next Gen), 60; **6** Daniel Suárez, MEX (Chevrolet Camaro ZL1 '24), 60; **7** Joey Logano, USA (Ford Mustang '24), 60; **8** Ty Gibbs, USA (Toyota Camry XSE Next Gen), 60; **9** Kyle Larson, USA (Chevrolet Camaro ZL1 '24), 60; **10** Chris Buescher, USA (Ford Mustang '24), 60.
Pole position: Logano.

Duel 2 (150.000 miles/241.402km).
1 Christopher Bell, USA (Toyota Camry XSE Next Gen), 55m 51s, 161.146mph/259.339km/h; **2** Austin Cindric, USA (Ford Mustang '24), +0.113s; **3** Denny Hamlin, USA (Toyota Camry XSE Next Gen), 60 laps; **4** John Hunter Nemechek, USA (Toyota Camry XSE Next Gen), 60; **5** Harrison Burton, USA (Ford Mustang '24), 60; **6** Zane Smith, USA (Chevrolet Camaro ZL1 '24), 60; **7** Brad Keselowski, USA (Ford Mustang '24), 60; **8** William Byron, USA (Chevrolet Camaro ZL1 '24), 60; **9** Chase Briscoe, USA (Ford Mustang '24), 60; **10** Justin Haley, USA (Ford Mustang '24), 60.
Pole position: Michael McDowell, USA (Ford Mustang '24).

NASCAR ALL-STAR OPEN, North Wilkesboro Speedway, North Carolina, USA, 19 May. 100 laps of the 0.625-mile/1.006km circuit, 62.500 miles/100.584km.
1 Ty Gibbs, USA (Toyota Camry XSE Next Gen), 37m 58.965s, 98.729mph/158.889km/h; **2** Darrell Wallace Jr, USA (Toyota Camry XSE Next Gen), +1.572s; **3** Josh Berry, USA (Ford Mustang '24), +2.009s; **4** Justin Haley, USA (Ford Mustang '24), +3.959s; **5** Noah Gragson, USA (Ford Mustang '24), +4.307s; **6** Alex Bowman, USA (Chevrolet Camaro ZL1 '24), +5.142s; **7** Chase Briscoe, USA (Ford Mustang '24), +5.604s; **8** Ryan Preece, USA (Ford Mustang '24), +7.105s; **9** Austin Dillon, USA (Chevrolet Camaro ZL1 '24), +7.334s; **10** Carson Hocevar, USA (Chevrolet Camaro ZL1 '24), +8.650s.
Fastest race lap Gibbs, 18.439s, 122.024mph/196.379km/h.
Pole position: Gibbs.

NASCAR ALL-STAR RACE, North Wilkesboro Speedway, North Carolina, USA, 19 May. 200 laps of the 0.625-mile/1.006km circuit, 125.000 miles/201.168km.
1 Joey Logano, USA (Ford Mustang '24), 1h 19m 57.335s, 93.802mph/150.960km/h; **2** Denny Hamlin, USA (Toyota Camry XSE Next Gen), +0.636s; **3** Chris Buescher, USA (Ford Mustang '24), +4.893s; **4** Kyle Larson, USA (Chevrolet Camaro ZL1 '24), +5.312s; **5** Ryan Blaney, USA (Ford Mustang '24), +5.451s; **6** Darrell Wallace Jr, USA (Toyota Camry XSE Next Gen), +7.453s; **7** Ross Chastain, USA (Chevrolet Camaro ZL1 '24), +9.222s; **8** Chase Elliott, USA (Chevrolet Camaro ZL1 '24), +10.218s; **9** Michael McDowell, USA (Ford Mustang '24), +10.666s; **10** Kyle Busch, USA (Chevrolet Camaro ZL1 '24), +11.310s.
Fastest race lap Larson, 18.362s, 122.536mph/197.202km/h.
Pole position: Logano.

Firestone Indy NXT Series

All cars are Dallara IL15-AER IL-2.

FIRESTONE INDY NXT SERIES, St. Petersburg Street Circuit, Florida, USA, 10 March. Round 1. 45 laps of the 1.800-mile/2.897km circuit, 81.000 miles/130.357km.
1 Nolan Siegel, USA, 52m 49.3943s, 92.005mph/148.068km/h; **2** Jacob Abel, USA, +1.3959s; **3** Louis Foster, GB, +1.8168s; **4** Michael D'Orlando, USA, +2.5480s; **5** Reece Gold, USA, +4.4578s; **6** Jonathan Browne, IRL, +7.9631s; **7** Caio Collet, BR, +8.3781s; **8** Myles Rowe, USA, +9.9905s; **9** Salvador de Alba, MEX, +11.7563s; **10** Christian Bogle, USA, +12.3531s.
Fastest race lap: Gold, 1m 05.0994s, 99.540mph/160.194km/h.
Pole position: Siegel, 1m 04.5759s, 100.347mph/161.493km/h.

FIRESTONE INDY NXT SERIES, Barber Motorsports Park, Birmingham, Alabama, USA, 28 April. Round 2. 35 laps of the 2.300-mile/3.701km circuit, 80.500 miles/129.552km.
1 Jacob Abel, USA, 45m 13.2293s, 106.810mph/171.894km/h; **2** Nolan Siegel, USA, +1.3326s; **3** James Roe, IRL, +1.9583s; **4** Caio Collet, BR,

+2.5617s; **5** Louis Foster, GB, +5.3211s; **6** Myles Rowe, USA, +6.4573s; **7** Michael D'Orlando, USA, +7.4590s; **8** Bryce Aron, USA, +10.2803s; **9** Callum Hedge, NZ, +10.4908s; **10** Salvador de Alba, MEX, +12.3402s.
Fastest race lap: Collet, 1m 12.5804s, 114.080mph/183.595km/h.
Pole position: Abel, 1m 11.3507s, 116.047mph/186.759km/h.

FIRESTONE INDY NXT SERIES, Indianapolis Motor Speedway, Speedway, Indiana, USA, 10/11 May. 2 x 35 laps of the 2.439-mile/3.925km circuit.
Round 3 (85.365 miles/137.382km).
1 Jacob Abel, USA, 48m 34.6690s, 105.437mph/169.684km/h; **2** Nolan Siegel, USA, +0.5470s; **3** Jamie Chadwick, GB, +2.0681s; **4** Callum Hedge, NZ, +3.6526s; **5** Myles Rowe, USA, +4.4706s; **6** Reece Gold, USA, +5.2579s; **7** Louis Foster, GB, +5.6844s; **8** Jonathan Browne, IRL, +7.3758s; **9** Christian Bogle, USA, +7.9286s; **10** Niels Koolen, NL, +9.0195s.
Fastest race lap: Abel, 1m 16.1813s, 115.257mph/185.488km/h.
Pole position: Abel, 1m 14.9358s, 117.172mph/188.571km/h.

Round 4 (85.365 miles/137.382km).
1 Louis Foster, GB, 45m 08.4692s, 113.464mph/182.603km/h; **2** Jacob Abel, USA, +2.3688s; **3** Caio Collet, BR, +9.6159s; **4** James Roe, IRL, +10.3576s; **5** Nolan Siegel, USA, +10.4305s; **6** Michael D'Orlando, USA, +11.0124s; **7** Myles Rowe, USA, +17.2272s; **8** Jonathan Browne, IRL, +21.1197s; **9** Salvador de Alba, MEX, +22.0160s; **10** Callum Hedge, NZ, +25.1580s.
Fastest race lap: Foster, 1m 16.4351s, 114.874mph/184.872km/h.
Pole position: Abel, 1m 15.0528s, 116.990mph/188.277km/h.

FIRESTONE INDY NXT SERIES, Detroit Street Circuit, Michigan, USA, 2 June. Round 5. 45 laps of the 1.645-mile/2.647km circuit, 74.025 miles/119.132km.
1 Louis Foster, GB, 56m 04.5065s, 79.206mph/127.470km/h; **2** Caio Collet, BR, +0.3608s; **3** Callum Hedge, NZ, +0.6771s; **4** Myles Rowe, USA, +0.9694s; **5** Jacob Abel, USA, +2.4544s; **6** Reece Gold, USA, +5.1069s; **7** Salvador de Alba, MEX, +5.8506s; **8** Josh Pierson, USA, +7.1979s; **9** Jonathan Browne, IRL, +9.9646s; **10** Michael D'Orlando, USA, +11.0418s.
Fastest race lap: Foster, 1m 06.1360s, 89.543mph/144.105km/h.
Pole position: Foster, 1m 05.1079s, 90.957mph/146.381km/h.

FIRESTONE INDY NXT SERIES, Road America, Elkhart Lake, Wisconsin, USA, 9 June. Round 6. 20 laps of the 4.014-mile/6.460km circuit, 80.280 miles/129.198km.
1 Jamie Chadwick, GB, 48m 03.0415s, 100.244mph/161.327km/h; **2** Louis Foster, GB, +0.8203s; **3** Jacob Abel, USA, +0.8439s; **4** Reece Gold, USA, +1.3684s; **5** Caio Collet, BR, +2.2711s; **6** Callum Hedge, NZ, +2.8936s; **7** Josh Pierson, USA, +3.6111s; **8** Bryce Aron, USA, +4.1967s; **9** Yuven Sundaramoorthy, USA, +4.6934s; **10** Nolan Allaer, USA, +5.3235s.
Fastest race lap: Abel, 1m 53.2301s, 127.620mph/205.384km/h.
Pole position: Chadwick, 1m 51.0333s, 130.145mph/209.448km/h.

FIRESTONE INDY NXT SERIES, WeatherTech Raceway Laguna Seca, Monterey, California, USA, 22/23 June. 2 x 35 laps of the 2.238-mile/3.602km circuit.
Round 7 (78.330 miles/126.060km).
1 Louis Foster, GB, 45m 22.3195s, 103.584mph/166.702km/h; **2** Caio Collet, BR, +8.2445s; **3** Jacob Abel, USA, +28.9764s; **4** Yuven Sundaramoorthy, USA, +29.9716s; **5** James Roe, IRL, +35.8921s; **6** Myles Rowe, USA, +38.0620s; **7** Christian Bogle, USA, +38.2935s; **8** Christian Brooks, USA, +46.2739s; **9** Jamie Chadwick, GB, +46.7545s; **10** Jack William Miller, USA, +52.8912s.
Fastest race lap: Foster, 1m 14.2070s, 108.572mph/174.730km/h.
Pole position: Foster, 1m 12.1760s, 111.627mph/179.646km/h.

Round 8 (78.330 miles/126.060km).
1 Louis Foster, GB, 44m 27.4314s, 105.715mph/170.132km/h; **2** Caio Collet, BR, +4.3962s; **3** Bryce Aron, USA, +22.0412s; **4** Yuven Sundaramoorthy, USA, +25.6155s; **5** Salvador de Alba, MEX, +31.4937s; **6** Jamie Chadwick, GB, +38.4999s; **7** Christian Brooks, USA, +40.6733s; **8** Christian Bogle, USA, +45.4593s; **9** Josh Pierson, USA, +46.8044s; **10** Jack William Miller, USA, +49.0732s.
Fastest race lap: Foster, 1m 13.6221s, 109.435mph/176.118km/h.
Pole position: Foster, 1m 12.4444s, 111.214mph/178.981km/h.

FIRESTONE INDY NXT SERIES, Mid-Ohio Sports Car Course, Lexington, Ohio, USA, 7 July. Round 9. 35 laps of the 2.258-mile/3.634km circuit, 79.030 miles/127.186km.
1 Caio Collet, BR, 44m 26.3447s, 106.703mph/171.722km/h; **2** Louis Foster, GB, +6.8091s; **3** Jacob Abel, USA, +13.0867s; **4** Callum Hedge, NZ, +22.5839s; **5** Christian Brooks, USA, +25.0708s; **6** Reece Gold, USA, +27.4623s; **7** Jonathan Browne, IRL, +29.4778s; **8** Nolan Allaer, USA, +31.1964s; **9** Josh Pierson, USA, +31.7475s; **10** Jamie Chadwick, GB, +37.3639s.
Fastest race lap: Collet, 1m 10.4485s, 115.386mph/185.696km/h.
Pole position: Collet, 1m 10.2879s, 115.650mph/186.121km/h.

FIRESTONE INDY NXT SERIES, Iowa Speedway, Newton, Iowa, USA, 13 July. Round 10. 55 laps of the 0.894-mile/1.439km circuit, 49.170 miles/79.131km.
1 Louis Foster, GB, 27m 28.5803s, 107.372mph/172.799km/h; **2** James Roe, IRL, +0.4867s; **3** Salvador de Alba, MEX, +1.9206s; **4** Callum Hedge, NZ, +3.1461s; **5** Christian Brooks, USA, +7.5854s; **6** Christian Bogle, USA, +9.1879s; **7** Jamie Chadwick, GB, +12.7265s; **8** Bryce Aron, USA, +13.5696s; **9** Jonathan Browne, IRL, +14.7625s; **10** Yuven Sundaramoorthy, USA, +15.1516s.
Fastest race lap: Caio Collet, BR, 19.2168s, 167.478mph/269.530km/h.
Pole position: Roe, 37.7248s, 170.625mph/274.595km/h (over 2 laps).

FIRESTONE INDY NXT SERIES, World Wide Technology Raceway, St Louis, Madison, Illinois, USA, 17 August. Round 11. 75 laps of the 1.250-mile/2.012km circuit, 93.750 miles/150.876km.
1 Louis Foster, GB, 43m 57.4339s, 127.965mph/205.940km/h; **2** Jacob Abel, USA, +3.3406s; **3** Yuven Sundaramoorthy, USA, +4.6040s; **4** Salvador de Alba, MEX, +4.7417s; **5** Callum Hedge, NZ, +9.5369s; **6** Bryce Aron, USA, +9.6889s; **7** Christian Brooks, USA, +9.7162s; **8** Christian Bogle, USA, +11.0267s; **9** Jordan Missig, USA, +11.2495s; **10** James Roe, IRL, +13.2118s.
Fastest race lap: Foster, 28.1012s, 160.136mph/257.713km/h.
Pole position: Foster, 54.8416s, 164.109mph/264.108km/h (over **2** laps).

FIRESTONE INDY NXT SERIES, Portland International Raceway, Portland, Oregon, USA, 25 August. Round 12. 35 laps of the 1.964-mile/3.161km circuit, 68.740 miles/110.626km.
1 Jacob Abel, USA, 38m 38.9698s, 106.713mph/171.738km/h; **2** Louis Foster, GB, +0.4103s; **3** Bryce Aron, USA, +1.2360s; **4** Caio Collet, BR, +1.7086s; **5** Christian Brooks, USA, +5.5380s; **6** Reece Gold, USA, +6.0540s; **7** Myles Rowe, USA, +8.0022s; **8** Yuven Sundaramoorthy, USA, +12.3771s; **9** Josh Pierson, USA, +21.9159s; **10** Jonathan Browne, IRL, +22.8894s.
Fastest race lap: Foster, 1m 03.3675s, 111.578mph/179.567km/h.
Pole position: Foster, 1m 02.1396s, 113.783mph/183.115km/h.

FIRESTONE INDY NXT SERIES, The Milwaukee Mile, Wisconsin State Fair Park, West Allis, Wisconsin, USA, 31 August. Round 13. 90 laps of the 1.015-mile/1.633km circuit, 91.350 miles/147.014km.
1 Louis Foster, GB, 41m 05.6760s, 133.375mph/214.647km/h; **2** Jacob Abel, USA, +4.3602s; **3** Salvador de Alba, MEX, +5.3458s; **4** Bryce Aron, USA, +5.9020s; **5** Jamie Chadwick, GB, +8.1072s; **6** James Roe, IRL, +9.9551s; **7** Yuven Sundaramoorthy, USA, +14.7102s; **8** Caio Collet, BR, +17.7830s; **9** Jonathan Browne, IRL, +25.5745s; **10** Christian Brooks, USA, +26.1991s*.
** 12s penalty to yield 3 positions for blocking*
Fastest race lap: Foster, 25.5372s, 143.085mph/230.274km/h.
Pole position: Foster, 48.3396s, 151.180mph/243.301km/h (over 2 laps).

FIRESTONE INDY NXT SERIES, Nashville Superspeedway, Lebanon, Tennessee, USA, 15 September. Round 14. 65 laps of the 1.330-mile/2.140km circuit, 86.450 miles/139.128km.
1 Louis Foster, GB, 31m 19.8694s, 165.554mph/266.433km/h; **2** Yuven Sundaramoorthy, USA, +0.3071s; **3** Caio Collet, BR, +1.7897s; **4** James Roe, IRL, +2.0898s; **5** Salvador de Alba, MEX, +2.9538s; **6** Michael D'Orlando, USA, +3.7591s; **7** Bryce Aron, USA, +5.0025s; **8** Jacob Abel, USA, +5.2964s; **9** Christian Brooks, USA, +11.5396s; **10** Josh Pierson, USA, -1 lap.
Fastest race lap: Abel, 26.2302s, 182.538mph/293.766km/h.
Pole position: Foster.

Final championship points
Drivers
1 Louis Foster, GB, 639; **2** Jacob Abel, USA, 517; **3** Caio Collet, BR, 436; **4** Callum Hedge, NZ, 332; **5** Salvador de Alba, MEX, 331; **6** James Roe, IRL, 316; **7** Jamie Chadwick, GB, 310; **8** Yuven Sundaramoorthy, USA, 309; **9** Bryce Aron, USA, 302; **10** Reece Gold, USA, 289; **11** Myles Rowe, USA, 285; **12** Christian Bogle, USA, 284; **13** Jonathan Browne, IRL, 279; **14** Josh Pierson, USA, 264; **15** Jack William Miller, USA, 216; **16** Christian Brooks, USA, 208; **17** Nolan Siegel, USA, 177; **18** Michael D'Orlando, USA, 171; **19** Nolan Allaer, USA, 158; **20** Niels Koolen, NL, 140; **21** Lindsay Brewer, USA, 102; **22** Jordan Missig, USA, 74; **23** Ricardo Escotto, MEX, 59; **24** Taylor Ferns, USA, 53; **25** Josh Mason, GB, 27; **26** Kiko Porto, BR, 18; **27** Jagger Jones, USA, 17.

Teams
1 Andretti Global, 428; **2** HMD Motorsports, 351; **3** Abel Motorsports, 310; **4** Andretti Cape Indy NXT, 167.

USF Pro 2000 Presented by Continental

All cars are Tatuus IP22-Mazda.

FOUNDATION BUILDING MATERIALS GRAND PRIX OF ST. PETERSBURG, St. Petersburg Street Circuit, Florida, USA, 9/10 March. 24 and 25 laps of the 1.800-mile/2.897km circuit.
Round 1 (43.200 miles/69.524km).
1 Lochie Hughes, AUS, 46m 38.3753s, 55.575mph/89.439km/h; **2** Christian Brooks, USA, +0.9900s; **3** Liam Sceats, NZ, +1.5954s; **4** Nikita Johnson, USA, +2.8931s; **5** Braden Eves, USA, +3.3554s; **6** Mac Clark, CDN, +4.1233s; **7** Hunter Yeany, USA, +4.8797s; **8** Frankie Mossman, USA, +5.4509s; **9** Nicolas Baptiste, CO, +6.3087s; **10** Ethan Ho, USA, +7.4192s.
Fastest race lap: Johnson, 1m 10.6266s, 91.750mph/147.658km/h.
Pole position: Hughes, 1m 10.1613s, 92.359mph/148.637km/h.

Round 2 (45.000 miles/72.420km).
1 Nikita Johnson, USA, 35m 48.4223s, 75.404mph/121.351km/h; **2** Lochie Hughes, AUS, +2.0391s; **3** Danny Dyszelski, USA, +5.1795s; **4** Frankie Mossman, USA, +8.7969s; **5** Christian Brooks, USA, +9.1515s; **6** Liam Sceats, NZ, +9.3744s; **7** Jace Denmark, USA, +10.8301s; **8** Braden Eves, USA, +11.2340s; **9** Mac Clark, CDN, +12.1391s; **10** Jorge Garciarce, MEX, +13.5855s.
Fastest race lap: Johnson, 1m 09.6979s, 92.973mph/149.625km/h.
Pole position: Hughes, 1m 10.163s, 92.356mph/148.633km/h.

CONTINENTAL TIRE GRAND PRIX OF LOUISIANA, NOLA Motorsports Park, Avondale, Louisiana, USA, 6/7 April. 3 x 18 laps of the 2.740-mile/4.410km circuit.
Round 3 (49.320 miles/79.373km).
1 Hunter Yeany, USA, 42m 10.7480s, 70.158mph/112.908km/h; **2** Nikita Johnson, USA, +0.2832s; **3** Jace Denmark, USA, +0.9589s; **4** Danny Dyszelski, USA, +1.9929s; **5** Mac Clark, CDN, +2.6015s; **6** Nicolas Baptiste, CO, +2.9561s; **7** Ricardo Escotto, MEX, +3.5489s; **8** Christian Brooks, USA, +4.6165s; **9** Frankie Mossman, USA, +5.3618s; **10** Simon Sikes, USA, +5.5601s.
Fastest race lap: Johnson, 1m 31.9438s, 107.283mph/172.655km/h.
Pole position: Denmark, 1m 31.0488s, 108.338mph/174.352km/h.

Round 4 (49.320 miles/79.373km).
1 Nikita Johnson, USA, 30m 26.8839s, 97.188mph/156.410km/h; **2** Hunter Yeany, USA, +3.5261s; **3** Simon Sikes, USA, +3.9747s; **4** Mac Clark, CDN, +4.6405s; **5** Nicolas Baptiste, CO, +8.2908s; **6** Ricardo Escotto, MEX, +8.7849s; **7** Jace Denmark, USA, +9.1880s; **8** Liam Sceats, NZ, +11.8949s; **9** Jorge Garciarce, MEX, +12.9280s; **10** Christian Brooks, USA, +13.8039s.
Fastest race lap: Johnson, 1m 31.4282s, 107.888mph/173.629km/h.
Pole position: Yeany, 1m 31.1144s, 108.260mph/174.227km/h.

Round 5 (49.320 miles/79.373km).
1 Nikita Johnson, USA, 27m 46.2074s, 106.561mph/171.493km/h; **2** Jace Denmark, USA, +2.8090s; **3** Hunter Yeany, USA, +6.0432s; **4** Simon Sikes, USA, +7.2428s; **5** Mac Clark, CDN, +7.9330s; **6** Ricardo Escotto, MEX, +13.3780s; **7** Christian Brooks, USA, +14.5706s; **8** Danny Dyszelski, USA, +15.9110s; **9** Frankie Mossman, USA, +16.4517s; **10** Lochie Hughes, AUS, +17.9910s.
Fastest race lap: Johnson, 1m 32.0523s, 107.156mph/172.452km/h.
Pole position: Johnson, 1m 31.4282s, 107.888mph/173.629km/h.

VP RACING GRAND PRIX OF INDIANAPOLIS, Indianapolis Motor Speedway, Speedway, Indiana, USA, 10/11 May. 3 x 25 laps of the 2.439-mile/3.925km circuit.
Round 6 (60.975 miles/98.130km).
1 Nikita Johnson, USA, 38m 21.4546s, 95.379mph/153.497km/h; **2** Liam Sceats, NZ, +4.0668s; **3** Lochie Hughes, AUS, +7.9214s; **4** Ricardo Escotto, MEX, +11.4461s; **5** Hunter Yeany, USA, +13.4478s; **6** Nicolas Baptiste, CO, +14.3210s; **7** Simon Sikes, USA, +14.6413s; **8** Christian Brooks, USA, +21.6504s; **9** Adam Fitzgerald, IRL, +27.3741s; **10** Jorge Garciarce, MEX, +27.5106s.
Fastest race lap: Johnson, 1m 23.1428s, 105.606mph/169.957km/h.
Pole position: Johnson, 1m 22.1036s, 106.943mph/172.108km/h.

Round 7 (60.975 miles/98.130km).
1 Liam Sceats, NZ, 36m 16.9099s, 100.836mph/162.279km/h; **2** Lochie Hughes, AUS, +0.6729s; **3** Jace Denmark, USA, +8.0660s; **4** Braden Eves, USA, +10.2437s; **5** Christian Brooks, USA, +17.9366s; **6** Nicolas Baptiste, CO, +20.3136s; **7** Danny Dyszelski, USA, +20.3949s; **8** Nicholas Monteiro, BR, +23.4376s; **9** Ethan Ho, USA, +23.7851s; **10** Frankie Mossman, USA, +24.5717s*.
** 5s penalty for avoidable contact*
Fastest race lap: Johnson, USA, 1m 22.7357s, 106.126mph/170.793km/h.
Pole position: Johnson.

Round 8 (60.975 miles/98.130km).
1 Simon Sikes, USA, 35m 03.3641s, 104.361mph/167.953km/h; **2** Nikita Johnson, USA, +0.7085s; **3** Lochie Hughes, AUS, +1.2748s; **4** Hunter Yeany, USA, +7.2038s; **5** Liam Sceats, NZ, +7.8854s; **6** Jace Denmark, USA, +8.1709s; **7** Christian Brooks, USA, +11.9298s; **8** Frankie Mossman, USA, +12.7331s; **9** Ricardo Escotto, MEX, +16.3552s; **10** Nicolas Baptiste, CO, +17.4495s.
Fastest race lap: Johnson, 1m 23.3885s, 105.295mph/169.456km/h.
Pole position: Johnson.

FREEDOM 90, Lucas Oil Indianapolis Raceway Park, Indianapolis, USA, 25 May. Round 9. 90 laps of the 0.686-mile/1.104km circuit, 61.740 miles/99.361km.
1 Braden Eves, USA, 36m 07.6239s, 102.538mph/165.019km/h; **2** Jace Denmark, USA, +0.6474s; **3** Lochie Hughes, AUS, +1.1658s; **4** Danny Dyszelski, USA, +1.8223s; **5** Bryce Aron, USA, +7.5001s; **6** Mac Clark, CDN, +18.1271s; **7** Nicolas Baptiste, CO, -1 lap; **8** Frankie Mossman, USA, -1; **9** Liam Sceats, NZ, -1; **10** Jorge Garciarce, MEX, -1.
Fastest race lap: Eves, 19.7522s, 125.029mph/201.215km/h.
Pole position: Eves, 39.0250s, 126.565mph/203.687km/h (over **2** laps).

ELITE ENGINES GRAND PRIX OF ROAD AMERICA, Road America, Elkhart Lake, Wisconsin, USA, 8/9 June. 3 x 15 laps of the 4.014-mile/6.460km circuit.
Round 10 (60.210 miles/96.899km).
1 Lochie Hughes, AUS, 31m 09.7351s, 115.929mph/186.569km/h; **2** Frankie Mossman, USA, +1.1382s; **3** Ricardo Escotto, MEX, +3.8787s; **4** Jace Denmark, USA, +4.1036s; **5** Christian Brooks, USA, +5.0151s; **6** Danny Dyszelski, USA, +6.4791s; **7** Nikita Johnson, USA, +12.4262s; **8** Liam Sceats, NZ, +12.6150s; **9** Jorge Garciarce, MEX, +14.5137s; **10** Mac Clark, CDN, +17.1838s.
Fastest race lap: Mossman, 2m 02.7319s, 117.740mph/189.483km/h.
Pole position: Hughes, 2m 02.6851s, 117.784mph/189.556km/h.

Round 11 (60.210 miles/96.899km).
1 Lochie Hughes, AUS, 41m 16.7671s, 87.516mph/140.843km/h; **2** Christian Brooks, USA, +1.1288s; **3** Liam Sceats, NZ, +5.4452s; **4** Jace Denmark, USA, +5.9615s; **5** Danny Dyszelski, USA, +9.6407s; **6** Braden Eves, USA, +10.0111s; **7** Jorge Garciarce, MEX, +10.2322s; **8** Logan Adams, USA, +11.4237s; **9** Cooper Becklin, USA, +11.8705s; **10** Tyke Durst, USA, +13.6103s.
Fastest race lap: Hughes, 2m 03.6084s, 116.905mph/188.140km/h.
Pole position: Simon Sikes, USA, 2m 03.0340s, 117.450mph/189.018km/h.

Round 12 (60.210 miles/96.899km).
1 Lochie Hughes, AUS, 36m 01.9575s, 100.259mph/161.351km/h; **2** Christian Brooks, USA, +0.2610s; **3** Jace Denmark, USA, +5.9148s; **4** Danny Dyszelski, USA, +6.8895s; **5** Simon Sikes, USA, +8.3600s; **6** Nikita Johnson, USA, +13.0757s; **7** Nico Christodoulou, CDN, +13.4663s; **8** Liam Sceats, NZ, +14.1896s; **9** Nicholas Monteiro, BR, +14.8492s; **10** Jorge Garciarce, MEX, +19.6355s.
Fastest race lap: Sikes, 2m 03.3561s, 117.144mph/188.525km/h.
Pole position: Hughes, 2m 03.4822s, 117.024mph/188.332km/h.

TATUUS GRAND PRIX OF MID-OHIO, Mid-Ohio Sports Car Course, Lexington, Ohio, USA, 6 July. 2 x 30 laps of the 2.258-mile/3.634km circuit.
Round 13 (67.740 miles/109.017km).
1 Nikita Johnson, USA, 40m 18.6270s, 100.827mph/162.266km/h; **2** Jace Denmark, USA, +1.3835s; **3** Christian Brooks, USA, +3.0223s; **4** Lochie Hughes, AUS, +4.2641s; **5** Simon Sikes, USA, +6.3839s; **6** Mac Clark, CDN, +23.6121s; **7** Frankie Mossman, USA, +25.1639s; **8** Jorge Garciarce, MEX, +39.3252s; **9** Ricardo Escotto, MEX, +39.6591s; **10** Nico Christodoulou, CDN, +39.8628s.
Fastest race lap: Sikes, 1m 17.9095s, 104.336mph/167.913km/h.

Pole position: Johnson, 1m 18.5055s, 103.544mph/ 166.638km/h.

Round 14 (67.740 miles/109.017km).
1 Nikita Johnson, USA, 46m 56.2628s, 86.591mph/ 139.355km/h; **2** Jace Denmark, USA, +0.9605s; **3** Danny Dyszelski, USA, +12.8065s; **4** Logan Adams, USA, +17.0605s; **5** Ricardo Escotto, MEX, +24.3028s; **6** Nico Christodoulou, CDN, +24.7614s; **7** Lochie Hughes, AUS, +25.1957s; **8** Simon Sikes, USA, +25.6737s; **9** Mac Clark, CDN, +25.8677s; **10** Alessandro De Tullio, USA, +26.2739s.
Fastest race lap: Denmark, 1m 18.8379s, 103.108mph/ 165.936km/h.
Pole position: Sikes, 1m 17.9095s, 104.336mph/ 167.913km/h.

CONTINENTAL TIRE GRAND PRIX OF TORONTO, Toronto Street Circuit, Ontario, Canada, 20/21 July. 2 x 25 laps of the 1.786-mile/2.874km circuit.
Round 15 (44.650 miles/71.857km).
1 Simon Sikes, USA, 32m 10.4143s, 83.267mph/ 134.005km/h; **2** Jace Denmark, USA, +0.3101s; **3** Ricardo Escotto, MEX, +4.3657s; **4** Alessandro De Tullio, USA, +7.0248s; **5** Lochie Hughes, AUS, +10.9789s; **6** Mac Clark, CDN, +12.3894s; **7** Jorge Garcíarce, MEX, +12.8183s; **8** Frankie Mossman, USA, +16.7637s; **9** Cooper Becklin, USA, +18.2421s; **10** Nicholas Monteiro, BR, +19.4226s.
Fastest race lap: Becklin, 1m 09.3552s, 92.705mph/ 149.195km/h.
Pole position: Danny Dyszelski, USA, 1m 10.6353s, 91.025mph/146.491km/h.

Round 16 (44.650 miles/71.857km).
1 Lochie Hughes, AUS, 35m 26.1941s, 75.600mph/ 121.666km/h; **2** Liam Sceats, NZ, +1.8768s; **3** Jace Denmark, USA, +2.2761s; **4** Mac Clark, CDN, +6.3724s; **5** Jorge Garcíarce, MEX, +8.5850s; **6** Frankie Mossman, USA, +8.8413s; **7** Nicholas Monteiro, BR, +11.8492s; **8** Simon Sikes, USA, +39.3858s*; **9** Cooper Becklin, USA, -1 lap; **10** Logan Adams, USA, -1.
** 20s penalty for avoidable contact*
Fastest race lap: Hughes, 1m 08.8901s, 93.331mph/ 150.202km/h.
Pole position: Hughes, 1m 09.1337s, 93.002mph/ 149.673km/h.

CONTINENTAL TIRE GRAND PRIX OF PORTLAND, Portland International Raceway, Portland, Oregon, USA, 23/24 August. 27 and 30 laps of the 1.964-mile/3.161km circuit.
Round 17 (53.028 miles/85.340km).
1 Nikita Johnson, USA, 40m 52.6210s, 77.835mph/ 125.264km/h; **2** Simon Sikes, USA, +0.6690s; **3** Frankie Mossman, USA, +6.6156s; **4** Ricardo Escotto, MEX, +22.2563s; **5** Glenn van Berlo, NL, +23.8351s; **6** Lochie Hughes, AUS, +28.0744s; **7** Danny Dyszelski, USA, +28.2931s; **8** Alessandro De Tullio, USA, +28.2959s; **9** Tanner DeFabis, USA, +1m 01.0779s; **10** Cooper Becklin, USA, +1m 11.0947s.
Fastest race lap: Sikes, 1m 19.8432s, 88.554mph/ 142.513km/h.
Pole position: Johnson, 1m 08.2603s, 103.580mph/ 166.696km/h.

Round 18 (58.920 miles/94.823km).
1 Nikita Johnson, USA, 34m 38.3689s, 102.057mph/ 164.245km/h; **2** Lochie Hughes, AUS, +1.5590s; **3** Simon Sikes, USA, +5.4937s; **4** Jace Denmark, USA, +7.5251s; **5** Glenn van Berlo, NL, +12.9555s; **6** Frankie Mossman, USA, +23.0996s; **7** Jorge Garcíarce, MEX, +24.0169s; **8** Danny Dyszelski, USA, +24.5320s; **9** Noah Ping, USA, +28.3753s; **10** Nicholas Monteiro, BR, +29.1505s.
Fastest race lap: Hughes, 1m 08.7417s, 102.855mph/ 165.528km/h.
Pole position: Johnson, 1m 08.4545s, 103.286mph/ 166.223km/h.

Final championship points
Drivers
1 Lochie Hughes, AUS, 395; **2** Nikita Johnson, USA, 355; **3** Jace Denmark, USA, 345; **4** Simon Sikes, USA, 272; **5** Liam Sceats, NZ, 256; **6** Christian Brooks, USA, 232; **7** Danny Dyszelski, USA, 230; **8** Frankie Mossman, USA, 222; **9** Ricardo Escotto, MEX, 218; **10** Jorge Garcíarce, MEX, 199; **11** Mac Clark, CDN, 187; **12** Braden Eves, USA, 170; **13** Nicholas Monteiro, BR, 162; **14** Hunter Yeany, USA, 148; **15** Nicolas Baptiste, CO, 143; **16** Logan Adams, USA, 114; **17** Tyke Durst, USA, 107; **18** Cooper Becklin, USA, 90; **19** Ethan Ho, USA, 80; **20** Alessandro De Tullio, USA, 66; **21** Adam Fitzgerald, IRL, 51; **22** Glenn van Berlo, NL, 50; **23** Nico Christodoulou, CDN, 48; **24** Arturo Flores, MEX, 39; **25** Charles Finelli, USA, 27; **26** Bryce Aron, USA, 26; **27** Shawn Rashid, USA, 19; **28** Tanner DeFabis, USA, 17; **29** Noah Ping, USA, 17; **30** Avery Towns, USA, 9; **31** David Morales, USA, 7; **32** Francesco Pizzi, I, 5.

Teams
1 Pabst Racing, 445; **2** Turn **3** Motorsport, 365; **3** VRD Racing, 241; **4** TJ Speed Motorsports, 238.

USF 2000
Presented by Continental

All cars are Tatuus USF-22-Mazda.

THE ANDERSEN COMPANIES GRAND PRIX OF ST. PETERSBURG, St. Petersburg Street Circuit, Florida, USA, 8/9 March. 2 x 20 laps of the 1.800-mile/ 2.897km circuit.
Round 1 (36.000 miles/57.936km).
1 Max Garcia, USA, 30m 04.6942s, 71.813mph/ 115.571km/h; **2** Evagoras Papasavvas, USA, +0.6444s; **3** Sam Corry, USA, +1.2325s; **4** Elliot Cox, USA, +2.3100s; **5** Michael Costello, USA, +2.9836s; **6** Nico Christodoulou, CDN, +3.3987s; **7** Quinn Armstrong, AUS, +3.9867s; **8** Jack Jeffers, USA, +4.3734s; **9** Ayrton Houk, USA, +5.4095s; **10** Joey Brienza, USA, +5.9574s.
Fastest race lap: Garcia, 1m 13.7918s, 87.815mph/ 141.324km/h.
Pole position: Garcia, 1m 13.3313s, 88.366mph/ 142.211km/h.

Round 2 (36.000 miles/57.936km).
1 Max Garcia, USA, 40m 34.2164s, 53.241mph/ 85.683km/h; **2** Sam Corry, USA, +0.0633s; **3** Evagoras Papasavvas, USA, +7.4807s; **4** Elliot Cox, USA, +9.6192s; **5** Nico Christodoulou, CDN, +10.5400s; **6** Thomas Schrage, USA, +10.6067s; **7** Quinn Armstrong, AUS, +10.8985s; **8** Joey Brienza, USA, +11.9810s; **9** Hudson Schwartz, USA, +14.4026s; **10** Xavier Kokai, AUS, +14.9029s.
Fastest race lap: Cox, 1m 13.5630s, 88.088mph/ 141.764km/h.
Pole position: Garcia, 1m 13.415s, 88.265mph/ 142.049km/h.

CONTINENTAL TIRE GRAND PRIX OF LOUISIANA, NOLA Motorsports Park, Avondale, Louisiana, USA, 6/7 April. 3 x 15 laps of the 2.740-mile/ 4.410km circuit.
Round 3 (41.100 miles/66.144km).
1 Max Garcia, USA, 24m 08.3397s, 102.158mph/ 164.408km/h; **2** Evagoras Papasavvas, USA, +3.3627s; **3** Joey Brienza, USA, +4.6856s; **4** Sam Corry, USA, +5.3514s; **5** Max Taylor, USA, +8.6765s; **6** Hudson Schwartz, USA, +10.9155s; **7** Ayrton Houk, USA, +19.0041s; **8** Quinn Armstrong, AUS, +21.0233s; **9** Carson Etter, USA, +21.5537s; **10** Maxwell Jamieson, USA, +24.9155s.
Fastest race lap: Garcia, 1m 35.7098s, 103.062mph/ 165.861km/h.
Pole position: Brienza, 1m 35.3141s, 103.489mph/ 166.550km/h.

Round 4 (41.100 miles/66.144km).
1 Sam Corry, USA, 28m 15.7305s, 87.254mph/ 140.422km/h; **2** Evagoras Papasavvas, USA, +0.6376s; **3** Max Garcia, USA, +1.1604s; **4** Hudson Schwartz, USA, +2.2529s; **5** Max Taylor, USA, +3.1044s; **6** Nico Christodoulou, CDN, +3.7134s; **7** Nicolas Giaffone, BR, +4.0613s; **8** Quinn Armstrong, AUS, +4.9524s; **9** Lucas Fecury, BR, +5.3046s; **10** Brady Golan, USA, +6.0389s.
Fastest race lap: Christodoulou, 1m 35.6070s, 103.172mph/166.040km/h.
Pole position: Garcia, 1m 35.3704s, 103.428mph/ 166.452km/h.

Round 5 (41.100 miles/66.144km).
1 Nico Christodoulou, CDN, 33m 47.4902s, 72.977mph/117.445km/h; **2** Evagoras Papasavvas, USA, +1.1898s; **3** Max Taylor, USA, +1.6189s; **4** Max Garcia, USA, +2.0418s; **5** Joey Brienza, USA, +3.0733s; **6** Hudson Schwartz, USA, +4.8718s; **7** Sam Corry, USA, +5.1858s; **8** Thomas Schrage, USA, +5.6385s; **9** Quinn Armstrong, AUS, +6.6045s; **10** Michael Costello, USA, +7.4444s.
Fastest race lap: Christodoulou, 1m 35.6877s, 103.085mph/165.900km/h.
Pole position: Garcia, 1m 35.4153s, 103.380mph/ 166.373km/h.

CONTINENTAL TIRE GRAND PRIX OF INDIANAPOLIS, Indianapolis Motor Speedway, Speedway, Indiana, USA, 10/11 May. 2 x 15 laps of the 2.439-mile/3.925km circuit.
Round 6 (36.585 miles/58.878km).
1 Max Taylor, USA, 24m 24.3016s, 89.945mph/ 144.752km/h; **2** Joey Brienza, USA, +4.0427s; **3** Evan Cooley, USA, +5.6893s; **4** Evagoras Papasavvas, USA, +6.8359s; **5** Sam Corry, USA, +12.1806s*; **6** Max Garcia, USA, +14.3639s; **7** Elliot Cox, USA, +16.7474s; **8** Brady Golan, USA, +22.2660s; **9** Tanner DeFabis, USA, +23.5567s; **10** Ayrton Houk, USA, +23.6047s.
** 5s penalty for causing an incident*
Fastest race lap: Cooley, 1m 26.6182s, 101.369mph/ 163.138km/h.
Pole position: Cooley, 1m 26.3485s, 101.686mph/ 163.647km/h.

Round 7 (36.585 miles/58.878km).
1 Max Garcia, USA, 26m 18.4257s, 83.441mph/ 134.286km/h; **2** Max Taylor, USA, +0.3779s; **3** Elliot Cox, USA, +0.6864s; **4** Ayrton Houk, USA, +1.7636s; **5** Nicolas Giaffone, BR, +2.4163s; **6** Hudson Schwartz, USA, +3.1764s; **7** Michael Costello, USA, +4.0620s; **8** Maxwell Jamieson, USA, +4.8568s; **9** Sam Corry, USA, +5.4540s; **10** Carson Etter, USA, +6.3418s.
Fastest race lap: Evan Cooley, USA, 1m 26.7595s, 101.204mph/162.872km/h.
Pole position: Cooley.

FREEDOM 75, Lucas Oil Indianapolis Raceway Park, Indianapolis, USA, 25 May. Round 8. 75 laps of the 0.686-mile/1.104km circuit, 51.450 miles/ 82.801km.
1 Tanner DeFabis, USA, 32m 00.6813s, 96.435mph/ 155.196km/h; **2** Nicolas Giaffone, BR, +1.2925s; **3** Evagoras Papasavvas, USA, +2.6219s; **4** Quinn Armstrong, AUS, +2.8277s; **5** Xavier Kokai, AUS, +3.4361s; **6** Elliot Cox, USA, +5.9069s; **7** Max Garcia, USA, +5.9070s; **8** Michael Costello, USA, +6.5212s; **9** Joey Brienza, USA, +9.3104s; **10** Hudson Schwartz, USA, +9.4712s.
Fastest race lap: DeFabis, 21.4929s, 114.903mph/ 184.919km/h.
Pole position: Giaffone, 42.3475s, 116.635mph/ 187.706km/h (over **2** laps).

ELITE ENGINES GRAND PRIX OF ROAD AMERICA, Road America, Elkhart Lake, Wisconsin, USA, 8/9 June. 2 x 9 laps of the 4.014-mile/6.460km circuit.
Round 9 (36.126 miles/58.139km).
1 Sam Corry, USA, 31m 08.6579s, 69.597mph/ 112.006km/h; **2** Joey Brienza, USA, +0.8723s; **3** Max Taylor, USA, +2.5379s; **4** Max Garcia, USA, +2.6075s; **5** Elliot Cox, USA, +3.1132s; **6** Ayrton Houk, USA, +5.5761s; **7** Hudson Schwartz, USA, +5.9010s; **8** Michael Costello, USA, +7.3774s; **9** G3 Argyros, USA, +7.4397s; **10** Lucas Fecury, BR, +7.8432s.
Fastest race lap: Corry, 2m 10.8739s, 110.415mph/ 177.695km/h.
Pole position: Garcia, 2m 09.7262s, 111.392mph/ 179.267km/h.

Round 10 (36.126 miles/58.139km).
1 Max Taylor, USA, 21m 17.8567s, 101.775mph/ 163.791km/h; **2** Michael Costello, USA, +0.5553s; **3** Joey Brienza, USA, +1.1385s; **4** Sam Corry, USA, +2.8705s; **5** Evagoras Papasavvas, USA, +3.0190s; **6** Max Garcia, USA, +3.4037s; **7** Nicolas Giaffone, BR, +4.4589s; **8** G3 Argyros, USA, +5.1332s; **9** Hudson Schwartz, USA, +7.3992s; **10** Ayrton Houk, USA, +9.0346s.
Fastest race lap: Taylor, 2m 10.1850s, 110.999mph/ 178.636km/h.
Pole position: Taylor, 2m 10.0591s, 111.106mph/ 178.808km/h.

TATUUS GRAND PRIX OF MID-OHIO, Mid-Ohio Sports Car Course, Lexington, Ohio, USA, 5/7 July. 18, 20 and 20 laps of the 2.258-mile/3.634km circuit.
Round 11 (40.644 miles/65.410km).
1 Max Taylor, USA, 39m 58.9008s, 60.994mph/ 98.160km/h; **2** Max Garcia, USA, +0.6031s; **3** Nicolas Giaffone, BR, +1.6299s; **4** Sam Corry, USA, +1.9658s; **5** Hudson Schwartz, USA, +2.2767s; **6** Elliot Cox, USA, +2.8546s; **7** Brady Golan, USA, +3.6299s; **8** Evagoras Papasavvas, USA, +4.0235s; **9** Joey Brienza, USA, +5.7331s; **10** Lucas Fecury, BR, +6.8071s.
Fastest race lap: Taylor, 1m 37.4193s, 83.441mph/ 134.286km/h.
Pole position: Papasavvas, 1m 23.5019s, 97.349mph/ 156.668km/h.

Round 12 (45.160 miles/72.678km).
1 Evagoras Papasavvas, USA, 29m 59.2965s, 90.355mph/145.413km/h; **2** Michael Costello, USA, +1.9659s; **3** Elliot Cox, USA, +2.4212s; **4** Max Garcia, USA, +3.8825s; **5** Max Taylor, USA, +3.3108s*; **6** Joey Brienza, USA, +5.9860s; **7** Nicolas Giaffone, BR, +6.5659s; **8** Sam Corry, USA, +7.2577s; **9** Ayrton Houk, USA, +8.8265s; **10** Hudson Schwartz, USA, +9.0568s.
** 1-position penalty for blocking*
Fastest race lap: Thomas Schrage, USA, 1m 22.8183s, 98.152mph/157.961km/h.
Pole position: Papasavvas, 1m 23.8281s, 96.970mph/ 156.058km/h.

Round 13 (45.160 miles/72.678km).
1 Max Taylor, USA, 36m 54.7407s, 73.406mph/ 118.136km/h; **2** Thomas Schrage, USA, +0.4468s; **3** Sam Corry, USA, +1.4749s; **4** Max Garcia, USA, +1.9525s; **5** Joey Brienza, USA, +2.1956s; **6** Nicolas Giaffone, BR, +2.5413s; **7** Hudson Schwartz, USA, +2.6523s; **8** Ayrton Houk, USA, +3.4362s; **9** Quinn Armstrong, AUS, +3.8481s; **10** Lucas Fecury, BR, +4.5851s.
Fastest race lap: Carson Etter, USA, 1m 23.7828s, 97.022mph/156.142km/h.
Pole position: Schrage, 1m 22.8183s, 98.152mph/ 157.961km/h.

CONTINENTAL TIRE GRAND PRIX OF TORONTO, Toronto Street Circuit, Ontario, Canada, 20/21 July. 20 and 19 laps of the 1.786-mile/2.874km circuit.
Round 14 (35.720 miles/57.486km).
1 Sam Corry, USA, 31m 49.1271s, 67.356mph/ 108.400km/h; **2** Max Taylor, USA, +0.5952s; **3** Max Garcia, USA, +1.7789s; **4** Evan Cooley, USA, +2.2559s; **5** Elliot Cox, USA, +3.0243s; **6** Nicolas Giaffone, BR, +4.6451s; **7** Hudson Schwartz, USA, +7.5831s; **8** Quinn Armstrong, AUS, +7.8655s; **9** G3 Argyros, USA, +8.3423s; **10** Joey Brienza, USA, +8.7433s.
Fastest race lap: Corry, 1m 12.7522s, 88.377mph/ 142.229km/h.
Pole position: Garcia, 1m 13.2411s, 87.787mph/ 141.279km/h.

Round 15 (33.934 miles/54.611km).
1 Evagoras Papasavvas, USA, 26m 27.1128s, 76.971mph/123.874km/h; **2** Liam McNeilly, GB, +0.4872s; **3** Sam Corry, USA, +2.3532s; **4** Max Garcia, USA, +2.6441s; **5** Max Taylor, USA, +4.0006s; **6** Elliot Cox, USA, +6.0717s; **7** Hudson Schwartz, USA, +8.8406s; **8** Joey Brienza, USA, +9.8213s; **9** Nicolas Giaffone, BR, +10.5935s; **10** Michael Costello, USA, +11.5840s.
Fastest race lap: Taylor, 1m 11.9873s, 89.316mph/ 143.740km/h.
Pole position: McNeilly, 1m 13.1595s, 87.885mph/ 141.437km/h.

CONTINENTAL TIRE GRAND PRIX OF PORTLAND, Portland International Raceway, Portland, Oregon, USA, 23/24 August. 24, 25 and 25 laps of the 1.964-mile/3.161km circuit.
Round 16 (47.136 miles/75.858km).
1 Michael Costello, USA, 40m 37.9146s, 69.604mph/ 112.017km/h; **2** Max Garcia, USA, +8.6360s; **3** Hudson Schwartz, USA, +9.5790s; **4** Nicolas Giaffone, BR, +12.1716s; **5** Quinn Armstrong, AUS, +12.9737s; **6** Evagoras Papasavvas, USA, +13.3702s*; **7** Sam Corry, USA, +13.9577s; **8** G3 Argyros, USA, +16.1331s; **9** Brady Golan, USA, +16.5936s; **10** Thomas Schrage, USA, +17.3018s.
** 10s penalty for avoidable contact*
Fastest race lap: Schwartz, 1m 27.0258s, 81.245mph/ 130.751km/h.
Pole position: Garcia, 1m 12.6461s, 97.327mph/ 156.632km/h.

Round 17 (49.100 miles/79.019km).
1 Max Garcia, USA, 31m 54.5496s, 92.325mph/ 148.582km/h; **2** Elliot Cox, USA, +0.6250s; **3** Thomas Schrage, USA, +0.9709s; **4** Max Taylor, USA, +1.3387s; **5** Evagoras Papasavvas, USA, +2.8809s; **6** Sam Corry, USA, +3.2534s; **7** Michael Costello, USA, +7.3221s; **8** Nicolas Giaffone, BR, +8.1713s; **9** Quinn Armstrong, AUS, +9.4396s; **10** Joey Brienza, USA, +11.6215s.
Fastest race lap: Schrage, 1m 12.1181s, 98.039mph/ 157.779km/h.
Pole position: Schrage, 1m 12.7643s, 97.169mph/ 156.378km/h.

Round 18 (49.100 miles/79.019km).
1 G3 Argyros, USA, 37m 17.9844s, 78.982mph/ 127.109km/h; **2** Max Garcia, USA, +3.0568s; **3** Nicolas Giaffone, BR, +4.3945s; **4** Thomas Schrage, USA, +6.1186s; **5** Joey Brienza, USA, +6.8043s; **6** Max Taylor, USA, +7.3369s; **7** Sam Corry, USA, +7.8320s; **8** Quinn Armstrong, AUS, +7.9193s; **9** Lucas Fecury, BR, +10.4832s*; **10** Carson Etter, USA, +25.6479s.
** 10s penalty for taking a short cut*
Fastest race lap: Michael Costello, USA, 1m 12.8761s, 97.019mph/156.138km/h.
Pole position: Schrage, 1m 12.1181s, 98.039mph/ 157.779km/h.

Final championship points
Drivers
1 Max Garcia, USA, 428; **2** Sam Corry, USA, 355; **3** Max Taylor, USA, 343; **4** Evagoras Papasavvas, USA, 326; **5** Joey Brienza, USA, 265; **6** Elliot Cox, USA, 264; **7** Nicolas Giaffone, BR, 245; **8** Hudson Schwartz, USA, 226; **9** Michael Costello, USA, 218; **10** Quinn Armstrong, AUS, 184; **11** Ayrton Houk, USA, 161; **12** Thomas Schrage, USA, 156.

Teams
1 Pabst Racing, 502; **2** Jay Howard Driver Development, 361; **3** VRD Racing, 341; **4** DEForce Racing, 210.

Atlantic Championship Series

Final championship points
Drivers (016)
1 Matthew Butson, USA, 492; **2** John McAleer, USA, 276; **3** Keith Grant, USA, 254; **4** Dudley Fleck, USA, 249; **5** Rich Zober, USA, 210; **6** David Grant, USA, 155; **7** Bill Munholland, USA, 116; **8** Clay DellaCava, USA, 71; **9** Tonis Kasemets, EST, 53.

Drivers (Open)
1 Nathan Byrd, USA, 427; **2** Paulie Gatto, USA, 308; **3** Steve Hamilton, USA, 226; **4** Jason Slahor, USA, 178; **5** Austin Holtgraewe, USA, 167; **6** Tim Pierce, USA, 160; **7** Charles Livingston, USA, 151; **8** Tyler O'Connor, USA, 55; **9** Rob Albani, USA, 40; **10** Glenn Cooper, USA, 37; **11** Bruce Hamilton, USA, 34.